THE WAY OF THE LORD JESUS

Volume Two

LIVING A CHRISTIAN LIFE

Vatican Council II, *Gaudium et spes,* 38 (in part) and 39:

Now, the gifts of the Spirit are diverse: he calls some to bear clear witness to the desire for a heavenly home and to keep that desire lively in the human family; he calls others to dedicate themselves to the earthly service of human persons, and by this ministry of theirs to prepare material for the heavenly kingdom. He frees all, however, so that—having set aside self-love and taken up and humanized all earthly forces—they can reach out toward that future when humanity itself will become an offering accepted by God.[14]

As a down payment on this hope and as nourishment for the journey, the Lord left to his own that sacrament of faith in which natural elements worked on by human hands are turned into his glorified body and blood—a supper of familial communion and a foretaste of the heavenly banquet.

39. *The New Earth and New Heaven*

We do not know the time for the consummation of the earth and of humanity,[15] nor do we know how the universe is to be transformed. As deformed by sin, the form of this world is passing away,[16] but we are taught that God is preparing a new home and a new earth where justice abides,[17] one whose happiness will fulfill to overflowing all the desires for peace which mount up in human hearts.[18] Then, with death conquered, the children of God will be raised up in Christ, and what was sown in weakness and corruption will put on incorruptibility;[19] then too, charity and its works staying in place,[20] the whole of the creation[21] which God created for humankind's sake will be freed from slavery to vanity.

We are warned that it profits one nothing if one gain the whole world but lose one's very self.[22] Still, the expectation of a new earth ought not to dampen but rather to enkindle our concern for cultivating this earth, where the body of the new human family grows, that body which already provides a sort of foreshadowing of the new age. So, although earthly progress must be carefully distinguished from the growth of Christ's kingdom, still, insofar as earthly progress can contribute to the better ordering of human society, it is very important to God's kingdom.[23]

For after we have promoted on earth, in the Spirit of the Lord and in accord with his command, the goods of human dignity, familial communion, and freedom— that is to say, all the good fruits of our nature and effort—then we shall find them once more, but cleansed of all dirt, lit up, and transformed, when Christ gives back to the Father an eternal and universal kingdom: "a kingdom of truth and life, a kingdom of holiness and grace, a kingdom of justice, love, and peace."[24] On this earth the kingdom is present in mystery even now; with the Lord's coming, however, it will be consummated.

14. See Rom 15.16.   15. See Acts 1.7.
16. See 1 Cor 7.31; St. Irenaeus, *Adversus haereses,* 5.36.1, *PG,* 7:1222.
17. See 2 Cor 5.2; 2 Pt 3.13.   18. See 1 Cor 2.9; Rv 21.4-5.   19. See 1 Cor 15.42, 53.
20. See 1 Cor 13.8; cf. 3.14.   21. See Rom 8.19-21.   22. See Lk 9.25.
23. See Pius XI, *Quadragesimo anno, AAS* 23 (1931) 207.
24. *Roman Missal,* Preface of the Feast of Christ the King.

Notices of Others' Rights in Certain Material

CONTENTS

PREFACE AND USER'S GUIDE

Like *The Way of the Lord Jesus*, volume one, *Christian Moral Principles*, this book is intended primarily but not solely for use as a seminary textbook. Also like that volume, it aims to treat its subject matter in accord with Catholic doctrine as it has been developed by the Second Vatican Council and recent papal teaching.

This volume treats the specific moral responsibilities common to all or most lay people and those common to clerics, religious, and lay people. A third volume is projected to deal with the special responsibilities of certain groups—physicians, lawyers, business people, and so forth—and a fourth, to treat the special responsibilities of clerics and religious.

Users of this volume might find it helpful to begin by reading the summaries at the beginning of each of the eleven chapters. While these do not briefly state all the main points, as the summaries at the end of volume one's chapters do, the summaries here do provide a look ahead by listing the matters treated in each chapter, and so complement the table of contents and the indexes. (Directions for using the indexes will be found on page 913.)

Like volume one's chapters, those of this volume are divided into questions, and, while most questions in this volume are longer than any in volume one, a complete question usually remains the smallest unit in which a reader can expect to find everything needed for an accurate understanding of any smaller unit. Generally, too, the introductory material at the beginning of questions and the numbered sections within them does not stand on its own, and so readers will do well to avoid drawing practical conclusions or launching criticisms on the basis of that introductory material (or the chapter summaries) considered in abstraction from the section, question, or chapter as a whole.

Personal Vocation and the Renewal of Moral Theology

Although this volume is meant to help Catholics shape their lives in accord with the faith they share, it is subtitled *"Living a Christian Life"* rather than *"Living the Christian Life,"* because Christian lives differ. Each saint is unique, and the uniqueness of the saints is not incidental to their sanctity. General moral norms are indispensable, but they are not sufficient to guide anyone's life. The Father, the Lord Jesus, and the Holy Spirit call each Christian to play his or her own part in their work of creation, redemption, and sanctification. To make known that personal calling and to enable each man, woman, and child to respond to it, God supplies each person with a unique set of gifts and opportunities. In these, each Christian can and should discern God's will; having discerned it, he or she should accept and fulfill it.

The whole of the unique life to which God calls each Christian is his or her personal vocation. Personal vocation was treated as a principle of Christian morality in volume one, especially in chapters twenty-three, twenty-seven, twenty-eight, and thirty-one. In this volume, specific responsibilities pertaining to personal vocation—to find, accept, and fulfill it—are treated in chapter two, question E. Moreover, throughout the present volume personal vocation serves as a principle, since a person's vocation determines how he or she must fulfill many responsibilities, especially affirmative ones.

Inadequately understood, *vocation* often has been limited to a Christian's calling by God to a certain state of life: priesthood or religious life, marriage, or a single life in the world. These alternative states of life are important elements of different personal vocations, but so are other sets of morally acceptable alternatives, such as the various kinds of work, association with others, hobbies, and so on. Indeed, each Christian's personal vocation embraces the whole of his or her life, not merely part of it, for God calls each believer to love and serve him with the whole of his or her heart, mind, soul, and strength. Thus, Vatican II adopts the inclusive understanding of vocation partly because it is conducive to the integration of faith and daily life, whose bifurcation, the Council teaches, "deserves to be counted among the more serious errors of our age" (GS 43).

The alternative to living one's whole life in response to one's personal vocation is instead to have some interests, make some commitments, and carry out some projects apart from faith in Jesus and hope for his kingdom. Even if such independent interests, commitments, and projects are morally acceptable in themselves, they are likely to be influenced by the prevalent cultural environment, which in affluent countries is a form of post-Christian, secular humanism. Due to that influence, interests, commitments, and projects which have not been integrated with faith and hope generate tensions and eventual conflicts with these principles of Christian living. Thus, John Paul II, in greatly developing Vatican II's teaching on personal vocation, treats it as an essential element in every Catholic's spirituality—as something on a par with prayer and devout reception of the sacraments.

But if personal vocation, understood in this way, is essential, why has the Church begun to stress it only recently? The answer is twofold.

On the one hand, while the inclusive concept of personal vocation has emerged only recently, what is grasped by that concept is entirely traditional. For the core of the inclusive understanding of personal vocation is simply this: at every juncture, one should ask, "What is God's will for me?" and, having discerned his will, one should accept it and strive to fulfill it faithfully. But, according to the New Testament, doing the Father's will is the principle of Jesus' life (see Jn 4.34, 5.30, 6.38; cf. Mt 26.39-42, Heb 10.7), and Jesus recognizes as kin those who follow the same principle (see Mt 12.50, Mk 3.35). Moreover, from the beginning, Christians have been exhorted to shape their entire lives by faith rather than by the prevalent cultural environment: "Do not be conformed to this world, but be transformed by the renewing of your minds, so that you may discern what is the will of God—what is good and acceptable and perfect" (Rom 12.2; cf. 1 Pt 4.2).

On the other hand, contemporary culture challenges Christians in a unique way. As the faith spread during Christianity's first millennium, it influenced culture, so that eventually most Christians' roles in the family, the economy, and civil society more or less belonged to their lives of faith. Moreover, throughout most of Christianity's first two millennia, few people had much choice about where they would live, what work they would do, or with whom they would associate. States of life involving virginity or celibacy for the kingdom's sake were considered personal vocations for those having the special gifts they require. But for others it was hardly necessary to discern a personal vocation; it was sufficient that they accept as God's will the responsibilities which were theirs willy-nilly. The contemporary world, however, presents Christians with a new situation. The secularization of culture in modern times gradually affected roles, first in the economy and civil society but more recently even in the family, opening the gap, which Vatican II deplores, between faith and daily life. Furthermore, many factors—such as scientific and technological progress, growing wealth, more complex social structures, and the liberal-democratic form of government—greatly increased the options available to people, especially those in the middle and upper classes in affluent societies. Such people no longer can live good Christian lives by passively accepting roles and responsibilities which are thrust upon them; they must reflect critically on culturally defined roles, examine their gifts and opportunities in the light of faith, discern what God asks of them, and commit themselves to doing it. Therefore, it has become necessary to stress personal vocation as the organizing principle of a good Christian life.

Vatican II calls for a renewed moral theology, which would deal more adequately with affirmative responsibilities by equally emphasizing two things: the nobility of the heavenly calling of Christians and "their obligation to bear fruit in charity for the life of the world" (OT 16). The preceding explanation clarifies one of the causes of the need for renewal perceived by the Council. Partly because the faithful had fewer options and many of their responsibilities pertained to culturally defined roles, classical moral theology—that is, the moral theology which developed after the Council of Trent and persisted until Vatican II—took most affirmative responsibilities for granted, and concentrated on clarifying the outer limits: mortal sin and its avoidance. Until fairly recently, such theology together with other means of spiritual formation—especially the instruction conveyed by the liturgy—provided most of the moral guidance which the faithful needed. But as secularization progressed and the faithful faced an increasing number of important choices, classical moral theology became less and less adequate, and its inadequacy became more and more obvious.

More guidance plainly is needed, especially with regard to affirmative responsibilities, whose articulation must take into account the diversity of personal vocations. Yet, while Vatican II calls for renewal in moral theology, the Council's documents include no systematic treatment of moral questions. Moreover, although Scripture, tradition, and current Church teaching, taken together, certainly contain, at least implicitly, everything Catholics need to shape their lives, the wealth of material must be gathered up and synthesized. The present volume presents the results of an attempt at the necessary synthesis, including the articulation of numerous affirmative norms with many of the nuances required by the diversity of personal vocations.

Christian Morality: Beyond Legalism and Secular Humanism

Classical moral theology was deficient not only in its treatment of affirmative responsibilities but in another, more serious way: the moral theologians failed to see clearly that moral norms are truths about what really is good for people or harmful to them. So, moralists treated the norms of morality as laws imposed by God, much as human laws are imposed by human authorities—a system of rules restricting individuals' freedom to live according to their personal preferences. Imbued with this view, both moral theology and pastoral practice sought to minimize what was regarded as the burden of morality, for example, by leaving those with erroneous consciences in good faith, so that they would not become disobedient to God's law. This legalistic approach tended to overlook the damage which people do to human goods when they act badly, even though in good faith.

A clear and consistent avoidance of legalism is especially important for contemporary moral theology because Christianity is in competition with secular humanism, which both claims to promote human goods in this world and ridicules the gospel for its otherworldliness. Indeed, by promising peace on earth together with freedom from injustice and misery, the various forms of secular humanism retain a residue of the gospel. At the same time, by accommodating the inclinations of fallen humankind, secular humanism offers redemption without the cross. Thus, it poses a powerful challenge to Christian faith.

This challenge also is unprecedented. Many world views differ from monotheism inasmuch as they developed without the light of divine revelation and so lack clear understandings of God the creator and human persons made in his image. Nevertheless, almost every world view acknowledged something divine, some more-than-human source of meaning and value. Therefore, most people have taken it for granted that human beings are aware of many values which no human has made or can change, and that these values always must be respected by humans in acting, lest their actions fail to mesh with reality and become self-defeating. However, guided by divine revelation, Jews, Christians, and Moslems have excluded from their world views all superhuman sources of meaning and value apart from God the creator. Consequently, when post-Christian humanism denies God, it makes a claim which is radically new in comparison with all previous human understanding and belief: that conscious thoughts, feelings, and choices of human persons—and, perhaps, of the higher animals—are the sole source of all meaning and value whatsoever.

According to this view, the material universe, by a blind and aimless evolutionary process, tosses up life, sentient life, and finally homo sapiens. Only with the higher animals and human beings, the secular humanist supposes, do good and bad emerge, as conscious beings feel differently about various experiences, develop interests, act on them, and use things, including their own bodies and one another, to pursue their ends. While secular humanists grant that there are values outside consciousness—such as health, human mental capacity, natural beauty, natural resources, efficient technologies, and excellent works of art—they tend to treat, and if consistent do treat, all these values as derivative from and instrumental to states of consciousness, so that only these latter can have independent and intrinsic value. For each individual, states of consciousness which he or she would rather experience than be without are good, and those which he or she prefers being without are bad. Consequently, according to a consistent secular humanism, all reasoning about values, including all moral arguments about right and wrong (good and evil, virtue and vice), ultimately hangs on the preferences of some individual or some particular group of individuals. While some of these preferences arise from nature—most everyone prefers feeling well to the miseries of ill health—some are determined by individual choice and others by cultural conditioning. Thus, this understanding of values and moral argumentation leads to the subjectivism and relativism prevalent today, including the subjectivist view that autonomous conscience is the ultimate standard of right and wrong, and the relativist view that a Christian can implement faith and love adequately by conforming to the contemporary standards of most respectable people in his or her society.

Christian teachers should recognize the seriousness of the challenge of secular humanism and bear in mind that only an authentic Christian humanism can compete successfully with it. The same insight is important to the faithful in living their Christian lives. Without it, they will mistakenly regard faithfulness as dehumanizing; when sacrifice becomes necessary, this mistake will sap their energy and undermine their will to persevere.

Thus, it is important for the faithful to understand that Christian moral norms are a matter of objective truth, to be embraced as a gift and lived with joy, not a matter of mere rules, to be applied or evaded legalistically. Accordingly, in this volume specific moral norms are proposed as truths about what is humanly good, so that the requirements of Christian life will be recognized as necessary for human flourishing, whose possibility is real though limited in this world, and whose perfection belongs to the hoped-for heavenly kingdom.

Unlike students of a textbook of classical moral theology, then, readers of this book will not find in it (any more than in the *Summa theologiae* of St. Thomas Aquinas) a spectrum of "probable opinions"—diverse rules legalistically conceived—among which faithful Catholics would be free to choose. For, inasmuch as morality is a matter of truth rather than of rules, a book of moral theology need not provide a survey of opinions marking the limits between the probably permissible and the certainly forbidden. Rather, it should provide clear and coherent guidance for living a Christian life, and readers should evaluate the guidance it provides by examining and reflecting on the theological sources it uses and studying the arguments it offers. Consequently, readers will find here grounds for accepting the norms proposed as true, and it will be up to each reader to think through the case for each norm.

If a norm and the case for it clarify what Christians should do and why, a reader will be able to understand it. But if not, the norm should not be treated as a more or less "probable theological opinion." Indeed, in a work of this scope, some mistakes are inevitable. Nevertheless, since the grounds for various norms often are independent of one another, readers who think one or another, or even many, of the proposed norms mistaken may find most others helpful.

Reply to an Anticipated Criticism

Many norms articulated in this volume are only implicitly present in the witnesses of faith, and on certain matters the norms proposed here are quite demanding in comparison with lenient "probable opinions" with which readers may be familiar. Thus, some readers are likely to feel that the guidance offered in this work creates fresh burdens and is rigoristic. Of course, no moral theology which avoids legalism can be called "rigoristic" in the technical sense, since rigorism properly so-called is a form of legalism which holds that the strictest opinion is the only safe one to follow. However, some may call this work "rigoristic" in a loose sense, meaning that it is too idealistic, since it makes no "realistic" concessions to the practices of contemporary society.

A reply must begin by putting this anticipated criticism into perspective. The moral theology for which Vatican II calls, one "more nourished by the teaching of sacred Scripture" (OT 16), cannot help but seem very demanding today.

For, on the one hand, the New Testament makes it clear that living a Christian life requires self-sacrifice and involves suffering: "If any want to become my followers, let them deny themselves and take up their cross daily and follow me. For those who want to save their life will lose it, and those who lose their life for my sake will save it" (Lk 9.23-24; cf. Mt 10.38-39, Mk 8.34-35, Jn 12.25-26). Cooperating in Jesus' work inevitably leads to suffering, since the world hates and persecutes faithful disciples (see Wis 2.1-20, Jn 15.18-21, Phil 1.27-30, 1 Pt 3.13-17, 1 Jn 3.16, Rv 13.10).

But, on the other hand, in all the affluent nations, contemporary community moral standards on many matters, most obviously but not only those touching on sex and innocent life, are quite permissive. While dissenting moral theologians have not unqualifiedly endorsed those permissive standards, their dissent has made permissiveness appear to be a legitimate option, and has clouded the consciences of a great many Catholics.

Consequently, at the present time any clear and full articulation of the authentic requirements of Christian life is bound to seem hard and unrealistic. That impression will be greater to the extent that those requirements are regarded, wrongly, as a burden imposed, rather than as necessary implications of sharing with the Lord Jesus in service to his kingdom—a communion of persons in which all the good fruits of human nature and effort will be found in their perfection (see GS 38-39). Willingly taken upon oneself, Jesus' yoke is easy and his burden light (see Mt 11.29-30), because for the wholehearted disciple the hard work of Christian life is, not the alienated labor of a slave, but the cooperation of a friend, who understands its point and hopes to share its fruit (see Jn 15.13-15).

Furthermore, insofar as Christians who try to fulfill their personal vocations are cooperating with Jesus, they are not left to their own resources. To take Jesus' yoke upon oneself is not to relieve him of it but to share it with him. Sharing it, his disciples also share his resources: "If you love me, you will keep my commandments. And I will ask the Father, and he will give you another Advocate, to be with you forever" (Jn 14.16). Again: "I appointed you to bear fruit, fruit that will last, so that the Father will give you whatever you ask him in my name" (Jn 15.16). It stands to reason that, since one's personal vocation is a God-given share in carrying out his plan, he will provide everything needed to fulfill it. Thus, for any who strive to do God's will, his grace is sufficient, and it is entirely realistic to follow Jesus in life and through death to the glory of his kingdom (see Heb 12.1-2).

Some Other Characteristics of This Work

One form grace takes is the divine gifts of faith, hope, and charity, infused into every Christian at baptism. As the exercise of these gifts is the heart of any authentic Christian life, the articulation of their normative implications must be the focus of a truly Christian, nonlegalistic ethics. Likewise, the truths embodied in the moral virtues must be articulated clearly, and their relationships to faith, hope, and charity explained, in order to provide helpful guidance for Christians who desire to live according to the calling and gifts they have received. Hence, this volume deals practically and synthetically with faith, hope, charity, justice, mercy, and the other virtues; they are used here, as they were by St. Thomas in the second part of the second part of his *Summa theologiae,* to illuminate and unify the many specific norms of Christian morality.

Another form grace takes is the continuing presence of Jesus to his disciples in their mutual help and support. The Church, including the blessed in heaven, sustains her members, and so they fulfill the law of Christ by bearing one another's burdens (see Gal 6.2). Any commitment to fulfill an element of one's personal vocation is a commitment to serve others in some specific way. Hence, this volume does not propose an individualistic ethic but an ecclesial and, more generally, a social ethic. So, in order to be fully practical, it incorporates canon law's relevant specifications of the responsibilities treated. Also, during the past century, the papal magisterium and Vatican II have articulated a substantial body of social doctrine, which theologians usually have treated apart from the rest of moral theology. This social doctrine is integrated into the moral theology of this volume, especially in chapters six through eleven. But not only there, for some important elements of it appear already in earlier chapters, especially in chapter two's treatment of the mission of the Church, apostolate, and personal vocation.

If some of those imbued with legalism will consider the guidance proposed in this volume rigorous, others who share that mentality will consider it lax. Those who confuse Christian morality with a law code to be imposed on the Church's halfhearted rank and file are likely to fear that the norms articulated here, which often are too complex and too qualified to serve as disciplinary rules, will be used to support rationalization. Of course, that may happen, but such a use of the book will be an abuse, to which any authentic moral theology is susceptible. Only those who sincerely desire to live a good Christian life can make proper use of a work which tries to clarify what that involves. As for those who lack that desire, they need conversion, not a list of simpler and stricter rules.

In this volume are treated all the specific moral norms which, even though constantly and most firmly taught by the Church, are now being questioned. What about the dissenting theological views? Their foundations were criticized in *Christian Moral Principles,* especially in chapters one, three, six, sixteen, twenty-three, and thirty-six. Someone who understands and accepts that criticism can apply it easily to dissenting opinions and arguments regarding the various norms; if someone does not understand it or rejects it, such an application would be unhelpful or unconvincing. Therefore, this volume generally makes no explicit mention of views which differ from clear and firm Church teaching. Nevertheless, they are taken into account insofar as greater effort and space are invested in explaining the norms from which dissent is most widespread.

As a theological textbook, this work attempts to be pastoral, not by treating every topic from the narrow point of view of the pastor's own duties, but by providing pastors with a body of knowledge which they should communicate in their preaching and teaching, as well as in counseling both in and outside the confessional. No theological textbook, however, can replace catechetical and homiletic materials, which must be carefully prepared and adapted to each particular class or congregation. So, this work is intended to serve as a pastoral resource, a reference book and aid to personal reflection.

Key to References within the Text

As has been explained, theological works should be grounded in sources beyond theology itself. So, nobody should *believe* theologians, including the author of this book. Instead, an individual should regard them as aids for his or her personal appropriation of the Church's teaching. Hence, those using this book will need to study its sources. Its chief sources are Scripture, the teachings of the Catholic Church, and the writings of St. Thomas Aquinas.

This volume is very large. If the sources cited to support the positions taken were not drastically limited, it would be far larger, but not, probably, much more useful. So, there is no attempt in each case to provide references to every source at hand, but only to those which seem directly relevant, and among those usually only to the most important sources.

Quotations from Scripture (except those within other quotations) are from the New Revised Standard Version of the Bible. References are made by means of the following abbreviations:

Acts	Acts of the Apostles	Dn	Daniel
1 Chr	1 Chronicles	Dt	Deuteronomy
2 Chr	2 Chronicles	Eph	Ephesians
Col	Colossians	Ex	Exodus
1 Cor	1 Corinthians	Ezk	Ezekiel
2 Cor	2 Corinthians	Gal	Galatians

Gn	Genesis	Phlm	Philemon
Heb	Hebrews	Prv	Proverbs
Hos	Hosea	Ps	Psalms
Is	Isaiah	1 Pt	1 Peter
Jas	James	2 Pt	2 Peter
Jb	Job	Rom	Romans
Jer	Jeremiah	Rv	Revelation
Jn	John (Gospel)	Sg	Song of Songs
1 Jn	1 John (Epistle)	Sir	Sirach (Ecclesiasticus)
Jos	Joshua	1 Sm	1 Samuel
Lk	Luke	Tb	Tobit
Lv	Leviticus	1 Thes	1 Thessalonians
Mal	Malachi	2 Thes	2 Thessalonians
1 Mc	1 Maccabees	Ti	Titus
2 Mc	2 Maccabees	1 Tm	1 Timothy
Mk	Mark	2 Tm	2 Timothy
Mt	Matthew	Wis	Wisdom
Phil	Philippians	Zec	Zecariah

DS refers to Henricus Denzinger and Adolfus Schönmetzer, S.J., *Enchiridion Symbolorum Definitionum et Declarationum de Rebus Fidei et Morum,* ed. 34 (Freiburg im Breisgau: Herder, 1967). This volume, as its title indicates, is a collection of "creeds, definitions, and declarations on matters of faith and morals." Texts are in chronological order. Two sequences of numbers appear in the margins; both are indicated in references in the present text. Quotations from this collection, unless otherwise noted, are from: *The Church Teaches: Documents of the Church in English Translation,* translated by J. F. Clarkson, S.J., J. H. Edwards, S.J., W. J. Kelly, S.J., and J. J. Welch, S.J. (Rockford, Ill.: Tan Books, 1973). In the translation texts are arranged topically rather than chronologically; a table (370-75) correlates with the earlier editions of DS.

For quotations from the Vatican II documents, the point of departure was a set of translations provided during the Council by the National Catholic Welfare Conference—the agency of the bishops of the United States, subsequently reorganized into the National Conference of Catholic Bishops and the United States Catholic Conference. Those translations were prepared quickly and were originally distributed as the Council completed its work on each document; later they were published in various forms, among which is a convenient, one-volume edition: *The Sixteen Documents of Vatican II and the Instruction on the Liturgy with Commentaries by the Council Fathers,* compiled by J. L. Gonzalez, S.S.P., and the Daughters of St. Paul (Boston, Mass.: Daughters of St. Paul, 1967). In each instance, the National Catholic Welfare Conference translation has been checked against the official text of the document, and amended or replaced whenever necessary to express more accurately the meaning of the Latin, and also to bring the English into accord with current usage—for example, with regard to inclusive language—

and the editorial style generally followed throughout this volume. References to the Vatican II documents use the abbreviations derived from the initial letters of the Latin text of each document, and then the numbers of the articles into which the documents were divided by the Council itself.

AA *Apostolicam actuositatem* (Laity)
AG *Ad gentes* (Missions)
DH *Dignitatis humanae* (Religious Liberty)
DV *Dei verbum* (Divine Revelation)
GE *Gravissimum educationis* (Education)
GS *Gaudium et spes* (Church in the World)
IM *Inter mirifica* (Communications)
LG *Lumen gentium* (On the Church)
NA *Nostra aetate* (Non-Christian Religions)
OE *Orientalium Ecclesiarum* (Eastern Churches)
OT *Optatam totius* (Priestly Formation)
PC *Perfectae caritatis* (Religious Life)
PO *Presbyterorum ordinis* (Priestly Life)
SC *Sacrosanctum Concilium* (Liturgy)
UR *Unitatis redintegratio* (Ecumenism)

Users of the Abbott-Gallagher edition should keep in mind that only the footnotes *italicized* in that edition are part of the Council documents. So, in that edition the Council's own notes usually have numbers different from those in the official texts.

S.t. refers to the *Summa theologiae* of St. Thomas Aquinas. This work is cited by its five main divisions: 1 (the first part or *prima pars*), 1-2 (the first part of the second part or *prima secundae*), 2-2 (the second part of the second part or *secunda secundae*), 3 (the third part or *tertia pars*), and sup. (the supplement compiled from an earlier work after Thomas's death). These main divisions are subdivided into questions (cited by q. with the question number), the questions into articles (cited by a. with the article number), and the articles into a body (c. for *corpus*) and replies to objections (cited ad 1, ad 2, and so forth). *S.c.g.* refers to St. Thomas's *Summa contra gentiles,* which is divided into four books and these into chapters. This work is cited by book and chapter, separated by a period.

Abbreviations in the Footnotes

AAS refers to *Acta Apostolicae Sedis,* the journal of the Holy See in which are published the official texts of documents issued by the popes and the Holy See's congregations. *AAS* began publication in 1909; its predecessor, from 1865-1908, was *Acta Sanctae Sedis* (*ASS*).

CIC refers to *Codex iuris canonici,* auctoritate Ioannis Pauli Pp. II promulgatus (Vatican City: Libreria Editrice Vaticana, 1983), which contains the law currently in force in the Latin Church. Quotations from the code, unless otherwise noted, are from *The Code of Canon Law: A Text and Commentary,* ed. James A. Coriden, Thomas J. Green, and Donald E. Heintschel (New York: Paulist Press, 1985).

EV refers to *Enchiridion Vaticanum: Documenti ufficiali della Santa Sede: Testo ufficiale e versione italiana,* 9 vols. (Bologna: Edizioni Dehoniane, 1965-85). References are to volume and page numbers, *not* to section numbers.

Inseg. refers to *Insegnamenti di Paolo VI,* 16 vols. (Vatican City: Tipografia Poliglotta Vaticana, 1963-78), or *Insegnamenti di Giovanni Paolo II,* 12 vols., most divided into 2 or 3 parts (Vatican City: Libreria Editrice Vaticana, 1978-89). These volumes include original-language versions of virtually all of the two popes' communications.

In Sent. refers to St. Thomas Aquinas, *Scriptum super libros Sententiarum magistri Petri Lombardi.* This work is divided into four books (1, 2, 3, or 4), each of which is divided into distinctions (d.), the distinctions into questions (q.), the questions into articles (a.), and the articles (sometimes, but not always) into little questions (qu'la). The ultimate unit is divided into a body (c.) and replies to objections (ad 1, ad 2, and so on). In some cases the text in *S.t.,* sup. is the same as that in *In Sent.,* and the reference to the former is provided in parentheses immediately after that to the latter.

OR refers to the English-language, weekly edition of the Vatican newspaper, *L'Osservatore Romano.* The reference includes the date of the issue cited and the relevant page number or numbers. When the Italian edition is cited, that is indicated in each instance, and the abbreviation *OR* is not used.

Pastoral Letters, ed. **Nolan,** refers to *Pastoral Letters of the United States Catholic Bishops,* ed. Hugh J. Nolan, 5 vols. (Washington, D.C.: National Conference of Catholic Bishops—United States Catholic Conference, 1983-89).

PE refers to *The Papal Encyclicals,* ed. Claudia Carlen, I.H.M., 5 vols. (1981; reprint, Ann Arbor, Mich.: Pierian Press, 1990). Quotations from papal encyclicals published before 1982, unless otherwise noted, are from this edition. In it, the encyclicals are numbered consecutively through the five volumes, and each is divided into numbered sections; in references, the number of the encyclical referred to appears first, followed by a period, and then the number or numbers of the relevant section or sections.

PL refers to *Patrologiae cursus completus: Series latina,* ed. J. P. Migne, 221 volumes (Paris: 1844-55). References include the number of the volume and column or columns.

PG refers to *Patrologiae cursus completus: Series graeca,* ed. J. P. Migne, 161 volumes (Paris: 1857-66). References include the number of the volume and column or columns.

The Rites refers to *The Rites of the Catholic Church as Revised by Decree of the Second Vatican Council and Published by Authority of Pope Paul VI* (New York: Pueblo, 1976). References are to the page numbers in this collected edition.

Vatican Collection, ed. **Flannery, 1:** refers to *Vatican Council II: The Conciliar and Post Conciliar Documents,* ed. Austin Flannery, O.P., new rev. ed. (Northport, N.Y.: Costello, 1992). *Vatican Collection,* ed. **Flannery, 2:** refers to *Vatican Council II: More Postconciliar Documents,* ed. Austin Flannery, O.P. (Northport, N.Y.: Costello, 1982). In each case, the relevant page number or numbers are indicated immediately after the colon.

Some Further Points to Note

Many popes and Vatican II have commended St. Thomas as a model for work in theology. The reflection carried on in *The Way of the Lord Jesus* began from his work. Both volumes are even more indebted to him than the numerous citations of his works suggest. Still, the writings of St. Thomas are not theological sources on a par with the teaching of the Church herself. On some important matters, the unfolding teaching of the Church seems to require positions incompatible with those of St. Thomas. In such cases, one must be a better friend of Thomas by disagreeing with him.

Another important theological source is the consensus of the approved authors. *Approved authors* means the authors of the standard manuals in moral theology which were in use in Catholic seminaries throughout the world prior to Vatican II. Despite the inadequacies of classical moral theology, the consensus of the approved authors on substantive issues has great weight inasmuch as popes and bishops authorized the use of their works for the training of priests. So, where the approved authors agree in proposing as certain a judgment on a moral norm or on the gravity of an act, the magisterium is firmly committed to that position. Therefore, this work regularly relies on the consensus of the approved authors. However, to avoid multiplying references, they usually are not cited as the authority for positions which are still commonly held by those Catholic moral theologians who do not dissent from the Church's constant and most firm teaching.

Since this volume presupposes *Christian Moral Principles,* familiarity with that volume is taken for granted throughout. Matters adequately treated in volume one are merely referred to here rather than treated again. In this volume, all references to volume one are indicated by *CMP,* always followed by a chapter number, often by a letter or number indicating the relevant question or appendix, and sometimes by a number indicating the relevant paragraph within a question.

By contrast, cross references within the present volume indicate no source and include the number of the chapter and letter of the question only if other than those in which the reference occurs.

Inevitably, in a work as large in scope as *The Way of the Lord Jesus,* some matters were treated in volume one which would better have been left for treatment here, particularly the treatment of the moral authority of law and some of the detail in the chapters on prayer and the sacraments. Also, some matters were not treated in volume one which should have been treated there, and so are treated here. This is particularly so of the treatment of hope and the Church's mission in chapter two of this volume, the first question of chapter four, and most of chapter six.

Acknowledgments

The acknowledgments section of the "User's Guide and Preface" of *Christian Moral Principles* explains the origin and sponsorship of the moral theology project which has resulted both in that volume and in this one. Dr. Robert J. Wickenheiser, President of Mount Saint Mary's College, has continued to encourage the work in every possible way.

This project also continues to depend on the substantial help of many persons. The greatest debt is to the three whose names appear on the title page. Joseph Boyle devoted about one hundred and twenty long days, spread over several years, to help with outlining most of the chapters, revising all of them, and drafting a few scattered sections. Jeannette Grisez, my wife, served as administrative assistant and secretary, helping with the work on a daily basis. Russell Shaw both commented in detail on all the chapters and made countless helpful suggestions for their revision; he also drafted the summaries.

Basil Cole, O.P., made suggestions in advance for the integration of canon law into the treatment and also commented on all the chapters. Patrick Lee researched recent theological literature in advance and also commented on all the chapters. John Finnis checked the references to and quotations from Denzinger-Schönmetzer and the documents of Vatican II, and made many helpful suggestions. Similarly, Robert G. Kennedy worked on the references to and quotations from Scripture, and Edward N. Peters on canon law. Joseph Casey, S.J., Kevin Flannery, S.J., and Peter Ryan, S.J., commented on all the chapters, providing many helpful criticisms and suggestions for improvement.

The following helped in lesser but significant ways with at least one, and in some cases with all, of the chapters:

Michael Carragher, O.P., Stephen B. Clark, Christopher Derrick,
Paul Flaman, John Geinzer, Robert P. George, James Hanink, Brian Harrison,
Mark Latkovic, Ronald Lawler, O.F.M. Cap., William Marshner,
William E. May, James T. O'Connor, Kevin Perrotta, Dermot Quinn,
Patrick Riley, Ray Ryland, William A. Ryan, Alan Schreck, Keith A. Snider,
and Thomas Weinandy, O.F.M. Cap.

Various drafts of most of the chapters were used as texts in classes at Mount Saint Mary's College and Seminary, and the seminarians and collegians participating in those courses helped to improve the work, as did the students who used chapter nine and related materials in the fall of 1991 in a course at the Franciscan University of Steubenville, Steubenville, Ohio.

Many thanks to all these persons for their help. Without it, this volume would be far more defective and less adequate than it is.

Mount Saint Mary's College
Emmitsburg, Maryland 21727-7799

22 November 1992
Solemnity of Christ the King

Jesus "for the sake of the joy that was set before him endured the cross, disregarding its shame, and has taken his seat at the right hand of the throne of God" (Heb 12.2).

CHAPTER ONE

FAITH, RELIGIOUS ASSENT, AND REVERENCE FOR GOD

Summary

People have a responsibility to seek faith, accept it as God makes it available, and guard it once they have it. But Christian faith is not individualistic. One only has faith by sharing in the Church's faith. Thus, fulfillment of the responsibility of faith requires giving the Church's teaching the assent it deserves.

There are good reasons to consider faith credible. There also are good reasons for confessing Christian faith as a Catholic, for today only the Catholic Church claims to possess the divine gift ensuring the gospel's integrity. The so-called logical case against faith does not tell against it, nor do certain practical challenges, which are partly true and partly false.

The gospel promises every blessing for which humans can hope, while the leading alternative to Christian faith, secular humanism, is not an appealing option. Unwillingness to give up sin is the only unanswerable reason for not believing.

Faith is primarily in God, but one cannot believe in God without accepting truths one knows him to reveal. The responsibility of faith should be fulfilled integrally. However, one should not accept theological doctrines with faith, since they can be mistaken. As for apostasy and heresy, they are grave sins against faith.

One should give religious assent to certain teachings of popes and bishops which are not infallibly proposed. The submission of religious assent is not obedience, and it is reasonable. Not all papal and episcopal statements call for religious assent, but the limits on the responsibility to give religious assent are themselves limited in several ways. Deliberate refusal to give the assent due is a grave matter, and sinful dissent—encouraging others to share in wrongful nonassent—is even more grave.

Believers should seek to understand their faith better through catechetical formation. When challenges to faith arise, a sound response should be sought. Faith also requires prayer and attention to Scripture, as well as attentiveness to the signs of the times.

Acts of worship are the chief way of honoring God. False worship and superstition must be avoided. Believers should profess their faith openly, while refraining from such things as blasphemy, testing God, and sacrilege.

Vows are promises to God. It is right to make vows prudently and to fulfill them; nonfulfillment may be a serious matter. Oath taking—calling God to witness to the truth of what one says—also can be appropriate, though statements in the New Testament opposing the practice indicate that, where one has an alternative, it should be preferred. Perjury is a grave matter.

Prologue to the Chapter

Christian faith is God's gift: "By grace you have been saved through faith, and this is not your own doing; it is the gift of God—not the result of works, so that no one may boast" (Eph 2.8–9). But a Christian's actions are not replaced by grace; rather, grace takes shape in works: "For we are what he has made us, created in Christ Jesus for good works, which God prepared beforehand to be our way of life" (Eph 2.10). The first of these good works is the act of faith itself.

Revealing himself, God enters into human history to save fallen humankind from sin and its consequences, and to call human persons to become members of the divine family. While people can choose to accept or to reject God's proposal, to reject it is to spurn God himself. Thus, faith is necessary for salvation: "The one who believes and is baptized will be saved; but the one who does not believe will be condemned" (Mk 16.16).[1]

In accord with Scripture, the Catholic Church teaches that faith is the beginning of salvation.[2] Indeed, it is the foundation and organizing principle for the whole of Christian life. As we shall see in chapter two, faith provides the content for hope, which motivates Christians to live for heaven and cooperate in the work of the apostolate. And as we shall see in chapter three, by incorporating fallen men and women into the new covenant, faith establishes the community which is fulfilled in eucharistic communion. Finally, as we shall see in chapter four, baptism and faith, as conversion from sin, initiate a process of growth toward holiness which must be lifelong.

If faith organizes the rest of Christian life, however, one might wonder: Given that someone has accepted the faith and through baptism become a member of the Church, how can he or she be irresponsible with respect to faith itself, as distinct from the rest of Christian life? The answer is that, although faith is a principle of Christian life which organizes all the rest, faith itself, as a human act, is a

---

1. The necessity of faith for salvation does not mean that all those who have not heard the gospel are lost; if they seek religious truth and are prepared to accept it, faith is implicit in that quest and readiness (see *CMP*, 30.2).

2. See DS 1528–32/799–801, 1562/822, 3010/1791, 3032/1811, 3035/1814; DV 5, DH 2–3. The faith which is the beginning of salvation is living faith, that is, faith motivated by the love of God poured forth in one's heart by the Holy Spirit (see *CMP*, 24.D). The Council of Trent teaches definitively that one who sins mortally after baptism can retain faith which is genuine although not living (see DS 1578/838). Such faith, remaining without love in the mortal sinner, can be called "dead faith." Insofar as it is dead, faith is not saving (see Jas 2.18–26; cf. DS 1544/808, 1577–78/837–38). But even one whose faith is dead should fulfill all the responsibilities pertaining to faith. Hence, in what follows *faith* must be read according to the context as referring sometimes (as here) to living faith and sometimes (as in specifying responsibilities) to faith prescinding from the distinction between living and dead faith.

commitment, and the commitment can be radically betrayed by sinning against faith. Moreover, faith itself generates responsibilities with respect to many actions closely related to the act of faith yet distinct from it.

Question A: What Theological View of Faith Does This Chapter Presuppose?

Adequately to appreciate one's responsibilities regarding faith and reverence toward God, one must understand and bear in mind several essential characteristics of faith. In first making the act of faith, one accepts God's offer of friendship and enters into communion with the divine persons. Hence, faith is much more than assenting to a set of propositions about God. Nevertheless, one cannot believe in God without believing the truth he reveals about himself and his saving plan for humankind. The communion into which one enters by faith includes other believers; it is ecclesial, not individualistic. Finally, faith is a fundamental option, which calls for faithfulness toward God.

1. Baptismal Faith Initiates a Personal Relationship with God

According to the New Testament, Christians by their faith not only accept a body of truth, but accept and live in an interpersonal relationship. Christian faith is life in Jesus, Son of God (see Gal 2.20).[3] Jesus brings those who believe in him into communion with the Father (see Jn 12.44–50, 14.1–11). Thus, faith and baptism into the divine family go together (see Mk 16.16; cf. Gal 3.26–27, Heb 10.22).

a) **Reverence and humility prepare humans to believe.** God creates all things and directs them to their proper fulfillment. His infinite majesty and mighty works as creator call for reverence. Those who are reverent not only stand in awe of God, honor him for his greatness, and acknowledge their dependence on him for every benefit, but humbly seek and accept their fulfillment according to his wise and loving plan. His plan, however, is to save fallen humankind by the gift of faith (see Eph 2.8–9); and so reverence and humility predispose men and women to accept faith when they learn that God has made it available.

b) **A preliminary faith in Jesus leads to saving faith.** The Council of Trent teaches that one receives saving faith (together with hope and love) only through Jesus, with whom one is united by baptism (see DS 1529–31/799–800). The rite of baptism makes it clear that those who come to be baptized seek God's gift of faith with a view to eternal life.[4] At the same time, though, faith in Jesus and acceptance of his message of salvation are prerequisites for the baptism of an adult (see Acts 2.41, 8.12, 18.8). Thus, baptism both presupposes faith and leads to it. The faith which baptism presupposes also is a fruit of the Spirit's work (see DS 1525/797, 1529/799, 3010/1791), drawing those who hear the gospel into a human relationship with Jesus. He, as man, brings his human brothers and sisters

---

3. See John L. McKenzie, *Dictionary of the Bible.* (New York: Macmillan, 1965), 268–69.

4. The baptismal rite formerly was clearer on this matter than now: see Joseph Ratzinger, *Principles of Catholic Theology: Building Stones for a Fundamental Theology,* trans. Mary Frances McCarthy, S.N.D. (San Francisco: Ignatius Press, 1987), 103–4.

into the covenantal communion with the Father which they seek in baptism and accept by saving faith.

c) **By baptismal faith, one commits oneself to the divine persons.** Just before new Christians are baptized, they (or the parents and godparents on behalf of babies) profess faith in each of the divine persons by responding to the parts of the creed, proposed as questions: "Do you believe in God, the Father almighty, creator of heaven and earth? . . . Do you believe in Jesus Christ, his only Son, our Lord . . . ? Do you believe in the Holy Spirit, the holy catholic Church . . . ?"[5] By answering "I do," those to be baptized commit themselves to the Father, Son, and Holy Spirit, much as a man and a woman commit themselves to each other in making their marriage promises.

d) **Baptismal faith establishes communion with God.** Baptism *in the name of* the Father, Son, and Holy Spirit is not only baptism by their authority but baptism *into* their family name.[6] Thus, baptism makes one an adoptive member of the divine family: "When we cry, 'Abba! Father!' it is that very Spirit bearing witness with our spirit that we are children of God" (Rom 8.15–16).[7] And as families live together, so the divine persons dwell in those who, having received the gift of faith, are faithful to it: "Those who love me will keep my word, and my Father will love them, and we will come to them and make our home with them" (Jn 14.23).

2. Faith Does Deal with Propositional Truths

When people become friends, an important part of their mutual gift of self is what they tell each other about themselves and their intentions. It is part of each one's acceptance of the other to believe and trust his or her self-communication (see *CMP*, 20.B). If neither believed what the other communicated, the two would not accept one another and could not be friends. God's revelation similarly includes propositions as an essential element, and Christian faith in God includes assent to them.

a) **Propositions are part of the way God reveals himself.** Propositions are contents of thought which are either true or false and can be expressed in language, usually in complete sentences. In saying something is so or ought to be done, one asserts a proposition; whenever people answer yes or no to whether something is so or ought to be done, they assert a proposition. God, in revealing himself through the prophets and through Jesus, says many things are so or not so, right or wrong; thus, part of the way in which he reveals himself is by asserting propositions. But these propositions are not the whole of revelation, for God also enters into human history and acts in it. Vatican II, therefore, teaches that God's "plan of revelation is realized by deeds and words having an inner unity: the deeds wrought by God in the history of salvation manifest and confirm the teaching and realities signified

---

5. See *The Rites*, 99–100, 146, 207, 222, 233, 245, 251–52.

6. See the Greek of Mt 28.19. Cf. W. F. Albright and C. S. Mann, *Matthew: Introduction, Translation, and Notes*, The Anchor Bible, 26 (Garden City, N.Y.: Doubleday, 1971), 362.

7. See *CMP*, 30.H. For the New Testament theology of Christian baptism as the communication of the Spirit, see David Michael Stanley, S.J., "The New Testament Doctrine of Baptism: An Essay in Biblical Theology," *Theological Studies* 18 (1957): 169–215.

by the words, while the words proclaim the deeds and clarify the mystery contained in them" (DV 2).[8]

b) Faith in God includes assenting to the truth of propositions. One cannot give God the submission of faith without assenting to the truth he has revealed (see DV 5; cf. DS 377/180, 3008–11/1789–92; *CMP*, 20.C).[9] Adults, in being baptized, and all Christians, in renewing their baptismal promises, assent to several propositions when they say "I do" in reply to the questions: Do you believe in the Father, in Jesus Christ, in the Holy Spirit? Similarly, the profession of faith in the Mass accurately reflects the true situation in that it affirms faith in God the Father, in the Lord Jesus, and in the Holy Spirit by affirming the central propositional truths of faith. It is only because what one believes in believing God includes this propositional element that "faith comes from what is heard, and what is heard comes through the word of Christ" (Rom 10.17).[10]

c) The propositional truths of faith really communicate God. It is a mistake to suggest, as some do, that Christian faith is believing in God rather than believing these propositional truths. Since God reveals these propositional truths and believing them belongs to faith, to refuse to believe the truths of faith would be to refuse to believe God himself. Moreover, the suggestion implies that propositional truths of faith are mere human thoughts or even mere sets of human words, altogether separate from God. But they are not mere thoughts or mere sets of words; they are what the words convey and the thoughts grasp. Neither mere conceptual formulations and verbal expressions of faith nor objects of faith entirely separate from God himself, they are God's self-expressions, by which he communicates himself, making known his saving plan and will (see DV 6). And how can God's self-expressions take shape in human propositions? Just as the Word takes shape in flesh; Jesus translates divine truth into human terms. Therefore, all who have faith in God should believe all the propositional truths which they recognize to be matters of faith.[11]

---

8. A valuable study: René Latourelle, S.J., *Theology of Revelation,* with a commentary on *Dei Verbum* (Cork, Ireland: Mercier Press, 1968), 313–488.

9. See Paul VI, General Audience (24 Apr. 1974), *Inseg.* 12 (1974) 368–69, *OR,* 2 May 1974, 1: "Baptism implies a precise and resolute doctrinal commitment. . . . You understand that, right from the first apprenticeship, doctrinal commitment is fundamental and solemn for those who wish to abide by the authenticity of the Christian profession; and that faithfulness to this commitment cannot be called obsolete and rigid integralism. It does not permit so-called pluralistic judgments."

10. John Lamont, "The Notion of Revelation," *New Blackfriars* 72 (1991): 335–41, cogently criticizes nonpropositional theories of revelation and defends a position quite similar to the one explained here.

11. St. Thomas, *S.t.,* 2–2, q. 1, a. 2, ad 2, points out that faith does not terminate in propositions (*enuntiabilia*) but in the reality, and some take this remark to mean that the propositional truths of faith are mere formulations, of limited and merely relative value. But that misinterprets Thomas's position (which is clear enough from aa. 1–2 as a whole): Although faith is in the primary truth (God), it takes propositional form, because realities are in a knower according to the knower's mode, and truth in humans is propositional; see Reginald Garrigou-Lagrange, O.P., *The Theological Virtues,* vol. 1, *On Faith,* trans. Thomas a Kempis Reilly, O.P. (St. Louis: B. Herder, 1965), 51–90. Propositions are not (as many since Kant suppose) constructs which express but also block some more direct experience or intuition of reality, but are the way by which human

d) One has responsibilities with regard to these truths of faith. Because the truths of faith are part of God's self-communication, it is impossible to believe in the God who reveals himself while denying these propositional truths. Still, most Christians are unaware of some truths of faith, and so believe in God without at once affirming every one of them. One should be ready to assent to truths of faith as one becomes aware of them, and should try to understand truths one explicitly believes and resist temptations to doubt them. At the same time, because the assent of faith should be refused to propositions which do not belong to faith, one should do what is necessary to discriminate between truths of faith and other propositions, even true ones.

3. Christian Faith Is Ecclesial, Not Individualistic

Union with Jesus makes the baptized children of God: "In Christ Jesus you are all children of God through faith. As many of you as were baptized into Christ have clothed yourselves with Christ" (Gal 3.26–27). Jesus, however, makes himself available as mediator between God and humankind, not by offering a separate relationship to each human person, but by establishing the community of the new covenant into which each person who is to be saved is called by a unique grace through personal faith.

The Church's preaching calls one to faith; baptism makes one a member of the Church, the communion of the new covenant; and the Eucharist perfects faith as one's commitment to communion not only with the divine persons but with other human persons.

a) The Church is not an optional association of Christian believers. Many who fully appreciate the importance of faith in Jesus nevertheless regard Church membership as entirely subordinate to personal faith. However, this view overlooks the intimacy between Jesus and the Church. Before his conversion, St. Paul "was violently persecuting the Church of God and was trying to destroy it" (Gal 1.13). But Jesus challenged him: "Why do you persecute me?" (Acts 9.4). This identification of the Church with Jesus is clarified in the Pauline writings: Christians are baptized into his one body, which is the Church (see 1 Cor 12.12–13; cf. Rom 12.4–5; Eph 1.22–23, 5.23–27; Col 1.18, 24).[12] Members of the Church are members of Jesus, living stones built into God's spiritual house (see Eph 2.19–22, 1 Pt 2.4–9). Thus, as there is only one Lord Jesus, there is only one Church, and this community formed by faith is "the household of God, which is the church of the living God, the pillar and bulwark of the truth" (1 Tm 3.15).

b) One has faith by sharing in the Church's faith. Jesus commissioned the apostles to preach the gospel throughout the world, so that all might believe and

---

persons identify with the realities they know. Faith is not peculiar in terminating in the reality rather than in propositions; the same thing is true, as Thomas expressly says, of science.

12. *CIC*, c. 96: "By baptism one is incorporated into the Church of Christ and is constituted a person in it"; c. 204, §1: "The Christian faithful are those who, inasmuch as they have been incorporated in Christ through baptism, have been constituted as the people of God." See LG 1, 7, 8, 11, and 31. On the Church as new covenant community according to the New Testament: Viktor Warnach, "Church," in *Encyclopedia of Biblical Theology*, ed. Johannes B. Bauer (New York: Crossroad, 1981), 101–16.

be baptized (see Mt 28.19–20, Mk 16.15–16). Tradition and Scripture, by which apostolic faith continues through the centuries, are committed to the Church (see DV 10). Those who accept the gospel come to the Church to seek saving faith in baptism; being baptized, "they have the duty to profess before others the faith which they have received from God through the Church" (LG 11). Thus, the Church's faith is the norm of personal faith (see C.5.h, below). For this reason, one fulfills one's responsibility of faith only by giving the Church's teaching the assent due it.

c) **The Church is not merely a means for reaching faith's goal.** Faith is a commitment to communion with the divine persons. The Eucharist concretely realizes this communion in the new covenant (see Mt 26.28, Mk 14.24, Lk 22.20, 1 Cor 11.25). The eucharistic communion of the Church on earth will be perfected in the eternal communion of heaven (see LG 9, 48).[13] Thus, the Church is not merely a convenient, but perhaps dispensable, means by which her members reach faith's goal. Rather, she is the kingdom in its incipient or embryonic form, and will attain her fullness in the glory of heaven (see LG 2, 48; *CMP,* 19.C and 33.E–F).

4. By Faith One Makes a Fundamental Option for Communion with God

Since faith is God's gift to created persons who are utterly dependent on him, it necessarily involves reverent obedience. One's initial act of faith is never left behind, for God's gift endures, and its free acceptance lasts as one's basic Christian commitment (see *CMP,* 16.G). Since the personal relationship with God that faith establishes should shape the whole of a believer's life, faith is a fundamental option. Closely related to faith, and flowing from it, are expressions of reverence, not only in acts of worship but in all other acts of Christian life bearing on the sacred.

a) **Faith in God involves personal submission to him.** Christian faith is characterized by humble and reverent submission, as Vatican II teaches: " 'The obedience of faith' (Rom 16.26; see 1.5; 2 Cor 10.5–6) is to be given to God who reveals, an obedience by which one entrusts one's whole self freely to God, offering 'the full submission of intellect and will to God who reveals' (Vatican I, DS 3008/1789)" (DV 5).[14]

Obedience often suggests submission to rules or laws, which may be arbitrary and are at best impersonal. The obedience of faith, however, is personal submission to God, in whom there is nothing arbitrary and who asks only for trust and love in response to his loving kindness and faithfulness. Still, the submission which faith requires would be unacceptable if it were submission to any human person or mere human society. It is right and good only because God creates out of love, creatures are wholly dependent on him, and faith is the acceptance of his gift of salvation

---

13. Ratzinger, *Principles of Catholic Theology,* 53: "The Church is *communio;* she is God's communing with men in Christ and hence the communing of men with one another—and, in consequence, sacrament, sign, instrument of salvation. The Church is the celebration of the Eucharist; the Eucharist is the Church; they do not simply stand side by side; they are one and the same."

14. John Paul II, General Audience (13 Mar. 1985), 5, *Inseg.* 8.1 (1985) 639–40, *OR,* 18 Mar. 1985, 12, considers this concise and rich statement of Vatican II to be a technical definition of faith.

and his invitation to share in his own blessedness—a blessing which surpasses all that even good created persons could naturally hope for.

b) **The act of faith is a Christian's fundamental option.** Abraham, the model of faith, listens to God, accepts his promises, and risks everything to act on them (see Gn 12–22; cf. Rom 4.1–3, Heb 11.8–19). Similarly, in making the commitment of baptismal faith, one renounces Satan and accepts Jesus, setting aside desires, goals, and commitments—such as greed for wealth, escapist pleasure seeking, and selfish ambition—incompatible with life in the new covenant because they are sinful. So faith requires Christians to undertake a new way of life, based on love, which fulfills all the commandments (see *CMP*, 30.I). Faith, therefore, is a fundamental option (see *CMP*, 16.G.3–6); it is *the* fundamental option of Christian life.

c) **The fundamental option of faith initiates an ongoing relationship.** This Christian fundamental option is not merely an option for moral goodness, but a personal commitment to God, revealing himself in Jesus, with whom one is joined by membership in his body, the Church. As a free choice, moreover, the act of faith endures, provided it is not revoked (see *CMP*, 2.E.6). But like the marriage promises a man and a woman make to each other, faith, as the acceptance of a personal relationship, must be implemented by many further choices that preserve and nourish it. Thus, responsibilities distinct from the act of faith itself must be fulfilled if faith is to survive and flourish as the basis of one's Christian life.

d) **Faith should be embodied and expressed in reverent actions.** Any authentic religion seeks to honor God by actions which embody and express reverence for him. For Christians, living in communion with God by faith, all such religious acts flow directly from faith. At the same time, they are distinct from it inasmuch as they involve more than the commitment of faith itself. Hence, besides persevering in the act of faith, one must fulfill responsibilities to profess one's faith, to think and speak reverently of God, and in other ways to act toward God with the reverence and humility which shape faith itself.

Question B: Why Reflect on the Responsibility to Keep One's Faith?

As a free human act, faith must be responsible; good reasons are needed for making and keeping this commitment. Questions C through G articulate some such reasons. Even while considering them, however, one must remember that faith is first, last, and always an undeserved gift of God.

Believers have no trouble understanding that those without faith should search for religious truth and consider why it would be good and right to become Catholics (see DH 1–3). But why should Catholic Christians, for whom this book is mainly intended, reflect on their own responsibility to believe? After all, the experience of friendship with God provides a much greater motive for cherishing faith than any reasons one can find, and every Christian is able not only to believe but to know God's personal love: "God abides in those who confess that Jesus is the Son of God, and they abide in God. So we have known and believe the love that God has for us" (1 Jn 4.15–16). Nevertheless, for several reasons, is important to think about why it is good and right to believe as one does.[15]

1. Understanding Enriches the Commitment of Faith

Most Catholics are baptized as infants, without making any personal choice. Even as adults, their commitment of faith usually is made and reaffirmed only in making choices to practice it, so that the reasons for believing as they do can remain unclear. But the reasons why one freely does anything are an important part of what one is doing. That is obvious when, for instance, an otherwise good act is done for a bad reason, for example, telling others the truth about their failings in order to hurt them. Conversely, when good acts are done for good reasons, the reasons are no less an important part of what one does. A good act is enriched when one has more good reasons for doing it. Thus, one can enrich one's act of faith, insofar as it depends on one's choice, by considering the reasons why it is right and good to believe.

2. Understanding Purifies Commitment

As with any other choice, the commitment to believe can be made on the basis of mixed motives, a combination of feelings both appropriate and questionable, of reasons both good and bad. Better understanding helps overcome faulty motives for believing, especially reasons which make Christian life a mere means to an inappropriate, ulterior end.

Among the bad reasons for believing are, first, social conformism for the sake of temporal advantages and, second, the prospect of hell misunderstood as an arbitrary punishment. The first exposes faith to shifting social pressures; the second breeds legalistic minimalism in those who are docile and rebellion in those who are spirited. As people and their circumstances change, faulty reasons for believing often turn into plausible excuses for abandoning faith.

Still, emotional motivations for doing anything always are mixed and usually can be allied to different sorts of reasons. Feelings of solidarity and fear naturally motivate faith, and inasmuch they are not reasons for believing, neither are they bad reasons. Moreover, the joy of solidarity in Christian communion and the fear of hell, when hell is correctly understood, normally are allied with sound reasons for faith. The presence in oneself or others of various emotional motives for faith should not cause embarrassment or lead to criticism. But it should spur one to examine one's feelings and reasons, and to integrate emotional motives with good reasons for believing.

---

15. If responsibilities are considered from a legal point of view, one finds no duty to believe, since one has no legal duties until one is under the law, and one comes under Jewish or Christian religious law only when one accepts God's revelation with faith. Thus, St. Thomas, *S.t.,* 2–2, q. 16, a. 1, points out that in the Old Testament there is no precept to believe. However, the moral responsibility to believe is presupposed by an upright commitment of faith. As one fulfills that responsibility, it remains in effect, continues to shape the commitment, and provides a reason to persevere in it.

3. Understanding Can Strengthen Commitment

Since faith is a commitment to renounce sin and live a holy life, every mortal sin in some way challenges faith, and mortal sin, unfortunately, seems not to be a rare occurrence. Thus, many Christians are tempted at some time to renounce their faith. Reflection on all the appealing aspects of the option of faith strengthens the will in its commitment, for the more one understands why it is good to believe, the less appealing are tempting alternatives. Moreover, misunderstandings can make it seem that faith is at odds with some other genuine human good—honesty, say, or concern for justice. Better understanding eliminates such false options by clarifying how Christian faith serves many human goods and is at odds with none. Eliminating false options strengthens the commitment of faith by making it clear that there is no sound reason to choose contrary to it.

4. Understanding Enables One to Give an Account

Christians who understand why it is good and right to believe as they do are equipped to fulfill another responsibility: to give an account of the hope that is in them (see 1 Pt 3.15). Hence, although the present work is not apologetics, questions C through G can help with the work of apologetics to which each Christian should contribute insofar as he or she can.

Question C: What Reasons Point to the Credibility of Catholic Faith?

There are good reasons, treated at length in books on apologetics intended to persuade nonbelievers, for judging Catholic faith credible. Here, space allows only a brief review, focusing on points which raise difficulties for many Catholics today.[16]

1. Reasons for Thinking That a Personal God Exists

A personal God is not only an uncaused cause, but a personal source of human beings' lives, related to them somewhat as a parent to children.

a) **It is reasonable to believe that there is a creator.** Propositions about most things can be understood without knowing whether the things are real (and the propositions true). Such things, considered in themselves, might exist or not; they are contingent beings. If they do exist, one naturally wonders why. An explanation

---

16. In addition to the works which will be mentioned in subsequent notes, the following are helpful for apologetics: St. Francis de Sales, *The Catholic Controversy,* trans. Henry Benedict Mackey, O.S.B. (Rockford, Ill.: Tan Books, 1989); E. L. Mascall, *The Secularization of Christianity: An Analysis and a Critique* (New York: Holt, Rinehart and Winston, 1966); Thomas Dubay, S.M., *Faith and Certitude* (San Francisco: Ignatius Press, 1985); William G. Most, *Catholic Apologetics Today: Answers to Modern Critics* (Rockford, Ill.: Tan Books, 1986); Peter Kreeft, *Fundamentals of the Faith: Essays in Christian Apologetics* (San Francisco: Ignatius Press, 1988). For a fuller treatment of many of the philosophical points covered briefly here, see Germain Grisez, *Beyond the New Theism: A Philosophy of Religion* (Notre Dame, Ind.: University of Notre Dame Press, 1975). Also see John Henry Newman, *An Essay in Aid of a Grammar of Assent* (Westminster, Md.: Christian Classics, 1973); Richard L. Purtill, *Reason to Believe* (Grand Rapids, Mich.: William B. Eerdmans, 1974).

begins to emerge as one sees how they depend on other things within the world; however, these in turn depend on still other things, and so they do not bring the search for an explanation to an end. Hence, the reality of contingent beings will be without an adequate explanation unless they depend on something real which depends on nothing else: a noncontingent being. But it is reasonable to think that the existence of contingent beings has an adequate explanation, since the alternative—to think it has none—unnecessarily leaves their reality partially unaccounted for. Therefore, contingent beings depend for their reality on something noncontingent: a reality which can explain the existence of contingent beings without itself calling for something further to explain it. This noncontingent source of the existence of contingent beings is called *the creator.*

b) **The creator must be unlike any contingent being.** Whatever can be understood of any contingent being leaves open the possibility that what is understood either is or is not real. That possibility, however, cannot be left open with respect to what is true of the creator. Therefore, whatever can be understood of any contingent being cannot be true of the creator: the creator must be unlike any contingent being. One understands what it is for contingent things to change and what it is for them to be unchangeable; neither change nor changelessness in any sense true of contingent things can be true of the creator. One understands what it is for human beings to be both bodies and spirits; the creator can be neither a body nor a disembodied spirit.[17] In sum, while contingent things point to a creator, what that creator is in himself remains unknown: "With regard to God, we cannot grasp what he is, but what he is not, and how other things are related to him" (*S.c.g.,* 1.30).

c) **It is reasonable to think of the creator as personal.** Things one freely chooses to bring about might exist or not; that they do exist depends on one's free choice. Similarly, contingent realities might exist or not, and that they do, depends on the creator. So, contingent beings depend on the creator somewhat as realities which come to be through human free choices depend on human agents. This suggests that the creator freely chooses to create certain contingent realities. But to act through choice presupposes the exercise of intelligence in view of a purpose. Therefore, although the creator must be entirely unlike a human being, one reasonably thinks of this source of contingent reality as an intelligently purposeful agent—a person.

d) **It is reasonable to consider the creator a personal God.** Their own intelligence directs human persons and communities toward fulfillment through freely chosen actions. But the realization of their hopes always depends on factors beyond human agents' control. Thus, when they enjoy something of what they hoped for, this fruit of their effort depends entirely on the creator, and only partly on themselves. Moreover, while human intelligence is like other contingent realities in having its existence from the creator, in another and special way it points to

---

17. This is not to deny the Church's teaching, based on Scripture, that God is an unchangeable spiritual substance (see DS 3001/1782), but to insist that nothing is truly said univocally of God and creature. A detailed treatment of how talk about God is meaningful: Grisez, *Beyond the New Theism,* 230–72.

a directive intelligence prior to itself. For human reasoning has practical principles by which one is alive to the various aspects of human fulfillment: life and health, esthetic experience and excellent performance, knowledge, marriage and children, and various forms of harmony or peace within oneself and with others (see *CMP*, 5.D; below, 9.A.1.j). These practical principles underlie all human interests in what is true, good, and beautiful. Unlike personal choices and the laws of society, people do not originate these principles; rather, they naturally come to know them, and so are endowed with them by the creator. Thus, human existence depends on the creator not only for its fulfillment but even for the principles underlying every possible plan for attaining that fulfillment.[18]

So, it is reasonable to think of the creator as a personal source of human existence who guides and cares for humankind, like the human parents to whom gratitude and reverence are due. Being due special gratitude and reverence, such a personal source of existence is a personal God: the mysterious Other to whom religious feeling and activity are directed.[19]

2. Reasons for Hoping and Expecting That God Might Reveal Himself

Those who work together in any way communicate personally with one another, especially when things are not going well. Children reach out to their parents for help and expect a personal response. Similarly, human beings, aware that they can attain no good except by cooperating with God, reasonably expect some personal communication from him, because several things make them aware of their need for it.

a) **Human beings are aware that they are at odds with God.** People are well aware that they sometimes act unreasonably, and do not perfectly follow the direction which, coming from God, is provided by the starting points of practical reasoning. Also, when their plans do not work out as they anticipate, they are not always ready to say, "God's will be done," but often look for ways to use God. So, human beings naturally do not expect God to be pleased with them. They realize that they are sinful and need his forgiveness, guidance, and strength to overcome their sins.

b) **Human beings need help to deal with other evils.** People quickly learn by experience that they cannot always overcome the wickedness of others—and often could overcome it only by wicked deeds of their own. Moreover, no human efforts are adequate to surmount natural disasters, such as accidents, disease, and death. Human beings need to become free of such evils, to be saved from them. Only God can help; one naturally calls on him.

---

18. A fuller development of the argument of this paragraph: Germain Grisez, Joseph Boyle, and John Finnis, "Practical Principles, Moral Truth, and Ultimate Ends," *American Journal of Jurisprudence* 32 (1987): 141–46.

19. For the point that human beings precisely in being created are personally related to their creator as God, see John Paul II, General Audience (13 Dec. 1978), *Inseg.* 1 (1978) 333–36, *OR,* 21 Dec. 1978, 1, 12; General Audience (2 Jan. 1980), 4, *Inseg.* 3.1 (1980) 14–15, *OR,* 7 Jan. 1980, 3.

c) **Human beings wonder what awaits them after death.** Human experience teaches that moral goodness and personal fulfillment in other goods do not always go together. In this world, indeed, moral goodness often leads to grief, and justice often is not done. Thus, life does not make complete sense if death simply ends it (see GS 18). Moreover, the specifically human activities of intellectual inquiry and free choice suggest that the human person is more than the body, which will suffer dissolution. So, death seems inappropriate for human persons, and it is hard for people to believe that they and everyone they love will simply cease to exist.[20] Thus, most human beings anticipate some sort of life after death and wish to know how to prepare for it. They think God could tell them.

3. Reasons for Believing That God Has Spoken

While not all religions claim that God personally reveals himself, the biblical religions (Judaism, Christianity, and Islam), which hold that the world was created from nothing, claim that God personally communicated with Abraham, Moses, the Hebrew prophets, and others. This claim must be considered in the light of the reasons, already outlined, for thinking a personal God exists, and for hoping and expecting that he might reveal himself. Such a consideration leads to several lines of reasoning which converge to support the claim of the biblical religions that God has spoken.

a) **The biblical religions offer a sound account of God.** Some religions think of the divine as impersonal, and some identify it with the world. Others propose a god or multitude of gods and goddesses so like humans that their existence, too, needs explaining. The biblical religions offer a description of God which adds to but does not contradict what reason can establish: that there is a creator who must be thought of as personal, but who is radically unlike a human person.

b) **The biblical religions offer a sound account of human persons.** Many religions propose a defective account of the human person. They have no place for freedom of choice, or they denigrate and try to set aside the bodily dimension of the human person. But the biblical religions say that God makes man and woman, who are complementary bodily persons, in his own image and likeness. This account is compatible with the facts that human persons are unities of body and spirit, are endowed with free choice, and, though irreducibly individual, can be fulfilled only in communion. For that reason, most who profess some form of biblical religion accept these facts about human persons, while most who hold a world view not grounded on divine revelation deny one or more, although all can be known by reason even without the light of faith.

c) **Biblical religion is true humanism.** Nonbiblical religions are genuine religions insofar as they propose ways of seeking communion with God (or "the gods"). Everything true and holy in each such religion is to be valued (see NA 2).

---

20. On the irreducibility of mind to physical entities and processes, see Stanley L. Jaki, *Brain, Mind and Computers* (New York: Herder and Herder, 1969); Mortimer J. Adler, *The Difference of Man and the Difference It Makes* (New York: Holt, Rinehart and Winston, 1967); idem, *Intellect: Mind Over Matter* (New York: Macmillan, 1990); Benedict M. Ashley, O.P., *Theologies of the Body: Humanist and Christian* (Braintree, Mass.: The Pope John Center, 1985), 307–32.

But the darker side cannot be ignored. Some religions make immoral demands (for example, by requiring human sacrifice), support unjust social structures (for example, by rationalizing a caste system), discourage people from struggling against evil (for example, by enjoining apathy), or aggravate human conflicts (for instance, by providing religious grounds for antagonism to certain kinds of people). While these evils also can infect the biblical religions as aberrations, none is characteristic of biblical religion. The writings contained in the Hebrew bible never debase the human person, but teach men and women their dignity and call them to integral fulfillment.

d) **The biblical religions forestall a problem of modern thought.** Various kinds of existentialism, seeking to preserve personal creativity, make meaning and value wholly subjective; Marxism and other evolutionist theories, locating the source of meaning and value in laws of nature and/or history, exclude free choice. In teaching that God is both the world's provident Lord and its transcendent cause, the biblical religions forestall this modern antithesis between moral objectivity and creative free choice. Against subjectivism, which easily turns into a nihilistic claim that life is meaningless, they teach that meaning and value are grounded in God's wisdom and love. Against determinism, they teach that humans can choose freely whether (and in some respects how) to cooperate with God. Moreover, since God is a transcendent cause, his creative causality can account for the reality of free choices without replacing them and explaining them away.[21]

e) **Biblical religion responds to human hopes and expectations.** In teaching that human persons must repent and oppose evil, but that evil can in the end be overcome only by God, the biblical religions take evil seriously and hold out hope for liberation from it. Genesis and Exodus illuminate the sinful human situation and make it clear that God is ready to intervene on behalf of those who call on him and trust him. Throughout Israel's history, God shows himself merciful and faithful. He also demands mercy and faithfulness of his people, and promises blessings on those who respond. The initial hope of God's people for liberation from their oppression in Egypt gradually develops into hope for complete salvation: a new and lasting covenant, open to all humankind, by which human misery will be healed, strife among peoples surmounted, and even death overcome.[22] Thus, the revelation claimed in common by all the biblical religions corresponds to the hopes and expectations, outlined above, that God might reveal himself.

f) **The biblical religions claim that God has worked miracles.** The biblical religions claim that miracles—"signs," "God's marvelous deeds"—point to God's self-revelation.[23] Some nonbelievers argue that the claim that God has worked miracles undercuts faith in revelation instead of supporting it, for they challenge

---

21. See *S.t.,* 1, q. 19, a. 8; q. 22, a. 2; John Paul II, General Audience (7 May 1986), 7–8, *Inseg.* 9.1 (1986) 1255–56, *OR,* 12 May 1986, 1.

22. On covenant, see *CMP,* 21.B–D; on the overcoming of strife, Is 9.4–7, 11.6–9; on the hope of life overcoming death, Dn 12.2; 2 Mc 7.9, 11, 23; 14.46.

23. On miracles see C. S. Lewis, *Miracles: A Preliminary Study* (New York: Macmillan, 1947); Robert D. Smith, *Comparative Miracles* (St. Louis: B. Herder, 1965); Louis Monden, S.J., *Signs and Wonders: A Study of the Miraculous Element in Religion* (New York: Desclée, 1966).

the very idea of a miracle, which they define as a violation of the laws of nature. However, miracles need not violate natural laws, for God can supplement natural causal factors without violating them.[24] Indeed, he must do that if he is to reveal himself, for, as creator of everything whatsoever, his personal communication will stand out from his constant creative work only if he brings about extraordinary occurrences to serve as signals. Miracles are such occurrences; they can be explained reasonably only as signs from God.[25]

g) **The claim that God has worked miracles is credible.** The Scriptures accepted by all the biblical religions in common narrate the history of a remarkable people who actually existed and had an impact on surrounding peoples. If all the miracles narrated in those Scriptures are regarded as unhistorical, what is left of that people's history becomes extremely difficult to understand and explain. Thus, the claim that God revealed himself and performed mighty deeds on behalf of that people is credible. Moreover, miracles still occur—for example, at Lourdes—while committed nonbelievers can only say: "Those strange events probably will be explained one day."[26]

4. Reasons for Believing that God Has Spoken in Jesus

The reasons for accepting the common claim of the biblical religions—that God has spoken—are reasons for preferring the Christian gospel to any view which simply rejects revelation. But the Christian gospel also proclaims that the self-revelation which God began by speaking to Abraham and others is completed in Jesus' life, teaching, death, and resurrection. There are several reasons for accepting this specifically Christian claim, too.

a) **Jesus fulfills the promises of the Old Testament.** Jesus' apostles and their associates, the source of the writings included in the New Testament, outline the case for this point, and later ancient Christian writers fully develop it. Considered by themselves, Jesus' life and teaching constitute a remarkably unified whole. Considered in the context of Old Testament expectations, they are a satisfying climax to the story of God's people; without this climax, the story seems truncated. Jesus fulfills the Old Testament by completing the development begun by the

---

24. Someone might object: God cannot supplement natural causal factors without making exceptions to, and so violating, laws of nature. This objection, however, assumes that the universe is a fully determined system. In the eighteenth and nineteenth centuries, many philosophers and scientists held that view, but hardly anyone does today. It would exclude free choice as well as miracles. Concerning it, see Joseph M. Boyle, Jr., Germain Grisez, and Olaf Tollefsen, *Free Choice: A Self-Referential Argument* (Notre Dame, Ind.: University of Notre Dame Press, 1976), 57–66.

25. A sound Catholic fundamental theology cannot claim that miracles are only incidental and dispensable: see DS 3034/1813; cf. LG 5; DV 4, 19; DH 11. Also see Grisez, *Beyond the New Theism*, 326–42; René Latourelle, *The Miracles of Jesus and the Theology of Miracles* (New York: Paulist Press, 1988).

26. On Lourdes see Patrick Marnham, *Lourdes: A Modern Pilgrimage* (New York: Coward, McCann and Geoghegan, 1981). Lourdes is cited here as an example not only because it is well known but because purported miracles there are investigated and carefully authenticated. Miracles also no doubt continue among all people who believe in genuine divine revelation—Jews, Christians separated from the Catholic Church, and Moslems.

Hebrew prophets, who looked toward the communion of all humankind in a new and lasting covenant with God.[27]

b) **The gospel responds very well to human needs and hopes.** More than any other ideology or religion—more than the other biblical religions—the Christian message of liberation and reconciliation realistically addresses the human situation and offers hope.[28] Jesus reveals God as the Father both of prodigal children and of a sinless Son who dies, seemingly forsaken, but is raised from the dead. The gospel proposes an ideal of a just and peaceful communion of all men and women, and provides confidence that evil need not triumph and can be overcome (see AG 8; GS 21–22, 41).

Insofar as overcoming evil depends on human effort, Jesus began the work, and the gospel tells those who believe in him to carry it on. In calling others to follow him, Jesus offers every human person, not some sort of demeaning way to avoid responsibility, but a noble role: an opportunity to live a worthwhile life and serve others. Therefore, more than any other ideology or religion, more than the other biblical religions, the Christian message of liberation and reconciliation realistically addresses the human situation and offers hope.

c) **The Church herself is a sign of the gospel's truth.** Confronted with the apostolic preaching of the gospel, a Jewish leader argued against trying to use force to suppress it: "If this plan or this undertaking is of human origin, it will fail; but if it is of God, you will not be able to overthrow them—in that case you may even be found fighting against God!" (Acts 5.38–39). That argument remains cogent for anyone who accepts the Old Testament and believes in God's providence. The argument set forth two possibilities; history shows which came to pass. For, even though the Christian Church throughout her history has suffered from tensions and divisions, she has remained recognizable as Jesus' body and bride.[29] The gospel's truth is manifest in the power by which missionaries' preaching and witness spread it through the world despite savage persecution. In her first few centuries, without using force and violence, the Church assimilated various cultures and transformed people's lives. Despite her sinful members, including some corrupt leaders and heretical theologians, the Church, unlike any merely human society, has survived two millennia in diverse historical situations (see DS 3013/1794). Moreover, unlike any nonbiblical religious community and the communities of the other biblical religions, the Church unites particular churches and congregations spread around the whole world and inculturated in many diverse forms. This remarkable unity is

---

27. This argument presupposes the reliability of the Gospels; for a scholarly defense of that presupposition, see René Latourelle, *Finding Jesus through the Gospels: History and Hermeneutics* (Staten Island, N.Y.: Alba House, 1979).

28. The development of the liberation theme in the Old and New Testaments is treated by the Congregation for the Doctrine of the Faith, *Instruction on Christian Freedom and Liberation,* 43–57, *AAS* 79 (1987) 571–78, *OR,* 14 Apr. 1986, 4–5; cf. Joseph Cardinal Ratzinger, "Freedom and Liberation: The Anthropological Vision of the Instruction 'Libertatis conscientia,' " *Communio* 14 (Spring 1987): 64–69.

29. See Pius X, *Editae saepe, AAS* 2 (1910) 361–62, *PE,* 176.7–8; Pius XI, *Ad salutem, AAS* 22 (1930) 211, *PE,* 207.15.

not sustained by any common political power or social interest, but only by the same faith, sacraments, and hope for the kingdom.

d) **The witness of Jesus' followers indicates the gospel's truth.** If what Christianity adds to the Old Testament were false, the way of Jesus would be contrary to God's revelation and to all true religion. Yet that way is at least as clearly a way of holiness as the way marked out in the Old Testament. For while the way of the Lord Jesus which the Church teaches is not easy and more people profess than practice it, many do live it splendidly, thus showing that Jesus lives in his Church and through her gives his followers the Holy Spirit's power. Even nonbelievers admire famous saints such as Francis of Assisi, Thomas More, Vincent de Paul, and Thérèse of Lisieux. But every Christian who renounces wealth, enjoyment, and status for a dedicated life of service makes Jesus' kingdom visible in this broken and suffering world.[30] And even those who fall short of putting belief into practice can bear witness to the truth of their faith by acknowledging themselves to be the sinners they are.

5. Why One Should Confess Christian Faith as a Catholic

Although God's revelation in Jesus is present wherever there is Christian faith, Christians are divided, and their disagreements extend to matters they consider essential to the integrity of Jesus' teaching and way of life. Yet Jesus promised to remain with his Church forever and to send his Spirit to teach her all truth (see Mt 28.20, Jn 16.12–15). So, despite the divisions among Christians, somewhere Christian faith must remain available in its integrity. The Catholic Church claims that she alone integrally preserves and hands on Christian faith. This claim is supported by the following line of thought.

a) **A divine gift ensures the gospel's integrity.** God's revelation in Jesus is given for people of all times and places, for all are called to share in the heavenly communion of divine and human persons which centers on Jesus. The fact that there is disagreement about essentials, nevertheless, makes it clear that particular Christians and groups of Christians can lose their hold on parts of the gospel while also confusing what belongs to it with what does not. In the absence of a special gift ensuring the gospel's integrity, revelation would become less and less available in the world. So, despite their differences, Christians agree that there is such a gift: the Lord Jesus does remain present in the Church, and the Spirit keeps intact Jesus' whole teaching and way of life (see Mt 28.18–20; Jn 14.15–21, 16.12–15). Where this gift is to be found is the issue on which Christians disagree.

b) **This divine gift belongs to the faith community as a whole.** Since particular Christians and groups of Christians can make mistakes in essential matters, the gospel can exist intact only in something common to all. Plainly, however, the whole of the gospel cannot be found in the bare minimum on which all Christians agree (the least common denominator of their faith), because they agree that they differ about essentials. It follows that the gospel in its integrity can exist in Jesus' Church

---

30. See René Latourelle, S.J., *Christ and the Church: Signs of Salvation,* trans. Sr. Dominic Parker (New York: Alba House, 1972). Taking and fulfilling the vows of poverty, chastity, and obedience thus is an important sign of the kingdom; see LG 44, PC 12–14.

as a whole only insofar as she is a whole by being a single, unified society. The divine gift which ensures the gospel's integrity must somehow belong to that social whole.

c) **This divine gift which belongs to Jesus' Church is not the Bible.** One reality which belongs to Jesus' Church as a social whole is the Bible (see DV 10). But although the Bible contains and presents what God wishes to reveal (see DV 11), it does not precisely contain revelation. For revelation is personal communication; as such, it is fully realized only in being received and remembered, appropriated and lived, and so cannot exist apart from the faith of believers.

Since the inspired books of the Bible include no table of contents for the whole Bible, Christians' common belief that certain books are inspired plainly has an extrabiblical ground in the Church's faith. Moreover, the idea that it is a matter of faith that all truths of faith are contained in the Bible is self-refuting, since there is no such claim in the Bible.

At first, God's revelation in Jesus lived in the minds and hearts of his disciples, and Jesus commissioned the apostles to preach it to others; only later did the faith of the early Church find expression in the writings which make up the New Testament.[31] Today, too, this revelation can exist only in the faith received and handed on by Christians, and the Bible can be interpreted rightly only in the light of their faith.

d) **This gift must be operative in official acts of the Church.** The integrity of the gospel is in the faith of Jesus' Church. Faith is present in each member of the Church, in each particular church, and in the universal Church as a whole. However, the faith of the Church as such can only be discerned in acts proper to the Church. And as the only acts proper to any human community are its official acts—those done by members of the community fulfilling their responsibilities as members—the Church's faith and teaching, as distinct from members' personal faith and pastors' personal teaching, can only be found in the Church's official acts, that is, in acts of faith and teaching proclaimed as expressing the faith of the Church as a social whole.

e) **It must be operative in new acts as well as in traditional ones.** Despite the divisions and separations from which Jesus' Church suffers, she still receives, proclaims, and hands on certain acts of faith which originated with the apostles and received normative expression in the early ecumenical councils. Protestants, Catholics, and Orthodox Christians believe their churches share by their official professions of faith in the living tradition of these acts of faith, and in doing so enjoy the gift of certain truth which the Lord Jesus wished his Church to enjoy.

These Christian churches are divided, however, not only from one another but internally, on matters they consider essential. Traditional professions of faith evidently cannot resolve the issues. To do so, therefore, new official acts are required, and no resolution can be accepted with faith unless it enjoys the gift which ensures the gospel's integrity. Thus, this gift must be operative, not only in

31. See DV 7, 18–19; Pontifical Biblical Commission, *Instruction Concerning the Historical Truth of the Gospels, AAS* 56 (1964) 712–18, *Catholic Biblical Quarterly* 26 (1964): 299–312.

traditional official acts of professing Christian faith, but in new acts of safeguarding and explaining that same faith, so that it will continue intact in its living tradition. The New Testament narrates one such official act, when the apostles and elders announced the resolution of a controversy: "It has seemed good to the Holy Spirit and to us" (Acts 15.28). Today, too, the divine gift which guarantees the gospel's integrity must be operative in official Church acts, including new ones resolving controversies.

f) **The Catholic Church exercises this divine gift.** Today, only the Catholic Church still claims to initiate such acts. She claims that the risen Lord Jesus authorized the apostles under Peter's leadership to preserve and spread the gospel to all humankind, that the pope and the other bishops in communion with him are the successors of Peter and the other apostles, that these successors still carry out Jesus' mandate to teach in his name—and, therefore, that in teaching officially on matters of faith and morals the pope and other bishops in communion with him can make decisive judgments with the infallibility which Jesus willed his Church to enjoy. (*Infallibility* in this context refers precisely to the gift which ensures the gospel's integrity; see *CMP*, 35.A and D.)

Of course, Christians who are not members of the Catholic Church deny that this argument establishes her unique claim, but nothing in Scripture falsifies it and some things in the New Testament support it.[32] Moreover, the divine gift which ensures the gospel's integrity must still operate somewhere, and it is only to be expected that those among whom it is operative should call attention to it. So, it is reasonable to accept the Catholic Church's claim, precisely because it is unique.

g) **This gift is operative only in certain teaching acts.** Only in certain of their acts do the pope and the bishops in communion with him teach in such a way that what they say is the teaching of the Catholic Church as a whole. Among these are acts by which they explicitly provide normative expressions of the Church's faith: solemn definitions on matters of faith or morals, either by the pope alone or by a council of the pope and the bishops in communion with him. But the day-to-day teaching of popes and bishops also can be recognized as the whole Catholic Church's teaching when three conditions are met: (i) the pope and the bishops in communion with him agree in the same position (ii) on some point of faith or morals and (iii) propose that position as divinely revealed, or as a truth which must be held as absolutely certain because it is required to safeguard and explain what is revealed.[33] The Catholic Church claims that the gift which ensures the gospel's integrity is operative in these two kinds of teaching acts: solemn definitions and other teaching acts which meet the three conditions (see DS 3011/1792; LG 25).

---

32. By studying the New Testament, Heinrich Schlier, an eminent Protestant Scripture scholar, was convinced of the soundness of the Catholic Church's claim; see his "A Brief Apologia," in *We Are Now Catholics,* ed. Karl Hardt, S.J., trans. Norman C. Reeves (Westminster, Md.: Newman Press, 1959), 187–215.

33. On these conditions, see John C. Ford, S.J., and Germain Grisez, "Contraception and the Infallibility of the Ordinary Magisterium," *Theological Studies* 39 (1978): 263–77; for a defense of this interpretation of LG 25: Germain Grisez, "Infallibility and Specific Moral Norms: A Review Discussion," *Thomist* 49 (1985): 248-87.

h) Christian faith is to be found intact in the Catholic Church. Since the divine gift which ensures the gospel's integrity is operative in the Catholic Church's official teaching acts, Christian faith is to be found whole and intact in the Catholic Church's faith. Thus, the Catholic Church holds, as it were in trust for every Christian and for all humankind, a precious principle of Christian communion: the integral deposit of faith, the whole revelation which God entrusted to Jesus, the complete Christian gospel (see 2 Tm 1.13–14; cf. UR 6; DV 10; GS 33, 62). Since that gospel is precisely what each Catholic as a Christian believes, Catholics reasonably accept the Catholic Church's faith as the norm of their personal faith.

It might be objected that the Church herself teaches that the supreme rule of faith is constituted by the inspired Scriptures together with sacred tradition (see DV 21). Does it not therefore follow that Scripture and tradition, not the Church's faith, should be accepted as the norm of one's personal faith? Tradition, however, *is* the Church's faith considered insofar as the Church exists throughout the generations, while Scripture, a privileged expression of that same faith, can be rightly understood only in the light of tradition (see DV 7–9).[34]

i) Christians who are not Catholics enjoy the gift of faith. God's revelation in Jesus also is present, although not integrally, in the faith of members of Christian churches and communions separated from the Catholic Church. Much else which enlivens and builds up Jesus' Church can also be found outside the Catholic Church's visible boundaries. The divisions among Christians are not total, and all who believe in Jesus and are properly baptized are truly Christians, living in a certain real, though imperfect, communion with the Catholic Church (see UR 3).[35]

34. The Catholic Church herself bears witness to the divine authority of the Scriptures: "Therefore, since everything asserted by the inspired authors or sacred writers must be held to be asserted by the Holy Spirit, we must acknowledge that the books of Scripture teach truth firmly, faithfully, and without error—truth which God for the sake of our salvation wished to consign to the sacred writings [note omitted]" (DV 11). The Latin of DV 11 does not require that the phrase, "truth which . . .," be taken as restricting the truths God consigns to Scripture to some subset of the propositions asserted by the sacred writers, and the records of the conciliar commission responsible for *Dei Verbum* (see *CMP*, 35, n. 17) exclude the restrictive interpretation.

35. Because the Church is the unique new covenant community, outside her there is no salvation, as Lateran IV solemnly teaches: "There is but one universal Church of the faithful outside which no one at all is saved" (DS 802/430). Vatican II reaffirms this definitive teaching (see LG 14, AG 7). But it must be rightly understood. Already in 1863, Pius IX, while absolutely rejecting indifferentism, teaches (as something taken for granted by both himself and the bishops) that those who are ready to submit to God but are separated from the true faith and Catholic unity by invincible ignorance can receive God's grace, live uprightly, and be saved (see *Quanto conficiamur moerore, Pii IX Pontificis maximi acta,* 3.1 [Rome: 1868], 612–14 [DS 2865–67/1677]; *PE,* 60.6–8). Also, in a 1949 decree approved by Pius XII, the Holy Office rejected a more restrictive interpretation (see DS 3866–73/—). What is new in Vatican II's teaching is the clarification that, although the one and only Church *subsists* in the Catholic Church (see LG 8, UR 4, DH 1), she also *embraces* in various ways all who "sincerely seek God and, moved by grace, strive by their deeds to do his will as it is known to them through the dictates of conscience [note omitted]" (LG 16; cf. GS 22). (On the meaning of Vatican II's "subsists in," see James T. O'Connor, "The Church of Christ and the Catholic Church," in *Faith and the Sources of Faith: Proceedings of the Sixth Convention of the Fellowship of Catholic Scholars,* ed. Paul L. Williams [Scranton, Pa.: Northeast Books, 1985], 41–57.) Thus, it remains true that there is no salvation outside the Church, but it is now recognized that those who are in good faith in not wishing to be

j) The Catholic Church admittedly is not perfect. It might be objected: Catholics have contributed to the divisions in Jesus' body, and the Catholic Church herself, as a human institution, must always be reformed, due to deficiencies not only in moral conduct and Church discipline but even in some formulations of teaching. All this is true (see UR 6). But deficiencies in moral conduct and Church discipline do not detract from the integrity of faith, while even deficiencies in the formulation of teaching either do not constitute erroneous teaching or, if they do, are present only in acts other than those described above (in g). The Catholic Church experiences human weakness and imperfection, but her faith remains whole because of the divine gift which ensures it.

k) The Catholic Church is not trying to usurp divine prerogatives. The pope and the bishops in communion with him believe that Jesus commissioned them to serve God's word by applying the rule of faith—namely, Scripture and tradition— and that he promised (and so surely provides) everything they need to carry out this service. They do not claim that the Church as a merely human institution possesses the gift which ensures the gospel's integrity, as if she had it under her control, but that the divine gift is operative in the Church, because she is enlivened and taught by the Holy Spirit, whom the Father and the Lord Jesus sent for this very purpose.

Nor do they claim that the divine gift belongs to them as private individuals or that it is operative in all their acts. Rather, they claim that when their official acts (under the specified conditions) manifest the Church's faith, those acts are guaranteed by the infallibility with which Jesus willed his Church to be endowed (see DS 3074/1839; LG 12, 25; DV 8).[36] In other words, the pope and the bishops in communion with him claim that when they do precisely what Jesus commissioned them to do, then they act in cooperation with him, so that "whoever hears them, hears Christ" (LG 20); they hold that such a cooperative act has the more-than-human characteristic of infallibility, not because it is theirs but because it also and at the same time is Jesus'.

Question D: What about the "Logical" Case against Faith?

Not only many nonbelievers but even some believers think there are no rational grounds for believing: the act of faith can only be a nonrational leap. Often such people assume that the so-called logical case against faith is overwhelming. If this view were sound, the act of faith, assuming it involves a free self-commitment, would not be a reasonable choice, and so would be morally irresponsible.[37]

---

inside the Catholic Church are not entirely outside her (see UR 3; *CMP,* 30.2). In view of every Christian's real communion with the Catholic Church, two propositions in the preceding argument which render it paradoxical actually are compatible: (i) the gift of infallibility which ensures the gospel's integrity belongs to Jesus' Church as a social whole, and (ii) only the Catholic Church's pastoral leaders claim to be able to initiate official teaching acts which can resolve controversies.

36. See *The Gift of Infallibility: The Official Relatio on Infallibility of Bishop Vincent Gasser at Vatican Council I,* trans. James T. O'Connor, with commentary and a theological synthesis on infallibility (Boston: St. Paul Editions, 1986).

37. Catholic teaching, definitively summed up by Vatican I, is that the assent of faith is free, and that although the truth of the mysteries of faith is not evident to natural reason, the evidences

The logical case against faith has four parts. (1) Faith is simply absurd, because it includes doctrines which are self-contradictory (for example, that God is three and one) or at odds with the facts (for example, that God is all-knowing, all-loving, and all-powerful, despite the plain fact of evil in the world). (2) Even if faith is not absurd, it is unreasonable, because it involves absolute conviction about matters on which opinions differ. (3) Even if it once was reasonable to believe, faith is now outmoded by modern science. (4) Although, despite everything, people still believe, that can be explained psychologically: faith is an illusion which human beings naturally develop to ease their anxieties and/or to control others.

1. Faith Is Not Absurd

Faith is mysterious but not absurd. Only if they are oversimplified do Christian doctrines seem self-contradictory or at odds with obvious facts.

a) God's inner reality is beyond human understanding. One thinks rightly about God only by keeping in mind that, as the ultimate source of everything else, he is quite unlike the world and the things human beings can comprehend, which only more or less share in reality, meaning, and value (see C.1.b, above). One can know what God is not, and how other realities are related to him, but one cannot know what he is in himself (see *S.c.g.*, 1.30). Thus, great theologians such as Augustine and Thomas Aquinas have been able to defend the mysteries of faith against the charge that they are self-contradictory.

For example, in saying that God is both "one" and "three," the doctrine of the Trinity does not use those words in a way which would imply the absurd statement that one equals three. Rather, while Christians, like Jews and Moslems, believe there is only one divine being (and reject the claims for all other gods), they also believe that this unique God, whose unity is unlike any which human beings comprehend, is three persons, whose personhood and distinction also surpass human understanding. This is mysterious, not absurd.[38]

b) God's ways cannot be judged by human standards. God's attributes are beyond human understanding. Most of his plan of creation and redemption is hidden even from believers (see Jb 38.1–42.6; cf. Rom 11.33–36). Therefore, it misses the point to try to judge his ways by applying human standards to what one thinks he is doing. For example, evil in the world seems inconsistent with what one believes about God only if it is assumed that an all-knowing, all-loving, and all-powerful God ought to eliminate evil but fails to do so. A Christian need not grant this assumption.[39] As with the problem of evil, so in other cases, Christian

---

of credibility are adequate to provide good reasons for believing: DS 3008–14/1789–94, 3017/ 1797, 3033/1812, 3035/1814. Some Protestants who think of faith as a nonrational leap regard it, not as a free human act, but as the effect of grace alone, and so do not see why it would be unreasonable and irresponsible to believe if the logical case against faith were overwhelming.

38. See Grisez, *Beyond the New Theism*, 370–73.

39. An excellent theological treatment of evil: Charles Journet, *The Meaning of Evil*, trans. Michael Barry (New York: P. J. Kenedy and Sons, 1963). Also: Jacques Maritain, *God and the Permission of Evil*, trans. Joseph W. Evans (Milwaukee: Bruce, 1966). A useful work with many fine insights and arguments, although not acceptable in every respect: Alvin Plantinga, *God, Freedom, and Evil* (New York: Harper and Row, 1974), 7–64.

doctrines seem at odds with the facts only on arguable assumptions, which believers need not grant. (The challenge to faith posed by the suffering of the innocent will be treated more fully in E.6.)

2. Faith Is Not Unreasonable

The second challenge to faith is based on a dilemma: If something is obvious or conclusively demonstrated, there is no need for faith; if it is neither obvious nor shown to be true, it is unreasonable to take it on faith. Those who pose this challenge conclude that Christian faith is unreasonable, because it requires absolute conviction about matters which are neither evident nor demonstrable beyond doubt, as can be seen, they argue, from the fact that many well-informed and educated people are unbelievers.[40] The response is that it is reasonable to believe God's self-revelation, and that Christian experience confirms faith.

a) **It can be reasonable to take something on faith as sure.** When others bear witness to something which they are in a position to know, one is right to be convinced of the truth of what they say, provided one has reasons to trust them and no good reason not to. Of course, there are limits to how sure one can be on this basis, for normally others cannot be trusted absolutely and can be mistaken. But if they were absolutely trustworthy and bore witness about matters concerning which they could not be mistaken, it would be entirely reasonable to believe their statements with absolute conviction.

b) **God cannot be mistaken about the matters he reveals.** Christian faith is quite different from belief in news reporters or experts, who provide impersonal information and judgments on matters of opinion. It is more like one's belief in other human persons or groups of persons who invite one to enter personal relationships. To accept others, one must believe what they say about their identity, intentions, and promises—matters about which they know directly and cannot be mistaken. But the content of Christian faith is God's invitation to communion, his plan for common life, and his promise of faithful cooperation with those who accept the invitation and agree to live according to the plan. God cannot be mistaken about these matters.

c) **God makes himself known as the source of faith.** The absolute certitude of faith is a fact requiring explanation. This certitude is a datum of experience of which each believer is immediately aware. Faith itself provides the explanation: Scripture and the Church's teaching make it clear that special divine action inspires and assists faith in those who come to believe (see Mt 16.17; Jn 6.44, 15.26; Rom 8.14–16; DS 3008/1789; DV 5). Hence, while the various truths of faith are mediated by others' testimony, faith's unique certitude shows that belief in those truths is immediately warranted by divine authority. If that were not so, faith would

---

40. Many philosophers who argue along these lines assume that if belief is not passively determined by evidence, it must be arbitrary. That dichotomy omits the real situation: belief is a moral act by which one more or less responsibly evaluates reasons and evidence which support but do not determine one's assent. See M. Jamie Ferreira, "Newman and the 'Ethics of Belief'," *Religious Studies* 19 (1983): 361–73; Patrick Lee, "Reasons and Religious Belief," *Faith and Philosophy* 6 (1989): 19–34.

be impossible, because for divine faith it is "necessary that revealed truths be believed on the authority of God who reveals them" (DS 3032/1811).[41]

d) **God is completely trustworthy.** Since God, who created everything, can do whatever he wills, plainly he can keep his promises. Moreover, God proved his love by revealing himself through Jesus' life, death, and resurrection. Assured of this love, believers also are sure that God will not betray them but will keep his promises (see 1 Cor 1.9, 1 Thes 5.24). Therefore, unlike human persons, God is completely trustworthy (see Dt 32.4; Ps 33.4, 145.13).

e) **Christian experience confirms faith.** In committing oneself to the faith, becoming a member of the Church, and so entering into friendship with Jesus as man, and through him into friendship with God, one experiences the real intimacy faith establishes. One's faith is confirmed by this experience, and one tastes something of what led Paul to exclaim: "I regard everything as loss because of the surpassing value of knowing Christ Jesus my Lord" (Phil 3.8). Thus, the absolute certitude of one's Catholic faith is analogous to that of a happily married woman in the sincerity of her husband's "I love you." But while any merely human partner can be untrue, Jesus cannot (see 2 Tm 2.11–13).

3. Faith Is Not Outmoded by Modern Science

Faith is not science, but it is not in conflict with science.[42] Any claim that the legitimate ways of reaching reality are limited to those called "science" is self-defeating, since that claim cannot be established by any science. Moreover, exclusive claims for scientific knowledge conflict with the reality of personal knowledge: one knows one's friends and is known by them in a way transcending what any scientist knows.

a) **Faith is not about the same thing as the natural sciences.** Modern physics, chemistry, biology, and so on do not deal with the same subject matter as faith, and so their methods and findings can neither conflict with faith nor replace (and so outmode) it. It is a sign of the harmony between faith and science that some able scientists are devout believers.

b) **History and archaeology have not undermined faith.** Faith bears on certain definite past states of affairs—for example, the exodus of the Jews from Egypt and Jesus' words and deeds—whose reality cannot be established by studies which prescind from the tradition of faith. Still, it is logically possible for historical and archaeological studies to make discoveries which would tend to undermine faith. But in fact such studies have not established anything inconsistent with the teachings of faith.[43]

41. According to Guy de Broglie, S.J., *Pour une théorie rationnelle de l'acte de foi*, 2éme partie (Paris: Institut Catholique, 1955), 166–70, the immediacy of faith is taught by St. Thomas and his classic followers. See also: Benoît Duroux, *La psychologie de la foi chez s. Thomas d'Aquin* (Tournai, Belgium: Desclée, 1963). A review of numerous theological accounts of the supernatural motive of Christian faith: Roger Aubert, *Le problème de l'acte de foi: Données traditionnelles et résultats des controverses récentes* (Louvain: E. Warny, 1945), 720–36.

42. See Stanley L. Jaki, *The Road of Science and the Ways to God* (Chicago: University of Chicago Press, 1978); Ashley, *Theologies of the Body*, 19–50, 253–344.

43. Some might argue that Scripture studies using the historical-critical method do undermine Christian faith. But they do so only insofar as they beg the question by proceeding from

Moreover, even if there were evidence which seemed to tell against some truth of faith, the argument never could be decisive. For instance, if someone claimed to have found Jesus' tomb and to have identified his remains, the argument for the claim necessarily would involve questionable assumptions going beyond the evidence.

c) **Secular culture which does conflict with faith is not science.** Of course, the social sciences, psychology, history, the humanistic disciplines, and the science and culture communicated through the mass media challenge Christian faith just insofar as they presuppose an alternative world view.[44] To that extent, however, they are not entirely detached scholarship, objective scientific inquiry, or reliable channels of information. Nonbelievers in the secular academic world and the media may be honest, but they naturally interpret everything in the light of some form of secular humanism which they apply to every problem society confronts.

d) **In particular, universal evolutionism is not science.** Holding that all reality undergoes evolutionary development, certain ideologies naturally deny those Christian doctrines which involve unchanging truths. However, such evolutionist theories also conflict with one another and cannot settle their conflicting claims by any scientific procedure. In fact, universal evolutionism plainly is philosophy, not science. Genuinely scientific theories are constituted of logically universal statements, which refer to some limited set of data and explain observed changes by the regular working of constant factors distinct from those data. But universal evolutionism tries to explain the whole of nature and history, not some limited set of data, and it denies that there are constant explanatory factors outside this subject matter.

4. Faith Is Not an Illusion Which Psychology Can Dispel

Christian faith does have an emotional appeal: it eases anxieties aroused by moral guilt and the prospect of death. But why must beliefs which answer to psychological needs be untrue? Psychological theories which try to explain faith as an illusion merely assume that what Christians believe is unreal. While nonbelievers think the anxieties eased by faith are mere symptoms of underlying psychological problems, Christians believe that sin and death should concern any sane person and that faith offers the only real hope of surmounting these evils.[45]

---

philosophical and theological assumptions which themselves have not been proved and which believers need not accept. See Joseph Cardinal Ratzinger, "Biblical Interpretation in Crisis: On the Question of the Foundations and Approaches of Exegesis Today," *This World*, no. 22 (Summer 1988): 3–19; Gerhard Maier, *The End of the Historical-Critical Method*, trans. Edwin W. Leverenz and Rudolph F. Norden (St. Louis: Concordia, 1977); Mary Ford, "Seeing, but Not Perceiving: Crisis and Context in Biblical Studies," *St. Vladimir's Theological Quarterly* 35 (1991): 107–25.

44. Against the notion that the social sciences and psychology somehow show that the word *God* cannot refer to a reality: John Bowker, *The Sense of God: Sociological, Anthropological and Psychological Approaches to the Origin of the Sense of God* (Oxford: Oxford University Press, 1973).

45. On excesses and abuses of psychology: Paul C. Vitz, *Psychology as Religion: The Cult of Self-Worship* (Grand Rapids, Mich.: William B. Eerdmans, 1977); William Kirk Kilpatrick, *Psychological Seduction: The Failure of Modern Psychology* (Nashville, Tenn.: Thomas Nelson, 1983).

Moreover, psychological theories which try to explain away faith as an instrument of social control can themselves be explained psychologically. For instance, some proponents of such theories had unfortunate childhood experiences with authority figures who behaved badly in the name of religion. Also, sinners naturally want to evade responsibility, and in doing so they deny as much of reality as necessary until, finally, "Fools say in their hearts, 'There is no God' " (Ps 14.1).

Question E: What about the Practical Challenges to Faith?

Besides the so-called logical case against faith, several challenges of a practical sort test or even weaken the faith of many Christians. Some of the more important are worth answering briefly here. (1) Christian teaching is correct in saying that this world is miserable, but in two thousand years Christianity has failed to make it much better. (2) Throughout modern times, Christianity has been losing ground to unbelief; perhaps the faith is a lost cause. (3) Faith's claim to have the absolute truth is closed-minded and leads to fanaticism and intolerance. (4) Faith always has led to infringements on people's freedom and still does. (5) Faith opposes worldly goods and enjoyments, and its otherworldliness distracts believers from the serious business of this life. (6) If evil in the world does not argue logically against faith, still the extent of human suffering, and especially the suffering of the innocent, suggests that God is not both loving and all-powerful.

If the role God gives his creatures in salvation history is minimized, as some forms of Protestantism have done and some Catholics do today, these practical challenges to faith are felt to be more threatening. Hence, the response must focus on the work people must do for their own salvation. That such work must be done does not imply, as some fear, that people can save themselves without grace or God's mercy; rather, it implies that God's mercy is so great that he wishes his gifts also to be the merits of those he saves (see DS 1548/810).

1. The Gospel Has Not Failed

Because secular humanism, both in its western liberal and its Marxist forms, does promise earthly freedom, prosperity, and peace, it is fairly judged on its failure to deliver. But the gospel does not promise to transform this world into a paradise. Although some foretaste of the blessings faith promises is given to believers, this life is primarily an opportunity for them to work out their salvation and to prepare material for Jesus' heavenly kingdom, whose completion is not of this world (see Jn 18.36; cf. 1 Cor 7.31, 1 Jn 2.15–17). Faith cannot be criticized for failing to deliver on a promise it never made.

Moreover, the gospel has borne much good fruit, as even fair-minded nonbelievers acknowledge, and no one can say what the world would be like today had Christian faith not been at work in it for two millennia.

2. The Gospel Is Not a Lost Cause

In the more developed and wealthy parts of the world, Christianity has lost ground during modern times to various forms of nonbelieving humanism. The question is: Why?

a) **Internal divisions which weakened Christianity can be overcome.** Divisions between the churches in the east and in the west, and the even deeper divisions between the churches of the Reformation and the Catholic Church, greatly weakened Christian missionary activity and led to fratricidal conflicts, including, though not exclusively, those of the European religious wars. Revulsion against these conflicts and the hope to end them played a large role in the development of nonbelieving humanism with its effort to separate everything of social and political importance from religion and make religious faith into a strictly private affair.

Today, however, the conflicts among Christians are no longer so sharp and bitter as they once were. Virtually all Christians today believe that their divisions are unacceptable and most are working to overcome them. While this ecumenical effort has begun slowly and will take time to bear its full fruit, it already has mitigated some of the bad effects of division, and promises to strengthen the social impact of Christian faith and lessen its vulnerability to nonbelief.

b) **Social and cultural transformation challenges faith.** The greatest loss, occurring during the nineteenth and twentieth centuries, accompanied the shift from a rural-agricultural to an urban-industrial social and cultural framework for individual and family life. Increased opportunities in urban-industrial life generate fresh temptations to seek fulfillment in possessions, self-indulgence, and status.

Even more important: the older, more stable framework in many ways supported Christian faith and life, whereas the newer, more mobile framework removes old supports and requires people to make many more major choices in organizing their lives. Unless all one's other major commitments are consciously made in order to live out one's faith, it is easily reduced to a single isolated interest among many, and the other interests, cultivated without reference to faith, eventually choke it out (see *CMP*, 28.D).[46]

c) **While the Catholic Church has not yet fully met this challenge, it can.** Until Vatican II, the Church's pastoral work in some ways failed to adapt to the changed situation. Recalling the truth that lay people, no less than priests and religious, make up the Church, the Council on this basis provides a fresh program for the Church's work. According to this program, all the Christian faithful are called to holiness by a personal vocation to dedicate every part of their lives—family, school, work, citizenship, leisure—to the Lord Jesus: to his gospel and to works of love (see LG 39–42, AA 2–8; *CMP*, 31.C–E). If this program is carried out with creativity and apostolic energy, the modern trend toward unbelief can be reversed.

d) **Despite appearances, secular humanism will not defeat Christianity.** The gospel appears to be losing ground to secular humanism. However, before the gospel was preached around the world, no one hoped for a world in which everyone would enjoy freedom, peace, and prosperity. It was Christian faith that first taught

---

46. See John Paul II, Homily at Mass at Osnabrück (Germany), 3, *AAS* 73 (1981) 67, *OR*, 1 Dec. 1980, 5: "Very few of us can still let ourselves be carried along today in the practice of faith simply by an environment of deep faith. We must rather decide consciously to want to be practising Christians, and to have the courage to distinguish ourselves, if necessary, from our environment. The premise for such a decided testimony of Christian life is to perceive and grasp faith as a precious chance of life, which transcends the interpretations and praxis of the environment."

humankind to hope for human fulfillment in a perfect community. The appeal of various forms of secular humanism is parasitic on this Christian vision. But they have not fulfilled, and simply cannot fulfill, the hope which Christian faith aroused. Apart from the residue of the gospel that they retain, these currently prevalent forms of humanism are impressive only because of their political, social, economic, and cultural power. Over the last two millennia, however, many empires and world views have enjoyed great power—until they faded away.

In different ways, and sometimes with violent persecution, the various forms of secular humanism attack the gospel, yet while Christianity has lost ground in the more developed and wealthy countries, it is becoming stronger in some parts of the world, and is nowhere dying out. But secular humanism is a house radically divided against itself (see G.1, below). Sooner or later, that house will fall, the modern age will end, and the next age will offer a fresh field for the seed of faith.[47]

3. Faith Is Not Closed-minded

Every morally upright commitment is important, as is every truth, and Christian faith is the most important commitment to the most important truth of all. In making an act of faith in Jesus and living according to it, one does not close one's mind but opens it to a whole dimension of reality which people without faith cannot enter. Yet faith does not bar believers from any dimension of reality that is accessible to nonbelievers.

a) **Christians, like others, sometimes are closed-minded.** Someone of weak faith is likely to be anxious, to lack confidence that the Holy Spirit will protect faith and continue to make it available despite every challenge. Moreover, if one's faith depends heavily on self-centered motives, elements of truth and goodness outside the Church are likely to appear as threats to be rejected rather than goods to be valued, welcomed, refined, nurtured, and integrated with one's faith to develop and perfect it. But such nervousness and narrowness are defects in one's personal faith rather than characteristics of Christian faith itself.

b) **Relativism and subjectivism are not the same thing as tolerance.** Some consider Christian faith intolerant simply because Christians affirm dogmas and hold objective moral norms rather than acquiescing in religious indifferentism and moral subjectivism. But every world view and way of life logically excludes alternatives. Relativists and subjectivists also have a definite world view and way of life; they too reject every position incompatible with their own. True tolerance is not indifferentism and subjectivism, but respect for those who hold another world view and way of life. Tolerance is readiness to presume good will in others and to put up with their conscientious behavior insofar as one's own conscience permits.[48]

c) **Relativism and subjectivism also can be closed-minded.** It is quite possible to be closed-minded in holding that one religion is as good as another and that whatever people think right actually is right for them. Relativists and subjectivists

---

47. See Rodger Charles, S.J., *The Church and the World,* Theology Today, 43 (Notre Dame, Ind.: Fides, 1973).

48. See Arthur Vermeersch, S.J., *Tolerance,* trans. W. Humphrey Page (New York: Benziger Brothers, 1913).

constantly talk about civility and moderation, but they are not immune from intolerance and fanaticism. Indeed, they are especially tempted to be arbitrary and self-righteous, precisely because they acknowledge neither a higher reality to which all realistic people must submit nor an objective moral standard by which all conscientious people must criticize themselves. Unable to call on their opponents to submit to principles which any reasonable person should accept (their views exclude such principles), relativists and subjectivists inevitably will be tempted to use nonrational methods—manipulation and even suppression—in order to prevail.

4. Faith Does Not Infringe on Freedom

Far from limiting freedom, faith in Jesus makes his disciples free (see Jn 8.31–36). With faith, individuals can escape from slavery to sin and to death's terror, and men and women together can escape mutual exploitation and enter into authentic, faithful communion. No longer living in conflict with reality and true fulfillment, Christians, if they are faithful, enjoy the freedom of the children of God (see Rom 8.21).

a) **Christians sometimes infringe on freedom.** Sometimes, though more in times past than today, Christians have resorted to unjust coercion and violated others' just liberty in the name of the gospel. Such abuses are at odds with Jesus' teaching and example, and are of no help in spreading and sustaining faith, for, as Vatican II teaches: "The truth cannot impose itself except by virtue of its own truth, as it makes its entrance into the mind at once gently and with power" (DH 1).

b) **Faith involves responsibilities, but imposes nothing on believers.** Like any way of life, the following of Jesus does limit one's freedom to do as one otherwise might. Part of this limitation concerns one's responsibility as a member of the Church to abide by her laws and obey her pastors. Nevertheless, as a Christian one may serve and pursue every human good, and one's responsibilities require of one little more than moral uprightness itself requires. As for any burdens involved in the authentic practice of faith, they are not impositions, for nobody can force anyone truly to keep the faith and remain within the Church's communion.

c) **The Catholic Church's authority does not impair freedom.** Someone who makes the commitment of Catholic faith and undertakes to live as a member of the Church is inconsistent in wishing to pick and choose among doctrines, moral teachings, and elements of Church order. In certain cases, the Church's pastors must call attention to such inconsistency. In doing so, they employ no coercion and impair nobody's religious freedom. Those disciplined remain free to speak and act as they think right, but they cannot truthfully continue to say what is no longer so, for example, that their opinions are in no way censurable or that they are Catholic theologians in good standing.

People who object to this actually are claiming for their particular group the right and power to overrule the Church's pastoral leaders on what the Church is to teach, how she is to worship, and so on. But the freedom of other members of the Church to be Catholics would be infringed if the Church's pastoral leaders were overruled.

5. Faith Calls for the Service of Human Goods in This World

Admittedly, an important strand of Christian theology has belittled many human goods. However, Christian faith serves not only the goods of religion and truth but the other goods as well. Moreover, it reinforces rather than weakens the responsibilities of Christians toward human goods in this world, inasmuch as faith and the hope flowing from it endow this life with eternal significance (see GS 34, 38–39).[49] Avoiding both fatalism and groundless optimism, Christian faith is realistic about what can be achieved in this world.

a) **Some theologies disparaged this-worldly goods.** Sometimes what really does belong to human persons and their fulfillment was confused with sin and so was mistakenly opposed. Moreover, a one-sided mysticism and exaggerated otherworldliness, drawn from Greek philosophy, led some Christians to view life in this world as nothing but a means for reaching heaven (see *CMP*, 34.A). Thus, Christian history includes strands of thought and feeling which slighted and sometimes even despised nature, this world, and the body, as if denigrating them were necessary to appreciate grace, heaven, and spiritual reality. In fact, though, the gospel teaches that the Word became flesh and will forever remain bodily, that every human good is to be redeemed and sanctified, and that service to human goods in this world is both the fruit of Christian love of neighbor and the material of the heavenly kingdom (see *CMP*, 34.E–G).

b) **Christian moral teaching promotes human goods.** Although the Christian way of life excludes that mutilated fulfillment in goods which cannot be attained without sin, this is for the sake of integral fulfillment in human goods, the complete realization of human dignity. For example, Christian morality excludes genital acts apart from marital intercourse in order to protect and foster several human goods: human life in its beginnings, faithful marital communion, the religious significance of the self-gift found in both virtuous sexual activity and abstinence for the kingdom's sake, and the integration of personality by which all the other goods related to sexuality can be harmoniously realized (see 9.E.6, below). Against the disintegrating effects of sin, Christianity provides the light and spiritual power to build up faithful persons and stable social bonds, especially those of the family, which are essential for individual fulfillment and social well-being.

c) **Faith is realistic about the pursuit of human goods.** Some religions outside the monotheistic tradition were fatalistic or quite pessimistic about the possibility of overcoming evils and realizing human goods, whether through human activity in this world or otherwise. The various forms of secular humanism, by contrast, are imbued with groundless optimism. They put too much trust in unaided human power to transform the world into an ideally good and happy community.[50] Christian faith avoids both pessimism and optimism; it is realistic and hopeful. With God's help, many evils can be overcome and many goods achieved even in this

---

49. Also see John XXIII, *Mater et magistra, AAS* 53 (1961) 460–61, *PE,* 267.254–57.

50. Paul VI, Christmas Message (1968), *AAS* 61 (1969) 54, *OR,* 26 Dec. 1968, 1, underlines the emptiness of contemporary aspirations: "We live in an era of hope. It is, however, a hope in the kingdom of this earth, a hope in human self-sufficiency."

world. But this world never will be an ideal community because, despite God's redemptive work in Jesus, sin and its consequences persist.[51]

6. Human Suffering Should Not Undermine a Christian's Faith

Suffering is an enigmatic fact which challenges every world view.[52] It is especially difficult to see any meaning or purpose in the suffering, sometimes excruciating and awful, of small children. And when one personally suffers or those one loves do, one wants to know why. But even more, one wants some *way* of dealing with suffering which holds out hope, based not on illusion but on *truth,* that a new and better *life* awaits one after death.

Jesus himself—the *way,* the *truth,* and the *life*—is the real Christian response to suffering. While his death and resurrection do not explain each particular instance, they do make it clear that God allows suffering for the sake of a great good, that the way to deal with suffering is to accept it with a love which overcomes hatred and sin, and that God responds to such love by making suffering end not in death but in new and perfect life.[53]

a) **Although evil is real, God is not responsible for it.** According to some world views, evil is not objectively real, but only relative and apparent. This conflicts with the fact that people cannot simply wish away sin and death or learn to see through them. According to other world views, evil is not only real, but something positive, real in the same way as good, and opposed to it. This conflicts with the fact that evil never is found by itself, but always in and with a good on which it is parasitical.

According to Christian faith, God made everything good, and evil arises only from a defect or mutilation in some thing (see *CMP,* 5.A). While that thing, as a positive reality, depends on God as its ultimate cause, a defect or mutilation does not need an ultimate cause in the same way. By misusing their freedom, created persons introduce evil into God's good creation. God permits this, because he can bring good out of evil, and because the freedom which created persons abuse is necessary for them really to love God and one another.

b) **Suffering in itself is not evil, but an experience of evil.** To suffer is to be aware of some particular evil, whether in oneself or in others, as repugnant. Suffering takes many forms, from the sensation of pain which arises from damage

---

51. John Paul II, Address to Congress on "Wisdom of the Cross Today", 2, *Inseg.* 7.1 (1984) 271, *OR,* 12 Mar. 1984, 3, speaks of Jesus' redemptive work and adds: "This is the foundation of the only 'humanism' possible, because it rejects both the pessimism of every Manichean direction, and the optimism of every immanentistic conception, primarily responsible for the tragedies of the modern world."

52. See John Bowker, *Problems of Suffering in Religions of the World* (Cambridge: Cambridge University Press, 1970).

53. On the Christian response to suffering as a practical challenge to faith, see John Paul II, *Salvifici doloris, AAS* 76 (1984) 201–50, *OR,* 20 Feb. 1984, 1–9. A valuable study clarifying Christian tradition on suffering: James Walsh, S.J., and P. G. Walsh, *Divine Providence and Human Suffering,* Message of the Fathers of the Church, 17 (Wilmington, Del.: Michael Glazier, 1985). Also see: C. S. Lewis, *The Problem of Pain* (New York: Macmillan, 1962); Peter Kreeft, *Making Sense out of Suffering* (Ann Arbor, Mich.: Servant Books, 1986); Russell Shaw, *Does Suffering Make Sense?* (Huntington, Ind.: Our Sunday Visitor Publishing Division, 1987).

to the body, through the emotion of grief over the loss of a loved one, to righteous indignation regarding unjust oppression. Insofar as suffering involves accurate knowledge and an appropriate reaction to some real state of affairs, it is not evil, which is a privation, but a positive reality, and in itself good. Suffering generally also serves the important function of motivating people, as pain motivates animals, to escape evil and/or struggle to overcome it.[54] However, insofar as suffering results from and manifests evil, it is felt to be repugnant, and so tends to be assimilated to evil and confused with it.

c) **God sometimes causes suffering as a punishment for sin.** Sin is the worst evil and the ultimate source of the other evils which afflict humankind. It gives rise to guilt and to the inevitable evil effects of sin, and these naturally lead to guilt feelings and other suffering—repugnant experiences whose positive reality, nevertheless, is good in itself. While God only permits, and does not cause, either sin or any other evil, he does cause the suffering which results from sin, just as he causes every positive reality apart from himself. During this life, suffering is an educative punishment, a symptom which sharply calls attention to what is really wrong, moves sinners to repent, and moves others to resist sin and deal with its consequences. In the next life, of course, those who persisted in evil will experience their own wretchedness, and their punishment no longer will be educative. However, their suffering will not be imposed on them by God (see *CMP*, 18.I); rather, their painful awareness of their situation will be the inevitable consequence of their own sins and of their true self-knowledge.

d) **God will overcome suffering and compensate the innocent.** Not all who suffer are being punished for sin, however, for the innocent also suffer. Generally, their suffering motivates them or others to pay attention to some evil and to deal with it. Moreover, by raising Jesus, God shows how he will overcome sin's terrible effects on all the innocent who suffer, and how their brief suffering in this world will lead to their everlasting joy in the next. Thus, it is far from clear that God should eliminate the pain and suffering of the innocent right now, rather than later.

e) **God sometimes permits suffering as an opportunity for love.** In three ways, the suffering of the innocent, especially of the helpless, offers others an opportunity for unselfish love. First, their poignant suffering should and often does move others to love them and struggle against the evils which make them suffer. Second, solidarity with the innocent who suffer with faith builds up one's own faith and intensifies the bonds of Christian community. Third, doing what one can to overcome suffering causes one to experience suffering, and this experience intensifies love. For in struggling against evil, one who wills to serve the good despite hardship comes to love more perfectly. That is so because it is more difficult to will

54. The evil of a heart attack is the destruction of part of the heart's tissue, not the pain in the chest which a conscious victim of heart attack experiences. (The pain causes heart attack victims to rest and seek help; if they felt no pain, death would be more likely.) Just as some people are blind or deaf, some lack the sense of pain, and that lack is a serious handicap; see Roger Trigg, *Pain and Emotion* (Oxford: Oxford University Press, 1970), 166. Similarly, the evil of being a sinner is not guilt feelings but the sin of which one is guilty, whether or not one suffers feelings of guilt. (Guilt feelings cause sinners to repent; if they feel no guilt, damnation is more likely.)

a good when that causes one to suffer than when it is easy and pleasant; thus, other things being equal, those who work to overcome evil would love less if they did not personally suffer by encountering and experiencing the evil they struggle against.

f) God's final word about suffering is Jesus himself. Someone whose Christian faith is whole and strong will find in it a satisfying response to the challenge of suffering. This response is not so much what one believes about Jesus as it is Jesus himself. For Jesus brings God near, shows his gentleness, and makes it clear that he desires human salvation and fulfillment, not sin and misery.[55] In Jesus' passion and death, God himself voluntarily experiences the consequences of sin by sharing in human sufferings. The suffering of the innocent might otherwise lead even believers to distrust or defy God, "But God proves his love for us in that while we still were sinners Christ died for us" (Rom 5.8).[56]

g) Christian hope makes even the worst suffering bearable. By Jesus' resurrection, God reveals the ultimate significance of suffering and death. Just as Jesus willingly suffered, because he looked forward to the joy of resurrection (see Heb 12.2), so Christians who are faithful can anticipate glory even amidst sufferings, and so can honestly say:

> When we cry, "Abba! Father!" it is that very Spirit bearing witness with our spirit that we are children of God, and if children, then heirs, heirs of God and joint heirs with Christ—if, in fact, we suffer with him so that we may also be glorified with him.
>
> I consider that the sufferings of this present time are not worth comparing with the glory about to be revealed to us. (Rom 8.15–18)

For those imbued with Christian hope, suffering in this life and even death itself become tolerable, for they are pangs of birth into everlasting life. The love which suffering can evoke is both a fruit of divine grace and a free and self-determining act of the will, which builds up a holy soul. The same holiness could not be attained without the suffering which evokes love.

This world is a soul-building shop: divine grace and human freedom forge souls on the anvil of suffering.

Question F: What Is the Only Unanswerable Reason for Unbelief?

The gospel calls for repentance, and one's repentance is not sincere unless one undertakes to lead a sinless life. But even though the gospel promises a wealth of true human goods as a motive to repent, it cannot promise what sin offers here and now. Thus, people can deliberately prefer darkness to light; unwillingness to give

---

55. See John Paul II, *Dives in misericordia,* 7, *AAS* 72 (1980) 1199–1203, *PE,* 279.66–79.

56. John Paul II, General Audience (30 Mar. 1983), 3, *Inseg.* 6.1 (1983) 855, *OR,* 5 Apr. 1983, 4, points out that without Christ, the cross is a scandal: "*The cross with Christ* is the great revelation of the meaning of suffering and of the value which it has in life and in history. He who understands the Cross, who embraces it, begins a journey very different from that of the process of contestation against God: in it there is found rather the motive of a new ascent to him on the way of Christ, which is, in fact, *the way of the cross.*"

up sin is their basis for unbelief.[57] It is unanswerable, not because it is an argument which cannot be answered, but because it is a nonrational commitment which is impervious to argument.

1. The Fallen Human Condition Resists Faith

Christian faith includes more than assent to true propositions; it is a commitment to follow Jesus. In this fallen world, however, those who consistently follow Jesus do not have easy lives. They must share in his cross as they cooperate in his uncompromising struggle against evil. Hence, typically, they have fewer material goods, fewer enjoyments in life, and less freedom to do as they please than if they compromised with evil. Accepting and holding fast to the cross is especially hard for the wealthy, self-indulgent, and powerful, whose faith is choked by the riches, pleasures, and cares of life (see Mt 13.22, Mk 4.19, Lk 8.14).

To follow Jesus means escaping from enslavement to disordered desires for riches, enjoyment, and status, and undertaking to live in obedience to God and in right relationships with and among men and women—the new covenant's communion with God and neighbor. This communion is Christian love, which takes shape in specifically Christian modes of response (see *CMP*, 26). Only gradually, however, do these becomes second nature, for they are not "natural" to fallen humankind. Thus, the fallen human condition resists faith's challenge. Many people are like the rich young man of the gospel (see Mt 19.16–22; cf. Mk 10.17–22, Lk 18.18–25): they experience a certain sadness and lethargy at the prospect of seriously undertaking to live the Christian life.

2. Faith Requires Renunciation of the Sinful Self

In every deliberate sin, freedom of self-determination is exercised contrary to what is known to be truly right and good. In sinning, sinners tend to regard moral truths legalistically, as if they were mere rules blocking them from doing as they please. Thus, deliberate sin seems to be self-affirming. Affirming the self and rejecting the limits which deny some forbidden fruit, sinners try to be autonomous, as only God really can be.[58]

Faith demands renunciation of this sinful self: pride must give way to humility. Humility is not self-depreciation, but readiness to accept everything good as God's gift and to thank him for it (see *S.t.*, 2–2, q. 161, aa. 2–3; *CMP*, 26.D). It is not self-negation, but escape from isolated and sterile autonomy into authentic self-fulfillment, to be realized and enjoyed in the only way possible: by sharing, as a member of God's family, both in his blessedness and in every human good. From

---

57. See John XXIII, *Ad Petri Cathedram, AAS* 51 (1959) 502, *PE,* 263.20: "Once we have attained the truth in its fullness, integrity, and purity, unity should pervade our minds, hearts, and actions. For there is only one cause of discord, disagreement, and dissension: ignorance of the truth, or what is worse, rejection of the truth once it has been sought and found. It may be that the truth is rejected because of the practical advantages which are expected to result from false views; it may be that it is rejected as a result of that perverted blindness which seeks easy and indulgent excuses for vice and immoral behavior."

58. See Congregation for the Doctrine of the Faith, *Instruction on Christian Freedom and Liberation,* 37, *AAS* 79 (1987) 568–69, *OR,* 14 Apr. 1986, 3.

the viewpoint of pride, however, humility seems to threaten the self. Thus, sinners who lack faith, as well as believers whose faith has been weakened by a habit of sinning, will be tempted to reject faith in order to avoid self-renunciation, that is, renunciation of their sinful selves (see Jn 3.16–21).

Question G: Why Is It Good to Be a Catholic Christian?

For those who accept the Catholic Church's faith as the norm of their Christian faith, the reasons why it is good to be a Christian serve as reasons why it is good to be a Catholic.

By themselves, considerations pointing to the credibility of Christian faith are not sufficient reasons to be a Christian—to make and keep the baptismal commitment, as faith requires. One makes this commitment and perseveres in it, as in any other, only for the sake of goods in which one hopes to share: in this case, the goods pursued by Jesus' covenantal community in following him.

1. Reasons to Regard the Secular Humanist Option as Unappealing

Today, most morally earnest Christians see some form of secular humanism as the only tempting alternative to their faith.[59] Secular humanists claim that Christian hopes are a naive illusion, mere wishful thinking like children's dreams of Christmas morning and the gifts Santa Claus will have left. Such wishful thinking, they maintain, is irrelevant for modern men and women, who realize that humankind's problems must and can be solved by autonomous human efforts. Nevertheless, despite technological progress, the human situation as a whole is not improving, and in some ways is worse than ever.[60]

a) **Secular humanism is a poor imitation of the gospel.** The appeal of secular humanism to the contemporary world transcends base motives only to the extent that it retains some residue of the gospel. Rejecting not only faith but what almost all men and women have acknowledged about God, secular humanists propose to fulfill the splendid hope which the gospel aroused and to do so without God. They expect merely human efforts and technology to bring about on earth an approximation to the heavenly kingdom.

---

59. See James Hitchcock, *What Is Secular Humanism? Why Humanism Became Secular and How It Is Changing Our World* (Ann Arbor, Mich.: Servant Books, 1982).

60. On the state of freedom in the contemporary world, see Congregation for the Doctrine of the Faith, *Instruction on Christian Freedom and Liberation, AAS* 79 (1987) 557–64, *OR,* 14 Apr. 1986, 1–2. John Paul II, Homily at Mass in Turin, 3, *AAS* 72 (1980) 289, *OR,* 21 Apr. 1980, 3, calls attention to fear of death, nuclear arsenals, and terrorism: "Incidents of this kind have always occurred, but today this has become a system. If men affirm that it is necessary to kill other men in order to change and improve man and society, then we must ask whether, together with this gigantic material progress, in which our age participates, we have not arrived simultaneously at the point of wiping out man, himself, a value so fundamental and elementary!" He also teaches, *Dominum et vivificantem,* 57, *AAS* 78 (1986) 881, *OR,* 9 June 1986, 12: "On the horizon of contemporary civilization—especially in the form that is most developed in the technical and scientific sense—*the signs and symptoms of death* have become particularly present and frequent." As examples, he mentions the threat of nuclear holocaust, death-dealing poverty and famine, abortion, wars, and terrorism.

However, their strategies for overcoming evil are unrealistic, and their promises to suffering humankind have proven empty. Most significantly, no secular humanist can come to grips with the greatest evils: sin and death. Virtually all of them reduce sin to nonmoral evil—psychological illness, ignorance, insufficiently evolved social structures, lack of adequate know-how, and so forth—and relinquish hope of immortality.[61]

b) **Secular humanism leads to moral irresponsibility.** While all secular humanists prize freedom in various senses, they reject the kind of freedom which is most essential for morality: freedom of self-determination. By denying the human capacity to make free choices, secular humanists undermine personal moral responsibility, and so make it easy to rationalize sins by blaming them on social structures, inadequate education, psychological problems, breakdowns in communication, and so on. Not thinking "My choice will make me be what I shall be" but "Factors beyond my control make me choose as I do," people influenced by deterministic ideas find it hard to resist the temptations to which fallen human beings always are exposed.

In this situation, people everywhere—in places still influenced by Marxist ideology as well as in those shaped by the liberal ideologies prevalent in affluent nations—are tempted to seek security in possessions and status. In both public and private life, lying and manipulative behavior, heedless and sometimes brutal competition, and exploitation of the weak by the strong are common. Anxiety also tempts people to seek escape in immediate distractions. Transient arrangements for quick gratification often are preferred to faithful relationships based on lasting mutual commitments.

c) **This moral irresponsibility undermines humanist aspirations.** Such moral irresponsibility undermines the earnest concern of secular humanists regarding the moral heart of humankind's problems: injustice. Hence, despite its aspiration for a better world, secular humanism lacks the moral resources to build a just and good society. Proponents of each form of secularism claim that their particular approach, if not frustrated by the proponents of alternatives and by the dead weight of tradition, would make the world peaceful, prosperous, and happy. However, the various forms of liberal secularism adopted by many people living in the wealthy nations rationalize abuses of liberty and unrestricted consumption of the world's goods, alongside neglect of those in dire need.[62] And while Marxism proposed to liberate the poor and oppressed, it only enslaved them the more.[63]

d) **Secular humanism does not respect human persons' dignity.** Every kind of secular humanism denies that there is any more-than-human and unchanging basis for meaning and value. Denying that there is a creator, secular humanists deny that people are endowed with inalienable rights. Most secular humanists therefore support various evil policies, such as legalized abortion and nuclear deterrence.

---

61. See Ratzinger, "Freedom and Liberation: The Anthropological Vision of the Instruction," 69–71.

62. See John Paul II, *Dives in misericordia*, 11, *AAS* 72 (1980) 1212–15, *PE*, 279.109–16.

63. See Congregation for the Doctrine of the Faith, *Instruction on Certain Aspects of "Theology of Liberation"*, 11.10–11, *AAS* 76 (1984) 905–6, *OR*, 10 Sept. 1984, 4.

Furthermore, even if secular humanism were able to achieve the better world it promises, that paradise would come too late for those who, in the meanwhile, are being deliberately killed or allowed to die miserably for the sake of "justice" and "freedom." To opt for any kind of secular humanism is to opt not for life but for death.[64]

2. The Blessings the Gospel Promises

The positive reasons why it is good to be a Christian are found in the blessings which the gospel promises to Jesus' faithful disciples.

a) Faith in Jesus is in human persons' ultimate self-interest. Self-interest often is equated with selfishness, but that is a mistake, since selfishness impedes friendship and other goods essential to real self-fulfillment. Unselfish people normally enter into good personal relationships in the hope of enjoying various goods together with others. The gospel itself appeals to true self-interest (see Mt 16.24–27, Jn 12.25–26).[65] Thus, although making and faithfully fulfilling the commitment of Christian faith may not be in one's temporal and earthly interest, it is in one's true and everlasting interest.

Faith in Jesus reconciles human persons to God, enables them to be his children, and holds out the hope of everlasting joy in heaven (see 1 Jn 3.1–2). Thus, faith is good for those who accept this great gift. It is also right to believe, for God is like a good parent to created persons. Good parents bring their children into existence out of love and unselfishly provide them with many other gifts. They ask little but to be loved in return. It is right that children revere such parents, express gratitude to them, and remain in loving communion with them. Thus, faith is right, because it responds affirmatively to God's will that human persons be in communion with him, and this pleases him.

b) Faith in Jesus also serves every other human good. Cooperating with Jesus' redemptive work, one is empowered by the Holy Spirit to live a meaningful and good life in this fallen world. Enlightened by faith, Jesus' disciples know the truth about the deepest and most important matters, a truth which liberates them both from the inadequacies of other world views and from the purposeless existence of those with no conscious world view. Able to love one another with genuine and unselfish love, Christians can enjoy the benefit of fellowship in the Church.

Sharing sacramentally in Jesus' gloriously risen and immortal body and blood, one can look forward confidently to personal, bodily life after death. Knowing that God loves and sustains what he has made (see Wis 11.24–26), one also can hope to find again in heaven, "cleansed of all dirt, lit up, and transformed," all the "good fruits of our nature and effort" which were nurtured on earth (GS 39). In other

---

64. Pius XII, *Summi Pontificatus, AAS* 31 (1939) 422, *PE*, 222.25, commented on the situation at the beginning of World War II in a way which remains valid: "No defense of Christianity could be more effective than the present straits. From the immense vortex of error and anti-Christian movements there has come forth a crop of such poignant disasters as to constitute a condemnation surpassing in its conclusiveness any merely theoretical refutation."

65. See *CMP*, 20.G; Paul VI, General Audience (9 Feb. 1972), *Inseg.* 10 (1972) 126, *OR*, 17 Feb. 1972, 12.

words, faith promises the renewal and completion in heaven of every good which the blessed wished to protect and promote in this world (see *CMP*, 34.E).

Question H: Which Truths Should One Accept with Catholic Faith?

As already explained (in A.1.c–d), faith primarily is in God, not in a set of truths. But because God reveals truths about himself and his plan for humankind, one cannot believe in him without being prepared to accept with faith every one of the truths he reveals.

1. One Should Believe the Truths the Church Proposes as Revealed

Since the Church's faith is the norm of personal faith, one's responsibilities with respect to propositional truths of faith are fulfilled by making sure one believes what the Church believes. Vatican I definitively teaches: "By divine and Catholic faith everything must be believed that is contained in the written word of God or in tradition, and that is proposed by the Church as a divinely revealed object of belief either in a solemn decree or in her ordinary, universal teaching" (DS 3011/1792).[66]

a) **One should believe every proposition asserted in Scripture.** Although Vatican I and Vatican II teach that the books of the Old and New Testaments in their entirety and in all their parts have been inspired by the Holy Spirit so that God is their author (see DS 3006/1787; DV 11), not every statement in Scripture expresses a revealed truth. Many express thoughts which the writer wishes readers to have in mind, but not necessarily to accept as true. For example, most statements in the book of Job are part of a lengthy dialogue, and the propositions they express clearly are not asserted by the book's author, whose assertions are limited to a few propositions, such as that the human mind is in no position to judge God's ways.

Only those propositions which the sacred writers assert—that is, propose for their readers' acceptance as certainly true—are also asserted by the Holy Spirit, who inspires the human authors and so speaks through them (see DV 11). Thus, of all the propositions in Scripture, the Church proposes as true on God's word only those which are asserted by the sacred writers.[67] In discerning what the sacred writers assert, the Church attends to "the content and unity of the whole of Scripture" and takes into account "the living tradition of the whole Church" along with "the harmony which exists among elements of the faith" (DV 12).[68]

---

66. To Vatican I's formulation, *CIC*, c. 750, adds: "It is manifested by the common adherence of the Christian faithful under the leadership of the sacred magisterium; therefore, all are bound to avoid any doctrines whatever which are contrary to these truths."

67. See DV 11; cf. Pius XII, *Divino afflante Spiritu, AAS* 35 (1943) 299–300, *PE*, 226.3–4; *CMP*, 35.B.

68. On Catholic hermeneutic of Scripture, see Ignace de la Potterie, S.J., "Interpretation of Holy Scripture in the Spirit in Which It Was Written (*Dei Verbum* 12c)," in *Vatican II: Assessment and Perspectives Twenty-five Years After (1962–1987)*, ed. René Latourelle, 3 vols. (New York: Paulist Press, 1988–89), 1:220–66.

b) One should believe the truths the Church teaches as revealed. Popes and bishops serve God's revealed word, which they are commissioned to hand on (see LG 25, DV 10). Their teaching is not their own, but only what they have received, which they must guard as inviolable and expound with fidelity.[69] Therefore, revelation itself "demands that, in full obedience of the intellect and will to God who reveals [note omitted], we accept the proclamation of the good news of salvation as it is infallibly taught by the pastors of the Church."[70] The Church teaches infallibly

> when the bishops scattered throughout the world but teaching in communion with the Successor of Peter present a doctrine to be held irrevocably. It occurs even more clearly both when the bishops by a collegial act (as in Ecumenical Councils), together with their visible Head, define a doctrine to be held [note omitted], and when the Roman Pontiff "speaks ex cathedra, that is when, exercising the office of Pastor and Teacher of all Christians, through his supreme apostolic authority he defines a doctrine concerning faith or morals to be held by the universal Church [note omitted]."[71]

Thus, Catholics not only should believe solemnly defined dogmas, but should accept with faith those teachings on matters of faith and morals which popes and bishops have concurred in proposing as divinely revealed.

2. One Should Accept on Faith Other Truths That Are Infallibly Taught

Faith also extends to truths which the Church finds it necessary to proclaim infallibly in order to safeguard and explain revelation, even if those truths are not, strictly speaking, revealed.[72] One obvious example is the Church's judgment concerning which writings make up the Bible and which do not.

Some theologians refer to the unconditional assent due such truths as *ecclesiastical faith*. Others reject this expression insofar as it suggests that a Catholic believes some truths with a faith distinct from faith in God revealing. Perhaps the best way of putting the matter is to say that one's faith in God revealing must extend beyond what, precisely, he has revealed, to include truths which cannot be denied without denying what he has revealed about the Church and his gift to her of

---

69. John Paul II, *Redemptor hominis,* 19, *AAS* 71 (1979) 306, *PE,* 278.72, explains that, just as Jesus proposed not a personal teaching but the Father's word (see Jn 14.24), so "it is required, when the Church professes and teaches the faith, that she should adhere strictly to divine truth."

70. Congregation for the Doctrine of the Faith, *Mysterium ecclesiae, AAS* 65 (1973) 402, Flannery, 2:432.

71. Congregation for the Doctrine of the Faith, *Mysterium ecclesiae, AAS* 65 (1973) 400–401, Flannery, 2:431–32. The first sentence closely follows LG 25. The internal quotation in the second sentence is from Vatican I's definition of the conditions under which popes teach infallibly (see DS 3074/1839). The Congregation for the Doctrine of the Faith also refers to Vatican II, LG 22 and 25.

72. Congregation for the Doctrine of the Faith, *Mysterium ecclesiae, AAS* 65 (1973) 401, Flannery, 2:432: "According to Catholic doctrine, the infallibility of the Church's Magisterium extends not only to the deposit of faith but also to those matters without which that deposit cannot be rightly preserved and expounded [note refers to LG 25]." See *CMP,* 35.D–E; Grisez, "Infallibility and Specific Moral Norms," 256–58.

infallibility. Faith therefore can extend to truths connected in the relevant ways with revelation insofar as they are guaranteed by the Church's infallibility.

3. One Should Fulfill the Responsibility of Faith Integrally

Nothing can justify setting limits to one's responsibility to accept every truth of faith. While doctrine develops and can be reformulated by the Church, legitimate development and reformulation does not call into question anything which Catholics as a whole previously held with faith.

a) One should expect temptations to set aside some truths of faith. In the fallen human condition, it is not uncommon to be misled more or less seriously or even to be betrayed by those one trusts. Hence, direct evidence—seeing for oneself that matters are as they are claimed to be—is important to one's sense of security. In making the act of faith and living by it, however, one stakes one's life on the truth one accepts as revealed by God. Direct evidence plainly would be most welcome, yet in many respects it is unavailable. Thus, it is necessary to overcome a considerable psychological obstacle in surrendering oneself to God. Furthermore, the requirements of faith sometimes are at odds with judgments one otherwise would make—especially judgments with practical consequences—and that, too, makes submission to divine authority, although reasonable, a difficult matter.[73]

b) Absolute submission to God in faith is reasonable. Questions C through E showed both that good reasons point to the credibility of the Catholic faith and that various arguments against it can be answered. Still, the claims of faith might seem excessive, as when St. Paul exclaims: "We destroy arguments and every proud obstacle raised up against the knowledge of God, and we take every thought captive to obey Christ" (2 Cor 10.4–5). If such absolute submission were to a merely human wisdom, it would be servile, but the unqualified obedience of faith is reasonable because the gospel is God's truth. Rather than enslaving those who accept it, faith in God's truth frees them from sin and death: "You will know the truth, and the truth will make you free" (Jn 8.32).

c) One should believe each and every truth of faith. Some truths of faith are less central than others, as Vatican II teaches: "There exists an order or 'hierarchy' of truths of Catholic doctrine, since they vary in their relationship with the foundation of Christian faith" (UR 11). This hierarchy must be taken into account in catechesis and ecumenical dialogue, because the more basic and important truths

---

73. Leo XIII, *Tametsi futura prospicientibus, ASS* 33 (1900–1901) 282, *PE,* 153.10, clearly explains why difficulty in submitting to divine authority is to be expected by those wishing to live an authentic Christian life: "It must therefore be clearly admitted that, in the life of a Christian, the intellect must be entirely subject to God's authority. And if, in this submission of reason to authority, our self-love, which is so strong, is restrained and made to suffer, this only proves the necessity to a Christian of long-suffering not only in will but also in intellect. We would remind those persons of this truth who desire a kind of Christianity such as they themselves have devised, whose precepts should be very mild, much more indulgent towards human nature, and requiring little if any hardships to be borne. They do not properly understand the meaning of faith and Christian precepts. They do not see that the Cross meets us everywhere, the model of our life, the eternal standard of all who wish to follow Christ in reality and not merely in name."

clarify the meaning of less central ones.[74] Nevertheless, even the least important truth of faith has the same warrant as the most important, and so "all dogmas, since they are revealed, must be believed with the same divine faith."[75]

Someone picking and choosing among dogmas must be using some principle to sort them out other than the evidence that they are indeed revealed. Such a person might, for example, be accepting those which seem plausible to a circle of friends or fellow theologians. If consistent, however, he or she accepts nothing precisely as revealed—accepts nothing with faith—and so does not have faith at all (see *S.t.*, 2–2, q. 5, a. 3).[76] Therefore, one should believe with the same faith all the truths which the Church teaches infallibly, because God guarantees the truth of them all.[77]

d) One should believe what Catholics formerly held with faith. Catholics in the past always took what they believed on God's word, especially his word in Jesus witnessed by the apostles. Faith today has the same source. Today, therefore, there can be no reason consistent with faith for calling into question anything which Catholics as a whole held with faith in earlier times.[78]

Someone might object: If that is so, religious knowledge does not progress like other kinds of knowledge, where mistakes in observation, errors in reasoning, and cultural limits are gradually overcome. The answer is: Doctrine does develop, but not in the same way as knowledge in other fields. Divine revelation and faith *are* unique. They do not originate in human observation and reasoning, and their truth transcends the cultural forms in which it was first expressed.

e) Development never falsifies what was believed in the past. The linguistic expressions used by the Church in her dogmatic formulations do not exhaustively

74. See *New Catholic Encyclopedia,* s.v. "hierarchy of truths," especially the quotation from Archbishop Andrea Pangrazio's Vatican II intervention proposing and explaining the notion of hierarchy of truths; Congregation for the Clergy, *General Catechetical Directory,* 43, *AAS* 64 (1972) 123, Flannery, 2:553–54; Secretariat for Promoting the Unity of Christians, "Reflections and Suggestions concerning Ecumenical Dialogue," 4.4.b, *EV* 3 (1968–70) 1626–27, Flannery, 1:545.

75. Congregation for the Doctrine of the Faith, *Mysterium ecclesiae, AAS* 65 (1973) 402, Flannery, 2:433, which on this point repeats the definitive teaching of Vatican I (DS 3011/1792).

76. Leo XIII, *Satis cognitum, ASS* 28 (1895–96) 721–23, *PE,* 138.9, clearly explains this point: nobody can reject any one dogma without falling into heresy and in principle rejecting the whole of revelation.

77. See Leo XIII, *Sapientiae Christianae, ASS* 22 (1889–90) 393–95, *PE,* 111.22–24; Pius XI, *Mortalium animos, AAS* 20 (1928) 12–14, *PE,* 201.9; Pius XII, *Orientalis ecclesiae, AAS* 36 (1944) 134, *PE,* 227.16.

78. Paul VI, *Petrum et Paulum, AAS* 59 (1967) 198, *The Pope Speaks* 12 (1967): 141, points out the seriousness of this temptation today: "Among our contemporaries, the religious sense which provides faith with a kind of natural foundation is growing weaker. But Catholic belief, too, is being contaminated. Ideas are appearing in the fields of exegesis and theology which have their origin in certain bold but misleading philosophical theories and which cast doubt upon or narrow down the full meaning of the truths which the Church has taught with her rightful authority. There is a pretense that religion must be adapted to the contemporary mind; the directive wisdom of the Church's teaching authority is scorned; theological inquiry is remodeled to suit the principles of 'historicism'; the divine inspiration and historical truth of Sacred Scripture are boldly denied: in short, God's People are being encouraged to adopt a new, so-called 'post-conciliar' attitude of mind."

encapsulate the revealed truth.[79] Therefore, while individuals on their own authority may not set aside the language the Church uses, the Church from time to time improves on it. Such improvements can even become necessary to defend the faith against errors and to expound it in fresh social and cultural contexts.[80]

Moreover, Christians today are in a position to articulate revealed truths in ways not available to the apostles, for the Church not only faithfully safeguards and hands on all that God revealed, but infallibly interprets it. So, as both Vatican I and Vatican II teach, the Church grows in her understanding of the realities and words which have been handed down (see DS 3020/1800; DV 8).

But the Church never can contradict the truth she has received from God. So, as Vatican I definitively teaches, the Church's dogmatic formulae should never be taken in a meaning different from the one the Church understood and understands in using them (see DS 3043/1818; cf. GS 62). It follows that legitimate and necessary development and reformulation of doctrine can never call into question anything which Catholics as a whole once have held with faith.[81]

4. One Should Not Accept Theological Explanations with Faith

To clarify the truths of faith and draw out their implications, theological reflection often joins them with other propositions which seem true. Reflection of this kind naturally leads to commonly accepted positions, which are handed on in the Church as a theological tradition. If not taught infallibly by the Church, such positions can be called *theological explanations*. Examples include the theory of the sacraments as signs, the theology of the condition of humankind's first parents insofar as it goes beyond what faith teaches in attributing perfections to them, and the explanation by analogy with human spiritual acts of the processions of the Word and the Spirit.

a) One should not overvalue any theological explanation. Inasmuch as they depend in part on propositions which are not divinely guaranteed, theological explanations should not be accepted with faith. Theological reflection is carried on not only by professional theologians, but by all thoughtful believers, including popes and other bishops as they preach and teach, and so the Church's teaching authority sometimes develops (or accepts and uses) theological explanations. But even such theological explanations as these could be mistaken, as has happened repeatedly, leading to doctrinal conflicts which divided some bishops from others.

---

79. See Paul VI, *Mysterium fidei, AAS* 57 (1965) 757–58, *PE*, 273.23–25; Congregation for the Doctrine of the Faith, *Mysterium ecclesiae, AAS* 65 (1973) 402–4, Flannery, 2:433–35.

80. In a famous passage in John XXIII's address at the opening of Vatican II, he distinguished between the truths of faith and the manner in which they are enunciated (see *CMP*, 20.2), but by no means condoned the questioning of anything the Church believed in times past. On precisely what Pope John said and what it meant, see the series of letters to the editor by John Finnis, *The Tablet* (London), 14 Dec. 1991, 1544–45; 4 Jan. 1992, 14; 18 Jan. 1992, 70–71; 1 Feb. 1992, 140; 8 Feb. 1992, 170.

81. For the criteria of authentic development of doctrine: John Henry Newman, *An Essay on the Development of Christian Doctrine* (Westminster, Md.: Christian Classics, 1968), 169–206. A general summary of the theology of development, with bibliography: *New Catholic Encyclopedia*, s.v. "doctrine, development of." See also Germain Grisez, "On Interpreting Dogmas: A Preliminary Analysis," *Communio* 17 (Spring 1990): 120–26.

b) **One should never believe professional theologians.** Reserve about a theological explanation should be all the greater if it has recently been developed and, even though accepted by many theologians, is not accepted by the Church's teaching authority. Such an explanation has not yet stood the test of criticism by Christians of diverse times, places, and conditions, and so is likely to be culture-bound by theology's contemporary situation. Moreover, while theological explanations proposed by the Church's teaching authority often call for religious assent, as will be explained, the views of theologians, considered simply as such, deserve acceptance only insofar as they are supported by cogent reasons and evidence drawn from faith, Church teaching, and truths which are self-evident.

5. One Should Not Accept Private Revelations with Faith

Throughout Christian history, some individuals have claimed to receive messages from God, the Virgin Mary, or other heavenly sources. In very many cases, such reports seem to be false. The pastors of the Church have accepted some as genuine, however, and in certain cases have themselves acted on such messages and commended their exhortations to the faithful. Theologians have called such accepted messages *private revelations.*[82]

However, such messages do not present any new doctrines, and the Church never proposes as a revealed truth any proposition contained only in them. Moreover, the Church's approval and implementation of such a message—for example, by establishing a new place of pilgrimage or a new feast—does not guarantee that everything contained in the recipient's report of the message is true. Therefore, no one should accept any private revelation with divine faith.[83] Rather, following the leaders of the Church, faithful Catholics take the word of the recipients of approved messages on human faith. Of course, in accepting and acting on these approved messages, one should subordinate whatever one does to the Church's teaching, liturgy, and law.

6. Apostasy and Heresy Are Sins against Faith Itself

Despite having heard the gospel and recognized its credibility, willful unbelievers sin against faith by refusing to assent to revelation because they do not wish to submit themselves and their lives to God. But even those who have received the gift of faith and personally committed themselves to it can sin directly against it; indeed, only they can commit the sins of apostasy from the faith and heresy.

a) **Apostasy—renunciation of the faith—is a very grave sin.** The sin of apostasy is committed by completely withdrawing one's commitment of faith and abandoning the Christian religion.[84] There is no more radical and total sin against faith. Other things being equal, those who commit it are more alienated from God than those who willfully rejected faith from the start (see 2 Pt 2.20–22).

---

82. See *New Catholic Encyclopedia,* s.v. "revelations, private."

83. What about the case of someone convinced that God has personally communicated something to himself or herself? That case is not under consideration here, since such people, convinced willy-nilly, need no help from moral theology.

84. See *CIC,* c. 751; *S.t.,* 2–2, q. 12, a. 1.

b) However, some fallen away Catholics are not apostates. Apostates know they should keep the faith yet freely choose no longer to be Christians, whereas some fallen away Catholics have not withdrawn their commitment of faith but only ceased trying to fulfill it. Others were baptized in childhood but never sufficiently formed in the faith to make a personal commitment to it; if they are willful unbelievers, their moral condition is like that of similar people who were never baptized. Others wish to be Christians, and are, but deny some truths which the Catholic Church proposes as divinely revealed; they are heretics, not apostates.

c) Heresy is sinful inconsistency with respect to the truth of faith. Catholics who have received the gift of faith in baptism and have personally made the commitment of faith can commit the sin of heresy. This they do by willfully denying or calling into question some proposition or propositions which they know are among those the Catholic Church believes and teaches—whether by solemn definition or by universal, ordinary teaching—to be divinely revealed.[85]

Those who commit the sin of heresy do not withdraw their commitment of faith. They believe in Jesus and wish to remain in covenantal communion with God. However, their action is not entirely consistent with their commitment of faith. For, although perhaps not holding any false theory of revelation and faith, heretics act as if they somehow had personal access to revelation, contrary to the truth: "So faith comes from what is heard, and what is heard comes through the word of Christ" (Rom 10.17). Although they were taught and accepted Catholic faith as God's revelation in Jesus, they no longer accept the Church's faith as the norm for deciding what propositions are divinely revealed, precisely because they do not care to accept as true all that the Church holds to be divinely revealed. Therefore, heretics assent to some truths of faith but deny others: "I find this acceptable, but I am not prepared to accept that" (see *S.t.*, 2–2, q. 5, a. 3).

d) One can commit heresy in one's heart by a single choice. Canon law limits heresy to the "obstinate" denial or calling into question of a truth which is to be believed with divine and Catholic faith. It might be supposed that "obstinate" implies prolonged persistence in a heretical opinion despite an admonition to give it up. Like any other sin, however, heresy can be committed without any outward act to provoke a challenge and without obduracy, that is, persistence in sin over time. *Obstinate* signifies that the sin of heresy is in purposely refusing to accept what one knows the Church holds to be divinely revealed.[86]

---

85. See *S.t.*, 2–2, q. 11, aa. 1–2. *CIC*, cc. 750–51, provides a definition of heresy which corresponds precisely to Vatican I's definitive teaching about what must be believed: DS 3011/1792.

86. See *CIC*, c. 751; cf. *S.t.*, 2–2, q. 11, a. 2, ad 3. James A. Coriden, "Commentary: Book III: The Teaching Office of the Church," in *The Code of Canon Law: A Text and Commentary*, ed. James A. Coriden, Thomas J. Green, and Donald E. Heintschel (New York: Paulist Press, 1985), 548, offers no support for his reading of "obstinate," summarized and rejected in the text. Against it, see standard commentaries on the corresponding canon of the 1917 code (1325, §2), which did not differ significantly on this point: Charles Augustine Bachofen, O.S.B., *A Commentary on the New Code of Canon Law*, vol. 6, *Administrative Law* (St. Louis: B. Herder, 1921), 335; Udalricus Beste, *Introductio in Codicem*, ed. 4 (Naples: M. d'Auria, 1956), 711–12. Of course, the canonical crime of heresy involves more than the sin of heresy; the Church cannot deal with heresy except when it is expressed, and does not treat anyone as a heretic without an appropriate process.

e) **Heresy is a very grave sin against faith.** To see the seriousness of heresy, it is essential to remember that propositions of faith are not mere sets of words, but are truths which the words express and which bring one into touch with divine reality. The heretic really rejects part of the reality which God wished to share with humankind in revealing himself. Moreover, that reality should be accepted inasmuch as God reveals it; thus, the heretic implicitly spurns God himself.[87]

Those who commit heresy sin even more gravely if they propagate their heretical opinion—that is, assert it in order to obtain other believers' assent—for doing that is a sin of scandal which also divides the Church.

f) **Nobody with Catholic faith simply loses it.** Because faith is God's gift and the believer's commitment, which of itself lasts if not withdrawn, nobody who has received the gift of Catholic faith loses it without grave sin. As Vatican I teaches, God "strengthens with his grace those whom he has brought out of darkness into his marvelous light (see 1 Pt 2.9), so that they may remain in this light"; thus, those who once accept faith under the Church's teaching authority "can never have any just reason for changing that faith or calling it into doubt" (DS 3014/1794, translation supplied; cf. DS 3036/1815). To deny this is to reject not only Vatican I but the Council's premise: that God is faithful and never abandons those who do not abandon him (see DS 3014/1794; cf. DS 1537/804).

Of course, only God can judge the responsibility of anyone whose faith appears to be lost. An apparent loss of faith may not reflect a free choice to abandon it, and, due to lack of sufficient reflection, a person may have mitigated responsibility even for a choice to reject the faith.

g) **Not all who deny revealed truths are heretics.** Those ready to believe whatever the Church clearly teaches to be revealed are not heretics even if they deny some revealed truth or call it into question. For example, suppose some nondefined moral teachings, such as the sinfulness of fornication, have been taught by the Church to be revealed. Then, someone who denied those teachings, not thinking that the Church has taught them to be revealed, would be in the situation described, provided he or she were prepared to submit to the Church's definitive judgment if and when it comes.[88] What of those who through an honest mistake deny what the Church does clearly teach to be revealed? They are not heretics, though they may be guilty of some other sin which led to their mistake. (Such people often are called *material heretics,* but this expression is easily misunderstood and best avoided.) Finally, those who continue to believe in their hearts while outwardly denying the faith—for example, to avoid martyrdom or to get a job from which believers are excluded—are not heretics. They commit the sin of outwardly denying the faith, which is a grave matter (see K.3.b, below), but not heresy.

h) **Not all willful rejection of a truth proposed infallibly is heresy.** Some truths closely connected with revelation, such as the proposition that certain books

---

87. A sign of the gravity of the sin of heresy is that one who commits it (or the even graver sin of apostasy) is automatically excommunicated: *CIC,* c. 1364, §1.

88. To say that such a person is not a heretic is not to say that he or she is blameless. Those who deny that the Church's teaching on the sinfulness of fornication pertains to faith should admit that it deserves religious assent, which will be treated in question I.

make up the canon of sacred Scripture, are infallibly taught by the Church. If such truths are not themselves revealed, their denial is not strictly speaking heresy. However, it is a serious sin against Catholic faith.[89]

Question I: Should One Assent to Teachings Which Are Not of Faith?

Using the word *believe* in a wide sense, one believes everything one accepts because the Church teaches it. In a strict sense, however, only that is believed which is accepted with faith. Yet popes and bishops often exercise their magisterium—that is, their role as Church teachers—by noninfallibly proposing teachings which are not matters of faith, but are somehow related to it. As has been said, one should not put one's faith in such teachings. Nevertheless, under appropriate conditions they should be accepted in the sense that one agrees with them, holds on to them, and acts in accord with them. *Religious assent* refers to this sort of submission of mind and will, which faithful Catholics give to authoritative teachings other than those calling for acceptance with faith (see *CMP*, 35.F–G).

1. Papal and Episcopal Teachings Can Call for Religious Assent

Vatican II teaches: "In matters of faith and morals, the bishops speak in the name of Christ and the faithful are to accept their teaching and adhere to it with a religious assent of soul. This religious submission of will and of intellect must be shown in a special way to the authoritative magisterium of the Roman Pontiff, even when he is not speaking ex cathedra" (LG 25).[90]

a) Popes and bishops cannot limit their teaching to matters of faith. If popes and bishops limited their teaching to matters of faith, there would be no need for religious assent. As a living community, however, the Church must think about many things beyond what she believes on God's word. Some are closely related to faith, others less so, but all are important if the Church is to think with one mind, as she must to carry on her common life (see *CMP*, 23.F). For the effectiveness of the Church's common action plainly presupposes a firm consensus, not only with respect to faith itself, but also with respect to many truths relevant to communicating it and bringing it to bear on contemporary situations.[91]

---

89. This is the common view among sound modern moralists. However, medieval theologians used *heresy* with a broader reference. St. Thomas, for example, considers it heresy willfully to hold any position once the Church makes it plain that the position has implications in conflict with divinely revealed truth (*S.t.*, 1, q. 32, a. 4; 2–2, q. 11, a. 2). In any case, this sin is very grave, for it is inconsistent with one's commitment of faith.

90. Vatican II nowhere uses the Latin phrase *assensus religiosus,* and in the passage quoted from LG 25 uses a single word, *obsequium,* to express what is meant by the English *assent* and *submission.* The relevant submission of soul—that is, of will and of intellect—is to the teaching proposed (the *sententiam*) insofar as the magisterium of the Church authoritatively proposes it (and so in the case of papal teaching is submission *Romani Pontificis authentico magisterio*). The very act, *to accept,* is to agree with (*concurrere*) and to hold fast to (*adhaerere*).

91. Leo XIII, *Sapientiae Christianae, ASS* 22 (1889–90) 393, *PE,* 111.18–19, argues from the need for solidarity in the apostolate to the Church's need to be of one mind: "To bring about such a union of minds and uniformity of action—not without reason so greatly feared by the enemies

b) **Religious assent is reasonable submission to the Church's teachers.** In giving religious assent, something is accepted on the authority of the pope or of one's bishop. Thus, one submits one's judgment to his. In doing so, one agrees with him about the point he teaches even if one would think it untrue except for his teaching. In this sense one submits one's mind and will to his.[92]

Someone might object: To submit one's judgment to another's in this way is unreasonable, since people ought to make judgments only in accord with relevant evidence and reasons. Part of the answer will be given below (in c): There are good reasons, grounded in faith itself, to submit one's judgment to that of the Church's teachers. The other part of the answer is that it is necessary to distinguish two senses of *in accord with relevant evidence and reasons.*

In one sense, judging in accord with relevant evidence and reasons means not accepting others' judgments when they conflict with something of which one is certain on the basis of compelling evidence and reasons. In another sense, it means never believing anyone, but only judging to be true that of which one is convinced apart from what anyone else says.

Since teachings to which religious assent is due are not matters of faith, one could not submit one's judgment to that of the Church's teachers if their teaching were inconsistent with evidence and reasons which convinced one, whether one wished it or not, of the opposite. But papal and episcopal teachings hardly ever raise problems of that sort. Rather, any teaching calling for religious assent either is supported by available evidence and reasons or, if not, is likely to be consistent

---

of Catholicism—the main point is that a perfect harmony of opinion should prevail; in which intent we find Paul the Apostle exhorting the Corinthians with earnest zeal and solemn weight of words: 'Now I beseech you, brethren, by the name of our Lord Jesus Christ, that you all speak the same thing, and that there be no schisms among you: but that you be perfectly in the same mind, and in the same judgment' (1 Cor 1.10). The wisdom of this precept is readily apprehended. In truth, thought is the principle of action, and hence there cannot exist agreement of will, or similarity of action, if people all think differently one from the other." Cf. Benedict XV, *Ad beatissimi Apostolorum, AAS* 6 (1914) 576–77, *PE,* 180.21–23.

92. Some people appeal to the so-called *sensus fidelium* to argue that if a large portion of those who identify themselves as Catholics hold some dissenting opinion, popes and bishops should submit their minds and wills to that group's opinion, rather than vice versa. This argument assumes that the dissenting opinion manifests a genuine sense of the faith. The *sensus fidei* (supernatural sense of the faith), however, is not something independent of the magisterium (see LG 12). For the distinction between the consensus of the faithful, which offers no criterion of moral truth, and the supernatural sense of the faith, see John Paul II, *Familiaris consortio,* 5, *AAS* 74 (1982) 85–86, *OR,* 21–28 Dec. 1981, 2; Aidan Nichols, O.P., *The Shape of Catholic Theology: An Introduction to Its Sources, Principles, and History* (Collegeville, Minn.: Liturgical Press, 1991), 221–31. In clarifying the distinction between the *sensus fidei* and the opinion of a large portion of the faithful, Congregation for the Doctrine of the Faith, *Instruction on the Ecclesial Vocation of the Theologian,* 35, *AAS* 82 (1990) 1565–66, *OR,* 2 July 1990, 3, points out: "Although theological faith as such then cannot err, the believer can still have erroneous opinions since all his thoughts do not spring from faith [note omitted]. Not all the ideas which circulate among the People of God are compatible with the faith. This is all the more so given that people can be swayed by a public opinion influenced by modern communications media." Some who appeal to the so-called *sensus fidelium* claim the support of Cardinal Newman, but that claim rests on misinterpretation; see James Quinn, S.J., "The Laity and Doctrine," *Homiletic and Pastoral Review* 91 (May 1991): 58–62.

with them. Accepting another's judgment on such matters cannot be ruled out as unreasonable unless it is unreasonable ever to believe anyone.

c) **Religious assent is rooted in divine faith.** The primary ground of the responsibility to give religious assent is the following fact, itself a truth of faith: God gives popes and bishops their teaching role, and the Holy Spirit helps them fulfill it (see *CMP*, 35.F). For someone who believes this, it is only reasonable to believe that, when popes and bishops fulfill their teaching role, God sees to it that those who submit their judgment to what is taught are not led into serious and harmful error.[93] Moreover, any teaching which calls for religious assent is at least partly drawn from truths of faith. If one believes the relevant truth of faith, one will be inclined to accept teachings drawn from it. Thus, in two distinct ways, religious assent is rooted in divine faith.[94]

d) **This assent is submission to teachings rather than to decisions.** Since religious assent involves submission of mind and will, it is easily confused with the obedience a Catholic also owes the pope and his or her bishop as governors of the Church community. However, insofar as the Church's pastoral leaders govern, they do not teach, for governing and teaching, although often closely related, are two different things.

In governing, the Church's pastoral leaders formulate directives concerning suitable ways for the members of the Church to act together in their common life and communicate those directives in the form of laws or policies or precepts. In teaching calling for religious assent, they try to discern what is true and communicate that judgment as a truth, although not as a matter of faith. Such teaching calls for acceptance as true, and so in giving religious assent a Catholic is accepting as true what the pope and his or her bishop teach, not obeying their directives to act or not act in certain ways.

e) **This assent is submission of will as well as of mind.** Since religious assent is not obedience, it requires more than mere outward compliance. Religious assent is submission in one's heart to the judgment of the teachers of the Church. This submission is of will as well as intellect for two reasons. First, when one would not make the same judgment oneself, one should be willing to follow the judgment of the pope or bishop as a teacher, but one can refuse to do so. Second, like truths of faith, truths which call for religious assent also make practical demands. Religious

93. For a fuller statement of this argument against theologians who claim that the Church's authority in teaching on moral issues must yield to ethical arguments, see J. L. A. Garcia, "Moral Reasoning and the Catholic Church," *New Oxford Review* 59 (June 1992): 13–17.

94. Congregation for the Doctrine of the Faith, *Instruction on the Ecclesial Vocation of the Theologian,* 23, *AAS* 82 (1990) 1560, *OR*, 2 July 1990, 3: "When the Magisterium, not intending to act 'definitively', teaches a doctrine to aid a better understanding of Revelation and make explicit its contents, or to recall how some teaching is in conformity with the truths of faith, or finally to guard against ideas that are incompatible with these truths, the response called for is that of religious submission of will and intellect (LG 25; *CIC*, c. 752). This kind of response cannot be simply exterior or disciplinary but must be understood within the logic of faith and under the impulse of obedience to the faith." In 15–17 (*AAS* 1556–58, *OR*, 2), of the same document, divine assistance to the successors of the apostles in their whole teaching role is emphasized as the ground for assent.

assent is given only if one both says yes and means it, in other words, only if one undertakes to act accordingly.[95]

2. Not All Papal and Episcopal Statements Call for Religious Assent

The responsibility to give religious assent has limits. Understanding the responsibility requires carefully distinguishing cases which fall within the limits from those which fall outside them.

a) **Religious assent is called for only under certain conditions.** One's responsibility to give religious assent comes into play only if the pope or one's bishop acts in his official capacity, proposes a teaching bearing on a matter of faith or morals, and calls for its acceptance as certain. Dealing with religious assent to papal teaching, Vatican II alludes to this last condition by saying such teaching must be sincerely adhered to according to the pope's "manifest mind and will, which he expresses chiefly either by the type of document, or by the frequent proposal of the same teaching, or by his manner of speaking" (LG 25).[96]

Thus, there are five kinds of cases in which one has no responsibility to give religious assent: (i) when popes and bishops express opinions on matters outside faith and morals, (ii) when they speak or write on matters of faith and morals but as individual believers or private theologians rather than in their official capacity, (iii) when they teach officially but only tentatively, (iv) when they put forward observations and arguments, without calling for their acceptance in themselves, but as incidental to a truth of faith or a teaching which calls for religious assent, or (v) when they give merely disciplinary directives, for example, that certain opinions should not be taught while certain others may be. In all these cases, one's responsibility is not to assent, but to listen respectfully, try to understand what the pastors are saying, and obey any disciplinary directives.[97]

b) **One sometimes owes assent to collective episcopal statements.** The teaching proposed in collective episcopal statements calls for religious assent if (as is often the case) it repeats teaching which otherwise calls for such assent, or if the statement is endorsed by the pope and/or by one's own bishop and its teaching

---

95. This submission of will in no way violates the freedom of the act of faith, about which the Congregation for the Doctrine of the Faith, *Instruction on the Ecclesial Vocation of the Theologian,* 36, *AAS* 82 (1990) 1566, *OR,* 2 July 1990, 4, teaches: "In fact this freedom does not indicate at all freedom with regard to the truth but signifies the free self-determination of the person in conformity with his moral obligation to accept the truth." Nor is the submission of will involved in religious assent in any way at odds with Vatican II's teaching on religious liberty (see DH 1–4, 7; cf. *CMP,* 3.B.9 and 3.G).

96. See *CIC,* cc. 752–53. Teaching documents issued by the various offices of the Holy See with express papal approval are acts of the ordinary papal magisterium, since in approving such a document the pope formally cooperates with the action of the relevant office.

97. Some reduce the responsibility to give religious assent to that of the respect which remains even in cases in which religious assent is not due. For instance, Coriden, "Commentary: Book III: The Teaching Office of the Church," 548, commenting on *CIC,* c. 752, translates *religiosum obsequium* as "religious respect." But *obsequium* means submission (although in this case not the submission of faith). For Vatican I (DS 3008/1789) and Vatican II (DV 5) describe the act of faith as "plenum revelanti Deo intellectus et voluntatis obsequium," which can hardly be translated "full *respect* of intellect and will to God revealing," and the formula for religious assent plainly is derived from the description of the act of faith.

meets the other conditions under which religious assent is required. Sometimes, when something contained in a collective episcopal statement troubles faithful Catholics, what troubles them is not proposed as certain, but only as a probable judgment. Such a judgment calls for respectful consideration but not for religious assent. If a collective statement—for example, a statement by a national conference of bishops—which is not endorsed by the pope should propose as certain a teaching on a matter of faith and morals which is compatible with but not included in other magisterial teaching, any Catholic troubled by the teaching should ask his or her own bishop what he intends to teach in a way that calls for religious assent.

3. Diverse Kinds of Teachings Call for Religious Assent

Not all teachings to which religious assent is due are of the same kind, but one cannot always tell which are which.

Sometimes the teaching is one which the Church proposes as revealed, so that it actually calls for the assent of faith. However, the teaching's status may not be clear to some Catholics, so that they mistakenly think it falls outside the ambit of faith. Still, as a constant and most firm teaching on a matter of faith or morals, it surely deserves at least religious assent.

Sometimes the teaching is not one which the Church proposes as revealed, yet in reality it pertains to revelation. Popes and other bishops not only teach the truths of faith which they have received, but clarify and defend them with the help of the Holy Spirit, bringing forth new things in harmony with the old (see LG 25; cf. DV 8, DH 1). At the leading edge of the development of doctrine and its expression, bishops (and even popes when not speaking *ex cathedra*) do not individually enjoy the gift of discerning infallibly what belongs to divine truth. Thus, while their newly developing teaching may in fact pertain to revelation, the manner in which it is proposed does not make clear that it does, and so it calls only for religious assent.[98]

Sometimes the teaching is a theological explanation. As has been explained, popes and other bishops not only hand on the faith but form a common outlook in the Church for the sake of solidarity in the common work of catechesis, evangelization, liturgical practice, and so on. Teachings noninfallibly proposed for this purpose often join truths of faith with other propositions which seem true.

4. The Limits of the Responsibility to Assent Also Are Diverse

While the responsibility to give religious assent is limited, so too are the limits themselves.

a) Mistakes in papal and episcopal teaching are not to be presumed. Teachings to which religious assent is due usually are truths, even if not truths of faith. In the few cases in which such a teaching is mistaken, the mistake is hardly likely to be obvious. Popes and bishops generally seek theological advice and study

---

98. *CMP*, 35.F–G, mainly considered this sort of case. Plainly, in some cases teachings of this sort are hard to distinguish from those infallibly proposed by the ordinary magisterium. Thus, it is easy to make the mistake of thinking that only religious assent is due the latter and that the assent of faith is reserved for truths which are clearly included in divine revelation by being witnessed in Scripture or solemnly defined by the Church (see *CMP*, 36.B).

it carefully before teaching on complex and difficult issues. If their authoritative teaching rejects some theological opinion, as it must if it concerns a question disputed among theologians, that is a better reason for thinking the theological opinion mistaken than for rejecting the papal or episcopal teaching.

Moreover, most Catholics have no more reliable way of interpreting Scripture or knowing and interpreting the Church's tradition than listening to and thinking with the magisterium. Very few are such experts in philosophy, science, or other fields of scholarship that they would really know that the Church's teaching depended on a mistaken premise from one of those fields, even should that occur. In practice, most of the faithful could question a pope's or bishop's judgment only by trusting some scholars in preference to others. But in doing that they would presume to make for themselves the judgment among experts which the pope and bishops are not only divinely authorized but better qualified to make.

b) **The limits of the responsibility to obey laws are not relevant.** Because giving religious assent to the teaching of popes and bishops is not obeying them as the Church's governors, the responsibility to assent is not limited by the limits of the responsibility to obey. It is a mistake to suppose that, because doubtful laws do not bind, teachings which seem doubtful do not call for assent. Quite the contrary. Propositions regarding faith or morals which otherwise would be doubtful deserve assent if the pope or one's own bishop teaches them as truths to be accepted as certain. Similarly, it is a mistake to suppose that epikeia (see *CMP*, 11.E.10–11) applies to the responsibility to give religious assent, or that teachings which some neglect are therefore invalidated as are laws which fall into disuse.

c) **Still, authoritative teachings can be known to be mistaken.** Teachings which otherwise would call for religious assent can, however, be known to be in error. The responsibility to give religious assent therefore is limited, and its limits vary with the diverse ways in which papal and episcopal teachings, although proposed as certainly true, can be mistaken. Needless to say, the existence of these limits in no way justifies radical theological dissent from the Church's constant and most firm moral teaching.[99]

d) **A more authoritative teaching can limit responsibility.** A papal or episcopal teaching might be incompatible with a truth of faith asserted in Scripture, solemnly defined, or already proposed infallibly by the ordinary magisterium. Then the act of faith of someone aware that this was so would block religious assent to

---

99. *Radical theological dissent* means the dissent of those theologians who not only both refuse to assent to the Church's constant and most firm teaching and propagate dissent from it but offer pastoral guidance to the faithful contrary to that given by the pope, and thus usurp his pastoral office (see *CMP*, 36). In doing so, they violate a norm stated by the National Conference of Catholic Bishops, "Human Life in Our Day," 53, in *Pastoral Letters*, ed. Nolan, 3:174: "Even responsible dissent does not excuse one from faithful presentation of the authentic doctrine of the Church when one is performing a pastoral ministry in her name." In his exchanges with the Congregation for the Doctrine of the Faith, Charles E. Curran, *Faithful Dissent* (Kansas City, Mo.: Sheed and Ward, 1986), 152–53, 212–13, 266, invoked these "Norms of Licit Theological Dissent," but omitted the crucial sentence. Radical dissent also is rejected explicitly by the Holy See: Congregation for the Doctrine of the Faith, *Instruction on the Ecclesial Vocation of the Theologian*, 27 and 33–34, *AAS* 82 (1990) 1561 and 1564–65, *OR*, 2 July 1990, 3.

that element of teaching. If the teaching of one's bishop (or of a group of bishops including one's own) which would otherwise call for religious assent were at odds with papal teaching, religious assent to the latter would block assent to the former, due to papal primacy (see DS 3059–64/1826–31). A teaching of a general council, such as Vatican II, even if not proposed as definitive, can be proposed infallibly inasmuch as it was previously defined or infallibly proposed by the ordinary magisterium. But if such a teaching does not pertain to faith, at least it calls for the religious assent due the teaching of the pope who confirms it, and so supersedes prior papal and episcopal teachings which otherwise would call for religious assent. However, elements of conciliar teaching which otherwise would call for religious assent could be superseded by subsequent papal or conciliar teaching.

e) **A contrary certitude can limit responsibility.** The responsibility to assent to authoritative teachings which are theological explanations can be limited in an additional way. Teachings of this kind depend partly on propositions which do not pertain to faith but seem true. But such propositions can be false, and someone who really knows the relevant subject matter can be certain they are. Such certitude limits the responsibility of religious assent, since one reasonably assents only to elements of a theological explanation which are consistent with other truths of which one is certain.[100] However, while a contrary certitude can block religious assent, the responsibility to assent is not blocked by considerations which merely raise doubts; thus, such assent is owed to many teachings which one otherwise would doubt.[101]

5. Within Due Limits, One Should Not Withhold Religious Assent

Where religious assent is known to be due, it is a sin to withhold it. Here this sin is called *deliberate nonassent.* To communicate such nonassent to others with

100. Congregation for the Doctrine of the Faith, *Instruction on the Ecclesial Vocation of the Theologian,* 31, *AAS* 82 (1990) 1562, *OR,* 2 July 1990, 3, allows for this limit by speaking of cases in which "the theologian's difficulty remains because the arguments to the contrary seem more persuasive to him [praevalere videntur]. Faced with a proposition to which he feels he cannot [non existimat se posse] give his intellectual assent, the theologian nevertheless has the duty to remain open to a deeper examination of the question." The translation, "seem more persuasive to him" is too weak; "seem to prevail" would be accurate, for the logic of the passage makes it clear that the contrary arguments must have apparent force sufficient to block assent. In volume one, this limit on the responsibility to give religious assent was overlooked (see *CMP,* 35.G).

101. Congregation for the Doctrine of the Faith, *Instruction on the Ecclesial Vocation of the Theologian,* 28, *AAS* 82 (1990) 1561, *OR,* 2 July 1990, 3: "Such a disagreement could not be justified if it were based solely upon the fact that the validity of the given teaching is not evident or upon the opinion that the opposite position would be the more probable." Francis A. Sullivan, S.J., *Magisterium: Teaching Authority in the Catholic Church* (New York: Paulist Press, 1983), 159, holds the view rejected here. While rightly arguing that *obsequium* is correctly translated as *submission* not *respect,* he mistakenly claims (164) that submission can be reduced to an attitude of docility, so that assent on the part of those not convinced of the truth of a teaching is not required by virtue of the Church's teaching authority (166). Thus, Sullivan reduces *obsequium* to the attitude one should take toward those official statements of popes and bishops which do not call for assent. The same author, "The Theologian's Ecclesial Vocation and the 1990 CDF Instruction," *Theological Studies* 52 (1991): 63, makes it clear that he continues to hold the position which the Congregation rejects. For a more adequate treatment of the responsibility of religious assent, see James J. Mulligan, *Theologians and Authority within the Living Church* (Braintree, Mass.: The Pope John Center, 1986), 95–118.

the intention of encouraging them to share in it is a more serious sin, called here *sinful dissent.*[102] Those who withhold assent from a truth of faith, mistakenly thinking that it calls only for religious assent, also are guilty of religious nonassent rather than of heresy, and propagating such an opinion is sinful dissent rather than propagating heresy.

a) **Deliberate nonassent is a grave matter.** As has been explained (1.c), religious assent, although distinct from faith in God, is an act of human faith grounded in divine faith. Thus, while the sin of deliberate nonassent is not directly against divine faith, it does violate (without withdrawing) the commitment of faith, insofar as that is a human commitment not only to God but to the covenantal communion which is the Church. Because of the seriousness of this violation in itself, and because it interferes with ecclesial solidarity, it seems that deliberate nonassent is a grave matter.[103] Two factors can aggravate its gravity: (i) if one denies not the teaching of one's bishop but papal or conciliar teaching, and (ii) if one persists in the sin after being warned by the Holy See or one's bishop.[104]

b) **To dissent sinfully is graver than merely to refuse assent.** Just as one can commit heresy in one's heart by a single choice, so the sin of deliberate nonassent can be committed simply by choosing not to submit to a teaching to which assent is due. However, sinful dissent is an even graver matter, since it gives others an occasion of sin and more seriously damages the solidarity of the Church.[105]

---

102. Logically, one might define *nonassent* as the omission of due assent and *dissent* as the assertion of a proposition incompatible with one to which assent is due. However, in both cases the sin is in the deliberate nonfulfillment of the responsibility to give religious assent (which, if it were given when due, would forestall the assertion of any incompatible proposition). Common use is followed here in referring to the communication of nonassent as *dissent,* since such communication plainly challenges the Church's teaching authority, whether or not it involves an explicit assertion of an incompatible position.

103. Papal teaching on the obligation to give religious assent is so insistent that it would be ludicrous to suppose that the popes have been dealing with a merely light matter. See Pius IX (DS 2879–80/1683–84, 2922/1722); Leo XIII, *Est sane, ASS* 21 (1888) 321–23 (cited in LG 20, n. 16 [86 in Abbott]); Pius XI (DS 3725/2253). Pius XII, *Humani generis, AAS* 42 (1950) 568, *PE,* 240.20, points out the seriousness of the obligation to give religious assent; he also explains that if a pope makes a point of settling a matter disputed among theologians, it can no longer be treated as an open question. Vatican II does not repudiate Pius XII's position on this matter, but cites as authoritative the passage which includes it (see OT 16, n. 31 [46 in Abbott]).

104. That the first factor aggravates the seriousness of deliberate nonassent is clear from Vatican II's statement of the obligation of religious assent in LG 25. That the second factor aggravates its seriousness is clear from the fact that after a warning, persistence in deliberate nonassent from papal or conciliar teaching is a canonical crime: *CIC,* c. 1371.

105. Congregation for the Doctrine of the Faith, *Instruction on the Ecclesial Vocation of the Theologian,* 30 and 40, *AAS* 82 (1990) 1562 and 1569, *OR,* 2 July 1990, 3 and 4, tells theologians to make known to the magisterial authorities any problems they have, thereby to work toward their resolution. In 27, 30, 34, and 39 (*AAS,* 1561, 1562, 1565, and 1568; *OR,* 3 and 4), the Congregation excludes publishing divergent opinions "as though they were non-arguable conclusions," "turning to the 'mass media'," "shaping a common opinion" at odds with the teaching proposed by the magisterium, and "opposing the Magisterium by exerting the pressure of public opinion, making the excuse of a 'consensus' among theologians, maintaining that the theologian is the prophetical spokesman of a 'base' or autonomous community which would be the source of all truth." Some theologians argue that the exclusion of dissent would prevent theological progress, but that argument is unsound in two ways. First, theologians can publish their views and arguments in

c) Not all who deny an authoritative teaching commit these sins. As explained above (2.a, 4.d–e), religious assent is required only under certain conditions, and the responsibility to give such assent is limited, because assent can be blocked. In that case, those who do not accept an authoritative teaching are not guilty of deliberate nonassent.

Moreover, even if many Catholics' adherence to dissenting positions is objectively indefensible, they do not commit the sin of deliberate nonassent if they really are convinced that on those issues the conditions requiring religious assent have not been met. And when ongoing, radical, theological dissent has caused great confusion in the Church, many Catholics may suppose that the conditions requiring religious assent are never met with respect to nondefined teachings which they personally do not find convincing. Of course, even if they do not commit the sin of deliberate nonassent, their error still might be culpable, as resulting from self-induced blindness due to previous sins (see *CMP*, 3.C.6–7).

d) Following subjectivist conscience is deliberate nonassent. The sin of deliberate nonassent is committed by those who rationalize their failure to assent as following their "conscience," using the word in a subjectivist sense. Conscience truly so-called is formed by moral truth, which can be known with certitude by the help of the Church's teaching (see *CMP*, 3.E–F).[106] "Conscience" in a subjectivist sense refers to one's own opinions and preferences, treated as more authoritative than any practical truth or requirement originating beyond oneself (see *CMP*, 3.G). But to treat one's own opinions and preferences as more authoritative than the Church's teaching is deliberate refusal to give that teaching the assent it deserves; and this refusal is only rationalized, not justified, by saying: "My conscience tells me it is right for me to do X, so it is right for me, no matter what the pope says!" While not the position of those convinced that in some instance the conditions requiring religious assent are not met, this is the position of those who do not care whether the conditions are met. Quite simply, these latter refuse assent on the

---

academic journals and present them at professional meetings, where they can state them as opinions or difficulties without asserting them unqualifiedly as truths; at the same time, they can warn the faithful that they should never use the authority of any theologian or group of theologians to justify a refusal to assent to papal or episcopal teachings; in this way theologians can do everything necessary to promote study and reflection without ever contradicting the teaching proposed by the magisterium. Second, throughout history, the greatest and most original theological work has been done by those explaining, developing, and defending truths of the Christian faith and way of life against nonbelievers and heretics. Dissenting theologians seldom manifest much originality and creativity; almost always they do little more than restate views and arguments which were already in circulation outside the Church.

106. Congregation for the Doctrine of the Faith, *Instruction on the Ecclesial Vocation of the Theologian*, 38, *AAS* 82 (1990) 1567, *OR*, 2 July 1990, 4, explains: "Finally, argumentation appealing to the obligation to follow one's own conscience cannot legitimate dissent. This is true, first of all, because conscience illumines the practical judgement about a decision to make, while here we are concerned with the truth of a doctrinal pronouncement. This is furthermore the case because while the theologian, like every believer, must follow his conscience, he is also obliged to form it. Conscience is not an independent and infallible faculty. It is an act of moral judgement regarding a responsible choice. A right conscience is one duly illumined by faith and by the objective moral law and it presupposes, as well, the uprightness of the will in the pursuit of the true good."

general principle that no one, not even those who speak in Jesus' name, can tell them what to do and what not to do.

Question J: How Should One Cultivate and Perfect One's Faith?

Although God's revelation in Jesus is the same gospel for all persons, times, and places, the community of faith must continually receive God's message, and each believer must appropriate it. In part, this is done through prayer: listening to God's word and responding to it in an ongoing, personal way. Faith also should be perfected by catechesis and study, and strengthened by struggling against difficulties as they arise. One also should attend to facts and possibilities relevant to putting faith into practice.

1. Instruction and Study Are Needed to Develop and Protect Faith

Even though the act of faith is not only a human act but a divine gift, and the content of faith surpasses human comprehension, one should strive to understand the whole of the Catholic faith as fully as possible and to reason within the framework of that faith. Objections and difficulties with respect to truths of faith should be considered thoughtfully, not merely repressed or brushed aside. This effort, necessary to develop and protect faith, requires lifelong docility and inquiry.

a) One should remain receptive to catechetical formation. Having accepted the person of Jesus by faith and turned to him with conversion of heart, one receives catechetical formation to know him better, to fully understand the gospel's promises and requirements, and to know how to follow the way Jesus marked out for his disciples.[107] Preparing for and following each of the sacraments, so that they can be fruitful, catechesis is not only for children, but for Christians of every age and condition. The faith of adults too "should continually be enlightened, stimulated and renewed, so that it may pervade the temporal realities in their charge."[108]

b) One should respond to challenges to one's faith. Faith is often challenged, either by the objections of others or by one's own experiences. Since the ground of faith, the all-knowing and all-truthful God revealing himself, provides a certitude superior to all others, no challenge really can call faith's truth into question. Thus, in the face of persistent challenges, one should not in any way qualify one's assent to relevant elements of faith; but because such challenges also are rooted in something real, simply repressing them or brushing them aside is unreasonable, and leads to dogmatism and obscurantism. To entertain such challenges without

---

107. The responsibility to be receptive to catechetical formation is part of the Christian's "grave obligation toward Christ, our Master, ever more fully to understand the truth received from him, faithfully to proclaim it, and vigorously to defend it" (DH 14).

108. John Paul II, *Catechesi tradendae,* 43, *AAS* 71 (1979) 1312, Flannery, 2:788; cf. 20 and 23, *AAS,* 1293–94 and 1296–97, Flannery, 2:774 and 776. Vatican II teaches that if Catholics neglect their training in the faith, they conceal God from others instead of revealing him to them (see GS 19). *CIC,* c. 229, §1, declares: "Lay persons are bound by the obligation and possess the right to acquire a knowledge of Christian doctrine adapted to their capacity and condition so that they can live in accord with that doctrine, announce it, defend it when necessary, and be enabled to assume their role in exercising the apostolate."

trying to respond to them, however, is to endanger, and eventually surrender, one's faith. Therefore, a sound and satisfying response to objections and difficulties should be energetically sought. Such a response takes into account and does full justice to whatever reality underlies the challenge, something which always can be done inasmuch as faith is not partisan but embraces truth and goodness integrally.

c) **Finding the response to challenges should be a communal effort.** Like so many other responsibilities of Christian life, this one is hardly likely to be fulfilled adequately unless Catholics really work together to fulfill it. In general, all believers should cooperate to sustain and build up one another's faith. If one's faith is challenged, one should communicate the problem accurately and confidently to someone capable of helping. Naturally, children will first go to their parents and teachers, parishioners to their pastors, and so on. But if a first attempt to solve a problem is unsuccessful, one should not let the matter drop, but should seek further help elsewhere. Someone from whom others seek help should take seriously the responsibility to provide it, seeking help in turn with regard to problems he or she finds too difficult. Those who think they have found sound and satisfying responses to challenges to their own faith should share them with others who might benefit.

d) **Uninvited doubts which are not difficulties are temptations.** When receiving Holy Communion, one may find oneself thinking: "Perhaps the host is nothing more than the wafer it appears to be." Every believer sometimes experiences such doubts, whose force comes from emotion rather than any defect in the commitment of faith. Faith's answer is already known to doubts of this kind, and they need not be treated as challenges to which a response must be sought.

Such spontaneous doubts cannot by themselves constitute the sin—against which Vatican I warns (see DS 3014/1794, 3036/1815)—of calling the faith into question. Rather, they are temptations, similar to other temptations to commit a sin of thought (see *CMP*, 15.F–G). Since they sometimes have their psychological origin in some unrepented sin, when they arise one should examine one's conscience. If one finds nothing there, one should pray for an increase of faith and turn one's thoughts to other matters. If the temptation persists, the problem is not moral but psychological, unless the temptation is diabolical, which always is possible but ordinarily should not be assumed (see *CMP*, 18.1).

2. Faith Requires both Attention to Scripture and Prayer

One person receives another's self-communication only in conversation: by listening attentively, pondering what the other wishes to share, and responding to it. Christian faith accepts God's personal self-revelation in Jesus. Scripture bears witness to revelation, and prayer responds to it (see *CMP*, 29.A). Thus, faith requires both prayer and attention to Scripture.

a) **These are necessary to receive and hand on faith.** The receiving and handing on of faith is tradition, the continuity of the communion of faith over time. One essential principle by which tradition develops in the Church, Vatican II teaches, is "the contemplation and study made by believers, who treasure these things in their hearts (see Lk 2.19, 51)" (DV 8). Believers contemplate God's word and study it chiefly by attending to Scripture, especially but not only when it is read in the liturgy. Furthermore, "prayer should accompany the reading of sacred Scripture, so that God and we may talk together; for 'we speak to him when we pray; we hear him when we read the divine sayings' [note omitted]" (DV 25).

b) One should deepen faith with liturgical and other prayer. Vatican II teaches that "when the Church prays or sings or acts, the faith of those taking part is nourished" (SC 33). The sacraments, especially, strengthen faith and express it (see SC 59). The contemplative dimension of each Christian's life is fundamentally the response of faith, hope, and charity to God's revelation and to continuing communion with the Father through Jesus in the Holy Spirit.[109] This dimension is deepened by listening to and meditating on the Word of God, and by individual, family, and group prayer, not least prayer of adoration for God's infinite majesty and of praise and thanksgiving for his revelation by which he gives himself to believers.[110]

c) One should strengthen one's commitment with explicit acts of faith. The commitment of faith is exercised and thus strengthened through deliberately recalling the truth of faith in general or one or more truths of faith in particular and renewing one's willing assent. Conscious and active participation in the liturgy includes such acts, not only in the Profession of Faith (the Credo) but also in the acceptance of the scriptural readings as the word of the Lord, the affirming *Amen* to the reality of the Eucharist as Jesus' body and blood, and so on. Many devotions also include explicit acts of faith—for example, the rosary begins with the Apostles' Creed. However, it is right and meritorious for every believer regularly to make personal, informal acts of faith, recalling the wonderful truths of salvation, cherishing them, and being animated by them.

d) One should nourish faith with prayer of petition. The requests for help which members of any community make of one another not only presuppose the bond of community, but also express and enhance the commitment to community and the confidence of those who seek and receive help.

Faith is one's bond of community with the divine persons, who alone can provide every good, and with the angels and the saints who are their intimate friends. Thus, asking help from the divine persons, either directly or through intercessors, presupposes faith: "Truly I tell you, if you say to this mountain, 'Be taken up and thrown into the sea,' and if you do not doubt in your heart, but believe that what you say will come to pass, it will be done for you. So I tell you, whatever you ask

109. Congregation for the Doctrine of the Faith, *Letter to the Bishops of the Catholic Church on Some Aspects of Christian Meditation, AAS* 82 (1990) 362–79, *OR,* 2 Jan. 1990, 8–10, 12, warns against dangers arising from the use of forms of meditation inspired by non-Christian religions, and teaches that Christian prayer always is rooted in divine revelation and seeks God by way of Jesus; the Congregation explains that authentic Christian personal prayer does not displace the sacraments, harmonizes with the liturgy, avoids impersonal techniques, does not focus on the self and on "experiences," does not prefer a mental void to Christian images and concepts, is accompanied by moral purification and the renunciation of selfishness, and bears fruit in works of love.

110. See Congregation for Religious and Secular Institutes, *The Contemplative Dimension of Religious Life, EV* 7 (1980–81) 470–73, Flannery, 2:245.

for in prayer, believe that you have received it, and it will be yours" (Mk 11.23–24; cf. Mt 17.20, 21.22; Lk 17.5–6).

Jesus frequently commended the faith of those who earnestly sought his help (see Mt 8.10; 9.22, 29; 15.28; Mk 5.34; 10.52; Lk 7.9, 50; 8.48; 17.19; 18.42). Prayer also nourishes faith.[111] Therefore, in both private and communal prayer, one should regularly and persistently beg God's help in every need. (On the necessary qualities of such prayer and the problem of seemingly unanswered prayers, see *CMP*, 29.D–E.)[112]

3. Faith Requires Attention to One's Situation and to Events In It

To live by faith is to live not only in accord with moral truth but in conscious cooperation with God's saving plan. But God's wise and loving providence embraces not only the general lines of salvation history but every detail of each creature's situation and every minute event affecting it (see Ps 145.8–20; Wis 8.1, 14.3–5; Mt 10.29–31; Rom 8.28). Thus, neither the Church as a whole nor her members nor families and other communities within the Church can learn all God wishes them to know about his plan and will by considering revelation alone. What can be called *situational factors*—that is, the actual situation and what is happening in it—must also be taken into account. Referring to some of these situational factors, John XXIII and Vatican II speak of the Church's duty to examine the signs of the times in the light of the gospel.[113]

Paying attention to situational factors does not mean relativizing faith or attempting to judge it by contemporary insights, attitudes, and values; the latter, rather, are to be judged by faith, whose light illuminates the contemporary world and makes its true significance appear. That significance must be grasped and acted upon.

a) **One should interpret situational factors by means of faith.** God's revelation in Jesus raises his servants to the status of friends: "I do not call you servants any longer, because the servant does not know what the master is doing; but I have called you friends, because I have made known to you everything that I have heard from my Father" (Jn 15.15). The providential plan of creation, redemption, and sanctification is revealed in Jesus (see Eph 1.9–10, Col 1.24–28).

This revelation provides Jesus' followers of all times and conditions with the general direction they need to play their own roles as God's friends and collaborators in carrying out his plan. Moreover, every good situational factor is just as it is because God wills it in accord with his plan, while no evil can occur unless God permits it for the fulfillment of his plan as a whole. Thus, faith can be used to

---

111. The parable of the dishonest judge (Lk 18.1–7), which teaches the need to pray persistently, ends by raising the question whether the Son of Man, when he comes, will find faith on earth (Lk 18.8). The implicit answer is: Only if Christians persistently pray. See Joseph A. Fitzmyer, S.J., *The Gospel According to Luke (X–XXIV): Introduction, Translation, and Notes,* The Anchor Bible, 28A (Garden City, N.Y.: Doubleday, 1985), 1177.

112. A brief, clear, and practical treatment of prayer: Vincent McNabb, O.P., *Faith and Prayer* (Westminster, Md.: Newman Press, 1953), 133–215.

113. See UR 4, AA 14, PO 9, GS 4; cf. GS 11, 44; M.–D. Chenu, O.P., "Les signes des temps," *Nouvelle revue théologique* 87 (1965): 29–39.

decipher the meaning of many situational factors which one can see as relevant to one's own responsibilities and choices (see AA 4).

In sum, only by using faith to interpret the signs of the times and similar situational factors does one pay attention to everything God wishes to communicate—that is, not only to his general revelation but to his special messages—so that one can play one's own part in carrying out his providential plan of creation, redemption, and sanctification.

b) Vatican II's teaching on the signs of the times should be a model. Vatican II teaches that to fulfill her mission the Church must scrutinize the signs of the times (see GS 3–4). These indicate God's presence and purpose in the happenings, needs, and desires of contemporary humankind, including Christians. The Council says the Church can decipher these signs because the Spirit of the Lord leads God's people. The decoding device is faith, which "throws a new light on everything, manifests God's design for the human person's total vocation, and thus directs the mind to solutions which are fully human" (GS 11).

The example of Vatican II should be followed in this matter. Not only the universal Church but particular churches, bodies within the Church (such as religious communities), and individual Catholics must read the indications of situational factors in order to discern and fulfill their missions or personal vocations (personal vocation will be treated in 2.E). The signs to be deciphered in each situation are those problems, opportunities, and resources relevant to decision and action. The needs, not only of Catholics but of anyone whom they are called to serve, help make clear God's plan and will. Faith guides this process of discernment, and the Holy Spirit helps one bring faith to bear on the facts of the situation.

c) Situational factors cannot falsify Christian principles. At each moment of decision, what one discerns as the significance of situational factors helps complete the message God wants to communicate to those who accept his revelation with faith. Thus, reading the signs of the times and other situational factors can be thought of as a continuing effort of faith to accept and act on God's living revelation. However, the true meaning of situational factors can be discerned only in the light of all the general principles of Christian doctrine and morality. Hence, no sound discernment of such signs can lead to judgments at odds with Christian principles. To suppose the contrary would be like supposing that correctly using a computer to solve particular problems could show that the mathematical principles on which all computation is based are themselves faulty.[114]

d) Groups should seek consensus in interpreting situational factors. Often Christian action on large-scale problems, such as socioeconomic reform, is seri-

---

114. Vatican II's method of reading the signs of the times in no way justifies the appeal, made both by some Latin American liberation theologians and by dissenting theologians in affluent nations, to contemporary Christian experience to try to justify moral views at odds with Catholic teaching. The Council's method proceeds neither solely by deduction from general principles nor solely by induction from experienced situations but by dialectical reflection on data in the light of faith. This process uses both deductive and inductive reasoning to arrive at synthetic insights, which make it possible to put faith into practice and transform existing situations according to God's plan and will.

ously impeded because those who should work together disagree in their interpretation of situational factors. Working from diverse and often incompatible analyses of the reality they confront, various dedicated individuals and groups proceed independently, often interfere with one another's efforts, and always fall short of the impact they would have if they could work together effectively. Plainly, in such cases all involved have the responsibility, which can be grave, to seek consensus in their analysis for the sake of solidarity in acting on behalf of the important goods they wish to serve.

Several steps should be taken in seeking this consensus. Since a correct reading of situational factors cannot conflict with Christian principles, the first step is to exclude interpretations which the magisterium, in reflecting on these principles and applying them, has rejected as unsound. The second step is for those concerned to engage in sincere dialogue, with the twin aims of developing points in which their understandings can complement one another and of overcoming differences insofar as possible. The third step is for those subject to some authority governing their action in the relevant field to subordinate their personal insights to the judgment of the proper authority. Of course, throughout this process, all involved should pray together for the light and healing of the Holy Spirit, who alone can overcome blind spots and biases.

Despite every effort, however, the consensus often will not be as complete and widespread as desirable. Yet those who see matters diversely will have to act on what they believe to be the sound interpretation of relevant situational factors, even when that means they will be working to some extent at cross purposes. When this happens, everyone concerned should be eager to remain united in charity (see Eph 4.3) and so should tolerate legitimate differences and strive to minimize conflict.

4. Failures to Cultivate and Perfect Faith Are Sinful

The importance of failures in these matters might lead one to suppose that they are likely to be mortal sins. In fact, however, they are more often venial, although such a failure can be a grave matter in particular cases.

a) Such failures are less important singly than cumulatively. Among the most basic and serious responsibilities of a husband and a wife are keeping their marital relationship always in mind, sharing their thoughts and feelings, listening to each other, working to overcome tensions, and being alert to each other's signs of need for help and affection. These responsibilities are so constant and pervasive that they cannot be fulfilled by any particular act but only by innumerable small, daily acts.

Most such acts, rather than being individually chosen, flow from and implement the marital commitment itself. So fundamental are those responsibilities that married people seldom are tempted to reject them entirely. Only a proposal to be unfaithful or to stop trying to fulfill the marital commitment carries with it the rejection of the fundamental responsibilities arising from marriage as a communion of persons.

It is much the same with one's responsibilities regarding faith. To know one's faith, to respond to challenges to it, to attend to God's word in Scripture, to converse with him in prayer, and to interpret the signs of his plan and will in the actual situation: these are similarly basic responsibilities. No particular act fulfills them completely, and no one ever rejects them entirely unless considering apostasy.

b) Most failures in these matters are venial sins. In a great many cases, the failure of individuals to fulfill these responsibilities is due to omission without choice. Such an omission cannot be a mortal sin (see *CMP*, 15.1). (The responsibility of parents with respect to their children's religious formation will be considered in 9.F.5.)

Even when an individual freely chooses not to perform a particular act suited to contribute to fulfilling these responsibilities, that choice is likely to be, at worst, a venial sin. For in these matters, many particular acts, considered in themselves, are morally optional—for example, praying at certain times of the day or using particular forms of popular devotion.[115] And others are morally required only inasmuch as one recognizes them as good and feasible and has no good reason for not choosing them. To deliberately omit such acts out of laziness, an incompatible inclination to amusement, or something of the sort would be a venial sin.

c) Mortal sins are possible in these matters. In some circumstances, however, one can have a grave responsibility in these matters to do something in particular, yet be tempted not to do it. For instance, someone struggling with a sin of weakness has a grave responsibility to pray persistently for God's grace, but may be tempted to give up the struggle and, in choosing to give in to that temptation, choose to stop praying. Again, a college or university student whose faith is challenged by his or her studies has a grave responsibility to seek help to resolve the difficulties, but may be tempted not to make the effort, and, motivated partly by rebellious feelings, may deliberately allow his or her faith to be subverted.

Question K: How Can One Properly Honor God and Show Reverence?

Acts of worship are the chief way of honoring God and manifesting humility, reverence, and devotion toward him. Chapter three will treat Catholic worship, centering, of course, in the sacrifice of the Mass and sacrament of the Eucharist. The present question is concerned only with those ways of honoring God and showing him reverence which, while presupposing and deepening faith, need not involve or be based on the central act of worship.

It will be useful to begin by considering the general human responsibility to worship God and the sins related to this responsibility. Then the many appropriate ways in which Catholics express their faith and honor God will be considered. Among these are making vows and taking oaths—practices which, used rightly, presuppose faith and reverently express it, and so manifest the honor in which God's people hold him.

115. See Gerald Kelly, S.J., "How Often Must We Pray?" *Review for Religious* 8 (1949): 289–96.

1. It Is Good and Right that Every Human Person Worship God

In himself, God is perfect goodness and love. He creates and orders the universe, including humankind, out of pure generosity. Human persons depend entirely on him; they cannot hope that any of their efforts will bear fruit without his help. For that reason, they should do what they can to please God and should seek his help constantly.

Moreover, everyone sometimes sins (as people have from the beginning) against God's wise and loving plan. In sinning, one becomes alienated not only from God but from others and even from one's own better self. One needs God's forgiveness and mercy. Thus, because it is both due God and in one's own interest, one should recognize the reality of God and the truth of the human relationship with him, will to act accordingly, and do appropriate acts precisely to express this recognition and will. This recognition and will, together with the appropriate acts which express it, constitute worship.[116]

a) **Human reverence and worship are strictly due God.** Considering who God is and what he has done, is doing, and promises to do for humankind, each and every human person has a strict obligation to give God the highest honor and to worship him. The Latin text of the opening of the Preface of the Mass beautifully expresses this point with regard to a central element of Christian worship, thanksgiving for God's saving work in Jesus: "It is indeed fitting and right, our duty and our salvation, always and everywhere to give thanks to you, Lord, holy Father, almighty and eternal God" (translation supplied).[117]

b) **Outward acts of worship are necessary for two reasons.** God neither needs nor desires creatures' worship as if he profited from it, but he does want real friendship with humankind, and desires the expression of human worship insofar as it is essential to that friendship. There are two reasons why it is essential. First, because humans are not pure spirits but bodily beings, their interior acts remain incomplete until expressed outwardly. Second, each human person lives, acts, and so relates to God, not as an isolated individual but together with others, and one simply cannot think and will with others except by using language and engaging in outward behavior.

c) **Worship of God is prayer, praise, and sacrifice.** While worship takes the different forms of prayer, praise, and sacrifice, these are not entirely distinct from one another. Prayer is the most basic form of worship. Worship is prayer insofar as it involves addressing God and, as it were, conversing with him (see *CMP*, 29.A). It is praise insofar as it expresses in words recognition of God's excellence. It is sacrifice insofar as it expresses the worshipers' self-gift to God by setting something valuable apart for him and dedicating it to him. The offering of sacrifice involves prayer and is generally accompanied by appropriate words and gestures.[118]

---

116. The treatment here of devotion, adoration, sacrifice, oblation, and thanksgiving is based on but adapts the treatment of St. Thomas: *S.t.*, 2–2, qq. 82, 84–86, and 106.

117. "Vere dignum et iustum est, aequum et salutare, nos tibi semper et ubique gratias agere, Domine, sacte Pater, omnipotens aeterne Deus."

118. St. Thomas, *S.t.*, 2–2, q. 86, a. 1, makes a further distinction between oblation and sacrifice: all sacrifices are oblations, but not all oblations are sacrifices. Whatever is offered in

d) Worship is usually thanksgiving, atonement, or petition. All worship is adoration insofar as it expresses reverence for God in words and/or deeds which manifest the worshipers' subordination to his majesty and their complete dependence on him. Sometimes worship is offered simply for the sake of adoration. But usually worshipers have a further reason; and thanksgiving, atonement, and petition are different reasons for worship. Worship is thanksgiving insofar as it responds with gratitude to the friendship and specific benefits God has given, atonement insofar as it heals friendship with God of wounds due to sin, and petition insofar as it relies on friendship with God to seek his blessings.

2. One Should Avoid Every Form of False Worship and Superstition

True Christian worship is based on and flows from the truth of faith and the hope of Christians, relying for salvation on God's providence and grace. People without faith and hope cannot express and rely on wholly authentic friendship with God.[119] Hence, they engage in some makeshift practices. Insofar as such practices misdirect the religious impulse toward some real, more-than-human power apart from God, that power can only be demonic.

Some of these practices survive or reappear from time to time in contemporary culture. Instead of taking the form of false religions, however, today they may present themselves as programs of self-improvement or psychological therapy, or as new forms of "spirituality." Whatever their guise, one must be careful to avoid any participation in false worship and superstition.

Catholics do not engage in false worship and superstition when they honor Mary, the other saints, and the angels in ways approved by the Church. Such honor is based entirely on communion with God, and so it is altogether subordinate to his plan, will, saving work, and grace. In no way does such honor put created persons in God's place; one gives them nothing and expects nothing from them apart from God. Still, even within the context of essentially Catholic worship, there can be superstition (which will be treated in 3.B.3.c, f).

a) Idolatry always is a very grave matter. Since it is a fundamental truth of faith that God is unique, it might be thought that only someone who commits the sin of apostasy can be tempted to worship any other power. In some situations, however, people might suppose they could gain something by worshiping demonic powers or something else believed to be real yet neither God nor demonic. Moreover, one could be tempted to participate outwardly, without inner assent and commitment, in the rituals of some form of false religion, witchcraft, or spiritualism

---

worship is an oblation; it is a sacrifice only when something is done to what is offered to set it apart as sacred. The destruction of the oblation is one, but not the only, way of setting it apart as sacred (see *S.t.*, 2–2, q. 85, a. 3, ad 3).

119. *People without faith and hope* here refers to a variety of people whose situations before God are very diverse. Some (only God knows which ones or how many) have refused the light; others have not adequately heard the gospel, but perhaps enjoy that implicit faith which can suffice for salvation (see LG 14, 16; AG 7; GS 22; *CMP*, 30.2). But even the latter are at a disadvantage insofar as they try to worship God in a fallen world without Jesus' teaching and example to guide them.

whose conception of the divine falsifies the very reality of God, for example, some kind of pantheism, polytheism, or nature worship.

The First Commandment proclaims God's exclusive lordship and forbids idolatry: the worship of any other power (see Ex 20.2–4, Dt 5.6–8). Plainly, deliberate worship of anything but God denies his unique sovereignty and is inconsistent with trust in him and loving communion with him. But even feigned worship of anything but God not only expresses and fosters false belief but is an act of infidelity to God. A person feigning worship of something known to be unreal offers to that nonentity the outward service which fidelity requires be given God alone.[120] Therefore, to engage in idolatry in either of these ways is a very grave matter, for it is a betrayal of covenantal friendship with God.

b) Divination seeks guidance from a higher power apart from God. Divination is any attempt to foresee future contingencies which human beings can know neither naturally nor by divine revelation. In taking seriously omens, astrology, automatic writing, or reading palms, cards, tea leaves, and so forth, people engage in divination. Implicit in these practices is recourse to something more than human which is assumed either to know the future, to determine it, or both. Such a higher power other than God would be either personal and demonic or some sort of impersonal, cosmic, ruling force which subjected human life to inexorable fate. In either case, something other than God is regarded as if it were divine, insofar as enlightenment is sought from it to supplement the guidance God has made available.

c) Magic seeks success from a higher power apart from God. *Magic* here refers not to entertaining tricks, but to any attempt to determine the future, that is, to succeed in getting certain results which are neither within human and natural power nor expected from God. Black magic (witchcraft, sorcery) explicitly seeks the help of demonic powers. Other magic is not so clearheaded, for the more-than-natural power is left vague and mysterious. Those who make serious use of lucky charms, formulas, amulets, and other vain observances to avoid bad luck and promote good luck rely on magic. Seeking power, as divination seeks guidance, from something more than human apart from God, magic treats this something as if it were divine. Its help is sought to supplement the help God offers those who ask it of him with faith.

d) Using means one considers natural is not divination or magic. People learn by experience to expect particular future events on the basis of particular natural signs (for example, the next day's weather from the sunset) and to anticipate causal consequences from superficial properties (for example, the medicinal effects of certain herbs). Such knowledge can be used to make accurate predictions without understanding the causal relationships involved. When the means of knowing or causing is not thought to involve a higher power other than God, there is no question of divination or magic. Thus, similar outward acts can have different religious significance depending on what factors a person believes to be operative. For instance, someone who uses a so-called divining rod to locate water may believe

---

120. On idolatry: *S.t.*, 2–2, q. 94; *The Interpreter's Dictionary of the Bible*, s.v. "idolatry."

either that the procedure works naturally though mysteriously or that some preternatural influence is involved. Moreover, practices considered by the expert to involve only natural factors can be taken by the less sophisticated as preternatural, and attributed either to God or to some other more-than-human principle.

e) The use of divination and magic is always a grave matter. These practices involve the failure to submit entirely to God and trust in his providence and care. Even if it is neither thought of as a demonic power nor actually worshiped, something else is treated as if it shared God's knowledge and power, and so as if it deserved to be worshiped. No clearheaded person can abide in covenantal communion with God while engaging in such practices or leading others to engage in them. Therefore, they are grave matters.

Nevertheless, some Catholics use or seriously rely on various forms of divination and magic without realizing what they are doing. Their sin can be venial due to insufficient reflection. Still, such venial sins seriously harm one's Christian life, since relying on what are at best illusory sources of knowledge and power displaces the efforts one should make, the natural means one should use, and, above all, the light and strength one should seek and accept from God.

Without taking these things seriously, other Catholics nevertheless involve themselves in them out of idle curiosity or for amusement. Though not gravely sinful in itself, this should be avoided, since it always unnecessarily toys with superstition, often supports frauds, and sometimes leads others into more serious involvement.[121]

f) Attempts to summon the ghosts of the dead also are excluded. Such attempts, called *spiritism* or *spiritualism,* always risk evoking demonic activity, and often are undertaken for the sake of divination and/or magic. The séances conducted by supposed mediums often involve religious elements whose doctrinal basis denies Jesus' divinity.[122] If Catholics undertake such practices to seek reassurance about the fate of their loved ones, they show lack of confidence in prayer and the rites of the Church, and manifest underlying defects in their faith. Those who seek guidance through a medium also show lack of confidence in divine guidance (see 1 Chr 10.13–14). Participation is a grave matter, and the Church warns her members to avoid having anything to do with such practices (see DS 3642/2182).

3. One Honors God by Professing the Faith

One's profession of faith acknowledges God as creator, redeemer, and sanctifier, and so honors him. In many situations, one should openly profess one's faith. While there are times when silence is justified, to deny one's faith or fail to profess it when appropriate is to be disloyal to God.

a) One should openly profess the faith. The profession of faith—its expression in language—is the specific way in which the act of faith is outwardly performed. For this reason, a formal profession of faith precedes baptism, and often

---

121. On divination and magic, see *S.t.,* 2–2, qq. 95–96.
122. See LG 49, n. 2 (228 in Abbott); *New Catholic Encyclopedia,* s.v. "spiritualists."

is renewed in the liturgy. But a profession of faith can be appropriate and sometimes necessary in the course of daily life.

Jesus teaches: "Everyone therefore who acknowledges me before others, I also will acknowledge before my Father in heaven; but whoever denies me before others, I also will deny before my Father in heaven" (Mt 10.32–33; cf. Lk 9.26). Just as family members and friends honor one another and deepen their mutual commitments by openly acknowledging their bonds of communion, so Jesus' followers honor God and deepen their faith by openly and proudly professing it. Someone ashamed to acknowledge the faith dishonors God, just as he or she would dishonor a relative or friend by failing out of embarrassment to acknowledge that person; and someone who denies the faith, as Peter out of fear denied his relationship with Jesus, would be disloyal to God, as Peter was disloyal to Jesus (see Mt 26.69–75, Mk 14.66–72, Lk 22.54–62, Jn 18.25–27).

Moreover, because God truly is supremely good, and faith affirms God's truth, the profession of faith manifests God's goodness, and so gives him honor he deserves (see *S.t.*, 2–2, q. 13, a. 1). Hence, whenever there is a choice between professing faith and denying it, it must be professed. (The profession of faith will be considered again in relation to the apostolic responsibility of Christian life in 2.B.2.c and 2.D.4.d–e.)

Sometimes, of course, Christians may be quiet about their faith without denying it. Provided they say nothing false and do nothing wrong, they often justifiably avoid calling attention to their faith in times of persecution. They may flee to avoid martyrdom and should not court it. Even in normal times, one whose faith is known need not profess it again (unless, of course, that is equivalent to denying it) if professing it probably will antagonize others rather than lead them to consider the gospel's truth.

b) Denial of faith and failure to profess it are grave matters. Believers can sin by denying their faith outwardly or failing to profess it openly when that omission is motivated by shame or is equivalent to a denial. One can be tempted to commit these sins against faith by shame or fear, for instance, by shame in the face of fellow students' or coworkers' manifest contempt for faith, or by fear of professors or managers who discriminate against outspoken believers. Faith can be denied by words or deeds, explicitly or implicitly; for example, in a time of persecution, those who avoid identification as Christians by pretending to share in the worship of a false religion deny their faith by deeds and implicitly.

In and of themselves, these sins of word and deed need not affect one's intellectual and volitional commitment of faith, but they do violate the covenantal friendship which faith establishes, dishonor God, and deprive other people of a witness of faith. For these reasons, Christians traditionally have cited Scripture to support their belief that salvation is at stake in these matters (see Lk 9.26, Rom 10.10) and have held that they must be prepared to die rather than deny the faith. Thus, these are grave matters.

+ + +

4. God's Honor Requires that One Think and Speak Reverently of Him

Like respect for human persons, reverence toward God is more than an attitude of mind and will. A reverent person does acknowledge God's infinite goodness and willingly accepts his sovereign majesty, but, more than this, thinks and speaks of him with due reverence.

a) **One should be reverent in thought and speech.** People's names rightly are used to address them, to speak well of them, and to recall (and sometimes bring to bear) their status and authority. Similarly, Christians rightly use God's name reverently to invoke and praise him, to urge others to act in ways pleasing to him, and to bring his power to bear against the powers of evil (see *S.t.*, 2–2, q. 90, a. 2). Again, just as one appreciates the good qualities of anyone whom one regards with appropriate respect, so one should be in awe of God's infinite greatness and should appreciate his perfect goodness. Moreover, just as respect can be shown for human persons by treating those dear to them and even their possessions with respect, so God is honored by thinking and speaking with appropriate reverence about everyone and everything which, by relationship to him, is sacred by somehow sharing in his holiness.

b) **Blasphemy is a sin against this reverence and is a grave matter.** One can sin by deliberately thinking or speaking in ways which involve contempt, scorn, disparagement, or abuse of God, and so dishonoring him directly in himself. One also can dishonor God indirectly, by thinking and speaking ill of sacred persons and things. Inasmuch as this sin violates the covenantal friendship which faith establishes, it not only is against reverence for God but against faith itself.

Jews and Christians universally have judged blasphemy to be a very grave matter (see *S.t.*, 2–2, q. 13, aa. 2–3).[123] Moreover, one is tempted to commit this sin because of hostility toward God, aroused by antagonism toward his plan and will, and such hostility presupposes some other serious sin (as will be explained in 3.A.4.a). Other things being equal, blasphemy directly against God most clearly dishonors him, and therefore such blasphemy is the worst sort. If expressed outwardly, it conflicts with the profession of faith, inasmuch as it calls in question God's supreme goodness (see *S.t.*, 2–2, q. 13, a. 1).

c) **The casual, irreverent use of God's name is not blasphemy.** The casual use of divine names and the names of saints or holy things to express negative feelings, without hostility toward God, bears an outward similarity to blasphemy. But when such expressions are used (as they commonly are in some social and cultural situations) without any thought of dishonor to God or any intent to detract from his goodness, they are profanity rather than blasphemy, and are venial sins of irreverence. Insofar as it is irreverent, however, profanity in speech should not be taken lightly.

In itself, profanity is more serious than thoughtless cursing of other persons without serious intent (Go to hell!), for such cursing is not irreverent toward God

---

123. It is a canonical crime to use media of social communication or a public speech or show to blaspheme: *CIC*, c. 1369.

but only disrespectful toward a created person. And both profanity and thoughtless cursing are more serious in themselves than the mere use of vulgar language, which is sinful only inasmuch as it needlessly annoys and distresses others.

5. God's Honor Can Require One to Desire Him to Show Himself

Respect for other persons leads to the desire that they manifest themselves in accord with their dignity when a situation calls for it. Similarly, reverence for God should lead Christians to ask him to show his power and goodness when they think his own honor and glory require it. This desire must be distinguished from the sin of testing God.

a) **Asking God to show himself and questioning him can be good.** One can want God to show his love, power, or other attributes for some good reason, including one's own consolation and the conversion of others, without in any way putting him to a test. Moreover, one can ask God for a sign of his will with respect to some choice to be made without putting him to a test, since what is doubted in such a case is not God's excellence but one's own judgment.

Again, as many passages of the Old Testament and episodes in the lives of saints make clear, people intensely involved in their relationship with God often express negative feelings toward him and question him, much as loving spouses and intimate friends do toward one another. Such expressions of feeling and questioning need not manifest irreverence, for they express desire for more perfect communion rather than doubt about God and his perfections.

b) **Attempting to put God to the test is always a grave matter.** People test others to establish their level of ability or attainment. In general, this practice is unobjectionable. Nor is there anything wrong with asking others to fulfill their commitments when the point is not simply to test them but to realize some common good, including the expression and experience of mutual love. But something is plainly wrong when someone tries to experiment with another's moral qualities and commitment: "If you really love me, you must prove it by doing this for me!" Similarly, one can put God to a test, or try to, either by expressly challenging him or by deliberately acting in a way which would be pointless except as a test (see *S.t.,* 2–2, q. 97, a. 1).

Since God has manifested his love and faithfulness, especially in Jesus, any testing of his good will toward humankind in general or oneself in particular presupposes lack of confidence in the new covenant communion, and so violates the Christian commitment of faith. Moreover, that God is omniscient and omnipotent are revealed truths. To call these attributes in question, as testing God does, manifests lack of faith. In any case, testing God seriously violates faith, since his majesty and goodness are beyond question, and so it always is a grave matter (see *S.t.,* 2–2, q. 97, a. 2).[124]

---

124. Many moralists say that there can be parvity of matter in virtually (or interpretively) testing God. But what they mean by *virtually (or interpretively) testing God* is leaving things to God when one can and should use available means. That can be done out of laziness, without any will to test God, and indeed with full faith in his excellence and with confidence in his loving care. The irreverence involved in such behavior can be slight and unintentional—thus the possibility of

6. God's Honor Requires that One Treat Sacred Things Reverently

One honors God by treating with reverence whatever is sacred. To violate the sacred is to commit sacrilege.

a) Sacred realities share in some way in God's holiness. Because the Lord is present in them, the eucharistic species are sacred. Because God's acts and words are present in them, the sacraments and copies of sacred Scripture are sacred things. Because of their baptism, God's people are sacred; because of their ordination or vows, priests and religious are sacred. Because of the use to which they are consecrated or dedicated, churches and blessed cemeteries are sacred places. Because the saints will rise to glory with Jesus, their relics are sacred. Sacramentals are sacred because they are blessed and designated for holy uses.

Christians should treat all these sacred realities with appropriate reverence and should distinguish them in practice from what is not sacred, in accord with the relationship of each to God by which it is holy (see *S.t.,* 2–2, q. 99, a. 1). Still, sacred persons, places, or other realities distinct from God should not be treated as if they were holy of themselves, as God is, for that would be to make idols of them.

b) Sacrilege dishonors God by dishonoring what is sacred. One commits sacrilege by violating a sacred reality, that is, by treating a person, place, or thing somehow set apart for God and his worship in a way inconsistent with the holiness which arises from his, her, or its specific relationship to God. In doing this, one acts irreverently toward God, which offends against the covenantal friendship established by faith (see *S.t.,* 2–2, q. 99, a. 2).

c) In several kinds of cases, a sacrilege is a grave matter. One way of violating a sacred reality is by treating it as if it were dishonorable (or, at least, not sacred) precisely for the sake of irreverence, for example, destroying an altar to show contempt for the Mass. Such sacrilege always is grave matter, since the intent is to dishonor God.

Another way is by committing another sin which somehow detracts from the holiness of the sacred reality, for example, fornicating with someone vowed to chastity or vandalizing a church. If the sin is grave and the violation of the sacred willingly accepted, even if not intended, the sacrilege also is a grave matter, since the irreverence, arising from the incompatibility between holiness and grave sin, is grave.

Still another way of violating a sacred reality is by deliberately administering or receiving a sacrament unworthily, or treating the eucharistic species as if they were not sacred. In such cases, even if no other sin is committed and the irreverence is only accepted as a side effect, not intended as an end or chosen as a means, the matter is grave because of the great irreverence such acts involve, inasmuch as the Holy Spirit acts in all the sacraments and Jesus is bodily present in the Eucharist. (Sacrilege against the Eucharist will be treated in 3.B.3.a).

d) The sacrilege of simony is always grave matter. To deal in spiritual realities, treating them as if they could be priced, is a sacrilege, for it involves the

---

parvity of matter. See St. Alphonsus Maria de Liguori, *Theologia moralis,* ed. L. Gaudé, 4 vols. (Rome: Ex Typographia Vaticana, 1905–12), 1:388–89.

will to equate the sacred with the profane. This sacrilege is called *simony* after the Simon who tried to buy from St. Peter the power to confer the Holy Spirit (see Acts 8.18–24). People commit this sin by offering a bribe to obtain a sacred office in the Church, extorting a payment from someone for a dispensation from a Church law, and so on. The sin is particularly grave because it violates the principle of spiritual goods: the gratuity of God's good will (see *S.t.,* 2–2, q. 100, a. 1).

Offering (and asking for) the ordinary stipends for saying Masses and performing other priestly duties is not simony; the stipend is compensation for the service, not a price put on the priceless spiritual good.[125] Similarly, buying and selling a blessed object or reliquary on the basis of its material worth is not simony, although charging for the blessing or for the relic would be.[126]

e) Sacrilege can be light matter. When a sacrilege is not grave for one of the reasons mentioned in (c) and does not involve simony, it can be light matter. For instance, those who without sufficient reason use a church for a profane but decent purpose violate its sacred character, but their irreverence, if not intended but only accepted, is not great. Using Scripture as material for humor unrelated to a religious purpose is irreverent, but need not be gravely so if God's word is not denied and the irreverence is not the point of the humor. Altar boys who drink the wine remaining after Mass misuse what belongs to the Church, but the theft is small and so the unintended irreverence is slight.

7. Making a Vow Is a Way of Worshipping God

As has been explained (in A.1), faith is more than intellectual assent, for it includes reverent submission to God and commitment to communion with the divine persons. A vow is a further promise to God, the making and fulfilling of which not only presuppose the covenantal relationship which faith accepts, but deepen that relationship, just as similar acts deepen purely human friendships.[127]

The most familiar vows are those by which some Catholics commit themselves to observe the three evangelical counsels of poverty, chastity, and obedience in an approved form of consecrated life. Such vows are called *public* because they are accepted in the name of the Church by a legitimate superior.[128]

However, the practice of making and fulfilling private vows can have a place in any Catholic's life, and the present treatment concerns only such private vows. One might, for example, vow to participate in daily Mass whenever possible, or to donate a certain part of one's income to the poor, or to forgo marriage in order to dedicate oneself more fully to a special vocation of service to some particular group of persons in need.

---

125. However, *CIC,* c. 947, warns: "Any appearance of trafficking or commerce is to be entirely excluded from Mass offerings."

126. *CIC,* c. 149, §3, and c. 1380, deal with simony; by the former, simonical provision of an office is invalid; by the latter, one who celebrates or receives a sacrament through simony is to be punished with an interdict or suspension. A study done before the 1983 code, but still helpful for its moral and canonical analysis of simony: Raymond A. Ryder, *Simony: An Historical Synopsis and Commentary* (Washington, D.C.: The Catholic University of America Press, 1931).

127. The treatment of vows here is based on but adapts that of St. Thomas, *S.t.,* 2–2, q. 88.

128. See *CIC,* c. 654 and c. 1192, §1.

a) **Vows are promises to God, but differ from promises to others.** To make a promise is not only to decide to do or omit doing something as another wants, but to bind oneself to carry out the decision, while communicating to the other person that one has made it and bound oneself (promises will be treated in 7.C.1). Those who promise put themselves in the position of not being able to change their decision without being unfaithful to the one to whom they made the promise. In all these respects, vows made to God are analogous to promises made to other people.

But vows differ from ordinary promises in four ways. First, one can promise another to do something morally wrong. But since God wants only what is good and since it is no gift to him to bind oneself to forgo doing something better than one might otherwise do, one can vow only what is both morally right and also better than what one might otherwise do. Second, in making promises to other persons, one benefits them by providing them with assurance about the future so that they can take advantage of knowing beforehand what one will do. But in making vows one cannot benefit God in that way, since he is all-knowing. Rather, one simply gives him the gift of the freedom to change one's mind in order to do what is especially good and pleasing to him. Third, the unfaithfulness to another human person in breaking a promise is not only disloyalty but unfairness, since the person is disappointed and loses the expected benefit. But since God cannot be disappointed or harmed, the unfaithfulness to him in breaking a vow is simply the irreverence and insult involved in taking back the gift one had given him. Fourth, promises among human individuals are expressed in language, sometimes in the presence of witnesses or in special, legal form. While vows can be expressed and witnessed, they need not be, since God knows one's heart, and one cannot evade responsibilities to him.[129]

b) **Not everything called a _vow_ will be treated here.** The word _vow_ is used to refer to a variety of promises made in a religious context. Thus, one speaks of _baptismal vows,_ although the baptismal promises to reject Satan and to serve God faithfully are essentially required by the commitment of faith, which is proper to baptism, and are more basic than any optional vow (see _S.t.,_ 2–2, q. 88, a. 2). Many people also speak of _marriage vows,_ because sacramental marriage is a sacred act carrying with it special religious responsibilities. However, the commitment to God involved in sacramental marriage is not optional but implicit in marital consent, which primarily is the commitment of the bride and groom to each other. In what follows, _vow_ refers only to optional promises made directly to God. (And, as stated above, only private vows are under consideration here; public vows will be treated in volume four.)

c) **Making vows prudently and fulfilling them is good and right.** Those who do something good in fulfillment of a vow determine themselves more firmly to that good than if they did the same thing without vowing it. Even more important, actions which fulfill vows are richer in meaning than they otherwise would be, for they have the added significance of a free gift to God. Just as gratuitous acts in

---

129. _CIC,_ c. 1191, §1, defines vow: "A vow is a deliberate and free promise made to God concerning a possible and better good which must be fulfilled by reason of the virtue of religion."

purely human friendships intensify commitment and nourish love, so vows intensify the commitment of faith and nourish charity toward God. To make a vow is to deepen one's intimacy with God by voluntarily binding oneself more firmly to some good which he wills.

d) **The power to make vows is subject to inherent limits.** Only those can make vows who can freely assume responsibilities, and they cannot do so without the reflection and freedom of choice necessary for grave moral responsibility (see *CMP,* 17.A–B). Moreover, as with other promises, one should not vow to do anything one cannot do. Besides, as no one can promise that someone else will do something, so one cannot bind anyone else by one's vow. For this reason, the vows of persons subject to authority can be nullified to the extent fulfilling them would be at odds with the authority's legitimate wishes.[130] An important instance of this occurs when a child subject to parental authority makes a vow whose fulfillment would conflict with what a parent otherwise would direct the child to do or refrain from doing; the parent can annul the vow.

e) **One should exercise prudence in making vows.** Because a serious responsibility is assumed in making a vow, vows should not be made hastily or lightly. Prudent persons considering making a vow, especially one binding under pain of grave sin, will consult an able confessor, spiritual director, or other holy and mature person about whether and how to proceed. Hesitation about making a vow does not manifest weakness of faith and fervor, but reverence toward God, for it shows that the promises one makes to him are taken seriously.

f) **In making vows, bargaining with God is to be avoided.** In purely human relationships, people often make promises (and threats) to motivate others to do as they wish. As an element of contractual arrangements among people with no common commitment beyond that to be fair to each other, such promises can be morally acceptable. However, they become manipulative when they interfere with and even displace common commitment; this reduces relationships, such as marriage, which should be loving communion, to practical arrangements for gratifying individualistic desires. In one's relationship with God, a merely contractual relationship is impossible: he gives every good—all one is and has—and, as his child, one is in communion with him. So, any attempt to bargain with God manifests serious defects in faith, hope, and love. Consequently, setting conditions on one's vows is wrong if it is an effort to bargain with God.[131]

Still, not all conditional vows involve bargaining with God. People in love sometimes make conditional promises, not to manipulate one another, but to propose plans for pursuing common interests which their loved ones may freely accept or reject. For example, a man might promise his wife: "If you will take the children to visit your parents, I will paint the interior of the house." Similarly, one rightly makes conditional vows to let God show whether he accepts the proposed

---

130. *CIC,* c. 1195: "A person who has power over the matter of the vow can suspend its obligation for as long as its fulfillment would prejudice such a person."

131. The failure of some Catholics to meet this requirement for good vows undoubtedly explains in part some Protestants' rejection of all vows—a position condemned by the Church (see DS 1622/865).

way of cooperating with him and intensifying one's relationship with him. For example, a person with certain skills might vow: "If you, Lord, provide such and such conditions necessary to put these skills to use in a certain form of apostolate, I will undertake that apostolic work and persevere in it until I complete it or die trying." But it remains wrong to make conditional vows in a bargaining spirit, especially if one foresees, as an honest and clearheaded bargainer would foresee, that one is likely to trust and love God less if he does not fulfill one's condition.

g) **The obligation assumed in making a vow has limits.** Since one freely binds oneself to what one vows, the obligation to fulfill the vow has all the limits set in making it. Moreover, just as with other promises, there is no responsibility to fulfill a vow if one discovers that one cannot rightly (or simply cannot) do so, if the condition on which or purpose for which the vow was made does not come about or ceases to exist, or if what one promised changes substantially, for instance, if in peacetime one vows to make a pilgrimage to the Holy Land at a certain time, but a war is raging when the time comes, so that fulfilling the vow would mean accepting substantial unforeseen burdens and risks.

h) **Vows can be dispensed, commuted, or fulfilled in alternate ways.** Just as human friends can release one another from promises and are prepared to do so if there is a good reason, so God can dispense vows. Bishops and all other pastors (and religious superiors in certain cases) can exercise this power in God's name with respect to any private vow provided they have a good reason and doing so does not infringe the rights of someone else concerned.

Those who can grant a dispensation from a vow also can commute the vow, that is, dispense from part of what was promised or substitute something less. Hence, someone with a good reason for not fulfilling a vow should request that it be commuted or, if necessary, dispensed.

Moreover, since what is important about a vow is the free gift of making it, one need not do precisely what was vowed, but is free to fulfill a vow by doing something else as good as or better, if that is possible in the nature of the case.[132]

i) **To break a vow is sinful.** It is a sin to break a vow, since the very act of vowing creates a responsibility to fulfill the vow out of faithfulness toward God. Having given him a gift, one acts unfaithfully in withdrawing it. Moreover, as making and fulfilling a vow presuppose, express, and deepen the covenantal friendship which faith establishes, so breaking a vow harms that friendship, just as wrongfully breaking a promise to a human friend harms the friendship.

Breaking a vow can be a grave matter, but need not be regarded as such in every instance.[133] While St. Thomas does not say explicitly how grave he considers breaking vows to be, he emphasizes that the demand of faithfulness to God, being

---

132. On the cessation, suppression, or dispensation of a vow and on commutation of the works promised, see *CIC*, cc. 1194–97. A study done before the 1983 code but still useful: James Martin Lowry, *Dispensation from Private Vows: A Historical Synopsis and a Commentary* (Washington, D.C.: The Catholic University of America Press, 1946).

133. The canonical definition of *vow* includes a statement of its obligation, but no precise indication of the gravity of that obligation: *CIC*, c. 1191, §1: "A vow . . . must be fulfilled by reason of the virtue of religion."

rooted both in his lordship and in the many gifts he has given, calls for the greatest fidelity to him; thus, one is most greatly obliged to God, and a vow to him is a very great obligation (see *S.t.*, 2–2, q. 88, a. 3). From this it seems to follow that deliberately failing to fulfill any vow would be a grave matter. Approved Catholic moralists, nevertheless, agreed that the responsibility of faithfulness which is assumed in making a vow is not always a grave one. They generally held that in making private vows, one can limit one's responsibility by intending only to bind oneself under pain of venial sin, and that even if in vowing one did not intend to limit one's responsibility, breaking a private vow admits of parvity of matter. Many also held that the obligation of a vow is determined by the seriousness of what is promised, and will be light if that is rather unimportant in itself.

8. One Honors God by Reverently Taking Oaths When Appropriate

God's truth and fidelity make his revelation credible and so make faith possible. These same divine characteristics lead those who believe in God to swear by him, that is, to call on him to guarantee their sincerity.[134] Familiar occasions for taking an oath are when entering on a public office or testifying in court. On these occasions and others when oaths are required, one should take them, and in doing so should bear in mind one's special obligation to be truthful.

a) **Rightly taking an oath is an act of faith and reverence.** In taking an oath, one calls on God to witness to and guarantee the truth of one's statements (for example, the testimony to be given) or the sincerity of one's promise (for example, to fulfill the duties of an office). Authentic oath taking involves a conditional readiness to accept justly deserved divine punishment for false swearing, a readiness often expressed elliptically by words such as "so help me God."

Underlying the practice of taking oaths are convictions basic to the act of faith itself: that God's truth and fidelity are beyond question, that he cares about and is involved in human affairs, and that sinners will be punished. Those who rightly take oaths hold these convictions and express them by their sincere oath taking. Moreover, to take an oath rightly is to submit to God's majesty and take seriously the special responsibility assumed in oath taking not to offend his holiness.

b) **In taking an oath, one assumes a new responsibility.** Someone who takes an oath to confirm his or her truthfulness assumes a new and grave responsibility toward God to be truthful. Special care must therefore be taken to be accurate in statements made under oath and to assert as certain only what one is certain of. In taking an oath to confirm the sincerity of a promise, one similarly assumes a new and grave responsibility toward God to be sincere.

Even so, this latter responsibility—to be sincere in promising—does not do away with the ordinary limits of sincere promises.[135] Thus, although confirmed by an oath, a promise to do something wrong or a promise extorted by fraud, force, or grave fear is null. Nor is there a duty to fulfill a promise, even though confirmed by an oath, from which one is released by the person for whose benefit the promise

---

134. The treatment of oaths here is based on but adapts that of St. Thomas, *S.t.*, 2–2, q. 89.
135. See *CIC*, cc. 1200–1203.

was made. Moreover, all other conditions which can limit the duty to keep sincere promises also limit the responsibility to carry out promises confirmed by oaths. Thus, such a promise need not be kept if the condition on which or the purpose for which it was made does not come about or ceases to exist, or if what was promised changes substantially, for example, if the nation to which citizens promised loyalty undergoes revolutionary changes in its constitution.

c) **It is often inappropriate to take an oath.** According to the New Testament, Jesus gave instructions to avoid not only false swearing but oaths in general, since a simple yes or no should suffice while anything beyond that comes from evil (see Mt 5.33–37; cf. Jas 5.12). Some have read this as an absolute prohibition of oaths. That view is unsound, however, both because it is inconsistent with other passages of Scripture and because the Christian tradition has approved of oaths.[136] What Jesus said about oaths must be read as excluding them generally but not absolutely. His point seems to be that among people who would consider oaths important, because they believe in God, mutual truthfulness should make oath taking unnecessary, and thus frequent use of oaths is bad, insofar as it supports practices of lying and deception.

Still, oaths are inappropriate in many cases. Invoking God's witness in insignificant matters dishonors him. Those who take oaths lightly show irreverence and seldom are careful enough about avoiding perjury. Moreover, in morally defective relationships which should either be terminated or radically renewed, oath taking as a substitute for mutual trust impedes the required conversion. Finally, in some cases it is wrong to make a true statement or a sincere promise, for example, if the statement defames someone or violates one's responsibility to keep a secret, or if the promise is to do something which should not be done. Swearing to confirm such a statement or promise is inappropriate inasmuch as it involves God in one's wrongdoing.

In some cases, legal documents and procedures offer an alternative to taking an oath: affirming under the penalty for perjury. Since oaths are excluded generally, though not absolutely, one should take such an option when it is available. This is easily done, by forming the general intention of affirming rather than swearing in such cases.

d) **Perjury is a grave matter.** Perjury is committed by someone who swears insincerely to the truth of what he or she believes false or to a promise he or she does not intend to keep. Those who commit perjury call on God to bear witness, but use his truth and faithfulness to guarantee their falsity and unfaithfulness. This dishonors God by attempting to make him a party to one's wrongdoing—something quite irreverent and inconsistent with covenantal friendship: "You shall not make wrongful use of the name of the Lord your God, for the Lord will not acquit anyone who misuses his name" (Ex 20.7, Dt 5.11; cf. Lv 19.12). Thus, in itself perjury always is a grave matter (see DS 2124/1174; *S.t.,* 2–2, q. 98, a. 3).

136. See W. D. Davies and Dale C. Allison, *The Gospel According to Matthew,* vol. 1 (Edinburgh: T. and T. Clark, 1988), 533–38; *New Catholic Encyclopedia,* s.v. "oaths."

Perjury often is grave matter for an additional reason: the inseparable injustice to others which it involves. This injustice lies in leading others to rely on one's insincerely sworn testimony or promises (see *S.t.*, 2–2, q. 70, a. 4). Also, in some instances, perjury causes others to be deprived of something due them: liberty, property, their good name, even life itself.

e) Breaking a promise sealed by an oath need not be grave. A promise sealed by an oath, whether made sincerely or not, is broken by not being fulfilled, provided the one who made it still owes it to the other party to keep it. But the oath confirming the promise directly bears on the act of promising, whose sincerity it guarantees, and only indirectly on the promise's fulfillment. Thus, even if a promise sealed by an oath is sinfully broken, the sin is not always perjury.

Perjury is committed in sinfully breaking a promise made under oath if, even while breaking it, one continues to take advantage of the confidence others bestowed because of the oath, for example, by covertly abusing a position of trust one has sworn to fulfill faithfully. But one does not commit perjury, and so does no irreverence to God, if in openly breaking the promise the confidence gained by the oath is surrendered. Breaking the promise is grave matter in these circumstances only if it would have been grave to break the same promise even if it had not been sealed by an oath. (The responsibility to keep promises and the sin of breaking them will be treated in 7.C.1.)

CHAPTER TWO

HOPE, APOSTOLATE, AND PERSONAL VOCATION

Summary

Christian hope has a twofold object: hope is *in* God because of his saving work in Jesus; it is *for* God's kingdom and fulfillment in it. Although hope, insofar as it is ecclesial, surely will be fulfilled, it nevertheless is compatible with frustration and failure.

Hope should be nurtured by meditation and prayer, and should be put into practice by living one's life for the kingdom. Not only hope but fear of hell should be correctly integrated into Christian life. Confirmation, the sacrament of personal vocation, empowers Christians to live in hope. Presumption and despair, as sins against hope, are very grave.

Jesus' mission was to establish a new human communion with God. While this mission was directed exclusively to serving the heavenly kingdom, the gospel also calls for radical social and economic reform. The Church's mission concerns exactly what Jesus' mission concerned—that is, every true human good, considered in relation to the kingdom—and expresses a preferential option for the poor, without taking the side of one class or another.

All Catholics have apostolic responsibilities, and indeed each one's whole life should be apostolic. Moreover, the essence of apostolic responsibility is bearing witness, so that only truly Christian words and deeds satisfy the responsibility. All Catholics likewise have responsibility for the Church's entire mission; and while clerics, lay persons, and religious meet this responsibility in diverse ways, their diverse apostolates nevertheless have certain common characteristics, including a constant readiness to suffer martyrdom, along with humility and love.

God calls every member of the Church with a personal vocation: a unique share in the Church's mission. Every Catholic should live his or her entire life in response to this divine calling, which includes both the commitments one should make and a suitable response to conditions beyond one's control. The responsibilities pertaining to vocation are threefold: to discern each of its elements, to accept the call it involves, and to carry it out faithfully. While faithfulness to vocation does not preclude change and creativity, it does require reaffirming commitments in the face of temptation and refusing to use bad means to good ends.

Question A: What Are the Essential Characteristics of
                Christian Hope in God?

In a loose sense, *to hope* for something merely means to wish for it with some fear that what one wishes will not come about. For example, a family planning a picnic hopes for good weather or a fat man hopes that his new diet will accomplish what none before has. *Hope* in this loose sense need not involve the idea of interpersonal relationship, but that idea is involved in *hope* in the precise sense relevant here. For here *to hope* means to count on another person to help one fulfill one's desire; one hopes in someone for something.

One of the first things people learn by experience is that they cannot achieve much by themselves. Throughout life, we need others' help to survive and flourish But others do not exist and act merely for our sakes, and so we soon discover that we cannot take them for granted. To be able to count on others, stable relationships, based on mutuality, are needed.

In entering into a lasting communion such as marriage, people commit themselves to one another for the sake of goods they wish to share in together. Their commitments are promises to fulfill their responsibilities, and one element of each party's motive for keeping his or her promises is anticipation of the benefits to be realized with the other's cooperation. Both confidently anticipate benefits because they mutually believe their promises to be sincere and count on their being kept. This *counting on* is their hope in one another, as distinct from their hope for the benefits anticipated.

Divine revelation and faith in God constitute a lasting communion, a covenant between God and human beings, based on mutual commitments (see *CMP*, 21.B). In revealing himself, God promises salvation from evil and a better life to those who agree to be his people. Moved by his grace, they in turn undertake to follow him exclusively and to keep his commandments (see Gn 17.1–14, Jos 24.14–27; cf. LG 9). Relying on God to be faithful in keeping his promises, his people hope in him for the salvation and better life they otherwise could not anticipate.[1]

This hope is not only a wonderful gift but an essential element in motivating Christians to give the highest priority in their lives to keeping God's commandments faithfully and doing what they must as his people (see Mt 19.16–22, Mk 10.17–22, Lk 18.18–23). In practice, one fails in hope by planning and living one's

---

1. This theme so permeates the Old Testament that no small set of texts reflects it fully. But the various aspects of hope emerge in the Psalms, and a few texts can serve as examples. God is the unique refuge of his people (16.1–2, 18.30–35, 31.1–2, 62.1–8); they must trust in his steadfast love (13.5, 31.14–24, 40.1–11) and anticipate salvation (3.8, 13.5, 36.5–10, 130.5–8) so confidently that they should be glad even as they wait (13.1–6, 33.18–22, 43.5). Also see Domingo Muñoz Leon, "La esperanza de Israel: Perspectivas de la espera mesiánica en los targumín palestinenses del Pentateuco," in *La esperanza en la Biblia,* XXX Semana Bíblica Española (Madrid: Consejo Superior de Investigaciones Científicas, 1972), 49–91. A source for this and the next question (but not always followed): St. Thomas, *Quaestio disputata: De spe.* Two useful studies: Charles A. Bernard, S.J., *Théologie de l'espérance selon saint Thomas d'Aquin* (Paris: J. Vrin, 1961); Jean Galot, S.J., *The Mystery of Christian Hope,* trans. M. Angeline Bouchard (New York: Alba House, 1977).

life as if one either were not really interested in what God promises, could do without him, could take him for granted, or could not count on him.

1. Christians Hope in God Because of His Saving Work in Jesus

As God's people of old counted on him as their covenantal partner to fulfill his promises, so Jesus' Church, God's new people, hopes only in him. The new covenant offers a new ground for hope: God's saving work in Jesus (see Ti 3.4–7; Heb 3.6, 6.17–20, 7.19, 10.23; 1 Pt 1.3–5). Christians have "a sure and steadfast anchor of the soul, a hope that enters the inner shrine behind the curtain, where Jesus, a forerunner on our behalf, has entered" (Heb 6.19–20).[2]

a) **God demonstrated his dependability by what he did in Jesus.** One of God's reasons for raising Jesus from the dead and giving him glory was to motivate faith and hope (see 1 Pt 1.20–21). By all he did in Jesus, God showed that his wise plan guides everything providentially to his people's good; they can count on it that nothing will be allowed to separate them from Jesus (see Rom 8.28–39). As God showed his merciful love by giving Jesus up to death to redeem humankind from sin, so one can count on that same love for salvation by Jesus' new life (see Rom 5.6–11). By what he did in Jesus, God showed his faithfulness, and so one can count on that same faithfulness to fulfill his promises. By raising Jesus from the dead, God showed his re-creative power, and so one can count on that same power for one's own resurrection (see Eph 1.8–14, Col 1.18–20).

In sum, by what he did in Jesus, God demonstrated that he knows how to save fallen humankind, wills to do so, will not change his mind, and cannot fail to save anyone who, hoping in him, cooperates with his grace.

b) **By working in Christians, the Holy Spirit nurtures their hope.** The Spirit of God works to accomplish salvation through Jesus (see Mt 1.18; 3.13–17; 12.28; Mk 1.9–11; Lk 1.35; 3.21–22; 4.14, 18; Jn 1.29–34). Jesus promises that the Father will give the Spirit to those who ask (see Lk 11.13). After Jesus' resurrection, God fulfills this promise by endowing Jesus' followers with the Spirit to complete the work of salvation in them and through their witness (see Jn 14.16–17, 15.26–27, 16.7–15, 20.21–23; Acts 1.8, 2.4). The Church enjoys the presence of the Holy Spirit and confers him on those who accept the gospel and enter into her communion (see Acts 2.14–42).

By the Holy Spirit's grace, Christians can abound in hope (see Rom 15.13). The Spirit's presence in the heart is a foretaste and guarantee of the heavenly glory for which one hopes (see 2 Cor 1.21–22, 5.5). This is so because the Spirit causes people to have and experience God's love (see Rom 5.5), enables them to live holy lives (see Rom 8.1–13), and so frees them from fear of hell and makes them experience themselves as the Father's loving children, destined to share in heavenly glory with Jesus (see Rom 8.14–17; cf. 1 Jn 3.1–2).[3]

2. A valuable study: Miguel Nicolau, S.J., "La esperanza en la Carta a los Hebreos," in *La esperanza en la Biblia,* 187–202.

3. Hope is treated in relation to the Christian's divine sonship in an excellent exegetical and theological commentary: Matthew Vellanickal, *The Divine Sonship of Christians in the Johannine Writings* (Rome: Biblical Institute Press, 1977), 331–51.

2. Christians Hope for God's Kingdom and for Fulfillment in It

Christian hope is for the coming of God's kingdom and for one's own salvation, that is, one hopes for the fulfillment of all things in Jesus and to be part of that new heavens and new earth. God promises these goods by Jesus' gospel and will fulfill this promise by restoring all things in Jesus (see LG 48).

a) Hope is for the life of the world to come. In accord with God's promise, Christians "wait for new heavens and a new earth, where righteousness is at home" (2 Pt 3.13). This new world is God's kingdom (see 1 Cor 15.50, 2 Tm 4.18); it already exists insofar as God's saving work in Jesus reconciles fallen humankind (see Mt 12.28; Lk 11.20, 17.20–21; Rom 6.5–14; Eph 2.6–7; Col 2.12, 3.1–4). However, one looks forward to the completion of God's plan, to the full experience of one's own share in his kingdom (see Mt 25.31–34, Rom 8.15–24, Col 3.4). This will be when Jesus comes again. All Christian hope focuses on this single future event: Jesus' coming in glory (see Mt 24.29–31, Mk 13.24–27, Lk 21.27–28, Acts 1.11, 1 Thes 4.13–17, Rv 22.20). On that day, he will radically transform the world by excluding all sin and all evil and establishing unbreakable communion with God (see 1 Cor 15.23–27, 2 Thes 2.1–12, 2 Pt 3.10–13, Rv 21.1–4).

Christian hope is not merely for the limited happiness possible in this passing world, but for perfect fulfillment in a lasting world, where all who are united with Jesus will live again after death, with life similar to that Jesus himself has enjoyed since God raised him from the dead (see 1 Cor 15.19–23, 1 Thes 4.13–14; GS 22). Finally, while one now lives "in the hope of eternal life that God, who never lies, promised before the ages began" (Ti 1.2), one looks forward to knowing God and Jesus so intimately that, like Jesus, one will become a mature member of God's family (see 1 Cor 13.11–12, 1 Jn 3.2), and so a sharer in divine glory (see 2 Cor 3.12–18; cf. Rom 5.2).[4]

b) Hope is for everything which contributes to eternal life. One hopes for the pardon of one's sins (see 1 Jn 1.9; DS 1678/898), because grave sin excludes a person from the heavenly kingdom (see 1 Cor 6.9–10; Gal 5.19–21; Rv 21.6–8, 22.14–15), which is the principal object of hope. One hopes for righteousness (see Gal 5.5), because a holy life is necessary for communion with God, and the kingdom will be unbreakable communion with God. One hopes for the resurrection of the dead (see 1 Cor 15.12–24), because only those who share in the bodily life of the risen Jesus will share fully in his kingdom, saved and glorified as complete human persons.[5] One hopes for the gift of the Holy Spirit, since he enables one to

---

4. A contemporary defense of the traditional Christian understanding of heaven: Peter Kreeft, *Heaven: The Heart's Deepest Longing*, expanded ed. (San Francisco: Ignatius Press, 1989).

5. Thus, according to St. Paul, although Christians are already children of God and coheirs with Jesus to his promised inheritance (see Rom 8.15–17), they also still "wait for adoption, the redemption of our bodies" (Rom 8.23), because only by that is their kinship with God complete. As St. Thomas points out, resurrection is necessary because disembodied existence is not sufficient for the salvation of the human person: "Now, since the soul is part of the human body, it is not the entire human being, and my soul is not I. So, even if the soul reached salvation in another life, neither I nor any human being would thereby do so" (*Super primam epistolam ad Corinthios lectura*, on 1 Cor 15.19).

serve the coming of the kingdom, and guarantees one's share in it (see Acts 1.4–5, Eph 1.13–14).

c) **Hope embraces human fulfillment in this world.** Jesus teaches his disciples to pray not only for the coming of the heavenly kingdom but for their daily bread (see Mt 6.10–11, Lk 11.2–3). While urging them to seek God's kingdom first, he promises with it the good things they naturally desire (see Mt 6.33). Classical theology acknowledged that Christians may rightly hope for human fulfillment in this world insofar as it is a necessary *means* to heaven. But Vatican II's teaching makes it clear that human fulfillment in this world is not only a means but a part of the heavenly kingdom. The Council teaches that all human hopes are embraced in Christian hope (see GS 1 and 21). This is so because the heavenly kingdom, while distinct from this world, is not separate from it; the kingdom already is present within or among Christians (see Lk 17.21).[6]

In faithfully fulfilling his or her personal vocation, which normally includes service to many goods of the temporal order, a person cooperates here and now with the Holy Spirit in building up the kingdom, that is, in doing the human work which God wants to precede his re-creative act. Like the elements prepared by human work for the Eucharist, the sacrament of heaven's present reality, all the good fruits of human nature and effort are materials prepared for the kingdom, so that the body of that heavenly communion grows day by day (see GS 38–39). Christians are like secular humanists in hoping for perfect human fulfillment, but differ from them in hoping for an everlasting communion among divine and human persons on an earth renewed by God's re-creative act, whose first fruit was Jesus' resurrection (see *CMP,* 34.E–F).[7]

d) **Hope is for heaven as a reward for doing God's will.** In doing the Father's will, Jesus suffered "for the sake of the joy that was set before him" (Heb 12.2), that is, for the kingdom which is the goal of the Father's plan of salvation. Christians hope that by following Jesus and sharing in his sufferings they too will share in his resurrection (see Phil 3.8–21). Apart from Jesus one can do nothing, but in him one can make one's personal contribution to the coming of the kingdom by bearing fruit which lasts (see Jn 15.5–17). These good works done in cooperation with Jesus are not useless (see 1 Cor 15.58; cf. Jn 14.11–12). They deserve the recompense which God promises to those who faithfully do his will (see Rom 2.6–7; 2 Cor 5.10; Heb 10.36, 11.6). While a good Christian life is not so much one's own as a grace which God gives (see Eph 2.8–10), still God is so generous that he wants his people to

---

6. The fullness of the kingdom is still to come; it depends entirely on God's grace; and it cannot be identified unqualifiedly with the Church. Nevertheless, the heavenly kingdom is being built by Jesus in the life of his Church on earth. Gerhard Lohfink, "The Exegetical Predicament concerning Jesus' Kingdom of God Proclamation," *Theology Digest* 36 (1989): 103–10, tellingly criticizes exegetical opinions which deny the presence of the kingdom, the role of human action in realizing it, and its social reality.

7. Congregation for the Doctrine of the Faith, *Instruction on Christian Freedom and Liberation,* 60, *AAS* 79 (1987) 579, *OR,* 14 Apr. 1986, 5, explains the distinction and relationship between earthly progress and the kingdom, and points out that apart from hope for the kingdom, there can be no true justice for either the dead or the living (but only the illusory prospect of perfect justice for some people in the future).

deserve his gifts (see DS 1548/810). It is right to hope that if one perseveres to the end, one will enjoy eternal life in heaven in consequence of keeping God's commandments and doing good with the help of his grace and in cooperation with Jesus (see DS 1576/836).

3. Hope Is Certain but Compatible with Frustration and Failure

Since Jesus' disciples have the Spirit as the guarantee of their inheritance (see Eph 1.13–14), their hope will not be confounded (see Rom 5.3–5). Still, Christians can expect to share in Jesus' inheritance only if "we suffer with him so that we may also be glorified with him" (Rom 8.17). Moreover, although it is necessary to do God's will in order to receive what he promises (see Heb 10.36), people sometimes are tempted to prefer their own wills. Thus, Christians work out their "salvation with fear and trembling" (Phil 2.12; cf. DS 1541/806), and the assurance of hope and clear awareness of the real possibility of failure paradoxically go together. Because the latter can easily obscure the former, it is important to see exactly what the assurance of hope consists in.

a) Hope's assurance is distinct from the certitude of faith. In the New Testament, faith and hope often are distinguished from each other (see 1 Cor 13.13; Col 1.4–5; 1 Thes 1.3, 5.8; Heb 11.1).[8] Following Scripture, the Church's teaching maintains this distinction (see DS 1526–31/798–800).

By faith, a person accepts the gospel, enters into the new covenant, and is certain of the truths God reveals: that he is preparing his heavenly kingdom, that he promises a share in it to all who are faithful to the covenant, and that he can and will fulfill his promise. Hope presupposes faith's certitude and commitment while adding to it a practical attitude of reliance on God. This makes the prospect of the kingdom's coming no mere theoretical possibility but a reality to live by.

This practical attitude has an absolute character. While sometimes called *certitude*, it might better be called the *assurance* of hope. This assurance presupposes the certitude of faith and adds to it: Christians *believe* in God and the sincerity of his promises, while they *rely* on God for his promises' fulfillment (see *S.t.*, 2–2, q. 17, aa. 5–7). But how can the absoluteness of hope as a practical attitude be consistent with fear that what is hoped for might not be realized?

b) Hope is communal as well as individual. To answer this question, it helps to notice that Christian hope is rooted in the Church as a communion. Often, hope is thought of as an individualistic virtue by which each Christian relies on God's mercy for personal salvation alone—a view which aggravates the paradox of hope's assurance, inasmuch as one knows both that one will not be saved without perseverance and that perseverance is not guaranteed (see Heb 10.26–36).[9] But

---

8. Still, this distinction is not so sharp as that made in most Catholic theology and some Church teaching. For biblical *faith* usually includes a reference to trust in God and often implies readiness to obey his commands. See O. Becker and O. Michel, "Faith," in *The New International Dictionary of New Testament Theology*, ed. Colin Brown, 3 vols. (Grand Rapids, Mich.: Zondervan, 1975–78), 1:587–606.

9. The Council of Trent teaches definitively: "If anyone says he has absolute and infallible certitude that he will certainly have the great gift of final perseverance, without having learned

hope should not be thought of as focused primarily on the salvation of each individual. Jesus' followers are joined together in communion with him, and being one ecclesial body enlivened by one Spirit, they share one hope (see Eph 4.4).

Thus, Vatican II teaches: "While she slowly grows, the Church strains toward the completed kingdom and, with all her strength, hopes and desires to be united with her King in glory" (LG 5; cf. LG 9, UR 2–3). The Church's teaching since the Council makes the point unmistakably clear: "The entire Church will reach its perfection on the day of the Lord's coming and will enter into the fullness of God: this is the fundamental objective of Christian hope and prayer ('thy kingdom come')."[10] Therefore, just as individuals have faith only by believing what the Church believes, so they hope only by sharing in the Church's hope. Personal hope is normal and healthy only when, being one with the Church's hope, it is enlivened by charity. Hope without charity is dead; hope with charity should transcend immature self-centeredness.[11]

c) **Insofar as hope is ecclesial, it surely will be fulfilled.** What the Church hopes for surely will be realized, since she hopes for nothing else than to be perfectly one with Jesus, and he always remains with her as her hope of glory (see Mt 28.20, Col 1.24–28).[12] Thus, even as the Church sails through the storms of history, she remains anchored firmly to Jesus in heaven (see Heb 6.19–20). Her perseverance is guaranteed. Now, just as an individual's faith cannot be mistaken insofar as it is one with the Catholic Church's faith, so an individual's hope cannot be frustrated insofar as it is one with the Church's hope. None will be lost who live faithfully in this community. All its living members will reach heaven, just as all who remain alive aboard a ship which comes safely to port surely reach their

---

this from a special revelation: let him be anathema" (DS 1566/826; cf. 1540–41/805–6). Still, hope nurtures perseverance: D. R. Denton, "Hope and Perseverance," *Scottish Journal of Theology* 34 (1981): 313–20.

10. Congregation for the Clergy, *General Catechetical Directory*, 69, *AAS* 64 (1972) 140–41, Flannery, 2:570. Note, also, that Mary, united with Jesus in glory, provides the Church with a perfect model of what she herself hopes to be (see SC 103; cf. LG 68). Thus, just as St. Paul hoped for his spiritual children (see 2 Cor 1.7), so faithful pastors hope for their flocks, parents for their children, and so on. On the communal nature of hope, see B. Olivier, O.P., "Hope," in *Theology Library*, ed. A. M. Henry, O.P., vol. 4, *The Virtues and States of Life*, trans. R. J. Olson and G. T. Lennon (Chicago: Fides, 1957), 91–92, 101–5.

11. The individualistic view of hope was supported by the teaching of St. Thomas that hope directly regards one's proper good and extends to others only insofar as one is joined to them by love (see *S.t.*, 2–2, q. 17, a. 3). This theological position no doubt is correct insofar as lifeless hope like lifeless faith can remain in mortal sinners, whom it can move toward repentance (see DS 1678/898, 2457/1407). While in mortal sin, one may be less interested in others' salvation but will not be less interested, unless one also despairs, in one's own.

12. Someone might object that inasmuch as faith teaches that the Church's full perfection in the glory of heaven will certainly come about, this cannot be the object of hope, but only of faith. The answer is that the certainty of faith that hope will be fulfilled is not inconsistent with hope, since its assurance is based on God's truthfulness and faithfulness in keeping his promises, on which the Church counts. That is why Christians continue to pray for the kingdom to come: its coming is certain only by the "necessity" of God's faithfulness in giving what he promises, which always nevertheless remains a free gift.

destination. But the Catholic Church offers adequate means for all her members to sustain their lives, and even to regain life when they lose it by grave sin (see UR 2–3). Thus, as a practical matter, each Catholic always has access to the means of being a living member of the community of faith and hope.

d) Hope guarantees only that God will do his part. Still, fear that one might not persevere is consistent with assurance that the Church's hope will be realized. So, the question remains: How is the paradox of hope's assurance resolved? The answer: By distinguishing between the conditions which are necessary for Christians to make the free choices they should make and their making of those choices. Hope guarantees the former, not the latter.[13]

The gospel proposes an appealing prospect of salvation. Faith accepts this prospect and the idea that it is available, and that acceptance leads spontaneously to the volitional act of hope: a lively interest in the coming of God's kingdom as something he guarantees to Christians and empowers them, with all the means necessary, to share in. This hope leads one to think practically about what one might do to hasten the kingdom's coming and to share in it. If choosing with some other intention or hoping in anyone but God, one might hesitate to choose and act rightly because that could be both costly and fruitless in relation to what one had in mind. Hope eliminates this source of hesitation. Choices can be made for the kingdom's sake with complete confidence—hope's assurance—that God will do his part and nothing else can nullify one's effort.

Yet, even though this assurance helps one choose rightly, it does not eliminate freedom. God will not fail to do his part, but he does not compel people against their free choice to do theirs. A person still can sin gravely and fail to use the means of salvation God provides.[14] Nor does this possibility in any way detract from the perfection of Christian hope, for although hope in God, like any other hope, is (in part) for oneself, it is not in oneself. While hoping in others (in this case, God) to do their part, one does not hope (except in a loose sense of *hope*) that one will do one's own part, but either does it or not.[15]

---

13. St. Thomas treats hope's assurance: *S.t.,* 2–2, q. 18, a. 4. A commentary: William J. Hill, O.P., "Appendix 7: The Certitude of Hope: Its Distinctive Nature," in St. Thomas Aquinas, *Summa theologiae,* vol. 33, *Hope* (New York: McGraw Hill, 1966), 161–66. The present treatment, however, differs from that of Thomas by regarding as intrinsic to hope the desire for the end which he treats as presupposed by hope; he develops his concept of hope by analogy with the sense appetite (emotion) of hope, and apparently never asks what sort of volitional act the desire for the end is: P. De Letter, S.J., "Hope and Charity in St. Thomas," *Thomist* 13 (1950): 231, 247–48. This gap is understandable in view of the context of theological discussion in which Thomas worked; that context has been examined by Servais Pinckaers, O.P., "La nature vertueuse de l'espérance," *Revue thomiste* 58 (1958): 405–42, 623–44.

14. Distinguishing God's grace, which is the object of hope, from human free acts, which are not the object of hope, the Council of Trent teaches about the gift of final perseverance: nobody should "feel assured of this gift with an absolute certitude" although "all ought to have most secure hope in the help of God. For unless men are unfaithful to his grace, God will bring the good work to perfection, just as he began it, working both the will and the performance" (DS 1541/806). The assurance of hope is not a guarantee that one will be faithful; despite God's grace, one still can be unfaithful.

15. Hans Urs von Balthasar, *Dare We Hope "That All Men Be Saved"? With a Short Discourse on Hell,* trans. David Kipp and Lothar Krauth (San Francisco: Ignatius Press, 1988), argues that

e) Human goods Christians hope for surely will be realized. As explained above, Christian hope embraces human fulfillment in this world, since this world is in continuity with the heavenly kingdom (see *CMP,* 34.E). Insofar as one acts on this hope, the good fruits of one's nature and effort are regarded as material for the kingdom. These objects of hope also share in hope's assurance; efforts to benefit one's neighbors and contribute to human fulfillment surely will succeed in the end. For this reason, "hope related to the end of time does not diminish the importance of intervening duties, but rather undergirds the acquittal of them with fresh incentives" (GS 21). However, just as Jesus' expectation that he would rise from the dead was consistent with his suffering and death, his disciples' expectation that the human goods for which they hope will be realized is consistent with failure in this world. Hope does not finally count on the effectiveness of human efforts but on God's re-creative act, which alone will fully overcome sin and its consequences.

Unlike the optimism of secular humanists, who dream of justice, peace, and plenty to be achieved progressively in the course of history, Christian hope should be soberly realistic about the prospects for a better world. The situation is like that of dedicated physicians, who, despite all their efforts—and even their successes—in protecting and promoting their patients' health, nevertheless know that eventually all will die. If they are Christians, such physicians expect human life finally to be saved, but only by God's act of raising the dead. Similarly, all hopeful Christians should strive earnestly to serve others and protect and promote human well-being, while knowing that the human goods they cherish will be saved and fully realized only in the kingdom. John Paul II explains this point clearly:

> Christian optimism [that is, hope], based on the glorious Cross of Christ and the outpouring of the Holy Spirit, is no excuse for self-deception. For Christians, peace on earth is always a challenge, because of the presence of sin in man's heart. Motivated by their faith and hope, Christians therefore apply themselves to promoting a more just society; they fight hunger, deprivation and disease; they are concerned about what happens to migrants, prisoners and outcasts (cf. Mt 25.35–36). But they know that, while all these undertakings express something of the mercy and perfection of God (cf. Lk 6.36; Mt 4.48), they are always limited in their range, precarious in their results and ambiguous in their inspiration. Only God the giver of life, when he unites all things in Christ (cf. Eph 1.10), will fulfil

---

the object of hope should include universal salvation; he quotes (212) Karl Rahner with approval for the position that there is a "*duty to hope for the salvation of all men*" (italics his). The arguments which von Balthasar offers for his position, however, actually are a priori arguments (as they must be, since there are no data on which to base an a posteriori argument) which succeed only if they show hell's impossibility and thereby disprove his other (and correct) thesis that one should regard hell as a real possibility for oneself. His thesis that all might be saved also implies that the scriptural witness to hell may be a bluffing threat, which in turn implies that the Holy Spirit may be bluffing, that is, lying. In von Balthasar's defense, someone might argue that according to him the scriptural witness to hell should be considered a warning rather than a threat, for he holds (165, cf. 49–58) "that God does not damn anyone, but that [if anyone is damned] the man who irrevocably refuses love condemns himself." But he also often (20, 21, 25, 34, 84, 166, 183, 186–87, 211) characterizes the scriptural witness to hell as a "threat." For an able critique of other aspects of this book of von Balthasar, see James T. O'Connor, "Von Balthasar and Salvation," *Homiletic and Pastoral Review* 89 (July 1989): 10–21.

our ardent hope by himself bringing to accomplishment everything that he has undertaken in history according to his Spirit in the matter of justice and peace.[16]

f) This assurance extends to goods one hopes for in this world. It is all well and good, someone might say, to be certain the human goods for which one hopes will be realized in heaven. But may not Christians also hope that goods important to them and those they love will be realized or preserved even in this world? The answer is: Yes, provided they seek first the kingdom, and hope for all these other goods only insofar as they belong to it. The point is not that one may hope for these goods only *if* God wills them, for he surely does, but that one must be ready to receive these goods *as* God wills them.

Suppose, for instance, a husband and father has cancer; his wife and children hope and pray he will recover. This hope is nothing other than their Christian hope, provided they count on God for this good and are prepared to accept it as he plans and wills to give it. For then they hope for their husband and father's recovery in this life provided it belongs to the coming of the kingdom, while at the same time being ready to accept God's will even if that is to save him from this evil, not now, but by resurrection. With this Christian hope, they will join in celebrating the sacrament of the anointing of the sick, so that he will be raised up from this sickness, whether from his hospital bed or from his grave.

4. Hope Is the Interest Which Motivates Every Act of Christian Life

While certain human acts, done with the help of grace, are necessary to prepare one to receive faith, hope, and charity, these three coprinciples of Christian life are acquired not by human acts but by the gift of the Spirit (see DS 1525–31/797–800; *S.t.*, 1–2, q. 62, a. 1; 2–2, q. 6, a. 1; q. 24, a. 2). Although faith, hope, and love very often have been thought of as if they were separate acts, St. Paul links them closely and dynamically, and treats faith as their basis (see Rom 5.1–5, Gal 5.5–6). So, it seems better to think of faith, hope, and love as concurring together in the single act of living faith (see *CMP*, 25.4).

On this view, unless hope is impeded by sins of presumption and/or despair, it always accompanies faith. Indeed, hope in God for the kingdom's coming motivates the act of faith: "The time is fulfilled, and the kingdom of God has come near; repent, and believe in the good news" (Mk 1.15). Hope also motivates every choice to do anything implementing faith. As a motive for the act of faith, hope is not a free choice distinct from the commitment of faith; and as a motive for every act of Christian life, it is not itself an act separate and apart from others. In fact, hope cannot be a choice, since hope bears on the ultimate end, which is sought for its own sake rather than for anything beyond itself, while every choice is of something which leads to what is beyond itself (see *S.t.*, 1–2, q. 13, a. 3).

Exactly what, then, is hope? It is the volition of the ultimate end of Christian life, the kingdom and Christians' sharing in it, which underlies and motivates the choices shaping Christian life, lived for the sake of the kingdom. In other words,

---

16. John Paul II, *Peace: A Gift of God Entrusted to Us!* (Day of Peace Message, 1 Jan. 1982), 12, *AAS* 74 (1982) 335–36, *OR*, 4 Jan. 1982, 7.

hope is, first of all, the *interest* which the Church as a whole and individual Christians have in realizing and sharing in the kingdom. Then, when the Church, communities within her, and individual Christians faithfully do God's will, hope is not only their interest in the kingdom's coming but the *intending* of that end for whose sake they make the Christian choices they make. Of course, in and of themselves, human acts could not realize the kingdom, but hope counts on God for the fruitfulness of the actions it motivates.[17]

Question B: How Should One Fulfill One's Responsibility to Hope?

Although it might be supposed that the responsibility to hope should be fulfilled by distinct acts of hoping, just as the responsibility to worship is fulfilled by distinct acts of worshiping, one cannot choose to hope as one can choose to worship (as has been explained in A.4). Still, there is a place for acts of hope, for hope can and should be nurtured by meditation. Hope also should be made specific in prayers of petition, exercised in shaping one's life, used to moderate fear, strengthened by receiving the sacrament of confirmation, and protected against sins which could distort or destroy it.

1. One Should Nurture Hope by Meditation and Concretize It in Prayer

People cannot live Christian life consistently unless they enjoy doing so, and no one will enjoy living Christian life without nurturing hope. This can be done by keeping in mind the truths which ground hope and by exercising it in praying for the things one needs. Since the Eucharist makes the kingdom present and provides a foretaste of it, devout participation in the Eucharist especially intensifies hope. Intense hope gives Christian life a characteristic balance of tranquillity and energy.

a) **One must nurture hope in order to enjoy following Jesus.** Just as competitors confident of winning celebrate their victory in their hearts even as they undergo the hardships of competing, so Christians whose hope is lively rejoice during this life. Jesus not only promises heavenly joy to those who suffer the consequences of following him, but calls for its anticipation: "Rejoice and be glad, for your reward is great in heaven" (Mt 5.12). St. Paul teaches that Christians always should call on God's help by constant prayer, rejoice in hope, be patient, and not be anxious (see Rom 12.12, Phil 4.4–6).

Since Christian joy presupposes hope, Jesus' and Paul's injunctions to rejoice can be fulfilled only by nurturing hope. But hope grows in a kind of virtuous circle: joy amid suffering helps faithful Christians endure what they must, this endurance

---

17. See Santiago Ramirez, O.P., *La esencia de la esperanza cristiana* (Madrid: Ediciones Punta Europa, 1960), 195–205. Readers interested in an analytic clarification of the distinctions between interest, intention, and choice (which are volitional) and other principles and elements of human action may find helpful the definitions and distinctions proposed by Germain Grisez, Joseph Boyle, and John Finnis, "Practical Principles, Moral Truth, and Ultimate Ends," *American Journal of Jurisprudence* 32 (1987): 99–120.

conforms their character to that of Jesus, and likeness to Jesus increases their confidence and further intensifies their hope (see Rom 5.3–4; cf. Phil 3.8–21). Consequently, hope must be nurtured until its liveliness bears fruit in an anticipation of heavenly fulfillment enabling one to rejoice amidst suffering.

b) Meditation on relevant truths of faith nurtures hope. Because acts of hope—prayers expressing the reasons for hoping in God as well as what is hoped for—presuppose the hope they express, they do not carry out hope as acts of worship carry out choices to worship. Still, they do intensify hope by recalling the truths of faith from which it most directly follows: that God promises the kingdom and that he can and will bring it about. Hope easily is weakened by forgetfulness of these truths and failure to give them explicit, real, and heartfelt assent; then interest in the kingdom, which always should be kept in mind as paramount, is overlooked even during deliberation concerning crucial decisions. To prevent this, one not only should use the short formulae of acts of hope, but should meditate on relevant passages of Scripture and the lives of the saints, and often engage in informal individual and communal meditation on the relevant truths of faith.

It is a serious psychological mistake to suppose that such meditation is unnecessary. Dedicated participants in other great enterprises seldom err in this way. Revolutionaries, for instance, sustain their courage by recalling their long-range goal while attending closely to anything which seems to promise its attainment. Christians, likewise, must foster hope, not allowing its expressions in prayer and worship to become merely verbal and formal, but making of each such expression an occasion for intensifying a vividly realistic faith in the kingdom and trust in the Holy Spirit's power to bring it about.

c) Prayer of petition presupposes and concretizes hope. Prayer of petition presupposes not only faith but hope: God is asked to help because he is counted on to do what is asked insofar as it will be truly good (see *CMP*, 29.E). For anything to be truly good, it must be in accord with God's providential plan, which culminates in the principal object of hope: the kingdom, in which all things will be fulfilled in the Lord Jesus. So, prayers of petition serve to spell out hope in detail, and to place the particular cares of one's life and times in the context of God's all-embracing plan and ultimate purpose.

In giving his disciples the Our Father (Mt 6.9–13; cf. Lk 11.2–4), Jesus ingeniously provides a summary and schema for all other acts of hope and prayers of petition. Calling on their covenantal partner ("Our Father, who art in heaven"), Christians express hope for the spread of the communion of faith ("hallowed be thy name") and the fulfillment of his saving plan ("thy kingdom come") through humankind's submission to his will ("thy will be done, on earth as it is in heaven"). The prayer also asks God for the essential means to live the Christian life ("give us this day our daily bread"), remission of past sins ("forgive us our debts, as we also have forgiven our debtors"), freedom from future sin ("lead us not into temptation"), and protection against the powers of evil ("deliver us from evil").[18]

---

18. The connection between hope and the Lord's Prayer was noted by St. Augustine: *Enchiridion de fide, spe, caritate* 114–26, *PL*, 40:285–86. St. Thomas, *Compendium theologiae*

d) One can nurture hope by devout participation in the Eucharist. The Mass not only recalls Jesus' sacrifice and makes it present for his followers to share in, but anticipates the heavenly banquet (see SC 8). The whole liturgy of the word and Eucharist is rich in the aspects of faith which most directly nurture hope.

The Communion rite especially can intensify both hope and the joy which flows from it. Beginning with the Lord's Prayer, it then goes on to ask the Father to "protect us from all anxiety as we wait in joyful hope for the coming of our Savior" and to ask Jesus to "grant us the peace and unity of your kingdom where you live for ever and ever." Holy Communion is the bread of everlasting life, the foretaste of heavenly glory, which it signifies and leads to (see Jn 6.35–40, 53–58; *CMP,* 33.E). So, freed from sin by the Lamb of God, "Happy are those who are called to his supper." Plainly, the experience of preparing for and receiving Communion will increase hope and joy for anyone who pays attention to what he or she is doing.[19]

e) As hope grows, one becomes more aware of God's providence. While hope is in itself volitional, it affects concrete awareness and feelings. The nurturing of hope increases the sense that God is not an absent parent but a loving and always present Father, guiding one step by step through life, providing whatever is necessary, and never permitting bad things to happen without some good reason. Rising to face the challenges of a new day, one knows that one works alongside Jesus and feels strengthened to do one's very best; lying down at night, one commends one's spirit to the Father and rests secure in his arms. Such a person lives without optimistic illusions, fully recognizing the general wretchedness of the human condition and the extremity of many particular situations. Yet he or she enjoys great energy and confidence, which block temptations to pessimistic fatalism. At the same time, profound peace of mind prevents a lapse into frantic zealotry.

2. One Should Put Hope into Practice by Living for the Kingdom

Since people always should do God's will and act for the kingdom's sake, hoping should be their intending of the end underlying each and every choice they make. Then they will essentially fulfill their responsibility to hope. To do this, all Christians together as one Church must carry out their common mission precisely in response to hope, while each must organize his or her life as a personal vocation, a personal share in the Church's common mission.

---

ad fratrem Reginaldum, 2 (*De spe*), provides a fuller explanation of the relationship between hope and prayer of petition (1–4) and the beginning of what would have been a rich commentary on the Our Father had he completed this work (5–10). Two recent commentaries on the Our Father support elements of the interpretation proposed here: W. F. Albright and C. S. Mann, *Matthew: Introduction, Translation, and Notes,* Anchor Bible, 26 (Garden City, N.Y.: Doubleday, 1971), 74–77; *Interpreter's Dictionary of the Bible,* s.v. "Lord's Prayer."

19. Many celebrants make small changes in the Communion rite which obscure its eschatological significance and thus detract from its effectiveness in nurturing hope. For example, some say "Happy are *we* who are called to *this* supper," thereby focusing attention on the present celebration instead of on the heavenly banquet; others pray for liberation from "unnecessary anxiety" or "useless worry," thereby focusing on temporal cares, regarding which one at times can worry usefully, instead of interest in heaven, concerning which only grave sin should make one anxious.

Question C will clarify the Church's mission; question D will treat the common responsibility to share in the Church's apostolate; and question E will treat each Christian's responsibility to find, accept, and fulfill his or her personal vocation. What follows is only an introduction to these important topics.

a) **Hope is not passive reliance on God but a principle of action.** Some Christians seem to think they can count on God for salvation while living like those who have no hope. This notion is altogether wrong, as the New Testament makes clear. Through Jesus' resurrection, God in his mercy "has given us a new birth into a living hope" (1 Pt 1.3), that is, a hope by which to live.[20] Throughout life, hope's assurance is to be realized, that is, made real through works of love and service. This requires being energetic in imitating those who lived their faith and so gained heaven (see Heb 6.9–12). Thus, one can hope for heaven only as a reward for doing God's will (see DS 1570/830, 1576/836). So, Paul prays that God who gave the Thessalonians hope through grace will comfort their "hearts and strengthen them in every good work and word" (2 Thes 2.17). And in prescribing armor for wide-awake Christians, ready for the struggle of life, he makes hope their helmet (see 1 Thes 5.8).

b) **The Church carries on Jesus' mission out of hope.** Hope, being primarily ecclesial, is operative in everything the Church does, for it is the intending of the end she has in view in carrying out her mission. To understand this truth about the Church, one must begin with Jesus. Coming into the world to do the Father's will (see Jn 4.34; *CMP,* 22.B), his mission is to save the world (see Jn 12.47; *CMP,* 22.C). The end for which Jesus acts, the kingdom fully realized by God's re-creative act, is to be the uniting of all things in himself (see Eph 1.9–10; LG 3; *CMP,* 19.B). This end is hope's precise object. Jesus is sent to fulfill hope, which he does: all God's promises find their yes in him (see 2 Cor 1.20).

Jesus consigns the completion of his work to the apostles, sending them into the world as the Father had sent him (see Jn 17.18). The Church does nothing without her Lord; he remains with her and sends his Spirit to teach and empower her. So, Jesus carries on his mission in and through his Church (see LG 4–5). Through the course of history, "the Church intends but one thing: to carry forward the work of Christ under the guidance of the befriending Spirit" (GS 3).[21]

c) **Vatican II teaches that hope calls for an apostolic life.** Hope, the Council teaches, not only motivates Christians to persevere through the struggle of an apostolic life but frees them from enslavement to wealth, so that they can "totally dedicate themselves to expanding God's kingdom and to shaping and perfecting the temporal order in a Christian spirit" (AA 4). Again, the Council teaches that the laity will show themselves to be children of the promise by making the most of the present and also waiting patiently for heavenly glory. It then urges:

---

20. See Bo Reicke, *The Epistles of James, Peter, and Jude: Introduction, Translation, and Notes,* Anchor Bible, 37 (Garden City, N.Y.: Doubleday, 1964), 79.

21. In addition to indications in Scripture and Vatican II, the nature of Jesus' mission and the homogeneity of the Church's mission with it is explained very well by Paul VI, *Evangelii nuntiandi,* 7–16, *AAS* 68 (1976) 9–16, Flannery, 2:714–18.

> They should not, then, hide this hope in the depths of their hearts, but should express it also through the structures of secular life, by a continual conversion and by wrestling "against the world-rulers of this darkness, against the spiritual forces of wickedness" (Eph 6.12). . . . The laity go forth as powerful proclaimers of a faith in things to be hoped for (see Heb 11.1) if they imperturbably combine with their life of faith the professing of that faith. (LG 35; cf. GE 2)

Vatican II refers in the passages cited to the laity, but this teaching applies equally to all the faithful.

3. Hope and Fear Should Be Correctly Integrated in Christian Life

Hope's assurance does not preclude every sort of fear. Hope not only is compatible with fear—of sin's occasions and of punishment for sin—but leads to it and even depends on it. Still, as love grows, anxiety about possible punishment lessens, and fear of what might lead to sin is purified of self-centeredness. Moreover, hope helps in overcoming the fears which inhibit one from living a Christian life. It is essential that these fears be conquered, for such a life is sure to involve suffering, perhaps even to the point of martyrdom.

a) Faith leads one to fear God and his just judgment. Faith holds out the prospect of heaven and leads one to hope for it, confidently counting on the wise, merciful, faithful, almighty Father. But faith also calls one to fulfill covenantal responsibilities, and warns that eternal death awaits those who separate themselves from God's love by mortal sin and die in it (see *CMP*, 18.G). This warning induces salutary fear of God, insofar as one thinks of hell as his just punishment of mortal sin. Jesus himself stirs up this fear: "Do not fear those who kill the body but cannot kill the soul; rather fear him who can destroy both soul and body in hell" (Mt 10.28; cf. Lk 12.4–5).

Jesus' warning does not mean that hell is imposed on sinners by God's choice. Its meaning instead is that God chooses to make created persons with freedom to love, that this freedom can be abused by sinning, that such abuse, when grave and persistent, inevitably results in hell, and that God reluctantly accepts this result only in the case of someone who refuses his help to forestall it (see *CMP*, 18.I).

b) Fear of hell always should be subordinated to hope. Sensible or imagined evils, being positive realities, directly arouse negative emotions, including fear. Thus, vivid descriptions of the torments of hell generate a powerful motive to avoid it. But even though that motive can be salutary, by itself it is inadequate, for two very different reasons.

First, while emotional fear of hell can motivate choices in accord with Christian hope, it also can motivate hatred of the gospel, regarded as threatening, and the choice to reject faith. Second, while merely emotional motives can be adequate to shape behavior which is naturally necessary for bodily well-being, no emotional motive by itself can shape human life toward its ultimate end, which, while including bodily well-being, goes beyond it to embrace the more-than-bodily aspects of heavenly fulfillment. Consequently, merely emotional fear of hell and desire for heaven need to be integrated with motivation of a higher order, that is, with volitional motivation.

Volitional motives—that is, interests and intentions—are specified by intelligible goods and evils. Unlike sensible or imagined evils, intelligible ones are not positive realities but privations. Thus, hell as an intelligible evil is not a set of sensible sufferings—which, indeed, are intelligibly good insofar as they reflect the real situation of the damned—but the permanent deprivation of both friendship with God and all the blessings of sharing in his kingdom. It is possible to understand a privation and take an interest in avoiding it, however, only insofar as one understands the good of which it is the privation and is interested in sharing in that good. So, the intelligible evil of hell cannot motivate people volitionally except insofar as they are interested in heaven and hope with Christian hope.

Therefore, since emotional fear of hell should be integrated with volitional motivation, and since volitional fear of the intelligible evil of hell necessarily presupposes hope, all fear of hell should be subordinated to hope.

c) **Fear of hell is essential for Christian hope.** For if one becomes forgetful of the possibility of hell and loses all fear of it, heaven seems a sure thing, with the bad result that it no longer is possible to have Christian hope for it or live a life shaped by that hope. Christian hope is the intention of the kingdom as one's end, and some good can be intended as an end only if one's action is expected to help bring about that good. Thus, someone confident of sharing in the kingdom no matter what, simply cannot intend it as an end and live for it, although such a person still may think about heaven for solace when loved ones die and during other times of suffering. In consequence, someone who forgets the possibility of hell ignores the kingdom when deliberating and making choices. Unable any longer to order his or her life to the kingdom, that person becomes motivated by other interests and desires, and these alien ends, pursued independently of faith and hope, make their own incompatible demands. Thus, the life of a Christian forgetful of hell becomes indistinguishable from the life of a nonbeliever.

Consequently, while properly Christian fear depends on hope, hope also depends on fear. And while hope for the kingdom always should dominate, fear of hell never should be entirely excluded. Thus, meditation on the last things, which appropriately begins from sacred Scripture, should reflect the balanced approach of the New Testament, which focuses on heaven but never entirely loses sight of hell.

d) **Love arouses a childlike fear of offending God.** While fear of hell always should remain, still the more a person loves God, the less he or she fears punishment. For the more God is loved, the less self-interested one is and the less inclined to commit mortal sins which deserve eternal punishment (see *S.t., 2–2*, q. 19, aa. 4, 6, 10). Hence, "perfect love casts out fear" (1 Jn 4.18), not by eliminating fear of hell and encouraging fearless sinning, but by liberating people from sin by the Holy Spirit's power (see Rom 8.12–17).

While fear of punishment, which can coexist with sin, decreases as love increases, another fear flows from love itself and grows with it. This is fear of what might lead to sin, not because sin deserves punishment, but because by sinning one offends the Father, whom one loves, and separates oneself from him. The more God is loved, the more one wants to do his will, and so the more one fears affronting him by sin. Moreover, aware from both personal experience and faith's teaching that one cannot save oneself, a person is motivated by this fear to cling tightly to God, just as small children cling tightly to their parent's hand when crossing a busy street. This childlike fear and reverence for God, which flow from love, enliven and reinforce hope by intensifying desire for heavenly communion and increasing confidence in the heavenly Father's care (see *S.t.*, 2–2, q. 19, aa. 5, 9).

e) **Hope in providence allays worries which inhibit good efforts.** In the fallen world, experience teaches that good efforts can go wrong and fail in many ways, and for many people this awareness has the bad result that well-grounded worries and anxieties paralyze them with discouragement or lead them to make "realistic" compromises between the good they desire and the mixture of good and bad they think they can achieve. However, faith teaches that God's wise and loving plan ensures the fruitfulness of the effort of those who do his will: "We know that all things work together for good for those who love God, who are called according to his purpose" (Rom 8.28). Hope's assurance is that those who love God can rely on his being on their side; Jesus' last word is: "And remember, I am with you always, to the end of the age" (Mt 28.20). Christians need not hesitate, feeling that God might not support their good efforts. Even if fear of failure is entirely realistic and good efforts seem to end badly, hope looks to the coming of the kingdom, in which all good human efforts will be fulfilled (see GS 38–39).

f) **Hope engenders faithfulness despite formidable threats.** Fears of losing status and possessions and of undergoing suffering and death tempt to infidelity. Christian life requires a faithfulness and heroism which are more than ordinary courage, for one must be ready to sacrifice every worldly good and endure every worldly evil to fulfill one's Christian responsibilities. Christian faithfulness flows from faith and love (see *CMP*, 26.G), but hope also engenders it. For by hope people count not on themselves but on God, aware that they always are in his providential care.

If one seeks the kingdom first, God meets all the needs about which one is likely to be anxious (see Mt 6.25–33). He can defeat every evil, no matter how fearsome: "In the world you face persecution. But take courage; I have conquered the world!" (Jn 16.33). Moreover, by hope one looks forward joyfully to glory, soon to be revealed, with which present suffering hardly deserves comparison (see Rom 8.18, 2 Cor 4.17). Thus, despite formidable obstacles and sufferings, "linked with the paschal mystery and patterned on the dying Christ, [the Christian] will hasten forward to resurrection in the strength which comes from hope" (GS 22).

g) **Hope underlies the courage required for martyrdom.** Martyrdom is laying down one's life in order to stand fast with Jesus and his Church. The martyr bears witness by faithful words, virtuous deeds, or both, and these lead to his or her death (see *S.t.*, 2–2, q. 124, a. 5). Thus, the martyrs include not only those killed for professing their faith but those who suffer death because, for Jesus' sake, they either refuse to do what is wrong or persist in doing what is right.

Martyrdom bears witness to faith, is a supreme work of love, and requires courage, but martyrdom and willingness to accept it also are special works of hope. Martyrs prize the heavenly glory for which they hope more than any other good, even life itself. Unwillingness to suffer martyrdom would mean setting a limit on fidelity to Jesus. Moreover, knowing their own weakness, people truly can be willing to accept martyrdom only insofar as they count on God to sustain them through tests they could not pass by themselves.

4. The Sacrament of Confirmation Is Especially Linked to Hope

Although the sacraments of baptism, confirmation, and the Eucharist all confer or increase faith, hope, and charity, in a special way baptism is the sacrament of faith, the Eucharist is the sacrament of love, and, similarly, confirmation may be considered the sacrament of hope.

a) **Confirmation empowers Christians to put hope into practice.** Confirmation introduces Christians, already living members of the Church, into her apostolate (see *CMP*, 31.C). According to the measure of their personal vocations, the confirmed become witnesses to Jesus and play their unique roles in his mission of salvation (see *CMP*, 31.D).[22] In fulfilling their share in the Church's mission, her members put their hope into practice. To do this, they need the gift of the Spirit, received in confirmation, who strengthens them by assuring them that he will bring them through to the end and by enabling them to experience, even in the midst of suffering, an anticipation of the joy of heaven. Of that strength and anticipated joy are martyrs made.[23]

b) **Confirmation is the sacrament of personal vocation.** The sacrament of confirmation provides the light and strength to discern, accept, and faithfully fulfill one's personal vocation (see *CMP*, 31.C). Thus, John Paul II teaches:

> Each one of you is individually called by Christ, called to be part of his Kingdom and to play a role in his mission of salvation. These are the great realities of your Baptism and your Confirmation. Having called you by name, God sends you forth to accomplish what he wants you to do. He says to each of you what he said to Jeremiah the Prophet: "I am with you to protect you."[24]

c) **One should receive the sacrament of confirmation.** At Pentecost, the apostles fearlessly began to proclaim salvation in Jesus the Lord (see Acts 2). The book of Acts as a whole makes it plain that the first Christians burned with zeal for the kingdom, which seemed to them not only entirely real but close. Consciously and constantly, the early Church lived in the intimate communion of the Holy Spirit, who guided, empowered, and made fruitful her life and missionary work. This sense

22. See Robert Christian, O.P., "Midway between Baptism and Holy Orders: Saint Thomas' Contribution to a Contemporary Understanding of Confirmation," *Angelicum* 69 (1992): 157–73.

23. See Louis Bouyer, *Le Consolateur: Esprit-Saint et vie de Grâce* (Paris: Les Éditions du Cerf, 1980), 113–33.

24. John Paul II, Homily at Mass for Youth (Dublin), 4, *Inseg.* 3.2 (1980) 463, *OR*, 15 Sept. 1980, 2 (without the words "your Baptism and"); also see Homily at Mass in Krakow, 3, *AAS* 71 (1979) 873–75, *OR*, 16 July 1979, 13. In his *Apostolic Letter on the Occasion of the International Youth Year*, 9, *AAS* 77 (1985) 602, *OR*, 1 Apr. 1985, 5, John Paul II points out that "before the Second Vatican Council the concept of 'vocation' was applied *first of all* to the priesthood and religious life, as if Christ had addressed to the young person his evangelical 'Follow me' only for these cases. *The Council has broadened* this way of looking at things. . . . Every human life vocation, as a Christian vocation, corresponds to the evangelical call. *Christ's 'Follow me' makes itself heard on the different paths* taken by the disciples and confessors of the divine Redeemer."

of the kingdom's reality and reliance on the Spirit are lively hope. Pentecost had made Christian hope come alive (see Rom 5.1–5, 8.12–17), and as the Holy Spirit was given at Pentecost to the whole incipient Church, gathered in the upper room, so he is given today in confirmation, in order to involve Christians more deeply in the Church and strengthen them to defend and share their faith by words and deeds (see *CMP*, 31.A).

Thus, to enliven hope by the fullness of the gift of the Spirit, every Catholic should receive the sacrament of confirmation.[25] Moreover, because the Spirit is not an object one possesses but a divine helper who dwells in one's heart, it is necessary to keep the sacrament of confirmation fresh by avoiding sins which would evict the Spirit and continuing to pray that he remain and perfect one's fellowship with Jesus and fellow Christians.[26]

5. One Should Not Sin against Hope by Presumption or Despair

Since faith underlies hope, hope can be undermined by doubting or denying relevant truths of faith. Here, however, presumption and despair are considered insofar as they are specific sins against hope, sins which can be committed without a prior error in faith or a sin against it.[27]

a) These sins must not be confused with various other things. It may be presumptuous, but it is not presumption against hope in God overconfidently to undertake something beyond one's ability—"to bite off more than one can chew." Nor is it presumption to plan to repent even as one sins; presumption is not a plan to repent but a substitute for repentance. Nor is presumption simply a choice not to repent a mortal sin; that is obduracy, which certainly is gravely sinful (see *CMP*, 18.E.3), but not a sin against hope.

It is not despair to be pessimistic about history and one's life insofar as their prospects depend on anything except God; such pessimism is entirely compatible with hope in God. Nor is psychological depression despair, for depression is a sickness from which the depressed suffer, while despair is a sin the despairing

25. There is an obligation to receive the sacrament of confirmation; *CIC*, c. 890: "The faithful are obliged to receive this sacrament at the appropriate time; their parents and shepherds of souls, especially pastors, are to see to it that the faithful are properly instructed to receive it and approach the sacrament at the appropriate time." However, the Church never has said how serious a matter it is for someone deliberately to neglect this sacrament. A study which remains useful though written before Vatican II and the 1983 code: J. Clement Bennington, *The Recipient of Confirmation: A Historical Synopsis and a Commentary* (Washington, D.C.: The Catholic University of America Press, 1952).

26. According to Jesus' promise, children of God who earnestly ask their heavenly Father for the Spirit will not be disappointed (see Lk 11.13). Not every Christian need experience what is sometimes called *baptism in the Spirit;* many great saints seem not to have had such an experience. However, the Church as a whole and every Christian do require the Spirit's caring presence and renewing action, and the charismatic renewal has enabled many to enjoy a vivid experience of the gift of the Spirit. See Francis A. Sullivan, S.J., " 'Baptism in the Holy Spirit': A Catholic Interpretation of the Pentecostal Experience," *Gregorianum* 55 (1974): 49–68.

27. This treatment of presumption and despair draws on St. Thomas (see *S.t.*, 2–2, qq. 20–21) in defining the two sins and their malice, but not in explaining their etiology and consequences. See *CMP*, 18.E.4–5, but note there a mistaken example of an expression of presumption: "I can always count on God's grace, and I will repent in my own good time."

commit. Nor is despair the fear which serious Christians, whether scrupulous or not, sometimes experience in considering their own sins and realizing vividly that their salvation is not guaranteed. Such fear not only is compatible with hope but presupposes it and is necessary to it, as has been explained (in 3.c, above).

Without really meaning what they say, people sometimes make statements which sound like presumption or despair. For instance, those who admit they are in mortal sin sometimes say, "God wouldn't send me to hell for this" or "God could never forgive me for this." But they may not clearly understand what they are saying or they may be expressing mere feelings without sinning against hope.

b) Presumption abuses hope by irresponsibly counting on God. Remaining interested in God's promises and counting on him to keep them, those who sin by presumption continue to hope and even, to some extent, to shape their lives by hope. But, not consistently putting hope into practice, they abuse it, expecting pardon without repentance and the reward for following Jesus without the cost of discipleship. This unrealistic expectation is the essence of presumption.

An element of pride underlies this sin. Rejecting God's terms for obtaining what he promises, the presumptuous expect to obtain it on their own. They suppose that God, like a blustery parent, threatens punishments which he will be too softhearted to carry out, and, like a permissive parent, accompanies his gift of freedom with a virtual guarantee to fend off the consequences of its irresponsible use. Such suppositions are inconsistent with faith, which not only depends on God's absolute truthfulness but also, assuring believers that God will do his part, calls them to do theirs, as grace empowers them to do.

However, the sin of presumption can be committed without denying any truth of faith. People determined not to fulfill the responsibilities of Christian life in some essential respect, yet, unwilling to face the prospective consequences, can resolve the tension by persuading themselves that somehow God will manage to save them despite themselves. This self-deception need not be logical enough to withstand critical reflection, since that is something the presumptuous manage to avoid.

c) Presumption threatens faith and weakens hope itself. Since the self-deception essential to presumption cannot withstand critical reflection in light of relevant truths of faith concerning the duty to cooperate with God's grace, this sin implicitly challenges previously sound faith. Absolute self-deception is beyond anyone's reach, and so the presumptuous may become aware of the inconsistency between what faith teaches about everyone's salvation and the subjective belief about their own to which they cling. The tension can be resolved by repenting the sin of presumption, by replacing presumption with despair, or by denying unwelcome truths of faith: that God is not only merciful but just, that unrepentant mortal sinners suffer everlasting loss, that some sins really are mortal, and so forth. In generating temptations to deny such truths, presumption threatens faith.

It also weakens hope. Rather than serving as the intention of all the choices which should make up Christian life, presumptuous hope renders many of them unnecessary and clears the way for a life-style apart from, and even sinfully at odds with, hope for the kingdom. Not being exercised, hope weakens as other interests grow strong. Eventually heaven, now taken for granted and regarded as irrelevant to present concerns, becomes a dim prospect, a mere fairyland which one used to yearn for but no longer finds exciting.

d) Despair destroys hope and gravely threatens faith. Despair is more radical than presumption, for the despairing entirely abandon hope of personally sharing in the kingdom. They will to be rid of interest in the kingdom and reliance on God, which they experience as burdens. Having sinned mortally, resisted the grace of repentance, and probably committed the sin of presumption—yet having exhausted their capacity for the self-deception it requires—despairing sinners finally throw off all restraint by convincing themselves: I have nothing more to lose; no matter what I do, I am a lost soul.

As with presumption, no error in faith need underlie this attitude. To sinners prepared to repent, hope is joy, for it provides both the reason for repenting and the assurance of the graces repentance requires and brings. But in those unwilling to repent, hope induces restlessness—the temptation, as it were, to repent—and blocks unconditional surrender to sin. Thus, hope seems a curse. Obduracy generates this problem. The presumptuous solve it by persuading themselves God will save them regardless of what they do, the despairing by persuading themselves he will not save them regardless of what they do. The self-deception of despair is made easier if hope has been weakened by presumption, so that what is lost in abandoning hope seems of little worth.

Those who despair are right in believing they cannot be saved if they remain sinners; they are wrong only in putting their status as sinners beyond the reach of God's grace. Still, if someone with faith despairs, faith is hardly likely to last, for such a person faces the awful prospect of hell and desperately needs to evade it. The only way of doing so consistent with despair is to deny the faith, beginning with the doctrine that hell awaits unrepentant sinners.

e) Presumption and despair are very grave sins. No one doubts that despair is among the gravest of sins, since it so strongly armors sinners against repentance and tempts them to abandon their faith. But presumption, while not so grave, also is a very grave and especially insidious sin, which blocks repentance, weakens hope, threatens faith, and tends toward despair and loss of faith.[28]

Someone might ask: If hoping, which is the Christian alternative to these sins, is not a free choice, and if these sins themselves necessarily involve self-deception, which hardly can be a freely chosen act, how can anyone commit them? The answer is that a mortal sinner's prior choice to resist the grace of repentance can extend into the voluntary acceptance of the self-deception involved in presumption and despair. This voluntariness, called *executive willing*, is sufficient for mortal sin (see *CMP*, 9.G.1–2). Thus, someone obdurate in mortal sin can commit these still graver sins without making additional free choices.

---

28. The pastoral defense against these sins is not to stress compassion and divine mercy one-sidedly, as has been done all too often since 1960, but to accompany the message about compassion and mercy with equally insistent teaching about the power and readiness of the Holy Spirit to liberate sinners and about their responsibility to cooperate with grace. A model is provided by John Paul II, *Dominum et vivificantem*, 42–48, *AAS* 78 (1986) 857–68, *OR*, 9 June 1986, 8–10.

Question C: What Is the Mission of the Church?

Since each Christian puts hope into practice by finding, accepting, and faithfully fulfilling his or her personal vocation, one's specific responsibilities in these matters must be considered in detail. Before doing so (in question E), however, it is necessary to treat those aspects of the apostolate common to all members of the Church (in question D), since a personal vocation is an individual's particular share in the apostolate. But because the apostolate carries out the Church's mission, that mission must be clarified first, beginning with Jesus' mission of salvation, which the Church carries on.

1. Jesus' Mission Was to Establish a New Human Communion with God

Jesus' whole mission was to prepare for and initiate God's ultimate saving work, the establishment of the heavenly kingdom. Yet the gospel of the kingdom's coming includes a call for radical social and economic reform.[29]

a) **Because of sin, humankind needs salvation by God's mercy.** God created human persons in order both to bless them with benefits suited to their nature and make them members by adoption of his own divine family. From the beginning, however, sin alienated humankind from God and led to conflicts among human beings themselves. Because of sin, human persons are doomed to suffering and death, and their desires are distorted: wealth, pleasure, and power often seem more appealing than goods like health and life, good work and truth, marriage and family, justice and friendship, which truly fulfill human persons (see *CMP*, 14.G–H). Moreover, because the protection and pursuit of those genuine goods often are impeded or blocked by others' sins and the consequences of sin, fallen men and women frequently are tempted to use bad means in the service of good ends; indeed, in the absence of hope, such wrongdoing sometimes seems necessary to salvage something from the wreckage of the broken world.[30] Without salvation by God's merciful forgiveness, humankind's situation is hopeless.

b) **Jesus' work will be completed by God's act of re-creation.** The Word became man to overcome evil. But overcoming evil did not lie in destroying it (which cannot be done, since it is a privation) nor in removing human persons from the midst of evil (which cannot be done, since it afflicts every person inwardly). Rather, Jesus' mission was to end humankind's alienation from God by establishing new communion with him, to heal humankind's divisions by inviting everyone into covenantal fellowship, to overcome death by providing the means to gain resurrection life, to rechannel disordered passions by the hope for authentic human fulfillment in the kingdom, and to send the Spirit with his gift of love, which enables those who believe in Jesus to follow him (see *CMP*, 22).

---

29. José Capmany, "La persona y el amor de Jesús en la ordenación social," *Scripta theologica* 14 (1982): 449–518, shows how the Church's increasing understanding of the integral sense of Jesus' saving work has affected her social teaching.

30. See Germain Grisez, "Practical Reason and Faith," *Proceedings of the American Catholic Philosophical Association* 58 (1984): 9–12.

Although everything Jesus did as man was God's saving work in him, this work enjoyed only limited success during Jesus' earthly life, and at the end it appeared a complete failure. Its full salvific significance appeared only when God responded to Jesus' sacrifice by raising him from the dead. That divine, re-creative act showed how the saving work begun in Jesus' human life and death will be completed by the Holy Spirit's power, when evil will be overcome in the new heavens and new earth (see *CMP*, 34.D–E).

c) **Jesus' mission exclusively served the heavenly kingdom.** Today, some argue that Jesus planned Israel's political liberation, while the traditional understanding of his mission is an ideologically biased, politically conservative misinterpretation, insofar as it omits his this-worldly concerns and focuses on repentance and the heavenly kingdom.

Many in Israel did want Jesus to be a this-worldly messiah, but he firmly rejected that role. Even while showing his concern for the suffering of his fellow Israelites, Jesus aimed at complete salvation through love and presented himself as the eschatological "son of man," concerned only for God's kingdom, not for any political society. Political rereadings of the New Testament do not interpret the texts reasonably, but replace their witness with a fictive history concocted to exploit Christian faith by putting it in the service of liberationist politics.[31]

d) **Yet Jesus' gospel calls for social justice and mercy.** The moral teaching of the Old Testament already clarifies many requirements for just social and economic relationships. Jesus perfects and radicalizes these, by teaching a mercy which goes beyond what is usually regarded as justice. Love of neighbor, and even of enemies, demands in practice that those who accept God's loving kindness extend it to others in concrete ways. Thus, Jesus identified himself with those in need and warned the wealthy and powerful that they were in danger of losing their souls. For this reason, the Church teaches: "The evil inequities and oppression of every kind which afflict millions of men and women today openly contradict Christ's Gospel and cannot leave the conscience of any Christian indifferent."[32]

2. The Church's Mission Concerns Exactly What Jesus' Mission Concerned

As an extension of Jesus' mission, the mission of the Church concerns what his concerned and only that. Vatican II teaches that this mission is one but complex:

---

31. See John Paul II, Address to the Bishops of Latin America, 4–5, *AAS* 71 (1979) 190–92, *OR*, 5 Feb. 1979, 2. Also: Oscar Cullmann, "Did Jesus Have Plans of Political Reform?" *OR*, 23 Feb. 1978, 6–7; 9 Mar. 1978, 6–8; Ernst Bammel and C. F. D. Moule, *Jesus and the Politics of His Day* (Cambridge: Cambridge University Press, 1984). One way of misunderstanding the New Testament is to read into it the Old Testament's theocratic politics; for a powerful theological critique of this mistake, see Hans Urs von Balthasar, "Considérations sur l'histoire du salut," *Nouvelle revue théologique* 99 (1977): 518–31.

32. Congregation for the Doctrine of the Faith, *Instruction on Christian Freedom and Liberation*, 57, *AAS* 79 (1987) 578, *OR*, 14 Apr. 1986, 5. Also, John Paul II, Discourse to the Bishops of India, 3, *Inseg.* 9.1 (1986) 260–61, *OR*, 10 Feb. 1986, 1, teaches: "Over and over again the Church proclaims her conviction that *the core of the Gospel is fraternal love springing from love of God.* The proclamation of the new commandment of love can never be separated from efforts to promote the integral advancement of man in justice and peace."

"For this the Church was founded: that by spreading the kingdom of Christ everywhere in the world for the glory of God the Father, all people might be made participants in saving redemption [note omitted], and through them the whole world might be ordered in reality to Christ" (AA 2).

a) **The Church's mission concerns every true human good.** The religious purpose of Jesus' mission was to reconcile sinful humankind with God and perfect its communion with him. This purpose also dominates the Church's mission. Reconciliation and communion in the body of Christ are the heart of the gospel which the Church preaches and the primary blessing which the Holy Spirit confers through her sacraments. Still, just as Jesus built up a network of disciples, cured the sick, and fed the hungry, the Church always has worked to build up her human communion and has shown her concern for education, caring for the sick, helping the poor, and promoting peace, justice, and other human goods.[33]

b) **Other human goods are not mere means to the religious end.** Someone might object that insofar as these goods are distinct from holiness and grace, they are mere signs or instruments of the Church's true concern, and so valueless except as means, to be used or set aside in the interests of her purely religious purpose. As a matter of fact, the Church's concern for goods other than religion does help fulfill her religious purpose. By putting love into action, this concern bears witness to the gospel's truth.

However, nothing belonging to the kingdom is a mere means. For the kingdom gathers in all good things and unites them to God in the fullness of Jesus: "For all things are yours . . . all belong to you, and you belong to Christ, and Christ belongs to God" (1 Cor 3.21–23; cf. Eph 1.10, Col 1.20). Thus, the Church always has taught that the kingdom includes not only the communion of sinless souls with God but the communion of human persons in immortal bodily life with Jesus and one another. Moreover, Vatican II teaches that the elements of the temporal order "are not only helps to the final end of human beings but have a God-given value of their own" (AA 7). The Council also teaches that the kingdom includes "all the good fruits of our nature and effort" (GS 39). In short, the kingdom is to include all good things, restored to one in Jesus: truly new heavens and a new earth, not merely a spiritual world. Hence, the Church's mission does not reduce all human goods other than religion to the status of mere means to holiness, grace, and the vision of God.[34]

---

33. John XXIII, *Mater et magistra, AAS* 53 (1961) 402, *PE,* 267.4, affirms that the Church's concern is not limited to the sanctification of souls but extends to the needs of daily life, and John justifies this concern by Jesus' example, for although "it was doubtless man's eternal salvation that was uppermost in his mind . . . he showed his concern for the material welfare of his people . . . as when he miraculously multiplied bread to alleviate the hunger of the crowds." Also see Congregation for the Doctrine of the Faith, *Instruction on Christian Freedom and Liberation,* 67, *AAS* 79 (1987) 583, *OR,* 14 Apr. 1986, 6, which argues from Jesus' example that Christians cannot ignore the poor who lack the necessities of life, and concludes: "This poverty is the result and consequence of people's sin and natural frailty, and it is an evil from which human beings must be freed as completely as possible."

34. GS 42 and its n. 11 (Abbott n. 132), which incorporates teaching of Pius XII, says that Jesus assigns the Church a "strictly religious" end. But GS 76, at the end, includes in the Church's mission the uncovering, cherishing, and ennobling of everything true, good, and beautiful in the

c) **The Church's mission is limited to what pertains to the kingdom.** While the Church's mission is not confined to strictly religious matters nor concerned with other human goods only as means to her religious purpose, still, like Jesus himself, the Church serves nothing but God's kingdom. Hope is her only interest; she intends nothing but its object: the kingdom. Thus, she cares for no human good except insofar as it contributes to the building up and coming of the kingdom. This not only is the teaching of the entire Christian tradition but of Vatican II: "While helping the world and receiving many benefits from it, the Church has a single intention: that God's kingdom may come, and that the salvation of the whole human race may come to pass" (GS 45).[35]

But if the Church's mission is limited to what pertains to the kingdom, what does that exclude? Evidently, not only the pursuit of wealth, pleasure, and power for their own sakes, but even the promotion of the most genuine human goods apart from their relevance to the kingdom. However, secularized society as such is concerned precisely with human goods as unrelated to the kingdom, for its interests are this-worldly and temporal, to the exclusion of Christian hope. The limitation on the Church's mission therefore means she should not act according to any secularized understanding of human goods, method of serving them, or plan for humankind's liberation.

d) **Like Jesus, the Church makes a preferential option for the poor.** As Jesus came to save sinners, not the righteous, the Church exists to mediate salvation, not to promote the greater flourishing of those already successful and happy. Vatican II teaches that the Church sees in the poor and suffering the likeness of Jesus and, like him, loves sinners and all who suffer from human weakness and the miseries of the fallen human condition (see LG 8).

Although this love is preferential, in aiming to give priority to more pressing human needs, the Church does not take the side of one class of people *against* others; her preferential love excludes nobody. On behalf of those suffering material poverty due to exploitation and oppression, the Church teaches the wealthy their responsibilities and thus works for social justice. But this work also seeks the true good of those who do injustice, by calling them to repentance and offering them liberation from sin.[36]

---

human community. The apparent contradiction dissolves if one takes into account that God's kingdom and righteousness—the strictly religious object of hope—includes the renewal of the entire fallen world, which embraces not only religion itself but every human good (see *CMP*, 25.B, 34.D–G).

35. For further substantiation of the account provided here of the Council's teaching on the Church's mission: Avery Dulles, S.J., "Vatican II and the Church's Purpose," *Theology Digest* 32 (1985): 341–52.

36. John Paul II, Discourse to the Cardinals (21 Dec. 1984), 9, *AAS* 77 (1985) 510–11, *OR*, 21 Jan. 1985, 7–8, cites LG 8, affirms that the preferential option for the poor always has been the Church's policy, and stresses that it cannot be exclusive since the message of salvation is addressed to every human being. He says that the option must be based on the gospel, not on alien ideologies, and warns that poverty of spiritual goods (under such an ideology) is even worse than material poverty. On the preferential option, also see Synod of Bishops, Second Extraordinary Assembly (1985), *Final "Relatio"*, 2.D.6, *EV* 9 (1983–85) 1778–79, *OR*, 16 Dec. 1985, 9; Congregation for

e) The Church's way of serving temporal goods is realistic. The gospel clarifies the requirements for human liberation. There are great evils in the world, and Christians must struggle against them. Sin is the source of misery and oppression; only love of neighbor rooted in love of God overcomes misery and begets social solidarity. Thus, the redemption of economic institutions and social structures requires conversion. If oppressors cease doing injustice, make restitution, and work for socioeconomic reforms, that is progress.

By contrast, destructive acts, so often claimed to be indispensable for human liberation, are not an effective means, for they do nothing to heal and build society into a communion of justice and love. Grandiose schemes for social change through revolution treat people as mere means to be used on the way to an imagined better future. Thus, the Church unhesitatingly rejects morally unrestrained class struggle as a tragic error which only increases misery.[37]

The gospel, far from being ineffectual, is realistic and effective, for it brings with it the Holy Spirit's power. True, oppressors can reject the grace of conversion and refuse to repent; Christianity offers no panacea. The struggle against sin and its consequences will meet with only limited success; the kingdom is not of this world. Even in the course of history, however, the Church's way of serving temporal goods contributes to human progress and liberation, for it deals with the human situation without illusions.[38]

3. The Church Carries on Jesus' Mission as a Complex, Integral Whole

God's saving work in Jesus bears on the whole of the human world and even on the cosmos, which somehow is implicated in the broken human condition (see Rom 8.18–23; cf. Hos 4.1–3). Thus, the Church's mission likewise extends to everything human and to the cosmos itself. This complex mission nevertheless is integrated into a unity.[39]

---

the Doctrine of the Faith, *Instruction on Christian Freedom and Liberation*, 68, *AAS* 79 (1987) 583–84, *OR*, 14 Apr. 1986, 6.

37. Injustice, however, inevitably leads to social conflicts, and Christians, taking a decisive stand on the side of justice, should cooperate in struggling for it: John Paul II, *Centesimus annus*, 14, *AAS* 83 (1991) 810–11, *OR*, 6 May 1991, 7.

38. Peruvian Episcopal Conference, *Document on the Theology of Liberation*, 52, *OR*, 4 Feb. 1985, 7: "An immanentistic messianism cannot but lead to the bitterest disappointments, but to renounce, from now on, any hope of improving this world means to deny the Lord's salvific power. The struggle against evil in this world is a human responsibility, helped by grace, but the definitive victory over evil and death is a gift from God for which we hope. It is reserved to him to put an end to history, just as it was he who began it." Also see Paul VI, *Evangelii nuntiandi*, 34–39, *AAS* 68 (1976) 28–30, Flannery, 2:725–27; Congregation for the Doctrine of the Faith, *Instruction on Certain Aspects of "Theology of Liberation"*, 11.11, *AAS* 76 (1984) 906, *OR*, 10 Sept. 1984, 4.

39. A useful history and analysis of magisterial teaching from Vatican II through *Evangelii nuntiandi* concerning the relationship between eschatological Christian salvation and human temporal progress: Bonaventure Kloppenburg, O.F.M., *Christian Salvation and Human Temporal Progress*, trans. Paul Burns (Chicago: Franciscan Herald Press, 1979). Also see: "Human Development and Christian Salvation (1976)," in International Theological Commission, *Texts and Documents: 1969–1985*, ed. Michael Sharkey (San Francisco: Ignatius Press, 1989), 145–61.

a) **The Church recognizes her mission's complex unity.** The complexity is recognized, although not explained as clearly as it might be, in recent Church documents. Vatican II teaches: "Christ's redemptive work, while essentially concerned with the salvation of humankind, includes also the renewal of the whole temporal order. Hence the mission of the Church is not only to bring to all people the message and grace of Christ, but also to penetrate and perfect the temporal order with the spirit of the gospel" (AA 5). The Synod of Bishops states: "Action on behalf of justice and participation in the transformation of the world fully appear to us as a constitutive dimension of the preaching of the Gospel, or, in other words, of the Church's mission for the redemption of the human race and its liberation from every oppressive situation."[40] And Paul VI teaches:

> The church proclaims liberation and cooperates with all those who are working and suffering on its behalf. She does not assert that her function is strictly confined to the religious sphere without regard for the temporal problems of men. But she reaffirms the primacy of her spiritual function and refuses to substitute for the preaching of the kingdom of God a proclamation of liberation of the merely human order. She declares that her advocacy of liberation would not be complete or perfect if she failed to preach salvation in Jesus Christ.[41]

b) **The Church's primary concern is each person's salvation.** Jesus' new covenant initiates the heavenly kingdom. It exists in the world and spreads through times and places. The Church is sent to preach the gospel, to manifest its truth in communal life shaped by love, to baptize those who wish to believe, and to teach believers everything Jesus commanded, so that they can live in and celebrate communion with the divine persons and one another. Because saved persons make up God's kingdom, the Church's hope requires that each human person's salvation be her primary concern. Thus, Vatican II teaches that in becoming man, the Son of God in a certain way united himself with every human being (see GS 22). From this teaching, John Paul II draws the conclusion:

> The Church therefore sees its fundamental task in enabling that union to be brought about and renewed continually. The Church wishes to serve this single end: that each person may be able to find Christ, in order that Christ may walk with each person the path of life, with the power of the truth about man and the world that is contained in the mystery of the Incarnation and the Redemption and with the power of the love that is radiated by that truth.[42]

---

40. Synod of Bishops, Second General Assembly (1971), *Justice in the World, EV* 4 (1971–73) 802–3, Flannery, 2:696. A helpful study of the meaning of this statement: Charles M. Murphy, "Action for Justice as Constitutive of the Preaching of the Gospel: What Did the 1971 Synod Mean?" *Theological Studies* 44 (1983): 298–311. Synod of Bishops, Second Extraordinary Assembly (1985), *Final "Relatio"*, 2.D.6, *EV* 9 (1983–85) 1778–79, *OR*, 16 Dec. 1985, 9, states the complexity; sets aside "false and useless oppositions between, for example, the Church's spiritual mission and the 'diaconia' for the world"; and affirms: "The salvific mission of the Church in relation to the world must be understood as an integral whole. Though it is spiritual, the mission of the Church involves human promotion even in its temporal aspects." But the document does not explain how these concerns are united.

41. Paul VI, *Evangelii nuntiandi, 34, AAS* 68 (1976) 28, Flannery, 2:725.

42. John Paul II, *Redemptor hominis, 13, AAS* 71 (1979) 282, *PE,* 278.37.

c) The Church's secondary concern is to make salvation integral. John Paul II teaches: "If the Church makes herself present in the defense of, or in the advancement of, man, she does so in line with her mission, which, although it is religious and not social or political, cannot fail to consider man in the entirety of his being."[43] The last phrase, "in the entirety of his being," shows why the Church's concern is not limited to personal piety, but includes social justice, peace, and the advancement of science and culture: these elements of the temporal order also belong to the fullness of human persons.

True, only individual human persons believe and hope in God, and love him and one another. But human persons complete one another in various forms of society, and are fulfilled by work and culture. Indeed, "man in the entirety of his being" refers even to the surrounding cosmos, for people cannot live without the natural world, in which humankind dwells as in a womb. Thus, everything else in visible creation pertains to human beings, and their salvation would be incomplete were not all things brought back to God in Jesus.

John Paul II's statement also indicates the precise way in which the Church's mission includes all these dimensions of persons. The Church becomes concerned with all the elements of the temporal order, which have their own value as created goods, insofar as they pertain to the fulfillment of human persons, and so are destined for a place in the kingdom, where all goods will be restored to God in Jesus (see GS 39, AA 7).

Question D: How Are Catholics' Apostolic Responsibilities the Same and Diverse?

In carrying out the Church's mission, each Catholic has a role to play: his or her personal vocation. But the diverse apostolates also have some common characteristics. This question treats the common characteristics, while question E will treat personal vocation.

1. Apostolic Responsibility Is Universal and Comprehensive

Vatican II teaches that the Christian vocation essentially is a calling to apostolate. *Apostolate* refers to each and every activity in the Church which is directed toward carrying out her mission (see AA 2). In respect to this calling, no member of the Church is ever off duty.

a) All Catholics, as members of a living body, should be active. Vatican II teaches: "It is incumbent on every disciple of Christ to do his or her share in spreading the faith" (LG 17; cf. AG 36). The Council also explains why everyone should help carry out the Church's mission: "Just as, in the structure of a living body, no part is merely passive, but each part shares in the body's workings as in its life; so, too, in the body of Christ, which is the Church, the whole body, 'each part working properly, promotes the body's growth in building itself up' (Eph 4.16)"

---

43. John Paul II, Address to the Bishops of Latin America, 2, *AAS* 71 (1979) 199, *OR*, 5 Feb. 1979, 4. Cf. John Paul II, *Redemptor hominis*, 15, *AAS* 71 (1979) 289, *PE*, 278.48; Leo XIII, *Rerum novarum, ASS* 23 (1890–91) 654–55, *PE*, 115.28–29.

(AA 2). The Church is Jesus' living body; her vital functions are his own priestly, prophetic, and kingly functions.

Every baptized person is a member of the Church, and every member should be ready to do, in ways appropriate for each, what the Church as a community is called to do: worship God and offer him gifts, receive and hand on his word, and serve and build up his kingdom.[44] Nor should anyone suppose that his or her potential contribution would be too insignificant to matter. Every organ's functioning is important to the whole body; as a natural body's head needs the body's feet, so Jesus needs his members (see 1 Cor 12.21–22, Col 1.24; CMP, 23.E).[45]

b) **One's whole life should be apostolic.** Every part of one's life should help to spread the faith, for one should do everything in Jesus' name (see Col 3.17; AA 4; CMP, 25.F, 27.E). Vatican II criticizes the tendency to divorce the rest of life from faith: "This split between the faith which many profess and their daily lives deserves to be counted among the more serious errors of our age" (GS 43). The Council calls for a vital integration of all activities—domestic, professional, social, and technical—with religious values, which should direct everything to the kingdom (see GS 43).[46]

c) **Apostolic responsibility is no less today than ever.** Since Vatican II, some have argued that it is an imposition on the religious liberty of others to insist on all the truths of faith and the uniquely integral goodness of Christian life. Some also think evangelization is no longer necessary because the Council made it clear that God saves all men and women of good will, whether conscious believers or not (see LG 16).[47]

Paul VI rejects such views as excuses for evading apostolic responsibility. He points out that proposing the gospel and the Christian way of life does not violate freedom of conscience but precisely respects and appeals to people's liberty. He argues that, although God "by extraordinary means" can save those who have not been evangelized, Jesus by his teaching and his life opened up the "ordinary way" of salvation. Moreover, Christians are called to bear fruit, and so their own salvation is imperiled if they fail to do so.[48]

It also is worth considering that apostolic work builds up the human communion of the new covenant, which is destined to last forever, and that people of good will who hear and consciously accept the gospel and Christian way of life enjoy great human fulfillment through their conscious relationship with Jesus and his Church—human fulfillment on which they would miss out if saved in some

---

44. See LG 31; CIC, c. 204, §1.

45. See Pius XII, *Mystici corporis Christi, AAS* 35 (1943) 204–21, *PE*, 225.25–59, at the heart of which (*AAS* 213, *PE*, 44) is the striking affirmation: "Christ has need of his members. . . . This is not because he is indigent and weak, but rather because he has so willed it for the greater glory of his spotless Spouse."

46. An emphatic reassertion of this conciliar teaching: John Paul II, *Christifideles laici, 59, AAS* 81 (1989) 509–10, *OR*, 6 Feb. 1989, 19–20.

47. On the possible salvation of people who have not heard the gospel, see *CMP*, 26.1; on the truth that outside the Church there is no salvation, see *CMP*, 30.2; 1.C.5.i, above.

48. Paul VI, *Evangelii nuntiandi*, 80, *AAS* 68 (1976) 72–75, Flannery, 2:755–57; cf. John Paul II, *Redemptoris missio*, 4–11, *AAS* 83 (1991) 252–60, *OR*, 28 Jan. 1991, 5–6.

other way. Moreover, Vatican II's teaching that God saves all people of good will does not imply that evangelization is unnecessary, since evangelization calls those who lack good will to conversion and provides them with powerful reasons to accept God's grace.

2. Only Truly Christian Action Fulfills Apostolic Responsibility

Although each Christian's whole life should be apostolic, it will be so only if made up of truly Christian actions. All such actions respond to grace and include prayer as their foundation. It is this witness by action flowing from communion with Jesus, not activism detached from him, which fulfills apostolic responsibility.

a) **The essence of all apostolic responsibility is to bear witness.** God's redemptive work is first, last, and always a merciful gift. Jesus' human witness proclaims God's kingdom and cooperates in receiving this gift on humankind's behalf. Questioned by Pilate about his kingship, Jesus says: "For this I was born, and for this I came into the world, to testify to the truth" (Jn 18.37). Those who believe in Jesus not only receive the gift of communion with God, but also become Jesus' allies insofar as he is a man.

As Jesus' mission is to bear witness, every Christian's mission is to cooperate in this witness, responding to God's truth and love by giving thanks to the Father, and sharing God's gift with others. Jesus told the apostles after his resurrection: "You will be my witnesses" (Acts 1.8; cf. Mt 28.18–20). Vatican II teaches that this mandate extends to all lay persons: "Every single lay person should stand before the world as a witness to the resurrection and life of the Lord Jesus and a sign of the living God" (LG 38).[49]

In sum, because apostolic activity shares God's gift with others, its essence is in bearing witness. This must not be confused with applying techniques for attaining certain specific human goals, even religious ones. Not just success but failure, too, affords opportunities to manifest hope, while successful efforts to attain human goals, including specifically religious ones, can be directed to ends other than the kingdom. Bearing Christian witness is thus very different from pragmatic activism.[50]

b) **Apostolic activity presupposes and increases life in the Spirit.** Since all true apostolate carries on Jesus' saving work, and since the most important element of this work is Jesus' prayer and self-offering to the Father, it would be a misunderstanding of the apostolate to try to spread the faith and serve the kingdom in others without nurturing one's own interior life.[51] People who try to give what they

---

49. *CIC,* cc. 209–10, states the obligation of all the Christian faithful without exception to remain in communion with the Church and pursue personal and ecclesial holiness; c. 211, states the fundamental responsibility to contribute to the Church's mission: "All the Christian faithful have the duty and the right to work so that the divine message of salvation may increasingly reach the whole of humankind in every age and in every land."

50. *CIC,* c. 673, illustrates this point with respect to religious life: "The apostolate of all religious consists first in their witness of a consecrated life which they are bound to foster by prayer and penance." Clearly, what is most important is not service of other kinds to one's neighbor, but the service Jesus came to render.

51. John XXIII, *Causa praeclara, AAS* 54 (1962) 568, *Catholic Documents* (London), 4, no. 33 (Jan. 1964), 9, points out that prayer and self-sacrifice are so much the essence of the apostolate

do not really have will neither build up the kingdom nor sanctify themselves. But those who truly live in Jesus not only bear fruit for him by carrying on his mission toward others but increase their life in the Spirit as, more and more, they engage their hearts, minds, souls, and strength in apostolic service.[52] For, although Jesus needs his members, none can contribute humanly to God's saving work without the Holy Spirit's grace. That is why Jesus, in sending the apostles, bestows the Spirit on them (see Jn 20.21–22, Acts 1.8). The Church, too, constantly prays that God will send his Spirit to make her mission fruitful, and one should join personally in this prayer. Life in the Spirit depends on docility to God's word and on prayer, penance, and worthy participation in the Eucharist.

c) **The apostle must be both adaptable and uncompromising.** Truly Christian apostolic activity imitates the Word. He emptied himself, identified himself with fallen men and women, claimed no privilege, used simple language, adopted the way of life of the most humble people, listened to what each person had to say, and conducted himself as a brother to everyone. But in no way did he water down or whittle away the truth, even though he was constantly under fire. Similarly:

> Our dialogue must not weaken our attachment to our faith. Our apostolate must not make vague compromises concerning the principles which regulate and govern the profession of the Christian faith both in theory and in practice.
>
> An immoderate desire to make peace and sink differences at all costs (irenism and syncretism) is ultimately nothing more than skepticism about the power and content of the Word of God which we desire to preach. The effective apostle is the man who is completely faithful to Christ's teaching. He alone can remain unaffected by the errors of the world around him, the man who lives his Christian life to the full.[53]

3. All Catholics Are Responsible for the Church's Entire Mission

It would be an error to suppose that clerics are responsible for what is of primary concern to the Church and lay persons for what is secondary. All Catholics have responsibilities with respect to the Church's entire mission.

a) **Not all are concerned in the same way with its distinct components.** John Paul II teaches:

> The *lay* state of life has its distinctive feature in its secular character. It fulfils an ecclesial service in bearing witness to, and in its own way recalling for priests, women and men religious, the significance of the earthly and temporal realities in the salvific plan of God. In turn, the *ministerial* priesthood represents in different times and places, the permanent guarantee of the sacramental presence of Christ, the Redeemer. The religious state bears witness to the eschatological

---

that one's life cannot be truly apostolic without them, but can be genuinely apostolic without external action.

52. See AA 4, which begins: "Since Christ, sent by the Father, is the wellspring and origin of the Church's whole apostolate, the success of the lay apostolate depends upon the laity's living union with Christ." Although not concerned with the laity, Vatican II's document on priestly life and ministry (see PO 12–14) clarifies the dialectic of interior life and apostolic service to be lived out, with suitable adaptations, in every Christian life.

53. Paul VI, *Ecclesiam Suam, AAS* 56 (1964) 647, *PE, 271.88.

character of the Church, that is, the straining toward the Kingdom of God that is
prefigured and in some way anticipated and experienced even now through the
vows of chastity, poverty and obedience.

All the states of life, whether taken collectively or individually in relation to
the others, are at the service of the Church's growth. While different in expression, they are deeply united in the Church's "mystery of communion" and are
dynamically coordinated in its unique mission.[54]

b) Clerics are ordained for sacred ministry in the Church. Those in holy
orders are ordained primarily for sacred ministry (see LG 31). They act in Jesus'
person when they establish the Church by proclaiming the gospel and when they
build her up by serving as teachers of the faith, as celebrants of the Eucharist and
ministers of the other sacraments, and as pastoral leaders (see LG 20–21, AG 39,
PO 2). Plainly, then, the primary responsibility of clerics bears on the primary
component of the Church's mission.

But they also have a twofold responsibility with respect to the temporal order.
First, they are rightly concerned with those temporal goods which are the means
for carrying out the Church's primary mission, for example, the Church's property.
Second, they have a wider responsibility concerning all temporal goods. This they
fulfill in and through their sacred ministry: by teaching the moral principles to be
followed in temporal affairs and by providing the spiritual aids by which the
temporal order can be restored in Jesus (see AA 7, 24).

c) Lay persons have special responsibility in the temporal sphere. The
laity's primary responsibility is to bear witness by holding fast to the faith, offering
their lives as a spiritual sacrifice, and growing in holiness (see LG 9–12). Lay
persons, "exercising an apostolate of evangelizing and sanctifying" (AA 6), complement those in holy orders in carrying out the Church's primary, saving mission,
which is "achieved by belief in Christ and by his grace" (AA 6). But besides their
role in bringing the gospel and holiness to others, they have a special responsibility
"of permeating and perfecting the temporal order with the spirit of the gospel" (AA
2). "In following out the Church's mission, the laity, therefore, exercise their
apostolate both in the Church and in the world, in both the spiritual and the temporal
orders" (AA 5). The temporal order includes everything of human value other than
the religious: the goods of life and family, work and business, culture, the arts and
professions, political institutions, international affairs, and so on (see AA 7). Thus,
lay people are properly and directly concerned with secular affairs. They are called
to "seek the kingdom of God by engaging in temporal affairs and by ordering them
according to the plan of God" (LG 31).[55]

---

54. John Paul II, *Christifideles laici*, 55, *AAS* 81 (1989) 503, *OR*, 6 Feb. 1989, 18. For the
legal distinction between clergy and laity, and between those in the religious state of life and others,
see *CIC*, c. 207.

55. See John Paul II, *Christifideles laici*, 14–15, *AAS* 81 (1989) 409–16, *OR*, 5 Feb. 1989,
4–5. *CIC*, c. 225, §1, states the general right and duty common to all Catholics to work "so that
the divine message of salvation becomes known and accepted by all persons throughout the world,"
and adds that the obligation on lay persons is more exigent if "people can hear the gospel and
know Christ only through lay persons." Idem, §2, states the special responsibility of lay persons:
"Each lay person in accord with his or her condition is bound by a special duty to imbue and perfect

d) Activity in the temporal sphere must be authentic apostolate. Christians must know and respect the proper principles of realities of the temporal order, because these principles direct action to the specific goods and human benefits of that order (see LG 36; GS 36, 43; AA 7). Christians also must know and respect the traditions of their own society, and live their faith within the framework of their own culture (see AG 21). How, then, will their activity in the temporal order differ from the outwardly similar activity of others, and so be authentic apostolate?

First, by conforming to Christian conscience, and thus insofar as possible healing and restoring the realities of the temporal order in the light of the gospel (see LG 36; AA 2, 7). Second, by ordering activities in the temporal order according to the demands of Christian love of neighbor, and so preparing material for the heavenly kingdom (see LG 34, 36; GS 38–39; AA 7). Third, by matching their apostolic deeds with apostolic words, using every opportunity to "announce Christ by words addressed either to nonbelievers with a view to leading them to faith, or to believers with a view to instructing, strengthening, and encouraging them toward a more fervent life" (AA 6; cf. LG 35). By differing from others' activities in these three ways, what Christians do bears witness to God's truth and love, and thus arouses hope, which draws people to the kingdom (see GS 93).

Therefore, even when lay people do their best, as they should, to protect or realize goods in the temporal sphere, they have a greater responsibility to bear witness to God's mercy and faithfulness in regard to humankind's integral liberation than to achieve that portion of it which can be realized within the fallen world's history. For the good fruits of human nature and effort, mutilated as they are by human sin, will be perfected only by God's re-creative act (see *CMP*, 34.E–G).

e) Religious meet their apostolic responsibility in a distinctive way. The religious state of life is not something "in between" the clerical and lay states.[56] Each religious is either a cleric or a lay person who adopts a distinctive style of Christian life, shaped by the evangelical counsels of poverty, chastity, and obedience (see LG 43). Thus, religious who are clerics are concerned with the two components of the Church's mission in the same ways other clerics are. Religious who are lay persons have diverse apostolic responsibilities proper to the diverse

---

the order of temporal affairs with the spirit of the gospel; they thus give witness to Christ in a special way in carrying out those affairs and in exercising secular duties." The development in Vatican II and since of the Church's teaching regarding the apostolate of the laity was prepared by various theological studies, among which one was most significant: Yves M. J. Congar, O.P., *Lay People in the Church: A Study for a Theology of Laity*, trans. Donald Attwater (London: Geoffrey Chapman, 1957).

56. *Religious state of life* is used here in the broad sense which includes not only the life of members of religious communities strictly so called but of the whole spectrum of those who commit themselves to live according to the counsels of poverty, chastity, and obedience in a way approved by the Church. Some suggest using *consecrated life* instead of *religious state of life* to make it clear that members of secular institutes and societies of apostolic life, as well as individuals consecrated as virgins, hermits, widows, and so on are included. However, although the life of a person committed to live according to the counsels is consecrated in a special way, every baptized person's life is consecrated (see PC 5). Hence, the substitution of *consecrated life* for *religious state of life* would lead to its own confusions.

forms of religious life. Some devote themselves almost entirely to prayer or various ecclesial ministries, while others share fully in the characteristic lay involvement in secular affairs, for example, teaching and health care.[57]

But all religious who faithfully fulfill their commitment to live according to the counsels have this in common: their lives manifest in an especially clear way the hope which should shape every Christian's life. For life according to the counsels closely imitates Jesus' life and makes it clear that the kingdom and its claims transcend all worldly values (see LG 44). The witness of poverty, chastity, and obedience is especially needed and powerful in secularized societies where many people, living without hope, care only for possessions, pleasure, and freedom to do as they please.

4. The Diverse Apostolates Have Certain Common Characteristics

Since the many members of Jesus' body enjoy diverse gifts and have different roles in building up the whole, the apostolate of each will be different from that of any other—a unique complex of good works to which God calls each one personally (see Rom 12.4–6; LG 12, AA 2–3). Therefore, the basic commitments of one's life, which organize the rest, help constitute one's personal vocation (see LG 11, 46; PO 6; GS 31, 43, 75). Question E will treat personal vocation. However, all apostolates have some common characteristics, and here these are considered insofar as all personal vocations share them.

a) **Putting faith into practice is the basic form of witness.** Jesus calls for the witness of a Christian life: "Let your light shine before others, so that they may see your good works and give glory to your Father in heaven" (Mt 5.16). John XXIII approvingly quotes St. John Chrysostom, who makes his point by overstating it: "There would be no need for sermons, if our lives were shining; there would be no need for words, if we bore witness with our deeds. There would be no more pagans, if we were true Christians."[58] Vatican II teaches: "Lay people fulfill the mission of the Church in the world mainly by that consistency of life with faith which makes them the light of the world" (AA 13; cf. AG 36). Plainly, this is true not just for the laity but for all Christians.[59]

b) **Apostolate of the word should complement the witness of life.** While emphasizing witness of life, Paul VI also forcefully teaches: "The meaning of a

---

57. Such involvement in the world is compatible with the renunciation of the world essential to the religious state of life, since life according to the vows excludes attachment to the world insofar as that attachment is sinful or an obstacle to growth in holiness, but does not exclude the concern for the world proper to the lay apostolate, which treats the world as potential material for the kingdom.

58. John XXIII, *Princeps pastorum, AAS* 51 (1959) 851–52, *PE*, 266.34; quoting St. John Chrysostom, *PG*, 62:551.

59. Paul VI, *Evangelii nuntiandi*, 21, *AAS* 68 (1976) 19, Flannery, 2:719–20, sketches a picture of Christians "radiating simply and spontaneously their faith in values which transcend common values and their hope in things which are not seen and of which even the boldest mind cannot form an image. By bearing such silent witness these Christians will inevitably arouse a spirit of enquiry in those who see their way of life. Why are they like this? Why do they live in this way?"

person's witness will be clarified by preaching, clearly and unambiguously, the Lord Jesus. The good news proclaimed by witness of life sooner or later has to be proclaimed by the word of life."[60] That is so because, while actions speak louder than words alone by verifying them, words communicate more than actions alone by clarifying them (see DV 2).

Everyone always should witness by good example, but the apostolate of the word should be exercised only as occasion permits. Then, however, there should be no hesitating. Plainly, this witness must be given when silence would amount to denial of the faith; but Vatican II goes further. Pointing out that lay apostolate is more than witness of life, the Council remarks that St. Paul's exclamation, "Woe to me if I do not proclaim the gospel!" (1 Cor 9.16), ought to echo in every Christian's heart (see AA 6). Every Catholic should speak to nonbelievers in order to lead them to faith, and to fellow believers in order to strengthen their faith.

For lay persons, the apostolate of the word is an especially pressing responsibility toward those "who can hear the gospel and recognize Christ only through the laity who live near them" (AA 13). Moreover, if bishops and priests call on lay people to help carry out the Church's official ministry of the word—evangelization and catechesis—they should serve to the best of their ability.[61]

c) **One should defend the faith when it is under attack.** Leo XIII exhorts Catholics to defend their faith amidst the pluralism of conflicting modern opinions. Citing the teaching of St. Thomas that all believers should defend the faith when it is endangered (*S.t.,* 2–2, q. 3, a. 2, ad 2), Leo adds:

> To recoil before an enemy, or to keep silence when from all sides such clamors are raised against truth, is the part of a man either devoid of character or who entertains doubt as to the truth of what he professes to believe. In both cases such mode of behaving is base and is insulting to God, and both are incompatible with the salvation of mankind.[62]

Arguing against softening the gospel to make it acceptable, Pius X points out that this strategy ignores the experience of the apostolic Church:

> If ever there was a time in which human prudence seemed to offer the only expedient for obtaining something in a world altogether unprepared to receive doctrines so new, so repugnant to human passions, so opposed to the civilisation, then at its most flourishing period, of the Greeks and the Romans, that time was certainly the epoch of the preaching of the faith. But the Apostles disdained such

---

60. Paul VI, *Evangelii nuntiandi,* 22, *AAS* 68 (1976) 20, Flannery, 2:720. Likewise, while Vatican II strongly commends witness "of the whole of a lay person's life flowing from faith, hope, and charity" (AA 16), the Council adds: "Then by the apostolate of the word, which is utterly necessary under certain circumstances, lay people announce Christ, explain and spread his teaching according to each one's situation and skill, and faithfully profess it" (AA 16).

61. See LG 33. *CIC,* c. 759, makes it clear that the laity always share in the responsibility of spreading the gospel by virtue of their Christian initiation and sometimes share in the clergy's apostolic responsibility because they are called on to do so: "In virtue of their baptism and confirmation lay members of the Christian faithful are witnesses to the gospel message by word and by example of a Christian life; they can also be called upon to cooperate with the bishop and presbyters in the exercise of the ministry of the word."

62. Leo XIII, *Sapientiae Christianae, ASS* 22 (1889–90) 390, *PE,* 111.14.

prudence, because they understood well the precept of God: "It pleased God by the foolishness of our preaching to save them that believe" (1 Cor 1.21).[63]

d) One always should be prepared to suffer martyrdom. While only those who actually lose their lives are counted as martyrs, their merit is not in their dying but in laying down their lives (see *S.t.,* 2–2, q. 124, a. 4, ad 4). Often those who die for Jesus suffer much else before that happens, and all who must suffer to profess and live Christian faith can and should commit themselves to persevere through everything, even until death. Vatican II therefore teaches that willingness to be a martyr is required of every Christian: "Though few are given this opportunity, still all must be ready for it: to confess Christ before others, and, amidst the persecutions from which the Church is never free, to follow him on the way of the cross." (LG 42; cf. *S.t.,* 2–2, q. 124, a. 1, ad 3).

Inevitably drawing attention from people of both good and ill will, a truly Christian life will provoke challenges. Christians must be prepared to explain the hope that is in them, accepting, as Jesus did, whatever suffering this entails (see 1 Pt 3.15–18). Moreover, readiness to lay down one's life as a martyr for one's fellow Christians a fortiori is readiness to part with one's wealth when they need help (see 1 Jn 3.16–18).

e) Heroism can be and often is a strict Christian duty. While many Christians have died for Jesus as a result of making a profession of faith or doing good works which they could have omitted without sin, there also are cases in which martyrdom cannot be avoided without grave sin; then one has a strict duty to be heroic by human standards.

This principle applies as well to readiness for martyrdom and every sort of suffering for Jesus' sake. For, "There is no act of perfection subject to counsel which does not come under precept in some circumstances as necessary for salvation; for example, as Augustine states, a man is bound by the necessity of preserving continence because his wife is absent or ill" (*S.t.,* 2–2, q. 124, a. 3, ad 1). Those who must make hard choices—for example, between wrongly cooperating in grave injustices and losing their possessions or their jobs, or between living in unchaste relationships and practicing lifelong continence—are called to heroism and are strictly obliged to respond to that call, thus bringing into play their readiness to accept martyrdom.

Denied release by a quick death from their slow martyrdom, they may have greater merit than those who actually give their lives. Yet the residual sinfulness and personality defects of such slow martyrs are likely to render their witness ambiguous, so that the nobility of their lives is less obvious than the nobility of the deaths of those who shed their blood.

f) Genuine and effective apostolate requires humility and love. Since the basic form of apostolate is the witness of life, all who share Jesus' mission must

---

63. Pius X, *Iucunda sane, ASS* 36 (1903–4) 524, *PE,* 166.26. Paul VI, General Audience (28 June 1967), *Inseg.* 5 (1967) 813, *The Pope Speaks* 13 (1968–69): 163, concerned about the impact of public opinion, warns against conformism: "In social conversation we are easily satisfied with accepting public opinion, or else we find it convenient to agree with the strongest, even if he isn't the most reasonable. We readily become conformists and part of the herd."

imitate all his virtues. But two, humility and love, are required for additional, special reasons.

Humility is necessary to receive, live by, and hand on a gospel which is not one's own but God's: his word, which one may not amend to please oneself or others, but must either serve faithfully or else betray.

Love is necessary to communicate the gospel's truth, as something one truly cherishes, to persons one truly loves, for their great benefit; to respect fully the human dignity and freedom of all, and so make available to them without pressure or manipulation Jesus' truth, which alone can vindicate their dignity and fulfill their freedom; to persevere in bringing God's truth to those who seem to reject it and even persecute anyone who tries to help them to know it; and to restore, maintain, and increase ecclesial unity, without which the gospel's credibility is diminished in many people's eyes.[64]

Question E: What Are One's Responsibilities in Regard to Personal Vocation?

Christians should put hope into practice by living for the kingdom. They do that by finding, accepting, and faithfully fulfilling their personal vocations, which are their particular shares in the apostolate. As a principle of Christian life, personal vocation is treated in volume one (especially *CMP*, 23.E, 27.B, 28.E, and 31.C). The present treatment will not repeat what is explained there, but will focus instead on one's specific responsibilities in this important matter.[65] Personal vocation should embrace every part of one's life, and care should be taken to discover and commit oneself to all its elements. Having done so, one should faithfully carry out one's vocational commitments.

1. One Should Live One's Life in Response to God's Vocation

Vocation means calling. God calls everyone to faith and holiness; he calls some in particular to priesthood or religious life. These, however, are not the only sorts of vocation, for there are genuine callings to states of life other than priesthood and religious life. But, more than that, God calls everyone (including those called to the priesthood and religious life) with his or her own personal vocation: a unique share in the Church's mission, a personal way of following Jesus.

a) **Jesus calls each of his disciples by name for a unique task.** Jesus himself had a personal vocation: the unique mission he received from his heavenly Father and carried out in the totality of his life, from childhood, through his baptism in the Jordan, and ending with his death on the cross (see *CMP*, 22.C).[66] Mary also had

64. See Pius X, *E supremi*, ASS 36 (1903–4) 137, *PE*, 164.13; Paul VI, *Evangelii nuntiandi*, 76–80, *AAS* 68 (1976) 67–75, Flannery, 2:751–57; John Paul II, Homily at Mass at College of St. Peter the Apostle (Rome), *Inseg.* 5.3 (1982) 842–46, *OR*, 27 Dec. 1982, 15.

65. What is said about personal vocation in volume one is confirmed by many recent documents of John Paul II. Besides those cited below, see: Meeting with the Youth of Madagascar, 5; *L'Osservatore Romano*, It. ed., 1 May 1989, 7 and A.iv (Fr. text); *OR*, 8 May 1989, 4.

66. See John Paul II, Homily in Miraflores Park (Cuenca, Ecuador), 7, *Inseg.* 8.1 (1985) 309, *OR*, 11 Mar. 1985, 5.

her own personal vocation: announced to her by Gabriel's message, accepted by her "Let it be done to me," and carried out through all the rest of her life.[67] Similarly, each and every Christian is hand picked, assigned a specific task in life, and personally called by Jesus to follow him in a unique way (see *CMP,* 23.E).

All Christians are called to holiness and to one and the same heavenly hope, but each also is called to a personal share in the Church's mission and given the special grace needed for that particular apostolic life, so that by living a life of witness, a prophetic life, he or she can cooperate with the Spirit in building up Jesus' body.[68] What God said to Jeremiah he says to each of Jesus' disciples: "Before I formed you in the womb I knew you, and before you were born I consecrated you; I appointed you a prophet to the nations" (Jer 1.5).

b) As they mature, persons normally develop a plan for their lives. Growing up, young people normally look to the future, anticipating fulfillment. They usually expect to marry, to work at some sort of gainful employment, to participate in civic affairs, to follow out various cultural and recreational interests, and so on. Needing to coordinate these diverse expectations, they rightly develop a plan for life.

In affluent societies, however, such a plan is all too likely to be self-centered, amounting to a set of egoistic goals—things to be owned, satisfactions to be enjoyed, positions and power to be obtained—together with a strategy for achieving them (see *CMP,* 28.D). Instead of shaping their lives in response to values and persons beyond themselves, many people merely aim at satisfying their desires, at trying to get what they want out of life.[69]

c) One's plan of life should be rooted in a sense of vocation. Idealistic young people see the matter differently. They are less concerned about what they will have, enjoy, and control than about what they will be (see GS 35). They too seek self-fulfillment, but they expect to attain it by self-giving, by sharing in the realization of genuine human goods in loving fellowship with others. They hope to contribute to others' well-being and to leave the world a better place than they found it. They want their relationships to be based on the mutuality of fairness and love. While, like their egoistic peers, they freely shape their own lives, their plan has the character of vocation, since they take into account and respond to the claims others make on them and to the appeal of objective values.[70] Such a life plan is not

---

67. John Paul II, Homily at Mass for Students of the Pontifical Minor Roman Seminary, 2, *Inseg.* 4.2 (1981) 1171, *OR,* 25 Jan. 1982, 5, teaches: "That was the moment of Mary's vocation. And the very possibility of Christmas depended on that moment. Without Mary's 'Yes', Jesus would not have been born." Also see Germain Grisez, "Mary and Christian Moral Principles," *Marian Studies* 36 (1985): 40-59; Benedict M. Ashley, O.P., "Moral Theology and Mariology," *Anthropotes* 7 (1991): 137–53.

68. See John Paul II, Homily at Mass at Bellahouston Park (Glasgow), 6, *Inseg.* 5.2 (1982) 2066–67, *OR,* 7 June 1982, 16, who uses Eph 4.7, 11–12 to illustrate this point; *Christifideles laici,* 58, *AAS* 81 (1989) 507–9, *OR,* 6 Feb. 1989, 19; cf. 1 Cor 12.7–11, Rom 12.3–8; LG 12, UR 2.

69. On plan of life and self-fulfillment, see John Paul II, *Apostolic Letter on the Occasion of the International Youth Year,* 3, *AAS* 77 (1985) 582–85, *OR,* 1 Apr. 1985, 2.

70. On plan of life as vocation, see John Paul II, *Apostolic Letter on the Occasion of the International Youth Year,* 9, *AAS* 77 (1985) 600–601, *OR,* 1 Apr. 1985, 4; Karol Wojtyla, *Love and Responsibility,* trans. H. T. Willetts (New York: Farrar, Straus, Giroux, 1981), 255–58.

so much a set of goals to be achieved as a set of commitments to be made (see *CMP*, 9.E and 23.E). It integrates various roles of service—in the family, at work, in the civic community, and so on—so that all the responsibilities a person assumes will be met.

d) **One discerns God's call in one's actual circumstances.** Some people imagine that many elements of life fall outside the area encompassed by God's call, as if they had nothing to do with his salvific plan. The supposition, in other words, is that God calls people to ways of life and service unrelated to their gifts, opportunities, and true personal fulfillment. If that were so, someone's real needs, well-integrated feelings, and decent aspirations could be more or less at odds with his or her vocation, and God's call could be an arbitrary demand to sacrifice true self-fulfillment.

This way of conceiving vocation is mistaken. It overlooks the fact that divine providence is all inclusive. God's salvific plan and will concern every aspect of each person's being and situation. One's gifts and opportunities are no accident: God provided them in view of his plan's goal, the kingdom, which includes each person's own true fulfillment and in no way conflicts with it. Since God's providential plan of creation and redemption includes everything about one and one's whole world, his call will in no way be at odds with one's gifts and circumstances, nor even with one's needs and feelings, except insofar as these are defective and need reformation for one's own good.

Therefore, John Paul II explains, what God calls one to can be discerned precisely in the facts of one's life and situation. " 'What is my vocation' means 'in what direction should my personality develop, considering what I have in me, what I have to offer, and what others—other people and God—expect of me?' "[71] When Christian young people in friendship with God pray, " 'What must I do?', what is your plan for my life? Your creative, fatherly plan? *What is your will?* I wish to do it,"[72] they will find the elements of God's reply in the appeal of values, the needs of others, and the gifts and talents they discover in themselves. Hence: "Examining these circumstances, the young person, boy or girl, constructs his or her plan of life and at the same time *recognizes* this plan *as the vocation to which God is calling him or her.*"[73]

2. One's Personal Vocation Should Embrace Every Part of One's Life

Although many Catholics today realize that it is a mistake to limit personal vocation to the calling some receive to the priesthood or religious life, not all appreciate the comprehensiveness of God's plan with respect to their lives. Inasmuch as the whole of life should be shaped by faith and hope, however, no part of it should remain outside one's vocational life plan.

71. Wojtyla, *Love and Responsibility,* 257.

72. John Paul II, *Apostolic Letter on the Occasion of the International Youth Year,* 9, *AAS* 77 (1985) 601, *OR,* 1 Apr. 1985, 4.

73. John Paul II, *Apostolic Letter on the Occasion of the International Youth Year,* 9, *AAS* 77 (1985) 602, *OR,* 1 Apr. 1985, 5.

a) **Personal vocation includes every sphere of activity.** Certainly, the great commitments which settle one's state in life—as cleric, religious, or married or single lay person—are important elements of personal vocation. But one's work—whether it be in homemaking, day labor, farm, factory, office, trade, profession, government, education, or whatever—also is a large part of life and offers its own opportunities for giving Christian witness, serving one's neighbor, and recapturing some part of the fallen world for Jesus' kingdom. Hence, although choice of work and commitment to an employer and a group of fellow workers are not so permanent and unconditional as to constitute a state of life, they are an important component of one's vocation.[74]

Similarly, in choosing where to live, a person undertakes the responsibilities of a citizen in that neighborhood, local community, and nation, and these civic duties must be fulfilled in a way which contributes to one's Christian apostolate. Even hobbies, forms of recreation, ways of vacationing, and so forth should be viewed as elements of vocation and carried on in accord with relevant norms.[75]

b) **Personal vocation includes every stage of one's life.** Personal vocation includes more than the life plan which a young person forms.[76] The small child who decides to obey parents and teachers in order to be more like the obedient Jesus makes a basic commitment of personal vocation. Though this commitment will develop and be further specified, it need not be replaced. Widows and widowers must ask anew what God's will for them is. Similarly, people who retire from their jobs have new opportunities for witness and service; they should continue to fulfill themselves and serve others by putting their gifts and resources to use, not simply filling their days with pastimes.

Thus, from childhood until death, an individual should listen for God's personal call, shaping and reshaping his or her life according to faith and hope, and living each day of it with love. In this way, one lives according to God's plan even when the immediate result seems to show that one had mistaken one's vocation. For instance, some are called to prepare for the priesthood, but not to be priests; to be

74. See John Paul II, Homily at Mass at St. Joseph Cafasso Parish, 4, *Inseg.* 4.1 (1981) 215–16, *OR,* 16 Feb. 1981, 6. Pius XI, *Quadragesimo anno, AAS* 23 (1931) 226, *PE,* 209.141, already pointed out: "The first and immediate apostles to the workers ought to be workers; the apostles to those who follow industry and trade ought to be from among them themselves." Although slightly marred by anti-Catholic polemic, the Protestant tradition offers a rich theology of work as an element of Christian vocation; see Lee Hardy, *The Fabric of This World: Inquiries into Calling, Career Choice, and the Design of Human Work* (Grand Rapids, Mich.: William B. Eerdmans, 1990), who points out (68–76) the convergence between that tradition and modern Catholic social teaching.

75. For example, John Paul II, Address at the World Organization of Tourism (Madrid), *Inseg.* 5.3 (1982) 1061–63, *OR,* 20 Dec. 1982, 5, 12, points out that vacation travel should be neither "a banal fact of consumerism" nor "a modern form of alienation, a waste of time and money"; it should be "more than a simple rest or kind of escape": "a pause to restore the psychophysical energies consumed in working," "a restorative activity, which should help [a man] to 're-create' himself through new experiences derived from upright and free choices," "a capacity for self-education and of culture," and "a privileged instrument for reinforcing and multiplying the mutual relations which enrich the human community" and "help to establish those ties of solidarity of which the present world, disturbed by wars, has such a great need."

76. See John Paul II, *Christifideles laici,* 45–48, *AAS* 81 (1989) 481–86, *OR,* 6 Feb. 1989, 15–16.

novices, but not religious; to be engaged, but not married. Often such experiences have an unforeseeable significance which only much later becomes clear. Discovering the limits of one's calling at a particular stage, one should thank God for the opportunity it has afforded to give witness and to serve, while at once trying to discover the next phase of his plan for one's life.

c) **Personal vocation includes education and preparation.** Human beings naturally desire to develop their capacities, to set goals and succeed in reaching them, to fulfill themselves and win others' respect. This natural desire motivates every serious effort to study, learn, and practice skills. While the pursuit of self-fulfillment can be selfish, it need not be. Paul VI explains:

> In God's plan, every man is born to seek self-fulfillment, for every human life is called to some task by God. At birth a human being possesses certain aptitudes and abilities in germinal form, and these qualities are to be cultivated so that they may bear fruit. By developing these traits through formal education of personal effort, the individual works his way toward the goal set for him by the Creator. . . .
>
> Self-development, however, is not left up to man's option. Just as the whole of creation is ordered toward its Creator, so too the rational creature should of his own accord direct his life to God, the first truth and the highest good. Thus human self-fulfillment may be said to sum up our obligations.[77]

Thus, every effort at self-development through education should be undertaken and carried out as part of one's vocation. Aptitudes and abilities should be appreciated as God's gifts, and their cultivation should be regarded as a responsibility to him.

This way of considering education has important consequences. Rather than doing their school work merely to avoid punishment or reach some extrinsic goal in the future, Christian children and young people should commit themselves to their studies insofar as these are an important part of the life to which God calls them now and a preparation for the service to which he will call them in due time. To the extent the educational system allows choices among programs and courses of study, students should select the options which will more fully develop their gifts and prepare them for greater service rather than those which seem easier or offer greater material rewards. Young people who have the opportunity for higher education should make the most of it for authentic self-development, not waste it in self-indulgence or regard it as a deferment of adult responsibilities.

d) **Repentant sinners always have a complete personal vocation.** While Christians who choose to live in mortal sin more or less completely reject God's call, others, perhaps partly due to poor catechesis, simply ignore their faith and hope in making plans which organize large parts of their lives. Their planning, directed to getting what they want without regard to what God wants, is at least venially sinful. But what becomes of the vocations of those who through sin make binding commitments they should not make or fail in ways that cannot be remedied to make commitments that should have been made? Suppose a young girl, careless

---

77. Paul VI, *Populorum progressio,* 15–16, AAS 59 (1967) 265, *PE,* 275.15–16.

about God's plan for her life, ignores her vocation to the religious life, marries, has children, and only then becomes devout. Has she missed her vocation, once for all? The answer is: No. God remains forever faithful; his gifts and calling are irrevocable (see Rom 11.29). But what God calls one to varies according to the particular circumstances of one's life. Having become a wife and mother, this woman is not free to abandon her responsibilities. She should recognize her marriage and parenthood as important parts of her vocation and commit herself to fulfilling them. As God calls those who have defrauded others to restitution, so he calls sinners who missed what would have been their vocation to that life of witness and service—that share in the Church's mission—available to them now, even at the eleventh hour. Hence, although a sinner may miss his or her vocation, a repentant sinner once more has a complete personal vocation.

This is not to say repentant sinners always are more blessed than if they had never sinned. Because of God's generous mercy, that sometimes might be the case; but it also may be that those who sin and repent, while blessed with many gifts, would have enjoyed far greater gifts had they never sinned.

e) **Conditions beyond one's control can pertain to one's vocation.** After speaking of the more obvious elements of vocation, such as work and state of life, John Paul II adds: "And I am thinking also of other situations: for example, of the husband who is left a widower, of the spouse who is abandoned, of the orphan. I am thinking of the condition of the sick; the old, infirm and lonely; and of the poor."[78] While many elements of one's vocation are undertaken by free choices, conditions of life beyond one's control can be elements of it insofar as they provide special opportunities to live according to faith.

Thus, although children have no choice about going to school, they can, as explained above, see their school work as an important part of their vocation, and can commit themselves to doing it for that reason. People who think they are called to marriage but do not find a suitable partner can and should consider their single state part of their vocation for as long as it lasts, even for the whole of their lives, and should make the most of it for witness and service.[79] The aging, as they lose their autonomy and become increasingly dependent on others, should neither exhaust themselves in a pointless struggle to retain what they must give up nor passively resign themselves to an empty existence. Instead, they should regard their situation as an opportunity to befriend those who care for them, to grow in meekness, to deepen the contemplative dimension of their lives, and to help others both by their prayers and by the witness of joyful hope.[80] Similarly, the vocation of someone injured in an automobile accident, permanently paralyzed from the neck down, and constrained to spend the rest of his or her life in bed would be the life of prayer and witness still possible even in that situation.

---

78. John Paul II, Homily at Mass at St. Joseph Cafasso Parish, 4, *Inseg.* 4.1 (1981) 215–16, *OR,* 16 Feb. 1981, 6.

79. See Pius XII, Address to Italian Women (21 Oct. 1945), *AAS* 37 (1945) 287, *Catholic Mind* 43 (1945): 708.

80. See Lucien Richard, "Toward a Theology of Aging," *Science et esprit* 34 (1982): 269–87.

3. One Should Take Care to Discover the Elements of One's Vocation

Since vocation is God's calling, its source is God's providential plan. Thus, one may not decide arbitrarily about any element of one's vocation. Rather, as John Paul II teaches: "Man must discover it—and discover it exactly."[81] He summarizes the process:

> To be able to discover the actual will of the Lord in our lives always involves the following: a receptive listening to the Word of God and the Church; fervent and constant prayer; recourse to a wise and loving spiritual guide; and a faithful discernment of the gifts and talents given by God, as well as of the diverse social and historic situations in which we live.[82]

One must not expect to hear God calling in some extraordinary manner; with the light of faith, personal vocation can be discovered in the sufficient signs by which God ordinarily makes his will known (see PO 11).

a) **The chief elements of one's calling are to particular roles of service.** Discovering a vocation is very different from merely knowing what one wants in life. People can know what they want and set out to achieve it without considering others or while viewing others' needs and interests as secondary, as mere helps or hindrances to self-fulfillment. In discovering the chief elements of his or her vocation, however, a person must consider others and accept the fact that an indispensable sign of being called to anything is a favorable response from the other or others who must decide whether to accept the offer. This is so because each and every Christian's vocation mainly is to use his or her gifts to serve others and build up the communion of faith, Jesus' body.[83]

Thus, God's plan for one's life is part of his larger plan for the life of the Church as a whole, and so one sometimes learns the limits of one's vocation by finding no response to one's readiness to make a commitment or even that a commitment already made cannot be fulfilled. For example, a man who thinks he may be called to the priesthood must try to find where he is needed. Only the particular needs of some concrete community will offer him a role of service; he has no vocation to the priesthood unless some bishop or religious superior accepts him as a candidate for ordination. Similarly, while those considering marriage may have good reasons for thinking that is God's will for them, they cannot be certain until they find someone with whom marriage is mutually agreeable. In general, proposals by members of the Church to use their charisms in particular ways are subject to the judgments of the Church's pastoral leaders.[84]

---

81. John Paul II, Homily in Miraflores Park (Cuenca, Ecuador) 9, *Inseg.* 8.1 (1985) 311, *OR,* 11 Mar. 1985, 6.

82. John Paul II, *Christifideles laici,* 58, *AAS* 81 (1989) 508, *OR,* 6 Feb. 1989, 19.

83. Whether they are exceptional and great or simple and ordinary, one's gifts are charisms, graces which the Holy Spirit provides for building up the Church; they always are to be exercised for service, subject to ecclesiastical authority. See LG 12; John Paul II, *Christifideles laici,* 24, *AAS* 81 (1989) 433–35, *OR,* 6 Feb. 1989, 8.

84. Paul VI, Address to the Rota, *AAS* 63 (1971) 139, *OR,* 11 Feb. 1971, 7, teaches: "Hence it is necessary to judge and differentiate between charisms in order to check their authenticity and correlate them with criteria derived from the teaching of Christ, and in accordance with the order which should be observed in the ecclesial community. Such an office pertains to the sacred

When the unwillingness of others to cooperate prevents Christians from committing themselves to something to which they thought they were called, they should accept that outcome as an inarguable sign of God's will. God calls no one to do what is impossible, and so in such a case it makes no difference to one's vocation whether the other acted rightly or wrongly. Even a wrong response, having been permitted by God, does not fall outside his plan; the insuperable obstacle of another's no makes it clear that God is calling one to something else. It is an error, then, for a man to be sure he has a vocation to marriage despite the fact that no woman will marry him and, even if proponents of women's ordination were correct in thinking it possible, it would be a mistake for a woman to think she clearly discerns a vocation to the priesthood so long as the Church does not accept women as candidates for ordination.

   b) **One should seek to serve those whose needs are great.** Since a personal vocation is a share in the Church's mission, and the Church has a preferential love for the poor, one should look for opportunities to serve those whose needs are unlikely to be met by others. The worst forms of poverty are spiritual: sin, ignorance of the gospel, lack of the sacraments, and so on.[85] Those who can should therefore consider serving in the ordained priesthood, the religious life, the foreign missions, religious education, and so on. Moreover, they should consider offering themselves where the need is great, rather than remaining in familiar, comfortable surroundings.

   The millions who are materially poor and oppressed also appeal to the Church's preferential love, and those who can do so should consider devoting at least part of their lives to helping them. Action to overcome structural injustices by morally acceptable means surely deserves special consideration, because of its potential for widespread benefits. Efforts to help individuals or small groups better their condition also are worthwhile. The benefits to persons are real and immediate, and the witness value of such service is clear.[86] Also, certain fields of activity deserve special consideration because they offer challenging opportunities for Christian witness: education, the media of communication, public affairs, and so forth.

   c) **Relevant facts about oneself and one's situation are signs.** Vocational and job counselors try to help young people learn about existing and likely future opportunities, their own abilities, and their not fully conscious interests and feelings. The goal is to help each client find a suitable place in the economy, a role the client can fulfill, and in this way also find personal fulfillment.

   Such data also are relevant to the effort to discover some element of one's Christian vocation, but they should be considered differently. Knowing by faith

---

hierarchy, which is itself established by a singular charism. So true is this, indeed, that St. Paul does not recognize as valid any charism that is not subject to his apostolic office (cf. 1 Cor 4.21, 12.4–5; Gal 1.8; Col 2.1–23)."

   85. See John Paul II, Homily at Mass in Calcutta, 7, *Inseg.* 9.1 (1986) 317, *OR,* 10 Feb. 1986, 13.

   86. Thus, an apostolate like that of Mother Teresa's congregation always will have great value. See AG 12, GS 88; Paul VI, *Populorum progressio,* 47 and 74, *AAS* 59 (1967) 280–81 and 293, *PE,* 275.47 and 74; Congregation for the Doctrine of the Faith, *Instruction on Certain Aspects of the "Theology of Liberation",* 11.2–3, *AAS* 76 (1984) 903, *OR,* 10 Sept. 1984, 4.

that nothing happens except by God's will or, at least, his permission, one will see the facts one faces as signs of his plan and will, to be interpreted in the light of faith (see 1.J.3). This means regarding one's gifts as talents by which God invites one to undertake a particular service, while limitations and defects (except insofar as they are handicaps to be overcome or sins to be repented) are recognized as indications that God is not calling one to certain forms of service. One also will be attracted by those possibilities which offer greater opportunity for witness and service to neighbors.

While hoping for self-fulfillment in serving God and neighbor, one will expect that reward to be complete only in the heavenly kingdom. This life offers only limited self-fulfillment, together with the suffering Jesus promised to all who follow him (see *CMP*, 26.K, 31.D).

d) **One should consider difficulties and obstacles only secondarily.** A vocation is the contribution one is called to make to the Church's mission: the building up of Jesus' kingdom. Those who keep this in mind in trying to discover the central elements of their vocations will be concerned primarily with the work to be done and only secondarily with the difficulties and obstacles, such as their deficiencies, the lack of necessary means, and the effort required.

Someone for whom these negative factors assume primary importance has forgotten that it is possible to draw on the Holy Spirit's resources by prayer. Counting on God and discovering some great service one might render, one will look for and usually will find ways of overcoming deficiencies and obtaining means. And one will be encouraged to accept the challenges of hard work and possible failure, confident that commitment and effort will not be fruitless for those who sincerely try to discover and do God's will. Even if one fails in this life, the attempt will bear witness to the kingdom and provide it with material which will be found purified and perfected in heaven (see GS 38–39).[87]

e) **A process of discernment is needed to discover one's vocation.** While God sometimes uses extraordinary means—an angelic visitation, a mysterious voice—to make his plan and will known to an individual, most people can discover their vocations by a process of discernment.[88] Vocational discernment means carefully gathering the relevant facts and then bringing to bear on them all the resources of faith, Christian morality, and Church order. One should take into account Jesus' advice—for instance, the counsels of poverty, chastity, and obedience—and seek the advice of trusted persons, such as parents, confessors, and devout friends. But nobody can discover someone else's vocation.[89] Even when all this has been done,

87. As St. Thomas points out (see *S.t.*, 2–2, q. 133, a. 1, ad 3), pusillanimity can originate from pride. Those who think they must accomplish everything by themselves underestimate what they really could do—with help. Conversely, Christians who abound in humility and hope seem reckless at times in their ambitious apostolic undertakings.

88. What follows regarding discernment uses but also modifies the classic treatment of St. Ignatius Loyola, *Spiritual Exercises*, 169–89, trans. Lewis Delmage, S.J. (New York: Joseph F. Wagner, 1968), 87–95.

89. Sometimes parents or others are confident that they know for certain what someone's vocation is. Unless they have received a private revelation, however, they have no way of discerning anyone else's vocation, because discernment presupposes awareness of one's own

therefore, an individual still must judge what he or she should do, sometimes determining between or among alternative possibilities, and always between accepting and not accepting something as an element of vocation.

One should pray for the Holy Spirit's guidance and sincerely try to prepare to receive and follow it. When this has been done, feelings play their proper part. All options but one eventually become less appealing, while that one seems definitely right. A sense of light, joy, and peace is experienced in recognizing God's will. (The discernment of vocation is treated more fully in *CMP*, 31.E; and below, 5.J.)

f) **Certain commitments should not be made without certitude.** To marry, to accept ordination to the priesthood, and to make final religious vows are commitments of a special kind. Not only is the matter very important for one's Christian life but the commitment is highly structured: one assumes a set of definite obligations to definite people over an indefinite future. The choice to be made definitively excludes its alternative. That choice, without further specification by additional choices, settles an important aspect of one's total vocation.

Once a commitment is made in these cases, one cannot significantly adapt the vocation to one's capacities, but must adapt oneself in every way possible to the vocational commitment. If therefore at the point of making such a commitment one is not confident it should be made, one should not make it. The process of discernment needs to be continued until every alternative to making the commitment—ordination, final vows, marriage to this person—loses its appeal and making it appears clearly to be God's call, recognized as such with a sense of light, joy, and peace.

Someone might say: If only one attractive option remains, there is no choice to make, and so, paradoxically, these most important commitments are made without any free choice. But that is not so. While someone who reaches the moment of making a major vocational commitment with the appropriate confidence no longer has any rational basis for not making it, nor even any feeling of attraction toward an alternative, such a person nevertheless knows that until the commitment is made, it can be declined; just as he or she also knows that, once the commitment has been made, other options will be foreclosed for the future, even if he or she then regrets making the commitment. This awareness of the unknown future naturally arouses some feelings of anxiety and reluctance, which the will must overcome to make the commitment. Thus, with respect to major vocational commitments, the confidence one should have and real freedom of choice are compatible. Consequently, while a commitment to a state of life should not be made so long as any doubt remains, it is a mistake to demand too much. A person who enjoys the necessary confidence that a commitment is God's will still experiences the general anxiety about the unknown future and the general reluctance about taking on a lifelong obligation which are felt by every thinking and responsible person.

feelings. Thus, such people's confidence in their judgment is an illusion, very likely rooted in their own subconscious feelings and wishes. Hence, when one is attempting to discern one's vocation, one should consider suspect the advice of those who think they know for certain that one should or should not make a certain commitment.

g) Other commitments may be made with less assurance. In the case of other important commitments, although an initial failure to discern should not lead to treating them as a toss up, a less definitive outcome can be accepted as a sufficient indication. Thus, the choice of a certain line of work should be an important vocational commitment; unlike choosing particular projects to carry out a professional commitment, that commitment itself is to the good or goods which the line of work serves, and to the persons who can be served in respect to the relevant good or goods. Yet no single choice fully specifies such a commitment, which must instead be developed through a series of choices.

A choice, for example, to go to graduate school (which is somewhat like a choice to enter a seminary or begin courtship with a particular person), ordinarily is not followed by a definitive commitment to a certain community for the remainder of one's professional life. Rather, the commitment is to a career, which requires one specification after another. In making these further specifications, the career can be adapted repeatedly to one's gradually emerging better self. And as one continues to discern and accept the career, one sometimes rightly returns to alternatives earlier rejected, and, seeing them now as appropriate parts of one's vocation, accepts them and commits oneself to them.

Hence, although commitments such as those to a certain profession are important in Christian life, less confidence is needed to make them responsibly. When a clear indication of which option better pleases one's better, Christian self emerges, this is sufficient. It is not necessary to continue until other possibilities lose their appeal and the one to be chosen emerges as uniquely appropriate, although that sometimes happens.

h) One should not try to discern too soon. People sometimes make the mistake of trying to discern too soon. For example, a woman who is a postulant in a religious order may or may not have a vocation to give her life in that community, but the commitment cannot be made until the time comes to make her vows. Yet she tries to discern now whether she is called to that vocation. Her effort is likely to fail, and if it seems to succeed may well lead to a false judgment, since she has not yet received the formation she will need before making the commitment.

Whether the postulant feels almost sure that she has a vocation or only thinks she might have one, her attitude should be: "I wish only to do God's will, and he seems to be (or might be) calling me to this form of religious life; so, I will follow his lead and prepare to commit myself to this." She ought to be confident that when the time comes the Spirit will give her the light she needs. Before then, she should be content to know only what she needs to know to live her life faithfully from day to day. Her current calling is to be a postulant and she should make the most of it. First-year seminarians who agonize over whether they should be priests make the same mistake; the time for that discernment is when they approach ordination to the diaconate.

Someone may object: But a final decision cannot be delayed that long. Far in advance, family and friends will be looking forward to the happy day. A certain momentum builds up, and, in practice, that will take the place of the necessary discernment. The answer is: To prevent that from happening, it is essential to make it clear to family and friends that no firm decision will be made until very shortly before the time comes to act on it.

i) One should recognize and accept one's present vocation. A related mistake is made by those who, aware that the time for discernment with respect to a major commitment has not yet arrived, assume that meanwhile they have no vocation. For example, a young man who thinks he is called to marriage and family life but has not yet found the right woman may fail to recognize his present responsibilities: to prepare himself to be a good husband and father, to save for a house, and so forth. At the same time, he should recognize that his present single state, which may continue until he dies, is part of God's plan for his life. He should accept and live it as an element of his personal vocation, making full use of the opportunities it offers for service and apostolate.

j) One should consider one's priorities critically. The less binding elements of one's vocation should be subordinated to others which are more important. Certain elements, such as a commitment to priesthood, religious life, or marriage, involve very important duties. Other important elements of vocation, such as those concerned with work, must be harmonized with such commitments. Hobbies, forms of recreation, and ways of vacationing should be selected and modified, without disregarding the genuine values involved, so as to harmonize with the central commitments and roles of service.

In discovering one's vocation, no already-existing duty may be ignored. For instance, a young man whose aged parents need his help and care may not ignore his responsibilities toward them when considering whether to get married. Still, duties should not be confused with attachments. While most people are attached to their family and home community, many have no duty to remain there. By mistaking such attachments for duties, people limit their availability and easily ignore important elements of their vocation.

4. One Should Accept Every Element of One's Personal Vocation

People have the right and duty to determine their own state of life and line of work, to decide where they will live, and to make many other large choices which will shape their lives.[90] As these and other elements of vocation are discovered, one should accept what one finds oneself called to and, having accepted it, should faithfully carry it out, as John Paul II teaches:

> It is precisely the principle of the "kingly service" that imposes on each one of us, in imitation of Christ's example, the duty to demand of himself exactly what we have been called to, what we have personally obliged ourselves to by God's grace, in order to respond to our vocation.[91]

90. See John XXIII, *Pacem in terris, AAS* 55 (1963) 261 and 263, *PE,* 270.15–16 and 25, for state of life and dwelling place, including migration. The Church's social teaching concerning work generally talks about people already engaged in a particular line of work, and so seldom treats this element of vocation as an area in which there are important options. However, although the right to choose one's line of work clearly is not absolute but conditioned in various respects, this element of personal vocation ordinarily is subject to the individual's responsible choice— obviously more so in advanced industrial economies than in less complex economies.

91. John Paul II, *Redemptor hominis,* 21, *AAS* 71 (1979) 318, *PE,* 278.87.

a) **Some elements of one's vocation need no commitment.** Besides his or her overarching commitments, a Christian should consider every lasting interest and ongoing activity in terms of vocation. Some of the less central lasting interests, such as hobbies, often develop unreflectively, perhaps beginning in childhood. Having come to see them as possible elements of vocation, one need only make sure that anything done in respect to them will contribute to one's Christian life and the harmonious fulfillment of one's total vocation.

Very often, people must accept rather than choose ongoing activities which make up an important part of their lives. Most children have little choice about whether to go to school; some people have no practical options about where to live; and some have no choice about what kind of work they will do. Even so, Christians can meekly accept these as elements of vocation which they simply cannot change, and can make the commitment to fulfill their unchosen responsibilities as part of what God calls them to. In this way they will fulfill their vocation in these respects, with the intention of bearing witness to Jesus and serving the needs of others.

b) **Failure to accept some element of one's vocation is a sin.** Since each person's vocation is to play his or her unique part in God's plan, failure to accept any element of one's vocation both impedes true self-fulfillment and evidences a defect in the meekness appropriate to those living in covenantal friendship with God. Moreover, since hope should shape one's life into apostolic service to the kingdom, and since personal vocation is one's unique share in the apostolate, failure to accept some element of a personal vocation betrays a defect in hope. How serious is such a sin? Its radical character suggests that it is grave, but the fact that the Church has not clearly warned against such sins suggests that any sin of this sort which is likely to be committed is only venial.

Perhaps the solution is that the responsibility to discover and accept one's personal vocation is a specifically Christian one, and a person becomes aware of such responsibilities less through applying general norms than through the dynamics of the Holy Spirit's law of love as it shapes his or her life (see *CMP,* 28.F). If so, those who gravely fail to seek and accept their personal vocations sin through lack of sufficient reflection, and so not mortally; while those who clearly discern God's call to do something are predisposed to respond as they should.

5. One Should Faithfully Fulfill All that Pertains to One's Vocation

Each element of one's vocation defines a set of responsibilities for witness and service which by definition should be fulfilled. Leaving aside the endless task of enumerating those responsibilities, what follows is intended to clear up a few confusions about what faithful fulfillment of vocational responsibilities means.

a) **Faithfulness means using everything one has to carry out one's vocation.** Since a Christian life properly organized by the principle of personal vocation includes every sphere of activity (see 2.a, above), it has a place not only for work and prayer, attending to the necessities of life, and sleeping, but for hobbies and recreation, celebrations, visits with friends, and so on. Because everything one has is a divine gift, to be used as God intends, all of it should be put to use, as efficiently and fully as possible, in carrying out one's vocational plan. Of course, if some activity fits in nowhere but seems genuinely worth doing, reflection and discernment can lead to the judgment that one's existing plan of life should be amended. What faithfulness excludes is holding anything in reserve for the use of an uncommitted part of the self, or thoughtlessly wasting material resources, energy, or time.

Many people, for example, waste much of their time and energy in pastimes which, while perhaps sinless in themselves, bear no real fruit either for themselves or others: daydreaming, useless worrying, idle chatter, and passive entertainment. Even fairly well-organized people often fail to make good use of the time and energy still available while they engage in some necessary activity, for example, by allowing their minds to wander as they shower and dress or by using a radio for passive entertainment as they commute. Committed Christians should discipline themselves to replace useless activities with others which not only promise real benefit but further one or another element of their vocation, and, whenever possible, should do two or more such things at once. For example, while occupied with necessary activities which leave the mind free, a person can make plans, think through a problem, or pray; while commuting, someone might listen to worthwhile tape recordings. The ideal of faithfulness is set by the exhortation: "Whatever you do, in word or deed, do everything in the name of the Lord Jesus, giving thanks to God the Father through him" (Col 3.17; see *CMP,* 27.E).

b) Faithfulness does not preclude change and creativity. Some elements of one's personal vocation involve morally binding promises or even unbreakable commitments. Moreover, faithfulness generally requires doing one's own duty rather than taking on responsibilities pertaining to others' vocations, for, as John Paul II teaches, "Confusion of charisms impoverishes the Church; it does not enrich it in any way."[92] Still, not all elements of one's vocation are unalterable, and faithfulness requires fulfilling one's vocation as it now is, not as it once may have been.

Again, while faithfulness means carrying out the responsibilities one has assumed, there may be various ways of doing that. Wishing to give better service, the faithful person does not always follow standard practices, but innovates, while respecting the requirements of morality and just law, as did the saints who founded new religious institutes to satisfy unmet needs.

Then too, in carrying out responsibilities, it often is necessary to undertake projects directed toward certain definite goals; but because projects are only means to the goods to be served, they often can be modified or abandoned without unfaithfulness, if they fail to serve the purposes they were meant to serve or if the purposes can be better served in other ways.

c) Faithfulness means reaffirming one's commitments against temptations. When a commitment is made, other possibilities are foreclosed. Encountering difficulties later or growing bored, one is likely to recall what was given up and imagine what might have been. The temptation arises to entertain the thought: I

---

92. John Paul II, Address to Ecclesiastical Assistants of International Catholic Associations, 4, *Inseg.* 2.2 (1979) 1391, *OR,* 7 Jan. 1980, 11.

wish I were not married (or married to my spouse); I wish I were not a priest; I wish I had not made these vows . . ..[93] Entertaining such thoughts is not a light matter but a grave violation of vocational commitment: "No one who puts a hand to the plow and looks back is fit for the kingdom of God" (Lk 9.62).

Although this sin's guilt no doubt is often mitigated by lack of sufficient reflection or full consent, the sin, if not repented, nevertheless generates inertia and sadness, and leads to a dispirited and plodding minimalism in doing one's duties. Since this state of soul is easily mistaken for depression or fatigue due to overwork, people often try to deal with it by seeking rest and distractions. Far from helping, such tactics only further weaken the commitment and make matters worse. The proper response is to recognize the seriousness of the sin, repent it, and reaffirm the commitment.

In doing so, one acts against one's feelings, and these should not be repressed; rather, discrepancies between feelings and commitments ought to be recognized as helpful clues to ways of thinking and acting which call for modification. Necessary changes should be made not only to fulfill vocational responsibilities more perfectly, but to make doing so more satisfying. For example, in order to better integrate feelings with a commitment, it sometimes helps to reorganize the activities which fulfill responsibilities, alternating sedentary work with physical exertion and solitary work with cooperative efforts.[94]

d) Faithfulness means not giving in to discouragement. The optimism inherent in contemporary secular humanist ideologies is both deceptive and contagious. It is deceptive because the fallen world cannot be perfected in the course of history. Of course, humankind can and should struggle against evil of every kind; this can achieve much good. Medicine, for example, can heal some illnesses and prolong life. Nevertheless, everyone will die, and only Jesus gives the medicine which cures death. The same urgency and the same poor prospects in the struggle against evil hold in every area of human endeavor, not least in politics. Yet Christians, infected with secular humanist optimism, often entertain false expectations concerning prospects for freedom, national and international economic justice, world peace, and so on.

When false expectations eventually encounter hard realities, optimism gives way to pessimism and cynicism. Then, rather than faithfully doing the good which is possible, even Christians often give in to discouragement and abandon their vocational commitments. To forestall this, they should live, not by optimism, which lacks realism about evil, but by hope, which counts on God to overcome it. While hope motivates efforts to overcome every evil and do every good possible in this world, it anticipates limited success and much frustration; but, counting on God for

---

93. The temptation also can arise in regard to professional and other work commitments, but these in the nature of the case are open to development and legitimate change, so that in regard to them one must distinguish between temptations to infidelity and thoughts about possibly appropriate modification.

94. See Kenneth C. Russell, "Acedia: The Dark Side of Commitment," *Review for Religious* 47 (1988): 730–37.

the ultimate overcoming of evil and the perfection of creation, hope never gives in to discouragement.

e) **Faithfulness means making the best of bad situations.** Often one can and should try to change a bad situation, but sometimes there either is no means or none whose use would be morally acceptable. Then a faithful person makes the best of the situation. There is an alternative: wasting time and energy analyzing the situation, even though one plainly cannot or should not try to change it; considering how the situation could be changed for the better by others who will not; complaining and wishing things were different; and omitting to do the good which is possible on the ground that it is so much less than what could be done *if only things were different.*

Especially tempted to fall into this sort of unfaithfulness are idealistic people with unselfish commitments: priests or religious whose dioceses or communities are in disarray, loving spouses whose partners are selfish, hard workers whose employers are poor managers, good students whose school is second rate, and so on. No situation in this fallen world is perfect, and there are constant temptations to indulge in an idealism which weakens faithfulness. The remedy is to remember that God calls one to do only what one can, by oneself and in cooperation with others. He does not expect one to accomplish what would be accomplished in a world not fallen; he alone can complete redemption by re-creation.

f) **Faithfulness means dynamic submission to God's plan and will.** Having suffered setbacks, even disastrous failures, those who try to fulfill the responsibilities of their personal vocations are likely to be told: "Practice resignation!" The advice is sound insofar as *resignation* means Christian meekness, which excludes rebelliousness against God. One must follow Jesus, who encountered much frustration in his earthly mission, but "learned obedience through what he suffered" (Heb 5.8; cf. Phil 2.6–8), and so fulfilled his mission and won glory. However, *resignation* also connotes passivity and despair, while faithfulness calls for a dynamic and hopeful attitude.

One's limitations, defects, setbacks, and failures should be interpreted as signs of something more important than the frustration of one's own desires: God's mysterious way of redeeming the fallen world. It is essential to bear in mind that faithfulness is more important than success, since whatever fragile and mutilated goods are achieved by faithfully fulfilling one's responsibilities are material for the heavenly kingdom. Hoping, one should actively bring one's own plans into harmony with what one learns is God's rather different plan, counting on him to purify and complete the fragments of good which one succeeds in realizing in this world (see GS 39).

g) **Faithfulness means abstaining from the use of morally bad means.** Even conscientious people may be tempted to violate moral norms when there is no other way of preventing some evil or achieving some good for their community (Church, country, company, school, family, and so on) or the people for whom they are responsible. For instance, some otherwise honest people regularly lie in the line of duty. Moreover, proportionalism rationalizes doing evil to attain good or prevent some "greater" evil. But the proportions of good and bad in options available for free choice never can be known, and so proportionalist judgments lack an objective basis (see *CMP*, 6.H.4–6).

Faithfulness never requires wrongdoing. To suppose it does impugns God's providence. A faithful person is not responsible for finding a solution to every problem, but only for doing what can rightly be done and hoping for the best. Witness and service are within one's power, but success in realizing good and preventing evil is not, since it depends on other factors, including the cooperation of other people. Moreover, God's redemptive plan, clearly revealed in Jesus' death and resurrection, does not ensure that all will go well in this world, but only that faithfulness will bear fruit by God's almighty mercy. Finally, then, only someone who hopes will act responsibly in the face of all setbacks and disappointments; for such a person counts on God to make his or her efforts fruitful, now or not now, as the case may be, but certainly in eternity.

h) Faithfulness means not counting the costs of doing one's duty. In evaluating projects, which are means to the goods one should serve, a person must count costs. Moreover, if it would be wrong to accept certain side effects of an act which otherwise would be required to fulfill a responsibility, the responsibility must be left unfulfilled. Often, however, it appears likely that fulfilling a responsibility will have side effects one finds repugnant but can rightly accept. The temptation then is to set aside the responsibility, on the excuse that the bad consequences of fulfilling it would be worse than the evil of not fulfilling it. But the two evils are compared not rationally but emotionally; here proportionalism rationalizes evasion of responsibility.

On this basis, pastors are tempted to be silent about truths which are out of season, parents to omit disciplining rebellious adolescent children, political leaders to tolerate the injustices of the powerful, and so on. Those who are unfaithful in this way often call such behavior "prudence," especially when they act on the basis of calculations about the harm to the institutions they serve rather than to themselves. This false prudence manifests weakness of hope. True prudence would determine how best to fulfill responsibilities while minimizing the bad side effects.

CHAPTER THREE

CHARITY, THE EUCHARIST, AND CHURCH MEMBERSHIP

Summary

To be in friendship with God it is not enough to be loved by him; one also must love him in return. This means striving to abide in and deepen communion with God, a responsibility fulfilled especially by worthy participation in the Eucharist, but also by all one's good acts, not least religious ones, including those pertaining to one's personal spirituality and one's duties as a Church member. Although hatred of God is possible, and is the worst sin, love of God does not require always having warm feelings toward him.

The principal act of Catholic worship is the Mass. One should participate devoutly in the Eucharist, while avoiding abuses such as the sacrilegious reception of Holy Communion. Sundays and holy days of obligation should be observed by participation in the Eucharist and other appropriate behavior and attitudes. However, eucharistic worship should not be limited to these days; on the contrary, in various ways the Eucharist should be extended throughout daily life.

The liturgy's other elements also are necessary or at least very worthwhile. Moreover, each individual should develop his or her personal devotional style, incorporating into it elements recommended by the Church.

In many cases one may pray in common with others who are not Catholics. But sharing in worship at odds with faith is wrong. Merely being present at others' worship, however, is not sharing in it.

Catholics should seek to build up the Church's unity, peace, and vitality. Dissent and pluralism about essentials are incompatible with the Church's well-being. Catholics should obey the pastoral leaders of the Church. Their authority extends to inner acts, but it is not totalitarian, and it does have limits. Schism is disobedience in its most extreme and radical form.

Catholics should support the Church and her life in many ways: prayer, mutual assistance, contributing services, helping to meet material needs, fostering vocations to the priesthood and religious life, contributing to missionary work, and revealing impediments to sacred commitments like holy orders and matrimony.

Catholics also should help to promote unity among Christians. This is not done by inviting non-Catholics to receive Holy Communion. Rather, the appropriate and efficacious means include prayer, one's own personal conversion and faithfulness, friendliness toward all Christians, and collaboration with them whenever possible.

Question A: How Can One Fulfill One's Responsibility to Love God?

God loves people unconditionally. Like the prodigal's father, the heavenly Father loves people even when they sin. Indeed, God loves the damned; they would cease to exist if he did not love them:

> You are merciful to all, for you can do all things,
> and you overlook people's sins, so that they may repent.
> For you love all things that exist
> and detest none of the things that you have made,
> for you would not have made anything if you had hated it.
> How would anything have endured if you had not willed it?
> Or how would anything not called forth by you have been preserved?
> You spare all things, for they are yours,
>   O Lord, you who love the living. (Wis 11.23–26)

But being loved by God is not enough to be in friendship with him, because friendship is mutual love. Consequently, one's first and greatest responsibility is to love God.

No single thing a person can do fulfills this responsibility. Still, worthy participation in the Eucharist is essential, since the Eucharist is related in a special way to charity.[1] Moreover, one not only shows love for God but safeguards it and grows in it by keeping his commandments. The present question deals with these matters in a general way, while the remaining questions of this chapter treat specific responsibilities with respect to the Eucharist, other acts of worship, and membership in the Church—the latter because the Church is the eucharistic community.

1. One Should Strive to Abide in and Deepen Communion with God

God's love is a gift which makes its recipients his intimate friends. One's proper responsibility with respect to charity is to strive to deepen this unique friendship

---

1. Someone might object: If worthy participation is essential, then people of good will who do not participate in the Eucharist without fault of their own are excluded from divine friendship. The answer: By their good will (which itself is a fruit of the Holy Spirit at work in their hearts) they intend to live in accord with the truth, and so at least implicitly wish and desire to do everything that God wills, which in reality includes their participation in the Eucharist. Hence, by their good will they do somehow participate in the Eucharist, are united by it with Jesus, and through him with the Father in the Holy Spirit, so that they do live in God's love. Although concerned with a different question, *Catechismus ex decreto Ss. Concilii Tridentini ad parochos (The Catechism by Decree of the Holy Council of Trent)*, Latin text with trans. by J. Donovan, 2 vols. (Rome: 1839), 2.4.50 (1:463, 465), explains how the Eucharist can be the source of every grace: "But we say that this Sacrament imparts grace, because even the *first* grace, which all should have before they [dare to receive] the holy Eucharist, lest they eat and drink judgment to themselves (1 Cor 11.29), is given to none, unless they receive in wish and desire this very Sacrament, for the Eucharist is the end of all the Sacraments, the symbol of ecclesiastical unity and brotherhood; and outside the Church grace is unattainable."

and to abide in the communion of love. The act by which this most especially is done is the sacrifice of the Eucharist, which normally should include devout reception of Holy Communion.[2]

a) **Charity is one's share in the life and love of the Holy Trinity.** God is a communion of three persons, perfectly one and perfectly distinct from one another, whose communion is divine love. Out of pure generosity, God creates human beings and offers them a share in his life. Through the Incarnation of the Word and Jesus' perfect sacrifice, "God's love has been poured into our hearts through the Holy Spirit that has been given to us" (Rom 5.5). What the Holy Spirit primarily gives those who accept God's love is the status of God's adopted children (see Jn 1.12, Rom 8.14–17). This status is a share in the divine nature (see 2 Pt 1.4); and, although at present Christians are only God's little children, divine love disposes them to the fullness of divine life (see 1 Jn 3.1–2). Thus, charity is not itself a human act, although it is related to human acts.[3] But this raises the question: Since people are responsible only for what they can do, if charity is not a human act, how can people have a responsibility to love God?

b) **One can and should grow in charity and abide in it.** In receiving God's commandments, the Israelites were exhorted to be faithful to the Lord: "Hear, O Israel: The Lord is our God, the Lord alone. You shall love the Lord your God with all your heart, and with all your soul, and with all your might" (Dt 6.4–5). Jesus endorses this commandment's primacy (see Mt 22.36–38, Mk 12.28–30, Lk 10.25–28) and further specifies the love for whose perfection it calls: Christians are to *abide in* the divine love with which God loves Jesus: "As the Father has loved me, so I have loved you; abide in my love" (Jn 15.9). With the grace of the Holy Spirit, a person can do something toward fulfilling these commands. Thus, one begins to fulfill the command to love God with one's whole heart, mind, soul, and strength by doing out of charity those human acts—first of all, the act of faith— which integrate one's entire self and all one's interpersonal relationships with the love of God in one's heart (see 1 Jn 2.3–6).[4] And one abides in the love with which the Father, Son, and Spirit love one another by remaining in Jesus' body, the Church, as a living member. For the Church is the community of the new covenant, in which divine-human communion is realized even now, although it will be perfected in heaven (see LG 7–9; *CMP*, 34.E).

---

2. A sound and very helpful treatment of the Eucharist, including history of the dogma and bibliography: James T. O'Connor, *The Hidden Manna: A Theology of the Eucharist* (San Francisco: Ignatius Press, 1988).

3. See *CMP*, 25.A; cf. *CMP*, 24.2, where charity is identified with sanctifying grace and the theory is proposed that it is an uncreated participation in the divine nature. Significantly, even St. Thomas, who holds that charity is a created disposition in the will, denies that it is in the will considered as a power of free choice, since choice as such is concerned with means: *S.t.*, 2–2, q. 24, a. 1, ad 3; cf. *New Catholic Encyclopedia*, s.v. "charity."

4. St. Thomas, *De perfectione vitae spiritualis*, 5, explains that to love God with one's whole heart is to order one's whole life to the service of God (in the language of 2.E, to organize it completely as vocation), with one's whole mind is to subject one's intellect entirely to faith in divine revelation, with one's whole soul is to relate all one's affection to God and love everything else in him, and with one's whole strength is to perform all outward words and deeds out of love.

c) **One does this in a special way by sharing in the Eucharist.** Vatican II explains the working of the Eucharist: "The renewal in the Eucharist of the covenant between the Lord and human beings draws the faithful into the compelling love of Christ and enkindles them" (SC 10). And John Paul II teaches: "Thanks to the Eucharist, the love that springs up within us from the Eucharist develops in us, becomes deeper and grows stronger."[5] These teachings can be explained along the following lines.

The new covenant primarily consists in the adoption or rebirth of human persons as members of God's family, and this is accomplished by the Holy Spirit's infusion of divine love into human hearts (see Jn 1.12 with 3.5; Rom 5.5 with 8.9–17; 1 Jn 3.1 with 4.12–16). Jesus is the mediator of this covenant; as the Word of God Incarnate he makes God present and accessible to humankind, and as man he leads his brothers and sisters into covenantal friendship with God by offering himself in a perfect and unending sacrifice (see Heb 9.15, 23–26; 10.11–22). When he offered this sacrifice to the Father at the Last Supper, Jesus made it clear that in sharing the bread and cup with his followers he shared his very body and blood with them, uniting them in human communion with himself and thereby in communion with God. Moreover, he commanded that his eucharistic words and deeds be repeated in his memory, so that he and his perfect sacrifice would be available to maintain and nurture the new covenant's divine-human communion. The faithful do this when they gather together as a church, presided over by the priest who acts in Jesus' person, and celebrate the sacrifice of the Mass. Therefore, by sharing in the Eucharist, one actualizes one's communion of love with the divine persons and experiences that communion, which is a foretaste of heavenly communion.

An analogy helps clarify this effect of the Eucharist: As the bond of marriage is realized and experienced in marital intercourse, so covenantal communion with God is realized and experienced in the Eucharist. In this sacrament, Christians are fully formed into Jesus' one ecclesial body and fully united with him. Since he is not only a man but the divine Word, Christians are thus intimately joined with the Father and the Spirit. In the Eucharist one is able to thank God, responding with, through, and in Jesus to the Father's love. Thanking God, one loves him the more, and so, in a virtuous circle of love, grows in charity, which is the communion for which Jesus prayed (see Jn 17.21–22; *CMP,* 33.D).

Hence, the Eucharist is the font of charity: it not only signifies the communion of divine and human persons, but realizes, nourishes, and allows people in a certain way to experience and rejoice in that communion.[6]

d) **To participate in the Eucharist is to engage in an act of worship.** In the Eucharist, Jesus makes his covenant-forming act present and enables those who participate to share in offering his sacrifice and themselves with it.[7] In doing this

5. John Paul II, *Dominicae cenae,* 5, *AAS* 72 (1980) 122, *OR,* 24 Mar. 1980, 6.

6. Because human friends are imperfect, human love primarily leads to desire for fulfillment. Because God is perfect in himself and his blessings are largely realized in Jesus, charity primarily leads to joy: see Paul VI, *Gaudete in Domino,* 7, *AAS* 67 (1975) 319–21, *OR,* 29 May 1975, 7.

7. "Taking part in the eucharistic sacrifice, which is the source and summit of the whole Christian life, they offer the divine victim to God, and, with that victim, themselves" (LG 11; cf. PO 2).

devoutly and worthily, as it should be done, a person offers the Father acceptable worship. And, as has just been explained, the Eucharist in a very special way makes one abide in God's love and deepens it. But the Eucharist has these effects, not only because it is the act of the worshipping community, but because this worship is a way of cooperating with God.

The participants' act unites them with Jesus' human act of self-sacrifice, to which God responds with his grace, forming and nurturing covenantal communion. Thus, the Eucharist is a source of charity because the Holy Spirit acts in it, as the epiclesis after the consecration in the third eucharistic prayer makes clear: "Grant that we, who are nourished by his [Jesus'] body and blood, may be filled with his Holy Spirit, and become one body, one spirit in Christ."

e) One's whole life should complete one's offering of the Eucharist. Jesus teaches: "If you love me, you will keep my commandments" (Jn 14.15) and "If you keep my commandments, you will abide in my love, just as I have kept my Father's commandments and abide in his love" (Jn 15.10; cf. 1 Jn 2.3–6, 3.21–24). This raises a question about the responsibility to love God: What is the relationship between keeping his commandments and the Eucharist? The answer is that both are essential and are parts of one whole.

On the one hand, one of the few new and specific commandments of Jesus is that his followers participate in the Eucharist: "Do this in remembrance of me" (Lk 22.19; cf. Jn 6.52–59, 1 Cor 11.24–25). On the other hand, as has been explained, eucharistic worship is an act of charity in a unique sense: not as a mere human act but in virtue of the Holy Spirit's action in the Eucharist. For those who share in it, participation in the Eucharist is the most central act, but not the only one, which carries out their commitment of faith.

By that commitment, analogous to the promises a man and a woman make when they marry, the baptized accept God's offer of communion in the new covenant. The Eucharist consummates the covenant as marital intercourse consummates marriage. However, as one cannot ignore what one's beloved wants, much less reject it, and continue to love, so one cannot love God unless one does his will (or, at least, what is honestly believed to be his will) throughout one's life.[8] Members of Jesus do this by living their lives motivated by hope and in accord with faith, always completing the Eucharist and preparing for it (see *CMP*, 33.D). But by trying to use one's whole life to complete and prepare for the Eucharist, one gradually integrates one's entire self and all one's interpersonal relationships with one's participation in the Eucharist, in this way gradually making one's whole heart, mind, soul, and strength instruments of the divine love which the Spirit pours forth in one's heart (see *S.t.*, 2–2, q. 24, aa. 4–5).

Thus, the devout reception of the sacraments and the practice of virtue must go together: the fundamental command to love God with one's whole heart, mind, soul, and strength is fulfilled only if one both participates worthily in the Eucharist and does one's best, with God's help, to keep all the commandments.

---

8. Thus, living faith works through love (see Gal 5.6); without a Christian life, faith is dead (see Jas 2.17–26).

2. All One's Good Religious Acts Help to Fulfill This Responsibility

The contemplative dimension of Christian life consists in all the upright, specifically religious acts one does. Its center is the Eucharist, but it includes the things pertaining to faith, hope, and repentance; the celebration of the other sacraments and the use of sacramentals; study of Scripture and meditation on it; and all one's acts of prayer and devotion.[9]

Plainly, the contemplative dimension, understood this way, is not reserved for an elite. Just as all Christians should share in the Eucharist, all also should live a full spiritual life including these other elements, which are necessary to link the Eucharist with the rest of Christians' lives—not only as individuals and families but as God's people united with him in the communion of the Church—and knit the whole into a eucharistic fabric, formed by God's love and in its service.

a) One should develop a personal form of spirituality. Christians' personalities and the things which make up their lives differ and so must be integrated with the Eucharist in somewhat different ways. Thus, while some elements of the contemplative dimension of Christian life are common to everyone—participation in the Eucharist and other things which the Church requires of all—many are variable and personal. Because a personal spirituality is so essential to connect the Eucharist with the rest of one's life, this responsibility will be treated later in the present chapter (C.2).

b) One should fulfill one's responsibilities as a Church member. Among one's religious responsibilities are those as a member of the Church. The Eucharist nourishes not an individualistic love of God (something quite impossible), but the new covenant communion, in which all who share in divine life abide with the divine persons. The Church, the communion of the new covenant in the world, is Jesus' bride, who will be joined forever with him in heaven. Thus, charity is implemented and increased by what one must do so that the Church can live and flourish. Therefore, responsibilities as a member of the Church also will be treated (in D).

c) One should fulfill one's responsibilities pertaining to faith. Responsibilities pertaining to faith also have a special importance in Christian life, for fulfilling them serves charity in a unique way. Faith is not simply one religious act among others to be done out of love; it is a person's basic commitment as a Christian, the fundamental option of Christian life (see 1.A.4, above; *CMP*, 16.G.3–7). As such, it is the foundation on which love builds.

By his self-revelation in Jesus' life and teaching, God offers human persons his friendship. Moved and helped by grace, an unbeliever can freely choose to accept this offer. Human goods, the overcoming of sin and death, initially motivate the choice to believe; but when someone who wishes to believe seeks and receives baptism from the Church, he or she receives not only faith but hope, along with the

---

9. On this meaning of *contemplative dimension,* see Congregation for Religious and Secular Institutes, *The Contemplative Dimension of Religious Life, EV* 7 (1980–81) 470–73, Flannery, 2:245.

supreme gift the gospel promises: the gift of the Holy Spirit, who pours forth charity into rightly disposed hearts (see DS 1525–32/797–801).[10]

Thus, in respect to one's free choices, charity presupposes faith. It is impossible either to grow in God's love or even remain in it without keeping the faith and fostering it. The responsibilities pertaining to faith, and certain closely allied responsibilities pertaining to reverence for God, were treated in chapter one.

d) **One should fulfill one's responsibilities pertaining to hope.** Like responsibilities pertaining to faith, those pertaining to hope have special importance because hope, like faith, is part of charity's foundation. Christians' do not love God as mature members of the divine family, for they are only God's little children. The Church is not the mature kingdom; she is its incipient stage, its seed. Thus, in this life, charity not only is a share in divine love but a disposition to fulfillment in heavenly communion. Without an interest in that fulfillment, one cannot be in communion with God now. Hope is that interest.

Moreover, as has been explained, charity grows as one's entire life is integrated with it by the living out of faith. Hope motivates people to do that by directing them to find, accept, and fulfill their shares in the Church's apostolate: their personal vocations. By always speaking and acting as personal vocation requires, a Christian approaches the ideal of doing everything for God's glory and in Jesus' name (see 1 Cor 10.31–11.1, Col 3.17), and so loves God with more and more of his or her heart. The responsibilities pertaining to hope and personal vocation were treated in chapter two.

e) **One should fulfill one's responsibilities pertaining to penance.** Some sins are grave matters, incompatible either with faith itself or with its specific requirements (see *CMP*, 16.G). To commit a mortal sin is to be unfaithful to God, to whom faith is a commitment of covenantal communion. But unfaithfulness to one's partner in a covenant plainly is incompatible with the unselfish love needed for friendship; and even though God, like the faithful spouse of an unfaithful married person, continues to love sinners, he can no longer cause them by his grace to share in his life, since their own wills are at odds with this communion. Thus, mortal sin is incompatible with charity (see *S.t.*, 1–2, q. 88, a. 2; 2–2, q. 24, aa. 11–12); one must avoid mortal sin to abide in God's love.

As for growing in God's love, that requires striving to overcome all sin and imperfection (see *S.t.*, 2–2, q. 184, a. 2). Only thus, gradually, are heart, mind, soul, and strength more and more put to work in the service of love. For this reason, responsibilities for avoiding sin and overcoming its effects also have a special relationship to charity. Chapter four will treat these responsibilities with respect to repentance and reconciliation.

---

10. Someone might ask: If what has been said above is true, how can the newly baptized share in God's love before participating in and receiving the Eucharist? The sacraments are organically related to one another: the Eucharist is incipient in baptism and penance, which bring or restore one to the communion of love which the Eucharist perfects and celebrates (see *S.t.*, 3, q. 73, a. 3; q. 75, a. 1; q. 79, a. 1, ad 1).

3. Love of God Requires Only What Is within One's Power

Not by their own ability but by God's grace, human persons can truly love God. Sometimes, however, people propose false ideals and say that only someone who realizes them truly loves God. Since these ideals simply cannot be met, the result is to confuse and discourage conscientious Christians. These false ideals should therefore be set aside.

a) **One cannot always feel warmly toward God.** Affectionate feelings toward human friends are appropriate, and so are feelings of love and joy toward God. But feelings are not directly within one's power. Sometimes one cannot help experiencing feelings of anger and even hatred toward friends and loved ones. In such cases, the genuineness of love is in what one wills, chooses, and does despite the feelings. The same is true of a relationship with God. One should try to integrate one's feelings with living faith; the practice of meditation helps in doing that. But even so, one does not always feel appropriately toward God. Not even true love for him eliminates all negative feelings.

b) **One cannot love God insofar as he is absolutely other.** Human friends love one another insofar as they are united and seek fulfillment together. A friend is truly loved if one desires and rejoices in his or her fulfillment, not simply as a means to one's own, but for the friend's sake. Still, in desiring a friend's good, one must desire one's own, since the friend desires and rejoices in one's fulfillment. Moreover, in loving a friend, one cannot help but desire and rejoice in the friendship's benefits to oneself. Thus, in loving a friend, one also loves oneself. The same is true of love of God.

Created persons do not really love God if they care about him only insofar as he serves their ends. Yet neither can they love him simply as a being perfect in himself, apart from the real relationship he establishes with them by revealing himself and inviting them to enter into covenantal communion.[11] A human person can only love the divine persons insofar as, united with them by faith, he or she hopes to live with them eternally, and so accepts their gift of a share in their own love. In accepting that gift, a human person perfectly loves himself or herself, since divine love is all-inclusive (see *CMP,* 24.E).

That is why the commandments of love include no injunction to love oneself (see Dt 6.5, Lv 19.18, Mt 22.37–39, Mk 12.30–31, Lk 10.27). The self-love presupposed by love of neighbor is immediately involved in love of God, not only entailed by it, as love of neighbor also is.

4. Hatred of God

Insofar as people hate something they call "God" but which is not truly God, they do not commit the sin of hating God, and may well be rightly hating something truly evil. Moreover, insofar as the truth about God is known, by faith or reason, he cannot be hated in himself, for he is all good and pure love. In gravely sinning, nevertheless, one violates God's wise plan and opposes his good will; and because

---

11. See *S.t.,* 2–2, q. 23, a. 1; P. De Letter, S.J., "Hope and Charity in St. Thomas," *Thomist* 13 (1950): 204–48, 325–52; cf. DS 2351/1327.

God's plan and will are not other than himself, committing a mortal sin can lead to the ultimate sin of hating God.

a) **Hatred of God underlies the sins against the Holy Spirit.** Someone conscious of being guilty of grave sin must make a choice: remain in sin or repent in the hope of being reconciled with God. If the choice is to remain in sin, one's very opposition to God may come to be regarded as a good, and God himself as an evil. Sinners might wish, for instance, that God did not exist as the source of moral truth or that his attributes could be changed to accommodate their sinful wills.

Just to the extent such wishes are endorsed by the free choices by which one persists in mortal sin, one hates God (see *S.t.*, 2–2, q. 34, a. 1). Such hatred need not involve hostile feelings; a sinner can endorse the wish that God not be God while emotionally regretting doing so, just as a professional killer can will to kill someone without feeling any animus toward the victim. Thus, hatred of God is a dimension of all the sins against the Holy Spirit: obduracy, presumption, despair, rejection of the known truth, envy of the grace others enjoy, and final impenitence which ends in hell (see *CMP*, 18.E).[12]

b) **Hatred of God is the worst sin.** Insofar as it is opposed to charity, hatred of God is in itself the worst sin (see *S.t.*, 2–2, q. 34, a. 2). But not all instances are equally evil.

The hatred of God by which Christians become apostates—and by which people who hear the gospel reject it in order to flee from the light—is greater than the hatred by which they previously committed less radical sins against the Spirit. Still, the guilt of such persons can be mitigated by lack of sufficient reflection (see *CMP*, 17.A).

Suppose someone, having sinned through weakness, even gravely, experiences thoughts and feelings of hatred toward God but, instead of consenting to them, repents of his or her sins: this person does not commit a mortal sin of hating God. And, not having committed some other mortal sin, one should not fear that one hates God merely because one sometimes has hostile feelings towards him, as already explained (3.a).

Question B: What Is One's Chief Responsibility in Regard to Worship?

By authentic acts of worship, human persons express, sustain, and deepen their true relationship with God. The general notion of worship and a Christian's specific responsibilities with respect to forms of worship which do not involve or presuppose the Eucharist were treated previously (in 1.K.1). Two matters remain to be considered: first (in this question), specific responsibilities with respect to the

---

12. As love of God leads to joy in his actual goodness and realized good will, so hatred leads to *acedia*: sadness in respect to these goods, now regarded as evils (see *S.t.*, 2–2, q. 35). *Acedia* makes faith and grace loathsome and thus provides the motivation to reject known truth and attack the grace other people enjoy. Thus, a more basic hatred of God and *acedia* together account for the fully developed hatred of the nonbelieving world toward Jesus and his disciples (see Jn 15.18–25).

eucharistic sacrifice and sacrament; then (in question C), responsibilities in regard to other aspects of spiritual life, which center in the Eucharist and complement it.

1. The Mass Is the Principal Act of Catholic Worship

Arising from faith and hope in Jesus, Christian worship can express and rely on authentic friendship with God. The primary and central act of this worship is the Eucharist, the sacrifice of Jesus and the sacrament of the communion in love of divine and human persons.

a) **The Eucharist is the primary act of Christian worship and love.** The "Eucharist contains the Church's entire spiritual good [note omitted], that is, Christ himself, our Pasch and living bread" (PO 5). Therefore, it "is the origin and summit of the whole Christian life" (LG 11). And because all other acts of a person's life should prepare for and flow from it (see *CMP*, 33.D), it holds primacy among all Christian acts.

While this primary act of Christian life is one, it has several distinct aspects. The Eucharist is at once and inseparably sacrifice (for it is Jesus' act of self-offering made present for his followers to join in) and sacrament (for it signifies and perfects the divine-human communion which Jesus establishes by his sacrifice). Its celebration is divine liturgy (for it offers God the best possible worship) and a banquet of human communion (for it unites Christians with their human Lord and, in him, both with the divine persons and with one another).[13]

Since the Eucharist embraces these distinct aspects, participation in the Eucharist does several things at once. One not only unites oneself with Jesus in offering his sacrifice but offers oneself together with him, thus worshipping the Father (see PO 5). Moreover, Jesus' sacrifice establishes the new covenant; and the Eucharist builds up and strengthens covenantal communion of the faithful in Jesus with God and so, in the Church, with one another.[14] Then too, even though the fullness of covenantal communion will be realized only in heaven, the Eucharist not only anticipates heavenly communion but nourishes and guards faithful souls until they are raised up to the glory of heaven (see *CMP*, 33.B–E). And finally, even now, believers "are through the reception of the Eucharist fully incorporated into the body of Christ. Thus, the eucharistic action is the center of the gathering together of the faithful" (PO 5).

b) **The Mass is the Eucharist in its proper setting.** Today, the words "Mass" and "Eucharist" often are used almost interchangeably. "Mass" is the wider expression, however, since it embraces the introductory rites and the liturgy of the word, as well as the eucharistic sacrifice and sacrament.

The penitential rite and the liturgy of the word not only prepare for the liturgy of the Eucharist, but are themselves acts which express one's true relationship with God. Repentance constitutes the necessary setting for the eucharistic celebration, inasmuch as it is essential to the covenantal communion which the Eucharist expresses and celebrates. The liturgy of the word and the eucharistic liturgy are

---

13. See SC 47; Paul VI, *Mysterium fidei, AAS* 57 (1965) 754, *PE*, 273.4–5.

14. See John Paul II, Homily at Mass for Agricultural Workers of Romagna (Cesena), 5, *Inseg.* 9.1 (1986) 1308–9, *OR*, 26 May 1986, 6–7.

integral parts of one action, so that, as Vatican II teaches, they constitute one act of worship (see SC 56).

2. One Should Participate Devoutly in the Eucharist

By virtue of baptism which unites them with Jesus, Christians share in Jesus' priesthood (see SC 14, LG 9–10, AA 3, AG 15). "They offer spiritual sacrifices to God through Jesus Christ, and they proclaim the perfections of him who has called them out of darkness into his marvelous light" (PO 2; cf. 1 Pt 2.5, 9). One with Jesus, Christians are united in his one body, the Church, and are privileged to offer both him and themselves to the Father, and to receive Jesus bodily in return. He thus fulfills his promise to abide in his disciples and to make them abide in him. Therefore, one should participate in the Eucharist with a twofold intention: to offer God authentic worship—Jesus' perfect and acceptable sacrifice—and to gain the best fruit of an act of love, namely, more perfect love. Fulfilling this intention requires devout participation: conscious, active, full, worthy, and reverent.

a) **Conscious participation requires understanding and attention.** While the liturgy of the word plainly calls for close attention, the whole liturgy communicates God's truth and love to those who participate attentively.[15] The Eucharist is a cooperative action; and the better it is understood, the more fully one can take part in it. Study of the rites and prayers is necessary to understand the mystery, that is, the sacred action. One should prepare for Mass and pay attention during it: this is conscious participation. Only in this way is Vatican II's teaching verified that "not only when things are read 'which were written for our instruction' (Rom 15.4), but also when the Church prays or sings or acts, the faith of those taking part is nourished and their minds are raised to God, so that they may offer him reasonable worship and more abundantly receive his grace" (SC 33).

b) **Active participation requires both will and performance.** Full cooperation in an action involves inwardly making one's own the willing by which the act is done and outwardly carrying out one's assigned role. Thus, one actively participates in the Mass by inwardly willing and outwardly behaving in certain appropriate ways. The appropriate willing is to will with Jesus to offer his self-sacrifice to the Father, and to will to offer with Jesus oneself: one's person, good works, and sufferings.[16] The appropriate outward behavior is to do all and only what pertains to one's particular role (see SC 28). Someone who has no special ministry actively

---

15. Full participation in the liturgy of the word requires not only that one hear or proclaim the word, but that one apply the gospel's eternal truth to the concrete circumstances of life, and put it into practice. See PO 4; John Paul II, Address to an International Congress of the Focolari "Parish Movement", 4–5, *Inseg.* 9.1 (1986) 1205–7, *OR,* 19 May 1986, 9.

16. See LG 11, PO 2; cf. Pius XII, *Mediator Dei, AAS* 39 (1947) 550–53 and 558–60, *PE,* 233.77–81 and 100–104. John Paul II, Homily at Mass at Alatri, 2, *Inseg.* 7.2 (1984) 312, *OR,* 17 Sept. 1984, 7, comments on Rom 12.1–2: "So, beloved brothers and sisters, Christian faith is above all *the offering of oneself* as a living sacrifice: because God, before everything asks for our heart; he awaits us, our person, our work, our sufferings. In this way is exercised the regal priesthood, to which the Second Vatican Council has invited everyone, including the laity." Mary's offering at the foot of the cross is a model of how one should join Jesus in his self-offering and offer oneself with him: see LG 58.

participates by following liturgical norms: making gestures, assuming postures, and joining in songs, responses, prayers, acclamations, and, when it is made, the profession of faith.[17]

c) **Active participation should be both earnest and meticulous.** Although some claim following liturgical norms inhibits active participation and fosters formalism, they are mistaken. Formalism must be avoided, of course, for it offers God nothing and is fruitless for those who are caught in it. The outward elements of active participation in worship must therefore be earnest, that is, honest and heartfelt. But the genuine alternative to formalism does not lie in bending or setting aside liturgical norms for the sake of spontaneity and creative self-expression. Rather, it lies in conforming one's mind and heart, as well as outward behavior, to Jesus' plan of worship as it is carried out in his Church.

Moreover, liturgical norms allow for and encourage spontaneity and creativity within certain definite limits. Exceeding those limits is not only unnecessary to avoid formalism but unjustifiable. The hierarchy must regulate the liturgy, both because it is the sacred action of Jesus with his entire Church, and because it embodies divine revelation and shapes the faith of those who participate.[18] "Therefore, no one else at all, not even a priest, may add, remove, or change anything in the liturgy on his or her own authority" (SC 22).

d) **Full participation includes Holy Communion and a Christian life.** Jesus himself commands his disciples to consume his flesh and blood (see Jn 6.53–58; cf. Mt 26.26–28, Mk 14.22–25, Lk 22.17–19). By receiving Jesus sacramentally, they perfect their communion with God and one another, and this growth of charity is the proper benefit to seek from participation in the Eucharist. Thus, it is appropriate that all Catholics who are properly prepared receive Holy Communion whenever they participate in the Mass.

Love of God cannot exist without love of neighbor, and so the divine-human communion nurtured by the Eucharist is real only if it extends to daily life. There love is expressed by apostolic witness and service to neighbor, through which people prepare further gifts to offer God as a spiritual sacrifice.[19]

In sum, the worthy reception of Communion "confers upon participation at Mass a value that is mature, complete, and binding on human life."[20]

e) **Worthy reception of Holy Communion requires a clear conscience.** The Eucharist is not just a banquet manifesting human fellowship. It is a sharing in the very body and blood of the Lord, which signifies and realizes the divine-human

---

17. See *General Instruction on the Roman Missal,* 2.14–17, Flannery, 1:165–66.

18. *CIC,* c. 838, §1: "The supervision of the sacred liturgy depends solely on the authority of the Church which resides in the Apostolic See and, in accord with the law, the diocesan bishop." Pius XII, *Mediator Dei, AAS* 39 (1947) 539–41, *PE,* 233.44–48, clearly explains the relationship between liturgy and faith. Liturgy is not a testing ground for possible propositions of faith, but rather embodies revelation and faith. Liturgical practice must conform entirely to the Church's dogmatic teaching, and must be regulated by Church authority to make sure that it does.

19. See *CMP,* 33.D; Congregation of Rites, *Eucharisticum mysterium,* 12–13, *AAS* 59 (1967) 548–50, Flannery, 1:110–12; John Paul II, Homily at Phoenix Park (Dublin), 5, *AAS* 71 (1979) 1072–73, *OR,* 8 Oct. 1979, 4.

20. John Paul II, *Dominicae cenae,* 9, *AAS* 72 (1980) 133, *OR,* 24 Mar. 1980, 8.

communion of charity (see 1 Cor 10.16–17, 11.23–29). Just as spouses unfaithful to their marriage promises are not entitled to marital intercourse, Catholics unfaithful to their commitment of faith to Jesus are not entitled to eucharistic Communion. If someone who has been unfaithful shares without repentance and reconciliation in the act of love, he or she only adds injury to injury. "Whoever, therefore, eats the bread or drinks the cup of the Lord in an unworthy manner will be answerable for the body and blood of the Lord" (1 Cor 11.27).

f) Reverent participation respects the holiness of the Eucharist. While an excessively formal attitude of reverence and awe toward the sacrifice of the Mass and the reception of Communion might reflect and foster inappropriate fear of God and self-depreciation, a casual attitude of relaxed informality during the Eucharist can reflect and foster forgetfulness of God's holiness and a lack of humility before him. Therefore, appropriate behavior is important in order to manifest and foster the reverence due the holy sacrifice and Holy Communion.

People participating in the Eucharist should dress modestly. They should make a reasonable effort to be present and seated on time. Members of the congregation should be friendly, but their conversation should be carried on outside the Church. For one should spend the moments before and after Mass in personal prayer or, at least, allow others to do so by avoiding unnecessary talk or any other behavior likely to distract them.

One should prepare reverently to receive the Lord's body and blood in Holy Communion.[21] As part of this preparation, the Church requires abstinence from all food and drink (except water and medicine) for at least one hour before the time of Communion.[22]

One should attend to and actively share in the prayers which precede and prepare for Holy Communion, for example, by expressing genuine faith when proclaiming the mystery of faith and genuine humility when saying: "Lord, I am not worthy."

In approaching the Blessed Sacrament to receive it, one should first adore the Lord. Where it is not the practice to receive kneeling, a sign of adoration, such as a bow, should be made, with due care to avoid disturbing the orderly procession to and from Communion.[23] Where the practice is approved, the host may be received in one's hand. In thereby showing one's dignity as a member of Jesus' body, one should at the same time show reverence by the care with which his body is handled.[24] Without going to extremes, as the scrupulous do, accidents involving

---

21. See Germán G. Suárez, O.M., "Teología de la preparación a la Comunión frecuente," *Teología espiritual* 17 (1973): 303–25.

22. The one-hour fast before receiving Communion is the bare minimum; the spirit of the law calls for a longer fast when possible. But the elderly and infirm, and those directly involved in their care, may receive even if they have not been able to fast for one hour: *CIC*, c. 919, §1, §3. Also, priests celebrating more than one Mass on the same day need fast only before their first reception of Communion: c. 919, §2.

23. Congregation of Rites, *Eucharisticum mysterium, AAS* 59 (1967) 560, Flannery, 1:122, makes it clear that to insist on kneeling to receive where this is not the practice is not an appropriate way to show reverence.

24. Congregation for Divine Worship, *Memoriale Domini, AAS* 61 (1969) 546–47, Flannery, 1:152–53.

the Blessed Sacrament, such as a dropped host, should be dealt with in a way which manifests faith in Jesus' presence and reverence for him.

Having received Holy Communion, one should make a sincere and appropriate thanksgiving, lingering with the Lord while taking leave of his bodily presence, much as loving spouses gently part after their intimate communion, rather than abruptly break it off. At a minimum, the quiet time between communion and the final prayer is to be used for this purpose, and no one should leave before the celebrant except for some urgent reason. This thanksgiving serves as a transition to the carrying on of one's daily life in Jesus, during the long intervals between brief moments of sacramental communing.[25]

3. One Should Avoid Abuses in One's Worship

Idolatry and the forms of superstition related to it (treated in 1.K.2) challenge God's unique majesty. But even without going so far, one can sin by receiving Holy Communion unworthily, by introducing superstitious elements into worship, and by other abuses.

a) **Receiving Holy Communion sacrilegiously is grave matter.** Because worthy reception of Holy Communion requires a clear conscience, someone in mortal sin is not eligible to receive. Doing so is the sort of sacrilege which is always grave matter.[26] For this reason, Jesus commands that those about to offer sacrifice first be reconciled with anyone with whom they are at odds (see Mt 5.23–24), St. Paul warns those about to receive Holy Communion to examine themselves (see 1 Cor 11.27–29), and the Council of Trent decrees: "Those who have mortal sin on their conscience, no matter how contrite they may think they are, must necessarily make a sacramental confession before receiving, provided that they have access to a confessor" (DS 1661/893).[27]

Someone conscious of mortal sin but lacking opportunity to confess may receive if, but only if, three conditions are met: there is a grave reason to do so, for example, not doing so would amount to publicly admitting a secret and shameful sin, with anticipated serious disgrace or dishonor (not just mild embarrassment); there is contrition for the sin, including a firm purpose of amendment and the intention to seek forgiveness in the sacrament of penance as soon as possible; and there is

---

25. An explanation and defense of thanksgiving after Communion is provided by Pius XII, *Mediator Dei, AAS* 39 (1947) 566–68, *PE,* 233.123–28, which ends beautifully: "The divine Redeemer is ever repeating His pressing invitation, 'Abide in Me.' Now by the sacrament of the Eucharist, Christ remains in us and we in Him, and just as Christ, remaining in us, lives and works, so should we remain in Christ and live and work through Him."

26. Even worse is maliciously to desecrate the Blessed Sacrament—to express contempt and hatred precisely contrary to the adoration and love due to Jesus present in the Eucharist. Actual desecration also is subject to a canonical penalty: *CIC,* c. 1367. It is worth noting that carelessness in handling the Blessed Sacrament is not desecration, but at worst a venial sin of irreverence. And only reasonable care is required, similar to the care one gives one's valuable personal possessions. If one is reasonably careful, it is scrupulosity, not reverence, to worry about whether a small particle of the Eucharist is lost.

27. See John Paul II, *Dominicae cenae,* 11, *AAS* 72 (1980) 138–39, *OR,* 24 Mar. 1980, 9; cf. *CIC,* c. 916.

earnest prayer, before receiving, for the grace required to make the contrition perfect (see 4.C.2.f–g).[28]

b) Receiving without observing the eucharistic fast can be grave. Traditionally, the eucharistic fast, required by the Church for the sake of reverence, was considered a grave responsibility which did not admit parvity. Now, since the requirement is more easily fulfilled, its violation is even harder to excuse. Still, some sound moralists now think this responsibility admits parvity of matter and hold there is no need to be concerned about mortal sin if the fast is not kept perfectly.

But someone who deliberately disregards the eucharistic fast out of irreverence for Jesus or contempt for the Church's law plainly is guilty of grave sin. And, knowing that the fast has been broken, whether by accident or on purpose, in a significant way, anyone as reverent and obedient as he or she should be, will not receive Holy Communion, except for a reason sufficient to justify an exception to the Church's law (see *CMP*, 11.G.6–7).[29]

c) To falsify Catholic worship can be a grave matter. Liturgical worship is the Church's act; Jesus and his members share in it. Since they act not simply as private individuals, but share in the Church's act, all who play a role in the liturgy act in an official capacity. Thus, anyone who makes unauthorized changes in the liturgy or encourages others to make them falsely offers as the Church's what in reality is only personal. Insofar as such falsification modifies authentic Catholic worship, it is a sort of superstition, for even if the unauthorized change is meant to contribute to genuine worship, the choice of falsification as a means is incompatible with the reverence essential to true worship (see *S.t.*, 2–2, q. 93, a. 1).

Sacramental simulation is a very grave kind of falsification. This occurs when a nonordained person tries to carry out the priest's role in the Eucharist, or a person who cannot validly absolve tries to hear a sacramental confession and/or impart sacramental absolution, or someone simulates the administration of any of the sacraments.[30]

But even in less serious cases where abuses do not render liturgical acts invalid, bending or setting aside liturgical norms, unless for some reason sufficient to justify an exception to the Church's law (see *CMP*, 11.G.6–7), violates the rights of anyone present who intends to participate only in authentic Catholic worship. Moreover, such violations sometimes embody deviations from Catholic faith, often generate conflict, and always set an example of disobedience to the Church.[31] Hence, the deliberate violation of liturgical norms harms the communion of charity which Jesus intended the Eucharist to perfect, and so is a grave matter.[32] Still, undoubtedly

28. See *CIC*, c. 916.

29. See I. Aertnys, C. Damen, and I. Visser, C.Ss.R., *Theologia moralis*, ed. 18, 4 vols. (Turin: Marietti, 1967–69), 3:222–25.

30. The latter sins are subject to canonical penalties: *CIC*, cc. 1378–79.

31. Many frequently violated liturgical norms are forcefully reiterated: Congregation for the Sacraments and Divine Worship, *Inaestimabile donum*, AAS 72 (1980) 331–43, Flannery, 2:93–102.

32. A matter in itself light would not receive the attention this one does from both the Council of Trent and the Church's law: DS 1613/856; *CIC*, c. 846, §1: "The liturgical books approved by

some people's guilt is mitigated by their lack of sufficient reflection due to widespread confusion and laxity in these matters.

4. One Should Observe Sundays and Holy Days of Obligation

While this section articulates the letter of the Church's law regarding Sunday observance—and no Catholic should take that law lightly—the right spirit is especially needed in fulfilling these responsibilities. Grudging participation motivated only by a concern not to violate the law is contrary to the Eucharist's meaning as an expression of gratitude and love. Thus, a joyful spirit of celebration, not mere dutifulness, is no less important for Sunday observance than it is for marital intercourse. For this reason, this section must not be considered apart from the context provided by the earlier parts of the chapter (especially A.1 and B.1).

Inaugurating the new covenant, Jesus commanded: "Do this in remembrance of me" (Lk 22.19; cf. 1 Cor 11.24–25). To fulfill their responsibility to worship according to Jesus' command, Christians always have gathered on Sunday, the day after the sabbath (see Acts 20.7). On that day, everyday work and business are put aside.

Certain important weekday feasts are celebrated in the same way as Sunday.

a) **Sunday is set aside for worship because of its Christian meaning.** People of virtually every culture set aside sacred times for worship, since it is owed to God and vital to the community's well-being. One of the commandments of the Mosaic covenant designated the time for worship: "Remember the sabbath day, and keep it holy. Six days you shall labor and do all your work . . . .. For in six days the Lord made heaven and earth, the sea, and all that is in them, but rested the seventh day; therefore the Lord blessed the sabbath day and consecrated it" (Ex 20.8–9, 11). Thus, sabbath worship and rest honored and gave thanks to God as creator of all good things.

Jesus commands his followers to celebrate the Eucharist (see Lk 22.19–20; cf. Jn 6.53–58, 1 Cor 11.23–25). In him, however, the fallen world becomes a new creation; thus, the "day" of his resurrection is not just the beginning of another ordinary week but the endless age after every earthly week. So, Christians began to celebrate the Eucharist on Sunday, neither to complete an earthly week (as the Jewish sabbath did) nor to begin a new earthly week, but to anticipate the everlasting rest of heaven, which will be the Lord's "day" in the fullest sense, when

---

the competent authority are to be faithfully observed in the celebration of the sacraments; therefore no one on personal authority may add, remove or change anything in them." Even approved extraliturgical devotions should not be mingled with the liturgy, since doing so goes beyond their properly subordinate role and imposes the devotional preferences of some on all. John Paul II, *Dominicae cenae*, 12, *AAS* 72 (1980) 142–46, *OR*, 24 Mar. 1980, 9–10, explains why participants in the Eucharist must subordinate themselves to it insofar as it is the common good of the Church. He allows that liturgical norms need not be fulfilled in situations where a valid celebration is possible only by setting them aside, yet he excludes making exceptions under normal conditions. The appropriate use of options provided in the books is not an exception to the law, but part of its fulfillment. Hence, the existence of various options constitutes no precedent for additional, unauthorized variations.

all God's work will be completed. Therefore, Sunday is the original and chief Christian feast.[33]

b) One should participate in Sunday and holy day Mass. Since divine law established the week as a regular cycle for work and worship, and since Christian eucharistic worship is so necessary to nurture the communion of love which is the Church, the Church always has considered participation in Sunday liturgy to be a serious obligation for all her members (see Heb 10.25).[34] On Sunday one should listen to God's word and participate in the Eucharist, in order to commemorate Jesus' passion, death, resurrection, and glorification (see SC 106). At various times and places, the obligation has been extended to include more or fewer other feast days: the holy days of obligation. The Church's law recalls this obligation: "On Sundays and other holy days of obligation the faithful are bound to participate in the Mass."[35]

c) Several conditions must be met to fulfill the obligation. Since the Mass is a unified act of worship, one should participate in a complete Mass (see SC 56). The obligation is not perfectly fulfilled by someone who comes late, leaves early, or participates in parts of two different Masses. One must be present to fulfill the obligation, because the Mass forms bodily persons into a worshipping community, and full participation includes receiving Holy Communion. Standing outside a Church too crowded to enter is sufficient for presence, but following a broadcast or telecast is not.

One must pay attention. Unintentional distractions do not violate this requirement, but deliberate turning of attention to other matters does. For example, intentionally thinking about business or a coming vacation would be incompatible with participation. Someone who slept soundly through the Mass would not meet the requirement at all.

Also, since the eucharistic liturgy signifies and builds ecclesial communion, it is fitting to participate whenever possible on Sundays and feast days in a Mass celebrated by one's bishop or parish priest (see SC 41–42), though the obligation is fulfilled by participating in any Mass in any Catholic rite.[36]

d) One may be excused or dispensed from this obligation. On particular occasions, one is excused from fulfilling this obligation if it cannot be done without great difficulty or harm to oneself or others, without omitting to serve an urgent

---

33. See Thomas K. Carroll and Thomas Halton, *Liturgical Practice in the Fathers* (Wilmington, Del.: Michael Glazier, 1988), 17–76, for a collection of materials bearing on the Lord's day.

34. Note the striking text from the *Didascalia* (a third-century book of Church order) quoted in PO 6, n. 31 (in Abbott, n. 82): "In your teaching tell the people to come to church and not to stay away. Tell them to come together always and not to constrict the church by staying away and so making the body of Christ a member short."

35. *CIC,* c. 1247. The holy days which are of obligation are listed in c. 1246, §1, but §2 authorizes conferences of bishops to abolish or transfer some of them to a Sunday with the prior approval of the Holy See.

36. See *CIC,* c. 1248, §1. In certain Eastern rites, the Sunday obligation may be fulfilled by participation in the divine praises (the choral office), since only one Mass is celebrated each Sunday, and not all can participate in it (see OE 15). However, for Latin rite Catholics, the Church's law specifically requires participation in Mass.

need of another or others, or without neglecting some other important duty. Among the most common excusing conditions are sickness or the need to care for children or others, travel or weather conditions which make going to church quite difficult or hazardous, and having to work during all the hours at which Mass will be offered. But conditions which would not keep people from doing what they routinely do or especially enjoy—for example, shopping or going to a party—can hardly excuse them from participating in Mass.

On particular occasions, the pastor of a parish or superior of a religious house in which one is staying can dispense one from this obligation or commute it, that is, allow the substitution of some other pious work. So, someone with a reason for wishing to miss Mass, but not a reason clearly strong enough to excuse doing so, should request a dispensation or commutation of the obligation.[37] For instance, an individual who wished to go backpacking over a weekend might ask to be dispensed entirely or to substitute a Mass on a weekday.

e) **Missing Mass without a good excuse is a grave matter.** Catholics always have considered themselves bound to participate in Mass on Sundays and holy days of obligation. Contrary to a lax opinion which Innocent XI condemned as at least scandalous and in practice pernicious, failure to keep Sundays and holy days is a grave matter (see DS 2152/1202). While it is true that some usually sound contemporary theologians deny that this is so, the Church's tradition and the ground of the obligation in both natural and divine law are cogent reasons for considering their view mistaken.

Nevertheless, there can be parvity of matter in respect to this obligation. Someone who comes a few minutes late or leaves right after Communion, or who dozes briefly but participates as well as possible in the central parts of the Mass, especially the consecration and Communion, substantially fulfills the obligation.[38]

f) **Incomplete participation in the Eucharist can be required.** Even if an unrepented mortal sin prevents the reception of Holy Communion, one still should fulfill the obligation of worship on Sundays and holy days. In such cases, a person should participate in the Eucharist incompletely, by assisting at Mass without receiving Holy Communion, for thus God is given the worship due him. Such incomplete participation remains beneficial to the participant, for even obdurate sinners can continue to enjoy the gifts of faith and hope, and so live in the fellowship of the Church. Their reverent, active participation in the Mass without Communion can help sustain what remains of their human relationship with Jesus, while their

---

37. See *CIC*, c. 1245. This canon refers to c. 87, which makes it clear that bishops could limit the power of pastors and superiors to dispense from this obligation.

38. Since no one has an obligation to do the impossible, those simply incapable of acts of worship—small children, the severely retarded, and so on—need not be brought to Mass. However, while merely ecclesiastical laws do not bind children under seven (see *CIC*, c. 11), divine law does. Small children and mentally handicapped persons should worship God in accord with their ability. Children should be taught early not only about Jesus and how to pray, but about the meaning of the Eucharist, and they should be encouraged to participate in the Mass as soon as they are able to do so. See M. Basil Pennington, *The Eucharist Yesterday and Today* (New York: Crossroad, 1984), 73–75.

faithfulness in fulfilling the obligation of worship can help dispose them to accept the grace of repentance.

g) **Sundays and holy days are to be saved for worship and leisure.** The Old Testament's ceremonial requirements strictly excluding work on the sabbath are not binding on Christians, for Sunday is not a symbol of God's rest after his work of creation (see *S.t.*, 2–2, q. 122, a. 4, ad 4).

Still, Christians should do their best to keep the Lord's day holy while fulfilling other serious responsibilities, since in celebrating Jesus' resurrection they anticipate the joy of heaven. As God's children who have been freed from sin, they should avoid it especially on Sundays and holy days. They also should avoid burdensome work on those days, in order to turn their hearts fully toward God and the hope of heaven. Thus, the Church's law concerning Sunday observance adds: Catholics "are also to abstain from those labors and business concerns which impede the worship to be rendered to God, the joy which is proper to the Lord's Day, or the proper relaxation of mind and body."[39]

Besides fulfilling the Mass obligation, it is appropriate to spend some time on Sunday in other religious acts, for example, reading Scripture or other edifying books, participating in evening prayer (vespers), reflecting on questions regarding personal vocation, and so on. Because the relaxation of mind and body must be proper to the Lord's day, and not every activity morally acceptable in itself is equally harmonious with that spirit of recollection and joy, Catholic families and individuals should make their own conscientious decisions about which recreational activities are and are not appropriate on Sunday.

Keeping Sunday holy requires a communal effort: everyone must try to avoid calling on others to do anything which would prevent them from keeping the Lord's day holy.[40]

h) **Unnecessary business or work on sacred days is to be avoided.** On Sundays and holy days, Christians should neither personally do nor require or encourage others to do any unnecessary business or work not in keeping with the character of the sacred day. The word *unnecessary* points to the fact that the duty is limited by other responsibilities. Business or work done for one's own true good or that of others is therefore permissible if it cannot be done some other time. For example, some people must work on Sunday so that others can engage in appropriate recreational activities.

Of course, any activity even venially sinful in itself can never be necessary and so will always profane a sacred day. There is, however, no simple way to say which kinds of business and work, sinless in themselves, are excluded. Each Christian has a responsibility (which probably few take seriously enough) to think carefully about this matter and make honest judgments. Those who are conscientious can occa-

---

39. *CIC*, c. 1247.

40. See John XXIII, *Mater et magistra*, AAS 53 (1961) 459–60, *PE*, 267.248–53; Franz X. Pettirsch, S.J., "A Theology of Sunday Rest," *Theology Digest* 6 (1958): 114–22; Kenneth C. Russell, "Reflections on *The Sabbath* (a review of *The Sabbath*, by Abraham J. Heschel), *Cross and Crown* 27 (1975): 18–24.

sionally soften the impact of their own judgments by seeking a dispensation from the obligation.

Considered in itself, violating this responsibility is a grave matter. Sundays and holy days of obligation are set apart to worship God and anticipate eternal rest. Deliberately doing business and work at odds with this purpose profanes this sacred time; it shows how little one loves God and cares about communion with him. Still, the matter of this sin is subject to parvity, and each person also must judge whether a particular violation would be a mortal or a venial sin. *Parvity* must not be pushed too far, however; there are outer limits. For example, it plainly would be grave matter to spend all day Sunday doing burdensome work which could as well be done some other day.

5. Eucharistic Worship Should Not Be Limited to Sunday

Besides Sundays and holy days of obligation, there are certain other times when eucharistic worship is required or appropriate.

a) **The Church invites all Catholics to daily Mass and Communion.** Jesus and his Church wish all Catholics to participate devoutly and fully in the Eucharist each and every day, in order to grow in the communion of charity, more strongly anticipate heavenly happiness, gain self-control, be strengthened to avoid mortal sin, and gradually overcome venial sin.[41] Although many people cannot participate daily, most could participate more often than they do. It is especially appropriate to make the effort during Lent and Advent, and on some of the more important feasts.

b) **The reception of Holy Communion is sometimes required.** The Church requires all Catholics who have made their first Communion to receive at least once a year. This precept must be fulfilled during the Easter season (in the United States, from the first Sunday of Lent to Trinity Sunday) unless one has a just cause for fulfilling it at some other time.[42]

Those who begin to be in danger of death, from any cause, are to receive the Eucharist as Viaticum, that is, so that the Lord will be with them on the way to their heavenly home (see 4.F.4.a).

c) **Failure to receive Communion when required is a grave matter.** These canonical norms merely articulate and specify the times when it is most necessary

41. See Congregation of the Council, *Sacra Tridentina synodus*, DS 3375–78/1981–83 (*AAS* 2 [1910] 894–98); Paul VI, *Mysterium fidei, AAS* 57 (1965) 771, *PE*, 273.66. See Joseph Nicholas Stadler, *Frequent Holy Communion: A Historical Synopsis and a Commentary* (Washington, D.C.: The Catholic University of America Press, 1947); Bertrand de Margerie, S.J., *Christ for the World: The Heart of the Lamb: A Treatise on Christology,* trans. Malachy Carroll (Chicago: Franciscan Herald Press, 1973), 485–512.

42. See *CIC*, c. 920. Children lacking the use of reason need not receive Holy Communion: DS 1730/933. Annual reception of Holy Communion is minimal; one's real responsibility, rooted in Jesus' own word, is wider though less clearly defined. This wider responsibility also is reflected in the Church's law (c. 898): "The faithful are to hold the Eucharist in highest honor, taking part in the celebration of the Most August Sacrifice, receiving the sacrament devoutly and frequently, and worshiping it with supreme adoration." Those who have already received Communion may receive a second time on the same day during a celebration of the Eucharist in which they actually participate: c. 917.

to fulfill Jesus' instruction about what is necessary for salvation, so that failure to fulfill them is a grave matter. However, this responsibility is not fulfilled by a sacrilegious Communion (see DS 2155/1205), and so, when those living in mortal sin are required to receive Holy Communion, they first should repent; but if unwilling to do so, they should not receive Holy Communion unworthily, since that does not fulfill the obligation and is an additional sacrilege.

d) **Sacramental Communion outside Mass unites one with the Mass.** Those who cannot assist at Mass nevertheless can participate in it by receiving Holy Communion outside Mass.[43] They should ask to do so if it is necessary to fulfill their Easter duty, if they are in danger of death, or if they otherwise would be deprived of Communion for a time they judge too long.

Those who cannot attend Mass but who nevertheless worthily receive Holy Communion and devoutly listen to or read the liturgical readings (and perhaps other parts) of the Mass, participate quite significantly. Some dioceses provide Sunday broadcasts or telecasts of Mass for shut-ins. The Church also encourages those who cannot assist at Mass on a Sunday or holy day to take part if possible in a liturgy of the word, celebrated according to the bishop's direction in a church or other sacred place, or to engage in prayer either individually, or as a family, or, if possible, as a group of families.[44]

e) **Spiritual Communion is a way of participating in the Eucharist.** Sometimes people cannot receive Communion because they have not fasted long enough or because of health problems or other obstacles. Others are prevented because they have not yet confessed a mortal sin of which they have repented. Yet active participation in the Mass not only is due worship of God and a way of nurturing fellowship with Jesus and the Church, but is an important way of safeguarding and growing in divine love. In these circumstances, spiritual communion is appropriate: one calls to mind one's faith in the Eucharist, wills to offer oneself to the Father in union with Jesus, and wishes one could receive him bodily. The Council of Trent teaches that those doing this, "with a living faith which works through charity (see Gal 5.6), . . . experience profit and benefit from it" (DS 1648/881).

Question C: What Other Forms of Worship Are Appropriate for Catholics?

While the Mass is a Catholic's primary and central act of worship, by no means does it replace or devalue other elements of the spiritual life. Rather, it calls for them, perfects them by uniting them with Jesus' death and resurrection, and integrates them into the living whole of divine-human communion.[45] Under certain conditions, one may even share with due care in the worship of those who are not Catholic.

43. See *CIC*, c. 918; *The Rites*, 459–64.
44. See *CIC*, c. 1248, §2.
45. See Gabriel M. Braso, O.S.B., *Liturgy and Spirituality*, trans. Leonard J. Doyle (Collegeville, Minn.: Liturgical Press, 1971), 165–208.

1. The Liturgy's Other Elements Are Necessary or Very Worthwhile

The other sacraments, the liturgy of the hours, and the sacramentals are closely linked with the Eucharist and directed toward it (see PO 5).

a) **The other sacraments are to be received when appropriate.** Like the Eucharist, to which each is related in its own way, the other sacraments establish or deepen communion with God and so build up the body of Jesus. Every sacrament is a form of divine worship (see SC 59), and one should receive each of them whenever appropriate.

Insofar as possible, the recipient of any sacrament and all involved in its administration and reception (for example, baptismal sponsors, witnesses to matrimony) should be attentive and play an appropriately active role. As with the Eucharist, this is more a matter of inward acts than of outward behavior.

b) **The Church calls all the faithful to the liturgy of the hours.** By the liturgy of the hours, the Church extends her worship, centered in the Eucharist, throughout the day (see *CMP*, 33.G). Sharing in this prayer thus helps integrate all one does with the Eucharist, and so to perfect it as spiritual worship. The liturgy of the hours also is a fine framework for individual and family prayer and devotions, and for examination of conscience.

The Church invites all the faithful to participate in the hours (see SC 84 and 100). Many easily could, at least by adopting one or two of the hours, preferably morning and/or evening prayer, as a regular form of household prayer.[46]

c) **Sacramentals extend the sacraments into daily life.** The sacramentals are significant acts variously related to the sacraments. For example, blessing oneself with holy water recalls one's baptism, while using it in blessing other things extends baptism, as it were, to objects which in various ways extend one's body. While not essential to divine worship, the sacramentals are practices of the Church which are effective by her prayer.[47] Central to all is the intercession of the Church, and some simply are prayers which the Church provides for particular benefits. Of these, some are incorporated in the rites of the sacraments, while others stand apart from the sacraments.

---

46. Regrettably few pastors instruct the faithful about this part of the liturgy and encourage them to share in it. About the value of participation by the faithful in general, see Paul VI, *Laudis canticum*, AAS 63 (1971) 534, International Commission on English in the Liturgy, *Documents on the Liturgy, 1963–1979: Conciliar, Papal, and Curial Texts* (Collegeville, Minn.: Liturgical Press, 1982), 1089. The Church invites all: *CIC*, c. 1174, §2. Since the point of the liturgy of the hours is to extend the Eucharist throughout the day, c. 1175 directs that "the true time of each hour is to be observed as much as possible." Dominic F. Scotto, T.O.R., *Liturgy of the Hours* (Petersham, Mass.: St. Bede's Publications, 1987), treats the history and importance of the liturgy of the hours and offers pastoral proposals to facilitate its celebration by parishes and families.

47. See *CMP*, 29.G.1–4; SC 60–61; *CIC*, cc. 1166–68. C. 1166 defines sacramentals as "sacred signs by which spiritual effects especially are signified and are obtained by the intercession of the Church." C. 1167 declares the exclusive authority of the Holy See in establishing, changing, doing away with, and interpreting sacramentals, and requires observance of approved rites and formulae. C. 1168 determines the minister of sacramentals by the norm of the liturgical books and the local ordinary's judgment.

Any prayer or blessing offered by the Church responsive to some need of an individual, family, or other group should be sought and used.[48] In this way, private devotion is more clearly and fruitfully linked with God's saving work in Jesus.

2. Individuals and Families Should Develop Their Own Devotional Style

The activity of the Church as a whole is not limited to the liturgy, and the spiritual life of her members is not limited to liturgical participation.[49] Each individual and family require other devotions and prayers which bring God's manifold gifts and mediate between the eucharistic center of communion with God in Jesus and day-to-day life transformed into "a living sacrifice, holy and acceptable to God" (Rom 12.1; cf. *CMP*, 29.F–H). Thus, every Catholic individual and family has the right and responsibility to develop and follow a singular form of spiritual life, provided it is in harmony both with the Church's teaching and with full participation in the liturgy.[50]

The requirements to read Scripture, pray, meditate, and examine conscience are dealt with elsewhere (especially 1.J.2, 2.B.1, 4.B.2.a–b, 4.C.2, 4.D.1.b–c, and 4.D.2). These things are fundamental to every individual's and family's spirituality. The present treatment summarizes only the Church's more important, current, specific recommendations concerning certain devotions, some liturgical and others not, which can hardly be omitted from anyone's spirituality.

a) **Eucharistic adoration outside Mass often is appropriate.** Since Jesus remains present as long as the consecrated species remain what they are, Catholics rightly adore him in the Blessed Sacrament, not only during but outside Mass (see DS 1656/888). This worship should be shown by genuflecting (or in some situations bowing) toward the tabernacle when entering and leaving church before and after Mass, or when visiting (even as a tourist) any place where the Blessed Sacrament is reserved, and by showing due reverence whenever the Sacrament is exposed, for example, in a public procession or in a sickroom where a patient is receiving Holy Communion.

It also is good to participate in such processions and in other optional devotions: eucharistic benediction, prayer before the Blessed Sacrament exposed, special services on the solemnity of Corpus Christi, eucharistic congresses, and so on.[51]

48. For blessings provided by the Church: *The Roman Ritual: Book of Blessings*, trans. International Committee on English in the Liturgy (Collegeville, Minn.: Liturgical Press, 1989). Many of these blessings can be administered by lay persons.

49. Vatican II (see SC 9, 12) endorses and briefly restates what Pius XII taught more fully in *Mediator Dei, AAS* 39 (1947) 530–37, *PE*, 233.23–37, where he warned against the danger of drawing pernicious conclusions from the Eucharist's objective excellence and power: Christian holiness is not to be reduced to liturgical participation; personal piety and a holy life also are necessary.

50. See *CIC*, c. 214. *Teaching* refers not only to doctrine but to moral norms and Church order, including the Church's liturgy and the norms governing it. Thus, Vatican II commends popular devotions "provided they accord with the laws and norms of the Church" (SC 13).

51. See Pius XII, *Mediator Dei, AAS* 39 (1947) 568–72, *PE*, 233.129–37; Congregation for Rites, *Eucharisticum mysterium*, 49–67, *AAS* 59 (1967) 566–73, Flannery, 1:129–36; *The Rites*, 484–96.

b) **The Church recommends devotion to Jesus' sacred heart.** Devotion to Jesus' sacred heart is rooted both in adoration of his living human body, insofar as it is the divine Word's flesh, and in the natural symbolism by which his living heart is a sign of his divine and human love. This love led Jesus to offer himself in redemptive self-sacrifice, which resulted in his death and the piercing of his heart, from which blood and water flowed. Raised to life again, he shares divine love with his followers through the "water" of the Holy Spirit and eucharistic Communion in his body and blood. Thus, devotion to Jesus' sacred heart embodies central truths of faith, focuses on God's love, makes amends for acts which answer Jesus' love with offenses, expresses adoration, thanks God for his mercy, and confirms the baptismal commitment to follow Jesus' way of the cross to heavenly glory.[52]

To implement this devotion liturgically, the Church celebrates the solemnity of the Sacred Heart on the Friday following the second Sunday after Pentecost. It is also recommended that all Catholics consecrate themselves to Jesus' sacred heart, observe the first Friday of each month by participating in Mass and receiving Holy Communion, display an image of the sacred heart in their homes and honor it by living under Jesus' lordship, and use approved prayers including the morning (or daily) offering and the litany of the sacred heart.[53]

Historically distinct in its origins but theologically closely related is the penitential practice of the way (or stations) of the cross, which consists in prayer and meditation on Jesus' suffering. The Church encourages this devotion by indulgences and by authorizing the formal erection of the stations.[54]

c) **The Church recommends veneration of Mary and all the saints.** Because the Church is a communion of love among created persons united with God, faithful Catholics always have venerated the Blessed Virgin Mary, the holy angels, the apostles, the martyrs, and other outstanding disciples of Jesus (see LG 50–51). This veneration involves several things: honoring their holiness, asking them to pray to God as one's intercessors, remembering their fellowship as one adores God, and rejoicing with them in his friendship. The saints' virtues should be imitated, and the help and protection of the angels should be sought. Still, it is possible to overdo such veneration, focusing devotion more on Mary or other saints than on God himself. The Church forbids such abuses and excesses, and Catholics not only should avoid them themselves but try to help others to correct them.[55]

---

52. The central doctrinal document on this devotion, which includes many references to prior elements of the Catholic tradition bearing on the matter: Pius XII, *Haurietis aquas, AAS* 48 (1956) 309–53, *PE,* 253. Essential elements of the devotion are not entirely optional (*AAS* 312, *PE* 10), because to reject them either would be to deny the union of Jesus' living heart with the person of the Word or to refuse to respond to God's redemptive love in a way proportionate to the precise mode in which he has chosen to express that love and make it effective.

53. For the sources of the various devotional practices and a survey of the documents which justify them, see Timothy T. O'Donnell, *Heart of the Redeemer* (San Francisco: Ignatius Press, 1992). A practical directory of sacred heart devotion: Walter Kern, *Updated Devotion to the Sacred Heart* (Canfield, Ohio: Alba House, 1975), 137–86.

54. See *New Catholic Encyclopedia,* s.v. "way of the cross."

55. The Church urges veneration of Mary and the other saints: see *CIC,* c. 1186. The Council of Trent (see DS 1821–25/984–88) and Vatican II (see LG 51) both defend the Catholic practice

d) Mary should be honored in an altogether special way. As mother of God, Mary was raised by his grace above every other created person; she was Jesus' first and best disciple; she maternally cooperates with him in his redemptive work; and she is the Church's heavenly mother, most splendidly fulfilled in that communion with God in which all the faithful hope one day to join her. Individuals and families should seek to imitate her *fiat* accepting her role in God's saving work, and should ask her intercession, confident that her motherly understanding and affection will lead her to act as mediatrix. Catholics can trust and love God more perfectly because of their affection for Mary and the encouragement which comes from the glory God has given her, a human person like themselves.[56]

e) The Church recommends the meditative recitation of the rosary. While outwardly emphasizing veneration of Mary, the rosary in reality leads through her to Jesus. The complete rosary essentially consists in reciting fifteen decades and meditating on the topic (the "mystery") assigned to each. Both the prayers and the topics of meditation have scriptural sources.

Someone correctly praying the rosary pays less attention to the framework of vocal prayer than the topics proposed for meditation. These include all the chief aspects of God's redemptive work: the Incarnation, Jesus' suffering and death, his resurrection and ascension, the sending of the Holy Spirit, and the first fruit (in Mary's glorification) of what God is doing through Jesus by the Spirit's sanctifying work. This meditative content sums up the eucharistic liturgy and the annual cycle of the Church's worship, and so the rosary can extend and prepare for the Eucharist much as the liturgy of the hours does.

Although the rosary lacks the richness of the liturgy of the hours, it has the advantage of simplicity. It is readily used by Catholics of all sorts in their individual, family, and communal prayer. The Church warmly recommends the rosary, and it is especially appropriate as a framework for the daily prayer of those unable to participate in the liturgy of the hours.

The morning, noon, and evening recitation of the Angelus also can be used to sanctify the parts of the day. The Angelus too summarizes God's saving work, since

---

of venerating Mary and the other saints, and direct bishops to eliminate abuses and excesses. *CIC,* c. 1187, directs that no act of public veneration be carried out except to those called *saint* or *blessed* by the Church's authority. Thus, one should publicly pray *for* rather than *to* others who lived and seem to have died in Christ. But privately—for example, within the family circle—Catholics rightly invoke the intercession of those friends and loved ones whom they are confident now live with the Lord.

56. See LG 65–68; John Paul II, *Redemptoris mater,* 38–47, *AAS* 79 (1987) 411–26, *OR,* 30 Mar. 1987, 11–14. Many of the principles underlying Vatican II's teaching on Mary are clearly and briefly stated by Pius XII, *Ad caeli reginam, AAS* 46 (1954) 633–37, *PE,* 251.34–45. Vatican II also vindicates using the title "mediatrix" of Mary, while carefully explaining that her role is subordinate to Jesus' unique mediation (see LG 62). Leo XIII, *Fidentem piumque animum, ASS* 29 (1896–97) 206–7, *PE,* 139.3, well accounts for the mediating role of Mary, following St. Thomas (*S.t.,* 3, q. 26, a. 1), who explains that it is compatible with the uniqueness of Jesus' mediation that others be mediators between God and human persons, insofar as they cooperate by preparing for or serving Jesus' work. Mary's unique cooperation, which she undertook by her *fiat,* is with the Incarnation itself, and so with the whole of Jesus' saving work and every grace he merited by it.

it recalls the Word's Incarnation and prays that "we may be brought by his passion and death to the glory of his resurrection."[57]

f) **Superstition in Catholic spirituality is grave in itself.** Genuine worship is based on the truth about God and creatures; it expresses love and reverence. It is superstitious to think God can be tricked or bargained with, that insincere outward religious behavior is sufficient to fulfill responsibilities to worship, or that religious feelings and experiences somehow make up for unrepented sins.

A manipulative attitude underlies the belief (involved, for example, in chain letters) that a certain number of prayers or a special form of religious practices will obtain favors, even apart from God's freely given mercy and faithfulness. Likewise, practices like lighting votive candles, carrying a rosary, and making the sign of the cross as a mere gesture cannot substitute for prayer. Such outward behavior should accompany prayer, not take its place.

When the Church disapproves alleged miracles and apparitions, continued devotion focusing on them is superstitious. To treat extraliturgical devotions as more important than the Eucharist and to evaluate the eucharistic liturgy by how it makes one feel are both mistaken attitudes, and both are superstitious.

In themselves, all forms of superstition show a false attitude toward God and a lack of genuine love and trust in him. Therefore, if freely chosen with sufficient reflection, superstitious practices are gravely sinful. Still, when their true character is clearly recognized, they are not likely to be very appealing. It seems likely, then, that people who sin in these matters often lack sufficient reflection and need catechesis to help them develop a more adequate understanding of religion.

3. Catholics May Worship with Others within Certain Limits

In general, those who worship together express unity as a worshiping community, common faith, and their specific commitment to their religious community and its form of worship. For this reason, one should never share in acts of worship inconsistent with Catholic faith.

Before Vatican II, the Church did not recognize and take into account the extent to which religious unity exists, especially among Christians, along with religious

---

57. On the rosary and the Angelus, see Paul VI, *Marialis cultus,* 40–55, *AAS* 66 (1974) 151–62; *The Pope Speaks* 19 (1974–75): 77–83. On the rosary as an element in sound spirituality: Louis Bouyer, Cong.Orat., *Introduction to Spirituality,* trans. Mary Perkins Ryan (Collegeville, Minn.: Liturgical Press, 1961), 87–94. The rosary is unique among extraliturgical devotions in the frequency and force with which the Church commends it. Leo XIII published an encyclical each year for sixteen years (1883–98) encouraging the rosary. *CIC,* c. 246, §3, and c. 663, §4, singles out the rosary for special mention in commending Marian devotion for seminarians and religious. Congregation for Bishops, *Ecclesiae imago (Directory on the Pastoral Ministry of Bishops),* 91, *EV* 4 (1971–73) 1322–25, *Documents on the Liturgy,* 838: "Among the devotions to be reverently preserved and spread among Christian families and communities, the holy Rosary of Mary stands out. It has been ceaselessly recommended by the popes as a kind of compendium of the Gospel and therefore as a model devotional practice recommended for the Church [note omitted] and splendidly confirmed by the practice of the saints." This document (see 90–91, *EV* 1320–25, *Documents on the Liturgy,* 837–38) also makes special mention of adoration of the Blessed Sacrament in and outside Mass, devotion to Jesus' sacred heart, veneration of Mary and the other saints, and the way of the cross.

divisions. But since the religious divisions between Catholics and other believers are not total, under certain conditions it is right to share in others' worship. Still, legitimate common worship cannot go beyond the unity actually existing between the other religious community and the Catholic Church. Thus, common worship should be avoided whenever it presupposes and expresses greater unity than really exists (see UR 8).

a) In many cases, one may pray in common with others. Although religiously divided in other respects, people who share belief in God often can pray together for common needs without introducing anything specific in which they differ. In praying with Jews or Moslems, for example, common scriptural material can be used. It is appropriate to join in such prayers, provided they involve nothing at odds with Catholic faith. Such authentic interfaith prayer is the work of the Holy Spirit, active in human hearts and moving humankind away from conflict and toward communion.[58]

As will be explained (in D.4.c), Catholics are encouraged to join in mutually acceptable prayer with Christians not in full communion with the Catholic Church. Moreover, aside from receiving communion (to be considered next), when a Catholic has a good reason to be present at the liturgical worship of other Christians, he or she may join in any of their prayers, hymns, and acts that are consonant with Catholic faith.[59]

b) One sometimes may seek grace through common worship. The validity of some sacraments requires that they be celebrated by a validly ordained minister. Since the Catholic Church recognizes the validity of orders and the other sacraments in the Eastern churches separated from the Catholic Church (see UR 15), participation in the liturgy of an Eastern church, provided one is welcome there, is encouraged if one otherwise would miss Mass on a Sunday or holy day of obligation. Such liturgical participation also fulfills one's Mass obligation whenever one has a good reason to be present at the liturgy of an Eastern church.

Moreover, when rightly participating in the eucharistic liturgy of an Eastern church, Catholics may under certain conditions receive Holy Communion.[60] The conditions are that the host church does not object, that Communion cannot otherwise be received, that receiving is necessary or would be to one's spiritual advantage, and that one avoids endorsing any false belief or acting as if existing differences were insignificant.[61]

---

58. See John Paul II, *Redemptoris missio*, 29, *AAS* 83 (1991) 274–75, *OR*, 28 Jan. 1991, 9.

59. See Secretariat for Promoting the Unity of Christians, *Ad totam ecclesiam*, 50, 59, *AAS* 59 (1967) 589, 591–92, Flannery, 1:498, 500.

60. See Secretariat for Promoting the Unity of Christians, *Ad totam ecclesiam*, 42, 44, 47, and 50. *AAS* 59 (1967) 587–89, Flannery, 1:496–98.

61. See *CIC*, c. 844, §§1–2. The canon also says (in §2) that under these same conditions Catholics may receive the sacraments of penance and anointing of the sick "from non-Catholic ministers in whose churches these sacraments are valid" (in practice, it seems, this means a priest of an Eastern Orthodox church). Since anyone can baptize, in case of necessity when an ordinary minister is not available Catholics may ask anyone available to baptize; for example, a Catholic woman suffering a dangerously premature birth rightly asks even a nonbelieving physician or nurse to baptize the child as soon as it is born (see c. 844, §1, and c. 861, §2).

c) **Mere presence at others' worship is not sharing in it.** Worship requires active participation of mind and will. Someone can be present without sharing in the worship of others. This is permissible for various reasons: to learn about other religions, to enjoy the esthetic values in their worship, and to fulfill various duties—by attending relatives' and friends' funerals and weddings, or being present at academic convocations, civic dedication ceremonies, and so on.

When present but not sharing in others' worship, it is right to show respect by silence and other signs, for example, sitting and standing when the worshipers do. But any specifically religious behavior should be avoided, since sincerely engaging in it would be participation, while engaging insincerely not only would be dishonest but would imply the profession of views contrary to Catholic faith.

d) **Sharing in worship at odds with faith always is a grave matter.** Someone who shares in worship professes the faith it embodies. Thus, Catholics who knowingly share in worship at odds with their faith either accept heresy (if they are sincere) or profess what they do not believe (if they are not). In either case, what they do is always grave matter.

Communion services and other sacramental rites requiring a minister with holy orders are necessarily at odds with Catholic faith when celebrated by someone not validly ordained. That is so not only if they embody a belief about the sacrament being administered different from the Catholic Church's faith, but even if they embody the Church's faith and are carried out with the right intention, for also embodied in every such sacramental rite are beliefs about the need for holy orders and the conditions for their validity. Participation, therefore, always is grave matter.

Catholics also should avoid sharing in prayers, hymns, and other acts involving anything at odds with their faith. Someone who makes little or no effort to judge what is and is not acceptable is negligent about preserving and professing the faith. Thus, when participating in the prayer and worship of Christians not fully in communion with the Catholic Church, one has a grave responsibility to discriminate carefully between what is and is not consonant with Catholic faith, and to avoid sharing in what is not.

Although lack of sufficient reflection undoubtedly lessens or eliminates the guilt of some who sin in this matter, such error threatens the integrity of personal faith and the effectiveness of witness to the gospel.

e) **Other prohibited sharing in worship also is grave matter.** Vatican II teaches that sharing in worship can be wrong even when it does not involve accepting falsehood: "Common participation in worship which harms the Church's unity, or involves . . . the danger of aberration in faith, of scandal and indifferentism is forbidden by divine law" (OE 26). Thus, the prospect of damage to the Church's unity or of any of these dangers limits the situations under which one may share in others' worship even when it is consistent with Catholic faith.

Catholics not only must avoid worship at odds with their faith but obey these additional norms regarding shared worship in order to promote genuine ecumenism and preserve the Catholic Church's existing unity. If the norms are widely ignored, real divisions will not be eliminated but will simply be made to seem insignificant even as they persist. Motivation to work for Church unity will be undermined, and

Catholics will more easily be led by subjective considerations to drift away from the Catholic Church and join some separated communion. Prohibited sharing in common worship therefore is a grave matter.[62]

Question D: How Should One Foster the Church's Unity, Peace, and Vitality?

Volume four will treat the special responsibilities of the Church's various sorts of members toward one another. Since individuals have different gifts (see Rom 12.4–8, 1 Cor 12.4–26), each member can build up the Church mainly by fulfilling his or her special responsibilities. The present treatment deals with only a few common responsibilities concerned with building up the Church by fostering her unity, peace, and vitality.

In considering these responsibilities, the various aspects of the Church's complex reality should be kept in mind. She is a communion of love among divine and human persons, and so must not be reduced to the measure of a merely human political society. She is a community of human persons with their human Lord Jesus and one another, and so responsible participation in the Church is just as demanding as membership in any human society. She is the sacrament of the kingdom for which Christians hope, and so should neither be simply identified with the kingdom nor regarded merely as an optional means to it. She is the herald of the gospel, sent by Jesus to the whole world, and so is never static, but always developing to embrace people of diverse cultures. She is the servant of all humankind, because she is the means of human cooperation in God's saving work, whose progress in the world is truly in humankind's interests and whose completion in heaven is humankind's only hope.

1. Catholics Should Keep in Mind What Truly Builds up the Church

To know how to build up a particular community, people must consider the sort of community it is and its purposes.

The Church is a uniquely intimate community: a communion of human persons with God, brought about by Jesus in the Holy Spirit.[63] The Church makes visible this communion with God, which he creates in and among human persons by revealing his truth and love in Jesus and offering sinful men and women the grace to repent and become members of the divine family. The Church, however, not only manifests divine-human communion, but is God's means of bringing it about. This she does chiefly by preaching the gospel, incorporating by baptism those who believe, and celebrating the Eucharist, which realizes Jesus' covenantal commu-

---

62. A sign of this is that the Church's law prescribes that anyone guilty of this sin is to be punished with a just penalty: *CIC*, c. 1365.

63. John Paul II, *Christifideles laici*, 18–20, *AAS* 81 (1989) 421–27, *OR*, 6 Feb. 1989, 6, beautifully articulates the reality of the Church as communion, which was taught by Vatican II and emphasized again by the 1985 extraordinary session of the Synod of Bishops. Also see Bruno Forte, *The Church, Icon of the Trinity: A Brief Study* (Boston: St. Paul Books, 1991), especially chapter three, "The Church as a Communion."

nion of God with his people. So, the Church can be called a *sacrament* of communion with God (see LG 1).

Being both divine-human communion and the sacrament of that communion, the Church is in many ways quite unlike a voluntary human association of free and independent individuals. She is far more like one body, a body with many members, each needing the others to form a living whole, and all utterly depending on their head (see LG 7). This image, the one body, is far more than a metaphor, since baptism really unites Christians with Jesus, and the Eucharist really enlivens them with his resurrection life.

Since God wills that everyone come to know his saving truth (see 1 Tm 2.3–6), the Church's communion potentially embraces the whole human family, restored to peace by being reconciled to God in Jesus and made part of God's family by the gift of the Spirit (see GS 92).

a) **One builds up the Church by seeing Jesus in her.** By laying down his life for the Church, Jesus shows his members how they should love her. He lives in the Church; he teaches, governs, and sanctifies through her pastors; he manifests himself also in every member's need for the others' loving care. As Jesus loved his sinful disciples and by the gift of the Spirit made them into a holy body for himself, so one should love the Church, including her human dimension, with the same love with which one loves Jesus himself.[64]

b) **Promoting and protecting the Church's unity build her up.** The Church's oneness ultimately is rooted in that of the Blessed Trinity, her one Lord, but it also involves unity of the hope of heavenly communion, to which the Trinity call humankind; of baptism, by which believers enter the Church; and of faith, which is the baptismal commitment (see Eph 4.4–6; cf. Jn 17.20–21, 1 Cor 12.4–7, Col 3.14).[65] Catholics will build up the Church if they "maintain the unity of the Spirit in the bond of peace" (Eph 4.3) by doing everything possible to protect and promote the Church's unity in faith and solidarity in hope, as well as striving to heal the Church's unity when it is injured.

c) **Democratic practices generally can build up a political society.** A political society organizes a group of people into a limited community for limited purposes. In many respects, members' interests are not common but potentially conflicting. Private interests also tend to distort public policies at the expense of the public interest. Moreover, every contemporary democratic society includes radical disagreements about the ultimate meaning of life, with the result that each such society's public policies reflect, not a single, sound world view, but a more or less

---

64. Paul VI, *Evangelii nuntiandi*, 16, *AAS* 68 (1976) 16, Flannery, 2:718: Some "declare that they are willing to love Christ but not the church. The absurdity of this distinction appears clearly from those words of the gospel: 'He who rejects you rejects me' (Lk 10.16 [and references to Sts. Cyprian, Augustine, and John Chrysostom]). How can anyone claim to love Christ without loving his church in face of that most striking testimony given by St. Paul: 'Christ loved the church and gave himself up for her' (Eph 5.25)." Also see Pius XII, *Mystici corporis Christi, AAS* 35 (1943) 238–39, *PE,* 225.92–95.

65. On Eph 4.3–6, see Markus Barth, *Ephesians: Translation and Commentary on Chapters 4–6,* Anchor Bible, 34a (Garden City, N.Y.: Doubleday, 1974), 457–72. A relevant magisterial exposition of Eph 4.3–16: Leo XIII, *Satis cognitum, ASS* 28 (1895–96) 720–23, *PE,* 138.9.

unstable consensus; and, while common experience and reason contribute to that consensus, so do common passions and sophistry.

Thus, upright members of a political society often can build it up by practices characteristic of democratic politics: electing public officials and/or otherwise helping to determine important matters of public policy, striving to protect their own interests against public encroachment and the interests of others, dissenting from and even struggling against official policies which seem unwise or unjust, and, above all, defending religious liberty against official attempts to decide ultimate questions.

d) **The Church is very unlike a political society.** As a uniquely intimate communion, established by God's grace, uniting human persons with God in Jesus, and in this way bonding them to one another, the Church is quite unlike any other community.[66] And to the limited extent she resembles other communities, the Church is more like the family than she is like political society.[67] The family is an intimate community involving its members in their whole being; they share a common life and should love one another in such a way that each one's interests are the interests of all the others. Even in the intimacy of familial communion, however, no member depends so totally on others as each and every Christian depends on the Lord Jesus.

Unfortunately, pervasive and longstanding clericalism, by reducing the laity to passivity and treating as normative forms of spirituality proper to priests and religious, has given Catholics a misleading experience of the Church. All too often the faithful feel themselves to be, not brothers and sisters joined in intimate communion and full cooperators in carrying out the Church's mission, but citizens in a rather weak monarchic or aristocratic political society, whose government lacks necessary checks and balances, and whose inefficient clerical and lay bureaucracy often is impervious to advice and criticism. Still, Catholics should not allow their experience of clericalism to obscure the Church's nature as intimate communion.

e) **Democracy in the Church is contrary to submission to the Lord.** Appropriately, some practices in the Church are similar to those of a democratic political society: inasmuch as the bishops united with the pope share authority with him, leadership is collegial (see LG 22); the faithful should contribute to each pastor's use of authority by making their needs and desires known, and appropriately expressing their opinions (see LG 37); and elective processes sometimes are used in the Church, and could be used more widely, as they sometimes have been in the past.

---

66. See Rudolf Schnackenburg, *The Church in the New Testament* (New York: Herder and Herder, 1965), 22–35 and 118–40.

67. Pius XII, Address to Members of the Tribunal of the Sacred Rota (2 Oct. 1945), *AAS* 37 (1945) 256–62, *Papal Teachings: The Church,* ed. Benedictine Monks of Solesmes, trans. E. O'Gorman, R.S.C.J. (Boston: St. Paul Editions, 1962), 597–602, provides a lucid explanation of the difference between the Church and a democratic polity. Cardinal Joseph Ratzinger, *Church, Ecumenism and Politics: New Essays in Ecclesiology* (New York: Crossroad, 1988), 191–203, explains the difference between political freedom and Christian freedom: the latter is full membership in God's household; the Christian's basic right is to the full faith.

Still, authority in the Church has a different basis and function from authority in a democratic political society. Jesus is Lord, and pastors govern in his name.[68] Their pastoral authority is a service entirely subordinate to the gifts of grace which God's people have received (see LG 18–19, DV 10).[69] By contrast, in a democratic political society, leaders govern in the name of the people.

Deliberation in the Church seeks to discern God's will through authoritative interpretation of revelation, consideration of the signs of the times in the light of faith, and so on. Deliberation in political society seeks to implement the people's common interests and to resolve their conflicts of interest fairly.

Plainly, therefore, just as the Church's government should not be a monarchy or an aristocracy, neither should it be a democracy. Democracy is appropriate in the rule of a community of equals, but not for leading God's people in their communion with their one Lord and with one another.[70]

f) **Pursuing special interests is at odds with unity of hope.** Since the Church's members have, and should use, diverse gifts, they also have diverse concerns and the right to pursue them (see LG 12–13). It does not follow, however, that they build up the Church by striving to pursue their individual or group concerns in competition with other segments of the Church, especially if in doing so they treat the Church's leaders as merely another interest group.

Unlike any political society, the Church has one common interest, the hope of heaven, which wholly embraces, yet transcends, all the other authentic concerns of her members. So, the true interest of each member and part of the Church is to build

68. John Paul II, Address to Bishops of Brazil, 6, *AAS* 82 (1990) 913, *OR,* 26 Feb. 1990, 2, explains that episcopal authority is not delegated by the people: "Being of sacramental origin, this authority is exclusively of divine origin, and remains such; it has no need, therefore, of ratification by anyone else." Politicizing the Church is not proper: "In that case the People of God would be placed on the same level as 'people' in a secular sense. That would in some way run the risk of subordinating the episcopal ministry to choices, even at the level of faith and Christian life, made on a human scale. We would have in that case a reversal of terms and values: instead of the People of God, God of the People."

69. See "The Priestly Ministry (1970)," 4–6, in International Theological Commission, *Texts and Documents: 1969–1985,* ed. Michael Sharkey (San Francisco: Ignatius Press, 1989), 23–66.

70. Even Jesus' teaching is not his own, and the Spirit does not speak on his own (see Jn 7.16, 16.13). Everything comes from the Father (see Jas 1.17–18). Congregation for the Doctrine of the Faith, *Instruction on the Ecclesial Vocation of the Theologian,* 39, *AAS* 82 (1990) 1568, *OR,* 2 July 1990, 4, teaches: "The Church, which has her origin in the unity of the Father, Son, and Holy Spirit (LG 4), is a mystery of communion. In accordance with the will of her founder, she is organized around a hierarchy established for the service of the Gospel and the People of God who live by it. After the pattern of the members of the first community, all the baptized with their own proper charisms are to strive with sincere hearts for a harmonious unity in doctrine, life, and worship (cf. Acts 2.42). This is a rule which flows from the very being of the Church. For this reason, standards of conduct, appropriate to civil society or the workings of a democracy, cannot be purely and simply applied to the Church. Even less can relationships within the Church be inspired by the mentality of the world around it (cf. Rom 12.2). Polling public opinion to determine the proper thing to think or do, opposing the Magisterium by exerting the pressure of public opinion, making the excuse of a 'consensus' among theologians, maintaining that the theologian is the prophetical spokesman of a 'base' or autonomous community which would be the source of all truth, all this indicates a grave loss of the sense of truth and of the sense of the Church."

up the whole by putting particular gifts at the service of other members and parts (see 1 Cor 12–14, 1 Pt 4.10–11). John XXIII teaches in respect to Jesus' peace: "Those who adhere to this peace must be ready to renounce their own interests and advantages for the sake of truth and justice, according to the words: 'Seek first the kingdom of God and his justice' (Mt 6.33)."[71]

g) Dissent leads to polarization and destroys the Church's peace. In a democratic society, it can be constructive to dissent from official policies and even to resist them, for they are grounded only in a human consensus, which may well be mistaken and at odds with the common good. But in the Church, whose policies are grounded on faith and directed toward salvation, these tactics are merely divisive. The Church does leave some matters open to controversy, and discussing them can be constructive if it helps determine the truth about some doubtful matter or the best solution to some problem. But dissent from constant and most firm teaching attacks truth, which is the principle of the Church's communion and common life:

> The Church "is like a sacrament, a sign and instrument, that is, of communion with God and of unity among all men" (LG 1). Consequently, to pursue concord and communion is to enhance the force of her witness and credibility. To succumb to the temptation of dissent, on the other hand, is to allow the "leaven of infidelity to the Holy Spirit" to start to work [note omitted].[72]

Such dissent also quickly leads to polarization. For those who do not accept the dissenting view must resist it for the sake of the authentic peace of the Church, a peace which, as John XXIII teaches,

> is not completely untroubled and serene; it is active, not calm and motionless. In short, this is a peace that is ever at war. It wars with every sort of error, including that which falsely wears the face of truth; it struggles against the enticements of vice, against those enemies of the soul, of whatever description, who can weaken, blemish, or destroy our innocence or Catholic faith.[73]

Contending over issues which bear on salvation itself, the opposed groups often disagree not merely about means, but about the Church's very purpose. Thus, the Church's peace is disturbed and her unity harmed.

h) Pluralism about ultimates destroys unity of faith. A legitimate pluriformity does exist in the Church and is to be maintained, for example, the diverse rites and spiritualities, and the many sound theologies reflecting on the one faith. Pluralism about ultimates is an entirely different matter. Even in political society,

---

71. John XXIII, *Ad Petri cathedram, AAS* 51 (1959) 518, *PE,* 263.95. Pursuit of partisan agendas against the program of the Church's pastors leads to excessive criticism. Of such criticism, John Paul II, *Redemptor hominis,* 4, *AAS* 71 (1979) 263, *PE,* 278.8, teaches: "Criticism too should have its just limits. Otherwise it ceases to be constructive and does not reveal truth, love and thankfulness for the grace in which we become sharers principally and fully in and through the Church. Furthermore such criticism does not express an attitude of service but rather a wish to direct the opinion of others in accordance with one's own, which is at times spread abroad in too thoughtless a manner."

72. Congregation for the Doctrine of the Faith, *Instruction on the Ecclesial Vocation of the Theologian,* 40, *AAS* 82 (1990) 1568, *OR,* 2 July 1990, 4.

73. John XXIII, *Ad Petri cathedram, AAS* 51 (1959) 517, *PE,* 263.93.

pluralism which leaves room for diverse world views can be dangerous insofar as it occasions relativism; yet it also is good insofar as it allows persons to seek and find the truth, especially religious truth, and freely commit themselves to it (see DH 2–3).[74] But in the Church such pluralism is entirely out of place, because only one world view is based on Jesus' gospel, which, as the Council of Trent definitively teaches, is the source of all saving truth and all sound moral teaching (see DS 1501/783; cf. DV 7). The Church hears this gospel with reverence and proclaims it with faith (see DV 1, DH 1), knowing well, as John XXIII teaches, "that there is no other truth than the one truth she treasures; that there can be no 'truths' in contradiction of it."[75] Therefore, pluralism about ultimates does not build up the Church: "The pluralism of fundamentally opposed positions instead leads to dissolution, destruction and the loss of identity."[76]

2. The Faithful Should Obey the Church's Pastoral Leaders

Because the Church, like any other society, has a definite structure, Church membership entails certain rights and duties.[77] All Catholics should obey the Church's pastoral leaders, the pope and their own bishops, for the same reasons loyal members of any society submit to their leaders' authority. Unlike other societies, however, the Church has a divinely given mission and structure (see CMP, 11.G), and these lead to special responsibilities with respect to obedience. The Church's unity, peace, and vitality are fostered by accepting and fulfilling these responsibilities.

a) **Faith and love ground the duty to obey Church authority.** The duty of obedience to Church authority has special grounds, over and above the moral basis for any genuine authority-obedience relationship. People enter into the Church's life by the baptismal commitment of faith, and it is this commitment, nothing less, which grounds their duty to obey the Church's precepts (see DS 1621/864). Even when those precepts might well be otherwise, they are to be treated reverently. Moreover, there is a special sense in which the Church's pastoral authority comes from God. The Father gives divine authority to Jesus, and he, to complete his saving mission, authorizes the apostles and their successors to exercise authority in his name (see Mt 16.19, 18.18, 28.19–20). As he obeyed the Father, so the faithful ought to obey the Church's pastoral leaders (see LG 37), out of love for Jesus and in order to build up his covenantal communion.[78]

---

74. For a further explanation of the expression "world view" used here, see New Catholic Encyclopedia, s.v. "Weltanschauung."

75. John XXIII, Ad Petri cathedram, AAS 51 (1959) 513, PE, 263.70.

76. Synod of Bishops, Second Extraordinary Assembly (1985), Final "Relatio", 2.C.2, EV 9 (1983–85) 1764–65, OR, 16 Dec. 1985, 7.

77. CIC, c. 96: "By baptism one is incorporated into the Church of Christ and is constituted a person in it with duties and rights which are proper to Christians, in keeping with their condition." A good summary of the authority-obedience relationship within the Church, renewed in terms of the concept of dialogue: Paul VI, Ecclesiam Suam, AAS 56 (1964) 657–58, PE, 271.113–15.

78. The duty to obey the pope and one's own bishop is analogous to the responsibility to give religious assent to their teachings which call for such assent. The two are linked in CIC, c. 212, §1: "The Christian faithful, conscious of their own responsibility, are bound by Christian obedience to follow what the sacred pastors, as representatives of Christ, declare as teachers of

b) Church authority extends to inner acts but is not totalitarian. Generally, a society's common good requires only cooperation in outward behavior. But, the Church's common good consists primarily in divine-human communion, which depends on interior acts of mind and will, and so her authority extends to her members' whole persons, including their interior acts.

Even so, the Church's pastoral authority is not totalitarian. For it is subordinate to faith and love, which redeem and perfect human persons, rather than subjecting them to some ideology, with its deceptive promises. Moreover, although pastoral authority sometimes is abused, when properly exercised it appeals solely to conscience, without the support of coercion, for the obedience of the faithful.[79]

c) The Church's leaders should exercise their authority reasonably. In the Church, as in any other society, the use of authority must safeguard the equal personal dignity of her members: "In virtue of their rebirth in Christ there exists among all the Christian faithful a true equality with regard to dignity and the activity whereby all cooperate in the building up of the Body of Christ in accord with each one's own condition and function."[80] That the Church is a communion of faith and love does not mean popes and other bishops may ignore the conditions necessary for the just use of authority in any human community. (On these conditions, see 7.E.3–4, below.)

Like any community's leaders, for instance, the Church's pastoral leaders can make wise decisions only if they deliberate well. The other members of the community should contribute to their deliberation by responsibly expressing their opinions on matters concerning the Church's good:

> The Christian faithful are free to make known their needs, especially spiritual ones, and their desires to the pastors of the Church.
>
> In accord with the knowledge, competence and preeminence which they possess, they have the right and even at times a duty to manifest to the sacred pastors their opinion on matters which pertain to the good of the Church, and they have a right to make their opinion known to the other Christian faithful, with due regard for the integrity of faith and morals and reverence toward their pastors, and with consideration for the common good and the dignity of persons.[81]

---

the faith or determine as leaders of the Church." On the specific authority-obedience relationship which obtains in institutes of the consecrated life, see PC 14; Congregation for Religious and Secular Institutes, *Evangelica testificatio,* 23–28, AAS 63 (1971) 509–13, Flannery, 1:691–94; *CIC,* c. 601 and c. 618.

79. See Pius XII, Address to Members of the Tribunal of the Sacred Rota (2 Oct. 1945), *AAS* 37 (1945) 256–62, *Papal Teachings: The Church,* 597–602; Paul VI, Address to the Prelates, Auditors, and Officials of the Tribunal of the Sacred Roman Rota, AAS 62 (1970) 111–18, *OR,* 12 Feb. 1970, 6–7.

80. *CIC,* c. 208.

81. *CIC,* c. 212, §§2–3; cf. LG 37. For a fuller statement of the right and responsibility of all the faithful to contribute to public opinion in the Church: Pontifical Commission for the Instruments of Social Communication, *Communio et progressio,* 116–21, AAS 63 (1971) 634–36, Flannery, 1:330–32. This document very forcefully states both the right and the responsibility: "Catholics should be fully aware of the real freedom to speak their minds which stems from a 'feeling for the faith' and from love" (*AAS* 634, Flannery, 330); "This free dialogue within the Church does no injury to her unity and solidarity. It nurtures concord and the meeting of minds by permitting the free play of the variations of public opinion. But in order that this dialogue may

d) The responsibility to obey Church authorities has limits. Beginning with a presumption in favor of obedience to pastors, one always should obey unless, after considering everything (including the grounds of that presumption), one judges it more probable that it would be wrong to obey or morally certain that obedience is not required. If the choice lies between obeying the Church's pastors and political authorities, the presumption in favor of the Church's authority should be maintained, since the Church should be loved more than one's country.

Yet a Catholic's responsibility to obey Church authorities is limited in four ways.

First, Church law and the precepts of Church authorities are hardly likely to require anything immoral; but if they did, one's responsibility to God—to avoid immorality—would prevail over the duty to obey.

Second, since the Church's pastors exercise authority for the sake of her proper mission, their decisions call for obedience only insofar as they direct members of the Church to act in ways relevant to that mission.

Third, conflicts of duties can demand that an individual not obey some precept otherwise calling for obedience.

Fourth, within the narrow limits of its legitimate use, epikeia applies to Church law (see *CMP*, 11.G.6).

e) Schism is disobedience in its most extreme and radical form. A schismatic intentionally rebels against hierarchical authority which he or she knows to be legitimately exercised. Instead of acting obediently as parts of the one body, schismatic individuals and groups act as if they were autonomous wholes, independent of the whole which is the Catholic Church; they commit the sin of schism by carrying disobedience so far that they purposely separate themselves from the Church's unity, which is realized by the submission of Jesus' members to him and by their communion with one another.

Since the pope is Jesus' vicar, Catholics who separate themselves from him divide themselves from Jesus and thus divide the Church. Schismatics refuse to be subject to the pope, either directly or by rejecting communion with those loyal to him. Thus: "Schism is the refusal of submission to the Roman Pontiff or of communion with the members of the Church subject to him."[82]

Those who simply disobey a precept or law, while acknowledging its authority, are not schismatic. Neither are those who refuse to submit to a particular ecclesiastical precept or law they believe to be illegitimate. Nor are religious who refuse to submit to their superiors but do submit to the pope and their own bishop. At the

---

go in the right direction it is essential that charity is in command even when there are differing views. Everyone in this dialogue should be animated by the desire to serve and to consolidate unity and cooperation. There should be a desire to build, not to destroy. There should be a deep love for the Church and a compelling desire for its unity. Christ made love the sign by which men can recognize his true Church and therefore his true followers (cf. Jn 17.21)" (*AAS* 635, Flannery, 331). Of course, such communications should be made through suitable channels and as one would make them to Jesus himself: "Let this [expression of opinion] be done, if the situation allows, through the institutions set up for the purpose by the Church, and always in truth, in courage, and in prudence, with reverence and charity toward those who by reason of their sacred office represent the person of Christ" (LG 37).

82. *CIC*, c. 751; c. 1364, §1, provides that a schismatic incurs automatic excommunication.

time of the Reformation, faithful Catholics who sided with the pope against their unfaithful bishops were not schismatic. While schismatics often are also heretics, it is possible to be in schism over matters of law and policy without rejecting any truth of faith.[83]

f) Disobedience to Church authority often is a grave matter. Because of its special grounds in faith and love, the responsibility to obey the decisions of Church authority is especially serious. Although this duty has the usual limits of all obedience, and although the sin of disobedience to Church authority admits of parvity of matter, in itself such disobedience is a grave matter. Plainly, there can be no parvity of matter in a regular practice of ignoring the decisions of Church authority or conforming to them only insofar as necessary to avoid sanctions or other unwanted consequences. Insubordination—refusal to recognize and accept the proper authority of ecclesiastical superiors—is a very grave matter, for it verges on schism and is opposed to the act of faith, insofar as that act is a human commitment to the Church as a covenantal communion.[84] Schism itself is an even graver sin for it is directly contrary to the Church's communion of love, which is her greatest good (see *S.t.*, 2–2, q. 39, a. 2, ad 3).

g) Contestation tends to schism and is a grave matter. In the years after Vatican II, Paul VI frequently deplored the widespread contestation which began with the Council and has continued since.[85] By "contestation" he meant active,

---

83. Among those who recently have been or appeared to be in schism: the Patriotic Association of Chinese Catholics, Marcel Lefebvre and his followers, the so-called Popular Church in Nicaragua, various groups (some reactionary and some revolutionary) which set themselves up as worshiping communities in defiance of their bishops, and the many families and individuals who reject papal authority and leave the Church. John Paul II, Letter to the Bishops of Nicaragua, *AAS* 74 (1982) 1108–13, *OR*, 6 Sept. 1982, 6–7, points out that the so-called Popular Church leads to the autonomy of the basic communities from the Church's legitimate pastors and teachers.

84. Those who not only disobey ecclesiastical laws or precepts but engage in contestation or persist in disobedience after receiving a warning from the Holy See or their own bishop are insubordinate. The gravity of persistence in disobedience is indicated by the fact that it is subject to canonical punishment: *CIC*, c. 1371, §2. The gravity of opposing Church authority also is made clear by c. 1373: "One who publicly either stirs up hostilities or hatred among subjects against the Apostolic See or against an ordinary on account of some act of ecclesiastical power or ministry or incites subjects to disobey them is to be punished by an interdict or by other just penalties."

85. See Paul VI, Homily at Holy Thursday Mass (3 Apr. 1969), *AAS* 61 (1969) 240–41, *OR*, 10 Apr. 1969, 4: "There is talk of renewal in the doctrine and in the conscience of the Church of God; but how can the living and true Church be authentic and persistent if the complex structure that forms it and defines it a spiritual and social 'mystical body', is today so often and so gravely corroded by dissent and challenge and by forgetfulness of its hierarchical structure, and is countered in its divine and indispensable constituent charism, its pastoral authority? How can it claim to be a Church, that is a united people, even though locally broken up and historically and legitimately diversified, when a practically schismatic ferment is dividing it, subdividing it and breaking it into groups which are more than anything else zealous for arbitrary and fundamentally egoistical autonomy, masked by Christian pluralism or liberty of conscience?" See also Paul VI's apostolic exhortation calling for an end of contestation: *Paterna cum benevolentia, AAS* 67 (1975) 5–23, *OR*, 26 Dec. 1974, 1–4. Also: Synod of Bishops, First General Assembly (1967), *Ratione habita, EV* 2 (1963–67) 1382–83, Flannery, 2:664, noted an element of this contestation: "Truths of the Faith are falsely understood or explained, and in the developing process of understanding doctrine its essential continuity is neglected." This document as a whole very straightforwardly and usefully faces the challenge of contestation in its doctrinal and theological aspects.

public insubordination. A notable example is the radical theological dissent from the Church's constant and most firm moral teaching. This dissent not only denies the truth of the teaching but challenges the hierarchy's pastoral authority by proposing dissenting opinions as norms which may be followed in practice (see *CMP*, 36.Int).

Often the challenge employs the methods of protest movements in political society, for example, using the communications media to foster dissatisfaction with existing laws and policies, forcing change by anticipating it, and pressuring leaders by conducting or threatening public demonstrations, withholding contributions, and so on. Those who engage in contestation lead others to refuse to accept hierarchical, especially papal, authority even to the point of rejecting it entirely, leaving the Church, and so ending in schism. Thus, contestation always is a grave matter, though not all who engage in it know what they are doing.

3. Catholics Should Support the Church and Her Life in Many Ways

The whole life of the Church is centered in the Eucharist, which calls every Catholic to active participation. Those who celebrate the Eucharist together are the People of God, the Church, and each of them should contribute to the Church's life and support her.

Chapter two included a treatment of common responsibilities with respect to the Church's mission. But all her members also have responsibilities with regard to her inner life. Some are common to all or almost all Catholics, and only these are treated here. Many others, including those of the Church's pastoral leaders, must be taken into account to provide balance to the responsibilities discussed here; they will be treated in volume four.

a) Everyone should pray for the Church. The Church is a creature of God's mercy. Depending totally on God for her salvific work, she has as her first need divine light and power. These necessary gifts cannot be taken for granted, as if they were the Church's permanent possessions. Rather, she receives them at each moment by the grace of the Holy Spirit, and so they are obtained only by united and persistent prayer. Thus, one should support the Church primarily by praying for her: that her pastors will fulfill their ministry, that her members will discern and accept the vocations to which God calls them, and so on.[86]

b) Christians should help one another follow Jesus faithfully. As members of a good family rally to the aid of any member whose life is in danger, so faithful Christians rally to the aid of any fellow disciple of Jesus whose spiritual life is in danger, for instance, they aid unwed mothers so that they are less tempted to have abortions and are better able to deal with their problems.

Speaking of the mutual help Christians owe one another in struggling against sin, Paul says: "Bear one another's burdens, and in this way you will fulfill the law of Christ" (Gal 6.2). This law is, primarily, the love given by the Holy Spirit, which

---

86. Paul VI, General Audience (2 Apr. 1969), *AAS* 61 (1969) 269–70, *OR*, 10 Apr. 1969, 3, asks for loyalty and prayer for the Church in her sufferings. United with Jesus, she shares in his sufferings, undergoing persecution, repression, and disloyalty, just as he did. Loyalty and prayer, not nervousness and discouragement, are needed in this situation.

makes Christians one body in Jesus. If members of the Church bear one another's burdens in struggling against sin, they fulfill this law in two ways: they put into action their fellowship as members of Jesus, and they overcome grave sin which alone drives out charity.

Societies generally stand by members whose welfare is gravely threatened in respect to commonly recognized values, but the less sympathetic a society is to Christian faith, the more it ignores many values essential to Christian life, fails to help protect them, and even attacks them. Thus, the special responsibility of Christians to give one another mutual support in avoiding and overcoming sin becomes more exigent as the surrounding culture becomes less sympathetic to faith.

An important but often neglected way to help others avoid and overcome sin is to admonish those who seem to be sinning. Every members' sins wound the Church, but she is harmed in a special way when pastors and other leading members of the Church seriously neglect their responsibilities, abuse their power, or commit shameful sins. Hence, every Catholic has a special responsibility to admonish such apparent sinners. To be successful and beneficial, admonition must be a work of Christian love, carried out with prudence (see 4.E.1.e, h).

c) **Every Catholic should contribute services when possible.** Dioceses and parishes depend heavily for their vitality on the contributed services of their members. Moreover, every service to the Church is a service to Jesus in his members. So, people asked by their bishops or parish priests to serve in some way should readily respond, unless prevented by other responsibilities. Canon law expressly states this responsibility in one specific matter: pastors are to use the services of clerics, religious, and lay faithful (especially, but not only, catechists) in the essential work of catechesis; "all of these are not to refuse to furnish their services willingly unless they are legitimately impeded."[87] If the bishop or pastor asks for assistance one cannot give, one should offer one's excuse and, if possible, help identify someone who can supply the needed service.

d) **If one can, one should help meet the Church's material needs.** The Old Testament precept of tithing does not bind Christians (see *S.t.*, 2–2, q. 87, a. 1), but the underlying moral responsibility to support religious activities remains. The Church needs material means for divine worship, apostolic and charitable works, and the support of her ministers. In accord with their ability, all who can should contribute goods or money to help meet these needs.

Still, those who can contribute nothing are fully entitled to the Church's services, and should neither hesitate to ask for them nor be denied them.[88] On the other hand, the right of ministers to support (see Mt 10.9–10, 1 Cor 9.11–14) and the Church's other needs justly require larger contributions from the wealthy. Even if they belong to wealthy parishes and dioceses, their contributions should be substantial, because there also are very poor dioceses and parishes, whose needs make a claim on the

87. *CIC*, c. 776.
88. *CIC*, c. 222, §1, and cc. 1260–63, spell out the general obligation of all the faithful to assist with the needs of the Church. C. 848 warns clerics not to deprive the poor of the sacraments; c. 1181 says that care is "to be taken in funeral rites against any favoritism toward persons and against depriving the poor of the funeral rites which are their due."

wealthier ones, all being joined in the Catholic Church's communion of love (cf. 2 Cor 8–9).[89]

Moreover, the People of God need facilities which are truly adequate for divine worship: church buildings that are beautiful, well-equipped, and well-maintained. Wealthy Catholics sometimes refuse to contribute for this purpose on the ground that they prefer to support charitable works. But this excuse is not valid for anyone who can do both things without neglecting some other responsibility, and most wealthy people can do both by forgoing goods and services they have no obligation to obtain and enjoy.

e) One should prudently fulfill the responsibility to contribute. Someone might object that people cannot be expected to contribute services and funds every time the pastor or the bishop asks, and no matter how questionable the project or proposed use of the money. Indeed, prudent judgments are required; time, energy, and resources should not be given to questionable purposes. But one need not support anything questionable; there are virtually unlimited opportunities to fulfill these responsibilities, because the Church has many unquestionable needs, not only in one's own parish, diocese, or nation but in the whole world.

Only when the Church's law or a precept of one's bishop so specifies is there a strictly defined duty to contribute services and money, and usually there is none. So, while those served by a parish should contribute their fair share to its support, other available resources can be used where one judges them to be most needed. Someone doing this will be fully justified in refusing requests which he or she judges to be less reasonable.

f) Everyone should protect the Church's honor. While avoiding triumphalism and being ready to acknowledge defects in the Church, Catholics should avoid slandering her and should be ready to defend her against lies and mistaken opinions. At all times they should bear in mind that their behavior is likely to be taken by outsiders as representative, and so should try not to do anything which would bring discredit to the household of faith. When the Church suffers from the shameful misdeeds of a leading member, no one should distance himself or herself from the shame by joining the company of scorners; rather, everyone should accept some share in the shame and work to heal the wound.

g) Everyone should foster vocations to the priesthood and diaconate. Since the ordained priesthood and diaconate provide the necessary ministries of the word and sacraments to the whole Church, every member shares a common duty to foster vocations to this service.[90] Everyone also should pray for priests and deacons, since these ministries are a divine gift to the Church, by which the greater gifts of the word and the Eucharist are available.

Catholics also can foster vocations by properly appreciating the specific dignity of holy orders, a consecration to act as Jesus' proxy, through whom he continues to teach, govern, and sanctify his Church. This is an entirely different matter from

---

89. Since those who contribute more are only doing their duty, they should not expect recognition or better treatment than those who lack means (see Jas 2.1–7).

90. See *CIC*, c. 233, §1.

trying to encourage vocations to the diaconate and priesthood by appealing to inappropriate motives, for example, desire for status, for a role of service other than that proper to ordained ministry, or even for sanctity, regarded as reserved for an elite. Such appeals encourage the illusions of some who are not truly called to the diaconate or priesthood, while repelling others who are.

h) **Everyone should foster and promote the religious state of life.** The way of life of those consecrated by profession of the evangelical counsels of poverty, chastity, and obedience has a special place in the life and holiness of the Church (see LG 43–44). All have a duty to promote this state of life.[91]

Encouraging vocations to religious life is one way to fulfill this responsibility. Another is by financial support, especially of those religious institutes whose needs are great because their apostolates are not self-sustaining or the number of gainfully employed members is inadequate to care for the growing number of elderly members, who gave years of service to the Church. Still another way is by constantly showing respect and Christian appreciation for those committed to religious life, while firmly rejecting anything which ridicules or belittles the three evangelical counsels or those committed to them.

i) **Everyone should contribute appropriately to missionary work.** By her very nature, the whole Church is missionary: Jesus sends her to carry on the mission given him by the Father (see AG 2, 35).[92] The most characteristic expression of the Church's missionary nature is her ongoing effort to implant herself among the peoples and groups where the faith has not yet taken root. Every member of the Church shares responsibility for this task. Everyone can and should offer prayers and do works of penance for this purpose, contribute materially to it as much as possible, encourage those called to give their whole lives to it, and be prepared to cooperate in other ways if the occasion offers (see AG 36).[93]

To be sure, God wills all to be saved, and draws toward himself even those who through no fault of their own do not know Jesus and his gospel (see LG 16, GS 22). But only those who do know Jesus and his gospel can be moved by the hope of heaven to live consistently in accord with moral truth despite the costs of doing so in this fallen world. Moreover, salvation—sharing in God's kingdom—is a truly personal relationship with God in Jesus, and with one's fellows in the human communion of the new covenant, Jesus' Church. People of whom it can only be said that they somehow belong to the Church despite never having heard the gospel can hardly play their full part in her life and are deprived of the benefits of conscious membership, especially the hope and joy of sharing in the Eucharist, and also the other helps to salvation available only in the Church. Thus, love impels every

91. See *CIC*, c. 574, §1. *Religious state of life* is used here in its broad sense, which includes the condition of members of secular institutes and societies of apostolic life.

92. See Manuel de Toya, O.P., "Visión misionera de la fe en el Nuevo Testamento," *La ciencia tomista* 95 (1968): 605–43.

93. *CIC*, c. 781: "Since the entire Church is missionary by its nature and since the work of evangelization is to be viewed as a fundamental duty of the people of God, all the Christian faithful, conscious of their own responsibility in this area, are to assume their own role in missionary work." For the specification of this role: Pius XII, *Fidei donum, AAS* 49 (1957) 238–44, *PE*, 257.48–67; John Paul II, *Redemptoris missio*, 77–82, *AAS* 83 (1991) 324–29, *OR*, 28 Jan. 1991, 16–17.

Christian to do his or her part in making Jesus and his gospel known to all who are still unaware of them (see LG 17).

Some today reject or disdain missionary work on a more profound basis. They claim that non-Christian religions offer equally valid, parallel ways of salvation for those who follow them faithfully. But this is not so. Not all the great religions can be equally valid, for they contradict one another on important matters, such as the significance of bodily life and death, the cause of human misery, and the way of being saved from it. Although non-Christian religions do include important truths and elements of real value, they also include important errors and defects. They do not have the whole truth about God as a communion of three divine persons, about human persons created in his image, about human freedom and sin, about the redemptive Incarnation and the sacraments, or about the heavenly kingdom for which everyone on earth should hope. False beliefs about these matters have bad consequences: moral errors and humanly destructive religious and social practices, which result in great miseries and hopelessness.[94]

j) Everyone should reveal impediments to sacred commitments. The commitments to marriage and the ordained priesthood are sacramentally consecrated; they establish sacred bonds between those who make them and Jesus present in his Church. On the reality of these bonds and the fulfillment of the attendant responsibilities, important spiritual effects depend: the genuineness of sacraments administered by a priest and the sanctification of marriage and family life. So, only those truly suited to be ordained or married should receive these sacraments.

The Church specifies certain conditions called "impediments" under which someone cannot or should not be married or ordained. A person who thinks there may be some impediment to a pending ordination or marriage should inform the pastor or local ordinary, who will apply the Church's law to determine whether or not there is an impediment.[95]

k) Every group should maintain its solidarity with the Church. Faithful Catholics often establish voluntary associations to promote common religious, charitable, and apostolic ends. Such groups should give primacy to helping their members respond to the universal call to holiness, and their purposes, organization, methods, and activities should be in accord with Catholic faith, moral teaching, and Church order. If they are, their members think and act with the Church, without imagining that only they fully grasp the gospel's truth and know how to put it into practice. These groups should bear witness to the faith, adapt themselves to the Church's apostolic goals, and work to further them. They also should maintain sincere and harmonious relationships with the Church's pastors. Communion with the pope and the local bishop should be shown by ready acceptance of their

---

94. A reply to the objection considered here: John Paul II, *Redemptoris missio,* 4–11, *AAS* 83 (1991) 252–60, *OR,* 28 Jan. 1991, 5–6; John Paul emphasizes that Jesus is the only savior, through whom not only faithful Christians but all people of good will reach heaven.

95. *CIC,* c. 1043 (with respect to sacred orders) and c. 1069 (with respect to marriage) state the universal duty to reveal impediments to the pastor or ordinary. While the canons do not say so, the importance of this duty suggests that failure to fulfill it without a just cause would be a grave matter.

teachings and pastoral initiatives. Moreover, without the authorization of the competent ecclesiastical authority, no group may use *Catholic* in its name.[96]

l) **Failure to support the Church can be a grave matter.** The Church does not tax her members as all political societies do. Nevertheless, supporting the Church in all the preceding ways—in particular, materially and by services when they are needed—is not something optional, up to each person's good will. Contributing support proportionate to one's ability to do so is a matter of strict justice, while not doing one's share takes advantage of other Catholics and impedes the Church from fulfilling her mission. The matter is grave, but subject to parvity.

Members of the Church should think carefully about this responsibility and make honest judgments about what they owe. While no general rule can say what that is, it is plain that one falls short gravely if one could contribute something but never contributes anything at all, if one's resources are growing steadily but one continues to make the same small contribution, and if one could easily contribute useful services but regularly avoids doing so.

In judging the material support owed the Church, one's means should be assessed by considering accumulated wealth or disposable income after paying taxes and meeting basic needs. Then one should contribute in proportion to one's means, taxing oneself, as it were, at progressively higher rates as one grows wealthier. In judging the supporting services due the Church, those who have more strength, ability, and leisure owe more than those weaker, less gifted, and more fully occupied with other responsibilities.

4. Catholics Should Help to Promote Unity among All Christians

Jesus' Church is the communion of the new covenant, ratified by his self-sacrifice. In the Eucharist, Catholics renew that sacrifice in order to share in it, and so to realize, experience, and nurture toward fulfillment in heaven the communion it establishes. As Jesus is the sole mediator between God and humankind, so there will be only one heavenly communion, and there is now but one new covenant communion present in the world. This unique Church of Jesus subsists in the Catholic Church, governed by the pope and the other bishops who are in communion with him.[97]

But Jesus' one Church is divided in the sense that many who are united with her insofar as they are properly baptized nevertheless are not in full communion (see UR 3, 22). Most form diverse churches or ecclesial communities, which the Holy Spirit uses as means for their salvation. Members of these Christian churches and communities enjoy many things which come from Jesus and lead back to him: the life of grace, other gifts of the Spirit, Scripture, and certain other elements. But all these things, which build up and enliven the Church, belong by right to the Catholic Church, and the fullness of the means of salvation can be obtained only in her (see

---

96. See *CIC*, c. 300; John Paul II, *Christifideles laici*, 30, *AAS* 81 (1989) 446–48, *OR*, 6 Feb. 1989, 9–10. Paul VI, *Evangelii nuntiandi*, 58, *AAS* 68 (1976) 46–49, Flannery, 2:738–40, critically treats so-called base communities; his main criterion is whether members of a group oppose or operate in harmony with their pastors.

97. See LG 8, UR 4; on *subsists in,* see 1.C.5.i with the accompanying note.

UR 3). Therefore, the perfect unity of Jesus' Church requires the full communion of all Christians in the Catholic Church.[98]

a) **There are several reasons for promoting unity among Christians.** The basic reason is that God wills it: the perfect communion with God and one another which human persons are called to enjoy in Jesus is the purpose of the whole divine plan of creation, redemption, and sanctification (see UR 2). But the present divisions are incompatible with this communion. They impede the sharing of goods among Christians: the Catholic Church is not built up, as she might be, by the gifts the Holy Spirit bestows on separated brothers and sisters, while the latter lack some essential truths of Christian faith and morality and are deprived of some means of salvation available in the Catholic Church (see UR 2–3).

The divisions also impede apostolate. Divided Christians cannot hand on God's truth and love to others as effectively as they could if they were in full communion. In addition, divisions weaken the defense of the faith against militant secularism.[99] Finally, since divisions arise through human failings while unity is a fruit of grace, the attainment of Christian unity would splendidly manifest the Spirit's power to overcome sin and give peace, and this would be a powerful incentive for the whole of humankind, imperiled by so many and such great divisions, to accept the gospel and seek salvation in Jesus.

b) **Catholics should foster unity by their own personal conversion.** Since the unity of Christians depends on their unity with God in Jesus, only more profound communion with the divine persons will unite Christians with one another (see UR 7, 24). Thus, there can be no true ecumenism without true conversion: turning from selfish attitudes and sin toward the Lord and his holy will. The first duty of Catholics toward ecumenical work is to renew the Catholic Church, beginning with themselves. For Jesus' radiance will shine more brightly on the Church's face in the eyes of other Christians and the whole world if each Catholic

---

98. Some will object to this way of putting the matter, for they "imagine that Christ's Church is nothing more than a collection (divided, but still possessing a certain unity) of churches and ecclesial communities" or "that Christ's Church nowhere really exists today and that it is to be considered only as an end which all churches and ecclesial communities must strive to reach." But these views are incompatible with Vatican II (see UR 2–4) and with the later teaching from which the quoted formulations are taken: Congregation for the Doctrine of the Faith, *Mysterium ecclesiae, AAS* 65 (1973) 397–98, Flannery, 2:429. Also John XXIII, *Ad Petri cathedram, AAS* 51 (1959) 512–16, *PE*, 263.65–87, argues that the Catholic Church is marked by unity lacking in other Christian communities, and so invites and exhorts Christians separated from the Apostolic See to return home. John hoped that Vatican II would facilitate this unity, as he made clear shortly before the Council's opening (*Aeterna Dei sapientia, AAS* 53 [1961] 799, *PE*, 268.62): "We are fully confident that this solemn assembly of the Catholic Hierarchy will not only reinforce that unity in faith, worship and discipline which is a distinguishing mark of Christ's true Church (DS 3008–14/1789–94), but will also attract the gaze of the great majority of Christians of every denomination, and induce them to gather around 'the great Pastor of the sheep' (Heb 13.20) who entrusted his flock to the unfailing guardianship of Peter and his successors (cf. Jn 21.15–17)."

99. John XXIII, *Aeterna Dei sapientia, AAS* 53 (1961) 802, *PE*, 268.77, emphasized this point, expressing the desire "to see the whole company of the redeemed in Jesus Christ's precious blood reunited around the single standard of the militant Church. Then let the battle commence in earnest, as we strive with might and main to resist the adversary's assaults who in so many parts of the world is threatening to annihilate our Christian faith."

aims at perfection, attends to the whole of revealed truth, uses every means of grace the Church offers, and faithfully fulfills his or her personal vocation (see UR 4).

c) **Catholics should pray for the unity of all Christians.** Since unity is a grace, it is necessary to ask God for it: "The actual effecting of this unity will not be brought about by human effort, but only by the goodness of that God who 'is not a respecter of persons' (Acts 10.34) and who 'puts no difference between us and them' (Acts 15.9)."[100] Catholics are encouraged to pray with other Christians for common concerns such as peace and justice, but above all for the unity of all Christians (see UR 8).

Prayer is especially suitable during the week of prayer for Church unity (18–25 January), when many Christians pray for this intention, and during the time from Ascension to Pentecost, when the members of the incipient Church begged the Spirit to confirm them in unity and in their mission. Any reading, prayer, or hymn expressing the faith and spiritual life common to all Christians may be used in such common prayer.[101]

d) **Catholics should foster unity by friendliness and collaboration.** Putting away past animosity, Catholics should avoid any word, judgment, or act unfair to other Christians, while recognizing and rejoicing in separated brothers' and sisters' graces and good works (see UR 4). One should respect Protestants proselytizing among Catholics, and not dismiss them contemptuously as "fundamentalists." Collaboration among divided Christians which puts Christian love into practice in service to others also nurtures love and so contributes to unity (see UR 12, GS 92). (Collaboration also is required in the conduct of ecumenical dialogue, but its norms will be treated in volume four, for they concern only one segment of the Church.)[102]

e) **Catholics should foster unity by remaining faithful.** Insofar as the Church is made up of sinners, she suffers from defects and always needs to be reformed (see UR 6). But neither the Church's defects nor the ecumenical movement, nor both together, should be used as an excuse for replacing elements of the Catholic Church's teaching, sacramental life, and essential structure with elements borrowed from other Christian churches. Far from fostering Church unity, such unfaithfulness would further wound it, for Christian unity must be in the truth. It will never be reached by tolerating differences on essentials or papering them over with compromises. The unity which, it might be supposed, could be reached quickly and easily by setting aside the question of truth would not be the genuine unity of Christians, which God wills. Authentic Christian unity must be in the truth—in Jesus who is

---

100. Pius XI, *Ecclesiam Dei, AAS* 15 (1923) 580–81, *PE,* 195.22.

101. See Secretariat for Promoting the Unity of Christians, *Ad totam ecclesiam,* 22–24 and 32–37, *AAS* 59 (1967) 582–83 and 584–86, Flannery, 1:491–92 and 494–95.

102. Some people think seeking converts to the Catholic Church is at odds with ecumenism, but that is a mistake. For ecumenism concerns only relationships with fellow Christians who are properly baptized and living as devout members of some Christian communion. Catholics may and should seek converts elsewhere as vigorously as ever. Moreover, fulfilling responsibilities with respect to ecumenism as part of a truly apostolic life is a good—and probably the most effective—way of attracting devout members of other Christian communions to seek full communion with the Catholic Church.

the truth (see Jn 14.6), in the Spirit who teaches all truth (see Jn 16.13), and in the Father whose word is truth (see Jn 17.17).[103]

f) Catholics should not invite others to receive Communion. Eucharistic sharing is not an apt means for promoting unity among Christians, because the Eucharist presupposes and expresses the unity to be sought. Indiscriminate eucharistic sharing could bring about an apparent unity, but would only impede true unity by leading to indifferentism.[104] So, just as care should be exercised about sharing in worship with others (see C.3, above), others should not be invited to receive Communion in the Catholic Church.[105]

Only in a few cases may Christians not in full communion with the Catholic Church receive Holy Communion. The exceptions, made case by case, are not based on the prospect of eventual Church unity, but on the spiritual need of the individual who asks to receive and on that person's already-existing, though imperfect, communion with the Catholic Church. That communion must include faith in the Eucharist: not just acceptance of the real presence in some sense, but acceptance of the Catholic Church's doctrine about it.[106]

103. John Paul II, Address to the German Bishops (Fulda), 4, *AAS* 73 (1981) 85, *OR*, 22 Dec. 1980, 9: "Unity, which comes from God, is given to us at the Cross. We must not want to avoid the cross, passing to rapid attempts at harmonizing differences, excluding the question of truth. But neither must we abandon one another, and go on our separate ways, because drawing closer calls for the patient and suffering love of Christ crucified. Let us not be diverted from the laborious way in order to remain where we are, or to choose ways that are apparently shorter and lead astray." John Paul II, *Reconciliatio et paenitentia*, 9, *AAS* 77 (1985) 204, *OR*, 17 Dec. 1984, 4: "The Church promotes reconciliation *in the truth*, knowing well that neither reconciliation nor unity is possible outside or in opposition to the truth." Paul VI, General Audience (20 Jan. 1971), *Inseg.* 9 (1971) 48–49, *OR*, 28 Jan. 1971, 1 and 12, explains that the faithfulness of Catholics is necessary for the ecumenical process, since unfaithfulness would separate them from Christ and so undermine true dialogue.

104. The argument against intercommunion is clearly stated by John Paul II, Address to Representatives of Various Christian Confessions, 6, *Inseg.* 8.1 (1985) 1327, *OR*, 3 June 1985, 8: "Is it truly to this sort of unity that the Lord invites us? Is it not a fact that—because faith is growing weaker—the world takes our differences less seriously regarding the sacramental nature of the Church, the minister and the Sacrament of the Eucharist itself? *If these differences . . . were no longer taken seriously, would they for this reason be overcome?* Wouldn't this be equivalent to lessening the suffering rather than healing the disease of a division which exists contrary to the will of Christ?"

105. *CIC*, c. 844, makes it illicit for Catholic ministers to administer the sacraments of penance, Eucharist, and anointing to non-Catholics unless, among other things, they "ask on their own" (§3). If Catholics invite non-Catholics to receive Communion, the latter are not asking on their own. So, they should not be invited.

106. See *CIC*, c. 844, §§3–4. These sections distinguish between (i) members of Eastern churches not in full communion with the Catholic Church and of certain other churches in the same condition as the Eastern churches and (ii) all other non-Catholic Christians. For the latter, there must be danger of death or other grave necessity, as judged by the diocesan bishop or conference of bishops, and inability to approach a minister of their own community. See also UR 8; Secretariat for Promoting the Unity of Christians, *In quibus rerum circumstantiis, AAS* 64 (1972) 518–25, Flannery, 1:554–59; further clarified in idem, *Dopo la publicazione, AAS* 65 (1973) 616–19, trans. as "Communication," *Documents on the Liturgy*, 343–45. This last document makes it clear that, except for members of the Eastern Orthodox churches, whose faith in the Eucharist can be presumed, Christians not fully in communion with the Catholic Church should never be given the Eucharist unless they personally profess their faith in it *in accord with Catholic doctrine*.

g) Thwarting authentic ecumenism is a grave matter. Not only is the Catholic Church firmly committed to the pursuit of unity among all Christians, but God wills that unity, and it is needed for the Church's more effective fulfillment of her mission. So, it is a grave matter to thwart authentic ecumenism either by deliberately failing to make one's proper contribution to it or by intentionally behaving in ways which impede true Christian unity. How? Since all can and should pray for Christian unity, anyone who refused to do so plainly would sin in this matter. Likewise, because false appearances of unity will impede the attainment of true unity, those who engage in forbidden eucharistic sharing and cultivate spurious consensus by false irenicism also sin.[107]

107. On false irenicism, see UR 11. Paul VI, General Audience (20 Jan. 1965), *AAS* 57 (1965) 245, *The Pope Speaks* 10 (1964–65): 143, points to the temptation which arises in the minds of good people but leads "to an attitude that is neither good, nor effective in removing the most serious of all the difficulties [in achieving unity], the doctrinal ones. We mean the temptation to lay aside controversial points; to hide, or weaken, or modify, or empty of meaning, or even deny those teachings of the Catholic Church that are not accepted today by our separated brethren."

CHAPTER FOUR

REPENTANCE, THE SACRAMENT OF PENANCE, AND THE STRUGGLE AGAINST SIN

Summary

As a result of sin, people are alienated from God, at odds with one another, and inwardly divided. Revelation therefore comes as an offer of salvation and a promise of reconciliation, while the call to faith—the commitment by which one accepts God's offer—also is a call to change one's life radically. It follows that the Church is a community of repentance and reconciliation.

Seen in this perspective, Christian asceticism aims at human fulfillment. Moreover, since the call to authentic repentance is essential to the gospel, one's responsibilities in this sphere should be gladly accepted. Still, sins and their effects last; they are not easy to overcome. Thus, the responsibilities to repent and be reconciled are continuous, while one's growth toward holiness is gradual and should be lifelong.

Besides the sacrament of penance and the acceptance of suffering with resignation, Christian life should include other penitential works. Some acts are more appropriately penitential than others, and the traditional triad of prayer, fasting, and almsgiving remain highly fitting. At the same time, one's personal penance should be supplemented by taking advantage of indulgences.

The sacrament of penance should be received when appropriate. That means rather often, even if one is not guilty of mortal sin, since the sacrament is effective in the struggle against venial sin. The sacrament requires self-examination and contrition for sins, and contrition includes the will to confess and a firm purpose of amendment, that is, the determination to avoid future sin. While penitents are free within limits to choose their confessors, they should do so carefully.

The confession of sins is essential to the sacrament of penance, and would be prudent even if it were not essential. All mortal sins committed after baptism must be confessed. Satisfaction for sins, the "penance" imposed by the confessor, also is essential.

Besides using the sacrament of penance, people should strive to overcome sin by prayer, self-denial, and serving others; the Eucharist is the basic way of

overcoming sin. Also, it is necessary to avoid or modify the occasions of sin and
to expect and resist temptations.

One's responsibilities for the moral welfare of others include admonishing
(traditionally called "fraternally correcting") those who seem to be sinning and
avoiding leading others into sin ("giving scandal").

Finally, it is necessary to see the whole of Christian life as a preparation for
death. This includes facing the likelihood of death realistically and humbly submitting to God's will. Christians should visit those who face death, and pray and
worship with them; and the dying should prepare themselves spiritually by receiving Holy Communion and the sacrament of anointing.[1]

Prologue to the Chapter

In revealing himself, God calls a fallen human race to intimate friendship.
Humankind is not a community living uprightly and at peace. Enslaved by sin and
suffering its consequences, men and women are alienated from God, at odds with
one another, and inwardly divided by the conflicting passions flowing from the
inescapable anxiety of persons who live in the shadow of death (see *CMP*, 14.G–H).
Revelation therefore comes to sinful humankind as an offer of salvation and a
promise of reconciliation, while the call to faith also is a call to change one's life
radically: "The kingdom of God has come near; repent, and believe in the good
news" (Mk 1.15). And since the prospect of death is bleak without the hope of
salvation, the alternative to repentance is horrible: "Unless you repent, you will all
perish" (Lk 13.3, 5).

Jesus came to save humankind from sin and all its consequences. Filled with the
Holy Spirit, he challenged evil and caused it to defeat itself (see Jn 3.16–21,
9.39–41), promised to send the Spirit to complete this process (see Jn 16.7–11),
and manifested God's will to overcome evil decisively by re-creation (see *CMP*,
20.F, 22.G, 30.A). When Jesus rose from the dead—with his humanity, which had
borne the full brunt of evil, re-created—he breathed the Holy Spirit on the apostles.
Then he sent them, as the Father had sent him, to carry on his redemptive mission
by healing evil at its very root: "If you forgive the sins of any, they are forgiven
them; if you retain the sins of any, they are retained" (Jn 20.23).

Thus, just as the Church is the community of faith (which receives and hands
on God's revelation of his own truth and love), of hope (which builds up God's
kingdom on earth for the sake of its perfection in heaven), and of love (which
celebrates in Jesus' Eucharist the divine-human communion established by his
redemptive sacrifice and resurrection), so the Church is the community of repentance and reconciliation: the minister of the Holy Spirit's renewal of the face of
the earth, a renewal he accomplishes by overcoming sin and preparing for
Jesus' return in glory.

---

1. Many of the topics treated in this chapter were treated in *CMP*, 32, which centers on the
sacrament of penance as an organizing principle of Christian life. So, although the present
treatment stands on its own, study or review of *CMP*, 32, will be profitable.

Question A: How Do Responsibilities in This Sphere Fit into Christian Life?

Each person's first response to God and turning toward him is a special grace and unique moment. But this initial conversion, the Church has always taught, usually is neither complete nor definitive, and the struggle against sin and tendencies to it must continue throughout life. Even after sins are forgiven, it is necessary to deal realistically and effectively with their effects on one's personality, interpersonal relationships, and relationship with the remainder of the created world. Moreover, responsibilities with respect to sin and its consequences do not end with oneself. Each Christian also must work for the renewal of the Church as a whole and do his or her part in the Church's service of reconciliation, so that Jesus' peace may reach out to embrace all humankind.

Today, the penitential dimension of Christian life—Christian asceticism—often is neglected. Many have discontinued or greatly reduced their use of the sacrament of penance and traditional penitential practices; some seem to ignore the whole sphere of responsibilities pertaining to repentance and reconciliation. The decline in ascetical practice points to a deeper crisis, affecting the very sense of God and of sin.[2] Many elements of the non-Christian, contemporary culture contribute to this crisis, and certain new forms of so-called spirituality, propagated even within the Catholic Church, rationalize abandonment of the whole Christian tradition concerning human free choice and moral responsibility, divine justice, and the conditions essential for genuine repentance. In light of all this, it is important to understand why it is as necessary today as ever to continue to turn toward God, struggle against sin, deal with its effects, and so help to make peace on earth.

1. Christian Asceticism Aims at Human and Personal Fulfillment

While everyone in the world experiences evil, the asceticism characteristic of some non-Christian religions is based on false interpretations of evil: the belief that matter, the body, and the very individuality of the person are evil in themselves, which leads to the notion that human persons are fulfilled only by escaping from the world, discarding their bodies, and ceasing to be the persons they are. Christian faith, by contrast, teaches that matter and individuality are goods created by God, while the evil disfiguring human nature and mutilating persons arises from the wrong free choices of creatures, including one's own sins. In the past, nevertheless, some Christians confused non-Christian with Christian asceticism. Such confusion can lead people to reject the asceticism they should practice.[3]

a) **Christian asceticism affirms life.** False asceticism is life denying. It points toward complete or partial annihilation of the human. By contrast, while Christian asceticism has been tainted by some mistaken and harmful excesses, it is essentially

---

2. See John Paul II, *Reconciliatio et paenitentia,* 18, *AAS* 77 (1985) 224–28, *OR,* 17 Dec. 1984, 6–7; Nicolò M. Loss, S.D.B., "La prospettiva di penitenza nella Bibbia," *Ephemerides liturgicae* 89 (1975): 220.

3. A helpful clarification of the essence of Christian asceticism: Hubert van Zeller, *Approach to Penance* (New York: Sheed and Ward, 1958).

life affirming.[4] For Jesus' salvation is not annihilation, but liberation and re-creation: "I came that they may have life, and have it abundantly" (Jn 10.10). Even when opposing the world and the flesh, the New Testament does not oppose a full human life, for then *the world* means humankind precisely as sinful and *the flesh* means the person precisely as enmeshed in sin.[5]

Moreover, Jesus by no means endorses death and other human miseries, which have their source not in God's good will but in creatures' sinful wills. These evil effects of sin become means of redemption only because, in assuming human nature in its fallen condition, the Word accepts them. Jesus does this in order to prepare humankind to receive God's re-creative gift of the Spirit, the gift that alone overcomes death and suffering.

b) Christian asceticism is a means to the kingdom. Christian penitential activity is shaped by faith, hope, and charity, but penance itself is not of the same order as those three gifts. As a person struggles against disease in order to live as only the healthy can, so a person struggles against sin in order to live a humanly and divinely full life as only the holy can. Thus, overcoming sin and its effects is not the ultimate purpose of penitential activities; rather, these aim at growth in holiness. All works of penance are for the sake of increasingly intimate communion with God and neighbor, and also for perfecting the peace of soul and harmony with God's good creation that sin had upset. Christian asceticism is a means to the kingdom, to its coming and to one's sharing fully in it. It accepts suffering and death as Jesus did and in unity with him: not as if they were good in themselves but insofar as accepting them is necessary for resurrection.

c) Christians need not reject any true good. Although the kingdom is more than human fulfillment—it is fulfillment in divine life—divine goodness and human goods are not at odds (see *CMP*, 24.E). In the kingdom, where one hopes to live a real, human, bodily life, as Jesus and Mary already do, all the good fruits of human nature and effort will be found again, freed of sin and completed (see GS 39). Those who denied and rejected their sinful selves for Jesus' sake and the gospel's will have saved their authentically human selves (see Mt 10.38–39, Mk 8.34–35, Lk 17.33, Jn 12.25). Thus, nothing good about human persons and communities, nothing which contributes to their reality and true fulfillment need be rejected.

In any human life, of course, it is necessary to choose, act for, and share in some human goods rather than others; moreover, Christian preferences, flowing from faith's understanding of what is required for human fulfillment, differ markedly from non-Christian preferences. Still, one need not and should not reject those goods which are given up for the kingdom's sake. For example, those called to virginity or celibacy should not regard marriage and parenthood as evils to be rejected, but should affirm them as great goods that they renounce only for the sake of other goods, seen by the eye of faith to be greater still.

---

4. See Louis Bouyer, Cong.Orat., *Introduction to Spirituality*, trans. Mary Perkins Ryan (Collegeville, Minn.: Liturgical Press, 1961), 134–41.

5. See John L. McKenzie, S.J., *Dictionary of the Bible* (New York: Macmillan, 1965), 280–82 and 942–44.

2:   Authentic Asceticism Is a Desirable Part of Christian Life

The previous section has clarified confusions about asceticism. But it also is important to see why people should joyfully accept their responsibilities in this sphere. Since repentance and penitential works would be unnecessary in a sinless creation, considered in and by themselves these are not unqualified goods. In the actual situation, however, repentance and penitential works really are good despite their lack of appeal. Rather than ignore, avoid, or rebel against them, one should gladly fulfill the responsibilities of the penitential dimension of Christian life, in which one is united with Jesus in submitting to God's judgment on sin. In penance one experiences in a special way God's saving love, revealed in Jesus' cross, and enjoys the fruit of repentance and penitential works: reconciliation and peace.

a) The call to repentance belongs to the gospel's good news. Authentic repentance is concerned with sin but should not be associated with it, though that is likely to happen in the subconscious mind. Repentance is to sin as appropriate treatment is to disease. Of course, it would be better if there were no diseases to treat, and likewise it would be better if there were no sins to repent. When one is sick, however, the alternative to treatment is not a healthy and comfortable life without treatment's burdens, but a life burdened and threatened by disease. And when one sins the alternative to repentance is not an innocent and peaceful life uncomplicated by repentance, but a life deformed by sin and increasingly enslaved by both sin itself and anxiety about death.

Repentance frees one from sin. Freedom from mortal sin is reconciliation with God and neighbor: the prodigal's return to his home, where his father receives him as a son and celebrates his return with a banquet (see Lk 15.22–24). The gradual overcoming of all other sin and sin's effects is growth in holiness, the building up of communion with God and neighbor. This communion is the central reality of God's kingdom, and so the gospel's good news of the kingdom's arrival also is a call to repentance: to come back to the Father's heavenly home, to remain at home, and to grow in familial solidarity. Repentance can indeed be painful, but its immediate fruits are joyful.

b) The sacrament of penance is a very easy way to deal with sin. While this may not seem true, a little thought makes the point clear.

Suffering from a fatal illness, such as AIDS, and offered, free of charge, a treatment which, while painful, took only a few minutes and assured complete and immediate recovery, any reasonable person would be happy to accept it. That is so even if people receiving the treatment had to promise never again to do what had brought on the disease. Likewise, anyone afflicted with a serious and chronic disease, such as diabetes, who was offered, free of charge, a treatment requiring only a few minutes every week or so, and was assured that the disease not only would be controlled but gradually cured, surely would want to receive that treatment and would cooperate with it.

Mortal sin is spiritual death, and venial sin is a serious, chronic spiritual disease; and spiritual disease and death are far more serious than mortal illness and chronic bodily disease. Considered in this light, the sacrament of penance plainly is a wonderful gift, one Jesus gave his life to win for his followers. Moreover, it manifests God's great gentleness and mercy, for its way of dealing with sin requires little from sinners in return for spiritual life and health.

c) **Authentic repentance is sure to be fruitful.** Repentance is not only the work of God's grace in sinners but their own free human act, motivated by the sure hope of God's merciful forgiveness. The Father's faithful love, so great that he gave his Son to reconcile humankind to himself, guarantees that he will receive with reconciling mercy anyone who turns to him, just as the father in the parable joyfully received his prodigal son (see Lk 15.11–32).[6] Confident, moreover, of the Spirit's power at work in oneself, one should be joyful in hope even while experiencing hardship (see Col 1.11–12). As Jesus "for the sake of the joy that was set before him endured the cross, disregarding its shame" (Heb 12.2), so the penitential dimension of one's life should be accepted for the sake of its fruit of holiness (see Heb 12.3–13; cf. Jas 1.2–4), which the gift of the Holy Spirit guarantees.

d) **In doing penance, Jesus' disciples can follow him joyfully.** Jesus not only preached penance but practiced it. Before beginning his ministry he received John's baptism, fasted, prayed, and overcame temptation (see Mt 3.13–4.11; Mk 1.9–13; Lk 3.21–22, 4.1–13). But even though he was sinless, Jesus was made "to be sin" (2 Cor 5.21), as Paul says, so that fallen humankind might be reconciled to God (see 2 Cor 5.18–21). His self-offering in obedience to the Father truly is redemptive (see *CMP*, 22.G, 22.2); therefore, it is the most perfect of all penances (see *S.t.*, 3, q. 15, a. 1, ad 5).

But Jesus' penance does not render one's own unnecessary: he suffered, leaving an example, that one should follow in his footsteps (see 1 Pt 2.21). Christians are called to cooperate in Jesus' redemptive work; to follow him is to deny oneself and take up one's own cross (see Mt 10.38, Mk 8.34, Lk 14.27). Thus, Christians, although degraded by sin, are ennobled, for they take part in Jesus' kingly work of conquering the reign of sin, beginning with its reign in themselves (see Rom 6.12; LG 36; *S.t.*, 3, q. 49, a. 1; q. 62, a. 5). God's grace is the greater in not only forgiving the sin but providing an opportunity for satisfaction that makes the repentant sinner more like Jesus.

Although Jesus' natural feelings resisted suffering and death, as he was about to die he experienced, due to his obedience, the joy of being in communion with the Father (see Jn 15.10–11). Similarly, when a person's natural feelings resist penance, he or she should accept it joyfully in solidarity with Jesus: "If we endure, we will also reign with him" (2 Tm 2.12).

e) **Repentance purifies and strengthens the Church.** Insofar as she is insep-arably united with Jesus, the Church is holy, but insofar as she is sinful in her members, she always needs to be purified (see LG 8, UR 6). Sin wounds the Church, but the penance of her sinful members not only reconciles them to her but heals the wounds they have inflicted on her (see LG 11).[7] Thus, the Church calls her members

---

6. John Paul II, *Dives in misericordia,* 1–8, *AAS* 72 (1980) 1177–1207, *PE,* 279.1–93, deals richly with divine mercy and includes a powerful synthesis of relevant scriptural sources.

7. John Paul II, *Reconciliatio et paenitentia,* 9, *AAS* 77 (1985) 203, *OR,* 17 Dec. 1984, 3, teaches: "The Church, if she is to be *reconciling,* must begin by being a *reconciled Church.* Beneath this simple and indicative expression lies the conviction that the Church, in order ever

"to purification and renewal so that the sign of Christ may shine more brightly over the face of the Church" (LG 15; cf. GS 43). For Catholics to correct what disfigures the face of the Church means removing the obstacle their sins place in the way of others' acceptance of the faith, thus making the Church a more effective sign of God's truth and love.[8] More broadly, the Church is a more effective sacrament—a sign and a means—of reconciling humankind to God and healing all human divisions as she herself is more perfectly united with Jesus through the healing of her inner tensions and divisions, caused by her members' sins.

3. Christians Must Struggle Hard against Sin and Its Effects

To appreciate the responsibilities pertaining to repentance and reconciliation, it is necessary to realize that sins are spiritual realities that last. They truly offend God while wreaking havoc in and beyond sinners. The struggle of Christians against sin is made still more difficult by diabolical adversaries, their own weakness, and the sinful world around them.

It would be contrary to God's wisdom and holiness for him simply to overlook or forget about evil, or to treat it as if it were good. His mercy cannot mean that he reconciles sinners to himself without their sins being overcome. Of course, the overcoming of sin is the work of God's grace, freely given because of his mercy and faithfulness; far from being a substitute for one's struggle against sin and its effects, however, grace is the power to win the battle.

a) Sins are spiritual realities that last. Insofar as they flow from free choices, human actions are not mere units of transitory behavior, which people do and then simply put behind them (see *CMP,* 2.H); rather, actions really constitute a person's life and self. Moral norms, furthermore, are truths, not mere rules, that guide human actions to the authentic fulfillment God plans and wills for creation as a whole and for each created person (see *CMP,* 3.A–B, 7.A, 7.E–F, 19.A–C, 23.F–G, 34.A, and 34.D–G). Sins, then, are choices contrary to what the sinner believes to be the moral truth. In every sinful choice, one makes oneself guilty, whether one feels guilty or not; and one remains guilty unless and until one has a real change of heart (see *CMP,* 13.A–B).

b) Sin offends God and causes widespread disharmony. Sins interfere with human fulfillment and disrupt human harmony on every level, as Vatican II teaches: "Often refusing to acknowledge God as their source, people have disrupted not

---

more effectively to proclaim and propose reconciliation to the world, must become ever more genuinely a community of disciples of Christ (even though it were only 'the little flock' of the first days), united in the commitment to be continually converted to the Lord and to live as new people in the spirit and practice of reconciliation."

8. In conformity with Vatican II's teaching (in LG 32–33, 39–42; AA 6), *CIC,* c. 210, prescribes: "All the Christian faithful must make an effort, in accord with their own condition, to live a holy life and to promote the growth of the Church and its continual sanctification." Sanctification is important for authentic ecumenism; John XXIII, *Paenitentiam agere, AAS* 54 (1962) 486, *PE,* 269.25, on the eve of Vatican II, called Catholics to penance, so "that the faith, the love, the moral lives of Catholics may be so re-invigorated, so intensified, that all who are at present separated from this Apostolic See may be impelled to strive actively and sincerely for union, and enter the one fold under the one Shepherd (cf. Jn 10.16)."

only their proper relationship to the ultimate end of the human person, but also their whole relationship to themselves, other people, and all created things" (GS 13; cf. *CMP*, 7.F).[9] Basically, however, sins explicitly or implicitly violate God's wisdom and love, and so alienate sinners from him. For those who have entered into a covenant with God, sin is unfaithfulness, as adultery is unfaithfulness to a spouse. Thus, although sins cannot harm God, they truly offend him inasmuch as they are against the good he wills (see *CMP*, 13.B–C). In sinning, one implicitly says to God: May thy will *not* be done on earth as it is in heaven!

The Bible expresses how offensive that is to God by speaking often of his wrath. While God's mercy is so great that repentant sinners need not fear that wrath, one must not forget Jesus' cross: revealing God's mercy, it also reveals just how seriously he takes sin.

c) **Malicious adversaries oppose every effort to overcome sin.** Vatican II reiterates the Church's teaching that humankind's fall was partly due to the Devil and that the Devil's continuing malicious action is one cause of the monumental conflict which makes up human history (see GS 13, 37). Christians do not enjoy total immunity from diabolical subversion (see DS 1668/894). Thus, the New Testament teaches them to prepare to fight: "For our struggle is not against enemies of blood and flesh, but against the rulers, against the authorities, against the cosmic powers of this present darkness, against the spiritual forces of evil in the heavenly places" (Eph 6.12; cf. 1 Pt 5.6–10). Since by themselves human beings are weaker than their diabolical adversaries, prayer for divine and angelic help is the chief means of carrying on this part of the struggle against sin.

d) **Fallen human nature is a handicap in the struggle against sin.** Honest people who desire to live uprightly often recognize in themselves a vulnerability to temptation and an inclination to sin arising from the fact that their feelings are not subordinate to reason (see Rom 7.23, Gal 5.16–17, Jas 1.14–15). The Church's teaching calls this experience "concupiscence" and explains that it is an effect of original sin which persists even in the baptized (see DS 1515/792; *S.t.*, 1–2, q. 82, a. 3; *CMP*, 14.G). Jesus makes it clear that people must take whatever measures are necessary to deal with this source of temptation (see Mt 5.29–30, Mk 9.43–47). St. Paul acknowledges the need to discipline himself much as an athlete in training does (see 1 Cor 9.24–27).

e) **Society conditioned by sin impedes one from following Jesus.** Original sin and subsequent actual sins not only affect those directly involved but distort social arrangements and practices, cultural processes and products, so that there

---

9. John Paul II, *Reconciliatio et paenitentia*, 15, *AAS* 77 (1985) 213, *OR*, 17 Dec. 1984, 5, points out that according to Genesis sin leads to human divisions, and then explains: "No one wishing to investigate the mystery of sin can ignore this link between cause and effect. As a rupture with God, sin is an act of disobedience by a creature who rejects, at least implicitly, the very one from whom he came and who sustains him in life. It is therefore a suicidal act. Since by sinning man refuses to submit to God, his internal balance is also destroyed and it is precisely within himself that contradictions and conflicts arise. Wounded in this way, man almost inevitably causes damage to the fabric of his relationship with others and with the created world. This is an objective law and an objective reality, verified in so many ways in the human psyche and in the spiritual life, as well as in society, where it is easy to see the signs and effects of internal disorder."

are real structures of sin (see GS 25). These structures are persisting realities shaped by sin; they, as it were, embody the sins which shaped them and conduce to further sins. For example, greedy choices lead to an unjust economic system in which the rich waste goods and pollute the environment, while the poor remain in desperate need. In some nations, certain families hold vast, undeveloped estates, thus shaping an agricultural system which allows many small farmers too little land to grow the food necessary to feed their families. Again, irresponsible choices about sexual activity—perhaps together with ill-conceived public programs of sex education, no-fault divorce, and so on—encourage a family structure in which children are deprived of the support and nurture of their fathers. Although such sociocultural structures of sin originate only in wrong free choices, the sins of individuals and groups, they extend far beyond the deeds and situations which give rise to them.[10]

Insofar as humankind is divided and afflicted by such structures of sin, it constitutes the sinful world, friendship with which is enmity toward God (see Jas 4.4). That world hates Jesus' loyal followers, who must remain in it without belonging to it (see Jn 15.18–19, 17.6–19). It presses everyone to conform to it, while the all-too-human tendency to conform impedes Christians from following Jesus or even thinking about their personal vocation. That is why Paul warns: "Do not be conformed to this world, but be transformed by the renewing of your minds, so that you may discern what is the will of God—what is good and acceptable and perfect" (Rom 12.2).

f) **Grace does not make overcoming sin painless and effortless.** As the parable of the publican and pharisee makes clear (see Lk 18.9–14), true repentance requires the acknowledgment that forgiveness depends on God's mercy. One would not be repentant in self-confidently supposing that one deserved acceptance in God's eyes. Indeed, it is a matter of faith that God's grace and mercy initiate and sustain whatever one does to overcome sin (see DS 373–96/176–99, 1521–25/793–97, 1530/800, 1551–54/811–14).

But it also is a matter of faith that grace does not replace human free choice and effort: "According to Catholic faith we also believe that after grace has been received through baptism, all the baptized, if they are willing to labor faithfully, can and ought to accomplish with Christ's help and cooperation what pertains to the salvation of their souls" (DS 397/200; cf. DS 1545–46/809, 1554/814, 1574/834). God's mercy is not merely a matter of writing off sins, as a creditor might cancel a debt (see DS 1561/821). Rather, God gives the sinner a new heart, which freely responds to his mercy (see Ps 51.10–12), so that those who were sinners can live as members of Jesus and act as befits God's friends (see Jer 31.31–34, Ezk 11.19–20, Jn 15.4–15).[11]

---

10. See John Paul II, *Reconciliatio et paenitentia*, 16, *AAS* 77 (1985) 213–17, *OR*, 17 Dec. 1984, 5–6; *Sollicitudo rei socialis*, 36–38, *AAS* 80 (1988) 561–66, *OR*, 29 Feb. 1988, 9–10.

11. Thus, Paul VI, *Evangelii nuntiandi*, 10, *AAS* 68 (1976) 11, Flannery, 2:714–15, teaches that while God's mercy and grace are freely offered to all, each person must attain a share in Jesus' kingdom and salvation "by force: 'men of violence take them by force' (cf. Mt 11.12, Lk 16.16) as the Lord says. They must achieve them by labour and sorrows, by a life lived according to the standards of the gospel, by self-denial and the cross in the spirit of the beatitudes of the gospel.

Therefore, the Council of Trent teaches that Christians not only must work out their salvation in fear and trembling, but "in labors, in sleepless nights, in almsgiving, in prayers and offerings, in fastings, and in chastity (2 Cor 6.3 ff.)"; they "should be in dread about the battle they must wage with the flesh, the world, and the devil" (DS 1541/806).

4. The Responsibilities to Repent and Be Reconciled Are Continuous

In one respect, repentance or conversion is unique and decisive. Hearing the gospel and moved by grace, people turn toward God, reject all the evil in which they are enmeshed and from which they suffer, believe, and receive new life: the light and power of the Holy Spirit to live in communion with God and his friends (see *CMP*, 20.C–D, 20.F, 24.D, 30.H–I). From this point of view, the gospel precisely is a call to repentance (see Mt 4.17, Mk 1.15), an offer of forgiveness, and a promise of the gift of the Holy Spirit (see Lk 24.46–49, Acts 2.38; cf. Jn 20.22–23). The response of faith is at once renunciation of sin and commitment to Jesus, as the baptismal promises make clear.

Of course, Catholics also acknowledge the possibility that those who have received salvation in Jesus can commit mortal sin, lose divine life, and so again need to undergo radical conversion (see *CMP*, 15.B–C, 32.A). But not everyone commits mortal sins, and normally the need for so radical a new conversion is not constant. It might seem, then, that one's responsibilities with respect to repentance and reconciliation are to be met only on a few special occasions. But that is not so. Every Christian always should be trying in several different ways to meet these responsibilities.

a) **One's basic act of repentance should be permanent.** The basic act of repentance sets God's prodigal children on their way toward their Father's house. A person has volitional sorrow for his or her own sins, arising from the choice to accept God's mercy and reject sin: "I will get up and go to my father, and I will say to him, 'Father, I have sinned against heaven and before you; I am no longer worthy to be called your son; treat me like one of your hired hands' " (Lk 15.18–19). No mere feeling, this free act is a self-determination of the personal, spiritual self.

Of itself, it persists unless there is a contrary choice. But such a choice would involve approving one's sins and so committing them anew. The basic act of repentance, by which a new and contrite heart is received, should therefore be permanent (see *S.t.*, 3, q. 84, a. 8). It should inform one's humble gratitude toward God, for, remaining of oneself a sinner, one is a repentant sinner only because of God's faithfulness and mercy. Great saints have expressed this awareness by identifying themselves as great sinners despite the remarkable gifts of grace they enjoyed.

b) **Growth toward holiness is gradual and should be lifelong.** In explaining the universal call to holiness, Vatican II points out that followers of Jesus, having become children of God and received a share in the divine nature, by God's grace

---

But above all each individual can achieve them by a total spiritual renewal of himself which the gospel calls *metanoia*, that is by a conversion of the whole man by virtue of which there is a radical change of mind and heart (cf. Mt 4.17)."

must "hold on to and complete in their lives this holiness they have received" (LG 40). This requires the Christian virtues and fruits of the Spirit. The Council adds: "Since truly we all offend in many things (cf. Jas 3.2), we need God's mercy continuously and must pray daily: 'And forgive us our trespasses' (Mt 6.12)" (LG 40).[12] Thus, continuous conversion is needed to overcome sin gradually. The overcoming of sin is growth in single-heartedness (see *CMP*, 26.I).

Continuous conversion is neither constant innovation nor repeated restoration. It is an ongoing effort to understand more correctly and fulfill more faithfully what was undertaken by the commitment of faith, to implement one's hope for the kingdom in an increasingly consistent way, and so to grow toward the ideal of perfection: to love God with one's whole heart, mind, soul, and strength, and to love one's neighbor as oneself (see *CMP*, 27.E).

c) **As holiness grows, residual defects continue to appear.** Growth toward the ideal of love is not simply a matter of gradually eliminating the major and minor sins that any healthy conscience can recognize by its awareness of the principles of natural moral law. It is intimate cooperation with the Holy Spirit in forming oneself to meet the demands of the specifically Christian commitments of one's personal vocation (see LG 41; *CMP*, 28.E). But even these commitments are at first imperfect, more or less limited and distorted by interests other than hope and motives other than charity; thus, it is necessary to struggle to respond consistently to one's vocation and to fulfill its commitments faithfully.

As the effort proceeds, more and more implications of the Christian modes of response gradually become clear, and awareness of one's shortcomings develops at an altogether new level (see *CMP*, 28.E–F). This is another reason why great saints consider themselves sinners: they expect to continue to discover their shortcomings in respect to Christian humility, meekness, detachment, mercy, and so on.

d) **The social dimension of penance cannot be definitively fulfilled.** God's grace frees Christians from the sinful world, but not from responsibilities toward that world. Like the sinless Lord Jesus, who entered the sinful world to save humankind, Jesus' followers must be peacemakers and liberators, extending God's peace to others (see *CMP*, 26.J). Unlike Jesus, however, repentant sinners owe it to God to have mercy on others, since they themselves gladly receive his mercy: "Forgive us our debts, as we also have forgiven our debtors" (Mt 6.12; see *CMP*, 26.H). On this ground, people should promote reconciliation by loving enemies and offering forgiveness to anyone who has wronged them. Moreover, justice is owed to anyone who suffers or has suffered injustices to which one has contributed, and on this ground, restitution must be made to those whom one has wronged (see 7.G, below).

On both grounds, furthermore, Christians' responsibilities to do penance and promote reconciliation include the duty to work for social justice: "to implement—

---

12. John Paul II, *Reconciliatio et paenitentia*, 4, *AAS* 77 (1985) 191, *OR*, 17 Dec. 1984, 2, similarly explains that while penance means the initial conversion of heart, penance also means doing penance, and this requires daily effort supported by grace: "Penance is therefore *a conversion that passes from the heart to deeds*, and then to the Christian's whole life."

by the way they live as individuals and as families, by the use of their resources, by their civic activity, by contributing to economic and political decisions, and by personal commitment to national and international undertakings—the *measures* inspired by solidarity and love of preference for the poor."[13] Plainly, these responsibilities which pertain to the social dimension of penance are ongoing; they never can be definitively fulfilled.

   e) **Penance will be incomplete until the whole Church is perfect.** A Christian's very identity as a member of Jesus depends on the Church as a whole, for Christians are to seek first the kingdom, and the Church is the incipient kingdom. The social responsibilities of penance and reconciliation cannot be met fully by any individual as long as the Church as a whole is not perfectly what Jesus planned and willed her to be. "But," as Paul VI teaches, "the actual image of the Church will never attain to such a degree of perfection, beauty, holiness and splendor that it can be said to correspond perfectly with the original conception in the mind of him who fashioned it."[14] Hence, a Christian has lifelong responsibilities to help and support fellow Christians in their work of repentance and reconciliation. No member of Jesus can rest until all are free of sin, and each should be able to say with Paul: "I am completing what is lacking in Christ's afflictions for the sake of his body, that is, the church" (Col 1.24).

Question B: What Are One's Responsibilities to Do Penitential Works?

   The essential act of penance is turning from sin toward God: emerging from darkness into light, from an unreal world of ideologies, rationalizations, and self-deceptions into the real world of which God is Lord, Jesus is Savior, and the Holy Spirit is Sanctifier. Having done that essential act of penance, however, penitential works are still necessary. But why is this so?

   Since sins offend God and cause multiple disorders, they deserve punishment. Punishment for sin, however, does not mean the same thing as society's punishment of wrongdoers. Society chooses something repugnant to the wrongdoer and imposes it as a punishment, but God does not choose and impose penalties for sin. Rather, he permits sin's bad consequences to impact upon sinners; this is like human punishment only insofar as it causes sinners to experience suffering which they deserve.

   Eternal punishment, hell, is the self-alienation from God and loss of human fulfillment resulting from persistence in mortal sin (see *CMP*, 18.H–I). Thus, while hell is entailed by mortal sin, this penalty is negated when the sin is forgiven. But other bad effects on the moral dimension of persons and their interpersonal communion—effects called "temporal punishment" insofar as they afflict the sinner without alienating him or her from God—remain (see *CMP*, 32.C). Therefore, one must do what one can—that is, do penitential works—to make up for

---

13. John Paul II, *Sollicitudo rei socialis*, 47, *AAS* 80 (1988) 581, *OR*, 29 Feb. 1988, 13.
14. Paul VI, *Ecclesiam Suam, AAS* 56 (1964) 612, *PE*, 271.10.

one's sins (see DS 1580/840, 1689/904, 1693/906). John XXIII approvingly quotes St. Augustine: "It is not enough for a man to change his ways for the better and to give up the practice of evil, unless by painful penance, sorrowing humility, the sacrifice of a contrite heart and the giving of alms he makes amends to God for all that he has done wrong."[15]

1. Penitential Works Must Be Rightly Understood

The idea of doing works of penance to make up, or offer satisfaction, for sins can be misunderstood. Although penance is a punishment or reparation for sin, those concepts must not be understood legalistically, as if sinners really compensated for their sins or had to suffer gratuitously. Penance rather should be understood as a constructive step for the repentant sinner. As John Paul II explains: "*To do penance* means, above all, to re-establish the balance and harmony broken by sin, to change direction even at the cost of sacrifice."[16]

a) **The responsibility to do penance extends beyond the sacrament.** Making satisfaction for sin belongs to the sacrament of penance; in the sacrament, a penance is imposed for this purpose (see DS 1692/905). But it is only a token of the will to make up for sin and overcome its residual effects in one's life. Above and beyond this token, everything voluntarily done to satisfy for sin and overcome its effects— and everything suffered in life with a heart submissive to God—is penance (see DS 1693/906; *S.t.,* sup., q. 15, a. 2).

b) **Penitential works cannot really compensate for sins.** Referring to the penance that the confessor assigns in the sacrament, John Paul II teaches:

> What is the meaning of this *satisfaction* that one makes or the *penance* that one performs? Certainly it is not a price that one pays for the sin absolved and for the forgiveness obtained: no human price can match what is obtained, which is the fruit of Christ's Precious Blood. Acts of satisfaction—which, while remaining simple and humble, should be made to express more clearly all that they signify—mean a number of valuable things: they are the sign *of the personal commitment* that the Christian has made to God, in the Sacrament, to begin a new life (and therefore they should not be reduced to mere formulas to be recited, but should consist of acts of worship, charity, mercy or reparation). They include the idea that the pardoned sinner is able to join his own physical and spiritual mortification—which has been sought after or at least accepted—to the Passion of Jesus who has obtained the forgiveness for him. They remind us that even after absolution there remains in the Christian a dark area, due to the wound of sin, to the imperfection of love in repentance, to the weakening of the spiritual faculties. It is an area in which there still operates an infectious source of sin which must always be fought with mortification and penance. This is the meaning of the humble but sincere act of satisfaction.[17]

---

15. John XXIII, *Paenitentiam agere, AAS* 54 (1962) 488, *PE,* 269.29; St. Augustine, *Serm.* 351.5.12, *PL,* 39:1549.

16. John Paul II, *Reconciliatio et paenitentia,* 26, *AAS* 77 (1985) 243, *OR,* 17 Dec. 1984, 9.

17. John Paul II, *Reconciliatio et paenitentia,* 31, *AAS* 77 (1985) 263–64, *OR,* 17 Dec. 1984, 12.

Thus, doing penance does not satisfy or make up for sin by making adequate compensation for it, but by exercising one's contrite will and maintaining it in one's renewed relationship with God.

c) **Penitential works must be united with Jesus' sacrifice.** As John Paul II also points out, solidarity with Jesus is the key to the effectiveness of any penance. People do not make reparation on their own but only through the Lord (see DS 1690–91/904). United with that of Jesus, one's satisfaction for sin really contributes to one's sanctification. For Jesus did not preempt his followers' responsibilities: without him one can do nothing, but in him one can and must bear much fruit (see Jn 15.4–6).

2. Some Acts Are More Appropriately Penitential than Others

Any virtuous act or suffering of a person in friendship with God can be a work of penance if united with Jesus' passion. That is clear from the prayer of the confessor for his penitent, now optional, which formerly ended every celebration of the sacrament of penance: "May the Passion of our Lord Jesus Christ, the intercession of the Blessed Virgin Mary, and of all the saints, whatever good you do and suffering you endure, heal your sins, help you to grow in holiness, and reward you with eternal life."[18] Still, the purpose of satisfying for sin is especially clear in accepting suffering and in acts such as prayer, fasting, and almsgiving.

a) **Prayer, fasting, and almsgiving are basic forms of penance.** Although recognizing other forms of penance, the Old Testament proposes three typical practices: prayer for the pardon of sin, fasting, and almsgiving (see Tb 12.8–10, Is 58.3–10). While Jesus condemns abuses in these practices, he teaches that, done rightly, they are meritorious and will receive the Father's reward (see Mt 6.1–18; cf. DS 1543/807).

Their point is clear enough in light of the fact that sin alienates the sinner from God, upsets the order of the self, and damages human community; but prayer draws one nearer to God, fasting imposes order on oneself, and almsgiving expresses love of neighbor which forms community. Again, there are three roots of sin: "the desire of the flesh, the desire of the eyes, the pride in riches" (1 Jn 2.16). These can be understood as unruly sensual appetites (to which fasting is an antidote), excessive desire for earthly goods (to which almsgiving is an antidote), and proud self-confidence that fails sufficiently to recognize dependence on God (to which prayer is an antidote).[19]

b) **Prayer is the best way to expiate sin and overcome it.** By prayer, the fundamental category of Christian action (see *CMP*, 29), God's revelation is constantly appropriated and brought to bear on life. Work and other action become prayer only if regularly shaped and enlivened by intervals of explicit, conscious prayer. As, for fallen men and women, the act of faith necessarily is an act of

---

18. *The Rites*, 363.
19. See John Paul II, Message for Lent (1979), 2, *AAS* 71 (1979) 346–47, *OR*, 12 Mar. 1979, 1; Homily in the Parish of John the Baptist on Via Giulia, 5, *Inseg.* 6.1 (1981) 642–43, *OR*, 16 Mar. 1981, 11; *S.t.*, sup., q. 15, a. 3. For a balanced, brief treatment of almsgiving, prayer, and fasting: Bouyer, *Introduction to Spirituality*, 176–83.

conversion from sin and toward God, so every sincere prayer is at least implicitly penitential: a work of acting against sin and making up for it. Jesus' model prayer includes specific petitions for forgiveness of sin and protection against temptation (see Mt 6.12–13, Lk 11.4); but with or without specific penitential content, prayer, both personal and liturgical, is the best sort of penance. Best of all is the sacrifice of the Mass.

Other penitential works are effective only insofar as they express conversion of heart, and conversion of heart begins and is maintained only in prayer. Moreover, since no human work really compensates for sin and any effort to overcome its consequences can only begin to do so, prayer is essential to invoke the help of the Holy Spirit, who accomplishes what one cannot do for oneself (see *CMP*, 29.C). So, for instance, prayer is necessary to overcome the world's disbelief, widespread avarice, and the conflicts threatening humankind.[20]

c) **Fasting subordinates sensuality and liberates spirituality.** Superficial satisfactions often make it difficult for people to exercise reasonable deliberation and free choice in shaping their personalities according to faith, hope, and charity, and bringing themselves into conformity with Jesus. Seeking to escape fear of death and other lesser anxieties by plunging into what is immediate and tangible, they all too easily begin to consider the unseen kingdom less real than the visible world and heaven a mere fantasy.

Fasting—that is, the deliberate renunciation not only of food but of other means of consumption, stimulation, and sensory enjoyment—frees the mind and heart for spiritual life, and so serves the penitential purpose of overcoming the residue of sin and strengthening a person to persevere in the purpose of amendment. Fasting serves prayer by facilitating it, while prayer complements fasting by making it fruitful (see *S.t.,* 2–2, q. 147, a. 1).[21]

Besides denying oneself what must be denied in order to avoid sin and fulfill the responsibilities of personal vocation, one should limit the enjoyment not only of food and drink, but of sleep, entertainment, play, and other forms of enjoyable experience. This is in order to redress the balance for previous self-indulgence, increase self-mastery over desires, and intensify the readiness to act according to the Christian modes of response and the hope for their promised heavenly fulfillment (see *S.t.,* 2–2, q. 147, a. 3).

d) **Self-denial purifies one's vocational commitments.** Following Jesus is fulfilling one's personal vocation. Yet initially the commitments that make up that vocation are imperfect. Young people study partly to display their talents for others'

20. See Pius XI, *Caritate Christi compulsi, AAS* 24 (1932) 185–88, *PE,* 213.15–21. This encyclical, published in 1932 in response to worldwide economic collapse, goes on to call for penance, and summarizes (*AAS* 191, *PE,* 28): "Prayer, then, and penance are the two potent inspirations sent to us at this time by God, that we may lead back to Him mankind that has gone astray and wanders about without a guide: they are the inspirations that will dispel and remedy the first and principal cause of every form of disturbance and rebellion, the revolt of man against God." The same theme is developed in Mary's messages at her various appearances of recent times.

21. See Paul VI, *Paenitemini, AAS* 58 (1966) 181, Flannery, 2:5; John Paul II, General Audience (21 Mar. 1979), *Inseg.* 2.1 (1979) 683–87, *OR,* 26 Mar. 1979, 1 and 12.

admiration, take jobs partly to gain wealth and status, and so on. Couples marry in the Lord, yet their good motives are mixed with not-yet-integrated desires for the pleasures of marriage and the comforts of family life. Men and women become priests or religious to serve Jesus and his Church in special ways, yet they also are motivated by elitism, role playing, and other unworthy concerns.

Since all such mixed motives eventually cause trouble, vocational commitments must be gradually purified and repeatedly reaffirmed. In some cases, faithfulness will be impossible otherwise, so that such purification eventually becomes a matter of urgent moral necessity. Progress can be hastened by deliberately frustrating the selfish and otherwise unworthy elements of one's motives as one becomes aware of them. This is done by acting contrary to the unworthy motive insofar as that promotes or is in harmony with the more appropriate motive, for example, giving up the pleasures of marriage insofar as that promotes or at least is in harmony with the real goods of marriage and family. Carried out in a penitential spirit, this practice is an important sort of fasting. Its specific fruit is the deepening and stabilizing of vocational commitments, so that in fulfilling them one more and more truly takes up one's cross and follows Jesus.

e) **Retreats and pilgrimages should combine prayer and self-denial.** Many common pious exercises are reducible to prayer and fasting, taking *fasting* in an inclusive sense. Retreats and pilgrimages, for example, are times for prayer whose success depends on self-denial: setting aside normal activities and distractions, choosing not to use available leisure in some other way, accepting the austerities of the retreat house, the inconveniences of travel, and so on. Like other penitential works, retreats and pilgrimages are useless unless one has a contrite heart.[22] If accompanied by most of the comforts and distractions of a vacation—although vacations also have their place—a retreat or pilgrimage hardly qualifies as penance.

f) **Almsgiving opens one to others and fosters communion.** There are at least two popular misunderstandings of almsgiving: that it is gratuitous condescension toward people whose claim to help is questionable and that it includes only handouts to relieve pressing immediate needs. These misunderstandings prejudice many against a practice which Jesus teaches is necessary for entry into his kingdom (see Lk 12.32–34).

Almsgiving should be understood as sharing what one has with others in need, out of love of neighbor (see 1 Cor 13.3). By almsgiving people open themselves to others, set aside the selfishness underlying their sins, and so cancel the boundaries between mine and yours. Those who give build up the communion of love, which is Jesus' body, and so give alms to him personally (see Mt 25.34–40).

Almsgiving is not limited to handouts to beggars, but extends to helping others meet any kind of bodily or spiritual need (see *S.t.,* 2–2, q. 32, a. 2). Hence, one gives alms in using time and talents to help others (as is done in every form of apostolate), offering them comfort when they suffer, and so forth.[23]

---

22. See Pius XII, *Le pèlerinage de Lourdes, AAS* 49 (1957) 612–15, *PE,* 259.35–42.

23. See John Paul II, General Audience (28 Mar. 1979), *Inseg.* 2.1 (1979) 724–29, *OR,* 2 Apr. 1979, 1 and 12.

Almsgiving in practice opposes both the quest for security in wealth and the false notion that what one has is absolutely and exclusively one's own, to do with as one pleases (see below, 10.E.5.b–e). It is an essential penitential practice inasmuch as it works against the harm sin does to genuine community while stimulating hope for the real security of heaven.

g) Work for justice can be a form of almsgiving. Some disparage conventional almsgiving, maintaining that such help, directed toward the materially poor, humiliates the recipients and even contributes to maintaining the unjust social structures and other oppressive conditions which underlie economic want. Two things must be said in response.

First, if motivated by charity, it is a form of almsgiving to get at the roots of social injustice by using any morally acceptable means which have a reasonable prospect of helping those suffering from poverty and oppression; indeed, this is better than other almsgiving insofar as it requires self-sacrifice and promises greater benefits for those who suffer. On the other hand, using morally questionable means to fight social injustice at best helps some at the expense of others, and so is contrary to charity; moreover, as a way of dealing with evil, it is self-defeating, for it extends and perpetuates sin, the ultimate source of all human suffering.

Second, until social injustice is entirely eliminated at the parousia, conventional almsgiving will remain necessary, for without it those who could meet others' desperate needs would leave them uncared for. Merely expressing righteous indignation about social injustices benefits nobody. It is no substitute for immediate help to individuals in desperate need.

h) Suffering willingly in union with Jesus is an excellent penance. While God's re-creative act will finally overcome all evil, in this life everyone suffers. This happens when one is personally *aware* of something bad while experiencing or undergoing it. But even though one's feelings rebel, this awareness itself actually is a good, for it is a grasp on reality as it truly is (see 1.E.6.b). Often suffering motivates people to do what is required to avoid or overcome evil; for example, the suffering alcoholism causes is a motive to avoid this form of self-destruction. Suffering is harder for those without faith, because they see no point in it. But faith views as a more or less direct consequence of sin everything else bad and the suffering it brings; and insofar as an individual's own sins deserve it, he or she should accept this consequence as punishment.

Many people nevertheless suffer undeservedly because of defects in their heredity or social situation, poverty, sickness, failure in the pursuit of good objectives, or other hardships. Especially if they suffer for doing what is right, they are like Jesus in suffering undeservedly, and they can be still more like him by accepting unavoidable suffering and offering it to the Father as a loving sacrifice. In this way, their suffering takes on a penitential value. For, united with Jesus' suffering, it atones for sin and merits God's re-creative act, which alone will repair all the horrible consequences of sin. John Paul II teaches:

> *In the cross, God has changed radically the meaning of suffering.* The latter, which was the fruit and testimony of sin, has now become participation in Christ's redemptive expiation. As such, it contains within it, already now, the announce-

ment of the definitive victory over sin and its consequences, by means of participation in the glorious resurrection of the Saviour.[24]

Thus, for Christians, willingly accepted suffering is a very appropriate penance.

3. One Should Do the Penance the Church Prescribes

The penitential works imposed in the sacrament of penance will be treated in the next question. Those to be considered here are the ones the Church prescribes by her general law and discipline.[25]

a) **Much of what is prescribed is required on other grounds.** The primary prescription is to do penance by faithfully fulfilling the commitments of one's personal vocation, accepting hardships patiently, and enduring life's inevitable anxieties. Those afflicted with infirmity, illness, poverty, or misfortune are called to offer their suffering with Jesus for the benefit of others as well as their own benefit. Beyond this, the Church urges every Catholic to perform some voluntary acts in response to the divine precept to do penance, and calls on priests and religious to satisfy the precept more fully.

To resist worldliness, people living comfortably in affluent societies should practice greater self-denial while at the same time helping people elsewhere in the world who suffer from material poverty. (Helping others can be and often is a duty in strict justice: see 10.E.5.b–d.) Using what is saved by self-denial for the benefit of others makes renunciation more meaningful, and so renders it not only easier but more joyful.

b) **The Church prescribes a minimal common observance of penance.** In the United States, Catholics are required to abstain from eating meat on Ash Wednesday and every Friday of Lent, and to fast on Ash Wednesday and Good Friday. Everyone over fourteen is bound by the law of abstinence, and adults are bound to observe the law about fasting from their nineteenth birthday until after their fifty-ninth birthday. While an exception to this minimal law may be made for a serious reason, arbitrarily ignoring it is a grave matter. Small children are not bound by it, but pastors and parents are to teach them a true sense of penance, which they should put into practice in some appropriate way.

All the Fridays of the year and all the weekdays of Lent (unless they happen to be solemnities) remain penitential time: works of penance, including fast and abstinence beyond the minimum required, are strongly recommended. Participation in daily Mass also is strongly recommended during Lent. Moreover, being required to fast and abstain less than they might be, Catholics in the United States are especially urged to practice almsgiving.

---

24. John Paul II, Address at Cottolengo Institute for the Sick and Aged (Turin), 3, *Inseg.* 3.1 (1980) 873, *OR,* 28 Apr. 1980, 5; also see his *Salvifici doloris,* 25–27, *AAS* 76 (1984) 235–42, *OR,* 20 Feb. 1984, 6–7.

25. See Paul VI, *Paenitemini, AAS* 58 (1966) 182–85, Flannery, 2:6–9; *CIC,* cc. 1249–53; adapted for the United States: National Conference of Catholic Bishops, *Implementation of the 1983 Code of Canon Law: Complementary Norms* (Washington, D.C.: United States Catholic Conference, 1991), 19, 29–34.

4. Personal Penance Should Be Supplemented by Indulgences

An indulgence is a remission of the temporal punishment due to sins already forgiven. As was explained in the introduction to this question, *temporal punishment* refers to certain effects of sins that can continue to afflict sinners even after the sins themselves are forgiven. Thus, indulgences are not concerned with the guilt of sin, which is the main concern of the sacrament of penance, but with punishment consequent on sin, also dealt with to some extent by penitential works. Indulgences are partial or plenary, depending on whether they free one from part or all of the temporal punishment due to sin.

An indulgence is obtained by a rightly disposed Christian who meets certain conditions set by the Church. The Church can grant indulgences because Jesus authorized her to bind and loose, thus giving her the power to apply his own merits and those of the saints.[26] Though a characteristic feature of Catholic penitential life (see *CMP*, 32.2), indulgences often are misunderstood, and many Catholics never take advantage of them.

a) **The merits of Jesus and the saints underlie indulgences.** Someone who dies in God's friendship but without having done sufficient penance by way of temporal punishment due to his or her sins will suffer a cleansing called "purgatory" after death (see DS 856/464, 1304/693, 1820/983). However, penitent Christians are not isolated individuals left to their own resources. Repentant and reconciled with the Church and with God, they are in solidarity not only with other members of the Church on earth but with Jesus and all who rejoice with him in heaven. Thus, those whose own penitential works are inadequate to deal with the temporal punishment due their sins can be helped by the merits of Jesus and the saints. Authorized by Jesus to administer the saving fruits of his sacrifice, the Church can apply those fruits and the merits of the saints to benefit repentant sinners and lighten their burden. The act by which the Church not only prays for repentant sinners but intervenes authoritatively on their behalf is called "granting an indulgence."

b) **Indulgences should be appreciated and used.** The main reason to use indulgences is that doing so helps overcome some of the consequences of sin, and so limits—and possibly even eliminates, for oneself or others—the purgation that otherwise might be necessary after death. Using indulgences also is a reminder of the seriousness of sin and of one's personal inability ever to make up for it. Indulgences build up the fellowship of the Church: they depend on, and so increase, one's solidarity with Jesus and the saints, while their use acknowledges the Church's authority to employ the keys to the kingdom of heaven. In offering indulgences for those in purgatory, furthermore, one exercises love toward them and so strengthens one's bonds with them. Finally, indulgences encourage the Church's members to meet her conditions in granting them, and that is spiritually beneficial.

26. For the preceding definitions of *indulgence, partial indulgence,* and *plenary indulgence: CIC,* cc. 992–93. The treatment of indulgences here is based mainly on Paul VI, *Indulgentiarum doctrina, AAS* 59 (1967) 5–24, Flannery, 1:62–79. See Basil Cole, O.P., "Whatever Became of Indulgences?" *Homiletic and Pastoral Review* 80 (May 1980): 60–68.

c) **To use indulgences, several things must be taken into account.** Rather than substituting for personal penitential works and sufferings, indulgences enhance their worth and effectiveness before God. To gain an indulgence, then, certain conditions must be met. Having done so, one may pray that the benefit of the indulgence apply to the dead who can use the help of other members of the Church to complete their purgation and enter into heavenly glory, or, except in a few cases where the indulgence can be applied only to the souls in purgatory, to oneself. (However, an indulgence cannot be gained for another living person.)[27]

d) **Many partial indulgences are gained very easily.** Indulgences are called either "partial" or "plenary" insofar as they offer remission of either some or all of the temporal punishment due sin.

While some remission of temporal punishment can be gained through one's own penitential acts, that remission often can be doubled by gaining a partial indulgence, which the Church attaches to various acts. For example, the Church offers a partial indulgence if one engages in various pious exercises and devotions, gives alms, denies oneself something licit, or in the course of one's daily work and suffering thinks of God with humble confidence and adds some invocation.

In order to gain partial indulgences, for himself or herself or on behalf of the dead, one who lives in friendship with God need only intend to do so. This option may be made generally and for the indefinite future, and also may be changed from time to time. Thus, someone who does penitential works and lives prayerfully can gain many indulgences every day without even thinking about doing so.[28]

e) **To gain a plenary indulgence, further conditions must be met.** To gain a plenary indulgence, one must be a member of the Church in good standing and in the state of grace, must do the specific work to which the indulgence is attached, and within several days before or after must receive the sacraments of penance and the Eucharist, and pray for the pope's intentions. It also is necessary to be free of all attachment to sin, even venial sin. The prayer for the pope's intentions need be no more than one Our Father and Hail Mary, and may be some other prayer. A single sacramental confession suffices to gain several plenary indulgences, but it is necessary to receive Holy Communion and pray for the pope's intentions to receive each.

If the conditions are not perfectly met, an otherwise plenary indulgence becomes partial. (But in some situations, confessors and bishops can mitigate the conditions for those who cannot fulfill them.) Except for the dying, who are offered a plenary indulgence at the moment of death, and who need not fulfill the usual conditions provided they have habitually prayed, only one plenary indulgence can be gained each day.[29]

f) **Not all these conditions are easily met.** There are many opportunities to gain plenary indulgences if one intends to do so, is not excommunicated, is living

---

27. See *CIC*, cc. 992–94.

28. See *CIC*, cc. 993–94 and c. 996; Apostolic Penitentiary, *Enchiridion of Indulgences,* 2nd rev. ed., trans. William T. Barry, C.Ss.R. (New York: Catholic Book Publishing, 1969), 15–40.

29. See *CIC*, c. 996, §1; *Enchiridion of Indulgences,* 25–27, 60.

in friendship with God, receives the sacrament of penance regularly and frequently, and offers some prayer for the pope's intentions each time one receives Holy Communion. But the requirement of total detachment from sin, including venial sin, may not be so easily met.

In praying that a plenary indulgence be applied to the dead, however, one might wonder: Must I be totally detached from sin to gain a benefit for a soul who is totally detached from it? It would seem not, since total detachment from sin seems to be a disposition for the remission of punishment rather than a condition for effective action on behalf of another. Hence, even those unwilling to give up some venial sin may be able to gain plenary indulgences on behalf of the dead.[30]

Question C: How Should One Use the Sacrament of Penance?

While baptism is the fundamental sacrament of conversion, the baptized have fulfilled their responsibilities in respect to their own baptismal conversion. Further responsibilities do flow from the baptismal commitment, but these embrace the whole life of faith (see *CMP*, 30.I), and so include all one's moral responsibilities. Every Catholic also has responsibilities with respect to the baptismal conversion of others, but these are responsibilities (already treated in 2.E) to accept and fulfill personal vocation as one's share in the Church's apostolate, in which the gospel's message of repentance is central. Hence, the sacramental focus of Christian responsibilities specifically related to repentance and reconciliation is not baptism but the sacrament of penance.

This sacrament is entirely subordinated to the Eucharist, the supreme sacrament of reconciliation. The Eucharist makes Jesus' perfect sacrifice always present in the Church, in order that his members may share in it and so be united with him, both in his redemptive act and in the resurrection life with which God answers it (see *CMP*, 22.G, 33.B). As the Council of Trent teaches, the Eucharist protects those who worthily participate in it from mortal sin and frees them from the guilt of venial sin (see DS 1638/875; *CMP*, 33.D). In sinning mortally after baptism, however, people not only offend God but betray their baptismal commitment to Jesus and wound his body, the Church. They remain members, but are moribund; that is why mortal sinners are deprived of Holy Communion.[31] But the absolution of the sacrament of penance transforms those dead in sin into revivified members of the Church, so that once more they can share fully in the Eucharist. In this way the

---

30. If this view is sound, the opportunity to help others greatly by forgoing what may be a relatively slight advantage to oneself argues in favor of forming the intention that any plenary indulgence one gains until the moment of one's own death be applied to that soul in purgatory who has the greatest claim on one's love.

31. John Paul II, Address to Bishops of Abruzzi and Molise, 4, *AAS* 74 (1982) 220–21, *OR*, 18 Jan. 1982, 7, quotes 1 Cor 11.27–29, and comments: "The theory according to which the Eucharist forgives mortal sin without the sinner having recourse to the sacrament of penance, is not reconcilable with the teaching of the Church. It is true that the sacrifice of the Mass, from which all grace comes to the Church, obtains for the sinner the gift of conversion, without which forgiveness is not possible, but that does not at all mean that those who have committed a mortal sin can approach Eucharistic Communion without having first become reconciled with God by means of the priestly ministry."

sacrament of penance plays an essential part in the reconciliation which the Eucharist perfectly realizes.[32]

It is true that someone with perfect contrition can be forgiven before approaching the sacrament of penance. But this is so only insofar as perfect contrition necessarily includes a desire to receive the sacrament, at least the desire implicit in any genuinely contrite heart to do whatever God wants in order to be reconciled with him (see DS 1543/807, 1677/898).

Therefore, the first responsibility with regard to the sacrament of penance is not to neglect it. In receiving the sacrament, there are further responsibilities: to do everything necessary to make its reception valid and fruitful, so that it will be a true renewal and deepening of the fundamental Christian conversion to God.[33]

1. The Sacrament of Penance Should Be Received When Appropriate

While only under certain conditions is there a strict obligation to receive the sacrament of penance, so that not doing so would be in itself a grave matter, a good reason for receiving it often exists, such that, in the absence of any contrary reason, the sacrament should be received.

Like all the sacraments, this one always is a true act of worship. Those who receive it not only confess their sins but are united with Jesus in confessing God's majesty and praising him for his mercy. Thus, whenever receiving the sacrament is appropriate, it should be received out of reverence and gratitude toward God, for the sake of its fruits for oneself, and as an act of witness and good example to others.

a) **Mortal sins should be confessed before receiving Communion.** In both penance and the Eucharist, Jesus makes himself present to his members in the Church through her human acts. He does this in order to rejoin them to himself (by the sacrament of penance) and to nurture their communion with him (by the sacrament of the Eucharist). But just as an amputated finger could not be nurtured without its first being rejoined to one's hand, so Jesus cannot nurture his members with his body and blood without first rejoining them to himself.

Worthy reception of Holy Communion therefore requires a clear conscience. The Church teaches that, before receiving, someone aware of having committed a mortal sin should purify his or her conscience by making a sacramental confession (see DS 1661/893).[34]

b) **Mortal sins must be confessed at least once a year.** The Church's law requires that Catholics confess at least once each year if they have committed mortal sins.[35] Since they also have the duty to receive Holy Communion at least

---

32. Although some deny it, many theologians support the view that the sacrament of penance remits guilt precisely insofar as it brings the sinner into touch with the Church's means of grace, and so provides him or her with God's grace. See Clarence McAuliffe, S.J., "Penance and Reconciliation with the Church," *Theological Studies* 26 (1965): 1–39.

33. A helpful guide to the use of the sacrament of penance: Thomas Weinandy, O.F.M.Cap., *Be Reconciled to God: A Family Guide to Confession* (Gaithersburg, Md.: The Word Among Us Press, 1988).

34. *CIC,* c. 916, allows for exceptional cases; see 3.B.3.a for the conditions under which someone who lacks the opportunity to confess a mortal sin may nevertheless receive Communion.

35. See *CIC,* c. 989.

once during the Easter season, this annual confession typically is part of the "Easter duty" for those who sometimes commit mortal sins and only minimally practice the faith. Those in danger of death also should receive Holy Communion as Viaticum, and they have a grave obligation to confess any mortal sin, if they can, before doing so.

Plainly, though, it is foolish to put off confessing mortal sins for as long as a year or until one is in danger of death. Reverence for God, concern for the Church wounded by one's sins, and reasonable self-interest should lead one to take the first opportunity to confess any mortal sin. A person who does not is likely to be tempted to commit additional sins and even to become obdurate.

c) **The sacrament of penance is effective against venial sin.** Called to holiness, which requires perfect, single-hearted love (see LG 40), all Christians likewise are called to complete sinlessness and have a strict obligation to struggle against venial sin, especially deliberate venial sin—the sort committed with sufficient reflection and full consent, which falls short of being mortal only because the matter is not grave. Regular, frequent reception of the sacrament of penance, with the right dispositions, is an especially effective means of carrying on this struggle (see *CMP*, 32.D).

Although venial sins can be forgiven in other ways, receiving the sacrament is a far richer Christian act than any other that is suited to the obligatory task of continuing conversion (see *CMP*, 32.D). Pius XII teaches that by frequent confession "genuine self-knowledge is increased, Christian humility grows, bad habits are corrected, spiritual neglect and tepidity are resisted, the conscience is purified, the will strengthened, a salutary self-control is attained, and grace is increased in virtue of the Sacrament itself."[36] These benefits, antithetical to any deliberate sin, are effects proper to the sacrament, aspects of the very conversion for the sake of which God has provided it.[37]

d) **The sacrament of penance should be received rather often.** In view of the foregoing considerations, and in the absence of any good reason to the contrary, people should receive the sacrament of penance as often as they find it helpful in their struggle against venial sin. For some that might be once a month, for others more often, perhaps every week. As a practical matter, omitting frequent confession usually means acquiescing in habits of deliberate venial sin and neglecting the responsibility to struggle against such sins. Although that neglect is not a grave matter, it is serious, because venial sins, especially deliberate ones, are important in themselves and often lead to mortal sins (see *CMP*, 18.C).

e) **It is good to participate in communal celebrations of penance.** The rite of penance as revised after Vatican II includes a normal form of communal celebration of the sacrament of penance culminating in individual confession and absolution of sins. A liturgy of the word and appropriate prayers and hymns in

---

36. Pius XII, *Mystici corporis Christi, AAS* 35 (1943) 235, *PE*, 225.88; cf. *CIC*, c. 988, §2.

37. See John Paul II, Address to Penitentiaries of the Major Basilicas, *AAS* 73 (1981) 204, *OR*, 23 Feb. 1981, 20; B. Kelly, C.Ss.P., "The Confession of Devotion," *Irish Theological Quarterly* 33 (1966): 84–90.

which everyone joins are part of it. It thus provides a richer liturgical setting for the sacrament and manifests its ecclesial nature more clearly. The revised rite also includes penitential services which are similar but do not incorporate confession and absolution. While those who participate in such penitential services do not receive the sacrament of penance, the nonsacramental service can prepare for the sacrament and also can help sinners dispose themselves to receive the grace of contrition when no priest is available to give sacramental absolution.

Both sacramental and nonsacramental communal celebrations build up the Church as a penitential community and take advantage of the power to convert which God's word possesses whenever people gather to listen to it. Not only is it good to participate in both types of communal celebration, sometimes that should be done, for example, if one ought to receive the sacrament and can only do that by participating in a communal celebration, or if, being unable to receive the sacrament of penance, one finds a nonsacramental penitential celebration conducive to sincere repentance.

2. Penance Requires Self-examination and Contrition for One's Sins

No one should approach the sacrament of penance out of mere routine or solely for extrinsic reasons like impressing or pleasing someone else. The only good reasons are to obtain forgiveness for mortal sins and to carry on an effective struggle against venial sin. To achieve these purposes, people must call their sins to mind, firmly reject them, and turn toward God.[38]

a) **One should try sincerely to be aware of one's sins.** People should live according to the moral truth written by God in the human heart and perfectly made known by the gospel. The Church's moral teaching makes moral truth more easily and precisely available. Living by these standards means using them not only to shape deliberations, choices, and actions, but to evaluate what one has done, so that any necessary adjustments can be made. Such retrospective evaluation is called *examination of conscience.*

It is best done daily, then recalled when preparing to receive the sacrament of penance (see PO 18). Before examining conscience, a person should pray for the light of the Holy Spirit, who alone can overcome rationalization and self-deception, uncover sin's roots, and make clear the true state of the heart.[39]

One should consider how well one's responsibilities are being fulfilled in regard to God, to moral truth, to other people, and to oneself. The examination should not be limited to private and family life, but should extend to work and community life, taking into account all the responsibilities pertaining to every aspect of personal vocation and the various projects intended to fulfill it. Not only what one has done, but what one has failed to do, should be considered, not least with respect to social responsibilities, whose neglect leads to personal, actual guilt for the injustices

---

38. *CIC,* c. 987, prescribes: "In order to receive the salvific remedy of the sacrament of penance, the Christian faithful ought to be so disposed that, having repudiated the sins committed and having a purpose of amendment, they are converted to God."

39. See John Paul II, *Dominum et vivificantem,* 44–45, *AAS* 78 (1986) 861–63, *OR,* 9 June 1986, 9.

existing in the various communities to which one belongs.[40] A reasonable effort should be made to recall and clearly discern any mortal sin which has been committed, anything which needs to be dealt with promptly (for example, an apology to be made, a neglect of duty to be remedied, an occasion of sin to be avoided), and failings in lesser matters where one is making a particular effort to do better.

b) **Neglect of examination can be a grave matter.** People may be tempted to avoid examination, for consciousness of sin causes painful feelings of guilt. But guilt feelings corresponding to reality are not bad. They signal one's true spiritual condition, as bodily aches and pains normally signal one's bodily condition. They can and should lead to seeking the needed and effective remedy: "If we say that we have no sin, we deceive ourselves, and the truth is not in us. If we confess our sins, he who is faithful and just will forgive us our sins and cleanse us from all unrighteousness" (1 Jn 1.8–9).

Neglecting to examine conscience when one thinks it essential for a good confession is itself a grave matter. In such a case, as much effort must be put into the examination of conscience as into any other important matter in life.

c) **The moral criticisms others offer should be considered carefully.** In the face of both charitable admonitions and angry words of condemnation, but especially the latter, a person is inclined to react defensively by seeking some self-justification or excuse; often one is tempted to counterattack by pointing out some fault in the critic. Instead, all such criticisms should be noted and reviewed calmly during the next examination of conscience.

One should first ask: Is the norm stated or assumed by the critic a true requirement of morality? Perhaps with the best of intentions, people sometimes try to impose false standards on others, and so it is a mistake to accept moral criticism uncritically. For example, if charged with being uncharitable, one must ask whether the standard of charity employed is drawn from the gospel or from a sentimental spirituality which disregards unpleasant and unpopular truths of faith. If the critic did apply a true moral norm, one should ask whether the application was sound or whether there may have been a mistake in applying the norm, perhaps due to a misunderstanding of one's behavior.

If a true norm has been correctly applied, however, the critic has done the valuable service of assisting one's self-examination, and deserves gratitude for it. Even if the critic has misunderstood behavior which did not involve the moral fault alleged, reflection on the criticism sometimes can help one to adapt one's manner of speaking and acting so that it will more accurately reflect and bear witness to one's faith and good will.

d) **One's sins should be rejected firmly with a truly contrite heart.** The sacrament of penance does not remove sins as, say, brushing teeth removes particles from them—in a merely mechanical manner. Nor is it a device for spiritual

---

40. As a model, see "Appendix III: Form of Examination of Conscience," at the end of "Rite of Penance," *The Rites,* 441–45. A sound and helpful (though somewhat incomplete) guide: Richard J. Rego, *A Contemporary Adult Guide to Conscience for the Sacrament of Confession* (St. Paul, Minn.: Leaflet Missal, 1990).

accounting, which simply cancels sins so they will not be charged to one's account. Rather, the sacrament is an interpersonal exchange between prodigal children and their heavenly Father, in a meeting mediated by the confessor acting in the person of Jesus. To this meeting, the sinner must bring not only honest awareness of his or her sins but a contrite heart.

Contrition is more than regret or sadness about sin. People often regret what they remain willing to do, but one repents only what one wishes one had not done and wills never to do again; people often are sad about what they could not help and others' sins, but one repents only sins for which one is responsible. Contrition is more than uttering the words of an act of contrition; a person can be contrite without using a formula, and if a formula is used, one must mean what it says. Normally, people with contrite hearts not only give outward expression to repentance, but feel shame and sorrow for their sins, and experience anxiety about their relationship with God.

Still, contrition must not be psychologized and understood in emotional terms. Essentially it is a change of heart: the heart that freely embraced sin now freely rejects it. Instead of feelings, it is a real will to be freed of all one's mortal sins and be reconciled with God—or, in the case of the venial sinner, to make progress in the struggle against sin and live more perfectly in communion with God.

e) Contrition includes the will to confess and to stop sinning. Contrition includes within itself not only the utter rejection of past sin, but a firm purpose of amendment and readiness to do whatever God wants in order to receive his forgiveness. Referring to cases in which a baptized person has committed a mortal sin, the Council of Trent teaches that contrition "is a deep sorrow and detestation for sin committed, *with a resolution of sinning no more."* It adds that contrition "is certainly a preparation for the remission of sins, if it be accompanied by trust in the divine mercy and a desire *of fulfilling the other conditions* necessary to receive the sacrament properly" (DS 1676/897, translation amended, emphasis added). Real contrition for mortal sin involves some kind of desire, at least implicit, for the sacrament of penance (see DS 1677/898). Thus, it requires a will to fulfill all conditions for receiving that sacrament worthily, among them confession of all mortal sins (see DS 1707/917), a real purpose of amendment, and readiness to make reparation for injuries and do penance. Lacking this will, contrition is insincere, and both feelings of sorrow and resolutions to change for the better are ineffectual.

f) To arouse contrition, one should excite one's faith and hope. True contrition presupposes faith, which teaches sinners the truth of God's faithfulness despite their unfaithfulness. Only faith makes plain the full significance of sin as an offense that, if venial, impedes growth in charity and, if mortal, precludes communion with the divine persons and makes the sinner worthy of hell. Contrition also presupposes hope. For hope motivates one to live the Christian life and repent of failures to do so. Even more to the point: as confidence in God's grace and mercy, hope is needed to seek forgiveness and undertake what must be done to obtain it.

Even mortal sinners usually can believe and hope as true contrition requires, since even mortal sin usually does not destroy the human relationship which faith and hope previously established with Jesus and his Church. Thus, the grace of the

Holy Spirit, who lives in Jesus' Church, empowers sinners to continue to believe and hope, and so to repent. This faith and hope leads sinners not only to reject their sins, as they might if these were extrinsic to them, but to reject themselves as sinners and to be ready to do what is necessary to obtain forgiveness.[41] At least implicitly, a human love of God and true contrition are already present in such a will, even if it is not yet free of sin.

g) **Of itself, the sinner's act of contrition remains imperfect.** Trent teaches that there can be genuine contrition short of perfect contrition. This genuine contrition is based on a true awareness of sin's evil and on salutary fear of punishment, and includes the intention to amend. It is a divine gift, a true work of the Holy Spirit, which leads sinners toward reconciliation by disposing them to seek forgiveness in the sacrament of penance. Of itself, however, the contrition in question is not perfected by charity, and so it is called "imperfect contrition" or "attrition" (see DS 1678/898, 1705/915).[42] Trent also teaches that contrition sometimes is perfected before the sacrament of penance is received, although not without some kind of desire to receive it (see DS 1677/898).

People certainly should strive to make contrition perfect. This involves considering that, as God's friendship is a great good, and the closer that friendship is the better, so alienation from God is a great evil, and even a slight loss of closeness to God is a very important loss. Contrition also can be intensified and purified by considering why God is lovable above everything and everyone else: his goodness, his faithfulness and mercy, and Jesus' love, which led him to die so as to save not only humankind in general but oneself in particular. But even if such considerations bring one to a more than merely self-concerned rejection of one's sins, they cannot guarantee that the contrition is motivated by charity, which is a more-than-human love of God, poured forth in hearts by the Holy Spirit (see Rom 5.5).

h) **One must ask God for perfect contrition as a gift of his mercy.** St. Thomas teaches that for those who have sinned mortally perfect contrition and the conferral of charity are mutually dependent: a mortal sinner cannot love God as a child of God should without becoming perfectly contrite, and cannot become perfectly contrite without again loving God as his child. The two things can come together either before the sacrament is received or when it is received, provided the sacrament is approached with the right intentions.[43] In either case, the mortal sinner

---

41. John Paul II, General Audience (14 Mar. 1984), 2, *Inseg.* 7.1 (1984) 682, *OR,* 20 Mar. 1984, 1, teaches the intimate unity of sin with sinner: "Our evil choices do not pass alongside us; they do not exist before us; they do not pass through us as though they were events which do not involve us. Our evil choices, inasmuch as they are evil, *arise within us,* solely from us."

42. Catholic theologians have long debated whether imperfect contrition (attrition) which does not include as a motive love of God for his own sake is sufficient within the sacrament of penance. This controversy was explicitly left open by a decree of the Holy See (see DS 2070/1146). For a helpful account of the history of the concepts and controversies over contrition and attrition: *New Catholic Encyclopedia,* s.v. "contrition."

43. Modern authors distinguish perfect from imperfect contrition (or attrition) primarily by the penitent's subjectively discernible motives. St. Thomas, however, focuses on the objective factor, namely, whether or not charity perfects the act: *S.c.g.,* 4.72; *S.t.,* sup., q. 1, a. 1; q. 6, a. 1; q. 18, a. 1. And according to Thomas, sanctifying grace, which he holds is inseparably linked with

can make an act of perfect contrition only by making as genuine an act of contrition as possible, while asking God in his mercy to perfect this contrition by renewing the gift of charity. Charity surely will be restored in the sacrament of penance to anyone who is sincerely contrite and acts on that contrition by properly receiving the sacrament, for God promises forgiveness through it: "Receive the Holy Spirit. If you forgive the sins of any, they are forgiven them" (Jn 20.22–23; cf. Mt 18.18; DS 1670/894).

i) **Venial sins cannot be forgiven without contrition for them.** Contrition for venial sin can be genuine without being all-inclusive. Just as people can be willing to commit certain venial sins but not others, so they can be sorry for and prepared to give up some venial sins but not all.

However, no one can be forgiven anything without contrition for it. Progress in the struggle against venial sin therefore presupposes real contrition, which must include a sincere will to love God more perfectly and the real determination to stop committing the sin. People who repeatedly confess the same venial sins, making no progress in overcoming them, need to consider both the sincerity of their contrition and the possibility that the problem is not really a moral one. If the sins are fully deliberate, the sincerity of their contrition is questionable; but if the contrition is real and the unwanted acts are not deliberate, they may be caused by psychological factors.

3. Genuine Contrition Includes a Firm Purpose of Amendment

Trent includes in the very definition of contrition the resolution not to sin again. A truly contrite person who considers the possibility of committing the same sin or any mortal sin in the future rejects the idea and is prepared to do what is necessary entirely to avoid mortal sin.

a) **Sin has not really been rejected if one does not mean to avoid it.** The purpose of amendment essential to contrition is completely different from a good resolution without real contrition. Rather than being a reluctant renunciation of sin, still regarded as desirable, purpose of amendment is part of a rejection of sin considered as entirely repugnant. To put the matter positively, the purpose of amendment rooted in real contrition is an aspect of becoming reconciled with God, because anyone who longs for the restoration of divine friendship—or, in the case of contrition for venial sin, for its growth—also wills to cling to that good and to remain with God, as the prodigal willed to remain with his father, always cherishing his love and never again rejecting it or even being less than wholehearted in accepting and responding to it.

Since genuine contrition includes such a purpose of amendment, someone who is not prepared to pay the necessary price to put sin aside, to make reparation for injuries caused to others, and to do what can be done to avoid sin in the future, is not really contrite. A person may feel guilty, regret having sinned, recite contrite words, and even make good resolutions; yet, lacking the will to do everything

---

charity, is not subjectively discernible in itself, but only imperfectly through its signs: *S.t.*, 1–2, q. 112, a. 5. On this view, followed here, sinners cannot *know* that their contrition is perfect.

possible to overcome sin in practice, he or she does not reject it in the way necessary for real contrition.

b) One must intend not to commit any grave sin whatsoever. Sometimes people enmeshed in a form of life involving grave sin detest the sin and wish to be reconciled to God, but recoil from paying the price. Believing or hoping that one day they will be able to give up the sin without so high a cost, they plan to amend their lives then: "Give me chastity, Lord, but not just yet"; "We look forward to better times, when it no longer will be necessary to lie and cheat in order to make a profit." This certainly is not as wicked as a will to persist in sin forever, yet even if the intention to amend in the future is real, it is not the purpose of amendment required for present contrition. Indeed, it is at least an early stage of the persistence in sin that can lead to hell (see *CMP*, 18.E).

Similarly, those who intend only to reduce the gravity or number of their mortal sins are not truly contrite. Even if it involves a sincere intention eventually to stop sinning entirely, such gradualism also involves a present will to commit a certain quota of sins.[44] And since a person who does not reject some kind of sin entirely is unlikely to resist temptations to commit it, a gradualist strategy does not work.

Spiritual counselors sometimes tell sinners to be patient with themselves and to exercise compassion toward themselves. Such advice would be sound and helpful if it meant only that sinners should be confident that they receive God's forgiveness when they are truly contrite and should not nurture hostile feelings toward themselves or judge their guilt greater than it is. However, the advice is ambiguous, and can be taken as a recommendation of gradualism; understood in that sense it should be rejected as pernicious. For sinners should not be patient with their sins, nor should they regard them as a pitiable misfortune; they should not calmly bear their guilt or consider it an affliction to be alleviated by gentle treatment. Instead, they should admit their guilt, firmly hope in the forgiveness and help of God, make the commitment to change which true contrition requires, and undertake to do whatever is necessary, no matter how difficult, to live holy lives.

c) Knowing one will sin again blocks purpose of amendment. A history of relapses and anxiety about the future are compatible with genuine contrition. Past experience can make one anxious and lead by way of self-observation to the belief that one probably will "fall into" sin again. However, nobody falls by accident into grave sin or even into deliberate venial sin: such sins are committed only by making free choices. A free choice is a choice that can be made or not; one makes it only inasmuch as one freely determines oneself to it. Since it is impossible to sin

---

44. See John Paul II, *Familiaris consortio*, 34, *AAS* 74 (1982) 123–24, *OR*, 21–28 Dec. 1981, 7. Summarizing the same teaching, John Paul II, Address to Priests Participating in a Study Seminar on "Responsible Parenthood", 4, *Inseg.* 6.2 (1983) 564, *OR*, 10 Oct. 1983, 7, forcefully recalls Catholic teaching concerning grace: "To maintain that situations exist in which it is not, *de facto*, possible for the spouses to be faithful to *all* the requirements of the truth of conjugal love is equivalent to forgetting this event of grace which characterizes the New Covenant: the grace of the Holy Spirit makes possible that which is not possible to man, left solely to his own powers. It is therefore necessary to support the spouses in their spiritual lives, to invite them to resort frequently to the Sacraments of Confession and the Eucharist for a continual return, a permanent conversion to the truth of conjugal love."

deliberately without free choice, someone who truly rejects any sin at present cannot possibly know he or she will deliberately commit that sin in the future.

Of course, a person can be aware that if everything in the future were to remain just as in the past, another relapse would occur. But purpose of amendment means readiness to do what is necessary, with the help of God's grace, so that the future will not be just like the past. Moreover, it presupposes hope by which one counts on God's grace rather than despairing of it. Thus, although a feeling of anxiety is compatible with a true purpose of amendment, someone who really is contrite wills to avoid every mortal sin (and any venial sin for which he or she is contrite), begs the Holy Spirit for the strength required to persevere despite temptation, and counts on him to provide that strength, although perhaps with deep feelings of self-doubt and anxiety about the future.

d) **One should persevere in repentance one day at a time.** While a purpose of amendment must refer to the indefinite future, in practice repentant sinners can mitigate their anxiety by focusing on their immediate responsibility: to seek the kingdom and resist temptation today. This strategy applies Jesus' advice regarding worry about the necessities of life:

> Your heavenly Father knows that you need all these things. But strive first for the kingdom of God and his righteousness, and all these things will be given to you as well.
>
> So do not worry about tomorrow, for tomorrow will bring worries of its own. Today's trouble is enough for today. (Mt 6.32–34)

By stirring up hope in God, putting one's affirmative responsibility first, and living each day as it comes, a person avoids the psychological burden of imaginatively coping all at once with the evil to be overcome during the rest of his or her life.

4. Within Limits, Penitents Are Free to Choose Their Confessor

Penitents have considerable freedom in the choice of their confessor, but certain limits must be observed in order to receive valid absolution. And while valid absolution is the main thing a penitent needs from the priest, prudent penitents carefully choose a regular confessor so as to gain the maximum benefit from receiving the sacrament.

a) **One is free to choose any legitimately approved confessor.** Not all Catholic priests are authorized to hear confessions, and not all those authorized may do so everywhere in the world. Apart from exceptional situations, to be considered next, someone who wishes to receive the sacrament of penance should approach only a priest in good standing who belongs to one of the rites fully in communion with the pope.[45] If such a priest is hearing confessions in a Catholic church or chapel, it can safely be assumed that he is authorized to do so. If not, one should ask him whether he is authorized to hear one's confession.

b) **In exceptional cases, the choice of confessors is wider.** If it is morally or physically impossible to approach a Catholic priest, the sacraments of penance, the

---

45. See *CIC*, c. 991; cc. 965–86 lay down the conditions under which priests are authorized to hear confessions.

Eucharist, and anointing of the sick may be received, when it is necessary or would be to one's spiritual advantage, from non-Catholic ministers in whose churches these sacraments are valid.[46] (This condition generally is met in the case of the Eastern Orthodox churches, whose priests have valid orders.)

Moreover, anyone in danger of death may choose to receive the sacrament of penance from any Catholic priest, even if an approved confessor is available. In such cases, even priests not in good standing are authorized to absolve penitents so that they will be prepared for death.[47]

c) **One should carefully choose one's confessor.** Saints have recommended regular confession to the same confessor, so that he will come to know one's heart and be able to provide wise, ongoing direction. This practice surely is good, provided it is possible to find a suitable confessor.

Some people seek a permissive confessor, so that confession will be as painless as possible; they want affirmation and support rather than correction and direction for growth in holiness. But it is self-defeating to choose a confessor on this basis, since no confessor can nullify the moral truth that sin violates. A confessor who does not adhere faithfully to the teaching of the magisterium and the laws of the Church cannot transform an evasive conscience into good faith. And one who does not urge and encourage penitents to live up to the gospel's severe demands provides little real help in the struggle against sin.

A Catholic should choose a confessor as a serious athlete would choose a coach: someone who has knowledge, experience, special skill in dealing with his or her personal aspirations, insight into his or her weaknesses, ability to communicate guidance clearly and effectively, the prudence to guide him or her step by step to steady improvement in performance, and the traits of personality and character which are necessary for the task at hand, though not always for a pleasant and easy relationship.

d) **One may walk out on an unsatisfactory confessor.** Someone who begins to receive the sacrament but finds reason to be dissatisfied with the confessor has no obligation to continue, but may excuse himself or herself and leave. One may, but need not, explain why one is doing so. Even in such a case, the priest is bound by the seal of confession.

5. Confession of Sins Is Essential to the Sacrament of Penance

While those about to be baptized must reject everything sinful in their former way of life and commit themselves to live in accord with the gospel, they need not confess their specific sins and how often they committed them. Why, then, may not those who sin after baptism also simply admit openly that they are sinful, be

---

46. See *CIC,* c. 844, §2.

47. *CIC,* c. 976, authorizes priests who otherwise lack the faculty to hear someone's confession to do so, both validly and licitly, provided that person is in danger of death, "even if an approved priest is present." This provision surely was not intended for the benefit of the priest authorized by it to absolve, but for the benefit of a person in danger of death: to encourage him or her to seek absolution from *some* priest by setting aside a legal condition which otherwise would limit choice.

contrite, and seek God's forgiveness directly, by asking it in their hearts, where nothing is hidden from him?

God does not will to save fallen humankind without its cooperation, but by using human actions as means of redemption—first Jesus' human actions, then those of the Church and her members (see *CMP*, 20.G, 30.C, 32.A). God's forgiveness comes to the sinner in the sacrament of penance insofar as the priest acts not in his own person—he too is only human and in need of forgiveness—but in the person of Jesus.[48] Because Jesus, who is God, really acts in and through the priest's action, there is no more direct way of seeking God's forgiveness than by using the sacrament of penance. The sacrament also has the advantage of providing a human encounter in which penitents know their sins are heard and absolved. Furthermore, the sins of those already baptized concern the Church in a way that prebaptismal sins do not (see DS 1671–72/895). Consequently, the Church must be involved actively in her members' reconciliation with God, and the priest functions as the Church's representative in this sacrament.

a) Confession is essential to the sacrament for two reasons. The sacrament of penance can be considered as both a court where sinners receive pardon and a clinic where they are spiritually healed. From both points of view, confession is essential. Willing that the Church hold the keys to the kingdom of heaven, Jesus authorized the apostles, and through them priests, acting in his person, to forgive or retain sins (see Mt 18.18, Jn 20.22–23). This requires submitting sins to the power of the keys for judgment, and so, as the Council of Trent definitively teaches, divine law requires that every mortal sin committed after baptism be confessed (see DS 1679/899, 1707/917).[49] Jesus also willed that the Church carry on his ministry of healing the spiritual disease of sin (see DS 813/437). This requires knowledge of the sinner's heart, so that fitting remedies may be prescribed.[50]

b) All mortal sins committed after baptism are to be confessed. After examining one's conscience, one is obliged to confess the mortal sins known to have been committed after baptism and since one's last good confession, stating each specific kind of sin and how often it has been committed (see *CMP*, 15.2). Having acknowledged a mortal sin and received absolution for it in a good confession, one need never confess it again. But if in good faith one receives absolution for a mortal sin without confessing it—for example, having forgotten

---

48. See Pius XI, *Ad catholici sacerdotii, AAS* 28 (1936) 13–15, *PE*, 216.20–21.

49. See *CMP*, 32, n. 6; Paul E. McKeever, *The Necessity of Confession for the Sacrament of Penance* (Washington, D.C.: The Catholic University of America Press, 1953). Against those who deny the definitiveness of Trent's teaching that integral confession is a matter of divine law, see Carl J. Peter, "Auricular Confession and the Council of Trent," *Proceedings of the Catholic Theological Society of America,* 22 (1967): 185–96, but note that Peter gratuitously substitutes the notion that divine law about integrity merely establishes a "value" for the plain meaning of Trent that it sets a norm—which, however, being affirmative admits exceptions when someone cannot fulfill it.

50. *CIC,* c. 959: "In the sacrament of penance the faithful, confessing their sins to a legitimate minister, being sorry for them, and at the same time proposing to reform, obtain from God forgiveness of sins committed after baptism through the absolution imparted by the same minister; and they likewise are reconciled with the Church which they have wounded by sinning." See John Paul II, *Reconciliatio et paenitentia,* 31, *AAS* 77 (1985) 258–59, *OR,* 17 Dec. 1984, 12.

to mention some mortal sin in confession—that sin must be confessed at the next opportunity.[51]

There is no strict obligation to confess something as a mortal sin if it is genuinely doubtful either whether it was in fact committed or whether one both judged the matter grave and made a free choice to commit it despite that judgment. Similarly, if having done one's best to make a good confession but subsequently growing doubtful about whether something was omitted which should have been confessed, one may presume that the confession was adequate, and the matter in question need not be confessed.

Since the point of confessing sins is to accuse oneself of them so that they may be absolved, confession should concern one's own sins, not others'; the essential features of the sins, not details irrelevant to the wrongness of what was done; and sins, not good works, temptations, or justifiable failures to do the physically or morally impossible in fulfilling responsibilities.

c) It is necessary only to do the best one can to confess mortal sins. Someone ready and willing to confess everything which can and ought to be confessed sometimes can receive the sacrament and enjoy its benefit without fully satisfying the requirement of confession.

In the first place, in trying to state the kinds of sins committed and their frequency, one need only express what is on one's conscience as accurately as one can and reply truthfully to whatever questions the confessor asks to clarify matters.

In the second place, no one is required to do the impossible. So, expressing one's sinfulness as best one can, at least by some sign or gesture, one may seek sacramental absolution even if there is no time to confess, or one cannot speak, or lacks privacy to communicate with the priest, or encounters a confessor with whom one has no common language.[52] Also, because a moral obligation not to do something makes doing it impossible, the requirement of confession is not violated by those who do not confess some sin because they honestly judge it would be wrong, for example, because there is good reason to think it would cause serious harm to them, to the confessor, or to some third party.

d) Legalistic evasions of the duty to confess must be avoided. Someone might be tempted to rationalize unwillingness to confess, treating it as if it were an impossibility, but that would be self-defeating. Honesty is essential in making judgments about the obligation to confess and in confessing. No one can deceive the Holy Spirit. Bad faith about any of the sacrament's essential requirements not only renders receiving it pointless and ineffective, but is the grave matter of a sin of sacrilege (see 1.K.6.b–c). Although often somewhat repugnant, and sometimes

---

51. See the definitive teaching of the Council of Trent: DS 1679–82/899–900, 1706–8/916–18; on the obligation to confess a forgotten sin: DS 2031/1111. *CIC*, c. 988, §1: "A member of the Christian faithful is obliged to confess in kind and in number all serious sins committed after baptism and not yet directly remitted through the keys of the Church nor acknowledged in individual confession, of which one is conscious after diligent examination of conscience."

52. *CIC*, c. 990, provides for confession through an interpreter, but does not require it, since penitents are not bound to make their sins known to others than the priest who absolves them. Similarly, if one lacks privacy, one is free to confess, but not bound to do so (see DS 1683/901).

extremely so, confessing shameful sins and receiving the confessor's instructions and admonitions are not really harmful. Thus, repugnance is not an adequate reason for judging it morally impossible to make a complete confession.

Moreover, if an opportunity later arises to confess a mortal sin which could not be confessed previously, one ought then to confess it.

e) Confession would be prudent even if it were not essential. Even if the confession of sins were not essential to the sacrament of penance, it still would be an appropriate practice. Partly because it is hard, an honest admission of wrongdoing helps make amends for the wrong done in any human interpersonal relationship. So, in the sacrament of penance, confession of sin by someone truly contrite is itself an important penitential act. Also, preparing to confess is conducive to contrition, including a sincere purpose of amendment. People often are reluctant to make a perfectly clean break with their sins, and if integral confession were not required, many would limit, and so corrupt, their contrition, settling for a feeling of repentance without its reality. Moreover, in confessing sins to someone else, a person precisely identifies them, and this facilitates leaving them behind and affirming the new person, freed from these sins, whom one intends to be.

f) Under certain conditions, general absolution may be received. Lack of time sometimes makes it necessary for a priest to administer general absolution to a large group of penitents without hearing their confessions. Sometimes, too, general absolution is administered when the strict conditions for licitly doing so are not met.[53] Since meeting the conditions is not the penitent's responsibility, even when general absolution is abused, it may be received without individual confession if one otherwise would be deprived of the sacrament for too long—for example, longer than one's usual interval between confessions—or would be deprived even once of Holy Communion.

But a person cannot validly receive general absolution unless truly contrite, and, as always, contrition includes purpose of amendment and willingness to confess all mortal sins. Those whose mortal sins are absolved without being confessed should therefore take the first opportunity to receive the sacrament in the normal way, and should then confess all previously unconfessed sins. General absolution should not be received repeatedly unless there is no opportunity to fulfill the obligation of making an individual confession.[54] Deliberate evasion of the respon-

---

53. See *CIC*, c. 961, for the conditions. In regard to the abuse of the rite, see Congregation for the Doctrine of the Faith, *Sacramentum paenitentiae*, 13, *AAS* 64 (1972) 514, International Commission on English in the Liturgy, *Documents on the Liturgy, 1963–1979: Conciliar, Papal, and Curial Texts* (Collegeville, Minn.: Liturgical Press, 1982), 951; "Reply to a Question about General Absolution," Flannery, 2:62–63; cf. John Paul II, *Reconciliatio et paenitentia, 33, AAS* 77 (1985) 269–71, *OR*, 17 Dec. 1984, 13; also, by curtailing use of the rite, various bishops have implied that it had been abused. Cardinal Joseph Ratzinger, "The Celebration of the Sacrament with General Absolution," *OR*, 12 Aug. 1985, 11, cogently argues that when some use general absolution as if it were a normal form they try to replace God's gift rather than ministering it, and arrogantly presume to act in Christ's name beyond their authorization to do so.

54. John Paul II, *Reconciliatio et paenitentia*, 33, *AAS* 77 (1985) 271, *OR*, 17 Dec. 1984, 13: "For the faithful, the use of the third form of celebration [the rite for reconciliation of several penitents with general confession and absolution] involves the obligation of following all the

sibility to confess mortal sins would make it pointless to go through the motions of receiving the sacrament.[55]

g) The sacrament always requires some kind of confession of sin. General absolution is not administered without asking penitents to give some sign that they desire it, for example, by kneeling, bowing their heads, or striking their breasts. By this sign they acknowledge in a generic way that they have sinned. Such a generic confession is sufficient for those whose consciences are not burdened with any mortal sin, and they need not confess their venial sins when they next receive the sacrament with individual confession.

A generic confession of sin also can suffice for the validity of the sacrament when someone conscious only of venial sins receives it with individual confession.[56] Since contrition, including the essential purpose of amendment, is absolutely indispensable for the sacrament, however, those whose consciences are clear of mortal sin must intend by confession, whether in merely generic or very specific terms, to acknowledge some real sin that they sincerely reject. That could be a mortal sin already confessed in an earlier, good confession, or a venial sin they have committed and intend to avoid in the future.

h) Penitents usually should confess rather specifically. Although someone with no mortal sin on his or her conscience can receive the sacrament with only a generic confession of venial sin, a person usually should confess specifically at least some venial sins for which he or she is contrite. The struggle against these sins will be more effective if one lays them out before one's confessor and receives advice about them.

Moreover, although not strictly obliged to confess doubtful sins, the penitent must firmly reject all mortal sins which might have been committed, and it is usually best to confess doubtful sins as doubtful, for the sake of peace of conscience and to receive any necessary instruction and clarification (although these also can be sought outside confession).

i) It can be necessary to confess sins already confessed. Growth in moral knowledge and sensitivity of conscience should not lead someone who tries to make a good confession and believes at the time that he or she has done so to doubt its validity later. But if one knows one has made a bad confession or a series of them—the outward behavior of receiving the sacrament having been vitiated by dishonesty and/or lack of true contrition—the obligation to confess all mortal sins committed since the last good confession remains to be fulfilled, along with confessing abuse of the sacrament.

j) It can be useful to confess sins already confessed. The case is very different with someone who on occasion—for instance, during a retreat, at a major turning

---

norms regulating its exercise, including that of not having recourse again to general absolution before a normal integral and individual confession of sins, which must be made as soon as possible." See DS 3835/—; *CIC*, cc. 962–63.

55. The intention of the individual to confess mortal sins not confessed when general absolution is received is necessary for its validity: *CIC*, c. 962, §1.

56. See Gerald Kelly, S.J., "The Generic Confession of Devotion," *Theological Studies* 6 (1945): 358–79.

point in life, or as death approaches—freely chooses to confess all (or the more serious) sins committed since childhood or since the last such inclusive confession. No one ever is obliged to confess again sins already confessed in a good confession, but this voluntary practice of a more or less inclusive retrospective confession can be spiritually profitable (see DS 880/470). It can help in deepening contrition, shaping one's plan for a penitential life over a longer period of time than one otherwise considers, and making up for possible deficiencies in earlier confessions—deficiencies which do not invalidate them, but which perhaps cause anxiety in a devout person.[57] In making such a confession, it is not necessary to confess everything previously confessed. But, of course, one must confess any mortal sin committed since one's last good confession.[58]

k) The seal of confession binds not only priests but everyone. The seal of confession guarantees Catholics the absolute secrecy of their sacramental confessions. Penitents are free to share their own secrets with others (though prudent penitents seldom do), but otherwise the seal of confession binds everyone.

People should do their best to avoid overhearing or in any way violating the privacy of another's confession, but if, aside from the penitent's own voluntary revelation, one somehow comes to know something about another's confession, there is a grave obligation not to say or do anything that might betray the secret, including even details such as the penance given.[59] One should proceed just as if nothing were known, and especially should never use what is known in any way that might embarrass or harm the penitent.

The faithful should insist that the arrangement of confessionals and the manner in which confessors speak safeguard each penitent's privacy. If a priest is observed saying or doing anything that might tend to violate the sacramental seal or even appear to violate it, he should be cautioned against doing so.

While revealing one's own confessional secrets to others does not violate the seal of confession, it can be gravely unjust to the confessor. For if what is said tends to harm him, the seal prevents him from offering the explanation or defense which would be appropriate in other circumstances. Therefore, penitents who talk about their experiences in the confessional should take special care to avoid the sin of detraction against the confessor.

6. Satisfaction for Sins Is Essential to the Sacrament of Penance

There is no eternal punishment for sins which have been forgiven (see *CMP*, 18.I), but, as the Council of Trent teaches, even then the sinner still deserves some

---

57. Those who suffer from scrupulosity generally are given special guidelines for their examination of conscience and confession. Usually they are advised not to confess anything doubtful and not to make an inclusive confession. Those who receive such direction from a confessor faithful to the Church's moral teaching and expert in dealing with scrupulosity should follow his advice with confidence.

58. See Benedict XIV, *Apostolica constitutio*, 16–17, *Benedicti XIV Bullarium*, 3.1 (Prati: 1846), 125–26, *PE*, 7.16–17.

59. See *CIC*, c. 983. A still helpful study, though written before Vatican II and the 1983 code: John R. Roos, *The Seal of Confession* (Washington, D.C.: The Catholic University of America Press, 1960).

temporal punishment. Thus, it is right that repentant sinners accept a penance: make some satisfaction for their sins. It also belongs to God's mercy to require such satisfaction, since in this way a sinner learns the seriousness of sin, is deterred from future and even more serious sin, is healed of the self-mutilation of sin by acts of virtue, and overcomes the bad habits acquired in living sinfully (see DS 1689–90/904, 1712/922).

a) **The Church has norms for determining a suitable penance.** Imposing penance pertains to the judicial aspect of the sacrament; it is an exercise of the confessor's duty to bind as well as loose (see DS 1715/925). Hence, a certain legal precision is appropriate in both the imposition and the carrying out of the penance. Sin upsets order in one's life and is a spiritual sickness; the penance should help to restore order and complete spiritual recuperation. It may take the form of self-denial, service to neighbor through works of mercy, or prayer; of course, in the latter case, prayer should be a genuine religious act, not mere recitation of formulas.

The penance not only should remedy weakness and help one live in a manner consistent with one's now contrite heart but should serve as atonement for sins. Thus, it should bear some relationship to the seriousness and specific kinds of those sins. But penances should not crush repentant sinners and be more burdensome than they can reasonably bear. Confessors should therefore impose "penances in keeping with the quality and number of the sins but with attention to the condition of the penitent."[60]

b) **One should accept and fulfill the penance imposed.** One's duty to accept and carry out exactly and fully whatever penance the confessor reasonably imposes is very like the duty to obey a just order of a court. While it need not be fulfilled at once (unless the confessor so specifies), neither should it be put off indefinitely. A substantial failure to carry out the penance imposed after confessing a mortal sin is itself a grave matter, unless the confessor made it clear that he did not intend the penance to bind under pain of mortal sin.

c) **Very often, the penance should be discussed with the confessor.** Occasionally a confessor proposes a penance one would find impossible or, at least, too difficult to carry out. Then one should explain the problem, preferably at once or before leaving the confessional, but if necessary by returning to the same confessor or going to another.

Although confessors, anxious not to be severe, more often propose routine and rather light penances, a person usually will benefit by being obliged to fulfill a more appropriate and substantial penance. If one commits oneself to it when contrition is lively, one will have the motivation to carry it out. Thus, one may plan a suitable and rather substantial penance, which one is confident one can and will fulfill, and suggest it to the confessor as a substitute for or supplement to the penance he proposes. (Penitents who have confessed a mortal sin and who suggest a more substantial penance may request that it be imposed only under pain of venial sin.) In planning a penance, one should consider what might be done on a regular basis

---

60. *CIC*, c. 981; cf. DS 1692/905; *The Rites*, 345–46, 351.

over a period of time—for example, until the next confession—because this is more likely to heal weakness and lead to virtuous habits.

7. Those Who Are Not at Present Repentant Should Not Despair

Some people know they are living in grave sin, experience its guilt, wish they could be freed of sin, more or less clearly recognize their peril, but are unwilling to amend their lives. Since they are not contrite, they are not disposed to receive the sacrament of penance validly, and so they are tempted to despair. John Paul II offers them the Church's encouragement:

> For all those who are not at the present moment in the objective conditions required by the Sacrament of Penance, the Church's manifestations of maternal kindness, the support of acts of piety apart from sacramental ones, a sincere effort to maintain contact with the Lord, attendance at Mass, and the frequent repetition of acts of faith, hope, charity and sorrow made as perfectly as possible, can prepare the way for full reconciliation at the hour that Providence alone knows.[61]

Thus, even the unrepentant should not abandon faith or give up hope.

Question D: What Other Means Are to Be Used to Overcome Sin and Its Effects?

Penitential works and the sacrament of penance constitute a great remedy for sin, but unless they are part of a spiritually healthy way of life, their effectiveness is lessened or even entirely blocked. Sin is overcome only by avoiding many temptations to commit it and choosing rightly when tempted to choose wrongly. Moreover, social divisions and conflicts, all more or less immediately following from sin, at least original sin, cannot be overcome without appropriate methods of reconciliation.

1. To Overcome Sin, One Must Pray, Practice Self-denial, and Serve Others

The most important elements of a spiritually healthy lifestyle, all absolutely essential to overcome sin and its effects, have been treated in previous chapters: faith and prayer, hope and personal vocation, charity and the Eucharist. These are the armor of God (see Eph 6.11–17). Self-denial also has been treated above insofar as it is one kind of penitential act. Thus, only certain aspects of prayer, participation in the Eucharist, self-denial, and personal vocation need be considered here, namely, those specifically relevant to avoiding or surmounting temptation, and bringing about reconciliation in society.

a) **The Eucharist is the basic way to overcome sin and its effects.** Since God's redemptive work reaches its culmination in the death and resurrection of Jesus, and this reality is made present in the Eucharist, worthy participation in the Eucharist is the basic means to overcome sin and all its effects. Indeed, daily participation in the Eucharist, while not obligatory in itself, can be a duty for those who find it a necessary measure to overcome sin.

---

61. John Paul II, *Reconciliatio et paenitentia*, 34, *AAS* 77 (1985) 272–73, *OR*, 17 Dec. 1984, 14.

The desire to participate in the Eucharist motivates one to seek absolution from past sins and avoid committing new ones, to be reconciled with others in order to participate with them in the Eucharist, and to live in charity with others so that the communal celebration of the Eucharist will express real communion. Receiving Holy Communion unites one bodily with Jesus and in him with others, and so completes and confirms the reconciliation with God and among human persons which is begun by the sacrament of penance and by mutual forgiveness.

Moreover, in the Mass one's prayers are consolidated with Jesus' prayer, which shaped his self-sacrifice, for one's liberation from sin and humankind's reconciliation. Participation in the Mass should therefore be the center of all one's prayers for everything necessary to overcome sin and its effects.

b) Prayer of petition should shape the struggle against sin. Humility is essential to victory in the struggle against sin. Without reliance on grace, a merely dogged struggle to resist temptation is sure to be self-defeating. Thus, the basic step is to admit that one's life is not in one's own control, and that only God can overcome sin and its consequences. By oneself one cannot live an upright life; but enlivened by the Spirit, one also can walk by the Spirit (see Gal 5.25). Thus, the first thing to do is ask for grace, the light and power of the Holy Spirit.[62]

Prayer should be in Jesus' name. Recognizing one's total dependence on God, one should pray humbly: " 'God opposes the proud, but gives grace to the humble.' Humble yourselves therefore under the mighty hand of God, so that he may exalt you in due time. Cast all your anxiety on him, because he cares for you" (1 Pt 5.5–7; cf. Jas 4.6–7). Realizing how imperfect one's own prayers are, one should seek the intercession of Mary and the other saints and angels. One should pray often and perseveringly, never giving up until what one seeks is obtained, and then changing petition to thanksgiving. One should pray not only for liberation from one's own temptations or for the strength to resist them, but for the conversion of others, especially insofar as that is necessary for complete reconciliation with them and for the overcoming of unjust social structures.

Insincere prayer is useless, and it is insincere apart from the determination to do everything possible to cooperate with God's grace. Rather than excusing one from using other means, prayer of petition should shape a determined and constant effort to use every other available means in the struggle against sin.

c) One must believe that such prayer will be effective. Asking for what one needs to be saved and praying in the way described—in Jesus' name, humbly, persistently, and sincerely—a person can be confident that God will hear the prayer and will give what is sought (see Mt 7.7–11; Lk 11.5–13, 18.1–8; Jn 14.13–14; 1 Jn 5.14–15). This confidence is the faith and hope that ensure that the prayer will be answered and the mountainous burden of evil removed:

> Truly I tell you, if you say to this mountain, "Be taken up and thrown into the sea," and if you do not doubt in your heart, but believe that what you say will

---

62. This point is central in a sound and very helpful booklet: Bert Ghezzi, *Getting Free: How Christians Can Conquer the Flesh and Overcome Persistent Personal Problems* (Ann Arbor, Mich.: Servant Books, 1982).

come to pass, it will be done for you. So I tell you, whatever you ask for in prayer, believe that you have received it, and it will be yours. (Mk 11.23–24; cf. Mt 21.21–22, Lk 17.6).

Quoting St. Augustine, the Council of Trent definitively teaches: " 'God does not command the impossible; but in commanding he cautions you both to do what you can and to pray for what you cannot,' and he helps you so that you can do it" (DS 1536/804, translation amended; cf. 1568/828).

Meditating on the example of saints who have won the victory over severe temptation is an important way to strengthen the necessary faith. Precisely for this reason, the Letter to the Hebrews devotes a whole chapter (11) to reviewing Old Testament models of faith and then draws the conclusion: "Therefore, since we are surrounded by so great a cloud of witnesses, let us also lay aside every weight and the sin that clings so closely, and let us run with perseverance the race that is set before us" (Heb 12.1).

d) **Self-denial is needed to overcome sin and foster reconciliation.** To avoid temptation, it is necessary to avoid occasions of sin, and that requires self-denial. Moreover, gaining strength to resist temptation calls for practice in mastering desires by voluntarily denying oneself the satisfaction of legitimate inclinations and giving up some legitimate comforts and rest. (Of course, voluntary self-denial must not be so great that it causes real harm to oneself or others.)

As will be explained below, justice cannot be achieved without mercy (see 6.F.4–5). So, to be reconciled with others, people usually must set aside some claims to strict justice and deny themselves the satisfaction of prevailing. (Obviously, this does not mean permissively encouraging others to persist in evil ways or sacrificing third parties by ignoring their rights for the sake of peace at any price.) Also, self-denial often is necessary to lessen others' anxieties and provide evidence of good will. It is partly because Jesus put this truth into practice that his self-emptying is effective in drawing people back to God.

e) **Service to others is necessary to overcome sin and its effects.** Essentially, efforts to overcome sin and foster reconciliation express the will to regain or strengthen communion with God. Yet reconciliation with God cannot exist by itself. Sin divides humankind into conflicting groups, divides every group into cliques, and divides every clique into self-centered individuals; but human fulfillment is possible only in the kingdom, where men and women form a single, reconciled, new covenant community in Jesus. Therefore, sinful self-love can be displaced only by proper love of self and love of neighbor, in which true love of God is realized.

Love of God and love of neighbor are inseparable. This is so not only because God loves humankind and every human person (and no one can love God while not loving those he loves), but because the Word became man. What one does for one's neighbors, one does for Jesus, and what one fails to do for them, one fails to do for him (see Mt 25.31–46). Thus, merely individualistic efforts to be purged of sin and achieve personal holiness fall short of fulfilling one's Christian responsibilities with respect to repentance and reconciliation.

f) **Work for justice should aim at reconciliation in the kingdom.** In working for reconciliation with and among others, one is precisely responsible for what

Christian love requires. Every effort to overcome sin and its effects on others should therefore be directed toward their true service: their fulfillment in Jesus. Striving to overcome social injustices thus requires the discernment of one's responsibilities through the consideration of one's personal vocation, and working for reconciliation in those ways to which one sees oneself called, and to which, very likely, one already has committed oneself.

Furthermore, it is necessary not only to seek to ameliorate the suffering of the poor and oppressed but to pursue this end as an apostolic work, offering credible witness even to the wealthy and oppressors, so that, if possible, they will be liberated from their profound spiritual misery and brought into the reconciled community. This is why efforts on behalf of social justice must not be subordinated to any movement or ideology that denies or ignores the reality of sin, calls on people to disregard their personal vocations, or proposes to overcome evil by destruction rather than repentance and healing.

g) **Love of others facilitates avoiding or overcoming temptations.** Someone fully occupied in serving others will not have time and energy to waste on temptations to self-indulgence, and so will not need to look for ways of keeping busy and avoiding daydreaming so as to block temptations.

For example, while children and young people striving to conquer temptations to unchaste thoughts and behavior should avoid sexual sins because they are contrary to reason and to love of God, they also should be busy serving others, especially by studying and working hard to prepare for the responsibilities of marriage and parenthood many soon will assume. If thus occupied, they will desire sexual self-control because it is essential: so that marital intercourse really will be a fully free act expressing love rather than a mere response to instinct, so that sexual love will be focused on the person they marry rather than responsive to anyone to whose sexual appeal they are exposed, and so that they will be responsible parents of children welcomed as God's gifts, not reluctant parents of unwanted children or calculating parents whose plan for self-fulfillment happens to include having some children, among many other goods. Lacking such love of others, however, young men and women hardly will have much success forestalling temptations by "keeping busy" and "avoiding daydreaming."

2. To Overcome Sin, One Must Keep Relevant Truths in Mind

Satan is the father of lies, but like most liars he can convince only those half-willing to be deceived, as the story of the serpent, Eve, and Adam makes clear (see Gn 3.1–6). Sin is a partial self-fettering of reason that always involves at least a temporary ignoring of truth. That can have many aspects, but a few truths always are relevant, and the struggle against sin and its consequences requires clarity about them, meditating on them, and recalling them—if possible to forestall temptation rather than resist it.

a) **Sin violates moral truth and blocks human fulfillment.** Even someone who believes sins offend God will find it hard, if not impossible, to resist temptation while retaining the childish attitude that sins are nothing more than naughtiness or rule breaking. A person who thinks that way will suppose that God's readily obtained forgiveness nullifies sin and its consequences so completely and easily that little if anything really is lost by sinning, provided it is quickly followed by contrite behavior. But every sin is contrary to some human good, and every choice to commit sin violates a moral truth pointing toward the integral fulfillment of human persons as individuals and in communion (see *CMP*, 7.F).

Although sometimes the damage is subtle, a little thought usually makes it clear how any kind of sin harms the sinner, other persons, or both. Even if they truly repent and are forgiven, sinners suffer irreparable loss: they waste part of their lives. Moreover, even the hidden sins of individuals have social repercussions that often are beyond remedy in this world. For sin which begins in the heart eventually affects behavior, and any sort of sinful behavior eventually harms others, at least by bad example, and so increases interpersonal disharmony, contrary to love of God and neighbor.

b) **Any sin is a great evil, and any grave sin is an immense evil.** Compared with pain, the loss of possessions, and even the loss of basic human goods such as health and life, any sin is a far greater evil, since it mutilates the sinner's heart and somehow wounds or impedes the growth of the kingdom. People living with faith and hope must pursue the kingdom and holiness, trusting God to make good all those evils which must be accepted rather than do the least moral evil.

Among sins, some are mortal, that is, incompatible with divine life (see *CMP*, 15.C). Heaven awaits those who persevere in love, hell those who do not (see Mt 25.31–46, Rom 2.6–8, 2 Cor 5.10, Rv 21.5–8). It might be tempting to imagine it possible to give in to the temptation to commit some mortal sin yet not really do so, because one's "fundamental option" remains sound, or because one would not sin if one were not so weak, or because one plans gradually to stop sinning. Such seductive thoughts, which undermine the will to resist temptation, must be set aside; they are groundless.[63]

What Scripture indicates about hell, moreover, should be understood as a warning, not a threat. Warnings and threats differ: parents who call children's attention to a dead animal in the road—"That young deer didn't look before running out"—are not threatening to run over them if they cross the highway carelessly, but warning them about what can happen if they are similarly careless. God warns that sinners can damn themselves; he does not threaten to impose hell on them (see *CMP*, 18.I). Since eternal punishment is not something God imposes, nobody should count on his mercy to forgo it, but only to provide the means necessary to forestall it.

c) **Redeemed by Jesus, one is God's child, living in his presence.** Enjoying the wonderful status of being God's children, Christians are to be sinless as Jesus is (see 1 Jn 3.1–10). They must bear in mind how far beneath their dignity it is to sin, and of how little real significance are material possessions, fleeting enjoyments, and worldly status. Moreover, Jesus has conquered the devil and the world. He paid the great price of redemption and in each Christian's baptism provides the

---

63. See John Paul II, *Reconciliatio et paenitentia*, 17, *AAS* 77 (1985) 223, *OR*, 17 Dec. 1984, 6; cf. *CMP*, 16.D–E, 17.E.

gift of the Holy Spirit. Strengthened by the Spirit, one shares in Jesus' power to overcome sin (see Rom 7.21–25, 1 Cor 15.56–57, 1 Jn 2.12–14). God's help is necessary, but those who ask for it receive it and can resist every temptation to commit mortal sin. To deny this would be to reject a defined truth of faith (see DS 1536/804, 1568/828).

Dealings with God should be something like those with a cherished guest—say, a dear, generous uncle—whom a person not only fears to offend but is anxious to please. God is not far away. One lives not only before him, but within him (see Acts 17.27–28); indeed, so long as one loves God, one's body is his dwelling place (see Jn 14.23, 1 Cor 6.19–20).

3. To Overcome Sin, Its Occasions Must Be Avoided or Modified

Occasions of sin are situations or actions which in some way conduce to a temptation to sin and which can be avoided or modified so that the temptation will be less likely and/or more easily resisted (see *CMP*, 32.E). Charity toward God, whom sin offends, as well as toward oneself and one's neighbors, whom sin harms, requires avoiding sin, and so requires the use of appropriate means to avoid it. Avoiding and modifying occasions of sin are such means. Anyone who really intends to vanquish sin will prefer to preempt it, if possible, by forestalling temptation or, at least, arranging matters so as to reduce the comparative appeal of the sinful possibility.

While there certainly are occasions of venial sins, for simplicity's sake only occasions of mortal sins will be considered here. The analysis may be applied, mutatis mutandis, to the occasions of venial sins.

a) Occasions of sin must be traced back to omissions or choices. In dealing with occasions of sin, the objective is to forestall the sin by altering the situational and behavioral context, with the good result that the temptation either will not arise or will not be so appealing. Occasions of sin are therefore morally significant because they should be avoided or modified. Now, nobody can be morally obliged to do anything unless there is an opportunity to make a free choice about it. To handle occasions of sin, then, one must look for the relevant omission or choice: What choice might be made that one is failing to make, or what choice might be avoided that is being made? Thus, the real occasion of sin is not so much the person, place, or thing which leads to sin as it is the omission or chosen action which one foresees, or should foresee, is likely to lead to temptation or intensify it.

Temptation is considering a possibility as an option for choice while being aware that it should not be chosen. How strong an appeal the tempting option makes depends partly on the intensity of the feelings urging that it be chosen and partly on the strength of the emotional and rational motives supporting choice of a morally acceptable alternative. To avoid occasions of sin, then, is to avoid choices and omissions likely to lead one to consider options which should not be chosen. To modify occasions of sin is to keep in view the goods a sinful choice would violate—since these provide the reasons for choosing rightly—while doing what one can before the temptation arises to weaken feelings supporting it and strengthen those supporting a morally good choice.

b) **Occasions of sin are either proximate or remote.** Many things which people rightly do carry with them some foreseeable likelihood of temptation to commit a sin of one kind or another. Since it cannot be forestalled entirely, everyone accepts a certain ordinary level of temptation, without regarding the actions or omissions that lead to it as occasions of sin. The question of occasions arises only when common human experience, one's own past experience, or some unusual feature of the situation calls attention to the fact that some choice or omission (usually, one of a recurrent type) will have as its side effect some temptation beyond the ordinary.

Even so, the occasion of sin may be only remote—not in time or place, but in the likelihood that the individual concerned will in fact yield to the accompanying temptation. One foresees temptation but judges that one will not sin. Still, aware that one might and sensitive to sin's great evil, one realizes it would be safer, and so preferable, to avoid the temptation if possible.

By contrast, if the foreseen temptation is such that the individual realizes he or she is somewhat likely to sin, the occasion is proximate. *Likely to sin* here does not mean more likely to commit sin than avoid it. It simply means that the temptation is foreseen as an important threat, such that one has serious doubts as to whether one will withstand it.

c) **Some occasions of sin can and should be avoided entirely.** Even apart from the side effect of temptation to commit another sin, the act or omission that is an occasion of sin sometimes is itself at least a venial sin. In such cases, it should be avoided both as a sin in itself and as an occasion of further sin. Plainly, too, even if it would be light matter in itself, it becomes grave matter if it is a proximate occasion of mortal sin. For example, a small overindulgence in alcohol is in itself light matter. But many people learn by experience that when slightly drunk they are strongly tempted to commit serious sins: to slander people they dislike, to become physically abusive, to waste large sums of money needed to fulfill important responsibilities, to risk their own and others' lives by driving, to entertain impure thoughts, and so on. For them, slightly excessive drinking that otherwise would be only a light matter becomes a grave matter as an occasion of sin.

What if an act or omission venially sinful in itself is judged to be a remote occasion of mortal sin? The teaching of classical moralists provides no clear answer. But since there never can be any acceptable motive for committing even the slightest venial sin, it seems that any occasion at all sinful in itself becomes grave matter insofar as it involves an absolutely unjustifiable risk of so great an evil as mortal sin. For example, the content of much of the popular media leads to temptations to commit various serious sins: of envy, greed, vanity, lust, and so on. Often, too, there are good reasons, such as the waste of time involved, for not making use of the media, so that doing so is venially sinful in itself. In these circumstances, it is unjustifiable to expose oneself or others (such as one's children) to content which might lead to a temptation to commit a mortal sin. Considering what is at stake, the matter seems to be grave.

Sometimes the act or omission that is an occasion of sin would otherwise be morally good but in no way obligatory. There is an alternative, also morally good, that could be chosen instead. In such cases, if the act or omission is a proximate occasion of mortal sin, it should be avoided by choosing the good alternative, while failing to avoid it is grave matter, due to the unjustifiable grave risk taken (see DS 2161–62/1211–12). For instance, if a salesman has a choice between different jobs, either of which would provide enough income to meet all his responsibilities, and he foresees that in one of the jobs he might well succumb to temptations to defraud customers while he will not experience similar temptations in the other, he should choose the latter job.

But if the occasion is remote and the act or omission would otherwise be morally good, there is some reason to take the risk and not so serious a reason for not taking it; and therefore taking it is not grave matter. Still, it would be more reasonable not to take it, and therefore it is light matter.[64] For example, a woman thinking of gambling a modest stake judges that doing so in itself would be justifiable as recreation and not wrong in other respects. However, while she never has risked too much, past experience leads her to think that she will be tempted to increase the stake to a point where her gambling would be gravely wrong. Having other options for recreation which carry with them no foreseen risk of temptation, she should not choose to gamble, even if she thinks she can deal with the temptation.

d) **Other occasions of sin should be modified to render sin unlikely.** Sometimes, however, it seems that an occasion of sin cannot be entirely avoided, for it appears that some other moral responsibility cannot be fulfilled without choosing the action or omission of which the temptation is a foreseen side effect.

If a proximate occasion of mortal sin is in question, however, the question to be settled, before judging that the other responsibility must be fulfilled and the risk accepted, is whether the responsibility remains compelling in this situation. Perhaps there is some alternative and satisfactory way of fulfilling it, or perhaps it is the sort of duty that yields when there is an important reason for leaving it unfulfilled. If so, this case really does not differ significantly from others in which there is a morally acceptable alternative, and choosing to risk mortal sin remains grave matter.

Still, the responsibility may be compelling, for example, a man's strict and urgent duty to support his family might require him to continue working with associates who have often led him into sin. In such a case, any doubts about the ability to withstand the foreseen temptation should be challenged and put to rest. No one sins without freely choosing to give in to temptation, and God promises the

---

64. Classical moralists differed with one another in strictness about the obligation to avoid occasions of sin; for a summary with some references, see Gerald Kelly, S.J., "Current Theology: Notes on Moral Theology, 1949," *Theological Studies* 11 (1950): 64–65. The positions proposed here might seem stricter than the strictest taken by classical moralists, but the comparison is not straightforward, because the classical treatment focuses on persons, places, and things which might lead to sin, but how they do so is not clear, while the present treatment focuses on actions and omissions among whose foreseen side effects are temptations. Consequently, the moral quality of the action, apart from the foreseen side effect of temptation, is even more crucial in the present treatment than it was in the classical treatment. For a good, brief, and practical summary for confessors of classical moral theology's treatment of occasions of sin: Gerald Kelly, S.J., *The Good Confessor* (New York: Sentinel Press, 1951), 79–86.

grace to make the right choice. Of course, people must do their part by taking whatever practical measures they can to strengthen themselves to meet the temptation's challenge, lessen its force, and so on.

4. Temptations Must Be Expected and Must Be Resisted as Soon as They Arise

Temptations occur when one thinks of the possibility of doing or saying or thinking something one ought not do or say or think (or not doing something one ought to do) as an appealing option available for choice. Prayer, self-denial, service to others, bearing relevant truths in mind, and avoiding occasions of sin are ways of forestalling temptations and/or preparing to resist them. Then, when temptation arises, it must be resisted: "Therefore take up the whole armor of God, so that you may be able to withstand on that evil day, and having done everything, to stand firm" (Eph 6.13). It is true by definition that temptations ought to be resisted: one ought to resist choosing as one ought not choose. But it is an informative and important moral norm that a person should anticipate temptations, be on guard, and begin to resist each temptation as it arises: "Discipline yourselves, keep alert. Like a roaring lion your adversary the devil prowls around, looking for someone to devour. Resist him, steadfast in your faith" (1 Pt 5.8–9).[65]

a) **The psychology of temptation requires prompt resistance.** Temptations arise only when the tempting possibility has some support from emotion: desire, fear, anger, hatred, laziness, and so on. But someone who has prepared for temptation also has emotions supporting the option of choosing rightly. Anticipating temptation and being on guard, one can choose at once to resist. Otherwise, even though not choosing at once to give in, one will begin to deliberate about doing so.

As this deliberation proceeds, the excluded option is imagined more vividly, and this fantasy intensifies supporting emotion, while emotions which support doing as one ought weaken. Sometimes this process interferes with deliberation to such an extent that free choice is precluded, and with it deliberate sin. (Of course, some past sin may have led to this situation or failed to forestall it.) But more often emotion only blocks full consideration of the reasons against giving in to temptation, and the sinful choice is made contrary to conscience. Although this is a sin of weakness, it nevertheless is deliberate, and is mortal if one remains aware when making the choice that the matter is grave (see *CMP*, 17.D–E). Prompt resistance could have prevented the sin.

b) **Resistance to temptation can be either direct or indirect.** Direct resistance to temptation is similar to the tactic used in a deliberative body by someone who forces an unwelcome proposal to a quick vote, thus defeating it before it gathers support. Sometimes, when tempted not to do something which should be done, one can choose to begin to do it at once; other times, tempted to do something which

---

65. On resistance to temptation: St. Francis de Sales, *Introduction to the Devout Life*, 5, trans. John K. Ryan (Garden City, N.Y.: Doubleday Image, 1972), 235–70; Alphonsus Rodriguez, S.J., *Practice of Perfection and Christian Virtues,* trans. Joseph Rickaby, S.J., 3 vols. (Chicago: Loyola University Press, 1929), 2:355–426.

should not be done, one can choose to begin doing the opposite at once. For example, someone tempted not to pay a debt can choose to pay it at once; someone tempted to lie his or her way out of a difficult situation can choose to tell the truth at once. Such choices resist temptation directly, and that should be done if possible—*possible* meaning the direct resistance is morally acceptable as well as otherwise possible.

But direct resistance is not always possible. A person might not have the means to pay the debt at once; in the difficult situation, someone might be bound to secrecy, so that not only lying but telling the truth is morally excluded. Then it is necessary to resort to indirect resistance. This is similar to the procedural tactic of a chairperson who forestalls deliberation on an unwelcome proposal by ruling it out of order and moving quickly to other business. To resist temptation indirectly, one simply sets the tempting suggestion aside and focuses attention on something legitimate (and, preferably, both interesting and entirely unrelated to the temptation).

c) **One should not try to resist temptation by oneself.** When direct resistance to temptation is impossible, indirect resistance sometimes breaks down, for a temptation might arise again and again despite the effort to set it aside. The situation is like that in a deliberative body where the chairperson's ruling that a proposal is out of order is appealed and overturned: debate begins despite the attempt to forestall it. Then there is need for reinforcement, the help and support of another.

Those who have humbly asked God for grace are borne up by his might. But God wills to carry on his redemptive work not only in and through Jesus' humanity but in and through the Church and her members, and not only by their prayer for one another, preaching, sacraments, and other official acts, but by their constant, mutual help, not least in turning from sin and resisting temptation: "Bear one another's burdens, and in this way you will fulfill the law of Christ" (Gal 6.2).

Thus, someone suffering temptation should seek the help of another member of a mutual support group, a spiritual director, a friend, a family member—in short, anyone who will understand the temptation and help resist it. Those called on for such help should give it if they can. The responsibility both to seek and give such help is grave if the temptation is grave matter.

d) **The persistence of temptation must be distinguished from sin.** Someone who fails to forestall temptations and/or prepare to resist them as can and should be done is guilty of that failure even if no temptations actually arise. Whether guilty of such prior failure or not, however, those who find themselves entertaining temptations and deliberating for and against giving in may wonder whether they have already sinned. It will seem so, for they are experiencing desire to do what is wrong and are more or less vividly anticipating the satisfaction of sinful inclination.

Still, these facts do not show that one has sinned deliberately. The inclination and its anticipated satisfaction can be merely emotional. And since a free choice is a fully conscious act of self-determination that ends deliberation, the fact that one is deliberating—even if one should not be—about whether or not to give in to a temptation shows that one has not yet given in to *that* temptation.

At this point, therefore, it is a mistake for a person, thinking he or she may already have sinned, to judge further resistance to temptation useless and give in.

Instead, the person should judge that he or she has not yet sinned, but is being strongly tempted to do so, and should set the temptation aside, if possible, or seek help to resist it.

5. One Should Work with Others to Overcome Sin and Its Effects

There can be no life of Christian faith, hope, and love of God without love of neighbor. In the fallen world, all responsibilities toward other people include aspects of the penitential dimension of Christian life. Relationships must be established and renewed in the face of selfishness, division, and conflict; justice must be done despite, and in reparation for, injustice; mercy must be practiced to bring others to reconciliation, heal the victims of sinfulness, and foster the fragile and imperfect peace possible in this world.

Thus, chapters six through eleven, which deal with many specific responsibilities flowing from love of neighbor and the requirements of justice, complement the present chapter; each of them in some way extends it.

Question E: What Are One's Responsibilities for Others' Moral Welfare?

A person's main responsibility with respect to the spiritual and moral well-being of others is to give them the example of Christian life and bear witness before them to Jesus' truth. This responsibility is met by discerning, accepting, and fulfilling one's personal vocation (see 2.E). Another important responsibility toward others is to help to assure them the full benefits of membership in the Church, by meeting one's own responsibility as a Church member (see 3.D). Moreover, as has just been explained, one should help others resist temptation and work with them to overcome sin and its effects.

Here it remains to treat only two other important responsibilities for the moral welfare of others: to admonish those who seem to be sinning and to avoid leading others into sin.

Since grave sin is incompatible with abiding in divine love, these responsibilities flow from a person's fundamental responsibility to love neighbors with that love which constitutes communion in Jesus (see 6.A). For this reason, moral theology traditionally took up admonishing (traditionally called "fraternally correcting") apparent sinners and avoiding leading others into sin in the treatise on charity (see *S.t.*, 2–2, q. 33 and q. 43). However, these responsibilities are appropriately treated in the present chapter, which deals with overcoming sin and its effects. For Christians should be concerned not only to overcome sin in their own lives but to help others overcome and avoid it.

In individualistic, post-Christian societies lacking both social solidarity and a sense of sin, indifference to others' true good and ethical subjectivism are so prevalent that the responsibilities to be treated here are generally ignored and sometimes even rejected: "Am I anyone else's keeper?" Jesus, however, loved his brothers and sisters too much to act as if he could be indifferent to their moral welfare, and every Christian is called to follow him in this matter as in others.

1. One Should Admonish Those Who Seem to Be Sinning

The responsibility to admonish is not the same as the responsibility which authorities as such have to direct and correct others, to maintain law and order. Rather, it is the responsibility everyone has to dissuade others from committing sins and encourage them to repent of sins they have not yet repented. (*Admonish* is used here to include the moral instruction an admonition sometimes involves and extends to the whole range of constructive moral criticism and advice.)[66]

Since the ground of the responsibility to admonish is love of neighbor—the will that others abide in God's love and not be separated from it by sin—authentic admonition is altogether different from reproof and criticism motivated by self-interest, frustration, or impatience with others' behavior. Love does not judge and condemn anyone, and is not meddlesome; rather, it is supportive and constructive. Thus, Christian admonitions must be directed to others' real benefit, and must be expressed with sympathy, thoughtfulness, and gentleness.

The New Testament indicates this responsibility in several places (see Lk 17.3, 1 Cor 6.1–6, Gal 6.1, 1 Thes 5.14, 2 Thes 3.14–15, Jas 5.19–20). Most familiar are the rather detailed directions for the specific kind of case in which one Christian considers himself or herself sinned against by another:

> If another member of the church sins against you, go and point out the fault when the two of you are alone. If the member listens to you, you have regained that one. But if you are not listened to, take one or two others along with you, so that every word may be confirmed by the evidence of two or three witnesses. If the member refuses to listen to them, tell it to the church; and if the offender refuses to listen even to the church, let such a one be to you as a Gentile and a tax collector. (Mt 18.15–17)

Any attempt to generalize from this raises many questions. Without judging others, as Christians are forbidden to do, how can one tell that it is appropriate to admonish them? Knowing oneself to be a sinner, can one presume to admonish others? Since the weak need support, is it appropriate to admonish those who seem to be sinning through weakness? Should someone be admonished about something that involves only light matter? Since the responsibility to admonish is affirmative, what are the circumstances in which it does not hold? When it does hold, how should one go about fulfilling it? Should only peers be admonished, or subordinates and superiors as well? Should one admonish nonbelievers as well as fellow Christians?

a) "Judge not" and "Admonish possible sinners" are compatible. Vatican II neatly formulates the prohibition against judging others: "God alone is the judge and searcher of hearts; for that reason he forbids us to make judgments about the internal guilt of anyone" (GS 28; cf. *S.t.,* 2–2, q. 60, a. 2, ad 1). This norm, however, does not preclude judgments necessary for determining that one should try to dissuade others from committing sins or to encourage them to repent if they have sinned.

---

66. A helpful study (though insensitive to the epistemological problems involved in judging whether to admonish): Joseph A. Costello, S.M., *Moral Obligation of Fraternal Correction* (Washington, D.C.: The Catholic University of America Press, 1949).

For, first, without judging others, one can take their own word for their state of conscience, and so can react to their statement that they are considering committing some sin or are unrepentant for a sin they have committed. People often do testify to their state of conscience, especially to associates and collaborators or those whose cooperation they are seeking. If one does not admonish such a person, he or she is likely to regard this reserve as approval and to be encouraged to commit or remain in the sin.

Second, without judging anyone's internal guilt, it is possible to judge that *what* others are doing is wrong. Perhaps, due to invincible ignorance or lack of freedom, they are not internally guilty; perhaps they are. But even if they are not, what they are doing can have moral significance for them and others, for instance, something done guiltlessly now may well become a source of later sin and often is a present injustice to others. So, one can react to what others are in fact doing, not reproaching them for immorality, but calling their attention to the apparent moral significance of their action.

Thus, the responsibility, stated precisely, is not to admonish sinners, but to admonish those who seem to be sinning. To evade this responsibility on the ground that one cannot fulfill it without being judgmental is to rationalize indifference and cowardice, rooted in the inadequacy of love of neighbor.

b) **Although one is a sinner, one can and should admonish others.** Not even grave sin entirely destroys sound judgment and natural good will toward others. Thus, a miserable but unrepentant grave sinner might humbly and sincerely warn someone else: "Do not ruin your life as I am doing." Still, a person who knows he or she is guilty of grave sin and is unrepentant is incapable of admonishing others as an act of charity, aimed at communion with them in Jesus. Before admonishing anyone, therefore, one should first examine oneself. If one needs to repent and accepts the grace to do so, then with charity one can admonish others: with the log removed from his or her own eye, a person will be able to see clearly to take the speck out of another's (see Mt 7.1–5).

Tempted to evade the responsibility to admonish, people often say: "I must not take a holier-than-thou attitude, since I am a sinner myself." If that truly expresses a salutary humility, however, it will not be used as an excuse for not fulfilling the responsibility. Of course, it could express the worldly prudence that people who live in glass houses should not throw stones; or it could register a refusal to undertake the reformation of life that is a condition for admonishing others charitably.

c) **Admonishing the weak is an important part of supporting them.** The point of admonition is to dissuade others from sinning and encourage them to repent if necessary. Understood in this way, admonishing someone who seems to be sinning, whether through weakness or not, in no way involves berating or attacking the person. Rather, it is moral support, especially appropriate for sinners through weakness, who often carry on a lonely struggle and welcome others' concern and help. Naturally, admonition of the weak should be accompanied by other appropriate elements of support, including prayer, especially prayer together, practical help to avoid occasions of sin, and affirmation of any good qualities and tendencies.

In relation to this and the preceding point it should be noted that the responsibility to admonish is incumbent on everyone and the act often should be mutual. St. Paul says, "Bear one another's burdens, and in this way you will fulfill the law of Christ" (Gal 6.2), precisely in stating the responsibility to admonish: "My friends, if anyone is detected in a transgression, you who have received the Spirit should restore such a one in a spirit of gentleness. Take care that you yourselves are not tempted" (Gal 6.1).

d) **The responsibility mainly, but not only, concerns grave matter.** The responsibility to admonish apparent sinners arises from charity: its point is to preserve or restore their communion in Jesus. Its appropriateness is clearest when someone seems to be sinning in grave matter, since mortal sin always is incompatible with charity, and sins involving grave matter are mortal if done with sufficient reflection and full consent.

Sometimes, though, sins in light matter can have serious implications for a person's Christian life and service to the kingdom. Venial sins in various ways lead to mortal sins (see *CMP,* 18.C), and so admonition can be appropriate when someone seems to be sinning dangerously in light matter, for example, when a child appears to be developing a habit of lying or cheating. Again, venial sins that irritate others can significantly reduce a Christian's apostolic effectiveness, and so can call for admonition, for example, when a priest is discourteous to parishioners.

In admonishing someone concerning a possible sin in light matter, however, it is important to maintain the right perspective. If, other things being equal, one is more ready to admonish when the apparent sin involves certain light matters than certain grave matters, one's motivation in admonishing is faulty. Again, hypocrisy rather than holiness is encouraged by systematically criticizing the superficial behavior of other people without leading them to consider their state of soul.

e) **The responsibility to admonish is limited by various conditions.** Admonition is not called for unless it clearly appears that someone either is about to sin or has sinned and not repented, and that the matter is grave or, if light, serious. Nor is intervention required unless likely to be beneficial. Thus, one need not admonish people who are no more likely to repent or avoid sin if admonished than if not—a group which includes both those likely to repent or avoid sin because of self-criticism and also those unlikely to accept admonition. A fortiori, if one judges that an admonition not only will be rejected but might provoke a sinner to become worse, one should not admonish (see *S.t.,* 2–2, q. 33, a. 6). In making such judgments, one's own limitations and relationship to the apparent sinner should be taken into account insofar as these affect the likelihood of admonishing fruitfully. However, one also must bear in mind that repentance is a fruit of grace, which always is available, and of freedom, which never is predictable.

Admonishing apparent sinners can be difficult, painful, and dangerous. Those admonished may strike back vindictively. In many more or less corrupt social situations, the personal nonconformity of faithful Christians is barely tolerated; if they criticize prevailing standards and call for reform, they are likely to find themselves isolated and excluded. But the responsibility to admonish flows from charity, and so one should be ready to pay the necessary price when there is hope of benefiting others.

Still, other responsibilities can limit this one. Sometimes action more drastic than admonishing is called for, because someone's seeming sins or crimes threaten to corrupt the innocent or endanger the common good. Then one should at once call the matter to the attention of the relevant authority rather than delay action while trying admonition. Again, one can judge that another affirmative responsibility takes precedence over this one. For example, employees with families to support sometimes rightly judge that they should not admonish their employers about matters that would call for admonition if they were free to risk their jobs.

f) **One should admonish subordinates, peers, and superiors.** Obviously, authorities should fulfill their responsibilities as such only in respect to subordinates. However, the responsibility under consideration here does not arise from a Christian's having authority over others but from charity, and it therefore extends to every neighbor, not only subordinates but peers and those in authority as well (see *S.t.*, 2–2, q. 33, a. 4).

All the same, the conditions limiting the responsibility to admonish apply differently to cases involving subordinates, peers, and superiors, and so often result in different judgments of conscience. Also, the right manner of fulfilling the responsibility is likely to vary depending on the relationship between the two parties. For example, in admonishing superiors a person must avoid even appearing to challenge their legitimate authority, for that is likely both to undermine it and to provoke a defensive reaction, which renders admonition ineffective.

g) **One should both evangelize and admonish nonbelievers.** Christian love should extend to nonbelievers, and so one should do what one can that they too may accept the grace God offers them, and both repent and believe. Sometimes considerations of prudence or the duties of a role impose limits on how a Christian can bear witness to nonbelievers; for example, a Catholic judge in a secularized nation cannot explicitly preach the gospel to nonbelievers appearing in court, but may have occasion to offer moral admonitions. However, if possible, nonbelievers should be asked to abandon their nonbelieving way of life and accept the gospel before they are admonished regarding this or that moral fault.

Of course, those who outwardly are nonbelievers, inwardly may be people who sincerely seek the truth and intend to live in its light, in other words, implicit believers (see LG 16, GS 22). Moreover, particularly in the field of social justice, one often has a responsibility to try to help nonbelievers see that they are wronging others and should not only desist but redress the wrong. But even so, it is preferable first to try to assure their share in the kingdom, and only then to seek the progress of earthly societies, even in goods as important as justice.

Thus, one can fulfill one's responsibilities to nonbelievers without judging them internally guilty of nonbelief by regarding both their nonbelief and the wrongs they do as apparent sins, and addressing both together. In bearing witness to the gospel before those who seem to be nonbelievers, one also will make it clear that the gospel affirms and undergirds moral norms they might be violating, and will encourage them to live up to such norms. At the same time, someone admonishing those who seem to be nonbelievers about their apparent injustices and other sins should not necessarily stop at ethical argumentation and exhortation; rather, he or she should if possible bear witness to the gospel, which alone can make the fullness of moral truth entirely intelligible, appealing, and existentially relevant to fallen men and women.

h) One should proceed in ways most likely to be beneficial. As a work of love, aimed at the apparent sinner's moral well-being, admonition must be done lovingly and in all respects in a manner likely to restore or maintain and strengthen communion in Jesus. Someone feeling even justifiable anger should regain his or her composure before offering an admonition, so that it can be given humbly, gently, kindly, and peaceably—in a word, as a true work of mercy.

Admonition need not always be done by words. Gestures, actions, or a manner that goads another's conscience are sometimes more effective. Even when words are appropriate, questions should come before assertions:

> Question a friend; perhaps he did not do it;
>   or if he did, so that he may not do it again.
> Question a neighbor; perhaps he did not say it;
>   or if he said it, so that he may not repeat it. (Sir 19.13–14)

Questions incite reflection, and so are more likely than assertions to be effective. They also reflect the reality that in admonishing one always addresses an apparent sinner whose internal guilt one cannot judge.

It also is important to choose the right time and place for an admonition; but this should not become an excuse for evading the responsibility by requiring an ideal situation that will never occur.

i) One usually should proceed in the order the gospel recommends. Generally, the apparent sinner should first be confronted alone, to protect reputation and honor while lessening embarrassment and defensiveness, thus increasing the likelihood of real benefit. An obvious application of this procedural norm is the rule common in almost every organization and society: someone who thinks others are acting wrongly should ordinarily begin by taking the matter up with them directly, and only afterwards, if necessary, call it to the attention of someone in authority; and when it is necessary to seek an authoritative intervention, he or she should ordinarily begin with immediate superiors.

Sometimes, however, a concerned group should act together because that seems more likely to produce good results, for example, a wife and children jointly confronting an alcoholic husband and father. Moreover, when the apparent sin is known to many and the hope of benefit is not lessened by a public admonition, one can start there, hoping to mitigate the scandal caused by the public wrongdoing (see *S.t.*, 2–2, q. 33, a. 7). Again, if there is solid hope of benefit, one should be prepared to go beyond initial, private admonitions and use public opinion to promote the moral well-being of apparent sinners, who sometimes can be shocked or shamed into repenting.

j) The responsibility to admonish apparent sinners can be grave. Sometimes, though judging that an apparent mortal sinner definitely should be admonished, a person fears the consequences, although he or she is morally free to accept them, or else is tempted by some selfish desire not to admonish. As has been explained, this responsibility is limited in several ways and must be carried out prudently. But where someone seems to be committing a mortal sin and the responsibility to admonish does exist, choosing not to do so is grave, inasmuch as it is a deliberate failure to act with love for a neighbor's salvation. Procrastination can lead to failure by omission without choice; this, of course, will not be a mortal sin.

2. One Should Avoid Leading Others into Sin

Leading others into sin usually is called "scandal" by Catholic moralists. The word will be used here, but it requires clarification.

Scandal has some irrelevant senses. In current English, the word often is used to refer to sins people consider especially shameful, whether or not they occasion anyone else's sin. In this sense, any public disgrace is a scandal. In the New Testament, Jesus, his gospel, and the cross are said to scandalize, inasmuch as they challenge people to faith and repentance, which some unfortunately choose to refuse. Sometimes, too, *scandal* in Scripture refers to any sort of obstacle presented by one person to another's doing what is right—in this sense Jesus called Peter a "scandal" (see Mt 16.23).[67]

Here, however, *scandal* has a precise sense, concerned with one agent's responsibility for another's sin. In this sense, nobody gives scandal to those who are either already fully determined to sin or entirely unlikely to sin.[68] Scandal is divided into active and passive. Scandal in the active sense can be defined in general as a sinful or inappropriate act (whether word, deed, or omission) that an agent foresees, or should foresee, is likely to be an occasion of sin for another or others. Passive scandal refers either to the sin occasioned by active scandal or to a sin occasioned by another's act that is neither sinful nor inappropriate.

The responsibility to be considered here concerns active scandal: one ought to avoid giving scandal to another. Although active scandal frequently overlaps with sinful cooperation, the two kinds of sin differ. Moreover, scandal can be given by sinful bad example without cooperating in any sin which it happens to occasion; and if others initiate sinful acts apart from anything one does, one can sinfully cooperate in their sins without giving scandal. (Cooperation with others' wrongdoing will be treated in 7.F, below.)

a) One can give scandal in many different ways. Another's sin can be occasioned by bad example, by advice and encouragement, by emotionally motivating the sin, by removing some impediment, by providing an opportunity, by

---

67. See Alphonse Humbert, C.Ss.R., "Essai d'une théologie du scandale dans les Synoptiques," *Biblica* 35 (1954): 1–28.

68. It does not follow that one need not be concerned about giving scandal to those one considers hopeless sinners or paragons of virtue. Not only should one abstain from such judgments but, since sin is a matter of free choice, in practice it cannot be known that others are, in fact, fully determined to sin or entirely unlikely to sin. One's loving efforts always could be a means of grace leading the former to repentance, and one's malice or negligence always could occasion the latter to fall from grace.

supplying material or resources, and so on. For moral analysis these differences are not so important as the distinction of the ways in which a person's will can bear on the scandalizing impact his or her act has on another:

i) One can give scandal (as Satan does) by acting with the precise intention that another sin, that is, that the other incur guilt and/or offend God (although it is not necessary to think of what one is doing in just those terms). For example, a delinquent boy, envying his parents' approval of his exemplary sister, might encourage the neighborhood Don Juan to seduce her, precisely so that she would lose her moral superiority.

ii) One can give scandal by acting with the precise intention that another do something sinful, not for the sin's sake but for the sake of some benefit expected in or from the sinful act. For example, a man invites a woman to engage in adultery, a lawyer advises a client to commit perjury, an officer orders his men to take no prisoners, a corporation seeking an unjust tax advantage offers legislators campaign contributions, and so on.

iii) Without intending someone else's wrongdoing in either of the preceding ways, one can give scandal by committing some sin even though it is foreseen, or should be foreseen, that this is likely to have the side effect of occasioning another's sin. For example, parents give scandal by committing sins in their child's presence although they realize (or are negligent in failing to realize) that the child is likely to follow their bad example. Again, political leaders who unjustly start a war give scandal by causing a state of affairs in which they know, or should know, that many combatants and noncombatants on both sides will commit sins they would not commit in a more normal, peacetime situation. Executives who share in perpetrating systematic economic injustices give scandal by reducing the victims of exploitation to a condition of wretched poverty which the executives know occasions sins of theft, prostitution, alcohol and substance abuse, abortion, and so on.

iv) One can give scandal by doing something otherwise morally acceptable, but inappropriate and sinful because one foresees, or should foresee, that it is likely to have the side effect of occasioning another's sin and one lacks an adequate reason for accepting this side effect instead of avoiding it by forgoing the act. For example, in St. Paul's day, Christians in Corinth could give scandal by buying meat that had been sacrificed to idols and serving it for dinner to certain fellow Christians; there was nothing inherently wrong in buying or eating such meat, but it was foreseeable that some guests, though believing it wrong to eat it, nevertheless would do so if it were served, and so would sin by acting against a sincere but mistaken conscience (see 1 Cor 8.7–13). A couple on a weekend camping trip can give scandal by engaging in otherwise legitimate marital intercourse without the privacy required to avoid arousing illicit desires in boy scouts camping nearby.

Scandal given in ways (i) and (ii) is called "direct" because the other's wrongful act itself is intended as an end or chosen as a means; scandal given in ways (iii) and (iv) is called "indirect" because the other's wrongful act is neither intended as an end nor chosen as a means but only accepted as a side effect.

b) One need not always avoid what will occasion others' sins. Since love requires dissuading people from sinning and encouraging them to repent, all the more does it require one to avoid leading them into sin. Since ways (i), (ii), and (iii) of giving scandal arise from the will either to scandalize or to commit some other sin that scandalizes, Christian love obviously excludes giving scandal in these ways. Moreover, way (iv) is defined so that it always is a sin: an act that otherwise would be good becomes sinful because, given the awareness that it is likely to occasion another's sin, one lacks an adequate reason to do it.

However, as that definition indicates, doing something not otherwise sinful but foreseen as likely to occasion another's sin may be permissible, provided there is an adequate reason for accepting this bad side effect. Then, even if one's act is the occasion of another's sin, the scandal is purely on the sinner's part; it is passive scandal of the second kind distinguished above.

c) **One may allow merely passive scandal to occur in two sorts of cases.** In two kinds of cases there can be an adequate reason to do something, otherwise morally acceptable, that one foresees is likely to be an occasion of sin for others.

First, when it is foreseen that the others will sin because of their own wicked character, for example, that preaching the gospel will lead those who reject it to commit sins of obduracy and malicious persecution. Their scandal is called "pharisaical"; a good act provokes their sin because they are predisposed to answer good with evil. As Jesus' example makes clear, nobody need forgo doing good merely to avoid such scandal. Love requires that sinners be encouraged to repent, but trying to avoid everything that occasions sinners' malice is neither necessary nor sufficient to lead them to repent.

Second, when it is foreseen that the others will sin because of their weakness or ignorance, the problem can be solved without forgoing the good act if something can be done to strengthen them against their weakness or remove their ignorance. If not, however, one might or might not have an adequate reason to accept the bad side effect. That will depend on how likely one's act would be to occasion others' sin, how serious their sin would be, how likely they would be to commit the sin apart from one's act, whether there is a good alternative besides simply doing or forgoing the otherwise good act, and the loss or harm to be suffered by others and/or oneself by forgoing it. In considering the last factor, a person should attend to the kind of loss or harm to be suffered, its extent, and its likelihood. Taking everything into account, he or she must decide whether to accept the bad side effect as the similar question, about material cooperation in another's sinful act, is decided (see 7.F, below).[69]

---

69. St. Thomas asks whether spiritual and temporal goods ought to be set aside to avoid passive scandal (*S.t.*, 2–2, q. 43, aa. 7–8). These questions bear on one of the relevant factors to be considered: what kind of loss or harm will result from omitting the good act. Part of his answer is undoubtedly correct: that we should not forgo or put off good acts necessary for salvation or for the fulfillment of grave responsibilities of office bearing on the temporal goods of the Church or civil society. However, he also supposes, perhaps too optimistically, that in other cases in which spiritual goods are at stake, the problem always can be solved, given good will on the part of those whose sin might be occasioned, by delaying the action for a time and doing what one can to allay the potential scandal. And he holds, perhaps mistakenly, that if such persons cannot be prevented from taking scandal, one must give up one's own temporal goods to avoid occasioning their sin.

d) Giving scandal can be either grave or light matter. In direct scandal—that is, ways (i) and (ii)—giving scandal always is grave matter if one intends to lead another into mortal sin, but in itself is light matter if only another's venial sin is intended.[70] In way (iii), giving scandal is grave if it is done either in committing a mortal sin or in committing what otherwise would be a venial sin while realizing that another is likely to be led to commit mortal sin. In the latter case, even though one's sin in itself would be venial, it is contrary to love to care less for a neighbor's moral welfare than for what motivates one's venially sinful act. If scandal given in way (iii) is not grave matter, it is, of course, light. In way (iv), if it is foreseen that one's act might lead another to commit only a venial sin, giving scandal is light matter; but if it is foreseen that another might commit a mortal sin, giving scandal is in itself grave. But it is subject to parvity if, while wishing and trying to avoid giving scandal, one nevertheless falls short of doing all that might rightly be done to avoid it (see *S.t.*, 2–2, q. 43, a. 4).

A mortal sin of scandal, like any other, involves not only grave matter but the choice to commit the sin despite awareness that the matter is grave. Thus, those who thoughtlessly give scandal in way (iv) do not commit a mortal sin. Even those who give scandal in ways (ii) and (iii) often are probably so intent on getting what they want that they do not attend to their responsibility for moral harm to others; they should, but do not, foresee that their acts might lead to others' sinning, and so are not capable of sufficient reflection.

In many cases, of course, sins of scandal in grave matter that are venial due to lack of sufficient reflection accompany mortal sins or result from previous, unrepented mortal sins which the sinner has rationalized to the point of being insensitive to others' moral well-being.

e) Sinners through weakness should beware of scandalizing others. People who commit mortal sins of weakness are not so obdurate that they lack conscience about the gravity of what they do and about their responsibility not to corrupt others. In giving in to a temptation to indulge their weakness, however, they also can be tempted to throw aside moral restraints and involve hitherto innocent persons in sin. Thus, teachers and parents sometimes not only give children bad example but even inculcate in them their rationalizations for sinning; various sorts of addicts sometimes initiate people previously uninvolved; and so on.

Jesus uttered a strong word about scandal: "If any of you put a stumbling block [*skandalon*] before one of these little ones who believe in me, it would be better for you if a great millstone were hung around your neck and you were thrown into the sea" (Mk 9.42; cf. Mt 18.6–7, Lk 17.1–2). While this warning is broad enough to apply to every case of scandalizing someone in grave matter, sinners through weakness should pay it special attention. Weakness may somewhat mitigate their own sin, but in no way does it lessen their responsibility for others' moral well-being.

---

70. When someone gives scandal in way (i), the malice motivating the act or the intention of some grave ulterior harm can and probably most often does make it grave matter. However, considered precisely in itself, deliberately leading someone to sin venially need not be incompatible with love of God and neighbor.

f) **Direct scandal always is a sin of scandal.** By definition, all scandal, even indirect, always is a sin. But certain cases of direct scandal require further discussion to exclude confusions and mistakes that would allow exceptions.

As was stated at the outset, it is impossible to scandalize someone who is determined to sin in any case. But it always is a sin of scandal to ask, advise, order, or in any other way lead others actually to commit particular sins they otherwise would not commit, even if they already were prepared to commit them and/or were guilty of similar unrepented sins. For example, not only those who offer themselves in prostitution but those who seek such service commit a sin of scandal, for, even if both parties to such transactions are prepared to sin, their determination to commit a particular sin of adultery or fornication depends on inducing the other party to cooperate.

Direct scandal, however, must be distinguished from asking, advising, ordering, or otherwise leading others to do something in itself right and good while foreseeing that they probably will sin, for example, calling for testimony by those one expects to commit perjury. Here, the other's sin need not be intended, but only accepted as a side effect of one's good act, for which there might be an adequate reason.

g) **Attempts to entrap wrongdoers should avoid scandal.** Scandal always is given if the entrapment is intended to encourage wrongdoers to engage in wrongful acts so that they will be caught, for example, if a bribe is offered to a public official, if someone posing as a prostitute solicits potential customers, and so on.[71] So, one should not take part in entrapment of this sort.

However, scandal need not be actively given, and the foreseen occasion of sin may be acceptable, if the trap is intended only to allow, not encourage, wrongful acts, for example, if police officers wear plain clothing or drive unmarked automobiles, if employers who suspect employees of theft covertly mark items likely to be stolen so that they can be identified, and so on. In such cases, the trap consists in not alerting those about to do wrong to the likelihood that they will be caught and punished. Those setting such a trap can consistently will that nobody do wrong, and so they need intend no more than to detect and prove any wrong that is done. Moreover, while such entrapment permits sinful acts which could be forestalled, there can be adequate reasons for permitting them: the hope that wrongdoers who are caught and punished will reform and that others will be deterred.

h) **People often give scandal by being too lax or too demanding.** Even without directing anyone to do anything evil, parents, teachers, administrators, military officers, and other kinds of superiors can give scandal by neglecting to exercise appropriate oversight and so exposing those under their direction to unnecessary temptation: to neglect their duties, cheat, treat one another unjustly, and so on. Superiors also can give scandal by making unreasonable demands,

---

71. Such entrapment is legal in many places and often is used in law enforcement; following this example, administrators of businesses and other organizations, and even parents, also resort to it. The good end of catching wrongdoers cannot justify the bad means of encouraging them to do wrong, nor is such encouragement justified by the fact that those entrapped were predisposed to do the wrong. The entrapment violates love of neighbor by encouraging a particular sinful free choice; love would instead hope for repentance and try to encourage it.

especially in competitive situations, foreseeing that some will resort to lying, cheating, stealing, taking unreasonable risks, and so on.

i) **To counsel the "lesser evil" can be to give scandal.** It is always direct scandal to encourage anyone to do any moral evil, however slight, so as to avoid any nonmoral evil, however great. Moreover, to intend that a lesser sin be committed so that a greater sin will not be committed is to intend the lesser sin, and so give scandal. Therefore, counseling someone to do a lesser evil can be permissible only if the counselor, rather than leading the wrongdoer to choose an evil he or she has not yet willed to do, only tries to persuade the wrongdoer to bring about less harm than he or she already has willed to bring about. The counseling must bear on the wrongdoer's outward performance with the intention of mitigating its harmful effects; and the advice—to do something less harmful—must be given in such a way that the counselor need not intend, but only accept, the wrongdoer's additional immoral choice to do the lesser *rather than* the greater evil. For example, a woman whose drunken, brutal husband often beats their son with a leather belt might dissuade him from using a baseball bat by saying: "Don't hit the boy with that bat! Beating him with your belt as you usually do is bad enough." A legislator may propose amendments to mitigate the injustice of a bad law which a legislature is about to approve. When Reuben's brothers were about to kill Joseph, he rightly advised them instead to cast him into a pit, from which Reuben hoped to rescue him (see Gn 37.20–22).[72]

Even so, counseling a lesser evil can scandalize others. For example, if a social worker counsels a group of promiscuous young men to limit themselves to monogamous relationships, their partners and other young people hearing about the advice are likely to take it as approval of fornication. Moreover, scandal apart, it can be wrong to advise someone to carry out a sinful choice in a less harmful way, for doing that can be unjust to particular people not otherwise at risk. For example, if a hostage, held by terrorists who are planning to destroy an airplane carrying three hundred people, suggests that it would be equally effective to destroy another flight carrying two hundred different people, the hostage does an injustice to the two hundred people put at risk by the advice, even though he or she intends to save one hundred lives.

Advising people whose sexual activities might transmit disease to reduce the risk by using condoms is seldom if ever a case of permissibly counseling the lesser evil. Publishing such advice or offering it indiscriminately gives scandal, for the advice encourages the choice of intercourse with a condom by some who are not already determined to engage in illicit sexual behavior or are determined only to engage in a specifically different immorality. Even if directed only to individuals

72. Classical moralists were not of one mind on the permissibility of counseling the lesser of two moral evils. Those who approved of counseling the lesser evil assumed as a condition: "if the other was already determined to carrying out the greater." See St. Alphonsus Maria de Liguori, *Theologia moralis,* ed. L. Gaudé, 4 vols. (Rome: Ex Typographia Vaticana, 1905–12), 1:353–54; cf. L. Bender, O.P., "Consulere minus malum," *Ephemerides theologicae Lovaniensis* 8 (1931): 592–614; E. T. Hannigan, S.J., "Is It Ever Lawful to Advise the Lesser of Two Evils?" *Gregorianum* 30 (1949): 104–29.

who have engaged regularly in sodomy, the advice gives scandal if it supports a choice to continue the practice. Moreover, using condoms may not lessen the harmful effects of habitual behaviors which risk transmitting disease, for even if the risk is reduced in particular instances, in the long run it may not be less and may even be greater. Condoms fail; habitually unchaste people are not likely to have the self-discipline needed for consistency in taking precautions; and the illusion of safety negates one motive for discontinuing the dangerous behavior.[73]

j) To tolerate evildoing can be to give scandal. *To tolerate evildoing* means refraining from trying to prevent *others'* evildoing even though one has some motive and capacity to prevent it. By definition, people cannot tolerate their own sin or any evildoing in which they participate. Also, toleration only permits evil; it must be distinguished from action that, however reluctantly and regretfully, contributes to evil.[74]

In some cases, toleration is obligatory: though having some motive and capacity to try to prevent others' evildoing, one has no morally acceptable way of doing so. For example, while able and inclined to suppress the activities of some false religion, public authorities might be obliged by respect for just liberty not to suppress it (see DH 2, 4).

But in other cases, where toleration is not obligatory, does or does not someone with a morally acceptable means of impeding others from doing evil give scandal by not trying to do so?

Since impeding others' evildoing by means that go beyond admonition and self-defense presupposes some kind of authority, scandal can be given by excessive toleration only when a person has some relevant authority. Plainly, if one fails to exercise authority and tolerates evildoing out of laziness, fear of unpopularity, cupidity, or some other base motive, the failure, which leaves scope for evil, constitutes scandal. Sometimes, too, the requirements of justice preclude toleration, because the evildoing involves harm to the innocent or to the common good.[75]

---

73. See Germain Grisez, "Is 'Safe Sex' a Lesser Evil? What the Bishops Really Said—and Did," *Crisis* 6 (Feb. 1988): 10–13. Condoms fail: Susan Harlap, Kathryn Kost, and Jacqueline Darroch Forrest, *Preventing Pregnancy, Protecting Health: A New Look at Birth Control Choices in the United States* (New York: The Alan Guttmacher Institute, 1991), 120, estimate that with average use of condoms, sixteen women per hundred will experience an unintended pregnancy during the first year of use.

74. Pius XII, Address to the Fifth National Convention of the Union of Italian Catholic Jurists, 5, *AAS* 45 (1953) 798, *The Pope Speaks* 1 (1954): 67, points out that no authority "can give a positive command or positive authorization to teach or to do that which would be contrary to religious truth or moral good." This address deals with toleration by public authority of error in religion and morality; in no way does it support the approval of public programs to instruct and/or assist wrongdoers in ways to mitigate the harmful consequences of their wrongdoing. It is worth noticing that people often do things which they know are immoral and disapprove of, and so, a fortiori, they sometimes formally cooperate in things they disapprove of; therefore, the fact that someone disapproves of that to which his or her action contributes does not show that the cooperation is only material.

75. It often is claimed that St. Augustine and St. Thomas Aquinas approved public authorities' toleration of prostitution, but the claim is questionable, because one of Augustine's texts used to support it was written before he became a Christian and one of the texts attributed to Thomas is not authentic: see Adélard Dugré, S.J., "La tolérance du vice d'après saint Augustin et saint

However, when toleration is neither obligatory nor precluded by considerations of justice, a good reason sometimes justifies it. For example, parents may be justified in tolerating some wrongdoing by their children so that they will learn by experience to take responsibility for their actions. When either tolerating evil or acting to impede it would be morally acceptable, discernment must determine which to choose.

Question F: What Should Christians Do to Prepare for Death?

Christian life as a whole is a preparation for death. Christians should live not only in hope of heaven but with the readiness to lay down their lives for others. Then daily living becomes, in imitation of Jesus, daily dying (see 2 Cor 4.7–12). The attitude of every Christian should be that of St. Paul in prison: "It is my eager expectation and hope that I will not be put to shame in any way, but that by my speaking with all boldness, Christ will be exalted now as always in my body, whether by life or by death" (Phil 1.20).[76]

Beyond that fundamental attitude, whenever a Christian faces death as a personal prospect, because of sickness, old age, or some external threat, both the individual and others concerned have some specific religious responsibilities. Central among these is the timely reception of the sacraments—penance, if necessary, Holy Communion, and anointing.

The sacrament of anointing, which is meant for all who are seriously ill, is closely linked with the sacrament of penance; the Council of Trent calls the sacrament of anointing a "culmination not only of penance but of the whole Christian life which itself ought to be a continual penance" (DS 1694/907; cf. *S.c.g.*, 4.73). According to this teaching, the sacrament shapes the whole of Christian life into a penitential preparation for dying in the Lord Jesus (see *CMP*, 32.H). Thus, in this chapter on the penitential dimension of Christian life it is appropriate to summarize the religious responsibilities involved in preparing for death.

1. One Should Face up to Death and Evaluate It in the Light of Faith

As John Paul II observes: "Our civilization tends to avoid the thought of death, because it does not wish to be disturbed from its dream of earthly contentment, as an exclusive value for man, *who is understood as an absolute subject.*"[77] By contrast, Christians should face death realistically and with hope.[78]

Thomas," *Gregorianum* 6 (1925): 442–46. In any case, a strong argument can be made that mere toleration of prostitution violates justice, because it allows the corruption and exploitation of girls and young women and involves grave risks to public health (including the health of the wives of men who use prostitutes), while public licensing and regulation are unjust because they involve the whole community in activity which not only is morally wrong and repugnant to many of its members but a paradigmatic instance of people using others.

76. On the meaning of sickness and death, see Leonard Bowman, *The Importance of Being Sick: A Christian Reflection* (Wilmington, N.C.: Consortium Books, 1976).

77. John Paul II, Homily at Liturgy of the Word at Milan Cemetery, 2, *Inseg.* 7.2 (1984) 1101, *OR,* 3 Dec. 1984, 6.

78. A source of the following treatment: Pius XII, Radio Address to the Sick of Italy and of the World (21 Nov. 1949), *AAS* 41 (1949) 610–14, *Catholic Documents* 3, no. 3 (1951): 15–17.

a) The likelihood of death should be faced realistically. The realistic acceptance of any prospective evil is difficult, and from an emotional point of view no prospective evil is greater than one's own suffering and death or that of a loved one. However, a person will not fulfill the other responsibilities involved in preparing for death without realistically accepting the likelihood of death as it approaches. The first responsibility in preparing for death is therefore to begin to face the fact and come to terms with it, for example, by frankly sharing one's feelings with loved ones and friends.

Kindly and firmly, family members, friends, and health care personnel should encourage and support a realistic estimate of the situation by anyone whose death is approaching. If someone who might still be able to make a free choice is in danger of death but not aware of it, those who know the true state of affairs should make sure he or she is informed. This of course calls for prudence and gentleness, and is best done by someone close to the individual. But it is a grave matter to allow anyone enjoying the use of reason to die without an opportunity to prepare for death, and an even graver matter to mislead someone about something so important.

b) Faith teaches that death in itself is a great evil. Faith clearly teaches that death is a consequence of sin and a punishment for it: death is the wages of sin (see Rom 6.23; cf. Rom 5.12–21; *CMP*, 14.H). Even after the death and resurrection of Jesus, which atones for sin, death remains humankind's last enemy, still to be overcome (see 1 Cor 15.26). It is unnatural, horrible, and final; human persons should not have to endure it (see GS 18; cf. 8.A.1.e).

c) Faith teaches that death in Jesus is the gateway to eternal life. By Jesus' death and resurrection, God has destroyed death; Jesus' victory over death is the triumphant message of the gospel. But Jesus is only the first to rise from the dead (see Col 1.18); those who eat his flesh will live forever (see Jn 6.51–58), and in the kingdom there will be no more death (see Rv 21.4). Whether one goes on living is not so important as whether one is united with Jesus (see Rom 14.7–9). The great evil of death is swallowed up by the hope of resurrection to heavenly glory, since Jesus' sacrifice and resurrection deprive death of its sting (see 1 Cor 15.54–56).

d) One should accept death, humbly submitting to God's will. While a person usually may, or even should, do what is possible to mitigate pain and delay death (see 8.F.3), faith empowers Christians to accept unavoidable suffering and death with hope. It also requires recognition that only God can determine the right time and conditions for each person's death. Christians should not face suffering and death like nonbelievers: cursing fate, resigning themselves to ultimate meaninglessness, or taking matters into their own hands by killing themselves so as to "die well." Jesus provides the model of dying truly well: "Father, into your hands I commend my spirit" (Lk 23.46; cf. Ps 31.5). Thus, when death approaches, Christians should abandon themselves and their loved ones to God's providence and mercy, confident that, being both wise and gentle, he will raise up to glory all who die in Jesus. Then death will be happy in the Christian sense.[79]

---

79. John Paul II, *Salvifici doloris,* 23, *AAS* 76 (1984) 232, *OR,* 20 Feb. 1984, 5, teaches: "Suffering as it were contains a special *call to the virtue* which man must exercise on his own part.

2. The Elderly Should Accept the Burdens of Old Age

Although old age has its proper blessings, it also is a time of fading. Daily life can become a burden as physical and mental powers decline and health deteriorates. Familiar activities become impossible; the aging person becomes dependent on others and is likely to be treated as a child. This situation itself is an element of vocation, an opportunity to practice resignation and forgiveness. Moreover, as people grow old and see many close friends and relatives die, the inevitability of death becomes plain. Knowing that death is imminent, they have a real advantage over younger people in preparing for it.[80]

3. One Should Visit and Pray with Those Who Face Death

Usually, people afflicted with serious illness or the infirmity of old age cannot engage in most of the activities they once enjoyed, and often others find it emotionally repugnant or practically difficult to spend much time with them. In danger of being, or at least of feeling, abandoned, such afflicted people usually need company and look forward to it. Those who visit someone facing death not only help him or her but are themselves helped to profit from the experience's lessons about life and death. Prayer and worship should be shared during such visits.

4. Those Who Face Death Should Prepare Themselves Spiritually

For Catholics, spiritual preparation for death centers on preparing for and receiving the sacraments with the best possible dispositions. Neither those facing death nor those concerned about them should put off seeking the sacraments. Vigorous action should be taken as needed to ensure that a priest comes in time; and, lest anyone die without the sacraments, it should be kept in mind that even a laicized priest or a non-Catholic minister of a church with valid sacraments (for example, a priest of an Eastern Orthodox church) should, if necessary, be asked to administer them.[81]

Throughout their lives penitents go from the sacrament of penance to lead lives of penance—lives of reparation for sin by renewal according to the gospel. The suffering they endure and the good they do are consecrated for their conversion, which is to end in eternal life. This consecration is renewed and completed as they receive the sacraments in preparation for death (see *S.t.,* sup., q. 29, a. 1; q. 30, a. 1).

a) **Anyone in danger of death should receive Holy Communion.** The Eucharist unites people with Jesus' death and resurrection. Received worthily, it guaran-

---

And this is the virtue of perseverance in bearing whatever disturbs and causes harm. In doing this, the individual unleashes hope, which maintains in him the conviction that suffering will not get the better of him, that it will not deprive him of his dignity as a human being, a dignity linked to awareness of the meaning of life. And indeed this meaning makes itself known together with *the working of God's love,* which is the supreme gift of the Holy Spirit."

80. See John Paul II, Address to the Elderly in the Cathedral of Munich, *Inseg.* 3.2 (1980) 1365–74, *OR,* 22 Dec. 1980, 6–8.

81. See *CIC,* c. 844, §2, and c. 922. While c. 292 prohibits a laicized Catholic priest from exercising the power of orders, it makes one exception: he may absolve someone in danger of death (c. 976).

tees eternal life. Thus, the Church requires that those facing death receive Holy Communion as Viaticum, that is, food for the journey to the next world. Viaticum should be received when a person becomes aware of the danger of death, even if he or she already has received on that day; fasting is not required. If the danger of death persists, the Eucharist should be received repeatedly as Viaticum, but not more than once daily.[82]

Of course, before receiving Viaticum, those in danger of death have the usual responsibility to examine themselves and receive the sacrament of penance if necessary. If a person facing death is able to make an inclusive confession—that is, a more or less comprehensive confession of sins committed throughout his or her life—and wishes to do so, that may produce great peace of conscience.

b) The sacrament of anointing is to be received promptly. The sacrament of anointing is for anyone who, having been baptized, is mature enough to have committed some sin (has the use of reason), and begins to be in danger of death due to sickness or old age (see SC 73; *CMP,* 32.H). Although it is reserved for those whose death is feared (see DS 1324/700), such fear normally arises at the beginning of any serious illness and with the early signs of decline common among those growing old. It is wrong to delay receiving the sacrament of anointing until death is near.[83] Promptly received, it can work powerfully on behalf of the restoration of health, since it is the Church's continuation of Jesus' work of healing. It also offers a special opportunity for a renewal of conversion, provides spiritual strength against Satan's assaults, and consecrates the whole process of suffering and dying.

c) This sacrament should be received with the right dispositions. Danger of death provokes a crisis, since a person easily is tempted to rebel against God or to lose confidence in his mercy. But someone in this situation also enjoys a special opportunity to renew faith, hope, and love. In receiving the sacrament of anointing, one should submit to God's will as Jesus did: "Father, if you are willing, remove this cup from me; yet, not my will but yours be done" (Lk 22.42). Having received the sacrament with the proper intentions, one should bear witness to faith and hope by the way one accepts God's will and offers whatever happens in union with Jesus' offering (see LG 11). 　　　　　　　　　　　　　　　　　　　　　　　　•

---

82. See *CIC,* c. 921. If necessary, Viaticum may be received under the form of wine alone: c. 925. Of course, the sick and dying are blameless if they cannot ask for the sacraments or if their request is not answered; chaplains, family members, health care workers, and others share responsibility to see to it that the spiritual needs of those in danger of death are met. If no priest is available to give Viaticum to a Catholic in danger of death, anyone having access to the reserved Blessed Sacrament should be asked to obtain It for the dying person. If such a person is conscious of grave sin and prepared to repent, he or she should pray for the Holy Spirit's help, make an act of contrition as perfect as possible (including the intention to confess if and when possible), and devoutly receive Holy Communion (see c. 916; 3.B.3.a).

83. See *CIC,* c. 1001, c. 1004, §1. For the history of the sacrament prior to Vatican II, see Paul F. Palmer, S.J., "The Purpose of Anointing the Sick: A Reappraisal," *Theological Studies* 19 (1958): 309–44. While the reception of the sacrament of anointing should not be delayed, it is an abuse to ask for or receive it for minor physical or psychological illnesses (see *CMP,* 32.H.5). A still useful study, even though written before Vatican II and the 1983 code: Charles George Renati, *The Recipient of Extreme Unction* (Washington, D.C.: The Catholic University of America Press, 1961).

d) This sacrament should be obtained for unconscious Catholics. This sacrament generally presupposes that the recipient is in grace. If possible, therefore, those in mortal sin should receive the sacrament of penance first. However, if someone is at least imperfectly contrite, the sacrament remits both sins and their residual temporal punishment (see DS 1696/909). Thus, whenever there is a reasonable presumption that an unconscious person in danger of death would desire this sacrament—and there normally is such a presumption in the case of any Catholic with the use of reason who has not explicitly refused it—a priest should be summoned to administer the sacrament.

e) This sacrament may and sometimes should be repeated. If a dangerously ill person recovers and then becomes dangerously ill again, the sacrament should be repeated. If an elderly or seriously ill person's condition deteriorates or becomes more critical, the sacrament also may be repeated, especially if some time has passed since its previous reception.[84]

---

84. See *CIC*, c. 1004, §2.

CHAPTER FIVE

SEEKING MORAL TRUTH: MORAL JUDGMENT AND PROBLEM SOLVING

Summary

Everyone naturally knows some moral principles, but not always what should be done in a given situation. To know that, moral principles must be brought to bear on the alternatives available for choice, and that requires practical reasoning guided by prudence.

Prudence presupposes experience and all the moral virtues, and is developed by seeking moral truth. Conscience, rather than being a substitute for such knowledge, is formed by this quest. Moral truth should be sought as the guide for one's every choice. To find the full moral truth necessary for living a Christian life, the light of the gospel is essential, and others' advice often is needed. Moral reflection should be thoroughgoing, taking every important factor into account.

Moral norms are important in several ways, and they are acquired from various sources. While experience of certain sorts is presupposed by the knowledge of moral truth, there are various erroneous theories of experience as the source of sound moral norms. One knows moral truths naturally and from revelation, and the Church's teaching articulates and confirms them.

Depending on the circumstances, there are several ways of solving problems about moral norms and their application. Doubts of fact sometimes need not be resolved, but ordinarily a reasonable effort should be made to do so.

Often one should look for options better than those immediately apparent. This requires asking oneself appropriate questions and trying to be inventive.

When facing a choice, a person should deliberate rationally despite emotional obstacles. But emotions are not to be ignored; in some situations they should be carefully examined, and their harmony with reason, or lack thereof, established. Since partiality can cause injustice, the Golden Rule should be used to exclude partiality. It may take several sorts of moral analysis to uncover partiality, however.

Depending on circumstances, there are various ways of dealing with residual doubts about norms, doubts about facts, and perplexity. Even the perplexed should do their best to act according to moral truth.

When a choice is necessary between morally acceptable options, discernment is needed. It involves attention to feelings and the comparison of different sets of emotional motives. It should be practiced in many cases, not just before making major commitments.

Most conflicts of duties should be forestalled or resolved. Impartiality and discernment are the keys to solving them.

In deliberating with others, one is fully responsible for one's own proper contribution, limited though this may be. Compromise is sometimes permitted, but one may not intend what one judges wrong. One also should help other participants to judge and act rightly.

Moral advisers should be both teachers and nondirective counselors, providing instruction as needed and promoting self-awareness and insight. They should never try to discern on others' behalf. Giving moral advice and exercising social authority are distinct functions, though sometimes the same person must do both. Moral advisers should never counsel the lesser evil, and those counseling people with a legalistic mentality have special responsibilities.

It should be noted that this chapter provides no support for proportionalism. Although several senses of *proportionate reason* are clarified here, all presuppose traditional morality.

Question A: Why Consider Responsibilities with Respect to Moral Truth?

This chapter considers responsibilities which concern the quest for moral truth. Yet everyone naturally knows some moral truth, so that at first it might seem pointless to pursue the quest. Why, then, must one seek to know moral truth? And how can one have choices to make in that quest—choices which must be made responsibly?

In fact, there is no need to seek the moral truth which is known naturally. But even though one naturally knows moral principles, what is to be done in a given situation is not always known. To know that, it is necessary to bring the principles to bear on the possibilities available for choice, and that requires reasoning. But the necessary reasoning does not always occur spontaneously; often it calls for choices.

Prudence facilitates moral reasoning, so that judging rightly what should be done becomes second nature for a thoroughly prudent person. However, prudence is not given by nature; it requires experience and all the moral virtues (see *S.t.,* 1–2, q. 57, a. 4; 2–2, q. 47, a. 15), which are stable dispositions of the will and emotions in line with moral truth. Moreover, because human nature is fallen, redeemed, and called to heavenly glory, the full moral truth needed to guide Christian life can be found only by using the light of the gospel (see *CMP,* 25.E).

1. To Develop Prudence, One Must Seek to Know Moral Truth

One must pay attention to one's responsibilities with respect to moral truth in order to fulfill them, and only in fulfilling them does prudence develop. As it does, less and less conscious effort to seek moral truth is required to know what one ought to do.

a) **Knowledge of moral truth and moral virtue presuppose each other.** A normal adult who is well integrated, well instructed, and holy is prudent, that is, morally wise (see *S.t.*, 2–2, qq. 47–51; *CMP*, 3.D). Prudent people spontaneously fulfill their responsibilities with respect to moral truth. When hesitation and deliberation occur, any inclination or suggestion to act inappropriately will lose its appeal to them or be set aside easily as soon as it is seen to be inappropriate. Hope for the coming of the kingdom and their own share in it pervades all their motivations, and vocational commitments shape their goals in this life. Very often, the right thing to do will be recognized without much effort, prescribed, willingly accepted in virtue of previous commitments, and so done without any need for a new choice. The choices a prudent person must make are among morally acceptable means, and they are guided by discernment. It follows that prudent persons' other virtues and their prudent judgments, which attain moral truth, are mutually interdependent. That raises the question: How can children develop prudence and the other virtues?

b) **To develop prudence, one should ask God for this gift.** Beginning with the infusion at baptism of faith, hope, and charity (see DS 1530/800), the whole of Christian life is the fruit of grace, and moral wisdom and other moral virtues are essential for living this life. Nobody develops prudence and the other virtues without God's help, which takes many forms, both extraordinary and ordinary. That is why Scripture says: "I prayed, and understanding was given me; I called on God, and the spirit of wisdom came to me" (Wis 7.7–8). Again: "If any of you is lacking in wisdom, ask God, who gives to all generously and ungrudgingly, and it will be given you. But ask in faith, never doubting, for the one who doubts is like a wave of the sea, driven and tossed by the wind" (Jas 1.5–6). Children, of course, are hardly likely to think about "prudence" and "virtue." But they can pray: "Jesus, teach me what I must do to please you and become like you"; and anyone who says this and really means it is asking in faith for wisdom.

c) **People who regularly choose as well as they can develop virtues.** Raising children well often is said to be forming them in the virtues. That raises the question: What is meant by *forming*?

Endowed with the gifts they received at baptism and helped by God's grace, Christian children whose characters are not yet fully formed can make morally good free choices, that is, they can freely choose in accord with judgments reached by practical reasoning which has been carried out as soundly as possible.[1] The practical reasoning of children who are brought up well is likely to be sound, and they also enjoy the advantage that morally good alternatives are presented to them in their most attractive light. But even if a child's moral reasoning is more or less

---

1. Virtuous persons often short circuit reasoning and judge by connaturality (see *S.t.*, 2–2, q. 45, a. 2). But to point this out would be no help to a child who needs to develop prudence and the virtues, since judgment by connaturality presupposes the mature virtue which the child must develop. Moreover, when one does not know what is right, "prudence" surely cannot provide the answer by substituting a judgment based on feelings and/or will for reasoning (see *CMP*, 3.D); cf. Pius XII, *Humani generis, AAS* 42 (1950) 574, *PE*, 240.33.

unsound and his or her moral judgments are sometimes false, the child can make good free choices, which begin the process of developing good character.

While sometimes a child's judgment concerns only whether or whom to obey, in other cases other moral questions are at issue—for example, how to behave in play situations—and no one involved in the child's upbringing happens to take much interest in them. How, then, does the child proceed? Helped by good example and instruction, children lacking mature prudence can understand the truth of many negative moral norms, and thus can know very well what they ought not to choose and do. Moral wisdom presupposes such knowledge, since prudent people simply refuse to consider options they know can never be rightly chosen. What moral wisdom supplies, and good children without it lack, is the ability to consider everything, think of new options, and, when two or more survive the test of negative norms, select the one which should be preferred.

When a child lacking mature prudence reaches his or her ultimate judgment prescribing a particular option—"This is what to do"—the judgment often falls short of full moral truth; a different option, usually one the child never thinks of, would be prescribed if he or she were morally more mature. Still, the child's will, not only exercised but formed in making such judgments and choices, need in no way conflict with moral truth and, indeed, can conform to it fully insofar as the child is aware of it. In sum, although their character is still undeveloped, children who choose in accord with moral truth as they know it already have good will, and that good will is the budding forth of virtue.

Thus, Christians have the core of the virtues insofar as they cherish the gifts they received at baptism and, having responsibly done their best to seek moral truth whenever they realize they should, choose in accord with their best judgment. As people carry out such morally good choices, other aspects of their personalities will gradually be drawn into line, errors in moral thinking will be corrected, and they will gain facility in carrying out right choices. In this way, people acquire virtues.[2]

   d) **One should attend to responsibilities regarding moral truth.** In sum, to develop virtues, people must do their best to know moral truth and choose in accord with it. But insofar as one is not already prudent, one can come to know moral truth only by deliberating and choosing to do the things by means of which it is most likely to be found. Therefore, a person has responsibilities with respect to the quest

---

2. As many commentators have pointed out, Aristotle has the notion of choice, but lacks the concept of *free* choice: see, for example, D. J. Furley, "Aristotle on the Voluntary," in *Articles on Aristotle*, vol. 2, *Ethics and Politics*, ed. Jonathan Barnes, Malcolm Schofield, and Richard Sorabji (New York: St. Martin's Press, 1978), 47–60. Aristotle thus misses both the self-developmental role of free choice and the responsibility each person has to acquire prudence. Some today, claiming to follow Aristotle, embrace act intuitionism, and mistakenly think that moral truth can be reached only by the virtuous person's prudence. Contrast this view with the account of prudence (and the reading of Aristotle) given by St. Thomas, according to whom prudence applies naturally known principles to particulars, and so always presupposes those principles, which also underlie the will's orientation to a human being's natural ends (that is, the basic human goods): see *S.t.*, 1–2, q. 10, a. 1; q. 47, a. 4; 2–2, q. 47, aa. 3, 6; *In Sent.*, 3, d. 33, q. 2, a. 4, qu'la 4. An incisive critique of act intuitionism: John Finnis, *Moral Absolutes: Tradition, Revision and Truth* (Washington, D.C.: The Catholic University of America Press, 1991), 101–5.

for moral truth; and their fulfillment requires reflecting on them. This chapter aims to encourage and assist in that reflection.

e) **The quest for moral truth often requires help and advice.** Someone might object: The kind of reflection described in this chapter is too difficult for most people. But individuals need not carry on such reflection all by themselves. The responsibility to seek moral truth by no means excludes, and sometimes actually requires, advice and help from others, for example, a parent, a priest, or some other intelligent, upright person.

Among the greatest obstacles to sound moral judgment are self-deception and rationalization. Self-deception occurs when emotion leads a person to overlook relevant facts or possibilities that otherwise would be obvious; rationalization occurs when the desire to evade responsibility for a wrong choice leads to fallacious reasoning. Talking over a problem of conscience with a sound adviser helps to prevent or overcome self-deception and rationalization, since one is forced to articulate the problem and one's thinking about it, and the adviser can call attention to overlooked facts and possibilities, question implicit assumptions, and criticize one's reasoning. Often, too, a sound adviser who is learned or experienced, or both, can help resolve doubts of fact, clarify relevant norms and their proper application, and so on—in short, help carry out many of the responsibilities described in the following questions.

2. Conscience Is No Substitute for the Quest for Moral Truth

Everything to be treated in this chapter could be dealt with in terms of conscience and its formation, since to form conscience is precisely to do what can be done to reach sound judgments concerning what choices to make. But the remainder of this chapter dispenses with the word *conscience*.

a) **To form conscience is to seek moral truth.** Today, *forming conscience* often is misunderstood or else understood too narrowly. Conscience, rightly understood, simply is a person's apprehension of moral truth considered insofar as it serves to direct particular choices or evaluate them retrospectively; in other words, it is one's last, best judgment of the moral truth about a choice one is about to make or has made in the past (see *CMP*, 3.B). Today, however, *conscience* often is used with subjectivist connotations, so that some people will expect a discussion of conscience to free them from "burdensome rules" rather than help them discover moral truth. It therefore seems preferable to talk, not about conscience, but about how to reach the moral truth concerning what is to be done.

b) **Everyone must engage in a personal quest for moral truth.** In treating formation of conscience, classical works on moral theology and spirituality treated some of the matters to be considered here, for example, methods for resolving doubts (probabilism and its alternatives) and the method of discernment. Since most of these works were addressed to priests, one might wonder: Why include this chapter in a volume on the moral responsibilities which everyone must fulfill? Is it not sufficient for moral theologians to discover the moral truth, priests to know it, and the faithful to follow their guidance? The answer is no, for at least two reasons.

First, by the time Vatican II began, it was generally agreed that the earlier approach to conscience formation involved confusions and abuses. The Council's teaching makes it clear that Catholics must avoid these. No longer acceptable is the legalistic outlook with which confessors and spiritual directors tried to tell people what would be permissible and forbidden, while the faithful felt free to do as they pleased within those boundaries. Today, all Christians are called on to try to reach moral truth as best they can so as to shape their lives as a whole by it (see *CMP*, 12.D, 12.1).[3]

Second, for many people, life today is more complicated than it used to be. There are more choices to be made, more alternatives to choose among, and more information bearing on those alternatives. No individual can be expert on all moral issues, and to some questions even the Church offers no answer. While people often should ask for and listen to others' advice, in the end each individual must make a personal effort to learn the moral truth relevant to his or her own life.[4] Therefore, no adviser should be expected to relieve one of the responsibility to find moral truth. Rather, an adviser should be looked to for enlightenment, not for a permission to do this or a prohibition against doing that.

Question B: What Are the General Norms for Seeking Moral Truth?

This question treats several general and very basic norms governing the whole process of seeking moral truth. Subsequent questions will focus on norms concerning problems which arise within the process.

1. The Quest for Moral Truth Requires an Appropriate Spirituality

In the fallen human condition, even the moral truth accessible to human reason often cannot be discovered without the help of revelation and faith (see DS 3005/1786). Moreover, besides the moral truth which everyone can know naturally, there is a specifically Christian morality and a specifically Christian prudence (see *CMP*, 3.D and 25.E).[5] Hence, moral truth should be sought with the help of faith.

---

3. See Germain Grisez, "Legalism, Moral Truth, and Pastoral Practice," *Anthropotes* 6 (1990): 111–21.

4. *CIC*, c. 229, §1, declares: "Lay persons are bound by the obligation and possess the right to acquire a knowledge of Christian doctrine adapted to their capacity and condition so that they can live in accord with that doctrine, announce it, defend it when necessary, and be enabled to assume their role in exercising the apostolate."

5. Paul VI, General Audience (26 July 1972), *Inseg.* 10 (1972) 772, *OR*, 3 Aug. 1972, 1, teaches: "Does a Christian morality exist? That is, an original way of living, which is called Christian? What is Christian morality? We could define it precisely in an empirical way by stating that it is a way of living according to the faith, in the light of the truths and example of Christ, such as we have learned from the Gospel and from its first apostolic irradiation, the New Testament, always in view of a second coming of Christ and a new form of our existence, the so-called *Parousia*, and always by means of a double aid, one interior and ineffable, the Holy Spirit; the other exterior, historical and social, but qualified and authorized, the ecclesiastical magisterium." See *CMP*, 25.E; Germain Grisez, "Practical Reason and Faith," *Proceedings of the American Catholic Philosophical Association* 58 (1984): 2-14.

While some of the ways in which faith is relevant will be treated in subsequent questions, three deserve attention here: commitment to discovering and following God's wise and loving plan, prayer for the Holy Spirit's help, and meditation on the models of Christian life.

a) One should commit oneself to discovering and doing God's will. For Jesus, doing the Father's will was the most basic need; it was his food (see Jn 4.34, 5.30, 6.38; cf. Mt 26.39, Mk 14.36, Lk 22.42, Heb 10.5–10). He taught his followers not only to pray that the Father's will be done (see Mt 6.10) but, above all, to do it (see Mt 7.21, 12.50; Mk 3.35), and he pointed out that determination to do God's will is required for discernment (see Jn 7.17). St. Paul likewise teaches Christians to offer their lives to God (see Rom 12.1); doing so, their minds are renewed so that they "may discern what is the will of God—what is good and acceptable and perfect" (Rom 12.2). Moral truth can hardly be found by someone who does not want to find it, but someone who consistently desires to do God's will can hope he will make it known.

Approaching the matter in this way forestalls a whole set of "problems of conscience" which vex those enmeshed in legalism and minimalism. Prompted by some merely emotional motive to do something—for example, to go as far as one may in expressing erotic affection—they try to settle every doubt about the precise point at which sin (or, more likely, mortal sin) begins. But someone concerned to discover "what is good and acceptable and perfect" sets aside emotional motives not integrated with reason as soon as doubts arise about the reasonableness of acting on them. Hence, the entire effort to find moral truth will center on the examination of possibilities which seem to implement one's faith and the commitments which make up one's personal vocation.

b) In seeking moral truth, one should ask for the Spirit's guidance. People sometimes think the Spirit's assistance is required only on some occasions but not all, or is far more needed at certain moments than others. That is a mistake. At every moment in the quest for moral truth the Holy Spirit's light is needed: so that one will remember to stop and think, to engage in even the most elementary moral reasoning, to pay attention to things one knows but tends to forget, and so on; and also to solve especially difficult questions and discover God's will in important matters, such as discerning elements of one's personal vocation among the available, morally acceptable options. Thus, it is a basic responsibility in the quest for moral truth to pray persistently and confidently for the light, needed at every juncture, which only the Holy Spirit can provide.

c) Jesus and the saints should be imitated. As the plan of a good life and noble character, moral truth finds its complete articulation only in a living person, and so the quest for moral truth necessarily includes imitating good people. Faith enables Christians to identify those they should imitate.

Jesus "fully reveals the human to human beings themselves and makes clear their most high vocation" (GS 22). He alone perfectly embodies the transforming effects of God's love on human life and character. Hence, people should put on Jesus' mind (see 1 Cor 2.16, Phil 2.5): meditate on the Gospels, try to perceive the relevance to their own lives of Jesus' way of thinking, speaking, and acting, and imitate him.[6]

The Church canonizes saints partly in order to propose them as models. Their lives and writings are a storehouse of case studies of people not so different from us who—despite their errors, sins, and failures—on the whole splendidly followed Jesus. Studying the saints and looking to the example of holy people of today often help one learn how to do specific things necessary to find moral truth: settle a doubt, look for a better alternative, discern, listen to others' advice but perhaps not follow it, and so on. So, part of studying how to follow Jesus is reading sound accounts of the lives of the saints, using worthwhile material about them available in other media, talking about them in the family and with friends, and so on.

2. One Should Maintain a Self-critical Attitude

One must seek wisdom—that is, full knowledge of moral truth—and prefer it to the satisfaction of any particular desire, or hostility, or laziness, or conformism. Since these feelings so often obscure moral truth, one can hope to find it only by maintaining a self-critical attitude.

a) **One should repent and ask the Holy Spirit for healing.** Insofar as they are in sin or remain emotionally attached to it, people not only cling to thoughts and feelings inconsistent with moral truth but are unreceptive to other thoughts and feelings without which they will probably not reach it, will perhaps not recognize it if it is reached, and will hardly welcome it if it is recognized. Sin leads them to shun the bright light of moral truth; living in sin, they prefer the shadows of self-deception and rationalization (see Jn 3.19–20).

Like a blind person unable to tell that he or she is in the dark, one cannot discover one's evasions of moral truth and root them out by any direct effort. The only way to get rid of them is by praying for the healing of the Spirit and making good use of the sacrament of penance, with sincere contrition for one's sins (see Ps 51.6–12; cf. 4.C.2.d–h).

b) **The ideologies that sustain sin should be rooted out.** Openness to reconsidering one's opinions is necessary, for, as Socrates said, "an unexamined life is not worth living." Someone who lives without self-criticism is content to believe whatever is convenient and to act on false opinions—to live in a cave, a world of shadows and illusions, rather than in the world of daylight and reality.[7] That is far worse than Socrates realized, for, unaware that each human person is called to be part of God's kingdom and contribute to its perfection, he had a very inadequate idea of what is lost when people willingly continue to dwell in darkness and the shadow of death.

Therefore, a person should be alert to tensions between his or her faith and kinds of actions approved or even enjoined by colleagues, friends, or society. In resisting

---

6. St. Thomas, *In symbolum apostolorum expositio,* a. 4, argues that Jesus' passion by itself suffices for the complete shaping of Christian life; to live perfectly is to love and hate what Jesus on the cross loved and hated, and no example of virtue is missing from the cross: charity, patience, humility, obedience, and so on; cf. *CMP,* 27.A.

7. Plato, *Republic* 8.514–17.

temptations or repenting sins, one can and should reflect on those elements of the group's beliefs and attitudes which make sinful acts seem acceptable or necessary, and should set about ridding oneself of them. They constitute an ideology which not only sustains some particular sin one might be tempted to commit but extends beyond it. Thus, one must try to discover other ways in which that ideology's false factual beliefs, inappropriate feelings, and mistaken evaluations might influence one's practical thinking, perhaps even on seemingly unrelated matters.

For example, suppose a college professor realizes that he has unfairly opposed the promotion of an able female colleague because of her gender. In repenting this sin, he ought also to examine the ideology leading him and other male colleagues to assume that their academic community is some sort of private club, meant to serve their interests, rather than a body dedicated to providing professional services to the institution's students and others. Again, suppose a woman has an abortion, deceiving herself that this is a valid exercise of her right to control her reproductivity, and repents of it; realizing she acquired her false notion of rights from certain leading feminists, she should examine their ideology to discover other ways in which it obscures her vision of moral truth.

3. One Should Seek Moral Truth to Guide Every Choice One Makes

An overarching norm is: people should try to know all the moral truth needed to guide each and every choice they make. This means discarding immature and conventional assumptions which would limit moral responsibility to some restricted set of choices.

a) No choice lacks moral significance. Nonbelievers recognize some moral limits, and those of good will accept the limits they recognize. But, generally recognizing no framework for their lives more basic than society's common good, nonbelievers tend to reduce morality to social constraints. In matters where there are none, they are likely to overlook moral issues.

The common good of the heavenly kingdom, not the common good of any this-worldly society, provides the framework for Christian life. This common good includes every authentic human good. Thus, morality does not concern some limited part of life but the whole of it. Hope is not one interest among others, but the overarching interest responding to the precept: "Seek first the kingdom" (see 2.A.4). Faith and its moral implications should shape Christians' daily work and play, business, politics, family life, and so on. It is necessary to look for the relevance of God's word to everything one does, not just those matters usually considered important moral questions.[8]

Yet even many Christians assume that various kinds of choices are outside the moral domain and free of moral significance. Children, for example, naturally suppose that morality concerns only those matters in which they either obey or disobey parents and others in authority. Some young people think it is permissible

---

8. John Paul II, *Christifideles laici,* 17, *AAS* 81 (1989) 418–21, *OR,* 6 Feb. 1989, 5, makes this point (quoting Col 3.17) and stresses especially the need for "unity of life," whereby everyday professional and social life is sanctified.

to do anything provided no one else is hurt. Some people take it for granted that morality concerns only serious matters, while playful acts are morally indifferent. Few people think omissions are morally wrong unless they violate clear duties. And some assume morality concerns only private life.

Of course, those who hold such views limit their search for moral truth to these matters. Plainly, however, nobody ever will find moral truth without looking for it. So, the views just cited should be set aside, as should others that tend to limit the field of moral responsibility by excluding some sorts of free choices.

b) **Social decision making is subject to moral evaluation.** Some people implicitly or explicitly assume that the moral standards governing private life are irrelevant to public affairs. The actions of nations and public officials are, they claim, exempt from the ordinary requirements of morality concerning killing, promise keeping, and so on. For example, some legislators say: "I am personally opposed to abortion, but as a public official I must defend its legality and vote to fund abortions." However, a moral norm applies to every action of the kind to which it refers; the actions of nations and public officials are not exempt (see *CMP,* 10.F).

Specifically referring to the relations political communities have to one another, John XXIII makes the point that the same morality applies to them as to individuals:

> This will be readily understood when one reflects that it is quite impossible for political leaders to lay aside their natural dignity while acting in their country's name and in its interests. They are still bound by the natural law, which is the rule that governs all moral conduct, and they have no authority to depart from its slightest precepts.[9]

Vatican II generalizes Pope John's point: all Christians should remember "that in every temporal affair they must be guided by a Christian conscience, since even in secular affairs there is no human activity which can be withdrawn from God's dominion" (LG 36; cf. AA 5, DH 14).

4. Moral Reflection Should Be Thoroughgoing

People trying to be morally responsible will engage in moral reflection upon becoming aware of the need to do so. Not yet perfect in holiness, however, they easily overlook the need for moral reflection and/or terminate it prematurely. Thus, one should be watchful regarding the need to begin moral reflection and ready to press it far enough to grasp the full moral significance of whatever one is considering doing.

a) **In many cases, one should reflect before acting.** With respect to the initiation of moral reflection, the rule for morally responsible but imperfect persons is: look before you leap. Often people are inclined to do something, even by purely spontaneous action without choice, when they should stop, reflect, and examine what would be involved. "Look before you leap" means that, before acting, and especially before making any choice, one should hesitate and investigate, reflect

---

9. John XXIII, *Pacem in terris, AAS* 55 (1963) 279–80, *PE,* 270.81. A similar point has been argued by philosophers with respect to people acting in professional roles: they remain morally responsible. See Albert Flores and Deborah G. Johnson, "Collective Responsibility and Professional Roles," *Ethics* 93 (1983): 537–45.

on exactly what one is about to do, and try to determine whether a different choice should be made.

Children, seeing others doing something, typically tag along or join in, simply because they want to be part of the crowd and fear being left out. Similarly, adults sometimes join organizations or accept jobs for reasons that are obvious and good, yet without investigating what the employing organization is committed to, what their duties will be, and so on. Again, people agree to buy things without considering costs, the probable effects of ownership on other things they value, and so on. In all such cases, lacking the prudence which would suggest the appropriate questions to ask, people should make a conscious effort to hesitate and investigate before doing anything out of the ordinary.

b) In reflecting, every important factor should be considered. Even after having hesitated and begun to deliberate, a person sometimes terminates moral reflection too quickly. For people spontaneously consider only those elements of the possible action which led them to hesitate and deliberate, while easily ignoring other elements which should be considered and which might even be more important than those taken into account. For instance, a boy told to come straight home from school may deliberate about going with a crowd instead, yet fail to ask himself what the crowd actually will do; a woman may hesitate about taking a new job because she is (reasonably enough) concerned about pay and security in comparison with her present job, yet not ask about exactly what her duties will be in this new job.

c) One always should think about prospective bad consequences. People sometimes terminate moral reflection too soon because they regard foreseen consequences as irrelevant or, at least, do not take them seriously enough. Thus, the morally responsible but imperfect person should bear in mind the maxim: always count the costs beforehand (see *S.t.,* 1–2, q. 20, a. 5).

A person should attend to the consequences of what he or she is doing even when following a moral judgment which is certainly true. Not even the probable consequences of refusing to violate a moral absolute should be ignored. Sometimes the bad consequences can be mitigated in some way, and, even if they cannot, others affected are due an explanation of why one is acting as one must, even while one prepares to accept and deal with any damage to oneself that might result.

d) One always should be looking for ways of doing good. Not every sin lies in choosing to do what should not be done; negligent failure to do what could and should be done also is a sin (see *S.t.,* 2–2, q. 54; cf. Mt 25.41–46).[10] So, doing one's clear duty and avoiding doing what is wrong are not enough. In some cases the failure to do something good which could and should be done results from overlooking facts which point to the possibility and need to do it. Thus, it is necessary to be sensitive to others' needs and to the opportunities to put one's possessions and gifts to work. The constantly changing facts of one's situation should be interpreted in the light of the gospel; God's will for oneself should be

10. Of course, if such failure neither involves a choice nor flows from a previous, unrepented mortal sin, it is only venially sinful (see *CMP,* 15.C.12–15).

discerned in them; and initiatives should be taken accordingly. In short, a morally responsible but imperfect person should bear in mind the maxim: do not wait for opportunities to do good to present themselves; anticipate them and go out to meet them.

Vatican II did that in noting the signs of the times: currently observable facts which need to be interpreted in the light of the gospel in order to discover God's presence and providence in history, so that the Church can do today what he wills (see UR 4, AA 14, PO 9, GS 4, 11, 44). Each individual Christian and each Christian community must continually do the same thing (see above, 1.J.3).

e) **Moral certitude suffices for choice and action.** A choice may be made and acted on by someone morally certain that doing so will be right, that is, in the absence of a well-founded or reasonable ground for doubting the correctness of the judgment. For even if some possibility of error remains, someone who is morally certain can proceed without being careless about the good or goods at stake, because inaction or further delay would impede serving some good or preventing some harm.[11]

But when is doubt no longer well-founded or reasonable? That is so when someone sees no positive reason for thinking his or her judgment is false, and self-examination and consideration of others' opinions fail to indicate that something has been overlooked or a mistake has been made in reaching the judgment. Even so, those who are morally certain may experience some feeling of uncertainty, especially if, as often happens, someone else disagrees with their judgment.

Of course, upon realizing that his or her prudence is inadequate to a problem, a person should look to the example of more mature and holy people. When something important is at stake, the question is whether, having the same level of certitude as oneself, such people do or do not proceed in a matter of the same kind.

Question C: How Can the Moral Norms Needed
for a Christian Life Be Acquired?

Moral norms direct free choices by indicating which choices are good, which bad; they are important for several reasons. Some current theories about the origin of moral norms in experience are mistaken. Everyone has some natural knowledge of moral principles, which faith clarifies and develops. Catholics should be docile to the Church's teaching authority and should study her social teaching. They should use their faith and the Church's teaching to criticize moral norms from other sources.

---

11. Pius XII, Address to the Rota (1 Oct. 1942), *AAS* 34 (1942) 339–40, *Canon Law Digest* 3 (1954): 607, explains: Moral certitude is "characterized on the positive side by the exclusion of well-founded or reasonable doubt, and in this respect it is essentially distinguished from the quasi-certainty which has been mentioned; on the negative side, it does admit the absolute possibility of the contrary, and in this it differs from absolute certainty. The certainty of which We are now speaking is necessary and sufficient for the rendering of a judgment, even though in the particular case it would be possible either directly or indirectly to reach absolute certainty." See Arthur Caron, O.M.I., "The Concept of Moral Certitude in Canonical Decisions," *Jurist* 19 (1959): 12–28.

1. Moral Norms Serve Several Important Functions in Moral Life

The obvious use of moral norms is to answer questions such as: What ought I to do? But they also are useful in three less obvious ways.

First, they can call attention to possibilities. A norm can awaken someone to the possibilities of making a commitment or doing something good which the person otherwise would not even think of. For example, "Workers should be paid a living wage" points to a responsibility shared by anyone whose actions affect wages and their purchasing power. Correctly understood, this norm can lead young people to consider a vocation to work for social justice, and can lead everyone to be more sensitive to the possibility of social injustice in everything he or she does.

Second, moral norms can call attention to overlooked moral issues. A norm can point out the moral dimension, otherwise at risk of being ignored, of a certain subject matter. For example, "You shall not covet your neighbor's house" (Ex 20.17) calls attention to the fact that a person might commit a sin of thought even without committing an overt sin against justice.

Third, moral norms can call attention to emotional biases. A norm can draw attention to emotional factors by which one might wrongly be led to make a choice. For example, "Do not repay anyone evil for evil" (Rom 12.17) directs Christians to consider whether a choice to punish a criminal is being made rationally or out of mere hostile feelings.

2. Certain Views of Experience as the Source of Moral Norms Are Mistaken

Experience of certain sorts not only contributes to moral insight but even is presupposed by knowledge of moral truth. In theories of morality, however, *experience* often refers either to awareness of people's actual standards and behavior (which can be described by polls and surveys, and studied by historians and social scientists) or to the process of trial and error by which people learn how to achieve concrete goals (and so acquire technical knowledge). Different theories propose experience in either or both of these senses as the source of sound moral norms. But neither awareness of people's actual standards and behavior nor expertise in achieving concrete goals provides dependable moral norms. Rather, any norms drawn from those sources must be criticized, using true moral norms as the standard. Moreover, so-called contemporary Christian experience reveals no new moral truths.

a) Valuable moral lessons sometimes are gained from experience. Something analogous to the process of trial and error often teaches morality, in the sense of calling attention to moral truths one has ignored, and so helps a person break out of self-deception and rationalization. If, furthermore, someone believes in providence and reflects on the matter in that light, it is clear that God has taught something through that experience. But the experience was not the norm's source but only the occasion for understanding it.

For example, having sold himself on the idea that there is nothing wrong with smoking marijuana, Bill, a bright college student, is brought up with a jolt when his grades drop and his scholarship is withdrawn. The experience may lead him to reflect, ask what God is trying to tell him, and come to see that substituting good feelings for reality is wrong. But Joan, who has a similar experience, is not interested in moral truth, and so she does not reflect and gain insight. Instead, she simply observes that she cannot have and do everything she wants, and so must choose between smoking marijuana and regaining her scholarship.

b) **Knowledge of moral truth presupposes certain sorts of experience.** First practical principles, although self-evident, are not intuitions: insights without data. Human beings have natural dispositions toward what will fulfill their potentialities, and these dispositions sometimes motivate behavior which occurs without deliberation or free choice. So, people become aware of these natural dispositions, and this awareness (which is a sort of experience) provides data for the insights by which certain of the first, self-evident principles are known, such as "Life is a good to be protected" and "Knowledge of truth is a good to be sought." Other principles, such as "Friendship is good" and "Peace of conscience is good" presuppose awareness of additional data, including tensions involving acts of the will.[12]

Moreover, to understand possible choices, another sort of experience is needed: awareness of human abilities and the opportunities for their exercise offered by various situations. Now, to formulate specific moral norms, it is necessary to understand possible choices, since the willing they would involve specifies kinds of acts whose moral character is indicated by the norms. Thus, while the truth of specific moral norms flows from that of moral principles (see *CMP,* 10.B, D), the understanding of those norms presupposes the experience required to understand the actions shaped by them.

c) **Moral truth must be used to judge the norms accepted in a society.** People often suppose moral norms to be like other social norms, for example, laws and rules of etiquette. Children, of course, acquire by experience many norms embodied in the culture in which they are raised. But that sort of experience cannot show that these norms are morally sound; it shows only that they are socially accepted. For instance, most children in ancient Greece and Rome, as well as in the United States before the Civil War, were brought up to think that owning other people is morally acceptable. But even though slavery was socially accepted and seemed to many people as natural as marriage, the norms embodied in cultures which accepted slavery were contrary to moral truth. That essential insight, nevertheless, was one which children could not gain from experience, that is, from their awareness of their society's standards. In other words, it is possible to learn by experience what people in fact do today and what contemporary society finds acceptable. But these are only states of affairs, to be judged by moral truth. They are not standards of morality superior to the principles and norms human beings naturally know—principles and norms reaffirmed and further specified by God's revelation, which is handed on by the Church's belief and teaching.[13]

---

12. See Germain Grisez, Joseph Boyle, and John Finnis, "Practical Principles, Moral Truth, and Ultimate Ends," *American Journal of Jurisprudence* 32 (1987): 108–9.

13. See Congregation for the Doctrine of the Faith, *Persona humana,* 3–4, *AAS* 68 (1976) 78–80, Flannery, 2:487–88.

Norms accepted in a given society at a particular time, such as those approving slavery, obviously can become irrelevant and out of date.[14] Failing to distinguish between such norms and moral truths, some people think contemporary experience provides a ground for criticizing the Church's moral teaching, including even certain moral norms asserted in Scripture and/or taught constantly and most firmly by the Church. If the distinction between moral truth and the norms accepted in a particular society at a particular time is kept in mind, one can see through this mistake. Neither the experience of people in former times, such as those in which slavery was accepted, nor the experience of people today is self-validating. Both must be judged by moral truth, which cannot be learned from such experience.

d) Trial and error teaches what works, but not whether that is good. Some people, including Marxists, claim truth is found only as it emerges from committed praxis. Others, including some moralists in the more prosperous nations, claim that moral norms are generalizations from people's experiences in trying to live fulfilling lives. Committed praxis and people's experiences in seeking to be fulfilled do indeed yield a certain sort of practical knowledge; it concerns how to pursue particular ends—for example, social revolution or individual satisfaction—and perhaps even how to be creative in transforming society and seeking personal fulfillment. However, practical experience does not provide any ultimate standard for judging that the ends pursued, the means used, or the types of creativity achieved contribute to integral human fulfillment.

Those claiming to derive moral truth in this way, from the experience of committed praxis or of the effort to live a fulfilling life, actually presuppose standards they never critically examine. Marxists, for example, presuppose certain moral truths: that many forms of modern economic activity are unjust and alienating, and many who exercise economic and social power unjustly oppress others. Since Marxism proposes to overcome social evils, its goals are assumed to be morally good. With the further assumption that the end justifies the means, the evidence of experience about what works is taken to reveal moral truth. However, in the light of moral truth the world for which Marxism hopes can be seen to be no less unjust in certain respects than the world it would replace; and the assumption that the end justifies the means has led Marxists to commit terrible violations of actual human persons' dignity and rights.[15]

Although their assumptions and goals are different from those of the Marxists, certain moralists in the affluent nations proceed in a similar way. The desirability of having satisfying experiences and avoiding suffering is taken for granted, while the prospect of a certain measure of satisfaction or misery is taken to be a proportionate reason for making exceptions to any moral norm as circumstances

14. In some societies, no distinction is made between law and morality. In societies in which the distinction is made, not everyone recognizes it or consistently attends to it. And even if a society other than the Church explicitly holds a norm to pertain to morality, that position can be mistaken, since no other society is divinely preserved from error in its moral judgments.

15. On the relationship between praxis and moral truth, see: Peruvian Episcopal Conference, *Document on the Theology of Liberation* (Oct. 1984), 43–49, *OR*, 4 Feb. 1985, 7.

may require.[16] When such ideas are vulgarized and put into practice, ordinary people assume that moral truths can be tested by experimentation; for example, someone might discover whether adultery is morally acceptable by trying it. Experiment and inductions from it, however, can only show what is, not what ought to be. They can be useful in working out technical rules, which guide action to reach concrete goals efficiently—for example, how to commit adultery without getting caught—but they are not useful in criticizing moral norms.

e) **Christian experience does not reveal new moral truths.** Pointing out that the Holy Spirit continues to work in all believers, some invoke the experience of contemporary Christians, the so-called sense of the faithful, as a source of moral truth (see note to 1.I.1.b). Experience indeed can lead Christians to understand more deeply the revealed truth they already accept by faith, and each Christian also needs experience to discover certain elements of God's plan for his or her life, for example, to discern the elements of personal vocation. But if the "sense of the faithful" is invoked against truths belonging to the moral order revealed by God and handed on in the Church, that is tantamount to claiming that this supposedly Christian experience is a fresh divine revelation, amending the revelation Christians of former times received and handed on. However, the notion that Christians today are receiving a fresh revelation through their experience is untenable: God revealed himself personally in Jesus, and made known in him the full mystery (see Jn 15.15, Eph 1.9–10, Heb 1.1–2; DV 4). That revelation develops through tradition, but neither needs nor is open to amendment by a fresh revelation.

3. One Should Learn the Moral Norms That Faith Teaches

People have some natural knowledge of God's plan for human fulfillment—namely, his law written in the human heart (see Rom 2.14–16; *CMP*, 7.A)—and this natural knowledge is purified and completed by divine revelation (see *CMP*, 7.B). This natural and revealed knowledge in turn provides the whole normative basis for a Christian's moral judgments. Since Christian morality and prudence exist, and since the gospel also clarifies and confirms many of the moral norms knowable by natural reason, one should try to learn all the moral norms which faith teaches.

a) **One should make a personal effort to appropriate God's word.** It is necessary to listen to the word of God, primarily by reading Scripture and participating attentively in the liturgy. Scripture should be interpreted rightly, by adhering to the Catholic tradition, setting aside the mistaken moral opinions God's people sometimes followed, and discerning the true moral order God reveals. It is summed

---

16. Not all proportionalists hold so simple a theory of value, but see, for example, John Giles Milhaven, *Toward a New Catholic Morality* (Garden City, N.Y.: Doubleday, 1970). Nevertheless, even the subtler forms of proportionalism fail to provide an acceptable theory of moral judgment (see *CMP*, 6). Moreover, every proportionalist must seek some way other than applying moral norms to determine both the goodness and badness of diverse consequences and how good or bad they are, and this need leads proportionalists, even despite themselves, toward subjective evaluation of consequences as experienced. See Bartholomew M. Kiely, S.J., "The Impracticality of Proportionalism," *Gregorianum* 66 (1985): 676–83.

up in the commandments to love God and neighbor, which are articulated in a special way in the Ten Commandments.[17]

Prayerful reflecting on revelation is needed in order to appropriate its truth, that is, to find the moral norms it contains and see their potential relevance for one's life. In appropriating moral truth in the light of faith, a person should be careful to distinguish absolute from nonabsolute norms, for example, the command not to commit adultery from the precept to obey civil authorities.

Someone sins who omits to learn the moral requirements contained in God's word and to engage in the prayer required to appropriate revealed moral truth. But probably such sins are almost always venial, since people who recognize a grave responsibility in these matters are unlikely to choose not to fulfill it.

b) One should be docile to the Church's teaching authority. Personal reading of Scripture and prayer are not enough. Individuals can go badly wrong, especially insofar as their personal inclinations are not those of saints. People should check their personal faith and insight into God's plan against the Church's faith and moral teaching. Vatican II teaches:

> In forming their consciences, the Christian faithful ought to give heed to the sacred and certain doctrine of the Church [note omitted]. For the catholic Church is, by the will of Christ, the teacher of the truth. It is her duty to give utterance to, and authoritatively to teach, that truth which is Christ, and also to declare and confirm by her authority principles of the moral order flowing from human nature itself. (DH 14)[18]

The responsibility to assent to the Church's teachings has been treated in a previous chapter (1.H–I).

c) The Church's social teaching should be studied. Some Catholics accept only some of the moral norms the Church teaches: those bearing on private life. But in shaping his or her Christian life a person also should apply the moral norms contained in the Church's social teaching:

> What good is it, my brothers and sisters, if you say you have faith but do not have works? Can faith save you? If a brother or sister is naked and lacks daily food, and one of you says to them, "Go in peace; keep warm and eat

---

17. See Patrick Lee, "Permanence of the Ten Commandments: St. Thomas and His Modern Commentators," *Theological Studies* 42 (1981): 422–43; Patrick D. Miller, Jr., "The Place of the Decalogue in the Old Testament and Its Law," *Interpretation* 43 (1989): 229–42; Reginald H. Fuller, "The Decalogue in the New Testament," *Interpretation* 43 (1989): 243–55.

18. It would be a mistake to suppose that Vatican II's formulation here supports the view that moral norms are extrinsic to the core of the gospel, "that truth which is Christ," so that the Church's moral teaching can be rejected without rejecting Christ himself. Many moral norms are revealed explicitly (see *CMP*, 7.B) and all of them are implicit in God's self-revelation in Jesus, since he perfectly instantiates human nature and humankind's divine vocation, fully revealing the human to humans (see GS 22). Thus, John Paul II, General Audience (24 July 1991), 3; *L'Osservatore Romano*, It. ed., 25 July 1991, 4; *OR*, 29 July 1991, 7, teaches: "One thing is certain—the life which Jesus Christ, and the Church with him, proposes to man is full of *moral demands* which bind him to what is good, even to the heights of heroism. It is necessary to observe whether, when one says '*no to the Church*', in reality one is not seeking to escape these demands. Here more than in any other case, the '*no to the Church*' would be the equivalent of a '*no to Christ*'. Unfortunately, experience shows that this is often the case."

your fill," and yet you do not supply their bodily needs, what is the good of that? (Jas 2.14–16)

While the Church's social teaching may seem quite theoretical, she does not offer it to project a better world for the sake of utopian speculation. The Church has no plan for an ideal sociopolitical order; instead she articulates relevant moral norms. Her social doctrine can become effective only if Catholics use these norms to judge the social situation confronting them, and then use that judgment as a basis for doing what they can to change the situation for the better.

Of course, it is necessary to distinguish between teachings proposed as certainly true and "prudential judgments," which popes and other bishops sometimes propose as guidance for the faithful without asking for or expecting their religious assent. While in some cases the latter are clearly labeled, in other cases their tentative character is indicated by various signs. For example, a judgment not proposed as certainly true might be expressed only informally or communicated only to some public authority, rather than published in a document addressed to the Church's teachers and/or members as such; it might take a new and very specific position on a particular situation, rather than recall and apply a common and constant Church teaching; it might use language which is indirect or tentative rather than straightforward and unqualified.[19]

4. One Should Criticize Other Norms in the Light of Faith

Although true moral norms are known by reasoning from naturally known principles (see *CMP,* 10) and are clarified, confirmed, and completed by divine revelation, Christians, like everyone else, also gather many norms from other sources. Referring to these, St. Paul teaches: "Do not be conformed to this world, but be transformed by the renewing of your minds, so that you may discern what is the will of God—what is good and acceptable and perfect" (Rom 12.2). Besides gathering norms from Scripture and the Church's teaching, therefore, a person must use those same sources to criticize the norms received from parents and teachers, and the norms proposed by society, for instance, those embodied in the customs of one's culture, the laws of political society, the norms of etiquette, standards suggested by psychology and the social sciences, and so on.[20]

19. An example: John Paul II, Message to Special Session of the United Nations for Disarmament, 8, *AAS* 74 (1982) 879, *OR,* 21 June 1982, 4: "In current conditions 'deterrence' based on balance, certainly not as an end in itself but as a step on the way toward a progressive disarmament, may still be judged morally acceptable." One can recognize that this statement does not propose a judgment as certainly true by the fact that it was addressed to the General Assembly of the United Nations rather than to the bishops and faithful of the Catholic Church, by its isolation in taking a more specific position on nuclear deterrence than that taken by any previous papal statement or Vatican II (see GS 80–81), and by its use of the indirect expression "may still be judged," which stops short of asserting the position expressed.

20. Leo XIII, *Aeterni Patris, ASS* 12 (1879) 104–5, *PE,* 80.10, points out that although ancient philosophers found some truths, these were mingled with many appalling errors, and that the early Fathers and Doctors of the Church "took up and investigated the books of the ancient philosophers, and compared their teachings with the doctrines of revelation, and, carefully sifting them, they cherished what was true and wise in them and amended or rejected all else."

It is wrong to follow other standards without criticizing them by faith. Nevertheless, some follow alien standards in a gross way: by using the rationalization that everyone is doing what they wish to do. And others subtly adopt worldly standards by gradually demanding less and less of themselves and of other people, so that eventually they come to think of true moral norms either as rigoristic or as ideals rather than binding norms.

Question D: How Can Problems about Norms and Their Application Be Solved?

Sometimes a person's own contrary inclination or someone else's suggestion leads the individual to question a moral norm he or she has in mind even though there is no reason to doubt its applicability or adequacy. In such cases, the person is being tempted to look for a way of evading a moral truth which is plain enough, and so he or she should choose according to the norm. On other occasions, though, no relevant norm is on hand, or an individual is unsure whether the seemingly relevant norm is applicable in this situation or is sufficiently specified in view of unusual circumstances. Then it is necessary to proceed step by step along the following lines.

1. In the Absence of a Norm, a Theological Consensus Should Be Followed

Relevant and definite norms proposed by the Church should be accepted; but when the Church's teaching leaves something open and a person is looking for a norm consonant with faith to guide some choice, the consensus of theologians should be followed if there is one.[21] *Consensus* here is used to mean general though not necessarily universal agreement. Of course, most people will need the help of someone with access to the literature of moral theology in order to discover whether such a consensus exists.

For example, Charles is considering donating a kidney to his brother, and there is no medical reason against his doing so. However, his wife, anxious about the risks involved, argues that for Charles to give up a kidney would be wrong—a bad means to a good end. The couple ask the hospital chaplain what the Church has taught on the matter. His reply: Nothing specific, but theologians who treat the question, including the more conservative ones, agree that kidney donation is not morally excluded in itself (see 8.G.1.e). Charles, however, also must consider whether it is fair for him, as a husband and father, to take the risks involved, particularly in view of his wife's reluctance.

---

21. "Consensus of theologians," of course, refers to that general agreement among theologians which can reasonably be taken as an indication of moral truth. The opinions of those who dissent from norms which the Church teaches constantly and most firmly cannot reasonably be trusted. So such opinions neither can constitute nor count against a useful consensus of theologians. Hence, the Congregation for the Doctrine of the Faith, *Instruction on the Ecclesial Vocation of the Theologian*, 39, *AAS* 82 (1990) 1568, *OR*, 2 July 1990, 4, warns against "making the excuse of a 'consensus' among theologians" in an attempt to justify opposition to the magisterium.

The reason for basing a judgment on theological consensus is not that theologians have any independent teaching authority in the Church.[22] While one should believe popes and bishops, whether with an assent of faith or with religious assent, theologians should be looked to for information and enlightenment rather than believed.[23] When the magisterium proposes no teaching on a moral question, however, and all or most of the faithful theologians who have examined it come to agreement about a norm, it is likely that they have discovered the truth as it appears in the light of faith.

2. One May Follow a Consensus in Applying and Specifying Norms

Sometimes, though in possession of a seemingly relevant norm, a person has reason to doubt its applicability or sufficient specificity (see *CMP*, 10.C). In such cases, too, a consensus can be helpful.

a) **A consensus about a norm's applicability may be followed.** Sometimes it is clear that a moral norm is true but not that it applies to the case at hand. Knowing that it always is wrong to kill the innocent, for instance, someone might wonder whether that absolute norm excludes a certain operation on a pregnant woman which will lead to the death of the unborn. If there is a consensus of theologians about the norm's application to the kind of case in question, that consensus may be followed. For example, there is a consensus that, when cancer of the uterus is life-threatening and less drastic treatment would be inappropriate, the removal of a pregnant woman's cancerous uterus is a permissible, indirect abortion.[24] So, whenever someone is in doubt about an operation which is clearly of that type, that consensus provides a solution.

b) **A generally accepted, more specific norm may be followed.** Sometimes the question is whether a norm is sufficiently specific. For instance, having made a promise, someone wonders whether it should be kept. Would it be right to make an exception here and now to the defeasible norm requiring promise keeping? In such cases, it may be possible to find a more specific norm, perhaps one often taken

22. No doubt, all Catholics who are sufficiently mature can participate in the magisterium, for example, by catechizing others who are less mature. But their participation has authority only insofar as they think with "the Church"—that is, express an authentic *sensus fidei*, among whose essential elements is agreement with the Church's pastoral leaders (see LG 12)—so that such participation never constitutes an independent magisterium. *CIC*, c. 812, requires that certain theologians have an official authorization to teach: "It is necessary that those who teach theological disciplines in any institute of higher studies have a mandate from the competent ecclesiastical authority." Theologians having the mandate participate in the magisterium in a certain way, but their teaching authority plainly is delegated, and when their opinions are at odds with received Catholic teaching, they deserve no credence.

23. The norm against believing theologians is relevant with respect to their opinions at odds with the Church's teaching: Congregation for the Doctrine of the Faith, *Haec sacra congregatio*, 2, *AAS* 68 (1976) 739, Flannery, 2:454–55, speaking of sterilization: "The congregation reaffirms this traditional Catholic teaching. It is aware that many theologians dissent from it, but it denies that this fact as such has any doctrinal significance, as though it were a theological source which the faithful might invoke, forsaking the authentic magisterium for the private opinions of theologians who dissent from it (LG 25)."

24. See John Connery, S.J., *Abortion: The Development of the Roman Catholic Perspective* (Chicago: Loyola University Press, 1977), 294–300.

for granted but seldom stated or else stated in various ways. For example, one may find that promise keeping in certain kinds of commercial matters admits of exception, provided those who break their promises fairly indemnify those to whom the promises were made. Again, one may find that promise keeping among friends admits of exception whenever the party who breaks a promise is morally certain the other party will consider the reason for breaking it sufficient.

3. Finding No Consensus, One Should Go Back to Moral Principles

Sometimes a person may have a problem about applying a norm but find no consensus; or one may suspect that a norm requires further specification but find no generally accepted, more specific norm to follow; or someone may have a moral problem and simply know of no relevant norm. For example, when the possibility of *in vitro* fertilization was first described, there was no norm to guide choices in regard to it. In all of these cases, it is necessary to refer to moral principles, for there is no other way to settle questions about the application of norms, to further specify norms, and to formulate entirely new ones (see *CMP,* 10.B).

a) The first step: clarify the action whose morality is in doubt. In referring to principles in order to determine the application of a moral norm or formulate a norm which is more specific or entirely new, it first is necessary to clarify the possible course of action about which there is doubt. This requires answering two questions.

First, what impact will the action have on various instances of basic human goods, either promoting or harming them in oneself and/or others? Often, it is easy to see an action's probable impact on instrumental goods, such as property, liberty, and natural resources. But it is necessary to look beyond these, to see what is at stake for those goods which are aspects of the being and flourishing of persons: life, truth, friendship, religion, and so on (see *CMP,* 5.D; 9.A.1.j, below).

Second, in making a choice, a proposal is adopted to do something for the sake of some benefit (see *CMP,* 9.C). Morally speaking, what is chosen is the means to the benefit, which is the end in view. To have an end in view in making a choice is to intend the benefit for whose sake the choice is made (see *CMP,* 9.D). Thus, in making any choice, one *chooses* precisely the content of the proposal adopted and *intends* precisely the anticipated benefit. But one also foresees effects other than the very carrying out of the choice and the benefits from doing so. These effects, foreseen but neither chosen nor intended, are *side effects.*

The difference between choosing a means, intending an end, and accepting side effects often is morally significant (see *CMP,* 9.F). Thus, the second question is: Which elements of the action's impact are included precisely in what I will choose if I choose to do the action or in the benefits I will anticipate, and which are neither included in the means or the end, but rather are part of what I will accept as side effects?

b) Next: apply moral principles to the act. Once the instances of basic goods on which an action bears and the voluntariness with which it bears on them are clearly understood, the action has been grasped precisely insofar as it is a moral act. Knowing clearly what is to be evaluated, one now must evaluate it by applying moral principles: the modes of responsibility and Christian modes of response.

The modes of responsibility articulate various conditions under which it is inconsistent with upright will to choose and/or accept side effects (see *CMP*, 7.G and 8). The Christian modes of response make it clear how human fulfillment can be served within the limits of the modes of responsibility and in accord with faith, that is, in the fallen and redeemed world in which one lives (see *CMP*, 25.F and 26). Thus, if the kind of act under evaluation is not excluded by any mode of responsibility and can implement one or more of the Christian modes of response, the act is morally appropriate for a Christian.

4. Examples Clarify This Procedure and Its Steps

It will help to consider in detail examples in which recourse to principles is required to solve problems of each kind: application of a norm, further specification of a norm, and development of an entirely new norm.

a) **An example of applying a norm.** Someone who is uncertain whether a particular act would be an act of killing an innocent person must analyze the choice to see whether or not the death is intended as an end or chosen as a means. Assuming the death is not intended as an end—for example, sought out of hatred—if the choice is to do something other than kill, then the norm prohibiting killing the innocent does not apply. The operation to remove a fallopian tube which might rupture as the embryo lodged in it grows was analyzed in this way, and it was concluded that the death of the unborn need not be intended as an end or chosen as a means.[25]

Of course, it also must be asked whether it is fair to accept the death as a side effect. In the case at hand, that presents no problem, assuming the unborn surely will die if not removed (see 8.D.3.d). But in cases of ectopic abdominal pregnancy, both mother and child sometimes can survive, so that the question of fairness requires independent consideration.

b) **An example of further specifying a norm.** In examining a classic example of promise breaking, St. Thomas formulates a norm more specific than that one should keep one's promise to return goods left in one's keeping. What if the party asking for the return of the goods wants to use them in an unjust revolution? Under that condition, the promise should not be kept and the goods should not be returned.[26]

---

25. While the classical moralists' analysis of so-called direct killing and that used in the present work agree with regard to removal of a fallopian tube which might rupture, they diverge on other cases: see 8.B.1.d–f and 8.D.3.d.

26. See *S.t.*, 1–2, q. 94, a. 4; cf. 2–2, q. 57, a. 2, ad 1; q. 120, a. 1. This solution sometimes is misunderstood as if Thomas had said that universal moral norms are subject to situational exceptions to be determined by some sort of intuition. However, his argument presupposes that the question is one of fairness (*naturalis aequalitas*) and proceeds by specifying a condition under which returning the goods on deposit would be "irrational." Moreover, Thomas does not treat prudence as an intuitive faculty which operates independently of propositional principles but as a disposition which enables a person easily and accurately to draw appropriate conclusions from such principles: see *S.t.*, 2–2, q. 47, a. 6.

Thomas does not fully articulate the analysis underlying this norm, but it can be supplied easily. Property is subordinate to basic human goods, including just peace. Breaking promises usually is wrong because it is unjust: it has bad side effects for interpersonal harmony (and often for other goods), and a person usually cannot accept these side effects without being unfair. But the proposal not to return the goods would be chosen in order to impede the revolution and so to protect just peace—a good shared by all members of the society. Without unfairness, the bad side effects of breaking the promise can be accepted. And, impeding an unjust revolution can implement Christian modes of response such as faithfulness and conciliatoriness. From these considerations, the more specific norm follows.

c) An example of developing a new norm. As it is actually practiced, *in vitro* fertilization seems morally objectionable because semen is obtained by masturbation and unwanted embryonic individuals are disposed of. But even leaving aside these acts, which are incidental to *in vitro* fertilization, an accurate analysis of the act and application to it of moral principles lead to a norm which excludes it as always wrong.

What exactly is the act of *in vitro* fertilization? It is not an act of sexual intercourse open to new life but a technological act resulting, when successful, in the production of a new human individual. It precisely aims at supplying someone with a baby by bringing a possible baby into being, and the choice of *in vitro* fertilization precisely is to (try to) produce a baby by this procedure. So, to choose to bring about conception in this fashion inevitably is to will the baby's initial status as a product.

How do moral principles apply to this act? Products as such are assigned their meaning and value by the human makers who produce them and the consumers who use them, and so the status of any product as such is subpersonal; therefore, the choice to produce a baby inevitably is a choice to enter into a relationship with the baby, affecting his or her very being, as with something subpersonal. This initial relationship, of those who choose to produce babies with the babies they produce, is inconsistent with, and so impedes, the communion which is appropriate in any relationship among persons touching on their basic goods.[27]

Of course, those who choose to produce a baby make that choice only insofar as it is a means to an ulterior end. They may well intend that the baby be received in an authentic child-parent relationship, in which he or she will live in the communion befitting those who share personal dignity. If realized, this intended end will be good for the baby as well as for the parents. But, even so, the choice to produce the baby is the choice of a bad means to a good end, because the baby's initial status as a product is subpersonal. The significance of this status is most clear

---

27. Thus, Congregation for the Doctrine of the Faith, *Instruction on Respect for Human Life in Its Origin and on the Dignity of Procreation: Replies to Certain Questions of the Day,* 2.5, *AAS* 80 (1988) 93, *OR,* 16 Mar. 1987, 6, states with respect to *in vitro* fertilization using an ovum and sperm of a wife and husband: "Such fertilization entrusts the life and identity of the embryo into the power of doctors and biologists and establishes the domination of technology over the origin and destiny of the human person. Such a relationship of domination is in itself contrary to the dignity and equality that must be common to parents and children."

when the laboratory's defective products are discarded and its surplus products used for lethal experiments.

5. People Can Solve Moral Problems by Referring to Principles

Can ordinary people solve moral problems by engaging in such analyses? Vatican II teaches:

> It is a matter for lay persons' well-formed consciences that the divine law be inscribed in the life of the earthly city. From priests they may look for spiritual light and nourishment. Lay people should not, however, expect their pastors always to be such experts that to every problem which arises, however serious, they can readily provide a concrete solution or that this is their mission. Rather, enlightened by Christian wisdom and giving attentive heed to the teaching authority of the Church [note omitted], let lay people take their own proper roles. (GS 43)[28]

Thus, the Council suggests that at least some people can carry through their own moral analyses, even in rather difficult matters. Many, of course, will need help.

Question E: How Can Doubts about Facts Be Resolved?

To find the moral truth and guide one's choice, it is not enough to know moral principles and norms. Everything relevant, whether actual or possible, also must be taken into account, even though it is not normative. For these are facts one faces and cannot ignore, since they help constitute the possibilities available for choice while also limiting them. Not knowing enough about some fact relevant to a moral judgment and not at once succeeding in getting the necessary information, one should engage in further investigation.

1. Sometimes It Is Not Necessary to Resolve Doubts of Fact

Doubts of fact need not be resolved if the facts will not change one's moral responsibilities. An important kind of case in which a doubt of fact is morally irrelevant occurs when someone chooses to do something immoral under a condition that might or might not obtain. Whether it does or does not, the person's moral responsibility is the same: a sin already has been committed. For example, if someone decides to commit adultery if an attractive opportunity arises, he or she already has committed it. If someone decides to lie under oath only if it is absolutely necessary, he or she already has committed perjury.

---

28. This conciliar teaching often is misinterpreted to suggest that the formulation of new specific moral norms may proceed independently of the Church's teaching authority and might reach conclusions at odds with it. This interpretation not only conflicts with GS 43 itself, but with the teaching of John Paul II, Address to Members of the Lay Apostolate (Liège), 10, *Inseg.* 8.1 (1985) 1546, *OR*, 15 July 1985, 9: "In fact, you are asked to form *good Christian judgment,* spiritual and pastoral discernment. As it applies itself to the complex realities of the world, this judgment presupposes respect for the laws specific to every discipline and true competence. But at the same time it presupposes that you are familiar with the Gospel, that you are guided by the spirit of the Church, subject to its Magisterium, that you have assimilated well the social doctrine of the Church, that you are moved by Christian charity, that you nourish your apostolic vigour with prayer and the sacraments (cf. AA 7)."

2. Reasonable Presumptions Should Be Made

When it is necessary to try to resolve a doubt of fact, the investigation should be shaped by two assumptions.

First, realizing that one is in doubt, a person may not simply presume that the "fact" in question is a fact. It must be proved or disproved before the doubt can be dismissed. For instance, if uncertain whether a debt was paid, one may not simply assume it was.

Second, if an act certainly has been done but one doubts whether it was done properly, one should begin by assuming it was, not allow a mere doubt to upset a settled situation. For example, if there is doubt about the validity of some legal act which certainly was done, validity is presumed while nullity must be proved.[29]

3. One Should Use Appropriate Methods and Seek the Help One Needs

In attempting to settle doubts of fact, the methods depend on the subject matter. Moral theology cannot teach these methods, since they belong to other disciplines.

When in doubt about a matter of fact, a person often will find it necessary and useful to obtain others' help. This will include trying to make sure the others are sufficiently familiar with the matter at hand and diligent in attending to the relevant facts. Also, because people's presuppositions affect their beliefs about matters of fact, the preferred helper in investigating matters of fact relevant to a moral judgment should be someone who shares one's Christian commitment.

4. Doubts about Positive Law Are Doubts of Fact

Doubts about the existence and applicability of norms of positive law are a special case of doubts about facts, since from the moral point of view the existence and applicability of legal norms simply are facts. The relevant moral norm is that just norms of positive law ought to be obeyed (see 11.D.1). This norm is defeasible when norms of positive law are inapplicable (see 11.D.2).[30]

5. One Need Make Only a Reasonable Effort to Resolve Doubts of Fact

How far must people go in trying to settle doubts about facts? Plainly, if concerned with grave matter, possible mortal sin, or a major choice such as a vocational commitment, their inquiry should be pushed much further than it otherwise would be. Still, there is no general answer to this question, since it

29. Note that this second presumption bears on acts and their moral, social, and legal meanings, not on products. If an automobile has been built and its builders doubt whether they bolted the steering mechanism together properly, they should check, not assume they did the job right. On these presumptions, see I. Aertnys, C. Damen, and I. Visser, C.Ss.R., *Theologia moralis*, ed. 18, 4 vols. (Turin: Marietti, 1967–69), 1:224–25; note that the third prudential principle they propose does not shape inquiry but directs judgment if inquiry fails to settle the doubt.

30. Epikeia as St. Thomas understands it (see *S.t.*, 2–2, q. 120) is concerned precisely with the defeasibility of this norm. Thus, although epikeia is concerned exclusively with positive law, the way one rightly judges that a positive law should not be obeyed is similar to the way one finds true exceptions to other defeasible norms. How this is done was discussed in D, above.

requires bringing prudence to bear on actual situations. Those who recognize their own limits can look for guidance to the example of mature, holy persons.

Question F: When and How Should Better Options Be Sought?

People engaged in deliberation often should look for alternatives besides those which spontaneously come to mind or are suggested by others. Although there is no way to guarantee that a better alternative will be found, there are certain things to do which can be helpful. Moreover, if alternatives are sought in the light of faith, some are likely to be found that would be either entirely unavailable or too unappealing to consider except in faith's light.

1. In Many Different Situations, One Should Look for Better Options

People very often tend to make the best of a situation, perhaps complaining ineffectually but not trying to change it or break out of it. Moreover, being reluctant to deliberate, many tend to choose what they take to be a morally good and appealing possibility without looking for alternatives. In following these tendencies, however, better possibilities often are overlooked; but someone who makes a practice of looking for better alternatives often will find them.

a) **Sometimes perplexity is resolved by finding a good alternative.** People are perplexed when it seems they will do something wrong or fail to fulfill some responsibility no matter what they do. This situation will be treated (in I.3, below). But such perplexity sometimes arises because the morally right—but unappealing—possibility has been excluded from consideration. Hence, the first and obvious thing to do when perplexed is to look for the overlooked morally acceptable alternative. For example, confronted by an implacable enemy bent on doing grave harm, George may seem to face a choice between doing whatever is necessary to dissuade that enemy (even by using morally excluded means) and surrendering (perhaps even cooperating in great moral evils to placate the enemy). Someone considering such a case in the light of faith sees an alternative: George could resist the enemy with morally acceptable means and explain the limits of his resistance by his faith. In this way, he would bear witness to the gospel and call his enemy to conversion, while praying both for that grace for his enemy and for success in his resistance with the limited means he is morally free to employ. Of course, he might fail, and failure will lead to some form of martyrdom. But for a Christian, martyrdom always should be acceptable. Again, a priest who thinks he must either tell a lie or give away someone's confessional secret perhaps has overlooked the possibility of saying: "As a matter of policy, I do not answer questions of that sort."

b) **When refusing to sin, one should try to mitigate any bad effects.** Even when it is necessary to refrain from something sinful, a person should look for an alternative better than simply not doing it. While considerations and feelings which might tempt one to do evil must be set aside, they should not be ignored. Perhaps the alternative which must be chosen can at least be altered by also doing something further. For example, Thomas More judged that he could not swear an oath he believed false. His refusal had bad effects both for himself and for his family. Not only did he refuse to swear the false oath, however, but he also tried to help his family understand why, sought to arrange for their safety, and asked God to mitigate the prospective harm.

c) **To resolve a conflict, one should consider yielding one's rights.** Sometimes finding a better alternative will resolve a seemingly intractable conflict among individuals or groups. For, in general, faith and hope make it clear that to overcome evil and promote good it is necessary and appealing to sacrifice what is due oneself in justice for the sake of peace, service to others, the spread of the gospel, and so forth. Thus, whenever conflicting claims raise questions of fairness, Christians must consider whether a solution can be found by not pressing their claims and instead yielding what they think they have a right to. For example, if three children disagree about fairly sharing a candy bar, one can solve the problem by giving parts of his or her share to the others until they are satisfied with their shares. And if the wealthy members of society choose to give up their wealth, even though they justly hold it, they can mitigate class conflict. In many cases, Christians should choose such merciful alternatives (see Mt 5.38–42, Lk 6.29–30; *CMP*, 27.F).

d) **To fulfill responsibilities, better alternatives should be sought.** Sometimes, finding an overlooked alternative will enable one to fulfill a responsibility that at first seems morally impossible to fulfill. For example, Sam, a salesman working for an unscrupulous contractor, thinks he must either defraud customers or fail to support his family. But Sam may find some honest way to use his talents and make an adequate living, perhaps by setting up a business that will help customers who have been defrauded to obtain the compensation due them.

Sometimes, even though finding a better alternative is not necessary to solve a moral problem, it is called for by some other moral responsibility. Whenever none of the options under consideration is appealing and well suited to implement one's faith and the other basic commitments made in harmony with faith, more adequate ways to implement them should be sought. For example, the head of a family who has a marginally adequate job and is offered another, better in some ways but not so good in others, should seek other possibilities, not simply choose between accepting and refusing that particular job offer.

e) **In important matters, many alternatives should be examined.** Sometimes, a better alternative should be sought even though the available alternatives include one or more good and appealing options. For even when the alternatives under consideration include morally acceptable and appealing ways of implementing faith or vocational commitments, people should try to widen the range of alternatives in important matters, and not simply choose among those which spontaneously come to mind or are suggested by others. For instance, if a woman is considering becoming a nun, she should examine a variety of forms of religious life and different communities. And a family seeking a place to live should consider a wide range of possibilities, taking into account how each would affect the family as a whole and each of its members.

2. To Find Better Alternatives, Several Things Should Be Done

No method can guarantee that alternatives will be found better than those which spontaneously present themselves. But it often helps to ask appropriate questions, and inventiveness can be cultivated; also, one should be realistic rather than wasting time thinking about impractical possibilities.

a) **One should ask oneself the appropriate questions.** When a person is not entirely satisfied with the alternatives already under consideration, the appropriate starting point of reflection is: I am about to make a choice which seems either at odds with goods in which I am rightly interested or hardly adequate to serve these interests. Is there nothing else I might choose which would be not only acceptable but appealing?

Lacking any special dissatisfaction with the alternatives already under consideration, the appropriate starting point of such reflection is: I am about to use my gifts and resources to do this, for the sake of realizing this good in such and such persons. Could I realize the same good in more people or more good in the same people, or even do both? Could I do a similar service where it is even more needed? For example, a young man, considering entering religious life to serve in Christian education, might find better alternatives by asking questions like the following: Where could I contribute most? Where could I help meet the greatest need for Christian education? These questions might lead him to consider various unfamiliar communities, such as those working in mission territories, whereas otherwise he might consider only a familiar one, with an apostolate in his home town.

b) **One should do what one can to be inventive.** It also is necessary to be inventive, as, for instance, St. Dominic was when, seeing the great need for the preaching and teaching of doctrine going unmet in his day by the diocesan clergy, he founded the Order of Preachers to meet it. Although there are no rules for being inventive—inspiration is a gift—people can dispose themselves to receive the gift. For instance, one can search one's memory, consult others, and look to somewhat analogous cases in biography, history, and fiction to discover possibilities which would otherwise be overlooked. Moreover, now and then one can retreat from constant activity to spend some quiet time in prayer and reflection, not pressing to solve problems, but making oneself ready to receive the Holy Spirit's suggestions.

In social and economic matters, an important source of better alternatives is the reflection in which individuals, groups organized for Christian social action, and other communities engage when examining the facts in the light of the Church's social teaching. While much of that teaching can seem inapplicable, many of its elements really can help a person see how certain general principles might apply to the particular situations he or she faces. In this way, an individual can think of fresh alternatives, options consonant with faith.

c) **Time should not be wasted on wishful thinking.** In looking for better alternatives, people often make the mistake of becoming fascinated with imaginable alternatives which are appealing but completely impractical. The tendency arises from a defect of hope: the realities one cannot change ought to be accepted as the conditions God has providentially provided (or, at least, permitted) and should trust that, with his help, all the good he wills can be done.

For example, a nun works out an elaborate plan about how she would run the parish if she were a priest; a married man daydreams about how pleasant his life would be had he married a different woman, when he should be thinking about how to make the best of his marriage. (On the sinfulness of such daydreaming by married persons, see 9.D.4.a.)

Again, a mother suffering from a disability can waste time and energy imagining how well she would care for her children if she were free of the disability, while failing to think of what she might really do to overcome her disability to some extent and care for the children as well as she can. Or a young priest might spend much of his time thinking about how he would assign the priests in the diocese and solve its major problems if he were the bishop. Perhaps his ideas not only appeal to him but are sound; but he is not the bishop, and he should instead be thinking about how to do the job he now has and perhaps making up, so far as possible, for the bishop's limitations.

In sum, while inhibitions should not be allowed to limit imagination's work of proposing alternatives for consideration, people should distinguish between proposals which are merely unconventional or somehow uninviting and those which are totally impractical, and waste no time discarding the latter.

Question G: When and How Should Emotions That Bear on Choices Be Criticized?

Emotions here refers to motives at the sensory level which are generically common to humans and other animals. Among them are desire, aversion, fear, anger, and the tendency to rest, which can be called "tiredness."[31] Emotions motivate behavior insofar as it is guided by sensory cognition, including awareness of the present situation, memories of past situations or elements of them, and imagination of possible situations. Usually, people are not conscious of their emotional motives. For example, in scratching one is moved by a desire to relieve an itch, but often one is unaware even of the itch and the scratching, much less of the desire; in driving an automobile, fear often makes one step on the brakes, but the fear is noticed only if the danger is unusual.

In general, there is nothing wrong with emotions, and while in themselves they are not rational, neither are they irrational. Every option considered in deliberation, including the possibility of not acting, is supported by some emotional motive making it at least somewhat appealing and bringing it to attention. No act, bad or good, can occur without some emotional motive, and good acts which succeed

31. Emotions here refers to what St. Thomas calls "passiones animae," which he treats both in general (see *S.t.*, 1–2, qq. 22–25) and in considerable specific detail (qq. 26–48). Sometimes *passiones animae* is translated *passions of the soul* and sometimes it is translated *feelings*, but the former expression has no other current use in English and the latter strongly suggests an object of consciousness. *Emotions* and *emotional motives* wrongly suggest intensity, and *emotion* often is used to refer to states of consciousness which are only contingently related to motivation: being joyful, sad, anxious, and so on. Moreover, St. Thomas does not identify tiredness as an emotion, because he assumes that the unmotivated state of an organism is to be at rest. However, healthy organisms which are awake need no motivation to engage in random movement as they constantly gather sensory information which specifies the emotions triggering functional behaviors, and so an emotion, specified by inner sensory awareness of the body's condition of fatigue, is required to trigger the functional behavior of finding a suitable place to rest and settling down for sleep.

normally result in emotional gratification. However, as everyone knows, emotions can deflect practical thinking and moral judgment, with the bad result that one judges wrongly about what is and is not to be done. Thus, examining emotions often can lead to insight into the motives supporting options under consideration in deliberation, and so can help one reach moral truth.

Sometimes troublesome emotional factors involve partiality in favor of oneself and those near and dear (question H will deal with such cases). At other times, the problem has to do with something other than partiality. The present question deals with cases of this latter kind.

1. One Should Deliberate Rationally Despite Emotional Obstacles

Emotional motivations can and often do interfere directly with the quest for moral truth by blocking consideration of some rational elements of the situation. Once these latter are considered, however, it becomes clear that a choice in line with those emotions would be simply unreasonable, that is, not in accord with any reason whatsoever.

a) **One should not be overly attached to existing situations.** Emotion often biases people in favor of the advantages of the status quo, so that they fail to consider an alternative, supported by reasons, involving something new. For example, Joe's job does not use his talents fully and certainly never will, but he ignores other employment opportunities, because the prospect of going to work in a new situation makes him anxious. Again, Jane is used to doing a job with familiar tools. A friend tells her the same job could be done more easily and effectively with a new tool which will quickly pay for itself. Comfortable with the familiar way of doing things, however, Jane does not find changing to a new way emotionally appealing, and so is inclined to ignore the advice. Her attitude is unreasonable: she should be openminded enough to check out what her friend is saying. If the evidence indicates that using the new tool really would serve her purpose better, emotional motives plainly should be set aside, inasmuch as choosing to act in accord with them would serve no rational interest whatsoever.

b) **One should not be overly attached to projects one has undertaken.** Commitments to basic goods and persons are one thing, the particular projects undertaken to fulfill them another. Commitments call for faithfulness, and a person's emotional investment in them supports fidelity. Projects should be rationally evaluated on the basis of their effectiveness, but a person's emotional investment in them can lead to unreasonable persistence. For example, Bishop Jones has devoted much time and many diocesan resources to a program for pastoral renewal. Once it is underway, it soon becomes clear that the program is not working well, and the Bishop wishes he had never undertaken it. However, he cannot bring himself to admit a mistake whose costly results should be written off. So, he ignores all bad news about the program and carries on with it. In general, people should consider reasons for revising or terminating projects rather than persist without a reason to do so.

c) **Longterm benefits and harms should not be ignored.** In relation to sensory cognition, what is more proximate is more real, and so emotion can fasten on short-term advantages and disadvantages and lead a person to ignore rational considerations about future prospects. For example, George is advised to undergo a dangerous operation but finds the prospect frightening, while the idea of delaying or forgoing it is not nearly so frightening; and so he is inclined to procrastinate. In such a case, it is necessary to evaluate the reasonableness of acting on the emotion —in George's case, fear—by asking about the risks and burdens of accepting the side effect. If the evidence is that it is riskier to put off the surgery than have it, George should consent to it even if the more remote risks of delaying or forgoing surgery remain emotionally less repugnant. Similarly, people often are so fascinated by the prospect of immediate satisfaction in a sexual relationship, experimentation with drugs, or something of the sort, that they thoughtlessly risk bringing lifelong misery on themselves and others.

d) Excessive concentration on a single goal should be avoided. Reason always requires giving appropriate attention to other matters besides those immediately at hand. However, emotion can lead to such great fascination with a particular goal that other responsibilities are slighted. Pursuing the objective takes concentration, which can reinforce emotion, leading to more intense concentration, and so on. For instance, Phyllis, having a good job and being eager to advance in it, becomes absorbed in its requirements and neglects her husband's needs, her own health, and even her religious duties, although aware that all these are at least as important to her as her work. In general, people should regularly take stock of their lives to make certain they are meeting all their responsibilities rather than becoming absorbed in one matter and slighting or overlooking others.

2. Emotions Should Be Questioned in Three Kinds of Cases

Sometimes an option for choice passes the test of rational reflection by application of sound moral norms, yet something still indicates that it might be a mistake to choose it. (When examining conscience, a person also often has occasion to question the role of emotions in choices recognized as sinful. But for simplicity's sake, the cases treated here will not be cast in terms of examination of conscience.) Three kinds of indications should lead anyone seeking moral truth to engage in further reflection, even though an option under consideration has passed every normative test suggested by previous questions.

a) Emotions should be questioned when one notices a sign of trouble. There are several common signs of trouble: a person feels uneasy with the alternative without seeing why, or someone else suggests that the prospective choice would be wrong but the individual fails to see any reason (or further reason) for thinking it so, or the choice does not seem to be the sort of thing a role model (a mature and holy person) would do.

b) Intense emotions and those inclining to partiality are suspect. Sometimes a person is aware that the option under consideration belongs to a class whose emotional motives often lack integration with reason. One should bear in mind that there are such classes of options and should be suspicious whenever a prospective option would be of such a kind. For instance, if a possibility has an unusually strong emotional appeal, the emotion should be examined. Again, if the option would have both benefits and harms, with the former accruing to oneself and those one loves, and the latter to others, one's emotional motives should be examined to see whether partiality is at work (such cases will be considered in question H).

c) **When the matter is important, one's emotions should be examined.** Sometimes there is neither a general reason for suspicion nor a sign calling for closer examination of emotional factors, yet because the choice is a major one—for example, a vocational commitment, a major project to implement such a commitment, an action which might lead to someone's death—one's emotional motives should not be regarded uncritically but carefully examined.

3. Examples Show How Emotional Motives Can Fruitfully Be Examined

When one option is supported only by emotions and the other by rational grounds as well, there is no need to examine one's emotions, since the modes of responsibility exclude acting on emotions against reasons. But sometimes both options are, or at least initially seem to be, supported by reasons which appear consistent with all relevant moral norms. Then it is necessary to examine the emotional motives which make each option emotionally repugnant or appealing, in an effort to try to discover how well those emotional factors harmonize with the reasons for and against each option.

Probably there is no way to provide systematic directions for reflection of this sort. However, examples can illustrate the process and show how, with its help, moral truth can be reached despite the influence of emotional factors.

a) **A case of purifying motives for a vocational commitment.** A man asks a young woman to marry him and she sees no reason not to; but, rightly, she does want to be sure. Although she loves the man, she asks herself what it is about him and her prospective life with him that makes marriage appealing. She realizes she was first attracted to him because she enjoys his company at entertainments and parties, and marriage appeals to her partly because she is unhappy living with her parents but cannot afford a place of her own. Being serious about her faith, she also realizes that marriage is a lifelong commitment, which probably will entail responsibilities toward children. Reflecting on this, she begins to wonder what sort of father the man will be, and even feels a certain distaste at the prospect of having him as her children's father. She now rightly judges: I ought to call off the wedding.

Similarly, a young man about to be ordained to the transitional diaconate should ask himself what makes the priesthood appealing to him. If he finds that it is the status priests enjoy in the Church rather than the opportunity to serve people by the ministry of the word and sacraments, he should not accept ordination on so unsound a basis. Indeed, if he cannot purify his motives, he should not seek ordination.

b) **A case of sorting out negative emotions.** A youth who has been acting arrogantly toward his parents calls home to announce that he is being held on a drug charge and asks his dad to bail him out. The father wonders what to do and talks the problem over with his business partner, who has done some drug counseling. This friend thinks it might be best not to post the bond: the jail in which the boy is lodged is not a bad one, and spending a few days there could bring him to face reality. The father is pleased with the advice: he has resented his son's arrogance and is angry with him for causing the family the trouble and embarrassment that will follow from the criminal charge. But the boy's mother is anxious about her son's being in jail and urges her husband to post bond at once.

His wife's pleas lead the father to realize the intensity of his anger and examine his emotional motivation more carefully. Is it the thought that his son may repent and reform which makes the idea of refusing to post bond appealing—or the prospect of his son's distress and humiliation? The father admits to himself that much of his anger is misdirected, and his emotions subside. Considering the matter more calmly, however, it still appears a good idea to refuse to post bond, so that the boy will learn that he must begin to take responsibility for his life. So the father judges: I ought to refuse my son's request to post bond, but I also must visit him in jail and do what I can to help him reform his life.[32]

c) **A case of seeing through and overcoming tiredness.** A mother is spending a quiet evening reading a long and difficult poem. Her small children have been tucked in bed, and she is relaxing with an after-dinner drink. Halfway through her reading, she realizes she has not heard the usual noises from the children's rooms and thinks perhaps she should check on them. But that would interfere with her appreciation of the poem, and so she is inclined not to do it. Still, she feels uneasy. Is it real anxiety about the children? No, it is more like a slight feeling of guilt. Then she realizes that what is holding her back actually is not interest in the poem; it is not as good as the critics say, and interrupting her reading for a few minutes will not significantly reduce her appreciation of it. Rather, relaxing and sipping her drink, she has begun to feel comfortable and tired, and that is why she was not inclined to check on the children. But, being a conscientious mother, who regularly masters emotions of that sort in caring for her children, she judges: I ought to check on the children and make sure everything is all right.

d) **A case of seeing through antipathy.** A family has been counting on a week's vacation at the beach. Just as they are about to leave, good neighbors down the hill are flooded out and appeal for help in cleaning up the mess. The family's vacation has been well earned, but their neighbors' need is urgent, since the disaster is so widespread that many people need help and little is available. The children are eager to go: they point out how pleasant it will be to relax on the beach, and how miserable the work at the neighbors' house will be, especially in such hot and humid weather. Mother favors helping the neighbors: she points out that they have been good neighbors and stand to lose thousands of dollars if the flood damage is not cleaned up promptly; moreover, the family can do without their planned vacation,

32. No doubt, the father's rightly chosen course of action could lead to apparent disaster, and, if it does, he is likely to say to himself: "I wish I had posted the bond! I did the wrong thing." But he should not say this, because he can know neither what would have happened had he posted the bond, nor all the effects of his actual choice, for some are hidden and others are still to unfold. Moreover, while understandable, the father's regret has no practical point, since he cannot change what he did in the past. In this respect, his situation is very different from that of Bishop Jones (in G.1.b), who can change what he is doing, and so should be open to evidence regarding the program's failure.

and they will get a good deal of exercise and a real change of pace by pitching in to help the neighbors. Father at first is reluctant to abandon the vacation, but he considers both sides. He has to admit to the children that he hates the prospect of the work, and, like them, would much rather spend the week lying on the beach. But in admitting that, he realizes that, except for their reluctance toward doing the work, he and the children would agree with mother and forgo the vacation. Knowing he should not allow his and the children's aversion to work to override the good reasons for helping the neighbors, father says: We're going to have to cancel the vacation.

e) **A case of examining fear and finding it wanting.** A young man is preparing to climb a mountain, when weather conditions turn bad. Veteran climbers begin calling off their plans to attempt the ascent. The young man knows the facts and understands their objective significance as well as the veterans do; but he is still inclined to go, although the risks of an accident are more than he anticipated. Let us assume that he has no family or other responsibilities to make it clear to him that taking the risk for the sake of the sport would be wrong. He asks himself: Does my boldness arise from my appreciation of the sport or from imagining myself bragging about making a climb veteran climbers were afraid to attempt? It seems to him that it is the former, not the latter.

Nevertheless, the young man ought to ask still another question: Am I inclined to attempt the climb because I am not sufficiently fearful of the risks? The answer will not be found by looking at his own emotions, since the fear he has provides no standard of its own adequacy. Rather, his best index to sufficient fear is that of the veteran climbers. Their fears of risks are well integrated with their appreciation of the values of the sport. The young man should judge: I ought not to attempt this climb today.

f) **A case of emotions transformed by faith.** A man fulfills his obligation to support his family by working as a guard, maintaining order in a striptease club, where he often is tempted to commit sins of impurity and sometimes has done so. He has not found another job that would enable him to support his family. His confessor suggests that the man should consider quitting his job at the club, but this advice seems unrealistic. The man obviously has a good reason for continuing to work at the club, but still he must ask himself exactly why he is inclined to continue in the job, while trying unsuccessfully to resist the temptations which are inevitable in that occasion of sin.

Like the young man in the mountain-climbing example, this man can inspect one of the two relevant emotional factors but not the other. For he can ask himself whether keeping the job appeals to him solely because of his emotions toward his family. Perhaps he actually rather enjoys the atmosphere of the club and is resisting detaching himself from it. Yet he finds that is not so: he really would be delighted to quit the club if he could find another job, even a harder one, adequate to support his family. However, the man cannot directly check another relevant factor: the adequacy of his repugnance to sin. Is this enough? He tries to judge that by looking to the example of saintly people, but, unlike the young mountain climber, he does not find a model with whom he identifies.

Continuing to fall into sin, praying for strength and light, the man begins, for the first time in his life, to read the New Testament. He reaches the fifth chapter of Matthew's Gospel and reads:

> You have heard that it was said, "You shall not commit adultery." But I say to you that everyone who looks at a woman with lust has already committed adultery with her in his heart. If your right eye causes you to sin, tear it out and throw it away; it is better for you to lose one of your members than for your whole body to be thrown into hell. (Mt 5.27–29)

Believing that this passage is addressed to him, he judges: I ought to quit the club and trust in God to give me some other means of supporting my family.

4. In All Such Cases, the Harmony of Emotions with Reason Is Judged

The problem in all of the examples was to become clear about the real thrust of emotional motivation which could have made reason swerve from its goal of moral truth. Moral truth is found by unfettered reason, and emotions in harmony with reason would not tend to fetter it.

Still, emotional factors and reasons are entirely different kinds of motives. What, then, does it mean to speak of harmony between emotions and reason, and how can they harmonize more and less well? The answer is that, since sentient nature is part of complete human nature, some of the emotions inclining one to consider options bear on concrete aspects of the anticipated states of affairs which one would intend in choosing those options. Bearing on an aspect of the anticipated benefit or harm, which is the possible reason for acting, these emotions are in harmony with reason and so can serve as a standard for judging whether the same is true of any other emotional motive operative in the same deliberation.

This answer can be explained as follows.

a) **The objects of reasons can include the objects of emotions.** Rationally motivated human acts aim to realize basic human goods in human persons or to prevent harms to such goods. (For simplicity's sake, preventing harms will not be mentioned in the remainder of this explanation, but it should be borne in mind as the alternative to realizing benefits.) The benefits at which acts aim are instantiations—that is, particular concrete realizations—of the goods. These instantiations perfect or fulfill persons, and so include both intelligible and sensible aspects. For example, health includes both an intelligible state of the organism and feeling well; friendship includes both an intelligible bond of communion and a sense of intimacy. The concrete, sensibly experienced aspects of benefits can be objects of the emotions necessary to motivate action to realize those benefits.

b) **Some emotional motives are entirely in harmony with reason.** Emotions respond to the whole complex reality of a concrete situation, and a situation in which a benefit is realized always includes much that is irrelevant to that benefit. Emotions of themselves, therefore, need not, and usually do not, focus exclusively on the sensible goods which contribute to the benefit supplying the reason to choose the action. For instance, John's emotions in buying an automobile may have more to do with how others will react than with his need for transportation. But some emotions do focus precisely on the sensible goods belonging to the benefit. For instance, when Mary chooses not to drink too much because she is concerned about her health, her anxieties about hangovers and other painful consequences focus precisely on a sensible aspect of the intelligible good. These emotions, concerned with and proportioned to the concrete aspects of the benefit at which an action aims, are entirely in harmony with reason.

c) **Such emotions are a standard for criticizing other emotions.** Emotional motives entirely in harmony with reason provide a standard which can be used to criticize other emotions. If some other emotion inclines one to consider the act worth doing but is at odds with the emotions providing the standard of harmony, that other emotion is not in harmony with reason. Also, if an emotion other than those which provide the standard inclines one to consider the act worth doing, and if in its absence one would not be inclined to do the act, that emotion is not entirely in harmony with reason, for it is not integrated with reason even though it does not conflict with it.

5. This Account Is Verified by Reconsidering the Previous Examples

Applying this general account to the six examples, it becomes clearer how emotional factors not in harmony with reason would have prevented reflection from reaching moral truth.

a) **The case of purifying motives for a vocational commitment.** The young woman thinking of marrying realizes that her emotional motives for marriage are inconsistent with the emotions she would have if she were about to marry for the sake of the benefits proper to marriage. That is why she begins to feel distaste for the prospect when she starts to reflect on what married life and parenthood with her fiance would involve. If she tells friends with a sound understanding of marriage she is not going through with the wedding because she would be marrying to escape her unhappy home situation rather than out of hope of a happy marriage, they will agree that her judgment is correct. Similar comments can be made on the case of the seminarian.

b) **The case of sorting out negative emotional motives.** The father of the youth arrested on the drug charge realizes that his resentment and anger are incompatible with the fatherly affection he would have if the appropriate benefit, his son's reformation, were the only motive inclining him to refuse his son's plea for help. But once insight into those hostile emotions neutralizes them, he recognizes that letting the boy stay in jail is motivated by the prospective benefit of doing so and by emotions conducive to acting effectively for its sake. These emotions, of concern for the boy, help the father think out more adequately the precise benefit to be pursued. Thus, he judges that he not only should refuse to bail the boy out of jail, but should do whatever he can to help his son reform his life.

c) **The case of seeing through and overcoming tiredness.** The mother reading the poem at first thinks that is a good enough reason for not checking on the children. And, according to the facts of the example, it would be. But she realizes that her inclination not to check does not arise from any need to concentrate on the poetry but from her tiredness. Having already made her own a desire to care for her children which is inconsistent with being swayed by that sort of consideration, she sees there actually is no reason not to interrupt her reading and check on the children.

d) The case of seeing through antipathy. The family looking forward to their vacation at the beach is motivated initially not to give up their plan both by the expected pleasure of the vacation—a motive fully in harmony with the benefit it promises—and by distaste for the work involved in helping the neighbors. They also are motivated to change their plan and help the neighbors by emotions of sympathy and neighborly solidarity. Seeing the antipathy to doing the work to be irrelevant to any prospective benefit, and so excluded from consideration, the father accepts his wife's application of the Golden Rule and judges the benefit to the neighbors more worth pursuing than the benefit to the family of taking the vacation. To go ahead with the vacation, he would have had to accept his and his children's antipathy to the work as an adequate motive for not responding to the neighbors' urgent need.

e) The case of examining fear and finding it wanting. The young mountain climber finds his desire to make the climb harmonious with his reason for doing so. But he cannot check his fear, or lack of it, against the fear that is normal in actions suited to realize the benefit of the sport of mountain climbing. The veteran climbers have developed that fear. They not only observe the weather conditions and consider the risks of having an accident, which being objective are the same for them as for the young man, but imagine themselves climbing under those conditions, attend to the fear they feel, compare it with the tension they normally experience as they set out for a climb, and recognize this fear is more than that involved in climbing for the sport of it. Thus, the example of the veteran climbers provides the young man with an indication of the sort of fear in harmony with reason. If he had the veteran climbers' maturity, he would see that for it to be reasonable to attempt the climb under the existing conditions would require some reason more than that provided by the sport, for example, the need to rescue others who mistakenly had attempted the climb. Lacking any such reason, the young man, if he understands the significance of the veteran climbers' reluctance to attempt the climb, will realize that his fear is not adequate to the actual danger.

f) The case of emotions transformed by faith. The man working at the striptease club, like the young mountain climber, finds nothing wrong with the element of his emotional motivation that he can check: his inclination not to quit his job is motivated by care for his family, not by the enjoyment of remaining in this occasion of sin. And, as the young mountain climber cannot check his fear, this man cannot check the adequacy of his repugnance to sin. However, insight into the gospel's significance for him arouses a hatred of sin, and a fear of hell, greater than he previously had, and at the same time arouses a new emotion harmonious with hope in God's help. If he were to remain in the club, his reason would have to be that care for his family required what hope now assures him is unnecessary.

+ + +

Question H: How Can Partiality Be Recognized?

Acts which would involve injustice often can be recognized by norms one already has on hand. They may be such that doing them is always wrong, and so would be wrong even if done to oneself, for example, killing an innocent person. They may be wrong because they fail to fulfill a recognized duty or violate a recognized right, for example, failing to do one's job or failing to pay someone an earned wage. Sometimes, though, an act would be unjust only because it would not be chosen except for feelings inclining to partiality. Only by attending to emotional motives is it then possible to avoid the false judgment that the unjust act should be done.

1. In Many Cases, Questions about Partiality Should Not Arise

Many people recognize hardly any moral issues besides fairness. They begin moral reflection on every question by asking: Can I make this or that choice without being unfair to anyone concerned? When thinking about what is fair, however, a person should consider only those options for choice which are morally acceptable in other respects. For example, fairness in making the "benefit" of abortion available to all is beside the point, both because abortion is unfair to the unborn and because it is the destruction of an innocent human life.

This point is equally valid, although perhaps less obvious, when the question of fairness concerns accepting side effects. Whenever one sins, even venially, there can be no valid reason for accepting any bad side effects whatsoever. Hence, whether or not partiality is involved, one always acts unjustly toward others if in sinning one accepts side effects which are harmful to them. For example, a couple who are fornicating and are worried about the possibility of passing on some disease should satisfy their concern to be fair to each other in this matter by avoiding fornication itself; parents who engage in idle gossip should satisfy their concern to avoid giving bad example to their children by breaking the habit of gossiping.

Of course, people examining their consciences should look for every aspect of moral evil in any sin, including any unfairness done to others in carrying out acts wrong in themselves.

2. In Two Ways, Emotions Inclining toward Partiality Can Cause Injustice

In one kind of case, the act distributes benefits among a group of people, and the question is whether inequality in distribution would be due to partiality or to some reason that justifies the inequality. Suppose a mother divides a candy bar among her three children and gives her son a bigger piece than she gives her daughters. Is this favoritism? Or is it a justified inequality—for example, is it the boy's birthday, or did he pitch in and do the girls' chores which they had neglected?

In another kind of case, the choice to do something would require accepting bad side effects for another or others. Would it be reasonable to accept those side effects, in pursuing the good for whose sake the act would be done, or unreasonable due to partiality? For example, if a garden is being ruined by rabbits and the owner considers using poisons to get rid of them, while accepting some risk of harm to the neighbors' pets, would it be unfair to use the poisons or may the risk be accepted?

3. The Golden Rule Should Be Used to Exclude Partiality

In cases of both kinds the Golden Rule should be applied to determine whether there is partiality. Each possibility can be tested in this way by considering it empathetically from the points of view of the various persons involved, imagining oneself in the place of each. The simplest cases concern instances of recurrent situations in which all involved play each role at different times: "How do you like it when someone does that to you?" In more complex cases, memory and imagination must be used to put oneself or someone near and dear into each role, thus applying the test for partiality to one's emotions about each possible solution: "How would you like it if someone followed that policy in dealing with your children?"

a) **To apply the Golden Rule, benefits and harms must be considered.** Since the point of applying the Golden Rule is to exclude partiality, no attempt should be made to apply it without first carefully considering the possible matters concerning which partiality could be at work. These are different potential benefits and harms to the different persons involved. Since one must be fair not only in what is intended and chosen but also in accepting whatever side effects are foreseen, all foreseen benefits and burdens of choosing and carrying out a possible action—or, alternatively, not choosing it, and perhaps choosing some alternative—should be considered. It is necessary to ask:

• Whom will this action benefit? Whom will it harm? If the act is not chosen, whom will that benefit and harm? And, likewise, for any alternative.

• Considering each benefit and harm, what sort of good is at stake? Is it a basic good of persons or an instrumental good? How extensive and serious will each benefit and harm be?

Reflecting as a Christian, a person must bring fully into play any specifically Christian benefits and harms. For instance, does doing or not doing an act, doing this or that, involve risk to someone's salvation? Does it involve harming or enhancing apostolic witness?

b) **Others' wishes sometimes are fairly ignored.** To the extent that a point of view is determined by immorality, it is of no help in reaching moral truth to take that point of view, whether the person holding it is subjectively guilty or not. Thus, in applying the Golden Rule, one should refuse to take into account the views of others insofar as these are morally unacceptable. Of course, such a refusal may be considered unfair by those concerned. For example, pederasts sometimes complain that a boy who refuses to accommodate them is unfair to them.[33] However, the boy's refusal need not be motivated by partiality, for it can be based on a prior moral consideration, the wrongness of sodomy, and an emotional detestation of it entirely in harmony with reason.

---

33. John Wilson, *Logic and Sexual Morality* (Baltimore: Penguin, 1965), 219–21, argues in support of that view.

Sometimes a person whose point of view is unwittingly determined by immorality indicates a preference which violates his or her own sincere but erroneous conscience. Someone trying to treat such individuals fairly should take as the measure for fairness that aspect of them believed to accord with moral truth. For example, a patient believes receiving a needed blood transfusion would be wrong, yet desires one; a fair person who considers accepting the transfusion the right thing to do will identify with the patient's desire for it, while a fair person who believes it wrong will identify with the patient's conscience on the subject. In general, one treats fairly those who are inconsistent within themselves by identifying only with those aspects of their personality and conflicting wishes which one believes to be in accord with moral truth.

c) **One can be unfair to others without harming them.** It is possible to be unfair to those to whom one has no established duty and does no harm. This happens when the general responsibility to use gifts in the service of others and build up the kingdom is imperfectly fulfilled because a person fails to choose impartially whom to serve and so fails to do good to some who would benefit if he or she were guided entirely by love of neighbor. For example, those influenced by racial preference act unfairly, though they harm no one, in donating exclusively to charities which serve people of their own race despite the greater needs of other people.

d) **The "veil of ignorance" is a use of the Golden Rule.** One technique for using imagination to put oneself in others' places has been called "stepping behind the veil of ignorance." A community's members are asked to imagine that they lose part of their memory, just enough so that they no longer know which role they play in the community. Then they are to make policies affecting all the members. For example, students, faculty, administrators, and service personnel at a college might engage in this exercise while jointly considering the school's budgetary policies concerning tuition, salaries, job security, living and working conditions, and so on. According to the rules of the game, each participant would share in policy making without adverting to whether he or she was the college president, the worker who cleans the latrines, a student without a scholarship, or a senior faculty member. The idea is to set aside, insofar as possible, factors like one's own social status, which often are obstacles to fairness.

4. Some Moral Problems Require Several Kinds of Analysis

Some complex cases, while involving considerations of fairness, also require criticism of emotional motives, and presuppose careful analysis of the action. For instance, the question of whether comatose patients ought to be fed and hydrated by tube involves all these elements.[34] This example is worth considering to illustrate how the different kinds of analysis complement one another. (For norms regarding accepting health care, see 8.F.3.)

---

34. See William E. May et al., "Feeding and Hydrating the Permanently Unconscious and Other Vulnerable Persons," *Issues in Law and Medicine* 3 (Winter 1987): 203–17; Germain Grisez, "Should Nutrition and Hydration Be Provided to Permanently Unconscious and Other Mentally Disabled Persons?" *Linacre Quarterly* 57 (May 1990): 30–43.

a) **An action can appear to be morally acceptable.** At the outset, stepping behind the veil of ignorance, people might say in all sincerity that if they were comatose, they would not wish to be kept alive indefinitely by tube feeding and would be willing to accept death. Thus, it seems that there need be no partiality motivating the judgment that a permanently comatose patient is not to be fed and hydrated. Moreover, discontinuing such care need not be carrying out a choice to kill. The care is expensive and seems to provide no benefit except to prolong a life which the patient will never again consciously enjoy; thus, it appears that the choice to discontinue can be made for the sake of using the resources for another good purpose, with the comatose patient's death accepted as a side effect.

b) **Reflection may show that some good has been overlooked.** In examining the goods at stake, however, one notes that survival is not the sole benefit. Feeding and hydrating, as well as other elements of life support—keeping the patient sheltered and clean—also express respect for his or her humanity and maintain human solidarity with the person. To see this point, it is only necessary to consider how decent people in earlier times did what they could to care for disabled, demented, and/or slowly dying family members. Feeling the bond of family solidarity to be an important good, not only for themselves but for the loved ones for whom they cared, they were willing to make considerable sacrifices for an aunt disabled by a stroke, a demented brother, or a slowly dying grandfather.

c) **Reflection may call the act analysis into question.** Perhaps the patient's death is not included in the proposal to avoid the costs of continuing care. But even so, feeding and hydrating are a rather small part of the total cost, whereas sheltering and keeping a comatose patient clean cost far more. However, virtually all the savings will be realized only after such patients die; and so it seems that the choice to discontinue feeding and hydrating, made to save the total cost of care, either is a choice to bring about death or a choice to discontinue care entirely, as would be done if the patient were already dead. The former clearly is wrong, and the latter much harder to justify than a simple choice to discontinue a burdensome treatment.

d) **Reflection can reveal that more people's interests are at stake.** The comparative burdens and benefits of caring for permanently comatose patients are very like those involved in caring for people of other kinds: the senile, the severely retarded, and the hopelessly insane. If it is right to adopt a social policy of discontinuing all care for the permanently comatose, it is hard to see why that policy should be limited to them (unless adopted on a discriminatory basis, as is suggested by the pejorative language, such as *vegetable,* which is applied to them). Moreover, it is not easy to diagnose the state of being permanently comatose, so in practice certain other severely debilitated patients are likely to be mistakenly identified as permanently comatose.

e) **The action is excluded because of its partiality.** While following someone's own wishes about care could be wrong for other reasons—for example, the person could be bent on suicide—it would not be unfair. So, there would be no partiality in a policy of not caring for permanently comatose persons who had made it perfectly clear in advance that, in order to avoid burdening others, they would not wish to be cared for in that condition. But what about those permanently comatose and other severely debilitated persons who did not make their wishes known?

However broad or narrow the class to be deprived of care might turn out to be, could the policy of withholding or withdrawing all care from such persons ever be fairly adopted in an affluent society? In a society with extremely limited resources, a community of hunter-gatherers, say, living from day to day on the very edge of survival, it might be, since in that situation caring for the severely debilitated would mean depriving others of the necessities of life. But it seems plainly unfair—another expression of carelessness about human dignity and solidarity—in a society which spends large sums of money on luxuries.

Question I: How Should Residual Doubt and Moral Perplexity Be Dealt With?

Sometimes, their best efforts to find moral truth having failed, people find themselves with residual doubt or, even worse, in perplexity, as if there simply were no morally acceptable alternative. How are these unsatisfactory states of conscience to be dealt with?

It should be recalled that, in charting the quest for moral truth, problematic possibilities supported by merely emotional motives were excluded at the outset. Hence, in what follows, any option under consideration is assumed to be interesting because it seems to promise some real benefit to oneself and/or others.

1. If Doubt about a Norm Remains, It Can Be Dealt with Responsibly

Doubt remains only if there is a positive reason for thinking a possible option would be wrong. What should be done if the kinds of reflection already treated in this chapter are insufficient to eliminate doubt about the objective moral character of an option under consideration?

When the problem is important, someone who has not already done so should seek the help of an adviser who can articulate moral principles, is skillful in moral analysis, and is morally upright and mature in virtue. But what if such a person cannot be found or else gives advice inadequate to resolve the doubt? In that case, the character of the alternatives determines how to proceed.

a) One should not act with residual doubt when one need not. If doubt remains, one should ask oneself whether there would be any clear responsibility to do the act if it were found to be morally acceptable. If there is at least one alternative which one is confident is morally acceptable, the answer is no. In such a case, the act should not be done, since that would mean running an unnecessary, and so unreasonable, risk of doing something objectively wrong—something, therefore, which might harm or interfere with the service of some human good or goods in ways real though not now obvious. For example, an engaged couple who reasonably wish to express their affection but are uncertain whether certain sorts of genitally stimulating behavior are permissible have a morally acceptable alternative: to express affection in ways they are certain are chaste. Having no moral responsibility to engage in behavior about whose morality they are doubtful, they should not.

b) In other cases, the more probably true norm should be followed. Sometimes, after all one's efforts, one remains unsure whether it would be right to choose a certain act, yet sure it should be chosen if it is right. For example, during the Nazi period, some conscientious Germans were uncertain about the moral permissibility of killing a tyrant, yet convinced that if such killing is permissible, they had an obligation to participate in a plot to assassinate Hitler. In such cases, the judgment should be followed which seems more likely to be true: that kind of act is permissible, or that kind of act is morally excluded. If it is judged more likely to be permissible, the risk of its being objectively wrong may be accepted, since this unavoidable risk is being taken only as a side effect of serving the relevant good or goods. For example, poor parents of hungry children are unsure whether they may rightly appropriate someone else's supply of food; but if they may, they plainly should, since in that way they can fulfill their grave obligation to care for their children. Thus, the parents should follow the judgment they think more likely true: it is (or it is not) right to take that supply of food.[35]

2. The Significance of Residual Doubts of Fact Varies in Different Cases

When unable to resolve a doubt about a morally relevant matter of fact, how one should proceed depends on the way in which the fact is related to one's moral responsibilities.

a) Those considering choosing moral evil should assume the worst. If a doubt of fact causes uncertainty about how seriously immoral an admittedly immoral act will be, it should be assumed that it is more immoral, not less. For even if one were certain about the fact and knew the act to be less immoral, there still would be no justification for doing it. If, therefore, one acts in the face of uncertainty about the fact which, objectively, could make the act still more seriously immoral, this willingness to do the greater wrong cannot be justified and one therefore is responsible for it. For example, if Samantha is not sure whether a form of birth prevention is contraceptive or abortifacient, she should assume it is abortifacient; if Robert is not sure whether the lie he is tempted to tell about someone will cause great or slight harm to that person, he should assume that the harm will be great.

b) In fulfilling responsibilities, one should take the safe side. People should prefer to err on the side of safety whenever two conditions are met: (i) a doubt of fact causes uncertainty about whether a certain way of acting will fulfill a clear responsibility to pursue some good or avoid some harm, and (ii) there is another morally acceptable way of acting which would more surely fulfill that responsibility. For example, the hunter who is unsure whether something moving in the bushes is an animal or a child should assume it is a child; the priest unsure whether the bread brought forward for consecration is valid matter should assume it is not; the

---

35. An exegesis of St. Thomas's account of conscience which comes to similar conclusions: Teófilo Urdanoz, O.P., "La conciencia moral en Santo Tomás y los sistemas morales," *La ciencia tomista* 79 (1952): 529–76.

physician unsure whether a new treatment will work should use a standard treatment he knows will work; a juror who remains unsure whether someone accused of a crime is guilty should assume the accused is innocent.

The reason for this norm is obvious: anyone who wholeheartedly intends an end is willing to use appropriate means to attain it; someone who fails to use appropriate means intends the end only halfheartedly at best. So, anyone conscientious and wholehearted about fulfilling responsibilities as he or she should be, will prefer to act in ways sure to fulfill them rather than ways which might well fail.[36]

Of course, this norm is defeasible. Sometimes acting on the safe side in respect to one responsibility necessarily entails acting on the risky side in respect to another, more compelling responsibility. Then it is necessary to take the risk of not fulfilling the responsibility which is less compelling. For example, fire fighters rightly use methods which are riskier to themselves in order more surely to fulfill their responsibility to rescue people trapped in a burning building.

c) **In considering doing good, one should hope for the best.** If a doubt of fact makes one uncertain whether an otherwise good act which is under consideration can be done successfully or is likely to produce the benefit anticipated, it should be assumed that it is worth trying. For example, people should try to obtain the education needed to perform valuable services to others, even though they cannot know whether they will succeed: Maria, who has the necessary gifts, should try to get a degree in medicine. Similarly, Mark should give his friend good advice, even though unsure whether the friend will understand, accept, and follow it.

This norm is not an absolute, since possible alternative good things one might try to do should be considered. Maria and Mark also must consider whether there are other opportunities for using their talents, time, energy, and resources. But Christians should be more ready than those without hope to try to do something good rather than conserve resources; God should be trusted to give success to the good works of one's hands, and even good efforts which fail in this world nevertheless will contribute to the kingdom (see GS 38–39).

People also should rely on God to provide for future needs, instead of anxiously anticipating them like those who, lacking faith, are driven by the insecurities of life to amass wealth and seek status (see Mt 6.25–34; *S.t.,* 2–2, q. 55, aa. 6–7). Moreover, if a possible act would carry out a vocational commitment, that is a further reason for trying it, despite doubts, and accepting the risk of failing. For in making the vocational commitment one already has pledged time, energy, and resources to implement it.

d) **Doubts about beneficial side effects do not impede choice.** If the doubt of fact is whether certain side effects will occur, consideration first must be given to whether these would be beneficial or harmful. If someone certain they would occur

---

36. Someone might suppose that the rule that one should take the safer course in such cases is at odds with the legitimate use of probabilism. However, that is not so, since probabilism, even if one accepts it within its proper domain, concerns doubtful laws, not uncertain facts. Indeed, the norm stated here is enunciated by St. Alphonsus Maria de Liguori, and the examples are based on his; see his *Theologia moralis,* ed. L. Gaudé, 4 vols. (Rome: Ex Typographia Vaticana, 1905–12), 1:21–24.

could rightly accept them, then uncertainty obviously does not bar the choice. The degree of probability may and can be taken into account in deliberation, just as all the other factors are taken into account in assessing the considerations in favor of that and other alternatives. For example, if Joe, a manager, can promote one of two otherwise equally qualified and deserving employees, Mary or Sally, he may take into account the small probability that the promotion would have good side effects for Mary and the greater probability that it would have good side effects for Sally, and judge it better to promote Sally than Mary.

e) **Doubts about harmful side effects may not be ignored.** If the side effects about which one remains uncertain would be harmful, the situation is more complicated. It is impossible to avoid all risks of harmful side effects, since every human act involves some. Sometimes it even is necessary to accept great risks incidental to one's efforts to realize goods or prevent other harms. But if the side effects are such that they could not rightly be accepted if they were certain to occur, the risk may not simply be ignored. Lacking an adequate reason to do the act and accept the risk, one obviously should not accept it.

f) **In taking risks, the risk itself becomes the side effect.** But if there is some reason—especially if it would be a clear duty—to do the act, supposing it to be a morally available option, taking the risk must be considered. One should estimate how likely it is that the harmful side effects will occur, and should regard that degree of probability as the side effect to be accepted if the choice is made. In evaluating the risk, the reasons why it would be wrong to accept the harm, supposing it were certain, must be applied to the risk itself. Obviously, the greater the risk of harmful side effects, the more important must be the reason to do the act.

For example, if Harry can support his family by working in a mine and so risking lung disease, and if it would be wrong for him to accept the prospective disease if he were certain to contract it, he must estimate the risk and evaluate it by the same considerations requiring him not to accept the disease if it were a certainty. (These include the good of his own life and the goods that make up the well-being of his family, as well as the modes of responsibility demanding reasonable effort and sacrifice in the pursuit of these goods, and faithful fulfillment of family responsibilities.) Again, if Harriet is considering a mountain ascent which entails a risk of injury or death, the estimated risk is the side effect she needs to evaluate. She should do this using the same moral considerations she would use to reject the harm (injury or death simply for the sport of climbing the mountain) as unacceptable if known to be certain.

It can be fair to accept some risk of harm to others, even though unfair to accept a greater risk of similar harm or a similar risk of greater harm. For example, if citizens and public officials are considering whether to build a nuclear power plant, they should neither ignore the risk of its malfunctioning, with grave consequences, nor simply reject the proposal as if those harms were inevitable. Rather, they should estimate the risk as accurately as possible and then evaluate its acceptability by the same moral considerations which plainly would exclude accepting such harms if they were certain to follow from approving the project.

3. Even the Perplexed Should Try to Act According to Moral Truth

Perplexity arises in situations of choice in which none of the available options seems morally acceptable. The perplexed person thinks: I will sin no matter what I do. The nature and unity of the principles of morality guarantee that perplexity always is resolvable.[37] Some philosophers deny this, however, holding that there are insoluble perplexities—morally tragic situations. Of course, some situations can be called "tragic" in the sense that the right choice is costly in terms of real human goods. But God's goodness and providence ensure that in every situation there is some way to avoid sin. So, it is certain on the basis of hope in God that there is always at least one right alternative, and in many cases it can be found (see F.1.a, above), even though it may be simply to abstain from action and accept the bad consequences. Yet it does sometimes happen that, even after a vigorous effort, no morally acceptable option is found. Then one can proceed as follows.

a) **If perplexed, one should examine one's conscience.** Perplexity sometimes arises because a person has made an immoral choice which he or she now takes as a given. For example, someone who has contracted to do something immoral (deliver a shipment of illegal drugs) may have to choose between two different immoral ways of fulfilling the contract (bribe customs officials or kill them). Thus, whenever perplexity arises, self-examination is necessary. If the situation is rooted in a prior immoral choice, it must be repented (in the example, give up dealing in illegal drugs).

b) **One's normative assumptions should be examined.** In some cases perplexity arises from erroneously absolutizing nonabsolute norms. For example, a young girl who thinks it always wrong to tell on other children may be perplexed because she also recognizes a responsibility to tell adults when another child is playing with matches and gasoline. In such cases, an appropriate specification of the relevant norm solves the problem. The girl needs to learn that it is not always wrong to tell on others.

Sometimes the alternative to the erroneously absolutized moral norm is a good act which should be done. Cecilia supposes she must keep promises even when the real need to do something else makes it wrong to do so. Having promised to take the children Christmas shopping on Saturday, she feels perplexed about her duty when grandpa needs to be taken to the hospital emergency room to have his chest pains checked out. Cecilia should see that this is a case where the general norm to keep promises must give way to a more specific norm.

Sometimes the alternative to the erroneously absolutized moral norm is to refrain from doing an immoral act. For example, Henry, an insurance adjuster with several children going to college, supposes he either must sin by obtaining bribes for settling cases unjustly or else will sin by failing to do his duty to educate his children. Henry must see that, even if times are hard and there is no other way to educate his children, his duty to do so is defeasible, and he may not fulfill it by arranging unjust settlements.

---

37. A helpful philosophical treatment of perplexity: Alan Donagan, *The Theory of Morality* (Chicago: University of Chicago Press, 1977), 143–53.

c) **One's application of moral absolutes should be examined.** In some cases, perplexity results from erroneous application of an absolute norm. For example, Mildred supposes that, since it is wrong to choose to kill, it also would be wrong to fulfill her duty to defend her children against attack by using possibly deadly force. If she discovers the root of this perplexity—for instance, by recognizing that she need not choose, but only accept, the foreseen harm as a side effect—her perplexity is dissolved (see *CMP,* 12.F).

d) **If choice is unavoidable, the lesser moral evil should be chosen.** The fact that a problem can be solved, objectively or considered in itself, does not mean every individual can solve it. In principle, perplexity always can be resolved—there are no morally tragic situations in which wrongdoing is inevitable—but, in practice, a person sometimes cannot here and now resolve perplexity, yet must make a choice. Then, among a set of possibilities all of which appear morally evil, the option which seems least evil in moral terms can reasonably be regarded as most nearly approximating what would be morally good.[38]

If, then, someone can resolve perplexity in no other way and must make a choice, it is morally good for him or her to choose what appears to be the lesser moral evil—not, however, insofar as it seems morally evil, but insofar as it is the option most likely to be good. In judging degrees of moral evil, the following criteria should be applied in the order given here: (i) whether the matter is grave or light; (ii) whether the sin would be against God or against human persons, whether against one's neighbor or oneself; (iii) among offenses against God, the seriousness of the irreverence, and among offenses against human persons, the extent of the harm.[39] If applying these criteria fails to solve the problem, the perplexed person does not sin in choosing the option which seems least repugnant.

Question J: How Should One Discern between or among Good Options?

After what is involved has been carefully analyzed, norms have been applied, and emotional motives have been examined, moral reflection sometimes reaches a confident judgment: both A and B are good, and one or the other is to be chosen. Still, both cannot be chosen, and God's plan for one's life is not yet fully clear: while knowing the moral truth about what one should *not* do, one still lacks the full moral truth about what *should* be done. In such cases, discernment is needed.

By definition, all the rational reflection possible has been done, and the relevant emotions already have been checked out and found in accord with reason.[40]

---

38. The judgment of least evil in moral terms is altogether different from the proportionalist attempt to weigh premoral values and disvalues: see *CMP,* 6.A–B.

39. See St. Alphonsus, *Theologia moralis,* 1:6. He also says (ibid) that one should avoid the transgression of natural law rather than of human or divine positive law. However, positive law only has moral force through a moral norm, and so the distinction between types of law seems irrelevant to determining which alternative would be the lesser moral evil.

40. St. Ignatius Loyola, *Spiritual Exercises,* 170, trans. Lewis Delmage, S.J. (New York: Joseph F. Wagner, 1968), 87–88, makes it clear that until all such tests have been passed, it is not time for discernment: "Authentic Christian choices necessarily pertain only to alternatives which

Discernment returns to emotions, this time seeking to determine how well possibilities otherwise judged good comport with the rest of one's individual personality. For emotions, even when fully integrated with reason, do not simply echo it. They also resonate to the bodily, organic, and psychic dimensions of the personality; and these, insofar as they are integrated with faith, also are parts of one's better, Christian self. So, emotions which resonate to them pertain to grace, indicate God's will for one's life, and rightly tip the balance among possibilities otherwise judged good.

1. To Discern Is to Compare Two Sets of Emotional Motives

There is a set of emotions related to faith and integrated with it, and these Christian emotions are aroused by prayer, worship, spiritual reading, and so on. (Because retreats provide, or should provide, extended opportunities for these activities, it is appropriate to make a retreat when an important discernment must be made.) The other set of emotions includes those bearing on the possibilities between which one must discern: whether to join this religious community or that (or become a religious or not), seek acceptance into a seminary program or not (or which one), marry or not (or this or that person), and so forth. These emotions are aroused by carefully and concretely considering as fully as possible what actually would be involved in the options under consideration. (It is assumed that the necessary investigating and information gathering already have been done.) Then one's Christian-faith emotions are compared with the sets of emotions related to each option—emotions which reflect not only the realities on which they bear but the reality of one's hidden self. What is involved here is not some sort of objective measurement, but the effort to perceive an inward harmony. If the emotions related to one option plainly harmonize better with one's Christian-faith emotions, that can be considered the option which pleases one's Christian self, and one should choose as pleases this self.

2. Discernment Should Be Practiced in a Wide Variety of Cases

Discernment not only is appropriate and often necessary in regard to certain important matters, such as vocation (see 2.E.3), but relevant whenever a person has reached the judgment that one of two or more morally acceptable but mutually incompatible possibilities is to be chosen.

a) **One should discern about many less important matters.** Some people would consider discernment beside the point in many situations, for example, when considering how to spend their holidays. At least in such matters, they think, a person may simply do as he or she pleases when facing morally acceptable alternatives. In one sense this is true, but in another it is not. The question is: Which

---

are good in themselves, or certainly not evil, and only those which are in harmony with the practices and procedures of our holy mother, the Catholic Church." The treatment of discernment here does not claim Ignatius' authority but is indebted to his work, especially to his idea of spiritual consolation as explained by Jules J. Toner, S.J., *A Commentary on Saint Ignatius' Rules for the Discernment of Spirits: A Guide to the Principles and Practice* (St. Louis: The Institute of Jesuit Sources, 1982), 94–121.

is the self being pleased—the better, more Christian self, or the not yet fully converted self? Since the former should be gratified and the latter overridden, it is important to settle this question even in less important matters. For instance, a man's emotions when at his best as husband and father are those he should use to evaluate his respective sets of emotions about taking a family vacation in the back country and at the beach. On that basis, he does right in proposing the vacation which "feels right."

b) Discernment often is needed to complete moral reflection. Discernment becomes necessary in the last stage of many of the types of cases discussed in previous questions. In particular, if other tests have been passed and one remains uncertain whether or not to accept some side effects, when both doing so and not doing so seem morally permissible, one must discern which is to be chosen. Consider the case of a pregnant woman whose uterus is affected by some pathology which would dictate its removal were she not pregnant but who might be able to sustain the pregnancy until the baby is viable. Having judged both options morally acceptable, and having examined her emotions bearing on each and found them sound, she must in the end discern which option is appropriate for her: surgery now or later. Here she will bring to bear not only her religious emotions but her family emotions, for example, toward her husband and other children if any.

3. The Effort to Discern Should Be Appropriate to the Matter

Suppose the effort to discern is not immediately successful, and neither option seems to fit better than the other. Indecisiveness, of course, can be a symptom of neurosis, but suppose that too can be ruled out. What to do then depends on the importance of the matter under consideration.

In less important matters, any option may be chosen: flip a coin, ask the next person one happens to meet, or use anything else as an index. That need not mean leaving the matter solely to chance, for, in these particular circumstances, the chance outcome also is an indication of God's will.

But if the issue is more important and its resolution can be delayed, one should engage in further deliberation: more inquiry about the options, more reflection on them, more discussion with others who share one's more basic commitments, and so forth. And the process of discernment should be prolonged with further prayer and consideration of what is involved in each option.[41]

---

41. Someone might object that the account of discernment proposed here seems to omit what is central: the Holy Spirit's action. Not so. Discernment begins with prayer, worship, and so on; when these activities are carried on by someone seeking to know God's will, they invite the Holy Spirit to shape the whole process and make it fruitful. Many writers on spirituality seem to assume that in any authentic discernment the Holy Spirit causes elements—either key data for the discernment, insight into the data, or both—which cannot be explained by secondary causes. That assumption, which often extends to the interior life as a whole, implies that in such matters the relationship between the Holy Spirit's action and secondary causes regularly is similar to the relationship which obtains when God does miracles in the physical world. Someone who does not share that assumption need not hold that the Holy Spirit *never* acts without using adequate secondary causes; rather, such a person can hold that sometimes there are miracles of grace—for example, when someone is converted from mortal sin to charity. Moreover, since God providentially plans and causes everything good, the possibility of explaining important occurrences in

Question K: How Should One Resolve Conflicts of Duties?

Duties in the strict sense are specific responsibilities to another or others, arising from a moral norm regarding action bearing on others, a just and applicable law, or a social role one is bound to fulfill. Sometimes, however, two (or possibly more) duties make conflicting demands: to be in two places at the same time, to use the same money for two purposes, or something of the sort. Sometimes, too, a duty conflicts with another affirmative moral responsibility; for example, somebody on the way to work notices a person who needs help and can only fulfill the common responsibility to help others by failing to fulfill the duty to be at work.

1. Duties Generally Take Priority over Other Responsibilities

Duties in the strict sense correspond to rights: the duty of parents to care for children corresponds to children's right to their parents' care; each persons's duty not to kill others corresponds to their right to life. Other responsibilities do not correspond to rights: the general responsibility to help others in need does not correspond to a right of this or that needy person to one's help; the responsibility of Christians to love enemies does not correspond to enemies' right to be loved; and the responsibility to avoid cruelty to animals does not correspond to a right to kind treatment. (Rights and duties will be treated more fully in 6.B.6, and the claim that animals have rights in 10.C.1.)

Conflicts between duties in the strict sense and other affirmative responsibilities are rather easily resolved. Since failing to do one's duty always is detrimental to others, the question is whether it is fair to leave the duty unfulfilled for the sake of fulfilling the other responsibility. The procedure already explained for applying the Golden Rule should be used. Because one's duty surely should be done unless the other responsibility overrides its claim, a doubt still remaining should be settled in favor of fulfilling the duty.

2. Most Conflicts of Duties Should Be Forestalled or Resolved

Some conflicts between duties in the strict sense are inevitable, but many should be foreseen and prevented, and others can be resolved.

a) In making commitments, conflicts of duties should be forestalled. Christians should bear in mind that fulfilling the duties that flow from their commitments is a serious responsibility toward others and part of their role in building up Jesus' body. Thus, they should avoid making commitments which they foresee they probably will be unable to fulfill in significant respects. For example, both men and women who marry and have children should avoid other undertakings likely to generate conflicts of duties at odds with a stable family life and the children's upbringing. God calls no one to inconsistent commitments. Thus, not only those called to be priests or religious but those with other callings—for example, to certain professional or civic roles—which they foresee would regularly lead to

---

spiritual life by secondary causes in no way excludes the Holy Spirit's action. All salvific divine causality is grace, whether or not its effect is a miracle of grace.

conflicts with the responsibilities of marriage and family life also are called to permanent or temporary celibacy for the sake of the kingdom.

b) One should give up less binding roles to fulfill others. If some of a person's roles based on breakable commitments regularly lead to conflicts with the duties of roles based on unbreakable commitments, the former should be given up for the sake of the latter. Thus, a man should give up a second job if it repeatedly conflicts with his family responsibilities and provides comforts rather than necessities of life; a woman should give up civic involvements if they regularly impede her from fulfilling her responsibilities as wife and mother.

c) One's life should be simplified to gain freedom to fulfill duties. It is common for people habitually to engage in certain activities which once had a legitimate place in their lives but now conflict with duties. For example, before taking on the responsibilities of a mature state in life, young people rightly have many activities: hobbies, certain forms of recreation, sports, friendships, and so on. But when a major commitment has been made, some of these activities, although good in themselves, can regularly conflict with duties. Plainly, in this situation, they should simplify their lives by changing their habits.

Similarly, the ownership of any kind of property entails the responsibility of caring for it and seeing that it is properly used (see 10.E.4.a, 10.E.5). Having obtained something for a good use, however, people tend to retain it even as their need for it declines. Very often, then, freedom to fulfill duties can be gained only by dispensing with something to which one has become attached, and the burdensome item of property should be disposed of unless retaining it is essential to fulfilling other responsibilities.

d) Some conflicts of duties can and should be resolved. Even people as careful as they should be to forestall conflicts of duties sometimes seem to encounter such conflicts. But a dutiful person often can find ways of resolving apparent conflicts so that no duty need go unfulfilled. When it appears that duties conflict, a person should look for an alternative to leaving either duty unfulfilled. Two things cannot be done at the same time, but it might be possible to transfer one to some other time; one cannot personally do something, but might be able to get someone else to take one's place.

Moreover, laws and social roles usually include implicit exception clauses, which under specific conditions limit duties. For example, the duty to attend Sunday Mass implicitly is limited by exceptions for cases in which doing so would endanger one's own health or that of others, interfere with taking care of a sick person, and so forth. One important form of exception clause is the possibility of obtaining a dispensation or permission from someone in authority, so that one is freed of the duty, for example, of participating in Sunday Mass (see 3.B.4.d).

3. Conflicts of Duties Are Solved by Impartiality and Discernment

If such efforts do not eliminate the problem, a person really does face a conflict of duties. Tempting as it might be to fulfill the duty whose nonfulfillment is likely to elicit a more unpleasant reaction, or to fulfill the duty one thinks looks easy and pleasant to fulfill, such motives should be recognized and firmly set aside.

a) **Partiality must be avoided.** Since the nonfulfillment of either duty will be detrimental to someone, the most important factor to examine is whether one is moved in one direction by partiality. Conflicts of duties are likely to be more or less recurrent, and someone who chooses with partiality to fulfill this or that duty almost surely will eventually do grave injustice to those he or she regularly fails to serve.

b) **One must discern which duty is more appropriate to fulfill.** If all the tests are passed, the problem of conflict of duties is exactly like any other case in which it is necessary to discern between two good options. Since no one ever is morally obliged to do the impossible, the situation is not one of perplexity. Because the fulfillment of either duty would be obligatory if it could be fulfilled, the choice to fulfill either will be morally good. Nonfulfillment of the other is not itself chosen. Rather, it is only a side effect of the good and morally required choice to fulfill the first.

c) **An overarching commitment provides the standard.** In carrying out this discernment, one's emotions about fulfilling and not fulfilling each of the conflicting duties should be considered and compared with one's more general emotions related to the object of the single commitment common to both. For example, if both duties pertain to professional life, discernment between the two should depend on a general sense of professional responsibility. But if the conflicting duties have no single principle short of faith itself, then one's religious emotions should be used as a standard, just as in making vocational commitments.

Question L: What Are One's Responsibilities When Deliberating with Others?

In general, of course, people's responsibilities with respect to moral truth are the same whether they deliberate individually or together. However, when sharing in decision making with others, a person faces a few special problems and temptations, and has some special responsibilities.

Their basic, general principle is that each participant in communal decision making is personally responsible for the common good, that is, the whole good that can be realized in and through the community's morally good cooperative action. While some may see their role merely as an opportunity to pursue or protect their personal or partisan interests, that attitude disregards the reality of the community and the right of all its members to their appropriate share in its common good. Thus, someone deliberating with others should try to determine how the community should act to realize its common good. Personal, party, or group interests should be pursued insofar as they can contribute to that common good and can be realized as parts of it, but not apart from or against the common good.

1. One Is Fully Responsible for One's Proper Contribution

Plainly, someone who shares the responsibility of making decisions for a group should seek moral certitude about what that group should do. In doing so, all one's relevant knowledge should be taken into account. Sometimes moral certitude can depend on human faith in others. While compromises often are warranted, a person may not consent to anything he or she judges wrong in order to reach them.

a) **Each principal participant should seek personal moral certitude.** In many cooperative projects, an individual can responsibly make a very limited contribution, leaving it to others to make sure the effort as a whole realizes its proper objective. That is so especially when many work together to make something or bring about some definite state of affairs: landing an army on a beach, building a barn, cleaning up the dinner dishes, moving a family, and so on. But when two or more deliberate and decide together, each principal participant must personally choose to promote or approve one option for common action, and so each should personally try to attain moral certitude concerning his or her personal choice. Therefore, when participating in a group's deliberation and decision making, a person should pay attention to and examine every step of the deliberation insofar as that is required for moral certitude concerning what personal position he or she should take on questions to be decided by the group.

Often, however, many members of a deliberative body fail to meet this responsibility. One or a few are deeply concerned about the body's common business, energetic in developing proposals and promoting their acceptance, and patient enough to carry on the body's work even when it becomes tedious; but others are inclined not to prepare for meetings, attend to the problems and available alternatives, question factual assumptions, look closely at the application of norms, come to meetings, persist when the hour grows late—in short, they are not inclined to contribute seriously to decision making by seeking moral certitude about what the group should do and doing what they can to win acceptance of their judgment.

Such persons usually are roused to action only upon perceiving some threat to their personal or partisan interests; otherwise, they tend to follow the lead of the few. Some follow one leader, others another, not because of confidence that their leaders have reached the truth of the matter, but because of emotional attachment, personal profit, or a merely general agreement with their opinions and policies. But because each person should seek moral truth to guide his or her personal choice concerning what proposal to promote or approve for common action, such docility and conformity are wrong precisely insofar as they replace the conscientious judgments people should make about how to use their personal power in the group's process.

For someone who reasonably foresees, or should foresee, that the community could do a grave injustice or suffer a serious harm if the common decision is not what it should be, abdicating personal responsibility in the common deliberation obviously is grave matter.

b) **Nothing relevant that one knows should be set aside.** While every participant in communal deliberation should direct his or her judgment by the requirements of the common good, it does not follow that each should judge exclusively on the basis of information and moral norms available and acceptable to all the others. Sometimes one person has some relevant knowledge which the other participants in deliberation are unaware of or deny. For example, one may possess secret information which may not be divulged or, as a Christian, may know a relevant moral norm that nonbelieving participants do not accept. In such cases, what is known should be taken fully into account, not set aside, as one considers what proposal the group should adopt to serve its common good. For one's duty is to try to identify the truth about what the community should do, and it cannot reasonably be expected that the truth will be identified if any relevant fact is ignored or any norm known to be true and relevant is set aside.

c) **Moral certitude can rest partly on human faith in others.** Although people should seek moral certitude concerning what proposal to support or approve, it does not always follow that they must personally examine, understand, and gain direct certitude about everything leading to the judgment favoring a particular proposal. Otherwise, nobody could serve responsibly in any deliberative body dealing with a wide range and quantity of business, for example, a national congress or parliament, or a provincial or state legislature. The necessary moral certitude sometimes can be achieved by believing others, either concerning what proposal to support or approve, concerning subordinate questions leading to that judgment, or concerning procedural matters.

If, however, an individual's judgment is based on human faith in another, he or she acts responsibly only if that faith is reasonable: there must be good reason to think that those trusted personally believe what they say and are likely to be correct. Many common motives for following leaders at best have no bearing on the reasonableness of trusting their judgment. Very often, it is unreasonable to accept another's judgment on faith until after examining, understanding, and gaining direct certitude about at least certain matters which led to it.

d) **One's role and corresponding responsibility may be limited.** Sometimes a person shares in a common deliberation not as a principal participant but only as a subordinate contributor. For example, an individual may be asked for his or her thoughts about a problem concerning which some authoritative body is deliberating, or may be asked by a superior for advice about a decision to be made. In such cases, the person's role in the decision-making process is limited, and his or her responsibility is only to carry out that role. Hence, it is not necessary to consider every alternative, investigate every doubtful fact, and so on. Rather, one need only attempt to understand the question as it is presented, consider it in the light of the common good of the community concerned, and offer the information and advice which appear appropriate.

Of course, when the matter seems very important or a seriously mistaken or wrong decision seems likely, a greater effort should be made, within the limits of one's responsibility, to bring about a sound outcome. But one should not feel responsible for communal decisions one cannot make, and so should not try to usurp others' responsibilities; rather, within the proper limits of obedience, a person should be prepared to accept the decision, even if he or she would have decided otherwise.

e) **In compromising, one may not intend what one judges wrong.** Sometimes, all of the proposals under consideration by a deliberative body are morally acceptable, and the issue is which is likely best to protect or promote the common good. In such cases, an individual should promote the proposal he or she judges best. But if it cannot gain approval by the body as a whole, one should compromise, that is, help to work out and join in approving what one considers the best alternative the body as a whole will approve. In compromising, however, consent may not be given to anything one considers to be wrong, even if that would serve as a means to gain support for a proposal one regards as urgently required by the common good.

Still, this must be distinguished from two other actions which sometimes are morally acceptable.

First, sometimes none of the alternatives for choice is morally acceptable. Then, a person may and should oppose what is morally worse even by voting for what is less bad, since it is not what is judged wrong which is intended but only the prevention of something more seriously wrong. For example, members of a legislative body may vote for a measure which partially rectifies some social injustice but also leaves it partially in place if their only alternative is to vote against the measure and let the injustice continue unrestricted.

Second, very often the question is whether to support or oppose a morally mixed omnibus proposal including both morally unacceptable elements and elements in accord with the true common good. In such cases, the proposal sometimes should be supported—its good elements intended while those which are morally wrong are only accepted as side effects. For example, members of a labor union perhaps should support a proposed contract they consider generally fair even if they judge that one category of workers will gain excessive advantages. Sometimes, however, the side effect cannot justly be accepted, and so such a proposal should be opposed. For example, members of the board of a professional association probably should oppose a proposed policy statement containing many sound and excellent elements but also including the authorization of a gravely unjust practice.

2. Other Participants Should Be Helped to Judge and Act Rightly

Insofar as the work of a deliberative body is a cooperative effort, a person not only should seek moral certitude for himself or herself but should try to help his or her colleagues judge and act rightly. It is necessary to take their beliefs and motives into account and proceed within their limits, but without saying or doing anything inconsistent with what one judges to be the truth and the true common good of the community.

a) **The case for what one judges right may be limited but not distorted.** Often it is clear that others will not accept some part of one's grounds for moral certitude about what proposal to support or approve; sometimes even stating such unacceptable elements evidently will do no good and, indeed, will draw opposition to what one judges true. Then such elements need not be stated. However, one should try to help others reach the truth on a basis one believes to be sound, and so the case for what one judges right may not be distorted by asserting anything believed to be false or invoking any motive not considered at least an element of a good reason.

b) **One may point out to others what consistency requires of them.** Sometimes others will not accept any good reason for adopting a proposal one judges should be adopted. However, consistency with their own convictions would lead them to support the proposal, though on grounds one judges unsound. In such cases, one may point out what consistency would require, for that need not involve asserting anything false or approving anything wrong.

Question M: What Are the Responsibilities of Moral Advisers?

All who preach the gospel and catechize provide moral advice, but their special responsibilities pertain to special roles in the Church, and will be treated in volume four. *Moral adviser* here refers to a more general and modest role, which most Christians sometimes must play, at least as parents, teachers, counselors, or friends. It is the role of helping someone who must make a choice but is uncertain about what is right.

1. Moral Advisers Should Be Both Teachers and Nondirective Counselors

There seem to be two possible, opposed conceptions of how to be a moral adviser. One is that, since moral truth is objective, the adviser should give instruction. The other is that, since moral principles are naturally known and moral problems arise largely from inner conflicts, the adviser, rather than offering instruction, should help the other party clarify his or her own insights, emotions, and desires.

Both views contain some truth, but neither by itself is adequate. As previous questions have shown, reaching moral truth does require knowledge of Church teaching and skill in its application. People with such knowledge and skill can and should teach others, helping them come to see moral truths they would not reach without help. But the process also requires clarification of emotional factors, recognition of various motives, and discernment. In respect to these latter factors the moral adviser rightly functions as a counselor who raises questions which only the person being advised can answer.

2. Moral Advisers Should Proceed Systematically

Although some problems are complicated and difficult, the general procedure appropriate for giving moral advice is rather simple.

a) **The moral adviser must understand the problem exactly.** Anyone proposing to give moral advice first should listen carefully and ask sufficient questions to understand the problem. Who must make the choice: the person seeking advice, or someone else, or some group? That individual or group alone, or as part of a larger decision-making body? What options are under consideration? What are the perceived advantages and disadvantages of each? Have other options been considered and discarded? Why does it seem that advice could be helpful?

Having gathered all the relevant information, the adviser can determine what sort of problem or problems need resolution: Is there a question about a moral norm, a problem about accepting side effects, a difficulty arising from a doubt of fact, a perplexity due to overlooking the morally right alternative, a matter of discernment, or some combination of these, or something else?

Of course, there are complex cases involving diverse problems, for example, the case of a divorced person who has attempted remarriage; here a moral adviser can help in appropriate ways. The relevant moral norms must be understood and correctly applied, and may not be overridden; but emotional factors also are important. While it is easy to exclude morally unacceptable options, careful discernment may be needed to discover precisely what should be done.

b) **The moral adviser should provide any needed instruction.** When the problem is wholly or partly due to ignorance—of a relevant norm, the correct application of a norm, the significance of a certain complex social or legal act, or something of that sort—the moral adviser must provide instruction. Advisers should be clear in their own minds about what is certainly true and essential to solving the problem, and should seek to win unqualified and firm assent to it. This is best done by laying out the grounds step by step, thus helping the one being advised to understand why the adviser thinks as he or she does.

Of course, not everyone can follow a complex line of reasoning, and, for faithful Catholics, not everything needs to be reduced to first moral principles. So, a Catholic moral adviser sometimes helps a fellow Catholic most effectively by simply clarifying the Church's teaching and its application. It is not enough, however, for moral advisers merely to assert what they are certain is true, offering only their personal credibility as a motive for believing what they say.

c) **The moral adviser should promote self-awareness and insight.** When appropriate, the adviser should lead the person being helped to examine and criticize his or her own emotions. But advisers should not rely too much on their own intuitions about the significance of emotional factors. They should ask questions, not try to substitute their judgment for that of the person seeking advice.

d) **Moral advisers should never try to discern on others' behalf.** While discernment presupposes faith, love, and knowledge of objective moral truths, in the end it depends on the individual's awareness of his or her own emotions as an index of his or her own better self and unique makeup. No one else has access to these emotions, and in cases of discernment moral advisers never should advocate one alternative over another. Rather, they should help those they are advising to prepare well, to consider all the relevant data, and to focus on the relevant emotions.

3. Moral Advice and Social Authority Should Be Distinguished

Many roles, such as those of parents and pastors, are complex: those who fulfill them must exercise social authority and also provide moral advice. This complexity easily can lead to confusion between the two responsibilities. However, moral advisers as such can only help others discover the moral truth; they cannot prescribe actions or give permissions.

a) **Sometimes the distinction is easily maintained.** If the one giving moral advice and the one receiving it both reflectively understand what they are doing at the level of moral truth, little difficulty arises, even if the process does not come to a satisfactory conclusion. Even though the effort has not entirely succeeded, the person receiving advice is aware of the responsibility to continue seeking the moral truth not yet found. Although the adviser may share in the teaching authority of the

Church and those being advised may appear to dissent wrongly, but in good faith, from the Church's teaching, both parties to the relationship are responsible to the truth and should conform to what they believe true in carrying out their vocational commitments.[42]

   b) **Moral advisers may not set aside their other responsibilities.** Of course, if someone giving moral advice also bears the responsibility of social authority, this latter responsibility must be fulfilled. For example, a parent instructing children about how they should treat one another also should take steps to see that they do not treat one another in grossly unfair ways. In such a case, a person holding social authority sometimes will require as a matter of obedience what the subject otherwise would consider it permissible either to do or omit; then the obedient subject will do what the moral advice did not show to be obligatory in itself. For example, after explaining why one child should allow the other approximately equal time on their shared bicycle, the parent may rightly (as authority) tolerate some unfairness. But if the moral truth is not grasped, the authority eventually must lay down the law.

   Sometimes, a person in social authority confronts a subject whose conscience conflicts with what the good of the society requires. It may happen that disobedience can then be tolerated, since, within limits, toleration safeguards individual dignity and conduces to peace, which also are genuine social goods. But if social authorities become convinced that the community's good demands conformity, they should prevent the subject from acting according to conscience if they can do so. Thus, even religious liberty is limited by the requirements of public order, as Vatican II teaches (see DH 7).

   c) **Those in a legalistic framework have special responsibilities.** While the present chapter's whole treatment presupposes the inadequacy of legalism, it may be helpful, by way of contrast, to consider the responsibilities of those operating within a legalistic framework.

   If those who give and receive advice both understand what they are doing legalistically, the adviser must proceed consistently according to that framework. Where doubts about norms are not resolved by the Church's teaching, they can be settled by a correct use of probabilism or an acceptable alternative, which will protect social order as well as individual liberty and good faith.[43] Legalistic moral advisers should not abuse their social authority by wrongly attaching sanctions to their moral advice; nor may they abuse their role as moral advisers by giving "permissions," as if moral questions were subject to their social authority.

---

42. *To be in good faith* means to intend to judge according to moral truth but fail to do so through an error not one's own fault (see *CMP*, 3.C). Some people who dissent from the Church's teaching on certain matters do so because they have accepted subjectivism with respect to those matters: the idea that what they consider right is right for them, and there is no objective moral truth. Having rejected moral truth, such people are incapable of good faith (see *CMP*, 3.G, 4.A, C). But in the case under discussion subjectivism on the part of those advised is excluded, because they are committed to discovering the moral truth. So, if their error is not their fault, they are in good faith, and really are acting in accord with moral truth insofar as it is accessible to them.

43. Concerning probabilism and its alternatives, see *CMP*, 12.D, 12.1–2, and nn. 9–10.

4. Moral Advisers of Legalistic People Have Special Responsibilities

Suppose an adviser understands matters at the level of moral truth while a person receiving advice understands matters legalistically: then the moral adviser who does not also have the responsibility of social authority should proceed entirely in terms of moral truth and should endeavor to lead the one seeking advice to understand matters this way.

If a moral adviser of someone imbued with legalism also has responsibilities as a social authority, these responsibilities must, of course, be fulfilled by giving appropriate directions. When subjects refuse to obey and wrongs are tolerated, advisers who also are social authorities should make it clear that, in not imposing sanctions, they are not extending approval to any action they believe is contrary to moral truth. In other words, advisers always should make it clear that an erroneous conscience, whose irreducible role is respected, is not the same thing as a correct conscience which will lead one following it to true fulfillment (see GS 16; *CMP*, 3.C). Failure to make this point clear risks scandalizing those who deserve sound moral advice, whether or not they are prepared to accept it.

5. Moral Advisers as Such Should Never Counsel the Lesser Evil

People are not led to moral truth by being advised to do lesser moral evils. For instance, "Practice contraception and avoid abortion!"—which until the 1960s was the teaching of proponents of birth control—might persuade someone to do a lesser moral evil, but such persuasion throws no light on the relevant moral truth. Thus, even if attempting such persuasion is justified in some case (see 4.E.2.i), it is not the business of a moral adviser and is likely to impede his or her proper work. Having undertaken to help another answer the question, "What is the right thing for me to do?" the advice to choose the lesser evil is almost sure to be taken as an indication that this is in complete accord with moral truth. Thus, someone who is both a moral adviser and a social authority, as parents are, has a reason not to attempt such persuasion even if it would be acceptable for someone whose only role was that of social authority, for example, a police officer or public health physician.

Question N: Does This Chapter Provide Support for Proportionalism?

This chapter has described various procedures, in addition to the rational application of norms to cases, to follow in the quest for moral truth. It might be supposed that some of these could be used to commensurate premoral goods and bads, thus making proportionalism a workable method of moral judgment. But that is not so.

1. Several of the Processes Described Here Examine Emotions

Proportionalists might imagine that the methods of criticizing emotions and discerning described here provide what they need to commensurate the goods and bads involved in different possible courses of action. However, these processes are not what proportionalism projects. They are not an attempt to commensurate various instantiations of goods that provide the reasons for free choices, but are concerned with criticizing emotions or perceiving the harmony of various groups of emotions with one another. If some set of emotions were to be used as a standard for selecting among options (as is rightly done in discernment) before making sure the options pass all rational tests (as must be done before discerning), one would in fact be accepting the maxim: abandon reason and follow emotions. That is not a moral norm but a recipe for immorality (see *S.t.*, 2–2, q. 47, a. 6).

2. This Chapter Clarifies Some Senses of *Proportionate Reason*

The treatment of conflicts of duties as well as several other segments of this chapter can be used to illustrate several different and legitimate senses of *proportionate reason* as it is used by traditional moralists. They said, for instance, that a proportionate reason is needed in order to accept bad side effects or divide goods unequally among members of a group entitled to share in them. The responsibility not to violate a moral absolute is a proportionate reason for accepting any side effects of avoiding its violation, however bad. The promotion and protection of basic human goods is a proportionate reason for sacrificing instrumental goods. Any moral responsibility to do something is a proportionate reason for accepting the side effects, provided accepting them is not conditioned by emotional motives unintegrated with reason, for instance, motives involving partiality. The discerned appropriateness of fulfilling one of two conflicting duties, assuming all prior tests have been passed, is a proportionate reason for not fulfilling the other.

3. All These Senses Presuppose Traditional Morality

The account of *proportionate reason* provided here is in perfect continuity with the tradition.

First, it makes it clear why classical moralists never supposed anyone could have a proportionate reason for violating a moral absolute. Insofar as the classical notion of proportionate reason depended on taking emotions into account, it was limited in application, for classical moralists realized that emotions, no matter how well integrated with faith and personal vocation, never can justify a choice to act against reason. Thus, as is done here, the classical moralists invoked proportionate reason only after other rational tests had been met.

Second, in offering the standard of proportionate reason, these moralists assumed that it would be applied by Christians of some maturity and integration: prudent persons who would intuitively apply the standard of their well-integrated emotions. That also is why it often is suggested that the example of good and experienced people be consulted to see what reason would be proportionate.

CHAPTER SIX

LOVE, JUSTICE, MERCY, AND SOCIAL RESPONSIBILITY

Summary

While the most basic Christian responsibility toward others is to love them, it is not always obvious what that requires. This chapter clarifies the question.

Jesus teaches that we should love our neighbors as ourselves, and love of neighbor is love of every human person. Jesus also teaches that we should love enemies as God does: we should seek reconciliation with them and not condition love upon their repentance; but we should not condone their wrongdoing.

Christian love exceeds the limits placed on other human love by hopelessness, indifference, individualism, and even death. Jesus' command to his followers to love one another as he loves them is truly new, and communion in Jesus is the source of this Christian love. But Jesus' commandment to love does not limit love to fellow Christians; it reaches out instead to all people. It is violated by hatred and evildoing toward others, though most kinds of sins against others admit parvity of matter.

Justice refers to several distinct realities, and there are narrower and broader concepts of justice. Still, some theories of justice are simply false, while some widely accepted accounts of justice—for example, that it consists in fulfilling agreements or in objective equality in exchange—are inadequate, even though in some cases they do point to useful standards. The principles of justice are moral rectitude and fairness.

Rights are not additional principles of justice but, rather, its consequences, and so rights are not treated as basic in Church teaching. The Church's teaching on rights mainly concerns natural rights.

A morally good life must be not only individual but communal. Communal responsibilities are generated by moral principles. The common good, understood in terms of basic human goods, and the good of each person are not at odds; instead, the common good and the individual's good include each other. But the common good of the new covenant community is a special case which takes priority over the good of each person and over every other common good.

In the present-day situation, secular humanism undermines social order; and the roots of sin—pride, avarice, and pleasure seeking—take special forms which account for the negative features characteristic of our culture. Individualism and collectivism, unrestrained capitalism and state socialism, have competed for political and economic dominance. The Church rejects the extreme elements of these approaches and supports private property together with social responsibility and a free economy together with the necessary public assistance for families and intermediate groups.

Justice and mercy are related, but mercy goes beyond justice by overcoming injustice, and must be practiced by Christians. Even so, mercy does not cancel out the objective requirements of justice. Works of mercy are works of love, and sometimes Christians should forgo rights for the sake of mercy. Peace is the fruit of justice which includes mercy.

Although Christians are not called to establish the kingdom of God on earth, still they should integrate social responsibility into their vocations. This includes promoting social justice and adopting a life-style consistent with social responsibility. One should act on behalf of justice in specifically Christian ways.

Question A: What Is the Primary Christian Responsibility toward Others?

Creating human persons in his own image and calling them by grace to heavenly communion, God wills that they constitute a single family in this world and begin now to treat one another as brothers and sisters. Love unites persons in communion, while perfecting each created member of the communion in his or her own distinct personhood. Because God calls human persons to divine-human familial communion, the first and greatest commandment is to love God and neighbor (see GS 24). Therefore, one's most basic Christian responsibility toward others is to love them. But what this requires is not always obvious and therefore must be clarified.

The present question does this by treating seven points. First, Jesus reaffirms the love commands of the Old Testament; second, he teaches his disciples to love enemies as God does; third, this love overcomes certain limits otherwise characteristic of human love; fourth, the specific character of Christian love arises from its origin in the communion of the divine persons themselves; fifth, nevertheless, Christian love does not exclude non-Christians; sixth, Christian love does exclude hatred and evil doing toward others; and, seventh, it also excludes all other sins against others; however, because of the possibility of parvity (littleness, slightness) of matter, one can love others even as one sins against them in small ways.

1. Jesus Teaches that One Should Love One's Neighbor as Oneself

Though differing in detail, the three synoptic Gospels agree that Jesus links two Old Testament commands: to love God with one's whole being and to love one's neighbor as oneself (see Dt 6.5, Lv 19.18, Mt 22.37–39, Mk 12.30–31, Lk 10.27). In thus linking love of neighbor with love of God, Jesus makes it clear that one has no more basic responsibility toward others than to love them.[1]

---

1. See G. Schneider, "agape, agapao, agapetos," in *Exegetical Dictionary of the New Testament,* ed. Horst Balz and Gerhard Schneider, vol. 1, *Aaron-Henoch* (Grand Rapids, Mich.: William B. Eerdmans, 1990), 8–12, for an analysis of the relevant New Testament vocabulary and

a) **Love underlies every responsibility toward others.** The commandments to love God and neighbor are stipulations of the covenant. To love God is to fulfill every covenantal responsibility toward him. But since God's people are his covenant partner, he has a special concern for their solidarity and flourishing. Therefore, the covenant also stipulates how members of the community are to strengthen it by their manner of treating one another. The many specific commandments with respect to neighbor identify things to be done or, more often, not done. The commandment to love one's neighbors concerns the inner principle, the community spirit, which should animate and motivate all that is specified and more. So, St. Paul points out: "Love does no wrong to a neighbor; therefore, love is the fulfilling of the law" (Rom 13.10; cf. Gal 5.14, Jas 2.8–13).[2]

b) **The required love is not emotional but volitional.** People who consistently act with good will gradually bring their feelings more and more into harmony with their will. Still, emotional love, the feeling or sentiment of affection, is not directly in one's power. It is impossible even for a saint to like everyone, and therefore the love one is required to bear toward others cannot be any such feeling as this. Rather, this love is volitional, and it has two aspects: positively, it is readiness and willingness to try to benefit others; negatively, it is unreadiness and unwillingness to harm them. Thus, Jesus closely links the command, "You shall love your neighbor as yourself" (Mt 22.39), with the Golden Rule, "In everything do to others as you would have them do to you" (Mt 7.12). According to Matthew, Jesus grounds the latter by saying, "for this is the law and the prophets" (Mt 7.12), and similarly says of the twofold love command: "On these two commandments hang all the law and the prophets" (Mt 22.40).

The Golden Rule formulated negatively—for example, "And what you hate, do not do to anyone" (Tb 4.15)—does not require doing good to others but only not hurting them. However, Jesus' affirmative formulation, tied to the command to love one's neighbor, calls for doing good; it plainly is violated by those who distance themselves from neighbors in need (see Lk 6.27–31, 10.29–37).[3]

c) **Perfect love of God does not limit true love of neighbor.** How can one love God with one's whole heart, mind, soul, and strength, and simultaneously love one's neighbor? Would not totally loving God leave no room for others? Plainly not: God commands nothing inconsistent, and both love commands are his.

---

bibliography. Victor Paul Furnish, *The Love Command in the New Testament* (Nashville: Abingdon, 1972), remains a useful treatment, although Catholic readers should notice that some of his assumptions are at odds with Catholic teaching.

2. On the relationship of the Ten Commandments in both Old and New Testaments to the law of love, see Patrick D. Miller, Jr., "The Place of the Decalogue in the Old Testament and Its Law," *Interpretation* 43 (1989): 229–42; Reginald H. Fuller, "The Decalogue in the New Testament," *Interpretation* 43 (1989): 243–55.

3. Joseph A. Fitzmyer, S.J., *The Gospel According to Luke (I–IX): Introduction, Translation, and Notes,* Anchor Bible, 28 (Garden City, N.Y.: Doubleday, 1981), 639, considers Lv 19.18 to be an alternative formulation of the Golden Rule, and yet thinks (639–40): "It is useless to try to establish that the positive form used by Jesus in Luke or Matthew is actually superior to the negative; it all depends on the context in which the rule is set." Nevertheless, as a matter of logic the affirmative formulation can refer to every choice, action, *and omission* which bears upon others, while the negative formulation cannot refer to omissions.

Unreserved love of God not only is compatible with love of neighbor but gives rise to it. Loving other persons is not appropriating them or being appropriated by them; rather, it is being in communion with them and regarding their good, including their love of others, as part of one's own good. True love for any person is a transitive relationship: in loving others, one has a reason to love those whom they love. This holds true for love of God: "Everyone who believes that Jesus is the Christ has been born of God, and everyone who loves the parent loves the child" (1 Jn 5.1). Moreover, someone who loves God wishes his will to be fulfilled; and God wills a perfect communion of all persons in divine-human love. Thus, a person who loves God must love others in a way which contributes to this communion. Consequently, if one loved God with one's whole heart, mind, soul, and strength, one would love oneself and others with the bounteous, faithful, and merciful love with which God loves each created person.[4]

The sacrament of the Eucharist concretely realizes love of God and neighbor in their unity with each other. In this sacrament, people are fully united with Jesus, and through him with his Father and their Holy Spirit; but eucharistic worship also forms human persons into a family of brothers and sisters in Jesus. While retaining and even perfecting one's distinct personality, one becomes in Jesus one flesh with others. In this way, people enjoy a foretaste of heaven, where they hope to live forever in intimate communion not only with the divine persons but also with other human persons.

d) **Love of neighbor should be benevolent, upright, and holy.** Jesus teaches that one should love one's neighbor as one loves oneself. Such love will be benevolent, not selfish. For one loves oneself for one's own sake, and so, loving neighbors as one loves oneself, a person will love them for their own sakes, not merely for his or her gratification or advantage. Moreover, people whose self-love is not mere egocentric feeling and partiality but benevolence efficaciously will what is good for themselves and avoid all sin; loving one's neighbors as oneself therefore means loving them uprightly and choosing to act for their true good, not merely wishing them well. Finally, in rightly loving oneself, one wills God's goodness for oneself but even more for him; thus, to love one's neighbors as oneself means loving them in God, and such love is holy (see *S.t.*, 2–2, q. 44, a. 7).

e) **Love of neighbor is love of every human person.** The gospel announces the coming of God's reign and a new covenant offered to all men and women (see Mt 28.19, Acts 10.34–43). Jesus teaches that everyone should be counted as a neighbor. Instead of making this point by proposing an argument in general terms, however, he uses a parable. Faced with a suggestion that the responsibility to love might be limited by restricting *neighbor* to some particular class of people, Jesus

---

4. John Paul II, Homily at Mass for the Family (12 Oct. 1980), 6, *Inseg.* 3.2 (1980) 847, *OR*, 20 Oct. 1980, 4, teaches a similar and even stronger thesis—that without love toward God, love of neighbor inevitably falls short: "This structure of the commandment corresponds to the truth of love. If God is loved above all things, then also man loves and is loved with the fullness of love accessible to him. If one destroys this inseparable structure, spoken of in Christ's commandment, then man's love will detach itself from the deepest root, will lose the root of fullness and of truth which are essential to him."

teaches that even a despised Samaritan makes himself a Jew's neighbor by acting toward him with love (see Lk 10.29–37). Thus, Jesus rules out using some predefined notion of neighbor as an excuse for limiting the circle of those whom one is prepared to love; he teaches instead that love of God calls one to act as a good neighbor toward any person found to be in need.

f) **Christian love preserves morally good priorities in loving.** Since the new covenant extends love to all, it might be supposed that, ideally, a Christian would acknowledge and follow no definite order of preference in affection for others and readiness to act in their interests. Imagining this actually to be the case, some argue that love of every human person is not a sound ideal, since one ought to love some people more than others, for example, one's own family more than total strangers.

Their argument mistakenly assumes that love which extends to all cannot at times prefer some to others. The universality of Christian love, however, is entirely compatible with observing certain priorities in loving. Indeed, of itself, Christian love necessarily involves two priorities: of God to self, since God's goodness is the principle of one's communion with him, and of self to others, since one's communion with God is the principle of one's communion with others in divine-human family life.[5] But because communion with God redeems, gathers up, and perfects all other upright relationships, Christian love also includes other priorities, which are essential to those relationships. Moreover, the divine-human communion of heaven will include all the good fruits of human nature and effort (see GS 38–39), among them all humanly good interpersonal relationships. Therefore, Christian life in this world, which prepares material for the heavenly kingdom, preserves and follows the order of preference in affection and beneficence toward others required by the various ways in which one already shares and can yet share in human goods together with others (see *S.t.*, 2–2, q. 26, aa. 6–7; q. 44, a. 8, ad 2).

To take an obvious and important example: just as marriage is a sacrament for Christian spouses through which their love for each other is caught up into divine love (see GS 48), so also in the order of charity the legitimate natural order of preference for one another—of husbands and wives, parents and children, sisters and brothers—remains intact. This order of love, however, must not be used as an excuse for evading responsibilities toward other, even distant, neighbors in need; a Christian should serve, not only those near and dear, but others too in accord with the specific requirements of his or her personal vocation.[6]

---

5. See *S.t.*, 2–2, q. 26, aa. 1–4. It might be objected that the command to love one's neighbor *as* oneself excludes a priority of self to neighbor. However, St. Thomas argues (a. 4, *sed contra*) that *as oneself* points to the priority by indicating that self-love is the model of love of neighbor, since the model exceeds the copy. To love others as oneself is to love them, not selfishly, but for their own sakes (which does not exclude the priority of self-love) and to will that they share in one's communion with the divine persons (which presupposes the self-love by which one wills to enjoy that communion).

6. What is asserted here about the order of charity generally follows what St. Thomas says about it in the cited articles. But the present treatment also purposely departs from his view in two respects. First, although one ought to be ready to accept the loss of one's life and of any lesser bodily good for the sake of others' salvation, it hardly seems meaningful to compare love of one's own body—which is part of oneself, not a distinct reality—with love of persons, whether oneself

2. Jesus Teaches His Followers to Love Enemies as God Loves Them

Some people today seem to think nobody has real enemies; rather, they suppose, all conflicts among people are due to psychological problems, breakdowns in communication, or other factors beyond anyone's control. This fading of a realistic understanding of human conflict is an aspect of the widespread denial of free choice and the loss of a sense of sin. Moreover, many people more or less consciously accept a subjectivist or relativist view which, while leaving room for quarrels, undermines the objective truth and justice by which upright people discern their real enemies.

Jesus neither suggests that one has no real enemies nor pretends that all conflicts among people are due to factors beyond anyone's control. He knows that sins generate real discord (see Jn 15.18–25). Some people seem to be enemies in the full sense: not men and women of good will. They hate others and wrong them, neither apologizing nor making amends for doing so. Someone who is hated and wronged can know that he or she has an enemy, even though it is impossible to read the ultimate truth of that enemy's heart. Nevertheless, Jesus teaches that one should love one's enemies and persecutors, following the example of the heavenly Father (see Mt 5.9, 43–48; Lk 6.27–36). According to this standard, it is necessary not only to avoid hating one's enemies but to treat them well. For that is how God treated alienated humankind: "God proves his love for us in that while we still were sinners Christ died for us" (Rom 5.8).[7]

a) **Forgiving enemies is not the same as excusing doers of harm.** While *forgive* and *excuse* often are used loosely, so that they become synonyms, the two can be distinguished in order to clarify an important point. Strictly speaking, it can be appropriate to excuse an act which in no way is sinful, but only a sin can be forgiven.

People often do harm without ill will, either incidentally to doing something good and right, or unintentionally, or through some understandable human weakness, such as an emotional outburst. Usually they make their good will and regret clear, for example, with an apology. The appropriate response is to acknowledge their effort to maintain good relations and accept any apology they offer, thus affirming the relationship.

While one should excuse doers of harm whose actions are excusable, that is not the same as forgiving enemies. Forgiveness does not imply that what was done was morally acceptable, unintentional, or a result of understandable weakness. Rather,

---

or others (see *S.t.*, 2–2, q. 26, a. 5). Second, since the goods which ground various special relationships with others differ in kind, not only in degree, it hardly seems possible to discern any single series of priorities among them which should be followed in every choice regardless of what is at stake (see *S.t.*, 2–2, q. 26, aa. 8–12).

7. See Benedict XV, *Pacem, Dei munus pulcherrimum*, AAS 12 (1920) 212, *PE*, 185.9: "Christian charity ought not to be content with not hating our enemies and loving them as brothers; it also demands that we treat them with kindness, following the rule of the Divine Master Who 'went about doing good and healing all that were oppressed by the devil' (Acts 10.38), and finished his mortal life, the course of which was marked by good deeds, by shedding his blood for them." A helpful study: José Antonio Llinares, O.P., "¿Como amar a nuestros enemigos?" *Ciencia tomista* 101 (1974): 191–213.

it presupposes that the act was objectively unjust, if not malicious. Thus, only what is not excusable needs to be forgiven. To forgive enemies is to seek to establish or restore good relations with people whose harmful actions seem to manifest malicious will.

b) **The old covenant set limits to the communion of love.** The Old Testament's requirement to love neighbors, although it extended to everyone living within the covenant community, even foreigners (see Lv 19.33, Dt 10.19), was restricted to that community: "You shall not take vengeance or bear a grudge against any of your people, but you shall love your neighbor as yourself" (Lv 19.18). This requirement of love transcends the "reciprocity ethic" (love those who love you), which Jesus criticizes by pointing out that even pagans and sinners do as much (see Mt 5.46–47, Lk 6.32–34). True, the Old Testament requires that good be done to personal enemies (see Ex 23.4–5, Prv 25.21–22); but the old covenant's love command did not extend to Israel's enemies. God's chosen people thought that if they were faithful to him, their enemies also would be his (see Ex 23.20–22, Dt 20.1–4, Jos 10.22–25, 2 Chr 20.29, Ps 44.1–8), and that good Israelites could even be obliged to obliterate enemy communities (see Dt 7.1–6, 20.16–18; Jos 6.16–21, 10.28–40, 11.10–23; 1 Sm 15.1–3).

c) **Jesus' gospel of God's mercy transcends these limits.** The new covenant does away with the barrier between God's people and the gentiles, reconciling the two groups to God through the cross, and joining them in a single fellowship (see Eph 2.14–20). In inaugurating this new covenant, Jesus teaches his disciples to love their enemies "so that you may be children of your Father in heaven; for he makes his sun rise on the evil and on the good, and sends rain on the righteous and on the unrighteous" (Mt 5.45; cf. Mt 5.9, Lk 6.35, Rom 12.17–21). By this teaching, Jesus makes it clear why Christians must love enemies as if they were friends: one must love enemies in order to be a child of God, who wills all sinners (including both one's enemies and oneself), to live as his family in heavenly communion (see *S.t.,* 2–2, q. 23, a. 1, ad 2). Conversely, someone who loves God can love his or her enemies, since to love God precisely is to be in communion with him, and those in communion with God, being his children, can imitate him.

d) **Jesus teaches that one must seek reconciliation with enemies.** In teaching that one must love one's enemies, Jesus makes it clear that this can mean more than blessing and praying for them, things which can be done without much personal cost. Loving enemies, Jesus teaches, means doing good to them, even despite the evil they have done and are likely to continue to do, for example, it sometimes means making loans to people who never reciprocate (see Lk 6.34–35). Justice without love often does little more than restrain hatred from doing more evil to enemies than one has suffered at their hands; at best, it excludes retaliation. Love, however, requires actively doing good to enemies.[8] It shows its salvific power by

---

8. For a comparison of this teaching of Jesus with teachings more or less approaching it: Pheme Perkins, *Love Commands in the New Testament* (New York: Paulist Press, 1982), 27–40. St. Paul also teaches beneficence toward enemies (see Rom 12.14–21). Paul's teaching should not be considered inconsistent because of his use of Prv 25.21–22—"If your enemies are hungry, give them bread to eat; and if they are thirsty, give them water to drink; for you will heap coals of fire

thus transcending the limits hatred sets and fulfilling the norm: "Do not be overcome by evil, but overcome evil with good" (Rom 12.21). In practice, this requires one to seek reconciliation and make peace: seek through kindness and generosity to bring persecutors to conversion and to resolve disputes peacefully.

e) **Love of enemies should not be conditioned on their repentance.** It might seem that enemies cannot be loved while they remain enemies, so that a person need only be prepared to love them should they ever seek reconciliation; for, it is argued, not even God can forgive sinners unless and until they repent. Against this argument: "God proves his love for us in that while we still were sinners Christ died for us" (Rom 5.8).

A person can forgive enemies, and, in doing so, try to serve as a channel of God's grace, evoking their repentance—assuming they really are guilty—by gently offering them forgiveness, just as God in Christ does with every sinner: "Just as the Lord has forgiven you, so you also must forgive" (Col 3.13). Therefore, people do not live by Jesus' teaching concerning love of enemies by waiting for them to ask forgiveness or show other signs of repentance, meanwhile refusing to love them. Rather, Jesus' teaching is lived only by following his example, as St. Stephen did in praying for those who were stoning him (see Acts 7.60).[9]

Even when enemies reject one's offer of forgiveness, it is possible to live in peace with everyone, insofar as it depends on oneself, and not try to avenge any wrong (see Rom 12.17–19, 1 Pt 3.8–14). It is true that love of enemies does not eliminate the requirements of justice, and that forgiveness cannot accomplish reconciliation unless it is met with willingness to make amends.[10] Still, people always can forgive enemies by praying that they will be moved to repentance, which will open the way to reconciliation (see Mt 5.44, Rom 12.14).

f) **Love of enemies does not condone any vice or sin.** It might seem to follow that love must accept everyone, even enemies, just as they are, and affirm them even in the error or sin which is present in them.[11] But the law of love does not require indiscriminate affirmation of everything about other persons (see *S.t.*, 2–2, q. 34, a. 3). One's love must be like Jesus'. He loves sinners and brings them into communion with himself in order to overcome their error and sin. When the scribes and pharisees bring a woman caught in adultery to Jesus, he not only saves her from being stoned to death but warns her not to sin again (see Jn 8.3–11). In a true sense,

---

on their heads"—for the context excludes interpreting "heap coals of fire" as suggesting a subtle way of executing revenge. *The New Jerusalem Bible*, n. j to Rom 12.20, offers a plausible exegesis: "The Christian takes vengeance on an enemy by doing good. The image of red-hot coals, symbol of burning pain, stands for the remorse which will bring the sinner to repentance."

9. Love of enemies aims at the conversion of persecutors and others engaged in injustice: see Luise Schottroff, "Non-Violence and the Love of One's Enemies," in Luise Schottroff et al., *Essays on the Love Commandment,* trans. Reginald H. Fuller and Ilse Fuller (Philadelphia: Fortress, 1978), 9–39.

10. See John Paul II, *Dives in misericordia,* 14, *AAS* 72 (1980) 1226–27, *PE,* 279.157.

11. This policy sometimes is proposed as being "nonjudgmental." But in practice nobody can observe it consistently, since consistently to affirm everything considered error and sin in others would involve affirming those whose statements and behavior are condemned as judgmental by proponents of the policy of being nonjudgmental.

Jesus is not judgmental: he sets aside the legalistic mentality, readily forgives sinners, does not condemn the world, and points out that those who refuse to acknowledge their sinfulness are self-condemned by the truth they violate (see Jn 3.16–21). But he realistically recognizes sinners as sinners and never accepts error as truth.

Similarly, if Christians' love of neighbor is genuine, it not only permits but requires them both to "hold fast to what is good" and to "hate what is evil" (Rom 12.9). Whatever is at odds with the perfect communion of heaven must be hated. Sinners, including oneself, can and should be loved insofar as Jesus has redeemed them and called them to everlasting life in himself; but something of their being, including one's own, *should* be hated: that by which they remain unrepentant sinners (see *S.t.*, 2–2, q. 25, a. 6).

Of course, it is impossible to read others' hearts. "God alone is the judge and searcher of hearts; for that reason he forbids us to make judgments about the internal guilt of anyone" (GS 28). The impulse to condemn any particular person except oneself as a sinner should be blocked by refusal to judge others. But that same refusal should block any sentimental tendency to acquit people of their apparent sins. Indeed, love forbids doing so, since acquitting those who really are sinners will encourage them to persist in their sins until they die in them.

3. Christian Love Transcends the Usual Limits of Human Love

In the fallen human condition, the love of human beings for one another not only can be negated by hatred but often is limited by hopelessness, indifference, selfish individualism, and death. Love of neighbor rooted in friendship with God goes beyond these limits; and the ways it does so shed further light on its unique character. (Bear in mind, too, that people who seem to be nonbelievers, if they are people in good faith and of good will, are in a fundamental sense Christians without knowing it, and can live in grace and act toward others with Christian love.)

a) Christian love transcends the limit set by hopelessness. The experience of fallen humankind points to the human impossibility of healing the wounds of evil. Without faith and hope, human beneficence therefore is limited either by resignation to evil or by denying its character as privation and responding to it on its own terms: doing evil to overcome evil (see *CMP*, 5.C). But hope anticipates the power and effectiveness of grace, and so love motivates energetic efforts to overcome evil, not only by knowledge, technology, and power, but also and chiefly by summoning sinners to repentance, offering morally good alternatives, and nurturing the tender beginnings of virtue.

Underlying love's transcendence of hatred is its transcendence of hopelessness: even if enemies are truly wicked, they need not remain enemies forever, for by God's grace they can repent and become friends. This conviction also underlies efforts to offer morally acceptable alternatives to those tempted to sin through weakness, for example, alternatives to abortion for those overwhelmed by the prospect of motherhood, alternatives to suicide for the depressed, alternatives to the escapism of alcohol and drugs for those without prospects for a decent life, and so on.

b) Christian love transcends the limits set by indifference. People naturally are attached to a small group of persons near and dear to them: family, friends, and, though perhaps more weakly, a wider circle, such as coworkers or compatriots. Without love, however, one simply would not care about most people; their personal suffering and sin would be of no concern. Individuals might do good to someone who happened to fall within the range of philanthropic projects launched to win honor for themselves or programs to mitigate social problems threatening their own security; but they seldom would have compassion for particular, actual persons or experience others' suffering as their own.

Faith and hope, however, make Christians aware that God calls every human being to the same heavenly communion to which he calls them; while love moves them to pray that all people will come to the knowledge of truth and be saved: "Your kingdom come, Your will be done, on earth as it is in heaven" (Mt 6.10; cf. 1 Tm 2.4). In this way love should overcome indifference to those nameless persons who do not belong to one's family, nation, business or professional group, or other community; it should make one aware that

> the obligation is pressing to make ourselves the neighbor of absolutely every person, and of actively helping others when they come across our path, whether they be old people abandoned by all, foreign laborers unjustly looked down upon, refugees, children born of unlawful unions and wrongly suffering for sins they did not commit, or the hungry who disturb our conscience by recalling the voice of the Lord: "Just as you did it to one of the least of these who are members of my family, you did it to me" (Mt 25.40). (GS 27)

The quotation from Matthew's Gospel points to the reality underlying compassion toward those to whom one otherwise would be indifferent: since the new covenant incorporates into Jesus' body all those he redeems, one does to him, and so also to oneself, what one does to them.

c) Christian love is not limited by an individualistic ethic. The same human sympathy and compassion which bind decent people to their family and friends also naturally lead them to help others with whom they come into *direct* contact when the need is obvious and moving. While there is, of course, nothing wrong with that, an individualistic ethic limits charity to such kindness, and also holds that charitable deeds are supererogatory (above and beyond every call of duty).

But Christian love requires concern for those whose needs are not so obvious and moving, for example, not only the man one is trying to help with his marriage problem but also his wife and children, not only the woman with a problem pregnancy but also her unborn child. Love also requires the fulfillment of social responsibilities, even when not fulfilling them harms nobody one knows (see AA 8, GS 30); for instance, one should conserve natural resources, vote conscientiously, avoid infecting others with diseases from which one suffers, and so forth; and Christian citizens of wealthier nations should do what they can to promote policies and programs to assist poorer nations.[12]

---

12. See John XXIII, *Mater et magistra*, AAS 53 (1961) 438–45, *PE*, 267.151–83.

d) **Christian love transcends the limit set by death.** Christian love is the communion of the new covenant. This communion, at once divine and human, begins on earth but will last forever in heaven. This love therefore transcends death. As the texts of the funeral Mass and the Masses in honor of saints make clear, the dead and living members of the new covenant continue to live with one another in Jesus. Not only should the dead be mourned and their memory honored—as every human community does—but one should pray for the souls in purgatory and ask the saints in heaven for their help. These works of love should include all the dead, even enemies, and not just loved ones and benefactors.

4. Jesus Teaches His Followers to Love One Another as He Loves Them

Jesus not only renews the Old Testament's commandment to love one's neighbor as oneself but adds to it the new commandment of Christian love.

a) **The love command of the new covenant truly is new.** While the love command of the new covenant is not new in calling for love of others, it is new inasmuch as it is a commandment to love *as Jesus himself does:* "This is my commandment, that you love one another as I have loved you" (Jn 15.12; cf. 13.34). So, it is specifically Christian. In Jesus' love, the Father's primordial and originating love is revealed: "Whoever has seen me has seen the Father" (Jn 14.9; cf. 1 Jn 4.7–21). Christian love, then, involves a sharing in divine love, the communion between the Son and the Father in the Spirit: "As the Father has loved me, so have I loved you; abide in my love" (Jn 15.9), and: "See what love the Father has given us, that we should be called children of God; and that is what we are" (1 Jn 3.1).[13]

Even as man, Jesus loves others more perfectly than they love themselves. For his human love is fully in accord with God's creative and redemptive love, while fallen human beings' love, even of themselves, never is perfect but always more or less defective, inasmuch as they settle in some respects for limited and merely apparent self-fulfillment rather than integral and true fulfillment.

b) **Communion in Jesus is the source of Christian love.** Though unable by themselves to love as Jesus does, Christians are joined with other disciples in a communion of love, whose principle is Jesus' divine love for those who believe in him (see Jn 15.9). They share in divine love because Jesus wins for them the "power to become children of God" (Jn 1.12); and, reborn as God's children, they can manifest divine love in their relations with one another: "Beloved, let us love one another, because love is from God; everyone who loves is born of God and knows God. Whoever does not love does not know God, for God is love" (1 Jn 4.7–8). Thus, loving one another as Jesus loves perfects his disciples' share in divine love: "No one has ever seen God; if we love one another, God lives in us, and his love is perfected in us" (1 Jn 4.12).

c) **Christians' love for others also must be like Jesus' human love.** By his own example, Jesus shows the practical significance of his new commandment of

---

13. See Edward Malatesta, *Interiority and Covenant* (Rome: Biblical Institute Press, 1978), 119–61, 253–82, and 293–324.

love: "This is my commandment, that you love one another as I have loved you. No one has greater love than this, to lay down one's life for one's friends" (Jn 15.12–13). Therefore, Christians must imitate Jesus' love in giving himself "to the end" (Jn 13.1). Thankful for what he has done, his followers must treat others in the same way: "We know love by this, that he laid down his life for us—and we ought to lay down our lives for one another" (1 Jn 3.16).

St. Paul also teaches that Christians fulfill the new "law of Christ" by bearing one another's burdens (Gal 6.2). The baptized become one in Christ, and all invidious distinctions among them are eliminated (see Rom 12.3–8, 1 Cor 12.12–27, Gal 3.25–28). It is not sufficient to believe in Jesus; his disciples also must be ready to suffer, following his example (see Phil 1.29–30). Instead of being self-indulgent and concerned about status, Christians are to serve one another (see Mt 20.25–28, Mk 10.42–45, Lk 22.25–27, Jn 13.12–16); only such love fulfills the law and builds up the communion in Jesus which will last forever (see Rom 12.9–13, 1 Cor 13, Gal 5.13–14, Phil 2.2–8).

5. This New Love Command Does Not Limit Love to Fellow Christians

It sometimes is suggested that, by comparison with the universality of the love of neighbor taught by the synoptic Gospels, the new commandment of love in St. John and St. Paul restricts love of neighbor by excluding outsiders and limiting love to members of the Christian community—the "brothers" who "love one another." Two things can be said about this view.

a) **Both love commands can be fulfilled at the same time.** St. Paul clearly implies that universal love of neighbor and special love of fellow Christians are distinct but compatible responsibilities. For he prays: "May the Lord make you increase and abound in love for one another and for all" (1 Thes 3.12; cf. 5.15), and he exhorts: "So then, whenever we have an opportunity, let us work for the good of all, and especially for those of the family of faith" (Gal 6.10). The clear implication is that there need be no conflict for Jesus' disciples between loving one another as Jesus loves them and loving all human beings as they love themselves.

The compatibility of the two love commands is easily explained. Abiding together in the mutual love of new covenant communion is possible and normal for those already united with Jesus, who share in his communion with the Father. Thus, it makes sense that members of the Church, who share together in the Eucharist, be addressed as a group and told to love one another. But since communion requires mutuality, it is not possible to abide in divine love with those who cannot reciprocate that love because they do not share in it, either not yet having entered into the communion of the new covenant or being alienated from it. Still, Christians can love those with whom they are not in communion as they humanly love themselves, praying that such people also will come to know Jesus or be reconciled with him. In other words, the new law of love is that of divine-human communion insofar as it is already realized, while the command to love one's neighbor as oneself implies the requirement to reach out to others with human love in order to extend and complete that communion.

b) **The new covenant's love also reaches out to all people.** Far from being limited, love which is in accord with the command to love others in Jesus and as he loves reaches out to people to whom one has no other predefined relationship and responsibilities. In Jesus, God offers grace sufficient for salvation to all who have not already died in their sins: "I, when I am lifted up from the earth, will draw all people to myself" (Jn 12.32).[14] As Vatican II teaches concerning human solidarity and the Incarnate Word: "He commanded his apostles to preach to all peoples the gospel's message so that the human race might become the family of God, in which the fullness of the law would be love" (GS 32). In this process of evangelism, the mutual love of Christians bears a primary and fundamental witness to God's love in Jesus; in doing so, it provides a challenge and opportunity to those who do not yet share in the new covenant communion: "The glory that you have given me I have given them, so that they may be one, as we are one, I in them and you in me, that they may become completely one, so that the world may know that you have sent me and have loved them even as you have loved me" (Jn 17.22–23).[15] Thus, far from excluding those who are not yet members, the perfection of love within the eucharistic community is Jesus' way of drawing all people to himself.

6. Hatred and Evildoing toward Others Violate the Love Command

Because love fulfills the whole law, every sin against others violates love. Many such sins will be treated in subsequent questions and chapters of this volume. Sins against the Church's unity, peace, and vitality—especially the sin of schism—violate love in an especially damaging way, for they are detrimental to new covenant communion subsisting in the Church; those sins were treated above (see 3.D.1.f–h, 3.D.2.e–g). Here are treated only the sins which directly oppose love of others in a radical way: hating them and evildoing motivated by hatred.

a) **To hate others is to will what is bad for them.** A person does not hate others in rejecting what truly is bad about them; in fact, such rejection is essential to loving them as they should be loved. Nor, in choosing to do something for some other reason, is it hating others to accept side effects—that is, foreseen but unintended consequences—which are bad for them, although such willing *can* be unjust, even gravely so. Feeling hatred toward others is not in itself the sin of hating them, since emotions arise spontaneously and occasion sin only insofar as one wills in accord with them; they must, however, be resisted, both by psychological means and by prayer for the Holy Spirit's healing grace.

To hate others is to will what is bad for them precisely insofar as it impedes, damages, or destroys something one believes to be part of their true good. For

---

14. See Rudolf Schnackenburg, *The Gospel According to John,* vol. 2, *Commentary on Chapters 5–12* (New York: Crossroad, 1987), 393–94. Cf. 1 Tm 2.4, which points to the universality of God's salvific will precisely to explain why Christians should pray for everyone, even those who persecute them; 1 Tm 4.10, which expresses, as a motive of apostolic effort, hope in God "who is the Savior of all people, especially of those who believe."

15. On Jn 17.21–23, see Rudolf Schnackenburg, *The Gospel According to John,* vol. 3, *Commentary on Chapters 13–21* (New York: Crossroad, 1990), 190–94.

example, to endorse feelings of anger or hostility by deliberately wishing that another die is to hate that person.[16]

b) One can hate others without being ready to act against their good. Choosing to bring about what is bad for others out of personal antipathy—for example, treating wrongdoers with cruelty that goes beyond just punishment—is action against their good. However, in many cases people harbor personal antipathy toward others, without being able (or ready) to do them harm; they may feel joy when some harm accidentally befalls the objects of their dislike or wish harm would befall them, yet be unready to do them that harm in view of the likely costs to themselves. Although it does not issue in any malevolent action, an act of will in accord with such antipathetic feelings is a sin of hatred in thought. For example, to wish that someone go to hell is a sin of hatred in thought. *Cursing* in the strict sense is the verbal expression of such a hateful wish.

Such sins of thought and speech can be mortal, if the usual conditions are met (see *CMP*, 15.C). They are more grave when committed against those who especially deserve love and honor, for example, parents (see Ex 21.15, 17; Lv 20.9). In some cases, though, sins of hatred are venial, either due to lack of reflection or choice, or because the evil wished is slight (see *S.t.*, 2–2, q. 76, a. 3).

c) In hating another, one may or may not seek some benefit. Sometimes a person hates others in the sense of wanting them to suffer some evil. No intelligible benefit for oneself or anyone else need be sought, and often none is; emotional satisfaction in the other's very suffering is an adequate motive. Such hatred can originate in different ways, for example, in envy (see *S.t.*, 2–2, q. 34, a. 6) or in the perception that others in some way oppose either oneself or some person or thing with which one identifies (see *S.t.*, 2–2, q. 108, a. 1).

Quite often, however, people will what is bad for others only as a means to some ulterior end. For example, if there is something to be gained by another's death or adversity, someone might will such evils for the sake of his or her own advantage. Such willing plainly is immoral; but does it constitute hatred of others? In one sense it does, in another it does not.

It is not hatred inasmuch as it is not motivated by personal antipathy, and so need not involve the desire that another suffer; a person might regret the evil he or she causes. But it plainly is hatred inasmuch as such willing is contrary to the love people should bear toward others. In short, such ill will toward others is not *affective* hatred (not motivated by personal antipathy), but it is *effective* hatred (a willing of evils for others).

Moreover, someone who hates others effectively is likely to develop emotional antipathy toward them. For instance, those who treat members of another nation, race, or sex unjustly often cultivate false images of them and nurture emotional hatred toward them, for then they can imagine that their victims deserve the treatment they get.

---

16. Anger is not necessarily bad, but one must handle it in a Christian way; see Bert Ghezzi, *The Angry Christian: How to Control—and Use—Your Anger* (Ann Arbor, Mich.: Servant Books, 1980).

7. Most Kinds of Sins Against Others Admit Parvity of Matter

Any sin against others involves either hating them, wrongly accepting what is bad for them, or failing to will what is good, and such willing either is at odds with loving them or manifests a serious defect in love. In general, therefore, sins against others are grave matter, the stuff of mortal sin. However, most also admit parvity (littleness, slightness) of matter, since on occasion the harm suffered or benefit lost can be so small as to be almost insignificant and hardly against the other person's will.[17]

a) **The tolerance of upright people sets the standard of parvity.** In small ways everyone fails in specific responsibilities toward others, and so nobody wishes to be held in all strictness to fulfill them. In fairness, therefore, neither should any reasonable person want others to be held strictly to fulfill every duty, no matter how insignificant, toward himself or herself. Consequently, in any type of situation, love of neighbor does not gravely require avoiding every harm and providing every benefit to others precisely as one should; rather, it only gravely obliges one to what is necessary to meet the standard of interpersonal conduct to which upright people generally would want and expect others in that kind of situation to be held. "Do unto others as you would have them do unto you" defines the full requirement of love, but "Do unto others as you would have them be held to do unto you" defines the limit beyond which the matter of a sin against another becomes grave.

b) **The standard of parvity must not be misunderstood.** The condition which sometimes mitigates wrongs done to others, so that there is parvity of matter, is easily confused with facile rationalizations of grave wrongs.

First, this mitigating condition is not met by mutual tolerance among wrongdoers which is not shared by people of upright will. Members of a particular community often condone certain unjust actions; they then are likely to ignore the harm their acts do to people outside their community. For example, competing businesses often do not wish to hold one another to high standards of honesty, so their managers rationalize the harm to customers by pointing out that their competitors are similarly dishonest: "Everybody does it." However, the harm customers suffer is not insignificant to the customers; and the managers want businesses held to higher standards of honesty when they, their loved ones, and friends are customers. So, the tolerance of competitors is not the proper standard for parvity of matter.

Second, the mitigating condition can make a kind of sin venial only insofar as its wrongness depends on its unfairness to the person harmed. Many kinds of acts,

---

17. The explanation here develops the insight of St. Thomas, *S.t.*, 2–2, q. 59, a. 4, who holds that to do what is unjust is of itself against love and so *ex genere suo* mortal sin. But to the argument that to do what is unjust in some small matter only minimally falls away from the standard, and so is tolerable and should be counted among minor evils, he replies (ad 2): "One who does an injustice in something small falls short of the complete idea of what it is to do the unjust, inasmuch as it can be considered not to be entirely against the will of the one who suffers this, for example if someone takes one apple from another or something like that, with respect to which it is likely that the other is neither harmed nor upset." Also see *S.t.*, 2–2, q. 66, a. 6, ad 3; q. 118, a. 4.

however, are wrong not only inasmuch as they are unfair but on other grounds, and the matter of such acts can remain grave on these other grounds even if everyone affected approves their being done. For example, the grave wrong of homicide is not only in its unfairness to the victim but in its violation of the basic good of human life. Thus, euthanasia remains grave matter even if everyone involved, including the person killed, regards it as an insignificant harm or even as a benefit. Similarly, a husband and wife who approve of each other's infidelity do not thereby render it light matter.

Question B: What Is Justice?

In fulfilling the whole law, love fulfills every requirement of justice. There are many theories of what justice is, and Jesus' teaching concerning love of neighbor provides a criterion for evaluating them: the Golden Rule. This criterion makes it clear that most theories of justice are either false or inadequate, while an adequate account will reduce all other criteria of justice to the Golden Rule itself and to other moral requirements governing even those actions that do not bear on others.

Scripture uses *justice* in a wide sense to mean goodness and holiness in general—Joseph was a just man (see Mt 1.19). Here, however, the word is used in its usual, narrower sense to refer to rightness in people's interactions and interrelationships. Even in this sense, *justice* expresses several closely related concepts rather than a single, simple concept. It is necessary to begin by making several distinctions and disengaging the three most important concepts. Then false accounts of justice must be examined and set aside. Next, several inadequate accounts can be criticized, and from that criticism the elements for an adequate account can be drawn. Finally, it is necessary to see how various kinds of rights are related to justice.

1. The Word *Justice* Refers to Several Distinct Realities

Considered from a moral point of view, people's interactions and interrelations involve four distinct but closely related realities that can be called "just" (or "unjust"). Here, these referents of *justice*—that is, the realities to which the word refers—are distinguished. (The corresponding referents of *unjust* or *injustice* are obvious, and readers can easily supply them.)

a) Justice belongs to certain objective situations. In one sense, *just* refers to an objective situation involving either an action affecting others or an interpersonal relationship that is as it ought to be. The just is what ought to be brought about (see *S.t.,* 2–2, q. 57, a. 1). *Justice* is used in this sense when someone says: "The stolen property has been restored and the thief tried and punished, so justice has been done." Again, if a man does what is objectively required toward another but does it with an immoral intention, people say: "He did the right (that is, the just) thing for the wrong reason." And when two children are dividing a candy bar and the perfectly just state of affairs would be pieces exactly equal in size, if one child accepts a slightly smaller piece, saying, "That's fair enough," the child refers to justice in this objective sense.

b) Justice belongs to certain morally good human acts. In a second sense *just* refers to the moral quality of a good act which bears on another or others and tends to bring about the objectively just: one speaks of a just choice or act as one speaks of a chaste choice or act. The word *justly* is used in this sense when someone says: "The jury's decision was fully in accord with the law and the facts, and so the members of the jury acted justly." Again, the child who settled for the slightly smaller piece of candy acted both justly and unselfishly. In what follows, the main focus is on justice in this sense, the justice of choosing and acting toward others.

c) Justice belongs to the character of certain persons. In a third sense *just* refers to a person whose just choices and actions have formed a character that disposes him or her toward, and facilitates, further just choice and action. *Justice* is used in this sense when someone says: "That judge and that jury are conscientious people, men and women of real justice!" Again: "That child, young as she is, has the virtue of justice." *Justice* in this sense is defined in a classical formula as "the enduring and unwavering willingness to give to all other persons what is rightfully theirs" (see *S.t.,* 2–2, q. 58, a. 1).

d) Justice characterizes certain societies and social structures. In a fourth sense *just* refers to the quality of interpersonal relationships which are harmonious rather than disturbed by wrongdoing and ill will. Thus, justice is found in a community whose members' just acts have provided their community with structures—laws, practices, and institutions—embodying their own habitual justice. The word *just* is used in this sense when someone says: "Good citizens seek to build a just society."

2. There Are Narrower and Broader Concepts of Justice

Justice is giving others their due, what is owed them (see *S.t.,* 2–2, q. 58, a. 1). But *giving others their due* can be understood in different ways: in a narrow sense, as fulfilling responsibilities defined by prior undertakings toward others; in an important, wider sense, as being fair to others, that is, acting in accord with the Golden Rule. And it can be understood even more inclusively: acting uprightly in any action bearing on others. In this broadest sense of *giving others their due,* all the goodness of a good act counts as justice insofar as that act has some bearing on others. So in this third sense, fulfilling duties and being fair are important parts of justice but not all of it.

a) Justice is fulfilling one's prior undertakings toward others. In making a promise, entering into a contract or covenant, or accepting a social role with its responsibilities, one usually owes the other or others that undertaking's fulfillment. *Duties* in a narrow sense refers to such obligations in justice.

Justice in its wider senses usually requires that such duties be fulfilled. But not always, for sometimes a promise is rightly broken or an undertaking is rightly left unfulfilled in some respects. For example, citizens rightly make exceptions to their allegiance to their country if it engages in an unjust war, and parents properly break their promise to take the children to the zoo on Sunday afternoon if the weather is cold and damp and one of the children seems to be coming down with the flu. It may also be just to leave such a duty unfulfilled in a particular case because one impartially judges that some other duty's conflicting demands ought to be fulfilled. (On resolving conflicts of duties, see 5.K.)

Something due because of one's own prior undertaking is an especially obvious requirement of justice. Supposing justice never to require anything except fulfilling duties of this sort, children (and even adults) therefore often deny its less obvious requirements. Thus, an adolescent is likely to rationalize disobedience, and so violate justice toward his or her parents, by saying: "I didn't choose my parents, so I don't see why I must obey them." Again, there is a political theory which maintains that citizens have no duty to obey laws they neither directly nor indirectly consented to (see 11.B.3.b, below).[18]

b) **Justice is being fair to others.** An injustice can be done without breaking any prior commitment, for example, robbing and killing a harmless stranger. In considering that act unjust, one presupposes a meaning of justice, based on equal personal dignity, which is wider than fulfilling one's prior undertakings. This meaning, recognized by most people if not all, is formulated in Scripture as the Golden Rule, which requires fair treatment of everyone without exception. Plainly, the robbery and killing are unfair—excluded by the Golden Rule—although they violate no prior undertaking to the stranger. Similarly, rebellious children and extreme libertarians nevertheless want the advantages of familial and political community for themselves, and if they occupied different positions in the family or society, they would want others to obey certain decisions to which those others had not consented.

Justice in this second sense also undergirds justice in the first sense. Since, in general, people want others to fulfill their undertakings, they generally violate the Golden Rule if they fail to fulfill their own. Yet there are times when the Golden Rule requires not fulfilling a prior undertaking. That is the case with citizens who set aside their oath of allegiance when their country engages in an unjust war: they would not want the citizens of another country to carry on a similar war against them. Again, if changed circumstances gave the children disappointed about missing the promised trip to the zoo a good reason for breaking some promise of theirs, they would not wish to be held to it.

c) **Justice is moral goodness as a whole in its bearing on others.** If *justice* is taken in the widest sense, even the requirement of fairness is not broad enough to cover all cases of injustice. In this widest sense, injustice is any immorality a person does precisely insofar as he or she knows, or should know, that it harms, is to the disadvantage of, or bears wrongly upon one or more other persons.

For instance, someone not only does wrong but wrongs others in knowingly leading them into sharing in wrongdoing, so that they give in to temptations they otherwise would not have experienced. This can happen where there is no prior undertaking or preexisting definite relationship—and without any unfairness, if the one who leads others into wrongdoing harms himself or herself in the same way, and they consent to the sin. For example, Jane, a drug addict, shares her supply

---

18. The American *Declaration of Independence,* 1776, invokes that theory in asserting that legitimate governmental authority rests on "the consent of the governed."

with a fellow addict, who otherwise might be driven to seek rehabilitation. It also can happen where a social institution embodies other immoral principles without violating the Golden Rule: John challenges George to a round of Russian roulette, to be conducted in a way involving no partiality. In such cases those who participate in the wrongdoing act unjustly toward one another even though they act impartially.[19]

d) Moral goodness in its bearing on oneself is not justice. It might be objected: If doing wrong that harms others is unjust to them even when it involves no partiality whatsoever, it could just as well be said that doing wrong which harms oneself is unjust to oneself. But no one says that. For example, nobody considers overeating unjust, except to the extent it affects someone other than the person who does it. This is because the ideas of justice and injustice always include a relationship with another or others (see *S.t.,* 2–2, q. 59, a. 3, ad 2). (Of course, people do say figuratively of those who fail to do something as well as they can that they are not doing themselves justice, or of those who modestly disclaim the praise due them that they are not being fair to themselves; but, as everyone recognizes, these are extended uses of *justice* and *fair*.)

3. Certain Theories of Justice Are Simply False

Proponents of some kinds of legal positivism more or less share the view of Thomas Hobbes that justice is nothing else than what the law actually requires.[20] As this account would have it, each society's justice is peculiar to it and relative to its particular system of law: justice changes as the law changes. Moreover, no law can be unjust, unless in conflict with some more basic law within the same system. This theory is at odds with faith's teaching that there is a moral law written on the human heart, clarified and interpreted by divine revelation (see Rom 2.15; *CMP,* 7.A–B). Closely akin to cultural relativism, it is vulnerable to the same critique (see *CMP,* 4.E).

According to utilitarianism, justice is whatever arrangement will bring about the "greatest good of the greatest number." The underlying assumption is that human interactions and relationships create a social situation as their product, and justice is the disposition of those interactions and relationships which, under the given conditions, is most likely to result in the best possible social situation.[21] This

19. This concept of injustice is analogous to the concept of sin, which is any immorality one does considered precisely insofar as it offends God (see *CMP,* 13.B.1). Thus, Scripture calls moral goodness as such "justice" ("righteousness") inasmuch as it is consonant with God's will. See H. Seebass and C. Brown, "Righteousness, Justification," in *The New International Dictionary of New Testament Theology,* ed. Colin Brown, 3 vols. (Grand Rapids, Mich.: Zondervan, 1975–78), 3:352–77.

20. A critique of some current forms of legal positivism: John Finnis, "Natural Law and Legal Reasoning," in *Natural Law Theory: Contemporary Essays,* ed. Robert P. George (Oxford: Oxford University Press, 1992), 134–57.

21. Today utilitarianism often takes other forms, for example, the economic analysis of law, as promoted by the Chicago school of economics and law. See Richard A. Posner, "Utilitarianism, Economics, and Legal Theory," *Journal of Legal Studies* 8 (1979): 103–40; he claims that the proper goal of the legal system is maximization of social wealth, that is, the state of affairs in which all goods are in the hands of those who value them most, where *value* is defined by

theory emerged as nonbelieving humanists shifted their hope from the heavenly kingdom to this world; it overlooks the truth that, so far as human efforts are concerned, human life and community do not draw their value from anything they produce. Rather, they have an ongoing and open-ended character, and, considered as materials for the heavenly kingdom, their value is inherent in them. Thus, utilitarianism is radically at odds with Christian faith and hope. Moreover, it offers no practical account of justice, since it requires that judgments be made by means of proportionalism, which is intrinsically incoherent (see *CMP*, 6.F).

4. Some Widely Accepted Accounts of Justice Are Inadequate

Besides theories of justice which are simply false, there are others which are true up to a point but inadequate. This is so because the reality of justice is complicated and the concepts of justice multiple, so that people often mistake the special features of what is just in particular kinds or aspects of interpersonal relationships for essential features of justice itself. To understand justice as fully and accurately as possible, these mistakes must be avoided.

a) **Justice is not reducible to fulfilling agreements.** This point was made (in 2.b, above), but it is worth adding another reason why this concept of justice is inadequate, namely, that some agreements, although knowingly and freely entered into, are unjust. For example, a woman whose automobile breaks down in a rough neighborhood, and who fears that she might be attacked or her car might be vandalized, may willingly agree to the demand by the driver of a passing tow truck to pay him fifty dollars more than he usually charges. The driver is plainly taking advantage of the woman's plight, and so the agreement lacks objective equality in exchange and is unjust. The same is true of any agreement in which one party takes advantage of another's special need.[22]

b) **Justice is not merely objective equality in exchange.** While objective equality in exchange might be necessary for justice in contractual arrangements, this requirement cannot be the fundamental principle of justice. For many questions of justice arise quite apart from any exchange, for example, questions about the justice to future generations of exhausting natural resources and to people around the world of polluting the environment. Moreover, even in exchanges, the comparative evaluation of what each gives and receives, which is necessary for determining equality, presupposes some just standard. But what can determine the justice

---

willingness and ability to pay in money. More recently, Posner has modified his position; see his *The Problems of Jurisprudence* (Cambridge, Mass.: Harvard University Press, 1990).

22. Leo XIII, *Rerum novarum*, *ASS* 23 (1890–91) 662, *PE*, 115.45, applies this to wage contracts: "Let the working man and the employer make free agreements, and in particular let them agree freely as to the wages; nevertheless, there underlies a dictate of natural justice more imperious and ancient than any bargain between man and man, namely, that wages ought not to be insufficient to support a frugal and well-behaved wage-earner. If through necessity or fear of a worse evil the workman accept harder conditions because an employer or contractor will afford him no better, he is made the victim of force and injustice." Paul VI, *Populorum progressio*, 59, *AAS* 59 (1967) 286, *PE*, 275.59, generalizes the norm, which he applies to contracts made between nations: "When two parties are in very unequal positions, their mutual consent alone does not guarantee a fair contract; the rule of free consent remains subservient to the demands of the natural law."

of a standard used to measure equality in exchange? Not the mere fact that it is accepted by the parties, since the same motives leading people freely to enter into unjust agreements can lead them to accept unjust standards for measuring equality in exchange.

In economic matters, market price often is used to measure equality in exchange. Of course, some participants can manipulate markets unfairly to their own advantage. But even if a market is not manipulated, there are three reasons why market price cannot always serve as a just standard.

First, some exchanges—for instance, those involved in friendships—involve goods such as affection and evils such as suffering for which there can be no market. Here it seems to be a just standard for equality in exchange that the parties receive what they merit by their contributions to the relationship.

Second, some exchanges involve goods such as persons or sexual acts for which there can, but should not, be a market. Here the market price, whatever it is, cannot settle what is just in the relationship, inasmuch as what is exchanged should not be treated as a commodity, and so should not be priced.

Third, the market itself often reflects injustices in the system of which it is a part. For example, when unemployment is high, the market price of a person's work often falls below what he or she needs to survive. Again, the market price of commodities exported by underdeveloped nations often is inadequate for them to import what they need. Here it seems that a just standard of equality must at least allow both parties to the relationship to continue living and contributing to it—in other words, justice will require that the weaker party receive enough in return to meet basic needs.[23]

Besides, the criterion of objective equality cannot be applied to those interpersonal relationships and interactions which do not involve an exchange. For example, something other than objective equality in exchange excludes killing strangers, since that exclusion does not originate in cooperative relationships involving exchange. Similarly, objective equality in exchange does not regulate the relations of parents to children; in treating their children as they should, parents do not benefit by receiving from their children goods and/or services objectively equal to those they provide, but by becoming good parents and enjoying the fulfillment proper to that role.

---

23. John Paul II, *Centesimus annus,* 34, *AAS* 83 (1991) 836, *OR,* 6 May 1991, 11, points out that "there are many human needs which find no place on the market," and explains: "Even prior to the logic of a fair exchange of goods and the forms of justice appropriate to it, there exists *something which is due to man because he is man,* by reason of his lofty dignity. Inseparable from that required 'something' is the possibility to survive and, at the same time, to make an active contribution to the common good of humanity." Again, in 40 (*AAS* 843, *OR,* 12): "Here we find a new limit on the market: there are collective and qualitative needs which cannot be satisfied by market mechanisms. There are important human needs which escape its logic. There are goods which by their very nature cannot and must not be bought or sold. Certainly the mechanisms of the market offer secure advantages . . .. Nevertheless, these mechanisms carry the risk of an 'idolatry' of the market, an idolatry which ignores the existence of goods which by their nature are not and cannot be mere commodities."

c) **Justice is not always determined by one's merits.** Some hold that, since justice consists in giving everyone what he or she deserves, its fundamental principle is merit. However, this view's plausibility depends on the ambiguity of *deserve*. In a broad sense, people deserve whatever is due them, and *desert* in this sense is coextensive with justice. In a narrower sense, people deserve something only if it is due them on a specific kind of basis, namely, performance that both meets some standard of excellence and has a social value; *desert* in this sense is merit, but it is not coextensive with justice.

Many responsibilities in justice do not depend on merit. Parents have great responsibilities toward their newborn babies, who plainly lack merit based on performance: babies do nothing to deserve the protection and care their parents owe them. Even in the wider political society, merit cannot be the sole standard for requiring contributions and distributing benefits. For some are incapable of contributing enough to earn even as much as they need to survive, yet if an affluent society neglects them and allows them to die, it violates justice.

In cases in which justice clearly consists in treating people according to merit, the responsibility can be reduced to the requirement of fairness, which is determined by the Golden Rule. For example, in a business organization, pay and promotions are given to motivate and facilitate the performance which the organization needs to achieve its purpose. So, those who work harder and more productively merit by making a greater contribution to achieving the business's purposes; they deserve more in the way of pay and promotions. If, in the absence of compelling reasons, salary increases and promotions instead go to those whose contributions are mediocre, the manager clearly is acting on the basis of favoritism, and so violates fairness. Therefore, other rational considerations being equal, fairness requires that all employees be treated according to their merits.

d) **Justice is not always a matter of satisfying basic needs.** Not only Marxists but many others hold that justice consists in members of a community contributing according to their abilities and receiving according to their needs.

Sometimes this plainly is so. For instance, when a man and a woman marry and have children, the family forms, as it were, one body. As with a natural body, where each part contributes as it can and receives, so far as the whole can manage, what it needs, so in the family each member should contribute as he or she can and receive from common resources what he or she needs, so far as the whole family can supply. The various human goods served by family life, together with the requirement of fairness, demand this unequal sharing of burdens and benefits because of the special kind of community a family is.

Indeed, even in the relationships between employers and employees, and between more and less developed nations, need certainly is a factor in determining what justice requires. Here too the goods at stake and the requirement of fairness demand that the needs of the weaker party be taken into account in setting the standard of justice in the relationship.

But need cannot be a principle of justice in every human interaction. The injustice of killing strangers, for example, does not arise from any need of theirs; in contracts between parties who cannot take advantage of one another, need is irrelevant to the standard for determining fairness in exchange; in a business partnership or an athletic association, the members' needs are not the right standard for distributing profits or praise.

e) Justice is more than equal distribution of benefits and burdens. Some people focus on justice as objective equality in the distribution of benefits and burdens among members of a group, especially a political society. This objective equality also is required by fairness under certain conditions, namely, if there is nothing that morally calls for inequality in distribution.

But this notion plainly does not cover all cases. Respecting the lives of strangers is not a matter of distributing anything—for example, the sanctity of life—whether equally or otherwise; parents who distribute everything equally to a newborn, a six-year old, and a teenager do not treat them justly; in business partnerships and athletic associations, differences in merit justify inequality in the distribution of benefits and burdens.

f) Justice is not reducible only to fairness. Even though most other proposed principles of justice, insofar as they are at all helpful, are reducible to fairness, fairness is not the only principle of justice. It is always a necessary condition, but not always sufficient, for justice. In other words, while no unfair act can be just, sometimes acts involving no partiality to anyone are unjust. For, as has been explained (in 2.c), one can do wrong, and harm others in doing it, without being unfair. That constitutes injustice in the broadest sense.

5. The Principles of Justice Are Moral Rectitude and Fairness

Partial accounts of justice describe it accurately only to the extent they specify applications of the fundamental conceptions of justice previously stated: in general, and most broadly, what the modes of responsibility (see *CMP,* 8) require in actions bearing on others; more specifically, the requirements of fairness, that is, the Golden Rule.

a) The inadequate accounts point to useful standards of justice. Provided a person acts fairly and violates no other mode of responsibility, justice is done whether or not there is balance in exchange, equality in distribution, giving and receiving in proportion to capacity and needs respectively, or treatment on the basis of any specific sort of merit. Still, in appropriate circumstances, each of these criteria can point to what fairness requires; rightly understood and applied, they are useful *standards* of justice. But because they are not *principles* of justice, their use must be governed by the Golden Rule and everything else required for actions to be upright, whether or not they bear on others.

b) The traditional kinds of justice presuppose the same principles. In the Church's teachings and in theological works, one often finds a distinction among various kinds of justice: legal, commutative, distributive, and social. They are not always understood uniformly within the tradition, but no matter how interpreted, they do not point to principles of justice independent of the Golden Rule and the other modes of responsibility.

Commutative justice, regardless of the precise definition given it, pertains to fairness in the interactions and interrelationships of two more or less equal parties.

Discussions of commutative justice refer to standards such as objective equality in exchange, contractual duties, and so on. As has been shown, all these are reducible to the Golden Rule. Similarly, distributive justice, regardless of the precise definition given it, requires fairness in the relationship between communities and their members. Discussions of it contain references to standards such as merit, need, and ability to contribute—all, again, reducible to the Golden Rule.

Legal—or, as it is sometimes called, "general"—justice has been interpreted in two quite different ways. One sees it as the complement of distributive justice: the duties a community's members have to it. The other considers it the underlying duty to respect and promote every common good, which gives rise both to communities and to cooperative relationships between and among individuals and groups.[24] Considered either way, legal or general justice cannot be reduced to the Golden Rule alone, since the Golden Rule presupposes an interrelationship requiring fairness, while legal or general justice not only requires fairness within relationships but obliges one to act as a responsible person in constituting and participating in various communities. This requirement, however, is reducible to other modes of responsibility (see *CMP*, 8). For, as will be explained (in C.1, below), it is the basic human goods and the modes of responsibility governing each person's action in respect to them which require individuals to form and participate in communities.

Social justice is never mentioned by St. Thomas; commutative and distributive justice, as he understands them, take in all social interactions and interrelationships. However, during modern times, commutative and distributive justice came to be understood more narrowly, so that they no longer seemed to require that all individuals and groups in a society direct their private actions bearing upon one another to the common good. This narrowing had the bad effect of seeming to imply that only justice in its narrowest sense—the duty to carry out one's prior undertakings—is required in private interrelationships and interactions. The magisterium therefore developed the idea of social justice in order to affirm the responsibilities and rights which were being ignored or denied. But since all of these responsibilities are reducible to the other kinds of justice as St. Thomas understood them, social justice does not presuppose any additional principle.[25]

---

24. See John Finnis, *Natural Law and Natural Rights* (Oxford: Oxford University Press, 1980), 184–88.

25. For the history of *social justice* and its meaning: Jean-Yves Calvez, S.J., and Jacques Perrin, S.J., *The Church and Social Justice: The Social Teaching of the Popes from Leo XIII to Pius XII (1878–1958)* (Chicago: Henry Regnery, 1961), 138–53; Jean-Yves Calvez, S.J., *The Social Thought of John XXIII: Mater et Magistra,* trans. George J. M. McKenzie, S.M. (Chicago: Henry Regnery, 1965), 94–99. Pius XI most clearly defines social justice in *Divini Redemptoris, AAS* 29 (1937) 92, *PE,* 219.51 (translation amended): "In reality, besides commutative justice, there is also social justice with its own set obligations, from which neither employers nor workingmen can escape. Now it is of the very essence of social justice to demand from each individual all [*id omne ab singulis exigere*] that is necessary for the common good. But just as in the living organism it is impossible to provide for the good of the whole unless each single part and each individual member is given what it needs for the exercise of its proper functions, so it is impossible to care for the social organism and the good of society as a unit unless each single part and each individual member—that is to say, each individual man in the dignity of his human

In any case, none of these distinctions is needed to deal with concrete questions of justice. That is clear from the historical changes in the interpretation of the kinds of justice, especially the magisterium's introduction of social justice, as well as from the fact that these various kinds of justice are all reducible to more basic principles. Since the distinctions are not needed, they will not appear in the remainder of this work except in references to the teaching of the Church or to other authors.

6. Rights Are Not an Additional Principle of Justice

One way of articulating the most general notion of a right is: a right is a relational moral attribute of a person or group which corresponds to a responsibility that another or others have toward that person or group. So, if X acts unjustly toward Y by not doing or doing A, then Y has a right that X do or not do A. (If Carl acts unjustly toward Jane by not paying her a certain sum of money, then Jane has a right to be paid that sum by Carl; since Carl acts unjustly toward Jane if he kills her, Jane has a right that Carl not kill her.)

Because there are different sorts of responsibilities toward others, there are different sorts of rights. As that suggests, rights are a consequence, not a principle, of what justice requires.[26] Thus, while the Church's teaching often refers to rights in order to call attention to the demands of justice, simply affirming rights does not clarify why justice requires what it does.

a) **Two distinctions with respect to rights must be kept in mind.** To understand the relationship between rights and justice, it is necessary to distinguish various sorts of rights corresponding to diverse responsibilities.

i) Some rights are natural but others are not. Since some responsibilities toward others are not specified by any choice or action either on their part or society's, some rights are natural, for example, the right of everyone not to be sexually assaulted and the right of children to be cared for by their parents (see *S.t.*, 2–2, q. 57, a. 2). But many responsibilities toward others do arise from some sort of mutual agreement or social choice, for example, the rights of parties to a contract or of citizens to be treated according to the law. These rights are not natural and sometimes are called "conventional" or "positive"; they include the rights conferred by law. In the United States, for instance: the right not to be tried for a felony without first being indicted by a grand jury, the right of those covered by Social Security to receive payments according to the law's provisions.

---

personality—is supplied with all that is necessary for the exercise of his social functions." This definition itself suggests that social justice involves no new principle of justice, but was needed because other traditional kinds had been narrowed to exclude some of justice's requirements. This narrowing was in part due to an ideological limitation of viewpoint to the contractual and individual; see, John Paul II, Address to the Workers of the Solvay Factory (near Livorno), 6, *AAS* 74 (1982) 599–600, *OR,* 5–12 Apr. 1982, 10. But it also was due to theoretical confusions; see Finnis, *Natural Law and Natural Rights,* 184–88, 196.

26. John XXIII, *Pacem in terris, AAS* 55 (1963) 264, *PE,* 270.28–30, teaches that rights and duties correspond in two ways: (i) in the same person, for example, one's right to life corresponds to a duty to preserve one's life; (ii) in different persons, inasmuch as a right in one person corresponds to a duty in others to recognize and respect it.

ii) Some rights are immunities; others are entitlements. Since some responsibilities toward others are fulfilled simply by not doing things which harm or interfere with them, some rights are immunities, namely, from that harm or interference. Since other responsibilities toward others are to do things that help or benefit them, other rights are entitlements, namely, to that help or benefit. Thus, the natural right not to be sexually assaulted is an immunity; the natural right of children to their parents' care is an entitlement. Similarly, the legal right not to be tried without being indicted is an immunity from that jeopardy, and the legal right to receive Social Security payments is an entitlement to that income.

b) **The Church's teaching mainly concerns natural rights.** In the Church's teaching, the concept and language of rights are used to articulate the requirements of justice in political society, especially but not exclusively with respect to economic matters. While social doctrine is of course concerned with legal rights, it has far more to do with injustices in laws, policies, and social and economic practices which directly and gravely violate human dignity and the natural rights of persons and families.[27] Therefore, the rights mentioned in the documents of the magisterium almost always are natural rights.

Vatican II speaks of "fundamental rights," in respect to which all persons are equal, as they are equal in basic dignity (see GS 29). Fundamental rights are a kind of natural rights: those which every human being has just insofar as he or she is a person, for example, the rights not to be killed, to be treated with respect, and to have and use a portion of subhuman creation to meet basic needs. These correspond to equally universal duties, which all human beings have toward one another. But fundamental rights do not include those natural rights corresponding to duties within specific relationships. The right of children to parental care, for instance, is natural but not fundamental, because it corresponds to the duty assumed by couples in becoming parents. (Obviously, in drawing this distinction, there is no suggestion that rights which are natural but not fundamental are unimportant or that violating such rights is not, in general, gravely wrong.)

c) **Rights are consequences, not principles, of justice.** Some natural rights that are immunities correspond to moral duties always and everywhere incumbent on everyone. These rights and duties are grounded in basic human goods and the modes of responsibility which exclude choices to impede, damage, or destroy them. So, to each moral absolute forbidding certain acts which affect others, there corresponds a right which everyone enjoys. Every society should recognize,

---

27. Leo XIII, *Rerum novarum, ASS* 23 (1890–91) 646, *PE,* 115.13, teaches: "A family, no less than a State, is, as We have said, a true society, governed by an authority peculiar to itself, that is to say, by the authority of the father. Provided, therefore, the limits which are prescribed by the very purposes for which it exists be not transgressed, the family has at least equal rights with the State in the choice and pursuit of the things needful to its preservation and its just liberty. We say, 'at least equal rights'; for, inasmuch as the domestic household is antecedent, as well in idea as in fact, to the gathering of men into a community, the family must necessarily have rights and duties which are prior to those of the community, and founded more immediately in nature. If the citizens, if the families on entering into association and fellowship, were to experience hindrance in a commonwealth instead of help, and were to find their rights attacked instead of being upheld, society would rightly be an object of detestation rather than of desire."

respect, and protect every person's inherent dignity, and so should do nothing which violates any moral absolute. What is at work here is justice in the widest sense.

Other natural immunities correspond to moral duties limited by other morally relevant considerations, and these rights and duties are grounded in other modes of responsibility, which lead to norms that generally but not always exclude doing certain harms to others. For example, the right affirmed by Vatican II to practice one's religion corresponds to political society's duty not to interfere with the free exercise of religion, but this duty itself is limited by the requirements of social peace and public morality (see DH 7). Similarly, one's right to one's property corresponds to the duty which others have to respect one's peaceful possession and use of it; but this duty itself can be limited by the fair claim which these others might have to one's property. Rights of this kind also belong to everyone, and should be respected by every society, yet their proper limits need to be recognized. In the instances cited, these follow from the way fairness and, in some cases, other modes of responsibility set limits to political society's tolerance of religious activity and to everyone's duty to respect others' property.

Some natural rights that are entitlements correspond to general, affirmative responsibilities always and everywhere incumbent on everyone. These rights are grounded in basic human goods and the modes of responsibility which require everyone to be prepared to cooperate with others and to treat them fairly (see *CMP,* 8.B, 8.E). Among these entitlements are everyone's right to be admitted as an equal into any human community unless its common good requires that he or she be excluded or be treated differently from other members. While such natural entitlements are conditional ("unless its common good requires . . . "), they are important, because they put the burden of proof on those who would exclude others or treat them unequally.

Other natural entitlements correspond to duties which some have toward others in specific kinds of relationships and which must be fulfilled in such relationships for the interaction to be fair and otherwise just. Thus, those to whom the duty pertains are not permitted to evade it. For example, children have a natural right, which is an entitlement, to be cared for; this right corresponds to the duty of their parents to care for them. People have a choice about whether to become parents, but if they enter into the relationship, they violate the Golden Rule in failing to care for their children. Another important instance is the right of workers to a living wage (on this right and the corresponding duty, see 10.A.3.f–g).

d) **In the the social teaching of the Church, rights are not basic principles.** Various documents of the magisterium, especially since the social encyclicals of John XXIII, speak of rights in ways which might be taken as suggesting that they are basic principles. For example, sometimes the magisterium speaks broadly about rights without specifying who has the duties corresponding to them.[28] Pope John, however, clearly teaches that both rights and duties flow from moral principles:

---

28. For example, John XXIII, *Pacem in terris, AAS* 55 (1963) 260, *PE,* 270.13, teaches that everyone has the right to a good general education, but does not consider who can and should provide it.

"These rights and duties derive their origin, their sustenance, and their indestructibility from the natural law, which in conferring the one imposes the other. . . . Every basic human right draws its authoritative force from the natural law, which confers it and attaches to it its respective duty."[29] Thus, the Church's teaching about rights presupposes a whole body of moral truth, including but not limited to the requirement of fairness.[30]

By proclaiming rights, recent Church teaching calls attention to areas of social life where people's real needs are not being fairly met and those who should meet them may not see their duties because they view justice too narrowly. Thus, sometimes the Church's teaching about rights points out that efforts should be made to discover what the requirements of justice are: to clarify what agent can and should meet people's needs. In some cases, fairness will require that the state step in and in others some other existing agent, while in still others it will be necessary to form some new community or modify an existing one.

Question C: How Does Community Generate Responsibilities toward Others?

Since justice and injustice always presuppose an interpersonal relationship, they plainly are related to community. Not all communities come into existence in the same way or have the same character. Responsibilities in all of them, however, flow from moral principles.

1. A Morally Good Life Must Be Not Only Individual but Communal

Human persons not only are individuals; together they make up communities. Much modern thought erroneously assumes that individuality is natural and community artificial. But our relationships are as primordial and real as our substantiality, and our communal reality is as natural and essential to our fulfillment as our individuality is. Vatican II teaches: "Humankind's social nature makes it evident that the progress of the human person and the advance of society itself hinge on each other" and affirms that "social life is not something added on to the person" (GS 25).[31]

a) **Human persons are created for communion.** That human persons are inherently interdependent is evident: a human is naturally a social animal. Human

---

29. John XXIII, *Pacem in terris, AAS* 55 (1963) 264, *PE,* 270.28, 30.

30. Like the duties to which they correspond, some rights inevitably conflict, and when they do, conflicts can be resolved only by reduction to more basic principles: goods and modes of responsibility. See Finnis, *Natural Law and Natural Rights,* 218–21.

31. The great emphasis in Catholic social teaching on the dignity of the person is entirely misunderstood if it is interpreted in an individualistic sense. Many passages make it clear that the true dignity of human persons is inseparable from their social nature; for example, John XXIII, *Mater et magistra, AAS* 53 (1961) 453, *PE,* 267.219, explains: "This teaching rests on one basic principle: individual human beings are the foundation, the cause and the end of every social institution. That is necessarily so, for men are by nature social beings." Of course, confirmed individualists find such passages paradoxical and are likely to suppose wrongly that the teaching is inconsistent.

sociability, moreover, transcends that of any other species, for language is a powerful and supple means of communication, enabling men and women to cooperate in endless and ever new ways. Indeed, they become self-conscious and establish their individuality only within interpersonal relationships.

Only divine revelation makes clear the full significance of human persons' social nature. The beginning of the book of Genesis tells how God created humankind male and female in order that man and woman, with their different gifts, might complement one another, and so form a communion. Interdependence—people's need for one another and their inability to fulfill themselves as isolated individuals—is clear: "It is not good that the man should be alone; I will make him a helper as his partner" (Gn 2.18). Subsequent chapters make it clear that sin underlies divisions among people and their difficulty in communicating with one another (see Gn 11.1–9). Thus, Vatican II teaches: "God did not create human beings for life in isolation, but for the formation of social union" (GS 32). This natural vocation to community belongs to human persons as made in God's image, foreshadows the revelation of their likeness in communion to the Trinity, and is the natural foundation for their calling to enter into communion with the divine family.[32] Consequently, human "solidarity must be constantly increased until that day on which it will be brought to perfection. Then, saved by grace, humankind will offer flawless glory to God as a family beloved of God and of Christ their brother" (GS 32).

b) The principles of morality are not individualistic. Integral human fulfillment, the ideal distinguishing moral good from moral evil, "is not individualistic satisfaction of desires; it is the realization of all the human goods in the whole human community" (*CMP*, 7.F.3). The modes of responsibility following from this first principle, especially the Golden Rule, exclude not only choices unnecessarily restricting concern about goods but also those which involve inadequate regard for other persons.

c) The basic human goods are not inherently individualistic. The good purposes for which people act have two aspects. One is that of a concrete goal, which appeals to imagination and feeling. The other is that of a benefit or set of benefits, which are hoped for inasmuch as they are intelligibly good. For example, the purpose of treating a throat infection with an antibiotic includes both the goal of eliminating the soreness and the benefit of restoring health by killing the bacteria. Concrete goals, insofar as they are the objects of imagination and feeling, are particularized: if achieved, they fulfill the emotional desire of an individual (or of a group bound together by feeling) to the exclusion of other individuals (or groups). The result is that, at the level of imagination and feeling, *your* goals are not *mine*, *their* goals are not *ours*.

Unlike concrete goals, however, hoped-for benefits, insofar as intelligibly good and volitionally pursued, are not particularized. These benefits are participations

---

32. See John Paul II, *Mulieris dignitatem*, 6–8, *AAS* 80 (1988) 1662–70, *OR*, 3 Oct. 1988, 3–4. Cf. Aristotle, *Nicomachean Ethics* 8.12.1162a16–18: "Between man and wife friendship seems to exist by nature; for man is naturally inclined to form couples—even more than to form cities."

in the basic human goods, which are the starting points of all practical thinking (see *CMP*, 5.B, 5.D, and 7.D). "Understandable goods do not have anyone's proper name attached to them" (*CMP*, 24.A.7). As a result, at the level of understanding and will, *your* benefits can be *mine*, *their* well-being can be *ours*.[33]

d) The basic human goods often must be pursued as common goods. The point to be explained here requires an understanding of *common good*. If an agent—a person or group—acts rationally for the sake of one or more goods, hoping that not only the agent but another or others will be benefited for their own sake, at least one good for which the act is done is common to the agent and the other or others to be benefited. (How this works out in various cases will be explained in 2, below.) *Common good* refers to such a good, whether one agent acts with the hope of benefiting another person or group, or two or more agents act together with the hope of mutual benefit. So, the point here is that the basic human goods often must be pursued through actions done in the hope of benefiting not only the agent but also another or others for their own sake.

The need to pursue the basic human goods as common goods is most obvious in the case of some of the reflexive goods. Take friendship: it can be realized—for example, in marriage and in the new covenant—only by persons who, regarding the very communion they share as inherently worthwhile, are ready to act for one another's benefit, even in the absence of any other self-interest.[34]

But the substantive goods, such as life itself and knowledge of truth, also generally are pursued as common goods. For example, people cannot survive unless others care for them when they cannot take care of themselves—during infancy, when they are sick, and so on. Nobody spends the whole of life as a solitary, and few people survive for long except as members of a community (a family or substitute for it), in which at least one member acts to ensure not only his or her own survival but the survival of the other members. Similarly, no one knows much that he or she does not learn from others. Almost all people's ideas and information come from others' thinking and observations, and are accepted on their word. Thus, human knowledge depends on a shared interest both in other persons and in the truth. That community of interest presupposes that acts of knowing and of communicating knowledge can benefit both the agent and others together.

2. Communities Are of Several Diverse Sorts

Persons who live together constitute a potential community; it becomes an actual community through action for a common good. Different ways of acting for a common good generate different sorts of community. Some are formed by mutual consent, others by unilateral initiative, and still others without any choice on the part of the persons involved.

a) Every interacting group of people is a potential community. Humankind as a whole is a potential community, insofar as all human beings are neighbors who

---

33. See Germain Grisez, Joseph Boyle, and John Finnis, "Practical Principles, Moral Truth, and Ultimate Ends," *American Journal of Jurisprudence* 32 (1987): 114–15.

34. For a fuller explanation of this point, see Finnis, *Natural Law and Natural Rights*, 141–44.

live on the same planet, are naturally related, and share common concerns. All men and women should treat one another justly in the broadest sense and also in the sense of acting fairly (or, at least, not unfairly) toward one another, whether or not any prior undertakings have been made. So, Vatican II teaches: "Every social group must take account of the needs and legitimate aspirations of other groups, and even of the common good of the entire human family" (GS 26).[35]

Any more limited group of people whose actions affect one another—say, a group of people riding on an elevator—also can be thought of as a potential community insofar as its members, like humankind as a whole, are thrown together and have some moral responsibilities toward one another. Still, groups in which the interrelationships of the members are not shaped by any member's action for a common good—say, the occupants of an elevator who jostle one another and look out only for themselves—remain only potential communities. In not acknowledging their common interests and finding suitable ways to live and work together, the members fail morally, for example, if the occupants of the elevator do not considerately make room for one another and try to make sure that each passenger reaches his or her destination. But until they begin to act for a common good, they are a community in potentiality rather than in actuality.

b) **Some organized groups are not really communities.** Particular groups of people can become organized either by mutual choices or by a unilateral initiative. Either way, a group can be organized for entirely self-interested reasons, in which case no real community is formed. For example, a man and woman can enter into an agreement to exchange sexual intercourse for money, each willing whatever benefit the other gains purely out of self-interest, not only without love but even without respect for each other. Again, if someone unilaterally does something that benefits another, but does it only for selfish reasons, that act does not establish community. For example, a politician who donates to charity solely to win votes does not form community with those whom the charity assists.

c) **A group of people becomes a community in one of four ways.** Particular groups can become true communities either (i) by the members' recognizing one another as persons and treating one another fairly, (ii) by mutual choices, (iii) by unilateral initiatives, or (iv) by the members' accepting responsibilities arising out of a natural human relationship.

i) Sometimes extrinsic conditions bring two or more persons together, so that their actions affect one another's interests. For example, a group of people find themselves on a crowded elevator; two students register for the same tutorial course. Without sharing any other common purpose, people in such a group can recognize their actual relationship and, although they make no mutual commitment, wish to live together in accord with the requirements of fairness. Insofar as they are shaped by this common interest, various individuals' actions establish among

---

35. John XXIII, *Mater et magistra, AAS* 53 (1961) 439–42, *PE,* 267.153–65; *Pacem in terris, AAS* 55 (1963) 292–96, *PE,* 270.132–45, calls attention to the worldwide social question, including the need for a public authority of the world community, with an appropriate relationship to nation states.

them a minimal community, which is shaped and limited by the conditions that hold its members together.

ii) Sometimes two or more persons make choices by which they accept responsibilities toward one another. For example, two people agree to play a game of tennis or a couple marry. Here, forming the community is itself a communal act, for those who belong to the potential community join together to bring about their community and perfect it.

iii) Communities sometimes are formed by a unilateral initiative: some persons make choices in virtue of which they accept and have moral responsibilities toward others, and these others come to have responsibilities even though they have not made any choice to enter into community. For example, a couple make choices that lead to their becoming parents, and so constitute a community of parents and children. The children have responsibilities toward their parents, even though they did not choose to be members of that community. Again, the Good Samaritan chooses to help an unconscious victim of crime, and so actualizes his potentiality to be the victim's neighbor. The person helped owes the Good Samaritan gratitude and has a special duty to return the favor should it be needed.

iv) Sometimes two or more persons find themselves naturally related in a way which entails responsibilities; by acknowledging and accepting these, they develop human community. For example, brothers and sisters find themselves intimately related in such a way that they not only should treat one another fairly but should love and help one another. Similarly, a woman who finds herself pregnant as a result of rape is a mother; she develops this parent-child relationship by accepting her responsibility not to destroy her child.

d) Communities established by mutual choices are of two sorts. Communities constituted in the second way—by *mutual* promises or commitments—again are of two sorts.

i) The community can be limited to cooperation in a specified act or set of acts for the sake of their specific purpose or set of purposes. The mutual choices are promises, which may or may not be legally binding, and interpersonal relationship between or among the community members is not sought for its own sake. Still, the common action of the agents constitutes community insofar as they seek to benefit one another not out of pure self-interest but out of willingness to join in a fair and otherwise just relationship. For example, two tennis players agree to play a fair game, a group of men form an equitable business partnership. While those involved in such relationships may not be interested in community for its own sake, they do form communities insofar as they wish not only to benefit themselves but to act justly toward one another.

Communities of this kind can and often do differ from one another in important respects. The community between the tennis players may be limited to playing that one game; yet it may involve legal obligations on both sides, for example, if the two are professional athletes and their agreement is a contract to play an exhibition game. Although also strictly limited in its purpose, the business partnership may be established by a complex legal agreement, with the expectation that it will last indefinitely.

ii) The community can be open-ended: it can extend to cooperation for the sake of sharing in some kind or kinds of good, where the sharing transcends the limits of the purpose or purposes of any particular act or set of acts. The action forming the community is not merely a means to some other good; and the interpersonal relationship itself is sought for its own sake and may be the primary good sought. Once a community of this sort has begun to exist, concrete purposes for at least some of its actions can be specified and altered without changing the community itself. Some very important communities are of this sort: friendships, marriage, and the Church.

Such a community sometimes can be established without any lasting, covenant commitment. For example, two people sitting next to each other on a long flight discover that they have much in common and agree not to watch the movie so that they can spend the time in conversation; they talk seriously about what is closest to their hearts and, though not expecting to meet again, briefly enjoy real friendship. However, open-ended communities tend of themselves to endure, and often are established by explicit commitments. For example, a man and woman marry, committing themselves to live together for the sake of their marital relationship itself, having children, and fulfilling their vocation.

e) **Communities established by a unilateral choice are open-ended.** When people make unilateral choices to benefit others, thus establishing community with them—as a married couple do when they have children—the community always is open-ended, since the good of the interpersonal relationship itself is not merely chosen as a means to an end but intended for its own sake. Even if, as in the case of the Good Samaritan, the relationship begins with one person's acting for a definite purpose to benefit another, that benefit is not the common good which the agent intends, because the agent does not personally share in it: the Good Samaritan does not recover from an attack as the robbers' victim does. The Good Samaritan intends to benefit the man he helps because he intends neighborliness or friendship with him as a common good, in which both share.

Someone might object that the community the Good Samaritan establishes with the victim is not open-ended in the same sense as the community parents establish with children. The Good Samaritan makes no lasting commitment, conducts no ongoing relationship, and serves only the limited purpose of rescuing the injured man. However, the Good Samaritan is not motivated to rescue him simply by that benefit to the victim. He is a Good Samaritan precisely because he cares about the victim for his own sake, and wants to be a good neighbor to him. In principle this intention is not limited by the particular benefit which it motivates the Good Samaritan to bestow. Of course, a good neighbor's responsibilities to strangers are not the same as those of parents to children, but both communities are open-ended insofar as they are defined, not by limited purposes extrinsic to the relationship, but by the good of the interpersonal relationship itself.

This point becomes clearer when the interpersonal relationship the Good Samaritan establishes is considered as a participation in the communion established by the new covenant. Jesus establishes this communion by his unilateral redemptive act, by which he intends to save other human individuals from sin and death, precisely so that they can share with him in heavenly communion. He commands his followers to extend covenantal communion to others, and uses the parable of the Good Samaritan to teach this lesson. In the parable, he makes the point that, by what the Good Samaritan did, he made himself the neighbor of the man who needed help—established community with him. In caring for the victim as he did, the Good Samaritan necessarily intended communion with him.

3. Moral Principles Generate Communal Responsibilities

Where people are constituted as a community in any of the ways described, their community-forming choices do not by themselves create new moral responsibilities; instead the choices bring about new responsibilities only by opening up fresh possibilities for pursuing human goods and bringing relevant moral principles to bear in fresh ways.

a) **Moral responsibilities flow from moral truth.** In communities formed and sustained by mutual consent, members obviously would have no communal responsibilities without their consent; yet their consent does not create their mutual responsibilities out of nothing. A moral responsibility is a claim made by moral truth upon one's choices, and the moral responsibilities of persons in community are claims made on them by the truth about the common good. Community-forming choices do not create any new moral truth but they do bring moral truth to bear in new ways, by creating opportunities for the community members to realize certain human goods together, and also by putting various of their goods at risk in new ways, so that they become vulnerable to one another's irresponsible behavior.

So, for instance, children can have serious responsibilities toward their parents, although they had no choice about being their children. Moreover, even after undertaking something by a promise or commitment, under some conditions one does not have a responsibility to fulfill it. This shows that the choice involved in the promise or commitment was not a sufficient condition of the moral responsibility.

b) **Fairness and other moral principles undergird communal duties.** The requirements of justice in the broadest sense and in the sense of fairness give promises and commitments their moral force (see B.4.a, above). Because many goods can be achieved only as common goods, one is obliged to enter into community when it is obligatory to pursue such goods. Even when it is optional, someone who decides to pursue them must undertake responsibilities toward others. If undertakings have been uprightly made, fulfilling them usually will benefit those to whom they were made, while failing to fulfill them generally will be unfair. That is why such choices can create responsibilities in justice in the narrowest sense, according to which justice simply is a matter of individuals and groups fulfilling their prior undertakings.

Since the responsibilities undertaken by a promise or a commitment arise from prior moral principles, sometimes they can be deliberately left unfulfilled without injustice (see B.2.a, above).

c) **Fairness is essential for all genuine community.** Although justice in the broadest sense extends beyond fairness, in a special way community rests on fairness as its foundation. As the Golden Rule makes clear, fairness is not simply a detached impartiality, a disengaged objectivity such as one brings to esthetic judgments. Rather, it is an impartial concern *for* all other people, modeled on one's concern for oneself and those near and dear. Such concern presupposes insight, not clouded by emotions such as self-hatred or unruly desire for immediate satisfaction, into the goods in which people must participate in order to be truly fulfilled. It also presupposes recognition of others as persons, distinct from oneself but sharing in the same inherent worth, and open to fulfillment in the same human goods.

It is impossible always to pursue every possible good for oneself or promote every good in those near and dear. But one should avoid doing anything to harm oneself and loved ones, unless there is an adequate reason for choosing to do something which causes harm incidentally, that is, as an unavoidable side effect. Thus, it is a pressing demand of fairness to be considerate of others, not intentionally to harm them or thwart their legitimate interests, and in making choices not to accept any side effects to others at odds with their upright will without good reasons for doing so—reasons they themselves, if they can grasp them and are reasonable, should appreciate and be able to accept.

If a group's members act thus toward one another, each can identify with the others in the way required for genuine community. Each can trust the community to safeguard his or her own interests, while the community can trust each member to serve common interests and set limits to the pursuit of individual interests. In this way, radical conflict is avoided and the basic harmony necessary for community is established.

Question D: Does the Common Good Take Precedence over the Good of Each Person?

The Church's teaching on social justice very often speaks of the common good of political society. In its name the Church rejects reducing justice to the mere fulfilling of contracts and other requirements of fairness in private dealing. For example, John XXIII teaches that "it is in the nature of the common good that every single citizen has the right to share in it—although in different ways, depending on his tasks, merits and circumstances. Hence every civil authority must strive to promote the common good in the interest of all, without favoring any individual citizen or category of citizen."[36] In trying to determine what justice requires, the limited interests of particular corporations, industries, classes, or any other parts of a political society cannot be given such weight that other parts are ignored.[37]

36. John XXIII, *Pacem in terris, AAS* 55 (1963) 272, *PE,* 270.56.

37. For example, John XXIII, *Mater et magistra, AAS* 53 (1961) 438–39, *PE,* 267.151, having stated other conditions for a sound economic and social policy, says: "But the justification of all government action is the common good. Public authority, therefore, must bear in mind the interests of the state as a whole; which means that it must promote all three areas of production—agriculture, industry and services—simultaneously and evenly. Everything must be done to ensure that citizens of the less developed areas are treated as responsible human beings, and are allowed to play the major role in achieving their own economic, social and cultural advancement."

At the same time, the Church's teaching treats the common good of political society as instrumental to the full good of persons: "The common good of society consists in the entirety of those conditions of social life under which men and women enjoy the possibility of achieving their own perfection in a certain fullness of measure and also with some relative ease" (DH 6; cf. GS 26, 74). Although social duties sometimes can require extreme self-sacrifice, people are not simply parts of society. The state exists for its citizens, not, as totalitarians imagine, citizens for the state (see 11.B.2.b, below).

Although both ways of talking about the common good are sound, they nevertheless can seem incompatible. According to the first, the common good seems to take priority; according to the second, the good of the individual. As what follows (in 2) will show, the inconsistency is merely apparent.

1. *Common Good* Will Be Understood in Terms of Basic Goods

Common good sometimes is used to refer to purely instrumental goods. For example, members of a family share their home, and members of a political society share a system of roads, parks, and so on. These things can be considered elements of the common good, taking *common good* in a wide sense.

In the following analysis, *common good* is used in a more restricted sense to refer only to one or more of the *basic* human goods (see *CMP*, 5.D; 9.A.1.j, below), considered insofar as they underlie community. So, unless the context makes the contrary clear, goods such as property and liberty (that is, freedom to do as one wishes) should not be understood in what follows as elements of the common good. This does not imply that property, liberty, and other instrumental goods are of little or no human significance. In truth, they are important: while property in itself does not perfect persons, it is a necessary means to pursuing most of the basic human goods which do; and while liberty is open to both good and bad use, without it people lack many opportunities to act intelligently and freely, and so cannot live decent human lives. Yet vital as they are, instrumental goods such as property and liberty simply are not the foundations on which human community can be built.

2. The Common Good and the Good of the Person Are Not at Odds

The ultimate principle for integrating the good of the individual and the common good is the relationship, clarified by God's self-revelation, which ought to exist between any communion of persons and the distinct individuals who share in it.

a) **Divine unity and the distinction of persons are not at odds.** The Trinity is not reducible to its members considered in their distinction from one another. Rather, the three divine persons, united in their mutual communion, are God, and God is perfectly one in his reality, goodness, and love. Yet the three divine persons really are distinct, not merely parts of a larger whole. Their distinct personhood is in no way diminished or lessened by their being together the one God.

b) **Human persons and society are to be like the Trinity.** God reveals that he has created human persons in his own image and likeness, made them by nature communal as he himself is, and called them to membership in his divine family (see GS 24). So, for humankind too, personal reality and fulfillment cannot belong to one individual apart from others. As Vatican II teaches: "God did not create human beings for life in isolation, but for the formation of social union" (GS 32). A human person can be fulfilled only by sharing in communion with the divine persons and other created persons:

> Indeed, the Lord Jesus, when he prayed to the Father, "that all may be one . . . as we are one" (Jn 17.21–22) opened up vistas closed to human reason. For he suggested a certain likeness between the union of the divine persons and the union of God's children in truth and charity. This likeness shows that the human person—the only creature on earth which God willed for its own sake—cannot fully find himself or herself except through a sincere gift of self. (GS 24)

In this passage, the phrase, "the only creature on earth which God willed for its own sake," calls attention to the fact that, although human persons are communal by nature, their distinct personalities, created by the divine persons on the model of their own selves, cannot be subordinated, as if they were mere parts or instruments, to any community.

c) **The common good and the individual's good include each other.** The common good is a good or set of goods in which a community's members share. Indeed, in the case of communities formed by their members' choices, the common good is that for whose sake the many individuals form the community and act together. And in choosing to act for the common good of any community, each member also at the same time acts for his or her own good, which can be called his or her "proper" good (from the Latin word *proprium*). *Proper* good here does not mean suitable or legitimate good, but simply the benefit he or she personally hopes to receive in and through the common action. Thus, rather than excluding the goods of a community's members, the common good embraces their proper goods just insofar as these are shares in the common good; from the point of view of the members of any society, its common good contributes to their proper goods.

d) **This relationship of mutual inclusion takes two different forms.** How the common good and the proper good of a community member include each other differs according to the different sorts of community.

i) In open-ended communities, the common good embraces the proper goods of community members primarily insofar as their very relationship and cooperation enable them to participate personally in various aspects of the basic good of communion of persons, such as justice, love, and peace, which, although they cannot be divided and appropriated, are needed by each member for his or her fulfillment. And the proper goods of each person include the common good inasmuch as persons are fulfilled only by their morally upright action and genuine, mutual self-giving, which constitute the justice, love, and peace of the community as a whole.

ii) In a community established to pursue definite and limited concrete goals, the common good and the proper good of a member embrace each other in two ways. First, the common good of justice in interrelationships and interactions within the community includes each member's being justly treated by the others, which contributes to his or her proper good, while the good of each member's just personal conduct helps make the community as a whole good. Second, insofar as attaining their common purpose allows the members to divide and appropriate the fruits of their effort, the common purpose includes the personal objective of each and pertains to his or her proper good insofar as achieving the purpose is a necessary means to the objective. For example, an investment partnership's common purpose of making profits embraces each partner's proper good insofar as profits are divided and assigned to each one's account, while each partner's purpose of making a profit includes the success of the joint enterprise insofar as that is a means to his or her profit.

3. Open-ended Communities Call for the Attitude of Solidarity

While *solidarity* appears in previous Church teaching, John Paul II uses the word in a refined and specific sense: that specific moral attitude or virtue by which individuals fulfill themselves by including the common good in their proper goods.[38]

a) **Solidarity is commitment to the common good.** The moral ground of every open-ended community is the essential incompleteness and interdependence of human individuals, their need for one another not merely to achieve specific and limited objectives, but for fulfillment as persons. Such interdependence requires sharing in goods precisely as common. The appropriate response to the requirements of the common good is not merely sympathy for others but solidarity—true self-giving which, if mutual, constitutes communion.

Solidarity, in the first place, is a firm and enduring commitment both to other persons and to the good, so that what is realized through common effort really will benefit others as well as oneself. This commitment implements love of neighbor, for it undertakes the work of love: to serve others rather than dominate them, to sacrifice oneself for them rather than exploit them. Solidarity is itself implemented not only by accepting and doing one's part in common action, but by encouraging others and supporting them in doing their parts, without infringing on their proper spheres of responsibility.

b) **This new concept is useful for the Church's social teaching.** While not ignoring the need for commitment to the common good, previous Church teaching has regularly taken it for granted, and has not introduced a concept specifying this basic commitment.[39] It is an act of justice, but since love of neighbor is necessary in order to do justice, solidarity more profoundly implements love. Also, whereas

---

38. See John Paul II, *Sollicitudo rei socialis,* 38–40, *AAS* 80 (1988) 564–69, *OR,* 29 Feb. 1988, 10–11. Solidarity is not to be confused with conformism; it has room for loyal opposition, since its focus is not on social authority structures as such, but on the common good which underlies them: see Karol Wojtyla, *The Acting Person,* ed. Anna-Teresa Tymieniecka, trans. Andrzej Potocki (Dordrecht: D. Reidel, 1979), 283–87.

39. Assuming it is informed by charity, the virtue of general (or legal) justice, as St. Thomas conceives it (see *S.t.,* 2–2, q. 58, a. 5), comes very close to what John Paul II calls "solidarity." However, this concept was lost in the later, tripartite division of justice, according to which legal justice, rather than ordering everything to the common good, merely orients the parts of a community to the whole, or even merely orients individual citizens in doing their duties toward the state. For a critique of this unfortunate development and a defense of the superior (and authentically Thomistic) position, see Finnis, *Natural Law and Natural Rights,* 184–86.

previous teaching neglected to clarify the relationship between commitments and the acts that implement them, John Paul II's teaching on solidarity clarifies the need for a firm and lasting self-determination, which shapes all of one's social action.

The word *solidarity* also has certain rhetorical advantages. It can be understood, at least to some extent, by persons who lack explicit Christian faith, yet it does not limit the required moral trait to a merely natural virtue, which would prescind from charity. Moreover, it connotes the social character of the very good to which it refers: persons existing in solidarity act together—in a real sense, the community acts. Thus, the word helps overcome the mistaken idea that even virtues concerned with actions bearing on others can be realized as character traits of isolated individuals.

4. The Common Good of the New Covenant Community Is a Special Case

The common good of the divine-human communion formed by the new covenant is related in a unique way to the personal good of each created member.

a) This common good takes priority over that of each person. Here it is true that the common good is greater and more God-like than the good of individual created persons. For the new covenant communion is the incipient kingdom, which includes divine persons as well as the complete personhood and fulfillment of the created persons who share in it.

But this priority of the good of the kingdom over the good of its members does not imply what an analogous priority would in any other community. Indeed, in a certain sense it is not a priority at all, for it does not mean that Christians are limited, damaged, restricted, or deprived of anything for the kingdom's sake. All that must be given up is sin and what really harms and limits a human person. Hence, one's total subordination, if it can be called that, to the kingdom's good (the fulfillment of all things in Jesus) will be one's own total fulfillment as well.

b) This common good takes priority over every other common good. Inasmuch as the kingdom includes and transcends every other true good of created persons, the common good of the new covenant community takes priority over every other common good. As Paul VI points out, Jesus attributes such essential importance to the kingdom that everything else becomes incidental: "The kingdom of God is to be considered, therefore, as the absolute good so that everything else is subordinate to it."[40]

However, this does not mean earthly affairs lack their proper autonomy: "If by the autonomy of earthly affairs we mean that created things and societies themselves enjoy their own laws and values which we must gradually discover, put to use, and regulate, then it is entirely right to demand that autonomy" (GS 36). Nor may faithful Catholics neglect their responsibilities toward the common goods of lesser societies: "Whoever in obedience to Christ seeks first the kingdom of God receives from that a stronger and purer love for helping all his or her sisters and

---

40. Paul VI, *Evangelii nuntiandi,* 8, *AAS* 68 (1976) 10, Flannery, 2:714.

brothers and for perfecting the work of justice under the inspiration of charity [note omitted]" (GS 72).[41]

5. Both the Common Good and the Good of the Person Take Precedence

In lesser, merely human communities, the common good should not take absolute precedence over the good of each person, as it does in the kingdom. Even in political societies, the good of the person *as a member of the society* is subordinate to the common good of the society as a whole; but this subordination does not imply that the attainment of collective ends can ever justify sacrificing what is essential to the whole fulfillment of any person.

a) **The good of the person as a whole takes precedence.** No mere human community's good includes the whole fulfillment of any of its members. That is why the Church regards political society's common good as comprised of goods instrumental to the fulfillment of persons. Such a society is not constituted to organize cooperation for the sake of that common good which ultimately and completely fulfills persons, and it may not even contribute in any positive way to that part of their fulfillment which is most important, namely, their relationship with God (see DH 3, 6). So, the common good of political society must be subordinated to its members' total fulfillment.[42] It follows that the authority of political society is strictly limited; beyond those limits, it should respect the freedom of persons (see DH 7).

b) **A society's good takes precedence over the good of its members.** Still, insofar as any society's members are its members and some aspect of their good is part of its common good, their good is subordinate to the common good.[43] For since their good in that respect cannot be realized apart from the common good, and since the common good also includes the good of every other member as such, their good cannot be realized fairly unless every other member of the society fairly shares in the common good. That is why the Church insists, against every kind of selfishness,

41. Ideally, there should be no conflict between Church and state (see GS 76). But in practice, as Leo XIII points out, *Sapientiae Christianae, ASS* 22 (1889–90) 387, *PE*, 111.6: "Instances occur where the State seems to require from men as subjects one thing, and religion, from men as Christians, quite another." Leo, of course, teaches that in such cases the laws of Jesus and the just claims of the Church take precedence (see *ASS* 387–89, *PE*, 6–11). Yet the Church cannot simply absorb the state and preempt its proper functions, for although the Church is the incipient kingdom, she is not the kingdom absolutely; because the heavenly kingdom will include not only the goods which the Church now includes, but every good fruit of the nature and efforts of all those who have feared God and done what is right (see LG 9, 16; GS 39).

42. Leo XIII, *Sapientiae Christianae, ASS* 22 (1889–90) 385, *PE*, 111.2, having affirmed the transcendence of human persons' last end, deduces the subordinate role of society: "But what applies to individual men applies equally to society—domestic alike and civil. Nature did not form society in order that man should seek in it his last end, but in order that in it and through it he should find suitable aids whereby to attain to his own perfection."

43. John Paul II, Address to Agricultural Cooperative (Faenza), 4, *Inseg.* 9.1 (1986) 1343, *OR*, 2 June 1986, 6, explains: "You know, therefore, that the good of the individual members can be made to coincide with that of all and that the common good is revealed to be greater than the sum of the individual goods; it is a good which surpasses in quality the sum of the single individual goods."

that the common good should prevail in society over individual, class, group, and other particular interests.

6. The Common Good Is Not an Independent Principle of Justice

The fact that human goods can and sometimes must be pursued, realized, and shared in as common goods underlies the possibility of communities of all sorts. In this sense, each community's common good is the principle of its very being, and so of all the moral responsibilities pertaining to it. However, the common good is not an independent normative principle—not, that is, a source of responsibilities over and above the basic human goods, the first principle of morality, and its specification by the modes of responsibility (see *CMP*, 10.3).

a) The moral principles of justice are sufficient. The common good provides the reason for developing or accepting common structures and participating in cooperative actions. But not all social structures and actions are just, and the common good's priority itself does not settle what is just; it only requires that the community's structures and actions be just. Their justice is determined by the moral principles previously explained (in B), which include the other modes of responsibility as well as fairness. Specifying all that people must do when acting in respect to others, these moral principles specify the duties arising from any undertakings, including one's social roles. Hence, the common good provides no additional principle of justice.

b) Common instrumental goods are not moral principles. An important part of what is often considered any society's common good consists in goods which are merely instrumental. For example, a dwelling place and its furnishings are part of a family's common good, and public lands, roads, and buildings are part of a political society's common good. But inasmuch as such goods are not basic human goods, the moral responsibilities which pertain to them are in no way grounded in them as principles, but instead are grounded in the basic human goods they serve.

c) The moral implications of different common goods are different. The moral implications of different common goods differ, not precisely insofar as they are common goods, but insofar as they involve different aspects of the various basic human goods pursued by communities of persons. This can be seen by comparing the common goods of different sorts of community. A family's common good includes the intimate communion of family life, sharing together in family prayer and apostolate, the health and safety of every family member, and the personal development of each as husband, wife, mother, father, son, daughter, sister, or brother. The common good of a political society includes the civic friendship of fellow citizens, defense against external enemies, maintenance of domestic tranquillity, promotion and regulation of economic activities, and so forth (see 11.B.2.a). Since the common goods of the two sorts of communities are so different, family responsibilities are very different from civic responsibilities. The same kind of difference appears in individuals' responsibilities insofar as they pursue different goods. For example, one's responsibilities with respect to taking care of health differ from one's responsibilities in respect to doing good work.

7. There Are Good Reasons to Speak of the Common Good

If what has been said is so, one might wonder: Why does the Church's teaching talk about the common good at all? Why not simply talk about justice, assuming that justice is rightly and fully understood?

a) **The common good is the principle of community.** No community can function unless one or more persons act for a common good. All responsibilities of community members as such depend on the community's common good. Thus, the concept of the common good is irreducibly necessary in any treatment of society and social responsibilities. Even if justice is rightly and fully understood, it is impossible to understand its requirements for a society and its members without focusing on and speaking of that society's common good.

Moreover, because many duties toward others presuppose community, people often try to rationalize violations of justice by ignoring or denying community. The Church therefore speaks constantly about the common good in order to recall attention to the reality of community, in this way reinforcing the responsibilities that follow from one's role in it, from fairness, and from other moral principles.

b) **Some exploit society for their own purposes.** Existing societies are not in all respects genuine communities; to some extent they are arrangements by which some dominate and/or exploit others. By calling attention to the common good, the Church speaks out against injustice and defends the dignity of those dominated and exploited. For instance, after pointing out that individuals, families, and various groups cannot carry on a full human life by themselves, and so need a wider community to pursue their common good, Vatican II teaches: "The political community, therefore, exists for that common good. In that common good it obtains its whole justification and meaning. From that common good it derives the right which is original and specific to it [its irreducible and proper place in an objectively right order]" (GS 74). From this principle, the Council goes on to draw the conclusion that the political community's authority should be employed in protecting the rights of individuals, families, and various other groups (see GS 74–75).

c) **Justice is seldom understood rightly and fully.** Oversimplifications of justice abound. One of the most common and important reduces it to a particular form of equality in exchange or in distribution, then uses this oversimplification to rationalize injustices. For example, some argue: The workers made a free contract to accept this particular (inadequate) wage, so they are not entitled to a living wage. Or: The handicapped and the elderly require a disproportionate share of the resources available for health care, so care for them should be strictly rationed. However, even if political society is in some sense constituted by mutual consent, it is not reducible to a mere contract (as is a community organized for specific purposes); moreover, it should respond to requirements of a people living together in a way fair to all, even if they are not members by an act of consent, for example, the retarded, small children, and those so disadvantaged they cannot participate in social affairs. Also, even if members of a political society are in some sense equal, it does not follow that the diversity of their needs may be disregarded in distributing benefits. Against the use of such oversimplified models to limit social responsibilities, therefore, the Church appeals to wider standards of justice, demanding their application throughout a society. The common good is a useful concept to express this appeal.

Question E: How Does the Social Situation Shape
One's Responsibilities?

Love of neighbor and the principles of justice (treated in A and B) underlie all Christian responsibilities toward others. But these responsibilities also have another starting point: the actual human condition occasioning many of them and frequently giving rise to temptations not to fulfill them.

If everything in the world were as it should be, questions about social responsibilities could be answered relatively easily. They are especially difficult because injustice is rampant. Nevertheless, conditions are quite different in the affluent countries of the West and in the rest of the world. Since most readers of this book are likely to be Catholics in the United States and other English-speaking countries, most of them affluent, the following description concerns the contemporary social situation considered from this point of view, taking other parts of the world into account only insofar as people in the affluent countries have responsibilties toward everyone else.[44]

As this is written, great changes are taking place in the world. Most Marxist governments have fallen, and the Soviet Union no longer exists. Nevertheless, it still is worth comparing and contrasting Marxism and Western secularism, both for the light this sheds on the latter and because even today Marxism remains a significant factor in some nations and in the thinking of some intellectuals.

1. Secular Humanism Undermines Social Order

Both Marxism and liberal secularism deny the reality of God and, in doing so, deny that there are meanings and values prior to human thinking, desires, and choices. According to both these forms of secular humanism, the ultimate source of the distinction between good and evil must be found within human beings themselves—in their thinking, desiring, striving, and social consensus. While the various forms of pragmatism which dominate philosophical thinking in the United States and other affluent nations differ greatly from Marxism in their details, they agree with it in reducing morality to effectiveness in bringing about desired outcomes—"good" results.

a) **Justice loses objectivity, and the ultimate appeal is to force.** This relativity of morality to human agents leaves no objective basis for resolving conflicts among groups with mutually incompatible goals. As John Paul II points out, many today assume that democracy presupposes agnosticism and relativism:

---

44. Catholic social teaching often refers to "the social question." Pius XII, *Sertum laetitiae, AAS* 31 (1939) 642 and 653, *PE,* 223.34, succinctly clarifies the meaning of this expression: "The fundamental point of the social question is this, that the goods created by God for all men should in the same way reach all, justice guiding and charity helping." Thus, for Catholics today who live in the affluent nations, consideration of the social question must focus on responsibilities toward those both in their own nations and throughout the world who lack the basic necessities of life.

Those who are convinced that they know the truth and firmly adhere to it are considered unreliable from a democratic point of view, since they do not accept that truth is determined by the majority, or that it is subject to variation according to different political trends. It must be observed in this regard that if there is no ultimate truth to guide and direct political activity, then ideas and convictions can easily be manipulated for reasons of power. As history demonstrates, a democracy without values easily turns into open or thinly disguised totalitarianism.[45]

Secular humanist parties or societies cannot rationally ground appeals to justice, but they can and often do appeal to "justice" for rhetorical or propagandistic purposes. John XXIII teaches:

> Yes, both sides speak of *justice* and *the demands of justice,* but these words frequently take on different or opposite meanings according to which side uses them. Hence, when rulers of nations appeal to *justice* and *the demands of justice,* they not only disagree on terms, but often increase the tension that exists between their States. And so the belief is engendered that if a nation is to assert its rights and pursue its own interests, there is only one way open to it: to have recourse to violence; ignoring the fact that violence is the source of the very greatest evils.
>
> Mutual trust among rulers of States cannot begin nor increase except by recognition of, and respect for, the moral order.
>
> But the moral order has no existence except in God; cut off from God it must necessarily disintegrate.[46]

b) The hope that motivates justice and mercy is rejected. The consequences of original sin are real: suffering and death, whose prospect leads to insecurity and disorderly emotions (see *CMP,* 14.G). Yet despite these consequences, men and women, helped by grace, can live uprightly, provided they have an adequate motive. Hope for heaven is that motive. When the relationship between the heavenly kingdom and life in this world is rightly understood, that hope provides a fresh incentive for fulfilling social responsibilities (see GS 21, 34, 39, and 43; *CMP,* 34.D–G). But all forms of secular humanism mistakenly reject hope for heaven as if it were an obstacle to human welfare in this world. More than a century ago, Leo XIII pointed out the result:

> The supernatural truths of faith having been assailed and cast out as though hostile to reason, the very Author and Redeemer of the human race has been slowly and little by little banished from the universities, the lyceums and gymnasia—in a word, from every public institution. In fine, the rewards and punishments of a future and eternal life having been handed over to oblivion, the ardent desire of happiness has been limited to the bounds of the present. Such doctrines as these having been scattered far and wide, so great a license of thought and action having

---

45. John Paul II, *Centesimus annus,* 46, *AAS* 83 (1991) 850, *OR,* 6 May 1991, 13.

46. John XXIII, *Mater et magistra, AAS* 53 (1961) 450, *PE,* 267.206–8. Congregation for the Doctrine of the Faith, *Instruction on Christian Freedom and Liberation,* 19, *AAS* 79 (1987) 561, *OR,* 14 Apr. 1986, 2, likewise teaches: "When man wishes to free himself from the moral law and become independent of God, far from gaining his freedom he destroys it. Escaping the measuring rod of truth, he falls prey to the arbitrary; fraternal relations between people are abolished and give place to terror, hatred and fear."

sprung up on all sides, it is no matter for surprise that men of the lowest class, weary of their wretched home or workshop, are eager to attack the homes and fortunes of the rich; it is no matter for surprise that already there exists no sense of security either in public or private life, and that the human race should have advanced to the very verge of final dissolution.[47]

2. The Roots of Sin Take Special Forms in the World Today

Underlying all social injustice is personal sin. When people deny God and objective moral limits, they tend to become selfish and to regard others as mere means to their own ends. The contemporary magisterium clearly explains the dynamics:

> Having become his own centre, sinful man tends to assert himself and to satisfy his desire for the infinite by the use of things: wealth, power and pleasure, despising other people and robbing them unjustly and treating them as objects or instruments. Thus he makes his own contribution to the creation of those very structures of exploitation and slavery which he claims to condemn.[48]

Power, wealth, and pleasure become idols. Sin's roots are in the quest for status, possessions, and enjoyment—in pride, avarice, gluttony, and lust (see *CMP*, 18.D). But these perennial roots of sin assume particular forms in contemporary, materialistic culture, which leaves little or no room for heaven and assigns ultimate value mainly to things which here and now mitigate painful feelings or provide sentient satisfaction.[49]

a) **Pride takes the form of self-assertion and individualism.** By clarifying the dignity of human persons and the crucial importance of each one's free choices, the gospel itself fosters regard for human individuals and provides a solid basis for their self-respect. Of course, the gospel also calls individuals to mortify their sinful selves and serve others out of love. Removed from its evangelical context, the Christian insight into each individual's worth is perverted to rationalize sin. Thus, post-Christian humankind is susceptible to a distinctive moral pathology: egoistic individualism, which exalts the well-being and satisfaction of individuals above every community, even the family.[50]

When colored by this pathology, pride is not expressed exclusively by the quest for positions of social superiority; also, and even more arrogantly, it is seen in every individual's effort to be his or her own sovereign. Thus, the contemporary attachment to liberty to do as one pleases: "No one can tell me what to do." This attitude leads to rejection of authority generally as well as unwillingness to accept any social responsibility toward people for whom one has no personal feelings. Other people are to be ignored except to the extent that they are relevant to one's own purposes

---

47. Leo XIII, *Quod Apostolici muneris, ASS* 11 (1878) 370–71, *PE*, 79.2.

48. Congregation for the Doctrine of the Faith, *Instruction on Christian Freedom and Liberation*, 42, *AAS* 79 (1987) 571, *OR*, 14 Apr. 1986, 4.

49. For a summary of twentieth-century materialism: Pius XI, *Ubi arcano Dei consilio, AAS* 14 (1922) 681–82, *PE*, 192.21–24.

50. A sociocultural critique of a widespread mode of individualism: Christopher Lasch, *The Culture of Narcissism: American Life in an Age of Diminishing Expectations* (New York: W. W. Norton, 1978).

or can be made so. Then they are to be dominated and manipulated, so that at least they will allow one to gain one's ends and at best will serve one's purposes.

b) Avarice takes the form of consumerism. Material goods should be used as means to pursuing and serving basic human goods. Avarice is the will both to have material goods beyond those needed to achieve one's good purposes and fulfill one's responsibilities, and to use the excess for emotional gratification—to compensate for a sense of insecurity or personal inadequacy—or for some other illegitimate goal (see *S.t.*, 2–2, q. 118, aa. 1, 6).

Avarice has been an engine of modern socioeconomic development. Artificial needs are created, that is, demands for goods and services which give transient emotional gratification but provide little or no real benefit to the consumer in terms of fulfillment in any basic human good.[51] Consumerism involves wasting resources without regard for the needs of others.[52]

Rejection of authority facilitates avarice, since those who do not acknowledge their responsibilities toward the common good are less inhibited in seeking to satisfy their individualistic cravings without regard to others' misery. At the same time, avarice reinforces rejection of authority, since waste, unlimited consumption, and the accumulation of possessions incline people to disregard the social responsibilities whose fulfillment authority coordinates.[53]

c) Pleasure seeking serves pride and avarice and also uses them. Natural pleasures have their limits, and the quest for them is the same today as always. But modern technology offers new opportunities for pleasure seeking, not least by providing more resources and leisure. Moreover, the abuse of drugs, both legal and illegal, offers new sensory satisfactions and makes it possible to suppress feelings which ought to motivate realistic efforts to deal with guilt and other evils.

Avarice uses pleasure seeking as a means, for example, by playing on this motive in advertising.[54] Rejection of authority facilitates pleasure seeking, since it enables people to set aside responsibilities that would limit self-indulgence. Pleasure seeking also reinforces rejection of authority, for self-gratification which has become habitual must be defended against any claims beyond the self.

51. For instance, advertising—often morally questionable on other grounds—frequently leads people to purchase new fashions or new models, when they could as well take care of and continue to use their serviceable clothing, appliances, automobiles, and so on. See John Kenneth Galbraith, *The Affluent Society*, 4th ed. rev. (New York: New American Library, 1985), 121–28.

52. See John Paul II, *Sollicitudo rei socialis*, 28–29, *AAS* 80 (1988) 548–51, *OR*, 29 Feb. 1988, 7.

53. It might be objected that the avaricious, rather than rejecting authority, strongly support law and order as safeguards of their wealth. However, the avaricious reject regulation of their own activities in accord with the common good; their selective support of the use of governmental power is not the same thing as submission to the moral claim of the common good, which alone is true acceptance of authority (see 11.B.3).

54. On the use of sex in advertising, see Eric Clark, *The Want Makers: The World of Advertising: How They Make You Buy* (New York: Viking, 1989), 113–18.

3. These Forms of Sin Explain This Culture's Characteristic Features

Afflicted with the same moral evils, the affluent countries of the West have common features in their social trends and conflicts, as well as in their anxieties. While every age and culture have their own moral defects—human history knows no golden age or paradise—the contemporary situation calls for a Christian response, and the magisterium sketches it in somber but accurate tones.

a) The moral quality of life is deteriorating in many ways. Among these social and cultural trends are the increasing incidence of violence against persons, including killing of the innocent (especially by abortion), sexual assault, and child abuse; decline of family life and abandonment of faithful relationships (indicated by increases of cohabitation and divorce); failure to care for the needy, even by their own families; the widespread abuse of mind-altering substances; the overwhelming of rational discourse by sophistry and outright lying in politics, the media, and even in supposedly scholarly works; the lowering of academic standards in many places; and decline in levels of skill and performance, as almost everybody wants more pay but few care about doing fine work and providing excellent service.[55]

b) Disregard of justice generates intractable social conflicts. Writing in 1922, Pius XI observed that disregard of justice causes "war between the classes, a chronic and mortal disease of present-day society, which like a cancer is eating away the vital forces of the social fabric." Likewise, he pointed out that political conflicts often originate in "desire for power and for the protection of some private interest which inevitably result in injury to the citizens as a whole."[56] True, in the United States and some other affluent nations whose economies support a large middle class, social conflicts do not occur in their classic form. Replacing such conflicts, however, are other injustices as great or greater: the urban poor are crushed or brutalized by wretched living conditions, people yet unborn are saddled

---

55. Papal documents repeatedly deplore the deterioration in the moral quality of life, and point to the link between self-indulgence and social injustice. Benedict XV, *Sacra propediem, AAS* 13 (1921) 38–39, *PE,* 189.18, calls unlimited desire for riches and thirst for pleasures the "stigma" of the epoch, and remarks that the wealthy "seem to wish to further excite the hatred of the poor by an unbridled luxury which accompanies the most revolting corruption." Pius XI, *Ubi arcano Dei consilio, AAS* 14 (1922) 678–79, *PE,* 192.14, laments "the morbid restlessness which has spread among people of every age and condition in life, the general spirit of insubordination and the refusal to live up to one's obligations which has become so widespread as almost to appear the customary mode of living. We lament, too, the destruction of purity among women and young girls as is evidenced by the increasing immodesty of their dress and conversation and by their participation in shameful dances, which sins are made the more heinous by the vaunting in the faces of people less fortunate than themselves their luxurious mode of life." John Paul II, *Sollicitudo rei socialis,* 28, *AAS* 80 (1988) 548, *OR,* 29 Feb. 1988, 7, similarly condemns "consumerism" for waste which deprives the poor of their fair share of goods and services originally meant for all: "This superdevelopment, which consists in an *excessive* availability of every kind of material goods for the benefit of certain social groups, easily makes people slaves of 'possession' and of immediate gratification, with no other horizon than the multiplication or continual replacement of the things already owned with others still better."

56. Pius XI, *Ubi arcano Dei consilio, AAS* 14 (1922) 677–78, *PE,* 192.12.

with a huge public debt, many potentially poor people are exterminated in the womb, and the working poor at home and abroad who contribute what they can to the nation's wealth are not paid a family wage as justice requires.[57]

c) **Anxiety is fueled by awareness of complicity in evil.** People in the affluent nations not only fear the potentially cataclysmic consequences of world politics based on mere power, but are anxious because their wealth and progress come about through morally defective economic structures (on sinful structures, see 4.A.3.e). Having described the former source of anxiety, John Paul II speaks of the latter:

> All this is happening against the background of the gigantic remorse caused by the fact that, side by side with wealthy and surfeited people and societies, living in plenty and ruled by consumerism and pleasure, the same human family contains individuals and groups that are suffering from hunger. There are babies dying of hunger under their mothers' eyes. In various parts of the world, in various socio-economic systems, there exist entire areas of poverty, shortage and under-development. This fact is universally known.
>
> The state of inequality between individuals and between nations not only still exists; it is increasing. It still happens that side by side with those who are wealthy and living in plenty there exist those who are living in want, suffering misery and often actually dying of hunger; and their number reaches tens, even hundreds of millions. This is why moral uneasiness is destined to become even more acute. It is obvious that a fundamental defect, or rather a series of defects, indeed a defective machinery is at the root of contemporary economics and materialistic civilization, which does not allow the human family to break free from such radically unjust situations.[58]

While not everyone in the affluent nations of the West shares in their wealth and power, anyone who does so enjoys advantages resulting from unjust social structures and should reflect conscientiously on the situation, in order to identify special responsibilities he or she may have to help rectify it.

d) **This somber analysis can be defended against criticisms.** The preceding analysis will be criticized by those who say it goes beyond the boundaries of moral theology and involves an overly pessimistic reading of sociological data. The contemporary social situation, some argue, is in general no worse, and in some ways is measurably better, than those of earlier times. The answer is that the recent magisterium (especially John Paul II) supports the main lines of the analysis, which, after all, is only a rough sketch, not a detailed description of all aspects of the current situation. The point of this sketch, moreover, is not to compare the state of the contemporary world with earlier situations, but to criticize the contemporary situation by Christian principles, in order to make it clear that many contemporary phenomena are morally defective.

---

57. John Paul II, *Centesimus annus,* 47, *AAS* 83 (1991) 852, *OR,* 6 May 1991, 13, teaches: "Even in countries with democratic forms of government, these [basic human] rights are not always fully respected. Here we are referring not only to the scandal of abortion, but also to different aspects of a crisis within democracies themselves, which seem at times to have lost the ability to make decisions aimed at the common good."

58. John Paul II, *Dives in misericordia,* 11, *AAS* 72 (1980) 1213–14, *PE,* 279.113–14.

4. The Church Rejects Individualism and Criticizes Capitalism

Individualism is a characteristic feature of the liberal secularism of the affluent nations of the West, and it has strongly influenced their capitalistic economies, while Marxism is characterized by collectivism. The Church's social doctrine analyzes these opposing ideologies and provides specific reasons for rejecting both as equally false, even if not always and in every respect equally pernicious in practice.[59]

The basis of the Church's social teaching is the requirement of love of neighbor and respect for the dignity of each human person. From this flows the anti-individualistic requirement of social solidarity: everyone should contribute to the common good, and private property entails social responsibility. From it likewise flows an anticollectivist requirement: individuals and small communities should be allowed to realize themselves by exercising their freedom, owning property, and fulfilling their responsibilities.[60]

This section deals with the Church's social teaching bearing on individualism and capitalism, the next with her teaching regarding Marxism and the socialist approach to economics.

a) **Individualism involves an inadequate notion of society.** Modern individualism is rooted in an ideological affirmation of freedom, according to which the free person should be a self-sufficient individual whose life is directed to getting what he or she wants in this world.[61] Individualism gives individual rights priority over social responsibilities. Political society then becomes either a mere arrangement lacking any common good whatsoever or, at best, something resembling a business partnership, whose participants primarily pursue their individual interests and have a common good only insofar as they share the commitment to be fair to one another.

In reality political societies are not like business partnerships, and they are not constituted by their members' mutual consent. Rather, any political society exists because families and groups of families live in proximity to one another, share many interests and other things in common, and therefore must recognize themselves as a community and accept their responsibility to cooperate for the sake of

59. John Paul II, *Sollicitudo rei socialis*, 41, *AAS* 80 (1988) 571, *OR*, 29 Feb. 1988, 11, explains the relationship between the Church's social doctrine (a "set of principles for reflection, criteria for judgement and directives for action") and the conflicting ideologies: "The Church's social doctrine *is not* a 'third way' between *liberal capitalism* and *Marxist collectivism*, nor even a possible alternative to other solutions less radically opposed to one another; rather, it constitutes a *category of its own*. Nor is it an *ideology*, but rather the *accurate formulation* of the results of a careful reflection on the complex realities of human existence, in society and in the international order, in the light of faith and of the Church's tradition. Its main aim is to *interpret* these realities, determining their conformity with, or divergence from, the lines of the Gospel teaching on man and his vocation, a vocation which is at once earthly and transcendent; its aim is thus *to guide* Christian behaviour. It therefore belongs to the field, not of *ideology*, but of *theology* and particularly of moral theology."

60. See Congregation for the Doctrine of the Faith, *Instruction on Christian Freedom and Liberation*, 73, *AAS* 79 (1987) 586, *OR*, 14 Apr. 1986, 6.

61. See Congregation for the Doctrine of the Faith, *Instruction on Christian Freedom and Liberation*, 13, *AAS* 79 (1987) 559, *OR*, 14 Apr. 1986, 2.

mitigating potential conflict and promoting other common goods, especially justice in their society itself (see 11.B.2.a).

Therefore, while citizens have many rights which political society ought to safeguard, including political and civil rights which set moral and legal limits to public authority itself, a political society's members should not regard it as a mere instrument for promoting their private interests. Rather, they should accept and fulfill their social responsibilities as an irreducible part of their true fulfillment as human persons living together in their national community.

b) Liberalism absolutized private property. In the economic field, eighteenth-century and nineteenth-century individualism was called "liberalism," because its proponents believed those engaging in economic activities should enjoy as much liberty as possible from social regulation, with government's main responsibility in the economic sphere being to protect the freedom of private enterprise and transactions. Liberalism tended to absolutize the right of private owners freely to use and dispose of property for their individual advantage, regardless of the needs of people toward whom they have no contractual duties. Liberals held that there are no natural economic entitlements for political society to recognize. They maintained that society should recognize only those entitlements corresponding to free undertakings in relationships established by mutual consent, and that laws should protect and facilitate the fulfillment of those rights and duties.

These theories provided the ideology underlying laissez faire capitalism and shaped its practices well into the twentieth century.[62] Still, some participants in capitalistic economies have recognized and tried to fulfill the social responsibilities of business, and a significant evolution of capitalism gradually occurred due to the pressures of opposing social and political forces.

c) Catholic social teaching requires social solidarity. The Church responded to economic liberalism by teaching that people have some natural entitlement rights. These include rights to a living wage, education, and so forth. Catholic social teaching urges that these rights be taken into account in social policy making. While defending private property, Catholic teaching also insists that God created material goods to fulfill the needs of every human person. As a result, ownership entails responsibility for the care and right use of material goods. Vatican II sums up this teaching:

> God has destined the earth and all it contains for the use of all human individuals and peoples, in such a way that, under the direction of justice accompanied by charity, created goods ought to flow abundantly to everyone on a fair basis [note omitted]. One must always bear this universal destination of

---

62. Paul VI, *Populorum progressio*, 26, *AAS* 59 (1967) 270, *PE*, 275.26, describes this ideology: "These concepts present profit as the chief spur to economic progress, free competition as the guiding norm of economics, and private ownership of the means of production as an absolute right, having no limits nor concomitant social obligations. This unbridled *liberalism* paves the way for a particular type of tyranny, rightly condemned by Our predecessor Pius XI, for it results in the 'international imperialism of money'." (The reference is to *Quadragesimo anno, AAS* 23 [1931] 212.)

goods in mind, no matter what forms property may take, as it is adapted, in accordance with diverse and changeable circumstances, to the legitimate institutions of peoples. For this reason, in using those goods, people should consider the exterior things which they legitimately possess not only as their own but as common, in the sense that their possessions should benefit not only themselves but others as well [note omitted]. (GS 69)[63]

The ultimate aim of a just property system in allocating ownership—that is, responsibility for the right use—of material goods is to satisfy fairly the needs of all insofar as that can be done. Thus, Catholic teaching, while defending private property, at the same time undercut what individualists regarded as their absolute right to private property and freedom of contract, and called on the state to make a special effort to defend the rights of the poor and disadvantaged.[64]

d) **Classical capitalism did not yield the benefits it promised.** Apologists for laissez faire capitalism claimed that it was justified by its good fruits. Noting the economic progress of capitalist nations, they attributed their achievements to free enterprise and competition in free markets. In response, Catholic social teaching pointed out that the ideal of free competition tends in practice to give way to economic domination. As the prosperity of the 1920s collapsed in the face of the economic crisis of 1929–31, Pius XI made the point: "Free competition has destroyed itself; economic dictatorship has supplanted the free market; unbridled ambition for power has likewise succeeded [that is, followed after] greed for gain; all economic life has become tragically hard, inexorable, and cruel."[65]

Recent Church teaching continues the critique of the laissez faire system. Paul VI, for example, points out that voluntary trade carried on only with a view to the immediate interests of the parties concerned often increases the disparity between rich and poor nations, and adds: "Market prices that are *freely* agreed upon can turn out to be most unfair. It must be avowed openly that, in this case, the fundamental tenet of *liberalism* (as it is called), as the norm for market dealings, is open to serious question."[66]

e) **The Church still regards capitalism with reserve.** While capitalism has evolved in some respects, even today libertarians (now often called "conserva-

---

63. On this Christian conception of property, see 10.D.1, below. For the background in prior papal teaching, see Calvez and Perrin, *The Church and Social Justice*, 190–225. A concise summary of this teaching from Leo XIII on: John Paul II, *Centesimus annus*, 30, *AAS* 83 (1991) 830–31, *OR*, 6 May 1991, 10. John Paul II, *Laborem exercens*, 18, *AAS* 73 (1981) 623, *PE*, 280.82, says that the "principle of the common use of goods" is the "fundamental principle of the moral order in this sphere," and (19, *AAS* 626, *PE*, 89) that this principle is "the first principle of the whole ethical and social order." Also see John Paul II, *Sollicitudo rei socialis*, 42, *AAS* 80 (1988) 573–74, *OR*, 29 Feb. 1988, 11–12.

64. Leo XIII, *Rerum novarum*, *ASS* 23 (1890–91) 658–59, *PE*, 115.37, having pointed out that public authority should defend everyone's rights, says: "Still, when there is question of defending the rights of individuals, the poor and badly off have a claim to especial consideration. The richer class have many ways of shielding themselves, and stand less in need of help from the State; whereas the mass of the poor have no resources of their own to fall back upon, and must chiefly depend upon the assistance of the State."

65. Pius XI, *Quadragesimo anno*, *AAS* 23 (1931) 211, *PE*, 209.109.

66. Paul VI, *Populorum progressio*, 58, *AAS* 59 (1967) 285–86, *PE*, 275.58.

tives," although not all conservatives are libertarians) still maintain an individual-istic ideology. Defending capitalism as the best way to satisfy people's needs while respecting their rights, they dislike both public regulation of economic activities and the Church's social teaching insofar as it calls for redistributive taxation, welfare programs, and so on. Consequently, while endorsing a free economy for the nations recently liberated from Marxism, John Paul II restates (in May 1991) the Church's critical evaluation of capitalism.

The Pope approaches the subject by pointing out that with Communism's failure a question arises: whether "capitalism should be the goal of the countries now making efforts to rebuild their economy and society?" The answer, he says, is affirmative, insofar as *capitalism* means "an economic system which recognizes the fundamental and positive role of business, the market, private property and the resulting responsibility for the means of production, as well as free human creativity in the economic sector."[67] But John Paul also makes it clear that the answer is negative insofar as *capitalism* means something else: "a method of upholding the absolute predominance of capital, the possession of the means of production and of the land, in contrast to the free and personal nature of human work";[68] a system which results in the alienation found in consumerism as well as in work "when it is organized so as to ensure maximum returns and profits with no concern whether the worker, through his own labour, grows or diminishes as a person";[69] "a system in which freedom in the economic sector is not circumscribed within a strong juridical framework which places it at the service of human freedom in its totality."[70]

5. The Church Rejects Marxism and Criticizes Democratic Socialism

The nineteenth-century stage in the development of the affluent nations pro-voked Marxism as a protest and counterproposal. It promised a better world in which injustice and alienation would be eliminated, people would enjoy peace and plenty, and other human interests would be facilitated. But Marxism is atheistic, deterministic, and materialistic; it denies God and rejects free choice, and with it the dignity of persons, and so the Church condemned it.[71] Moreover, its wonderful promises proved empty, and instead of liberating people, it enslaved them.[72]

---

67. John Paul II, *Centesimus annus,* 42, *AAS* 83 (1991) 845, *OR,* 6 May 1991, 12.

68. John Paul II, *Centesimus annus,* 35, *AAS* 83 (1991) 836, *OR,* 6 May 1991, 11.

69. John Paul II, *Centesimus annus,* 41, *AAS* 83 (1991) 844, *OR,* 6 May 1991, 12.

70. John Paul II, *Centesimus annus,* 42, *AAS* 83 (1991) 846, *OR,* 6 May 1991, 12. See also John Paul II, *Sollicitudo rei socialis,* 20–22, *AAS* 80 (1988) 536–40, *OR,* 29 Feb. 1988, 5, where the "system which is historically inspired by the principles of *liberal capitalism*" is treated as the ideology of the bloc in the West, and the Church's continuing "critical attitude" toward it as well as toward Marxist collectivism is explained.

71. Vatican II, without using the word *Marxism,* firmly rejected it by saying: "In her loyal devotion to God and to humankind, the Church has already repudiated and cannot cease repudi-ating, sorrowfully but as firmly as possible, those pernicious doctrines and actions which contradict reason and the common experience of humanity, and dethrone human beings from their native excellence" (GS 21), and by appending to this a note—n. 16 (Abbott n. 47)—containing references to encyclicals of Pius XI, Pius XII, John XXIII, and Paul VI in which Marxism is condemned.

72. See Congregation for the Doctrine of the Faith, *Instruction on Certain Aspects of the "Theology of Liberation",* 11.10, *AAS* 76 (1984) 905–6, *OR,* 10 Sept. 1984, 4. For an earlier brief

In the social and economic sphere, the Marxist alternative to individualism and capitalism is collectivism and state socialism. This approach has influenced parties on the left in the democratic nations, although they downplay Marxism's philosophical foundations and distance themselves from totalitarianism.

a) **The Church rejects collectivism or state socialism.** Inasmuch as the Church rejects individualism and laissez faire capitalism, it might seem that she supports the opposite ideology. However, the Church steadfastly rejects collectivism as well as individualism, state socialism as well as laissez faire capitalism.

State socialism attacks private property, which the Church's teaching defends, and tries to overcome its abuses with a system of public ownership. Collectivism eliminates the multitude of independent socioeconomic communities—corporations, trade unions, cooperatives, and so on—and replaces them with centralized management of productive goods and undertakings.

Contrary to this ideology, the Church holds that, besides the family and the state, there is need for many intermediate communities of various kinds and sizes; for a community directed toward some modes of cooperation for some goods will be more or less unsuited to organize and integrate cooperation in other ways and toward other goods, and indeed no society short of God's kingdom can integrate all possible ways of cooperating for all the goods of persons. Consequently, without a complex socioeconomic structure, including a variety of intermediate communities, people cannot pursue their whole human vocation and fulfill it.[73]

b) **Every society should respect the liberty of its members.** State socialists argue that political society not only should regulate the economy but should itself be the economic agent, whenever it can play that role efficiently, even though that will eliminate private enterprise and collectivize the means of production. The Church rejects this conclusion. The material results of economic activity do not exhaust the good it serves; economic activities also are important because individuals, families, and voluntary associations participate as agents in achieving those results, and so engage in intrinsically valuable human deliberation, choice, and action (see GS 34–35). Thus, even if political society could satisfy all needs for material goods and do it efficiently—and the experience of societies which tried this approach indicates that it cannot—the Church resists that approach for the sake of the greater participation possible when diverse communities pursue goods by organizing and integrating cooperation in various ways.[74] Consequently, every society must respect those liberties of its members—both of individuals and of smaller communities within it—which fall beyond the society's fair claims on them (see DH 1, 7).

c) **Larger societies should help smaller ones attain their ends.** Insisting on social solidarity, the Church proposes a nonindividualistic alternative to collectivism. It is that larger societies, with resources (such as revenues from taxation)

---

and scathing summary of Marxist praxis, see John XXIII, *Ad Petri Cathedram, AAS* 51 (1959) 526, *PE*, 263.130.

73. See John XXIII, *Mater et magistra, AAS* 53 (1961) 414–18, *PE*, 267.53–67.

74. See, for example, John Paul II, *Laborem exercens,* 13, *AAS* 73 (1981) 608–12, *PE*, 280.58–62.

unavailable to the smaller communities within them, can and should help these smaller communities survive and pursue their own good purposes. The ideal relationship is analogous to that of good parents to their growing children: rather than trying to live their children's lives, the parents provide the regulation, support, and encouragement that children need to live their own lives. This relationship of political societies to the smaller communities within them, which involves both respecting their liberty and helping them, is called "subsidiarity." The principle of subsidiarity, which resists centralization and excludes collectivism, can be formulated this way: the larger society should not absorb the functions of smaller communities when the latter, given suitable help, can fulfill these functions; rather, the larger society should help smaller communities within it to carry out their proper functions.

Here *subsidiarity* (drawn from the Latin word *subsidium,* which means help) does not mean the smaller community is politically or juridically subordinate to the larger, although that may be so. Rather, it means that the larger community supports smaller ones within it in their proper activities (in practice, *supports* often means subsidizes with grants of money, but in principle it refers to any kind of help, including regulation and coordination with other segments of the society).[75]

d) **Even democratic societies violate the principle of subsidiarity.** While rejecting Marxism as such, the democratic governments of the affluent nations of the West have used some of the questionable methods of socialism in dealing with the socioeconomic problems of public welfare. Thus, John Paul II points out that the so-called welfare state (also called the "social assistance state") tends to violate the principle of subsidiarity "to the detriment of both economic and civil freedom":

> By intervening directly and depriving society of its responsibility, the Social Assistance State leads to a loss of human energies and an inordinate increase of public agencies, which are dominated more by bureaucratic ways of thinking than by concern for serving their clients, and which are accompanied by an enormous increase in spending. In fact, it would appear that needs are best understood and satisfied by people who are closest to them and who act as neighbours to those in need. It should be added that certain kinds of demands often call for a response which is not simply material but which is capable of perceiving the deeper human need. One thinks of the condition of refugees, immigrants, the elderly, the sick, and all those in circumstances which call for assistance, such as drug abusers: all these people can be helped effectively only by those who offer them genuine fraternal support, in addition to the necessary care.[76]

75. Pius XI, *Quadragesimo anno, AAS* 23 (1931) 203 (DS 3738/——), *PE,* 209.79 (translation amended), formulates the principle and characterizes its violation as a grave evil: "Just as it is gravely wrong to take from individuals what they can accomplish by their own initiative and industry and give it to the community, so also it is a wrong and at the same time gravely harmful and disruptive to right order to assign to a larger and higher association what smaller and subordinate organizations can do. For every social activity ought of its very nature to furnish help to the members of a social body, and never destroy and absorb it." See Calvez and Perrin, *The Church and Social Justice,* 121–24, 328–37.

76. John Paul II, *Centesimus annus,* 48, *AAS* 83 (1991) 854, *OR,* 6 May 1991, 13–14.

Thus, the politicizing of the economy characteristic of even democratic socialism is unacceptable.

e) **In the poorer nations, Marxism retains its appeal.** In the world's poorer nations, governments fail to vindicate many people's rights to the minimum necessities for a decent human life. Their suffering is extreme, and promises of amelioration through social and economic development have not been fulfilled. Knowing that affluent people are immeasurably better off, that the technology exists to meet everyone's basic needs, that international economic arrangements going back to colonial times—and perhaps even earlier—have been unjust, and that huge resources still are being devoted to armaments, such people long for liberation with a hope grounded in a genuine sense of their own dignity. This sense often is inspired at least in part by the gospel and the ideal of human communion it proclaims. Such people will no longer passively submit to crushing poverty and its wretched consequences.[77] But desperate people naturally grasp at almost any chance of rescue. Thus, liberationist movements influenced by Marxism retain their appeal in some parts of the world.

6. The Church Rejects Egalitarianism

Collectivists have always idealized absolute equality: nobody a king, everybody a comrade. Noting that inequalities limit individual freedom, many individualists also have endorsed egalitarianism. The Church, however, rejects it, because some of the differences which result in inequalities are essential to the complementarity of persons united in genuine community. Moreover, denying that equality is an absolute value, the Church condemns the use of inherently immoral means to eliminate even unjust inequalities.

Egalitarians idealize absolute equality as a standard of perfect justice. But the Church, while holding that all persons are equal in dignity and fundamental rights, also teaches that "rightful differences exist among people" (GS 29). She rejects the ideal of absolute equality and affirms the legitimacy of differences among people in rights which are not fundamental, because she sees the positive value for human community which is present in the existence of many persons with different gifts to be used for building up the whole.[78]

While egalitarians idealize equality in the belief that all differences in social status offend the dignity of persons, the Church holds that not only what human persons have in common but also what is proper to each, sin and other evils

77. See GS 63; Congregation for the Doctrine of the Faith, *Instruction on Certain Aspects of the "Theology of Liberation"*, 1.1–9, *AAS* 76 (1984) 878–79, *OR*, 10 Sept. 1984, 1.

78. Leo XIII, *Quod Apostolici muneris*, *ASS* 11 (1878) 372, *PE*, 79.5: The socialists' habit "is always to maintain that nature has made all men equal, and that, therefore, neither honor nor respect is due to majesty, nor obedience to laws, unless, perhaps, to those sanctioned by their own good pleasure. But, on the contrary, in accordance with the teachings of the Gospel, the equality of men consists in this: that all, having inherited the same nature, are called to the same most high dignity of the sons of God, and that, as one and the same end is set before all, each one is to be judged by the same law and will receive punishment or reward according to his deserts. The inequality of rights and of power proceeds from the very Author of nature, 'from whom all paternity in heaven and earth is named' (Eph 3.15)."

excepted, belongs to personal dignity. God's good creation embraces both common human nature and diverse personal gifts, and both are necessary to interpersonal communion. Moreover, the Church denies that subordinates are inferior as persons to their superiors. Hence, the Church's position is that injustices resulting from differences in social status cannot be overcome by disregarding or circumventing differences in people's gifts, but only by reforming practices which wrongly exploit such differences.[79]

7. Catholics in Affluent Nations Should Work for Social Justice

The preceding sketch makes clear the need for justice in the world and the great difficulties in the way of doing anything constructive about it. But the contemporary situation also has other features. People today have an altogether new degree of awareness of the situation. The problems are discussed daily in the mass media, and it is easy to learn a great deal about any specific problem if one cares to. Moreover, many Catholics in affluent Western nations have more gifts and capabilities for action than ever before. These include education, material means, leisure, some influence on government, and the ability and freedom to organize. They also have at their disposal modern transportation and communication, modern statistics and social analysis. Thus, it is hard to excuse ignoring the misery of many people in their own nations and throughout the world, as if all of them were well and happy (see AA 8). The world in effect has shrunk, and it is harder than ever to ignore the hundreds of millions of neighbors who lie injured or dying in various sorts of ditches.

Still, all too many Catholics in the affluent nations are lulled by individualism and self-satisfaction into a general and pervasive indifference to their responsibilities with regard to social justice. This indifference is sinful, and the sin is extremely serious, even if it falls short of being a mortal sin for those who never actually choose to ignore their responsibilities contrary to a conscience sufficiently aware of the matter's gravity.

Question F: How Are Justice and Mercy Related in Practice?

Christians who love others will fulfill every responsibility toward them (see Rom 13.8–10, Gal 5.14, Jas 2.8–13). Thus, everything one owes anyone—beginning with what is owed others in justice—is demanded by the responsibility to love others as Jesus does (see Jn 13.34). Yet justice is not enough; in practice, love must go beyond it and become mercy. But because mercy transcends justice, it might be

---

79. Leo XIII, *Rerum novarum*, *ASS* 23 (1890–91) 648, *PE*, 115.17, teaches: "It must be first of all recognized that the condition of things inherent in human affairs must be borne with, for it is impossible to reduce civil society to one dead level. Socialists may in that intent do their utmost, but all striving against nature is in vain. There naturally exist among mankind manifold differences of the most important kind; people differ in capacity, skill, health, strength; and unequal fortune is a necessary result of unequal condition. Such unequality is far from being disadvantageous either to individuals or to the community. Social and public life can only be maintained by means of various kinds of capacity for business and the playing of many parts; and each man, as a rule, chooses the part which suits his own peculiar domestic condition."

supposed that the requirements of justice can be fulfilled perfectly without mercy or even that mercy somehow sets aside justice. However, God is both just and merciful, and Christians are called to imitate him.

1. Fallen Humankind Often Evades the Requirements of Justice

While people have special responsibilities to other members of their limited communities—family, neighborhood, political society, and so on—they ought to regard all others as members, however distantly related, of one great family. For that is the truth of the matter: comprising a single species, human persons share the earth as their common home, and are all called to be children of God; yet they usually do not regard one another as brothers and sisters.

a) People tend to evade justice by restricting community. History, anthropological studies, and everyday experience teach that human beings of all times and places strongly tend to suppose that the requirements of justice apply only within their limited communities, excluding others and even denying their very personhood. For instance, many people of European origin who settled in the Americas regarded the indigenous peoples and the blacks transported from Africa as subhuman, and some people today adopt a similar attitude toward the unborn. Even when the humanity of others is acknowledged, various groups struggle for competitive advantage, so that many people who should form or participate in communities settle for arrangements short of real community. For example, more able people discriminate against those subject to some disability, members of one race or sex treat those of another as inferior, and so on.

b) The ultimate source of this narrowing down is sin. Sin, beginning with original sin, produces conditions in which it often is hard to act justly. In the fallen human condition, it seems virtually impossible to respect everyone's rights, since evildoing by others must be expected and concupiscence inclines everyone to selfishness. Still, violating others' rights remains wrong.[80]

In many cases, respecting everyone else's rights would make a group vulnerable to others' evildoing. For example, in some situations a tribe or nation must either unjustly dominate its neighbors or risk being unjustly dominated by them. In situations of scarcity, too, respecting others' rights often endangers one's own survival: in a famine, those who do not wrongly take the food from others' mouths

---

80. Pius XI, *Quadragesimo anno, AAS* 23 (1931) 219–22, *PE*, 209.132–35, describes a specific form of the process sketched here in general. Concupiscence inclines people to prefer the passing goods of this world to the lasting goods of heaven; hence, there develops an unquenchable thirst for riches which leads people to break God's laws and violate their neighbors' rights. Historically, several factors—the instabilities of the modern economy, the special opportunities it offers, the advantages of corporate organization, and inadequate governmental regulation—led increasing numbers to pursue profit without regard to the impact of their activity on other people. Pius then succinctly describes (*AAS* 221, *PE*, 134) the process of moral deterioration: "Those first entering upon this broad way that leads to destruction (cf. Mt 7.13) easily found numerous imitators of their iniquity by the example of their manifest success, by their insolent display of wealth, by their ridiculing the conscience of others, who, as they said, were troubled by silly scruples, or lastly by crushing more conscientious competitors." The same analysis underlies the magisterium's recent social teaching; see, for example, Paul VI, *Populorum progressio*, 49, 58–59, 66, 75–76; *AAS* 59 (1967) 281–82, 285–86, 289–90, 293–95; *PE*, 275.49, 58–59, 66, 75–76.

are likely to starve. In all cases, respecting others' rights would require the stronger and more able to restrain themselves from satisfying their desires at the expense of the weaker and less able. Today, for instance, if the rich and powerful accepted structural changes in the economy so as to allocate to the weak and poor a share of the world's resources corresponding to their basic needs and the fruits of their work, those with more would have to surrender, at least for a time, some of their security and comfort.

2. Mercy Goes Beyond Justice by Overcoming Injustice

A generous act goes beyond what justice requires, but it does not violate justice unless generosity toward one person is at another's undue expense. Merciful acts, similarly, transcend the demands of justice without violating them.

a) God's mercy is his goodness overcoming evil. Apart from what he has gratuitously promised, God owes no creature anything; everything he does in respect to creatures is thus pure generosity. Usually, however, his act of creating is not said to be merciful, since it did not overcome any prior evil. Rather, *merciful* said of God points to his saving will (see *S.t.*, 2–2, q. 30, aa. 1, 4). God's mercy is his steadfast love, by which he continues to love his creatures despite their sins and does everything necessary to save fallen humankind. This steadfast love overcomes sin, the greatest evil, and so is the greatest mercy.

b) Human love, confronting evil, similarly takes the form of mercy. For humans too, mercy resembles the generosity by which people give gifts to their friends and loved ones. It is a form of benevolence, an expression of love, by which people go beyond the requirements of justice and give something gratuitously. For instance, giving a friend a certificate for dinner for two in a restaurant and giving such a certificate to a poor, elderly couple whose social security check has been delayed are both acts of generosity: justice requires neither gift, and love motivates both.

Mercy, however, is different from other forms of benevolence in that it responds to evil (see *S.t.*, 2–2, q. 30, a. 1). A merciful person gives another something not owed precisely in order to overcome something bad: feeding the poor and hungry couple is a work of mercy, because it does something to help them. Similarly, in response to others' sins, the merciful bring about undeserved reconciliation with those who wrong them by granting forgiveness rather than exacting retribution.

c) Mercy transcends compassion by motivating effective action. Mercy must not be confused with the mere feeling of pity which does nothing effective about misery (see Jas 2.15–16) or with that sentimentalism which condones sin so as to spare people the pain of guilt. As John Paul II teaches:

> The true and proper meaning of mercy does not consist only in looking, however penetratingly and compassionately, at moral, physical or material evil: Mercy is manifested in its true and proper aspect when it restores to value, promotes and draws good from all the forms of evil existing in the world and in man.[81]

---

81. John Paul II, *Dives in misericordia*, 6, *AAS* 72 (1980) 1199, *PE*, 279.63. A few paragraphs earlier (*AAS* 1197–98, *PE*, 59), he explains that mercy is love dealing with evil: "Mercy—as Christ

3. Misconceptions about Justice and Mercy Must Be Set Aside

Mercy presupposes that a person depends on others for benefits to which he or she has no right. Assuming that such dependence is incompatible with equal personal dignity, many people suppose that mercy is at odds with justice. But this misconception flows from a mistaken ideal of individual autonomy and requires no refutation. Neither does the misunderstanding which confuses mercy with so-called charitable deeds which actually express pride, a desire for honor, and/or self-righteous condescension.

Other misconceptions concerning justice and mercy, however, are subtler and require clarification.

a) Justice does not demand that wrongdoers be repaid evil for evil. Some people think mercy somehow sets aside justice because they share a widespread misconception: that justice demands retaliation in kind—evil for evil. This misconception often is a premise, for example, in arguments for capital punishment. But justice does not require evil for evil. It demands only a restoration of a fair balance sufficient to deprive wrongdoers of the advantage they have taken over the law abiding, to mitigate conflict, and to establish harmony. None of these requires repaying evil with evil. "An eye for an eye and a tooth for a tooth" did set some limits to retaliation, but a vengeful attitude distorts justice rather than embodying it.[82] Punishment motivated by hostility is not just.

b) Justice does not forbid giving what is unmerited. Some people think mercy violates justice by providing benefits to the undeserving. But merit is only a nonabsolute standard of justice, not one of its principles. Moreover, the most plausible kind of merit to use as a standard of justice is virtue: the morally good deserve more, the bad less. But recompense for such merit, which depends entirely on God's grace, belongs mainly to him rather than to human beings, who are incapable of making the necessary judgments. Thus, it is a mistake to reduce justice to merit and use that conception to exclude mercy. One should not wait for others to become good enough to deserve forgiveness, nor should help be given only to the "deserving" poor, although the kind of help to be offered people depends, of course, on their needs and capacities to use the sorts of help which can be given.

c) Mercy does not cancel out the objective requirements of justice. Although mercy does offer forgiveness or some other unmerited benefit, it does not do this to evade the demands of justice, but to open the way to reconciliation and help those who suffer. The aim is that, with the healing and building up of the bonds of community, the requirements of justice might be met. John Paul II teaches:

> You know, in fact, that Christian love animates justice, inspires it, discovers it, perfects it, makes it feasible, respects it, elevates it, surpasses it; but it does not exclude it, does not absorb it, does not replace it, but rather presupposes it

---

has presented it in the parable of the prodigal son—has the interior form of the love that in the New Testament is called *agape*. This love is able to reach down to every prodigal son, to every human misery, and above all to every form of moral misery, to sin."

82. See Mt 5.38–42; John Paul II, *Dives in misericordia,* 12, *AAS* 72 (1980) 1215–16, *PE,* 279.120–22.

and demands it, because true love, true charity, does not exist without justice. Is not justice perhaps the minimum measure of charity?[83]

Thus, mercy never overrides justice. Forgiveness, for instance, is not a matter of overlooking sin. Although forgiveness can anticipate contrition, reconciliation still requires contrition, which is genuine only if it involves the will and real effort to make amends, insofar as possible. Thus, mercy does not condone or ignore the evil which it forgives.[84]

d) Mercy is not unilateral and condescending. It often is supposed that the benefits of acting mercifully necessarily are one-sided, and that mercy can be shown only by the virtuous toward sinners, the rich toward the poor, the strong toward the weak, and so forth; thus, it seems impossible for the merciful entirely to avoid condescension, which affronts the dignity of those to whom mercy is shown. Some therefore resist the idea that mercy should be shown to those in need, insisting instead that justice alone is enough.

However, mercy must be shown to those in need and their dignity also must be preserved; and both things can be done at the same time. Those who are shown mercy can respond in kind. This is so because, although human persons cannot reciprocate God's mercy, mercy among human persons never is truly realized without mutuality. Mercy is love dealing with evil and suffering, and every human being suffers from sin and its consequences, and needs the help of others. Alcoholics Anonymous, for example, has learned not only that the active alcoholic needs the help of recovered alcoholics to recover, but that the recovered alcoholic must serve others in order to maintain his or her own sobriety.

Everyone needs others' forgiveness and sometimes desperately needs their generous help. Therefore, mercy fully succeeds only when enemies mutually forgive one another, and when those who care for others' needs receive care when they need it. Moreover, perfect mercy means that those who receive benefits show mercy to their benefactors, for example, when the hungry who are fed love their benefactors despite their defects. Far from being an obstacle to justice, mercy fosters communion of persons equal in dignity, thus leading them to achieve that equality in respect to various goods which justice requires.[85]

To suppose that those who receive mercy are thereby necessarily degraded betrays a false sense of values. Being in need is not shameful, while proud individualism, which assumes that nobody ever should depend on others, is the very antithesis of Christian humility. Indeed, those who show mercy also must be humble, and their mercy bears witness to the dignity of those to whom they show it:

> The *raison d'être* of our charity is the inalienable dignity which we acknowledge in every human being, created in the image and likeness of God, loved by God, saved by God, adopted by God as a son, and identified with Christ himself. We

---

83. John Paul II, Address to the Workers of the Solvay Factory (near Livorno), 10, *AAS* 74 (1982) 602, *OR,* 5–12 Apr. 1982, 11.

84. See John Paul II, *Dives in misericordia,* 14, *AAS* 72 (1980) 1226–27, *PE,* 279.157.

85. See John Paul II, *Dives in misericordia,* 14, *AAS* 72 (1980) 1222–24, *PE,* 279.141–49.

cannot resign ourselves to leave this brother, who has such a value in God's eyes, in misery, in abandonment, in loveless solitude. Our charity goes beyond the emotional pity which is undeniably a natural door for charity. It goes beyond horizontal solidarities. It is based on that transcendence which we recognize in each one of our brothers. Our brotherhood has its source in God. Such is the witness that you must bear, loud and clear, in the Church, like a light that one cannot put under a bushel, like a torch that must shine in the eyes of men. And at the same time, in all humility, we keep our awareness of being only servants.[86]

4. Christians Must Exercise Not Only Justice but Mercy

The gospel proclaims not only God's merciful forgiveness of sin, but a new, universal, and permanent covenant. Jesus calls every human person to accept this covenant and enter into God's heavenly kingdom. Those who do so accept the responsibility to show others the same mercy God has shown.

a) **The gospel rejects the strategy of limiting human community.** Rather than restricting community, mercy expands it, for mercy is the form love takes when it confronts and overcomes evil. Jesus teaches that each of his followers should be ready to be everyone else's neighbor: that is exactly the point of the parable of the Good Samaritan (see Lk 10.29–37). He calls all who accept the gospel to share in and contribute to his work of divine mercy, to undo and overcome sin and its effects not only in themselves but in the whole world. "Christ's messianic program, the program of mercy, becomes the program of his people, the program of the Church."[87] Moreover, inasmuch as true community is, not a mere arrangement to avoid needless conflict among individuals who remain autonomous, but a genuine sharing of life, it is not enough to avoid harming others. For inasmuch as the new covenant is communion of human persons in Jesus with God, how one cares for one's neighbors' needs is how one treats Jesus himself: "Just as you did it to one of the least of these who are members of my family, you did it to me" (Mt 25.40; cf. AA 8, GS 27).[88]

b) **Mercy is the justice of Jesus' kingdom.** Having received God's mercy and entered into the new covenant community, a person must extend forgiveness and community to others.

> The "Golden Rule" occurs in Matthew—and even more directly in Luke—in the context of the Beatitudes, of a forsaking of claims of distributive justice, of the love of one's enemies, of the demand to be 'perfect' and 'merciful' as the heavenly Father is. For this reason, gifts received from the Father are precisely what a Christian may expect from his neighbor and what he should give to his neighbor.[89]

---

86. John Paul II, Address to the Pontifical Council "Cor Unum", 5, *AAS* 77 (1985) 478, *OR*, 7 Jan. 1985, 4.

87. John Paul II, *Dives in misericordia*, 8, *AAS* 72 (1980) 1205, *PE*, 279.86.

88. See Joachim Jeremias, *The Parables of Jesus*, 2nd rev. ed. (New York: Charles Scribner's Sons, 1972), 202–10.

89. Hans Urs von Balthasar, "Nine Theses in Christian Ethics," in International Theological Commission, *Texts and Documents: 1969–1985*, ed. Michael Sharkey (San Francisco: Ignatius Press, 1989), 111; also see Paul Ricoeur, "The Golden Rule: Exegetical and Theological Perplexities," *New Testament Studies* 36 (1990): 392–97.

One is strictly obliged to love enemies because, needing and receiving God's mercy, one is bound to extend the same mercy to others (see Mt 5.7, 6.14–15; Mk 11.25; Lk 6.35–37; Eph 4.32; Col 3.13). The parable of the unmerciful servant makes this point: those who receive God's mercy sin if they do not show mercy to others, and God will judge them justly (see Mt 18.23–35). Thus, Jesus taught his disciples to seek and expect God's mercy only on condition that they extend mercy to others: "Forgive us our debts, as we also have forgiven our debtors . . .. For if you forgive others their trespasses, your heavenly Father will also forgive you; but if you do not forgive others, neither will your Father forgive your trespasses" (Mt 6.12, 14–15; cf. Lk 11.4). Within the community of the new covenant, whose members must treat every human person as a neighbor, the requirements of mercy are requirements of justice.[90]

c) **Mercy's requirements are not morally optional for Christians.** While people often owe others forgiveness and help, apart from the new covenant these social responsibilities extend only to fellow members of various communities (compatriots, colleagues, relatives, and so on), and there is no need to go beyond the boundaries of existing community.[91] Reaching beyond those limits in some exceptional case is a purely gratuitous gesture.

For Christians, however, doing what is necessary to overcome evil is never gratuitous. Jesus makes it absolutely clear that everlasting punishment awaits those who fail to serve his needs manifested in the hunger, thirst, homelessness, naked- ness, sickness, and ill treatment of those regarded as the least important of his brothers and sisters (see Mt 25.41–46). So, the works of mercy are obligatory, and it is wrong to think of mercy's requirements as if they were supererogatory (that is, above and beyond the requirements of duty).[92]

It might be objected that sinners have no right to be forgiven and those with needs have no right to more help from anyone than justice requires of that person. The answer is: The duties of mercy do not correspond to any rights which anyone has apart from God's mercy to every human person. Since God has in fact shown mercy toward all, however, the Golden Rule requires everyone who accepts that mercy to show similar mercy to others. Thus, within the community of the new covenant, whose members must always be ready to welcome new members, sinners have a right to be forgiven by fellow sinners, and those with needs have a right to more help than justice otherwise would require. Yet those to whom mercy is shown

---

90. See Jeremias, *The Parables of Jesus,* 210–14. Also see Antonio Di Marino, S.J., "L'epi- keia cristiana," *Divus Thomas* (Piacenza) 55 (1952): 396–424, for a treatment of the specifically Christian sense of *epikeia* as a virtue of moderation in judgment.

91. The principle that those who receive God's mercy must extend mercy to others is not peculiar to the New Testament (see Sir 28.1–4), but its range of application is determined by the extent of the covenant: "Remember the commandments, and do not be angry with your neighbor; remember the covenant of the Most High, and overlook faults" (Sir 28.7; cf. Lv 19.18).

92. St. Thomas, *Super evangelium S. Matthaei lectura,* on Mt 22.39, generalizes from the conclusion of the parable of the Good Samaritan to define the concept of neighbor in the love commandment, saying that "under the name 'neighbor' is included whoever ought to do mercy to us or whomever we ought to do mercy to." Thus, the responsibility of mercy is not supererogatory but strictly prescribed by the law of love.

are not entitled to it in such a way that mercy loses its gratuitous character. For those who are shown mercy are indirect beneficiaries of God's entirely gratuitous mercy, since those who show mercy do so only by first sharing in God's mercy and then handing it on.

Someone glad to receive God's forgiveness would fail to treat others according to the Golden Rule if he or she were to withhold mercy from them. It is significant that in Luke's Gospel, Jesus' reaffirmation of the Golden Rule is at the heart of his teaching that Christians should love enemies, and the passage (Lk 6.27–36) culminates: "Be merciful, just as your Father is merciful" (Lk 6.36).[93] One fails to give others what they should be given by not forgiving their trespasses as God forgives one's own and by not meeting their needs as one hopes God will meet one's needs. Therefore, "the words of the Sermon on the Mount: 'Blessed are the merciful, for they shall obtain mercy' (Mt 5.7), constitute, in a certain sense, a synthesis of the whole of the good news, of the whole of the 'wonderful exchange' (admirabile commercium) contained therein."[94]

5. Love Should Be Put into Practice in Doing Works of Mercy

Christians have responsibilities toward others which cannot be recognized independently of faith and hope, and cannot be fulfilled without love: the responsibilities of the mercy which is the justice of Jesus' kingdom. Catholic moral theology usually has treated some of these in a general way, under the heading of *almsgiving*. Insofar as almsgiving is a form of penance, it was discussed above (in 4.B.2.f–g). The responsibilities of mercy, which are far more extensive than what most people would call "almsgiving," will be treated in their specific variety in subsequent chapters, but there are a few general norms.

a) **Works of mercy should be works of love toward those helped.** Knowing they cannot use their resources for any better purpose than to meet others' needs, loving givers appreciate the opportunity to come closer to others and build up the communion of love. Thus, a person must not only help others but must do so in a specifically Christian manner:

---

93. John Paul II, *Dives in misericordia*, 4, *AAS* 72 (1980) 1191, *PE*, 279.36, teaches: "Love, so to speak, conditions justice and, in the final analysis, justice serves love. The primacy and superiority of love vis-à-vis justice—this is a mark of the whole of revelation—are revealed precisely through mercy. This seemed so obvious to the psalmists and prophets that the very term justice ended up by meaning the salvation accomplished by the Lord and his mercy [note omitted]. Mercy differs from justice, but is not in opposition to it if we admit in the history of man—as the Old Testament precisely does—the presence of God, who already as Creator has linked himself to his creature with a particular love." See also 14, *AAS* 1221–28, *PE*, 139–61. John XXIII teaches that peace requires justice animated and perfected by love: *Pacem in terris, AAS* 55 (1963) 265–67, *PE*, 270.35–38.

94. John Paul II, *Dives in misericordia*, 8, *AAS* 72 (1980) 1206, *PE*, 279.88. The Pope goes on (*AAS* 1206, *PE*, 89): "This exchange is a law of the very plan of salvation, a law which is simple, strong and at the same time 'easy.' Demonstrating from the very start what the 'human heart' is capable of ('to be merciful'), do not these words from the Sermon on the Mount reveal in the same perspective the deep mystery of God: that inscrutable unity of Father, Son and Holy Spirit, in which love, containing justice, sets in motion mercy, which in its turn reveals the perfection of justice?"

One should consider in one's neighbors the image of God in which they have been created, and also Christ the Lord to whom is really offered whatever is given to a needy person. The freedom and dignity of the person being helped should be respected with the utmost sensitivity, and the purity of one's charitable intentions should not be stained by seeking one's own advantage or by fondness for domination [note omitted]. The demands of justice should first be satisfied, lest what is due in justice be offered as if it were a charitable gift. Not only the effects but also the causes of evils should be removed. Help should be given in such a way that the recipients may gradually be liberated from dependence and become self-sufficient. (AA 8)

Of course, people should not be given "help" which in reality would harm them, for example, by supporting their self-destructive behavior or irresponsibility. So, alcoholics and other addicts should be encouraged to do what is necessary to overcome their addiction, not helped to maintain it. And everyone capable of working ought to do the work necessary and possible to obtain the necessities of life: "Anyone unwilling to work should not eat" (2 Thes 3.10).[95]

b) *Works of mercy* should not be understood narrowly. In the narrowest sense, almsgiving is the act by which money or goods are compassionately given to a needy person for God's sake (see *S.t.,* 2–2, q. 32, a. 1). But the tradition broadens the notion by listing both corporal and spiritual works of almsgiving or mercy (see *S.t.,* 2–2, q. 32, a. 2). The corporal works are feeding the hungry, giving drink to the thirsty, clothing the naked, sheltering the homeless, visiting the sick, ransoming the captive, and burying the dead. The spiritual works are instructing the ignorant, counseling the doubtful, admonishing sinners, bearing wrongs patiently, forgiving offenses, comforting the sorrowing, and praying for the living and the dead.

Even these lists are not exhaustive. The full range of *works of mercy* can be understood only by considering that all of them implement Christian love of neighbor. Now, since the object of love is not limited to this or that kind of good, all one's resources—not only money and material goods, but talent, time, energy, and so on—can and should be used to implement it. Therefore, the general norm for works of mercy is that all the members of Jesus' body should make their resources of every kind available for the benefit of other members, actual or potential, of that same body.

c) Christians should rejoice in doing works of mercy. With respect to works of mercy, St. Paul teaches: "Each of you must give as you have made up your mind, not reluctantly or under compulsion, for God loves a cheerful giver" (2 Cor 9.7). The giver's spontaneity and cheerfulness are signs of love.

Created persons have only what they have received as God's gifts; those with greater gifts hold them in trust to serve others' needs. Thus, loving givers are cheerful, for they are both pleased by others' good, which they seek, and fulfilled personally in discharging their trust. They do not perceive those in need as inferiors, but as fellow members of Jesus who deserve care and help.

---

95. See Paul VI, *Populorum progressio, AAS* 59 (1967) 266, *PE,* 275.18.

Moreover, Christians realize that the fabric of communion built up here on earth by their giving to others and receiving from them will last forever in heaven. Universal self-sufficiency would not make for community, but the universal dependence of created persons on God, together with their mutual interdependence, do.

d) Need is not the sole criterion for Christian love. Since mercy focuses on meeting others' needs, Christian love might be thought to demand what Marxists think justice demands: to each according to need. But the Marxist is mistaken in suggesting that justice can be measured by needs. Mercy includes justice, and God's mercy is the standard for Christian mercy. Rather than distributing his gifts solely according to the criterion of need, however, God gives greater gifts to some than to others. In this, he acts according to his overall plan for the kingdom (see Rom 9.14–18, 1 Cor 12.4–11, Eph 4.11–13; DS 1529/799; LG 12, AA 3, AG 23; *S.t.*, 1–2, q. 112, a. 4).

Moreover, while the New Testament makes it clear that Christian love should extend to absolutely everyone, it also requires particular regard for communities in which one has specific responsibilities, even though fulfilling these sometimes is inconsistent with the criterion of need; for example, it insists upon the special duties each person has to his or her own family (see A.1.f, above; Eph 5.21–6.9, Col 3.18–4.1). Why does the New Testament maintain such priorities? Evidently because God's love is wider even than his mercy. His plan includes not only redemption—the meeting of all the needs which result from sin—but the ongoing work of creation: bringing still more persons into being and more perfect fulfillment. Thus, while procreation and other good creative human activities do not meet needs, Christian love by no means excludes them.

e) Love requires that surplus be used to meet others' needs. All people naturally love themselves and some others, and so use their resources to satisfy their own needs and the needs of their loved ones; decent people also acknowledge duties in strict justice and fulfill them. While Christian love does not exclude these uses of resources, it changes their meaning: in meeting needs out of Christian love, one always cherishes and builds up Jesus' body, for now oneself and one's neighbors are not loved as isolated individuals or as members of some merely human community, but as members or potential members of the communion of the divine family. For this same reason, however, whenever one has surplus resources, love requires using them to meet the needs of other members or potential members of Jesus' body (on the meaning of *surplus,* see 10.E.2).

In a world without sin and the misery following from it, people might have surplus which they could justly keep for themselves or share with others just as they pleased. But in the actual world, fallen and redeemed, mercy must be done, using every gift and surplus resource. Of course, both surplus and need are matters of more and less, not only in the sense of being greater or smaller in quantity, but also in the sense of varying qualitatively in degree. Clothing which a person never will wear again is surplus in a stronger sense than clothing he or she occasionally wears but could do without; someone with nothing at all to wear needs clothing in a stronger sense than someone whose clothing is threadbare. And this is true not only of money and material resources but all one's resources—the talents, time, and energy which even those materially poor can employ to meet others' needs.

f) Christians should forgo rights for the sake of mercy. In the fallen world, where both society's members and its structures are afflicted with evils, rights which would obtain in an unfallen world sometimes should not be asserted. For example, in an unfallen world, people who applied their work to their fair share of natural resources might have a right to the whole product. But in the world as it is, where some people are in dire need and social structures favor the rich and powerful, that right cannot be maintained intact, since part of the fruit of honest work always is urgently needed to mitigate suffering and struggle against injustice. Thus, a Christian conception of justice which incorporates mercy requires that, in the service of others, individuals forgo what otherwise would be their rights (see *CMP*, 27.F).

g) To omit works of mercy is a refusal to abide in love. Individuals, families, and other groups should take a conscientious approach to the question of the disposability of their more or less surplus resources and the urgency of others' more or less compelling needs. Plainly, however, when someone's surplus (in a strong sense) matches another's extreme need, that individual either meets the need or refuses to love (see GS 69). People who fail in this matter, Jesus warns, "will go away into eternal punishment" (Mt 25.46).

This is not a threat that Jesus will impose punishment on the uncharitable; it is simply a warning that refusing to act as a member of Christ toward his other members, actual or potential, is of itself incompatible with sharing in the communion of divine family life: "How does God's love abide in anyone who has the world's goods and sees a brother or sister in need and yet refuses help?" (1 Jn 3.17). It cannot, for faith without the works of mercy is dead (see Jas 2.13–17). Someone really prepared to enter into the intimacy of the heavenly kingdom will treat others as brothers and sisters even now, while someone who ignores others' needs is not prepared to enter into the intimacy of the heavenly kingdom. Thus, Jesus does not threaten anyone but simply clarifies the full meaning of omitting works of mercy.

6. Christians Should Respond with Gratitude to Benefactors

Christian love requires those who receive mercy to be grateful toward those who have shown them mercy. As those who have gifts to offer can manifest and increase love by doing works of mercy, so those who benefit can intensify communion by their gratitude. Strictly speaking, gratitude is due only for a kindness that goes beyond the demands of justice (see *S.t.*, 2–2, q. 106, a. 1); but since the grateful heart responds to the good will of others more than to the benefit received (see *S.t.*, 2–2, q. 106, a. 5), Christians should respond with gratitude to anyone who treats them with love, even if everything done happens to be required by justice.

Gratitude should be manifested by words of thanks and praise, but also by good deeds, if possible by responding with a greater good than the one received (see *S.t.*, 2–2, q. 106, a. 6). Christian gratitude often takes the form of praying for benefactors' salvation and trying to help them to grow in holiness by encouraging them to do still greater works of love.

Usually, ungratefulness is not a mortal sin; it would be only if it resulted from inner contempt, or took the form of returning serious evil for good, or involved a grave failure to answer mercy with mercy when a benefactor in turn needed help (see *S.t.*, 2–2, q. 107, aa. 2–3). Nevertheless, since Christians build up the fabric of communion in Jesus by giving to and receiving from one another, the loving gratitude of those who benefit from works of mercy is as important as the love of those who do the works.

7. Peace Is the Fruit of the Justice Which Includes Mercy

The preceding account of the relationship between justice and mercy helps clarify what the Church has in mind in talking about peace. Peace is not mere absence of conflict; it is the tranquillity of order, that is, the harmony resulting when people and other realities are as they ought to be.[96] It is the communion that should be realized within any community of persons, ultimately among all humankind, and of humankind itself with God.[97] The obstacles to this communion are already-existing evil and continuing injustice. So, only justice which includes mercy can lead to peace (see GS 78).

By his cross, Jesus reconciled humankind to God and laid the foundation for everlasting peace. "For this reason, all Christians are urgently summoned 'to live the truth in love' (Eph 4.15) and to join with all true peacemakers in pleading for peace and bringing it about" (GS 78). Ultimately, however, peace is not of this world: Since "human beings are sinful, the threat of war hangs over them, and hang over them it will until the return of Christ" (GS 78). The enduring reality of evil and its exacerbation by continuing injustice will always stand in the way of the attainment of peace. Still, it is worth pursuing, since justice ought to be done; and doing it does have some fruit in this world; more importantly, doing justice contributes material for the kingdom, in which alone peace will be fully realized, when the Lord returns and hands over the kingdom to his Father (see GS 38–39).

Question G: How Does Christian Love Shape Social Responsibility?

Christian love requires not only fulfilling all specific responsibilities toward others, but understanding and approaching the whole area of social responsibilities in a specifically Christian way. The true objective must be kept in view: not to establish the kingdom on earth, but to do what can be done within an integrated Christian life to promote the kingdom, which is not of this world. In so doing, one

96. See St. Augustine, *De civitate Dei* 19.13; cf. Paul VI, Christmas Message (1966), *AAS* 59 (1967) 77, *The Pope Speaks* 12 (1967): 47: "Peace is not a primary good, but a resultant and derivative good that infers and requires a prior good. This prior good is precisely order, justice, the harmony of things."

97. Thus, for St. Thomas, the essence of peace is the harmony within human persons, among them, and with God which is the fruit of charity (see *S.t.*, 2–2, q. 29, aa. 1, 3). Pius XI, *Ubi arcano Dei consilio, AAS* 14 (1922) 685–86, *PE,* 192.33–36, clearly articulates the concept of peace of Christ, a work of justice perfected by charity and reconciliation.

also will make the most authentic possible contribution to overcoming injustice or at least mitigating it, and building a better world.[98]

Influenced by the optimism of various forms of secular humanism, many Christians have projected a utopia comparable to those imagined by utopian nonbelievers. Since such thinking loses touch with reality, those who indulge in it are prone to turn the fulfillment of social responsibility into many large ideas and much empty talk.

What follows is intended to be realistic and practical. Although it may strike some as rather negative, minimal, and pessimistic, it is better—since only God can bring on the dawn of justice and peace throughout the world—to light one small candle from the light of Christ than to work for the world's illumination by other lights, which never will overcome the darkness of sin or do away with the shadow of death.

1. One Is Not Called to Establish the Kingdom on Earth

Christians, and the laity in a special way, are called to work for the renewal of the whole temporal order (see AA 5, 7; 2.D.3.c, above). The Church's social doctrine provides them with necessary guidance: norms for criticizing existing structures and guiding practical efforts to reform them. Misunderstanding both these norms and their mission, those with scope for action on behalf of social justice may suppose they not only should try to develop and carry out appropriate, although more or less limited, projects, but should even attempt to work out an overall plan for a better world, with a view to transforming the contemporary world into a good and just global community, a Christian counterpart of the secular humanists' utopias.

This aim is illusory. Secular humanistic approaches to human misery are stimulated by a residue of Christian hope: secular humanism of every kind anticipates the establishment of an ideal human community in this world. In this anticipation, modern secular humanism is remarkably like the outlook of Jesus' time: the expectation of an earthly kingdom was so strong that right up to Jesus' ascension the apostles continued to ask him: "Lord, is this the time when you will restore the kingdom to Israel?" (Acts 1.6). Against this persistent and recurrent expectation of an earthly kingdom, faith teaches that earthly progress must not be confused with the growth of God's kingdom (see GS 39). A perfect human community will come to be only with the parousia. Meanwhile some men and women will not be people of good will: weeds will grow with wheat until the harvest (see Mt 13.36–43).[99]

---

98. A relevant and helpful work: Donal Dorr, *Spirituality and Justice* (Maryknoll, N.Y.: Orbis Books, 1984).

99. John Paul II, *Centesimus annus*, 25, *AAS* 83 (1991) 823–24, *OR*, 6 May 1991, 9, teaches: "When people think they possess the secret of a perfect social organization which makes evil impossible, they also think that they can use any means, including violence and deceit, in order to bring that organization into being. Politics then becomes a 'secular religion' which operates under the illusion of creating paradise in this world. But no political society—which possesses its own autonomy and laws [note omitted]—can ever be confused with the Kingdom of God. The Gospel parable of the weeds among the wheat (cf. Mt 13.24–30, 36–43) teaches that it is for God

Therefore, the only complete better world, the only real universal communion (of all willing to share in it), the only true civilization of love is the kingdom—and it is not of this world.[100] This is the authentic Christian counterpart of secular utopias. Faith therefore teaches Christians to seek "a better country, that is, a heavenly one" (Heb 11.16) and offers no alternative. Since the only realistic plan for a perfect world is God's plan for bringing on the kingdom, any plan for such a world which Christians try to fabricate will result from confusing their limited role with that of divine providence. Moreover, since God's plan is certain to succeed while any alternative is certain to fail, the Christian rejection of these alternatives is rooted not in pessimism but in hope. Jesus articulated God's plan when, anticipating the joy of hope's fulfillment, he proclaimed the Beatitudes, which both "prevent us from worshipping earthly goods" and "divert us from an unrealistic and ruinous search for a perfect world, 'for the form of this world is passing away' (1 Cor 7.31)."[101]

2. One Should Integrate Social Responsibility into One's Vocation

The Church's social teachings require that people participate in morally upright ways in action for social justice and forbid abandoning the public domain. Those teachings should be used to understand public issues, evaluate possible ways of dealing with them, and guide one's actions in respect to them.

Although mercy requires that the demands of justice not only be fulfilled but exceeded, Christians sometimes organize their lives without considering their responsibilities in respect to social justice. Treating these responsibilities as an afterthought is a mistake, however, since they affect every area of one's life, and also make their own specific demands.[102]

a) One should commit oneself to promoting social justice. Taking into account the contemporary situation—the misery of many people and the persistence of unjust structures—is important for many decisions, especially those by which people commit themselves to elements of their personal vocations (see 2.E.3.b). Every Christian has gifts suitable for promoting social justice; a few have the extraordinary gifts needed for social leadership, while others have the common gifts needed to contribute in various ways to the struggle against unjust structures and particular social evils. Of course, not everyone is called to be an activist; a

---

alone to separate the subjects of the Kingdom from the subjects of the Evil One, and that this judgment will take place at the end of time. By presuming to anticipate judgment here and now, man puts himself in the place of God and sets himself against the patience of God."

100. John Paul II, *Sollicitudo rei socialis*, 48, *AAS* 80 (1988) 583, *OR*, 29 Feb. 1988, 13, teaches: "The Church well knows that *no temporal achievement* is to be identified with the Kingdom of God, but that all such achievements simply *reflect* and in a sense *anticipate* the glory of the Kingdom, the Kingdom which we await at the end of history, when the Lord will come again."

101. Congregation for the Doctrine of the Faith, *Instruction on Christian Freedom and Liberation*, 62, *AAS* 79 (1987) 581, *OR*, 14 Apr. 1986, 5.

102. *CIC*, c. 225, §2, declares: "Each lay person in accord with his or her condition is bound by a special duty to imbue and perfect the order of temporal affairs with the spirit of the gospel; they thus give witness to Christ in a special way in carrying out those affairs and in exercising secular duties."

contemplative nun can make a unique contribution. In fulfilling their personal vocations, however, Christians are not pursuing merely individualistic self-fulfillment, but are making their proper contribution to the kingdom. Each therefore is called to further social justice in accord with his or her personal vocation.[103]

By committing oneself to one's vocation and carrying it out, then, one fulfills one's social responsibilities to the whole world as well as possible (see GS 43). It follows that those who seek, accept, and faithfully fulfill their personal vocations should not feel guilty when faithfulness to their vocation precludes doing on behalf of social justice something which plainly needs doing. The remaining unmet needs of the Church and the world devolve upon others, and should be consigned by prayer to God's mercy.

b) One should adopt a style of life suited to social responsibility. People living in comparative comfort in an affluent society are tempted to quiet their consciences by verbally espousing liberal causes, lending token support to ineffectual social movements, vehemently condemning powerful agents of putative injustice such as multinational corporations, and making other gestures, all the while ignoring the injunction: "Let us love, not in word or speech, but in truth and action" (1 Jn 3.18).[104] Instead of following so conventional and hypocritical a path, a person should talk less and practice a more genuinely Christian style of life, which will enable him or her to do for others what really can be done, even though it may seem likely to make little difference to the massive injustices crushing the less fortunate.

This means setting aside individualism and adopting the attitude of solidarity with the poor and oppressed. One should be ambitious to serve others, not jealous of one's personal freedom to do as one pleases. Consumption should be limited to what is truly necessary to maintain oneself and fulfill the responsibilities of one's personal vocation. As John Paul II teaches: "We must find a simple way of living. For it is not right that the standard of living of the rich countries should seek to maintain itself by draining off a great part of the reserves of energy and raw materials that are meant to serve the whole of humanity."[105] People should restrain their impulses to seek sensory gratification, in order to gain the freedom and power to make the sacrifices and endure the sufferings inevitably involved in pursuing justice and doing works of mercy.

---

103. Congregation for the Doctrine of the Faith, *Instruction on Certain Aspects of the "Theology of Liberation"*, 11.3, *AAS* 76 (1984) 903, *OR,* 10 Sept. 1984, 4: "All priests, religious and laypeople who hear this call for justice and who want to work for evangelization and the advancement of mankind, will do so in communion with their bishop and with the Church, each in accord with his or her own specific ecclesial vocation."

104. Paul VI, *Octogesima adveniens,* 48, *AAS* 63 (1971) 437–38, *OR,* 20 May 1971, 9, teaches: "Let each one examine himself, to see what he has done up to now, and what he ought to do. It is not enough to recall principles, state intentions, point to crying injustice and utter prophetic denunciations; these words will lack real weight unless they are accompanied for each individual by a livelier awareness of personal responsibility and by effective action. It is too easy to throw back on others responsibility for injustice, if at the same time one does not realize how each one shares in it personally, and how personal conversion is needed first."

105. John Paul II, Homily in Yankee Stadium, 6, *AAS* 71 (1979) 1172, *OR,* 22 Oct. 1979, 5.

c) **There are various ways of working for social justice.** The Church enjoins the laity to participate in public affairs: "May all Christians be aware of their special and personal vocation in the political community" (GS 75; cf. AA 7, 14; GS 43).[106] A person may well be able to work as a civil servant and in some situations even to seek and hold an elective office: "Catholics skilled in public affairs and adequately enlightened in faith and Christian doctrine should not refuse to administer public affairs, since by doing so in a worthy manner they can further the common good and at the same time prepare the way for the gospel" (AA 14). Also, available political means should be used to oppose officially sanctioned injustices, such as legalized abortion (see 11.D.6).

It also is possible for a person to contribute to social justice by accepting appropriate roles, available to a faithful Christian, in small-scale organizations. These roles include participation in religious confraternities of a traditional sort— for example, a St. Vincent de Paul society—and in civic communities, such as a local citizens' association. They also include work in diverse sorts of voluntary associations formed precisely for social action, for example, the various groups that make up the prolife movement in the United States and various other nations. When such associations are sound, they have several marks: the full and active participation of their members, democratic processes, a focus on efforts to raise consciousness concerning the injustices they strive to overcome, and, in some cases, carrying on projects to change unjust policies and structures.

The opportunities to work for social justice offered by small-scale communities and voluntary associations should not be scorned as insignificant. Working in these ways, an individual can do some good, help some people, and overcome some injustices. Such work can be an effective apostolate and can provide material for the heavenly kingdom (see GS 38–39).

d) **Only good means may be used to promote social justice.** In taking on and fulfilling roles and responsibilities, a person sometimes may tolerate and even materially cooperate in injustices (see 7.F.4–5). But there are limits. For example, justice demands that those seeking office not purchase the support of special interest groups by promising them unfair advantages. Moreover, moral absolutes must never be set aside: since they mark out and safeguard certain important rights of every person, they cannot be violated without violating the dignity of persons.[107]

---

106. John Paul II, *Christifideles laici*, 42, *AAS* 81 (1989) 472–73, *OR*, 6 Feb. 1989, 14, teaches: "Charges of careerism, idolatry of power, egoism and corruption that are oftentimes directed at persons in government, parliaments, the ruling classes, or political parties, as well as the common opinion that participating in politics is an absolute moral danger, do not in the least justify either scepticism or an absence on the part of Christians in public life."

107. John Paul II, Homily at Mass for Youth (Belo Horizonte, Brazil), 5, *Inseg.* 3.2 (1980) 8, *OR*, 14 July 1980, 1, teaches: "Sharing as priest, bishop and cardinal the lives of innumerable young people at University, in youth groups, in excursions in the mountains, in clubs for reflection and prayer, I learned that a youth begins to grow old in a dangerous way, when he lets himself be deceived by the facile and convenient principle that 'the end justifies the means'; when he adopts the belief that the only hope of improving society is to promote struggle and hatred between social groups, that it is to be found in the Utopia of a classless society, which very soon reveals itself as

An individual may not make moral compromises to gain or hold a position of power or influence, even in order to use it to do good. Because such positions often cannot be obtained or held without unjust dealing or violations of moral absolutes, moral limits sometimes put such positions beyond the reach of a faithful Christian or require abandoning them—as St. Thomas More did.

3. One Should Act in Specifically Christian Ways to Promote Justice

Many people think of social justice as an objective which can be promoted in only one way, and suppose that way to be common to nonbelievers and Christians alike. But faithfulness to Jesus, who proclaimed the truth and bore consistent witness to it by his action, requires Christians to proceed as he did. If they do, their efforts to promote social justice will be a genuine apostolate and will markedly differ from nonbelievers' efforts.

a) One should work for justice by going to the roots of injustice. Strategies aimed at intensifying enmity in order to destroy those who do injustice plainly are wicked, since greater hatred is worse in itself and is an added obstacle to repentance. While certain kinds of pressure can be used rightly to rectify unjust social, political, and economic structures, such activities should be subordinated to a general strategy of peacemaking, based on trust in the power of God's grace to make truth and love effective.

The roots of injustice are personal sins, and the conversion of sinners builds up the kingdom as nothing else does. The magisterium teaches:

> The acute need for radical reforms of the structures which conceal poverty and which are themselves forms of violence, should not let us lose sight of the fact that the source of injustice is in the hearts of men. Therefore it is only by making an appeal to the *moral potential* of the person and to the constant need for interior conversion, that social change will be brought about which will truly be in the service of man [note omitted].[108]

Only an approach which strives to remedy the spiritual poverty of those who do injustice, as well as the material poverty of those who suffer it, is adequate to an authentic Christian preferential option for the poor, that is, a commitment most vigorously to serve those whose needs are greatest (see 2.C.2.d).[109] So, in a Christian strategy for promoting justice and peace, the first and indispensable

---

the creator of new classes. I became convinced that only love draws closer things that are different, and brings about union in diversity."

108. Congregation for the Doctrine of the Faith, *Instruction on Certain Aspects of the "Theology of Liberation"*, 11.8, *AAS* 76 (1984) 905, *OR*, 10 Sept. 1984, 4.

109. John Paul II, *Centesimus annus*, 57, *AAS* 83 (1991) 862, *OR*, 6 May 1991, 15, teaches: "Today more than ever, the Church is aware that her social message will gain credibility more immediately from the *witness of actions* than as a result of its internal logic and consistency. This awareness is also a source of her preferential option for the poor, which is never exclusive or discriminatory towards other groups. This option is not limited to material poverty, since it is well known that there are many other forms of poverty, especially in modern society—not only economic but cultural and spiritual poverty as well." Cf. John Paul II, Discourse to Cardinals, Members of the Roman Curia, and Pontifical Household, 9, *AAS* 77 (1985) 510–11, *OR*, 21 Jan. 1985, 7–8.

element, the foundation of every other effort, is to know what justice requires, to bear witness to it in ways appropriate to one's personal vocation both by speech and by action (accepting as a consequence inevitable personal suffering for justice' sake), and to pray for the conversion of those who violate the requirements of justice, beginning with oneself.[110]

b) **The very sharing of Christian faith powerfully promotes justice.** Christian faith provides an adequate rationale to repent and do justice, and the hope that follows on faith is adequate to motivate a life in accord with faith's requirement of love. Thus, justice is promoted by sharing Christian faith with those who sin against justice, as well as by sharing faith and hope with those who are the victims of injustice. Faith in providence and awareness of human free choice liberate such people from the idea that their condition depends on mere luck or blind fate, and raises their consciousness of their own dignity. Hope provides them with motivation for building up the kingdom, which enables them to struggle perseveringly against injustice without hatred, selfishness, and the use of immoral means, and even to intercede, as Jesus did, for those who treat them unjustly.

c) **Justice should be advocated even when it seems impractical.** Politics is the art of the possible, and nonbelievers naturally limit the possible to what is *humanly* possible. In the making of public policy and in every other practical affair, they therefore limit the options under consideration to those which are feasible; and often all such options make seemingly necessary compromises with well-established conditions of injustice or else with powerful countermovements which are themselves unjust.

In bearing witness to the gospel, however, one should assume that whatever is right, even if it is humanly impossible, is possible to God and worth pursuing. So, prejudices about feasibility should be set aside while every problem and movement is examined creatively in the light of the gospel, so that a truly just option can be articulated and advocated. Doing so not only bears witness to the truth but makes a unique contribution to public debate, by setting out the radical standard of justice as a possibility to be considered seriously, not ignored as impractical.

d) **One should not despair of the fruitfulness of one's efforts.** Quite often, one's best efforts on behalf of justice and peace will appear to meet with little or no success. Even when something is accomplished, the good outcome is likely to be vulnerable and temporary.

Nevertheless, Christians ought to do their best to achieve the good they can. For whatever is achieved really will benefit those who suffer from injustice and its consequences. And, as John Paul II teaches:

> However imperfect and temporary are all the things that can and ought to be done through the combined efforts of everyone and through divine grace at a given moment of history, in order to make people's lives "more human", nothing will be *lost* or *will have been in vain.* This is the teaching of the Second Vatican Council, in an enlightening passage of the Pastoral Constitution *Gaudium et*

110. An example of the execution of this strategy: *You Reject Them, You Reject Me: The Prison Letters of Joan Andrews,* ed. Richard Cowden Guido (Manassas, Va.: Trinity Communications, 1988).

Spes: "After we have promoted on earth, in the Spirit of the Lord and in accord with his command, the goods of human dignity, familial communion, and freedom—that is to say, all the good fruits of our nature and effort—then we shall find them once more, but cleansed of all dirt, lit up, and transformed, when Christ gives back to the Father an eternal and universal Kingdom . . . .. On this earth the Kingdom is present in mystery even now." (GS 39)[111]

4. Each Christian Should Shape His or Her Life by Moral Truth

In what follows in this volume, relevant moral absolutes will be laid out clearly, not because Christian morality is merely or even mainly negative in its bearing on others, but because it is determinedly concerned to respect and protect the dignity of every person. There also will be many affirmative norms, more or less exigent. But all these together still will not tell anybody exactly how to fulfill his or her personal responsibilities. As Vatican II teaches, the Church's teaching always provides necessary principles, but it does not always provide solutions to concrete problems (see GS 33, 43). So individuals must apply the affirmative norms to the possibilities in a situation, in order to arrive at an ultimate practical judgment of Christian prudence as to what is to be done. Hence, for this part of the book to be fruitful, it will be necessary to make use of chapter five.

---

111. John Paul II, *Sollicitudo rei socialis,* 48, *AAS* 80 (1988) 583, *OR,* 29 Feb. 1988, 13 (translation of quotation from GS 39 supplied).

CHAPTER SEVEN

EQUAL DIGNITY, COMMUNICATION, INTERPERSONAL RELATIONSHIPS, AND RESTITUTION

Summary

The dignity of human persons is rooted in their relationship to God. While love excludes discrimination which violates that dignity, love also distinguishes among persons in accord with their dignity. Thus the errors of social stratification and egalitarianism are both profoundly mistaken. It is always grave matter to violate others' dignity, for to do so is to hate them; nor may power be used for domination. Women and men have equal dignity as persons but complementary gifts.

All communication should be open to community, and all parties to communication should submit themselves to truth. There are responsibilities on the side of those who receive communications as well as on the side of those who communicate. Truthfulness is an obligation in each and every communication. Unloving communication is wrong because it damages communion. This rules out such things as boasting, false modesty, flattery, and detraction. But lying and other deceptions in communication also are incompatible with love, including love of enemies, and so are wrong. The various justifications advanced for lying in some circumstances, and even for "mental reservations" which are intended to deceive, do not stand up under examination. At best, lying as a "lesser evil" can be subjectively blameless.

Although there is an obligation to keep promises, sometimes promises lose their obligatory force and need not be kept. Similarly, there is a limited responsibility with respect to secrets. While this responsibility can have different bases, secrecy often is good, and should be respected. The responsibility nevertheless is limited, and sometimes secrets need not, or even should not, be kept. The Golden Rule is useful in judging the limits of the responsibility.

Fulfilling one's vocation often requires forming or joining voluntary associations. The specific purpose of a structured voluntary association should be respected, and it is unjust for some members of an association to impose a change of purpose on others. Friendship, a form of voluntary association, is intrinsically good and valuable for Christian life, and should be sought and offered. Friends have certain specific responsibilities to one another: to communicate their real and full selves, to give one another precedence in the order of charity, to defend one another's reputation and honor, and so on.

Authority and obedience are essential to all communal actions, and do not preclude equal personal dignity. But some conceptions of obedience are contrary to personal dignity, as are some notions of authority. The force and the limits of authority are determined by its moral ground; the exercise of both authority and obedience should be shaped by the common good.

Formal cooperation in others' wrongdoing is always wrong, but material cooperation is sometimes, though not always, permissible. The Golden Rule provides guidance in determining whether to cooperate. Discernment is necessary when both cooperating and not cooperating are good. In some cases, the Church's leaders can authoritatively decide.

Restitution restores justice in an unjust state of affairs. An obligation arising from the good of justice as interpersonal harmony, it can be required by diverse specific conditions. Usually, however, just restitution does not make things exactly as they were. The Golden Rule must be applied to determine what restitution is required; and not just those obliged to make restitution but those to whom it is owed should be just and merciful.

Question A: How Is Equal Dignity Consistent with Diversity in Social Status?

Similarity in common humanity and difference in individuality both are necessary conditions for people to associate with one another. Since both factors, humanity and individuality, are present in all human persons, respect for human dignity must respond appropriately to both.

Christian love builds up on earth a network of relationships which will last forever in heaven. Love therefore responds to all persons in the same way, inasmuch as every person shares the same human nature and divine calling, and to each person in different ways, inasmuch as each has different gifts and needs; it is entirely self-consistent in doing this. Thus, in its own unique way, love transcends two defective ways of dealing with people's sameness and difference: structures of dominance, which violate the equality of persons as human, and processes of impersonal leveling, which violate the uniqueness of persons as individuals. God-given sameness in humanity forestalls the need to pursue equality by eliminating differences; God-given differences in people's gifts provide opportunities for them to fulfill themselves in communion by mutual self-giving.

1. Two Opposed Social Realities Block This Reconciliation

In the fallen human condition, not only do individuals treat one another unjustly, but societies are shaped by structures at odds with basic human rights (on sinful structures, see 4.A.3.e). While rightly opposing such structures, the movement on behalf of the absolute equality of individuals also attacks the dignity of persons, since their unique gifts belong to their personhood and are essential to their fulfillment.

Both social realities—unjust social structures and the movement toward absolute equality—develop their own pervasive attitudes, characteristic practices, and antagonistic ideologies. In confused and watered-down forms, both often affect different portions of people's thinking and action without their being aware of it. It is important to understand them in their pure forms, however, in order to see their essential inadequacy and be equally ready to resist both.

a) **Social stratification violates the equality of persons as human.** Many social relationships have been and are shaped by institutionalized domination. A caste system is an obvious example; so are men's domination over women, colonial powers' domination over native peoples, slavery, and the legal nonpersonhood of the unborn. Such structures infringe on the fundamental human rights of those subjected to domination. Those who benefit from the injustice rationalize it by claiming that relevant differences between themselves and those whom they dominate mark objective degrees of humanity or human excellence, and that just social order requires social stratification reflecting their own inherently superior worth. Supported by ideology (racism, colonialism, or some other specific form of what in general can be called "an ideology of social stratification"), such social structures deny the equality as human beings of those who are dominated—deny that the dominated as persons have inherent worth transcending their social function or the value others attribute to them. Indeed, the ideology of stratification inevitably tends to reduce those dominated to the status of nonpersons or second-class persons.

b) **Egalitarianism ignores the dignity of persons as different.** The ideal of most secular humanists, not only collectivists but many liberal democrats, is not only to do away with every structure based on domination but to make all persons equal by making their social roles as alike as possible and disregarding the remaining differences. But differences among people's natural endowments and attainments tend to lead to differences in social status, and people's different situations also differentiate their opportunities. Thus, this ideal leads to egalitarianism and sociocultural homogenization: the impossible project of eliminating everything which requires differences in social roles—except, of course, for those factors reflecting people's merely subjective preferences (see 6.E.6). In the pursuit of this ideal, egalitarians regard differences among people's natural endowments, even those such as gender which serve fundamental human goods, as mere obstacles to universal equality and equal rights.

2. Love Responds to Every Person's Equal Dignity

Created in the image and likeness of God and endowed by nature with the capacities to reason and make free choices, human persons enjoy precisely the same essential dignity (see DH 1, GS 12–17).[1] Moreover, the importance of differences in status resulting from the fallen human condition is greatly reduced insofar as

---

1. Only the essential dignity shared by every human being is under consideration here. This must be distinguished from moral goodness and holiness acquired by cooperating with God's grace, which sometimes also is called "dignity"; see William E. May, *An Introduction to Moral Theology* (Huntington, Ind.: Our Sunday Visitor Publishing Division, 1991), 19–22.

redeemed humans become children of God (see GS 22). To this all human beings are called, and love should extend even to those who seem to have rejected this calling, in the hope that they too will accept it. Thus, the same Christian love should embrace Jesus and every human person.

a) **The dignity of persons is rooted in their relationship to God.** Holding that human persons enjoy a spark of the divine, the Stoics already affirmed the dignity and fellowship of every member of the human family. But Christian faith knows a deeper ground for human dignity and communion:

> The dignity of the person is manifested in all its radiance when the person's origin and destiny are considered: created by God in his image and likeness as well as redeemed by the most precious blood of Christ, the person is called to be a "child in the Son" and a living temple of the Spirit, destined for the eternal life of blessed communion with God. . . .
>
> In virtue of his personal dignity the human being is *always a value in himself and for himself,* and as such demands being considered and treated as a person and never as an object to be used, or as a means, or as a thing.[2]

The phrase, "child in the Son," points to Christian faith's special basis for affirming the same essential dignity in every human being. St. Paul clarifies it: "In Christ Jesus you are all children of God through faith. . . . There is no longer Jew or Greek, there is no longer slave or free, there is no longer male or female; for all of you are one in Christ Jesus" (Gal 3.26, 28).[3]

b) **Love excludes discrimination which violates dignity.** For egalitarians, equality among people is a goal to be attained by eliminating or ignoring differences. By contrast, the revelation that their divine origin and calling constitute the deepest basis of human persons' dignity makes it clear that the equality which is important is not a goal to be reached but something God freely gives in creating, redeeming, and sanctifying human persons. That common dignity is the bedrock on which equality in fundamental rights rests: "The dignity of the person constitutes *the foundation of the equality of all people among themselves.* As a result all forms of discrimination are totally unacceptable."[4]

Christian love rejects the discrimination which faith finds unacceptable. Vatican II teaches:

> The disposition of a human person toward God the Father and his or her disposition toward fellow human beings are so connected that Scripture says: "Whoever does not love does not know God" (1 Jn 4.8).
>
> The foundation therefore is taken away from any theory or practice which leads to discrimination, between one person and another or between one nation and another, with respect to human dignity and the rights flowing from it. (NA 5)

---

2. John Paul II, *Christifideles laici,* 37, *AAS* 81 (1989) 461, *OR,* 6 Feb. 1989, 12.

3. However, Gal 3.28 should not be used as a proof text to deny the appropriateness of differences in the roles of men and women or their complementarity, since the verse, read in context, plainly means to exclude only the relevance of such differences for a Christian's relationship to God; see Thomas Hopko, "Galatians 3:28: An Orthodox Interpretation," *St. Vladimir's Theological Quarterly* 35 (1991): 169–86.

4. John Paul II, *Christifideles laici,* 37, *AAS* 81 (1989) 461, *OR,* 6 Feb. 1989, 12.

Consequently, love requires avoiding "every form—whether social or cultural—of discrimination with respect to the fundamental rights of persons, whether on the basis of sex, race, color, social condition, language, or religion" (GS 29). This list is not exhaustive; other factors often are used to rationalize injustices, among them differences in nationality, wealth, health, physical or mental capacity, age, and personal appearance.[5] Also, with respect to the rights flowing from human dignity, love rejects discrimination not only between individuals and peoples, but also between any other communities, classes, or groups whatsoever.

c) **Love distinguishes among persons in accord with their dignity.** Not all distinctions among persons violate their dignity. It often is right to treat people who have different needs differently, for example, parents rightly spend more money on the medical care of sickly children than healthy ones. Society also rightly treats criminals differently from the law-abiding. Their dignity as human beings should not be violated, but they may be punished in ways, such as imprisonment, which otherwise would violate fundamental rights.

Different people have different weaknesses and experience different temptations. Whether caused by natural factors or by culture, morally burdensome characteristics for which individuals are not responsible should not be used as an excuse for discriminating against them, and doing so would be similar to discriminating on the basis of race, religion, and so on. In this sense, sexual orientation should be included in the list of bases of unjust discrimination. However, in speaking of sexual orientation, many people actually mean readiness to engage in homosexual activity, and in this sense *sexual orientation* should not be listed among the bases of unjust discrimination. For homosexual activity is gravely wrong (see 9.E.3.e, 9.E.6) and so, like any other kind of grave wrong, provides a reasonable basis for dealing differently with those who voluntarily engage in it, both for their own good, the protection of other individuals, and the well-being of society as a whole.

5. With regard to nationalism and racism, see Paul VI, *Populorum progressio,* 62–63, *AAS* 59 (1967) 287–88, *PE,* 275.62–63. With regard to those who are not physically or mentally normal, the Holy See, *Document for the International Year of Disabled Persons,* I.1, 3, *EV* 7 (1980–81) 1044–47, *OR,* 23 Mar. 1981, 6, teaches clearly: "The first principle, which is one that must be stated clearly and firmly, is that the disabled person (whether the disability be the result of a congenital handicap, chronic illness or accident, or from mental or physical deficiency, and whatever the severity of the disability) *is a fully human subject, with the corresponding innate, sacred and inviolable rights.* This statement is based upon the firm recognition of the fact that a human being possesses a unique dignity and an independent value, from the moment of conception and in every stage of development, whatever his or her physical condition. . . . A perfect technological society which only allowed fully functional members and which neglected, institutionalized or, what is worse, eliminated those who did not measure up to this standard or who were unable to carry out a useful role, would have to be considered as radically unworthy of man, however economically successful it might be. Such a society would in fact be tainted by a sort of discrimination no less worthy of condemnation than racial discrimination; it would be discrimination by the strong and 'healthy' against the weak and the sick." With regard to potential discrimination on the basis of age, see John Paul II, Message to the World Assembly on the Problems of the Aging Population, 1, *AAS* 74 (1982) 1173–75, *OR,* 30 Aug. 1982, 4–5.

3. Love Appreciates Persons' Diverse Gifts and Potentialities

Loving everyone in Jesus with the same Christian love means acknowledging the same human dignity shared by all who are called to be God's children and avoiding all discrimination with respect to every basic human right. But the same love extends to each person's whole being, including all his or her diverse gifts and potentialities. Thus, St. Paul wrote his famous treatment of love (1 Cor 13) precisely to explain how communion should exist in Jesus' one body, the Church, among members with diverse and complementary gifts which are to be exercised in an orderly and harmonious way.

Love appreciates differences, perfects them even as it unites those who differ, and motivates different people to use their various gifts in fulfilling the diverse, complementary responsibilities pertaining to their personal vocations. Thus, St. Paul teaches:

> Now there are varieties of gifts, but the same Spirit; and there are varieties of services, but the same Lord; and there are varieties of activities, but it is the same God who activates all of them in everyone. To each is given the manifestation of the Spirit for the common good. . . .
>
> For just as the body is one and has many members, and all the members of the body, though many, are one body, so it is with Christ. For in the one Spirit we were all baptized into one body—Jews or Greeks, slaves or free—and we were all made to drink of one Spirit. (1 Cor 12.4–7, 12–13)

While Christian love honors every excellence and respects those holding legitimate authority (see *S.t.*, 2–2, q. 102, a. 1; q. 103, a. 1), it cannot treat differences of gifts, services, and good works as if they marked degrees of personal superiority and inferiority. For every gift, service, and good work is valuable in its own proper way, a way incommensurable with any other, and each makes its unique, indispensable contribution to the common good (see 1 Cor 12.14–26).

4. Love Precludes Using Power for Domination

In the one body with its many members, each member has its own role and enjoys its own excellence (see 1 Cor 12.14–26). Excellence implies power, and this immediately raises the question of how domination can be avoided. The answer is that the law of love requires those who should cooperate in open-ended communities (see 6.C.2) to submit to one another out of reverence for Christ (see Eph 5.21). The power each person has because of his or her gifts is to be used for others' benefit: "Like good stewards of the manifold grace of God, serve one another with whatever gift each of you has received" (1 Pt 4.10; cf. GS 32). Indeed, love requires those with greater power to use it, not for domination, but to serve others more effectively (see Mt 20.25–28; Mk 9.35, 10.42–45; Lk 22.25–27; Jn 13.12–15). For instance, husbands are to love their wives as Jesus loved the Church in laying down his life for her (see Eph 5.25).[6]

6. On this verse, John Paul II, General Audience (11 Aug. 1982), 4, *Inseg.* 5.3 (1982) 205–6, *OR*, 16–23 Aug. 1982, 1, comments: "Love excludes every kind of subjection whereby the wife

Such love precludes domination, for nobody lays down his or her life for a nonperson or a second-class person.

5. To Violate Others' Personal Dignity Is Grave Matter

The gospel is opposed to social stratification, which misinterprets differences among persons as if they marked degrees of dignity of human beings as such, consigns supposedly inferior persons to roles of menial service, and reduces the common good to what is fulfilling for those who supposedly are superior.

The gospel likewise is opposed to egalitarianism, which fails to appreciate the value of differences among persons, prefers the individualistic pursuit of fulfillment to mutual service, and reduces the common good to the sum of the goods of individuals.

In their extreme forms, both an ideology of social stratification and egalitarianism lead to treating persons as things, to be used or enjoyed. Stratification does this by rationalizing dominance and denying that all human beings are equal; egalitarianism does it by disregarding valuable differences among persons and substituting individualism for mutual service, so that true community becomes impossible and interpersonal relationships are reduced to mere arrangements for mutual exploitation. Either approach is at odds with the dignity of persons as individuals and the communion to which they are called. Acting according to either approach therefore is inconsistent with love of neighbor, and so is grave matter.

a) Treating others as property violates their personal dignity. The clearest case of treating persons as property is the form of slavery in which masters own slaves just as they own animals. Under this arrangement, it is often legal for masters to dispose of their slaves at will, beat them, sexually use and abuse them, mutilate them, deprive them of marriage and family life, and even exercise the power of life and death over them. While these plainly are grave injustices, the underlying wrong is the attempt to reduce the very person of the slave to the condition of an object of possession, use, enjoyment, and disposal—a thing without his or her own ends, a mere means to the master's ends. Vatican II includes slavery in the group of sins against reverence for the human person characterized as *infamies* (see GS 27). It not only violates the dignity of enslaved persons but violates love, for one cannot love another as oneself and abide with him or her in Christ while at the same time treating that other as a thing.[7]

---

might become a servant or a slave of the husband, an object of unilateral domination. Love makes the husband simultaneously subject to the wife, and thereby subject to the Lord himself, just as the wife to the husband. The community or unity which they should establish through marriage, is constituted by a reciprocal donation of self, which is also a mutual subjection." For a fuller development of this point, see 9.D.2; John Paul II, *Mulieris dignitatem,* 10 and 24, *AAS* 80 (1988) 1674–77 and 1710–12, *OR,* 3 Oct. 1988, 5 and 11.

7. Several New Testament passages seem to take for granted slavery's moral acceptability, for example: "Slaves, obey your earthly masters with fear and trembling, in singleness of heart, as you obey Christ . . . .. And, masters, do the same to them. Stop threatening them, for you know that both of you have the same Master in heaven, and with him there is no partiality" (Eph 6.5, 9). What is one to make of such passages? First, the Christians of the first centuries lived in an extremely antagonistic society, whose institutions they could not change; thus, while they took

b) **Certain other actions are very similar to enslaving people.** Today everyone condemns slavery, and people in most parts of the world do not have the opportunity or motivation to commit the sin of enslaving another or holding a slave. However, it still is possible to be tempted to violate human dignity radically, in ways sharing more or less fully and plainly in the malice of slavery, and so human persons continue to be treated as things. Human individuals, including embryos produced in laboratories and still-living aborted babies, sometimes are used as material for experimentation or as a source of tissues and organs for the benefit of others; children, including babies conceived and gestated by contract, are bought and sold; women are sold or held captive and used, through systems of organized prostitution and otherwise; workers, particularly some migrant laborers and illegal immigrants, are exploited as fully as possible and receive only the minimum necessary to keep working.

These things usually are done without legally categorizing persons as property, yet those exploited are treated as things for others' use and enjoyment, contrary to justice and love. In every such case, the offense against the person is so direct and so great that the sin plainly is very grave.

c) **To violate others' dignity is to hate them.** Even without being treated as things in such gross ways, people can have their dignity violated by discrimination or the refusal to recognize their unique gifts and acknowledge their individual value. It is an important part of each person's good to be a member of genuine communities in which his or her humanity is honored and his or her special gifts are appreciated and helped to flourish. To deny others' equality as human beings or their gifts as unique individuals is contrary to this good; doing so by a deliberate act of will is contrary to love, and so is a form of hatred.

For instance, racism, even in the absence of animus against individuals, is radically contrary to love for members of a race considered inferior, since it negates their equality in humanity and implicitly conflicts with willing their full sharing in human communion. But an egalitarianism which goes so far as to despise the diverse gifts of different sorts of people—for example, the kind of feminism which refuses to recognize and appreciate the different values inherent in being a man and being a woman—also rejects their true fulfillment and manifests hatred by preferring a multitude of equal individuals to a communion of many members in one body, in which each member uses his or her special gifts in the service of others.

---

established injustices for granted, that must not be interpreted as condoning them. Second, while the master-slave relationship is not explicitly condemned by any New Testament writer, neither does any defend it. Moreover, the teaching that being a slave does not exclude one from the new covenant (see 1 Cor 7.21–24, 12.13; Gal 3.28; Col 3.11; Phlm 15–17) and that masters must treat slaves fairly (see Col 4.1; cf. Eph 6.9) calls for a change in the lived relationship between masters and slaves, and implicitly calls into question the conventional structure with its radical injustice. Third, the New Testament focuses on a more basic and widespread servitude: slavery to sin (see Rom 6.17) and its overcoming by the obedience of Jesus, who, though divine, accepted the role of a slave (see Phil 2.6–7). Thus, New Testament advice to slaves emphasizes Christian patience and mercy, which imitate Jesus in suffering injustices without hatred and returning loving service for the injustice suffered (see 1 Pt 2.18–25).

6. Women and Men Are Equal in Dignity but Complementary in Gifts

Men have dominated women in most societies and cultures, and an ideology of social stratification has rationalized it: precisely as persons, it has been assumed, women are inferior to men and naturally suited to be their subjects.[8] The feminist movement originated in understandable and justified reaction to that injustice. However, some feminists are egalitarians; they not only denounce the injustice of male domination but deny the personal significance and social value of the difference between man and woman. Such feminism is appropriately called "radical," to distinguish it from sound efforts to end male dominance and achieve justice for women.

Radical feminists regard sexuality as merely biological, and demand for women not only equality in fundamental rights but the greatest possible sameness in every social role and activity. So, for instance, radical feminists in general reject the complementarity of men and women in marriage and family life, while Catholic radical feminists claim the Church's teaching is inconsistent in affirming women's dignity and equality with men while denying them ordination to the priesthood. But the Church's teaching on the significance of sexual differentiation shows how love reconciles diversity in gifts and social roles, on the one hand, with equality in human dignity and in every fundamental right, on the other.

a) **Men and women are alike in dignity, complementary in function.** Recent popes insist both that men and women have the same dignity and that the difference between the sexes has personal and social value:

> The Church deems that a woman, as a person, enjoys a dignity equal to that of a man, but is ordained by God and by nature for different tasks, which perfect and complete the work assigned to man. A similar dignity, a complementary function: one can summarize in this expression the principle in the light of which the problem of woman's work should be examined.[9]

---

8. John Paul II, *Mulieris dignitatem*, 10, *AAS* 80 (1988) 1674–77, *OR,* 3 Oct. 1988, 5, points out that the domination of men over women is a result of sin, and in this sense a divine punishment (see Gn 3.16), but no less unjust on that account, and concludes: "The overcoming of this evil inheritance is, generation after generation, the task of every human being, whether woman or man. For whenever man is responsible for offending a woman's personal dignity and vocation, he acts contrary to his own personal dignity and his own vocation."

9. John XXIII, Address to a Congress of the International Federation of Young Catholic Women, *AAS* 52 (1960) 392, *The Pope Speaks* 6 (1959–60): 331. In *Pacem in terris, AAS* 55 (1963) 267–68, *PE,* 270.41, John notes with approval: "Women are gaining an increasing awareness of their natural dignity. Far from being content with a purely passive role or allowing themselves to be regarded as a kind of instrument, they are demanding both in domestic and in public life the rights and duties which belong to them as human persons." Vatican II (see GS 29) also teaches the sameness of women and men in human dignity. Prudence Allen, R.S.M., *The Concept of Woman: The Aristotelian Revolution 750 BC–AD 1250* (Montreal: Eden Press, 1985), 292–315, shows that Hildegard of Bingen (1098–1179) worked out the complementarity of woman and man; but Aristotle's view that woman is inferior insofar as different from man prevailed in theology until recently.

And what is a woman's complementary function? It is the counterpart of a man's calling to fatherhood and to fatherlike responsibility for those who depend on him in various relationships: "Every woman is made to be a mother: a mother in the physical meaning of the word or in the more spiritual and exalted but no less real sense."[10]

b) Not every social role is equally suitable for men and women. Discrimination against women, including that denying them an equal opportunity to participate in professional and social life, is unjust. But affirming equal human rights nevertheless is compatible with rejecting egalitarianism:

> The equalizing of rights must not degenerate into an egalitarian and impersonal leveling. Egalitarianism, which is blindly pushed forward by our materialistic society, is little concerned with the specific welfare of persons, and contrary to appearances it takes no notice of what is suitable and what is not suitable for women. It thereby runs the risk either of 'virilizing' women or of depersonalizing them.[11]

For example, while fathers should share in the care of their small children, the primary responsibility in this matter naturally falls to mothers; and while women can help deal with challenges which must be repelled by physical force, generally men are better suited by nature to organize such actions and execute them.[12] Such differences do not imply that individuals of either sex are less capable on the whole than those of the other, but that individuals of both sexes are naturally needed to fulfill complementary social roles.[13]

10. Pius XII, Address to Italian Catholic Women, *AAS* 37 (1945) 287, *Catholic Mind* 43 (1945): 708. Similarly, John Paul II, Address to Participants in the Fifth International Congress of the Family, 2, *Inseg.* 3.2 (1980) 1084, *OR,* 29 Dec. 1980, 7, teaches: "Some [married women] are tempted to seek a solution in movements which claim to 'liberate' them, although it would be necessary to ask what liberation it is a question of, and not to mean by this word emancipation from what is their specific vocation as mothers and wives, or imitation, leading to uniformity, of the way in which the male partner finds fulfillment." A helpful philosophical-theological critique of radical feminism: Ronda Chervin, *Feminine, Free and Faithful* (San Francisco: Ignatius Press, 1986).

11. Paul VI, Address to the Members of the Study Commission on the Role of Women in the Church and in Society, and the Committee of the International Women's Year, *AAS* 68 (1976) 200, *OR,* 12 Feb. 1976, 3–4.

12. See Benedict M. Ashley, O.P., *Theologies of the Body: Humanist and Christian* (Braintree, Mass.: The Pope John Center, 1985), 434–36. For a cogent criticism of feminists' refusal to recognize and appreciate innate differences between men and women, and the deleterious effects of this refusal on marriage and the family, see Michael Levin, *Feminism and Freedom* (New Brunswick, N.J.: Transaction Books, 1987), 16–97 and 264–96.

13. Alice Schlegel, *Sexual Stratification: A Cross-Cultural View* (New York: Columbia University Press, 1977), 356, concludes on the basis of studies in comparative anthropology: "It is clear that in all known human societies, gender provides the basis for a fundamental division in social function. In no society to date do men take primary responsibility for the care of young children, nor do women take a principal role in organizing and implementing activities of offense and defense, although the degree to which the opposite sex is involved in these activities varies greatly from society to society. Even where division of labor by sex is minimal or nonexistent . . ., this division of function occurs [note omitted]. Division of function, however, does not necessarily lead to stratification; rather, it can lead to balanced complementarity."

c) **Women are justly excluded from ordination to the priesthood.** The Church believes it impossible to ordain women as priests. It is not that women as persons or as Christians suffer from some defect in human nature or in divine grace. They, no less than men, are created in the image of God and called to be created anew in the likeness of the Word Incarnate. But Jesus, the divine bridegroom, has entered into covenantal communion with the Church as his bride (see Eph 5.22–33; Rv 19.7–8, 21.9, 22.17), and women as female are not suited to represent Jesus within the assembled Church in his spousal relationship with her: "It is *the Eucharist* above all that expresses *the redemptive act of Christ the Bridegroom toward the Church the Bride*. This is clear and unambiguous when the sacramental ministry of the Eucharist, in which the priest acts *'in persona Christi'*, is performed by a man."[14]

Underlying this argument against women's ordination is the premise, defended at length by John Paul II, that the difference between man and woman is of more than biological significance, because it is an unalterable determining condition of their complementarity and fundamental vocation to fulfill themselves and each other in and by their mutual self-giving.[15] God makes use of this significance of the difference between the sexes both in revealing himself in Scripture and in communicating himself by means of the sacraments of the Eucharist and holy order. If a woman were to act as Jesus' proxy in the performance of the Eucharist, his husbandlike relationship with his wifelike Church would not be expressed, so that the very meaning of the Eucharist for everyone who participates in it would be obscured and rendered ambiguous. Whereas all members of the Church, including those in sacred orders and other men, must share in her feminine role as bride, united with her Lord in the one-flesh communion of his body, all would instead be led to think of themselves as a multitude of individual partners with the Lord "in the mystery of redemption."[16]

---

14. John Paul II, *Mulieris dignitatem,* 26, *AAS* 80 (1988) 1716, *OR,* 3 Oct. 1988, 12. Cf. Congregation for the Doctrine of the Faith, *Inter insigniores, AAS* 69 (1977) 98–116, Flannery, 2:331–45; Jean Galot, S.J., *Theology of the Priesthood* (San Francisco: Ignatius Press, 1984), 251–67; Ashley, *Theologies of the Body,* 530–31, 560–61.

15. See John Paul II, *Mulieris dignitatem,* 6–7, *AAS* 80 (1988) 1662–67, *OR,* 3 Oct. 1988, 3–4; the Pope also explicitly asserts complementarity of women and men precisely insofar as they are persons: *Christifideles laici,* 50, *AAS* 81 (1989) 489, *OR,* 6 Feb. 1989, 16: "The condition that will assure the rightful presence of woman in the Church and in society is a more penetrating and accurate consideration of the *anthropological foundation for masculinity and femininity* for the purpose of clarifying woman's personal identity in relation to man, that is, a diversity yet mutual complementarity, not only as it concerns roles to be held and functions to be performed, but also, and more deeply, as it concerns her nature and meaning as a person."

16. See the draft document prepared by a committee of the National Conference of Catholic Bishops, "Partners in the Mystery of Redemption: A Pastoral Response to Women's Concerns for Church and Society," *Origins* 17 (21 Apr. 1988): 757, 759–88. It might be objected that it would be no less fitting for a woman to act *in persona Christi* than for men to share in the Church's feminine role as his bride. However, members of the Church as such do not represent anyone, and so no special symbolic significance attaches to their masculinity or femininity. Moreover, inasmuch as God has chosen to play the role of husband in establishing covenantal communion with humankind, there is no alternative to male Christians sharing in the Church's feminine role, but there is an alternative to the ordination of women.

7. Love Responds to Differences Due to Limitations and Defects

Not all important differences among people are based on their possessing different gifts or powers to serve one another. Some are based on limitations and defects: the helplessness of a baby, the handicap of a maimed or retarded person, the misery of a poor family, the wretchedness of an unrepentant sinner, the obtuseness of an unbeliever, and so on. Viewed without love, such differences can provide motives for discrimination or opportunities for exploitation; viewed with love, they provide opportunities for service, which builds up Jesus' body. Thus, loving parents, teachers, nurses, pastors, and so on find their own fulfillment in the services they render, rather than in domination, and come to appreciate the value of others' needs for the growth of communion in love.

Question B: What Are One's Responsibilities in Communicating?

Revelation and faith, together with the conversation with God called "prayer," initiate and maintain the interpersonal communion of the covenant (see DV 2–5, GS 19; *CMP,* 29.A). Similarly, the self-expressions which people exchange ground and build up human community: "Communication is more than the expression of ideas and the indication of emotion. At its most profound level, it is the giving of self in love."[17] Thus, communication involves not only language but actions insofar as these communicate to others and, through being perceived and interpreted, affect interpersonal relationships.

All interpersonal relationships should be material for the kingdom (see GS 38–39). Moreover, many other responsibilities toward others presuppose and build on the fulfillment of responsibilities in communicating. So, these are among the first of one's duties of Christian love toward others.

1. Some Responsibilities Are Common to Both Partners in Communication

In some situations, such as communication through the mass media and letter writing, one party actively communicates and the other receives the communication; in others—dialogue or conversation—the partners alternate in playing both roles. But in either case, all involved have certain common responsibilities to fulfill if their communication is to serve the relevant goods.

a) **All communication should be open to community.** Every act of communicating and receiving communication tends to draw the parties into an interpersonal relationship or to carry on and perhaps deepen an existing relationship. If the acts are motivated by charity, they will be open to genuine community and will tend to establish or build it up. But, if partners in communication do not act in ways open to genuine community, that will be because their acts somehow are not loving. Either the other party is considered an enemy and genuine community is intention-

17. Pontifical Commission for the Instruments of Social Communication, *Communio et progressio,* 11, *AAS* 63 (1971) 598, Flannery, 1:297; cf. GS 23.

ally excluded (for example, family members engaged in a quarrel seek to defend their self-interests and hurt one another), or the other party is considered an inferior person and genuine community seems impossible (for example, those caring for children, the sick, the elderly, and so on try to keep them calm and manageable rather than seeking mutual understanding as a basis for cooperation); or, again, the other party is regarded as a mere means to some specific end, and genuine community is considered irrelevant (for example, an advertiser may seek only to motivate people to buy a product or service, whether or not that really is in their interest); or, finally, the other party is regarded with indifference, and genuine community seems pointless (for example, people who wish to keep their distance encounter one another at a party, while traveling, or in other situations where they are required to converse).

   b) All parties to communication should submit themselves to truth. As creatures, human persons are utterly dependent on God. Their freedom and action presuppose realities whose meaning and value cannot be changed. Therefore, human fulfillment requires knowing and conforming to the truth, and especially to the truth about what is good. But since genuine community is cooperation in seeking common fulfillment, it depends on submission to truth. Consequently, since all parties to communication should be open to genuine community, they should submit themselves to truth. The alternative is pursuing what they want regardless of truth, caring about no common good beyond themselves, and so, while using means of communication, failing to promote genuine community.

   c) In communicating, one should be pleasant and courteous. All communication should be open to community, and mutual good will and honor are essential for that purpose. Pleasantness in speech and manner manifests good will and the desire to please others. Marks of courtesy—polite words, gestures, and other actions—manifest not only respect for persons insofar as they are persons, but the honor appropriate for each in accord with his or her social status, the relationship of persons, and other circumstances (see *S.t.*, 2–2, q. 114, a. 1). Hence, in communicating, people should always be courteous and pleasant (see Col 4.6), unless it is unavoidable to sadden others or there is some reason for not trying to please them.

   Norms of etiquette, differing in various social and cultural milieus, define modes of expression and practices which, partly by their inherent characteristics and partly by social convention, are pleasant and courteous. Sometimes, to be sure, there are morally compelling reasons for violating them: conventions occasionally are inconsistent with truth or moral goodness, and unconventional behavior sometimes may be appropriate in efforts to reform sinful social structures. In the absence of any morally sound reason for acting contrary to the norms of etiquette accepted in one's present social situation, however, a person ought to observe them, since this manifests good will and appropriate respect and honor for others. Unconventional behavior intended precisely to show hatred toward others or dishonor them gives offense which is hardly likely to be experienced as insignificant, and so is almost always a grave matter.

   d) In conversation, the principles of dialogue should be observed. The principles of dialogue are conditions which must be met for conversation to further genuine communion. Dialogue requires clarity in expression, meekness and patience in the exchange, mutual confidence, and prudent consideration for one another's characteristics and circumstances. Here "truth is wedded to charity and understanding to love."[18]

All participants must respect one another as persons responsible to the truth and bound to act in accord with conscience. They should seek to come together in truth and to find grounds for willing cooperation. Each should assume that all have something to contribute, that all can benefit from what others have to give, and that all must judge for themselves what they can accept from others. Participants should presume that another's communication is well intentioned, and each should try to grasp the elements of others' communications in their total personal context, that is, in the light of all the factors which actually determine and limit their meaning. Each party should declare honestly and without compromise what he or she thinks true, while expecting and encouraging others to do the same; there should be no excessive eagerness to eliminate differences, since these must not be suppressed but transcended by means which respect responsibility to truth and personal freedom. Participants in a dialogue should treat differences and oppositions as important, and deal with them patiently.

e) One always should communicate with the appropriate care. Genuine communication can serve various good ends. It can aim primarily at establishing or carrying on interpersonal relationships, or, though open to community, it can be directed toward cooperation in pursuing particular technical goals or realizing goods such as knowledge and esthetic experience. Since circumstances affect whether and how well a communication succeeds, people deliberating about whether to communicate should consider the time, place, and other circumstances which would make communicating most effective.

Yet communication frequently occurs spontaneously and without its being directed to any good end. Such idle talk often imposes on others, and it always wastes time and offers an avoidable occasion for other sins. Jesus warns that "on the day of judgment you will have to give an account for every careless word you utter" (Mt 12.36). So, a person should never engage in communication without directing it, either by habitual intention or actual deliberation, toward some good end—which, of course, can be the building up of community and friendship by simple sociability.

Most people sometimes are tempted to evade burdensome duties and escape pressing problems by taking refuge in pointless conversation, rationalizing this as sociability or a way of fulfilling some responsibility or solving some problem. Indecisive leaders, anxious to avoid commitment and conflict, often waste many people's time in meetings which nearly all the participants recognize as useless. A person should be alert to the danger signs, for example, that more time than usual

---

18. Paul VI, *Ecclesiam Suam, AAS* 56 (1964) 645, *PE,* 271.82; the four requirements of dialogue are stated: *AAS* 644–45, *PE,* 81. The requirements are set out and explained more fully, but with a specification to a limited field, by the Secretariat for Nonbelievers, *Humanae personae dignitatem, AAS* 60 (1968) 692–704, Flannery, 1:1002–14.

is being absorbed in conversation while work is piling up, or that repeated discussions are covering the same ground without making any progress.

f) **Communication should respect community's extent and limits.** Without privacy, interiority and intimacy are impossible; so, privacy is necessary to develop and maintain the individual identities of persons and communities. Since communication directed to good ends serves community, all who engage in it should bear in mind the extent and limits of the community relevant to that communication. That includes maintaining the community's privacy and protecting the secrets pertaining to other communities. The latter responsibility will be treated in detail (in C.2).

g) **Everyone should bear in mind communication's imperfections.** Few attempts at communication succeed entirely. Natural limitations, errors, moral failings, and the defects of language and other media ensure that many communications will fail entirely or succeed only partially, and that partially successful communications often will lead to such great misunderstandings that those who attempted to communicate regret having done so. It is important to keep this fact in mind, for it should limit attempts to communicate, qualify confidence that a communication has been received, and color the interpretation of any response or action based upon it.

2. One Has Responsibilities in Receiving Communications

Since all communication should further community, a person should be appropriately receptive to efforts to communicate, but should resist abuses of communication.

a) **Sincere efforts to communicate should be accepted and acted on.** Others' sincere efforts to communicate serve community: they either seek help in pursuing some good, offer some benefit, or both. Within the limits of time and energy set by individual capacities and prior responsibilities, a person should be open to further community, and that requires listening to others, attempting to understand what they wish to communicate, and appropriately taking it into account. Initially trusting others, a person should try to understand their motives. If they seem sincere, he or she should be ready to receive not only help, confirmation, and support, but also expressions of need, challenges, and demands to change.

In sincerely attempting to communicate, people give themselves, and a person accepts them with love only if he or she regards them as important, that is, really listens to and hears them. Sometimes that means agreeing with them, accepting what they offer, and giving what they ask; but, when that is not possible or right, really listening to others means at least considering their communication and allowing it to make whatever difference is judged appropriate, which usually at least includes some response to show that the communication was received and considered.

b) **One should resist manipulation but not foreclose communication.** It often happens that those addressing one appear not to care about community. They may seem to consider one an enemy or inferior person, or wish to use one as a mere means to their own ends, for example, a salesperson appealing to base or irrelevant motives. Then it is necessary to deal with the reality, take the apparent manipulation into account as a given fact, and not be credulous or susceptible.

At the same time, charity rules out passing ultimate judgment on those communicating in such ways and condemning them. Communication with them should not be entirely foreclosed. At a minimum, that requires being ready to accept a sincere communication if it eventually is made. Beyond that, unless there is some reason not to do so, people should respond to those who seem to wish to manipulate them by pointing out how their behavior is perceived and calling on them either to show that the perception is mistaken or to act differently.

c) **Others should not be encouraged to communicate wrongfully.** A person encourages others to communicate in three ways: by asking questions or otherwise inviting them to communicate, by willingly receiving their efforts to communicate, and by responding affirmatively. In all these ways it is possible to encourage others to communicate wrongfully. Expressing idle curiosity, for example, may encourage others to lie or reveal secrets that they should keep. Listening patiently, providing an audience, or responding affirmatively can encourage many kinds of wrongful communication, including blasphemy, sinful proposals, defamation, detraction, flattery, boasting, derision, salacious stories, gossip, and idle talk. At a minimum, an affirmative response to such communications should be avoided; they should not even be received unless this must be done incidentally to fulfilling some other responsibility; and, in the absence of some reason for not doing so, a person should let those who communicate wrongfully know how their action is perceived and should call on them to desist and repent.

d) **One should be careful about what one takes from the mass media.** In choosing what to receive from the mass media, people should consult available sound criticism and rating services (see IM 9). They should register disapproval of anything clearly and seriously offensive to Christian faith or morals while expressing appreciation for what is sound, constructive, and well done (see IM 14).[19] Apart from specific objectionable content, television and radio programs are likely to mediate a world view incompatible with Christian faith and its implications.[20] Researching the public's motives and using technologies for manipulating them, many commercial producers seem interested only in maximizing profit by gaining as large an audience as possible and preparing it to receive and act on the

---

19. See Pius XII, *Miranda prorsus; AAS* 49 (1957) 782, 787, 794, 795, 796, 801–3; *PE,* 260.67, 85, 125, 129, 133, 158–66. Pontifical Council for Social Communications, *Pornography and Violence in the Communications Media: A Pastoral Response,* 27; *L'Osservatore Romano,* It. ed., 17 May 1989, A.3; *OR,* 5 June 1989, 11, proposes a relevant norm: "The general public also needs to make its voice heard. Individually and collectively, concerned citizens—including young people—should make their views known to producers, commercial interests and public authorities." While specifically concerned with the problem of stemming the tide of pornography and violence in the media, this norm is at least as binding in reference to media content at odds with truths of faith and requirements of social justice.

20. For a brief, scathing critique of both public and commercial broadcasting systems, see Pontifical Council for Social Communications, *Aetatis novae,* 1.5; *L'Osservatore Romano,* It. ed., 18 Mar. 1992, 4; *OR,* 18 Mar. 1992, 6. Also see William F. Fore, *Television and Religion: The Shaping of Faith, Values, and Culture* (Minneapolis: Augsburg, 1987), 15–71.

commercial message.[21] Publicly sponsored productions sometimes promote secularist ideologies and partisan political views. People either should abstain from viewing or listening to programs corrupted in any of these ways or should take care to do so critically and only occasionally, while counteracting their subconscious psychological influence by regular reading of Scripture, prayer, and meditation.

The professional skills, technology, and vast resources often devoted to communication through the mass media give it a level of technical excellence and impact beyond the reach of communication of other kinds: ordinary lectures and homilies, letters and memoranda, amateur productions, and so on. Therefore, people must make a special effort to take a critical approach to the messages conveyed by the mass media, while inappropriate standards, drawn from media, should not be applied to communications of other kinds. If the latter require of recipients more attention, patience, and effort to understand, they also contribute to interpersonal communion in ways the mass media will never replace.[22]

3. One Has Responsibilities in Communicating to Others

To communicate sincerely to others is to express oneself and give oneself in love. Since such self-expression and self-giving further genuine communion and so build up the kingdom, that good should be kept in view.

a) In communicating, one should strive always to be constructive. Since communication should be self-expression in love, only that should be communicated which will benefit others and build up genuine community. In every communication, one should try to manifest love, respect, and due honor, not only for those who are addressed but toward everyone mentioned: "Love one another with mutual affection; outdo one another in showing honor" (Rom 12.10); "Let no evil talk come out of your mouths, but only what is useful for building up, as there is need, so that your words may give grace to those who hear" (Eph 4.29). Put negatively: one should not indiscriminately communicate everything to everyone and should never communicate anything maliciously to anyone. That which others are not likely to be able to receive and benefit from should not be communicated, nor should what will needlessly annoy or harm anyone, nor what will manifest secrets which should be kept, nor what is simply useless and time wasting.

b) In each and every communication, one should be truthful. Only truthful expressions really express oneself and allow others the access to oneself which genuine community requires. Hence, people always should communicate truthfully. Truthfulness is especially important for Christians, because they can spread the truth of the gospel and do their part in building up the kingdom only by testifying to truth, and their testimony will be more effective if absolute truthfulness in other matters puts their trustworthiness beyond doubt.

Since people communicate not only by words but by deeds, truthfulness is required not just in linguistic expressions but in all actions done with the intent of

---

21. See Jerry Mander, *Four Arguments for the Elimination of Television* (New York: William Morrow, 1978), 134–53.

22. See Pontifical Council for Social Communications, *Aetatis novae*, 2.7, 4.16; *L'Osservatore Romano*, It. ed., 18 Mar. 1992, 4–5; *OR*, 18 Mar. 1992, 6, 8.

communicating something (see *S.t.,* 2–2, q. 111, a. 1). For instance, Judas was untruthful by feigning friendship and loyalty after deciding to betray Jesus (see Mt 26.25, 49). Forgery, plagiarism, counterfeiting, and deceptive impersonation are only some of the many kinds of untruthful communication by deeds.

The importance of certain subjects provides additional and more serious reasons for truthfulness concerning them. For example, to enter into communion with God and abide in it, people need to know the truth about matters of faith and morals; therefore, untruthfulness about these matters gravely violates charity. Similarly, both love of neighbor and justice require truthfulness about matters which may influence important decisions and other matters in which falsity can cause someone serious harm.

c) **Courtesy need not be incompatible with truthfulness.** It might be objected that constructive communication requires courtesy, and courtesy can be incompatible with truthfulness, since good manners sometimes call for expressions at odds with a person's actual feelings. For example, letters must be addressed "Dear so-and-so," a "How are you?" must be answered "Very well, thank you," and corrupt superiors must be addressed with deference and honor. However, such customary, polite usages give many expressions and practices meanings different from those they would seem to have to someone unfamiliar with the relevant requirements of etiquette: polite expressions do not correspond to feelings, but to the dignity of persons and the formal implications of the involvement of each in a social situation in accord with his or her place in the network of social relationships. Thus, even if polite expressions and practices involved untruthfulness at some earlier time, the established conventions now can be followed in truthful communication. For example, dinner guests can follow customary form in expressing appreciation for hospitality by saying that it was a "fine meal and enjoyable evening" even if they think the food was poor and the conversation boring. Indeed, such expressions and practices usually should be used for courtesy's sake, and someone generally may use them appropriately even though foreseeing that, as a side effect, people unfamiliar with the conventions may be deceived.

d) **One should strive to overcome self-deception and ideology.** Unless people are honest with themselves, they hardly can be honest with others. The requirement of truthfulness in communication, therefore, demands that a person face up to the truth about himself or herself, and avoid self-deception and rationalization. Similarly, communities to which one belongs sometimes have their ideologies or communal rationalizations, and if one acquiesces in them, one is sure to communicate their falsifications rather than the truth. Hence, the effort must be made to overcome or resist not only personal but social evasions and distortions of the truth; for example, men should try to overcome the ideology which rationalizes domination of women, and women should try to resist radical feminism.

e) **One should try to be accurate, clear, and reasonable.** Good communication is hard work; laziness often tempts people to shirk it. Often, real communication is not the easiest way of achieving a desired objective; a person can be tempted to employ the easier expedient of manipulation. Thus, laziness and expediency lead to careless inaccuracy, exaggeration, lack of needed qualifications, stronger assertions than are warranted, and negligent failures to clarify one's meaning—all of which defeat the purpose of communication, which should contribute to authentic communion among persons. Consequently, love of neighbor requires serious efforts to be accurate and clear. Likewise, those who seek genuine community must use only what they think are sound arguments pointing to true conclusions, and must propose only good reasons for doing what they believe right.

f) **One should make good use of the media of social communication.** The media of social communication can be and often are used to convey unsound arguments intended to gain people's assent to certain positions (propaganda), to persuade them to act in desired ways (manipulative advertising), and so on.[23] Through right use of the media, however, it is possible to multiply the good one does in communicating something worthwhile to communicate to many people (see IM 2). So, one should learn how to gain access to the media and use them in ways available to the public at large, for example, by providing suitable material, writing letters to editors and managers, and so on.[24]

It is important to contribute to the formation of sound public opinion on matters of social justice. Of itself, it does not benefit those who are neglected or oppressed to raise consciousness about their suffering. Yet this is an indispensable means of stimulating social deliberation and encouraging action, whether the action will mitigate suffering directly or lead to the necessary, more radical reform of sinful social structures.

4. One Should Support a Presumption Favoring Freedom of Communication

Since communication is essential to cooperation and very important for building up every sort of community, it is an extremely valuable instrumental good. While sincere communications often express errors and seem to create problems, they also reveal aspects of situations which require attention if real progress is to be made and communion in the truth achieved. Moreover, indications that communication is not succeeding or is counterproductive usually call for renewing communication in a more thoughtful manner, rather than discontinuing or suppressing it. Consequently, those involved in every human association should begin with a presumption favoring freedom of speech and other modes of communicating.

Of course, like any instrument, communication can be abused, and even its right uses can have such bad side effects as to require some limitations. Nevertheless, apparent abuses of communication often turn out to be defects caused by factors other than bad will, and attempts to prevent bad side effects of one sort by imposing limits on communication are likely to have bad side effects of a different, and

23. On manipulative advertising, see Eric Clark, *The Want Makers: The World of Advertising: How They Make You Buy* (New York: Viking, 1989), 59–124, 163–201.

24. By the same token, abuses of the media of social communication are likely to be a grave matter; thus, *CIC,* c. 1369, prescribes: "A person who uses a public show or speech, published writings, or other media of social communication to blaspheme, seriously damage good morals, express wrongs against religion or against the Church or stir up hatred or contempt against religion or the Church is to be punished with a just penalty."

perhaps even worse, sort. Usually, therefore, it is better that necessary limits on communication be self-imposed by those involved in any association rather than established and enforced by authority. Therefore, people should support a strong, though rebuttable, presumption against inhibiting communication, not only in political society but in the family, the Church, and, indeed, in every community and relationship.

This presumption, however, must not be misunderstood. It is rebuttable, and should not impede safeguards of morally justified privacy and secrecy, or restraints on expression involved in immoral and socially damaging activities, such as the production and dissemination of pornography.[25] Moreover, even within its proper limits, the presumption against authoritative restriction of communication establishes only a liberty, which individuals must use responsibly, not a right to communicate in careless and harmful ways.

5. Unloving Communication Damages Communion and So Is Wrong

Since communication should be a giving of self in love, it should establish and build up community among persons. Any manner of communicating, truthful or not, is wrong if it falls short in love and needlessly impedes or harms interpersonal communion. Contention and sowing discord do this directly. But true communion also is damaged indirectly, but no less seriously, if, in communicating about persons (oneself and others) and about groups (those to which one belongs as well as others), a person does not express the truth or expresses it without love.

Damaging communications about persons and groups bear upon their reputation and/or honor. Individuals need a good reputation to enter into community and participate fully in it. Communities need a good reputation to hold their members and function effectively for them, and also to enter into and participate fully in wider communities. Worthiness of honor and its due recognition, whether enjoyed by individuals or by groups, are nothing but the reality and mutual acknowledgment among individuals and communities of their same fundamental human dignity, their legitimate differences in status, and their true social value, a value following from their real gifts and accomplishments, especially their moral goodness and holiness. Thus, individuals' and groups' reputations and honor are important not only for themselves but for every community in which they take part.

Boasting, false modesty, and hypocrisy, which bear upon one's own reputation and honor, violate the sincerity and openness with others that are so necessary for genuine community. Detraction, insult, and ridicule attack others in their reputation or honor. Flattery is a method of manipulating others for one's own ends, in violation of true community.

a) **Boasting, in itself a light matter, is more serious than it seems.** Provided there is some reason for doing it, there is nothing wrong in calling attention to one's genuine good qualities and accomplishments or the valuable possessions of oneself

---

25. The United States Supreme Court's jurisprudence regarding freedom of speech—see, for example, *Michael Barnes* v. *Glen Theater, Inc.* (21 June 1991), 115 L. Ed. 2nd 504–31—rather than regarding speech as an instrumental good seems to assume that it is valuable in itself. This assumption tends to absolutize freedom of speech to the detriment of other moral and social values.

or one's group (this is sometimes inaccurately called "boasting"). Boasting in a correct, but wide, sense involves doing the same thing out of vainglory—merely to win honor, without regard to the praise of God and the good of one's neighbor (see *S.t.*, 2–2, q. 132, aa. 1, 5). And it is boasting in the proper and strict sense to be less than perfectly truthful while engaging in self-glorification or the glorification of one's community (see *S.t.*, 2–2, q. 112, a. 1).

Boasting is a light matter in itself and even when the truth is stretched, though it can be grave if it springs from or is part of some mortal sin, for example, if it manifests gravely sinful pride or is part of an attempt to seduce someone or to compete unfairly for an important job (see *S.t.*, 2–2, q. 112, a. 2; q. 132, a. 3). However, even boasting which is not a grave matter is more damaging to community than it seems, for it focuses attention on goods insofar as they are one's own, rather than gifts of God to be used for the kingdom. Thus, it almost always fosters individualistic competition and status seeking rather than solidarity and service, and it arouses others' envy without encouraging their emulation.

b) False modesty, in itself a light matter, also can be serious. The opposite of boasting in the strict and proper sense is false modesty: a person untruthfully belittles himself or herself. Personal false modesty can be part of a manipulative strategy to move others to respond with praise and honor or a device of the lazy to avoid using their gifts in service. False modesty about a community to which one belongs—for instance, exaggeration of the Church's human defects—can serve as a rationalization for not fulfilling one's responsibilities in the community or for rebelling against its authority. In itself a light matter, false modesty, like boasting, can be grave if it springs from or is part of some other act which is grave matter, for example, if it is used to evade a grave duty or to encourage schism.

c) Hypocrisy can be either a grave or a light matter. If those who lack virtue and holiness simulate what they lack, they practice hypocrisy, seeking by mere outward show to keep their reputation and to receive undeserved honor. As deceptive communication, all hypocrisy is at least venially sinful. The New Testament, however, condemns as a most grave sin a certain kind of hypocrisy: the pretense of sincere faith by those who sinfully reject or pervert Jesus' gospel. While the enormity of their sin lay in their unbelief more than in their pretense,[26] hypocrisy nevertheless can be a grave matter even without rejection of faith. For those who are role models, sinning gravely in ways others can observe, while hypocritically maintaining that their behavior is not sinful, clearly is grave matter, because it is scandalous. Hypocrisy also can be a grave matter because of an ulterior purpose, for instance, when it is part of a strategy of pursuing some status for oneself at odds with the common good or of manipulating and dominating others in order to use them for some selfish or ideological goal incompatible with the kingdom (see *S.t.*, 2–2, q. 111, a. 4).

Still, even though a person may be guilty of other grave sins when sinning by hypocrisy, the hypocrisy itself is not a grave matter if the pretense of goodness has

---

26. See Wolfgang Beilner, "Hypocrite," in *Encyclopedia of Biblical Theology: The Complete Sacramentum Verbi,* ed. Johannes B. Bauer (New York: Crossroad, 1981), 390–92.

some reason compatible with charity, for instance, to avoid distressing loved ones or to avoid disgrace for one's sins of weakness. Furthermore, manifesting a sincere aspiration and commitment to a holiness not yet achieved is not hypocrisy at all. Nor is it hypocritical to teach and support norms and ideals one believes true but fails to put into practice. A parent or a pastor who says, "Do not imitate my bad example, but instead live by my sound teaching," does not commit the sin of hypocrisy but rather mitigates a possible sin of scandal.

d) **Flattery and ingratiation also can be either grave or light.** Praising and complimenting people truthfully, and in general trying to please them, are in themselves courteous and friendly acts which strengthen community and encourage others in what is good. But insincere praise, unwarranted compliments, and attempts to please which are not in order are sinful flattery and ingratiation. These sins can be grave—for instance, praising others' grave sins (perhaps by saying how "courageous" they are to commit them)—or if the flattery and ingratiation are part of a grave sin (see *S.t.,* 2–2, q. 115, a. 2).

Even when these sins are not grave, they manipulate people and feed their vanity, rather than establishing genuine community and calling others to authentic commitment to the goods to be served by cooperation. More specifically, those who are dominated often use flattery and ingratiation to gain favor and maintain a semblance of community with their unjust masters, whom they actually despise; whereas, love of neighbor requires those who are unjustly treated to admonish their oppressors (see 4.E.1) or at least to avoid obsequiousness, which only confirms oppressors in sin.

e) **Contention and quarreling can be either grave or light matter.** Sometimes truth and goodness require a person to disagree with others, to refute them, to challenge their proposals, and to say what offends them—and to do these things with a sharpness and precision which make clear what is at stake and how important it is. If what is necessary is done as gently and courteously as possible, the act really is loving and conducive to true communion. Some will call it "divisive," but they are wrong.

Someone who falls short of this ideal through passion, not with respect to the substance of what is said but only with respect to the manner of saying it, sins by violating gentleness and courtesy but the violation in itself is only a light matter (see *S.t.,* 2–2, q. 38, a. 1). Even so, the sin is serious insofar as it hinders genuine dialogue and is likely to provoke a defensive response, which easily evades truth and sound argument by dismissing what has been said as "uncharitable polemic."[27]

The sins of contention and quarreling are another matter and are inherently more serious. They involve disagreement, challenge, refutation, and offense, not in the service of truth and goodness, but quite apart from them, and perhaps even directly against them. If contention is against truth or justice in an important way, it plainly is a grave matter (see *S.t.,* 2–2, q. 38, a. 1). Likewise, quarreling is a grave matter

---

27. See Germain Grisez, "Charity and Dissenting Theologians," *Homiletic and Pastoral Review* 80 (Nov. 1979): 11-21.

if it manifests a real lack of charity, as when the intent is to bring contempt on someone (see *S.t.,* 2–2, q. 116, a. 2).

Even the sins of contention and quarreling can be light matter, however, provided they do not express bad will toward opponents and are not opposed to truth or justice in any important matter. That often is the case, for instance, with barroom arguments and quarrels among children over petty issues, where any anger and hatred involve only transitory feelings. Still, even such contention and quarreling plainly have a negative impact on community, and often are the occasion of far more serious sins: fights in which real harm is done, infidelities, and so on.

f) Gossip provides a context for serious sins against others. It is a normal and valuable exercise of community for members of a group to exchange information about the personal doings and concerns of other members just insofar as doing so arises from love and contributes to cooperation and help for those in need. When it does not arise from love and merely serves curiosity, however, it is gossip: idle talk which treats those discussed as objects of astonishment, amusement, and so forth.

Gossip is sinful, for it is idle talk, not directed toward building up community. Still, it is light matter in itself, for although it does not spring from love, it need not, and often does not, manifest hatred or cause harm, but only wastes opportunities for more constructive conversation or other worthwhile activity. Nevertheless, simple gossip sometimes offers the occasion for serious sins of calumny and detraction, which constitute malicious gossip; whenever that danger is recognized, gossip should be considered a grave matter.

g) Detraction, which wrongfully sullies reputation, is of itself grave. Good reputation is the object of a basic human right (see GS 26). That individuals and communities often spend large sums of money—in law suits, advertising, and so on—to vindicate, promote, or acquire a good name shows how much they care about reputation and suggests how important it is. People need their good name in order to enter into and participate fully in various communities, and so to share in most human goods; while the good name of communities is important not only for analogous reasons but also for their relationship to their own members. So, any act that destroys or damages the reputation of an individual or community is important. Christians are warned: "Do not speak evil against one another" (Jas 4.11); and the sin of sullying another's reputation is among those typical of pagans and of degenerate people of the end time (see Rom 1.30, 2 Tm 3.3).[28]

Detraction (also called "defamation") is any act of communication that wrongfully sullies an individual's or group's reputation. It takes two forms: lying and communicating truths which should not be communicated. The former is called "calumny"; the latter is simply called "detraction." Because of the good at stake and the violation of justice and love involved, all detraction, even that involving no lie, is of itself grave matter, although it admits of parvity of matter.[29]

---

28. *CIC,* c. 220, prescribes: "No one is permitted to damage unlawfully the good reputation which another person enjoys." Also see c. 1390.

29. A helpful study: Kenneth B. Moore, O.Carm., *The Moral Principles Governing the Sin of Detraction and an Application of These to Specific Cases* (Washington, D.C.: The Catholic University of America Press, 1950).

Sometimes people engage in detraction—especially, but not only, calumny—precisely *in order to* sully the reputation of their victim. They may do this simply out of hatred; or they may do it for an ulterior end, such as gaining an unfair advantage. In either case, the detraction carries out an intention to cause the victim significant harm; thus, it violates love and does not admit of parvity of matter (see *S.t.*, 2–2, q. 73, a. 2).

Sometimes, however, the detraction is indirect: people do not intend but only foresee the harm their wrongful communication will do to someone's reputation and accept it. This sort of indirect detraction admits of parvity of matter when the foreseen harm is slight. For instance, to protect themselves, wrongdoers often not only lie but imply that witnesses against them are lying; their lies are calumnious, although not intended or expected seriously to harm the witnesses' reputations. Again, for mere amusement and without intending harm, gossips often wrongly broadcast truths that hurt others' good names, but in some cases the harm is slight.

h) **Calumny—detraction by lies—is committed in different ways.** While the lie constituting calumny can be a straightforward assertion, lacking and known to lack any basis in fact, often it is less blatant, but no less calumnious, and all the more effective in sullying reputation: something false is not asserted unqualifiedly but proposed as a suspicion ("I think the boss is taking kickbacks"); or something likely is asserted unqualifiedly ("The Admiral's wife has been cheating on him"); or something with some basis in fact is exaggerated ("The Catholic Church always has persecuted her great theologians"); or a truth is communicated in an intentionally deceptive way, for instance, by omitting the context that would make it harmless ("He referred to his opponent as a 'black beast'!" [when the phrase was used to translate *bête noire*]). Sometimes—for instance, in a letter of recommendation—where it is expected that those who merit praise will be praised enthusiastically, faint praise is used deceitfully to damage a reputation; in such cases, the faint praise is calumny.

Since moral character is central to good name, calumnies often concern alleged immorality. However, other defects can be the subject of calumny, for instance, untruthful criticisms of people's professional competence or job performance can gravely damage their reputations even though no moral fault is imputed to them. In some situations, a person's reputation can be harmed even by lies about something which is not truly bad but only despised by a certain circle; for instance, employees of a laxly managed organization can damage an unusually competent executive's reputation by exaggerating his or her strictness in a complaint to higher management.

Calumny is committed on different occasions and in various media. Scholars can commit it in scholarly works, journalists in publications or broadcasts, politicians in campaigning, propagandists in publicly criticizing opponents, competitors in speaking confidentially about one another to those who will evaluate them, subordinates by whispering lies about authorities in order to undermine them, authorities in discrediting people who oppose them, and so on.

i) **Sometimes truths that harm reputation should be communicated.** As stated in paragraph (g) above, not only calumny but simple detraction—harming reputation by truths that should not be communicated—is sinful. The problem arises because people often do not respond appropriately to the truth about others: instead, they easily become excessively defensive, or lose respect, or draw unwarranted inferences. For example, an accurate account of the past crimes of a small businessman who has completely reformed will cause many not to trust him; publication of the transcript of a woman's narration of her experience of being raped could diminish some people's respect for her; a report that a candidate for public office once needed treatment for depression could lead many voters to the unwarranted conclusion that he or she would be undependable.

Reflecting on such cases, in which communication that harms a reputation is sinful, sheds light on cases in which the truth should be communicated even though harm to reputation is foreseen: here, others need to know the truth in order to be able to do what is appropriate. Whenever a person judges that, except for the foreseen harm to reputation, the damaging information should be communicated, he or she must judge whether in fact the obligation to communicate the information remains despite the side effect. If the conclusion is that it does, the individual can and should reveal to others what they need to know, without intending to harm the person whose reputation will be harmed.

Some sorts of cases typically require this. One knows someone is doing wrong, and tells someone else in confidence in order to enlist help in correcting the apparent sinner. One knows someone has committed a crime and reports it to the authorities. One knows an innocent person is accused of something and reveals who is guilty, in order to free the innocent from blame. One knows someone is professionally incompetent or does poor work, and warns others who might be badly served. One knows someone is making a major mistake—such as preparing to marry a person in ignorance of that person's very serious shortcomings—and communicates what is known to prevent the mistake. Those who share authority over someone—parents over children, supervisors over employees, and so on— have information which others who share that authority need in order to exercise it properly, and so they compare notes and share their information. One knows about defects in a candidate for a public office rendering him or her less worthy or suitable for it, and makes them known to other voters.

j) Sowing discord is an especially serious form of detraction. Good repute in one another's view has a special character for the participants in any emotionally close relationship, such as a friendship; here, things which might not affect reputation with others can matter greatly, while what might greatly affect reputation with others can make little difference. All the same, continuing closeness among friends and intimates depends on their continuing to enjoy good repute in one another's eyes. Sometimes, however, people deliberately try by detraction to sow discord between or among friends or intimates, for example, to break up a marriage or alienate coworkers. One method is the poison-pen letter or anonymous telephone call; another is tale bearing—repeating to one person what another said about him or her.

While people often sow discord out of envy and hatred, sometimes they do so for the sake of an ulterior end. In either case, sowing discord directly attacks the goods of friendship, faithful companionship, and peace in intimate community. Therefore, it is an even graver matter than detraction otherwise is. Still, it is not sowing discord to communicate a truth which should be communicated, for example, the truth about a seducer to someone being seduced, in order to break up the immoral relationship.

k) Insult offends honor and signals a defect in community. An insult is a consciously offensive communication dishonoring and humiliating someone or some group. Insult bearing on moral qualities or sin is called "contumely" (see *S.t.,* 2–2, q. 72, a. 1, ad 3). An insult can be used simply to express hostility, not precisely to dishonor, and an insult chosen precisely to dishonor can be used as a means to an ulterior end, for example, to elicit a violent reaction, to distract attention from something else, to lessen an authority's effectiveness, and so on. In all cases, those who engage in insults show that they reject or do not desire authentic communion with those they insult.

Insults can be communicated directly to the persons or groups to be dishonored or to others in solidarity with them. Language can be used or, with or without language, gestures and actions. Even pointedly omitting customary signs of respect which are plainly called for can serve to insult.

Where there is some form of social stratification, it is not uncommon for those who dominate to make a practice of insulting their subjects, at least partly as a means of asserting superiority and demanding submission. Systematically dishonoring and humiliating someone with insults involving immodesty or bearing on his or her gender or sexual characteristics is a form of sexual harassment.[30]

l) Insult strictly so called is in itself grave. Although it admits of parvity of matter, an act of insulting is in itself grave. Since such an act never can be good, whenever it is foreseen that serious offense will be taken, an insult is not light matter. Again, insults are grave matters if they are precisely intended to dishonor someone or some group, whether the insult is chosen simply out of hostility or as a means to some further end (see *S.t.,* 2–2, q. 72, a. 2). Thus, Jesus says that "if you insult a brother or sister, you will be liable to the council; and if you say, 'You fool,' you will be liable to the hell of fire" (Mt 5.22).

Any practice of insulting, including that involved in sexual harassment, plainly is a more serious matter, other things being equal, than an isolated act of insulting. Moreover, insults very often are mixed with other sins against those offended: an attempt to dominate, violation of economic rights, physical abuse, immodesty, defiance of authority, and so on.

Angry people frequently insult others without reflecting and choosing to do so; even if the matter is grave, such acts lack the subjective elements required for mortal sin. Also, language and behavior insulting in some contexts sometimes can be used sinlessly in others to communicate a legitimate point or as humor. However, the latter possibility often is used as a pretext for rationalizing insult, especially but not

---

30. This form of sexual harassment usually involves other wrongs as well, and not all forms of sexual harassment involve insult. Many involve either sexual assault (see 8.G.2) or immodesty (see 9.E.9.d). While any sort of harassment by definition involves a practice or systematic pattern of behavior, the single actions involved in harassment always are wrong in themselves.

only in the form of ridicule, under the guise of humor ("kidding"). This dishonest practice is especially common in families and other groups of intimates or close associates, where those who are dominant use it to express contempt for others or humiliate them.

m) Generally, one should suffer detraction and insult patiently. People whose reputation and honor are offended often become very angry, hate the offender, and are tempted to retaliate. Giving in to this temptation violates the Christian norms of meekness, mercy, and peaceableness, which require resignation, forgiveness, and efforts toward reconciliation with the offender.

While retaliation always is excluded, however, mere stoic silence in the face of such offenses can be inappropriate, and an active defense or response can be morally required. That is so, for instance, when responding actively might lead the offender to repent, or is necessary for the sake of the common good, or so that one will not be prevented from fulfilling serious obligations to others. When it is necessary to deal actively with detraction or insult, what is done should be limited by the good end in view, with preference given to action which is likely to restore harmony with the offender.

6. Lying and Other Deceptions in Communication Are Always Wrong

It is a basic norm of all communication that all parties submit themselves to truth (see 1.b, above). Lying and other deceptions are intentional untruthfulness: they express outwardly something at odds with one's inner self and attempt to lead others to accept it. Thus, they divide the inner and outer selves of those who engage in them, contrary to their own self-integration and authenticity, while impeding or attacking the real community that truthful communication would foster, even when deception seems necessary. Therefore, lying and other deception in communication are always wrong.[31]

Although some lies are not seriously immoral, truthfulness, even when there is no question of grave matter, is more important than people usually realize. Untruthfulness often has cumulative consequences: habitual indifference to truth by individuals and erosion of trust in society. People begin by excusing lies to protect the innocent from malicious enemies and to safeguard inviolable secrets; they end, as experience plainly shows, immersed in disinformation and insincerity in every sort of public and private communication.

a) Untruthfulness is at odds with a Christian's new life in Christ. In his deepening of the commandments, Jesus calls for such perfect truthfulness that oaths would be unnecessary: "Let your word be 'Yes, Yes' or 'No, No'; anything more

---

31. St. Thomas argues that every lie is a sin: since linguistic expressions naturally signify what one has in mind, it is unnatural and wrong to use them to signify something at odds with what one has in mind (see *S.t.*, 2–2, q. 110, a. 3). This argument often is taken out of context and criticized as a perverted-faculty argument. However, communication is a social practice directed toward self-expression and communion; and previous arguments (in q. 109 and q. 110, a. 1) make it clear that Thomas thought that abusing the practice violates both the integrity between one's inner self and one's expressed self, and the solidarity between one's self and others.

than this comes from the evil one" (Mt 5.37). Other New Testament teaching makes it clear that Jesus' new way of life excludes untruthfulness and explains why:

> Now this I affirm and insist on in the Lord: you must no longer live as the Gentiles live, in the futility of their minds. They are darkened in their understanding, alienated from the life of God because of their ignorance and hardness of heart. They have lost all sensitivity and have abandoned themselves to licentiousness, greedy to practice every kind of impurity. That is not the way you learned Christ! For surely you have heard about him and were taught in him, as truth is in Jesus. You were taught to put away your former way of life, your old self, corrupt and deluded by its lusts, and to be renewed in the spirit of your minds, and to clothe yourselves with the new self, created according to the likeness of God in true righteousness and holiness.
>
> So then, putting away falsehood, let all of us speak the truth to our neighbors, for we are members of one another. (Eph 4.17–25)[32]

Lying is part of the fallen human condition, but not of the condition of humankind renewed in Jesus (see Col 3.9). As Jesus is truth (see Jn 14.6) and "no deceit was found in his mouth" (1 Pt 2.22; cf. Is 53.9), so Christians are to live according to truth, putting aside whatever follows from ignorance of God's truth and from hardheartedness. Christian love requires truthfulness with one's neighbor "for we are members of one another"; the quality, and perhaps the very existence, of communion in the new covenant is at stake whenever one communicates with one's neighbors.

   b) Lying to enemies is incompatible with loving them. Although most Catholic theologians have considered the prohibition of lying a moral absolute, there is a lesser but significant school of thought holding that lying sometimes can be justified, particularly when it is a question of lying to an enemy, who has no right to the truth, in order to protect the innocent from harm.[33] The classic example is: May a person not lie to a murderer who is seeking a potential victim?

   It seems correct to hold that the Christian answer is no (see *S.t.,* 2–2, q. 110, a. 3, ad 4). Since the truth is to be spoken with one's neighbor, a person must not lie even to enemies, for enemies too are neighbors. Of course, silence is not lying, and enemies need not be provided with the truth of which they can be expected to make bad use. But even someone certain he or she was speaking with a person intent on committing murder would not be acting as love requires if, judging that person to be beyond repentance, he or she resorted to lying in an effort to save the potential

---

32. This passage clarifies how sinners, by sexual immorality and other sins as well as lying, violate both their own integrity and genuine interpersonal communion, and thus become unauthentic when measured by the standard of truth in Jesus: see Markus Barth, *Ephesians: Translation and Commentary on Chapters 4–6,* The Anchor Bible, 34A (Garden City, N.Y.: Doubleday, 1974), 499–513.

33. See Boniface Ramsey, "Two Traditions on Lying and Deception in the Ancient Church," *Thomist* 49 (1985): 504–33; Julius A. Dorszynski, *Catholic Teaching about the Morality of Falsehood* (Washington, D.C.: The Catholic University of America Press, 1948), 15–37. The view that it can be justifiable to deceive an enemy who has no right to the truth sometimes but not always has been accompanied by a definition of *lie* which excludes such deception; see Michaël Ledrus, S.J., "De mendacio," *Periodica de re morali, liturgica, canonica* 32 (1943): 5–58, 123–71; 33 (1944): 5–60; 34 (1945): 157–209.

victim's life. Rather, treating as neighbors both the potential victim and the enemy would require not giving the information and, usually, explaining why: "I will not answer your question and help you do wrong; instead, for your soul's sake, I ask you to repent of your wicked intent." Such an answer might or might not succeed, but it is a work of hope, while lying is an act of desperation.

Some recent authors have used the historically factual example of agents of a totalitarian power who asked those in charge of an institution to identify certain children who would be sent off to a death camp. Was it not entirely right to protect the children by lying? Could that have been even a venial sin? Yes, it could have been a sin; objectively, it was not right.[34] The appropriate Christian response would have been to refuse submitting insofar as it involved even the smallest sin, to resist injustice by every morally acceptable means, and to be prepared to die if necessary—preferably in place of those to be sent to the death camp, but even with them—in witness to the falsity of that ideology and to the truth of the gospel, which the ideology's proponents sought to supplant.

It might be objected that, had it been feasible, it would have been morally acceptable and perhaps even obligatory to defend the children with force—if necessary, deadly force—against the agents of the totalitarian power (see 8.C.1.d–e); thus, it is paradoxical that it was not right to lie to them. This objection might be cogent if the malice of lying and killing lay exclusively in their injustice to those deceived or killed. But that is not the case; indeed, lying, while always wrong, does not always violate any right of those deceived. One cannot lie, however, without choosing the self-alienation which, opposed as it is to self-integration and authenticity, is sufficient to make lying wrong; but deadly force can be used to defend the innocent without choosing the death which, because it is opposed to life, makes intentional killing always wrong. Moreover, using deadly force in defense does not impede community as lying does. For attempting to deal with the agents of a totalitarian power by lying maintains a semblance of community based on false ideology and blocks the development of real community based on the common good. Indeed, the lies of the oppressed are an important element in their reluctant submission to an unjust regime which might well be unable to withstand united, courageous, and open resistance.[35]

---

34. Someone might argue that God commended lying in such circumstances by blessing the midwives who lied to Pharaoh (see Ex 1.18–21). The reason for the blessing, however, is that the midwives "feared God" (Ex 1.21); that was why they first acted with heroic virtue in grave matter by refusing to kill the innocent: "But the midwives feared God; they did not do as the king of Egypt commanded them, but they let the boys live" (Ex 1.17). The midwives' self-defensive lying was a distinct, subsequent, and entirely incidental act, whose venially sinful character would not have negated their heroism and merit in God's eyes. In any case, the scriptural witness should be considered as a whole, and Old Testament examples from the perspective of New Testament teaching; see, for example, D. W. Wead, "Lie, Lying," in *The International Standard Bible Encyclopedia,* ed. Geoffrey W. Bromiley, 4 vols. (Grand Rapids, Mich.: William B. Eerdmans, 1986), 3:128–29.

35. In this way, Adam Michnik, *Letters from Prison and Other Essays,* trans. Maya Latynski (Berkeley, Cal.: University of California Press, 1985), 3–15, explains why he refused to sign a declaration of loyalty to Poland's Jaruzelski government. In an introduction to Michnik's book (xxx), Jonathan Schell sums up the approach of the Workers' Defense Committee, which was the

c) **Mental reservation with the intent to deceive is a lie.** Catholic theologians in modern times envisaged situations in which secrets could not adequately be protected by remaining silent, rebuffing an inquiry, or distracting the inquirer. While most held that lying is always wrong, it was suggested that in such situations mental reservation might be used, that is, a person might employ an expression that would not convey what had to be concealed, while mentally qualifying its meaning in such a way that, if taken with that qualification, it would express truth. As understood by the speaker, the statement would express something in accord with what he or she actually had in mind; but as understood by the hearer, it would not manifest the secret the speaker was obliged to protect.

It seems, however, that *mental reservation* itself has two meanings.[36]

In one sense, it refers to expressions which can obscure the truth even if no one is deceived, and so can be effective without expressing an assertion believed to be false.[37] The use of such expressions is not lying. Quick-witted individuals use ambiguity in this way. For example, a woman, attending an office party given by her employer and finding the entertainment offensive, politely excuses herself: "I am sorry I cannot stay for the rest of the evening, for I suddenly feel sick to my stomach," thinking her excuse cannot be held against her but its ambiguity will not be missed. Moreover, many statements are generally recognized as ambiguous: "Mr. Jones is not available just now," "Mrs. Jones is not at home," and even, in certain contexts, "I don't know." Likewise, social conventions provide many expressions which, while always manifesting respect for persons, often mask actual sentiments (see 3.c, above).

In another sense, however, *mental reservation* refers to studied ambiguities which cannot effectively obscure the truth without deceiving, and so cannot be used without intent to deceive. Such a mental reservation depends for its success entirely upon the false sense of the expression, whose true sense remains irrelevant to the

---

antecedent of Solidarity: "Its simple but radical guiding principle was to start doing the things you think should be done, and to start being what you think society should become. Do you believe in freedom of speech? Then speak freely. Do you love the truth? Then tell it. Do you believe in an open society? Then act in the open. Do you believe in a decent and humane society? Then behave decently and humanely."

36. Innocent XI condemned a form of mental reservation (DS 2126–27/1176–77), called "strict" or "pure" (as against "broad") mental reservation. The point here is to reject both strict or pure mental reservation and any broad mental reservation that involves speaking contrary to one's mind with (at least a conditional) intent to deceive. There is no feasible way to compare the position defended here with the "traditional view on broad mental reservation," since the Catholic moralists (approved authors) who accepted some such practice disagreed among themselves on exactly what it is and how far it licitly extends; see Dorszynski, *Catholic Teaching about the Morality of Falsehood,* 27–28, 61 (especially n. 84), and 68 (point 7 and n. 12). However, the position defended here certainly is more restrictive than treatments of broad mental reservation by some usually sound authors. See, for example, I. Aertnys, C. Damen, and I. Visser, C.Ss.R., *Theologia moralis,* ed. 18, 4 vols. (Turin: Marietti, 1967–69), 2:391–95.

37. St. Thomas, *S.t.,* 2–2, q. 110, a. 3, ad 4, says it is permissible to hide the truth prudently under some concealment ("sub aliqua dissimulatione"), but, unfortunately, does not explain what that means. What he says could refer to the kind of expressions described here, and so proponents of more permissive accounts of mental reservation cannot claim his authority against the view taken here.

communication. Thus, it both expresses something at odds with what one has in mind and carries out the intent to deceive, and so is a lie.[38]

d) **Not all deceptive actions are dishonest communications.** Since actions are more ambiguous than words, an ambiguous action which probably will deceive others often at the same time signifies something that is true. For example, a young woman traveling alone who acts as if she is part of a family group both truthfully signifies that she is not receptive to advances by strangers and deceives those who might otherwise attempt to take advantage of her (see *S.t.*, 2–2, q. 111, a. 1, ad 1). Again, a waiter who is politely pleasant to boorish, irritating customers, or a teacher who is grieving for a recently deceased parent but tries to smile cheerfully in class does not express his or her present feelings but does honestly manifest something else: the will to relate to others in an appropriate and constructive way.

Moreover, in some sorts of situation, no question of honesty arises: deceptive acts are done but are neither intended nor understood as self-expressive, since everyone involved understands, and perhaps even agrees, that deception may be practiced. In such cases, people can intend to deceive others without violating truthfulness; for example, there is no untruthfulness when entertainers create illusions, players in games bluff or opposing armies in war feint, and so on.

e) **Lying to protect secrets should be unnecessary.** Many examples meant to show that a lie (or a mental reservation) is necessary to protect a secret instead show the difficulty involved in rebuffing enemies. For example, a priest called to testify in court about something he was told under the seal of confession usually can protect the secret by a mental reservation which does not involve deception or by refusing to testify. However, he may suffer legal penalties unjustly imposed by a government that does not respect the inviolability of the sacrament of penance.

In some cases, a simple refusal to answer a question will reveal the answer. For example, suppose a priest agrees to testify on behalf of innocent people accused of a crime that they did not confess it to him; if he then refuses to comply with another defendant's similar request, his refusal would reveal that individual's secret. Such cases can and should be forestalled by consistently maintaining secrecy. If a priest always refuses as a matter of policy to talk about what he has heard or not heard in confession, his refusal to answer any particular question will not reveal any secret. But even someone who has failed to follow a sound policy about secrets can avoid

---

38. Two theological arguments that lying sometimes is permissible deserve brief replies. First, in trying to elude pursuers, various saints are said to have spoken with a mental reservation which could not have protected them had they not succeeded in intentional deception. For example, St. Athanasius, asked by those seeking him where to find Athanasius, is said to have replied: "He is not far off!" These examples, even if historically accurate, do not falsify the position taken here, because saints sometimes commit venial sins, not all saints have believed that lying is always wrong, and a saint who believed that lying is always wrong may well not have had a precise concept of lying, and so might have told a clever lie in a well-intentioned effort to dissimulate without lying. Second, Dorszynski, *Catholic Teaching about the Morality of Falsehood*, 69–72, 75, plausibly argues that conceptions of broad mental reservation typical of the approved authors allow speech contrary to one's mind, and so make an exception to the norm forbidding lying. However, the issue concerns behavior which at worst is light matter for sin, and so there is no great difficulty in thinking that the approved authors go too far in their various theories of mental reservation.

revealing a secret by saying: "Hitherto I answered questions of that sort, but I have come to realize that doing so is not good, and so I have adopted a policy of refusing to answer any question of that kind. Therefore, I refuse to answer, and you can draw no conclusion from my refusal."

Of course, priests and others morally bound to protect confidences can use legitimate mental reservations, that is, those that are effective even if they deceive nobody. For example, asked whether he knows that a woman has certain failings, a priest can say: "I have nothing to tell you about that aspect of her life" or "I really cannot say whether or not she has those failings" or, in some contexts, "I do not know"—all of which can express a refusal to answer with sufficient ambiguity that, without actually deceiving anyone, the priest probably can evade punishment for not answering. The regular use of such language to express ignorance as well as to hold back reserved information and reject prying questions maintains its useful ambiguity, so that it can continue to protect secrets effectively without actually deceiving questioners.

f) Lying and other deception in communication can be grave matter. While the commandment, "You shall not bear false witness against your neighbor" (Ex 20.16; cf. Ex 23.1; Dt 5.20, 19.15–19), specifies a particularly noxious form of lying, not just perjurers but other liars can sin gravely (see 1 Tm 1.10, Rv 21.8). Thus, if someone deliberately deceives another about an important subject—for example, a matter of faith or morals, or something on which an important decision will be based—the lie or deceptive deed is a grave matter, even if the ulterior purpose is not to harm anyone, but to bring about something regarded as a greater good.[39]

Moreover, since lying is sinful in itself, a person never can be justified in accepting any bad side effect of a choice to lie. Therefore, if someone foresees that serious harm can result from his or her lie or deceptive deed, that deception is a grave matter, whether the serious harm foreseen is intended as an end, chosen as a means, or only reluctantly accepted.[40]

Further, the Golden Rule requires that the seriousness of harm to be expected from lies be evaluated from the perspective not of the liars but of those deceived

---

39. In public discourse, such lying is widespread and very damaging. For example, in today's world, more sophisticated and better informed people, not only proponents of totalitarian ideologies, often suppose that they may lie in public statements, media campaigns, and even scholarly publications ("simplify matters too complex for ordinary people to handle") in order to lead the public to accept and support ideals, policies, and programs which those who think themselves more enlightened and/or expert judge to be good, right, and necessary. John XXIII, *Ad Petri Cathedram, AAS* 51 (1959) 500, *PE,* 263.11, condemns this kind of deception: "Anyone who consciously and wantonly attacks known truth, who arms himself with falsehood in his speech, his writings, or his conduct in order to attract and win over less learned men and to shape the inexperienced and impressionable minds of the young to his own way of thinking, takes advantage of the inexperience and innocence of others and engages in an altogether despicable business."

40. Among serious lies, one should notice that under certain conditions, lying to a prospective spouse can invalidate a subsequent marriage (see *CIC*, c. 1097, §1), and that lying by someone wishing to enter religious life can invalidate admission to a novitiate (see *CIC*, c. 643, §1, 4–5). Also, certain lies to Church authorities which injure another's reputation and certain lies involving Church documents constitute the canonical crime of falsehood (see *CIC*, cc. 1390–91).

and others affected. Liars often exaggerate the good their lying will do and belittle its harmfulness to others; but those who imagine they tell only "white" lies often judge that they themselves have suffered significant harm when others tell them similar lies.

Like other kinds of immoral action, lying is a mortal sin only if it is freely chosen in grave matter with sufficient reflection. Pathological liars perhaps lack freedom of choice in this area; small children certainly lack both freedom of choice and sufficient reflection; and many usually honest people sometimes lie, at least in certain sorts of situations, without deliberating.

g) **Supposedly helpful lies manipulate others and often harm them.** Sometimes people lie because they think it will help others and harm no one. For example, health care workers sometimes lie to a patient when they think the truth would be psychologically harmful or the lie helpful to the patient, and family members sometimes lie to one another to prevent the sadness or anxiety a truthful account of bad or threatening news would cause. Even when they are light matter, such lies are contrary to the goods which communication serves. Helpful liars manipulate those to whom they lie, usually overconfidently presuming that they know what in fact they cannot know: that those they try to deceive cannot deal with reality, cannot make good use of the freedom only truth can give, and will not suspect or even detect the deception, lose trust, and suffer more than if they had not been lied to. Indeed, because of their impact on freedom and/or the consequence of suspicion, supposedly helpful lies can cause great, even though unintentional, harm.

Such a lie plainly is grave matter if it deprives someone of an important truth to which he or she has a right, for example, when lying to a dying person is likely to prevent him or her from preparing for death. Still, in such a case, while the lie is grave matter, the liar usually does not foresee the possible harm, and so lacks sufficient reflection.

h) **Humorous lies manipulate others and often offend their dignity.** Many moralists think humorous (jocose) lies have little or no moral significance. This opinion may be based partly on a confusion between telling humorous fictional stories not intended to deceive anyone (these are not lies, and can be morally acceptable) and humorous lies properly so called. The latter do aim to deceive someone, although usually only temporarily, and generally in the context of playful mocking or teasing ("kidding"). For instance, someone first tells a credulous person something astonishing, embarrassing, or frightening but untrue, and by this deception provokes an emotional reaction; then the joker manifests the truth and at least implicitly ridicules the reaction.

Although the humorous lie usually is not a grave matter, its moral significance is obvious: like every other lie, it manipulates others. This fact also explains why humorous liars typically victimize people whom they regard as inferiors (and thus offend their dignity): adults often tell such lies to children, male superiors to female subordinates, the sophisticated to the simple, and so on.

i) **Lying as a "lesser evil" is at best subjectively blameless.** People often try to excuse or justify lying in a difficult situation by arguing that it was the "lesser evil." This could have any of four meanings. First, offered by someone who thinks that lying sometimes is justified, the argument could be that the lie in question was morally acceptable. But, assuming the preceding arguments are correct, lying never is justified. Second, it could be a proportionalist argument that the norm prohibiting lying is subject to justifiable exceptions. But proportionalism is unacceptable as a theory of moral judgment (see *CMP*, 6). Third, it could be an argument that a venial sin of lying is excusable to avoid great harm. That is true if *excusable* means that, although the lying remains a sin, it is easily forgiven; but it is false if it means the moral evil of a venially sinful lie is less than any nonmoral evil, however great. Fourth, it could be an argument that the choice to lie was justified, inasmuch as the individual was perplexed in conscience, that is, he or she honestly thought the only alternative to lying was to choose some greater moral evil, such as violating a duty to keep a secret. This argument can be sound inasmuch as a choice made in perplexity can be subjectively blameless (see 5.I.3.d). Still, it is never objectively true that the only alternative to lying is to choose some greater moral evil, and so the person who was perplexed in conscience either failed to think of the morally acceptable alternative or mistakenly judged it morally evil.

Question C: What Are One's Responsibilities with Respect to Promises and Secrets?

It takes more than communication to form and maintain communion among persons. The bonds of communion are determined and developed by promises and their fulfillment, while the boundaries of various communities are marked by appropriate confidentiality. Promises and secrets are important instruments which love uses to form and articulate interpersonal communion in a multiplicity of communities.

1. There Is a Defeasible Responsibility to Keep Promises

A promise is a deliberate and free expression both of an intention to fulfill another's hope and of the acceptance of the added responsibility which follows from expressing an intention to do so.[41] Promises can be unilateral, but many promises, such as those involved in most legal contracts, are bilateral or even multilateral.

---

41. The intention to make a promise should carry with it the acceptance of the obligation to keep it, but the intention to promise does not create that obligation out of nothing. The obligation flows from the goods at stake, including friendship and/or justice, and the requirement of fairness: see John Finnis, *Natural Law and Natural Rights* (Oxford: Oxford University Press, 1980), 298–308. Whenever in expressing his or her intentions a person knows that doing so will arouse others' hopes, that person has some responsibility in fairness not to disappoint those hopes. In making a promise (whether or not one uses the words *I promise*), one intentionally arouses or nurtures another's hope and explicitly accepts the obligation not to disappoint it. Thus, in promising, by focusing attention on the consciousness of responsibility not to disappoint another's hope, a person greatly increases the extent to which friendship or justice is at stake, and so also intentionally increases the responsibility to fulfill the promise. Because of this deliberate increasing of responsibility through explicit reflection on it, one obligates oneself in promising in a sense quite different from that in which a responsibility not to disappoint others is assumed when, without making a promise, one raises their hopes merely by declaring one's intentions.

Promises enable two or more persons to will together over some stretch of time; such union of wills is necessary for dependable cooperation, which, in turn, is necessary for effective community of every sort. Love requires Christians to build up community, and so it requires them to make and keep promises.

a) To make a binding promise, certain conditions must be met. Since a promise is a deliberate and free act, only those capable of such acts can make binding promises. For this reason, children who do not yet have the use of reason cannot make promises, while immature or unsophisticated people cannot make binding promises about matters beyond their competence. Coercion, including psychological pressure, invalidates any promise made due to it, because in limiting the options available for free choice coercion excludes the free self-giving required to form or build up community.

If someone makes a promise which would not have been made except for deception or fraud, those who deceived or defrauded have no right that the promise be kept. The duty to keep it is nullified by a requirement of fairness: people may not by wrongdoing acquire claims upon those they wrong.

Since a promise expresses the intention to fulfill another's hope, nobody can make a promise to which no hope corresponds. Sometimes the hope comes first: one party desires something, asks another for it, and receives a promise in response. For example, an employee asks his or her employers for a salary increase, and the employers say they will give it if certain conditions are met. Sometimes the offer of a promise arouses a hope that completes and validates the promise: one party proposes a promise of something to another, that proposal arouses a response of hope, and communicating that response (sometimes by a merely tacit consent) consummates the promise. For example, a mother tells her children she will take them to the zoo Sunday afternoon if they finish all their homework by then, and as a result the children count on her for the enjoyable excursion.

Since a promise also expresses a responsibility to fulfill its corresponding hope, a binding promise cannot be made while simultaneously implying there is no responsibility to keep it, for example, by saying it would be wrong to do so.

b) In making promises, one should be truthful. Since a promise is a communication, making promises plainly involves the same responsibility to be truthful that holds for every communication. But since a special responsibility is accepted in making a promise, there also is a special responsibility to be truthful, for deception in making a promise involves a will which is inconsistent with the will to keep them.

c) In making promises, relevant conventions should be observed. Since a promise is a communicative expression, it often is impossible to make a promise without more or less carefully observing relevant conventions. Some may be informal, for example, languages provide various expressions suitable for making promises. Others are formal: legal systems establish conditions for making many promises, especially bilateral ones that constitute contracts.

When relevant conventions must be observed in order to make binding promises, they plainly should be observed, and deliberate failure to do so is deception in simulating a promise. But even when a binding promise can be made without observing relevant conventions, they should be observed unless there is a reason to set them aside; for this makes the promise more effective, by making it clearer that a promise is made and defining more precisely what may be hoped for and what must be done to fulfill that hope.

d) Promises sometimes lose their obligatory force. Many promises, especially bilateral ones, are made subject to expressed conditions; and, since a promise expresses an intention, its obligatory force is limited by such expressed conditions. Therefore, promises lose their obligatory force if the conditions are not met.

Since no one ever is obliged to do what is impossible or morally wrong, this happens if one discovers that a promise simply cannot be kept or can be kept only by doing something morally wrong. And, since a hope corresponds to a promise, it also happens if the person or persons who would benefit from the keeping of the promise both are competent judges of their own interests and make it clear that they do not care whether the promise is kept. Similarly, those who would benefit from the fulfillment of promises can freely choose to accept something else in place of what was promised or even entirely to concede their claim to it.

Very often, those who make promises would not do so if they then knew something of which they are ignorant—especially, but not only, if they foresaw changes in circumstances which make carrying out the promise more onerous than expected. Someone might argue that, since ignorance takes away freedom, promises that would not be made except for ignorance necessarily lack obligatory force. In making promises, however, people are aware that they may be ignorant of some facts and do not completely foresee the future; yet within some limits of error and ignorance, they express their intention nevertheless to do what they promise. In the nature of the case, the limits cannot be specified in advance; instead, when the problem arises they are determined by what is fair, all things considered. Thus, a promise does not lack obligatory force merely because it would not have been made except for ignorance, but it does lose obligatory force if unforeseen conditions render keeping the promise unfairly burdensome.

Sometimes those concerned, after being fully informed, agree in judging what are fair limits to unforeseen burdens, or at least agree to accept a mediator's judgment. In any case, a conscientious promiser begins with the presumption that fair limits have not been passed and the promise should be kept, and considers the obligation extinguished only when morally certain that it has been.

e) Breaking a promise sometimes but not always is a grave matter. Provided a promise retains its obligatory force, its breaking or neglect is inherently wrong. But how wrong? No general answer is possible, since many factors have a bearing on the extent to which people want and expect those who have made promises to be held to them; these factors include the character of the relationship between the parties as well as the magnitude of disappointment, loss, and/or harm which will result from breaking the promise. However, it is clear that breaking a promise sometimes is light matter. Indeed, since promises often lose their obligatory force, a culpable failure with little adverse impact seldom seems worth distinguishing from a reasonable judgment that the promise was not binding. Still, if significant loss or harm will result, failure to keep a promise surely is a grave matter.

2. There Is a Limited Responsibility with Respect to Secrets

Secret does not refer here to everything any individual or society wishes to hide, but only to something that someone or some group has some *morally acceptable reason* for hiding. Concealment to facilitate wrongdoing is not in question here.

a) **Secrecy can be good insofar as community is rightly limited.** Since communication builds up community, it is clear that sincerity, openness, and generosity in communicating generally are good. The goodness of secrecy, which presupposes outsiders—those to whom what is hidden is not communicated—is not so clear. However, secrecy obviously is important for intimate communion, such as that between spouses, by enabling the partners to reveal themselves more fully than they would or rightly could to others. And, in general, secrecy is important for building community, for it allows those voluntarily entering or participating in it to exercise freedom in revealing themselves, as they must do in order to give themselves to others. Moreover, all communities except that of the new covenant are rightly limited in various ways, and secrecy protects individuals' and communities' identities, by restricting access to themselves and to what is their own.

In the fallen world, secrecy often is necessary for additional reasons. It facilitates the doing of good acts without mixed motives, which is why Jesus urges that prayer, fasting, and almsgiving be done in private (see Mt 6.1–6). Again, it is a necessary condition for communities to pursue or protect various goods: it protects plans, ideas, and strategies against those who might use them unfairly; it protects things such as deliberations or preparatory drafts that might be misunderstood or maliciously used; it protects property that might be unjustly taken. Hence, individuals sometimes rightly keep secret what they share in any particular community, and communities sometimes rightly keep secret what they share with one another.

b) **The responsibility regarding secrets can have different bases.** Since *secret* here refers to something an individual or group has a morally acceptable reason for keeping hidden, the first and general basis for the responsibility with respect to any secret is the good directly at stake and the requirement of fairness: one wants to keep one's own secrets and so should protect and respect others'.

A second basis for responsibility with respect to certain secrets is that valuable interpersonal relationships depend on trust that those secrets will be kept. On this basis, there is a special duty with regard to the secrets of sacramental confession (see 4.C.5.k), intimate communication between husband and wife or between friends, professional secrets, secrets children confide to parents, and so on.

These basic duties often are reinforced by a promise, whether unilateral or contractual, by a law or other social norm, or by both a promise and a social norm.

c) **Secrecy often is qualified and cannot be presumed.** The responsibility to keep a secret often is qualified, so that its basis is satisfied and it is not violated if the secret is divulged within certain limits. For instance, someone troubled in conscience about a matter involving some secret generally could discuss the matter in confidence with a confessor or moral adviser without violating secrecy. Again, professional colleagues who can fulfill their professional responsibilities only by collaboration usually do not violate professional secrecy by sharing secrets and the responsibility to keep them.[42] Again, spouses and intimate friends often can share in confidence secrets which pertain to other relationships, without endangering any relevant good or violating the real meaning of any reinforcing promise or norm.

Also, when a group of people engages in private in some common deliberation or action, no member should presume that other members will consider the action secret. Some may have good reasons for concealing the action and others for revealing it. If the latter have not promised confidentiality and the group as such does not have a norm requiring secrecy, those who desire it should not presume it.

d) **This responsibility can be violated in diverse ways.** Plainly, the responsibility to keep secrets can be violated both by purposely or carelessly divulging a secret in one's possession and by failing to take appropriate precautions to protect it. But the responsibility with respect to secrets has another dimension: the duty to respect others' secrets and not seek access to them. It can be violated in many ways, for example, asking prying questions, eavesdropping, covertly using electronic listening devices, peeping, opening and reading others' letters, searching through others' personal papers and effects, and extorting information by drugs or torture.

e) **The responsibility to protect and respect secrets is limited.** Leaving aside the secrecy of sacramental confession (see 4.C.5.k), under certain conditions a person should divulge or seek access to secrets.

Of course, secrecy has some generally recognized limits. The good and acceptable reason for hiding something usually only obtains within limits, and beyond these, the trust required for valuable relationships is not undermined if a secret is revealed. Moreover, when something formerly secret has been divulged, it is no longer secret; when persons or groups are willing that their secrets be divulged, others no longer need keep them; and when concealment becomes a means of wrongdoing or its morally acceptable reason otherwise ceases, the moral responsibility with respect to secrets also ceases.

Even when some persons or groups continue to have a good and morally acceptable reason for wishing to conceal something, others sometimes can have a good and morally binding reason to reveal or investigate it. For different agents' responsibilities can differ, both because of their different roles and duties, and because of differences in what they know or believe as a basis for acting.

Thus, citizens who know that some of their leaders are preparing secretly to wage war and believe them to be acting rightly must protect the secret, while other citizens convinced the leaders are acting illegally and wrongly could be obliged to communicate what they know to other leaders or even the public at large. People who know they are innocent can have good reason to protect certain secrets, but authorities (parents, superiors, managers, police, and so on) who must deal with wrongdoing can have an obligation to seek access to those secrets in order to distinguish between the guilty and the innocent. Victims of a deadly disease which

---

42. The seal of confession is not an exception, because the confessor never need violate it to fulfill his professional responsibilities. If he needs help to deal with a difficult question, he can obtain it without revealing the penitent's identity; if the penitent's identity must be revealed to deal with a canonical problem, the confessor may not proceed without the penitent's full and free consent.

in most circumstances is not contagious can have good reasons—such as fear of others' irrational reactions—to keep their condition a secret from most people, but physicians and others with public health responsibilities can have an obligation to divulge the secret, if that is necessary to stop the spread of the disease.[43]

f) The Golden Rule should be used in judging secrecy's limits. Still, the responsibility to protect and respect secrets should be presumed to remain unless it is overridden by some clear responsibility to the contrary. Judging oneself to have a duty that cannot be fulfilled without divulging or seeking access to some secret, one should consider the basis of the responsibility to keep or to respect the secret, including any relevant promise, law, or other social norm, and the various goods at stake. In doing so, it is important not to overlook indirect effects, for example, the effect which setting aside secrecy in some instances may have upon a whole set of professional relationships. Having considered all these things, one should ask oneself which is in accord with the Golden Rule, respecting the secret or fulfilling the other duty. One should divulge or seek access to the secret in order to fulfill the other duty if, and only if, one judges that doing so is in accord with the Golden Rule.

g) Even beyond the limits, one must take care to act justly. Even when one should seek access to some secret, one may not be indiscriminate in the means used. Of course, means evil in themselves may not be used, for example, lying or torture. But even a means not intrinsically evil may be unfair because unnecessarily invasive or otherwise repugnant to those affected. Moreover, the information legitimately acquired may not be divulged or used unfairly. Again, even when some secret should be divulged, a reasonable effort should be made to mitigate harm. The secret may be divulged only to the extent necessary, and a person doing so should be considerate in the method and circumstances. Furthermore, in most cases when one should seek access to or divulge some secret, one should regret having to do so, and the regret should be communicated.

h) The responsibility of secrecy is in itself a grave matter. If the right of secrecy obtains, its wrongful violation always is an injustice and often has ill effects for valuable interpersonal relationships. If the violation is chosen out of hatred or as a means to some grave evil, or if it is likely to cause significant harm, the matter is grave. Still, the violation can be light matter, since secrecy sometimes serves rather insignificant goods or serves more important goods in marginal ways. For example, family members and intimate friends sometimes keep gifts and pleasant news secret from one another for a time in order to enhance enjoyment or celebrate a particular occasion. Such secrets serve an important good, the love among friends and family members, but only in a small way; and so it is not grave matter to violate secrecy in such matters, for example, for an older child to reveal plans the parents are making for a surprise party on a younger child's birthday.

i) Secret information unjustly exposed may not be unfairly used. People often unjustly seek access to or divulge secrets as a means to some further injustice,

---

43. See, for example, Gene Antonio, *The AIDS Cover-Up? The Real and Alarming Facts about AIDS,* 2nd ed. (San Francisco: Ignatius Press, 1987), 141–51, 177–78.

and then it is obvious that the information may not be used to accomplish that unjust end. Again, the point of secrecy often is to block potential injustices, and these obviously remain injustices for anyone whom the secret's exposure enables to commit them.

Nevertheless, once secret information is unjustly exposed, it sometimes can be used fairly, especially by third parties. For instance, if someone wrongly reveals plans for a surprise party, others can rightly change their own plans for a celebration on the same occasion. Still, unjustly exposed information sometimes cannot be fairly used, even by a third party, although it could be fairly used if justly obtained. For example, in a contest to solve a problem, no competitor can fairly use information gained from anyone's wrongful violation of another competitor's secrets, although the same information could be fairly used had it become available in some other way. Thus, whenever secret information is unjustly exposed, one should consider whether a prospective use of it is fair, taking into account how it became available.

Question D: What Are One's Responsibilities in Voluntary Associations and Friendships?

Responsibilities in the Church, the family, and political society are treated in other chapters (3.D, 9, and 11). Commitment is required for full participation even in these three communities, but involvement in other associations, to be treated here, is voluntary in a stronger sense (see GS 25). Either they are friendships, grounded in natural affinities but willingly cultivated for their own sake, or they are more structured associations, deliberately formed to promote more or less well-specified common interests.

Associations of the latter kind are many and diverse. They include religious societies such as orders and congregations, charismatic communities, sodalities, informal Bible study groups; charitable organizations such as St. Vincent de Paul societies, the Red Cross, shelters for the homeless; political and patriotic associations such as political parties, civic associations, groups concerned with specific rights; economic associations such as businesses, cooperatives, trade unions, professional societies, consumer clubs, automobile associations; cultural and re-creational associations such as universities, schools, communal libraries and museums, theater companies, athletic leagues and teams, collectors clubs, the Boy Scouts and the Girl Scouts; health and welfare organizations such as hospitals, organizations to deal with specific diseases, Alcoholics Anonymous chapters, volunteer fire companies, hospices.

Most responsibilities regarding voluntary associations will not be treated in this question, but many of these—including responsibilities regarding communication, promises, secrets, and the exercise of authority and the practice of obedience—which hold in every interpersonal relationship, are treated in other questions of this chapter. Some others, proper to particular associations, have the force of positive law (see *CMP*, 11.D–E). This question deals only with certain responsibilities in regard to and within voluntary associations: namely, those which pertain either to all voluntary associations, or to all associations of the more structured sort, or to all friendships.

1. Some Responsibilities Pertain to All Voluntary Associations

Because friendships and associations of the more structured sort differ greatly, few specific responsibilities pertain to both. But these few are important.

a) One should subordinate voluntary associations to faith. Obviously, a person should not join any voluntary association whose specific purpose is at odds with the truth of faith or is morally wicked. But the point here is broader. Faith, as fundamental option, should overarch one's whole life, and involvements in voluntary associations should be subordinated to faith in a particular way. Either they should be elements of personal vocation, coordinated with its other elements, or they should be subordinated to personal vocation as a whole, so that they do not conflict with it in any way but rather make their contribution to its faithful fulfillment. For example, a friendship or participation in a religious community should be an element of one's personal vocation; membership in a consumer cooperative or a country club should be subordinated to one's personal vocation.

This responsibility is blatantly violated by those who regard their membership in the Church and their practice of the faith as only one part of their lives as a whole, more or less coordinate with other parts—for example, work, politics, and leisure—carried on through other associations in virtually complete isolation from faith (see GS 43). Sociologically, of course, being a member of the Church is distinct from and parallel to being an employee of a business or a member of a political party or fraternal association. Psychologically, each of these involves an individual with a distinct group of people, makes a distinct set of demands, and offers a distinct set of satisfactions. But hope's absolute primacy in Christian life—"Strive first for the kingdom of God" (Mt 6.33)—requires a person to go beyond the sociological and psychological appearances, and subordinate every other aspect of life to membership in the Church, understood not merely as a human community, but as the People of God, the communion of divine and human persons.

This responsibility also is violated, though not so blatantly, by involvement in voluntary associations in ways that otherwise would be morally good but somehow detract from or conflict with responsibilities flowing from personal vocation.[44] For instance, active involvement in groups dedicated to good causes unrelated to one's personal vocation diverts one's time, energy, and other resources from the fulfillment of vocational responsibilities. Again, certain ways of cultivating and carrying on friendships, which in themselves would be good, sometimes can create difficulties for a person's marriage and family life or someone's life as a priest or religious, and so every friendship must be shaped to harmonize with such fundamental elements of personal vocation.

b) Communal selfishness in such associations should be avoided. Because human goods are not in themselves individuated and human persons are social by nature, very few people are so egoistic that they consistently pursue only their

---

44. *CIC,* c. 278, §3, makes this point with respect to clerics.

individual satisfaction. Indeed, except for those who are deeply and thoroughly wicked, blatant egoism ordinarily appears only in intimate relationships, such as those within the family, and egoistic selfishness in other contexts is more likely to be due to psychological weakness than to moral fault. Everyone, however, is tempted to social selfishness: the restriction of love and community by unreasonable partiality to his or her own family, nation, or other group. Thus, selfishness, as the contrary of Christian love and justice, often takes a nonegoistic form, and is found in the commitments, structures, policies, attitudes, practices, and actions of various communities.

Examples make the point clear. Friends can be generous to one another but selfish by developing their relationship for mutual escapist gratification at the expense of mutual help in living good lives and growing in holiness.[45] Associates in a business enterprise can make great personal sacrifices for the company's success yet disregard the impact of their business on the economy as a whole. Parents can devote themselves to their children while the family as a whole violates the rights of neighboring families. Monks can fulfill their vows personally yet care more about their monastery's prestige than about their apostolic responsibilities.

Sometimes it is impossible to be part of a voluntary association without endorsing and serving its communal selfishness; for example, some businesses require all their employees to cooperate in practices unfair to customers or competitors, and some civic associations are open only to those who agree to protect the privileges of one region against the common good of the wider community. In such cases, a person should not enter the association or else should leave it upon discovering its inherently selfish character. Sometimes, to be sure, it is possible to participate in a community without formally cooperating in communal selfishness, but even so, one should do what one can to reform what needs reforming in the association and shape all its activities in accord with the requirements of justice and love.

2. Some Responsibilities Pertain Specifically to Structured Associations

Like friendships, the more or less structured voluntary associations one forms and joins to promote specific common interests are rooted in the social nature of human persons.[46] However, such associations aim less at the good of community itself than at other goods which members hope to realize through their cooperative activity. Thus, specific responsibilities in respect to such associations flow mainly

45. C. S. Lewis, *The Four Loves* (New York: Harcourt, Brace and World, 1960), 115–23, points out and analyzes an allied danger: strengthened in self-confidence by mutual affirmation, otherwise humble individuals belonging to a circle of friends often become overconfident about their shared values and views, with the bad result that they develop a supercilious attitude toward people outside the circle.

46. Indeed, the right to found and act in voluntary associations is a natural right: see Leo XIII, *Rerum novarum, ASS* 23 (1890–91) 664–68, *PE*, 115.49–57. The Church also expressly recognizes that the faithful have that right—see *CIC*, c. 215 and c. 298; cf. AA 19—with respect to the sorts of associations appropriate to promote the various specific interests (spiritual, charitable, apostolic, and so on) of members of the Church as such.

from the practical requirements of their more or less specified purposes, rather than from the requirements of the interpersonal relationship itself (see GS 30–31).

a) One should form or join associations to fulfill one's vocation. Often, participation in voluntary associations to promote specific common interests is not morally optional but required, for in many cases it otherwise is impossible to fulfill one's personal vocation.[47] Although the costs of involvement, in money, time, and energy, may discourage one from forming or joining appropriate associations, one should do so. And even though an association's purpose could be promoted as well, or perhaps better, by the political society, subsidiarity (see 6.E.5.c) requires trying to fulfill responsibilities through voluntary associations whenever this is reasonably possible.

When there is a choice to be made among various voluntary associations serving the same interests, a person should prefer the one which offers most for meeting his or her vocational responsibilities. For example, someone seeking graduate or professional training should judge first which school's program is likely most fully to develop his or her abilities, then try to find the means, and if possible make the necessary sacrifices, to go to that school, rather than preferring one with an easier program, or located in a more attractive place, or able to offer funding. Again, those seeking employment should decide which job to accept by first considering how best to use their gifts for service and to meet other vocational responsibilities, such as those to family; only then should they take into account factors such as the work's pleasantness or its location.

b) Sometimes groups rather than individuals should associate. Because individualism is so pervasive, there is a tendency to suppose that only individuals can and should form and act in voluntary associations. Sometimes, however, the specific purpose would be better served by an association of couples, families, or groups of some other sort, in which case the individualistic assumption ought to be set aside. For example, sometimes couples or families, rather than their members as individuals, can better associate to promote goods such as growth in spiritual life or recreation.

c) One should participate actively in voluntary associations. In a typical voluntary association, a few members are energetic and dedicated while many take a much less active role. Within limits, this situation is inevitable and indicates no moral fault, provided a fair relationship obtains between the contributions members make and the benefits they receive. Fairness must take into account not only the strict proportion between contributions and benefits, but also other factors, such as differences in members' abilities to contribute, subjective differences in the value or burdensomeness to different members of objectively similar contributions and benefits, and the limits of the association's capacity to distribute burdens and benefits.

---

47. John XXIII, *Pacem in terris, AAS* 55 (1963) 262–63, *PE,* 270.23–24, not only teaches the right to found and act in voluntary associations, but insists on the urgency of doing so, and adds (24): "Such groups and societies must be considered absolutely essential for the safeguarding of man's personal freedom and dignity, while leaving intact a sense of responsibility [note omitted]."

Even when all the factors which justify differences among members' contributions are considered, however, it can be clear that many benefit without doing their fair share. Often, a voluntary association lacks effective means of compelling them to do so. Therefore, members must be conscientious in judging how much to contribute and contributing it.

Moreover, there often is a responsibility to contribute more than would be one's fair share, as determined by the distribution of burdens and benefits. For if involvement in the association is, as it should be, a way of fulfilling one's personal vocation, and if that cannot better be done by withdrawing from the association (and perhaps joining another), one should participate sufficiently so that the association will succeed and the prospective benefits will be realized, and so should contribute proportionately more when others fail to do their fair share.

Again, an individual member of an association bears some responsibility for its actions. When those more active fail to direct these actions rightly, one must intervene, if there is a morally acceptable way of doing so, either to remedy the situation by becoming more active or to separate oneself from the association. Someone who does neither thing accepts responsibility for the association's wrongdoing and failure to fulfill its good purpose.

One or more of the preceding considerations can require a person to accept the responsibility of leadership in a voluntary association. Someone who does so, or who accepts that responsibility without being obliged to, should fulfill it conscientiously, taking care to promote the common good rather than his or her personal or party interest, and to treat other members fairly.

In all these matters, people are inclined to resent having to contribute more than others and to hate those whose benefits outweigh their contributions. However, such situations should be accepted as part of the fallen human condition, in the awareness that one participates in this relationship for the sake of the kingdom, and is required to practice mercy, the justice of the kingdom, instead of insisting on the justice proper to the association itself.

d) Each association's specific purpose should be respected. A structured voluntary association's specific purpose is the primary element of its constitution and one factor determining its identity. Still, constitutions sometimes are unwritten, usually are somewhat vague, and always are capable of being ignored. It is not uncommon for an association's resources and capacities to be used to pursue objectives outside its purpose, and indeed for members to be interested in such goals. Often, too, the temptation to proceed in this way is aggravated by the fact that the association's members have other bonds with one another; they may be relatives, fellow members of some other association, or friends, or they may become friends or form a party within the association itself.

However, inappropriate use of an association's capacities and resources lessens its effectiveness in respect to its specific purpose. If participants have rightly associated to promote that purpose, they act wrongly in lessening its effectiveness. Moreover, while all members share the association's specific purpose, not all are likely to be interested in any extrinsic objective. Thus, action for such an objective will be divisive; and it will be unfair to those members, even if few, who are not interested in the extrinsic objective, because it will use the association's resources and capacities in ways that will reduce the benefits which would accrue to them if its specific purpose were respected.

Therefore, in any structured voluntary association, members should carefully distinguish between their special bonds arising from solidarity in pursuing the association's common good and bonds originating elsewhere, and should not allow the latter to determine their participation in the association or their position on issues that arise within it. Each member should be careful to initiate and support only proposals for action in accord with the association's specific purpose. So, one should not try to persuade the garden club to take a stand against abortion or the right-to-life group to participate in a project to line the suburb's streets with oak trees. Moreover, one should resist others' attempts to divert associations from their specific purposes.[48]

e) Amending an association's constitution can be unjust. Sometimes, attempts to alter an association's purpose involve efforts to amend its constitution. Often, of course, there are good grounds for supporting an amendment that clarifies and refines an association's purpose without substantially altering it; but one which radically changes an association's purpose, even if technically legitimate, can be incompatible with the common good and unfair. That will be so if the association could still serve its original purpose, but the change will interfere with serving it, and members who joined and contributed on the basis of that purpose oppose the change because they remain committed to the original common good. In such a case, the change will be detrimental to some members, and cannot be justified by the association's common good; rather, it is grounded in the particular good of some members (even a large majority) to the detriment of the good of others (even a small minority). Thus, the change is not an act of the association.

It might be objected that there need be no unfairness in such a case, since those amending the constitution are in reality terminating the original association and establishing a new one, leaving the minority free to form their own new association along the lines of the original one. If that is so, however, the original association's assets should be disposed of according to the constitution's provisions or divided fairly between the two groups; the majority evades this responsibility by taking over for its own purpose the original association's assets, including its very structure and history.

f) One should carry on one's apostolate in every association. In every association, a Christian should live according to his or her faith and, when occasion

---

48. John Paul II, *Laborem exercens,* 20, *AAS* 73 (1981) 631, *PE,* 280.98, lays down the norm in the specific case of unions and politics. Unions must be concerned for the wider common good: "However, the role of unions is not to 'play politics' in the sense that the expression is commonly understood today. Unions do not have the character of political parties struggling for power; they should not be subjected to the decision of political parties or have too close links with them." By saying "too close links," John Paul plainly grants the legitimacy of some forms of involvement by a union in politics, namely, those essential for it to pursue its proper purpose, which is the common good of its members as such. What the norm excludes is any politicization of unions which diverts them from their proper end.

offers, be prepared to bear witness to it explicitly. Cooperating in the association's good work with members whose motives are morally faulty often can serve as an important means or preparation for evangelization. For instance, students with true Christian motivation, working closely with teachers and fellow students motivated mainly by the desire for status and money, have a special opportunity to bear witness to the gospel.

In the context of many associations (for example, school, work, and neighborhood), those who share apostolic consciousness and commitment should associate together, if only informally; this sometimes can be an ecumenical group. In this way they can lend one another moral support and share their observations, judgments, and suggestions for action. Thus, without defining themselves as a party within the politics of the association, they can work together more effectively in carrying out their apostolic commitment.

3. Some Responsibilities Pertain Specifically to Friendships

Unlike more structured voluntary associations, which are deliberately formed and directed toward more or less limited purposes, friendships are not chosen as means to other ends. Rather, they depend on natural affinities and are cultivated, at least in part, for the sake of the communion itself. Of course, friends must have some common interest—for example, studies, work, prayer, a sport, the common concerns of a neighborhood—and common commitment to pursue such an interest can cause a friendship to develop spontaneously, without even being chosen. But a friendship is not restricted by any such common interest; it can embrace any and all of the friends' interests.[49]

Friendship's starting point is that certain individuals who share a common interest attract and are attracted by each other, feel mutual sympathy and affection, and enjoy being together. They reveal themselves to each other by sharing their feelings and personal information, especially about their hopes and commitments, admire each other's good qualities, discover some significant agreement in values (and generally in basic convictions and commitments), are hopeful about each other's potential for communion and growth, and begin to give each other gifts and confer mutual benefits.

In giving gifts and conferring benefits, friends, in the sense under consideration here, do not choose to do these things as means to any ulterior end. Rather, friendship begins precisely insofar as each looks to the other's well-being, not seeking any personal advantage except the mutual advantage inherent in and flowing from the association itself. Jonathan, for instance, valued David's well-being for David's own sake, and so sought to protect and benefit David, seeking nothing for himself except his share in their very friendship and in the common good of Israel, to which they both were committed, by being David's friend and

---

49. For an introduction with references to classical works, see *New Catholic Encyclopedia*, s.v. "friendship," but the author is mistaken in supposing that ideal friendship means the disappearance of "I" and "thou." That is an ideal for neo-Platonists but not for Christians, whose model of friendship is the Trinity. A generally sound treatment of the psychology of friendship: Ignace Lepp, *The Ways of Friendship*, trans. Bernard Murchland (New York: Macmillan, 1966).

having David as his own friend; David was disposed and acted similarly toward Jonathan (see 1 Sm 18–20). In this way they together brought into being their friendship, a communion in which the "I" of each for himself and the "you" of each for the other by no means disappeared, but were sharpened and intensified, by being joined in their common "we," that is, in the bond of friendship itself and in their fulfillment together in the other goods, such as the welfare of Israel, in which they shared as friends.

Friendship requires reciprocity, and reciprocity often is easier between two individuals than among three or more, or between communities. Friendships of two individuals are therefore comparatively common and are what people usually think of as friendship. However, a friendship can be a circle of three or more persons, and communities can be friends, for example, two married couples or two whole families can develop a genuine friendship.[50] But for simplicity's sake, what follows will be formulated in terms of the friendship of two individuals.

The idea of friendship can be realized more or less clearly, completely, and purely in different instances, depending on the psychological health, maturity, and moral character of the persons involved. Hence, in some cases the norms that follow are open to qualifications when applied to actual friendships, which are likely to be limited in various ways.[51]

a) Friendship is intrinsically good and valuable for Christian life. Any friendship of the kind under consideration here is an instance of a basic human good, and so is good in itself. Friendship also is necessary for the full development and perfection of human persons, who are created for communion. Moreover, it facilitates the apostolate, for Christians have many opportunities to share their faith, like other things they value, with their friends, who, due to friendship, are disposed to be receptive. Finally, friendships are among the good fruits of human nature and effort destined to last forever (see GS 38–39). Therefore, while children and others subject to authority cannot be commanded to form friendships, parents and other authorities should do what they can to encourage and support authentic friendships.

b) One should seek and offer friendship. While friendship, especially in its beginning, is a gift more than an achievement, in view of its value people should dispose themselves for this gift. Children often seek and offer friendship very simply: "I would like to be your friend. Will you be my friend?" Adults, having learned to be cautious in interpersonal relationships generally, are less trusting. Yet even if they are right to be so, childlike directness is appropriate when friendship seems possible, since such directness effectively tests the apparent possibility, verifying it when genuine, and discarding it when not.

Fear of the possible humiliation of being rejected, anxiety about the possible pain of being wounded in consequence of entrusting oneself to another, and reluctance to accept the responsibility of reciprocating others' gifts and benefits are

---

50. Lewis, *The Four Loves,* 92–102, obviously taking as his model friendships among groups of kindred spirits in a more or less academic community, regards the circle of friends as the typical form of friendship.

51. On friendship in antiquity, the Bible, and the early Church: *Theological Dictionary of the New Testament,* s.v. "philos, phile, philia."

motives for not seeking and not accepting friendship. These concerns do warrant some caution: "When you gain friends, gain them through testing, and do not trust them hastily" (Sir 6.7). But loneliness, which also is painful, can be overcome only by friendship and other forms of authentic intimacy, not by the superficial relationships and distractions many people try to use for the purpose. The responsibilities of friendship can be great, but they are not burdensome, because they are lightened by love. Moreover, the benefits of friendship outweigh its costs, first, because one need do nothing to earn friendship's greatest benefits, which flow from it insofar as it is a natural good and gift of God, and second, because the gifts friends must give each other mainly are goods which are not diminished by being shared. In any case, given the role of friendship in moral and spiritual life, a person should be ready to pay the necessary emotional and practical price to seek and offer it.

c) **One should make oneself available for friendship.** Focusing too exclusively on definite ends to be realized through interacting and cooperating with others leads one not to pay attention to them as whole persons, existing in themselves, with their own, not-yet-completely-defined potentiality for growth and perfection. But that attention is necessary for the beginning of friendship. Therefore, a person should try not to experience and think of others exclusively in terms of their practical importance, but to regard them contemplatively, as realities in themselves, having a certain beauty, even if damaged and incomplete, as the unique images of God that they are.

Making oneself available for friendship, however, should not be confused with creating an illusion of friendship. Without dishonesty, people can and should be affable and obliging in every social relationship, including those that are purely practical. However, certain expressions and ways of behavior are signs of interest in the relationship itself rather than in anything to which it would be instrumental. For example, it violates not only truth and justice but friendship itself to elicit confidential information by feigning personal interest in a couple's family and home in order to develop a relationship for some ulterior end, such as making a sale, for this renders the essential language of friendship ambiguous and makes it more difficult for people to accept other, sincere expressions of availability for friendship.

d) **Friends should communicate their real selves.** Because friendship is a communion of persons precisely in their personhood, it depends upon the mutual giving of true selves. Friends cannot cultivate their oneness without mutually understanding each other from within. They should trust each other and communicate without reserve what constitutes themselves.

That does not mean friends should tell each other everything they think and feel, everything they do, every secret they have. Such total communication not only is impossible, but in particular cases would be wrong. Friends, even more than others, should not scandalize each other, betray others' secrets to each other, bore each other with constant and pointless self-revelation, or waste each other's time in idle talk.

But they should confide in each other not only their deep convictions and commitments but their doubts and weaknesses, and should allow their habitual attitudes and feelings to show, so that each can grasp the other's self-understanding, motivations, and potential for growth. In their intimate communication, they not only should avoid deception and dishonesty but should let down their guard, put aside the personae which may be appropriate in other situations, and allow themselves to appear as they are.

e) Friends should facilitate and protect their communication. The communication essential to friendship is thwarted if attempts to communicate are not properly received. One friend's self-revelation must be treated by the other as a gift, not received skeptically and critically examined for subconscious motives. If there is to be any psychological analysis, the friend whose motives are in question must initiate and lead the discussion. When each becomes the object of the other's examination and insight—for example, by employing techniques of psychoanalytical interpretation—mutual objectification has replaced mutual self-giving.

When friends make themselves vulnerable to each other, each must protect the other's exposed self. Because friendship depends on self-revelation in trust, friends have a special responsibility to safeguard what is entrusted to them; betrayal of a friend's trust violates the special good of the friendship itself. Although secrets sometimes should not be kept, wrongly revealing a friend's confidences, other things being equal, is far more likely to be grave matter than revealing the secrets of someone not a friend (see Sir 27.16–18).

f) Friends rightly enjoy precedence in the order of charity. Like family relationships, friendship is a natural good of human persons, a good healed and perfected by grace. Genuine friendships rightly nurtured belong to one's personal vocation, and so friends, like family, should receive preference in one's care and beneficence. Of course, that is no license for unfair favoritism.

Every person sometimes has some very great need which nobody but a friend can meet. Friends should be prepared to meet such needs if they can, and may rightly subordinate other responsibilities, except those to family members, just as they should when family members have similar needs.

g) Friends should defend each other's reputation and honor. Individuals seldom can defend themselves adequately against unjust attacks on their reputation and honor; their attempts are likely to be dismissed as self-interested, and even to enhance an attack's significance. It also is difficult to proclaim one's own goodness without seeming immodest and to struggle with dishonorable opponents without seeming to share their bad qualities. Moreover, and most important, rather than protecting their own interests at the expense of further alienating the enemy, Christians are constrained by love to respond to unjust attacks in a way likely to promote the enemy's spiritual welfare. Therefore, Christians are especially vulnerable to enemies who seek to destroy reputation and honor.

While such attacks sometimes can be tolerated, damage to reputation and honor sometimes will seriously impair a person's ability to fulfill his or her personal vocation and serve others faithfully. In such cases, an effective response is needed. Friends should undertake that defense, which is more effective if they act promptly and on their own initiative, without waiting to be asked.

h) Friends should not allow conflicting interests to divide them. People often think friends have all things in common, but that is not true. The distinct selves do not merge into one; each friend has his or her own personal vocation and life to live. Therefore, friends have different interests and goals, and it is almost inevitable that these sometimes will conflict. Then friends can be tempted to try to force each other to subordinate their legitimate but conflicting interests to their bond of friendship or else to let their differences divide them. Doing the former means failing to fulfill responsibilities to the goods that underlie the conflicting interests, as well as abusing the bond of friendship by making it into an instrument of self-interest; while giving in to the latter temptation means forgoing the good of the friendship.

But that is wrong—unreasonable because unnecessary. Even when their interests conflict, one friend can still will the other's goods without willing contrary to his or her own; for their personalities remain distinct, and the distinction itself is essential to the good of friendship. For example, athletes who are friends have conflicting interests when competing against each other. But it is not necessary that they stop trying to excel or that they cease being friends. Instead, both can do their best, each wishing the other to do likewise, and both rejoicing in the victory of either. All conflicting interests that could strain friendships can be dealt with in this way, provided friends recognize their responsibility to be themselves, not merely other selves of their friends.

i) One should avoid confusing friendship with comradeship. People closely associated in the pursuit of specific goods—for example, fellow soldiers, members of a school class, coworkers—often develop group spirit and more or less strong emotional bonds. These bonds are very similar to those of friendship, and friendships often spring up among comrades; but the possible coincidence of the two sorts of relationship does not mean they are identical, and it is an error to confuse them. Comrades who are not friends are not interested in each other as whole persons and do not desire their relationship for its own sake, but only for the sake of legitimate self-interest and the specific good they serve together.

Those who confuse comradeship with friendship are likely to make two additional kinds of mistakes. First, they may wrongly suppose that comradeship should have the same moral status in life as friendship, and so commit themselves too much to comrades, allowing them an unwarranted priority in the order of charity, and communicating with them more unreservedly than they should. Second, wrongly expecting comrades to fulfill all the responsibilities of friendship, they may make unreasonable demands and suffer avoidable disappointments.

j) One should avoid confusing friendship with romantic relationship. Like the inclination that leads to friendship, erotic inclination, which leads to romance, is universal. However, while everyone may and should seek and offer friendship, only spouses and single persons with marriage in view should nurture a romantic relationship (see 9.I.1.c–d, 9.I.2.b). Yet even in those who are neither married nor free to marry, inclinations toward friendship and romance often are commingled and easily confused, with the bad results that possible friendships are mistakenly treated as occasions of sin, actual friendships are spoiled by becoming occasions of sin, couples in love fail to cultivate friendship, and romantic relationships are wrongly nurtured as pseudofriendships.

Although the integrated emotions of a mature person serve his or her commitments, healthy emotions initially serve biological needs, and, biologically, the most fundamental interpersonal relationships are those between spouses, parents and children, and brothers and sisters. Hence, the affectionate feelings characteristic of these relationships no doubt color all interpersonal emotions. Some call all such feelings "erotic," and if the word is taken in that broad sense, no doubt it is true that all affection for others is basically erotic. A romantic relationship, however, involves erotic love in a narrower sense. It is the feeling which includes sexual desire but tends not only to sexual satisfaction, which can be entirely self-centered, but to a fuller union of two bodily persons, who thus belong to each other more or less permanently, enjoy each other, and delight in each other's enjoyment.[52]

Whenever a relationship begins and develops between two unmarried persons who either are not free to marry or are of the same sex, they need to know whether it is romance or friendship. Several characteristics distinguish the two.

While both erotic love and love of friendship draw persons together into intimate communion, the two nevertheless differ, since erotic love draws a couple toward bodily union, while friendship moves friends toward a union of minds and hearts, which employs bodily contact only incidentally to manifest affection. A sign that a relationship is really friendship, rather than something else, is that the parties to it focus, not on the experience of being together, but on a union realized mainly by conversation and by engaging together in activities both morally good and immediately rewarding—eating meals, playing, traveling, worshipping, and so forth.

Thus, a couple involved in a romantic relationship must be together in order to touch each other; friends share common interests beyond themselves and enjoy seeing each other both to pursue those interests and to communicate more perfectly than is possible by letters and telephone calls. Even slight bodily contact between romantic lovers often leads to genital arousal; the contact of friends does not. Romance is of two persons only, and is exclusive and jealous; friendship can expand to three or more, and is compatible with and unthreatened by a friend's other intimate relationships, including an erotic one. Romance is fascinating and absorbing; friendship does not distract from other interests and concerns. Romance happens to people who "fall" in love; friendship grows between people who cultivate it. If these distinguishing characteristics are kept in mind, one can avoid confusing friendships and romantic relationships involving erotic love.

k) In practice, one should distinguish erotic love from friendship. In the absence of the marks of erotic inclination, mutual attraction and affection, even sudden and strong, should be recognized as the basis of possible friendship, and

---

52. Lewis, *The Four Loves,* 131–60, very well articulates the concept of erotic love, though he too sharply distinguishes it from its nucleus of sexual instinct. While it is true that full-blown romance is not essential for sexual desire and enjoyable intercourse (including marital intercourse of couples who do not marry "for love"), even those who have intercourse with prostitutes prefer it to masturbation for the sake of the psychological satisfaction of being united with another person: an illusion of romance.

these feelings should be welcomed, not only in oneself but in others, such as one's children.

However, it is not unusual for inappropriate erotic feelings to arise, especially in a child or young person, toward a new acquaintance or a friend, whether of the same or the opposite sex. One should recognize such feelings when they arise, acknowledge them to oneself, and not act on them (or allow children to act on them). Generally it is not necessary to judge that the relationship itself is an occasion of sin and to give it up. But one should carry it on only within the limits—for example, of time, place, situation, and frequency of meetings—consistent with self-control and the gradual elimination of the inappropriate feelings.

Acknowledging erotic feelings to the other party in such a case is a bad idea. Not infrequently it leads to the discovery that the feelings are mutual or to arousing an erotic response, and that discovery or response intensifies the feelings. So, inappropriate erotic feelings almost never should be acknowledged to the one who has aroused them. They should be kept to oneself or confided to another—which for children could be a parent or elder sibling, for happily married persons their spouse, or for others a spiritual director or friend.

Couples who experience appropriate, mutual erotic inclination, whether they are married couples or unmarried but free to marry, should realize that erotic love, while good and splendid, is insufficient as a basis for a lifelong relationship. Hence, while nurturing romance, they should recognize the distinct value and conditions of friendship, and do what they can to cultivate it too.

However, couples who are not friends and who experience inappropriate erotic inclination should recognize that their attraction offers no basis for friendship and should not try to cultivate the relationship as a friendship—"Although we cannot rightly be lovers, we will continue to see each other as 'friends' "—since in making such an attempt they remain unnecessarily in an occasion of sin.

l) **Friends should encourage each other's growth toward holiness.** All Christians, of course, not only should avoid leading others into sin but should encourage their growth toward holiness. Friends, however, have special opportunities, and so special responsibilities, in this matter.

Unlike erotic lovers, who tend, especially in the early days, to see each other through rose-colored glasses, friends perceive each other in their true colors, defects and all, and understand each other's inward motivations. So, they are in an unusually good position to mirror each other honestly and to uncover what self-deception hides. At the same time, knowing that they are loved for themselves and as the persons they are, friends are in an unusually good position to gain insight from their friends, to accept their advice, to respond well to their admonitions. Moreover, the stability and mutual tolerance characteristic of friendship make it possible for friends to learn by trial and error how best to help and support each other, and so their efforts to do so can grow in effectiveness. Then too, the mutual affection of friends motivates them to please each other by changing in appropriate ways. Therefore, each has a special power, and so a special responsibility, to promote the other's moral development. Without being asked, friends should give each other good advice, which naturally will include any necessary admonition, delivered in a form as painless as possible.

Friends should encourage each other's spiritual growth in other ways, which are equally if not more important. Conscientious people take their own good qualities for granted but are acutely aware of their sins, defects, and weaknesses. Seeing all this as it is, friends, in motherly fashion, can focus on what is good and its potential for growth, confirm its reality, endorse it, rejoice in it, honor and praise it, and so nurture its unfolding. For this reason, friends can help each other almost irreplaceably in discerning elements of vocation and inventing and revising projects to fulfill vocational commitments. Moreover, when one friend falls into sin, and is shamed and dishonored, the other can and should support recovery by acknowledging the truth without pretense, yet loyally remaining a firm friend, showing that no such wound is beyond healing, and so serving as an image and medium of God's forgiving and healing grace.

Finally, friends should support each other both by praying together and by praying individually for each other and for the grace to be good friends.

m) One should never entirely terminate any friendship. Often, the interest which friends take in each other eventually lessens; and many friendships are disrupted by circumstances, such as one friend's moving to a distant place or making some major commitment whose responsibilities make it difficult or impossible actively to carry on the friendship. Such developments nevertheless are compatible with maintaining the friendship as a communion of good will, affectionate memory, and prayer for each other. Termination of friendship is something else: a deliberate attempt to destroy a relationship, or what one regards as the remains of a relationship, which has been damaged by the other party. Motivated by anger or hatred aroused by conflict or betrayal, such an attempt not only violates the seventh mode of responsibility (see *CMP*, 8.G), but the requirement of Christian love to forbear, forgive, and make peace.

Question E: How Should One Exercise Authority and Practice Obedience?

The kingdom is the common object of hope, the common good, for which all Christians should cooperate with God and with one another. Each Christian has a unique vocation; each, as a particular member of Jesus' one body, can make an irreplaceable personal contribution. But since all vocations are parts of the Church's single mission, all must work together. Moreover, in the pursuit of human goods, Christians must cooperate with others insofar as possible.

Common action depends on unity in decision and in execution. The unity in decision of a cooperating group is the exercise of authority; its unity in execution is the practice of obedience. Therefore, Christians must rightly exercise authority and practice obedience. Human authority comes from God, and obedience to it should be religiously motivated, as the New Testament teaches: "There is no authority except from God" (Rom 13.1), and "Be subject to one another out of reverence for Christ" (Eph 5.21). In pointing to authority's moral foundation, this teaching illuminates both its moral force and its moral limits.

1. Authority and Obedience Are Essential to All Communal Actions

While authority and obedience often are misunderstood as dominance and submission, authority is the capacity to make decisions on behalf of a community and obedience is the cooperation of members of a community in carrying out its acts. Thus, the functions of authority and obedience to it are present even in a community without a leader. For example, one day at lunch four students plan to go camping together on the weekend. They settle everything by unanimous consensus: Charlie will arrange for transportation, George will purchase food, John will rent equipment, and Phil will obtain permits and maps. In agreeing to these plans, the four students form a community and exercise authority on its behalf. As each carries out his task, whether he finds it enjoyable or onerous (so that he wishes he had not agreed to do it), he obeys the group's decisions. Without authority, Charlie, George, John, and Phil could not have their plan to do what is necessary to go camping together; without obedience, they will not cooperate effectively in carrying out their plan. This example makes it clear that authority and obedience are necessary if there is to be any community and cooperation whatsoever.

2. Authority and Obedience Do Not Preclude Equal Personal Dignity

Authority and *obedience* have bad connotations, partly due to abuses of authority, which give even its right use a bad name. Another reason, however, is that authority and obedience necessarily limit people's freedom to do as they please, and this freedom is overvalued by contemporary Western culture. While most people realize that some authority and obedience are inevitable, many, cherishing the ideal of autonomy, think authority and obedience are at best necessary evils, so that the less, the better.

a) **Some conceptions of obedience preclude personal dignity.** Some religions and philosophies maintain, contrary to Christian faith, that the destiny of human persons is to lose their individual identity and selfhood, to be swallowed up in one ultimate reality. Obedience seems good precisely insofar as it negates the self in order to overcome diversity and the plurality of responsible agents. Again, some philosophical and religious anthropologies hold that some human individuals are naturally inferior to others—there are natural slaves, women are inferior to men, and so on—and inferiors can share in moral responsibility only by submitting to superiors. On this view, the obedience of some reflects their personal inferiority and incapacity for full human responsibility. Moreover, some take the obedience of small children as their model for all obedience, but small children really are incapable of shaping their own lives, and so their obedience substitutes for more mature responsibility.

Such conceptions conflict with personal dignity. Obedience as self-negation entirely excludes the dignity of persons, and obedience based on slavish or childish submission structures relationships among responsible adults at the expense of equality in personal dignity. Nevertheless, elements of such conceptions sometimes color Christian thought and discourse about authority and obedience, so that they are badly misunderstood and, in some ways, wrongly valued.

b) The ideal of autonomy makes obedience seem a necessary evil. While false evaluations of authority and obedience are one factor which, by way of reaction, provokes the utopian ideal of entirely eliminating them from human association, other factors also nurture the ideal of absolute autonomy (complete self-rule). These include concupiscence, which inclines fallen men and women to resent having to conform to reality and to wish instead that reality could be made to conform to them; and a false paradigm of perfect personhood as absolute self-sufficiency, based on a misunderstanding of divine unity and perfection, and contrary to the Christian conception of God as a Trinity of persons whose fullness of life is their communion with one another.

The ideal of personal autonomy is taken for granted in contemporary, liberal societies, as if it were a self-evident truth. While accepting authority and obedience to limit social conflict, people think that, ideally, individuals should be free to do as they please. In exercising such liberty, it is supposed, people will adopt various styles of life and will fulfill themselves by their individualistic creativity. Authority and obedience appear to be only necessary evils which are to be minimized as much as possible.

c) Usually, some must exercise authority on behalf of a group. Sometimes it is right for certain people to impose their judgment on others without appealing to their freedom but simply by constraining them, for example, parents who stop babies from harming themselves, those who restrain the insane, police who lock up criminals. While parents and the rest do have authority, it is not exercised by these justified impositions; those subjected to them have no opportunity to obey or disobey, and so the duty to obey does not come into play.

The authority-obedience relationship is different: those involved are cooperating, and so they necessarily share moral responsibility. This sharing, which requires the authority of unified decisions, is necessary for the fulfillment of human persons. One might suppose that the necessary authority always should be by consensus. However, God gives different powers and gifts to different individuals so that they complement one another, make up social wholes, and realize most human goods by cooperatively carrying out their different roles (see GS 24–25; A, above). Not all the members in most communities are equally capable of exercising authority, and so it is necessary that some take the initiative in action while others freely follow their leadership (see *S.t.,* 2–2, q. 104, a. 1).[53] Thus, authority must be exercised by some, and others must obey them. Except in cases in which authority is exercised by consensus, this need, together with the requirement of fairness, provides the specific moral basis of authority and the duty to obey it (see *CMP,* 11.B).

d) This providential plan for human cooperation has positive value. Human persons are ennobled by being empowered to share not only in God's being but in his intelligence, freedom, causality—and authority. Still, this relationship does not

---

53. See Leo XIII, *Quod Apostolici muneris, ASS* 11 (1878) 372–74, *PE,* 79.5–8.

ennoble those in authority at the expense of those who obey. Rather, both are ennobled, since no true authority-obedience relationship exists without free choices on both sides to sustain it and carry out what it requires.

Then too, all who are able to act with mature responsibility exercise authority in respect to those matters in which their initiative is appropriate for effective cooperation. In a democratic society, for example, legislators decide about laws which all (including themselves) must obey, but citizens at large decide who will hold elective offices. Also, the same persons can exchange initiative in different relationships: the Catholic woman who also is a judge obeys her pastor in parish affairs, but he obeys her when he serves on the jury in a case tried in her court.

e) God's authority respects human dignity. The dignity of human persons depends on God: his initiative in creating humankind in his image, redeeming disobedient humankind, and calling each human person not only to fulfillment in human goods but to a share in the divine nature (see 2 Pt 1.4; GS 14–17, 22). God reveals himself and offers his covenant, but he forces no one to accept it; rather, he makes it clear that in doing so human beings will be enabled to cooperate in carrying out his plan, which includes their own true fulfillment. Thus, God appeals to people's freedom for the obedience of faith, which consists in accepting and doing his word (see Gn 22.15–18, 1 Sm 15.22, Heb 11.8). Mary illustrates the point: God does not use this most excellent of created persons in a merely passive way. He makes his will known to her, and she cooperates in his work through her free acts of faith and obedience (see LG 56). Thus, the Christian conception of divine authority is that of an initiative that appeals to freedom and respects the dignity of those who obey, while the Christian conception of obedience is that of reasonable and free submission.

f) Obedience ought to be given through human authorities to God. The ideal of autonomy is a distorted shadow of a Christian conviction about personal dignity: it is not fitting that those redeemed by Jesus—and sharing in the freedom of God's children, the dignity of his kingly people—should be servile to other human persons.[54] However, authority-obedience relationships do not have this result.

In the perspective of faith, the moral order, grounded in God's wisdom and goodness, undergirds authentic authority and obedience, which shape cooperation toward true human fulfillment. Thus, human authorities should be obeyed insofar as their commands make a moral claim, which can be accepted out of love for God. Because authority's legitimate commands make a moral claim, however, it does not follow that every human authority is God's personally authorized agent.[55] In practice, the most important consequence of authority's source in the moral order (and ultimately in God) is that those exercising it must respect others' dignity and those subject to it can obey without compromising their own dignity.

---

54. See Pius XI, *Quas primas, AAS* 17 (1925) 601–2, *PE,* 197.19.

55. See John XXIII, *Pacem in terris, AAS* 55 (1963) 269–72, *PE,* 270.46–54. Of course, genuine prophets, priests, and rulers of God's people of the old covenant and the ordained when acting in *persona Christi* under the new covenant are God's authorized agents; but other human authorities receive power from God through the natural law, not through divine positive law; for an explanation of this point, see 11.B.3.a.

g) **Jesus is the model and ultimate motive for Christians' obedience.** Jesus' whole life and death were shaped by obedience to the Father (see Heb 5.8, 10.5–7). "Though he was in the form of God, [Jesus] did not regard equality with God as something to be exploited" (Phil 2.6); so he was obedient even unto death, and therefore is exalted in the divine glory that is rightly his (see Phil 2.8–11).[56] St. Paul points this out precisely to explain to Christians how they should relate to one another: "Let each of you look not to your own interests, but to the interests of others. Let the same mind be in you that was in Christ Jesus" (Phil 2.4–5). Thus, subordination need not mean inferiority: even at the end of time, when God's plan reaches its completion, the Son, without derogating from his own lordship, will subject himself to the Father. That God may be all in all, however, everything must first be subjected to the Lord Jesus (see 1 Cor 15.24–28). This requirement of the kingdom's coming is the ultimate theological reason for obedience: "Be subject to one another out of reverence for Christ" (Eph 5.21; cf. 1 Pt 2.13).

3. The Moral Ground of Authority Determines Its Force and Limits

The fact that human authority comes from God sometimes is misinterpreted in a way that tends to absolutize certain authorities, especially public officials. Properly understood, however, the origin in God of human authority as such means only that every true authority is morally grounded. Although this does give it a force beyond what society can confer, whether by the power to compel compliance, by the weight of public opinion, or by the desires and interests of those who obey, the moral ground of authority also establishes authority's limits.

a) **Obedience should be ready and generous, not minimalistic.** A minimalistic attitude regards authority's prescriptions as a mere set of rules, to be satisfied only as necessary and evaded if possible. Some people comply with authority only insofar as they think it in their own interests to do so, but since authentic human authority is morally grounded, this is not true obedience. Thus, compliance merely to avoid punishment is not really obedience—submission to the moral claim of authority—nor is complying only in proportion to the authority's personal appeal and psychological persuasiveness.

Christians who rightly appreciate authority's moral grounding obey legitimate authorities, including those who cannot enforce their commands and those who make compliance psychologically difficult by their irritating or inept style of leadership. Truly obedient, such Christians are ready to comply, not waiting until the authority spends extra time and effort exhorting and admonishing them. They often go beyond the letter of what is prescribed in order to fulfill its evident purpose, while never using the letter to thwart authority's intent.

b) **Human authorities are subject to God and called to serve.** Since all human authority is morally grounded, none is unlimited. Before those in authority command anything, they first must be submissive to God's plan and will (see Wis

---

56. A helpful essay on *obedience* in Scripture: Alois Stöger, "Obedience," in *Encyclopedia of Biblical Theology,* 616–20. Jesus' obedience to the Father expresses his love as Son: Peter McDonald, "Obedience: The Supreme Image of Divine Love Itself Appearing," *Priests and People* 3 (Feb. 1989): 41–46.

6.1–8). They must obey their own legitimate superiors and the just law governing their exercise of authority. Moreover, they must be careful, for their responsibility is greater than that of those who obey them: authorities are responsible not only for the actions they command but for the action of commanding as well. Then too, since there are many human authorities in diverse relationships and for different matters, authorities must recognize and remain within their proper limits.

Christian hope should operate in the shaping of Christians' cooperation in authority-obedience relationships. Then both the exercise of authority and the practice of obedience are subordinated to the responsibility which Christians have to contribute to fulfilling the Church's mission. Just as Jesus is the model of obedience, so he is the model of authority; he regarded it as an element of his mission as servant, and he calls Christians to exercise authority as a service (see Mt 20.25–28, Mk 10.42–45, Lk 22.25–27, Jn 13.12–15). Thus, those in authority sin if they take advantage of their leadership role to practice favoritism or otherwise abuse their position, whether on their own behalf or on behalf of others.

c) **Authority extends only to morally acceptable courses of action.** Since all human authority is from God, who does no evil, there is no authority to command anything wrong. True human authority, being morally grounded, extends only to what is morally right. When people in authority command something wrong, faithful Christians do not obey them but do what is morally right: they obey God (see 1 Mc 2.19–22, Acts 5.29). Withholding obedience in such a case is not disobedience: the command has no authority, and obedience is not due it (see *S.t.*, 2–2, q. 104, a. 5).

In practice, it follows that someone exercising authority should require only what he or she is sure is right, while someone called on to obey a command about whose rightness he or she is in doubt must try to resolve the doubt. Sometimes one's own reflection or the advice of others will accomplish that. Authorities should be prepared to help, and should not regard reasonable requests for such help as resistance. If reflection does not lead to the judgment that the command certainly or more probably should *not* be obeyed, the presumption is on the side of the authority: one should obey, since otherwise one would fail to cooperate responsibly for the good at stake (see *CMP,* 12.C).

d) **Compliance sometimes should extend beyond the duty to obey.** One sometimes has a responsibility to conform to orders or precepts even though they are not rightly made by legitimate authorities. (Such conformity, strictly speaking, is not obedience, since obedience is given only to what morally deserves it: rightly made decisions of legitimate authorities.) There are several sorts of cases. Sometimes an authority makes an unreasonable demand, but compliance is in one's own true interests (including one's interests in fulfilling various responsibilities). In such cases, compliance is in order if this can be done without doing something wrong. Again, those in authority sometimes violate the rights of some members of the community, yet certain aspects of the common good of some other community call for docile compliance. Again, sometimes one should comply with directives which promote both good and bad purposes, doing so for the sake of the good even though such precepts are not truly authoritative insofar as they fall short of justice. Finally, one sometimes should comply with precepts which are unjust in allocating burdens and benefits, because not doing so will intensify rather than mitigate injustice. (The proper response of citizens to unjust laws is treated in 11.D.3.)

4. The End of Authority and Obedience Should Shape Their Use

Authority and obedience have as their end the common good: human fulfillment in and through cooperative action. Just as authority's moral grounding determines its force and limits in general, the common end of authority and obedience determines the right manner of exercising authority and practicing obedience.

a) Authorities should conform to their own directives. Those who think of authority as power over others in effect deny that authorities are bound by their own directives; as they see it, authorities are above the law because no one can force them to observe it. However, the moral basis of any genuine use of authority is that the one in authority reasonably decides what is required to attain the common good and justly commands it. Thus, authorities who do not willingly conform to their own directives, when these bear on their actions, manifest either unreasonableness in their directives, unfairness in setting requirements, or both. St. Thomas applies to such authorities Jesus' reproof of hypocrites who pronounce but do not perform (see Mt 23.3, 23–28; *S.t.,* 1–2, q. 96, a. 5, ad 3).

Even if they cannot be held to obedience, those who exercise authority should set an example of conformity to their own directives, whenever these are relevant to their personal actions. They are truly obedient in doing so, for they submit to the same moral requirement that binds others and are subject to God who is its source.

Moreover, when authorities give directions which do not apply to their own activity, they should not command what they would regard as unreasonable if they were among those asked to obey. It also is a sign of a right attitude in those in authority that they readily and generously obey others to whom they are themselves subject.

b) Authorities should listen to those whose action they direct. The purpose of authority is not served unless those exercising it make reasonable choices among morally acceptable ways of acting for the common good. Since authorities must be certain to command nothing wrong, they should listen carefully to moral misgivings, whether their own or others', about any of the possibilities they are considering, and should try either to resolve such concerns or to avoid the option which provokes them.

Moreover, to make a reasonable choice, an authority must be aware of the possibilities, and generally some possibilities will only emerge in listening to those whose action is directed. For in acting, people often hear or think of some new possibility or, at least, of a significant variation on a familiar way of doing things. Further, no authority can make a reasonable choice without considering the advantages and disadvantages of each possibility, and usually those who will have to carry out what is commanded are uniquely able to predict some advantages and disadvantages. Finally, an authoritative decision is similar to an individual's discernment in that rational reflection can leave two or more possibilities for choice (see 5.J). Then those in authority rightly take the feelings of the members of the social body as one sign of which option will best shape cooperation.[57]

c) Those subject to authority should truly submit to it. In some communities, such as democratic political societies, many participate in various ways in the exercise of authority. Even then, though, not all who must obey participate directly in making decisions. It would not be good if they did, for then either the whole society would spend all its time making decisions, or decisions would be poorly made by those whose gifts and responsibilities lay elsewhere. Also, while those who do not make decisions can play an important part in the work of authority by contributing to the deliberative process, they should not suppose themselves always entitled to know everything on which the authority's decision is based. Sometimes the common good or the rights of individuals require keeping relevant information secret.

Having made their appropriate contribution, those not in authority should not try in other ways to influence a decision, and should submit to every rightly made decision of any legitimate authority. The first step toward rebellion is to put pressure on a legitimate authority properly engaged in making a decision by suggesting that it will be obeyed reluctantly if it is unpopular. If people next attack unwelcome but rightly made decisions—for example, by saying the authority failed to listen to them—they foment rebellion; and they engage in it if they seek to nullify a rightly made decision which they dislike by encouraging disobedience.

d) Rebellion against rightful use of authority has two main sources. Among the reasons why people rebel against decisions that deserve obedience, two stand out. First, some simply do not recognize and accept authority's moral foundation; either they are not committed to the common good or they are not fair-minded or both. Second, while accepting authority's moral foundation, some in particular situations reduce the common good to some more limited good they desire to see achieved. Having their own conception of what should be done, they are not open to the possibility that some other course of action may be as good or even better. And so they think the authority's decision is less good than it should be, judge it unreasonable, and are likely to say it is against their conscience. While presuming to judge the authority's decision erroneous, they cannot know it to be so, and they should realize that the authority simply has made a decision different from the one they would have made. Instead they act disloyally and thereby impede members of the community, including themselves, from fulfilling their personal vocations. The remedy is hope, which enables one to obey legitimate authority just as it motivates the fulfillment of one's personal vocation: with creativity, without giving in to discouragement, with active self-surrender, and without counting costs.

e) The responsibility to obey has limits. Obedience should be given only to genuine authority, and authority is limited in two ways. First, authority extends

57. The responsibilities stated here underlie provisions of the Church's law that make clear the importance of distinguishing between deliberation and decision, and the responsibility of authorities to take seriously others' participation in deliberation: see *CIC,* c. 127. Also see *The Rule of St. Benedict,* trans. Anthony C. Meisel and M. L. del Mastro (Garden City, N.Y.: Doubleday Image, 1975), 51 (ch. 3).

only to morally acceptable courses of action. Second, it extends only to what serves the common good of the community whose cooperative action it directs. So, for instance, civic authority has nothing to say about the Church's liturgy except insofar as liturgical actions could disturb the peace, disrupt traffic, or something of the sort. Similarly, the Church's pastoral authority does not extend to political matters, such as selecting public officials. Still, because the Church has the right and duty to teach the moral truth about political actions as about others, her pastors can rightly teach that public office should not be entrusted to those who support patently unjust laws and public policies.

The moral obligation to obey has other limitations. Even when a genuine authority operates within its proper limits, conflicts of duties can require an individual not to obey some precept which otherwise would call for obedience. Also, within the narrow limits of its legitimate use, epikeia applies to every kind of human law (see *CMP*, 11.E.10, 11.G.6). Still, a person should begin with a presumption in favor of obedience: one obeys unless one judges that doing so would more probably or certainly be wrong.[58]

f) Disobedience can be a grave sin. Within the limits of the responsibility to obey, disobedience can be, but is not always, a grave matter. Sometimes disobedience is grave because it directly and seriously damages or impedes the common good and sometimes because it concerns a matter already grave by divine or natural law, for example, a liturgical requirement for the validity of a sacrament or a criminal law forbidding doing what would gravely harm someone. But obedience also is a grave matter if the authorized policy settles questions which otherwise will lead to contention, discord, and conflict among various groups or factions in the community, thus seriously impairing its solidarity in pursuing its common good. Suppose a just statute is enacted to regulate labor-management relations and eliminate disruptive disputes: all parties have a grave obligation to comply with the law and cooperate in making it work. In such questions, law often indicates the gravity of obedience by assigning a significant penalty for disobedience. Moreover, even apart from the matter at stake, disobedience is grave if it expresses deliberate contempt for authority, for example, the disobedience of those who make it a policy to obey only when they either fear the consequences of disobeying or find what authority commands to be agreeable.

g) Abuse and abdication of authority can be equally grave sins. Authorities can abuse their proper role in several ways. They can knowingly command something wrong or something beyond their proper sphere; in making their decisions and issuing commands, they can violate authority to which they themselves are subject; they can unfairly shape their decisions by personal preferences; they can make hasty and ill-considered decisions; they can fail to listen as they should to those whose action they direct.

Authorities also can abdicate their responsibility: by postponing difficult decisions which need to be made, by shaping decisions in ways that give unfair

---

58. The judgment that one should not obey is an act of conscience, which is altogether different from an individualistic assertion of a personal preference, all too easily rationalized as "letting my conscience be my guide."

advantage to the resistant and rebellious, and by omitting to exercise authority for fear of expected bad consequences which they could rightly accept.

Abuses of authority often are felt to be a more serious matter than its abdication, which generally is less noticeable and less obnoxious to those jealous of their personal liberty. However, both not only adversely affect the common good toward which the authority should direct cooperative action, but damage the bonds of community and make loyalty and obedience more difficult. Thus, abuse and abdication of authority can be equally grave matters.

Question F: When Should One Cooperate with Those Who Are Doing Wrong?

Cooperation often refers to the action of a group of more or less coequal participants, each making a distinct and appropriate contribution in pursuit of a common end. In such cooperation, involving the exercise of authority and the practice of obedience, one fulfills one's responsibilities toward others by personally doing what is right and avoiding scandal.

Sometimes, though, *cooperation* refers not to communal action but to the subordinate action of one who contributes something to the wrongdoing of another, who is the principal agent pursuing his or her proper good. In this sense, cooperation is either formal or material. (This distinction has been treated in *CMP,* 12.G, and so need only be summarized here.) Formal cooperation always is morally excluded. Material cooperation is sometimes justifiable, sometimes not, depending on the acceptability of the side effects.

1. Formal Cooperation in Others' Wrong Acts Is Always Wrong

Cooperation is formal in the following three kinds of cases: (i) one intends or one's purpose includes that another commit a sin; (ii) one shares the other's wrong intention, in the sense that the proposal one adopts—that is, precisely what one chooses to do—includes something (and perhaps everything) objectively wrong in the other's proposal; or (iii) one's proposal includes the other's successfully carrying out an objectively wrong choice.

In all these cases, one wills moral evil; thus, formal cooperation of all three kinds is always wrong. It occurs in the first way, for example, when a misguided counselor encourages a person to commit embarrassing sins, imagining that this will lead to his or her spiritual growth; in the second way, when a nurse who favors abortion volunteers her service in an abortion clinic, in order to help women seeking abortions to get them; in the third way, when an inspector takes bribes to approve faulty construction, wishing the fraud to succeed so that the bribery will not be exposed.

Formal cooperation with others' sinful acts can be by means of an omission. For instance, a police officer who ignores criminal activities in order to obtain a percentage of the proceeds intends the success of the criminal acts; thus, he or she formally cooperates with them by omitting the police work that would impede them.

2. Formal Cooperation Is Not Limited to Private Life

People sometimes formally cooperate in others' sinful acts in fulfilling their professional roles. Legislators who support what they recognize to be an unjust war want their nation to win; thus, they formally cooperate in treating the enemy nation unjustly. Again, a hospital administrator acts on a proposal which includes the purpose of some patients that they be sterilized when he or she decides that the obstetrics department will offer sterilization and sees to it that all patients about to be sterilized fulfill the usual requirement to give their informed consent. In doing so, the administrator formally cooperates with sterilization, even if he or she finds it repugnant, disapproves of it, and tries to dissuade patients from undergoing it.[59] It is a rationalization of such cooperation, not a justification, to claim that its point is respect for the consciences of those who judge sterilization morally acceptable. For anyone else's state of conscience is irrelevant to the administrator's own act, which includes seeing to it that each sterilization is both consented to and effectively carried out.

3. Cooperation That Is Not Formal Is Called "Material Cooperation"

A person materially cooperates with the objectively wrong acts of others by doing something which helps them carry out their choices (and which may even be absolutely necessary to their doing so), while intending as one's own end and choosing as one's own means something which neither is nor includes their objectively immoral actions or proposals, or their sinning. In material cooperation, these results are only accepted as side effects of carrying out one's own choice. For example, an engineer who keeps the utilities working in a hospital where abortions are done, only to make a living and further the other good things done there, materially cooperates with those abortions. Again, a locksmith forced at gunpoint to help robbers break into a bank's safe and carry out the money only materially cooperates in the robbery, although the locksmith's actions are essential to the robbery's success. Legislators who, having tried and failed to exclude abortion funding from a general appropriation bill, then vote for the bill only to bring about the good things it will fund materially cooperate in the abortions the appropriation will pay for.

Whenever there is a morally acceptable way to prevent another's unjust action, anyone noticing this possibility has reason to intervene: the prevention of the injustice and protection of the good at stake. Thus, a choice not to intervene is cooperation by omission, and it is material, if not formal, cooperation.

4. Material Cooperation Is Sometimes, but Not Always, Permissible

Obviously, if the act by which a person materially cooperates is itself sinful, the material cooperation also is sinful. But even if that act otherwise would be morally

---

59. One can do an act of which one disapproves, sinning against one's conscience. By the same token, one can formally cooperate with an act which one disapproves. See Germain Grisez, "Public Funding of Abortion: A Reply to Richard A. McCormick," *Homiletic and Pastoral Review* 85 (June 1985): 46–47.

acceptable, the material cooperation sometimes is not permissible. Material cooperation in others' objectively wrong acts involves accepting as side effects of one's own acts both their contribution to the wrongdoing and its harmful effects; however, one is responsible not only for what one intends and chooses, but also, though not in the same way, for what one accepts as side effects (see *CMP,* 9.F). In materially cooperating in others' wrong acts, therefore, a person bears some responsibility, and it is necessary to consider whether one is justified in accepting the bad side effects or not.

The engineer, the locksmith, and the legislators of the preceding examples may well be justified in their material cooperation. But suppose the owner of a gun store happens to learn that a regular customer uses guns and ammunition purchased there to fulfill contracts for murder. In continuing to sell the merchandise simply for the sake of profit, the owner would only materially cooperate in bringing about the victims' deaths, but would hardly be justified in accepting that side effect.

Assuming cooperation is material and the act by which it is carried out otherwise would be morally good, the question is whether one has an adequate reason to do that act in view of its bad side effects. Often, one bad side effect of material cooperation is the temptation to cooperate formally. For someone who begins by cooperating materially in many cases already has or soon develops an interpersonal relationship with the wrongdoer and thus is led to deeper involvement, including a sharing of purposes. For example, whenever friends, relatives, or members of any group or society materially cooperate, solidarity inclines them to hope for the success of the wrongdoing which they are helping. Thus, material cooperation easily becomes the occasion of the sin of formal cooperation. Then it should be dealt with in the same way as other occasions of sin (see 4.D.3), and may be excluded on this basis alone.

5. The Golden Rule Helps Determine Whether to Materially Cooperate

If material cooperation is not excluded as an occasion of sin, the problem is that one's own interests in doing what constitutes material cooperation are more or less in conflict with the interests of others who will suffer bad side effects. In such cases, the Golden Rule provides the test. (On the use of the Golden Rule to exclude partiality, see 5.H.3.)

To make the test, it is necessary to take into account not only what one's own cooperative act would be in itself (precisely what one would intend as an end and choose as a means), but all the morally relevant circumstances:

• Is there a morally acceptable option other than doing the act and materially cooperating, on the one hand, and, on the other, simply omitting the act so as to avoid the side effects? Plainly, someone who cannot fulfill some important responsibility except by materially cooperating with another's wrongdoing has more reason to do so than someone with a morally acceptable alternative.

• What kind of loss or harm will result from the wrong act in which one would materially cooperate, how extensive will it be, how certain is it to occur, and who will suffer it?

- What other bad side effects will follow from doing the action that involves material cooperation? What kind of loss or harm will result from them, how extensive, how certain, and who will suffer it?

- What kind of loss or harm will result from forgoing the otherwise good act, how extensive, how certain, and who will suffer it?

- If one does not materially cooperate, will that prevent the wrong? Or will the wrongdoer nevertheless be able and likely to act?

Because mercy is the justice of the kingdom, a Christian reflection before applying the Golden Rule brings fully into play the specific claims of love. Hence, in considering various losses and harms, one always should ask:

- Does this loss or harm involve a probable and avoidable risk to anyone's salvation? For instance, if the wrongdoer is not in good faith and material cooperation is avoided, is he or she likely to repent and reform?

- Will accepting this loss or harm seriously impede one from finding, accepting, or in some respect fulfilling one's personal vocation?

- Will accepting it impair the witness that should be given by oneself or one's community to God's truth and love?

Answering all these questions as well as possible does not settle whether one should materially cooperate or not, but it does gather together an adequate description of the alternatives. The Golden Rule must be applied to this description in order to exclude either the alternative of materially cooperating or that of forgoing the act involving material cooperation, if, as often is the case, one of those alternatives cannot be chosen without partiality.[60]

6. If Cooperating and Not Cooperating Are Both Good, One Must Discern

The presupposition here is that the cooperation in question is not formal but material, and that, in all respects other than its side effect of helping another's sin with its bad effects, the act by which one materially cooperates is morally acceptable. Having judged that the action is not excluded on other grounds (for example, as an occasion of sin), carefully applied the Golden Rule, and concluded that neither doing nor forgoing the action would be wrong, one can conclude that both alternatives are good, insofar as they agree with right reason. Which to adopt is then a matter for discernment. In discerning, love is allowed to have the last word, for discernment rests on emotions integrated by one's commitments of faith and

---

60. Classical modern moral theologians offered opinions on many recurrent kinds of actions involving material cooperation. See, for example, seventeen pages of "examples of licit and illicit cooperation" in Bernard Häring, C.Ss.R., *The Law of Christ: Moral Theology for Priests and Laity,* trans. Edwin G. Kaiser, C.Pp.S., 3 vols. (Westminster, Md.: Newman Press, 1961–67), 2:500–517. The opinions Häring proposes on most of the examples, considered just as he frames them, seem sound, although sometimes additional circumstances could be specified in which they would be unsound. However, many of the norms ("principles") which Häring provides for judging material cooperation are questionable unless they are understood as defeasible indications of judgments to be made by applying the Golden Rule.

personal vocation, and these commitments spring from and express Christian love (see 5.J).

7. The Church's Leaders Can Authoritatively Decide in Some Cases

In trying to put the Church's social teaching into practice, Catholics often must work closely with people who have radically erroneous world views. Perhaps they have good will and pursue good immediate ends, but they also may use objectively bad means and/or pursue objectively wrong long-term ends. Collaborating with them in doing otherwise good acts thus involves the problem of material cooperation. Whether this is acceptable and appropriate is a judgment primarily to be made by lay people who have responsibility in the particular field involved. Still, as John XXIII teaches, they must

> act in accordance with the principles of the natural law, and observe the Church's social teaching and the directives of ecclesiastical authority. For it must not be forgotten that the Church has the right and duty not only to safeguard her teaching on faith and morals, but also to exercise her authority over her sons by intervening in their external affairs whenever a judgment has to be made concerning the practical application of this teaching.[61]

Thus, when the Holy See or one's bishop (usually in concert with other bishops of a region or nation) provides authoritative direction regarding material cooperation in social and economic matters with those acting wrongly in some respects, that direction should be followed.

Question G: What Are People's Responsibilities with Regard to Restitution?

The concept of restitution is analogous and can be used in a range of senses. Here it is understood in a sense broader than it has in classical moral theology. Making restitution can promote many goods, but it always contributes to that justice which is a mode of harmony among persons and the foundation of friendship and genuine community. Restitution, broadly understood, can be due on many diverse grounds. Sometimes just restitution restores a situation to what it had been, but restitution also can be due when that is impossible; and, even when possible, restoring the situation may not be appropriate. While law, custom, and other factors can help determine what justice requires by way of restitution, the only adequate standard for settling that question is the Golden Rule, directly applied to all the relevant facts. In making restitution, Christians should try not only to mitigate or overcome the harm or deprivation being unjustly suffered but to restore or build up interpersonal harmony and trust. For the sake of that same good, those to whom restitution is due should cooperate with those making it.

---

61. John XXIII, *Pacem in terris, AAS* 55 (1963) 300–301, *PE,* 270.160. Underlying the possibility that the Church's leaders might authoritatively judge the suitability of material cooperation in some cases is the necessity that, for effectiveness in the social apostolate, Catholics maintain solidarity.

1. In an Unjust State of Affairs, Restitution Restores Justice

When an unjust state of affairs results from something that has been done or has happened, the injustice should be rectified. Restitution is one of the various kinds of acts which do this. It is not the same as making satisfaction for wrongdoing, though wrongdoers who bring about unjust states of affairs usually should make restitution. St. Thomas has an analogous concept of restitution, which classical moral theologians tended to narrow.

a) **Different kinds of requirements of justice presuppose injustice.** Justice requires respect for others' fundamental rights (for example, not to enslave them) and fulfillment of commitments (for example, fidelity to treaties with them). These and many other requirements of justice presuppose only goods; they do not presuppose anything disordered. But some requirements of justice, including restitution, do: they are requirements precisely to undo, overcome, or forestall various aspects or results of injustice.

It is helpful to distinguish three other kinds of requirements from restitution. One deals with an unjust state of affairs by requiring that those with gifts and resources use them to meet the needs of victims of injustice. A second kind tends to undo or overcome injustice by requiring that something come about in the unjust moral agent: someone who has done an injustice must repent and do penance for the sin. A third calls on persons or communities whose proper role it is to deal with injustice to fulfill their responsibilities: when big brother mistreats little sister, a parent should intervene; when a crime is committed, the police should arrest the criminal.

b) **Restitution differs from other acts which rectify an injustice.** Like the first kind of requirement—that those with gifts and resources help meet the needs of victims of injustice—restitution's point is to rectify injustice by benefiting its victims. Restitution differs, however, in that it concerns rectifying the injustice precisely insofar as it involves two particular parties: the one suffering it, and the one involved in either its coming about or its continuing to exist. Suppose Sally is extremely wealthy and her college roommate, Jane, is very poor: when the pen Jane needs to write her final examinations is stolen and she has no way of obtaining another, Sally should give or lend Jane a pen or the money to buy one. But that is not restitution, unless Sally stole the pen or (perhaps innocently) accepted it as a gift from the thief. On the other hand, if Jane, in a moment of weakness, steals a bottle of perfume from Sally's ample stock, but repents and returns it, that is restitution, even though Jane's resources are meager and Sally would hardly miss the perfume.

Unlike the second kind of requirement—to repent and do penance—the point of restitution is not to straighten out the unjust moral agent, but to rectify the injustice which is being suffered.[62] If Sam is caught committing burglary, no doubt he should repent and do penance, and perhaps he should be punished, but he cannot make restitution of the goods he failed to steal; if Harold succeeds in burglary but

---

62. For this distinction, sometimes insufficiently noted by the classical moralists, see St. Thomas, *In Sent.*, 4, d. 15, q. 1, a. 5, qu'la 1.

returns the stolen goods solely to avoid being caught, he remains an unjust person—he still needs to repent and do penance—but he has made restitution.

Like the third kind of requirement (that those officially responsible for dealing with injustice do so), restitution rectifies injustice insofar as it affects others. But it differs in rectifying only injustice which is being suffered, whereas those responsible for dealing with injustice generally take a more inclusive approach, for example, the police not only try to return stolen cars to their owners but to catch car thieves and prevent and deter thefts. Also, those officially responsible for dealing with injustice should rectify injustices because that is their social role, not because a particular unjust state of affairs somehow involves them personally.

Thus, restitution can be provisionally defined: one party owes another restitution whenever, under all the existing circumstances, the first party ought to try to mitigate or overcome some harm or deprivation being suffered by the second for this reason: that the first party either was involved in the coming about of that harm or is in possession of something which the second should have.

c) **This provisional definition differs from that of St. Thomas.** St. Thomas builds up an analogous concept of restitution, beginning from the situation in which one person, having something which belongs to another, returns it. According to this view, even returning to the owner a borrowed item or something left for safe keeping is restitution (see *S.t., 2–2, q. 62, aa. 1, 6*). The provisional definition proposed above is not so broad, since it presupposes an existing injustice. However, it can be broadened by saying that actions necessary to forestall potential injustices constitute restitution whenever omitting them would be an injustice requiring restitution. Thus, returning a borrowed item or a deposit when appropriate can be regarded as restitution, since not doing so would unjustly deprive the owner of it and require restitution in the stricter sense.

d) **Some classical moralists' concepts of restitution were too narrow.** In modern times, many approved authors of moral theology texts narrowed down the concept of restitution in one or more of three ways.

First, their focus on reconciling sinners in the sacrament of penance led many of them to think about and discuss restitution in the context of the requirements for contrition and absolution. In itself, this was reasonable, since sinners who owe restitution are not really contrite unless willing to make it insofar as they can. However, classical moralists mistakenly tended to think that, since readiness to make restitution is necessary for contrition, someone involved in the coming about of an injustice need not make restitution except to the extent he or she needs to be contrite. Many therefore ignored, denied, or limited the responsibility of restitution in cases involving unjust harm brought about by a person who sinned but not mortally, or who sinned mortally but without foreseeing the harmful consequences, or who even sinned mortally and foresaw harmful consequences but did not precisely intend the unjust state of affairs which actually resulted.[63]

---

63. See Aertnys, Damen, and Visser, *Theologia moralis,* 2:274–76; see Henri J. Renard, S.J., "An Approach to the Problem of Restitution," *Modern Schoolman* 36 (1958–59): 77–89, for an enlightening contrast between such an approach and that of St. Thomas.

Second, some of these moralists also at times thought of restitution as restoration, a view criticized below (in 4); they then assumed that when restoration is impossible, restitution is unnecessary.

Third, some also misunderstood a point St. Thomas makes: restitution is an act of commutative justice (that is, the establishment and maintenance of a fair balance between two parties) rather than of distributive justice (the fair sharing of benefits and burdens among members of a community) (see *S.t.*, 2–2, q. 61; q. 62, a. 1). As was explained in the previous chapter (see 6.B.5.b), many classical moralists narrowed down the concepts of commutative and distributive justice. As part of that narrowing, they supposed that the two kinds of justice never are in play in the same act.[64] For example, some thought that, because distributive justice requires fair sharing of civic responsibilties in levying and paying taxes, commutative justice is irrelevant to taxation; and from this they concluded that repentant tax evaders need not make restitution to the government.

Assuming, however, that the tax payments required by law really are a citizen's fair share of the burden of financing governmental activities, fairness to the community surely requires that tax evaders pay what they owe; for they should have paid it when due, and successful tax evasion does not undercut the ground of their obligation (see 11.E.2). (If it did, the government would be unjust in requiring those whom it detects evading taxes to make good.) Of course, it might be said that this obligation is not precisely the duty of restitution, but an analogous responsibility pertaining to distributive justice, as the duty of restitution does to commutative justice. However, following the view of St. Thomas, it can be said instead that the duty to pay taxes is at one and the same time a matter of distributive and commutative justice.[65] For, once distributive justice has determined what share is fair, the government, acting on behalf of the community as a whole, and the taxpayer are two parties between which balance must be reached by transferring precisely that fair share, no more and no less.[66] If the government mistakenly takes too much, the taxpayer is entitled to a refund, just as if the government were a private business billing for its service. By the same token, if a citizen evades just taxes, they still are due to the government, no less than if an individual evades paying a private contractor's fair bill.

---

64. However, some were clearer on this matter: see Aertnys, Damen, and Visser, *Theologia moralis*, 2:263, n. 3.

65. St. Thomas points out that distributive and commutative justice are in play in the same act, using the example of a distribution which gives an individual less than his or her fair share (see *S.t.*, 2–2, q. 62, a. 1, ad 3). And since commutative justice by definition exists in a two-sided relationship, it cannot be present in the government's relation to a citizen without being present in that citizen's relationship with the government.

66. See Aertnys, Damen, and Visser, *Theologia moralis*, 2:263; also see 2:311–12, where two opinions are presented, one requiring restitution for tax fraud, the other only compliance with the law's requirements in the matter.

2. The Good of Justice as Interpersonal Harmony Requires Restitution

Generally, restitution remedies some harm beyond the injustice itself. When individuals or communities suffer injustice by something another moral agent does or by being deprived of something, restitution usually helps the victim protect or pursue some good. For example, when Jane's stolen pen is returned, she can use it to write her final examinations. This remedy of harm certainly underlies and contributes to the force of the obligation to make restitution. However, restitution can be required even though it will not remedy any harm beyond the injustice itself. For example, if Sally, the wealthy roommate, neither needed nor especially cared for the stolen bottle of perfume, and would readily have given it to Jane had she asked, Jane's returning the perfume does not help Sally protect or pursue any good; yet the perfume's theft made Sally the victim of an injustice by violating her right of ownership, and that right was vindicated when Jane returned the perfume. That restitution can be required even when it remedies no substantive harm makes it clear that the essential ground for the obligation resides in some good other than the proper good of the victim of injustice.

Restitution always contributes to justice—that interpersonal harmony which is the foundation of friendship and genuine community. If one of two parties involved in an actually or potentially unjust state of affairs should do something to rectify or prevent the injustice, doing it eliminates a likely source of conflict from their relationship. For those who should rectify or prevent an injustice but fail to do so cannot have good will toward those who suffer it, and the latter also have a motive for bad will toward the former. Thus, persisting injustice interferes with love of neighbor and so with the building up of the kingdom. Consequently, restitution essentially is necessary for the sake of friendship, genuine community, and the kingdom.[67]

3. Diverse Specific Conditions Can Require Restitution

As has been explained, individuals and communities can be required to make restitution in two general types of cases. In one, they have been involved in the coming about of an actual or potential injustice; in the other, they possess something alienated from its owner. Both general types are clarified by further specifications, which also make it clear that in many cases the general obligation to make restitution is reinforced by other specific responsibilities.

The point here is *not* that the obligation to make restitution is the same regardless of its grounds. Differences in the grounds on which restitution is required do affect how much restitution is due (see 5, below). The point is simply to clarify those diverse grounds.

a) Mortally sinful unjust deeds require restitution to their victims. The most obvious species of case in which involvement in the coming about of an injustice generates an obligation to make restitution is that in which the injustice has been

---

67. A similar explanation of the requirement to make restitution: St. Thomas, *In Sent.,* 4, d. 15, q. 1, a. 5, qu'la 2.

caused by a moral agent's mortal sin of injustice against its victim. With sufficient reflection and full consent, John wounds, sexually abuses, cheats, slanders, or in some other way harms Mary; the harm Mary suffers plainly is John's fault; therefore, John should do what he can to remedy that harm.

In cases of this kind, the sinner's responsibility to repent reinforces the duty to make restitution. Not only did John's sin involve a grave defect of good will toward Mary; for him to continue to allow her to suffer the harm his mortal sin has caused will be inconsistent with a good will toward her, and he cannot repent without changing his bad will to good. Therefore, unless John chooses to do what he can to make restitution, he has not really repented.

This is so even if his bad will now has a different object than when he committed the injustice against her. Of course, he may have willed to harm her then and may will that she continue to suffer the harm now (the injustice is motivated by hatred and the object of John's bad will remains the same); yet it may be that he did not hate her, yet willingly and unfairly accepted harm to her as a side effect of a choice with some other motive, and that he now has still another motive for refusing to make restitution. The object of John's bad will is different; he may sincerely regret having harmed Mary in the first place and may only reject the self-sacrifice required to remedy that harm. But he has not entirely changed his bad will to good, and so his change of heart is not the moral reversal necessary for repentance.

Thus, when one person or community willingly harms another person or community by a mortal sin of injustice, the requirement to do something by way of restitution does not depend on whether the harm was intended as an end, chosen as a means, or only wrongly accepted as a side effect. Nor does it depend on whether the sinner foresaw the precise harm suffered by the victim, though how much and what sort of restitution is required might vary with the extent to which the harm was foreseen or should have been.

Those who formally cooperate in a mortal sin of injustice against some individual or community obviously incur the basic responsibility—to be willing and ready to make restitution to the victim—for the same reason the principal agents incur it. So do those who materially cooperate in a mortally sinful way, provided the grave wrongness of their material cooperation resides at least partly in their willingness to accept the injustice.

Of course, whether cooperators in injustice actually will be required to make restitution and, if so, how much of the burden they must bear, will depend on whether and to what extent the principal agent and/or other cooperators fulfill their responsibility to rectify the injustice. Once sufficient restitution has been made by any responsible party or parties, the victim no longer suffers harm, and so nobody owes further restitution, although those responsible still might have accounts to settle among themselves (see *S.t.*, 2–2, q. 62, a. 7, ad 2).

If a victim of an injustice has received full compensation from his or her insurer, mortally sinning perpetrators of the injustice owe restitution to the insurer.

b) Other sinners can owe restitution for injustices their sins cause. Obviously, in cases similar to those just considered except that parvity of matter in the injustice makes the sin venial and the duty of restitution light, the logic of the responsibility—the reasons for it and its conditions—are the same as has been explained. For gravity or parvity of matter does not affect the relationships between those involved in an unjust state of affairs, between sinners' wills and those wills' objects, and so on.

In cases similar to the preceding kind except that lack of sufficient reflection and/or full consent makes the sin venial, the sinner nevertheless should be willing to make at least some sort of restitution to the victim, and the responsibility can be grave. For example, Harold, engaging in thoughtless gossip, slanders Irene by spreading the story that she is committing adultery, and the slander threatens her marriage. Learning that the story is false and that Irene is suffering harm due to his slander, Harold plainly has a grave obligation to do what he can to reassure Irene's husband that she is faithful. Yet, when Harold spread the story, he thought it true, bore no ill will toward Irene, and did not foresee what would happen; his sin of slander was venial due to lack of sufficient reflection. Again, Irene's husband, George, mistakenly identifies Pete as the supposed adulterer, takes him by surprise, beats him, and seriously injures him. In attacking Pete, George knows that what he is doing is gravely wrong, but, being very short-tempered and on medication prescribed to ease his stress, he never considers any alternative to beating Pete, such as not doing so. Although George's sin was venial due to lack of full consent, when he learns from Harold that Irene never committed adultery, George certainly should do what he can to ensure Pete's recovery.

Since Harold's and George's responsibility to make restitution is greater than their responsibility to repent their previous sins of injustice, the former responsibility plainly does not follow from the latter, and the latter does not significantly reinforce the former. However, Harold and George could and should be better men, and Irene and Pete suffer injustices resulting from actions which Harold and George would not have done had they been more prudent and self-controlled. Since their moral failings led to the injustices, Harold and George ought to rectify them, and the gravity of what Irene and Pete have suffered makes the duty of restitution grave.

Does it follow that one has a grave obligation to make restitution whenever one's sin in any way causes an injustice? No. Under the circumstances, the very fact that Harold's and George's actions caused grave harms as they did is a sufficient basis for a reasonable person to apply the Golden Rule and judge that the two men should make restitution. But circumstances vary, and the ways in which one party's sin contributes to the injustice suffered by another also vary.

c) **Without sinning, one can incur the duty to make restitution.** As was explained above (in 1.c), restitution in the broad sense does not presuppose an actual injustice. If harm has been done, the action required to remedy it can be considered restitution if omitting that action would be an injustice requiring restitution. There are various ways in which moral agents can blamelessly bring upon themselves the duty to make restitution in this wider sense.

First, both individuals and communities can do something sinlessly while foreseeing harms or risks of harms to others as side effects. However, those side effects sometimes are fairly accepted only if the moral agent compensates those who suffer harm. The compensation constitutes restitution in the broad sense, since failure to make it would be an injustice requiring restitution in the stricter sense.

An important species of this first way of blamelessly incurring the duty of restitution is the justified breaking of a promise which calls for compensation. Dynamo Electric promises to complete a job by a certain date but subsequently finds itself unable to make the deadline without taking a ruinous loss. Breaking the promise is justified, but Dynamo must pay damages specified in the contract. Again, Sam, Dynamo's owner, promised to take his children to the zoo on Saturday, but breaks his promise in order to play golf with a very important potential customer. Sam is justified in disappointing the children, but should make it up to them, for example, by bringing home a special treat.

Second, without any sin on their own part, both individuals and communities can owe restitution for another moral agent for whose actions they somehow are responsible or whose responsibilities they inherit. For example, even parents who do their best to bring their children up well nevertheless should do something by way of restitution if one of their misbehaving children ruins the tire on a neighbor's car by pounding a nail into it. Heirs should begin by paying the decedent's just debts, and so, though without personal fault, owe restitution, insofar as the estate suffices, to anyone to whom the decedent should have made it but did not.

Third, unjust relationships between two members of a community resulting from a distributive injustice can call for restitution. For example, if a baby sitter who likes one twin and dislikes the other unfairly divides a treat which the parents had left for both, the favored child, though blameless, should remedy the injustice. Again, Sally and Jane, the wealthy and poor roommates, invite all the women on the corridor to a party; Sally is too busy to go shopping, and Jane uses her whole semester's spending money for the party supplies considered appropriate at their school. As cohostess, Sally should contribute her fair share by reimbursing Jane for at least half the cost.

d) **There are several species of the duty to return property to its owner.** Just as the general duty of restitution for harms divides into several species, so does the general duty to return property.

Plainly, those who wrongly take another's property or formally cooperate in its taking must return it or make good the loss. Wrongful material cooperators whose cooperation was sinful precisely by being participation in the injustice share the responsibility of restitution. In both cases, the duty of restitution extends beyond what was taken, to losses the owner suffered due to the wrongful taking, for example, interest which would have been earned on stolen money or the cost of temporarily replacing a stolen automobile.

But other wrongful material cooperators and even other sinners whose sinful acts contributed to the wrongful taking also can have a duty to make good the loss, just as they can have a duty to remedy other unjust harms to which they have contributed. For example, a house guest, warned to lock up because burglaries are common in the area, forgets the warning and leaves the house wide open while going for a walk. The house is burglarized, and the host suffers a loss not covered by insurance. The negligent guest should do something—precisely what is another question—toward making good that loss.

Those entirely blameless also can be obliged to restore to the owner property which is wrongly taken by a third party. Steve steals a necklace and gives it to his friend, Gloria, for her birthday. Gloria accepts it innocently, but later learns it was stolen. She must return it to the owner. Again, Dan borrows Ella's camera to use on a vacation trip, takes all due care, but surrenders it to an armed robber. Dan should do something to make up for the loss (see *S.t.*, 2–2, q. 62, a. 6).

Also, finders of lost property usually should return it to the owner or turn it in to some agency responsible for doing so, such as the police or a lost-and-found office.

Of course, people who innocently find themselves in possession of stolen property or who happen to find lost property have a much more limited responsibility of restitution than do those who wrongly take another's property. The former need compensate the owner neither for consequential losses nor for their own use (even consumption) of the property during any time they honestly believed it was theirs to use. Moreover, when such innocent people return property, the owner should compensate them for their trouble and expense, and this payment is not morally optional, as is an unpromised reward given as a token of gratitude.

4. Just Restitution Usually Does Not Make Things Be Just as They Were

When Jane returns the bottle of perfume she stole from Sally, even before her roommate notices that it is missing, her act of restitution restores the objective situation to just what it had been before the theft.[68] But usually when restitution is required, such a restoration is impossible, and even if possible, the duty of restitution may require something else. For the duty of restitution is to do what is just now, not undo what has been done.

a) Restitution often is due even though restoration is impossible. Wrongdoers who owe restitution sometimes rationalize that, since the wrong they did cannot be undone, they need only repent. For example, George, having injured Pete, might say he is sorry but cannot undo the beating or the injury, and so need make no restitution. However, since Pete is unjustly suffering harms—hospital bills, lost pay, pain, and so forth—due to the injury, George must do what he can to remedy the ongoing injustice.

In general, those who have done any injustice should ask themselves what they can do, not to make things as they were, but to make things as they should be now. Thus, when Tim, a married man, seduces Ann, to whom he pretends to be single, and she becomes pregnant, Tim does not make restitution by paying for an abortion, but by doing what he can to see to it that she and the child are cared for properly. And although Bob, a repentant thief, has no way of locating the stranger from whom he stole a camera, restitution remains possible: Bob should give what he owes as

---

68. Must Jane tell Sally what she did? In general, no, and doing so might only cause Sally unnecessary distress. Still, Jane could have an obligation of some sort to tell Sally. For example, Jane might judge that telling Sally is necessary to put an end to the temptation to steal her things.

alms for his victim's spiritual welfare and thus rectify the injustice, whether the victim is alive or dead (see *S.t.,* 2–2, q. 62, a. 5, ad 3).[69]

b) **Even when restoration is possible, justice may not require it.** Frank steals a pair of tickets to a World Series game from the handbag of a coworker, Cindy. Thinking she has lost the tickets, Cindy plans a party for the evening of the game, inviting everyone in the office. Frank repents but realizes it is too late for Cindy to change her plans. Is his duty of restitution to return the tickets to Cindy's handbag? It may instead be to compensate Cindy for the market value of the tickets, and for her time and trouble obtaining and searching for them. For if Frank returns the tickets, he does not remedy the harm he has done to Cindy; rather, he presents her with an additional problem and causes her further distress. Thus, compensation in money more likely will fulfill what justice now requires.

Moreover, sometimes justice does not require those who innocently obtain stolen property or find lost property to return it to its owner, as will be explained (see 10.E.5.g, 10.F.1.e).

5. The Golden Rule Must Be Used to Judge What Restitution Is Required

It is impossible to articulate an adequate set of specific norms for making restitution. Various norms of morality, law, and custom can be helpful, but they always admit of exceptions, and sometimes fall short of requiring what really would be fair. Hence, to determine what restitution should be made, the Golden Rule must be directly applied. In applying it, many things should be taken into account, but wrongdoers who owe restitution should be ready to suffer the consequences of making it. Discussion with the wronged party or mediation often helps to reach a fair judgment. In making restitution, Christians should be willing to do more than justice requires, for very often only mercy can satisfy the wronged party and make reconciliation possible.

a) **The norms for making restitution are helpful but inadequate.** The norm requiring that one who wrongfully takes another's property should return it seems clear and simple. But stolen property should not be returned when, in unusual circumstances, doing so would gravely harm rather than benefit the victim of injustice (see *S.t.,* 2–2, q. 62, a. 5, ad 1). And, as the example of the stolen tickets makes clear, something other than the simple return of stolen property may be more adequate as restitution. Thus, one should not return stolen property without considering whether fairness requires something else. To make that judgment, the Golden Rule must be applied.

Moreover, every specific moral norm regarding restitution can be fulfilled only insofar as possible, and *possible* always refers not only to physical but to moral

---

69. Some classical moralists mistakenly generalize from this kind of case, in which giving alms is appropriate restitution, to suggest almsgiving as an *alternative* to restitution, without reference to the victim of injustice. This mistaken suggestion obviously results from confusion between making restitution and doing penance for sin. Almsgiving often is a suitable penance but is appropriate as restitution only when it is the best way of remedying the injustice suffered by the victim.

possibility. For example, if Herb cannot both relieve his parents' extreme need and return money he has stolen from someone who is *not* in extreme need, he should do the former rather than the latter (see *S.t.,* 2–2, q. 62, a. 5, ad 4). And in general, one cannot tell what is morally possible without comparing responsibilities and judging what is fair, which, once more, means applying the Golden Rule.

Laws often provide norms for restitution. The law of torts is especially concerned with this problem, but other parts of the law sometimes specify duties of restitution. If legal requirements are just, those who owe restitution not only should comply with them but should do so promptly rather than delay until they are compelled to comply (see *S.t.,* 2–2, q. 62, a. 8). However, in any particular case, even just laws, and all the more so unjust ones, can require more or less than what is really just, and so their demands are subject to moral review.

Indeed, the restitution required by law often is inadequate, because laws are limited in many ways: they can deal only with major injustices, only the provable aspects of harm, only the harms which lawmakers recognize, and so on. Often, for instance, those who become prosperous after a bankruptcy have moral responsibilities, unenforceable at law, to repay certain creditors, such as those suffering serious, ongoing harm directly resulting from the bankruptcy. Like laws, customary norms and the rules of etiquette often provide helpful indications of what wrongdoers should do by way of restitution. By themselves, however, these indications are no more adequate than legal requirements. Therefore, the requirements of restitution set by law, custom, and etiquette always must be reviewed by a moral judgment as to what is fair, which, again, means following the Golden Rule.

b) In applying the Golden Rule, many things should be considered. Many factors can affect what is appropriate by way of restitution, and the following list is not exhaustive. However, generally these questions should be considered.

• What is the harm or loss which calls or might call for restitution? In answering this question, one should consider not only the immediate effects of any unjust act, but consequential damages. For example, if money is stolen and retained for some time, the loss suffered not only is the amount taken, but the interest it could have earned or the benefits which would have been gained by spending it. If an automobile is damaged, the loss is not only the cost of having it repaired but the time and trouble required to do so. Also, one should distinguish between harm to or loss of actual goods, on the one hand, and, on the other, deprivation of potential ones, since, other things being equal, the former is worse than the latter (see *S.t.,* 2–2, q. 62, a. 4). Then too, past, present, and future harm or loss should be considered distinctly, since past harm may call for compensation, present harm effective remedy, and future harm preventive measures.

• What might be done to compensate for, remedy, or prevent that loss or harm? Since the unnecessary continuation of an injustice increases it, in considering this question, one should take into account the urgency for action to mitigate or prevent injustice, and should seek ways to rectify it quickly if that can be done. But one also should consider not only what can be done now but what might be done in the future, since those who cannot make adequate restitution now should commit themselves to fulfilling the responsibility if and when they can. Moreover, what is difficult and repugnant should not be ruled out as impossible; fairness can require wrongdoers to suffer much more in making restitution than their victims have suffered due to the injustice.

• However, since some possible ways of making restitution might be morally impossible, one must ask: Would doing this violate any absolute moral norm? If so, that alternative must of course be excluded. But nonabsolute norms also can affect the moral possibility of alternatives. So, one must ask: Would this way of making restitution conflict with some other responsibility? Would it be likely to have other bad side effects? If so, what would they be? How likely? Who would suffer them?

• Although restitution, unlike penance, rectifies actual or potential injustice, whether and how a moral agent owes restitution depends, among other things, on whether and how that agent was responsible for the injustice. So, in addition to questions about the injustice suffered and possible ways of rectifying it, one must ask: Is restitution owed because a wrong was done, and, if so, precisely how was the wrongdoer responsible for the harm or loss? As has been explained (in 3, above), diverse specific grounds require restitution. Cases in which the ground is a sin of injustice or some moral fault must be distinguished from those in which the duty of restitution is incurred blamelessly. Among the former, grounding in a mortal sin of injustice against the victim must be distinguished from grounds in lesser faults, among which, again, factors affecting the degree and sort of moral responsibility should be distinguished.

• Since the point of restitution is not to make things be precisely as they were, but to do what is just now, one cannot entirely ignore the significance of the burdens and benefits of possible forms of restitution to those making restitution and those receiving it. Therefore, depending on the ground requiring restitution, another question is more or less relevant: What are the comparative capacities of those involved to bear the burdens and forgo the benefits? The less morally responsible an agent owing restitution is for the actual or potential injustice to be rectified or prevented, the more relevant this question becomes.

• Often, two or more moral agents, whether by cooperating formally or not, contribute to some harm or share in possessing something which requires restitution, and so share the responsibility to make it. In such cases, it is important to ask: Did both or all incur the duty of restitution on the same specific ground or on different grounds? When some of those involved became liable by a mortal sin of injustice against the victim, their duty of restitution obviously takes priority over the duty of those whose responsibility is less. Still, those with a prior and greater responsibility to make restitution often are less ready to fulfill it and more able to evade it. So, one also must ask: To what extent have others rectified or prevented the injustice, and, if they have not done what they should, to what extent can they be induced or compelled to do so?

• Finally, even after making a reasonable effort to look into some of the preceding questions, one very often is not sure of the answers. Residual doubts should be taken into account in judging what fairness requires. Hence: If any of the relevant facts is in doubt, how would one or the other resolution of the doubt affect a fair judgment as to what should be done?

c) **Wrongdoers should not consider difficult restitution impossible.** Having harmed others and through malice, selfishness, or weakness deprived them of what is due, wrongdoers often are quick to exclude appropriate restitution as impossible, when in reality it is both physically and morally possible, though difficult. Wrongdoers certainly should not consider too great, and so morally impossible, any burden required for their own repentance and reformation. Nor, if the party to whom they owe restitution is reasonable, should they consider too hard any restitution required to regain trust and achieve reconciliation.

Sometimes criminals (and even their moral counselors) think restitution is unnecessary because it cannot be made without accepting punishment for the crime. For example, a repentant rapist, Charlie, learns that he has harmed his victim, among other ways, by leading her husband to doubt her fidelity. Charlie must do what is necessary to put that doubt to rest, even if that will lead to his being convicted of the crime. He should not excuse himself by saying the burden of accepting his punishment is too great. Since he deserves the punishment, the burden of accepting it cannot be unfair, and so he must not exclude the necessary act of restitution as excessively burdensome.

d) **Discussion and mediation often clarify what is due as restitution.** Very often, those who owe restitution can easily apply the Golden Rule by communicating with the party to whom it is due, expressing appropriate repentance or concern, affirming their determination to do the right thing, and asking: What do you think that would be? When such a discussion leads to a mutually acceptable solution— assuming both parties are competent judges of their own interests and free from undue pressures—that solution is precisely what justice now requires. Resolving the problem by communication and cooperation also contributes greatly to restitution's essential purpose: reconciliation and the building up of community. Justice and mutual benevolence beget peace.

When direct communication is impossible or fails, mediation often helps. Someone who is intelligent, fair-minded, and trusted by both parties can gather the relevant information and apply the Golden Rule, communicating with the parties not only to enlist their acceptance of the solution but to take advantage of their help in reaching it. In this way the mediator helps the parties to develop a good relationship. Sometimes, difficult and complex cases can be mediated satisfactorily by the parties' lawyers, provided they are skillful negotiators and not unduly eager for litigation.

Considering how much good is realized when an issue regarding restitution is resolved by discussion and mediation, it is apparent why it generally is inappropriate for Christians to use an adversarial procedure, such as a lawsuit, especially when that involves submitting their relationships with one another to the judgment of nonbelievers (see Mt 5.25).

e) **In making restitution, Christians should do more than justice requires.** There is another, related reason why taking the initiative in using legal processes to settle issues about restitution is unsatisfactory from a Christian point of view.

Since law can require only what is necessary to vindicate rights, it often falls short of the requirement of Christian mercy. God owes sinful humankind nothing, yet in Jesus he makes satisfaction for all humankind in order to reestablish communion. Christians must imitate and actively share in God's mercy, and so extend it, in order to extend that communion, to enlarge and build up the kingdom. Whenever possible, they should do enough to satisfy those to whom they owe restitution, even when that requires going the extra mile, so that restitution's essential end of mutual good will and peace will be realized.

6. Those to Whom Restitution Is Owed Should Be Just and Merciful

Not only those who owe restitution but those who deserve to receive it should act fairly and mercifully, so that the rectification of the injustice suffered by the latter will contribute to genuine community.

a) They should not take advantage of those who owe them restitution. Laws and customs which are in general just sometimes require more than is fair by way of restitution. In such cases, those owed restitution should decline the excess, since accepting it would be unjust.

Occasionally, too, the party owing restitution offers more than is fair. If made for some reason—for example, to demonstrate good will—such an offer can be accepted as a gift. But if it is made by mistake or due to emotional pressure, fairness requires declining the excess.

If the law provides well for those who deserve restitution in cases of a certain kind, injured parties whose cases fall into that category very often see that as an opportunity to obtain a large award, whether or not that is fair. This is especially so if the restitution would be paid by an insurance company. Plainly, however, injured parties should make a careful judgment as to what is fair and seek no more; and exaggerating the injury or otherwise lying to obtain more than is fair clearly is an additional, grave injustice.

May an injured party seek punitive damages when the law permits? Certainly yes, if, as sometimes happens, fair restitution can be obtained only by seeking such damages. Perhaps yes in other cases. On the one hand, when a law provides for punitive damages, lawmakers presumably had in view some just end other than restitution, so that a plaintiff seeking punitive damages presumably serves a public interest and receives just compensation for doing so. On the other hand, injured parties must consider their responsibilities in both fairness and mercy before seeking punitive damages beyond what would suffice for fair restitution.

Rejecting an offer of restitution which one realizes is fair and using legal processes to seek more is an abuse of these processes and a further grave injustice. Indeed, suing is wrong not only when the plaintiff seeks excessive restitution, but when other factors render the lawsuit unjust: a fair settlement could be reached out of court, the burdens of the legal process on the defendant will be unfairly great, the plaintiff seeks restitution only as revenge, and so forth.

b) Those owed restitution also should be merciful. Like those who owe restitution, those entitled to it should seek above all to achieve mutual good will and peace. Thus, unless other responsibilities require them to insist on everything to which they are entitled, they should be ready to mitigate the burden on the party making restitution, especially when that might facilitate or confirm repentance, bear special witness to the gospel, or offer some other significant benefit in terms of Christian values.[70]

---

70. For an interesting application of the Christian principle of mercy to both those owing and those deserving restitution in a specific type of case: James Druckenbrod, "Medical Malpractice: A Christian Ethical Perspective," *Linacre Quarterly* 58 (Nov. 1991): 13–33.

CHAPTER EIGHT

LIFE, HEALTH, AND
BODILY INVIOLABILITY

Summary

Human life is sacred because of the relationship of human persons to God. God makes human persons in his own image and prohibits killing them. Life is a human person's concrete reality, and bodily life is an intrinsic good of persons. No bad condition can lessen its goodness and sanctity.

It is always gravely wrong to intend to kill the innocent, either as an end or as a means. (*Innocent* is a technical term referring to everyone except those found guilty of capital crimes and enemy combatants in war.) Catholic tradition and the magisterium exclude all exceptions; and this prohibition extends to suicide and euthanasia. Intentionally killing the innocent is always grave matter.

Sometimes, however, though by no means always, it is morally acceptable or even obligatory to accept death or the risk of death as a side effect. (Choosing precisely to risk death, however, is never morally acceptable, since that is choosing to kill.) It is in this context, morally speaking, that deadly force sometimes may be used for defensive purposes. Its use, nevertheless, is limited by fairness and mercy.

The Church's affirmation of the personhood of the unborn is reasonable, while arguments against their personhood are not persuasive. Since every human individual should be treated as a person from fertilization, the moral norms protecting others' lives apply to the unborn. Abortion is morally excluded not only when it involves intentional killing (as it generally does) but also, ordinarily, even in the small number of cases when the child's death is accepted as a side effect. Some methods of so-called contraception are in fact abortifacient and are to be rejected along with other forms of abortion.

But even true contraceptive acts, considered in moral terms, are contralife, since one who chooses to contracept chooses to prevent a new instance of the basic human good of life. Thus, contraception is always wrong, and choosing to use contraception is grave matter.

Health is not pleasure and felt satisfaction, nor should the idea of health be expanded to take in total human well-being. Rather, health is well-integrated, harmonious, psychosomatic functioning. One should take reasonable measures to protect and promote health, both one's own and others', especially one's family's. In deciding whether to accept or reject medical treatment, the benefits and burdens should be evaluated by moral standards, and the decision should be made in light of personal vocation. Psychoactive substances should be used rightly—to promote healthy functioning—and should not be abused.

There also are various other responsibilities toward persons as bodily: to maintain bodily integrity in harmony with health (sterilization as a method of birth control always is wrong, but organ transplants can be right or wrong, depending on their relationship to relevant goods); not to engage in sexual assault, which always is grave matter; to shape all other bodily contacts by justice and charity (this rules out prizefighting and any other intentional bodily injury in sports); and to respect the space and mobility of other persons.

Question A: Why Should Human Life Always Be Treated with Reverence?

The pagans of ancient times lacked the concept of *person,* which was developed by Christians to articulate the mysteries of three persons in one God and a divine person who also is human. From its theological roots, the concept gathered meaning in its application to human individuals, considered as beings made in God's image and called to be his children. To call a human individual "a person," then, is to say more than that he or she is a member of the species *homo sapiens; person* connotes the dignity, the intrinsic worth, of a human being as a subject of rights and responsibilities.

Because most contemporary secular humanists regard consciousness as the source and bearer of all intrinsic values, they tend to identify the human person with the conscious human subject, and to regard the body as something other than the person himself or herself: something personal insofar as each individual depends on his or her own body, but something subpersonal insofar as the body is outside the consciousness, whose material substratum and instrument it is.

This view of the human person, the body, and their relationship has direct implications for moral questions regarding acts which affect human persons as bodily. If a living human individual is not yet conscious or never again will be conscious, it is not a person, according to a consistent secular humanist view, but a potential person or a vegetable. Moreover, if bodily life is not intrinsically good but is valuable only as a necessary condition for preferred conscious states, when suffering prevails over satisfaction in a person's experience, his or her quality of life is poor; and if there is no prospect of its improving, he or she is better off dead. Thus, to many people influenced by secular humanism, abortion and euthanasia seem entirely reasonable, while Christian morality on these matters seems to them irrational. In the same perspective, it seems that feeling well is the most important part of health, with the result that health care transcends pain relief only if shortsightedness is avoided and a long-term view taken.

Nevertheless, because human life is a basic human good (see *CMP,* 5.D), one need not be a believer to appreciate its value. In practice, even secular humanists usually take life's intrinsic goodness for granted, though they deny it in theoretical reflection and may act contrary to it in particular instances. In the tradition of faith common to Jews and Christians, human life not only is good but sacred. To speak of the sacredness or sanctity of human life presupposes its intrinsic goodness but also says something more: not only that it deserves special respect but that it participates in various ways in God's own holiness.

Scripture makes it clear that the life of human persons, made in God's image, is sacred. The ultimate basis for the human body's sacredness lies in this: the Word of God became flesh and calls humankind into bodily solidarity with himself. Moreover, the person as bodily is social, and the human body is the medium through which the rest of material creation will belong to the heavenly kingdom. Therefore, human life always should be treated with reverence, and every person's life, health, and bodily integrity and inviolability are to be fostered and respected.

1. Human Life Is Sacred Because of Its Relationship to God

God makes it clear that all human beings are related to him in a special way. Sin disrupts humankind's relationship with God, and death results from sin, but the Incarnation enables human persons to hope for resurrection and everlasting life.[1]

a) God makes persons in his own image and prohibits killing them. God creates human persons in his own image and likeness, not only insofar as they are intelligent and free, but also insofar as they are made for communion with one another, empowered to procreate, and given dominion over the rest of the material world (see Gn 1.26–30).[2] Many other philosophical and religious views sharply contrast spirit with matter, and regard matter as bad in itself or as the source of evil; but Scripture makes it clear not only that the material world is good but that with the creation of man and woman, the whole created world, including human persons' relationships with other things, is very good (see Gn 1.12, 18, 21, 25, 31).

Since human persons are the image of God, he treats human life as sacred, requires that men and women themselves respect life's sanctity, and encourages them to procreate:

> For your own lifeblood I will surely require a reckoning: from every animal I will require it and from human beings, each one for the blood of another, I will require a reckoning for human life. Whoever sheds the blood of a human, by a human shall that person's blood be shed; for in his own image God made humankind. And you, be fruitful and multiply, abound on the earth and multiply in it. (Gn 9.5–7)

Thus, because of their similarity to God, human persons' lives are to be treated with reverence.

b) Sin alienates humankind from God and leads to death. God makes people in his own image and likeness so that they will be capable of friendship with him. Although human persons do not entirely cease to be in God's image even when they sin mortally, they do abandon the friendship with God for which he made them.

---

1. On *life* in the Bible, see H.-G. Link, "Life," *The New International Dictionary of New Testament Theology,* ed. Colin Brown, 3 vols. (Grand Rapids, Mich.: Zondervan, 1975–78), 2:476–84.

2. See John Paul II, *Mulieris dignitatem,* 6–7, *AAS* 80 (1988) 1662–67, *OR,* 3 Oct. 1988, 3–4; General Audience (14 Nov. 1979), *Inseg.* 2.2 (1979) 1153–57, *OR,* 19 Nov. 1979, 1, 16.

Spiritual alienation from God, the Lord of life, has inevitable bad effects on the human person as a whole, and God warned the first humans that sin would lead to their death (see Gn 3.3).[3] Genesis makes it clear that death means the destruction of bodily persons: God tells the first couple they will have a hard life "until you return to the ground, for out of it you were taken; you are dust, and to dust you shall return" (Gn 3.19).

Now, if sin, by alienating bodily persons from God, brings about their destruction, their concrete reality as bodily beings can hardly be incidental to their relationship with God. So, because God made human persons for communion with himself, their lives are sacred.

c) **God wants not death but life for human persons.** Like other intelligible evils, death is not a positive reality created by God; rather, it is the privation of life (see *CMP,* 5.A). Moreover, although death is a punishment for sin, it should not be regarded as arbitrarily imposed on sinners. Death is by no means what God wants for the bodily persons he created:

> God did not make death,
> and he does not delight in the death of the living.
> For he created all things so that they might exist;
> the generative forces of the world are wholesome,
> and there is no destructive poison in them. (Wis 1.13–14)

Thus, death is opposed to God; it is part of sin's affront to him. Therefore, despite sin, to live and to hand on life remain great goods for human persons, and God promises blessings to those who obey him:

> See, I have set before you today life and prosperity, death and adversity. If you obey the commandments of the Lord your God that I am commanding you today, by loving the Lord your God, walking in his ways, and observing his commandments, decrees, and ordinances, then you shall live and become numerous, and the Lord your God will bless you in the land that you are entering to possess. (Dt 30.15–16)

And so God exhorts his people: "Choose life so that you and your descendants may live" (Dt 30.19; cf. Prv 8.34–36, Sir 15.16–20, Jer 21.8).

The possibility of choosing life is a real one, more so than God's people of the old covenant ever knew. God is stronger than death, and he refuses to tolerate it. Jesus' resurrection guarantees that human persons united with him also will rise from the dead and live forever in their own bodies (see 1 Cor 15). This promise of resurrection makes it clear that, despite death, God intends life for human persons. Moreover, Christians' hope for everlasting bodily communion in Jesus with God brings out a further dimension of his relationship with human persons and the sacredness of human bodily life: the human body is made for communion, not only among human persons but even with God.

---

3. For an account of how sin leads to death and a criticism of the view that human beings would have died even had they not sinned, see *CMP,* 14.H, including nn. 27, 28. Though not entirely consistent with Catholic teaching, a helpful attempt to explain how sin has inevitable bad effects on the person as a whole is found in R. W. L. Moberly, "Did the Serpent Get It Right?" *Journal of Theological Studies,* n.s., 39 (1988): 1–27.

d) **The Incarnation gives human life its ultimate sanctity.** The divine Word gives human life its ultimate sanctity by becoming flesh (see Jn 1.14). This sanctification of living human flesh is not limited to Jesus' individual body. Jesus says: "I am the living bread that came down from heaven. Whoever eats of this bread will live forever; and the bread that I will give for the life of the world is my flesh" (Jn 6.51). Thus, the Eucharist extends the Incarnation's sanctification of life to human persons who are Jesus' members: "The bread that we break, is it not a sharing in the body of Christ? Because there is one bread, we who are many are one body, for we all partake of the one bread" (1 Cor 10.16–17). Through communion with Jesus, Christians share in divine life, and their bodies are temples of the Holy Spirit (see 1 Cor 6.13–20). Even more than God's people of the old covenant, therefore, Christians have good reason to treat human life with reverence.[4]

e) **Despite hope, death remains in itself a great evil.** While death is a consequence of sin, it is not itself an existential evil (a privation in the moral order); yet it is inherently bad, since it deprives people of the good of life (see *CMP*, 5.H). Insofar as death is the necessary path to resurrection and everlasting life, Christians should be ready to suffer it; indeed, they rightly look forward to death as their ultimate way of offering themselves to God in union with Jesus.

But it does not follow that hope of resurrection takes away the evil proper to death. "The last enemy to be destroyed is death" (1 Cor 15.26) remains true until the end of time, for only then will death be destroyed. Hope presupposes realism about the great evil of death. Rather than taking away death's inherent badness, hope honestly acknowledges that loss of life is a great evil; only then does it go beyond this hard truth, counting on God to destroy death by his re-creative act (see GS 18). Therefore, Christians should not suppose that death really is not so great an evil and that in practice they need not take life's goodness and sanctity with utter seriousness.

The secularized climate of opinion encourages this mistake. Lacking the hope of resurrection, nonbelievers can be led by dread of death to utter despair. But if they resist, they usually go to the opposite extreme, and fail to appreciate how great an evil death is. Committed to the view that everything good must end, they consider death merely the boundary of the life process; and because everyone's life eventually becomes unpleasant, they regard death as a potential friend, the final solution to life's problems.[5] Usually, then, nonbelievers who resist despair are

---

4. Canon law manifests in many ways the importance of respecting human life and bodily integrity; subsequent notes call attention to some canons having specific relevance. One general indication: *CIC*, c. 1041, lists among those irregular (permanently impeded) as regards the reception of holy orders: "(4) a person who has committed voluntary homicide or who has procured an effective abortion and all persons who positively cooperated in either; (5) a person who has seriously and maliciously mutilated himself or another or a person who has attempted suicide." Moreover, c. 1044, §1, 3°, provides that those mentioned in both (4) and (5) are among those irregular as regards exercising orders already received, and c. 1047, §§2 and 3, provides that the impediment specified by (4) can be dispensed only by the Holy See.

5. The contemporary nonbeliever's view of death is essentially similar to that rejected in Wis 1.16–2.24; see David Winston, *The Wisdom of Solomon: A New Translation with Introduction and Commentary*, Anchor Bible, 43 (Garden City, N.Y.: Doubleday, 1979), 111–23.

oblivious not only to human life's sanctity but even to the full moral significance of acts against it. For they not only ignore the relationship of humankind with God, which gives human life its sanctity, but also deny the essential badness of human death, which gives acts against human life a unique evil.

Christians who live in cultures largely shaped by nonbelief must be careful not to adopt this non-Christian attitude toward life and death. In particular, they should not mingle it with elements of a Christian conception of hope or allow false optimism about life and death to lessen their appreciation of life's goodness and sanctity.

2. Human Life Always Retains Its Intrinsic Goodness and Sanctity

Bodily life is a good intrinsic to human persons—part of their very reality—not something extrinsic and valuable only as a means to other human goods. Therefore, life retains its sanctity even for those who suffer under various bad conditions.

a) **Human life is a person's concrete reality.** The human person is neither the body nor the soul taken separately, but a unity of these coprinciples. Vatican II clearly affirms the unity of the human person: "The human person is a unity of body and soul" (GS 14). Because of this unity, a person's body is not something he or she has, but a constitutive part of what he or she is. In explaining the sanctity of human life, John Paul II points out an important consequence of the person's unity:

> All human life—from the moment of conception and through all subsequent stages—is sacred, because human life is created in the image and likeness of God. Nothing surpasses the greatness or dignity of a human person. Human life is not just an idea or an abstraction; human life is the concrete reality of a being that lives, that acts, that grows and develops; human life is the concrete reality of a being that is capable of love, and of service to humanity.[6]

For any living being, to be is to live, and to die is to cease to be. Hence, "human life is the concrete reality of" human persons, who are by definition rational, sentient, *living* bodies.[7]

b) **Salvation requires resurrection.** That human persons really are organisms, not spirits temporarily encased in flesh, is confirmed by the doctrine of the resurrection of the body, as St. Thomas clearly explains: "Now, since the soul is part of the human body, it is not the entire human being, and my soul is not I. So, even if the soul reached salvation in another life, neither I nor any human being would thereby do so."[8] A separated soul is not a human person but a spiritual

---

6. John Paul II, Homily at Capitol Mall (Washington, D.C.), 3, *AAS* 71 (1979) 1271, *OR,* 5 Nov. 1979, 7.

7. See *S.t.,* 1, q. 18, a. 2; in its most proper sense, *to live* simply means to exist in a nature that has capacities for self-movement; less strictly, *to live* refers to vital functions: to take nourishment, to grow, to reproduce, to sense, to choose, and so on.

8. St. Thomas, *Super primam epistolam ad Corinthios lectura,* commenting on 15.19. Thomas says that "the soul is part of the human body," because he holds that the soul is the "form" of the human body, that is, an intrinsic principle of the living, bodily person (see *S.t.,* 1, q. 76). This position is more than a philosophical-theological doctrine, for against theories of the soul in conflict with the faith, the Council of Vienne (1312) and the Fifth Lateran Council (1513) taught that the soul is really and of itself the form of the human body (DS 902/481, 1440/738), thus

element which survives a person's death; and while this spiritual element has consciousness and will, so that it is a "self," the whole person will exist again only when he or she is raised up.[9] Thus, the resurrection really is necessary to overcome the evil that a human person suffers in dying.

For those who die in grace, resurrection will perfect them precisely as bodily persons (see 1 Cor 15.42–44, 53). The dogma of the Assumption of the Blessed Virgin Mary further confirms this, inasmuch as that teaching prescinds entirely from the question whether she actually died, and focuses exclusively on the fact that at the end of her earthly life, she was assumed body and soul into heavenly glory (see DS 3903/2333; LG 59).

c) **Bodily life is an intrinsic good of persons.** Since a person is an organism whose life is his or her concrete reality, bodily life is an intrinsic good of the person. Life is not an instrumental good, with a merely relative value, varying with its usefulness for pursuing or protecting other personal ends. Therefore, to maintain that under some conditions human life loses its value and may be disposed of without violating its sanctity implies that human persons, instead of being bodily realities, are nonbodily selves which have and use bodies. This view occasionally is stated explicitly:

> Physical nature—the body and its members, our organs and their functions—all of these *things* are a part of "what is over against us," and if we live by the rules and conditions set in physiology or any other *it* we are not men, we are not *thou*. When we discussed the problem of giving life to new creatures, and the authority of natural processes as over against the human values of responsibility and self-preservation (when nature and they are at cross-purposes), we remarked that spiritual reality and moral integrity belong to man alone, in whatever degree we may possess them as made *imago Dei*. Freedom, knowledge, choice, responsibility—all these things of personal or moral stature are in us, not *out there*. Physical nature is what is over against us, out there. It represents the world of *its*. Only men and God are *thou;* they only are persons.[10]

---

insisting on the unity of the bodily person. A helpful exposition of this anthropology with a critique of certain recently proposed revisions to it: Augustine Regan, C.Ss.R., "Human Body in Moral Theology: Some Basic Orientations," *Studia Moralia* 17 (1979): 151–88.

9. Congregation for the Doctrine of the Faith, *Letter on Certain Questions Pertaining to Eschatology, AAS* 71 (1979) 941, Flannery, 2:501, affirms that the Church understands the resurrection of the dead in which she believes "as referring to *the whole person*," and then goes on (502): "The Church affirms that a spiritual element survives and subsists after death, an element endowed with consciousness and will, so that the 'human self [ego humanum]' subsists, though lacking meanwhile the complement of its body [the translation omits this phrase]. To designate this element, the Church uses the word 'soul', the accepted term in the usage of Scripture and Tradition." In identifying the soul with *ego humanum*, the Congregation does not contradict St. Thomas, for the Congregation uses *ego* to refer to a subject of intellectual and volitional acts ("an element endowed with consciousness and will"), while Thomas uses *ego* to refer to a complete person. Thomas, of course, also holds that the separated soul is a subject (see *S.t.*, 1, q. 89); and the Congregation, by describing the separated soul as a "spiritual element," makes it clear that the whole person, destroyed by death, cannot again exist except by resurrection.

10. Joseph Fletcher, *Morals and Medicine: The Moral Problems of: The Patient's Right to Know the Truth, Contraception, Artificial Insemination, Sterilization, and Euthanasia* (Boston: Beacon, 1960), 211. Fletcher was not a Catholic, but a similar though more nuanced view appears in recent works by some Catholic moralists. For example, Timothy E. O'Connell, *Principles for*

Here the line between the personal and the subpersonal, the intrinsically good and the instrumentally good, plainly is drawn in the wrong place: between God and the spiritual part of human persons, on the one hand, and, on the other, human bodies and the rest of physical nature. Scripture, tradition, and the Catholic Church's constant and most firm teaching draw that line between God, angels, and human bodily persons, on the one hand, and, on the other, the remainder of the material world.[11] Human persons can rightly use the latter for their own fulfillment, but may not treat their own or other persons' bodies as mere instruments or objects for use.

d) No bad condition can lessen the goodness and sanctity of human life. Disease, debility, and mutilation reduce participation in the good of life, yet a person's life remains an intrinsic, not instrumental, good, so that its goodness and sanctity are unaffected by such conditions. Some people deny this, thinking life not to have its full value close to its beginning or end, or to lose its value if the quality of a person's functioning and experience is poor because of disease, disability, or the wretchedness of extreme poverty. Today many even unquestioningly assume a standard for human bodily perfection and suppose that people who do not meet it should never have been born or are less worthy of respect.[12] However, the Church plainly teaches that human life has the same goodness and sanctity "*in every phase of development,* from conception until natural death; and *in every condition,* whether healthy or sick, whole or disabled, rich or poor."[13]

e) Life is good apart from its being a condition for fulfillment. Not everyone who supposes the goodness and sanctity of life to depend on some condition means to deny the unity of the human person and assert that the person's body is part of physical nature "over against us." Some take a different tack, arguing that even though human life is a good intrinsic to persons, it is valuable only insofar as it is a condition for a person's integral fulfillment; that aside, it is without value.

This argument is unsound. It is true that life will be most good as a constituent of everlasting life, but faith makes it clear that goodness belongs to human life even

---

a Catholic Morality (New York: Seabury, 1978), having said (59) that the body "is the 'belonging' of a person and yet also *is* the person," at once goes on to treat the person as a metaphysical principle of which one is not even directly aware, describes "the person himself or herself—the I" as a "dimensionless pinpoint around which everything else revolves," and concludes (59–60): "So I do not assert my personhood, and the personhood of all human beings, because I can see that personhood. No, that personhood is subject, not object to be seen. Rather I assert the existence of personhood because I am *aware* that it is the subject implied by and experienced in the contemplation of all objects. In the terminology of Karl Rahner, personhood is not something we consider; rather it is the 'condition of the possibility' of all things that we consider." Thus, under the influence of Kant's dualism, the human person is reduced to the transcendental ego. By contrast, see Robert M. Cooper, "Do 'I Own My Body'?" *Anglican Theological Review,* 55 (1973): 420–33.

11. On the anthropology implicit in sacred Scripture, see Wulstan Mork, O.S.B., *The Biblical Meaning of Man* (Milwaukee: Bruce, 1967), 1–125.

12. See Barbara M. Stafford, John La Puma, and David L. Schiedermayer, "One Face of Beauty, One Picture of Health: The Hidden Aesthetic of Medical Practice," *Journal of Medicine and Philosophy* 14 (1989): 213–30, for some of the historical roots of this quite relative standard.

13. John Paul II, *Christifideles laici,* 38, AAS 81 (1989) 463, *OR,* 6 Feb. 1989, 12.

apart from its ultimate fulfillment. For even the life of the damned remains in itself a good, as is shown by the fact that God does not annihilate them.[14]

3. Reverence for Human Life Requires More Than Not Killing People

Because a human person's life always retains its goodness and sanctity, it always must be treated with reverence. To see what that means, it is necessary to take into account the social character of bodily life, the human body's central place in God's plan for material creation, and the relationship which health, bodily integrity, inviolability, and physical mobility have to a person's life.

a) Persons as bodily are social. Although human beings are more than bodily realities, they are organisms which reproduce sexually, and as such are not only individuals but members of a natural community sharing in a common life. They do not communicate and give themselves to one another through some purely spiritual meeting of souls, but in and by bodily performances and contact. Bodily life and functioning, therefore, are important not only insofar as life is the very reality of the person, but insofar as the body is the medium of interpersonal communion in and through which persons fulfill themselves.[15]

Furthermore, human sexual capacity does not acquire its personal meaning solely from the interpersonal communion which it enables a couple to realize and celebrate.[16] Rather, human biological fecundity is of itself personal and interpersonal, because by it persons hand on personal life to new persons.[17] Thus, the sanctity of life embraces life in its transmission, and reverence for life must respond to that fact.

b) Persons as bodily fulfill both themselves and the world. All work and play involve bodily performances which affect the surrounding world. In this way, human persons both fulfill their capacities and endow the world with human

14. Annihilationism is incompatible with the biblical evidence: E. J. Fortman, S.J., *Everlasting Life after Death* (New York: Alba House, 1976), 169–70. See also *S.t.,* 1, q. 104, a. 4.

15. See John Paul II, General Audience (9 Jan. 1980), *Inseg.* 3.1 (1980) 88–92, *OR,* 14 Jan. 1980, 1, 20; General Audience (16 Jan. 1980), *Inseg.* 3.1 (1980) 148–52, *OR,* 21 Jan. 1980, 1, 12.

16. The view rejected here is implicit in the claim that the teaching of *Humanae vitae* against contraception involves "biologism." The truth is that the denial of the personal significance of human biological fecundity implies dualism. That denial and its implication of dualism are found in the so-called majority working paper of Paul VI's Pontifical Commission on Population, Family, and Births, *Documentum syntheticum de moralitate regulationis nativitatum,* 2.4: "Ipsum donum mutuum per totam vitam perdurat, foecunditas biologica non est continua et est subiecta multis irregularitatibus, ideo in sfaerem humanam assumi et in ea regulari debet." Since nothing assumes what it already is or has of itself, those who wrote that "biological fecunity ought to be assumed into the human sphere" clearly presupposed that the biological fecundity of human persons is not per se human. See Germain Grisez, "Dualism and the New Morality," *Atti del congresso internazionale Tommaso d'Aquino nel suo settimo centenario,* vol. 5, *L'agire morale* (Naples: Edizioni Domenicane Italiane, 1977), 323-30.

17. Vatican II (see GS 51) teaches that human sexuality and reproductive capacity marvelously surpass those found in lower forms of life; John Paul II, *Familiaris consortio,* 11, *AAS* 74 (1982) 92, *OR,* 21–28 Dec. 1981, 3, explains that human "fertility is directed to the generation of a human being, and so by its nature it surpasses the purely biological order and involves a whole series of personal values."

significance (see 10.A.1, 10.B.3). The human goods that are realized in the process are more than expendable means for reaching heaven; they are material for the kingdom, where they will be found perfected and glorified (see GS 38–39). Moreover, through bodily performances, human persons bring the rest of material creation to its fulfillment: "The human person is a unity of body and soul. By one's bodily condition, one gathers in oneself the elements of the material world, so that, through the human person, these elements reach their most exalted condition and raise their voice in free praise of the creator" (GS 14). Therefore, the good of life embraces the bodily functioning that is essential to the various activities by which human persons both fulfill themselves and bring the world to its own fulfillment.

c) **Reverence for life entails many responsibilities.** Since human life is an intrinsic good of persons, the requirements of reverence for life include a moral absolute forbidding the intentional killing of the innocent. And since life is a person's concrete reality, love for persons requires expressing reverence for life by cherishing it. This means at least not killing people through negligence. But since life is vulnerable and everyone's life is threatened in many ways—by natural forces and animals, by sickness and accident, by one's own foolishness or carelessness, and by the malicious or careless acts of others—cherishing life also means that one should act to protect oneself and others against loss of life. Being affirmative, this responsibility is limited by other responsibilities; but when anyone's life is threatened, there often is a strict and grave obligation to do what one can to protect it.

Protecting and promoting health also are part of reverencing life, since life is diminished and threatened by ill health. And since every bodily organ and part is personal, reverence for life requires respect for the body's integrity. Further, since bodily contact among persons often is meaningful and sometimes helpful or harmful, reverence for life requires due care in all bodily contact with others. Finally, since every organism needs its own space and must move about, human persons need both room and mobility; and so reverence for life also includes respect for others' space and freedom to move about.

4. The Will's Orientation toward Human Goods Determines Morality

The moral character of actions often depends on whether they carry out an intention bearing on the good of life or carry out some other intention, with the foreseen effect on life accepted as a side effect. For example, it is morally evil to choose to kill oneself even to further a good cause, but freely accepting death (as Jesus did) can be morally excellent; it is bad to choose to contracept, but avoiding pregnancy by abstaining from sexual intercourse always is obligatory outside marriage and can be obligatory within marriage; it is bad to withhold medical treatment in order to hasten death, but it can be good to administer drugs for pain relief even if their use also shortens life.

Many people presently feel that such distinctions are unintelligible. More or less explicitly, they assume that the goodness or badness of actions depends on whether or not they are effective in bringing about results which are wanted or unwanted (see *CMP,* 6). But the morality of actions depends more on the heart from which they flow than on the results to which they lead (see *CMP,* 7). Someone who loves neighbors and loves self in communion with God and neighbor will avoid intending ends or choosing means whose intending or choosing would be at odds with that love of God, neighbor, and self.

Since a human being's life is his or her concrete reality, intending a person's death as an end in itself or as a chosen means to some other end is always inconsistent with volitional love for that person.[18] True, before making a choice, one also should consider the foreseeable results of adopting and carrying out each possible alternative, since a loving heart seeks to benefit persons and not harm them. But such a heart often must accept some result which it would not intend or choose, because love for life or some other human good calls for the action or inaction which brings about that result.

In studying the following questions, therefore, it should be kept in mind that the will's orientation, in intending and choosing, toward life and other basic human goods makes an act be the kind of moral act it is.[19] Thus, it will not seem surprising that similar behaviors with similar results often constitute acts differing in moral quality.

Question B: Is It Always Gravely Wrong to Intend to Kill the Innocent?

People seldom desire that they themselves or those they love be killed, and so, with the Golden Rule in mind, everyone thinks killing human beings is generally wrong. But sometimes killing seems justified, for example, when it is the only way to resist a wrongful attack. Also, many people today think that one can be justified in killing oneself or someone else, either to end suffering or to prevent some other evil or achieve some good. Some also think circumstances can mitigate the gravity of killing, since not all who take life act with the same malice.

To resolve these issues, it is necessary first to understand what *intend* and *innocent* mean. Then one must see why it is always wrong to intend to kill the innocent, why this matter does not admit parvity, and how subjective factors can reduce the guilt of an act of killing.

---

18. Killing in war and as capital punishment require special treatment. Since they are authorized by public authority, they will be treated in 11.E.3 and 11.E.1.j, where the treatment here will be presupposed, and no exception to it will be made.

19. St. Thomas often makes the point, for example: *S.t.,* 2–2, q. 64, a. 7, "Moral acts receive their species according to that which is intended"; see 1–2, q. 72, a. 8, on the specification of sins; cf. John Finnis, "Object and Intention in Moral Judgments According to Aquinas," *Thomist* 55 (1991): 1–27. This position must not be confused with subjectivism. A subjectivist thinks that an act, while being what it is in itself, can be either good or evil depending on one's thoughts, feelings, or wishes regarding it. By contrast, the position proposed by St. Thomas and accepted here is that, while thoughts, wishes, and feelings about an act sometimes can affect one's subjective responsibility in choosing it, a human act has an inherent goodness or badness which cannot be affected by such subjective factors. Intentions intrinsically constitute moral acts inasmuch as these acts are the carrying out of choices; but the acts constituted by intentions are either good or evil by their conformity or lack of conformity to right reason, that is, to practical reason, unfettered by nonrational factors, bringing to bear the truth about what is humanly good.

In studying this question, it should be borne in mind that even those who do not intend to kill can wrongly bring about death, freely accepting it as a side effect of some action they should not do. That a killing is not intentional does not mean it is morally acceptable. It could be gravely evil. (That evil will be treated in the next question.)

1. To Will Death as an End or as a Means Is to Intend to Kill

Intend sometimes refers exclusively to the willing of an end, as distinct from the choice of a means, but sometimes it refers both to the willing of an end and the choice of a means, as distinct from accepting foreseen side effects. Here, *intend* is used in the latter, more inclusive sense. In this inclusive sense, *intentional killing* is synonymous with another expression sometimes found in the Church's teaching: *direct killing.*

a) Death can be desired without being willed as an end or as a means. *Desire* can refer to either an emotion or a will act, and in both senses there can be a desire for death which has nothing to do with intending to kill.

At the level of imagination, death can be thought of as if it were sleep or rest, and so it can be emotionally attractive, especially as an escape from weariness and suffering. Such an emotional desire for death, whether one's own or another's, is a natural reaction which is good in itself. People often experience it without being tempted, much less willing, to kill.

At the level of reason and will, also, there can be a wish for death in the absence of an intention to kill. Such a wish can respond to a judgment that death, whether one's own or another's, would be good insofar as it would end misery—for example, the suffering of a terminal illness—and/or release the soul into the afterlife. If that judgment neither presupposes nor tends toward any choice to do anything which might bring about or hasten death, the wish which it specifies need not be a moral fault. Indeed, often it is virtuous, as when devout, elderly people pray that God will soon call them to their heavenly reward.

But not all desires for death are so benign. Temptation often begins with desire, and if someone becomes aware of a temptation to intend or wrongly accept death, deliberately entertaining the desire shares the moral character of the tempting proposal. Moreover, a wish for someone's death can be a hypothetical will to kill the person: "I would kill him if I dared." Such a wish is a sin of thought, as is considering killing or loss of life with satisfaction and approval: "I wish he would have a fatal heart attack," "I am glad she murdered him," or "That stroke got him out of my way; it was indeed a stroke of good luck." Of course, like any other sin, such sins of thought cannot be mortal without sufficient reflection and full consent, either at the time or in some previous, unrepented mortal sin from which they flow.

b) One can knowingly cause something without intending it. Since God makes human beings in his own image, what he reveals about his own willing sheds light on human willing. Although it is not explicit in Scripture, revelation's teaching concerning God's goodness and providence points to a distinction between his doing something properly and per se and his doing it only permissively. This distinction is pivotal in one of the Council of Trent's canons: "If anyone says that it is not in man's power to make his ways evil, but that God performs the evil works just as he performs the good, not only by allowing them but also properly and per se [*non permissive solum, sed etiam proprie et per se*] . . .: let him be anathema" (translation amended).[20] Corresponding to this distinction in God's willing is the distinction between a human person's doing something intentionally and causing something nonintentionally in bringing about a side effect. Unlike God, one causes things nonintentionally in bringing about unforeseen effects; but like God, one also causes something nonintentionally when, in doing something else, one foresees and permits it as a side effect, which one does not cause properly and directly.

In making a choice, one intends as one's end the satisfaction or benefit desired for oneself and/or others in and/or through carrying out the choice. One chooses as a means something in one's power—some performance or omission—thought more or less likely to bring about the intended end. But it also is more or less clearly foreseen that, either possibly or surely, the performance or omission will have various good or bad consequences distinct from its intended end, and in making the choice these good or bad consequences are accepted, gladly or reluctantly as the case may be, as side effects. For example, a gluttonous man who chooses to drink and eat excessively foresees and accepts hardening of his arteries, damage to his liver, and so on, without either intending or choosing these consequences. Again, a woman afflicted with stuttering who chooses to testify at a trial in order to serve justice clearly foresees that she will stutter but only accepts the stuttering as a side effect.

c) **This distinction applies even in matters of life and death.** Jesus went up to Jerusalem to celebrate the Passover; in doing so, he freely accepted his own death, but he neither intended it as an end nor chose it as a means (see *CMP*, 22.F–G). Sometimes, too, the very same sort of performance or omission could belong to two acts that could cause another's death, but which have very different moral significance, depending on what choice the performance or omission executes, that is, depending on whether the death is chosen as a means or only accepted as a side effect of choosing something else. For example, a father trapped on the thirtieth floor of a burning building who throws his child out a window with no expectation that the child will survive could either have chosen the child's death as a means of being rid of unwanted responsibility or have accepted that death as a side effect of saving the child from the engulfing flames. Again, an overworked nurse at the scene of a disaster who does nothing to prevent the prompt death of some severely injured victims could choose their death to end their misery or accept it as a side effect of caring for others with better chances of survival.

d) *Choosing to kill* **is not always explained in the same way.** According to the analysis of action used in this work, choice is the adoption of a proposal. A person deliberates about doing something considered possible and interesting much as members of a deliberative body debate motions. Adopting a proposal to do

---

20. DS 1556/816. Even God foresees and permits evils that he does not directly will (see *S.t.*, 1, q. 49, a. 2; 1–2, q. 79, aa. 2–4; *S.c.g.*, 1.96, 3.71). To deny this would be to deny at least one of three propositions, all of which pertain to faith: that God's will is perfectly holy, that his providence is all-embracing, and that some creatures have sinned with the result that evil is real.

something is making a choice, just as adopting a motion by voting is the group's reaching a decision. The doing (whether performance or omission) carries out the choice, much as the executive carries out a legislative body's enactments. Carrying out the proposal has foreseen consequences neither included in the proposal nor sought for their own sake: these are the side effects that an individual or a group accepts (see *CMP,* 9.F).

On this analysis, choosing to kill is adopting a proposal precisely to kill or to do something understood in such a way that its meaning includes bringing about death. For example, people who choose to shoot someone in the heart or to administer a lethal dose of opiates ordinarily understand what they choose as ways of ending life, and when a proposal is so understood, its very meaning includes bringing about death.

Some classical moralists, however, think of choice as if it were merely the releasing, the 'positing,' of the outward performance or omission.[21] Then, considering the performance or omission in terms of objective causality in the world, they define what is chosen by its immediacy and perhaps also by its regularity as a result of that objective causality.

On this theory, choosing to kill (direct killing) is choosing to do or omit something that straightaway leads to death. For example, people who choose to shoot someone in the heart or knowingly to take a lethal dose of opiates posit a cause (the bullet entering the heart or the opiates affecting the nervous system) that straightaway leads to death. For these moralists, such performances or omissions seem to be plain instances of intentional (direct) killing, and the choices executed by such performances always are choices to kill.

e) **The two approaches can differ in identifying intentional killings.** The two approaches agree that the distinction between intentional (direct) and nonintentional (not direct) killing is morally significant. Moreover, in many cases they reach the same judgments. For example, on both approaches, a Mafia hit-man intentionally (directly) kills his victims to earn his fee; Jesus freely accepted death but did not intentionally (directly) kill himself; and a surgeon who removes a cancerous uterus gravid with a twelve-week fetus in order to prevent the cancer's spread accepts but does not intend the certain consequence of the death of the unborn (does not directly kill the baby).

---

21. Careful discrimination between what is chosen as a means and what is accepted as a side effect is essential for using the principle of double effect. For clear indications that mediation in the order of physical causality was pivotal for some authors, see John Connery, S.J., *Abortion: The Development of the Roman Catholic Perspective* (Chicago: Loyola University Press, 1977), 131–32 (Vasquez) and 188 (Lugo). For a historical summary of double effect, see Joseph T. Mangan, S.J., "An Historical Analysis of the Principle of Double Effect," *Theological Studies* 10 (1949): 41–61; J. Ghoos, "L'Acte à double effet: Étude de théologie positive," *Ephemerides theologiae Lovaniensis* 27 (1951): 30–52. In support of the view adopted in the present work: Joseph M. Boyle, Jr., *"Praeter Intentionem* in Aquinas," *Thomist* 42 (1978): 649–65; idem, "Toward Understanding the Principle of Double Effect," *Ethics* 90 (1980): 527–38; John Finnis, *Moral Absolutes: Tradition, Revision, and Truth* (Washington, D.C.: The Catholic University of America Press, 1991), 37–40, 67–77.

But the two approaches can lead to differences in applying the distinction between intending death (directly killing) as a means and accepting it as a side effect, and so in identifying certain deadly deeds as instances of intentional (direct) killing. For example, some classical moralists thought that using deadly force in defense against an unprovoked attacker constitutes intentional (direct) killing (which, however, they considered justifiable).[22] No doubt, understanding *choosing to kill* as they did, they thought that a woman who puts a bullet through a would-be rapist's head when that is the only way to stop his attack must intend the rapist's death (directly kill him). However, according to the analysis of action used in this work, that woman could shoot the rapist in the head in carrying out a proposal to defend herself against rape, only accepting his foreseen death as a side effect rather than intending it (directly killing him).

Those who hold the classical moralists' view will object that it makes no sense to say someone could choose to shoot someone else in the head without intending to kill (directly killing) that person. The objection begs the question, because it presupposes the classical moralists' concept of intention (directness). The analysis employed here has a different concept of intention (directness): people intend only what they choose as a means or seek as an end (people directly do only what carries out or is shaped by an intention). The rapist's death is not what is chosen as a means or sought as an end when the woman shoots him in the head to stop his attack (the shooting is not direct killing). Her end is to avoid being raped; her means is to prevent the would-be rapist from carrying out the behavior which would constitute rape. The nonhomicidal character of her intention (that this shooting was not a case of direct killing) would be manifested if the shot resulted in an incapacitating wound rather than death, and the woman, rather than shooting the wounded man again, promptly summoned an ambulance and, while awaiting it, did everything she could to save his life.

f) The word *direct* in this context has misleading connotations. The connotations of the word *direct* partly explain why the theory rejected here has seemed plausible to many people. However, as was noted above, the magisterium uses *direct* to mean *intended as an end or chosen as a means*.[23] In reading Church teaching which uses *direct* in this sense, therefore, one must take care not to import any notion of behavioral or physical directness, such as that expressed by *straight-away*, or any other notion of temporal immediacy or spatial proximity. Moreover, to avoid confusion, it would be best not to use *direct* to mean *intended as an end or chosen as a means*. From now on in this book, *direct* will not be used in that

22. See I. Aertnys, C. Damen, and I. Visser, C.Ss.R., *Theologia moralis,* ed. 18, 4 vols. (Turin: Marietti, 1967–69), 2:143, for references to some who held this view (n. 1), which, however, some classical moralists also opposed (n. 2). St. Thomas, *S.t.,* 2–2, q. 64, a. 7, provided the original treatment of double effect in explaining how a person defending himself or herself could justly bring about an attacker's death.

23. See Pius XII, Address to the Italian St. Luke Guild of Physicians, *Discorsi e radio-messaggi* 6 (1944–45): 191; quoted in Congregation for the Doctrine of the Faith, *Declaration on Procured Abortion,* n. 15, *AAS* 66 (1974) 735, Flannery, 2:452.

sense except in translations of Church teaching and, in quotation marks, when referring to the theory rejected here.

g) Omissions can be a means of intentional killing. Someone can intentionally kill another by an omission. If a person can do something necessary to sustain life, but deliberately omits to do it in order that death will ensue, that omission, morally speaking, is a means of intentional killing. For example, if Mark, a diabetic who is disappointed in love, decides to end his life by omitting the insulin injections he needs for survival, that omission is a means of intentional killing and constitutes suicide. If the Joneses, deciding they do not want their handicapped newborn child, direct the nursery to withhold food in order to make sure the baby dies, that omission is a means of intentional killing and morally constitutes murder, regardless of how the law and its officers view the act.[24]

2. *Innocent* Here Is Used as a Technical Term

Innocent often refers to those who are free of personal moral guilt: "as innocent as a baby." Since all adults are sinners, none is innocent in this sense. In the present context, though, *innocent* is used in a technical sense to refer to everyone but those who either have been found guilty of a capital crime or are carrying on an unjust war. Thus understood, *innocent* may seem to name a mere construct without any intelligibility of its own; but this concept of innocence has significance which is clarified by considering how it developed in Scripture and tradition.

a) *Innocent* first refers to those not guilty of capital crimes. The sacred writers of the Old Testament propose as a divine command, "You shall not kill" (Ex 20.13, Dt 5.17),[25] and as a norm for judicial processes, "Keep far from a false charge, and do not kill the innocent and those in the right" (Ex 23.7). From this narrow context, the Old Testament extends the use of *innocent* to refer to every member of the community who might be a victim of wrongful killing, and forbids the shedding of "innocent blood" (see Dt 19.10, 19.13, 21.8–9, 27.25; Jer 7.6, 19.3–5, 22.3; and so on).

b) *Innocent* also refers to noncombatants in an enemy population. In the Old Testament, Israel seems to be enjoined to kill its enemies in war. Indeed, the command to kill appears to embrace the whole populations of the nations Israel displaces (see Dt 7.1–2, 13.12–18, 20.16–18; Jos 6.18–21, 10.40, 11.14; 1 Sm 15.2–32; and so on).[26] In the New Testament, however, killing in war is nowhere treated. Moreover, the gospel recognizes no unalterable human enemies, for it calls all humankind into Jesus' kingdom. Hence, some Christians believed that killing

---

24. Because the killing is intentional—the Joneses want food withheld precisely as a means of ensuring the child's death—its wrongness does not depend on the child's condition: whether he or she would survive and flourish with care or is certain to die in a few minutes regardless of what is done. This point about intentional killing must be kept in mind when considering other examples in this question.

25. The text of the New Revised Standard Version uses *murder* but *kill* is offered in a note as an acceptable variant.

26. Norbert Lohfink, " 'Holy War' and the 'Ban' in the Bible," *Theology Digest* 38 (1991): 109–14, explains that the Old Testament shows that Israel gradually extricated itself from supposedly sacred violence.

in war is never justifiable (see 11.E.3.e). However, as Christians exercised political authority, they developed the theory of justifiable war. Its key idea is that when just social order is gravely challenged by those ready to use unjust force, war can be justified, somewhat as capital punishment is, but only within strict moral limits (see 11.E.3.b–c).

Perhaps the most important of these limits is that in war it is necessary to distinguish between those involved in using unjust force (enemy combatants) and the rest of the enemy's community (noncombatants among an enemy's population). In articulating this distinction, *innocent* was extended to refer to noncombatants.[27] Thus, according to the Christian view of humankind as called to be the one People of God, noncombatant members of an enemy society are innocent in much the same sense as members of a society's own population who have been found guilty of no capital crime.

c) **Only criminals and enemy combatants are not innocent.** It is clear from the preceding that, in the Christian tradition on the morality of killing, the original core of the idea of innocence is immunity from capital punishment, not moral innocence. The behavior of enemy combatants threatens just social order, and they are easily assimilated to criminals: although they may be neither morally nor legally guilty, they pose a threat similar to that posed by criminals. Hence, killing them is considered justified, and they are not called "innocent." Apart from these two specific groups—criminals found guilty of capital crimes and enemy combatants in a justifiable war—all others are juridically innocent. Their activities are not gravely harmful to just social order, and so all who uphold that order must treat their lives as inviolable.

3. It Is Always Wrong to Intend to Kill the Innocent

The preceding points clarify both the precise meaning of *intending* to kill and the very inclusive reference of the word *innocent*. It now remains to explain the specific moral norm that excludes acts of killing shaped by an intention to kill an innocent person, and to show why this norm admits of no exceptions whatsoever.

a) **Divine revelation teaches that killing the innocent is wrong.** The prohibition against killing the innocent is central to the Noachic covenant: "Whoever sheds the blood of a human, by a human shall that person's blood be shed; for in his own image God made humankind" (Gn 9.6). The sacred writer considers this covenant binding on all humankind, so it clearly is not meant to articulate a mere cultural convention. Thus, as St. Paul points out, by the law written in their hearts, even those ignorant of the law of Moses know the wrongfulness of murder (see Rom 1.29–32, 2.14–15). "You shall not kill" also is one of the stipulations of the second table of the Sinai covenant (see Ex 20.13, Dt 5.17). Jesus teaches that people

---

27. See, for example, Hermann Busembaum, in St. Alphonsus Liguori, *Theologia moralis,* ed. L. Gaudé, 4 vols. (Rome: Ex Typographia Vaticana, 1905–12), 1:663, who teaches that it is licit to kill enemies in a just war precisely insofar as necessary for the purpose of the war, but that one may not directly take the lives of innocents. He clarifies the concept of *innocents* in this context by means of a list: "children who cannot bear arms, women, old men, religious, clerics, foreigners, merchants, and rustics."

must keep these commandments to enter eternal life (see Mt 19.16–18, Mk 10.17–19, Lk 18.18–20).

Developing Jesus' teaching concerning the primacy of love, the New Testament explains why these commandments remain valid: love of one's neighbor sums them up and fulfills them (see Rom 13.8–10; cf. Mt 22.40). Hence, murderers even now do not have eternal life abiding in them (see 1 Jn 3.15); unless they repent, they will end "in the lake that burns with fire and sulphur, which is the second death" (Rv 21.8).

Thus, the serious wrongness of killing the innocent follows not only from the inherent goodness of human life but from the order of creation (humans made in the image of God) and the purpose of redemption (the covenant communion, which will be perfected in heavenly communion, to which humankind is called). The order of creation and the purpose of redemption are central to divine revelation. Hence, Scripture makes it clear that divine revelation teaches that killing the innocent is wrong.[28]

b) Catholic tradition and the magisterium exclude all exceptions. While admitting that divine revelation generally excludes killing people, some will argue that nothing in Scripture shows the norm to be exceptionless. However, Scripture should be read in the light of the Church's tradition and under the guidance of the magisterium.[29]

The *Catechism of the Council of Trent* provides a neat summary of the tradition. The commandment forbidding killing "was the first prohibition issued by the Almighty" after the deluge; "amongst the precepts of the Old Law first expounded by our Lord, this is the first" which he mentioned, and in explaining it, "our Lord points out its twofold obligation": prohibitory and mandatory. The Catechism's exposition of the prohibitory part begins by listing kinds of killing not forbidden by the commandment: killing of animals, execution of criminals, killing an enemy in a just war, killing by accident rather than by intent or design (though such killing also can be wrong), and killing in self-defense. Setting aside these kinds of killing, "the prohibition embraces all others, with regard to the person who kills, the person killed, and the means used to kill."[30]

---

28. For an additional theological reflection on relevant texts of Scripture, see Augustine Regan, C.Ss.R., "The Worth of Human Life," *Studia Moralia* 6 (1968): 215–25.

29. See DV 10 and 12. Vatican II, by referring in DV 10 to Pius XII, *Humani generis, AAS* 42 (1950) 568–69 (DS 3886/2314), *PE*, 240.21, indicates the proper exegesis of its very compact statement on the role of the magisterium in interpreting the word of God. DV 10, interpreted as it should be in the light of Pius XII's more ample exposition, has very important implications for moral theological method: see *CMP*, 1.C. Some today ignore these implications and treat Scripture in isolation from the magisterium; see, for example, Josef Fuchs, S.J., "Christian Faith and the Disposing of Human Life," *Theological Studies* 46 (1985): 672–77. A critique of this way of using Scripture: Germain Grisez, "Moral Absolutes: A Critique of the View of Josef Fuchs, S.J.," *Anthropos* (now *Anthropotes*) 1 (Oct. 1985): 186–92.

30. *Catechismus ex decreto Ss. Concilii Tridentini ad parochos (The Catechism by Decree of the Holy Council of Trent),* Latin text with trans. by J. Donovan, 2 vols. (Rome: 1839), 3.6.1–8 (2:125–31). This catechism is not cited as if it were by itself especially authoritative, but for its clear and brief formulation, which exemplifies the Catholic tradition.

In the recent magisterium, Pius XII precisely restates the traditional teaching:

> As long as a man is not guilty, his life is untouchable, and therefore any act directly tending to destroy it is illicit, whether such destruction is intended as an end in itself or only as a means to an end, whether it is a question of life in the embryonic stage or in a stage of full development or already in its final stages.[31]

Hence, if sacred Scripture is read as it should be, in the light of tradition and the magisterium, intending to kill the innocent is clearly seen to be always wrong.

Although this moral norm has not been solemnly defined, it is certainly a divinely revealed truth infallibly taught by the ordinary magisterium (see *CMP*, 35.E). So, every Catholic should assent to it with faith.

c) **Even if not unjust, suicide always is objectively wrong.** Suicide, that is, a person's intentional killing of himself or herself, often is unjust, inasmuch as it unfairly leaves unfulfilled the individual's duties toward other individuals, communities, or society at large, or imposes unreasonable burdens on them. Even apart from its possible injustice, however, suicide is wrong insofar as it involves the intention to kill an innocent person. For this reason, the Catholic moral tradition treated suicide as a species of wrongful killing (see *S.t.,* 2–2, q. 64, a. 5).[32] Vatican II makes the same point by listing "voluntary suicide" among the "infamies" that are "opposed to life itself" (GS 27). Moreover, since each created person is responsible to God to use the gift of life in his service, suicide "is to be considered as a rejection of God's sovereignty and loving plan."[33]

A movement is now under way on behalf of suicide and assisted suicide, and their legalization, for the terminally ill and others suffering protracted and severe pain. Killing in such circumstances, its proponents argue, is necessary to eliminate suffering—that is, as euthanasia—and for the sake of death with dignity. However, even in these circumstances, intentional killing remains wrong, and the good purposes it is meant to serve should instead be pursued by providing better and more appropriate care, including adequate pain relief.[34] Christians, moreover, should remember that their dignity is God-given and unaffected by suffering, debility, and death, and that these evils, insofar as they are unavoidable, should be meekly accepted, courageously borne, and devoutly offered to God along with Jesus' suffering and death, with the confident hope of sharing in his resurrection.[35]

31. Pius XII, Address to the Italian St. Luke Guild of Physicians, *Discorsi e radiomessaggi* 6 (1944–45): 191; quoted in Congregation for the Doctrine of the Faith, *Declaration on Procured Abortion*, n. 15, *AAS* 66 (1974) 735, Flannery, 2:452.

32. An excellent exposition and defense of the traditional teaching: Augustine Regan, C.Ss.R., "Moral Argument on Self-killing," *Studia Moralia* 18 (1980): 299–332.

33. Congregation for the Doctrine of the Faith, *Declaration on Euthanasia, 3, AAS* 72 (1980) 545, Flannery, 2:512.

34. See Congregation for the Doctrine of the Faith, *Declaration on Euthanasia, AAS* 72 (1980) 545–51, Flannery, 2:512–16; Germain Grisez and Joseph M. Boyle, Jr., *Life and Death With Liberty and Justice: A Contribution to the Euthanasia Debate* (Notre Dame, Ind.: University of Notre Dame Press, 1979), 139–49, 171–83, 412–14. Also see *Euthanasia and Clinical Practice: Trends, Principles and Alternatives,* The Report of a Working Party (London: The Linacre Centre, 1982).

35. See John Paul II, *Salvifici doloris, AAS* 76 (1984) 201–50, *OR,* 20 Feb. 1984, 1–9, for a splendid clarification of the Christian meaning of human suffering; also see 4.F.1, above.

People who think their lives are not worth living sometimes choose to end them by a calculated omission. For example, precisely in order to end a psychologically repugnant life, someone paralyzed from the neck down may refuse to eat or demand that a life-sustaining respirator be removed. Again, someone grieving over the loss of a spouse may reject medical care, not burdensome in itself and necessary to sustain life, in order to "rejoin" his or her beloved. Since the choice in such cases is to bring about death, the act is suicide.

Sometimes, hoping to make a political point, people bring about their own deaths by fasting or by other self-destructive acts, such as setting themselves afire. The end may be important and the act selfless, but if such a person chooses to kill himself or herself, the act is suicide: a bad means to the good end.

   d) **Apparent exceptions in the Old Testament can be explained.** As already mentioned, the Old Testament's rules for war appear to require the killing of whole populations, including the noncombatant members of the nations Israel displaces. Also, Abraham apparently rightly chose to kill an innocent in following God's command to sacrifice Isaac as a burnt offering (see Gn 22.2–18). Such passages can be used to argue that Scripture admits exceptions to the norm excluding the killing of the innocent.

   However, the Old Testament's rules for war need not be read as assertions by the relevant human authors that the killing of innocents is morally required. Read as they should be, in the wider context of the Bible as a whole, these rules only show what the Israelites of early times believed to be God's will, and so were bound in conscience to do, but they do not reflect the moral truth. The New Testament, read in accord with Christian tradition and the magisterium's interpretation, makes it clear that God never willed the killing of the innocent (see *CMP,* 8.H.7–9). The story of Abraham's test might be explained along the same lines: though his obedience to what he took to be God's will was exemplary, his conscience was blamelessly in error, for in reality God never ordered him to sacrifice Isaac.

   St. Thomas proposes a different account of those Old Testament passages that appear to make exceptions to the norm excluding the killing of the innocent, as well as to other precepts of the Decalogue. He holds that to obey specific divine commands, as Abraham and other Old Testament saints did, is to do a moral act different in kind from choosing to carry out a similar performance for some other reason, so that Abraham, for example, did not consent to homicide (see *S.t.,* 1–2, q. 94, a. 5, ad 2; q. 100, a. 8, ad 3).[36]

   e) **Moral reflection clarifies the reason why the norm is exceptionless.** Rather than being a merely instrumental good, life is a basic human good, one of the intrinsic aspects of a person's reality and fulfillment (see *CMP,* 5.D and, above, A.2.c). Anyone moved by anger or hatred to regard someone's life as if it were an evil and so to will as an end that person's death, violates the seventh mode of

---

36. Whether one agrees that someone could will to carry out a divine command to kill without intending to kill, it is clear that Thomas meant to allow no exceptions to the norm excluding killing the innocent. For a critique of arguments for the opposite view, see Patrick Lee, "Permanence of the Ten Commandments: St. Thomas and His Modern Commentators," *Theological Studies* 42 (1981): 422–43.

responsibility (see *CMP*, 8.G); and anyone moved by desire for some ulterior end to choose to destroy someone's life as a means to that end violates the eighth mode of responsibility (see *CMP*, 8.H). A will that violates either of these modes of responsibility cannot be consistent with a will to integral human fulfillment: to will that someone be deprived of life is inconsistent with willing that he or she share in integral fulfillment (and this remains true even for killers who think their victims eventually will be raised from the dead to enjoy everlasting life in heaven). The same point can be expressed in terms of love: to will that someone be deprived of life is inconsistent with love of neighbor toward him or her.[37] So, one may never will as an end (contrary to the seventh mode) or choose as a means (contrary to the eighth mode) to kill anyone.

Some argue that while the death of the innocent always is bad, killing an innocent person sometimes is morally justified, since the alternative is to accept something even worse in its impact on the genuine human well-being of the individual killed and/or other persons. For instance, starving a grossly defective baby to death (while administering drugs to prevent suffering) saves the child a miserable life and relieves others of the great and prolonged burden of caring for it. Again, if a group of people adrift at sea are starving, killing and eating the weakest (who would die soon in any case) can preserve the lives of the rest until rescuers arrive. Spies who kill themselves can both avoid torture and prevent the enemy from acquiring secret information which would cost many lives. The dying who have fulfilled their moral and spiritual obligations sometimes could avoid great pain and forestall temptations to rebel against God's will by choosing a speedy and easy death.

This argument is an example of proportionalism or consequentialism (criticized in *CMP*, 6). Its central defect is that it assumes what cannot be known: that the repugnant alternative to killing is worse than the killing itself. To the extent examples lend plausibility to the argument, that is because they highlight factors which strongly impact on one's feelings. In such cases, then, admitting exceptions to the norm excluding killing the innocent means subordinating rational judgment to emotion. That is simply to abandon morality.[38]

4. Intentionally Killing the Innocent Always Is Grave Matter

Although it is always wrong to intend to kill the innocent, not all acts of killing have the same malice. For example, a hit-man's cold-blooded murders plainly are far worse than the act of a wife who reluctantly gives a lethal dose of drugs to her terminally ill husband after he has begged her repeatedly to do so. Also, people tempted to kill sometimes use means which may not be deadly or decide to kill

37. Since the salvation of baptized infants is certain, if choosing to kill them were not inconsistent with loving them, it would be loving to kill them. However, since killing destroys a bodily person, loving the baptized infant is inconsistent with intending his or her death, and since proportionalism is erroneous (see *CMP*, 6), even the goodness of eternal salvation cannot "outweigh" the evil of killing the child.

38. For recent defenses of moral absolutes, see Finnis, *Moral Absolutes;* William E. May, *Moral Absolutes: Catholic Tradition, Current Trends, and the Truth,* The Père Marquette Lecture in Theology, 1989 (Milwaukee: Marquette University Press, 1989).

only under some condition they hope will never be fulfilled. Such cases raise the question whether there might not sometimes be parvity of matter in the intentional killing of the innocent.

a) Intentional killing always is incompatible with love. Many harms to others—for example, taking property—admit of more and less; they can be so slight as to be insignificant. But killing entirely deprives a person of bodily life. It does not admit of more and less, and so there can be no insignificant degree of it. Most acts of intentional killing obviously are incompatible with love, for they are done either out of emotional hatred or for some ulterior end, for whose sake the person to be killed is treated as a disposable thing. But even intentional mercy killing or suicide motivated by feelings of sympathy or sadness is incompatible with volitional love, since willing that someone be deprived of the intrinsic good of life is incompatible with willing his or her complete good.[39]

The cold-blooded hit-man and the sympathetic wife will the same thing in one respect: both choose to kill. In this respect, the gravity of what they do is the same. However, they also will different things insofar as they choose for the sake of entirely different ends. In this respect, the gravity of what they do is not the same, for his selfish motivation adds to the gravity of what he chooses, while her misguided affection limits the badness of her willing to her choice of killing as a means.

b) Killing remains grave even if one's intention is conditional. Sometimes people intend to kill only if a certain condition, not in their own power, is fulfilled. For example, a man gambles everything he owns, intending to kill himself if he loses; a woman, holding up a bank, says: "Give me the money or I'll kill you," and means it. Both hope the condition will not be fulfilled; they would rather not kill. But both do intend to kill if the condition happens to be fulfilled. Since what is willed is the same as it would be if the intention were unconditional, the matter of the sin remains grave. For gravity is determined by what the agent wills (the object of the moral act), not by conditions and limits on the carrying out of a choice.[40]

c) Killing remains grave even if one uses means that may not work. Sometimes, intending to kill yet emotionally ambivalent or afraid to do a patently deadly deed, people use means that may or may not be effective. For example, a woman decides to commit suicide and takes several sleeping pills, not knowing whether the dose will be lethal; a man deliberately delays summoning help when his wife suffers a sudden seizure, hoping she will die but fearing she may recover. Assuming that what is willed in such cases is the same as what would be willed if more certain and straightforward means were used, the matter of the sin remains the same. For the gravity of the matter is determined by the harm the agent wills, not by the harm he or she is likely to effect.

---

39. *CIC,* c. 1397, lists homicide among the few offenses against persons which remain canonical crimes.

40. On conditional intention, see John Finnis, Joseph M. Boyle, Jr., and Germain Grisez, *Nuclear Deterrence, Morality and Realism* (Oxford: Oxford University Press, 1987), 81–86.

d) Other factors can mitigate the guilt of intentional killing. The gravity of the matter is only one factor in determining a person's guilt in committing a sin. Subjective factors can limit responsibility, and circumstances can mitigate the sin's seriousness. Since killing is so manifest an evil and is naturally highly repugnant to normal people, many who purposely take life no doubt act with limited responsibility. Someone who commits suicide in a desperate attempt to escape the anguish of profound depression perhaps has no more moral responsibility for his or her own death than someone who suffers a fatal heart attack.[41]

People can do deadly deeds without any free choice whatsoever, their behavior motivated exclusively by feelings. For example, without hesitation, deliberation, or choice, a jealous lover might kill in anger or a depressed person jump out a window. Since these deadly deeds occur without choice, they are not in themselves morally significant. If those who do them bear any moral responsibility, it is for previous acts and/or omissions that somehow set the stage.

Those who intentionally kill an innocent person also may lack sufficient reflection when they choose to kill (see *CMP*, 17.A). In some cases, even in a matter as elemental as killing, a person's conscience could be in blameless error. For example, bad advice could persuade the parents of a severely handicapped newborn that depriving the baby of food and water in order to end his or her life would be a legitimate decision to limit care.[42] In other cases, unusual pressures could distract someone from the grave moral wrongness of killing, so that in choosing to kill he or she does not violate conscience but sets aside only nonmoral considerations, such as fear of bad consequences; perhaps that sometimes happens when depressed people kill themselves. Lack of sufficient reflection lessens or eliminates a person's guilt for a choice to kill, except insofar as the defect in conscience is his or her own fault.

Even if someone freely chooses, contrary to conscience, to commit the grave sin of killing an innocent person, moral immaturity, emotional instability, and other subjective factors can affect his or her understanding of the wrongness of what is done (by limiting insight into the evil of killing) and/or his or her strength of will (by limiting the alternatives considered and the intensity of each option's appeal). Also, as noted above, the end which a person has in view can limit or add to the gravity of the act, and other circumstances can have a similar effect. Hence, the guilt of diverse, mortally sinful acts of intentional killing varies greatly, both according to the extent to which the killer's will embraces the evil and according to the gravity (understood by the killer) of the evil willed.

---

41. *CIC,* c. 1184, which specifies those to whom funeral rites are denied, significantly omits those who have committed suicide, no doubt because psychological insight into the mental processes leading people to commit suicide indicates that such persons should not be considered manifest sinners. Of course, no one who contemplates suicide should suppose that a free choice to kill oneself could fail to be a mortal sin.

42. John Paul II, Address to the Eleventh European Congress of Perinatal Medicine, 4, *AAS* 80 (1988) 1426, *OR,* 2 May 1988, 11, teaches: "It must clearly be reaffirmed that every life is sacred and that a possible deformity can never justify a death sentence, not even when it is the parents themselves, in the throes of emotion and disappointed in their expectations, who request euthanasia by means of suspension of treatment and nourishment."

Question C: When Is It Wrong to Accept or Risk Death as a Side Effect?

People intentionally kill only in willing death as an end or choosing it as a means. So, even if one knowingly brings about someone's death as a side effect, one is not responsible for *intentional* killing if one neither wants the death nor chooses to kill. However, since side effects can be avoided by choosing not to do the act of which they are consequences, a person has some responsibility for any death foreseen as resulting, or possibly resulting, from carrying out a choice.

Accepting death as a side effect means making and carrying out a choice to do something other than kill and with a purpose other than death, but with the expectation that a death, one's own or another's, will result. *Risking death as a side effect* is similar, but the expectation is that someone's death might result.

Responsibility in accepting or risking death as a side effect is not always guilt, because such a will is not always wrong. Jesus freely accepted death, and every Christian should be prepared to follow him and die a martyr. Moreover, it is impossible to avoid all foreseen risks to life, since virtually any form of work, play, travel, or other activity carries some risk. The question is: What factors distinguish between cases in which it is wrong to accept or risk death as a side effect and those in which it is morally acceptable or even obligatory?

1. Norms for Accepting or Not Accepting Death as a Side Effect

It always is wrong to accept one's own or another's death as a side effect of doing something that would be wrong in any case. The instance in which it clearly is praiseworthy to accept death as a side effect is that in which one's own death is accepted in the line of duty or in doing some work of mercy. In other cases, fairness usually excludes accepting another's death as a side effect of doing something otherwise morally good or even obligatory. But another's death sometimes may be accepted as a side effect, for example, of the defensive use of deadly force. Still, it is not always right to accept death as a side effect even of efforts to serve genuine human goods or prevent real human evils.

a) **Accepting death as a side effect of any sin is wrongful killing.** If it is foreseen that a prospective act will cause someone's death, that is a reason not to do it. The act, then, cannot rightly be chosen unless one has a morally acceptable reason to do it. But although a person can have strong motives, including reasons, to sin, there never can be a morally acceptable reason to do so. Therefore, one is guilty of wrongful killing whenever, in doing something that is sinful even apart from its deadly effect, one accepts someone's death. For example, if Frank, accused of murdering Rosa, lies to save his life, knowing the lie will lead to Marvin's death, Frank is guilty of Marvin's death, since the lie is wrong in itself, and so cannot be chosen for any reason whatever that would justify accepting anyone's death.

b) **Unfairly accepting another's death is wrongful killing.** If it is foreseen that a prospective act, even though otherwise morally acceptable, will result in someone's death, the question is whether accepting that death is fair and merciful. If not, one should forgo the act in order to avoid the incidental death; and if one chooses to do it, the choice is wrongful killing. For example, Mary, a fire fighter, jumps out a window into a net to save herself, leaving to the flames a child whom she could and, given her duty as a fire fighter, should have saved. She does not intend but only accepts the child's death, and her self-preserving act otherwise would be morally good. But since the child's death results from Mary's dereliction of duty, she is guilty of it. Again, Sam, who has a wife and several small children, has acquired a place on a life raft by a fair lottery, but voluntarily gives it up to a single woman and goes down with the ship. If Sam's act were not unfair to his dependents, it could be a heroic act of mercy; but this self-sacrificing act of his involves unfairly forsaking his wife and children, and so he should not accept his own death. His "heroic" act is wrongful killing of himself. (In both of these cases, the effect which strong emotion and confusion have on moral judgment and choice plainly could mitigate the sinfulness of the acts of wrongful killing.)

c) **Sometimes death may or should be accepted as a side effect.** If there is a morally acceptable reason to accept one's own or another's death as a side effect of doing something both morally good in itself and in accord with justice and mercy, one may, and sometimes even should, accept it. For example, the Uganda martyrs had a strict obligation to accept their own deaths as a side effect of refusing to do something wrong in itself: sodomy. Maximilian Kolbe mercifully accepted his own death as the side effect of saving a fellow prisoner's life, while the fellow prisoner, in order to return to his wife and family, fairly took advantage of Kolbe's offer, accepting the saintly priest's heroic death in doing so.

Mary, the fire fighter, should have accepted her own death, if necessary, to save the child, for saving the child was her duty. Similarly, some crewmen on the Titanic rightly accepted their own deaths in fulfilling their duty to save the passengers; some passengers whose responsibilities allowed them the freedom to sacrifice themselves also rightly accepted their own deaths in order to save others, although they could have saved themselves; and some other passengers acted fairly in taking their places on the lifeboats and accepting the death of those for whom there was no room.

d) **Deadly force sometimes is rightly used for defensive purposes.** Wrong-doers confronted with others' legitimate use of force plainly have no right to defend themselves. Innocent victims, whenever possible, should evade or deflect attacks, summon the proper authorities, or defend themselves by means unlikely to cause serious harm. Sometimes, however, people can defend themselves and/or others against unprovoked violations of person or property only by using means they expect to result in the death of the agent or agents of the violation.[43] Assuming the death is not intended as an end (for example, to satisfy vengeful anger) or chosen

---

43. Those who classify killing in self-defense as "direct" killing are compelled to make the justification of any such killing hinge on the moral status of the attacker as a so-called materially unjust aggressor, and in this way to bring the attacker into the class of the noninnocent. However, according to the preceding analysis, since the attacker is neither a criminal found guilty of a capital crime nor an enemy combatant in a just war, he or she must be considered innocent. The justification of killing in self-defense, therefore, depends entirely on the goods of the various persons at stake and the fairness and mercy with which a defender acts with regard to them.

as a means (for example, to forestall future threats), it may be accepted as a side effect of the use of the minimum adequate defensive force, provided one acts both fairly and mercifully in accepting it.

For example, bank guards, fearing the fire power of Ma Fia, an armed robber, and believing they cannot safely stop her except by shooting her in the chest, rightly do so and accept her death as a side effect of carrying out their duty to guard the bank (including its employees and customers) while also protecting their own lives. Similarly, a woman who can safely and surely stop a man from raping or kidnapping her daughter only by slicing his throat rightly accepts his death as a side effect of her protective act. In these cases, the defenders' responsibilities preclude forgoing the use of the necessary, deadly force: the bank guards and the mother would be derelict in their duties, not merciful, if they were unwilling to accept the deaths they expect to result from their defensive acts.[44]

   e) **Fairness and mercy limit defensive uses of deadly force.** If the violation is not to persons—for example, interference with something essential for some-one's survival, a direct threat to life or limb, an attempt at rape or kidnapping—but solely to property, fairness precludes the defensive use of deadly force. People universally value their own lives and the lives of those they love above any piece of property which is not essential for survival, and so the Golden Rule forbids accepting another's death as the side effect of using deadly force to prevent, for instance, nothing more than a thief's escape with one's wallet and jewelry.

Someone might object that fairness here must take into account the injustice the thief is doing: surely, a mugger's victim may use force with the intention of disabling him. True, but even if the injustice is taken into account, the Golden Rule forbids killing the thief: nobody would want a loved one—a friend, a child—who went astray and committed such a crime to suffer death at the victim's hands.[45] Moreover, the objection depends on a claim about the injustice the thief is doing: but thieves are not always morally responsible for their actions.

In many cases, one's own life cannot be sacrificed without unfairness to others, such as dependents, or detriment to the common good. But when no duty requires the use of deadly force in personal self-defense, mercy, the justice of the kingdom, should prompt one to suffer death rather than defend oneself by means that would bring about the death of an assailant, for whose eventual salvation one should hope. The model is Jesus, who, striving to overcome the wounds of sin and its conse-

---

44. It might be objected that such examples, and by implication the norms they illustrate, are morally irrelevant and otiose, since in such a situation a person can hardly engage in rational deliberation and make a free choice. However, it is good for anyone who wishes to do what is right in every situation to know sound norms applicable to such emergencies. Sometimes there is time for reflection, and in any case an advance commitment to act on sound norms both contributes to good character and predisposes to appropriate action in emergencies, in which grave conse-quences other than moral guilt might follow from doing the wrong thing or being inhibited from doing the right thing.

45. Although many modern moral theologians considered killing in defense of property justified, the position taken here agrees with the earlier tradition; see Shaun J. Sullivan, O.F.M., *Killing in Defense of Private Property: The Development of a Roman Catholic Moral Teaching, Thirteenth to Eighteenth Centuries* (Missoula, Mont.: Scholars Press, 1976).

quences by love, did not wish to be defended against unjust arrest, suffering, and death by the wounding of those sent to arrest him.[46]

2. Norms for Risking Death as a Side Effect

Simply riding in an automobile puts life at risk. Yet not even those who engage in the most hazardous work—for instance, test pilots and the technicians who defuse terrorists' bombs—straightforwardly accept death as a side effect; they only risk it, while expecting, hoping, and doing their best to survive. Risking death is conditionally accepting it: "Doing this, I know that death will ensue if things go badly, and I accept that." Thus, the same principles that determine the moral character of accepting death as a side effect determine the morality of accepting a risk to one's own life or another's. But the application of the principles is more complicated, partly because risks of death vary so greatly.

Often they are rightly ignored. Many everyday actions, good and bad, carry with them low-level risks of death, others' or one's own. Thinking about such risks ordinarily nurtures fruitless anxiety, so in practical reflection there is no obligation to bear them in mind, investigate them, or take them into account. Moral questions about risking death arise only if a risk comes to attention, either spontaneously or by someone's pointing it out, as a reason for not making a choice one otherwise might make.

a) Risking death as a side effect of any sin is always wrong. If a person becomes aware that carrying out a choice would involve a risk to anyone's life, that is a reason not to do it, and the act cannot rightly be chosen without some other good reason for doing so. But there cannot be a good reason to commit any sin. Therefore, deliberately accepting any risk to anyone's life in doing something otherwise sinful aggravates the seriousness of the sin. For example, people who wish to keep their weight down but eat too much—venially sinful gluttony (see *S.t.,* 2–2, q. 148, a. 2)—and are warned that they are risking untimely death from arterial disease, commit a more serious sin if they do not try to change their habits and deliberately go on taking this unjustifiable risk to life.

b) One should strictly observe traffic laws. Like all laws, traffic laws must be interpreted reasonably, and doing so takes into account customs, with limits generally marked by a certain level of law enforcement, which diverge from the written law (see 11.D.1.c–d). Still, when reasonably interpreted, traffic laws generally are just and applicable, and then any disobedience to them is sinful (see *CMP,* 11.E). The risk of serious harm, including personal injury and even death to oneself and others, increases if they are disobeyed, and, being a side effect of sinfully violating the laws, it cannot be rightly accepted and increases the moral

---

46. See St. Ambrose, *De officiis* 3.4.27, *PL,* 16:153; St. Cyprian, Letter 60 (to Pope Cornelius), in S. Thasci Caecili Cypriani, *Opera omnia,* ed. W. Hartel, Corpus Scriptorum Ecclesiasticorum Latinorum (Vienna: 1871), 3.2:693 (cited in National Conference of Catholic Bishops, "Challenge of Peace: God's Promise and Our Response," 113, in *Pastoral Letters,* ed. Nolan, 4:524); St. Bernard, *De praecepto et dispensatione,* 7.13, *PL,* 182:869. St. Thomas (and classical moral theology), on the contrary, thought that one should use deadly force, if necessary, in self-defense and accept an assailant's death, "because one has a stronger duty to take care of one's own life than another's" (*S.t.,* 2–2, q. 64, a. 7). This view, however, seems to overlook mercy.

significance of any violation. Pius XII, pointing out that everyone has a "grave duty to respect the lives of others," concludes: "The often dramatic consequences of violating the traffic code give its observance an extrinsic obligatory character far more serious than people generally think."[47]

c) **Fairness can require that a risk of death not be accepted.** Sometimes one's responsibilities to others make it clear that it is unfair to accept a risk of death to them or even to oneself. Clearly, for instance, business partners who market a product whose use might lead to fatal accidents, while warning their own loved ones not to use it, unfairly risk customers' deaths. High public officials whose death would be detrimental to the common good take unfair risks if they evade their body guards out of mere bravado or annoyance with constant, close protection.

If someone doubts whether it is fair to risk his or her own or another's death, and has no moral responsibility to take the risky alternative even if it is permissible, its riskiness is a reason not to take it, and so it is wrong to do so. Plainly, for example, those who drink heavily and drive act unfairly, since they are severely impaired. But if a person is only slightly intoxicated and it will be inconvenient to avoid driving, he or she might doubt whether it would be fair to take the risk. In such cases, the question is whether there is a morally acceptable alternative to taking the risk, supposing it permissible to do so; if there is, the risk should be avoided.

However, if someone doubts whether it is fair to risk his or her own or another's death, yet would have a clear moral responsibility to take the risky alternative assuming it is permissible, the risk should be accepted. For example, John can earn a good living only in a hazardous occupation. He marries, and the couple begin having children. John's wife worries about him and urges him to quit; he wonders whether it is fair to her to continue his hazardous work. But he judges that, in order to provide his children with better opportunities, his responsibilities would require him to keep the job, assuming that would not be unfair to his wife. So, he should dismiss his doubts about fairness to his wife and take the risk.

d) **Sometimes significant risks of death should or may be taken.** Physicians, nurses, police officers, lifeguards, fire fighters, priests, and so on undertake important duties toward others. At times, they must risk their own lives to fulfill those duties; and if, motivated by fear, they avoid doing so, they are derelict in their duty and sin gravely through cowardice. But if they do take necessary risks, they are only doing their duty with appropriate courage, and are not heroes in the same sense as those who do brave deeds beyond the call of duty.

Suppose someone is aware that a prospective act, not his or her duty but otherwise morally acceptable, would entail a risk to life; suppose, too, that he or she is certain that accepting the risk would not be unfair; then this individual should examine the motives inclining him or her to choose that act. Sometimes feelings unintegrated with faith and personal vocation may be at work. For instance, a young

---

47. Pius XII, Address to Delegates Attending the Second World Congress of the International Highway Federation, *Discorsi e radiomessaggi* 17 (1955–56): 275; *The Pope Speaks* 2 (1955): 335. Also see Daniel L. Lowery, C.Ss.R., "Moral Code for Motorists," *Liguorian* 48 (Feb. 1960): 1–8.

man offered a hazardous job at high pay should not take it solely out of a desire for the money; but he may accept the job if he needs the money for some good purpose or judges the work to be an important service to others. Again, a young woman might think of taking up sky diving merely in order to experience the thrill of this sport. On that basis, it would be wrong to take the risks involved. But she might have a sound reason for choosing a somewhat risky sport, for example, as a form of recreation which she thinks would help her overcome extreme shyness and meet some suitable young men, and so carry out what she thinks is her vocation to marriage. On that basis, assuming there is no other reason to avoid the risk, she may take it.

e) **Wrongly accepting risks to life seems always to be grave matter.** Whenever an act involves a risk to another's life and is certainly unfair, the matter seems to be grave, since people regard risk to life as significant. Even if the risk is only to one's own life but taking it certainly is unfair, the potential effect on others must be significant, and so the matter of the act seems to be grave.

It also seems that other cases in which someone admits it is wrong to accept a risk to life—excessive eating by the obese, smoking, unnecessary driving when slightly intoxicated, and so on—should be considered grave matter, since it is hard to see how someone who loves himself or herself and others can deliberately accept a risk to life, even if it is slight, while recognizing the wrongness of doing so.

Nevertheless, the Church's teaching hardly touches explicitly on these sins and nowhere makes it clear that they are always grave. In the absence of clear Church teaching, one hesitates to assert that any kind of act never admits parvity. Thus, unless accepting a risk to life is plainly wrong and the risk is so great that almost everyone considers it significant, someone might be able to judge honestly that the matter is light.

3. Choosing to Risk Death Is Always Gravely Wrong

It is one thing to accept a risk of death as the side effect of some other act, but quite another to choose precisely to risk death, whether one's own or another's, as a means to some ulterior end. This latter choice always is wrong, and gravely so.

a) **Choosing to risk death is choosing to kill.** People sometimes precisely choose to risk their own lives out of bravado or for thrills. For example, young people play "chicken": driving vehicles down the center of a road toward a head-on collision, with the understanding that the first driver to turn away shows lack of courage. In doing this, they choose the risk to their own lives (and accept the risk to others') as a means to their end. Again, managers of some spectacles want performers to risk their lives in order to attract larger audiences through the morbid fascination of a dangerous performance.

In all such cases, where the risk to life is included in the proposal adopted by choice, the choice is gravely evil; it actually is a conditional will to kill, since the choice is of death if the risk should materialize, a contingency outside the power of the one making the choice, assuming the risk is real.

b) **Not all death-defying acts carry out a choice to risk death.** Sometimes an action involves a risk to life that enhances its value, yet the action can be chosen for a good reason, with the risk to life only accepted as a side effect, not chosen as a means. For example, because of the danger involved, high-wire performers who work without a net both require great skill and provide a more exciting performance. In choosing to work without a net, they can be choosing the more difficult, and so inherently more entertaining and rewarding, art; they need not be choosing precisely to risk life as a means to excite and entertain. The former choice is significantly different from that of a daredevil whose performance involves no special skill, but derives its value as entertainment entirely from the fact that the stunt may end in disaster. Here the choice is to risk life (to kill himself or herself if the stunt is unsuccessful) in order to attain an ulterior end (fame and fortune if the stunt succeeds).

Question D: Is Abortion Always the Wrongful Killing of a Person?

Abortion sometimes is used to refer to any ending of a pregnancy, whether induced or a miscarriage, before the unborn can survive. But insofar as a miscarriage neither is nor presupposes any human act, it is a medical problem, posing no moral questions other than those relevant to any sort of fatal accident, for example, whether it was due to carelessness.

Considered as a human act, abortion is the deliberate ending of pregnancy before the unborn can survive, or, later, by a method chosen with the intention that the unborn not survive. It is not abortion to induce birth when the child is expected and intended to survive. (The morality of inducing birth should be judged in each case by the norms for accepting a risk to another's life.)

In principle, the morality of killing the unborn is the same as that of killing people already born.[48] Yet abortion presents two special difficulties. First, questions are raised about the status of the unborn: Are they really persons? When do people begin? Second, questions are raised about the application of relevant norms: In difficult cases, how can one act with proper regard for the lives of both the child and the mother? How does the distinction between intentional killing and accepting death as a side effect apply to acts that lead to the death of the unborn?[49]

+ + +

48. A treatment of various aspects of abortion: Germain Grisez, *Abortion: The Myths, the Realities, and the Arguments* (New York: Corpus Books, 1970); note, however, that this work not only is outdated in some respects by subsequent developments but superseded both by the line of argument offered here for the personhood of the unborn and by more adequate research in some areas by others; for example, see Connery, *Abortion,* for the history of Catholic teaching on abortion.

49. Many documents of the magisterium deal with abortion; see, for example: Congregation for the Doctrine of the Faith, *Declaration on Procured Abortion, AAS* 66 (1974) 730–47, Flannery, 2:441–53; Ad Hoc Committee on Pro-Life Activities, National Conference of Catholic Bishops, "Pastoral Guidelines for the Catholic Hospital and Catholic Health Care Personnel" (11 Apr. 1973), in *Pastoral Letters,* ed. Nolan, 3:370–74.

1. It Is Reasonable to Hold that Human Persons Begin at Fertilization

Vatican II, pointing out that God has given human persons the responsibility of safeguarding life, draws the conclusion: "Therefore from the moment of its conception life must be guarded with the greatest care, while abortion and infanticide are unspeakable crimes" (GS 51). The Congregation for the Doctrine of the Faith points out that the Council's teaching only summarizes and reaffirms unbroken Christian tradition: "The tradition of the Church has always held that human life must be protected and cherished from the beginning, just as at the various stages of its development."[50] So, John Paul II says nothing new in repeating over and over that human life is inviolable from the moment of conception.[51]

a) **Personhood is not a status that other people confer.** Persons exist only with other persons, and the social recognition of one's personhood leads to social respect for one's essential dignity and the fundamental rights flowing from it. Noting these facts, some draw the conclusion that personhood is a social status, rather like family membership or citizenship, which parents or society can confer or refuse to confer.[52] However, the conclusion does not follow. While it is true that personhood does have important social implications, not everything social is subject to human determination, for human society itself presupposes persons and their essential attributes, including their equal personal dignity and fundamental rights. Moreover, the view that other people confer personhood conflicts with faith's teaching that God creates all human persons in his own image and likeness, and destines each for a personal relationship with himself: "Before I formed you in the womb I knew you, and before you were born I consecrated you" (Jer 1.5; cf. Ps 139.13, Is 49.1, 2 Mc 7.20–23, Gal 1.15).

b) **Personhood is not an attribute attained by development.** Human individuals can claim and exercise their rights as persons only after becoming aware of their own interests. Some argue from this fact for a developmental view of

---

50. Congregation for the Doctrine of the Faith, *Declaration on Procured Abortion*, 6, *AAS* 66 (1974) 733, Flannery, 2:443. Canon law emphasizes abortion's seriousness by treating it as a special crime: *CIC*, c. 1398: "A person who procures a completed abortion incurs an automatic excommunication." Accomplices incur the penalty if the abortion would not have been done without their cooperation: c. 1329, §2. Although the Church always has held that it is grave matter to destroy unborn life at any stage of development, canon law has not always treated abortion at the early stages as a crime: see Roger John Huser, O.F.M., *The Crime of Abortion in Canon Law: An Historical Synopsis and Commentary* (Washington, D.C.: The Catholic University of America Press, 1942), 30–78.

51. For examples of such statements, see A.2.a, A.2.d, above. Besides the works cited in subsequent notes, for arguments to support the view that the person begins at conception, see Francis C. Wade, S.J., "Potentiality in the Abortion Discussion," *Review of Metaphysics* 29 (1975): 239–55; John Gallagher, C.S.B., *Is the Human Embryo a Person? A Philosophical Investigation* (Toronto: Human Life Research Institute, 1985); Germain Grisez, "When Do People Begin?" *Proceedings of the American Catholic Philosophical Association* 63 (1989): 27–47.

52. See, for example, Pierre de Locht, "Discussion," in *L'Avortement: Actes du Xème colloque international de sexologie* (Louvain: Centre International Cardinal Suenens, 1968), 2:155; Louis Beirnaert, S.J., "L'avortement: est-il un infanticide?" *Études* 333 (1970): 520–23; Mary Warnock, "Do Human Cells Have Rights?" *Bioethics* 1 (1987): 2.

personhood: that it begins only after birth, when a child becomes self-conscious, aware of his or her own future, and concerned about it. Until that happens, according to this view, unborn and even newborn babies are only potential persons.[53] This argument also is fallacious. Human individuals can be persons with a right to life before they are aware of that right and able to claim it. So, unborn and newborn babies are not potential persons; they are actual persons, although they are only potentially self-conscious and concerned about their future as adults.

Both this notion of personhood and the previous one also miss what *person* usually means in ordinary language, where the word refers to newborn babies and the severely retarded as well as to normal, grown men and women.[54] One can see

---

53. A leading proponent of this view: Michael Tooley, *Abortion and Infanticide* (Oxford: Oxford University Press, 1983). Throughout his book, Tooley also proceeds on an implicit presupposition that the developmental view is to be preferred because it leads to what he thinks his readers will consider to be more satisfactory results than any alternative view. For an explicit argument along the same lines, see Daniel Callahan, *Abortion: Law, Choice and Morality* (New York: Macmillan, 1970), who embraces the developmental view (although he does not face its implications for infanticide): "Abortion is an act of killing, the violent, direct destruction of potential human life, already in the process of development. That fact should not be disguised, or glossed over by euphemism and circumlocution. It is not the destruction of a human person—for at no stage of its development does the conceptus fulfill the definition of a person, which implies a developed capacity for reasoning, willing, desiring and relating to others—but it is the destruction of an important and valuable form of human life" (497–98; cf. 384–89, where he first adopts the developmental notion of personhood). Callahan likes this view partly for the precise reason that it "provides a way of weighing the comparative value of the lives at stake" (396). This argument is an instance of consequentialism (criticized in *CMP*, 6). As usual, the consequentialist who provides the scales determines the outcome of the weighing: for Callahan, the "body-life" of the potential person is easily outweighed by the "person-life" of the pregnant woman in "a huge number of situations" (496; cf. 398, 498).

54. Both *Webster's Third New International Dictionary* and the *Oxford English Dictionary* say that a standard use of *person* is to refer to a living, human individual. Criticizing Grisez, *Abortion: The Myths, the Realities, and the Arguments,* for holding that a person is "nothing more than a living human individual," Michael J. Coughlan, *The Vatican, the Law and the Human Embryo* (Iowa City, Iowa: University of Iowa Press, 1990), 61, says: "In fact Grisez seems to think that where we draw the line between persons and non-persons is almost arbitrary: 'Anyone with sufficient ingenuity in metaphysical argument should be able to construct some sort of plausible theory of personality according to which any one of us will turn out to be a non-person' [reference to p. 306].' Why, then, does Grisez think that his definition should be given preference? Because, he suggests, it is given in *Webster's Dictionary* as the oldest meaning of the word, and because it is a more comprehensive definition than later alternatives, such as 'a being characterised by conscious apprehension, rationality and a moral sense'. Public policy for a pluralistic society ought to accept the more comprehensive view, he argues [reference to pp. 418f.]." However, as here, the reference to the dictionary definition of *person* in *Abortion* is part of a more extensive argument, and both that reference and the consideration about comprehensiveness occur in a jurisprudential argument (418–19), more than one hundred pages after the conclusion of the argument for the personhood of the unborn (306), from which Coughlan's quotation is drawn. He simply ignores the argument itself, which begins (273) with the heading: "Is the Aborted Embryo or Fetus a Human Being?" Moreover, the sentence before the one Couglan quotes (from 306) is: "If a utilitarian theory is accepted, not only the personhood of the unborn, but the personhood of all of us is put in jeopardy"; thus, instead of saying "Grisez seems to think that where we draw the line between persons and non-persons is almost arbitrary" Couglan should have said: "Grisez argues that once utilitarianism is accepted, the drawing of the line between persons and non-persons becomes arbitrary."

why *person* is used as it is by considering how people think and talk about themselves. They regularly speak in ways that show they think of their personhood, not as an acquired trait, but as an aspect of what they are. When someone says "I was born at such and such a time and place," the word *I* refers to the same being the speaker now is. This way of talking shows that the concept of person connotes an essential property, which implies that whatever has it necessarily has it and never exists without it. Hence, what people usually think of as an individual person simultaneously comes to be and becomes a person, and cannot cease to be a person without ceasing to be the individual he or she is.[55] To use *person* in a different, special sense, and to say that unborn and newborn babies are only potential persons, as proponents of the developmental view do, is to manipulate language and discriminate against those who have not developed sufficiently to be aware of their right to life.[56]

c) **Human persons are not realities other than their living bodies.** Human persons can do things—think, make free choices, put things to use—which show that they are more than bodies. Moreover, not only Christians but most other people think a person's soul (or spirit or ghost) somehow continues to exist after death. On the basis of such facts, some think human persons are spiritual realities essentially other than their living bodies, and they argue that, although abortion destroys a living human body, it does not destroy a person.[57] This argument also is fallacious. Persons can be more than their bodies without being realities other than their bodies, since a whole can be more than one of its parts without being a reality other than that part.

Bodily life is an intrinsic good of persons (see above, A.2). Certainly, human persons are more than their bodies, and so persons cannot be identified exclusively with their bodies. Yet experience shows that one is not a reality other than one's living body, since one is the subject of one's bodily properties, processes, sensations, and feelings, just as truly as one is the subject of one's intellectual knowledge, choices, and more-than-bodily use of things to achieve one's purposes.[58] Therefore,

55. To develop this argument, see David Wiggins, "Locke, Butler and the Stream of Consciousness: and Men as a Natural Kind," *Philosophy* 51 (1976): 131–58, and the works Wiggins cites in his n. 33; James W. Anderson, "Three Abortion Theorists: A Critical Appraisal" (Ph.D. diss., Georgetown University, 1985), 176–201; Michael Lockwood, "Warnock versus Powell (and Harradine): When Does Potentiality Count?" *Bioethics* 2 (1988): 187–213; idem, "Hare on Potentiality: A Rejoinder," *Bioethics* 2 (1988): 343–52.

56. Stephen D. Schwarz, *The Moral Question of Abortion* (Chicago: Loyola University Press, 1990), 86–112, develops some other lines of argument against the developmental view, and points out some implications of using for personhood criteria that are subject to degree. On this, also see Grisez and Boyle, *Life and Death with Liberty and Justice,* 229–36. Two criticisms of the earlier version of Tooley's argument will repay study: James G. Hanink, "Persons, Rights, and the Problem of Abortion" (Ph.D. diss., Michigan State University, 1975), 42–172; Gary M. Atkinson, "Persons in the Whole Sense," *American Journal of Jurisprudence* 22 (1977): 86–117.

57. See Joseph Fletcher, *Morals and Medicine* (Boston: Beacon, 1954), 152, 211–13; Tooley, *Abortion and Infanticide,* 64, 103, 130, 154–55, 163–64, 175–76.

58. Some philosophical arguments against dualism (the view that human bodies are not persons): B. A. O. Williams, "Are Persons Bodies?" in *The Philosophy of the Body: Rejections of Cartesian Dualism,* ed. Stuart F. Spicker (New York: Quadrangle/New York Times Books, 1970), 137–56; Gabriel Marcel, *The Mystery of Being,* vol. 1, *Reflection and Mystery* (Chicago:

that persons transcend bodies does not provide any ground for supposing that in destroying a living human body abortion destroys something other than a person.

   d) **A personal soul should be considered present from conception.** Relying on Aristotle's biology, St. Thomas thought that an active power in the semen gradually forms a new living individual out of only potentially living matter (the menstrual blood) and that the developing body is not ready to be informed by a personal soul until at least forty days after conception.[59] While Aristotle's biology is universally rejected today, some nevertheless appeal to the theory of St. Thomas in support of the premise that, since the soul is the substantial form (that is, intrinsic, constitutive, determinative principle) of the living body and a substantial form can exist only in matter able to receive it, the personal soul can exist only in a highly organized body. They add a further premise, that specifically personal acts—thinking, making free choices—depend on sense organs and a brain. So, they conclude, an early embryo cannot be a human person, but is really only a prepersonal entity, which substantially changes into a person when the sense organs and brain begin to develop. (Against St. Thomas, they go on to assume that abortion of a prepersonal entity might be justified.)[60]

   Even after being born, however, babies at first show no signs of being able to think and make free choices. The beginning of the brain's development is not yet the bodily basis required for specifically personal acts but only its precursor. If this precursor satisfies the requirements of the theory of St. Thomas, there is no reason

Henry Regnery, 1960), 127–53; Grisez and Boyle, *Life and Death with Liberty and Justice,* 70–71, 375–79, 402; J. M. Cameron, "Bodily Existence," *Proceedings of the American Catholic Philosophical Association* 53 (1979): 59–70. On Kant's form of dualism and some related theories: Joseph M. Boyle, Jr., Germain Grisez, and Olaf Tollefsen, *Free Choice: A Self-Referential Argument* (Notre Dame, Ind.: University of Notre Dame Press, 1976), 110–21.

   59. Congregation for the Doctrine of the Faith, *Declaration on Procured Abortion,* 7, *AAS* 66 (1974) 734, Flannery, 2:443, points out that "the various opinions on the infusion of the spiritual soul did not cast doubt on the illicitness of abortion. It is true that in the Middle Ages, when the opinion was generally held that the spiritual soul was not present until after the first few weeks, a distinction was made in the evaluation of the sin and the gravity of penal sanctions. In resolving cases, approved authors were more lenient with regard to that early stage than with regard to later stages. But it was never denied at that time that procured abortion, even during the first days, was objectively a grave sin." A reading of Connery's detailed history, previously cited, substantiates this assertion. And it stands to reason that through the centuries in which all Christians considered both contraception and abortion grave sins, theoretical doubts about the personhood of the early conceptus made little practical difference to judgments about the immorality of attempts to terminate pregnancy at that stage.

   60. Joseph F. Donceel, S.J., "Immediate Animation and Delayed Hominization," *Theological Studies* 31 (1970): 76–105, argues for this view. Also see Thomas A. Shannon and Allan B. Wolter, O.F.M., "Reflections on the Moral Status of the Pre-Embryo," *Theological Studies* 51 (1990): 603–26, who attempt to support the theory by appealing to additional supposed facts, some drawn from the work of Norman M. Ford, S.D.B., which will be criticized below, and others from sources such as Carlos A. Bedate and Robert C. Cefalo, "The Zygote: To Be or Not To Be a Person," *Journal of Medicine and Philosophy* 14 (1989): 641–45, whom Shannon and Wolter use to support their view that the zygote does not contain sufficient genetic information to "develop into an embryo that will be the precursor of an individual member of the human species" (608). However, Antoine Suarez, "Hydatidiform Moles and Teratomas Confirm the Human Identity of the Preimplantation Embryo," *Journal of Medicine and Philosophy* 15 (1990): 627–35, argues cogently that recent research contradicts the Bedate-Cefalo thesis.

why precursors at earlier developmental stages should not also satisfy them. But modern biology makes it clear that each embryonic individual has from the outset its specific developmental tendency, which includes the epigenetic primordia (the sources for the development) of all its organs. Therefore, if the soul can exist only in a matter able to receive it, that fact does not mean that a human zygote cannot have a personal soul.[61] It follows that the supposition that the human embryo is at first a prepersonal entity, which only later becomes a person, posits two entities where only one is necessary to account for the observed facts. But entities are not to be multiplied without necessity. Consequently, the view that the embryo becomes a person when the brain begins to develop should be rejected, and the personal soul should be considered to be present from conception.[62]

   e) Absence of brain functioning is compatible with personhood. Some argue by analogy that, since brain death is sufficient to mark the death of the person, the onset of brain function is necessary to mark the person's beginning.[63] Some who propose this argument may think the irreversible loss of cerebral (higher brain) functions marks the person's death, but that view is vulnerable to the same

---

61. Against Donceel's theory, Benedict Ashley, O.P., offers cogent criticism: "A Critique of the Theory of Delayed Hominization," in *An Ethical Evaluation of Fetal Experimentation: An Interdisciplinary Study,* ed. Donald G. McCarthy and Albert S. Moraczewski, O.P. (St. Louis: The Pope John Center, 1976), 113–33. Ashley points out that Donceel drastically understates the case when he says that St. Thomas knew well that the early embryo was not yet a fully organized body. In fact, following Aristotle, Thomas thought that life originates from the semen and the menstrual blood, that neither is alive, and that the very limited, active instrumental power in the semen only gradually organizes the blood into a body that can begin to grow and nourish itself. But Thomas also held that God's infinite power accomplished instantaneously in the conception of Jesus what the semen's power normally takes forty or eighty days to do. Thus, it seems that Thomas accepted Aristotle's theory of the person's becoming, not because he thought that matter cannot receive a personal soul until it has the organs required for the sensory basis of spiritual activities, but only because he thought that the semen's power is so limited that it cannot bring about the epigenetic primordium of the personal body until forty or eighty days. Against some more recent arguments for delayed animation, see Augustine Regan, C.Ss.R., "The Human Conceptus and Personhood," *Studia Moralia* 30 (1992): 97–127; Stephen J. Heaney, "Aquinas and the Presence of the Human Rational Soul in the Early Embryo," *Thomist* 56 (1992): 19–48.

62. Moreover, to maintain his hypothesis, Donceel is forced to add another. He stresses ("Immediate Animation," 85) that the soul, as form, cannot be the efficient cause of the embryo's development, rather, the soul is the term of the generative process. St. Thomas thought that the father imparted instrumental efficacy to the semen, and that the semen remained present as the active principle of development. Since that hypothesis plainly is mistaken, Donceel offers another: somewhat as in evolutionary development of humans from lower forms of life, God is the proper efficient cause of embryonic development, creatively transforming the parents' contributions until the material is ready to receive a personal soul, which he then also creates. Donceel also claims (92–96) that historical evidence shows that delayed hominization was given up under the influence both of the erroneous biological theory of preformation and of Cartesian dualism. This is not so: Grisez, *Abortion,* 171–72.

63. A clear statement of this argument: Robert M. Veatch, "Definitions of Life and Death: Should There Be Consistency?" in *Defining Human Life: Medical, Legal, and Ethical Implications,* ed. Margery W. Shaw and A. Edward Doudera (Ann Arbor, Mich.: AUPHA Press, 1983), 99–113.

criticisms as the developmental view of the person's beginning. However, only the irreversible loss of all brain functions is reasonably taken as marking the death of the person.[64]

When *brain death* is correctly understood, the argument by analogy fails, because it depends on the assumption that the absence of brain functioning has the same significance at life's beginning as at its end. This is false, for when the whole brain is dead, there is no principle to integrate the functioning of the organism, and so the organism has ceased to be; therefore, the person is dead. By contrast, before the brain develops—even in the zygote (that is, the new, one-celled individual resulting from the fertilization of the ovum by a sperm)—something does integrate the whole embryo's organic functioning, and so a unified human individual is developing. As the development of the whole goes on, so does the development of its integrating principle (whatever that is at various stages), until, finally, the mature brain integrates the mature individual's functioning.

f) Absence of familiar personal qualities is compatible with personhood. Many arguments against the personhood of the unborn depend on common sense assumptions. For example, someone indicates some clear and striking difference between the early embryo and any experientially typical person, even a newborn: "The fertilized egg is much smaller than the period at the end of this sentence," or "It has no eyes, no ears, no mouth, no brain, and, like a parasite, draws nourishment from the pregnant woman's blood." Pictures or drawings of very early embryos support such statements (just as pictures of twelve-week and older embryos support statements that they are persons), and this evidence is thought to show that the embryo becomes a person only after a period of development.

Such arguments are persuasive because they use imagery and directly affect feelings. Usually, in judging whether or not to apply a predicate to an experienced entity, one does not examine it to see whether it meets a set of intelligible criteria; instead, one judges by appearances, using as a guide past experience of individuals of that kind. Thus, people unfamiliar with snow and ice would find it strange that they are considered to be forms of water. The early embryo, usually never experienced, falls far outside the range of sensory standards for recognizing people; the test of appearances suggests that this strange entity is not a person. People react to images of early embryos as they might when seeing persons of a different race for the first time in their lives: those strangers surely are not people.

This argument can be answered only by dealing with its instances. In each case it is necessary to point out that, while the particular difference is striking because of the normal limits of human experience, entities that are different in that way certainly are living, human individuals.[65] Then it can be pointed out that to deny that these individuals are persons simply on the basis of their small size or odd appearance would be discriminatory.

---

64. See Grisez and Boyle, *Life and Death with Liberty and Justice,* 59–78; Benedict M. Ashley, O.P., and Kevin D. O'Rourke, O.P., *Healthcare Ethics: A Theological Analysis,* 3rd ed. (St. Louis: Catholic Health Association of the United States, 1989), 366–68.

65. Schwarz, *The Moral Question of Abortion,* 70–85, skillfully treats several versions of the common sense argument, and in doing so provides a model for treating others.

g) **A person normally begins at conception.** The preceding considerations show that human personhood cannot reasonably be denied of any living human individual; and the observed facts, as summarized by a biologist, show: "Fertilization in mammals normally represents the beginning of life for a new individual."[66] Therefore, conception, in the sense of fertilization—when the sperm and the ovum fuse—normally should be regarded as the beginning of a new person. But why *normally* and not *always?* Because the complications which sometimes arise require certain qualifications.[67]

Sometimes an early embryo divides and identical twins (or even more than two identical individuals) are formed. Moreover, abnormal fertilization can result in a hydatidiform mole: a growing mass of tissue, genetically distinct from the mother, but without the organization required to develop into a baby.[68] While admitting that every living human individual is a person, some cite these and other facts in arguing that new human individuals do not begin at conception, when the sperm fertilizes the ovum. Instead, they say, conception results in a mass of separate and distinct cells from which a human individual arises only at the primitive-streak stage of development, when the embryo is implanted in the wall of the womb, and the new individual or individuals take definite shape with recognizable boundaries: a right side and a left side, a front and a back, a head end and a lower end. After that, the number of individuals will not change unless some die.[69] Hence, they conclude, new human individuals, which are persons, begin two to three weeks after conception.

The first thing to notice is that the phenomena from which this argument begins are exceptions. Most unborn babies with their accessory tissues develop from a single zygote and are alone in developing from that zygote. So, in most cases individuality appears to begin at fertilization and to be continuous. Moreover, the facts do not support this theory's assumption that fertilization and subsequent cell division keep giving rise to really distinct individuals until a small army of them form the true human individual.

66. This statement appears at the beginning of a recent, masterful, fifty-page summary of what is currently known about mammalian fertilization: R. Yanagimachi, "Mammalian Fertilization," in *The Physiology of Reproduction,* ed. E. Knobil et al. (New York: Raven, 1988), 135.

67. For a good, slightly fuller statement of these arguments and replies to them, using somewhat different materials than those used here, see Albert S. Moraczewski, O.P., "Personhood: Entry and Exit," in *The Twenty-fifth Anniversary of Vatican II: A Look Back and a Look Ahead,* ed. Russell E. Smith (Braintree, Mass.: The Pope John Center, 1990), 87–96.

68. Suarez, "Hydatidiform Moles and Teratomas," 629, describes the origin of such moles: "Hydatidiform moles of the complete type (CHM) arise from androgenetic eggs (i.e., from eggs with two paternal nuclei). Most CHM arise from fusion of an egg and sperm followed by duplication of the sperm genome and loss of the female nucleus. A smaller number of CHM arise by dispermy (two sperms enter into the egg) and loss of the female nucleus [citations of supporting scientific articles omitted]."

69. The fullest articulation of this line of argument: Norman M. Ford, S.D.B., *When Did I Begin? Conception of the Human Individual in History, Philosophy and Science* (Cambridge: Cambridge University Press, 1988). An excellent critique of Ford's book: Anthony Fisher, O.P., "Individuogenesis and a Recent Book by Fr. Norman Ford," *Anthropotes* 7 (1991): 199–244. Also see Nicholas Tonti-Filippini, "A Critical Note," *Linacre Quarterly* 56 (Aug. 1989): 36–50.

When a new human divides into identical twins, one may speculate that perhaps the fertilized ovum contained primordia for two individuals from the outset. Even if not, however, such twins can be explained by saying that two generations have occurred rather than one, the first by the usual process of sexual reproduction, and the second by an unusual process of asexual reproduction: either the first individual reproduced by giving up part of itself, or the original individual ceased to be when it split, and two new individuals came to be. There is no logical or biological reason to reject this explanation.[70]

Some will object: But if this is so, when a couple have identical twins, they are really the grandparents of one or both of the babies, which is indeed odd. It is odd, but this oddity does not show that the explanation is faulty. Rather it shows that, while the facts provide some basis for saying that couples are "grandparents" of their identically twin offspring, there also are good reasons to follow ordinary usage and call them "parents." But neither word's meaning and connotations are entirely suited to the actual situation, which, being unusual, is bound to vex common sense.

A hydatidiform mole is a new organic individual, genetically both human and unique, but it is not a new human being. Why not? A sperm and an ovum are two distinct organisms, each an individual cell with its own membrane. A sperm loses its membrane when it enters the ovum; the ovum quickly reacts; the two cells fuse into one, and the process of development begins.[71] The sperm and the ovum no longer exist as distinct entities; the activated ovum is a new, biologically human individual.[72] If it has in itself the epigenetic primordia of a human body normal enough to be the organic basis of any intellectual act whatsoever, this new individual is a person. But the activated ovum lacks these primordia if it includes in itself anything predetermining it to develop into a hydatidiform mole.[73]

---

70. The fact that individual plants remain individuals although they could be divided and grafted shows that there is nothing logically or biologically absurd in an organism remaining substantially the same although it could have been divided into two or more individuals of the same kind or combined with another or others. On this and other facts used by Ford and others to argue against the individual's beginning at fertilization, see Thomas V. Daly, S.J., "The Status of Embryonic Human Life: A Crucial Issue in Genetic Counselling," in *Health Care Priorities in Australia: 1985 Conference Proceedings*, ed. Nicholas Tonti-Filippini (Melbourne, Australia: St. Vincent's Bioethics Centre, 1985), 45–57.

71. See Ford, *When Did I Begin?* 102–8. If two or more sperm enter before the ovum reacts, the resultant individual, which may be a hydatidiform mole, cannot develop normally. A factual description of the fusion of sperm and ovum and the initial development of the new individual: R. G. Edwards, *Conception in the Human Female* (London: Academic Press, 1980), 593–605.

72. For a detailed defense of the position that the new individual begins at this point, not at syngamy, see: St. Vincent's Bioethics Centre Working Party, "Identifying the Origin of a Human Life: The Search for a Marker Event for the Origin of a Human Life," *St. Vincent's Bioethics Centre Newsletter* 5.1 (Mar. 1987): 4–6; T. V. Daly, S.J., "Individuals, Syngamy and the Origin of Human Life: A Reply to Buckle and Dawson," *St. Vincent's Bioethics Centre Newsletter* 6.4 (Dec. 1988): 1–7.

73. An analogous account, presumably, can be given of any embryo having so abnormal a genetic structure or organization that it is intrinsically predetermined never to develop a brain. This seems true, too, of an ovum developing parthenogenetically; however, if some parthenogenetically developing human ovum had in itself the necessary epigenetic primordia, it too would be a person. What about an anencephalic baby? In most cases the cause of anencephaly is unknown, and cases vary greatly: D. Alan Shewmon, "Anencephaly: Selected Medical Aspects," *Hastings*

Nor does the fact that the embryo proper first becomes recognizable at the primitive-streak stage show that a substantial change brings the person into being only at this stage. For this line of argument is simply an appeal to common sense: everyone whom one knows has at least a recognizable, definitely shaped body; but prior to the primitive-streak stage, one cannot point out the embryo's head end and lower end, its front and back, its right and left sides; so, prior to this stage there is no "real" human individual. Like all appeals to common sense, this argument is based on appearances. It does not show that a substantial change occurs at the primitive-streak stage, for it does not show that either a new individual or the epigenetic primordia of a developed human person are absent at fertilization.

h) Personhood is not disproved by a high mortality rate. Arguing that pregnancy losses before implantation are frequent, some theologians object to basing moral norms on the supposition that the new person begins at conception: "Will [today's moral theologian] be able to admit that 50 percent of the 'human beings'—real human beings with an 'immortal' soul and an eternal destiny—do not, from the very start, get beyond this first stage of a human existence?"[74]

The premise probably is false, since no one has shown that pregnancy losses are so high. However, even if the premise were true, the argument proves nothing. For many natural pregnancy losses are due to such severe chromosomal defects that the individual probably lacks the epigenetic primordia for a body normal enough to be the basis for any intellectual act (in which case, as explained above, these are not losses of human beings). Then too, for most of human history the infant mortality rate was very high. Are we to say that during that time infants were not persons? Theologically, moreover, the argument is presumptuous, since neither revelation nor reason shows that God cannot provide appropriately for those who never come to the use of reason.

2. Every Human Should Be Considered a Person from Fertilization

Someone might object: Since there are so many complicated arguments on this matter, perhaps room remains for further questions about whether every human should be considered a person from fertilization. But this objection lacks force. There is no end to the raising of theoretical questions, but there are very strong factual and theoretical grounds for thinking that almost every human person once was a fertilized human ovum. The counterpositions are weak. There is no room for practical doubt.

To be willing to kill what for all one knows is a person is to be willing to kill a person. Hence, in making moral judgments people should consider the unborn persons from the beginning, their lives instances of innocent human life. As the

---

Center Report 18.5 (Oct.–Nov. 1988): 11–19. Even if such a baby now lacks (but previously had the primordium of) the bodily basis of some intellectual act, he or she is a brain-damaged person, just as is the adult whose higher brain functions are irreparably lost. The facts appear to show that the anencephalic baby is a brain-damaged person, and so in practice such babies should be regarded as persons with a right to life.

74. Donceel, "Immediate Animation," 100, quotes this from Karl Rahner, *Schriften zur Theologie,* 8 (Einsiedeln: 1967), 287 (*Theological Investigations,* vol. 9, *Writings of 1965–67: I,* trans. Graham Harrison [New York: Herder and Herder, 1972], 226).

magisterium teaches: "From a moral point of view this is certain: even if a doubt existed concerning whether the fruit of conception is already a human person, it is objectively a grave sin to dare to risk murder."[75]

3. The Norms Protecting Others' Lives Apply to the Unborn

Given the preceding answer to questions about the personhood of the unborn, only someone prepared to discriminate against them will deny that killing an unborn human individual is as bad as killing anyone else, and accepting or risking such an individual's death is as serious as accepting or risking anyone else's death. Thus, the magisterium often treats the killing of the unborn as an instance of the killing of the innocent (see the statement of Pius XII, quoted in B.3.b, above).

Moreover, John Paul II sometimes focuses on the peculiar malice of abortion and articulates the various aspects of its immorality:

> God willed the loving union of husband and wife to be the source of new life. He wishes to share, as it were, his creative power with husbands and wives, endowing them with procreative power. God desires that this tremendous power to procreate a new human life should be willingly and lovingly accepted by the couple when they freely choose to marry. Parenthood has a dignity all of its own, guaranteed by God himself. On my part I owe it to my Apostolic Office to reaffirm as clearly and as strongly as possible what the Church of Christ teaches in this respect, and to reiterate vigorously her condemnation of artificial contraception and abortion.
>
> Yes, from the moment of conception and through all subsequent stages, *all human life is sacred,* for it is created in the image and likeness of God. Human life is precious because it is a gift of God, whose love knows no limit; and when God gives life, it is forever. Whoever attempts to destroy human life in the womb of the mother, not only violates the sacredness of a living, growing and developing human being, and thus opposes God, but also attacks society by undermining respect for all human life. I want to repeat here what I stated when visiting my homeland: "If a person's right to life is violated at the moment in which he is first conceived in his mother's womb, an indirect blow is struck also at the whole moral order, which serves to ensure the inviolable goods of man. Among those goods, life occupies the first place. The Church defends the right to life, not only in regard to the majesty of the Creator, who is the first Giver of this life, but also in respect of the essential good of the human person."[76]

Both contraception and abortion are wrong, but abortion destroys the life of an actual person made in God's image, attacks society by undermining respect for all

---

75. Congregation for the Doctrine of the Faith, *Declaration on Procured Abortion,* 13, *AAS* 66 (1974) 739, Flannery, 2:446. The point is further explained (in n. 19, *AAS* 738, Flannery, 452): the question of the moment when the spiritual soul is infused "is a philosophical problem from which our moral affirmation remains independent for two reasons: (1) supposing a later animation, there is still nothing less than a *human* life, preparing for and calling for a soul in which the nature received from parents is completed; (2) on the other hand it suffices that this presence of the soul be probable (and one can never prove the contrary) in order that the taking of life involve accepting the risk of killing a man, not only waiting for, but already in possession of his soul."

76. John Paul II, Homily at Mass for Families (Cebu City, Philippines), 5–6, *AAS* 73 (1981) 365–66, *OR,* 2 Mar. 1981, 5, emphasis in *AAS*.

human life, and strikes a blow at the whole moral order, which protects not only life but every other basic human good.

a) **Abortion usually is intentional killing of the unborn.** An abortionist intends to kill the unborn baby. Usually, he or she does not will the baby's death for its own sake; the abortionist's immediate end is to provide the service sought by those who wish to terminate pregnancies, and that generally is a means to the ulterior end of being paid. Of course, performing abortions sometimes is required as part of a medical-training program. But regardless of their exact ends, abortionists regularly use techniques chosen to ensure the baby's destruction. Regarding a live birth as an unfortunate complication, they sometimes fulfill their undertaking by disposing of the tiny newborn in a way that will guarantee his or her prompt death.

Men who urge an abortion, arrange it, or pay for it usually intend the baby's death. While some are concerned for the woman and are trying to help her obtain what she wants, many consider cheap and easy abortion a welcome alternative to self-sacrificing love. Many men involved in abortion are irresponsible husbands or lovers, who have negligently generated a child whom they do not wish to support and father; others are trying to cope with the consequences of some other man's irresponsibility, while minimizing their own burden.

Women who seek an abortion also usually intend the baby's death. Most do not will that death as an end, for they do not simply hate the new life growing within them. But they have reasons for wishing they were not pregnant, reasons which sometimes are in themselves sound: health concerns or the desire to avoid hardship for existing children in an impoverished family. Most often, the woman is not prepared to accept the responsibilities of motherhood or, if she already has children, does not wish to add to her responsibilities. Perhaps she wanted to have a baby but now knows or fears that the baby she bears is suffering from some serious disease or defect, and so wishes to terminate this pregnancy and try again. Perhaps she was taken advantage of or even raped, perhaps she was betrayed by an unfaithful lover, perhaps she used contraceptives unsuccessfully. Regardless of the circumstances which led to the pregnancy, however, completing it, giving birth, and then giving up the baby are repugnant to the woman. The alternative of quickly getting rid of the child seems preferable.

Thus, a woman contemplating abortion usually has an ulterior end, good or bad, for wishing to undo the pregnancy, make everything (insofar as possible) as it was, and go on with her life just as if another new life had never been growing within her. Willing that ulterior end, she considers the proposal of pregnancy termination and adopts it by a free choice, knowing what this proposal really involves.

Of course, a pregnant woman, particularly one of low intelligence or little sophistication, can be so misinformed or confused that she truly believes that new life does not begin at conception; she simply does not grasp that her pregnancy means a child is growing within her. Thinking perhaps that the abortion will only bring on a delayed menstrual period or get rid of some sort of prepersonal beginning of life, she truly misunderstands what she is doing and is not merely engaging in self-deception and rationalization. In choosing abortion, all such a woman really intends is the prevention of a new person's coming to be: contraception. Also, women often choose abortion with great anguish and reluctance, under pressure from a social worker, a parent, a husband, a lover, an employer, a landlord, her own desperate need; reluctantly consenting to abortion, a woman may suffer it with great anguish as the only way to avoid what appears to be some disaster.

The point here is not to judge and condemn women undergoing abortion or others involved. It is simply that if they know the truth, that the abortion will destroy the life of a baby, those who choose abortion or formally cooperate in it usually intend the baby's death.[77] Almost always there are other ways to forestall or deal with the problems which lead to the choice of abortion, but they would require self-control and self-sacrifice, and it is easy to see these as greater evils than ending incipient life "when necessary."

b) Sometimes intentional abortion does not involve intentional killing. As explained above (in B.1), according to the analysis of action used in this work, intentional killing as a means is choosing (adopting a proposal) to kill or to do something understood in such a way that its very meaning implies bringing about death. By contrast, many classical moralists thought that "direct" killing as a means is positing an action that straightaway brings about death. In their view, all "direct" abortion is "direct" killing of the innocent. But on the view taken in this work, someone might choose to abort without choosing to kill.

For example, suppose a woman suffering from kidney disease becomes pregnant and wants to avoid the health problems that will result from carrying the child; or a woman becomes pregnant as a result of rape and wants to be freed of her ongoing suffering. In either case, and perhaps in a few others, in seeking abortion the precise object of the pregnant woman's choice might be, not the baby's death, but the termination of pregnancy as the necessary means to the end in view: a benefit expected to flow from the baby's removal rather than from the baby's death or any consequence of it. On this assumption, the proposal adopted is, not to kill the unborn baby, but to have him or her removed from the womb, with death as a foreseen and accepted side effect. An abortion carrying out such a choice would not be an intentional killing.

Someone might object that this analysis opens the way for everyone involved in abortions, even abortionists, to say they do not intend the baby's death, but only accept it as a side effect of terminating pregnancy. Many involved already claim abortion is only pregnancy termination and deny that they are killing babies; however, what matters is, not what anyone says, but what is really included in the proposal adopted when abortion is chosen as a means to some ulterior end. For reasons already sketched out, most people choosing abortion probably do regard killing the baby as necessary to their end; they consider the alternatives, find getting rid of the baby less repugnant than any other option, and rationalize choosing that

---

77. Through 1963, the Planned Parenthood Federation of America published a pamphlet, *Plan Your Children for Health and Happiness,* which contained the truthful statement: "An abortion requires an operation. It kills the life of a baby after it has begun." The 1964 revision omitted this statement, and Planned Parenthood subsequently became a leading proponent and supplier of abortion.

option as a lesser evil. Furthermore, nonintentional killing is one thing, justifiable killing quite another.

c) **Abortion, even if not intentional killing, usually is wrong.** Even if the proposal adopted in choosing abortion does not include the baby's death, that death almost always is unjustly accepted. People are generally prepared to sacrifice anything but their moral integrity to save their own lives or the life of someone they love, and they generally want others on whom they and their loved ones depend to pay a very high price rather than accept their death. So, it is unfair to accept any innocent person's death, especially that of a dependent, in order to avoid lesser burdens, including those imposed by pregnancy and giving birth, short of a threat to the mother's own life.[78] Therefore, even if an abortion to bring the experience of rape to an end or to solve some health problem posing no immediate threat to the mother's life does not carry out a choice to kill the unborn, it still involves wrongfully accepting the baby's death.

Some deny this conclusion, especially with respect to cases of rape.[79] Women who have been victims of this crime have suffered a very great wrong. However, if pregnancy results, the unborn baby is entirely innocent of any wrong. Terminating the pregnancy neither corrects nor limits the wrong done by the rapist, but only adds wrong to wrong. Justice forbids this, while mercy demands that the wrong already done be limited and overcome, so far as possible, with healing love. People plainly should extend this love to women who are victims of rape, and the latter should extend it to the new person, if one comes to be as a result of the crime.

Women who have been raped need to reaffirm their own worth rather than allowing what they have suffered to deprive them of their sense of self-worth and integrity. This requires correctly drawing the line between evil and good: the rapist's act was evil, but the woman who is raped remains good, and the baby, though unwelcome, proceeds in part from her, is innocent, and so belongs on her side of the line. To reaffirm herself, she must accept the baby's goodness, with the conviction that nothing that happened can make her and her baby bad.[80] Nurturing the baby until its birth, she can then decide whether or not to continue to accept the responsibilities of motherhood.

---

78. Judith Jarvis Thomson, "A Defense of Abortion," *Philosophy and Public Affairs* 1 (1971): 47–66, tries to challenge this conclusion; for critiques of her work, see Grisez and Boyle, *Life and Death with Liberty and Justice,* 205–7; Michael Davis, "Foetuses, Famous Violinists, and the Right to Continued Aid," *Philosophical Quarterly* 33 (1983): 259–78; Francis J. Beckwith, "Personal Bodily Rights, Abortion, and Unplugging the Violinist," *International Philosophical Quarterly* 32 (1992): 105–18.

79. Because of the inadequacy of consent due to immaturity or other causes, any true victim of incest is a victim of rape. Those who consent to incest with full voluntariness are not victims but initiators of it or conspirators in it.

80. For some psychological evidence that abortion is not beneficial to victims of rape and incest: Sandra Kathleen Mahkorn, "Pregnancy and Sexual Assault," and George E. Maloof, "The Consequences of Incest: Giving and Taking Life," in *The Psychological Aspects of Abortion,* ed. David Mall and Walter F. Watts (Washington, D.C.: University Publications of America, 1979), 53–110. For some first-person accounts by victims of rape or incest who underwent abortion: David C. Reardon, *Aborted Women: Silent No More* (Chicago: Loyola University Press, 1987), 206–18.

d) Sometimes the baby's death may be accepted to save the mother. Sometimes four conditions are simultaneously fulfilled: (i) some pathology threatens the lives of both a pregnant woman and her child, (ii) it is not safe to wait or waiting surely will result in the death of both, (iii) there is no way to save the child, and (iv) an operation that can save the mother's life will result in the child's death.

If the operation was one of those which the classical moralists considered not to be a "direct" abortion, they held that it could be performed. For example, in cases in which the baby could not be saved regardless of what was done (and perhaps in some others as well), they accepted the removal of a cancerous gravid uterus or of a fallopian tube containing an ectopic pregnancy.[81] This moral norm plainly is sound, since the operation does not carry out a proposal to kill the child, serves a good purpose, and violates neither fairness nor mercy.[82]

At least in times past, however, and perhaps even today in places where modern medical equipment and skills are unavailable, certain life-saving operations meeting the four conditions would fall among procedures classified by the classical moralists as "direct" killing, since the procedures in question straightaway would lead to the baby's death. This is the case, for example, if the four conditions are met during the delivery of a baby whose head is too large. Unless the physician does a craniotomy (an operation in which instruments are used to empty and crush the head of the child so that it can be removed from the birth canal), both mother and child eventually will die; but the operation can be performed and the mother saved. With respect to physical causality, craniotomy immediately destroys the baby, and only in this way saves the mother. Thus, not only classical moralists but the magisterium regarded it as "direct" killing: a bad means to a good end.[83]

However, assuming the four conditions are met, the baby's death need not be included in the proposal adopted in choosing to do a craniotomy.[84] The proposal can be simply to alter the child's physical dimensions and remove him or her, because, as a physical object, this body cannot remain where it is without ending in both the baby's and the mother's deaths. To understand this proposal, it helps to notice that the baby's death contributes nothing to the objective sought; indeed, the procedure is exactly the same if the baby has already died. In adopting this proposal, the baby's death need only be accepted as a side effect. Therefore, according to the analysis of action employed in this book, even craniotomy (and, a fortiori, other

81. See United States Catholic Conference, *Ethical and Religious Directives for Catholic Health Facilities* (Washington, D.C.: United States Catholic Conference, 1977), directives 13, 16, and 17. On ectopic pregnancies, also see T. Lincoln Bouscaren, S.J., *Ethics of Ectopic Operations,* 2nd ed. rev. (Milwaukee: Bruce, 1944).

82. Obviously, if the embryo could be transplanted from the tube to the uterus and both persons saved, it hardly would be fair to allow the baby to die: Thomas J. O'Donnell, S.J., *Medicine and Christian Morality,* 2nd ed. rev. (New York: Alba House, 1991), 166–67.

83. The magisterial teaching is in nineteenth-century decrees of the Holy Office, regulating what can be taught safely in Catholic schools; see DS 3258/— (the 1889 decree), which refers to a prior, similar decree, confirmed by the pope (*ASS* 17 [1884] 556); DS 3298/1890a (confirmed by the pope, 25 July 1895).

84. See Joseph M. Boyle, Jr., "Double-effect and a Certain Type of Embryotomy," *Irish Theological Quarterly* 44 (1977): 303–18.

operations meeting the four stated conditions) need not be direct killing, and so, provided the death of the baby is not intended (which is possible but unnecessary), any operation in a situation meeting the four conditions could be morally acceptable.[85]

e) Sometimes the baby's life should be given priority. Sometimes three conditions are simultaneously fulfilled: (i) some pathology threatens the life (or at least seriously impairs the health) of a pregnant woman, (ii) an operation or treatment that is not intentional killing of the baby would benefit her, and (iii) the operation or treatment would lead to the baby's death (or at least risk his or her life). When these three conditions are met, many people are quick to judge that the operation or treatment is morally acceptable; even classical moralists often will agree with them, provided "direct" abortion is not in question. However, justice or mercy can require that the pregnant woman and those caring for her give priority to her baby's life.

As already explained (in c, above), if the mother's life is not at stake, it is unfair to accept the baby's death. So, if the pathology only impairs the mother's health, an operation or treatment that surely will result in the baby's death is not morally acceptable. For example, abortion to ameliorate a kidney disease posing no immediate threat to the mother's life cannot be justified. Nor is the removal of the pregnant woman's diseased uterus acceptable if it can safely be delayed or an alternative safely used with a prospect of the baby's survival. Fairness even can exclude an operation or procedure involving only a risk to the baby's life, if that risk is great and the prospective benefit to the mother is uncertain or if the risk to her involved in omitting the operation or procedure is not so great.

Again, in a situation in which the lives of both a pregnant woman and her child are at stake and both cannot be saved, if an operation can be performed with a prospect of saving one or the other, fairness can require the procedure more likely to save at least one. Proceeding in a way which surely will result in the baby's death and offers only a limited chance of saving the mother may well be unfair discrimination, when the alternative would surely result in the mother's death, with a better chance of saving the baby. (The point here is not to assert what fairness *does* require, but what it *might* require. An actual judgment must take into account not only the good of life, but other goods, including those instantiated in the mother's relationships to that child, to other children, and so on.)

Moreover, even if it otherwise is fair to accept or risk the unborn baby's death as a side effect of some appropriate operation or treatment of a pregnant woman, she may be free to offer her own life or risk it to save her baby or prevent risking its life. If such self-sacrifice is not morally excluded—for example, by her other responsibilities—a Christian mother rightly does this work of mercy for her child.

f) Prenatal testing and counseling with a view to abortion are wrong. Medical diagnosis and treatment of the unborn are good, and may be obligatory,

---

85. If the analysis proposed here should lead in practice to a judgment in conflict with the Church's teaching, I would follow and urge others to follow the Church's teaching. If the teaching is open to refinements in respect to its application, these must be completed by the magisterium.

provided they are undertaken for the child's benefit and meet the norms which govern therapeutic efforts in other cases: proper consent, the avoidance of unreasonable risks, and so on. Examinations and tests which do not benefit the child but are done merely to allay the parents' anxiety or satisfy their curiosity can be justified only if they involve no significant risk to the child. However, prenatal testing "done with the thought of possibly inducing an abortion depending upon the results" is gravely wrong.[86] The wrong involved is that of abortion itself, for abortion is conditionally intended by someone who chooses prenatal testing with a view to terminating the pregnancy if the test results are of a certain kind. The same wrong is done by those who formally cooperate, including advisers who suggest or condone abortion when counseling people about the results of prenatal tests.

g) **Artificially produced embryos should be treated as persons.** Sometimes human ova are fertilized in laboratories to produce human embryos, with a view to implanting them in women who want to have babies.[87] Sometimes spare embryos or ones that are or may be abnormal are disposed of or used for experimentation. Because treating those admitted to be persons in this way plainly would be unjust, the sole ethical defense of such actions is that artificially produced human embryos are only "potential human beings." However, since every human individual should be considered a person from fertilization, these actions really involve intentionally killing the innocent or unfairly accepting their deaths.

h) **Many other risks to the unborn should not be accepted.** The norms for accepting risks to others' lives also hold for the unborn. No risk may be accepted in choosing to do something that would be wrong even apart from that risk. So, intemperate behavior is a more serious matter for a pregnant woman insofar as it involves a risk to her unborn child than for someone not pregnant. Also, one may not unfairly accept risks to others. So, a pregnant woman may not accept risks to her unborn child unless she has an adequate reason for doing so, and others (such as her husband) should cooperate with her in order to lessen the risks to the child.

4. To Use Certain Methods of "Contraception" Is to Procure Abortion

Since abortion is possible only after conception has occurred, it is essentially different from contraception. Although contraception also is morally wrong, it is

---

86. See Congregation for the Doctrine of the Faith, *Instruction on Respect for Human Life in Its Origin and on the Dignity of Procreation: Replies to Certain Questions of the Day,* 1.2, *AAS* 80 (1988) 79–80, *OR,* 16 Mar. 1987, 3.

87. In itself, this procedure is morally wrong: see Congregation for the Doctrine of the Faith, *Instruction on Respect for Human Life in Its Origin and on the Dignity of Procreation: Replies to Certain Questions of the Day,* 2.B.4–5, *AAS* 80 (1988) 90–94, *OR,* 16 Mar. 1987, 5–6; *In Vitro Fertilisation and Public Policy,* Evidence Submitted to the Government Committee of Inquiry into Human Fertilisation and Embryology by the Catholic Bishops' Joint Committee on Bio-Ethical Issues, on Behalf of the Catholic Bishops of Great Britain (London: Catholic Information Services, May 1983); William E. May, "Catholic Teaching on the Laboratory Generation of Human Life," in *The Gift of Life: The Proceedings of a National Conference on the Vatican Instruction on Reproductive Ethics and Technology,* ed. Marilyn Wallace, R.S.M., and Thomas W. Hilgers (Omaha, Neb.: Pope Paul VI Institute Press, 1990), 77–85.

not morally equivalent to abortion; abortion is far graver, because it is the destruction of an existing person, in violation of his or her right to life. Hence, it is important to recognize that certain choices to use so-called contraceptives really are choices to kill the unborn after fertilization.

a) **Not all ways of preventing birth constitute contraception.** People often use abortion as a backup after trying but failing to prevent conception. In such cases, it is clear that conception has occurred, and that the further intervention attacks the new life. But some people also resort to abortion when they omit contraception and fear pregnancy. The recourse to abortion can be very early, even before evidence of conception is available, and can involve scraping the lining of the uterus with an instrument (dilatation and curettage), evacuating the uterus (so-called menstrual extraction), or abortifacient drugs (the "morning-after pill").

At least sometimes, too, some so-called contraceptive techniques, though used before intercourse, prevent birth by interfering with the reproductive process after fertilization. This is how intrauterine devices work, not always but certainly often, and the same is true, though probably less often, of the various oral contraceptives (forms of the birth control pill).[88] All such methods are partly abortifacient, not merely contraceptive.

b) **It is unjust to use possibly abortifacient "contraceptives."** If, knowing the facts, someone chooses to prescribe, use, or encourage the use of such a method, the intention can be simply to prevent birth, whether the objective is accomplished by preventing conception or by killing the conceptus. But since the conceptus should be considered a person, that is a conditional intention to kill an innocent person.

Someone might argue that, if a method of birth prevention sometimes prevents conception and sometimes prevents implantation, the intention in choosing it could be to prevent conception, and its possible interference with the reproductive process after conception could be accepted as a side effect. Even if such a method can be chosen in this way, however, it is not possible justly to accept as a side effect the death of an individual whose conception is not prevented. For contraception itself always is wrong, and so one cannot justly choose to use it while accepting the possibility of killing someone as a side effect.[89]

---

88. Susan Harlap, Kathryn Kost, and Jacqueline Darroch Forrest, *Preventing Pregnancy, Protecting Health: A New Look at Birth Control Choices in the United States* (New York: The Alan Guttmacher Institute, 1991), state that when not effective in some other way, intrauterine devices work "by initiating a local inflammatory response to a foreign body, which inhibits implantation should fertilization occur" (27), combined oral contraceptives "change the uterine lining to inhibit implantation should fertilization occur" (27), the progestin-only pill works by "inhibiting implantation" (28), contraceptive implants work by "inhibiting implantation of a fertilized ovum" (28), and progestin-only injectables work in ways "similar to those of the minipill and implants" (29). See Ashley and O'Rourke, *Healthcare Ethics*, 3rd ed., 278–79; Kristine M. Severyn, "Abortifacient Drugs and Devices: Medical and Moral Dilemmas," *Linacre Quarterly* 57 (Aug. 1990): 50–67; Rudolf Ehmann, "Problems in Family Planning," *Anthropotes* 7 (1991): 100–101.

89. Suppose the same pill were used, not as a contraceptive, but in a way morally acceptable in itself, for example, to treat a disease of the uterus of a married woman. Would its possible abortifacient action be acceptable as a side effect? O'Donnell, *Medicine and Christian Morality,*

Question E: Why Is Contraception Always Wrong?

There are two reasons why Catholics should believe that contraception is always wrong. First, the Church teaches it. Indeed, because the Church has proposed this teaching constantly and most firmly, her infallibility in day-to-day teaching on matters of faith and morals appears to guarantee it (see *CMP*, 35.D–E).[90] Second, in his work on the theology of the body, John Paul II has provided careful analyses of the relevant scriptural data and drawn the conclusion that the moral norm excluding contraception "belongs not only to the natural moral law, but also to the *moral order revealed by God:* also from this point of view, it could not be different, but solely what is handed down by Tradition and the Magisterium."[91]

The point of the present question is not so much to show the truth of this teaching as to offer a particular way of understanding why it is true. Of course, a person can reject this explanation and others yet still accept what the Church teaches.

In the present question, contraception will be considered only insofar as it is a contralife act. Contraception within marriage and its relationship to marital love will be explained (in 9.E.1.a, 9.E.1.f, 9.E.2.e, 9.F.1.e, 9.F.1.g).

1. Contraception Traditionally Was Rejected as Contralife

Until they began to accept contraception, Roman Catholic, Orthodox, and Protestant Christians all considered sexual activity outside marriage seriously sinful.[92] Hence, theological attempts to justify contraception focused on its use within marriage. Because these attempts occasioned the major papal declarations on this subject, current Catholic teaching about it regularly refers specifically to marital acts and distinguishes contraception from natural family planning, which married couples can rightly practice. Historically, however, much of the Christian tradition condemned contraception as a contralife act without distinguishing between its uses by married couples and by others.[93]

2nd ed. rev., 229, thinks so. However, it seems more reasonable to say that the seriousness of the disease, the greatness of the risk, treatment options, and possible abstinence from marital intercourse should be considered, and a judgment made on the same basis as in other cases involving risks to life.

90. See John C. Ford, S.J. and Germain Grisez, "Contraception and the Infallibility of the Ordinary Magisterium," *Theological Studies* 39 (1978): 258–312; Germain Grisez, "Infallibility and Specific Moral Norms: A Review Discussion" (a reply to Francis A. Sullivan, S.J.), *Thomist* 49 (1985): 248–87.

91. John Paul II, General Audience (18 July 1984), 4, *Inseg.* 7.2 (1984) 103, *OR,* 23 July 1984, 1. The development in the Church's teaching on religious liberty provides no precedent for change in her teaching on contraception; see Brian W. Harrison, *Religious Liberty and Contraception: Did Vatican II Open the Way for a New Sexual Ethic?* (Melbourne, Australia: John XXIII Fellowship Co-op, 1988).

92. A contemporary study by an evangelical Protestant opposing contraception and invoking the witness of the Protestant tradition against it: Charles D. Provan, *The Bible and Birth Control* (Monongahela, Pa.: Zimmer, 1989).

93. See John T. Noonan, Jr., *Contraception: A History of Its Treatment by the Catholic Theologians and Canonists* (Cambridge, Mass.: Harvard University Press, 1965), 91, 93, 98, 99, 100, 136–37, 144, 146, 160, 168–69, 173–78, 215, 232–37, 360–64. While Noonan's work is useful, his interpretations are not always sound. For example, he is mistaken in thinking that St.

For example, a canon concerning contraception, *Si aliquis,* was included in the Church's universal law from the thirteenth century until 1917: "If anyone for the sake of satisfying sexual desire or with premeditated hatred does something to a man or to a woman, or gives something to drink, so that he cannot generate, or she cannot conceive, or offspring be born, let that person be treated as a homicide."[94] This canon does not say contraception is homicide; the tradition made no such mistake.[95] Rather, the canon says that those who use contraception commit a sin analogous to homicide.

Of course, contraception and abortion often have been condemned together. For example, in dealing with marriage, the Catechism of the Council of Trent teaches that "married persons who, to prevent conception or procure abortion, have recourse to medicine, are guilty of a most heinous crime, for this is to be considered an impious conspiracy of homicides."[96]

2. Contraception Always Is Contralife

Contraception can be carried out by a variety of methods, and outward behavior similar to that involved in contraception sometimes has an entirely different moral significance. So, contraception must be understood accurately, in terms of the intention involved. That intention is to impede a new instantiation of the good of human life. Therefore, contraception always is contralife.

a) **Contraception is not defined by a pattern of outward behavior.** The act of contraception is not tied to any one pattern of behavior. There are various ways to contracept and many outward performances that could, but need not, be ways of contracepting. On the one hand, many people mistakenly rely on contraceptively useless techniques and engage in the behavior they involve. Morally speaking, such behavior, because it is chosen to contracept, is a way of contracepting. Also, the use of barriers, drugs, and withdrawal are different more or less effective behaviors often chosen to contracept. On the other hand, some outward performances which usually are ways of contracepting can be chosen for other reasons. For instance, to treat a pathological condition, women who never engage in sexual intercourse sometimes take the same drugs others use for contraception. Fertile women who do engage in sexual intercourse also can take the same drugs without contracepting,

---

Thomas requires procreative intent for entirely sinless sex within marriage. See Germain Grisez, "Marriage: Reflections Based on St. Thomas and Vatican Council II," *Catholic Mind* 64 (June 1966): 4-19. Also see Fabian Parmisano, O.P., "Love and Marriage in the Middle Ages," *New Blackfriars* 50 (1969): 599–608 and 649–60.

94. *Decret. Greg. IX,* 5.12.5, *Corpus iuris canonici,* ed. A. L. Richter and A. Friedberg (Leipzig: 1881), 2:794: "Si aliquis causa explendae libidinis vel odii meditatione homini aut mulieri aliquid fecerit, vel ad potandum dederit, ut non possit generare, aut concipere, vel nasci soboles, ut homicida teneatur." The dropping of *Si aliquis* from canon law in 1917 probably was due to the extensive and much needed simplification accomplished at that time by its first codification, which involved a clearer standard distinguishing appropriate objects of legislation from subjects suitable for moral teaching.

95. The norm was introduced into canon law by Burchard of Worms, who placed it, not in the book on homicide (vi), but in that on fornication (xvii): *PL,* 140:933.

96. *Catechismus ex decreto Ss. Concilii Tridentini,* 2.8.13 (1:651, translation amended).

when they do so as therapy and only accept—perhaps gladly, perhaps reluctantly—temporary sterility as a side effect.

b) Contraception is defined by what one wills as an end or means. In teaching that contraception always is morally excluded, Paul VI defines it in terms of intention: "any action which either before, at the moment of, or after marital intercourse, is specifically intended to impede procreation—whether as an end or as a means."[97] He could not have accurately defined contraception in any other way, for only certain intentions can render the various things people do ("any action") contraceptive.

Sometimes the prospect of a new person's coming to be is repugnant in itself to people who plan to engage in sexual intercourse; they therefore intend as an end something they consider a good: that new life not begin. More often, though, people have a reason to avoid having a baby: they are not married or do not have the means to care properly for a baby (or another baby), they have other responsibilities to fulfill or interests to pursue, their health may be impaired, and so on. In such cases, preventing the beginning of a new life is not willed as an end, but it is willed, for it is chosen—sometimes reluctantly to avoid some serious problem—as a means of facilitating sexual intercourse by forestalling its possible reproductive consequence.

Thus, to contracept a person must think that prospective sexual intercourse might cause a new life to begin, and that this possible effect can be impeded by some other behavior he or she could perform. The choice is to perform that other behavior; the relevant immediate intention (which may or may not be directed toward some further purpose) is that the new life not begin.

Here and in what follows, *begin* and *come to be* refer both to the initiation of the life of a person and to the person's continuing existence. So, contraception aims to impede both the initiation of life and the being of the individual whose life might be initiated if it were not impeded.

c) A contraceptive act is distinct from any sexual act. Usually, contraception is closely related to a sexual act. Thus, it is often thought of as if it were itself a sexual act, and its morality often is treated as an issue of sexual ethics.

However, contraception is different from sexual acts, such as heterosexual intercourse, sodomy, masturbation, and so on. Someone who both engages in sexual intercourse and contracepts does two distinct things. On the one hand, with contraceptive intent, a woman may take the pill regularly or a man have himself sterilized, yet fail to find a desirable and willing partner with whom to engage in sexual intercourse. On the other hand, a couple tempted to fornicate has two choices to make, not one: whether to fornicate, and whether to contracept. They may decide

---

97. Paul VI, *Humanae vitae,* 14, *AAS* 60 (1968) 490, *PE,* 277.14 (translation amended). In criticizing an earlier version of the argument offered here, Janet E. Smith, *Humanae Vitae: A Generation Later* (Washington, D.C.: The Catholic University of America Press, 1991), 355, says: "If one intends to do something that violates nature (contraception does), one acquires an evil will. But what one intends to do (the external act) is defined as good or bad independently of any act of the will." This criticism overlooks the fact that Paul VI, in order to reject every sort of contraception, was compelled to define it in terms of the intention to impede procreation.

to fornicate and not contracept, perhaps agreeing that if pregnancy occurs they will get married. Thus, while contraception presupposes at least the belief that a possible act of sexual intercourse might be fruitful, those who choose to contracept plainly do so by a choice distinct from the choice to engage in sexual intercourse, and the behavior carrying out a choice to contracept is distinct from, though usually closely associated with, the behavior essential to sexual intercourse.[98]

   d) **Considered in moral terms, every contraceptive act is contralife.** Considered as a technological intervention in a biological process, contraceptive behavior need only prevent the fertilization of an ovum by a sperm. From that point of view, eliminating the possibility of a conception by successful contraception does not bear on any human individual's life; it is not as if a possible baby were waiting somewhere to be conceived. However, considered as a moral act—that is, considered in moral terms, whether as morally good or as evil—contraception carries out a choice specified, just as other choices are, by a possible future state of affairs which the agent intends to influence by means of his or her act. Those who choose to contracept often also intend some further good, for example, not to procreate irresponsibly, with bad consequences for already-existing persons. But in choosing contraception as a means to this further good, they necessarily imagine a new person coming to be if he or she is not prevented, they want that imagined person not to be, and they efficaciously will that he or she never be.[99] That will is a contralife will. Therefore, considered as a moral act, each and every contraceptive act necessarily is contralife.

   Moreover, in and of itself, a contraceptive act is nothing but contralife. For, being distinct from any sexual act that occasions it, a contraceptive act cannot be considered part of that sexual act, even if the outward behaviors involved in the two acts are closely associated. Contraception is related to sexual acts only

---

98. Ashley and O'Rourke, *Healthcare Ethics,* 3rd ed., 296, merging contraception with the sexual acts it facilitates, assert that contraception by married couples "is at worst a sin of weakness." That might be true of couples who usually try to avoid contraception but occasionally succumb to passion and engage in *coitus interruptus.* But couples who systematically practice contraception, using methods which require a steady will, hardly are committing a sin of weakness; indeed, one factor which occasioned the crisis over contraception in the Catholic Church in the early 1960s was the marketing of antiovulant drugs, which could not be used without denying the wrongness of contraception or admitting a sin which, unlike a sin of weakness, is unrelated to the ebb and flow of passion.

99. In her criticism of an earlier presentation of this argument, Smith, *Humanae Vitae,* 363, argues "that couples, in fact, are not undergoing such a thought process. Is it not possible that some, and perhaps most, contraceptors reason in this way: 'It would be best for us not to have a baby (or another baby) at this time. Let us find some way of rendering ourselves infertile (as we are periodically during a month anyway) and thus we can continue to engage in sexual intercourse responsibly'?" She overlooks the fact that the couple's choice to find some way to render themselves infertile is an efficacious will to prevent the baby "it would be best for us not to have." Moreover, while recent Church teaching has focused on contraception in marriage and rejected it primarily because it renders a married couple's intercourse nonmarital (an aspect of contraception's wrongness treated in 9.E.1.a, f, below), the strand of Catholic tradition rejecting contraception as contralife (summarized above, in 1) should not be casually brushed aside by anyone who respects the Church's teaching authority.

instrumentally, inasmuch as it lessens the likelihood of pregnancy, which otherwise might be a motive to refrain from sexual intercourse.[100]

e) Avoiding conception by abstinence need not be contraception. Some couples abstain from sexual intercourse at times when they believe conception is likely and engage in it only when they think conception unlikely. It certainly seems that those who act in this way do not want to have a baby and are doing what they can to avoid having one. Many therefore argue that they have exactly the same intention as those who choose to contracept.

In reply, it must be admitted that the intention could be the same. Imagine two couples, both of whom have had one child and, preferring greater freedom to enjoy their hobbies, decide they want no more. One couple opt for the pill. The other reject the pill because of its possible health hazards, and choose periodic abstinence for its technical advantages: it is cost free, effective, without bad side effects, and so on. Both plainly have the same intention, and it is contraceptive.[101]

However, the intention of those who avoid conception by abstaining from sexual intercourse need not be contraceptive. It helps to recall that when all Christians considered contraception sinful, they also considered fornication and adultery sinful, partly because they might lead to pregnancy. Thus, at that time, when everyone considered marriage the only appropriate situation in which to have and raise children, avoiding conception was assumed to be a good reason for couples not living together in marriage to abstain from intercourse. Moreover, when circumstances such as a wife's health or a family's poverty required a conscientious married couple to avoid having a child or another child, the Church encouraged them to abstain from marital intercourse. Nobody suggested people in either situation were practicing contraception.

It is easy to see why. In the case of unmarried couples, abstaining from intercourse carried out a proposal, not precisely to prevent the beginning of new life, but to refrain from committing fornication or adultery while at the same time avoiding pregnancy out of wedlock. Similarly, married couples who abstained did not intend precisely to impede procreation; rather, their abstinence carried out a proposal not to cause a complex foreseen state of affairs, including not only a

---

100. This being so, one cannot argue (as some Catholic proponents of contraception more or less clearly do): Since marital intercourse is good, contraception involved in it can be acceptable. If the contraceptive act and the marital act were one and the same human act, that argument might succeed, since that one act could be analyzed as an act with two effects. However, the principle of double effect is not correctly used to justify what is done in one act by the good features of another, distinct act.

101. John Paul II, Address to Participants in a Course on Natural Family Planning (14 Dec. 1990), 5; *L'Osservatore Romano*, It. ed., 15 Dec. 1990, 6; *OR*, 17 Dec. 1990, 3, having stressed the importance of proper moral instruction for the practice of NFP, adds: "In short, it allows people to see that it is not possible to practice natural methods as a 'licit' variation of the decision to be closed to life, which would be substantially the same as that which inspires the decision to use contraceptives: only if there is a basic openness to fatherhood and motherhood, understood as collaboration with the Creator, does the use of natural means become an integrating part of responsibility for love and life." Also see, John Paul II: General Audience (5 Sept. 1984), 4, *Inseg.* 7.2 (1984) 322, *OR*, 10 Sept. 1984, 10.

prospective child's coming to be but, at once and inseparably, the bad consequences which made it reasonable for them to avoid having that child.

Now, when married couples today choose to avoid conception by periodic abstinence, their intention can be similar to that of couples who in former times abstained continuously. While they abstain during fertile times in order not to cause a pregnancy, however, their intention does not preclude intercourse during times they identify as infertile; and if they choose to have normal marital intercourse at those times, their intention in doing so plainly cannot be to impede the beginning of a new life, since the infertility is due to natural conditions, not to their marital intercourse.[102]

Thus, the willing that relates to the prospective baby's not coming to be need not be the same in (i) the choice of any method of contraception (including sexual abstinence with contraceptive intent) as in (ii) the noncontraceptive choice to avoid conception by abstinence. In (i), the intention precisely is to prevent a baby from coming to be. Even when that is willed for the sake of some good ulterior end, such as avoiding bad consequences which should be avoided, those who make this choice do not want a baby, in the precise sense that their choice bears on the baby's not coming to be as a means to their good ulterior end. But in (ii)—the non-contraceptive choice to avoid conception by abstinence—the couple do not choose the baby's not coming to be as a means to anything. Rather, their choice is to refrain from intercourse insofar as it might cause a state of affairs which would include not only a baby's coming to be but other things which they think it reasonable, and perhaps obligatory, to avoid. Those who make this choice do not want to cause that state of affairs as a whole; rather than choosing the baby's not coming to be, they only accept it in choosing not to cause the state of affairs which would include it.

This makes a great difference if pregnancy does occur. Since couples who noncontraceptively abstain to avoid conception never precisely will a prospective baby's not coming to be, they do not have to change their wills to accept or love the unexpected baby. They may be emotionally upset upon learning they are having a baby for whom they were not planning, but, whatever their feelings, the baby is not unwanted in the morally relevant sense. For, using the word *want* to refer to efficacious volitions, which are morally determinative, rather than feelings, which are important but not morally determinative, the baby does not come to be as unwanted, since his or her coming to be is not contrary to the parents' intention. The unexpected pregnancy may even fulfill their emotional desires and volitional wishes for a baby, so that they can truthfully say: "Although we were practicing

---

102. Paul VI, *Humanae vitae*, 16, *AAS* 60 (1968) 492, *PE*, 277.16, teaches that contraception and natural family planning are completely different, because only contraception obstructs the natural unfolding of the generative process. He concludes: "If therefore there are well-grounded reasons for spacing births, arising from the physical or psychological condition of husband or wife, or from external circumstances, the Church teaches that married people may then take advantage of the natural cycles immanent in the reproductive system and engage in marital intercourse only during those times that are infertile, thus controlling birth in a way which does not in the least offend the moral principles which We have just explained [note omitted]."

periodic abstinence because we thought we should not have a baby just now, we are glad we are going to have this baby, for we really wanted it."

Thus, there is a real and very important difference between not wanting to cause a baby, which is common to both (i) and (ii) above, and not wanting the baby whom one might cause, which is true of (i) but not of (ii).

f) Preventing conception due to rape need not be contraception. In choosing to prevent a conception that might result from rape, someone could be choosing to contracept. This plainly is so when an administrator of an institution housing men and women incapable of giving consent to sexual intercourse makes little or no effort to prevent their copulation but takes measures to prevent pregnancies.

However, other sorts of cases must be considered. Rape is the imposition of intimate, bodily union upon someone without her or his consent, and anyone who is raped rightly resists so far as possible. Moreover, the victim (or potential victim) is right to resist not only insofar as he or she is subjected to unjust force, but insofar as that force imposes the special wrong of uniquely intimate bodily contact. It can scarcely be doubted that someone who cannot prevent the initiation of this intimacy is morally justified in resisting its continuation; for example, a woman who awakes and finds herself being penetrated by a rapist need not permit her attacker to ejaculate in her vagina if she can make him withdraw. On the same basis, if they cannot prevent the wrongful intimacy itself, women who are victims (or potential victims) of rape and those trying to help them are morally justified in trying to prevent conception insofar as it is the fullness of sexual union.[103]

The measures taken in this case are a defense of the woman's ovum (insofar as it is a part of her person) against the rapist's sperms (insofar as they are parts of his person). By contrast, if the intimate, bodily union of intercourse is not imposed on the woman but sought or willingly permitted, neither she nor anyone who permits the union can intend at the same time that it not occur. Hence, rape apart, contraceptive measures are chosen to prevent conception not insofar as it is the ultimate completion of intimate bodily union but insofar as it is the beginning of a new and unwanted person.

3. Contraception Is Always Wrong

The argument here is straightforward: Contraception always involves a choice to impede new human life; life is one of the basic human goods (see *CMP*, 5.D);

---

103. While victims of rape rightly try to prevent conception considered as the ultimate completion of the intimacy wrongly imposed on them, if the attempt fails, there is no justification for abortion, because a new person then exists with his or her own life and right to it. Hence, it would be wrong for a woman anticipating rape to use an abortifacient, such as an intrauterine device, or for a physician to do a dilatation and curettage on a victim of rape to prevent the implantation of an embryo if there is one. If rape is anticipated, however, a diaphragm and/or spermicide may be used; and, provided their effect probably will not be abortifacient, antifertility drugs may be used before or after the rape, even with a slight risk of abortion accepted as a side effect. See Joint Committee on Bioethical Issues of the Bishops' Conferences of Scotland, Ireland, England and Wales, "Use of the 'Morning-After Pill' in Cases of Rape," *Origins* 15 (13 Mar. 1986): 633, 635–38; "A Reply: Use of the Morning-After Pill in Cases of Rape," *Origins* 16 (11 Sept. 1986): 237–38; Ashley and O'Rourke, *Healthcare Ethics,* 3rd ed., 286–90.

the seventh and eighth modes of responsibility exclude choosing to impede any of the basic human goods (see *CMP*, 8.G–H). So, contraception is always wrong.[104] However, several objections to this argument call for replies.

a) The life contraception prevents is an instance of a basic good. Homicide plainly attacks an instance of the basic good of life, the given reality of an actual person. But contraception only prevents the coming to be of a new person, the realization of the potentiality to cause human life. So, some will object, the argument against contraception is fallacious; it equivocates on *life*, they will say, since the life prevented by contraception is not a real instance of the basic good of life.

To answer this objection, one must bear in mind that the basic human goods are morally relevant precisely insofar as they can be intelligible ends of acting on which the will bears when one makes choices. Considered in this way, *life* refers to the same thing whether one chooses to prevent conception or, by abortion, to prevent the birth of a baby already conceived. Indeed, sometimes people who do not want a baby choose at one and the same time both to try, by practicing contraception, to prevent the unwanted baby's coming to be and, if contraception should fail, to resort to abortion. Conversely, a couple about to marry who choose a home partly because it has a room suitable for a nursery act for the same good as when, during a subsequent pregnancy, they choose and buy the things they need for their baby. Both before and after he or she is conceived, the hoped-for child for whom they prepare is no mere abstraction. Nor is the unwanted child whose life someone seeks to prevent by using contraception. For both the hoped-for child and the unwanted child specify will acts, whose moral significance as prolife and contralife they thereby determine.

b) In general, human acts bear on possible, not actual, goods. In bearing on a possible instance of human life, rather than anyone's actual life, contraception does not differ from other human acts. Choices concern only what is within human power; but since nobody can do anything about what has been or already is, all human acts affect only the future. Homicide does not destroy the victim's entire life; his or her past and present are beyond harm. Homicide only prevents the victim from having a future. So, the homicidal will, like the contraceptive will, is only against life that would be, not against life that is. Of course, there remains a difference: the prospective life that homicide cuts off is continuous with the present, actual life of the person killed, whereas the prospective life prevented by successful contraception is not continuous with anyone's actual life. However, the prospective life which a failed attempt at contraception sought to prevent is continuous with the actual life of the unwanted child.

104. National Conference of Catholic Bishops, *To Live in Christ Jesus: A Pastoral Reflection on the Moral Life* (Washington, D.C.: United States Catholic Conference, 1976), 18, teaches: "In contraceptive intercourse the procreative or life-giving meaning of intercourse is deliberately separated from its love-giving meaning and rejected; the wrongness of such an act lies in the rejection of this value [note omitted]." An argument against contraception grounded in its opposition to the good of life can be articulated without articulating the general theory of basic human goods and modes of responsibility: Germain Grisez et al., " 'Every Marital Act Ought to Be Open to New Life': Toward a Clearer Understanding," *Thomist* 52 (1988): 369–90.

c) **Contraception is wrong even if it is not unjust to any person.** Of course, nobody can do an injustice to a possible person who will never come to be. Therefore, some will object, contraception need not involve any injustice to anyone, and so, they will say, the will it involves, though necessarily contrary to the basic human good of life, need not be wrong.

Part of the answer to this objection is that one's will can be unjust without one's actually doing an injustice to anyone. For example, if a woman who is the beneficiary of her husband's life insurance plans to kill him on Saturday to collect the insurance, her will is contralife and unjust even if he dies in an automobile accident on Friday. Although not in exactly the same way, the will of someone practicing contraception also is unjust. For every method of contraception, even sterilization, has a failure rate.[105] When the attempt at contraception does not succeed, an unwanted baby comes to be, and then abortion may be considered. But even if the baby is accepted and loved, he or she began life as someone unwanted. So, to choose contraception knowing that it might fail and a baby might come to be as unwanted is to be willing to put another in a position no reasonable person would wish to be in. Therefore, choosing contraception is an injustice, even if it succeeds and the harm remains in one's heart.

d) **Even if contraception is not unjust, it is wrong as suicide is.** The other part of the answer to the preceding objection is that not all moral evils are injustices. A deliberate suicide's will to destroy his or her own life is a grave moral evil, even if no injustice is done to anyone. Similarly, contraception is wrong inasmuch as it carries out a will to prevent life. Christians generally are acutely aware of the wrong of deliberate suicide, because they see it as a violation of the stewardship which God gives each human person over his or her life. The will to prevent life is likewise irreverent toward God, the Lord of life, with whom couples are called to cooperate in responsibly procreating new persons for the kingdom.[106]

---

105. Harlap, Kost, and Forrest, *Preventing Pregnancy, Protecting Health,* 120, having defined *failure rate* as the percentage of women experiencing an unintended pregnancy in the first year of use and *perfect use* of a contraceptive method as "correct and consistent" use (which, in the case of sterilization, presumably means following instructions exactly) estimate that with perfect use vasectomy has a one-tenth of one percent failure rate (one woman per thousand becomes pregnant during the first year after the sterilization), that the failure rate of tubal sterilization with perfect use or vasectomy with average use is twice that, and that the failure rate of tubal sterilization with average use is one-half of one percent (one woman per two hundred becomes pregnant during the first year).

106. John Paul II, Address to Participants in a Study Seminar on "Responsible Parenthood" (17 Sept. 1983), 1, *Inseg.* 6.2 (1983) 562, *OR,* 10 Oct. 1983, 7, points out that each person comes into existence through God's personal creative love, and that married couples only share in God's work, and adds: "When, therefore, through contraception, married couples remove from the exercise of their conjugal sexuality its potential procreative capacity, they claim a power which belongs solely to God: the power to decide *in a final analysis* the coming into existence of a human person. They assume the qualification not of being cooperators in God's creative power, but the ultimate depositaries of the source of human life. In this perspective, contraception is to be judged objectively so profoundly unlawful as never to be, for any reason, justified. To think or to say the contrary is equal to maintaining that in human life situations may arise in which it is lawful not to recognize God as God."

Of course, contraception differs from suicide, since contraception, rather than destroying an actual person, prevents a person's coming to be. Still, the similarity between suicide and contraception is closer than might seem. Modern individualism usually obscures life's unity as it flows from parents to children, but this continuity is real and is experienced vividly by a man and a woman who are in love and who joyfully receive the gift of a child as the fruit of their love and its embodiment. Thus, although a choice to contracept intends to forestall the new person, still it also is a choice to limit the continuity of real human life. For, in preventing the baby whom they project and reject, those who choose to contracept limit their own lives as they tend to become one and to flow beyond themselves. It is as if, by contracepting, they commit a kind of limited suicide; they choose to cut off their life together, as they are about to hand it on, at the precise point at which a new person might emerge.

e) Even those who should not procreate should not contracept. Sometimes couples have morally compelling reasons not to have a baby. For example, they may not be married or, if married, they may not have the capacity and the resources to care properly for a child (or, perhaps, another child). In such cases, it would be gravely irresponsible, and so gravely wrong, to risk pregnancy. Therefore, some will object, such couples should choose contraception, even if it is contralife, as the lesser evil.

Three things must be said in answer. First, the argument is an example of proportionalism, which is not a workable method of moral judgment (see *CMP*, 6.F). Second, couples who cannot responsibly engage in sexual intercourse open to new life always have an alternative to contraception: they can and should abstain from any intercourse which would involve wrongly accepting the possibility of pregnancy. Third, if such a couple choose contraception, they irresponsibly risk pregnancy, because contraceptives sometimes fail.

As has been explained (in 1.e), avoiding conception by abstinence need not be contraception. Thus, married couples may be able to practice periodic abstinence (see 9.F.1.e–j). A man and a woman who are not married to each other should not engage in sexual intercourse in any case; if they not only do so but practice contraception, they only facilitate one immorality by another. Moreover, using contraception aggravates rather than mitigates the sinfulness of fornication, since to the specific malice of fornication it adds that of a contralife will and the associated injustice to the unwanted child if contraception fails.

f) Contraception should not be promoted to solve social problems. Taking a wider perspective, many proponents of contraception claim that excluding it means accepting both large numbers of teenage pregnancies among the poor in affluent nations, with consequent welfare costs and child neglect, and unchecked growth of population in the poorer nations, with consequent poverty and misery. So, they argue, contraception must be accepted and even promoted in order to solve these social problems.

That argument is another example of the proportionalist fallacy. Like many proportionalist arguments, it ignores the bad effects of the course of action it defends. In the first place, promoting contraception, especially among the young, condones and even encourages immoral sexual activity. Even if contraceptives are provided and used, this activity also will lead to many pregnancies, since all methods of contraception have a failure rate. Moreover, the children who come to be as unwanted are likely to be aborted, or neglected and abused, because, unlike children who are unplanned by people open to new life, they were rejected in advance. Furthermore, promoting contraception may lead to even more pregnancies than otherwise would have occurred. For while some people can use contraception consistently and effectively, most cannot, because its use facilitates the habitual satisfaction of sexual desire without regard to the reasonableness of doing so, and people with a habit of satisfying desires without regard to reason find it hard to resist even when they recognize special reasons for doing so.

The argument also evades the true issue raised by delinquency, poverty, and misery: the need to recognize and rectify social injustices. Moreover, it assumes that the poor could not and would not practice self-control and be responsible parents if they understood their situation better, had more reason to hope for their children's future, and knew how to practice morally acceptable birth regulation.

Proponents of contraception will say that self-control never will solve the problem. There are two answers to that. First, even granting their narrow view of "the problem," one can see that contraception never will solve it either, and, as already explained, can even make it worse. That is why those who promote contraception to solve social problems generally also promote sterilization and abortion, and sometimes support public programs that manipulate and even pressure people into accepting these techniques of controlling the birthrate. Second, the real problem is the fallen human condition, which has no human solution.

Sound approaches can only mitigate the evils from which humankind suffers. In procreating as in other matters, irresponsibility will always be a part of life. The morally sound and Christian response is not to try to overcome this evil by means of contralife technologies, but to encourage and help people to live decent human and Christian lives. Such encouragement and help should include teaching natural family planning, which also may be propagated through government programs (see GS 87). To encourage responsible parenthood without contralife approaches is to build a better world, because it promotes true human development, in which economics serves people instead of subordinating them to economics.[107]

107. John XXIII, *Mater et magistra, AAS* 53 (1961) 445–48, *PE*, 267.185–99, well articulates the Church's response to the questions raised by increases of population: all people and nations should work together for social justice, couples should act responsibly, and no immoral means should be used. Also see: Holy See's Intervention at International Conference on Population, *OR,* 20 Aug. 1984, 4–5; Submission of the Catholic Church to the XXII CIOMS Conference, *OR,* 18 July 1988, 8–11; National Conference of Catholic Bishops, "Statement on Population" (12 Nov. 1973), in *Pastoral Letters,* ed. Nolan, 3:380–83. The views of those who advocate population control also have been challenged on factual and theoretical grounds as scientifically defective; see, for example, Julian L. Simon and Herman Kahn, eds., *The Resourceful Earth: A Response to Global 2000* (Oxford: Basil Blackwell, 1984); Jacqueline Kasun, *The War against Population: The Economics and Ideology of World Population Control* (San Francisco: Ignatius Press, 1988), 21–77. Kasun also shows (115–55) some of the bad effects of government efforts in the United States to limit adolescent pregnancies.

4. Choosing to Use Contraception Always Is a Grave Matter

Certain statements of national episcopal conferences published after *Humanae vitae* suggest that the practice of contraception need not always be a grave matter.[108] Moreover, in recent years, even some bishops and theologians who affirm that contraception is always wrong have urged pastoral approaches which seem reasonable only if the sin of contraception can admit parvity of matter.[109] However, there are cogent reasons for holding that contraception never is a light matter, even though contraception, like any other sin, is not always mortal, since lack of sufficient reflection or consent can limit its guilt.

a) **The received teaching insisted on the gravity of the matter.** By referring to homicide, the canon, *Si aliquis,* which was included in the Church's law for many centuries, and the Catechism of the Council of Trent, which shaped the instruction of Catholics for several centuries, plainly considered contraception a grave matter. Classical theologians uniformly considered it grave and excluded the possibility of parvity. Within the context of his wider teaching on marriage, Pius XI reaffirms the received teaching on contraception:

> Any use whatsoever of matrimony exercised in such a way that the act is deliberately frustrated in its natural power to generate life is an offence against the law of God and of nature, and those who indulge in such are sullied with the stain of a grave wrong [gravis noxae labe commaculari].
>
> We admonish, therefore, priests who hear confessions and others who have the care of souls, in virtue of Our supreme authority and in Our solicitude for the salvation of souls, not to allow the faithful entrusted to them to err regarding this most grave law of God; much more, that they keep themselves immune from such false opinions, in no way conniving in them.[110]

Thus, Pope Pius makes it clear that contraception in marriage is always grave matter, by predicating not only wrongness but gravity of it in a logically universal proposition: "Any use *whatsoever* of matrimony."

b) **Recent teaching should be read as reaffirming this point.** In *Humanae vitae,* Paul VI precisely reaffirms the Church's constant teaching on contraception, and in doing so refers explicitly to Pius XI's universal proposition.[111] Perhaps to avoid seeming to confuse grave matter with mortal sin, he does not repeat Pius XI's

---

108. The Austrian bishops (21 Sept. 1968), although they held that the systematic exclusion of procreation from marriage because of an egotistical attitude would be a grave matter, said expressly: "Not lastly, we wish to point out that the Holy Father does not speak of grave sin in his encyclical. Therefore, if someone should err against the teaching of the encyclical, he must not feel cut off from God's love in every case, and may then receive Holy Communion without first going to confession" (*Humanae Vitae and the Bishops: The Encyclical and the Statements of the National Hierarchies,* ed. John Horgan [Shannon, Ireland: Irish University Press, 1972], 61).

109. See Ashley and O'Rourke, *Healthcare Ethics,* 3rd ed., 295–97. Such pastoral approaches, which also are applied to other sins, raise a general problem (treated in *CMP,* 17.E). Their application to contraception is criticized by Grisez et al., " 'Every Marital Act Ought to Be Open to New Life': Toward a Clearer Understanding," 418–23.

110. Pius XI, *Casti connubii,* AAS 22 (1930) 560 (DS 3717/2240), *PE,* 208.56–57 (translation amended).

111. Paul VI, *Humanae vitae,* 11 (*"quilibet matrimonii usus"*) with n. 12, AAS 60 (1968) 488, *PE,* 277.11 ("each and every marriage act").

"stain of a grave wrong." Still, he nowhere denies it. So, one reasonably interprets what he does say as including a reaffirmation of previous teaching that contraception always is grave matter. Two further considerations support this interpretation.

First, in his pastoral exhortation to married couples in *Humanae vitae,* Paul VI not only urges them to seek strength in prayer and the Eucharist, but exhorts them to make use of the sacrament of penance.[112] Since only mortal sins must be confessed, this exhortation suggests that Paul VI considered contraception a grave matter and assumed that it ordinarily is a mortal sin even for those struggling to avoid it.

Second, if Paul VI thought that contraception is only a light matter, one must suppose he would have said so, in order to relieve many Catholic couples of grave burdens of conscience and save the Church as a whole from much tension. Indeed, he would have been irresponsible and inept if, judging contraception a light matter, he omitted to say so clearly. But Paul was a conscientious and capable pastor who agonized for years over various questions regarding contraception. So, he plainly did not believe he could say that it can be a light matter, any more than he believed he could say it can be morally acceptable.

Even granting for the sake of argument that Paul VI could not make up his mind on the question of gravity, the whole tradition summed up by Pius XI and reaffirmed over and over by John Paul II witnesses to contraception's gravity. Indeed, had contraception not always been considered grave matter, the tradition could and would have left open the question of its intrinsic immorality.

c) **Some acts of contraception are not mortal sins.** As with any other case in which the matter of a sin is grave, contraception is a mortal sin only if the two subjective conditions, sufficient reflection and full consent, are met—in other words, only if someone chooses to contracept despite his or her judgment that it is gravely wrong in itself to do so, or that it is gravely wrong to act against the Church's teaching on the matter (see *CMP,* 17.A).

Given the definition of contraception, people cannot practice it without choosing precisely to prevent conception. But only God knows how many violate a judgment of conscience which meets the requirement of sufficient reflection. Despite all that has been said to the contrary, even nonbelievers can understand why contraception is wrong, and the Church's teaching has been widely publicized. Yet the gravity of the matter is not obvious, and both theological dissent and pastoral neglect nurture

---

112. Paul VI, *Humanae vitae,* 25, *AAS* 60 (1968) 499, *PE,* 277.25. In his pastoral guidance, John Paul II, *Familiaris consortio,* 34, *AAS* 74 (1982) 124, *OR,* 21–28 Dec. 1981, 7, likewise envisages "a progress that demands awareness of sin, a sincere commitment to observe the moral law, and the ministry of reconciliation." Summarizing the same teaching, John Paul II, Address to Participants in a Study Seminar on "Responsible Parenthood" (17 Sept. 1983), 4, *Inseg.* 6.2 (1983) 564, *OR,* 10 Oct. 1983, 7, recalls Catholic teaching concerning grace and the sacraments: "To maintain that situations exist in which it is not, *de facto,* possible for the spouses to be faithful to *all* the requirements of the truth of conjugal love is equivalent to forgetting this event of grace which characterizes the New Covenant: the grace of the Holy Spirit makes possible that which is not possible to man, left solely to his own powers. It is therefore necessary to support the spouses in their spiritual lives, to invite them to resort frequently to the Sacraments of Confession and the Eucharist for a continual return, a permanent conversion to the truth of conjugal love."

confusion in many people's minds. Moreover, mere guilt feelings, together with awareness of violating the Church's "official teaching," do not show that someone has the awareness of grave matter required for sufficient reflection. Indeed, many Catholics say their choice to use contraception is not contrary to their conscience. Of course, that assertion could manifest self-deception and rationalization rather than a genuine judgment of conscience (see *CMP*, 3.C.6–7).[113]

Question F: What Are One's Responsibilities with Respect to Health?

An accurate and clear understanding of health itself is necessary to grasp responsibilities in respect to it. With that foundation, it usually is easy to see what measures should be taken to protect health. When life is at risk, however, specific norms are needed to guide the decision whether to accept medical treatment. People should not intentionally or unreasonably do anything which harms health and should use psychoactive substances rightly, not abuse them.

Individuals should fulfill all these responsibilities with respect to their own health; but they also have a social dimension, inasmuch as people, especially members of families, should care for one another and cooperate in protecting and promoting this good.

1. Health Is a Certain Part of the Good of Human Life Itself

Health can be misunderstood in different ways, with the bad result that suitable means to promote it are not used, while means suitable for promoting health are mistakenly used to try to solve other problems. To understand responsibilities with respect to health, one must understand clearly what it is.

a) **Health is well-integrated, harmonious, psychosomatic functioning.** As sentient organisms, human persons have many capacities, both organic and psychic, which can function or fail to function, and which can function in diverse ways. If one or several of these capacities are impeded from functioning or function in a

---

113. John Paul II, Address to Second International Congress on Moral Theology, 4; *L'Osservatore Romano,* It. ed., 13 Nov. 1988, 4; *OR,* 19–26 Dec. 1988, 7, restates Vatican II's teaching on conscience (see GS 16) and firmly rejects the subjectivist notion that conscience itself creates moral norms. He then draws consequences which he says are to be stressed: "Since the *Magisterium of the Church* was created by Christ the Lord to enlighten conscience, then to appeal to that conscience precisely to contest the truth of what is taught by the Magisterium implies rejection of the Catholic concept both of the Magisterium and moral conscience. To speak about the inviolable dignity of conscience without further specification, runs the risk of grave errors. There is a great difference between the person who falls into error after having used all the means at his or her disposal in the search for truth, and the situation of one who, either through simple acquiescence to the majority opinion, often deliberately created by the powers of the world, or through negligence, takes little pains to discover the truth. . . . The Church's Magisterium is among the means which Christ's redeeming love has provided to avoid this danger of error. In his name it has a real teaching authority. Therefore, it cannot be said that the faithful have embarked on a diligent search for truth if they do not take into account what the Magisterium teaches, or if, by putting it on the same level as any other source of knowledge, one makes oneself judge, or if in doubt, one follows one's own opinion or that of theologians, preferring it to the sure teaching of the Magisterium."

way not coordinated with others, the person as a whole suffers some form of disability or disease. But if the various human capacities are actuated in such a way that they contribute to and do not impede one another, every capacity can develop and be actuated as fully as the total potentiality of the rational, sentient organism allows. Then the person as a whole is fully functioning with well-integrated, harmonious functions: he or she is healthy.

b) **Health should not be reduced to pleasure and felt satisfaction.** Normally, pleasure and felt satisfaction of all sorts are experiences of healthy functioning, while severe or prolonged pain and undue emotional distress (as distinct from appropriate pain, sadness, or fear) are experiences of disability, disease, or threats to health. However, both healthy and unhealthy functioning can occur without manifesting themselves directly in conscious experience. Moreover, pain in the strict sense, the sensation of pain, is an important element of healthy functioning, because it signals incipient harms and stresses, and motivates appropriate organic and psychic adjustments. For instance, the pain felt upon touching a hot stove makes one pull one's hand away, preventing serious damage; the pain felt in a strained joint makes one rest it and allow it to heal. Thus, pleasure and felt satisfaction are aspects of healthy functioning, but not the whole of it; pain as a sensation also is an aspect of healthy functioning; and undue emotional distress is only one part of unhealthy functioning.

People often do confuse feeling good with being well and feeling bad with being ill. But this is a confusion, for it mistakenly reduces realities to appearances.

c) **Health should not be expanded to include total human well-being.** Health, understood as well-integrated, harmonious psychosomatic functioning, is analogous to the goods of other aspects of the person: knowledge and wisdom, the moral virtues, and various skills and cultivated talents. The concept of health also sometimes is used metaphorically in descriptions of the integrity of human persons as they were created by God: sin "wounds" and grace "heals" human nature. Thus, *health* is easily expanded to embrace all human goods and to refer to the integral flourishing of persons; at the same time, many evils from which people can suffer are confused with diseases.

However, very different acts are appropriate for promoting good psychosomatic functioning and other human goods in the intellectual, moral, and cultural orders. Hence, the concept of health should not be expanded to include all aspects of human well-being.[114]

d) **Health is both good in itself and instrumental to other goods.** As understood here, health is not a human good separate from life itself. Human life has several dimensions—the organic, psychic, intellectual, moral, and cultural—and can be realized both more and less fully. Health is the fullness of life in its physiological and psychic dimensions, as distinct from the others. Consequently, health shares in the sanctity of life; wrong choices that destroy, damage, or impede health violate life.

---

114. Many definitions of *health* err on this side; for examples, see the treatment of health and disease in Ashley and O'Rourke, *Healthcare Ethics,* 3rd ed., 20–35.

While, health, as part of the good of life, is good in itself, not merely a means to other goods, it also is a means—a more or less important condition for the intellectual, moral, and cultural fulfillment of the person. This fact provides additional reasons for protecting and promoting health, but it also dictates that the ways chosen to serve it be consonant with these other goods. Moreover, health's instrumental value should not be exaggerated; it does not guarantee the other goods, and its absence does not always greatly detract from them. For example, when ill health is not the consequence of a person's ongoing wrongdoing, deteriorating health and moral growth can go together.

2. Reasonable Measures Should Be Taken to Protect and Promote Health

Within the framework of one's personal vocation as a whole, one should act for one's own health and that of others, especially of family members and neighbors.

a) **Responsibility for health begins with oneself and one's family.** Because health is well-integrated psychosomatic functioning, and such functions always go on and always are subject to disturbing factors, there is a constant need in every person's life for action to protect and promote health. People have the greatest motivation and opportunity to attend to this need in relation to themselves and those with whom they live. Hence, the responsibility for each person's health primarily falls on that person, assuming he or she is competent, and on those on whom he or she closely depends: family members, neighbors, and so on.

While health itself is realized mainly in individuals, it also exists in communities insofar as they constitute unified, psychosomatic systems; for example, a couple can function well reproductively and a group can interact well psychologically. When health itself is communal, cooperation for its sake clearly is essential. But even insofar as health is an individual good, its protection and promotion generally require social efforts. For example, eating is a family activity, and all members of a family must cooperate so that the meals they share will meet the needs and promote the health of every member. Again, the Golden Rule often requires neighbors to advise and encourage one another to do what is healthful, and to help one another avoid or overcome illnesses and other threats to health.

b) **Choices concerning health should take other goods into account.** Partly because health is an aspect of the basic good of life and a means to other goods, but also partly because many people excessively fear death and greatly esteem health care technology, people in affluent nations sometimes tend to think of health as if it were the most important value. As a result, they assume that other goods must yield to health's paramount claims, and so deliberate and make choices regarding health without duly considering their other responsibilities. Important as it is, however, health is only one good among others, and Christians should harmonize choices concerning health with other elements of their personal vocations. This seldom means that health should be neglected entirely, but it often demands that the means used to protect and promote health be selected and limited to avoid interfering with other areas of life. Of course, one's total vocational responsibilities also can call for special care for one's health; for example, a couple with several young children have a special duty to take good care of themselves so that they will be fully capable of caring for each other and raising their children.

c) **One should pursue the reality, not merely the feeling, of health.** Because pain is an important warning signal, no unusual, intense, or persistent pain or other sign of abnormal functioning should be ignored. One should try to find the cause of pain and other symptoms, deal with the real problem they represent, and in this way also eliminate the pain. However, since it is easy to confuse health's reality with its appearance, many people are less interested in being well than in feeling well, and so they fail to do what they should to protect and promote health. They pay little attention to diet, exercise, and so on, while neglecting preventive measures and checkups. They wait until symptoms become troublesome before doing anything about a health problem, and at that point seek technical health care assistance, which they think of mainly as a technology to eliminate or mitigate pain. More interested in gaining relief from the symptoms than in curing the underlying disease, however, they follow the plan of treatment prescribed only until they feel better instead of doing all that they know they must if they are to recover fully.

d) **One should moderate the satisfaction of natural tendencies.** Like animals of other kinds, humans have natural tendencies: drives or appetites to eat, drink, move about, rest, and so on. But unlike other animals, humans should moderate the satisfaction of these tendencies, with a view not only to health but to their own total good and that of the communities in which they participate. Yet it can be difficult to maintain even the moderation of appetites required for health, inasmuch as the distortion of human emotional responsiveness due to original sin often causes people to experience excessive anxiety, tiredness, and desire for immediate satisfaction (see *CMP,* 14.G). Hence, one must discipline one's natural tendencies according to a reasonable plan, which will take health requirements into account in the context of one's whole vocation. The habit of such moderation is the virtue of temperance (see *S.t.,* 2–2, q. 141, a. 6).

Given the basic practical insight into the good of health, experience teaches, within limits, what is moderate: it is a matter of common sense to stop eating before one becomes ill, to feed children enough so that they grow, and so on. But common sense is not always adequate to the new problems which affluence creates by enabling people to make more choices between healthier and less healthy styles of life, including food, drink, and exercise. Moreover, modern knowledge of nutrition, exercise, and other factors affecting health greatly increases people's capacity to judge accurately what is moderate. Hence, although it remains the same in principle, temperance now requires taking into account and acting on all available, relevant, and reasonably credible information. For example, given what is now known about the causes of heart and arterial disease, temperate people today will adopt certain restrictions on their diet which sound reason would not have dictated in earlier times.

e) **One should use other means to protect and promote health.** Besides moderating the satisfaction of natural tendencies, one can and should take advantage of modern knowledge and technical means to pursue health, even when the relevant action does not spring from any spontaneous appetite. Thus, one's regimen should include the use of some leisure time for exercise appropriate in amount and type (see GS 61). Elementary rules of hygiene should be learned and followed in order to avoid infectious diseases, food poisoning, damage to teeth, and so on. One should avail oneself of technical means: inoculations, medical and dental checkups, and so forth.

f) One should employ the health care system appropriately. The health care system of professional physicians, hospitals, and so on can be an important help in fulfilling one's responsibility to protect and promote one's own health and that of one's dependents. It should be used not only to deal with health problems after they arise, but to anticipate and prevent them insofar as possible.

Nevertheless, physicians and psychologists cannot solve all life's problems. If a person has guilt feelings because he or she has sinned, repentance and reconciliation, not tranquilizers or psychotherapy, are the answer. If a married couple's sexual relationship is not going well because of selfishness, kindness and self-denial, not sex therapy, constitute the proper remedy.

But for genuine health problems, technical and professional advice, prescriptions, treatments, and surgery often are indispensable. Even so, a person should not assume a completely passive role, abdicating his or her own responsibility and expecting or allowing health care professionals to do everything necessary. Instead, patients should be the primary agents of their own health care.

g) One should take responsibility in using the health care system. People should make it clear to health care professionals that they regard them as helpers. This includes insisting on being told the truth about their condition and prospects. The professional is the authority in the sense that he or she has competence based on extensive education and experience; it would therefore be presumptuous, foolish, and self-defeating to ignore the professional's observations, practical reasoning, and advice. But the person seeking help is the authority in the sense that he or she is both the employer of the professional and the subject of the treatment process, with every right to determine what morally acceptable end will be pursued and which of the available and technically feasible means he or she will personally accept.

Therefore, physicians, hospitals, and so on should be chosen carefully. While seeking advice in order to learn about technically feasible possibilities and their advantages and disadvantages, people should make their own judgments and choices. If a health care professional advises doing something morally wrong in itself, that advice should be rejected, and the relationship probably should be terminated. If, as is generally the case, the advice is not morally objectionable in itself, one should consider it carefully, keeping in mind the wider responsibilities of one's life, which no one else can fully appreciate.

Partly because people who seek health care services often abdicate personal responsibility and assume the passive role of patients, health care professionals have tended to assume too much responsibility for decision making. As a result of this and other factors, they often are held legally liable for any unsatisfactory outcome of treatment. Partly to shield themselves from legal liability, however, many health care professionals proceed defensively and order more tests and treatments than necessary, rather than drawing a reasonable line and accepting reasonable risks. Hence, one also should be alert to the possibility that one is receiving excessively cautious advice, and should take responsibility for refusing tests and treatments recommended by health care professionals only, or primarily, to protect themselves from potential legal liability.[115]

Moreover, some professionals recommend major surgery and other complex and costly treatment which equally competent professionals consider unnecessary or no more promising than simpler alternatives. Therefore, if it seems reasonable to follow professional advice, but doing so would involve great burdens, a second opinion should be sought from an independent, equally competent professional source, and in discussing the matter one should inquire particularly about the advantages and disadvantages of any reasonable alternatives.

Someone who judges that professional advice should be accepted should listen carefully to any instructions and ask questions regarding his or her role in the treatment process until entirely clear about his or her personal responsibilities. Then those responsibilities should be fulfilled conscientiously.

3. Norms for Deciding Whether to Accept Health Care

People ordinarily encounter no special moral difficulty in reaching a decision to accept or refuse treatment that would protect or promote their own or a dependent's life or health. However, when life is at risk, many people need more specific norms than those already stated. The norms articulated here also may be helpful in less serious situations.

Although professional nurses participate in medical treatment, medical care can be distinguished from basic nursing care: the latter includes those forms of care which a reasonable person who is sufficiently alert and able could and would provide for himself or herself, or which a good mother could and would provide for her baby. This distinction is important for two reasons. First, basic nursing care has a special importance in maintaining human solidarity with those unable to care for themselves; to deny anyone such care when it could be given implies that the individual is no longer regarded as a person. Second, in calculating the costs of medical treatment and considering how much treatment is anyone's maximum fair share, the cost of basic nursing care should not be included; someone who wants to argue that society cannot afford to feed, house, and tend nonproductive consumers, such as the severely retarded and insane, should not try to make the case by reclassifying basic nursing care and its cost as medical treatment.

Nevertheless, when basic nursing care is provided together with medical treatment, the two become intertwined and the boundaries between them blur. Rather than attempting to distinguish sharply between medical treatment and basic nursing care, the following analysis deals with health care as a concrete reality, but pays special attention to the value of human solidarity.

---

115. James Druckenbrod, "Medical Malpractice: A Christian Ethical Perspective," *Linacre Quarterly* 58 (Nov. 1991): 17–26, offers sound insight regarding the relationship between medical malpractice and distortions in the physician-patient relationship.

a) **All prospective benefits should be considered.** Attempts to maintain life can be excessive and unreasonable, since some motives for seeking health care are not reasons for doing so. People can be motivated by excessive fear of sickness and unwillingness to accept the inevitability of death; pride can motivate them to try to make themselves function perfectly. Such motives can lead to selfish use of health care facilities and services: a form of greed that wastes scarce resources.

Still, since life is a basic human good (as has been explained in A.2) and since health is an aspect of the good of life (1.d, above), a reason never is lacking to seek or accept any kind of care at all likely to protect life or promote health.

Some are quick to call health care "futile" if it does not offer hope of curing or significantly improving the functioning of a dying, comatose, or seriously disabled person.[116] That view, however, rests on an assumption, usually unstated, that life and health are good only as instrumental to quality of life: functioning at some arbitrarily determined level. Usually the level chosen is that at which a person is conscious or likely to gain (or regain) consciousness, along with experience such that continuing consciousness probably will seem preferable to oblivion. However, because life is good for the human person as a bodily being, not only as a conscious subject (see A.2, above), care that keeps someone alive, no matter what his or her condition, really does benefit that person, even if only in a small way. Therefore, health care is not strictly speaking futile (that is, utterly useless) if it sustains life even for a short time or in any way mitigates a disease or handicap.[117]

Providing life-sustaining health care also can realize other values. Rightly motivated care maintains human solidarity with those cared for: it affirms their dignity as persons, manifests benevolence toward them, and maintains the bond of human communion with them. Some will deny that maintaining human solidarity with an unconscious person in any way benefits him or her. However, unconscious people plainly can be burdened insofar as they can suffer indignities; by the same token, they can be benefited by being cared for out of a love which respects their dignity.

---

116. Many deny that keeping people alive benefits them when there is no prospect that they will ever gain or regain the use of their specifically human capacities. For example, Kevin O'Rourke, O.P., "The A.M.A. Statement on Tube Feeding: An Ethical Analysis," *America*, 22 Nov. 1986, 322, focusing on the tube feeding of comatose persons, argues that it is useless to sustain life unless doing so helps a person to pursue "the purpose of life," and writes: "In order to pursue the purpose of life, one needs some degree of cognitive-affective function." Richard McCormick, "The Defective Infant (2): Practical Considerations," *The Tablet* (London), 21 July 1984, 691, makes a more general assertion along similar lines: "Life is a value to be preserved precisely as providing the condition for other values and therefore in so far as these other values remain attainable. To say anything else is, I submit, to make an idol of mere physical existence." McCormick's question-begging dichotomy between regarding life as merely instrumental and treating it as an idol leaves no room for the truth: life is one basic human good among others.

117. Thus, John Myers, Bishop of Peoria, "Advance Directives and the Catholic Health Facility," *Origins* 21 (3 Oct. 1991): 279, points out with respect to providing food and water: "Artificial nutrition and hydration are useful for the provision of nutrients and useless when they fail to provide nutrients; they are not useless when they fail to secure complete recovery from some symptom, pathology or condition extrinsic to the need for nutrients."

Moreover, the bond of human communion can be maintained with permanently unconscious persons despite their inability to enjoy the good experiences normally characteristic of this bond as it exists among conscious persons. For while interpersonal communion normally has psychological components on both sides, essentially it is a moral reality, maintained by fidelity of will and action. Just as a couple eagerly expecting their baby's birth establish a parental relationship with him or her, a husband faithful to his comatose wife maintains marital communion with her. In doing so, he truly benefits not only himself (by continuing to be a good husband) but her, although she cannot consciously enjoy and respond to this benefit. Similarly and generally, families and larger communities that faithfully care for their unconscious members maintain human communion with them and thereby benefit not only themselves (by continuing to be loving families and genuine communities) but their unconscious members.

b) Some motives for forgoing health care are not good reasons. Fearing an unfavorable diagnosis, people often delay seeking care for themselves or their dependents because they shrink from the bad news or else from the burdens associated with needed care. Such motives are merely emotional. Considered simply as such, emotional repugnance is not a rational motive, and so cannot provide a reason to forgo health care. A person who feels repugnance toward doing what would protect life or promote health must discern that feeling's relationship to intelligible goods.

Sometimes, experiencing and/or anticipating much suffering and little or no enjoyment, people who are seriously ill or disabled seek their own early death. They have a reason to forgo care, for in that way they avoid experiences which they find repugnant. However, it is a bad means, since it amounts to killing themselves, and so is morally wrong, as suicide always is, regardless of the ulterior end or method. Similarly, people sometimes choose to forgo or terminate care of a dependent in order that the person will die, thus forestalling the burdensome consequences of his or her continuing life. This is a choice to kill, and so is morally wrong, even if motivated by the desire to prevent suffering: so-called mercy killing.

In refusing or limiting health care for themselves or others, people sometimes wrongly accept death without intending it. Perhaps a person who still has grave responsibilities to fulfill refuses some life-sustaining treatment because he or she unreasonably fears the pain it would involve. Or a couple are told that their newborn daughter will be severely retarded and also needs expensive surgery, not covered by insurance; if the baby were not going to be retarded, they would be ready to spend the money, but they decide to refuse the surgery and allow the girl to die, discriminating against her because of her handicap.

c) The burdens of health care can provide an adequate reason to forgo it. Life is like other basic human goods: it does not override every other good, nor does it always deserve preference. There always are reasons not to do something that would protect life or promote health, since health care always involves burdens. Hence, sound judgment requires identifying both the prospective benefits and burdens of possible forms of care. In this matter, the Holy See teaches:

It is also permissible to make do with the normal means that medicine can offer. Therefore one cannot impose on anyone the obligation to have recourse to a technique which is already in use but which carries a risk or is burdensome. Such a refusal is not the equivalent of suicide; on the contrary, it should be considered as an acceptance of the human condition, or a wish to avoid the application of a medical procedure disproportionate to the results that can be expected, or a desire not to impose excessive expense on the family or the community.[118]

Therefore, burdens that attach to the care itself can provide adequate reasons to forgo it. These burdens can be grouped in three categories:

i) Care imposes economic costs and utilizes facilities and services which usually could be put to other good uses.

ii) Many things which can be done for the sake of health also can have bad side effects for health itself. Surgery always carries some risks of death and/or disability; medications often interfere with various functions. Examinations and treatments often are painful, and pain can interfere with good functioning, especially at the psychic level.

iii) Many things which can be done for the sake of health have bad side effects for other human goods. They may restrict one's inner life and activity, prevent one from moving about freely, isolate one from family and associates, and so on.

d) Moral standards should be used to evaluate benefits and burdens. Occasionally a possible treatment—for example, of a married person's sexual dysfunction by training sessions with another partner—is morally wrong in itself, and so should be excluded regardless of its prospective benefits and even apart from any burdens it might involve. But when it is not wrong in itself either to accept some form of health care or forgo it, the benefits and burdens must be evaluated. Unless these are measured by moral standards, however, there is no rational way to commensurate them, since they are diverse instances of values. Therefore, relevant moral standards must be employed.

e) One should judge in the light of one's whole personal vocation. In judging whether to accept or refuse a possible or proposed form of health care for oneself, the first consideration ought to be what decision, if any, is dictated by one's religious responsibilities or duties toward other people. Sometimes these demand that the care be accepted despite its burdens: one must make one's peace with God, do one's duty toward one's dependents, perhaps complete important work. At other times, fairness toward other people who would bear the burdens of the care requires forgoing it despite prospective benefits. Even if fairness does not dictate accepting or refusing care, mercy can point to the appropriateness of forgoing it in order to avoid burdens to others, including its costs.

If the preceding considerations do not lead to a decision and one is confident that both options remain morally available, the next step is to examine the motives inclining one to each. Merely emotional motives, such as anxiety, should be set aside in favor of reasons. Since reasons support both options, either can be good,

---

118. Congregation for the Doctrine of the Faith, *Declaration on Euthanasia*, 4, *AAS* 72 (1980) 550–51, Flannery, 2:515–16.

and one must discern between them. In doing so, the consonance of each with one's entire personal vocation should be tested.

When all the goods at stake are considered in this light, it sometimes is reasonable to judge that other goods should take priority over health.[119] Moreover, there are persons, especially the dying who have no special responsibility to try to prolong life, who may see no reason why they must accept the burdens of life-sustaining care. If they neither will death as an end nor choose it as a means, but prefer to accept it rather than accept the burdens of some or all kinds of care, they may forgo the burdensome care.

f) Adults should consider appointing an agent for health care decisions. Parents or guardians make health care decisions for children, and competent adults can make them for themselves. In times past, when an adult no longer could make such decisions, usually few of them remained to be made, and the family and their physician ordinarily had no difficulty arriving at a consensus. Now, however, this approach often no longer works well because of many factors: advances in medical technology require more decisions and more complex ones; with changes in health care delivery, physicians, administrators, and others unfamiliar with the patient and the family are likely to be involved; concerns about potential liability for malpractice can lead to care which is excessive in some respects; families sometimes lack the stability and solidarity necessary for sound decision making; disagreements among those involved regarding moral norms and their application sometimes block consensus; and so on. Thus, many prudent Christian adults have good reasons to seek some way of determining how decisions regarding their health care will be made if, at some future time, they become unable to make them. The matter has been confused, however, because proponents of euthanasia, exploiting concerns about possible excessive treatment and using *death with dignity* as a slogan, have advocated the so-called living will—an advance directive to limit health care—as a step toward the legalization of euthanasia.[120]

While it would be possible to make a morally acceptable advance directive similar to the so-called living will, doing so does not determine adequately how health care decisions will be made if one cannot make them. Most such directives take effect only if one is terminally ill, but many people not terminally ill are unable to make vital decisions. Moreover, such directives must either deal with few

119. For example, Pius XII, Address to an International Congress (responding to questions proposed by Dr. Bruno Haid), *AAS* 49 (1957) 1030, *The Pope Speaks* 4 (1957–58): 396, dealing with three moral questions about the use of respirators, points out that one normally is not required to use extraordinary means of preserving life, since a strict obligation to use them "would be too burdensome for most men and would render the attainment of the higher, more important good too difficult. Life, health, all temporal activities are in fact subordinated to spiritual ends." Pius apparently means that dying patients may be spared the respirator if that will help them to make their peace with God, for he goes on at once to treat the administration of the sacraments. This teaching does not imply that there is a hierarchy of value among the basic goods considered in themselves, but that priorities among them are established by unfettered practical reason and reflected by the commitments which shape an upright person's life; see Germain Grisez, Joseph Boyle, and John Finnis, "Practical Principles, Moral Truth, and Ultimate Ends," *American Journal of Jurisprudence* 32 (1987): 137–41.

120. See Grisez and Boyle, *Life and Death with Liberty and Justice,* 14, 100–107.

potential problems or resort to dangerously vague language or both, because it is impossible either to know now what decisions will be needed in the future or to gather in advance the information required to make prudent decisions.[121]

A more adequate and prudent approach is to designate someone, usually a mature, dependable family member or close friend, as one's agent or proxy, to make necessary health care decisions on one's behalf if one cannot decide for oneself, and to designate a second similar person as alternate to fulfill that role if the first is unable, unwilling, or unavailable. Only persons should be chosen who accept relevant moral truths and who can be trusted to apply them prudently. It is important in naming these persons to do all that is required so that the designation will be legally effective, and expert advice may be necessary for this purpose. Copies of the document, with an indication of how the original can be obtained, should be given to those designated and others who should be aware of it: physicians, family members, friends, and so on.[122]

In making a document of this sort, some people add to it specific instructions regarding particular procedures, for example, not to resuscitate. In general, doing this is unwise, because problems cannot be resolved prudently until they arise and relevant information is available. Instead, those who designate agents should discuss any special concerns with them and, if it seems appropriate, confer jointly with them and those who might help clarify areas of concern, for example, a sound adviser about moral questions or a physician about medical information.

In some jurisdictions, nevertheless, various provisions or limitations in the law may make it appropriate for a person designating an agent for health care decisions to provide some specific instructions in the document. On the one hand, instructions excluding options which are never morally acceptable—sterilization, abortion, actions or omissions intended to cause or hasten death—may be necessary or appropriate to ensure that an agent's morally sound decisions will be respected. On the other hand, instructions explicitly authorizing an agent to reject or withdraw certain forms of life-sustaining care may be necessary to empower him or her to make those decisions if appropriate. For example, the law may presume that agents are not authorized to deny services which every patient can reasonably expect; but, in a spirit of Christian mercy, someone might prefer to save others the costs and burdens of care if it ever happens that he or she is unconscious and there is no reasonable hope of recovering consciousness. To ensure that an agent will be able to carry out that wish, it might be necessary to include in the document an appropriate, specific instruction.[123]

121. For a critique of a proposed Uniform Rights of the Terminally Ill Act, see Committee for Pro-Life Activities, National Conference of Catholic Bishops, "The Rights of the Terminally Ill" (2 July 1986), *Origins* 16 (4 Sept. 1986): 222–24.

122. See New York State Catholic Conference, *New York State's Health Care Proxy Law: A Catholic Perspective* (Albany, N.Y.: New York State Catholic Conference, 1991); The Massachusetts Catholic Conference, *The Health Care Proxy Bill: A Catholic Guide* (1 Dec. 1991); Medical Ethics Commission, Archdiocese of Chicago, *Commentary: Illinois Durable Power of Attorney for Health Care* (5 Nov. 1991).

123. With such an instruction, might not the agent refuse even ordinary means? A trustworthy agent will not automatically refuse anything, but will judge which means are extraordinary and

g) Others sometimes should limit health care for the dying. Not infrequently, dying people have not determined in advance how decisions will be made to govern their care. Then, when they either can no longer make such decisions or express their wishes, their families and those helping to care for them must judge whether various kinds of care are appropriate in view of the burdens they entail and the benefits they promise. Very often, their judgment will favor continuing the care. By applying the Golden Rule, however, those concerned sometimes rightly judge that it would be too burdensome to the patient or unfair to others to initiate or continue some elements of care.

Sometimes good care for those whose death is imminent includes doing something which will shorten their lives. Assuming there is no special reason to prolong life—for example, to allow the person an opportunity to prepare spiritually for death—and death is not intended, that may be done which is in the patient's real interest, even if it will result in earlier death. For example, if no other means of making a patient comfortable is available and sedation will not prevent him or her from fulfilling exigent responsibilities, the narcotics necessary to suppress pain may be administered, even if doing so will shorten life.[124] Again, terminal patients may be cared for at home or in a hospice, where they can be near their loved ones and costs are lower, rather than in a hospital or other fully equipped facility, where their lives could be prolonged.

People often hesitate to direct discontinuing some means of life support—a respirator, say—whose discontinuation will lead promptly to death, even though they would unhesitatingly refuse to initiate its use if that were the question before them. If the reason for not using some means would be its obvious burdensomeness, that same reason justifies discontinuing it; the reluctance is an irrelevant feeling which should be set aside.

h) Others ordinarily should care for the severely handicapped and comatose. Supplying food and water to comatose persons is not in itself costly or otherwise significantly burdensome. Rather, it is the care as a whole that is expensive and the condition as a whole that others find burdensome. Hence, the choice to withdraw elements of life-sustaining care which are not significantly burdensome in themselves, either to the patient or to others, sometimes amounts to a morally excluded choice to kill. But even if death only is accepted as a side effect,

---

which ordinary, all things considered, and accept ordinary means as long as there are any. When the benefit which is decisive in entitling a person to care is that it maintains human solidarity, that person (or his or her agent if so authorized) need not accept the care, since one can forgo the care without depriving oneself of human solidarity, much as one spouse, though entitled to the other's company, may forgo it when the latter wishes to work abroad for a year. Thus, in such a case and some others, people are entitled to care which they (and authorized agents making decisions for them) are not obliged to accept. If they (or their properly authorized agents) forgo that care out of mercy, the moral goodness of their refusing it does not imply that noncompetent persons without authorized agents may be deprived of similar care: see h, below.

124. See Pius XII, Address Responding to Questions Proposed by the Italian Society of Anesthesiology (24 Feb. 1957), *AAS* 49 (1957) 147, *The Pope Speaks* 4 (1957–58): 48; cited by Congregation for the Doctrine of the Faith, *Declaration on Euthanasia, AAS* 72 (1980) 548, Flannery, 2:514.

the choice to discontinue life-sustaining care as a whole, unless made to fulfill some other, overriding responsibility, is a choice to break off human solidarity and discontinue care.

In choosing to forgo care and accept one's own death in order to avoid burdening others with the expense of care to which one is entitled, a person acts with mercy toward them. But no one can be merciful on others' behalf, and so, unless authorized by someone to do so, one cannot exercise mercy for him or her by avoiding burdening oneself and/or others with care to which he or she is entitled. On the contrary, that is treating the person as a useless object, to be disposed of as cheaply and expeditiously as possible. Therefore, those elements of care that are not very burdensome in themselves ordinarily should be provided even to persons who will never recover consciousness. Even assuming (not conceding) that there is little or no benefit to them in prolonging their lives, it remains of great benefit, to them and everyone concerned, to treat them as persons to the end. Hence, the Golden Rule, especially when informed by Christian love, requires that no one be left entirely without care except in extreme situations, for example, disasters in which it simply is not possible to care for everyone.[125]

i) **The preceding norms clarify *ordinary* and *extraordinary*.** In its effort to articulate norms for accepting and forgoing various forms of health care, Catholic moral theology has spoken of "ordinary means" and "extraordinary means."[126] In practice, an ordinary means is identified simply by determining what means is morally required. Hence, using this expression adds nothing to—and is less helpful than—the expressions used in the specific norms already articulated.[127]

Medical progress lessens the burdensomeness of many procedures and forms of health care, so that those extraordinary in the past often are morally required today. For example, before antiseptic procedures, even simple surgery involved a grave risk to life, and therefore many moralists reasonably held that a surgical operation was an extraordinary means. It is fallacious to use their opinion today to argue that

---

125. Cf. 5.H.4, above, where this matter also is treated. See U.S. Bishops' Pro-Life Committee, "Nutrition and Hydration: Moral and Pastoral Reflections," *Origins* 21 (9 Apr. 1992): 705–12. Also see Germain Grisez, "Should Nutrition and Hydration Be Provided to Permanently Comatose and Other Mentally Disabled Persons?" *Linacre Quarterly* 57 (May 1990): 30–41; while others should care for such persons, those making decisions on their behalf sometimes may judge that fairness requires that the means used in their care be limited, for example, that they not be sustained indefinitely in intensive care facilities (41–42). Orville N. Griese, "Feeding the Hopeless and the Helpless," in *Conserving Human Life,* ed. Russell E. Smith (Braintree, Mass.: The Pope John Center, 1989), 149–232, treats the matter in detail, using the method of classical moral theology, and arrives at similar conclusions.

126. See Daniel A. Cronin, "The Moral Law in Regard to the Ordinary and Extraordinary Means of Conserving Life," in *Conserving Human Life,* 33–76. A brief history of the ordinary-extraordinary means distinction: Gary M. Atkinson, "Theological History of Catholic Teaching on Prolonging Life," in *Moral Responsibility in Prolonging Life Decisions,* ed. Donald G. McCarthy and Albert S. Moraczewski, O.P. (St. Louis: The Pope John Center, 1981), 95–115.

127. Congregation for the Doctrine of the Faith, *Declaration on Euthanasia,* 4, *AAS* 72 (1980) 549–50, Flannery, 2:515, acknowledges that to say that one need not use "extraordinary" means "is perhaps less clear today, by reason of the imprecision of the term and the rapid progress made in the treatment of sickness." The document proceeds to recommend judgment by comparison of burdens and benefits.

surgery needed to save the life of a handicapped newborn may rightly be forgone, when the motive is the anticipated burdens of the handicap, rather than of the surgery, to the child and others. Surgery that would routinely be performed on a child without a handicap does not become an extraordinary means in the case of a handicapped child.

4. One Should Not Intentionally or Unreasonably Do What Harms Health

Since health is part of the basic human good of life, it shares in life's sanctity. Intentional acts contrary to health are always wrong, and unfairly or otherwise unreasonably accepting side effects harmful to health also is wrong.

a) One should never intentionally harm anyone's health. It is always wrong to seek as an end or choose as a means to some other end to destroy, damage, or impede any instance of a basic human good (see *CMP*, 8.G–H). That is done in intentionally harming one's own or another's health. So, one may never intentionally harm anyone's health. For example, one should not try to pass on a disease to others out of resentment toward them or toward society at large. One should not purposely weaken others physically or psychologically in order to take advantage of them or gain a competitive advantage. One should not go on a hunger strike to debilitate oneself (much less bring about one's death) as a means of gaining political leverage for some good cause.

By contrast with the morally unacceptable hunger strike, however, a person could engage in a hunger strike—better called a "fast"—as a morally upright symbolic gesture. In this case, the choice would be, not to debilitate oneself, but only to show seriousness about one's cause by frustrating the natural desire to eat, much as in fasting penitentially. Someone engaging in such a morally acceptable fast would limit it to avoid the risk of death or serious harm to health, and any bad effects for health would only be accepted as side effects, not intended (see *S.t.*, 2–2, q. 147, a. 1, ad 2).

b) One should not unfairly accept bad side effects to others' health. It always is unjust to accept any bad side effect for others in making a choice that is itself wrong. So, for example, those who defraud others by selling them useless or unnecessary medications or surgery not only are guilty of the fraud but of any bad side effects which might follow from using the medication or having the operation.

But even if what is done is good in itself, a person should take into account its potential impact on others' health, and use the Golden Rule to judge the acceptability of any foreseen bad side effects. For example, those handling food should be conscientious about hygienic measures necessary to prevent contamination, those with communicable diseases should try to avoid spreading them to others, those camping in the wilderness should not pollute streams from which others might drink. People should not encourage others' intemperance, for example, by serving them too many drinks out of misguided hospitality or sending them gifts of foods in which they tend to overindulge. People should not interfere with others' needed rest, for example, by noisy partying.

c) **One should reasonably avoid bad side effects to one's health.** To do anything wrong in itself while foreseeing possible bad side effects to one's own health also is wrong. For example, to engage in illicit sex with the possibility of contracting a sexually transmitted disease is doubly wrong.[128] Moreover, even if what is done is not wrong in itself, a person must have an adequate reason to accept bad side effects to his or her own health. People who take steroids for muscle building violate this norm; so do those who, out of vanity, fail to dress appropriately against bad weather.

Nevertheless, for a good reason, bad side effects to one's own health may be accepted. For example, those ministering to or caring for the sick should take all reasonable precautions but, having done so, may and often should accept serious risks. People who cannot earn a living except by work hazardous to their health also may accept the health risks involved and usually are morally required to do so.

d) **Work should be arranged to avoid bad side effects to health.** Many jobs involve health and safety hazards which can be eliminated or at least lessened by precautions. Also, any kind of work can be carried to the point at which the worker's capacities are exhausted and he or she suffers or at least risks physiological or psychological harm. Greed or other motives sometimes tempt not only employers and managers but workers themselves to exceed reasonable limits and neglect reasonable precautions. Therefore, a person should apply to work the norms that bad side effects to others' health should not be unfairly accepted and bad side effects to one's own should reasonably be avoided. Not only the need for the results of work and desire to profit from it but the nature of the work, the conditions under which it is done, and each worker's personal limitations should be taken into account in judging what precautions to take and what limits to set in order to meet the norms of avoiding unreasonable harm or risks to health.[129]

e) **Participation in experimentation can be good or bad.** Sometimes experimentation, especially of a psychological kind, involves acts wrong in themselves, for example, lying or deliberate arousal of illicit sexual desire. Participating in such experiments never is justified. But even if experimentation involves nothing wrong in itself, it can be objectionable because of bad side effects. Not all medical and other scientific experiments involve health risks for participants, but many do, and no one should volunteer for or agree to participate in any experiment without obtaining full disclosure of any possible health risks, as well as of the experiment's potential benefits, and the alternatives to cooperating in it.[130]

---

128. Harlap, Kost, and Forrest, *Preventing Pregnancy, Protecting Health,* briefly describe the variety, ease of transmission, and seriousness of many sexually transmitted diseases; for example, more than twelve million episodes occur per year in the United States (41); "following a single act of unprotected intercourse with an infected man, an estimated 50 percent of women will contract gonorrhea" (43); and "STDs can have serious health consequences for the carrier, both in the short term and in the long term" (42).

129. See Leo XIII, *Rerum novarum, ASS* 23 (1890–91) 660–61, *PE,* 115.42.

130. On medical experimentation, see Ashley and O'Rourke, *Healthcare Ethics,* 3rd ed., 234–41; Lino Ciccone, *Salute e malattia: Questioni di morale della vita fisica (II)* (Milan: Edizioni Ares, 1986), 270–319. The principles underlying the moral norms in this matter are articulated by

If there are risks, a person may reasonably participate for either of two reasons: first, if he or she is ill, no proven treatment is available or effective, and the experimental treatment offers a sufficient prospect of benefit to make it seem right to accept the bad side effects or risks; second, if the experiment promises substantial benefit to others, the individual has no special responsibility to avoid the risks of participating, and he or she does so in the hope of helping others, as an act of mercy.

f) **Such risks may be accepted for others only in their own interests.** People making decisions for someone who is not competent—for instance, parents for a child—may accept any risks to health involved in experimental treatment when the treatment offers sufficient prospect of benefit to the dependent person himself or herself. However, they may not accept any significant risk (that is, any risk beyond the level of life's common risks) to a dependent's health for the sake of an experiment's possible benefit to others. For parents and others in charge of the noncompetent have a special responsibility to act in their personal interests, not to subordinate them to others. Nor can such subordination of a dependent's interests be an act of mercy, since mercy is self-sacrifice, not imposing sacrifice on someone for whom one is responsible.

This norm applies to the human conceptus from the beginning, since the conceptus should be considered a person whose life is as sacred as anyone else's. Therefore, as Paul VI teaches, one may not "be a party to experiments on the human embryo or foetus, even for the progress of science, not even if this being was destined, for natural reasons or through men's criminal act, to perish before seeing the light of day."[131]

5. Psychoactive Substances Should Be Used Rightly, Not Abused

Psychoactive substance here refers to anything introduced into the body for the purpose of affecting the nervous system and how one feels. Substances introduced for other purposes, even if they have an incidental psychoactive effect, fall outside this definition.

People use many things to affect their state of consciousness: tea and coffee, aspirin and other pain killers, sleeping pills, tranquilizers and antidepressants, tobacco, alcoholic beverages, marijuana, cocaine, heroin, LSD, PCP, and so on. Some psychoactive substances can be used reasonably, in accord with health and other goods, but all of them also can be abused.

There is a huge and ever-growing body of information concerning the use and abuse of psychoactive substances. No attempt will be made here to summarize the data. Rather, norms applicable to any psychoactive substance will be articulated, distinguishing between reasonable use and abuse.[132]

Pius XII, Address to the First International Congress on the Histopathology of the Nervous System (13 Sept. 1952), *AAS* 44 (1952) 779–89, *Catholic Mind* 51 (May 1953): 305–13.

131. Paul VI, Address to Fifth International Congress of Psychosomatic Obstetrics and Gynecology, *AAS* 70 (1978) 99, *OR*, 1 Dec. 1977, 12; see Congregation for the Doctrine of the Faith, *Instruction on Respect for Human Life in Its Origin and on the Dignity of Procreation: Replies to Certain Questions of the Day*, 1.4, *AAS* 80 (1988) 81–83, *OR*, 16 Mar. 1987, 3.

132. Ciccone, *Salute e malattia*, 321–515, provides an extensive treatment of problems concerning drugs, alcohol, and tobacco.

Of course, as in other matters, people who regard morality legalistically will tend to rationalize abuse by interpreting what they are doing as reasonable use. Nevertheless, people who sincerely desire to do what is right will find the following norms helpful for guiding their choices.

a) **Psychoactive substances may be used rightly to promote health.** Assuming that their use is not excluded by bad side effects (a matter to be considered below), psychoactive substances can be used reasonably whenever the psychoactive effect itself contributes to healthy functioning by mitigating the bad physiological or psychological effects of some condition of consciousness.

For example, sometimes the cause of pain is unknown or cannot be remedied: some kinds of headaches, the pain of terminal cancer, and so on. Such dysfunctional pain interferes with psychic and even with organic functions, and so, in itself, is unhealthy. In such cases, pain relievers are reasonably used to mitigate the pain and promote a more healthful level of functioning. Many other psychoactive substances can be used reasonably in analogous ways. Tranquilizers, antidepressants, and sleeping pills can ameliorate abnormal emotional states which interfere with normal psychological functioning and rest. Mild stimulants—such as the caffeine in tea, coffee, and cola drinks—can help people overcome feelings of lethargy and fatigue in order to stay awake, concentrate, and function more effectively.

Alcoholic beverages sometimes are used in religious rituals, such as the Eucharist, or consumed as appetizers, foods, or medications; in such cases, their effect on consciousness can be irrelevant, and then they are not used as psychoactive. When consumed to affect feelings, as they often are, alcoholic beverages can be used reasonably in limited amounts as a mild depressant: to quiet excessive emotions, to shift from the intense effort of the working day to social intercourse and rest, or to reduce nervousness and inhibitions in order to facilitate intimacy and celebration.

b) **Psychoactive substances should be used when appropriate.** Sometimes people unreasonably hesitate to make appropriate use of such substances, particularly pain killers. Perhaps they confuse right use with abuse, or falsely believe that Christian asceticism requires suffering pain even when there is a reason to seek relief. Perhaps they have an excessive and misplaced fear of addiction. For example, terminal cancer patients sometimes refuse, or are denied, the pain relief they need to function as well as possible in doing the good things they still can do and having the worthwhile experiences they still can have. In any case, a psychoactive substance should be used when there is a reason grounded in an intelligible good to use it and no reason not to do so.[133]

---

133. See Pius XII, Address Responding to Questions Proposed by the Italian Society of Anesthesiology, *AAS* 49 (1957) 129–37, *The Pope Speaks* 4 (1957–58): 33–49; Pius XII, Address to the International College of Neuro-Psychopharmacology (9 Sept. 1958), *AAS* 50 (1958) 694–95, *The Pope Speaks* 5 (1958–59): 438; cf. John C. Ford, S.J., "Chemical Comfort and Christian Virtue," *American Ecclesiastical Review* 141 (July-Dec. 1959): 361–79. Acute Pain Management Guideline Panel, *Acute Pain Management in Adults: Operative Procedures: Quick Reference Guide for Clinicians,* AHCPR Pub. No. 92–0019 (Rockville, Md.: U.S. Department of Health and Human Services, 1992), 2, states: "The obligation to manage pain and relieve a patient's suffering is an important part of a health professional's commitment. The importance of pain management

c) **Any merely emotionally motivated choice to use is an abuse.** Sometimes, however, people choose to use psychoactive substances without any reason, that is, without having any intelligible good in view. They do not seek to alter the way they feel in order to improve their general or psychological functioning in some respect; rather, the altered state of consciousness becomes an end in itself, and the use of the substance is, at least to some degree, a flight from reality into an artificially generated experience. The motive is a merely emotional urge to experience the feeling of excitement, euphoria, or escape. But someone who chooses to satisfy an urge also must be aware of some reason not to satisfy it, for there would be no need to choose unless one were aware of an eligible alternative. So, such a choice to use a psychoactive substance follows an emotional urge against a reason, and that violates the third mode of responsibility (see *CMP*, 8.C). Consequently, such a choice always is morally bad, and carrying it out always is an abuse.[134]

d) **Using psychoactive substances without a reason is always wrong.** Since rightly using, and not abusing, psychoactive substances is a matter of regulating sensory desires by reason, it pertains to temperance (see *S.t.*, 2–2, q. 141, aa. 1–3). In regulating some tendencies—to eat, to rest, to move about—temperance is moderating the satisfaction of a tendency that normally contributes to health. Hence, one need not have a reason for satisfying those tendencies, and temperance requires only that their satisfaction be limited by rational considerations. In regulating the urge to use psychoactive substances, however, temperance moderates the satisfaction of a different sort of tendency. For if any use of any psychoactive substance is motivated, not by an intelligible good, but precisely by an urge to experience an altered state of consciousness, that act, as experience indicates, always harms two basic human goods: healthy functioning and the interpersonal communion of friendship or association.

The bad effects on healthy functioning are obvious and easily understood; those on friendship or association are more subtle. However, there plainly is a difference between, say, drinking which serves sociability and drinking to get drunk. Even if several people set out to get drunk together, the goal of each is his or her own conscious state, which neither is shared with nor communicable to anyone else, and so for these people to get drunk together actually is not a social activity directed toward a common good. By contrast, if several people, having set out to celebrate an occasion or engage in conversation, drink only to facilitate their common activity, their incommunicable states of consciousness must remain subordinate to

---

is further increased when benefits for the patient are realized—earlier mobilization, shortened hospital stay and reduced costs. Yet clinical surveys continue to show that routine orders for intramuscular injections of opioid 'as needed' result in unrelieved pain due to ineffective treatment in roughly half of postoperative patients."

134. John Paul II, Address to Youth (Montreal), 6, *Inseg.* 7.2 (1984) 457, *OR,* 1 Oct. 1984, 10, emphasizes the contrast between self-discipline and escapism, and thus implies that the criterion for the right use of psychoactive substances is service of intelligible human goods: "In times of darkness, do not seek an escape. Have the courage to resist the dealers in deception who make capital of your hunger for happiness and who make you pay dearly for a moment of 'artificial paradise'—a whiff of smoke, a bout of drinking or drugs. What claims to be a shortcut to happiness leads nowhere. It turns you away from that intelligent self-discipline which builds up the person."

their interpersonal communion; and, if one party's drinking begins to interfere with communication, the others will consider that an unfortunate excess.

Reflection can clarify the harm to healthy functioning and to friendship or association which experience suggests.

The temporary or even lasting negative effect on healthy functioning is obvious in some cases: for example, when people use drugs or alcohol to experience a "high," their normal psychological functioning and motor skills are impaired, their vital functions are strained, and so on. But even when the effect is not obvious, using any psychoactive substance either suppresses or intensifies some function, and doing either thing, in the absence of any reason, is unreasonably to detract from one's healthy functioning—the former directly, the latter indirectly (because intensifying one function detracts from others and/or from the harmony among them).

As for the harm to friendship or association: immediately and in itself, any use of a psychoactive substance, not for an intelligible good, but precisely for the experience, alienates oneself from one's own body. This is so because the substance only affects the state of consciousness by first affecting the body, so that in using the substance one is using one's body to affect one's conscious state; but the body, rather than participating in any good, is treated as if it were a mere instrument, distinct from one's conscious subjectivity and at its service. Of course, this self-alienation from the body in no way affects the metaphysical unity of one's person, since nothing a person does can alter his or her metaphysical constitution. Nevertheless, it is an existential dualism between the body and the conscious self, that is, a division between the two insofar as they are coprinciples of integrated, acting person. But a person's capacity to embody himself or herself completely in his or her acts is necessary for the self-giving involved in the communication which establishes and nurtures interpersonal communion. Hence, to choose to use a psychoactive substance precisely for the experience is to accept damage to the capacity of one's bodily self for interpersonal communion. But to damage an intrinsic and necessary condition for attaining a good is to damage that good itself. Thus, in choosing to use a psychoactive substance, not for the sake of some intelligible good, but precisely for the experience, a person accepts damage to the basic human good of friendship or association.

Consequently, in the absence of a reason to use a psychoactive substance, there always is a reason not to use it: the damage such use does to healthy functioning and to the body as a capacity for interpersonal communion. Any choice to use such a substance not motivated by a reason (that is, not made in view of an intelligible good), therefore, is intemperate and morally bad, and any such use is abuse.

e) **The use of psychoactive substances can have bad side effects.** The use of some psychoactive substances not only impedes healthy functioning but involves risks to the user's state of health and even to life. For example, using tobacco is causally related to various forms of cancer and other diseases; cocaine kills some users; LSD and PCP can cause lasting psychotic conditions; excessive use of alcohol can cause liver damage.

Many psychoactive drugs are addictive for most people (alcohol is not addictive for most but plainly is so for some). Ordinarily, the regular, and often increasing, use of psychoactive drugs to feed addiction not only impairs functioning, and so of itself is unhealthful, but carries further risks to health.[135]

At a certain level, the use of many psychoactive substances allows a person to remain conscious and active but causes the lessening or loss of rational control over emotions and actions, a condition not only unhealthy but an occasion of other sins.

The use of many psychoactive substances interferes with acknowledging problems and dealing with them realistically and effectively. For example, pain relievers often mask the symptom of a disease, with the bad result that treatment is delayed; tranquilizers can reduce realistic anxieties about situations demanding effective action; alcohol use sometimes diminishes feelings of guilt about other sins.

Many psychoactive substances can reduce psychic functions and performance below the level appropriate for someone who either is engaging in particular activities or should be prepared to do so: alcohol impairs the ability to drive, pain relievers can render a terminally ill person unable to participate in the sacraments or conduct necessary business, and so on.

Some uses directly affect other people in ways they find offensive; for example, many people object to smoking.

Many uses violate laws that appear to be essentially just, and which are meant to deal with serious social problems and to limit great harm to many people. Violating these laws contributes to a more or less extensive network of criminal activities, some involving murder, kidnapping, corruption of public officials, and other very serious evils.

f) Reasons for using such substances are not always adequate. While a person might have a reason to use some psychoactive substance, in many cases the bad side effects should exclude doing so. People recovering from surgery should at times tolerate some pain so that they can exercise appropriately and cooperate in other ways in their own care; recovered alcoholics should entirely forgo the use of alcohol rather than fall back into addictive behavior. If using tobacco as a stimulant ever is rational, the financial cost, the impact on others who find it objectionable, the probability of addiction, and especially the bad effects on users' health surely are stronger reasons for not using it.[136] Some people claim that marijuana, like alcohol, can be used reasonably as a psychoactive substance, but the analogy with alcohol is questionable. Moreover, even setting aside other considerations, the social problems resulting from violating laws regarding marijuana should exclude any unlawful use.[137]

---

135. National Conference of Catholic Bishops, "Pastoral Message on Drug Abuse," *Origins* 20 (22 Nov. 1990): 390–92, summarizes the risks and consequences of addiction to some widely abused substances.

136. Ciccone, *Salute e malattia,* 502–3, argues cogently that significant, habitual use of tobacco, as against occasional light use, is grave matter, and that its basic gravity often is aggravated by circumstances. It does not argue against the truth of this judgment to point out that saints in times past used tobacco, since they did not know the effects of using tobacco. Of course, unless and until the magisterium proposes as certain a norm excluding the habitual use of tobacco, Catholics must form their consciences by personally examining the arguments.

137. Thomas C. Kane, O.P., "Current Issues in Moral Theology: The Marijuana Problem," *American Ecclesiastical Review* 160 (Jan.–June 1969): 129, suggests that the smoking of a

Some people try psychoactive substances out of curiosity, but, considering the side effects, that is a good enough reason only for someone engaged in serious research. In general, it is reasonable to accept the costs and risks of any sort of experimentation only if there are good reasons to think that it will make a real contribution to human knowledge and well-being.

Among the reasons given for using various psychoactive substances are enhancing esthetic experience, deepening intimate community, and providing a religious experience. It is true that some of these substances can be used for such purposes, for example, a limited amount of alcohol can be used to enhance a group's social functioning. But these reasons often seem to be rationalizations, for they refer only to the felt side of intelligible goods. For instance, even if it provides an extraordinary, temporary feeling of closeness, using a psychoactive substance, unless it really contributes to functioning, does nothing to form or strengthen the commitments and real cooperation which are the core of genuine community.[138]

g) Self-examination is needed regarding one's motives in this matter. Self-deception is rampant in the use of psychoactive substances. Even those who consider their use reasonable should regularly examine themselves to make sure that they actually are motivated by the reason, not some merely emotional motive. Of course, if addiction sets in, clear thinking and discernment become more difficult. So, a person should review his or her use of psychoactive substances from time to time and seek advice about it from mature friends and/or professionals who are temperate in the matter.

h) Because of bad side effects, abuse often is grave matter. In and of itself, the use of a psychoactive substance without a reason need not be seriously harmful to the user or anyone else. Hence, the immorality need only be light matter. However, accepting the bad side effects of abuse very often makes the act grave matter. In discussing the gravity of such a sin, traditional moral theology focused on the excessive use of alcohol and on only one bad side effect: drunkenness deprives one of rational control. The consequences of this loss of control also were noted: the occasions of sin it involves, and its tendency to interfere with the fulfillment of important responsibilities (see *S.t.*, 2–2, q. 149, aa. 1 and 4; q. 150, aa. 1–2). However, other psychoactive substances often have the same effect, and several other bad side effects seem serious enough to make the abuse of a psychoactive substance a grave matter: serious risk to life or health, either directly or as a result of potential addiction, significant inconvenience to other people, violations of law that contribute to organized criminal activity, and so on. Thus, if a serious side effect is foreseen, it seems clear that any abuse of any psychoactive substance should be considered a grave matter.

Of course, as with any other form of immorality, grave matter here is one thing, mortal sin another. Habitual abuse affects clear thinking and self-control so that,

---

marijuana cigarette for the sake of curiosity or occasionally cannot be a grave matter, but he fails to consider whether the act is immoral in itself and ignores laws bearing on it.

138. Paul VI, Address to Persons Engaged in Anti-Drug Campaign, *Inseg.* 10 (1972) 1284–85, *OR*, 4 Jan. 1973, 3–4, points out that mystical and religious claims made for drug use are fraudulent, since people using drugs do not yield good fruits in works of charity, social service, and so on.

with respect to many of their particular acts, alcoholics and drug addicts perhaps do not have the sufficient reflection and full consent without which there is no mortal sin (see *CMP*, 17.A–C). Still, as the habit is being formed, abusing a psychoactive substance can be a mortal sin even though it is a sin of weakness (see *CMP*, 17.D–E).

i) **Alcoholics and drug addicts should seek or accept treatment.** Although some people gravely abuse alcohol and/or other psychoactive substances without becoming addicted, the signs of addiction eventually do appear in many others. The abuser experiences a craving, similar to intense hunger, and regularly indulges to satisfy it. This activity no longer is incidental to eating, recreation, and so on, but becomes an important, if not the central, concern of daily life and begins to impinge on the fulfillment of responsibilities. Abusers also become increasingly preoccupied with ensuring an adequate supply, while usually they deny having any problem.

When these signs appear, family, friends, employers, and other associates should not encourage and support addicts by helping them hide their addiction and manage their lives more or less satisfactorily despite it. Instead, everyone concerned should press the addict to abandon self-deception and rationalization, admit the underlying problem, and deal with it.[139]

By the time alcoholics and drug addicts admit their problem, they often are unable to stop without medical treatment and other support, and in many cases probably lack moral responsibility for their addictive behavior. However, they are likely to have more or less lucid and unpressured moments, when they know they should seek help and could choose to do so. Rejecting such an opportunity can be a mortal sin even if the addictive behavior no longer is.

Those who enter into treatment should recognize that, while it can provide indispensable help, it cannot substitute for their own responsibility and effort. Follow-up is essential to avoid renewing the addiction, and Alcoholics Anonymous and analogous programs seem useful for many people. Such programs involve a series of steps toward spiritual renewal; in carrying them out, Catholics, of course, should seek sound pastoral guidance and recommit themselves to their faith and its practice, including regular and devout reception of the sacraments.[140]

Question G: What Other Responsibilities Are There toward Persons as Bodily?

Other actions, besides those impinging on life and health, can adversely affect the person precisely as bodily. These include mutilation (removing some of the

---

139. Very helpful for both the addicted themselves and others concerned: Roy Barkley, *The Catholic Alcoholic* (Huntington, Ind.: Our Sunday Visitor Publishing Division, 1990). Though explicitly dealing with alcoholism, much of Barkley's analysis and advice is applicable to other addictions.

140. See *New Catholic Encyclopedia*, s.v. "alcoholism"; John C. Ford, S.J., "Depth Psychology, Morality, and Alcoholism," *Proceedings of the Catholic Theological Society of America* 5 (1950): 64-149; idem, "The Sickness of Alcoholism: Still More Clergy Education?" *Homiletic and Pastoral Review* 87 (Nov. 1986): 10–18.

body's parts and functions), assault (hostile contact with the body), and physical constraint (inhibiting the body's movement).

Political societies sometimes make use of such practices to punish people. Here, however, mutilation, assault, and physical constraint will be treated as personal and interpersonal acts.

The morality of actions which mutilate or otherwise harm the body, or risk doing so, parallels the morality of actions which cause or risk death. Thus, questions about the morality of actions which cause any kind of bodily harm usually can be answered by applying the analysis which would apply to them if they caused death; in doing so, one must, of course, make the same crucial distinctions between what is sought as an end, chosen as a means, and accepted as a side effect. Still, sometimes basic goods other than life are at stake, and some specific kinds of acts deserve special attention.[141]

1. Bodily Integrity Should Be Maintained in Harmony with Health

Affirmative responsibilities for maintaining bodily integrity fall under the responsibilities with respect to health treated in the previous question. Thus, the issues to be treated here concern only the morality of acts that remove a bodily part, a physiological or psychic function, or both.

a) **Bodily integrity is a good of persons in two ways.** In desiring their bodies to be good, people want two things: beauty and health. So, the body's integrity is good in two ways: insofar as the body expresses the person and is necessary for communication (lack of integrity is disfiguring and repulsive); and insofar as the body functions as a living whole (lack of integrity reduces or eliminates some capacity, and so detracts from health).

Many acts which detract from the body's integrity affect both goods at once; for example, amputating a limb is both disfiguring and disabling.

b) **Acts that detract from neither good are morally acceptable.** Acts that remove parts of the body without affecting either of the relevant goods affect bodily integrity only materially, and so do not of themselves raise any moral issue. For example, it is not morally problematic to trim nails or hair in accord with prevailing styles and to remove a normal appendix to prevent possible future appendicitis.

Acts intended to improve appearance that do not detract from any capacity also are morally acceptable in themselves, for example, removing excess fat. Even a materially disfiguring procedure which does not affect any function is morally acceptable if it enhances appearance according to the standards of one's culture, for example, stretching the lips or ear lobes. Yet a procedure which does not affect any function and is favored in some cultures—tattooing, for instance—can be offensive to others and so have an antisocial significance, by virtue of which it becomes morally wrong.

Because pain is not an intelligible evil but only a sensible one (see *CMP*, 5.B), people may purposely inflict it on themselves, provided they do not detract from

---

141. One source, not always followed, for what follows: Gerald Kelly, S.J., "The Morality of Mutilation: Towards a Revision of the Treatise," *Theological Studies* 17 (1956): 322–44.

their comeliness or health, for some good end: penitential practices of scourging oneself or wearing a hair shirt, psychological experimentation with the sensation of pain, and so on. (Inflicting pain on others raises a question about bodily contact; see 3.c–d, below).

c) **Acts which intentionally detract from either good are always wrong.** For the sake of self-punishment or revenge, people motivated by negative feelings sometimes seek as their end to detract from their own beauty, health, or bodily integrity, or that of someone else, by removing some bodily part or suppressing some physiological or psychic capacity. Including, as they do, the will to damage an intrinsic good of the person, such acts are always wrong.

Sometimes people choose to do such things as a means to some ulterior end. Mutilation or its threat is used to coerce someone; a dying, but not yet dead, person's body parts are taken for transplant. People sometimes disable themselves to arouse others' pity and motivate almsgiving; choir boys were castrated so that their voices would not change and they could go on singing; misunderstanding Jesus' figurative speech, some Christians mutilated themselves to avoid temptation.

Although intended for good ends, such acts also include a choice to damage an intelligible good, and so they are always wrong.[142]

d) **Detriment to function sometimes may be accepted.** It can be morally good and even obligatory to remove a part of the body essential to some physiological or psychic function, when doing so of itself also protects or promotes health; the detriment to function may not be intended as a means to the other end, but may only be accepted as a side effect.[143] For example, a person sometimes should consent to the cutting off of an infected or cancerous limb or nonvital organ when that is necessary to prevent the infection or cancer from doing great harm to the body as a whole. Indeed, this is so even when the part removed is itself healthy, if removing it has natural consequences which are necessary for the health of the body as a whole and which cannot be brought about in another way. For example, a man suffering from breast cancer may consent to the surgical removal of his normal testicles in order to stop the hormones which are aggravating the cancer.[144]

However, even if detriment to function is not willed as a means but only accepted as a side effect, it would be wrong to accept any great and/or lasting detriment if

---

142. It is a canonical crime to mutilate or seriously wound a person: *CIC*, c. 1397.

143. This norm has been called "the principle of totality": mutilation is morally permissible when it is necessary for the good of the whole body. See John Gallagher, C.S.B., "The Principle of Totality: Man's Stewardship of His Body," in *Moral Theology Today: Certitudes and Doubts,* ed. Donald G. McCarthy (St. Louis: The Pope John Center, 1984), 217–42, for an analysis of relevant papal texts and references to many theologians. Actually, the so-called principle of totality is merely an instance of double effect, but the physical "directness" of the causing of harm and physical "indirectness" of the causing of benefit led theologians (and the magisterium) to suppose that a special principle is needed. By using the distinction between what is intended and what is accepted as a side effect to analyze problems of mutilation, one can solve issues (such as those concerning transplantation) that are perplexing if it is supposed that the "principle" of totality is irreducible to more basic principles.

144. See Pius XII, Address to Congress of Urology (8 Oct. 1953), *AAS* 45 (1953) 674, *Papal Teachings: The Human Body,* ed. Benedictine Monks of Solesmes, trans. E. O'Gorman, R.S.C.J. (Boston: St. Paul Editions, 1960), 278.

the benefit to health could be achieved in some less damaging and/or less permanent way. For example, the surgical destruction of portions of the brain, with severe detriment to normal psychic functions, is not a reasonable way to treat behavior problems that can be dealt with adequately by psychoactive drugs; removing a fertile woman's uterus is not a reasonable way to deal with a disease that could be treated successfully without sterilizing her.

To improve appearance, a person may sacrifice something of his or her bodily integrity and accept the consequent detriment to function as a side effect. For example, a man whose ears are unusually large but functional may have them cosmetically remodeled even at some small sacrifice of function; a young woman may choose to have healthy tissue removed from her unusually large breasts.

e) The preceding norms can be applied to organ transplantation. The norms already articulated make it clear that the morality of removing parts of a human body depends on the act's relationship to the relevant goods: healthy functioning and beauty.

Since donating parts of one's remains after death detracts from neither of these goods, a person can rightly make such a donation for others' benefit. Since donating blood under the conditions set by sound medical practice does not harm the donor and involves very little risk, a person not only may but should donate blood if others need it and there is no special reason not to give it.[145]

However, since both eyes are necessary for some visual functions, such as depth perception, a living person would damage his or her vision by donating a cornea for transplant. Hence, someone who chose to make or carry out such an organ donation would be choosing to detract from his or her own or another's health as a means to the good end, for example, benefiting someone else. Since such donations are bad means to a good end, they always are morally wrong.

Someone might argue that a donor could rightly make such a choice in a spirit of self-sacrifice. After all, did not St. Maximilian Kolbe give up his very life to save a fellow prisoner? But the analogy fails, because Kolbe, while freely accepting death, did not choose to end his own life; he suffered death in place of his fellow prisoner, and in doing so lost his life, but he did not transfer his life to the other man. By contrast, the organ donor does transfer his or her own organ and its function to the other person, and so must freely choose to end or damage his or her own function in choosing to give away the organ whose function it is.[146]

---

145. John Paul II, Address to the First International Congress of the Society for Organ Sharing, 5; *L'Osservatore Romano*, It. ed., 21 June 1991, 5; *OR*, 24 June 1991, 2, treats organ donation as an expression of love and solidarity: "A transplant, and even a simple blood transfusion, is not like other operations. It must not be separated from the donor's act of self-giving, from the love that gives life. The physician should always be conscious of the particular nobility of this work; he becomes the mediator of something especially significant, the *gift of self* which one person has made—even *after death*—so that another might live."

146. John Paul II, Address to the First International Congress of the Society for Organ Sharing, 4; *L'Osservatore Romano*, It. ed., 21 June 1991, 5; *OR*, 24 June 1991, 2, states the norm: "A person can only donate that of which he can deprive himself without serious danger or harm to his own life or personal identity, and for a just and proportionate reason. It is obvious that vital organs can only be donated *after death*."

While choosing to give part of one's body to another is wrong when the very giving of the part involves giving up or detracting from some function, it can be right when it only entails a moderate risk of future detriment to function. In the second case, the potential loss of function is not part of the chosen means but only is an accepted side effect. For example, assuming that donating one kidney for transplant does not lessen kidney function, with detriment to one's health generally, a person may do so, even though accepting a risk to health in the event he or she contracts a kidney disease later.[147]

Can mercy call for donating a kidney? If someone has no moral responsibility not to accept the health risks and other side effects of the surgery, if the other's need is great, and if the possibility of success is good, he or she could have such a Christian responsibility. As with other responsibilities of mercy, of course, only the person who would make the sacrifice can judge in a particular case whether or not it is called for.

f) Sterilization as a method of birth control is always wrong. No benefit to the person as a whole can justify any procedure which brings about sterility and is chosen for that very purpose. In no way does sterility as such truly benefit anyone; it only facilitates sexual intercourse—the distinct act in and through which some benefit is expected—by excluding conception. Thus, the intention in choosing sterilization is contraceptive, and the sterilizing act is at best a bad means to a good ulterior end. Moreover, because sterilization involves bodily mutilation and is usually irreversible, it is, other things being equal, more seriously wrong than other methods of contraception.[148]

People with a legalistic mentality sometimes suppose there is an easy out for Catholic couples who accept the Church's teaching on contraception, yet want no more children and do not wish to abstain during the fertile period: let one spouse be sterilized and that spouse (or both) confess the sin; then the couple can engage in intercourse whenever they please without worrying about pregnancy or feeling guilty about contraception. The trouble with this supposed solution is that a sin is not simply a technical violation which can be repaired by going to confession. The

147. See Ashley and O'Rourke, *Healthcare Ethics,* 3rd ed., 304–12, for further discussion and references to other theological work on organ donation. They correctly point out (306) that functional integrity (as distinct from anatomical integrity) is a key factor for the morality of transplants between living persons. For the value of an organ, such as a kidney, is not simply its material reality but its capacity to function for the good of the person as a whole. Ciccone, *Salute e malattia,* 210–69, who treats organ transplantation more fully, also accepts the principle of functional integrity (222). Augustine Regan, C.Ss.R., "The Basic Morality of Organic Transplants between Living Humans," *Studia Moralia* 3 (1965): 338–41, rejects functional integrity, but Regan's criticism confuses the natural teleology of bodily parts with their relationship to the relevant goods. Regan's own attempted justification (348–61) depends on extending the principle of totality to include the whole good of the person not only as an individual but as a participant in interpersonal communion. That argument fails inasmuch as the principle of totality is not a fundamental moral standard but rather is reducible to an adequate analysis of relevant acts in terms of what is intended and what is accepted as a side effect.

148. See Paul VI, *Humanae vitae,* 14, *AAS* 60 (1968) 490, *PE,* 277.14; Congregation for the Doctrine of the Faith, *Sterilization in Catholic Hospitals, AAS* 68 (1976) 738–40, Flannery, 2:454–55; cf. Ashley and O'Rourke, *Healthcare Ethics,* 3rd ed., 271–78.

choice of sterilization, like any sin, is a self-determination, an existential self-mutilation more profound than the physical self-mutilation of sterilization; and this self-determination lasts until the person repents. Consequently, unless those who have tried to solve their problems by means of sterilization are truly contrite—"I wish I had not done that, and if I had it to do over, I would never make that choice"—confession is fruitless for them.

But sometimes people do sincerely repent being sterilized. Like those who repent any other sin, they can be absolved and spiritually healed, so that they can live in grace again. Must they now either abstain entirely from marital intercourse or try to have the sterilization reversed? While Church teaching does not deal explicitly with this question, general principles point to a negative answer, at least for most cases. On the one hand, having repented sterilization, married couples have the same right to intercourse and reasons for it which other couples have after the wife's menopause. On the other hand, there usually are good reasons not to try to have the operation reversed: doing so involves costs and other burdens, the attempt often fails to restore fertility, and even if it were to succeed, many such couples would have no moral obligation to try to have a child.[149]

Nevertheless, those who repent of being sterilized should consider their responsibilities conscientiously. Some couples will rightly judge that they still should have one or more children if they can, and that they can and should accept the burdens of an attempt at reversal.

Moreover, if repentant couples enjoy without restraint the freedom sterility has given them, they might sin by deliberately thinking: "I am glad and would do it again." Realizing this danger, many repentant spouses will rightly judge and mutually agree that, in order to maintain and confirm their repentance and verify its sincerity to themselves and each other, they should abstain during periods which would be fertile except for the sterilization.[150]

2. Sexual Assault Is Always Grave Matter

Sexual assault is a special type of offense against the bodily person. While there is a wrongness common to every instance of this sin, in many cases additional factors aggravate its specific wrongness. Not all sexual assaults are offenses by men against women. All persons capable of the required deliberation and choice can commit this offense against any other person's bodily self. In ordinary language, *assault* connotes perceptible violence, but that is not essential to sexual assault as understood here.

The sin of sexual assault is one thing; the sin of an illicit sexual act is quite another. Here, only the former is treated; the latter will be treated below (in 9.E). Hence, the following treatment of sexual assault must be accurately understood: acts not morally objectionable precisely as sexual assaults very often are morally wrong as sexual acts.

---

149. See Thomas J. O'Donnell, S.J., "Repentance Following Directly Willed Contraceptive Sterilization," *The Medical-Moral Newsletter* 26 (Jan. 1989): 4.

150. See John F. Kippley, *Sex and the Marriage Covenant: A Basis for Morality* (Cincinnati: The Couple to Couple League International, 1991), 208–15.

While many acts described as sexual harassment constitute sexual assault, the two are not identical. On the one hand, *harassment* connotes a pattern of behavior with the intention to disturb or annoy, while a sexual assault can be a single act done without any such intention. On the other hand, sexual assault is a kind of bodily contact, while sexual harassment need not involve contact. Thus, other acts which sometimes constitute sexual harassment are treated elsewhere (see 7.B.5.k–l and 9.E.9.d).

a) **Sexual assault is defined by four conditions.** Sexual assault is (i) intentional contact (ii) by one person with another's body (iii) that either is sexually motivated or is with the genital parts or both (iv) without appropriate consent by the person whose body is touched.

i) Sexual assault is *intentional contact,* not contact which is the side effect of some other act, for example, pushing through a crowd or standing in the aisle of a crowded bus.

ii) Sexual assault is contact with *another's body,* because, although one can wrongly touch one's own body, such wrongful touches do not constitute assault. Since a married couple are two in one flesh, truly one body, their unloving sexual contacts with one another do not constitute sexual assault as defined here, but a distinct type of sin, which will be treated below (in 9.E.1.a and 9.E.2.g).

iii) When the other three conditions are met, sexually motivated contact with *any* part of another's body is sexual assault. For example, patting another's arm as a first step in making a sexual approach or pinching another's buttocks as a way of seeking sexual satisfaction can be sexual assaults. When the other conditions are met, genital contact which is not the side effect of some other morally good act always is sexual assault. A woman's breasts count as genital organs, since they contribute both to her reproductive role, to the erotic arousal of others, and to her own gratification.

iv) What is required for *appropriate consent* depends both on whether the contact is sexually motivated and whether it is with the genitals. If the contact is sexually motivated and is with the genitals, the consent required for it not to be sexual assault is actual informed consent. If the contact is sexually motivated but is not with the genitals, or if it is not sexually motivated and is with genitals, the required consent can be either actual informed consent or reasonably presumed consent. Examples of appropriate consent to nonsexually motivated genital contact are a person's actual informed consent to the genital contact involved in a medical examination and babies' reasonably presumed consent to the genital contact involved in bathing them. Examples of reasonably presumed consent to sexually motivated nongenital contact are manifestations of erotic affection by a person attempting to establish a romantic relationship with someone who seems interested and willing: warmly holding the other's hand, squeezing the other's shoulder, kissing, and the like.

b) **Consent to sexually motivated contact involves four conditions.** Appropriate, expressed consent to sexually motivated contact requires four things: it must be (i) plainly expressed either by words or by deeds, (ii) based on an understanding of the significance of the contact, (iii) given with full voluntariness, and (iv) given to the contact precisely *as* sexually motivated.

Hence, consent to sexually motivated contact is not appropriate and the deliberate contact is sexual assault if the consent (i) is presumed to genital contact on the basis of ambiguous signs, (ii) is given by a child or a severely retarded or demented person who does not understand the contact's significance, (iii) is given out of fear or by someone deprived of the use of reason (for example, due to severe intoxication), or (iv) is given for a nonsexual purpose when the contact is wholly or partly sexually motivated, for example, consent to a medical examination from which the examiner seeks sexual gratification.

When these four conditions are met, consent is adequate so that contact does not constitute assault even though the consent is elicited by prolonged cajoling, a threat to break off a romantic relationship, or a promise (whether sincere or deceitful) of payment or some other benefit. Moreover, consent can be fully voluntary even though a person who otherwise might resist consents when sexually aroused, fatigued, excited due to a celebration or travel, or intoxicated but still able to distinguish between right and wrong.

c) **Contact carried beyond the limits of consent becomes assault.** People often give consent to some limited sexually motivated contact without giving consent to further sexually motivated contact, for example, consent to kissing but not to genital touches, or consent to genital touches but not to sexual intercourse. Since sexually motivated contact naturally progresses toward completion, a person who gives appropriate consent to any sexually motivated contact implicitly consents to further contact unless he or she clearly sets a limit. For example, unless a woman at some point makes it clear that she does not consent to the further step in the progression, if she allows a man to fondle her breasts she consents to his fondling her vulva, and if she allows him to fondle her vulva she consents to sexual intercourse. Nevertheless, if at some point she expresses her nonconsent to further contact, that further contact becomes sexual assault, and if that unwanted contact is sexual intercourse, it is rape.

d) **Sexual contact with a prostitute can be assault.** Although a prostitute undergoes sexual contact in exchange for payment, contact with a prostitute sometimes satisfies the definition for sexual assault. For in a particular case a prostitute may not consent to sexual contact or it may be carried beyond the limits consented to. Moreover, a prostitute's consent is not fully voluntary if he or she is too immature, mentally disturbed, drugged, terrorized by an exploiting handler, or motivated by extreme need. In such cases, contact with a prostitute is wrong not only insofar as it is a certain kind of sexual sin—for instance, adultery or sodomy—but also insofar as it is a sexual assault.

e) **Sexual assault violates the person in a unique way.** Since the human body is personal, it is more than a physiological-psychic functional system which a person has and uses. A body is not something a person possesses but is an integral part of that person's self. If it were something other than the self, two persons' bodily contact never could constitute personal unity between them. But since one's body is integral to one's person, it is part of the capacity to give oneself to others in ways that establish and build up communion with them. Such self-giving takes diverse forms, including friendly facial expressions and gestures, handshaking, embracing, and marital intercourse.

As a capacity for self-giving, the body requires special respect, since one can give oneself only if free to do so or to refrain. Among the forms of bodily self-giving, sexual self-giving is uniquely intimate. Hence, the body as a capacity for sexual self-giving has a unique inviolability. Therefore, sexual assault always violates the person, is never considered insignificant by the one who is assaulted, and so is always grave matter.

In many cases, people choose with sufficient reflection to commit some other grave sexual sin and then voluntarily, although without further deliberation and choice, carry out a sexual assault. For example, an unmarried man and woman sinfully engage in mutually agreeable erotic play, the woman makes it clear that she wishes to stop short of intercourse, and the man rapes her. Whether or not he planned and chose to rape the woman, he is guilty of that sexual assault inasmuch as he did choose to engage in gravely immoral sexual play with her and voluntarily pressed it to completion without her consent (see the analysis of executive willing in *CMP*, 9.G.1–3).

Obviously, the man's sin of rape in such a case, while mortal, is less wicked than it would be had he planned and chosen the rape, and the woman also bears some responsibility for the rape insofar as she cooperated in the sin that led to it.

f) Many added factors can aggravate sexual assault's wrongness. The wrongness of sexual assault usually is increased by various specifications and/or circumstances of the act. Generally speaking, sexually motivated assault at least incipiently carries out some other sexual sin. For example, the assailant who touches another's genitals acts out a fantasy of fornication, adultery, or sodomy. Moreover, sexual assault can lead to sin by the person assaulted and others who observe the act.

Even in its more ordinary and less extreme forms, sexual assault has bad psychological effects and impedes or damages community: it causes anxiety, embarrassment, and humiliation to those assaulted and fuels group antagonisms, for example, the antagonism of some women against men in general. Then too, the high incidence of sexual assault renders all bodily contacts ambiguous and so discourages people from legitimate communicative contacts, for example, embracing others to welcome, comfort, or reassure them. Moreover, many people suffer anxiety due to potential sexual assault. For example, children's sense of security even with their own parents can be damaged by reports of parents sexually abusing children.

In its more egregious forms, sexual assault often has more serious consequences for its victim: immediate bodily harm, unwarranted loss of reputation, risk of contracting sexually transmitted diseases, depression and other serious psychological trauma, and harm to an existing intimate relationship or to the potentiality for such a relationship. When a man rapes a woman, she often suffers several or all of the preceding bad consequences; sometimes she also suffers loss of her virginity and/or involuntary pregnancy. Thus, it is easy to see why most people consider such rape the paradigm of sexual assault, a wrong comparable to homicide and, in some cases, even worse.

g) **Other behavior should not be confused with sexual assault.** Behavior that could be an act of sexual assault but in fact is not should be distinguished from true sexual assault. So, people should not be judged to be engaged in sexual assault if their behavior leads to bodily contact which may well be unintentional. Even if people intentionally make bodily contact that in some way is inappropriate, their acts should not be considered sexual assault unless the contact is genital or its sexual motivation is clear. For example, jocular patting or pinching of buttocks that is not sexually motivated is not sexual assault. Such contact can be grave matter if it is an occasion of mortal sin or is seriously repugnant and insulting. But it also can be virtuous when it occurs as innocent, playful contact among relatives and friends.

3. Justice and Charity Should Shape All Other Bodily Contacts

Because bodily contact is contact with the person, it seldom is insignificant. It can communicate for good or ill; it can be helpful; it can harm some intelligible good or cause pain.

a) **Bodily contact often can be fairly accepted as a side effect.** Some bodily contact with others is merely a side effect of moving about and occupying legitimate space. For example, a person takes his or her assigned seat in an airplane, and in doing so touches another's arms and/or legs. Such contacts are ruled by fairness: they are morally acceptable insofar as they are necessary for legitimate purposes and not harmful, painful, or damaging to the other person. One may push through a crowd if necessary to reach a legitimate destination, but may not injure others in doing so.

b) **Communicative contacts are subject to special norms.** Some bodily contacts with others are meant to be communicative: tapping someone on the shoulder to get his or her attention, shaking hands, sexual intercourse, lightly spanking a small child. Because these are so various, it is impossible to make a general moral judgment on them. To all such contacts, the general norms of communication apply (see 7.B). For instance, if meant to be communicative but not sexual, contacts such as embracing and joining hands must meet the standards of communication by being sincere and restrained, so that those making them neither pretend interpersonal communion that does not really exist nor press such communion on individuals unwilling to share in it. To some of these contacts, the norms of sexual morality also apply (see 9.E). Since pain is not an intelligible evil, parents may inflict it on small children—for instance, by lightly spanking them—to teach them to avoid certain behavior, provided the act that causes pain does no real harm (see *S.t.,* 2–2, q. 65, a. 2).

c) **Contacts intended for other ends can be either good or bad.** Bodily contact, when not meant to be communicative, sometimes is intended to benefit or cooperate with another in some way: the contacts of people working or playing together, of health care personnel with patients, of a rescuer with the person rescued. Such contacts, not wrong in themselves, can be wrong because the touching is part of some wrong act, for example, cooperation in injecting illicit drugs. They also can be unfair, because against the reasonable will of those touched or someone responsible for them: health care imposed on competent persons against their wishes, assisting a handicapped individual who prefers to struggle alone, restraining someone else's child instead of leaving it to the parents to do so.

Some intentional bodily contacts are neither communicative nor intended to benefit or cooperate with those touched, but are intended for some other purpose. In some cases, the contact is made by handling or striking the body of someone who is unfairly harming, threatening, or blocking another or others. For example, one might strike a mugger in self-defense or push aside someone blocking legitimate access to a building. In such cases, the minimal necessary violence, if fairly exerted, is justified.

In other cases, the person with whom the contact is made is not wrongly harming, threatening, or blocking anyone, but his or her body is used as a means for one's own purposes. Usually such contact is so repugnant that nobody would consider it insignificant. For instance, a mugger assails a man to make him a docile robbery victim, an investigator experiments on an aborted but still living baby, a transplant team takes a woman's organs while she might still be alive, a police officer inflicts pain on prisoners to coerce them into disclosing information (torture used as a means). Such acts are seriously unfair, and the matter is always grave.

d) **Contacts willed for the sake of harm constitute grave matter.** Some bodily contacts are motivated by anger or hatred and are intended to inflict pain, cause harm, or even destroy life, health, or beauty. For example, a frustrated motorist runs over a traffic officer; a man vents his anger by beating his wife; a jealous lover throws acid in a rival's face. All such acts are wrong, not only because of the motive but because of their impact on the bodily person. People do not regard any of these acts as insignificant, even if only slight pain or harm results. Therefore, all such acts are grave matter, and the more serious of them, which carry some risk of death or permanent disability, approach the gravity of intentional killing.

e) **Prizefighting cannot be justified and should not be supported.** Prizefighters cooperate in setting up and carrying on their fights; provided they abide by the rules they agree to, they do not act unfairly in inflicting harm on one another. However, when they punch each other, they do intend the harm they inflict, because it is the means to weakening and perhaps knocking out an opponent and thus winning the fight. In this respect, prizefighting differs from sports such as football, in which the bodily contact involved can achieve the game's purpose without inflicting any harm, so that players need not intend the harm they foresee as possible or even likely when they make violent contact with other players. Moreover, the harm fighters seek to inflict on one another is serious enough that nobody suffering such harm in other contexts would consider it insignificant. Therefore, prizefighting cannot be justified, and is grave matter. People should not cooperate in or encourage such activity.[151] Nor should they either wager on or watch prizefights,

---

151. See Joseph Farraher, S.J., "Notes on Moral Theology," *Theological Studies* 24 (1963): 64–69; Aertnys, Damen, and Visser, *Theologia moralis*, 2:136, including n. 25.

since doing so is likely to lead to a temptation to will that one of the fighters harm the other, and yielding to that temptation would be a sin of thought in grave matter.

f) This norm can be generalized to apply to other sports. The norm regarding prizefighting can be generalized to apply to any sport in which the intentional infliction of bodily harm is essential. Moreover, in any sport whatever, any choice to harm an opponent in order to better the chance of winning is grave matter, since every competitor regards as significant any harm suffered that is likely to affect a contest's outcome. When rooting for their favored team, spectators should refrain from willing that players on the other side be injured.

4. Others' Space and Mobility Should Be Respected

As sentient and mobile organisms, people need both space in which to exist and freedom to move about, but plainly it is possible to infringe on others' space and inhibit their movements. Doing either is likely to lead to bodily contact, and so the morality of respecting space and mobility is very closely related to the morality of bodily contact.

a) People have their proper space in different ways. One way in which people have a certain space is by legitimately occupying a piece of land or some structure. They may own it or have the owner's authorization to use it, or may be legitimately using a public area or piece of unclaimed territory. People occupy their space by being actually or habitually present in it and/or by indicating in some way—by a sign, a fence, an enclosure, or the like—that others are unwelcome to enter without invitation or authorization. For instance, in a public park where there are plenty of picnic tables, each family or group's space includes the whole table it uses; in a territory occupied by various nomadic tribes, each tribe's space is an area sufficient for it to carry on its own activities without interference.

Besides the space people have by occupying land and structures, everyone has a certain proper space. At a minimum, it is the space his or her own body occupies, but in uncrowded conditions it includes sufficient surrounding space to avoid unwelcome bodily contact or other incursions on privacy. For example, on an uncrowded public vehicle, each passenger's space is that required to avoid unnecessary touching. In a park where couples are strolling and talking, each couple's space is that required to maintain insofar as possible the privacy of conversations.

b) One can infringe on others' space without actually entering it. Someone infringes on others' space not only by actually entering it but by doing anything that inhibits or adversely affects their use and enjoyment of it. For example, using herbicides or insecticides which wind and water carry onto others' property infringes on it. Again, causing sound—for instance, by playing loud music—which annoys others by carrying into their homes or work places infringes on them. Such infringements are not always recognized as such by law, but that does not mean they are morally negligible.

c) One should not infringe unfairly on others' space. Not all entering of another's space is infringing on it, for some entry can be reasonably presumed to be welcome or, at least, acceptable. For example, walking up to and knocking on someone's door for any legitimate purpose is not an infringement on the occupant's space. Nor are all infringements unfair. For instance, someone who walked into another's unoccupied home in a life-and-death emergency to use the telephone would infringe on the resident's space but do so fairly.

If someone unfairly infringes on another's space, the matter is grave but admits parvity. For example, in a neighborhood of private homes in which people usually do not trespass, walking between homes along a property line can unfairly infringe on the residents' space, but generally such trespassing is considered insignificant unless damage is done, and so, even if unfair, can be light matter.

d) One should not unfairly inhibit others' moving about. People can inhibit others' movements in two ways: by excluding them from some space or by confining them within some space. Either can be justified. For example, one rightly excludes uninvited strangers from entering one's home, and rightly holds a burglar until the police arrive. In general, parents may inhibit their small children's movements for any reason, and anyone may rightly restrain another from committing a crime or may temporarily prevent another from doing violence to himself or herself. Apart from these cases, however, fairness sets narrow limits on the right to interfere with another's physical freedom.

A person wrongly excludes another or others from some space in wrongly claiming space that is not his or her own or trying to control space beyond his or her legitimate authority. The seriousness of this offense depends on how extensive the limitation is, the significance of the activity it impedes, and so on. Thus, it can be either grave or light matter.

Confining others unfairly prevents them from engaging in the whole range of activities otherwise open to them. Confinement can range from temporarily preventing someone from leaving a building, to preventing people from emigrating, to kidnapping. People aware of undergoing deliberate unfair confinement never consider it insignificant. Thus, the matter is always grave.

e) Added factors aggravate the wrong of unfairly holding someone. While unfairly detaining persons always is a grave offense against them, further factors often aggravate the wrong. The confinement frequently involves wrongful bodily contact which sometimes also leads to bodily injury, often causes psychological distress, sometimes causes other serious harm to those confined and their loved ones, sometimes prevents those confined from fulfilling important responsibilities, and sometimes is an element of another grave wrong to the person, such as sexual assault, robbery, or detaining for ransom. The last, kidnapping, frequently involves many of the other aggravating factors, and therefore is considered one of the most serious offenses against persons as bodily beings, comparable in its gravity with murder and rape.[152]

+ + +

---

152. Fraudulently or forcibly kidnapping or detaining someone is a canonical crime: *CIC*, c. 1397. C. 1089 makes the kidnapping or detention of a woman an invalidating impediment to marriage; the impediment ceases only after the woman is separated from the man so that she can freely choose, without force or fear, whether to marry him.

CHAPTER NINE

MARRIAGE, SEXUAL ACTS, AND FAMILY LIFE

Summary

Every marriage is a permanent and exclusive union. Traditional theology treated marriage simply as an instrumental good, but recent Church teaching points beyond that view, to the view that marriage itself is a basic human good. While marital communion can exist without parenthood, having and raising children is nonetheless the specific, intrinsic perfection of marriage, which shapes it as an open-ended community formed by the self-giving of marital consent. The good of marriage itself implies that marriage is permanent and monogamous. The inadequate motives of some who enter into marriage do not affect its properties.

The Church's practice (for example, in granting annulments and dissolving nonconsummated marriages) is consistent with this theology of marriage. Annulment is not a form of divorce but a judgment that a particular marriage never existed. When a couple have consented to marriage but not yet consummated it by conjugal intercourse, their relationship is not yet fully constituted as a marriage. At the same time, the Church rejects the view that adultery justifies divorce and holds that even nonsacramental marriage is indissoluble. Solving some apparent puzzles in this area requires recognition that there are such things as imperfect marriages—unions which both are and are not marriages.

Marriage is sacred in itself and also within the old covenant. But every marriage of a baptized couple also is an enduring sacrament, which confirms marriage's unity and indissolubility while both preparing for and participating in heavenly communion. Christian couples should regard marriage as a vocation; and the family should function as a kind of domestic church.

Within the framework of the divine design for marriage, each couple should build a unique marital and family communion by satisfying various responsibilities. Papal teaching on the husband-wife relationship is consistent; John Paul II's emphasis on the spouses' *mutual* subjection does not contradict the tradition. The equality and differences of husband and wife can and should be harmonized. Both spouses should maintain and perfect their marital love, and should be companions in the whole of life. At the same time, being male and female differentiates spouses' responsibilities, though excessive differentiation of roles should be avoided. The father-husband has a special role in decision making: ordinarily, as a service to the family, to make decisions in situations where one person must exercise authority for the family.

Married couples should engage in chaste sexual acts, in which sexual pleasure is subordinated to communion; they should abstain when there is a reason to abstain. Spouses should cooperate lovingly in marital intercourse, and marital sexual acts short of intercourse can be appropriate. But married persons should not engage in other sexual acts, nor should the unmarried engage in any sexual act. Although sexual arousal, and even satisfaction, can occur blamelessly without an intentional sexual act, nevertheless all intentional sexual acts violating the marital good are grave matter. With the help of grace it is possible for Christians to pursue chastity and attain it.

Spouses have responsibilities with regard to children. They should procreate responsibly, in light of their vocation to marriage, using only upright methods to carry out their conscientious judgments; in this connection, birth regulation by periodic abstinence is not contraception. Parents should raise their children to be good Christians. They should treat children fairly. They should exercise parental authority, while bearing in mind that it is limited by the true good of children. They should recognize and fulfill their responsibility in regard to religious formation, and indeed should bring Christian principles to bear on the whole upbringing of children: their use of media, schooling, education in sexuality, hobbies and friends, and so on.

For their part, children should honor, help, and obey their parents. The family should be a community of love and service, where, for example, crises like the death of a family member and pregnancy out of wedlock are dealt with in a responsible, Christian way.

If a marriage is troubled, some sin or sins usually underlie the situation, and this requires repentance and mutual forgiveness on the spouses' part. They also should take the necessary steps to deal with nonmoral sources of trouble. Sometimes spouses may, or even should, initiate a marital separation, subject to the Church's authority; but even separated persons still have many marital and familial responsibilities. Where troubles relate to a doubt about the validity of a marriage, the doubt can and should be overcome. So-called internal forum solutions to marriage cases solve nothing; Catholics in bad marriages should recognize the truth of their situation and act accordingly.

Couples preparing for marriage also have responsibilities. To begin with, a person should discern whether he or she has a vocation to marriage and, if so, should begin to respond by developing chaste friendships. Those with marriage more immediately in prospect should seek suitable partners; they should not carry on untimely romantic relationships, however, and they should consider as potential partners only those who are truly available and morally well qualified. An engagement should be the result of both romance and reflection—the romantic element should of course be chaste. Upon becoming engaged, the couple should begin immediate preparation for marriage by seeing a priest at once and jointly settling several important questions. Wedding arrangements should serve the relevant goods and not impose unreasonable burdens on anyone concerned. Far more important than planning the wedding's details is preparation—not least, spiritual preparation—to fulfill the responsibilities of married life.

Question A: Why Is Every Marriage a Permanent and Exclusive Union?

Although marriages are communities formed by mutual consent, still marriage is rooted so deeply in human nature that it is found in every age and culture. Anthropologists studying a culture do not ask whether its members marry but what special characteristics marriage has in that society. In doing so, they refer to something recognizable in any society by its constant characteristics: it is the more or less stable heterosexual relationship recognized by society as the community in which it is appropriate for a man and a woman to engage regularly in sexual intercourse, and to beget and raise children.[1]

The marriage of two baptized persons is a sacrament (see C, below). However, not only do the spouses' responsibilities in marriage as such also pertain to sacramental marriage, they underlie the responsibilities which are proper to it; and of course not all Catholics are married to baptized persons. Therefore, before considering a Christian couple's special responsibilities, it is useful to consider why indissolubility (which excludes divorce) and exclusivity (which excludes polygamy) are essential properties not only of sacramental marriage but of all marriage as God meant it to be.

This question treats (1) the intrinsic goodness of marriage; (2) the complex structure of this good, which includes both the couple's relationship and the potential of their communion for parenthood; (3) the properties of indissolubility and exclusivity; and (4) the fact that those attempting marriage cannot alter these properties.

1. Marriage Is Not Merely Instrumentally but Intrinsically Good

Every community joins people in cooperation for a common good, and a community's appropriate constitution and characteristics are determined by that common good and by the ways in which its members can cooperate for it. To understand the moral responsibilities of marriage, one therefore must begin by identifying its common good. Any such attempt, however, encounters a long theological tradition, which distinguished several goods and ends of marriage and which requires critical reflection in order to clarify the single, unified common good of marriage.

---

1. G. Robina Quale, *A History of Marriage Systems,* (New York: Greenwood Press, 1988), 305, summarizes: "Marriage *is* an alliance before it is anything else. It is an alliance between the two who are marrying. It is an alliance between families who become more closely linked . . .. Marriage is the means by which the larger social system recognizes not only the mother, but also the father of the children whom the mother bears. Marriage acknowledges each as the other's partner in bringing children into the world and raising them. Marriage is also the means by which the larger social system seeks to control the expression of the powerful instincts of sexual attraction."

Scripture suggests that marriage is intrinsically good. But St. Augustine, while defending the goodness of marriage, held that it is an instrumental good, and this view influenced subsequent theological reflection. St. Thomas not only accepted it but distinguished between the ends of marriage, classifying them as primary and secondary. This line of theological reflection never achieved an entirely harmonious synthesis of all the facets of Christian marriage.[2] The Church's teaching in modern times implied that marriage is more than an instrumental good, and, during the twentieth century, the Church's doctrine on marriage has developed. As a result of this development, marriage no longer is seen as a means to ends beyond itself; rather, its intrinsic goodness has been clarified, and its various goods and ends can now be seen as aspects of its intrinsic goodness.

Since intelligible goods which are intrinsically, not merely instrumentally, good, are basic human goods (see *CMP,* 5.D), the result of this development in Catholic teaching about marriage can be summed up by saying that marriage itself is a basic human good.

a) Scripture suggests that marital communion is intrinsically good. The book of Genesis includes two accounts of the creation of man and woman. According to one, God first creates the man, observes that it is not good for him to be alone, and so creates the woman from part of the man's body; when God presents the woman to him, the man at once recognizes her as his appropriate partner, as part of himself (see Gn 2.18–23). From this, the sacred writer concludes: "Therefore a man leaves his father and his mother and clings to his wife, and they become one flesh" (Gn 2.24).[3] Here, the contrast between the man's initial loneliness ("not good") and the fulfillment of marriage that motivates him to leave his father and his mother implies that marital communion is in itself good.[4]

---

2. A study of the history of teaching on the ends of marriage, from Scripture through John Duns Scotus: Claude Schahl, O.F.M., *La doctrine des fins du mariage dans la théologie scolastique* (Paris: Éditions Franciscaines, 1948).

3. While St. Paul understands "they become one flesh" as referring to sexual intercourse (see 1 Cor 6.15–16), it refers, not to that alone, but to the total communion of the married couple by which they are, as it were, one person; see Maurice Gilbert, S.J., " 'Une seule chair' (*Gn* 2, 24)," *Nouvelle revue théologique* 100 (1978): 66–89. Thus, the communion of married life is actualized and experienced not only in chaste marital intercourse but also, when intercourse is fruitful, in having and raising children, and in domestic life as a whole. On this point, also see Pierre Grelot, *Man and Wife in Scripture* (New York: Herder and Herder, 1964), 35–36, 123–24. The whole of Grelot's beautiful little book might well be read as background for this chapter.

4. John Paul II, General Audience (9 Jan. 1980), 2 and 4, *Inseg.* 3.1 (1980) 89 and 90, *OR,* 14 Jan. 1980, 1, teaches (sec. 2): "When God Yahweh says that 'it is not good that man should be alone' (Gn 2.18), he affirms that 'alone', man does not completely realize this essence [the very essence of the person]. He realizes it only by existing *'with some one'*—and even more deeply and completely: by existing *'for some one'."* The Pope explains (sec. 4): "Precisely by traversing the depth of that original solitude, man now emerges in the dimension of the mutual gift, the expression of which—and for that very reason the expression of his existence as a person—is the human body in all the original truth of its masculinity and femininity." This is what John Paul calls the "nuptial" meaning of the body: sexual differentiation manifests that God has made the man and the woman for each other, so that, inasmuch as they are incomplete and able to exercise freedom of self-determination, these bodily persons can complete each other by their mutual self-donation. A helpful commentary on this aspect of John Paul II's teaching: Alfredo Martínez Albiach, "Teología del sexo," *Burgense* 23 (1982): 425–53.

According to the other account, man and woman were created together in God's image and blessed: "So God created humankind in his image, in the image of God he created them; male and female he created them. God blessed them, and God said to them, 'Be fruitful and multiply, and fill the earth and subdue it' " (Gn 1.27–28). Here, the fact that man and woman are created together in God's image suggests that their very communion pertains to the natural perfection of human persons.[5] But this account raises the question: Precisely how is marriage related to the blessing of offspring?

b) St. Augustine held that marriage is an instrumental good. In a work defending the goodness of marriage against those who despised and denigrated it, St. Augustine explicitly denied that marriage is good in itself: "Surely we must see that God gives us some goods which are to be sought for their own sake, such as wisdom, health, friendship; others, which are necessary for something else, such as learning, food, drink, sleep, marriage, sexual intercourse."[6] For Augustine, marriage is good because it makes possible both the propagation of the human race, in which the good of friendship is realized, and the fidelity of chastity, by integrating sexual desire into legitimate activity (and so providing a "remedy for concupiscence"); for Christians, he holds, the good of marriage also is in the sanctity of the sacrament, that is, in marriage's indissolubility.[7] Augustine also holds that marital intercourse is justified only when either intentionally directed to procreation or necessary, because of human weakness, to maintain marital fidelity.[8]

Nevertheless, perhaps because the Church's teaching and practice never excluded the marriage of persons known to be infertile, Augustine begins his exposition of the goodness of marriage:

5. Vatican II teaches that "God did not create the human person as a solitary," and, having quoted "male and female he created them" (Gn 1.27), explains that the two sexes' "companionship produces the primary form of interpersonal communion. For by their innermost nature human beings are social, and unless they relate themselves to one another they can neither live nor develop their gifts" (GS 12). This gloss on Gn 1.27 implies that marriage is not merely an instrumental good: the companionship of man and woman belongs to humankind as image of God and is the primary form of one of the essential, intrinsic aspects of human fulfillment.

6. St. Augustine, *De bono coniugali* 9.9 (*Saint Augustine: Treatises on Marriage and Other Subjects,* trans. Charles T. Wilcox, M.M., et al. [New York: Fathers of the Church, 1955], 21–22).

7. See St. Augustine, *De bono coniugali* 24.32 (*Treatises on Marriage and Other Subjects,* 47–48). Augustine explains the creation of woman as helper, *De Genesi ad litteram* 9.5.9 (*St. Augustine: The Literal Meaning of Genesis,* trans. John Hammond Taylor, S.J. [New York: Newman Press, 1982], 75): "Now, if the woman was not made for the man to be his helper in begetting children, in what was she to help him? She was not to till the earth with him, for there was not yet any toil to make help necessary. If there were any such need, a male helper would be better, and the same could be said of the comfort of another's presence if Adam were perhaps weary of solitude. How much more agreeably could two male friends, rather than a man and woman, enjoy companionship and conversation in a life shared together."

8. See St. Augustine, *De bono coniugali* 6.6, 10.11 (*Treatises on Marriage and Other Subjects,* 16–17, 24). John T. Noonan, Jr., *Contraception: A History of Its Treatment by the Catholic Theologians and Canonists* (Cambridge, Mass.: Harvard University Press, 1965), 131, claims that Augustine did not invent his understanding of the procreative good but took it from Philo and the Stoics; and while some of Noonan's interpretations are questionable, he provides (76–81) enough evidence to make it clear that, without explicitly stating it, several other Fathers of the Church shared the view that marriage is only an instrumental good.

This does not seem to me to be a good solely because of the procreation of children, but also because of the natural companionship [*societas*] between the two sexes. Otherwise, we could not speak of marriage in the case of old people, especially if they had either lost their children or had begotten none at all. But, in a good marriage, although one of many years, even if the ardor of youths has cooled between man and woman, the order of charity still flourishes between husband and wife.[9]

Unfortunately, this point, which manifests a certain tension in Augustine's thinking, is left undeveloped.

Had Augustine developed this insight, he might have resolved the tension by synthesizing the good of the natural society between the sexes with the other three goods—offspring, fidelity, and sacrament—and articulated a more adequate view of the communion of married life as a whole.[10]

c) St. Thomas held that marriage has primary and secondary ends. About three centuries after Augustine, St. Isidore of Seville set out what became the standard schema in Catholic theology for treating the *purposes,* as distinct from the *goods,* of marriage. Following Scripture, Isidore distinguishes three reasons (*causae*) for marrying: first, for the sake of offspring ("Be fruitful and multiply"); second, for the sake of a helper ("It is not good that the man should be alone"); and third, on account of incontinence ("It is better to marry than to be aflame with passion").[11]

About five centuries later, in his *Commentary on the Sentences,* St. Thomas, drawing on Aristotle, developed this schema by distinguishing between marriage's primary and secondary ends. Thomas, explaining the sense in which marriage is natural, says its principal end is the good of offspring and its secondary end is the mutual help which the spouses give each other in domestic life. Marriage is natural in respect to its primary end, since nature intends that children be not only born but brought up, and this requires the lasting tie between the parents in which marriage consists. Marriage also is natural in respect to its secondary end:

> For, just as natural reason dictates that people dwell together, since individuals are not self-sufficient for everything that pertains to life—which is why human beings are said to be political by nature—so, of those activities which are required for human life, some are better suited to men and others to

9. St. Augustine, *De bono coniugali* 3.3 (*Treatises on Marriage and Other Subjects,* 12).

10. Indeed, Augustine may have had a glimmer of insight into the unity of the good of marriage, for the present summary of his view is drawn from his work titled, *De bono coniugali* (*On the* Good *of Marriage,* not: *On the* Goods *of Marriage*). John J. Hugo, *St. Augustine on Nature, Sex and Marriage* (Chicago: Scepter, 1969), 129–36, points out that in this work Augustine is not talking about multiple ends of marriage but multiple goods, and even asserts (133): "St. Augustine, then, does not distinguish a hierarchy of ends within marriage: the one good of marriage is three-faceted." Likewise, following Augustine, the Council of Florence speaks, not of three goods, but of the threefold *good,* of marriage (*"triplex bonum matrimonii"*) (DS 1327/702). Also see: Augustine Regan, C.Ss.R., "The Perennial Value of Augustine's Theology of the Goods of Marriage," *Studia Moralia* 21 (1983): 351–78.

11. See St. Isidore, *Etymologiae* 9.7.27, *PL,* 82:367.

women, so that nature inclines toward a certain association [*associatio*] of man with woman, which is matrimony.[12]

While Thomas does not usually list remedying concupiscence among the ends of marriage, he does teach that, after original sin, marriage serves to curb concupiscence, especially in Christians, to whom the marital sacrament gives healing grace.[13]

The distinction between primary and secondary ends was vital for Thomas in dealing with one problem: how to reconcile Old Testament polygamy with natural law. His solution is that polygamy did not violate the primary end, and so could be permitted, although it interfered with the secondary end.[14] By using the distinction and hierarchy of the ends of marriage in this way, Thomas confirms Augustine's view that marriage is not good in itself but only as instrumental to the procreation and raising of children.[15]

Nevertheless, in the very place where he deals with the problem of polygamy, Thomas reveals complexities in his thinking. For, in coordinating the ends with the goods of marriage, he says that the principal end pertains to the human couple according to their generic nature, which they share with other animals, and thus *having and raising children* is a good of marriage. The secondary end of marriage, which pertains to the human couple precisely as human, is cooperation in the activities necessary for life; thus, the spouses owe each other *fidelity,* which is another of the goods of marriage. Beyond these two natural ends, marriage among Christians has the end of signifying the union of Christ and the Church, and so the *sacrament* is a good of marriage.[16]

Thomas thus coordinates the good of fidelity with the secondary end, cooperation in daily life, which he says belongs to marriage as specifically human. This suggests a question: Is this cooperation, when carried on with fidelity, a good intrinsic to marriage itself? While Thomas never raises this question, an affirmative answer to it seems to be implicit in the explanation he offers (in the *Summa*

---

12. St. Thomas, *In Sent.,* 4, d. 26, q. 1, a. 1 (*S.t.,* sup., q. 41, a. 1), cf. *In Sent.,* 4, d. 33, q. 1, aa. 1–2 (*S.t.,* sup., q. 65, aa. 1–2). Unfortunately, after his first attempt in his youthful *Commentary on the Sentences,* Thomas never wrote a full treatment of marriage.

13. See St. Thomas, *In Sent.,* 4, d. 26, q. 2, aa. 1–3 (*S.t.,* sup., q. 42, aa. 1–3); cf. *In Sent.,* 4, d. 34, q. 1, a. 2, ad 3 (*S.t.,* sup., q. 58, a. 1, ad 3); *In Sent.,* 4, d. 34, *expositio textus* (after a. 5, but not included in *S.t.,* sup.). The curbing of concupiscence is an essential, secondary end of marriage: *In Sent.,* 4, d. 40, q. 1, a. 3 (*S.t.,* sup., q. 54, a. 3); cf. *In Sent.,* 4, d. 30, q. 1, a. 3 (*S.t.,* sup., q. 48, a. 2).

14. See St. Thomas, *In Sent.,* 4, d. 33, q. 1, aa. 1–2 (*S.t.,* sup., q. 65, aa. 1–2).

15. In explaining how the good of offspring makes marriage both a useful good and virtuous, St. Thomas, *In Sent.,* 4, d. 31, q. 1, a. 2, ad 6 (*S.t.,* sup., q. 49, a. 2, ad 6), says: "Marriage, through being directed to offspring, is useful, and nonetheless virtuous (*honestum*), inasmuch as it is rightly directed." On this analysis, just as eating, which is only instrumentally good, becomes good in itself insofar as it is temperate, so marriage and the marital act, which are instrumental goods, become good in themselves insofar as they are realized through virtuous acts, and these acts are virtuous because they rationally order these instrumental goods to the ultimate end.

16. See St. Thomas, *In Sent.,* 4, d. 33, q. 1, a. 1 (*S.t.,* sup., q. 65, a. 1). This coordination of ends with goods makes it clear that the primacy of the primary end is not in value, since Thomas previously explained that the sacrament is the most excellent good of marriage: *In Sent.,* 4, d. 31, q. 1, a. 3 (*S.t.,* sup., q. 49, a. 3).

theologiae, written many years after his *Commentary on the Sentences*) of how Mary and Joseph were truly married. There he says that marriage has its first perfection from its form—the intrinsic principle which makes it what it specifically is—and he describes this form as the "indivisible joining of souls, by which each spouse is bound to maintain unbreakable fidelity with the other" (*S.t.,* 3, q. 29, a. 2, c.).[17] Moreover, while Thomas does not list friendship among the ends or goods of marriage, he says, in arguing for the indissolubility of marriage, that there seems to be maximum friendship between husband and wife, since they share not only marital intercourse but the whole of domestic life (see *S.c.g.,* 3.123).

d) **The Church teaches that there are three *reasons* to marry.** The *Catechism of the Council of Trent* was first published under the authority of St. Pius V in 1566; during the next four centuries, this book had a very great direct and indirect effect on day-to-day catechesis throughout the Catholic Church. Taking up the question, "Why a man and a woman should be joined in marriage," the catechism gives a fresh restatement of traditional doctrine. The three purposes are presented, not primarily as ends (*fines*) which God had in view in instituting marriage, but as reasons (*causae*) which people should have in view in giving their marital consent:

> The first reason, then, is this very society of the two sexes, sought by an instinct of nature, entered into with the hope of mutual help, that each, assisted by the work of the other, may be able more easily to bear the hardships of life and stand up under the weakness of old age.
>
> Another reason is the desire for procreation, not so much, however, to leave behind heirs to inherit property and wealth, as to bring up worshipers in the true faith and religion. . . . And this was also one reason why from the beginning God instituted marriage. . . .
>
> A third reason was added to the others after the fall of our first parent, when, on account of the loss of the righteousness in which man was created, appetite began to resist right reason: namely, that anyone who is aware of personal weakness and wishes to avoid the struggle with the flesh may use the remedy of marriage to avoid sins of lust. . . .
>
> These therefore are the reasons, and those who wish to contract marriage piously and religiously, as becomes the children of the saints, should propose one or more of them to themselves.[18]

Thus, the "natural companionship [*societas*] between the two sexes," which St. Augustine recognized as a good of marriage but failed to incorporate into his

---

17. The form of a natural thing, such as a plant or animal, is the source rather than the end of its actions. Thinking about marriage, as he does the other sacraments, with concepts drawn from natural philosophy, Thomas overlooks the fact that, since each marriage is constituted by the mutual consent of the parties, its form can be its end. In other words, if one asks a couple who are getting married, "Why are you doing this?" they can answer, "In order *to be married,*" including within that end everything good which pertains to marriage: living together, enjoying marital intercourse, having and raising children, fulfilling their Christian vocation, and so forth.

18. *Catechismus ex decreto Ss. Concilii Tridentini ad parochos (The Catechism by Decree of the Holy Council of Trent),* Latin text with trans. by J. Donovan, 2 vols. (Rome: 1839), 2.8.13–14 (1:648, 650; translation supplied). The catechism adds that other decent motives for marrying, compatible with those stated, need not be condemned, for example, Jacob was not condemned for choosing Rachel on account of her beauty.

synthesis, finally finds its place in the Church's teaching: "this very society [*societas*] of the two sexes, sought by an instinct of nature." Moreover, this explanation of the purposes of marriage significantly differs from that of St. Thomas. Obviously, the first two purposes' order is reversed, so that offspring, the primary end in Thomas, becomes the second reason to marry. Less obviously, but even more significantly, the purpose which in Thomas is the secondary end is transformed in becoming the first reason to marry.

In Thomas, the secondary end of marriage is the mutual help which the spouses give each other, not the association (*associatio*) of man and woman to which nature inclines. Of course, since marriage essentially is that association, Thomas must refer to it in showing how marriage is natural, but his argument presupposes that domestic life as an end of marriage is extrinsic to its essence. In the catechism, however, the first reason to marry primarily is "this very society of the two sexes, sought by an instinct of nature"—that is, marriage itself—not merely the mutual help for which the couple hope, although that help is included in this reason for marrying. Thus, in teaching that the first reason to marry is "this very society of the two sexes, sought by an instinct of nature," the catechism implies that marriage itself is a purpose to marry, since "this very society" refers to marriage itself. This, in turn, implies that marriage is intrinsically good, and that Augustine was mistaken in classifying marriage as an instrumental good, along with learning, food, drink, and sleep.[19]

e) In the twentieth century, the Church's teaching on marriage developed. Since canon lawyers deal with issues about the validity of marriages, and a putative marriage's validity or invalidity is settled when the wedding ceremony ends, canonists necessarily think of marriage as it then is, rather than as an ongoing communion. Only after the wedding, however, do the couple begin to actualize any of its ends. So, despite the development in catechesis, theologians, many of them canonists, tended to maintain the view that the ends of marriage are extrinsic to its essence.[20]

Moreover, to deal with marriage cases, canon lawyers need a definite and clear statement of the purpose of marriage, and the 1917 *Code of Canon Law* supplied one: "The primary end of matrimony is the procreation and raising of offspring; the secondary, mutual help and the remedy for concupiscence."[21] Interpreting this statement with a legalistic mentality, theologians read it as decisive with regard to all issues about the meaning and value of marriage. Consequently, the view that marriage and marital intercourse are only instrumental goods became more dominant than ever.

---

19. Also see Leo XIII, *Arcanum, ASS* 12 (1879) 395, *PE,* 81.26, where the end of the divine institution of marriage is said to include not only "the propagation of the human race, but also that the lives of husbands and wives might be made better and happier . . . in many ways: by their lightening each other's burdens through mutual help; by constant and faithful love," and so on—and "for the good of families."

20. See John C. Ford, S.J., "Marriage: Its Meaning and Purposes," *Theological Studies* 3 (1942): 338–64.

21. *Codex iuris canonici* (1917), c. 1013, §1 (translation supplied).

However, that view's very dominance provoked the emergence of an antithesis: Even if the primary end of marriage and marital intercourse is the procreation and raising of children, still marriage has an intrinsic value and meaning, the spouses' union in mutual love, and, since chaste marital intercourse expresses this value and meaning, it too has an inherent significance.[22] The two views' incompatibility and the plausibility of the second led to a development in Catholic teaching on marriage.[23]

f) **Pius XI began this development in *Casti connubii*.** Published at the end of 1930, *Casti connubii* not only reaffirms the truths about marriage which the Church had always taught but adds to previous teaching. While saying nothing inconsistent with canon law's statement of the ends of marriage and even citing it—but only to make the point that the primary end includes the raising of children, not merely procreation—Pius does not use the ends to organize his treatment; instead, he uses the three goods: offspring, fidelity, and the sacrament. In the good of fidelity, Pius implicitly includes conjugal love, for he lists the *fostering* of conjugal love among the secondary ends of both marriage and the marital act.[24]

Moreover, in explaining fidelity, he teaches that conjugal love underlies its realization—conjugal love "pervades all the duties of married life and possesses a certain primacy of nobility in Christian marriage"[25]—and thus suggests that conjugal love brings about the intrinsic perfection of marital communion. Distinguishing authentic conjugal love from lust, sentiment, and empty talk, Pius explains that true love is expressed by action, which must go beyond mutual help and have as its primary purpose that the spouses help each other grow in virtue and holiness.[26] Pius then adds:

> This mutual moulding of husband and wife, this determined effort to perfect each other, can in a very real sense, as the Roman Catechism [the *Catechism of the Council of Trent*] teaches, be said to be the chief reason and purpose [*causa et ratio*] of matrimony, provided matrimony be looked at not in the restricted

---

22. See Dietrich von Hildebrand, *In Defence of Purity: An Analysis of the Catholic Ideals of Purity and Virginity* (New York: Longmans, Green, 1931), 16–27; *Marriage* (New York: Longmans, Green, 1942). Since the first of these works was published in German in 1927 and the second in 1929, they could have influenced the drafting of *Casti connubii*. Even if they did not, however, von Hildebrand's books no doubt articulated ideas already in circulation; see Noonan, *Contraception*, 494–95. Von Hildebrand's position should not be confused with that of theologians, such as Herbert Doms, whose views will be considered shortly, for, while the latter drew on von Hildebrand's work, they attacked elements of Catholic teaching which he respected and tried to safeguard.

23. A detailed study of the work of the twentieth-century magisterium on marriage: Ramón García de Haro, *Matrimonio e famiglia nei documenti del magistero: Corso di teologia matrimoniale* (Milan: Edizioni Ares, 1989). A study making clear the dialectical tension which led to development: Francis W. Carney, *The Purposes of Christian Marriage* (Washington, D.C.: The Catholic University of America Press, 1950). A study of the development: Alain Mattheeuws, S.J., *Union et procréation: Développements de la doctrine des fins du mariage* (Paris: Éditions du Cerf, 1989), 50–204.

24. See Pius XI, *Casti connubii*, AAS 22 (1930) 561, *PE*, 208.59.

25. Pius XI, *Casti connubii*, AAS 22 (1930) 547–48, *PE*, 208.23 (translation supplied).

26. See Pius XI, *Casti connubii*, AAS 22 (1930) 548, *PE*, 208.23.

sense as instituted for the proper conception and education of the child, but more widely as a communion, companionship, and association of life as a whole.[27]

In this way, Pius not only recalls the catechism's teaching but implies that Christian marriage is in itself a vocation and way of holiness. Thus, he supplies another ground for questioning the view that marriage is good only as instrumental to offspring.

g) Pius XII rejected a misconception of the communion of married life. Some theologians, purportedly developing Pius XI's remark that marriage can be looked at "more widely as a communion, companionship, and association of life as a whole," launched a frontal assault against the canonical statement of the ends of marriage.[28] They were dissatisfied with the view that marriage is a merely instrumental good and wished to affirm its intrinsic value. However, being thoroughly imbued with the prevailing legalistic mentality, they assumed at the outset that the ends of marriage are extrinsic to it. This led them to deny that procreation is the primary purpose of marriage and to assert that the intrinsic meaning and immediate purpose of marriage is the spouses' very one-flesh unity.[29] Moreover, these theologians not only affirmed the intrinsic meaning and value of the marital relationship, detached from its ordination to reproductivity, but offered an analogous account of conjugal intercourse.[30]

Although those engaged in this line of theological reflection were groping toward a resolution of longstanding tensions, they oversimplified the problem by reducing the communion of married life to the intimate relationship of husband and

27. Pius XI, *Casti connubii, AAS* 22 (1930) 548–49, *PE,* 208.24 (translation amended).

28. For a summary of this line of theological reflection and references to relevant works: John C. Ford, S.J., and Gerald Kelly, S.J., *Contemporary Moral Theology,* vol. 2, *Marriage Questions* (Westminster, Md.: Newman Press, 1964), 20–35; for a fuller treatment and a measured critique: Carney, *The Purposes of Marriage,* 203–61.

29. The most influential work along these lines was Herbert Doms, *The Meaning of Marriage,* trans. George Sayer (New York: Sheed and Ward, 1939). Doms presupposes that children are extrinsic to the good of marriage, and regards them as accidental to its intrinsic meaning: "Men and women are drawn together by their desire for completion. They want as persons only to fulfil each other. But thanks to nature they tend, when they do this, to procreate new human beings" (36). He rejects (87) the primacy of procreation: "The constitution of marriage, the union of two persons, does not then consist in their subservience to a purpose outside themselves, *for* which they marry. It consists in the constant vital ordination of husband and wife to each other until they become one. If this is so, there can no longer be sufficient reason, from this standpoint, for speaking of procreation as the primary purpose (in the sense in which St. Thomas used the phrase) and for dividing off the other purposes as secondary." He then suggests (88) that it would be best to give up talking about primary and secondary purposes.

30. Thus, Doms, *The Meaning of Marriage,* holds (85) that the *immediate* purpose of the marital act "is the realisation through fusion of bodies of the real two-in-oneship of husband and wife" and that procreation is only an ulterior, *biological* purpose, which he contrasts with the ulterior, *personal* purpose of the fulfillment of the spouses as persons. In laying his foundation for this claim, Doms idealizes the marital act, for example (48): "For these reasons the normally performed sexual act is an act which employs all the powers of husband and wife on every plane of their being. Spirit, mind, body, everything is given to another person in a common act with the highest degree of intensity." Moreover, Doms explicitly denies (222) "that the relationship of husband and wife has its foundation in a single principle of generation," dismissing this as an echo of "the 'scientific thought' of the Middle Ages, long since discarded by modern biology."

wife, considered in abstraction from potential parenthood, which they brought in almost as an afterthought.[31] Interpreted in the perspective of the standard account of the ends of marriage, this new theology rejected the primary end and absolutized the secondary end.[32] Thus, in 1944 the Holy Office (since renamed "Congregation for the Doctrine of the Faith"), with the confirmation of Pius XII, declared inadmissible the opinion of those who "either deny that the primary end of marriage is the generation and education of children, or teach that the secondary ends are not essentially subordinate to the primary end, but are equally principal and independent."[33]

Pius XII thus made it clear that an adequate account of the intrinsic value of marriage could not displace parenthood from its central position. There remained only one alternative: to treat parenthood as part of the communion of married life.

h) Vatican II articulated an integrated view of marriage and family. Rather than reducing marriage to its essence, which is fully realized when the wedding ceremony ends, Vatican II regards it as an ongoing community. The Council considers marriage globally, entitling its central treatment, the first chapter of the second part of *Gaudium et spes:* "Fostering the Dignity of Marriage and the Family."[34] In the chapter's central article (GS 49), the Council repeats and develops Pius XI's teaching about conjugal love, presenting it as the vivifying source of the whole communion of marriage and family life.

Thus, conjugal love, while never identified as an *end* or *good* of marriage, becomes the integrating principle of the whole chapter: marriage and the family are a "community of love" (GS 47); marriage itself is an "intimate community of conjugal life and love" (GS 48); conjugal love "is uniquely expressed and perfected through the marital act" and such acts "signify and foster that mutual self-giving by which spouses enrich each other with joyful and grateful hearts" (GS 49); the fruitfulness of marriage is treated as the fulfillment of conjugal love (see GS 50); and the problem of birth regulation is seen as one of harmonizing conjugal love with respect for life (see GS 51).

In this way, the Council presents marriage as a unified reality, continuous with the family, good and holy in itself, and bearing within itself its various goods and ends, whose riches it diffuses widely:

31. See the summary which Doms, *The Meaning of Marriage,* provides of his position (94–95); after defining marriage as an indivisible, indissoluble, intimate community of life specifically differentiated by sexual intercourse, and after listing its benefits to the spouses, he adds (95): "It tends also to the birth and education of new persons—their children. The child assists their own fulfilment, both as a two-in-oneship and as separate individuals. But society is more interested in the child than in the natural fulfilment of the parents and it is this which gives the child primacy among the natural results of marriage."

32. Doms, *The Meaning of Marriage,* often puts matters in a way which supports this reading; see, for example, 210–13.

33. DS 3838/2295; for an English translation of the decree and bibliography regarding it, see Ford and Kelly, *Marriage Questions,* 27–30.

34. A valuable commentary on this chapter of *Gaudium et spes*: Marcellinus Zalba, S.J., "De dignitate matrimonii et familiae fovenda (ad cap. I partis II Const. de Ecclesia in mundo commentarium," *Periodica de re morali, canonica, liturgica* 55 (1966): 381–429.

> God himself is the author of matrimony, endowed with various goods and ends, all of which are of the greatest importance for the continuation of the human race, for the personal development and eternal destiny of the individual members of the family, and for the dignity, stability, peace, and prosperity of the family itself and of human society as a whole. (GS 48)

When the Council says that God endows marriage with its "various goods and ends," a note supplies references to the places where the three goods are treated by St. Augustine, the Council of Florence, and *Casti connubii*. It also supplies one reference to a passage bearing on the ends of marriage (*S.t.*, sup., q. 49, a. 3, ad 1), where St. Thomas, answering an objection to his thesis that the sacrament is the chief of the marriage goods, explains that the good of offspring holds primacy in one way but not in another. The Council's notes supply no reference to canon law or any other source setting a hierarchy among the ends of marriage. Moreover, the Council refrains from speaking of primary and secondary ends of marriage, thus avoiding the suggestion, associated with that terminology, that marriage is instrumental to ends extrinsic to it.

However, Vatican II by no means repudiates the truth contained in the traditional theology of the primary end of marriage. Immediately after the sentence quoted above mentioning the goods and ends of marriage, the Council adds: "By their own natural character, the institution of marriage and conjugal love are directed to the procreation and raising of children and find their culmination in this" (GS 48). This formulation avoids the suggestion that marriage and conjugal love are means to the end of offspring, and points instead to the view that having and bringing up children normally belong to the full unfolding of marriage and conjugal love themselves.[35]

Vatican II then goes on at once to treat mutual help, too, not merely as the division of labor appropriate in the household insofar as it is an economic unit, but as the proper unfolding and perfecting of the conjugal covenant itself: "Thus the man and the woman, who by their conjugal covenant 'are no longer two, but one flesh' (Mt 19.6), by the intimate conjoining of their persons and their actions provide each other with mutual help and service, experience a sense of their oneness, and achieve it more fully day by day" (GS 48). In this way, the Council

---

35. It is often said that Vatican II deliberately set aside the traditional hierarchy of the primary and secondary ends of marriage. But it is more accurate to say that the Council avoided the terminology of primary and secondary ends, which suggested that marriage is only instrumentally good, and developed traditional teaching by relating conjugal love to the various ends (while leaving open the possibility of regarding these as intrinsic elements of the good of marriage considered as a unitary good). See Congregation for the Doctrine of the Faith, *The Book "Human Sexuality"*, *EV* 6 (1977–79) 1132–33, Flannery, 2:507–8, which refers to the underlying conciliar documents; John Paul II, General Audience (10 Oct. 1984), 3, *Inseg.* 7.2 (1984) 846, *OR*, 15 Oct. 1984, 8. Karol Wojtyla, *Love and Responsibility*, trans. H. T. Willetts (New York: Farrar, Straus, Giroux, 1981), 66–69, explains that conjugal love as a virtue is not to be confused with one of the purposes of marriage, mutual help, but is the source from which flow all the benefits of marriage: procreation and raising of children, mutual help, and the remedy for concupiscence. While conjugal love is the source (efficient cause) of all the ends, they specify it and in that sense are its ground: see Guy de Broglie, S.J., "Le fondement de l'amour conjugal," *Doctor communis* 23 (1970): 192–216; Alberto Ablondi, "Famiglia: comunità di vita e di amore," *Lateranum* 45 (1979): 230–44.

includes mutual help within the very communion of married life, much as the *Catechism of the Council of Trent* did by absorbing it into the "very society of the two sexes, sought by an instinct of nature."

i) Recent Church teaching maintains Vatican II's integrated view. Laying the foundation for his reaffirmation of the Church's teaching on contraception, Paul VI avoids any suggestion that marriage is good only as instrumental to offspring and nowhere speaks of its "primary end." Instead, neatly summing up Vatican II's integrated vision, he teaches that married love originates from God, who is love, and who instituted marriage to effect in human beings his loving plan: "As a consequence, husband and wife, through that mutual gift of themselves, which is specific and exclusive to them alone, develop that communion of persons, in which they perfect each other, so that they may cooperate with God in the generation and rearing of new lives."[36]

Similarly, John Paul II, in responding to the work of the 1980 session of the Synod of Bishops on marriage and family, begins his exposition of the Church's teaching on marriage by pointing out that, because human beings are created in the image of God who is love, the fundamental vocation of every human being is to love. Since human persons are bodily, their bodies must share in love as they realize their vocation in one of two specific ways: marriage, and virginity or celibacy. He then draws the conclusion:

> Consequently, sexuality, by means of which man and woman give themselves to one another through the acts which are proper and exclusive to spouses, is by no means something purely biological, but concerns the innermost being of the human person as such. It is realized in a truly human way only if it is an integral part of the love by which a man and a woman commit themselves totally to one another until death.[37]

After explaining that such self-giving excludes the option to change one's mind, he adds: "This totality which is required by conjugal love also corresponds to the demands of responsible fertility."[38] Thus, John Paul II first describes marriage, without mentioning parenthood, as one way of realizing the human vocation to love, next emphasizes the totality of self-giving required by conjugal love, and only then points out that this totality is itself completed by the procreation and raising of children.

Vatican II's development of Church teaching concerning marriage received legal force in the 1983 *Code of Canon Law.* The 1917 code's statement of the primary and secondary ends no longer appears; in its place in the 1983 code is the first section of the first of the canons on marriage: "The matrimonial covenant, by

---

36. Paul VI, *Humanae vitae,* 8, *AAS* 60 (1968) 485–86, *PE,* 277.8 (translation amended). A helpful study: Settimio Cipriani, "Alcune riflessioni Bibliche sulla 'Humanae vitae'," *Lateranum* 44 (1978): 3–31.

37. John Paul II, *Familiaris consortio,* 11, *AAS* 74 (1982) 92, *OR,* 21–28 Dec. 1981, 3. This chapter includes many quotations from and references to *Familiaris consortio;* to understand the document more adequately, one may find helpful the sound commentary: *Pope John Paul II and the Family,* ed. Michael J. Wrenn (Chicago: Franciscan Herald Press, 1983).

38. John Paul II, *Familiaris consortio,* 11, *AAS* 74 (1982) 92, *OR,* 21–28 Dec. 1981, 3.

which a man and a woman establish between themselves a partnership of the whole of life, is *by its nature ordered toward the good of the spouses and the procreation and education of offspring;* this covenant between baptized persons has been raised by Christ the Lord to the dignity of a sacrament."[39]

j) Marriage is one of the basic human goods. Intelligible goods which are intrinsically good are basic human goods (see *CMP,* 5.D). One way of identifying a basic good is to consider people's actions and ask, "Why are you doing that?" Persisting with that question eventually uncovers a small number of basic purposes of diverse kinds. These purposes arouse interest because their intelligible aspects are instantiations of the diverse basic goods. If engaged couples are asked why they are preparing to marry, they give many different answers, but often say something like: "We are in love and want to spend the rest of our lives together, and we feel we are ready to settle down and have a family." That can be restated in abstract terms: the couple not only are drawn together by erotic emotion but will to form a lasting marital communion, which they expect will be fruitful.

Reflection on that answer makes it clear that marriage is a basic human good. First, marriage is an intelligible good: although emotion motivates people, as it does other animals, to mate, a person can be interested in marrying before embarking upon a romantic relationship with anyone. Second, people can wish to be married for its own sake, in the sense that they judge marriage to be potentially fulfilling and so choose to do what is necessary or useful to establish and maintain marital communion.[40]

Reflection also clarifies how the basic good of marriage includes parenthood. In the long theological tradition, *offspring* and *the procreation and raising of offspring* often were used interchangeably in referring to the chief good or primary end of marriage.[41] However, the two expressions differ in meaning, and the latter, rather than the former, accurately expresses that good and end. For, while children,

---

39. *CIC,* c. 1055, §1 (emphasis added); cf. LG 11, 41; AA 11; GS 48. A very extensive commentary on the canons on marriage in the 1983 code: Luigi Chiappetta, *Il matrimonio nella nuova legislazione canonica e concordataria: Manuale giuridico-pastorale* (Rome: Edizioni Dehoniane, 1990).

40. Someone might object: Since virginity and celibacy for the kingdom's sake pertain to the vocations of some Christians, marriage cannot be a basic human good, for, if it were, such Christians would be called to renounce part of integral human fulfillment. The answer: Although marriage is a basic human good, not everyone need participate in it by being married; integral human fulfillment means, not the same mode of participation by every individual in every good, but the realization of all the human goods in the whole human community: *CMP,* 7.F.3; cf. *S.t.,* 2–2, q. 152, a. 2, ad 1. Those called to virginity or celibacy for the kingdom's sake can participate in the good of marriage in several ways: as children of their own parents, as pastors of families, as collaborators with parents in the education of their children, and so on.

41. For example, compare St. Thomas, *In Sent.,* 4, d. 26, q. 1, a. 1 (*S.t.,* sup., q. 41, a. 1), with *In Sent.,* 4, d. 33, q. 1, a. 1 (*S.t.,* sup., q. 65, a. 1). Often, *offspring* is used (as in *Casti connubii,* quoting St. Augustine) when referring to the good and *the procreation and raising of offspring* when referring to the end (just as in c. 1013 of the 1917 code). Of course, *offspring* can be used as an abbreviated way of saying *the procreation and raising of offspring.* However, the latter expression cannot substitute for the former used in its proper sense, and Vatican II and subsequent papal teachings often use the latter expression or others which explicitly refer to parenthood or some aspect of it.

as distinct persons, are good in themselves and should be loved for their own sakes, procreating and raising children, as activities in which the husband and wife cooperate, not only benefit the children but fulfill the couple. Insofar as it fulfills the couple, parenthood—having a family—is not an extrinsic end to which one-flesh unity is instrumental, but a realization of its potentiality.[42]

In marrying, of course, many people not only intend the good of marriage but have subjective purposes in view: sexual satisfaction, financial security, social status, and so on. But the fact that marital communion can be regarded as instrumental to other goods does not argue against its status as a basic good, since other basic goods also can be regarded as means. For example, although friendship is good in itself, many people carry on friendships for the sake of their moral and spiritual benefits, and while good work is of itself fulfilling, many people pursue excellence in work as a means to earning more money.

In sum, marriage is a basic human good, and the married couple's common good is, not any extrinsic end to which marriage is instrumental, but the communion of married life itself. The *communion of married life* refers to the couple's *being* married, that is, their being united as complementary, bodily persons, so really and so completely that they are two in one flesh. This form of interpersonal unity is actualized by conjugal love when that love takes shape in the couple's acts of mutual marital consent, loving consummation, and their whole life together, not least in the parenthood of couples whose marriages are fruitful. Thus, in considering marriage as a basic human good, none of its traditional ends and goods is set aside; rather, all of them are included in the intrinsically good communion of married life itself.[43]

---

42. The basic goods, grasped by insights which are principles of practical reasoning, also are the objects of natural inclinations; among these goods, which pertain to natural law, St. Thomas lists the union of male and female, raising children, and so on, corresponding to that inclination which human beings have in common with other animals: *S.t.,* 2–2, q. 94, a. 2. Unfortunately, however, Thomas did not complete the part of the *Summa* in which marriage would have been treated, and so never developed this insight.

43. For further clarification of the notion of *basic goods:* Germain Grisez, Joseph Boyle, and John Finnis, "Practical Principles, Moral Truth, and Ultimate Ends," *American Journal of Jurisprudence* 32 (1987): 102–15. But the lists of basic human goods provided both there and in *CMP,* 5.D, omitted the good of marriage because of the supposition that in respect to the marital communion itself marriage could be reduced to the reflexive good of friendship and in respect to having and raising children to the substantive good of life and other basic goods. The reduction of the good(s) of marriage to other basic goods, however, is unsatisfactory for three reasons. First, in marrying, people seem to intend only one many-faceted good rather than several distinct goods. Second, since the good of anything is the fullness of its being, and since basic goods of diverse sorts are irreducible to one another, either there is one basic human good proper to marriage or marriage is not one reality; but recent Church teaching, which resolves the tensions in the tradition, presents an integrated view of marriage; therefore, marriage is one reality having a basic good proper to it. Third, while marital friendship and fidelity might be reducible to the reflexive good of friendship, the core of the good of marital communion is the good which Augustine calls the "*sacramentum.*" (Thomas argues that, if the goods of marriage are considered in themselves, this good is the most essential, since marriage cannot exist without it: *In Sent,* 4, d. 31, q. 1, a. 3 [*S.t.,* sup., q. 49, a. 3].) Now, this good, the couple's one-flesh unity itself, is not reducible to the existential good of friendship, for, while the couple's consent gives rise to the marital bond, it transcends the moral order: unlike a friendship, a marriage is indissoluble.

Still, those who wish to defend all the truth contained in the traditional theology of marriage might object to this account of marriage as a basic human good: "It sounds suspiciously like the erroneous theology of marriage condemned by Pius XII." This objection is answered by the whole of the next section, which explains how parenthood is essentially involved in the good of every marriage, even in that of an infertile couple.

2. Marriage Is a Special Kind of Open-ended Community

The spouses' interpersonal communion and their parenthood are something like the crypt of a church and the upper church which is built upon it. Sometimes a crypt is built and used as a church in the expectation that eventually it will be the foundation for a grander, upper church. Still, the eventual upper church is not an extrinsic end to which the crypt is only instrumental; rather, the upper church will complete the structure of which the crypt is the first and basic part. But even though the plan for the upper church determines the plan for the crypt, if the upper church never is built, the crypt can serve as, and really be, an entirely adequate church for those who worship in it.

In somewhat the same way, the valid marriage which exists when the wedding ceremony ends is of its very nature part of a larger whole. Always and everywhere, marriage is the relationship recognized as appropriate for begetting and raising children. Parenthood is not the end of marriage to which conjugal communion is instrumental; conjugal communion is intrinsically good. But conjugal communion is designed to be, and normally is, an intrinsically good part of a larger, intrinsically good whole: the family.

Thus, parenthood is the intrinsic fulfillment of the intimate union of persons and actions. Because parenthood fulfills marriage, it shapes the spouses' interpersonal communion; and the way children come to be sets requirements for marriage as a whole, among them that it be an open-ended community. Nevertheless, while having and raising children perfects marital communion, the latter can exist and fulfill the spouses even if the former is impossible. For marriage realizes the potentiality of man and woman for unqualified, mutual self-giving, which they undertake and begin by the very act of marital consent.

a) **Having and raising children perfects marital communion.** Vatican II teaches that parenthood is a *gift* which fulfills the husband and wife precisely insofar as they are a married couple:

> Marriage and conjugal love are by their nature ordained toward the begetting and educating of children. Children are really the supreme gift of marriage and contribute in the highest degree to the welfare of their parents. The God himself who said, "It is not good for man to be alone" (Gn 2.18), and "who made man from the beginning male and female" (Mt 19.4), wishing to share with human beings a certain special participation in his own creative work, blessed male and female saying, "Increase and multiply" (Gn 1.28). (GS 50)

Marriage and conjugal love "are by their nature ordained toward" children, "the supreme gift of marriage"; but inasmuch as marriage is a basic human good, it is not instrumental to having and raising children (see 1.j, above). Children are neither the end to which marriage is a means, nor a means (perhaps only optional) to the couple's perfection as such or as individuals, nor a mere result of interpersonal love.

What then is the relationship between marriage as a communion of persons and parenthood? Having and raising children are the ultimate realization and fulfillment of the good of marital communion itself, as John Paul II makes clear. He richly develops a theology of marital intercourse and of marriage as a personal self-gift resulting in an intrinsically good communion of persons; according to this theology, marriage and the marital act are not merely instrumental goods. But he also teaches that marital love should be fruitful, if possible, because, without openness to parenthood, conjugal love itself cannot be authentic.[44]

   b) Parenthood is the specific, intrinsic perfection of marriage. Biologically, every animal, whether male or female, is a complete individual with respect to most functions: growth, nutrition, sensation, emotion, local movement, and so on. But with respect to reproduction, each animal is incomplete, for a male or a female individual is only a potential part of the mated pair, which is the complete organism that is capable of reproducing sexually. This is true also of men and women: as mates who engage in sexual intercourse suited to initiate new life, they complete each other and become an organic unit. In doing so, it is literally true that "they become one flesh" (Gn 2.24).

Thus, while marriage is not merely instrumental to having and raising children, still children do not perfect marriage accidentally, as furniture and decorations perfect a church. They perfect marriage intrinsically: "Marriage and conjugal love are *by their nature* ordained toward the begetting and educating of children" (GS 50, emphasis added). A man and a woman as individuals cannot have and adequately care for children; they fulfill their potentiality to do so by becoming a couple, and the community they thus form differs specifically from other communities, which enable people to cooperate for other common goods.

   c) This specific perfection shapes marriage as a community. A community's specific perfection is its common good as a whole or, at least, a part of it. The common good or goods of any community determine its structure and form of cooperation (see 6.C.2). Therefore, although marriage cannot be reduced to parenthood, its ordering toward the begetting and raising of children determines the conditions for the unity and cooperation of a married couple. Vatican II explicitly points out this essential relationship:

> By their own natural character, the institution of marriage and conjugal love are directed to the procreation and raising of children and find their culmination in this.
>
> *Thus,* the man and the woman, who by their conjugal covenant 'are no longer two, but one flesh' (Mt 19.6), by the intimate conjoining of their persons and their actions provide each other with mutual help and service. (GS 48, emphasis added)

---

44. See John Paul II, *Familiaris consortio,* 14, *AAS* 74 (1982) 96–97, *OR,* 21–28 Dec. 1981, 3; cf. Karol Wojtyla, *Love and Responsibility,* 224–36.

By using the word *thus* (*itaque*) as connective, the Council makes it clear that the married couple's communion and cooperation are shaped in view of potential parenthood.[45]

d) **The way children come to be sets requirements for marriage.** Offspring come to be within the marital community by a process in which the two partners contribute elements to form a new individual, who then is differentiated and separated from his or her parents. This process is complex and lengthy.

Humans are sentient creatures, whose physiological and psychological capacities develop only gradually with many years of nurture and training. With the help of education, humans also transcend the sentient world, so that by knowledge and belief they live within the whole of reality, and by love and freedom enter into interpersonal communion, and help to shape themselves and others by a lifelong series of free choices. Finally, to live fully in the natural and social worlds, bodily persons must receive, share in, and expand culture: they must learn to use language and tools, develop their creative capacities, and acquire sufficient material goods to survive and hand on life to a new generation.

The complexity of the genesis and development of new persons is mirrored in a married couple's interpersonal communion. Not limited to the physiological initiation of their offspring, their unity should be not only in flesh but in mind and heart—in every power. And because the development of human persons takes so long, conception resulting from marital intercourse is only the beginning of a marriage's fulfillment in children, a fulfillment which develops gradually over many years.[46]

e) **Parenthood requires that marriage be an open-ended community.** In open-ended community, the members value their interpersonal relationship for its own sake, not merely for the sake of some limited goal or set of goals they pursue together; moreover, not only do they will to cooperate fairly with one another, but

---

45. This was the truth, denied by Doms and others, on which the Holy Office insisted (see 1.g, above). Expanding on and restating the 1944 decree, Pius XII, Address to the Italian Catholic Union of Midwives, *AAS* 43 (1951) 848–49, *Catholic Mind* 50 (1952): 60, stated the point affirmatively: "The truth is that matrimony as a natural institution, by virtue of the will of the Creator, does not have as its primary, intimate end the personal improvement of the couples concerned but the procreation and the education of new life. The other ends, though also connected with nature, are not in the same rank as the first, still less are they superior to it. They are subordinated to it. This holds true for every marriage, even if it bear no fruit, just as it can be said that every eye is made for seeing although in certain abnormal cases, because of special inward and external conditions, it will never be able to see." Apart from the instrumentalist implication of the analogy—a sterile marriage has intrinsic value which a blind eye lacks—this statement is precisely true.

46. John Paul II, Address to Young Married Couples at Taranto, 4; *L'Osservatore Romano,* It. ed., 30–31 Oct. 1989, 7; *OR,* 11 Dec. 1989, 5, teaches: "With marriage, dear couples, you have begun the realization of a great project: *fusing* your persons to the point of becoming 'one flesh', and giving birth, from this stupendous union, to *life,* to *human life.* You are collaborators of the Creator in the propagation and rearing of human life. Conjugal love *opens of its nature into paternal and maternal love.* As you know, however, being a father or mother goes beyond the mere physical fact and becomes a *spiritual begetting.* This is your educative task! You are called to pass on to the fruit of your union not only material goods but also spiritual goods and those virtues, ideals and moral values, which are *their most precious heritage."*

each loves the others for their own sakes (see 6.C.2.d, 6.D.2.d). So, if parents love children for their own sake and do not consider them merely a goal whose attainment is instrumental to their self-fulfillment as spouses, their relationship with the children is that of open-ended community. But parents *should* love children for their own sake. As persons, children cannot rightly be treated as mere means to others' perfection, and so should be received as a gift and loved for themselves, not sought and used as a means to their parents' fulfillment.

As has been explained, a married couple's fulfillment in parenthood intrinsically perfects their spousal relationship. When a couple have children, a man who is not a good father is not a good husband, and a woman who is not a good mother is not a good wife. For spouses who also are parents, the spousal and parental relationships are not entirely separate; the former includes the latter. So, to form open-ended community with their children, husband and wife must form open-ended community with each other.

Hence, in entering marriage, the man and the woman should will their marital communion for its own sake, willing also to each other every good relevant to this relationship. But, insofar as the marital communion is the source from which new persons emerge, every good of the person can become relevant to marriage. Thus, spouses should will each other's complete perfection as persons. Consequently, while remaining distinct persons, the married couple should also be a uniquely intimate and all-embracing interpersonal communion, as it were, one person.

In sum, a married couple should not regard the long process of a child's development as a large, joint project to be successfully completed but as the fulfillment of their open-ended community with the child, loved for his or her own sake. Spouses thus should will their own marital communion as something good in itself, and in doing so mutually will their complete perfection as persons, each in this way loving the other for his or her own sake.

f) **Marital communion can exist without parenthood.** Although the requirements of parenthood shape marriage as a community, the Church always has held in practice that elderly couples and others who know they are sterile can marry.[47] Vatican II teaches clearly concerning the marriage of the sterile: "Marriage to be sure is not instituted solely for procreation" (GS 50), and draws the conclusion: "Therefore, marriage persists as a companionship and communion of the whole of life, and retains its value and indissolubility, even if offspring are lacking" (GS 50).

To understand this, it helps to notice that marital communion already exists when a couple marry and begin to live together, for, though shaped by its ordination to children, marriage must exist before it is perfected by actual parenthood. If a couple know or come to learn that they never will be able to have children, their marital communion is no less real and no less fulfilling as a communion of complementary persons, even though it always will lack the fulfillment of parenthood. For while marital communion is unlike friendship in that it fulfills a man and a woman precisely insofar as they can be together the principle of new persons, it also is like friendship by being fulfilling for them in itself, apart from the fruitfulness of their

47. On sterility, see *CIC*, c. 1084, §3.

cooperation. God created man and woman for this communion: "It is not good that the man should be alone; I will make him a helper as his partner" (Gn 2.18). In marital communion, man and woman image their creator: "God created humankind in his image, in the image of God he created them; male and female he created them" (Gn 1.27). "So," Jesus teaches, "they are no longer two, but one flesh" (Mt 19.6, Mk 10.8).

Therefore, since marital communion itself fulfills the spouses, a couple can enter marriage for the sake of this fulfillment, even if they cannot attain the ultimate common fulfillment enjoyed by couples whose marital intercourse is fruitful. Given man and woman as they are and the good of marriage as it is, sterile couples can commit themselves to sharing in the good of marriage within their mutually understood and accepted limitations, and cooperate in many appropriate ways to carry out their commitment.

g) Marital consent is the self-giving which forms marital communion. Vatican II teaches that conjugal "love is an eminently human one since it is directed from one person to another through an affection of the will; it involves the good of the whole person" (GS 49).

The "affection of the will" essential for conjugal love is the same reality essential for the very existence of marriage: marital consent.[48] Although erotic desire and feelings of affection usually accompany volitional love, a couple can marry without these but not without mutual volitional love. When the couple marry, their love leads them "to a free and mutual gift of themselves" (GS 49).[49] In other words, it takes shape in the commitments "whereby spouses mutually bestow and accept each other" and so form the conjugal covenant (GS 48). The bride and groom bestow themselves by committing their bodily selves to marital communion and thereby undertaking its responsibilities. Each accepts the other by trusting his or her expressed commitments and, acting on that trust, bestowing himself or herself.

Of course, except for communities which are initiated unilaterally, any open-ended community, such as a genuine friendship, is constituted by mutual self-bestowal, in the sense that those involved will the relationship as something good in itself and thus will one another's good, not selfishly, but for the other's own sake. However, the mutual self-giving which constitutes marriage differs from that

48. The Church teaches that consent makes the marriage; see DS 643/334, 756/397, 1327/702, 1813/990, 3701/2225; Paul VI, Address to the Roman Rota, *AAS* 68 (1976) 206–7, *OR,* 26 Feb. 1976, 3–4; *CIC,* c. 1057, §1.

49. Marital consent is the mutual commitment of the couple to be married. Since this consent is to an open-ended community which embraces all the goods of the person, it is appropriately said to be mutual self-giving. Thus, *CIC,* after stating in c. 1057, §1, that the consent of the parties makes the marriage, adds in §2: "Matrimonial consent is an act of the will by which a man and a woman, through an irrevocable covenant, mutually give and accept each other in order to establish marriage." This statement of the object of marital consent agrees with the position of St. Thomas, *In Sent.,* 4, d. 28, a. 4, c. (*S.t.,* sup., q. 48, a. 1, c.): marital consent is not precisely consent to future sexual intercourse (and so marriage is not a contractual exchange of rights over each other's bodies for the purpose of marital intercourse) but is simply consent to *marriage,* a communion of husband and wife which is oriented to the whole of married life, which, of course, normally includes marital intercourse.

constituting other open-ended communities. Friends will every good for each other, but they need not actually cooperate except with respect to those particular projects which from time to time they find mutually agreeable. Married couples, by contrast, commit themselves to the common life suited to parenthood, and so they must cooperate constantly with respect to the whole range of basic human goods. For this reason, conjugal love as the will to be married is appropriately said to be *total*.[50] (It does not follow that spouses are morally bound to share every commitment and cooperate in every project: see D.5.c–d, below.)

3. The Good of Marriage Implies that Marriage Is Permanent and Exclusive

Because a commitment to any open-ended community involves willing its good in a way that transcends any specified goal, it is not limited in time. Usually, however, such commitments are not exclusive and do not require constant mutual service until death. For example, people can and often do carry on two or more friendships simultaneously by means of occasional communication and contact, and a genuine friendship can effectively cease, without being destroyed, when the friends lose touch with each other.

Jesus teaches that marital commitment should be different. It is a commitment to a unique kind of communion, which, he explains, follows from God's own creative plan for man and woman. He concludes: "So they are no longer two, but one flesh. Therefore what God has joined together, let no one separate" (Mt 19.6, Mk 10.8–9).[51] Since Jesus refers to God's original plan, this teaching concerns marriage as such, not only Christian marriage as sacramental. Consequently, in marrying, a man and a woman form an exclusive and indissoluble union, whether it is a sacramental marriage or not.

Some today argue that Jesus' teaching concerning indissolubility should be understood only as a moral norm: spouses ought not to divorce, and they sin in doing so; but, having repented the sin, they are able to remarry—in other words, divorce is wrong but possible. However, the impossibility of divorce is implied by Jesus' teaching that attempted remarriage after divorce results in adultery.[52] So, Catholic tradition interprets that teaching not only as a moral norm but as a

50. Paul VI, *Humanae vitae*, 9, *AAS* 60 (1968) 486, *PE*, 277.9, first characterizes married love as fully human inasmuch as it is a compound of sense and spirit, and above all an act of free will; then he characterizes marital love as all-embracing: "It is a love which is *total*—that very special form of personal friendship in which husband and wife generously share everything, allowing no unreasonable exceptions and not thinking solely of their own convenience. Whoever really loves his partner loves not only for what he receives, but loves that partner for the partner's own sake, content to be able to enrich the other with the gift of himself."

51. Some exegetes hold that Jesus' scriptural premise (drawn from Gn 2.24) was intended to explain sexual desire or love, not indissolubility. However, Angelo Tosato, "On Genesis 2:24," *Catholic Biblical Quarterly* 52 (1990): 389–409, cogently argues that the verse was a gloss of the late Persian period intended to ground a newly developed norm "which was generically anti-polygamous and implicitly antidivorce" (409). Still, Tosato points out (405, n. 43) that the Old Testament norm is not yet the absolute norm which Catholic tradition finds in the New Testament.

52. See Mk 10.11–12, Lk 16.18, 1 Cor 7.10–11. On the so-called exception clause (Mt 5.32, 19.9) and Pauline privilege (1 Cor 7.15), see B.3–4, below.

revelation of the intrinsic indissolubility of marriage: an attempt to remarry is wrong because divorce is impossible. Vatican II's teaching concerning not only Christian marriage but marriage in general sums up this traditional way of understanding indissolubility:

> The intimate partnership of married life and love has been established by the creator and qualified by his laws, and it is rooted in the conjugal covenant of irrevocable personal consent. Hence, by that human act whereby the spouses mutually bestow and accept each other, a relationship arises which by divine will and in the eyes of society too is durable. In view of the good of society as well as that of the spouses and their offspring, this sacred bond does not depend on human decision. (GS 48)[53]

Several considerations (articulated in a, b, c, and d) help to explain why marital communion's intimate and all-embracing character calls for a commitment that is both truly mutual and entirely dependable. Additional considerations (articulated in e, f, and g) help clarify why the marital union is exclusive and indissoluble, so that it "does not depend on human decision."[54]

a) Erotic love and affection call for exclusivity and permanence. To begin with, even if erotic desire is no part of a couple's motivation in marrying, marital intercourse normally involves and intensifies erotic love, and such love tends to expand into conjugal affection, which permeates the whole relationship. This affection presses for exclusive and permanent union, as everyone recognizes and Scripture attests:

> Set me as a seal upon your heart, as a seal upon your arm;
> for love is strong as death, passion fierce as the grave.
> Its flashes are flashes of fire, a raging flame.
> Many waters cannot quench love, neither can floods drown it. (Sg 8.6–7)

In contemporary Western countries, likewise, people in love typically are jealous and, divorce statistics notwithstanding, most brides and grooms *want* their marriages to last. These demands made by erotic love and conjugal affection for exclusive and lasting union are among their good, God-given characteristics, corresponding to the reality that the man and the woman complete each other to

---

53. The Latin is "non ex humano arbitrio pendet," which is not accurately translated by "no longer depends on human decisions alone" (see both Abbott and Flannery), since that wrongly suggests that the already-constituted bond partly depends on human decisions. The Council of Trent likewise clearly teaches (on the basis of Gn 2.23–24, Mt 19.6, and Mk 10.9) that the bond of marriage, even if it is not sacramental, is in itself perpetual and indissoluble; see DS 1797–99/969; cf. Pius IX, DS 2967/1767; Pius XI, DS 3711/2235. On the Church's teaching on the indissolubility of sacramental marriage, see C.3, below. When the Church speaks of the *bond* of marriage, that expression must not be misinterpreted in accord with individualistic assumptions, as if the man and the woman were complete and self-enclosed realities, tied together by the bond, a third something extrinsic to both of them. Rather, the bond is the marriage itself, the union of the two persons, each incomplete in himself and in herself, but now forming one new and complete reality (two in one flesh); thus, the bond is what is proper to married couples as distinct from otherwise similar unmarried couples.

54. Divorce has increased with secularization, but other socioeconomic factors also have been at work; see Roderick Phillips, *Putting Asunder: A History of Divorce in Western Society* (New York: Cambridge University Press, 1988).

become one flesh.[55] Hence, if a couple entering a putative marriage limit their commitment to allow either for similar relationships with others or for divorce, these limitations compromise the erotic and affective elements of marital love.

b) Polygamy is disadvantageous to the multiple partners and others. In a polygamous marriage, two or more persons share one common spouse. Polyandry, the form of polygamy in which one woman has two or more husbands, plainly has serious disadvantages, for it is found in very few cultures.[56] Polygyny, the form of polygamy in which one man has two or more wives, has been practiced in many cultures. However, it has disadvantages for most men, for except in transitional social situations in which women substantially outnumber men, it is unavoidable that polygyny either remain the prerogative of a few wealthy and dominant men, or deprive many men of wives, or require that most men delay marriage. Children of the multiple unions also are likely to suffer, for when they are numerous and/or dwell in separate households, they do not receive a full share of their father's attention and guidance.

Furthermore, polygyny deprives the conjugal relationship itself of mutuality. Husbands with multiple wives, generally of different ages, can hardly treat all with equal regard and affection. Unless all the wives accept lack of reciprocity and unequal treatment with self-abasing resignation, jealous rivalry is likely.[57] In any case, this absence of mutuality can seem fair only if everyone concerned assumes women are inferior to men, for, as St. Thomas observes, "among husbands having plural wives, the wives have a status similar to that of servants" (*S.c.g.,* 3.124). Polyandry imposes an analogous lack of mutuality on the multiple husbands of a single wife.

The incompatibility of polygamy with conjugal mutuality is not accidental, but results from its distortion of the essential requirements of unqualified commitment to the good of marriage. Completing each other to become, as it were, one person, spouses need each other but no third party. Indeed, if either carries on a similar relationship with someone else, the couple's communion will be destroyed or else limited to a less full unity or potential for unity, actualized only discontinuously by the spouse involved in the other relationship. It is no more possible to become as it were one person (one flesh) with two or more others simultaneously than it is to engage simultaneously in marital intercourse with two or more partners. Consequently, if either party in entering a putative marriage limits his or her commitment

---

55. See Pius XII, Address to Newlyweds (29 Apr. 1942); *Discorsi e radiomessaggi* 4 (1942–43): 53–57; *Papal Teachings: Matrimony,* ed. Benedictine Monks of Solesmes, trans. Michael J. Byrnes (Boston: St. Paul Editions, 1963), 346–48.

56. See George Peter Murdock, "World Ethnographic Sample," *American Anthropologist* 59 (1957): 686.

57. In a sympathetic study of the subject, Jessie L. Embry, *Mormon Polygamous Families: Life in the Principle* (Salt Lake City: University of Utah Press, 1987), 193, points out: "They would not have considered living the principle if they had not felt that they would be blessed and receive rewards in an afterlife. The ability to overcome problems of husbands dealing with more than one wife, wives dealing with co-wives, and children dealing with an extended family was possible because of that same faith. Religious motivations enabled them to deal with or suppress expected jealousies and disagreements that would occur in any family, especially where there were more than one wife." Cf. St. Thomas, *In Sent.,* 4, d. 33, q. 1, a. 1 (*S.t.,* sup., q. 65, a. 1).

to allow for one or more similar relationships with others, the commitment, which should be a mutual and unconditional self-bestowal, will be neither mutual nor unconditional.

c) **Divorce almost always harms children and often is bad for women.** The proper raising of children to maturity requires contributions from both parents, cooperating together in solidarity. Divorce almost always minimizes, and often virtually eliminates, the psychological and moral contribution of one of the parents. The children often suffer material deprivation, and the burden of providing single-handedly for their basic needs which must be borne by the parent who cares for them generally detracts from other aspects of nurture. Thus, children of divorced parents are likely to suffer more or less serious psychological and economic insecurity. Public programs to mitigate the economic effects of divorce on children burden society at large with the responsibilities the parents have failed to fulfill.[58]

d) **The self-giving of marital union calls for indissolubility.** Since they complete each other to become, as it were, one person, a man and a woman truly joined in marital communion cannot attempt to divide without severe trauma, analogous to, and in some respects even worse than, the loss of a substantial part of one's own body. Of course, every married couple must accept the fact that death eventually will divide them. However, if they anticipate that they might intentionally attempt to separate from each other, they either must be prepared to cause the trauma divorce would involve or must will to limit their unity in order to avoid that trauma. But doing either is at odds with conjugal love. If, therefore, in attempting

---

58. Theologians and canonists who question the indissolubility of marriage often formulate the issue in terms of a dichotomy between the good of the institution and that of the person. Paul F. Palmer, S.J., "When a Marriage Dies," *America,* 22 Feb. 1975, 128, rightly points out: "It might be argued that the enlightened theologian of today cares more for the happiness of people than he does for marriage as an institution. But when the institution is dissolving, as witnessed by the three million American Catholics who have divorced and remarried, there must be a lot of unhappy people, including a host of unhappy children." U.S. Congress, House Select Committee on Children, Youth, and Families, *U.S. Children and Their Families: Current Conditions and Recent Trends, 1989,* 101st Cong., 1st Sess., Sept. 1989, 52–53 and 116–18, reports that in the United States: in 1988, 21.4 percent of all children under 18 were living with their mother only; in 1985, only 37 percent of women with children under 21 whose fathers were absent received child support payments from the absent fathers; and in 1987 more than half of all children living in female-headed households lived below the poverty line, *even after more than 42 percent of such children received government payments.* Also see U.S. Bureau of the Census, *Family Disruption and Economic Hardship: The Short-Run Picture for Children,* Current Population Reports, series P–70, no. 23 (Washington, D.C.: U.S. Government Printing Office, 1991). A number of authors who do not believe marriage indissoluble point out various aspects of the harm divorce causes to the couple, their children, and others: Joseph Epstein, *Divorced in America: Marriage in an Age of Possibility* (New York: Dutton, 1974); Diane Medved, *The Case against Divorce* (New York: Donald I. Fine, 1989); Lenore J. Weitzman, *The Divorce Revolution: The Unexpected Social and Economic Consequences for Women and Children in America* (New York: Free Press, 1985); Terry Arendell, *Mothers and Divorce: Legal, Economic, and Social Dilemmas* (Berkeley, Cal.: University of California Press, 1986); Tracy Barr Grossman, *Mothers and Children Facing Divorce* (Ann Arbor, Mich.: UMI Research Press, 1986); Judith S. Wallerstein and Sandra Blakeslee, *Second Chances: Men, Women, and Children a Decade after Divorce* (New York: Ticknor and Fields, 1989), especially the summary of conclusion, 297–308.

to marry the parties reserve the right to divorce, they act inconsistently with the conjugal love necessary for marriage.

Another consideration lies in the fact that, even though a new person begins at conception, still the child's full emergence as a mature person takes many years. During all these years, any threat to the marital communion will be a radical threat to the child's own development. Hence, if the parties in attempting to marry allow for breaking off their marital communion, they endanger the good of any children they might have, and that is inconsistent with the love they should have toward those children.

Besides, becoming, as it were, one person to beget and raise their children, the spouses must provide each other with constant mutual service in a common life, including communication and cooperation with respect to the whole range of goods to be shared with their children. This requires that both contribute wholeheartedly and unconditionally. When people attempt to dissolve marriages, however, it becomes clear how impossible it is to divide and reappropriate what each contributed to so intimate a community. Hence, if in marrying the parties anticipate the possibility that the marital communion might be terminated, they will tend to fashion a less intimate relationship, and their self-gift will be limited and qualified.

Finally, spouses who regard divorce as an option are likely to manipulate each other by threatening it. The relationship not only is destabilized in this way but, often, reduced to a pragmatic arrangement rather than a genuine community.[59]

e) **The couple cannot make marital union exclusive and indissoluble.** Couples considering marriage can understand and accept that the good of marital communion calls for a truly mutual and entirely dependable relationship, and so can wish to form a union with these characteristics. At the same time, however, they will be aware of a seemingly insurmountable obstacle to making an absolutely irrevocable commitment: while it is possible for people to commit themselves for life and sincerely desire never to change their minds, even so no one can choose today not to change his or her mind tomorrow. Common experience illustrates this truth: people can wish for and pledge undying friendship, but cannot preclude a future choice to end a relationship which either or both parties have come to consider undesirable. Hence, even if couples planning to marry understand and accept that the good they desire calls for a truly mutual and entirely dependable relationship, they will realize, if they are clearheaded, that they themselves cannot make their marital union exclusive and indissoluble. If the union they are about to form is to have these properties, they will see, it cannot be by their own wills but must be by virtue of something about one-flesh union itself which they must accept,

---

59. Pius XII, *Sertum laetitiae, AAS* 31 (1939) 640–41 and 651, *PE,* 223.25, quotes Leo XIII, *Arcanum, ASS* 12 (1879) 396, *PE,* 81.29, on the bad consequences of divorce: "Because of divorce, the nuptial contract becomes subject to fickle whim; affection is weakened; pernicious incentives are given to conjugal infidelity; the care and education of offspring are harmed; easy opportunity is afforded for the breaking up of homes; the seeds of discord are sown among families; the dignity of woman is lessened and brought down and she runs the risk of being deserted after she has served her husband as an instrument of pleasure. And since it is true that for the ruination of the family and the undermining of the State nothing is so powerful as the corruption of morals, it is easy to see that divorce is of the greatest harm to the prosperity of families and of states."

so that, once they enter into that union, nothing they subsequently choose or do will be able to divide them from each other and/or unite them simultaneously in a similar union with someone else.

f) Marital union in itself is exclusive and indissoluble. Since the good of marriage calls for exclusivity and indissolubility, couples considering marriage who understand and accept what marital union requires will reasonably suppose that their prospective marriage, though formed by their consent, somehow will be exclusive and indissoluble in itself. Of course, they can forgo the good of marriage, either by remaining single or by excluding something essential to the relationship; but if they do choose to marry they should assume that their marriage will be exclusive and indissoluble even if one or both should later change their minds and wish they were not married.

The same argument can be put another way. A couple who wish to marry should enter into an exclusive and permanent union. However, people cannot commit themselves to marriage as an exclusive and permanent union unless they believe it has these properties. But they will not reasonably believe this if it is not so.[60] Thus, people can marry as they should only if marriage of itself excludes polygamy and divorce. Now, people can marry as they should. Therefore, marriage of itself, independent of the will of those who enter into it, is exclusive and indissoluble.[61]

g) Further considerations help to clarify marriage's indissolubility. Marital consent is a mutual self-giving to form, as it were, one new person. In giving such consent, the parties do more than make a contract: they enter into a covenant.[62] By a covenant, members of different families or larger communities try to form a community whose ties will be as close as those joining blood relatives. In the context of salvation history, the notion of covenant takes on greater depth from God's faithfulness. Unlike human freedom during this life, God's freedom of choice does not imply potential infidelity; for, although God commits himself with sovereign liberty, once he has done so, the relationship into which he enters endures forever. For Jews and Christians, therefore, their covenant with God remains

60. While in general people can reasonably believe propositions which are not so, and while people can unreasonably draw false conclusions from first principles of practical reasoning, people cannot *reasonably* believe implications of a first principle of practical reasoning—marriage is a good to be pursued—if those implications are not true.

61. If the argument proposed here is sound, one can know, even without faith, *that* marriage in itself is exclusive and indissoluble, but one cannot fully understand *why* it has these properties. For the argument proceeds from the requirements of the good of marriage and the limited ability of human freedom to meet these requirements to the supposition that they are met by an objective principle which transcends human freedom. This argument leaves the cause of indissolubility opaque, since it does not demonstrate the property directly from the nature of marital communion itself. However, such direct demonstration is impossible, since marital communion, like the person as such, is not confined to one order of reality. See Germain Grisez, *Beyond the New Theism: A Philosophy of Religion* (Notre Dame, Ind.: University of Notre Dame Press, 1975), 230–40 (on the limits of reductionism) and 353–56 (on the inherent mysteriousness of human community, inasmuch as it transcends the distinction of orders of reality).

62. See Paul F. Palmer, S.J., "Christian Marriage: Contract or Covenant?" *Theological Studies* 33 (1972): 617–65; idem, "When a Marriage Dies," 126–28. While the word *contract* still appears in the Church's law regarding marriage, *covenant* now is used in crucial canons: *CIC*, c. 1055, §1; c. 1057, §2.

forever, and even if men and women are unfaithful, God sustains the relationship. But since marriage itself is a covenant and is involved in the covenant with God (as will be explained in C.1.d), marriage also participates in the absolute indissolubility of relationships constituted by divine freedom.[63]

Even when a man and a woman do not wish to marry, if they agree to have sexual intercourse and their intercourse results in the birth of a child, their consent and sexual intercourse have brought about a certain permanent bond between them (although not the bond of marriage). They can wish they were not parents and neglect their responsibilities, but, regardless, they remain the child's parents and are bound by parental duties. Moreover, the child binds them indissolubly together: the child embodies their unity, and their duties to him or her entail duties toward each other.

When a man and a woman do consent to marriage and enter into communion open to new life, they form not only a bodily union with inescapable moral implications but a full communion of persons: a communion of will by mutual, covenantal commitment, and of organism by the generative act they share in.[64] They may later regret having formed this union, but they cannot undo their real oneness. As the elements constituting each of them an individual person are divided only by death, so only death ends the one-flesh unit they constitute in marrying.

4. Individuals' Intentions Do Not Affect Marriage's Properties

Although marriage is a basic human good, people often marry for other reasons or due to merely emotional motives. While some motivations are incompatible with the good of marriage, so that the putative marriage is only a quasi-marital arrangement, many inadequate motives are compatible with the good of marriage and the consent necessary to marry validly. Moreover, the differences in marriage customs in various cultures do not exclude any couple who wish to marry from the possibility of valid marriage.

a) People often get married with inadequate motives. Ideally, people who marry would understand the good of marriage and its properties, intend to participate together in that good, and so commit themselves to a lifelong and exclusive communion of love. They would will their marital union for its own sake and unselfishly will each other's fulfillment in it, integrating all other relevant interests and emotional motives with this volitional, conjugal love.

However, many people, perhaps most, marry with mixed motives not entirely integrated with unselfish mutual love. Many are motivated by passion; even if they marry with the hope of achieving chastity, their sexual desire will only gradually be integrated with conjugal love. Others are more interested in the security and comfort of a household than in marital communion and its fulfillment in parenthood. Indeed, some people choose to marry without at all intending as an end the

63. See J. R. Lucas, "The 'Vinculum Conjugale': A Moral Reality," *Theology* 78 (1975): 226–30.

64. St. Thomas, *In Sent.*, 4, d. 27, q. 1, a. 1, qu'la 2, ad 3 (*S.t.*, sup., q. 44, a. 2, ad 3), says that "the joining of a man and a woman in matrimony is maximal, since it is both of souls and of bodies."

good of marriage itself, since none of their motives are reasons or emotions integrated with unselfish love; their choice is to use marriage as a means to other ends.

Many people do not believe marriage is an exclusive and indissoluble union, and their choice to marry takes for granted the possibility of polygamy and/or divorce. Some know about the properties of marriage but only reluctantly accept exclusivity and/or indissolubility, since they would rather make a less wholehearted commitment. Some know about the properties of marriage but reject one or both, perhaps intending to carry on extramarital relationships or to divorce if the marriage does not go well.

Some people act as bride or groom in a marriage ceremony while deliberately rejecting not only one or both of the properties of marriage but elements essential to the good of marriage itself. For example, they may agree in advance always to prevent conception, or not to live together, or to maintain their relationship only as a temporary expedient, perhaps as a way of meeting some legal requirement concerning taxes or immigration.

b) Some inadequate motives are incompatible with valid marriage. Various things other than the motives of those involved can invalidate their attempt to marry, for example, incapacity or invalidating impediments created by law. Apart from these, the validity of marriage depends solely on the reality of mutual consent to marriage.[65]

To be real, consent must be sincere: it must express a commitment to enter into marriage and undertake its responsibilities. People can exclude indissolubility by so entirely subordinating the relationship they enter to extraneous motives that the relationship is regarded as a mere means to be used or to be set aside as those motives indicate. Moreover, if someone deliberately wills anything inconsistent with elements essential to the good of marriage itself, he or she makes no commitment to marry, and so does not give sincere consent. Something inconsistent with an element essential to the good of marriage can be willed by prior mutual agreement or by one party's unilateral reservation.

A couple may carry out the formalities required for marriage, while one or both intend only to pursue some specific goal or set of goals, rather than enter into an open-ended relationship. Their relationship is very like a business partnership. Perhaps, agreeing to exclude children, the couple "marry" to provide the woman with financial support and the man with sexual satisfaction—an arrangement similar to prostitution. Or perhaps they plan to work together for the *things* each desires: a sexual partner, certain emotional satisfactions, a home and other possessions, a certain social status, and even a child or children (considered as desired objects to be possessed and enjoyed). Such a relationship is not truly a marriage, but is only quasi-marital. At least one, if not both, in no way wills the other's fulfillment and that of their child or children for their own sakes, in a way

---

65. *CIC*, c. 1060, sets down a presumption which must be borne in mind in any discussion of factors which might render a marriage invalid: "Marriage enjoys the favor of the law; consequently, when a doubt exists the validity of a marriage is to be upheld until the contrary is proven."

transcending specific goals; in entering the relationship, at least one partner does not give himself or herself to the other to form marital communion. Instead, the couple at best mutually concede rights to various kinds of service, and if they anticipate becoming parents, at least one of them wants a child or children primarily as a means to some selfish end.

Such relationships plainly are only quasi-marital relationships; they are not exclusive and indissoluble valid marriages. Thus, the intentions of those entering into them do not affect the properties of marriage.

c) **Many inadequate motives are compatible with valid marriage.** Sincere mutual consent to marriage, which is sufficient for validity, expresses a choice to marry, and that choice is specified by the concept of marriage. This concept neither depends on each couple's subjective motives for choosing to marry nor on their drawing up a list of mutually agreeable conditions for their particular partnership. Rather, couples who consent to marriage understand it as a social reality whose elements and conditions are already settled. They find it available, just as people find other social realities, such as language, which they can use or not, but cannot arbitrarily change.

Since the choice to marry is specified by this understanding of marriage as a given, a couple who sincerely consent to marriage determine themselves to the essential elements of the good of marriage. Provided their subjective motives are not incompatible with the choice to marry, so as to exclude mutual commitment and sincere consent, they really do what they choose to do, and so they validly marry.[66] Thus, even if a couple get married, intending as their end not the good of marriage but some other good or motivated by mere emotion, still, provided they sincerely consent to marry, they will the good of marriage. They will it in making the choice which their consent expresses, for that choice is a commitment to fulfill the responsibilities of marriage and parenthood. By that commitment, they establish open-ended community, and in this way they will their marital and parental relationships for their own sakes. In doing so, they also will the good of the other persons involved for their own sakes, and thus mutually give themselves to form marital and familial communion.

d) **Various cultures' customs are compatible with valid marriage.** Since a couple's choice to marry is specified by their understanding of marriage as a given,

---

66. *CIC,* makes this point with respect to the marriages of Catholics: "Error concerning the unity, indissolubility or sacramental dignity of matrimony does not vitiate matrimonial consent so long as it does not determine the will" (c. 1099); outward consent is presumed to express internal consent (c. 1101, §1); "But if either or both parties through a positive act of the will should exclude marriage itself, some essential element or an essential property of marriage, it is invalidly contracted" (c. 1101, §2). The truth these canons articulate does not hold only of the marriages of Catholics, for it follows from the nature of human free choice and the fact that marriage has an objective reality, independent of people's thoughts about it and motives for entering into it; this objective reality is more or less available to all men and woman in the institution of marriage which they find as a given in their society. While the reality of marriage is completely available in the institution of Christian marriage in the Catholic Church, the intrinsic elements of the good of marriage itself, though not its essential properties, are available in virtually any society, as will be explained in d.

it might seem that customs in various cultures render valid marriage impossible for people in many times and places. For, it might be argued, marriage customs vary just as languages do, marriage in all non-Christian societies is dissoluble, and many societies also approve polygyny.

In reality, marriage is subject to much less cultural variability than language is. Language is a system of signs used to communicate meanings having no necessary connection with those signs; so, while individuals cannot make language mean whatever they wish, communities do gradually invent and change their languages. Marriage, by contrast, is a basic human reality, rooted in natural inclinations and directed by a self-evident principle of practical reasoning. As a result, the essential elements of the good of marriage always are included in marriage as it is given in a society: marriage always and everywhere is the more or less stable heterosexual relationship that society recognizes as the community in which it is appropriate for a man and a woman to engage regularly in sexual intercourse, and to beget and raise children.

Of course, each society develops various customs and practices which both implement couples' choices to mate and have children, and regulate the relationship between marriage and other elements of the society, not least economic ones. Such regulations often create conditions, not implied by the good of marriage itself, for the validity of marriage in a particular society. For example, just as the Church requires for validity that Catholics be married before their bishop or pastor, or someone delegated by him,[67] other societies require formalities such as approval by some authority, a contract between the families, or the carrying out of some religious rite. Despite the great variability in such customs and practices, however, a valid union remains possible for couples who can and do mutually consent to marriage.

In some societies, male dominance has led to so radical a depersonalization of women that marriage customs and practices suggest a woman's consent is irrelevant to the validity of marriage. For example, it might appear that in exchange for two cows, a father gives his daughter to a man who wants a mate, and the girl no more consents to the arrangement than the cows do. If so, the society's depravity prevents the man and the woman from marrying, because mutual consent is absolutely essential for marriage. Instead of being married to the man, the woman is prostituted to him and enslaved by him; rather than engaging in intercourse with a husband, she is the victim of rape. Nevertheless, even if a society considers a marriage valid without the woman's consent, in particular cases a woman might consent by finding the arrangement made by her father satisfactory and willingly cooperating with it. If so, despite the society's depravity, the couple marry validly.

As for the exclusivity and indissolubility of marriage, these are not elements of the good of marriage itself; rather, they are essential properties, that is, requirements for fully realizing that good in and through ongoing marital and familial communion. But even though essential, they are not self-evident elements of the good of marriage itself, and are inevitably obscure to fallen humankind. Hence, except in

---

67. See *CIC*, c. 1108; this requirement admits certain exceptions.

Christian societies, the given reality of marriage often does not include exclusivity and seldom or never includes indissolubility. How this fact affects marriage will be treated below (in B.4).

e) **Inadequate motives endanger the good of marriage.** Plainly, people who do not know about the properties of marriage and so fail, through no fault of their own, to commit themselves to a permanent and exclusive union are hindered from realizing fully and stably the good of marital and familial communion. But even if people know about marriage's essential properties and accept them, their inadequate motives for choosing to marry often lead to trouble. Emotional motives not subordinated to unselfish mutual love often lead to sexual abuse within marriage, irresponsible procreation, and even infidelity. If some other purpose in life is a person's reason for marrying, he or she will always be tempted not to fulfill marital responsibilities except insofar as that other purpose requires.

Thus, even if inadequate motives are consistent with sincere consent, so that the marriage is valid, these motives threaten marriage. Therefore, not only should people choose to marry because marriage is good in itself; in choosing to marry, they should subordinate their other motives for marrying, insofar as they can, to this uniquely appropriate one.

Question B: Is This Theology of Marriage Consistent with the Church's Practice?

Various objections can be made against the view that not only the sacramentality of Christian marriage but the good of marriage as such requires that it be an exclusive and permanent union. Here, only specifically theological objections will be considered, in order to clarify what already has been explained and to defend the Catholic Church's consistency in her teaching and practice.[68]

The theological objections can be summed up as follows. The Church dissolves nonconsummated marriages, grants annulments to couples who everyone thought were married, and dissolves nonsacramental marriages. These practices seem to make significant exceptions to indissolubility. Moreover, they are not recent inventions, but have their roots in the New Testament. For Jesus' "absolute" prohibition of divorce is reported in Matthew's Gospel with what appears to be an

---

68. A brief statement of the standard objections: Karl Lehmann, "Indissolubility of Marriage and Pastoral Care of the Divorced Who Remarry," *Communio* 1 (1974): 219–42. A more extensive summary of dissenting opinions involving the standard objections: Richard A. McCormick, S.J., *Notes on Moral Theology: 1965 through 1980* (Washington, D.C.: University Press of America, 1981), 84–86, 332–47, 372–81, 544–61, 826–41. A reading of these summaries of opinion makes it clear that all of the dissenters either assume that marriage is dissoluble (that its dissolution is wrong but possible, so that remarriage also is wrong but possible) or have a very legalistic conception of the moral norms which flow from marriage's indissolubility; that is, they think of these norms as rules to be applied and mitigated, not as moral truths necessitated by the covenantal reality of marriage. Many also take for granted a proportionalist conception of moral judgment. These elements of their view already have been dealt with in question A or in volume one; what remains to be done in this question is to dispose of the common arguments which attempt to appeal to theological sources against the Church's actual teaching on marriage's properties.

exception clause, and St. Paul apparently allowed converts from paganism to consider themselves free of their uncooperative pagan spouses.

1. The Church Is Coherent in Dissolving Nonconsummated Marriages

The Church holds three things: (i) that marriage is indissoluble, (ii) that the parties' consent to marry, given under appropriate conditions, makes the marriage, and (iii) that even after the parties have given valid consent, their marriage can be dissolved, provided they have not consummated it by marital intercourse.[69] These three propositions seem incompatible, and some suggest the incompatibility must be resolved by denying that marriage is indissoluble. However, (i) and (iii), considered by themselves, are consistent. And so the apparent incompatibility can be resolved, without qualifying marriage's indissolubility, by explaining the sense in which consent *by itself* makes a marriage and showing that there remains a sense in which consummation by marital intercourse also is necessary for a marriage's full reality.

a) **"Consent makes marriage" must be understood in context.** Historically, different marriage customs existed among the various peoples who became Christian, and during the first millennium the Church as a whole had no commonly agreed procedure for the marriage of Christians.[70] Around the end of that time, various theories suggested different elements as partly or wholly constituting marriage: a formal engagement or other promises to marry in the future (perhaps sealed with an oath), the payment of a dowry (sometimes carried out in a way that made marriage appear to be the selling of the woman), the parties' consent to marry (sometimes exchanged years before they would begin to live together), a nuptial Mass, the priest's blessing (or, at least, his presence), the bride's going to her new home (or being carried there), and the first act of marital intercourse.

Theologians and canonists addressed the question, and two main theories emerged: (i) that the parties' consent by itself, given under appropriate conditions, is sufficient to make a marriage and (ii) that both the parties' intention to marry and intercourse are necessary to make a marriage.

In favor of (i) was that consent plainly is necessary (both theories require it), while intercourse is inherently ambiguous, since unmarried couples can engage in it without thereby becoming married. But against (i) was a longstanding practice in the Church: after a man and a woman consented to marriage but before they engaged in marital intercourse, either might enter a monastery and take solemn

---

69. See *CIC*, c. 1056; c. 1057, §1; c. 1142. C. 1061, §1, defines consummation by stating that a marriage is said to be "consummated if the parties [having exchanged valid marital consent] have performed between themselves in a human manner the conjugal act which is per se suitable for the generation of children, to which marriage is ordered by its very nature and by which the spouses become one flesh."

70. For the history summarized here, see George Hayward Joyce, S.J., *Christian Marriage: An Historical and Doctrinal Study,* 2nd ed. rev. (London: Sheed and Ward, 1948), 39–67; E. Schillebeeckx, O.P., *Marriage: Human Reality and Saving Mystery,* trans. N. D. Smith (New York: Sheed and Ward, 1965), 287–97; Theodore Mackin, S.J., *Marriage in the Catholic Church: What Is Marriage?* (New York: Paulist Press, 1982), 145–75.

vows, and the other was considered unmarried and free to marry. In favor of (ii) was that it reflected the common understanding of Jesus' teaching, according to which indissolubility is grounded in the one-flesh communion formed by the spouses when they come together (see Mt 19.4–6; cf. Mk 10.6–9). But against (ii) were both the truth of faith that although Mary was always a virgin, she and Joseph really were married, and Roman law's view of marriage as a voluntary association formed by the parties' mutual consent.

Alexander III (pontificate 1159–81), in resolving problems about particular cases, moved toward a practical resolution of the theological and canonical debate. He took the position that consent by itself makes marriage, but that until marriage is consummated, the profession of public vows by either party dissolves it. This practical resolution, however, left the theoretical problem unresolved.

b) Consummation is necessary for marriage's full reality. This problem can be clarified by recalling that marriage is a covenantal community. The parties to a covenant first undertake their mutual responsibilities and then seal their relationship by a cooperative performance (see *CMP*, 21.B). For instance, each Christian is initiated into the new covenant in two stages: baptism and faith make the individual a Christian, while participation in the eucharistic sacrifice and Holy Communion perfect his or her participation in the Church's covenantal communion with Jesus.

Thus, viewing marriage as a covenant, it is necessary to distinguish between (i) the moral bond which a man and a woman form in undertaking the roles and responsibilities of husband and wife and (ii) the one-flesh communion they form by beginning to live together as a married couple. The word *marriage* refers to both. The consent of the bride and the groom establishes the moral bond; but that consent is to enter into one-flesh communion, and so, insofar as *marriage* refers to the latter, it begins only when the couple come together, thus sealing their marital covenant. Now, the husband and the wife do not come together in one-flesh unity until they engage in marital intercourse. Thus, although the consent which the couple give in marrying is *to form* a permanent and exclusive union, the reality having these properties—marriage as unbreakable covenantal communion—is fully constituted only with the first act of marital intercourse.[71]

Thus, John Paul II explains that marital consent is a sacramental sign by reason of what it signifies:

> However, this sacramental word is, *per se,* merely the sign of the coming into being of marriage. And the coming into being of marriage is distinguished from its consummation to the extent that without this consummation the marriage is not yet constituted in its full reality. The fact that a marriage is juridically

---

71. In speaking of the coming to be of marriage, Vatican II (GS 48) treats "the conjugal covenant" and "irrevocable personal consent" as identical (cf. *CIC*, c. 1057, §2). However, the Council does not thereby imply that the consent of the bride and the groom fully constitutes the conjugal covenant; consummation, fulfilling consent, also is necessary. To deny this would be to assert that Vatican II implicitly contradicts the Council of Trent's definitive teaching that solemn religious profession dissolves a true marriage which has not been consummated (see DS 1806/976).

contracted but not consummated (*ratum—non consummatum*) corresponds to the fact that it has not been fully constituted as a marriage. Indeed the very words "I take you as my wife—my husband" refer not only to a determinate reality, but they can be fulfilled only by means of conjugal intercourse. This reality (conjugal intercourse) has moreover been determined from the very beginning by institution of the Creator: "Therefore a man leaves his father and his mother and cleaves to his wife, and they become one flesh" (cf. Gn 2.24).[72]

c) **Mary was a true wife though she always remained a virgin.** Catholic tradition understands Scripture (see Mt 1.16–25) as teaching that Joseph and Mary were validly married, and the faith likewise teaches that their marriage could not have been consummated by conjugal intercourse, since Mary always was a virgin.[73] These truths of faith pose no problem for John Paul II's explanation of the role of consummation in constituting marriage. For, according to that explanation, although Mary and Joseph were not two in one flesh, they were truly married, precisely in the sense that any bride and groom are married at the end of the wedding ceremony, when they have consented to marriage but not yet consummated it. The decision of Mary and Joseph not to consummate their marriage in no way violated the good of marriage. Moreover, even though their non-consummated marriage never was "fully constituted as a marriage," it was a true and ongoing covenantal communion, which was uniquely fulfilled: by the fruit of Mary's womb, to whom Joseph, her husband, truly became father by consenting to God's will for their marriage.[74]

2. The Church's Annulment Process Is Not a Form of Divorce

Catholics who are separated or civilly divorced and wish to marry again often are encouraged to seek a declaration of nullity from a Church court. If they receive an affirmative response, they are free to marry in the Church, just as people who receive a civil divorce are free to marry in any civil society which recognizes that divorce. It might seem that the Church's annulment process is the equivalent of civil divorce, but it is not.

---

72. John Paul II, General Audience (5 Jan. 1983), 2, *Inseg.* 6.1 (1983) 42, *OR*, 3–10 Jan. 1983, 7.

73. On the reality of the marriage of Mary and Joseph, see Leo XIII, *Quamquam pluries, ASS* 22 (1889–90) 66–67, *PE*, 110.3. Mary's perpetual virginity pertains to faith on the basis of Scripture and very rich and extensive tradition; see Michael O'Carroll, C.S.Sp., *Theotokos: A Theological Encyclopedia of the Blessed Virgin Mary,* rev. ed. (Wilmington, Del.: Michael Glazier, 1983), 357–62. The New Revised Standard Version translates Mt 1.25: "but had no marital relations with her until she had borne a son"; however, the meaning of the Greek preposition (*heos*) translated *until* does not imply that Mary and Joseph engaged in marital intercourse after Jesus' birth.

74. John Paul II, *Redemptoris custos*, 7, *AAS* 82 (1990) 13, *OR*, 30 Oct. 1989, 2, teaches: "The *Son of Mary* is also *Joseph's Son* by virtue of the marriage bond that unites them: 'by reason of their faithful marriage *both of them* deserve to be called Christ's parents, not only his mother, but also his father, who was a parent in the same way that he was the mother's spouse: *in mind,* not in the flesh' [note omitted]. In this marriage none of the requisites of marriage were lacking: 'In Christ's parents all the goods of marriage were realized—offspring, fidelity, the sacrament: the *offspring* being the Lord Jesus himself; *fidelity,* since there was no divorce' [note omitted]." Cf. *S.t.,* 3, q. 29, a. 2.

a) **An annulment states that an apparent marriage never really existed.**
While a civil divorce and a Church annulment are alike in facilitating a new
relationship that will be regarded by the relevant law as marriage, the two processes
are entirely different in their presuppositions and significance. Civil divorce
presupposes that marriage is a legal relationship subject to the state's authority, that
a true marriage existed, but that civil authority terminates it. Annulment presupposes that the previous relationship, which appeared to be a marriage, really was
not—that even if the partners entered the relationship in good faith and did all they
believed necessary to marry, they did not succeed in marrying because of some
defect in their consent, capacity to marry, or potential to fulfill the responsibilities
of marriage. The Church's annulment process, therefore, focuses on the question:
When this couple appeared to marry, did they really marry or not? When someone
seeking an annulment receives it, the response does not say, "You married, and your
marriage is dissolved," but, "In reality, you were not married." Strictly speaking,
the Church never annuls a marriage but only finds that an apparent marriage never
existed and declares that fact by issuing a decree of nullity.

b) **The annulment process is not changing into a divorce process.** Apparently well-informed Catholics today sometimes claim that some tribunals, especially in the United States, actually grant divorces but call them annulments to keep
up appearances. To this, at least two things must be said. First, to some extent the
claim depends on hasty interpretation of the fact that the number of annulments has
increased considerably. Much of the increase can be explained by wider awareness
of the possibility of annulment, greater efficiency in the Church's courts, an
increase in the number of invalid marriages due to inadequate premarital catechesis
and dissent from Catholic teaching regarding marriage and its essential properties,
and legitimate development, based on Vatican II's teaching on marriage, in the
understanding of the requirements for a valid marriage. Second, perhaps in some
cases the annulment process has been abused, either by someone seeking an
annulment or by a tribunal, so that valid marriages have been declared null. But
abuses do not constitute the Church's practice, and any decree of nullity resulting
from an abuse is worthless.

3. The Church Rejects the View that Adultery Justifies Divorce

According to Matthew's Gospel, Jesus seems to qualify his teaching excluding divorce by making an exception in favor of a man who dismisses his wife
because of "unchastity" (see Mt 5.32, 19.9). On this basis, many non-Catholic
Christians believe that divorce on the ground of adultery is possible, and that
at least an innocent or repentant party may remarry. The Catholic Church firmly
rejects this view.

a) **Jesus made no exception in favor of the ground of adultery.** Critical
opinion today supports the position that *unchastity* (*porneia*) in the so-called
exceptive clause refers, not to adultery, but to some sort of sexual irregularity or
wrongful sexual intercourse.[75] Precisely what the clause refers to is disputed, but

---

75. For helpful summaries of exegetical views, including some others less favored than those
mentioned here, with references to the leading proponents of each view, see Pierre Adnès, S.J.,

one plausible interpretation is that it concerns incestuous unions which pagans considered marriages but Christians held to be invalid.[76] Another, older Catholic reading is that the clause admits divorce in the sense of separation but not the dissolution of a marriage which would open the way to another marriage.[77]

   b) **The "exceptive" clause does not qualify Jesus' teaching.** On both of those interpretations, and some other possible ones, the exceptive clause can be understood as clarifying Jesus' teaching without making an exception to the indissolubility of marriage.

   If *unchastity* refers to relationships considered by pagans to be marriages but considered by the evangelist to be illicit unions, the clause means only that some putative marriages are null.[78] Perhaps people entered them in good faith before their conversion, but, becoming aware that these relationships could not be true marriages, Christians should rectify matters by divorce—*divorce* as understood by civil law.

   If *divorce* refers to separation without the dissolution of the marriage, the "exceptive" clause was merely dealing with the new problem to which Jesus' teaching gives rise precisely because it is unqualified. Jewish and Roman practices of divorce and remarriage forestalled questions about the obligations of people abandoned or betrayed by their spouses. But for those who accepted Jesus' teaching as unqualified, the question inevitably arose: What then? On this interpretation, Matthew's Gospel reports Jesus' teaching with a clarification similar to that which St. Paul makes: "To the married I give this command—not I but the Lord—that the wife should not separate from her husband (but if she does separate, let her remain unmarried or else be reconciled to her husband), and that the husband should not divorce his wife" (1 Cor 7.10–11; cf. Rom 7.2–3).

   c) **The Church's teaching on this matter is definitive.** Some development did occur before the Church reached her clear teaching and firm discipline entirely excluding adultery as a justification for divorce, and the Eastern Orthodox churches

---

Le mariage (Tournai: Desclée, 1963), 23–28; Schillebeeckx, *Marriage,* 142–55; for a briefer summary of the main views: Benedict T. Viviano, O.P., "The Gospel According to Matthew," in *The New Jerome Biblical Commentary,* ed. Raymond E. Brown, S.S., Joseph A. Fitzmyer, S.J., and Roland E. Murphy, O.Carm. (Englewood Cliffs, N.J.: Prentice Hall, 1990), 642–43.

   76. John P. Meier, *Matthew* (Wilmington, Del.: Michael Glazier, 1980), 53, explains: "All too common in the eastern Mediterranean, such marriages were forbidden by Lev. 18:6–18. Some rabbis allowed a Gentile to maintain the incestuous union when he entered Judaism, and similar problems about these unions arose when Gentiles became Christians. The problem is mentioned in Acts 15:20, 29; 21:25; and 1 Cor 5:1. In all these texts *porneia* is used to describe the incestuous marriage. The 'exceptive clause' is thus the exact opposite of a relaxation of Jesus' radical morality."

   77. See DS 1327/702 (Council of Florence); St. Thomas, *Super evangelium S. Mattthaei lectura,* on 5.32 and 19.9. This classical reading can be sustained by modern critical exegesis; see Quentin Quesnell, S.J., "Made Themselves Eunuchs for the Kingdom of Heaven (MT 19, 12)," *Catholic Biblical Quarterly* 30 (1968): 335–58; Quesnell points out (347–48) that the reading is found as early as St. Clement of Alexandria.

   78. Schillebeeckx, *Marriage,* 148, explains: "*Porneia,* then, was a marriage that was null and void according to the Jewish law, and thus also according to the canon law of the primitive church following the apostolic decision of Acts xv.20–29." But Schillebeeckx goes on (154) to favor the position that the clause refers to separation without remarriage.

eventually thought it possible to divorce in cases of adultery.[79] However, the Western church settled the question during the Middle Ages. Thus, in 1439 the Council of Florence taught that adultery justifies only permanent separation, not divorce and remarriage (see DS 1327/702). Later, against Protestant claims to the contrary, the Council of Trent solemnly condemned anyone who says the Church erred in having taught and in teaching that marriage *cannot* be dissolved even on account of adultery (see DS 1807/977).

Although this canon of Trent's does not explicitly define the indissolubility of marriage, it does so implicitly, for, as Pius XI teaches:

> If therefore the Church has not erred and does not err in teaching this, and consequently it is certain that the bond of marriage cannot be loosed even on account of the sin of adultery, it is evident that all the other weaker excuses that can be, and are usually brought forward, are of no value whatsoever.[80]

4. A Nonsacramental Marriage Is Indissoluble If It Is 'Perfect'

St. Paul teaches that a Christian married to a nonbeliever should not divorce if the nonbelieving spouse is willing to maintain the marriage (see 1 Cor 7.13). "But if the unbelieving partner separates, let it be so; in such a case the brother or sister is not bound. It is to peace that God has called you" (1 Cor 7.15). On the basis of this passage, the Church's canon law and the Holy See have developed the so-called Pauline and Petrine privileges.[81] These constitute a practice by which the Church often permits a Catholic to marry despite the fact that either that Catholic or the

---

79. It often is argued that various Church Fathers and councils permitted divorce on the ground of adultery, but much of the material on which such arguments depend need not be interpreted as approving remarriage following divorce after a valid marriage was consummated, and so can be read as entirely compatible with the Church's teaching and practice. See Anthony J. Bevilacqua, "The History of the Indissolubility of Marriage," *Proceedings of the Catholic Theological Society of America* 22 (1967): 253–308; Gilles Pelland, S.J., "Le dossier patristique relatif au divorce: Revue de quelques travaux récents," *Science et esprit* 24 (1972): 285–312, 25 (1973): 99–119; E. Hamel, "The Indissolubility of Completed Marriage: Theological, Historical, and Pastoral Reflections," in *Contemporary Perspectives on Christian Marriage: Propositions and Papers from the International Theological Commission,* ed. Richard Malone and John R. Connery, S.J. (Chicago: Loyola University Press, 1984), 181–200; Henri Crouzel, S.J., "Remarriage after Divorce in the Primitive Church: A Propos of a Recent Book," *Irish Theological Quarterly* 38 (1971): 21–41 (the book criticized is Victor J. Pospishil, *Divorce and Remarriage: Toward a New Catholic Teaching* [New York: Herder and Herder, 1967]).

80. Pius XI, *Casti connubii, AAS* 22 (1930) 574, *PE,* 208.89. It often is pointed out that Trent purposely avoided condemning the practice of certain Eastern churches. However, while Trent was careful not to affront those churches, the canon to which Pius XI refers, read in the context of the Council's whole doctrine on marriage (DS 1797–1812/969–82), clearly entails that the practice of the Eastern churches *is not in accord with the truth which Trent defines.* One especially must consider the other canon concerning indissolubility: "If anyone says that the marriage bond can be dissolved by reason of heresy, domestic incompatibility, or willful desertion by one of the parties: let him be anathema" (DS 1805/975). Since this dogmatic definition bears directly on indissolubility and directly condemns the opinion that marriage is dissoluble on any of the leading grounds other than adultery, arguments supporting dissolubility based on the indirectness of the other canon only reach cases involving adultery. But few if any Catholics who today offer such arguments conclude that marriage is dissoluble *only* on the ground of adultery.

81. See Joyce, *Christian Marriage,* 469–99.

person he or she wishes to marry was previously *nonsacramentally* married to a third party.[82]

Many today argue that this implies that all nonsacramental marriages *can* be dissolved, and that to say they are "indissoluble" only means, at most, that they *should not* be dissolved. Contrary to this view, the Church maintains, in accord with Jesus' teaching, that marriage as such, not only Christian marriage, is inherently indissoluble.[83]

In an attempt to reconcile the Pauline and Petrine privileges with the indissolubility of marriage, theologians and canonists have distinguished between intrinsic and extrinsic indissolubility. The argument is that, while nonsacramental marriages are intrinsically indissoluble (so that no merely human power can dissolve them), they are extrinsically dissoluble by divine power, exercised vicariously by the pope. But this way of accounting for the theological data is unsatisfactory insofar as it implies that the good of marriage can be disposed of as a mere means to a religious end extrinsic to marriage itself.

Instead of using a distinction between intrinsic and extrinsic indissolubility, it seems better to take account of inherent differences in marital relationships arising from differences in the objects of the consent which constitutes marriage, and on this basis to distinguish between 'perfect' and 'imperfect' marriage. Given this explanation, the Church's practice based on St. Paul's teaching does not imply that nonsacramental marriages are therefore dissoluble, but rather that imperfect marriages, although dissoluble, are valid marriages.

a) The Church holds nonsacramental marriage indissoluble. Pius XI, commenting on "What God hath joined together let no man put asunder," states the Church's position:

> Wherefore, Our predecessor Pius VI of happy memory, writing to the Bishop of Agria, most wisely said: "Hence it is clear that marriage even in the state of nature, and certainly long before it was raised to the dignity of a sacrament, was divinely instituted in such a way that it should carry with it a perpetual and indissoluble bond which cannot therefore be dissolved by any civil law. Therefore although the sacramental element may be absent from a marriage as is the case among unbelievers, still in such a marriage, inasmuch as it is a true marriage there must remain and indeed there does remain that perpetual bond which by divine right

---

82. See *CIC*, cc. 1143–50, with the commentary by Thomas P. Doyle, O.P., in *The Code of Canon Law: A Text and Commentary*, ed. James A. Coriden, Thomas J. Green, and Donald E. Heintschel (New York: Paulist Press, 1985), 814–19; Congregation for the Doctrine of the Faith, "Privilege-of-the-Faith Cases: Instruction and Procedure" (6 Dec. 1973), *Canon Law Digest* 8 (1973–77): 1177–83 (see related material, 1184–88); Ignacio Gordon, S.J., "De processu ad obtinendam dissolutionem matrimonii non sacramentalis in favorem fidei," *Periodica de re morali, canonica, liturgica* 79 (1990): 511–76; *New Catholic Encyclopedia*, s.v. "marriage, canon law of"; Donald J. Gregory, *The Pauline Privilege: An Historical Synopsis and Commentary* (Washington, D.C.: The Catholic University of America Press, 1931). Anyone who might be able to take advantage of this practice of the Church should contact the diocesan tribunal or consult a Catholic pastor, who will help to initiate the necessary canonical procedure. Any marriage in which *either* party is not baptized is nonsacramental: since the non-Christian spouse cannot share in the sacrament, which is the marriage covenant itself, neither can the Christian spouse.

83. See DS 1797–99/969; GS 48; *CIC*, c. 1134; cf. St. Thomas, *S.c.g.*, 3.123.

is so bound up with matrimony from its first institution that it is not subject to any civil power. And so, whatever marriage is said to be contracted, either it is so contracted that it is really a true marriage, in which case it carries with it that enduring bond which by divine right is inherent in every true marriage; or it is thought to be contracted without that perpetual bond, and in that case there is no marriage, but an illicit union opposed of its very nature to the divine law, which therefore cannot be entered into or maintained [note omitted]."

And if this stability seems to be open to exception, however rare the exception may be, as in the case of certain natural marriages between unbelievers, . . . that exception does not depend on the will of men nor on that of any merely human power, but on divine law, of which the only guardian and interpreter is the Church of Christ.[84]

Thus, the Church holds that her practice, developed on the basis of St. Paul's teaching (see 1 Cor 7.15), does not imply that nonsacramental marriages as such are dissoluble. Rather, the practice is based on the belief that God himself wills an exception, which the Church interprets and applies.

b) Some licit nonsacramental unions are dissoluble. Assuming that the Pauline and Petrine privileges are based on an exception to the indissolubility of marriage, one wonders: How *can* God will this exception? Surely, the requirement of indissolubility is not merely a divine law imposed on human beings. Rather, it follows from the nature of man, woman, and marital communion as God creates them. It seems inconsistent and in violation of the principle that grace perfects rather than negates nature to suppose that, although from the beginning God designs marriage to be indissoluble, yet for the benefit of Christians he wills certain nonsacramental marriages to be dissolved through the Church's vicarious exercise of his authority.[85]

To solve this puzzle, it helps to notice that Pius VI, in the passage Pius XI quotes, overgeneralizes in writing that every marriage is either "really a true marriage, in which case it carries with it that enduring bond which by divine right is inherent in every true marriage; or it is thought to be contracted without that perpetual bond, and in that case there is no marriage, but an illicit union opposed of its very nature to the divine law, which therefore cannot be entered into or maintained." This dichotomy leaves no room for the marriages of people in Old Testament times, which, while surely not merely illicit unions, were "thought to be contracted without that perpetual bond" to which Jesus recalled attention. Indeed, it is possible

---

84. Pius XI, *Casti connubii, AAS* 22 (1930) 551–52, *PE, 208.34–35.*

85. Such a view can seem satisfying only if the problem is considered legalistically. Similar legalism leads some to argue: if nonsacramental marriages can be dissolved by the Church, they can be dissolved by others if there is an adequate reason to do so. It also leads some to argue: since the Church can dissolve nonsacramental marriages and nonconsummated sacramental marriages, surely the Church can dissolve any marriage. For a clarification of legalism and an argument for excluding it from the whole of pastoral practice: Germain Grisez, "Legalism, Moral Truth, and Pastoral Practice," *Anthropotes* 6 (1990): 111–21. Schillebeeckx, *Marriage,* 158, manifests dissatisfaction with the legalistic view of the Pauline privilege by suggesting that the marriage dissolves itself, for "there must have been a kind of *error substantialis* (fundamental mistake) in the conclusion of the contract if the non-Christian no longer desired to live with a believer in marriage."

to hold that those marriages were in truth both valid and dissoluble, for, according to one school of theological opinion which the Church has never rejected, the people of Old Testament times did not sin when they remarried after divorce.[86]

c) **God permits fallen humans to marry imperfectly.** The theologians who held that the marriages of people in Old Testament times were both valid and dissoluble posited an explicit divine dispensation to account for their dissolubility. However, Scripture offers no evidence of such a divine dispensation, and, except in Christian societies, humankind as a whole understands marriage much as the people of the Old Testament did. Couples consent to marriage as it is understood in their society, and in the fallen human condition other societies share the hardness of heart (see Mt 19.8, Mk 10.5) which accounted for Moses' acceptance of divorce. Some non-Christians may believe that marriage should not be dissolved, and a particular non-Christian couple may hope their own marriage will be a lifelong union; but marriages of non-Christians in societies where divorce is accepted usually are "thought to be contracted without that perpetual bond."

No Catholic theologian or canonist supposes that all these marriages are invalid, nor does anyone suppose that all these couples receive a divine dispensation. The common view is that these nonsacramental marriages are valid and indissoluble, even though the parties do not know about indissolubility, consent to marriage as they find it in their society, and can be divorced and remarried validly in the Catholic Church if they meet the conditions for a Pauline or Petrine privilege. This view, however, suffers not only from its legalistic explanation of the so-called privileges, but from its supposition that the free choices of people consenting to marriage understood in their society as dissoluble nevertheless regularly constitute indissoluble unions. This is implausible, for the consent constituting marriage is a free choice, and people can choose to do only what they believe they can do.[87]

---

86. See St. Thomas, *In Sent.*, 4, d. 33, q. 2, a. 2, qu'lae 2–3 (*S.t.*, sup., q. 67, aa. 3–4). St. Thomas presents this view as a probable opinion, though he prefers a different account.

87. Pietro Gasparri, *Tractatus canonicus de matrimonio*, ed. nova, 2 vols. (Vatican City: Ex Typis Polyglottis Vaticanis, 1932), 2:27–29 (§§ 806–7), articulates the argument for the supposition that people consenting to marriage understood in their society as dissoluble constitute indissoluble unions: (i) people who marry intend true marriage, and that is marriage as God instituted it, namely, an indissoluble union; (ii) to suppose the contrary would be to suppose that all the marriages of nonbelievers, of Greeks, of Calvinists, and so on are invalid; (iii) it also would be contrary to the favor of the law that marriage enjoys; and (iv) it is not in accord with the fact that most people getting married are not then thinking about divorce or a second marriage. To (i): People who marry do intend marriage as God instituted it in the sense that they intend as their end the good of marriage to which a basic precept of practical reason points; however, they intend marriage as they find it in their society in the sense that they choose to marry and consent to marriage only as they know it and consider it possible for themselves. One must grant that the objective requirements of the end cause the intention of it to imply a will toward indissolubility and unity; however, one must deny that consent to marriage thought to be dissoluble is an efficacious will to form an indissoluble union. And it is consent, not the intention of the good of marriage as an end, which makes marriage. To (ii): One can grant that to suppose the contrary is to suppose that all those marriages are invalid as perfect marriages; still, one can hold that in general those marriages are valid as imperfect marriages. To (iii): It is contrary to the favor of the law that marriage enjoys to suppose that any particular putative marriage is not a true marriage and to put the burden of proof on the one who holds it valid; however, it is not contrary to the

A more plausible account is that such marriages are valid but imperfect precisely as marriages, and are divinely permitted inasmuch as God allows fallen human beings to continue to participate in the good of marriage despite their hardness of heart, that is, their inability, due to original sin, to comprehend, commit themselves to, and live up to marriage's essential properties of indissolubility and exclusivity. Their marriages lack permanence and exclusivity, not because marriage as such can be dissoluble and nonexclusive, but because imperfect marriages lack these properties. And imperfect marriages lack them because the marital consent which constituted them was defective, not due to personal bad will of the parties but due to fallen humankind's hardness of heart.[88]

d) Imperfect marriages both are and are not marriages. People lacking the light of the gospel consent to marriage as they find it in their society. This always includes the essential elements of the good of marriage itself. Intending this, they *intend* the good which is the object of that first principle of practical reason grounded in the natural human tendency to mate, have children, and bring them up. However, marriage as they find it and consent to it does not include marriage's essential property of indissolubility and sometimes does not include exclusivity. Such couples form a relationship which participates in the good of marriage, yet

---

favor of the law that marriage enjoys to hold on the basis of a general principle (the relationship between a free choice and its specifying object) that people who do not think marriage is indissoluble do not consent to indissoluble marriage. (In other words, this element of Gasparri's argument begs the question of principle at issue by invoking a presumption which properly concerns the judgment of particular cases according to relevant principles.) To (iv): One can grant that most people getting married do not expressly condition their consent on dissolubility and that this fact is decisive for people who marry as Catholics and for anyone else who enters marriage in a society that holds marriage indissoluble; however, since people who live in a society that holds marriage dissoluble take dissolubility for granted, they can consent to marriage only as they know it, and so they constitute only dissoluble unions.

88. John T. Noonan, Jr., *Power to Dissolve: Lawyers and Marriages in the Courts of the Roman Curia* (Cambridge, Mass.: Harvard University Press, 1972), 341–92, narrates the development of canon law and the Holy See's practice in regard to the dissolution of nonsacramental marriages. Plainly, the actual rationale of those who brought about the development has been legalistic, based simply on the pope's vicarious power. The explanation proposed here in terms of the category of imperfect marriage, therefore, is only theological, not historical. Someone might point out that the *CIC*, c. 1086 and c. 1125, prevents a Catholic from entering a nonsacramental valid marriage unless (c. 1125, 3°) both parties have been "instructed on the essential ends and properties of marriage, which are not to be excluded by either party." (This provision is new; it was not included in the corresponding canons in the 1917 Code—c. 1061 and c. 1070.) From this it could be argued that if couples really meet this requirement in entering a nonsacramental marriage, it would not be dissoluble according to the theological explanation in terms of imperfect marriage, but would be according to the legalistic rationale in terms of the pope's vicarious power. So, the argument would conclude, the explanation in terms of imperfect marriage does not account for possible cases to which the Church's present practice could extend (and to some cases to which it already has extended). The answer is that the fault need not be with the explanation: it is possible that the Holy See's practice should not extend to certain cases encompassed by the legalistic rationale (and, since the details of the Holy See's practice rest neither on any solemn definition nor on any teaching of the universal, ordinary magisterium, the practice can be based on a doctrinal mistake). Even so, in practice faithful Catholics will proceed in accord with the judgments of the appropriate authorities of the Church; a theological theory such as that proposed here should not be followed in practice against the judgment of the pope and/or bishops in communion with him.

also falls short of the requirements of that good, and so does not perfectly realize it. Their willing is inconsistent, since their consent falls short of the commitment necessary to realize fully their intention to share in the good of marriage. Such inconsistent willing brings into being a relationship that both is and is not a marriage. And that relationship is dissoluble, not insofar as it is a marriage but insofar as it is not.

Someone might object: It is absurd to say that a relationship both is and is not a marriage, since it either does or does not meet the essential conditions for marriage; and if it does not, it is not a marriage at all and should be called an "illicit union," not an "imperfect marriage." This objection would be sound if marriage were a natural species, since each natural entity must belong to some definite species and, logically, cannot do so without having all the essential properties of that species. But while marriage is natural insofar as it is a basic human good, it is a moral species insofar as its instances come to be by choices specified by intellectual judgments, with the result that relationships constituted by commitments specified both by true beliefs about the good of marriage itself and by erroneous beliefs about its essential properties neither fail entirely to realize that good nor realize it perfectly.[89]

89. Still, someone might ask: Are two pagans who marry, thinking divorce possible, *truly* married or not, prescinding, now, from questions about their personal responsibility. The answer: They are truly married, yet their marriage is essentially defective, and they are not married precisely insofar as it is defective. Gregory XIII explained that "connubia inter infideles contracta, vera quidem, non tamen adeo rata censeri, ut necessitate suadente dissolvi non possint" (DS 1988/—). Canonists often use *ratum* as if it were synonymous with *sacramental,* but even if the two words have the same reference, they do not have the same sense: *ratum* means *settled, unalterable,* or *firm.* Neither Pope Gregory nor the canonists explain *why* only a sacramental marriage is *ratum.* But if those who attempt marriage in good faith while believing it dissoluble form true but imperfect marriages, one can see why such marriages are not *rata* and so are dissoluble, although marriage as such, not only sacramental marriage, is essentially indissoluble. Noonan, *Power to Dissolve,* 239–301, narrates the history of canonical jurisprudence which has been based on the dilemma that the marital consent of nonbelievers and Protestants who think divorce possible must be presumed not to exclude indissolubility, and that the contrary presumption would imply that all such marriages simply are invalid. The explanation developed here escapes between the horns: intending to marry, not merely to enter into some lesser relationship, people in good faith who are not in a position to understand marriage as indissoluble can marry; but not rightly understanding marriage, they cannot consent to, and so do not form, a perfect marriage. Noonan goes so far as to say at one point (274): "Policy had hardened to the point where intent to marry indissolubly appeared to be a presumption required by the infallibility of the Church." This statement of Noonan's, however, interprets the thrust of an argument of Pius VI in a letter to the Bishop of Prague (which Noonan quotes on the same page), and this argument expressly concerns the *validity* of the marriages of non-Catholics who believe that divorce is possible. On the theory that such marriages are imperfect, they would be valid but dissoluble—a possibility Pius VI did not consider (and that Noonan does not articulate). Finally, it is important to note that nothing in Noonan's account supports the view that the Holy See's practice and judgments in this matter meet the conditions for infallible teaching by the ordinary magisterium, which include both the proposal of the teaching as something which must be held as absolutely certain and the moral unanimity of the whole college of bishops (see *CMP,* 35.D).

Question C: What Difference Does the Sacrament Make to Marriage?

The principle of the sacramentality of marriage is the new covenant, by which God forms with humankind an exclusive, everlasting, and bodily communion (see *CMP*, 19, 34). It is exclusive, because Jesus, the incarnate Word of God, joins God with his people in the unique communion that will become the heavenly kingdom. This communion will last forever, because God is perfectly faithful and the blessed will sin no more. This new covenant is bodily, because those who enter into it not only share in Jesus' divine life and cooperate with him in human acts but share in his risen bodily life. By participating in the Eucharist, they begin now to live in glorious bodily communion with him, and, if faithful, they will do so forever.

In the beginning, marriage already had a sacred character, which was enhanced under the old covenant. Jesus renewed the sacredness of marriage and perfected it, with the result that the marriages of Christian couples are sacramental, signifying the union of Jesus with his Church. Thus, Christian marriage, which contributes directly to the new covenant's fulfillment, has a special firmness: by the light of their faith, the spouses are enabled to understand the absolute indissolubility of their marriage and the ultimate, salvific significance of that indissolubility. Moreover, by the grace of the sacrament, the spouses are empowered to persevere until death in faithful conjugal love, so that every Christian husband and wife not only should but can recognize, accept, and manifest the indissolubility and exclusivity of their sacramental marital communion.[90]

1. Marriage Is Sacred in Itself and within the Old Covenant

Marriage in itself is not purely secular. In several respects, marriage was sacred from the beginning, as the Old Testament makes clear; its religious significance does not begin when Jesus makes it a sacrament of the new covenant. Thus, following previous popes, Pius XI teaches "that there is a certain sacredness and religious character attaching even to the purely natural union of man and woman," which arises from its divine origin, its ministry of begetting and raising children for God, and its effect of joining the couple in communion with God.[91]

a) **Married life is cooperation with God in creating persons.** Marriage is sacred because of its divinely assigned mission: to hand on God's gift of life and raise children for him.[92]

---

90. An excellent work treating many aspects of the sacramentality of marriage more fully than is possible here: Peter J. Elliott, *What God Has Joined: The Sacramentality of Marriage* (Staten Island, N.Y.: Alba House, 1990).

91. Pius XI, *Casti connubii, AAS* 22 (1930) 570, *PE,* 208.80. Leo XIII, *Arcanum, ASS* 12 (1879) 392, *PE,* 81.19, teaches that marriage not only is a divine institution but "was from the very beginning a kind of foreshadowing of the Incarnation of his Son" (the wedding of the divine with the human), so that it is inherently religious and a sort of sacrament even within the old covenant and among nonbelievers.

92. Paul VI, *Humanae vitae*, 1, *AAS* 60 (1968) 481, *PE,* 277.1, begins: "Humanae vitae tradendae munus gravissimum."

Among the works of God's creation, human persons are special, since they are made in God's image and likeness (see Gn 1.26–27). Creating man and woman to complement each other by becoming one flesh (see Gn 2.18–23), God blesses them: "Be fruitful and multiply, and fill the earth and subdue it" (Gn 1.28). Parenthood is the handing on of God's image:

> When God created humankind, he made them in the likeness of God. Male and female he created them, and he blessed them and named them "Humankind" when they were created.
> When Adam had lived one hundred thirty years, he became the father of a son in his likeness, according to his image, and named him Seth. (Gn 5.1–3).

With fertility, God empowers men and women to cooperate in his creative work. When Eve bears Cain she says: "I have produced a man with the help of the Lord" (Gn 4.1), and the heroic mother of seven sons recalls their origin from God: "It was not I who gave you life and breath, nor I who set in order the elements within each of you" (2 Mc 7.22; cf. Jb 31.15, Jer 1.5).

Children are born for God and belong to him (see Ezk 16.20–21). Forming them, God makes them for his own glory (see Is 43.6–7). Since he created man and woman, and directed them to one-flesh communion, God is entitled to the fruit of their union: "Godly offspring" (Mal 2.15). It follows that children are a divine heritage and reward (see Ps 127.3–5). In the perspective of the Old Testament, fertility manifests God's love and is a great blessing (see Gn 12.2, 17.16, 26.24; Ps 113.9, 128.3–4), while sterility is a privation (see Gn 30.1, 1 Sm 1.6).

Vatican II sums up the matter by teaching that marriage is a special participation in God's own creative work; the couple "cooperate with the love of the creator and the savior, who through them will enlarge and enrich his own family day by day" (GS 50). The Council also teaches that human life and the couple's role in transmitting it should be understood and evaluated in the perspective of eternity, for these realities are not limited to this world alone (see GS 51).

b) God reveals his creative love in the communion of man and woman. God creates out of gratuitous love, to manifest his goodness and share his happiness with created persons (see *CMP,* 19.A). So, created reality as such is, in a wide sense, a sacrament, inasmuch as it is a visible sign of God's love. Within this sacrament, human persons, as male and female, manifest God's goodness in a special way, for he creates them in his own image and likeness (see Gn 1.26–27). This image consists not only in the spiritual powers of knowledge and freedom, but in the communion of persons that man and woman form. God calls men and women to communion, and they fulfill themselves by freely giving themselves to each other (see Gn 2.18–24). As John Paul II explains: "Mankind, to resemble God, must be a couple, two persons moving one towards the other, two persons whom perfect love will gather into unity. This movement and this love make them resemble God, who is Love itself, the absolute Unity of the three persons."[93] Thus, by sexual

---

93. John Paul II, Homily at a Mass for Families (Kinshasa, Zaire), 2, *AAS* 72 (1980) 425, *OR,* 12 May 1980, 4; cf. John Paul II, General Audience (14 Nov. 1979), 3, *Inseg.* 2.2 (1979) 1155–56, *OR,* 19 Nov. 1979, 1, 16; John Paul II, *Familiaris consortio,* 11, *AAS* 74 (1982) 91–93, *OR,* 21–28

differentiation, the human body, male and female, reveals creation as the fundamental gift, divine love as the source of this gift, and God's plan for the man's and the woman's mutual self-giving.[94]

c) **Marriage is an integral part of the sacrament of creation.** Because of the human body's God-given significance, which John Paul II calls its "nuptial meaning," married couples by their bodiliness, sexual differentiation, and bodily communion constitute a visible sign of the mystery of God's truth and love.[95] In the original innocence in which God created them, human persons were without shame, because they did not regard one another as objects, but experienced their sexuality's nuptial significance, and so not only felt themselves to be, but were in truth *in their very bodiliness,* subjects of holiness. John Paul II explains:

> The words of Genesis 2.24, "a man . . . cleaves to his wife and they become one flesh", spoken in the context of this original reality in a theological sense, constitute marriage as an integral part and, in a certain sense, a central part of the "sacrament of creation". They constitute—or perhaps rather, they simply confirm, the character of its origin. According to these words, marriage is a sacrament inasmuch as it is an integral part and, I would say, the central point of "the sacrament of creation". In this sense it is the primordial sacrament.[96]

Thus, from the beginning of creation, marriage expresses God's plan that humankind should "be holy and blameless before him in love" (Eph 1.4) and should not only manifest divine goodness, as all creation does, but personally share in God's love and freely respond to it. As Jesus points out, God himself joins husband and wife together so that their union is holy and indissoluble (see Mt 19.6, Mk 10.9).[97]

d) **Marriage is analogous to God's covenant relationship with Israel.** To clarify the covenant relationship between God and Israel, the prophets use the marital relationship, which naturally expresses God's love and calls for human self-giving. Israel slipped into the practices of paganism, whose gods begot rather than created, and whose worship involved fertility rites. So, although Israel's Lord

---

Dec. 1981, 3. Also Paul VI, Address to Members of "Equipes Notre-Dame", 3, *AAS* 62 (1970) 429, *OR,* 14 May 1970, 8, teaches: "The duality of sexes was willed by God so that man and woman together might be the image of God and, like him, a source of life."

94. See John Paul II, General Audience (9 Jan. 1980), 2–5, *Inseg.* 3.1 (1980) 88–91, *OR, 14* Jan. 1980, 1, 20.

95. See John Paul II, General Audience (20 Feb. 1980), 2–5, *Inseg.* 3.1 (1980) 429–31, *OR,* 25 Feb. 1980, 1, 12. *Sacrament* is used here not in the specific sense in which it refers to the seven signs instituted by Christ and administered by the Church, but in a wider sense, in which it refers to the mystery of God, hidden from eternity, considered in its very relevation: see John Paul II, General Audience (20 Oct. 1982), 7–8, *Inseg.* 5.3 (1982) 860–61, *OR,* 25 Oct. 1982, 3, 11.

96. John Paul II, General Audience (6 Oct. 1982), 6, *Inseg.* 5.3 (1982) 700, *OR,* 11 Oct. 1982, 2.

97. Origen, *Commentaries on Matthew,* 14, 16, in *The Faith of the Early Fathers,* vol. 1, selected and trans. W. A. Jurgens (Collegeville, Minn.: Liturgical Press, 1970), 211, articulates this aspect of marriage's natural sacramentality: "Certainly it is God who joins two in one, so that when He marries a woman to a man, there are no longer two. And since it is God who joins them, there is in this joining a grace for those who are joined by God. Paul knew this, and he said that just as holy celibacy was a grace, so also was marriage according to the Word of God a grace. He says, 'I would that all men were like myself; but each has his own grace from God, one in this way, another in that' (1 Cor 7.7)."

is the creator, who altogether transcends sexuality, Israel's sin against the covenant is a kind of adultery or harlotry. God's response, despite justified outrage at the offense, is absolute faithfulness and readiness to forgive (see Hos 1–3). The law forbade a man who divorced his faithless wife to take her back (see Dt 24.1–4), but God recalls Israel, his faithless wife, to her first love, which she experienced toward him in the desert (see Jer 2–3). Even when Israel suffers the consequences of her infidelity, consequences likened to the curses of sterility and early widowhood, she is encouraged to hope (Is 54.5–8; cf. Ezk 16 and 23). When men divorce their Jewish wives to marry pagans, Israel's infidelity to God becomes intertwined with men's infidelity to their wives. So, when men ask why God no longer accepts their sacrifices with favor, the answer is:

> Because the Lord was a witness between you and the wife of your youth, to whom you have been faithless, though she is your companion and your wife by covenant. . . . So look to yourselves, and do not let anyone be faithless to the wife of his youth. For I hate divorce, says the Lord, the God of Israel. (Mal 2.14–16)

Thus, once the marital relationship is recognized as analogous to God's covenantal relationship with Israel, marriage itself is seen to be a covenant, which God witnesses and guarantees.[98]

In this way, within the old covenant, marriage became a sign of God's covenantal relationship with his people, and each couple's marital relationship began to be seen as sharing in the sacredness and indissolubility of that salvific relationship.

2. Every Marriage of a Baptized Couple Is an Enduring Sacrament

While marriage is sacred in itself and within the old covenant, the marriage of two baptized Christians enjoys an additional sacredness, for it is one of the seven sacraments of the new covenant, and so is both a sign of God's saving work in Jesus and a means by which that work is effective in the lives of the faithful who do what they can to cooperate with it (see DS 1310–11/695, 1606–8/849–51, 1800/970).

a) **Christian marriage is a communion within the new covenant.** The Church teaches that marriage is one of the seven sacraments of the new covenant (see DS 718/367, 761/402, 794/424, 860/465, 1601/844, 1801/971). Enumerating the sacraments, the Council of Florence interprets Scripture and ties the sacramentality of marriage to Jesus' union with the Church: "The seventh is the sacrament of matrimony which is a sign of the close union of Christ and the Church according to the words of the Apostle: 'This is a great mystery—I mean in reference to Christ and to the Church' (Eph 5.32)" (DS 1327/702).[99]

---

98. See John Paul II, General Audience (22 Sept. 1982), *Inseg.* 5.3 (1982) 517–22, *OR,* 27 Sept. 1982, 1, 8; General Audience (12 Jan. 1983), *Inseg.* 6.1 (1983) 100–104, *OR,* 17 Jan. 1983, 3, 12.

99. The word *this* in Eph 5.32 may refer to the one-flesh unity of husband and wife referred to by Gn 2.24, which is quoted in Eph 5.31. On that reading, the one-flesh communion formed by husband and wife points ahead, even in the beginning, to the communion of the new covenant, and so begins to manifest (in an obscure way) the mystery of God's eternal plan to unite all things in Christ (see Eph 1.9–10, Rv 19.7). See Markus Barth, *Ephesians: Translation and Commentary on Chapters 4–6,* The Anchor Bible, 34A (Garden City, N.Y.: Doubleday, 1974), 641–47, 720–38. However, neither Florence nor Trent claims that Eph 5.32 by itself *asserts* the sacramentality of

The Council of Trent summarizes Jesus' teaching on marriage and then goes on to explain precisely why matrimony is a sacrament:

> Moreover, Christ himself, who instituted the holy sacraments and brought them to perfection, merited for us by his passion the grace that brings natural love to perfection, and strengthens the indissoluble unity, and sanctifies the spouses. The Apostle Paul intimates this when he says: "Husbands, love your wives, just as Christ also loved the Church, and delivered himself up for her" (Eph 5.25); and he goes on to add: "This is a great mystery—I mean in reference to Christ and to the Church" (Eph 5.32).
>
> Therefore, since matrimony under the law of the gospel is, because of the grace given through Christ, superior to the marriage unions of earlier times, our holy Fathers, the councils, and the tradition of the universal Church have always rightly taught that matrimony should be included among the sacraments of the New Law. (DS 1799–1800/969–70, translation amended)

According to this teaching, Christian marriage is a sacrament because it is a covenantal communion within the new covenant and an effective part of it.

b) Sacramentality renders perfect marriage practicable. The teaching of the Church that the marriage of a Christian couple is a sacrament means it is not only a sign imaging Jesus' union with the Church but an effective sign, one by which the Holy Spirit acts to build up and strengthen the communion of the new covenant. The couple receives the Holy Spirit's grace through Jesus to enable them to live their own marital communion, including its development into parental and familial communion, as their small portion of the Church united with Jesus, and thus to enjoy in their marriage the fruits of Jesus' sacrifice.[100] Trent mentions marital love brought to perfection, indissoluble unity, and personal sanctification through their common life. John Paul II explains this point:

> Through the sacrament, Christ establishes a permanent presence in every marriage relationship, through which the partners must establish with Christ the Redeemer an uninterrupted, open and sincere dialogue which opens them to his healing, restoring and always sanctifying grace. Without this door open to the Redeemer, who "has become our wisdom and also our justice, our sanctification, and our redemption" (1 Cor 1.30), it is not possible to build a Christian marriage, that is, the intimate and continuous union of life in complementarity between a man and a woman (Charter of the Rights of the Family, Preamble B), which is at the same time an effective channel of supernatural life.[101]

---

marriage. The Church's doctrine that marriage is a sacrament follows from Eph 5.32 when it is considered *together with* other data: Jesus' teaching about the indissolubility of marriage in the beginning, the real efficacy of God's redemptive work in him, Scripture's witness to the sacredness of marriage even under the old covenant, Jesus' use of the marriage and wedding feast analogy to describe the new covenant, and his participation in the wedding feast at Cana. On the history of the development of doctrine on the sacrament of marriage, see G. Le Bras, "La doctrine du mariage chez les théologiens et les canonistes depuis l'an mille," *Dictionnaire de théologie catholique,* 9.2:2123–2317.

100. See John Paul II, *Familiaris consortio,* 15, AAS 74 (1982) 97, *OR,* 21–28 Dec. 1981, 3–4. On the family as the domestic church, see 5.b–c, below.

101. John Paul II, Address to Those Engaged in Marriage Apostolate (3 Dec. 1983), 3, *Inseg.* 6.2 (1983) 1241, *OR,* 6 Feb. 1984, 8. Also, John Paul II, Homily During Mass for

The Lord Jesus' participation in each Christian marriage is not simply a fact reinforcing the requirement of fidelity to marriage as indissoluble but a gift empowering fallen men and women to meet this requirement. Thus, Jesus' restoration of marriage not only recalls his followers to their responsibilities but renews and strengthens them with the Holy Spirit's power so that they can realize and enjoy the benefits of marriage as God meant it to be.

c) **The sacrament endures throughout the marriage.** The sign in which the sacrament consists is the conjugal bond itself, that is, the Christian marital communion of the two persons.[102] Since this marital communion is initiated by the spouses' mutual covenantal consent, the sacrament cannot come to be without that consent. However, marital communion, and thus the sacrament, is fully constituted only when the marriage is consummated by conjugal intercourse, so that the couple become two in one flesh (see B.1.a–b, above). Once constituted, this one-flesh union lasts until one of the spouses dies, and so the sacrament of marriage, which begins on the wedding day, continues throughout the couple's life. Concerning this, Pius XI approvingly quotes St. Robert Bellarmine:

> The sacrament of matrimony can be regarded in two ways: first, in the making, and then in its permanent state. For it is a sacrament like to that of the Eucharist, which not only when it is being conferred, but also whilst it remains, is a sacrament; for as long as the married parties are alive, so long is their union a sacrament of Christ and the Church.[103]

It follows that a couple who strive to fulfill their responsibilities are never without the help and the confirming power of the Holy Spirit given in the sacrament. Indeed, Pius XI follows St. Augustine in teaching that, just as those who apostasize carry

---

Families (Faenza), 6, *Inseg.* 9.1 (1986) 1352–53, *OR,* 2 June 1986, 8, teaches: for Christian couples "to marry is above all an act of faith; it is the bringing of their human love into the supernatural order; it is the entrusting of their love to God, so that God himself will watch over it, guaranteeing it with his grace and blessing. According to the words of the Divine Master himself, it is not so much they who join themselves, but rather the Heavenly Father. Their principal duty is to preserve this union. They will succeed in so far as they recall that God has constituted himself guarantor of that union, and, consequently, in so far as they turn to him with full and unlimited trust in moments of difficulty."

102. John Paul II, Address to Two International Groups of Researchers (3 Nov. 1979), 4, *Inseg.* 2.2 (1979) 1032–33, *OR,* 3 Dec. 1979, 15, teaches: "Certainly, every sacrament involves participation in Christ's nuptial love for his Church. But, in marriage, the method and the content of this participation are specific. The spouses participate in it as spouses, together, as a couple, so that the first and immediate effect of marriage ("res et sacramentum") is not supernatural grace itself, but the Christian conjugal bond, a typically Christian communion of two persons because it represents the mystery of Christ's incarnation and the mystery of his covenant. The content of participation in Christ's life is also specific: . . . it is certainly a question of the normal characteristics of all natural conjugal love, but with a new significance which not only purifies and strengthens them, but raises them to the extent of making them the expression of specifically Christian values."

103. Pius XI, *Casti connubii, AAS* 22 (1930) 583, *PE,* 208.110. See Leonard F. Gerke, *Christian Marriage: A Permanent Sacrament* (Washington, D.C.: The Catholic University of America Press, 1965), for a full exposition of this point and a defense against contrary theological opinions. Gerke also argues (119–28, 138–54, 155, 157) that the actions of married life, and especially conjugal intercourse, are the permanent, visible, sacramental sign, and that these sacramentalized acts, rightly done by those in grace, give grace.

the baptismal seal with them, so even those who commit adultery carry the sacrament with them, although now it marks their infidelity rather than channeling their faith and love.[104]

To understand the persistence of the conjugal bond, and so of the sacrament, it is necessary to bear in mind what this bond is. It is not a legal fiction nor is it only a moral obligation, although legal and moral consequences flow from it; it is not the biological process of mating nor the fact of parenthood, although those realities of the natural order fulfill it. Essentially the bond is the two persons' real union in which they become, as it were, one new person—a new reality affecting the man and the woman insofar as they belong to both the order of nature and the moral order. The enduring sacrament, thus, is the marital union of the man and the woman, by virtue of which they, as husband and wife, together are a married couple.[105]

d) The sacrament is not something added to a Christian marriage. Since the sign in the sacrament of matrimony is the very union of the man and the woman whereby they are a married couple, the Church teaches "that among Christians every true marriage is, in itself and by itself, a sacrament; and that nothing can be further from the truth than to say that the sacrament is a certain added ornament, or outward endowment," such that a Christian couple could form a marital covenant without by that very fact receiving the sacrament.[106]

To understand this point, it helps to bear in mind that the baptism of the man and the woman made them individually, but in their whole personal being and permanently, members of the Church, thus bringing them into her covenantal union with Jesus. Hence, when in marrying the couple become, as it were, one new person, their marital communion also exists within the Church, and their marital covenant belongs to the new covenant. Their marriage therefore is sacramental precisely because their conjugal communion itself, without anything further, not only signifies the union of Jesus with his Church but develops that union.[107]

3. The Sacramentality of Marriage Affects Its Properties

The sacramental character of Christian marriage confirms the properties that belong to marriage as such: unity (the necessity of monogamy) and indissolubility (the impossibility of divorce).

---

104. See Pius XI, *Casti connubii, AAS* 22 (1930) 555, *PE,* 208.41; St. Augustine, *De nuptiis et concupiscentia* 1.10, *PL,* 44:419–20.

105. Pius VIII, *Traditi humilitati, Bullarii romani continuatio,* 9 (Prato: 1856), 26–27, *PE,* 30.10, teaches that the conjugal union itself is the sacrament: "It is agreed that the union of marriage signifies the perpetual and sublime union of Christ with his Church; as a result, the close union of husband and wife is a sacrament, that is, a sacred sign of the immortal love of Christ for his spouse." Cf. John Paul II, General Audience (5 Jan. 1983), 4–7, *Inseg.* 6.1 (1983) 43–45, *OR,* 3–10 Jan. 1983, 8.

106. Leo XIII, *Arcanum, ASS* 12 (1879) 394, *PE,* 81.24. Cf. DS 2966/1766; Pius XI, *Casti connubii, AAS* 22 (1930) 554, *PE,* 208.39; *CIC,* c. 1055, §2. An important and sound theological treatment of this matter: Carlo Caffarra, "Marriage as a Reality in the Order of Creation and Marriage as a Sacrament," in *Contemporary Perspectives on Christian Marriage,* 117–80.

107. See John Paul II, *Familiaris consortio,* 13 (the paragraph beginning "Nam per baptismum" or "Indeed, by means of baptism"), *AAS* 74 (1982) 95, *OR,* 21–28 Dec. 1981, 3.

a) The sacrament confirms marriage's unity and indissolubility. Marriage's natural sacredness, its sacramentality in the wide sense, already puts the bond initiated by the spouses' covenantal commitments beyond their own power. Several Fathers of the Church, in particular St. Augustine, conceived of indissolubility as an enduring *moral* obligation (already in pagan Rome, *sacramentum* meant a sacral obligation), which was strengthened in the case of Christians by their marital union's function as a sign of the absolutely unbreakable union of Christ with his Church.[108] Despite these Fathers' lack of clarity about the more-than-moral indissolubility of marriage as such, their insight into the relationship between Christian marriage and the new covenant provided a sound basis for subsequent development.

In clarifying her teaching concerning the sacraments against heretical opinions, the Church, beginning in the twelfth century, explicitly taught that the marriage of a Christian couple is a sacrament alongside baptism and the Eucharist, which are not only sacred signs but effective means of grace (see DS 718/367, 761/402).[109] Around the same time, papal judgments clarified the fact that nonconsummated marriages and marriages of non-Christians might be dissolved but the consummated marriage of a Christian couple is absolutely indissoluble (see DS 754/395, 755/396, 768–69/405–6). In 1201, Innocent III also interpreted the one-flesh communion to which Jesus pointed as excluding polygamy, and explained the practice of polygamy in the Old Testament as a divine concession no longer available to Christians (see DS 778/408).[110]

b) The Church teaches infallibly on marriage's properties. Subsequent Church teaching infallibly proposed this developed understanding of the sacrament of matrimony and its properties of unity and indissolubility.

A thirteenth-century profession of faith already specified that Christian marriage excludes polygamy (see DS 860/465). The Council of Florence taught that marriage is "indissoluble because it signifies the indivisible union of Christ with the Church," and explained that while a married person is allowed to separate from an adulterous spouse, he or she may not remarry "since the bond of a marriage lawfully contracted is perpetual" (DS 1327/702). The Council of Trent definitively teaches Christian

---

108. See Schillebeeckx, *Marriage,* 280–87.

109. The doctrine on sacramentality was anticipated in the long tradition. Early in the second century, St. Ignatius of Antioch, *Letter to Polycarp* 5, *PG,* 5:723, says Christians should marry with their bishop's decision, so that their marriage will be according to the Lord and not according to desire. (Schillebeeckx, *Marriage,* 245, minimizes the significance of this passage.) Again, the third letter of Cyril to Nestorius, included in the proceedings of the Council of Ephesus, includes a striking passage (in *Decrees of the Ecumenical Councils,* ed. Norman P. Tanner, S.J., vol. 1, *Nicea I to Lateran V* [London: Sheed and Ward, 1990], 58, lines 23–39) explaining that the purpose of the Incarnation is to "bless the beginning of our existence," by undoing the effects of sin, and that for this reason the Lord in his new covenant "blessed marriage and, when invited, went down to Cana in Galilee with his holy apostles."

110. One need not accept this explanation, but may hold the more likely view that polygamy never was willed by God but only tolerated, as divorce was: see Joyce, *Christian Marriage,* 579–80. St. Thomas offers a clear summary of the developed, Catholic understanding of the sacrament of matrimony, with its implications for the unity and the indissolubility of every consummated Christian marriage, omitting only the significance of consummation: *S.c.g.,* 4.78.

marriage's unity by condemning the opinion that divine law allows Christians to have many wives simultaneously (see DS 1802/972). Trent, likewise, teaches that the indissolubility of marriage already was expressed in the account of creation (in Gn 2.23–24), and more openly revealed by Jesus (in Mt 19.6, Mk 10.9; see DS 1797–98/969). Then, in a paragraph already quoted, Trent teaches that Christ's grace in Christian marriage confirms its indissolubility (see DS 1799/969); the Council then goes on with definitive canons to condemn both the opinion that marriage can be dissolved on account of heresy, domestic incompatibility, or willful desertion, and the opinion that the Church errs in teaching that marriage cannot be dissolved on account of adultery (see DS 1805/975, 1807/977).

During the centuries after Trent, all Catholic bishops, by the manuals of moral theology they approved for seminarians and the catechisms they approved for the faithful, proposed *as based on Scripture* the same teaching about marriage's unity and indissolubility, and Catholics accepted this teaching with faith as an essential element of the moral order revealed by God.[111] Even without Trent's solemn definitions, such unanimity in the Church's faith and teaching would suffice to manifest their infallible character (see LG 12 and 25).

c) **Today's magisterium reaffirms the same truths.** As twentieth-century secular, and even religious, opinion rejected the traditional conception of marriage, Pius XI clearly and strongly reaffirmed both that Jesus' teaching excludes polygamy among Christians and that divine law decrees that not even the Church can dissolve sacramental marriages.[112] Vatican II counts polygamy and the "plague of divorce" among the deformations which obscure the dignity of the institution of marriage (GS 47); the Council also teaches both that the mutual consent which gives rise to the conjugal covenant is irrevocable and that—for the good of the couple, of children, and of society—the sacred bond of marriage, once it exists, does not depend on human choice (see GS 48).

Developing the teaching of Vatican II and gathering the fruits of the 1980 Synod of Bishops, John Paul II teaches that conjugal communion, which has its natural basis in the complementarity of man and woman, is perfected by the sacrament. He proceeds not only to reaffirm the rejection of polygamy and divorce but to clarify the reasons why they are incompatible with Christian marriage.[113] The same teaching also is embodied in the Church's law.[114]

111. See Joyce, *Christian Marriage*, 400–409, for a summary of acts by the Holy See since Trent defending the absolute indissolubility of sacramental marriage.

112. See Pius XI, *Casti connubii, AAS* 22 (1930) 547 and 552–53, *PE*, 208.21 and 35–36.

113. See John Paul II, *Familiaris consortio*, 19–20, *AAS* 74 (1982) 101–4, *OR*, 21–28 Dec. 1981, 4–5.

114. *CIC*, c. 1056: "The essential properties of marriage are unity and indissolubility, which in Christian marriage obtain a special firmness in virtue of the sacrament"; c. 1057, §2: "Matrimonial consent is an act of the will by which a man and a woman, through an irrevocable covenant, mutually give and accept each other in order to establish marriage"; c. 1134: "From a valid marriage arises a bond between the spouses which by its very nature is perpetual and exclusive; furthermore, in a Christian marriage the spouses are strengthened and, as it were, consecrated for the duties and the dignity of their state by a special sacrament"; and c. 1141: "A ratified and consummated marriage cannot be dissolved by any human power or for any reason other than death."

d) The persistence of the sacrament also confirms indissolubility. Like the other sacraments, matrimony is a complex, cooperative act, uniting the recipients' covenantal commitments with the human redemptive act of Jesus and the Holy Spirit's work of healing and sanctification (see *CMP*, 30.B). Jesus' teaching reveals what marriage was meant to be in the beginning and how hardness of heart subverted it. By the sacrament, "freeing man from his hardness of heart, he makes man capable of realizing this truth in its entirety."[115] Inasmuch as the sacrament endures, Jesus' active presence within each marriage also endures, as Vatican II teaches:

> Christ the Lord abundantly blessed this many-faceted [conjugal] love, welling up as it does from the fountain of divine love and structured as it is on the model of his union with the Church. For as God of old made himself present (cf. Hos 2; Jer 3.6–13; Ezk 16 and 23; Is 54) to his people through a covenant of love and fidelity, so now the savior of men and the spouse (cf. Mt 9.15, Mk 2.19–20, Lk 5.34–35, Jn 3.29; cf. also 2 Cor 11.2; Eph 5.27; Rv 19.7–8, 21.2, 9) of the Church comes into the lives of married Christians through the sacrament of matrimony. He abides with them thereafter so that, just as he loved the Church and handed himself over on her behalf (cf. Eph 5.25), the spouses may love each other with perpetual fidelity through mutual self-bestowal. (GS 48).

Because a Christian marriage as a sacrament is a lasting cooperation with Jesus' redemptive act, the spouses are bound by their conjugal covenant not only to each other but to the Lord Jesus, who is a party to their marriage. Now, "if we are faithless, he remains faithful—for he cannot deny himself" (2 Tm 2.13). Thus, Jesus' involvement provides an additional reason why the husband and wife cannot dissolve the bond by mutual consent. But more than that, it guarantees the Holy Spirit's presence, and so confirms indissolubility by a fidelity which the couple achieve only by accepting it as a gift of grace.[116]

4. Marital Communion Participates in Everlasting Heavenly Communion

The first principle of Christian life is charity, the communion of love that the three divine persons are—God *is* love—and which they graciously will to extend to include created persons (see *CMP*, 24.B). Hence, the overarching responsibility for Christians is to abide in God's love and to love one another with the same love with which Jesus loves them. Because of Jesus' presence in the sacrament of marriage, Vatican II teaches: "Authentic married love is caught up into divine love and is governed and enriched by Christ's redeeming power and the saving activity of the Church, so that the spouses may be efficaciously led to God and helped and strengthened in their sublime mission as father and mother" (GS 48). Indeed, the divine-human communion, the new and everlasting covenant centering on Jesus in glory, actually is realized in and through the communion of Christian marriage and its fulfillment in a Christian family, which unites human persons not only with one

---

115. John Paul II, *Familiaris consortio,* 13, *AAS* 74 (1982) 94, *OR*, 21–28 Dec. 1981, 3.

116. An excellent scriptural study on this theme: Guy Bourgeault, S.J., "Fidélité conjugale et divorce," *Science et esprit* 24 (1972): 155–75.

another but, through their baptismal and eucharistic Communion with Jesus, with the divine persons.

Of course, the same might be said of any good interpersonal relationship among Christians, for example, a personal friendship, a community of religious, an association of teachers and students, or even a business partnership. However, the interpersonal communion of marriage involves a special bodily aspect, and in Christian marriage this aspect is intimately related to its sacramentality. Now, no good fruit of human nature or effort will be absent from the heavenly kingdom (see GS 39). Therefore, the bodily aspect of Christian marital communion also contributes to the new covenant communion and in some mysterious way will last forever in heavenly communion.

a) **Every human good realized on earth will last forever.** God calls men and women to cooperate with him in completing his work of creation and preparing for his ultimate act of re-creation, by which his plan for the whole created universe will be brought to fulfillment. Carried out through love, the secular activities of Christian life, including those proper to marriage and family life, prepare material for the heavenly kingdom (see LG 31, 34; GS 38). When God creates the new heavens and new earth and Jesus hands over his kingdom to his Father, not only love itself but all its good fruits—the material prepared for the kingdom—will endure, and so every good that fulfills human nature and effort will find its place in that everlasting heavenly communion (see GS 39). While the ways in which people now act for and experience these goods may not be appropriate in heaven, the positive reality and goodness of all the fruits of human nature and effort will find a place in heaven, but freed from the evil which now mutilates them, glorified, and transformed to overcome the limitations which make them, as yet, imperfect (see GS 39).

Considered in this light, Christian life lived in grace is seen to be already life in the heavenly kingdom, although not experienced as such; at present the kingdom is incipient but incomplete, and so its coming remains the object of hope and prayer. How the good fruits of one's day-by-day life belong to the kingdom even now and how they will be transformed are mysterious; indeed, even how the bodies of Christians belong to the kingdom and will be transformed by resurrection defies imagination (see 1 Cor 15.35–50). But resurrection life, which already somehow exists, will perfect bodiliness, not eliminate it, fully "clothe" those who are saved, not denude them (2 Cor 5.1–5).

Perhaps an analogy will help. Christians who live now according to God's plan revealed in Jesus are related to the coming heavenly kingdom somewhat as God's people of Old Testament times were related to the Church established by Christ. The people of that time already belonged to the Church and cooperated in the gradual Incarnation of the Word; the writings of the Old Testament contain material which the Holy Spirit has reworked, clarified, and completed in the New. Similarly, those who live according to God's plan in the present age prepare material for the everlasting kingdom.

b) **Eucharistic bodily communion in Jesus will last forever.** The sacrament of the Eucharist is both the principle and a paradigm of what is happening in the whole of Christian life: it transforms natural materials refined by human work into the glorified body and blood of Jesus, and builds up the divine-human communion which is to last forever (see GS 38). The Eucharist is not merely a sign of what will be; for although the sign it involves will drop away, the Eucharist truly realizes what will be: divine-human communion in and with Jesus. Of course, Christians do not yet fully experience the communion they enjoy in the sacrament; they still can lose this communion through sin, and the communion does not now have the effects it will have on their bodies, which remain subject to weakness, suffering, disease, and death. But in heaven, these negative features and limits will drop away, and the *sacrament* of the Eucharist will be no more. Only the positive reality of interpersonal communion, now present but veiled in the sacrament, will remain as the unending heavenly wedding feast.

The human dimension of the communion established by the Eucharist involves not merely a spiritual union of mind and will, through cooperation in faith with Jesus' redemptive act, but bodily union with and in the glorified body of the risen Lord: "Those who eat my flesh and drink my blood abide in me, and I in them" (Jn 6.56). Since the interpersonal communion established by the Eucharist will last forever, and since it has a bodily dimension, this human bodily communion with and in Jesus also will last, and, indeed, will be the foundation for the relationship: "Just as the living Father sent me, and I live because of the Father, so whoever eats me will live because of me" (Jn 6.57). In a very real sense, and not merely metaphorically, the Eucharist builds up the Church as one body: "The bread that we break, is it not a sharing in the body of Christ? Because there is one bread, we who are many are one body, for we all partake of the one bread" (1 Cor 10.16–17). This one body of Jesus will include in their gloriously risen bodily reality all who abide in him until death. Hence, without losing their distinct personalities, all human persons who are saved will forever share together completely in a one-flesh communion with and in Jesus (see *CMP,* 19.E, 33.C, 34.E.7).

c) **Bodily marital communion contributes to heavenly communion.** In general, the sacraments are remarkably consonant with the requirements of human nature. This is no accident. God created human nature for the kingdom, and so it includes what was necessary on humankind's part for God's revelation which initiates the kingdom, for the Word's Incarnation and redemptive act which definitively establish it, and for the Spirit's work of sanctification and re-creation which are perfecting it. Marriage fits this pattern: it is a natural sacrament, renewed by Jesus to be an unbreakable communion and an effective means of sanctification. The covenant of sacramental marriage flows from the covenant Jesus established on the cross and continually renews in the sacrament of the Eucharist.[117] Thus, Jesus' new covenant is dynamically present *within* marriage itself, as John Paul II teaches:

> Not only does the Covenant inspire the life of the couple, it fully partakes in that life, injecting its own energy in the lives of the spouses; it "models" their

---

117. See John Paul II, *Familiaris consortio,* 57, *AAS* 74 (1982) 149–50, *OR,* 21–28 Dec. 1981, 11.

love from within; they love one another not only *as* Christ loved, but, mysteriously, *with* the very love of Christ, as his Spirit is given to them . . . in the measure in which they let themselves be "modelled" by him (cf. Gal 2.25; Eph 4.23). At Mass, through the ministry of the priest, the Spirit of the Lord makes the body and blood of the Lord from bread and wine; in and through the sacrament of marriage, the Spirit can make the very love of the Lord from conjugal love; if the couple let themselves be transformed, they can love with the "new heart" promised by the New Covenant (cf. Jer 31.31; *Familiaris consortio,* no. 20).[118]

An important similarity between the new covenant and the marital covenant is that both communions are one-flesh unities, real and objective sharings in a common, bodily life. Marriage, however, is very limited, since it joins only two persons on the basis of each one's natural incompleteness with respect to the single organic function of reproduction. By contrast, the bodily communion built up by the Eucharist joins in Jesus all who share in the one bread with respect to the entire, glorious life which they hope to live in him forever.

Still, if Christian marriage is considered insofar as it depends on Jesus' covenant present in the Eucharist, it is clear that the marital covenant as a sacrament realizes in a specific way Jesus' new covenant. Hence, the married couple as such, in their very one-flesh union, also are united in Jesus with each other and with other Christian couples and individuals. In this way, marital communion, in its bodily aspect, not only signifies but is part of the communion of the new covenant.

d) Marital communion will be perfected in heavenly communion. Since none of the fruits of human nature and effort will be lost, the good of marriage, its very one-flesh communion, certainly will be preserved and perfected in the heavenly kingdom. And since the bodily communion of heaven cannot be dissolved, one-flesh marital communion, insofar as it already is a material element of the kingdom, also cannot be dissolved.

Still, "in the resurrection they neither marry nor are given in marriage, but are like angels" (Mt 22.30; cf. Mk 12.25, Lk 20.34–36); moreover, death does dissolve a marriage, so that widows and widowers are free to remarry (see 1 Cor 7.7–9; DS 1353/—). How, then, can the one-flesh communion of marriage endure forever? The answer is that it cannot endure insofar as it is based on sexual differentiation, is limited to couples, and is fulfilled by having and raising children. Rather, it will endure in the resurrection without these limits and will be perfected within the greater one-flesh communion of the blessed in and with the Lord Jesus.[119]

---

118. John Paul II, Address to the "Equipes Notre-Dame" (23 Sept. 1982), 2, *Inseg.* 5.3 (1982) 543–44, *OR,* 15 Nov. 1982, 6. Also, John Paul II, General Audience (4 July 1984), 6, *Inseg.* 7.2 (1984) 10, *OR,* 9 July 1984, 8, teaches that by virtue of the sacrament, the practice of conjugal life becomes liturgical: "In that [sacramental] sign—through the 'language of the body'—man and woman encounter the great 'mystery' in order to transfer the light of that mystery—the light of truth and beauty, expressed in liturgical language—to the 'language of the body', that is, to the language of the practise of love, of fidelity, of conjugal honesty, that is, to the ethos rooted in the 'redemption of the body' (cf. Rom 8.23). In this way, conjugal life becomes in a certain sense liturgical."

119. John Paul II, General Audience (16 Dec. 1981), 4, *Inseg.* 4.2 (1981) 1138, *OR,* 4 Jan. 1982, 2, teaches: "We must think of the reality of the 'other world' in the categories of the rediscovery of a new, perfect subjectivity of everyone and at the same time of the rediscovery of

The ethical requirement of exclusivity belongs to marital communion according to its natural basis, and so also characterizes the sacrament. With death, however, the sacrament gives way to the greater reality to which it points. Hence, widows and widowers can remarry without violating marital communion, yet married couples should regard their love, not as transitory, but as undying.[120]

e) **Virginity or celibacy complements the sacrament of marriage.** Virginity or celibacy for the kingdom's sake also signifies and anticipates heavenly communion. The Church definitively teaches that it is better and more blessed to remain in such Christian virginity or celibacy than it is to be joined in sacramental marriage (see DS 1810/980; OT 10; cf. LG 42, PC 12, PO 16). Still, as John Paul II teaches: "Virginity or celibacy for the sake of the Kingdom of God not only does not contradict the dignity of marriage but presupposes it and confirms it. Marriage and virginity or celibacy are two ways of expressing and living the one mystery of the covenant of God with his people."[121]

Although those who receive and respond to the gift of virginity or celibacy do not violate the basic human good of marital communion, they do forgo it, leaving unfulfilled the instinct of nature toward sexual union and parenthood.[122] By their extraordinary renunciation, they bear powerful witness to the kingdom's definitive value.[123] In Jesus' striking phrase, they make "themselves eunuchs for the sake of the kingdom of heaven" (Mt 19.12). Moreover, while their way of life is not a sacrament of the bodily intimacy of resurrection life, it is a sign of the inclusivity of the communion of the blessed in Jesus and of his absolute centrality in the kingdom of heaven.

Thus, virginity or celibacy for the kingdom and the sacrament of marriage are necessary and complementary signs. Marriage manifests that heaven will be an

---

a new, perfect intersubjectivity of all. In this way, this reality signifies the real and definitive fulfilment of human subjectivity, and, on this basis, the definitive fulfilment of the 'nuptial' meaning of the body. The complete concentration of created subjectivity, redeemed and glorified, on God himself will not take man away from this fulfilment, in fact—on the contrary—it will introduce him into it and consolidate him in it."

120. Pius XII, Address to the World Union of Family Organizations (16 Sept. 1957), *AAS* 49 (1957) 900–901, *The Pope Speaks* 4 (1957–58): 289, teaches: "Far from destroying the bonds of human and supernatural love which are contracted in marriage, death can perfect them and strengthen them. It is true that legally, and on the plane of perceptible realities, the matrimonial institution does not exist any more, but that which constituted its soul, gave it strength and beauty—conjugal love with all its splendor and its eternal vows—lives on just as the spiritual and free beings live on who have pledged themselves to each other." What Pope Pius says here about conjugal love must be developed in view of Vatican II's teaching (in GS 38–39) that not only does charity itself subsist but its work—all the good fruits of human nature and effort—which will be found again, transformed, in heaven.

121. John Paul II, *Familiaris consortio*, 16, *AAS* 74 (1982) 98, *OR*, 21–28 Dec. 1981, 4. In the same place, John Paul also reaffirms the superiority of the charism of virginity or celibacy for the kingdom's sake to that of marriage.

122. See Paul VI, *Sacerdotalis caelibatus*, 50–56, *AAS* 59 (1967) 677–79, *PE*, 276.50–56; also see Paul M. Quay, S.J., *The Christian Meaning of Human Sexuality* (Evanston, Ill.: Credo House, 1985), 85–99.

123. See OT 10; also Jean Galot, S.J., "La motivation évangélique du célibat," *Gregorianum* 53 (1972): 731–57.

intimate, interpersonal, communion in which human bodily persons will find their fulfillment; virginity or celibacy manifests that heavenly communion will be inclusive, rather than exclusive, and will surpass the limitations of the most intimate communion men and women can experience in this life.[124]

5. Special Responsibilities Pertain to Marriage as a Sacrament

The remainder of this chapter will treat the many responsibilities of Christian spouses and parents, considering these responsibilities insofar as they flow from faith and love. Here it is necessary only to consider some arising directly and immediately from the sacramentality of Christian marriage.

a) **Christian couples should regard marriage as a vocation.** Consent to marriage and commitment to fulfill the responsibilities flowing from it determine a very large part of a married person's life. Since the whole of Christian life should be lived according to faith, couples should undertake and live their married life as a very important part of their Christian vocation. Because marriage is a sacrament, it is all the more clear and important that no one should suppose he or she could undertake or live it independently of faith, hope, and love (see GS 48; cf. LG 41). Thus, Vatican II treats marriage as a vocation (see GS 48, 49, 52; cf. LG 35).[125] Hence, all the responsibilities regarding personal vocation (treated in 2.E) should be considered to pertain to marriage as a sacrament.

In affluent contemporary societies, the view is widespread that marriage is only an arrangement for attaining specific goals; this is radically at odds with regarding marriage as part of one's Christian vocation. Such an arrangement, which falls short of authentic marital communion, is only a means for satisfying individuals' desires by carrying out their agendas and achieving specific objectives. True marital communion is not a mere means, though, but a human good in itself, willed by each spouse unselfishly for the other's good as well as his or her own. Such marital communion, as a lasting reality, must not be evaluated by its usefulness or satisfactoriness; rather, it must be sought and accepted as a blessing, cherished for itself, and nurtured. To fulfill the responsibilities of marriage as a sacrament, therefore, Christian spouses should undertake married life as a deliberate response to God's call, give their marital consent as a yes to God's will that they become and remain one, always regard each other as God's gift, anticipate any children they

---

124. St. Thomas, *In Sent.*, 4, d. 38, q. 1, a. 5, holds that marriage and virginity are complementary signs, but he explains the complementarity in a different way.

125. John Paul II, *Apostolic Letter on the Occasion of the International Youth Year,* 9, *AAS* 77 (1985) 602, *OR,* 1 Apr. 1985, 5, points out that "before the Second Vatican Council the concept of 'vocation' was applied *first of all* to the priesthood and religious life, as if Christ had addressed to the young person his evangelical 'Follow me' only for these cases. *The Council has broadened* this way of looking at things. . . . every human life vocation, as a Christian vocation, corresponds to the evangelical call. *Christ's 'Follow me' makes itself heard on the different paths* taken by the disciples and confessors of the divine Redeemer." This teaching makes clear the error of Hans Urs von Balthasar, *The Christian State of Life,* trans. Mary Frances McCarthy (San Francisco: Ignatius Press, 1983), 421, in denying that marriage can be a vocation: "No sound and balanced Christian will ever say of himself that he chose marriage by virtue of a divine election, an election comparable to the election and vocation experienced or even only perceived by those called to the priesthood or to the personal following of Christ in religious life."

might have as God's children entrusted to their care, and subordinate to this vocational perspective their particular desires and specific goals: sexual and emotional satisfaction, a home and other possessions, an approved social status, and even the self-fulfillment to be found in parenthood.

b) The family should function as a little Church within the parish. From the beginning, the Church welcomed and incorporated not only individuals but entire families and households (see Acts 11.13–14; 16.15, 31; 18.8; 1 Cor 1.16, 16.15). Indeed, we know from the New Testament that early Christian congregations sometimes were based on households, and this seems to have been the norm during the first three centuries.[126] When persecutions or other adversities made parish life impossible, the Church often survived in Christian households.

Today, too, just as the parish is a local church within the diocese, so the Christian family is a little church within the parish. For, as the Greek word for church, *ekklesia,* suggests, a church is a community called together by God,[127] and a Christian family should be such a community, inasmuch as Christians should marry and have children according to God's plan and in response to his vocation. Joined to Christ by baptism and consecrated by the sacrament of matrimony, the two or three (or more) family members are gathered in Jesus' name, and he lives in their midst (see Mt 18.20). For this reason, Vatican II refers to the family as the "domestic Church" (LG 11; cf. AA 11).[128] John Paul II explains:

> The meaning of this traditional Christian idea is that the home is the Church in miniature. The Church is the sacrament of God's love. She is a communion of faith and life. She is a mother and teacher. She is at the service of the whole human family as it goes forward towards its ultimate destiny. In the same way the family is a community of life and love. It educates and leads its members to their full human maturity and it serves the good of all along the road of life.[129]

Hence, the couple and their whole household not only should work together to build up the wider society (see AA 11) but, as Christians, should "work for the upbuilding of the people of God through their marriage and their family."[130]

c) The sacrament of marriage shapes this miniature Church. Like every sacrament, marriage looks back to the new covenant as Jesus established it, instantiates that covenant at present, and points forward to that covenant as it will be fulfilled in heaven (see *S.t.,* 3, q. 60, a. 3).

Considering the covenant as a reality established by Jesus' death and resurrection, the couple should recall and bear witness to it, and so carry out their part in

---

126. See Gregory Dix, *The Shape of the Liturgy,* 2nd ed. (London: Dacre Press, 1945), 12–35.

127. See John Paul II, General Audience (20 July 1991); *L'Osservatore Romano,* It. ed., 21 July 1991, 4; *OR,* 22 July 1991, 11.

128. Helpful theological studies: Domenico Sartore, C.S.I., "La famiglia, chiesa domestica," *Lateranum* 45 (1979): 282–303; Jean Beyer, S.J., "Ecclesia domestica," *Periodica de re morali, canonica, liturgica* 79 (1990): 293–326; Vigen Guroian, "Family and Christian Virtue in a Post-Christendom World: Reflections on the Ecclesial Vision of John Chrysostom," *St. Vladimir's Theological Quarterly* 35 (1991): 327–50.

129. John Paul II, Homily at Mass in Belmont Racecourse (Perth), 3, *Inseg.* 9.2 (1986) 1782, *OR,* 9 Dec. 1986, 21.

130. *CIC,* c. 226, §1.

Jesus' prophetic office.[131] They should nurture their own faith and, in fidelity to their vocation as parents, hand it on intact to their children. Moreover, by living their specific form of family life, good Christian families become witnesses to love and life, give testimony to their faith and hope, and so challenge other families to accept, or more perfectly share in, these gifts (see GS 48). This witness is especially needed at a time when the values of secularism permeate so many families, with the bad result that they either fail to develop the Christian virtues of self-sacrifice, fidelity, and chastity, or else set them aside while seeking a specious happiness in consumerism, individualistic liberation, and ephemeral pleasure.

Considering the covenant as a reality instantiated in their marital communion, the couple should put into practice the merciful love which forgives and redeems, serve and build up communion among God's people, and so carry out their part in Jesus' kingly office.[132] The Christian family does this by walking in the Spirit and fulfilling the new law of love. Charity indeed must begin at home, in each family member's generous and unselfish quest for the others' good; but it must extend beyond the family circle to the Church at large, and then to all men and women, who also are called to enter the kingdom and find their fulfillment as members of God's family.

Considering the covenant as the heavenly communion in which their marriage will find its ultimate fulfillment, the couple should unite the whole of their married and family life to Jesus' sacrifice, gratefully offering it to God as material for the kingdom and so carrying out their part in Jesus' priestly office.[133] The persisting sacrament of marriage, developing and completing for the married couple the graces of baptism and confirmation, enables family life as a whole to be an effective means of sanctification.[134] Still, love remains imperfect and sin always is possible,

---

131. Focusing primarily on the prophetic responsibility of the family, John Paul II, *Christifideles laici,* 62, *AAS* 81 (1989) 514–15, *OR,* 6 Feb. 1989, 20, teaches: "The *Christian family,* as the 'domestic Church', also makes up a natural and fundamental school for formation in the faith; father and mother receive from the Sacrament of Matrimony the grace and the ministry of the Christian education of their children, before whom they bear witness and to whom they transmit both human and religious values. While learning their first words, children learn also the praise of God, whom they feel is near them as a loving and providential Father; while learning the first acts of love, children also learn to open themselves to others, and through the gift of self receive the meaning of living as a human being. The daily life itself of a truly Christian family makes up the first 'experience of Church', intended to find confirmation and development in an active and responsible process of the children's introduction into the wider ecclesial community and civil society. The more that Christian spouses and parents grow in the awareness that their 'domestic church' participates in the life and mission of the universal Church, so much the more will their sons and daughters be able to be formed in a 'sense of the Church' and will perceive all the beauty of dedicating their energies to the service of the Kingdom of God." Also see John Paul II, *Familiaris consortio,* 51–54, *AAS* 74 (1982) 142–47, *OR,* 21–28 Dec. 1981, 10–11.

132. On the kingly responsibility of the family, see John Paul II, *Familiaris consortio,* 63–64, *AAS* 74 (1982) 155–58, *OR,* 21–28 Dec. 1981, 12–13.

133. See John Paul II, *Familiaris consortio,* 13, *AAS* 74 (1982) 95, *OR,* 21–28 Dec. 1981, 3. Verbally, the Pope associates *prophecy* with the sacrament's anticipatory aspect, but he is not here concerned with the threefold office. On the priestly responsibility of the family, see *Familiaris consortio,* 55–62, *AAS* 74 (1982) 147–55, *OR,* 21–28 Dec. 1981, 11–12.

134. Leo XIII, *Inscrutabili Dei consilio, ASS* 10 (1877) 590, *PE,* 78.14, teaches that the benefits of the sacrament extend to the children: "Our Lord Jesus Christ, by raising to the dignity

so that family members not only can but should obtain forgiveness and reconciliation in the sacrament of penance, and should deepen and perfect their communion with one another and with the divine persons by participating in the Eucharist. Family prayer, devotions, and the use of sacramentals prepare for the Eucharist and prolong it within the household. By joining together constantly in petition, praise, and thanksgiving, the members of the family maintain unbroken dialogue with God. Families inevitably are anxious and troubled about many things; only by regular prayer can they keep other things in their proper place, subordinate to the quest for God's kingdom.

Question D: What Are the Responsibilities of Spouses toward Each Other?

This question will articulate and explain the general principles of the mutual responsibilities of the spouses, as well as the specific norms for their relationship of friendship, their common domestic life, and their different, complementary roles as husband-father and wife-mother. The specific norms concerning marital sexual activity, having children, and raising them will be treated in subsequent questions (E.1–2 and F).

1. Each Couple Should Build a Unique Marital and Familial Communion

As has been explained, marriage is not a project, directed toward achieving some definite, limited goal or set of goals, but a form of human and Christian life, a vocation to lifelong love and the service of new life. No two couples bring to marriage and family life exactly the same gifts and limitations, the same opportunities and problems. Each husband and wife should work together creatively in the effort to build the best marriage and family they can. Moral norms provide only a necessary framework for this creative effort.

a) **The divine design for marriage is not a detailed plan.** While all good marriages are similar in essentials, each differs in details. Just as each person has a unique personal vocation, marked out by his or her special set of gifts, limitations, and opportunities, so each couple who share together the vocation of marriage and parenthood must accept and fulfill it in their own way. As John Paul II teaches:

> God, who called the couple *to* marriage, continues to call them *in* marriage [note omitted]. In and through the events, problems, difficulties and circumstances of everyday life, God comes to them, revealing and presenting the concrete 'demands' of their sharing in the love of Christ for his Church in the particular family, social and ecclesial situation in which they find themselves.[135]

---

of a sacrament the contract of matrimony, in which he would have his own union with the Church typified, not only made the marriage tie more holy, but, in addition, provided efficacious sources of aid for parents and children alike, so that, by the discharge of their duties one to another, they might with greater ease attain to happiness both in time and in eternity."

135. John Paul II, *Familiaris consortio,* 51, *AAS* 74 (1982) 143–44, *OR,* 21–28 Dec. 1981, 10. Note John Paul's affirmation of the *ongoing* character of the couple's vocation.

The couple should take into account both the opportunities and challenges of their whole sociocultural situation, and should make the most of their gifts to cooperate with God in creating their own, unique good marriage. In doing this, they of course should pray regularly, both individually and together, seeking light concerning God's will for them and inspiration concerning how to fulfill it creatively.

b) **Christian couples should not think of marriage as a joint project.** Ignoring or rejecting God's plan for marriage and family, many people consider marriage merely a joint project undertaken by a man and a woman to obtain some of the things they happen to want out of life. On this view, couples may decide for themselves, by mutual agreement, whether to have children, how long their relationship will last, and even whether it will allow for extramarital intimacies. This view errs not only by arbitrarily setting aside essential elements of the framework which God's plan provides but by arbitrarily limiting the couple's cooperation to a joint effort to achieve a limited set of definite goals. Having set such limits, a couple will look about for techniques for achieving a happy marriage, and, when seemingly insoluble problems arise, will be likely to conclude that their marriage has "broken down." Christian couples, by contrast, should regard the problems which inevitably arise in marriage and family life as material they must use creatively to become what God calls them to be.

c) **They should be cautious in following guidance, advice, and models.** Christian couples can obtain helpful guidance from sources which accurately articulate God's design for marriage and family life, and provide suggestions about some of the problems they are likely to encounter. A priest or other counselor working within a sound framework also may be able to help them to deal with difficulties. But many books and articles on marriage, as well as many psychologists and marriage counselors, presuppose the false view described above and embody it in their advice. Couples should be wary not only of guidance and advice clearly inconsistent with Christian moral norms, but of anything or anyone purporting to teach an art or set of techniques for a good marriage. Marriages are not machines, to be tuned up occasionally and repaired when broken, and anyone claiming to offer this kind of service for marriage should not be trusted.

Moreover, young people should not imitate too closely even virtuous and happily married Christian couples. While their example should be followed in essential matters, the details of their lives and ways of doing things may not be appropriate for others. Therefore, each married couple should try to understand the norms for marriage and family life, and think carefully and continually about how best to fulfill God's design in their unique communion.

2. Papal Teachings on the Husband-Wife Relationship Are Consistent

Christian faith makes it clear that one member of a communion of persons can hold primacy without compromising the equal dignity of the others: the Father, being first in the Holy Trinity, sends the Son and the Spirit to carry out his plan for humankind, but the three persons are coequal in divinity and all its attributes. In accord with this model for interpersonal relationships, the New Testament and

Christian tradition present marriage as a union of persons, equal in personal dignity and fundamental rights, but with complementary roles and a certain primacy for the husband.[136]

Until recently, papal teaching emphasized the wife's duty of obedience; but John Paul II focuses on the spouses' *mutual* submission. The rhetorical expressions of previous and present papal teachings of course reflect very different social contexts; but the propositions taught should be regarded, not as inconsistent, but as different elements of truth, to be integrated into a single, coherent view.

a) The New Testament suggests the complexity of the relationship. Some New Testament passages, dealing explicitly with the relationship between husbands and wives, indicate that husbands hold primacy, for example: "Just as the church is subject to Christ, so also wives ought to be, in everything, to their husbands" (Eph 5.24).[137]

Other passages, dealing not with marriage but with the relationship between man and woman in general, point to their equal dignity. While there are differences, "Nevertheless, in the Lord woman is not independent of man or man independent of woman. For just as woman came from man, so man comes through woman; but all things come from God" (1 Cor 11.11–12). Again: "There is no longer Jew or Greek, there is no longer slave or free, there is no longer male or female; for all of you are one in Christ Jesus" (Gal 3.28).[138]

b) Past papal teaching emphasized the wife's subordination. For example, facing emergent feminism, Pius XI used Ephesians 5.22–23 to reaffirm that marriage rightly "includes both the primacy of the husband with regard to the wife and children, the ready subjection of the wife and her willing obedience."[139] He criticized "false teachers" who

> do away with the honorable and trusting obedience which the woman owes to the man. Many of them even go further and assert that such a subjection of one party to the other is unworthy of human dignity, that the rights of husband and wife are equal; wherefore, they boldly proclaim the emancipation of women has been or ought to be effected.[140]

c) John Paul II emphasizes the mutual subjection of the spouses. Commenting on Ephesians 5.21–33, John Paul II states that the exhortation to husbands to

---

136. For sources in Scripture and tradition, see Stephen B. Clark, *Man and Woman in Christ: An Examination of the Roles of Men and Women in Light of Scripture and the Social Sciences* (Ann Arbor, Mich.: Servant Books, 1980), 47–100, 281–97.

137. Cf. 1 Cor 11.3, Col 3.18, Ti 2.4–5, 1 Pt 3.1.

138. Moreover, Jesus' teaching on marriage, by excluding polygamy and divorce, rectifies injustices to women tolerated by the old covenant, and his way of dealing with and relating to women breaks with customs of the time and shows that he does not wish them to be second-class members of the new covenant. See Congregation for the Doctrine of the Faith, *Inter insigniores*, 2, *AAS* 69 (1977) 102–3, Flannery, 2:334–35; John Paul II, *Mulieris dignitatem*, 12–16, *AAS* 80 (1988) 1681–92, *OR*, 3 Oct. 1988, 6–8.

139. Pius XI, *Casti connubii, AAS* 22 (1930) 549, *PE*, 208.26.

140. Pius XI, *Casti connubii, AAS* 22 (1930) 567, *PE*, 208.74. John XXIII, *Ad Petri Cathedram AAS* 51 (1959) 509–10, *PE*, 263.53, sums up the tradition: "Within the family, the father stands in God's place. He must lead and guide the rest by his authority and the example of his good life."

love their wives as Christ loved the Church calls not only on husbands but on all men to adopt Jesus' style in dealing with women. He then goes on:

> The author of the Letter to the Ephesians sees no contradiction between an exhortation formulated in this way and the words: "Wives, be subject to your husbands, as to the Lord. For the husband is the head of the wife" (5.22–23). The author knows that this way of speaking, so profoundly rooted in the customs and religious tradition of the time, is to be understood and carried out in a new way: as a *"mutual subjection out of reverence for Christ"* (cf. Eph 5.21). This is especially true because the husband is called the "head" of the wife *as* Christ is the head of the Church; he is so in order to give "himself up for her" (Eph 5.25), and giving himself up for her means giving up even his own life. However, whereas in the relationship between Christ and the Church the subjection is only on the part of the Church, in the relationship between husband and wife the "subjection" is not one-sided but mutual.[141]

John Paul goes on to argue that the mutual subjection of the spouses is a gospel innovation which definitively challenges succeeding generations: "Saint Paul not only wrote: 'In Christ Jesus . . . there is no more man or woman', but also wrote: 'There is no more slave or freeman'. Yet how many generations were needed for such a principle to be realized in the history of humanity through the abolition of slavery!"[142]

John Paul's interpretation of Ephesians makes it clear that the latter is neither countenancing male domination nor imposing a one-sided subjection of wives to husbands. The sacred writer's intention, rather, is to call Christian spouses to live their marriage relationship in mutual self-sacrifice, following Jesus' example. This responsibility differs for the spouses only insofar as their characteristic temptations are different: men are tempted to abuse and neglect their wives, and so are admonished to love and care for them; women are tempted to respond to their husbands' shortcomings by rebelling against them and acting autonomously, and so are admonished to obey.

d) It should not be supposed that John Paul II rejects the tradition. Because the popes, assisted by the Holy Spirit, try to articulate the same faith, in the absence of compelling evidence new teaching should not be thought to contradict old. Thus, if possible, the different papal teachings should be understood as compatible, and a careful reading shows that they can be.

Pius XI, in his doctrinal encyclical on marriage, makes it clear that a husband should respect his wife's equal personal dignity and should not dominate her. Subjection "does not deny or take away the liberty which fully belongs to the woman" as a human person; it does not imply that she has the status of a minor; it

---

141. John Paul II, *Mulieris dignitatem,* 24, *AAS* 80 (1988) 1711, *OR,* 3 Oct. 1988, 11. In many respects anticipating John Paul's interpretation of the relevant verses, on the basis of careful exegesis: Stephen Francis Miletic, *"One Flesh": Eph. 5.22–24, 5.31: Marriage and the New Creation* (Rome: Editrice Pontificio Istituto Biblico, 1988), 99–120.

142. John Paul II, *Mulieris dignitatem,* 24, *AAS* 80 (1988) 1712, *OR,* 3 Oct. 1988, 11. Also see John Paul II, General Audience (11 Aug. 1982), *Inseg.* 5.3 (1982) 204–7, *OR,* 16–23 Aug. 1982, 1, 16.

requires her to obey as a companion equal in dignity, not as an inferior.[143] Thus, the husband's headship in the family no more demeans his wife than Christ's headship in the new covenant community demeans the Church.

John Paul II, in his apostolic letter offered as a meditation on the dignity of woman, points out that male domination of women is due to their vulnerability and is a product of original sin. At the same time, he insists on "the specific diversity and personal originality of man and woman." Women rightly resist being dominated, John Paul argues, but that just resistance "must not under any condition lead to the 'masculinization' of women. In the name of liberation from male 'domination', women must not appropriate to themselves male characteristics contrary to their own feminine 'originality'."[144]

This affirmation of the difference between men and women implies the legitimacy of sexually differentiated roles in marriage. John Paul does not spell out that implication, but it is hardly reasonable to suppose that he should have done so, since the document deals with the spouses' roles only insofar as that subject is relevant to woman's dignity. Moreover, John Paul treats the different roles of the spouses in his apostolic exhortation on marriage and the family.[145]

Therefore, one cannot read into John Paul's teaching the denial of a wife's duty to obey her husband without supposing him to be saying that wives need *not* be subject to their husbands. However, the Pope does not say this, even when he compares male domination to slavery.[146] Rather, emphasizing that a husband should love his wife in a self-sacrificing way, he asserts that the subjection should be *mutual*. The unstated implication is that while a wife need not submit to her husband's selfish domination, she remains subject to his rightly exercised authority.

---

143. Pius XI, *Casti connubii, AAS* 22 (1930) 549, *PE,* 208.27. It is worth noticing that this teaching has deep roots in the tradition. For example, St. Thomas, *In Sent.,* 4, d. 38, *expositio textus,* ad 2, argues that wives are not property and must not be subordinated as slaves are; in *S.t.,* 1, q. 92, a. 3, he interprets the symbolism of Eve being formed from Adam's side to mean that a wife neither should dominate nor be enslaved, but should be her husband's companion.

144. John Paul II, *Mulieris dignitatem,* 10, *AAS* 80 (1988) 1676, *OR,* 3 Oct. 1988, 5. Similarly, Pius XII, Address to Italian Women (21 Oct. 1945), *AAS* 37 (1945) 285–87, *Catholic Mind* 43 (1945): 706–8, very clearly articulates both the equal dignity of persons of both sexes and their personally and socially important differences; he insists, at the same time, that men and women can neither maintain nor perfect their dignity unless they respect and fulfill their differences.

145. See John Paul II, *Familiaris consortio,* 22–25, *AAS* 74 (1982) 106–11, *OR,* 21–28 Dec. 1981, 5–6. In the last paragraph of the passage cited, the leadership role of the husband-father is sketched out: "In revealing and in reliving on earth the very fatherhood of God (cf. Eph 3.15), a man is called upon to ensure the harmonious and united development of all the members of the family: he will perform this task by exercising generous responsibility for the life conceived under the heart of the mother, by a more solicitous commitment to education, a task he shares with his wife (cf. GS 52), by work which is never a cause of division in the family but promotes its unity and stability, and by means of the witness he gives of an adult Christian life which effectively introduces the children into the living experience of Christ and the Church." This sketch emphasizes the husband-father's service to his family, and the exercise of authority insofar as it is necessary to carry out the service is implied by the reference to the fatherhood of God.

146. A sound exegesis of Gal 3.28 does not argue for the elimination of complementary, sexually differentiated roles; see Thomas Hopko, "Galatians 3:28: An Orthodox Interpretation," *St. Vladimir's Theological Quarterly* 35 (1991): 169–86; cf. Clark, *Man and Woman in Christ,* 137–63.

3. Marriage Itself Has Two Aspects Which Must Be Harmonized

Much of the new emphasis in John Paul II's teaching can be explained by his concern to vindicate the dignity of women against male domination. When a man dominates his wife, his abuse of his role upsets the harmony between two essential aspects of marriage: (i) communion of two persons alike in dignity and rights, and (ii) collaboration of two bodily persons complementary in capacities and functions. When the couple subject themselves to each other out of reverence for Christ, these two aspects are entirely harmonious.

a) **Marriage should be a communion of persons equal in dignity.** Although essentially different from any other human relationship, marriage is like friendship: the spouses enter it freely and as equals, and undertake to form an open-ended communion and to cooperate in mutually fulfilling activities. Each therefore is entitled to the other's respect, love, support, and availability for the interpersonal relationship. Pius XI teaches that the spouses' equality "must indeed be recognised in those rights which belong to the dignity of the human soul and which are proper to the marriage contract and inseparably bound up with wedlock. In such things undoubtedly both parties enjoy the same rights and are bound by the same obligations."[147] In this equality, conjugal rights are included, as St. Paul teaches: "For the wife does not have authority over her own body, but the husband does; likewise the husband does not have authority over his own body, but the wife does" (1 Cor 7.4). Moreover, consent to marriage includes a commitment to friendship, because the spouses should unselfishly will each other's personal good in every respect.

b) **Marriage unites a man and a woman precisely as such.** If two persons of different races become friends, that difference need not shape their relationship; eventually they may not even think about it. But two persons can become one flesh in marriage only because they are a male and a female who can join together as a single principle of reproduction. In this relationship, then, the biological realities, including the fact that only the wife can bear and nurse babies, belong not only to the order of nature but to the moral order, for they are part of the capacity of human persons to act for and share in a human good. This good, the marital union itself, is most fully realized in the emergence of children. Therefore, the biologically necessary differentiation of roles in bearing and caring for children serves the good of marriage. Moreover, the biological differences between woman and man lead to differences in other characteristics, which, though often only a matter of degree, are important. Hence, spouses' complementary sexuality does shape their relationship.[148]

147. Pius XI, *Casti connubii, AAS* 22 (1930) 568, *PE,* 208.76. This equality of rights is articulated in Church law; *CIC,* c. 1135, declares: "Each of the spouses has equal obligations and rights to those things which pertain to the partnership of conjugal life" (cf. c. 1111 of the 1917 code).

148. John Paul II, General Audience (18 May 1983), 2, *Inseg.* 6.1 (1983) 1262, *OR,* 23 May 1983, 3, commenting on Gal 3.28, explains: "Obviously Paul does not deny the existence of differences among people. What he wishes to say is that these differences can no longer be a motive for division, because Christ has unified all in his person." Alice S. Rossi, "A Biosocial

c) **The spouses' equality and differences can be harmonized.** If marriage is considered *instrumental* to procreation, as much Catholic theology considered it until recently, the functional difference between the spouses seems more important than their mutual communion, which presupposes their equal personal dignity. On the other hand, if marriage is considered a merely consensual relationship similar to other friendships, as it is by many feminists, the spouses' equality seems more important than their complementarity, and may even seem to require that their functional differences be minimized as much as possible. Traditional theology does more justice to equal personal dignity than feminism does to complementarity, but both views subordinate one aspect of marriage to the other.

However, if marriage is understood as Vatican II and John Paul II understand it, it is seen to be a unique kind of communion and form of cooperation. The spouses establish their marriage by mutual, free consent, but in consummating it they truly become one flesh, that is, they form as it were one new person, and so they are perfected in their communion as they cooperate in the service of new life. The two aspects of marriage, distinguished at the beginning of this section, are harmonized, for the spouses' complementarity as coprinciples in procreation is part of their very being as two persons joined in one flesh.

4. Both Spouses Should Maintain and Perfect Their Marital Love

Although the two aspects of marriage are inseparable, each entails specific responsibilities. Insofar as marriage is a communion of persons equal in dignity and rights, both spouses have exactly the same responsibilities: to maintain and increase unselfish love. Neither should use the other as a mere means to selfish ends, and each should faithfully serve the common good even when the other fails to do so.

a) **The will to be married to this person is central to marital love.** Someone whose expectations in making a choice are disappointed usually does nothing wrong in wishing he or she had not made it. But the choices a couple make in consenting to marriage are different, because, once they have consummated their union, its reality no longer depends on their wills and acts. Since only death can part them, the couple should conform their wills to the reality of their union, and love each other unwaveringly. Although conjugal love has other aspects, it is primarily the couple's intention in marrying to share together in the good of

---

Perspective on Parenting," *Daedalus* 106 (Spring 1977): 2, points out "a tendency in much contemporary thinking to confuse equality with identity and diversity with inequality. But where age and sex are concerned, diversity is a biological fact, while equality is a political, ethical, and social precept [note omitted]. Marxist theory notwithstanding, there is no rule of nature or of social organization that says men and women have to be the same or do the same things in order to be socially, economically, and politically equal. . . . [T]he particular version of egalitarianism underlying current sociological research on, and advocacy of, 'variant' marriage and family forms is inadequate and misleading because it neglects some fundamental human characteristics rooted in our biological heritage." For a survey of data regarding men's and women's differences: Clark, *Man and Woman in Christ,* 371–465. Also worth critical study: Walter J. Ong, *Fighting for Life: Contest, Sexuality, and Consciousness* (Ithaca, N.Y.: Cornell University Press, 1981), 51–115; Jean Vanier, *Man and Woman He Made Them* (Mahwah, N.J.: Paulist Press, 1984), 49–55.

marriage. The first responsibility of both spouses, therefore, is to maintain their will to be married to each other.

Directly contrary to that will is any wish not to be married or not to be married to this person. Even though such wishes come spontaneously to mind when marital disappointments and difficulties occur, spouses should recognize them as the primary temptation against conjugal love, and reject them as bad thoughts (see *CMP*, 15.E–F).

Intentionally to entertain such thoughts seems to be a grave matter. For, although classical moralists failed to identify this kind of sin, it is clear that any married person's wish not to be married or not to be married to his or her spouse seriously damages marital love. In fact, it is likely to lead to adultery and is certainly the first step in any attempt to dissolve a marriage by divorce. Like any other sin, of course, this one is not mortal unless, aware of a grave obligation *not* to entertain such wishes, one nevertheless chooses to do so; but even if the sin is only venial, it paves the way for infidelity and divorce.

b) **Marital love requires the will to be friends, not just partners.** Business partners cooperate in pursuing at least one common good: the profits they hope to divide. They need be interested in one another only to the extent necessary to collaborate in their limited enterprise; they should will to be fair to one another, but their obligations extend no further. By contrast, the common good of friends is their friendship itself; each finds personal fulfillment in being a friend and having a friend. Interested in one another as complete persons, they desire their mutual perfection in all the goods of both. Their mutual self-giving must go beyond fairness, to a generosity that does not count costs and benefits (see 6.C.2.c–d).

The good of marriage is the spouses' very communion. Husband and wife should seek their personal fulfillment in being good spouses and parents. They should desire each other's complete good. Like other friends, spouses should measure their responsibilities to their common life, not by requirements of fairness, but by their capacity to benefit each other. So, they should not reduce their communion to mere partnership by demanding rights or by withholding marital affection and service in order to enforce claims. Nor should they try to divide their responsibilities according to a strict formula. Rather, they should lighten their burdens by sharing them as fully as possible, gaining satisfaction in fulfilling them skillfully, and using generosity to express love.

c) **Spouses should strengthen marital love by nurturing affection.** Husband and wife can strengthen their mutual good will by exercising it in ways which intensify the corresponding emotion: conjugal affection. They can do this not only by marital intercourse and the sexual play leading to it but by many light expressions of erotic affection, and also by doing what they can to retain their sexual appeal for each other. Moreover, they should continually engage in the acts appropriate in any friendship: conversation to share concerns and feelings, gift giving, reminiscing and planning, celebrating together, and so on.[149]

---

149. See Paul M. Conner, O.P., *Married in Friendship* (London: Sheed and Ward, 1987), 101–69, for a helpful reflection on marital friendship and its cultivation.

To claim the right to marital intercourse while neglecting other expressions of affection tends to damage rather than strengthen conjugal love. Spouses who fail to listen sympathetically and help each other whenever possible do not meet essential requirements of friendship. Friends do not criticize each other harshly, and never do so in others' presence; neither should spouses. Also, like good friends, spouses should notice each others' good points, compliment each other, express gratitude, and support good resolutions and efforts at self-improvement.

Taking each other for granted or neglecting the things which contribute to mutual personal attractiveness tends to weaken affection. Therefore, with due regard to the requirements of modesty and other circumstances, spouses should show each other their love regularly in different ways, and do the other things in their power to nurture affection and maintain their mutual attractiveness.

No single act of this kind is essential, and so it is only light matter to be negligent at times about this responsibility; but it would be a more serious matter to choose, as some spouses do when quarreling, to express hostility either by withholding manifestations of affection or by purposely making themselves unattractive. Of course, such a choice sometimes is not a mortal sin inasmuch as sufficient reflection is lacking.

d) Spouses should not intentionally hurt or slight each other. Anger and hatred tempt people intentionally to hurt or slight one another. The more intimate and important the relationship, the more serious it is to give in to such a temptation. Between spouses, any intentional hurt or slight (as distinct from a spontaneous expression of negative feelings) not only harms affection but manifests ill will at odds with conjugal friendship. If such behavior is fully deliberate, which it often is not, the harm to marital communion is likely to be significant, and so any intentional hurt or slight between spouses is a grave matter. When committed by spouses who are parents, sins of this kind almost always also harm their child or children in various ways, and this side effect adds to their seriousness.

Even if not fully deliberate, intentional hurts and slights can seriously wound conjugal love, and so it is very important not only to avoid mortal sin in this matter but to reflect and choose to avoid the sin entirely. It does not follow that spouses should hide their anger and hostile feelings toward each other. While not acting on such feelings, they often do well to articulate them, for example, by saying in a restrained voice: "I am feeling irritable today and finding it hard to keep my temper" or "When you do that in a situation of such and such a kind, it really hurts me, and I cannot help feeling angry." Expressing feelings in this way sometimes fulfills the responsibility to admonish (see 4.E.1), and it also pertains to the openness and sharing which should characterize any friendship.

Spouses also should avoid fueling each other's anger. A mild and soothing answer, a joke, or an affectionate word or gesture often can forestall a quarrel. When a quarrel does break out, both spouses should try to stop acting on their hostility, if necessary by remaining silent or taking a walk until feelings subside. It never helps to bring up past mistakes and faults or to widen the conflict by expressing animosities toward in-laws. If a quarrel concerns a real issue, its discussion should be postponed to a definite time but not evaded. After a quarrel, both spouses should admit their faults, ask pardon, forgive each other, put the hurt behind them, and try to be gentle and considerate. (These matters will be treated more fully in H.1.)

e) **If spouses do not serve love, their relationship degenerates.** If spouses do not do what they should to foster love, their motivation for fulfilling their roles as husband and wife inevitably changes. Acting to get what he or she can out of the relationship, each sees that expected benefit, not as part of the common good of the marriage, but as part of his or her good as a separate individual. No longer intending the common good of marriage but still desiring each other's cooperation, the spouses are reduced to insincere appeals to love or to straightforward bargaining for the services each desires. Plainly, insofar as they are insincere, they manipulate each other. But even when bargaining honestly, they fall into a practice of mutual manipulation, insofar as each appeals to the other's selfishness and makes clear the price to be exacted if he or she fails to cooperate. Fair-minded spouses may try to carry on their relationship as if it were a business partnership, but since the goods pertaining to marriage cannot be divided and enjoyed by each individually, both inevitably feel cheated.

While both spouses can engage in manipulation, rewarding and punishing each other, they do so in different ways, each perverting his or her distinctive marital role. For example, the wife may withhold marital intercourse or refuse to cook dinner; the husband may resort to physical abuse or spend his evenings away from home. For sheer survival, however, wives generally depend more on their husbands' performance and forbearance than vice versa, and this difference is accentuated when the wife is pregnant or nurturing small children. Therefore, as sin drives out love, a wife all too often learns by experience what is meant by the scriptural passage which John Paul II cites in explaining male domination: "Your desire shall be for your husband, and he shall rule over you" (Gn 3.16).[150]

f) **Intentional manipulation of one's spouse can never serve love.** Spouses engage in intentional manipulation when they try to motivate each other by appealing to selfishness instead of to the common good of marriage. In many cases, manipulation is mutually selfish, but sometimes one spouse, having the common good more at heart, might be tempted to use manipulation to compel the other to serve it. For example, a wife whose husband is self-absorbed and uninterested in conversing about matters of common concern might try to compel him to be more forthcoming by having dinner alone before he arrives home, and leaving him to eat by himself, so that he will experience something of the loneliness she feels. But her manipulative tactic is not likely to work, for what is defective is her husband's love, and love cannot be elicited by such tactics. If she manages to make her husband feel lonely, he also will feel resentful, with the bad result that, even if he should decide to humor his wife by talking with her during dinner, his will toward genuine communion will not have increased.

g) **Behavior which seems manipulative may not really be so.** Not all behavior which could be manipulative need be chosen with a manipulative intent. Very often, what is required by marital and family responsibilities also is morally obligatory

---

150. See John Paul II, *Mulieris dignitatem,* 10, *AAS* 80 (1988) 1674–77, *OR,* 3 Oct. 1988, 5.

on other grounds. For example, an alcoholic should do what is necessary to overcome his or her addiction, not only because it is inconsistent with being a good spouse and parent but also because it violates other goods, such as health. Perhaps a man no longer cares about his wife and their children, but still cares about his own health. Like any true friend, the alcoholic's wife also will be concerned about the self-destructiveness of his habit. Therefore, while she appeals to his self-interest in appealing to this motive, she is not being manipulative, since this element of his self-interest also is morally obligatory for him, and in no way at odds with marital and parental love.

Moreover, if one spouse is not loving and the marital good is damaged, the other should try to serve it faithfully as well as possible under the circumstances. That service often will impact adversely on the spouse who is at fault, with the good result that he or she may realize how much is at stake and be moved to repent. For example, a wife whose alcoholic husband abuses her and the children might lock him out of the house, not only to protect herself and the children, but to stop him from so grossly violating his marital and familial responsibilities, and to prevent the further erosion of her own affection toward him. Though foreseeing that he will be embarrassed and inconvenienced, she need not intend to motivate him merely by appealing to his self-concern. Rather, she can hope he will realize that her locking him out, precisely because she is a good wife and mother, will deprive him of benefits he would fully enjoy if he were a good husband and father.

In general, a loving but firm effort by one spouse to serve the common good of marriage and family in ways which have only an incidental negative impact on the other is not manipulative. Far from being wrong, such an effort often is obligatory, and it also can be constructive, by motivating the spouse who is at fault to repent. This result can be foreseen, even hoped for, without manipulative intent, as a desirable side effect.

5. Spouses Should Be Companions in the Whole of Life

Besides the mutual responsibilities pertaining to marriage as a consensual communion of persons—a special kind of friendship—the spouses also have mutual responsibilities related to their cooperation in the specific good of marriage as a one-flesh communion open to new life. To the extent this good requires, a married couple should live together and be companions in the whole of life.[151] Still, not all interests and responsibilities of married persons pertain to marriage, so each spouse can have other responsibilities which legitimately limit the extent of marital cooperation.

a) Spouses should live together in order to realize the marital good. Friends need not, and ordinarily do not, live together; to carry on their friendship, they need only communicate from time to time. By contrast, in order to realize the marital good, which is the union of two in one flesh, a married couple need a home in which to live together. They should work together to meet this need, because the home embodies marital commitment and gives it cultural expression. Husband and wife

---

151. *CIC*, c. 1055, §1, indicates this duty: "The matrimonial covenant, by which a man and a woman establish between themselves a partnership *of the whole of life* . . ." (emphasis added).

also should be available to each other more or less continually, not only for marital intercourse, but to care for each other and maintain their relationship by regular communication.[152] Moreover, for full and effective cooperation in raising children, a common household is essential.

Concretely, what each married couple must do to fulfill this norm will vary. Different couples, without in any way violating the good of marriage, can realize it in somewhat different ways and to somewhat different degrees. A couple with small children should, if possible, spend some time at home together with them virtually every day, while childless couples and those whose children are grown could discern that they are called to work in different cities. Accepting this vocational requirement, they could agree to establish two residences, and actually live together only when their other responsibilities permitted.

Plainly, if either spouse refuses without adequate reason to share a common household with the other, he or she gravely violates this responsibility. But spouses can fall short of fulfilling it perfectly in many less serious ways. For example, if a husband unnecessarily fails to come home in time for dinner, the couple's common life suffers to the extent they do not share that meal together. Again, a childless couple violate this norm if they live in the same apartment and sleep in the same bed but do little else together, because they are preoccupied with their separate jobs and other activities. In such a case, if neither raises any objection, their failure to share more fully in a common life is not in itself grave matter; but if it continues for long, it can pose a serious threat to their marriage, and accepting that threat will be a grave matter.

b) The norm that the couple should live together admits exceptions. Like any affirmative responsibility, the duty of spouses to live together is limited by their other responsibilities. Sometimes a husband can fulfill his duty to provide for his family only by work which requires him to spend most of his time far from home. Sometimes a spouse's health or responsibilities toward parents impose a temporary separation. Again, civic obligations, such as the duty of military service, can take precedence over the responsibility to live together.

Even when required and fully justified by other responsibilities, any prolonged separation is detrimental to a couple's cooperation, especially in caring for children, and can threaten the marriage itself. So, unless their other responsibilities require them to accept a prolonged separation, couples should keep separations brief (see 1 Cor 7.5). At such times they should maintain regular communication and make special efforts to remedy the bad effects of separation when they can be together again.

If either spouse intentionally does grave harm to the other or otherwise gravely damages the marital good, a temporary or permanent separation may be justified or even morally required. Cases of this kind will be treated below (in H.2).

c) A married couple need not share all commitments and projects. Spouses must harmonize their other vocational commitments with marriage and parent-

---

152. *CIC*, c. 1151, prescribes: "Spouses have the duty and the right to preserve conjugal living unless a legitimate cause excuses them."

hood; thus, no married person is truly called to anything which would displace marriage and regularly render it impossible to fulfill its responsibilities. However, the faithful fulfillment of the marital commitment and its ensuing responsibilities need not exhaust a married person's gifts and resources. The personal vocation of someone who is married can include elements neither included in nor consequent upon his or her marriage and family life.

Thus, one spouse sometimes can rightly make a commitment which the other does not share, implement that commitment with appropriate projects, and so carry on activities outside the cooperation of the common life of marriage and family. Still, since married persons should be companions in the whole of their lives, each spouse should take an interest in all of the other's activities, will the other's good even in those things that fall outside their cooperation, and be supportive in such matters when possible. Moreover, in carrying out commitments not shared by their spouses, married persons should shape their activities so that they will not disrupt marital and familial cooperation.

Consequently, neither spouse should resist the other's desire to develop legitimate interests compatible with the good of marriage (including the well-being of any children). Conversely, neither may pursue personal fulfillment in activities in any way incompatible with that good.

d) A couple may agree to limit their marital cooperation. Some individual interests and activities of married persons need not conflict in any way with their responsibilities as spouses and parents. Within wide bounds, both spouses can rightly engage in personal prayer and devotions, keep in touch with personal friends, do their own exercises, read in areas of their own interests, and so on. Each should respect the other's freedom in regard to such personal activities, provided they are good in themselves and in no way interfere with the fulfillment of marital and familial roles. So, for example, a wife who insisted that her husband say the rosary with her although he preferred to pray the liturgy of the hours would be unjust in imposing her devotional preference on him. The same must be said of a domineering husband who forbids his wife to carry on a wholesome friendship which she is careful to keep from infringing on her responsibilities to him and the children. On the same basis, if a couple are childless or their children are grown and the wife wishes to engage in work outside the home, her husband has no right to insist she not do so in order that he can be their sole provider.

In other cases, individual interests and activities could conflict with a married person's responsibilities as spouse or parent. Usually, the best course is to forestall the conflict, either by giving up the troublesome interests and activities or by postponing marriage, or even entirely forgoing it. But in some cases, a couple can cooperate to prevent the conflict, and they may undertake by mutual agreement to do so. For example, a woman might hesitate to accept a proposal of marriage because she wishes to care for her aged parents, who otherwise would be forced to live in a nursing home. Her commitment to her parents could seriously limit her ability to cooperate in marital and familial activities. However, the couple can marry, with the understanding and agreement that she will care for her parents as long as necessary, and that her commitment to do so will limit their marital life and activities, even to the extent of limiting marital intercourse to delay having children. In general, a couple can agree, whether before marriage or later, to limit cooperation in common activities in order to allow for other elements of each spouse's personal vocation, provided neither wills anything inconsistent with the good of marriage.

e) **Limits to marital cooperation often violate the good of marriage.** Even though couples sometimes can rightly agree to limit marital cooperation, individual spouses and even couples often wrongly limit it and so violate the good of marriage. A limitation that could be rightly established only by mutual consent may not be unilaterally imposed. For example, a married woman whose work requires her to be away from home for weeks at a time wrongly pursues her professional career without her husband's consent. Again, couples who mutually agree to limit marital cooperation, not so that they can fulfill other elements of their vocations, but simply to satisfy selfish desires, are not committed to marriage as they should be. For example, a couple who marry but avoid pregnancy so that both can work until they have many nonessential things plainly prefer having things to fulfilling their marital communion by procreating and raising children.

Even spouses who rightly agree to limit marital cooperation should be prepared to set aside the agreed-upon limits if they would prevent them from fulfilling some pressing responsibility as spouses or parents. For example, the couple who marry with the understanding that the wife will take care of her aged parents should not rule out the possibility that her marital responsibilities might prevent this, for instance, if her husband should become ill, so that she would have to work full time to support them. Again, a couple who agree to put off having children should take into account the possibility of unplanned pregnancies and be ready to accept the responsibilities of parenthood. If in such cases married persons fail to set aside other things in order to fulfill their duties as spouses or parents, they violate the good of marriage.

6. Spouses Should Accept Their Sexually Differentiated Roles

By differentiating the sexes, God plainly intends to differentiate the spouses' roles; and because this natural differentiation serves the good of marriage and family, it should be endorsed willingly, not resisted and limited as much as possible. Still, how the two roles are differentiated can vary to some extent, and spouses should not too rigidly divide the activities pertaining to each role.[153]

a) **Being male and female differentiates the spouses' responsibilities.** If the spouses do not fulfill their respective roles, children cannot be born, survive, and

---

153. In a study in social psychology, Robert S. Weiss, *Staying the Course: The Emotional and Social Lives of Men Who Do Well at Work* (New York: Free Press, 1990), 121–22, explains "the traditional principles of the marital division of labor," which have been accompanied by "the principle of helping out"—that either spouse helps the other insofar as possible whenever necessary. He argues (262–64) that the traditional distinction of roles remains sound and workable, while attempts to attain fairness by equalizing the spouses' tasks are unworkable and psychologically harmful. He concludes (264): "Best is if instead of trying to achieve equity each partner simply pitches in wholeheartedly, doing what needs doing. With this commitment the traditional division of labor, liberally modified by the principle of helping out, and adapted to the tastes and skills of the husband and the wife, can be satisfactory to both partners."

be adequately raised. Only the wife can bear and nurse children, and while engaged in that process she inevitably becomes both vulnerable and dependent. The husband, most likely larger and more muscular, and little affected by the reproductive process, can move about comparatively freely, and is in a position to protect and provide for his wife and children. Therefore, the good of marriage requires that each spouse accept his or her role and fulfill its responsibilities.[154] Thus, concerning the raising of children, Vatican II teaches:

> The active presence of the father is highly beneficial to their formation. The children, especially the younger among them, need the care of their mother at home. This domestic role of hers must be safely preserved, though the legitimate social progress of women should not be underrated on that account. (GS 52)

Like any other moral requirement, this one, though rooted in biological necessities, can be violated; for example, women have abortions, and men abandon their families.

If the wife-mother does accept her role and fulfill it consistently, she nurtures her children for many years. In doing this, she must accept each child as he or she is, support her children's gradual development, and work along with the natural forces that make for their healthy growth. Not only physiologically but psychologically, women naturally are adapted to this nurturing role (see 7.A.6.b). In accepting and carrying it out, the wife-mother shapes her own personality and character so that she continues to treat her children in a characteristically motherly way even when they are grown. Her motherliness also affects her other interpersonal relationships, not least that with her husband.

b) Jewish and Christian faith has shaped the paternal role. Biologically, it is possible for primate males, including men, to impregnate females but do little or nothing to protect and care for them and their offspring.[155] Indeed, in some societies and cultures, fathers have been minimally involved in family life or else involved in so domineering a way that women and children were regarded as property, to be used, abused, and even killed at the whim of the husband and father.[156]

The Old Testament presents a distinctive understanding of God as a Father whose chief characteristics are faithfulness and loving-kindness, and this Father became the model for Jewish and Christian fatherhood. Hence, the Jewish or

---

154. Alice Schlegel, *Sexual Stratification: A Cross-Cultural View* (New York: Columbia University Press, 1977), 36, concludes on the basis of anthropological studies: "Women's role as childbearer has no alternative in the foreseeable future. In women's understandable haste to move into the larger world, it is tempting to devalue this role. If we do this, we do ourselves, as individuals and as a society, the greatest disservice. The personal gratifications of parenthood, and the well-being of children, depend upon some sense of satisfaction with nurturant roles. The problem we face is to create social arrangements that allow for both care of children and greater freedom for mothers from childbearing responsibilities." The whole chapter (1–40), outlining a theory of sexual stratification, repays careful reading.

155. Peter J. Wilson, *Man, the Promising Primate: The Conditions of Human Evolution* (New Haven: Yale University Press, 1980), 71, says: "Simply stated, an adult female will be naturally transformed into a social mother when she bears a child, but there is no corresponding natural transformation for a male."

156. See Leo XIII, *Arcanum, ASS* 12 (1879) 387–88 and 390, *PE,* 81.6–7 and 14.

Christian father is expected to be involved in his family, to be present to protect and care for his wife and children, and to carry out his responsibilities faithfully. He also is expected to respect the personal dignity of other family members, to treat them not only firmly but gently, and to subordinate his individual interests to the good of the family as a whole.[157]

If the husband-father fulfills his role, he deals with the wider world outside the home in order to obtain the necessities of life and defend his family against threats to its security. In doing this, he must set and pursue goals, make and execute plans, and strive to meet standards for success. Like his wife, the husband also is naturally adapted for his role, and its fulfillment shapes his personality and character. In fathering his children, he communicates knowledge and techniques they need in order to deal with the wider world, sets standards for them, and criticizes their performances.[158] His fatherliness also affects his other relationships, including that with his wife.

   c) **Fatherliness and motherliness are not mutually exclusive.** Although the two complementary roles are sharply differentiated at their biological roots, this is not the case with the personality and character traits pertaining to each. Fatherliness and motherliness are not contraries, completely exclusive of each other; rather, they more or less overlap in each and every parent.

   Still, the development of children not only calls for the fulfillment of both roles but for their differentiation. Children need both to be accepted and nurtured, and to be challenged and held to standards, and in any given instance these two activities are in tension. Both parents can and should share to some extent in doing both things, but neither can do both fully at the same time. Therefore, the spouses must accept different responsibilities and carry them out consistently for the good of their children.

   Moreover, childless couples can live a real married life, rather than merely sharing life as friends, only by developing their specific masculine and feminine potential and acting toward each other in sexually differentiated and complementary ways.

   d) **Not all social embodiments of sexual-role differentiation are bad.** Obviously, spouses often reject the responsibilities proper to their roles or fail to carry them out. Since the biology of the reproductive process allows men more opportunities to abuse their role, husbands and fathers often lead the way in irresponsibility by being unfaithful, employing physical violence, exacting services and privileges by means of implicit or explicit threats, and deserting. Male domination of women has shaped some aspects of every culture and every society's institutions. Abuses

---

   157. John W. Miller, *Biblical Faith and Fathering: Why We Call God "Father"* (Mahwah, N.J.: Paulist Press, 1989), shows that the Jewish and Christian conception of fatherhood is a cultural achievement deeply rooted in divine revelation and argues cogently that Christians should strive to protect and promote the father-involved family. Cf. Christopher Dawson, "The Patriarchal Family in History," in *The Dynamics of World History*, ed. John J. Mulloy (New York: Sheed and Ward, 1956), 156–66.
   158. See Basil Cole, O.P., "Réflexions pour une spiritualité masculine," trans. Guy Bedouelle, O.P., *Sources* (Fribourg) 12 (Mar.–Apr. 1987), 49–55.

of the husband-father role, as well as the corresponding embodiments of the perversion of the wife-mother role, demand reform.

Still, it is a mistake to try to do away with everything embodying the two roles' differentiation.[159] Their conscientious fulfillment by both spouses is essential to actualizing the great human good of familial communion. Lacking support from institutions in fulfilling their complementary roles, spouses are unlikely to fulfill them. Moreover, whether or not institutions are supportive, spouses inevitably shape culture in accord with the differentiation of their roles when they fulfill them properly. Therefore, while reform of sexually differentiated roles should be promoted, attempts to minimize these roles should be resisted.

e) Excessive differentiation of roles should be avoided. Exaggerating the sexual differentiation of roles, beyond what is required by the good of marital and familial communion, can have adverse effects on the realization of other goods capable of contributing to the well-rounded fulfillment of the spouses, whose whole being is not absorbed in marriage and family life. Sometimes, for example, the education of girls has been so completely ordered to their role as wives and mothers that they have been denied education and cultural benefits equal to those afforded boys. That injustice should be rectified (see GS 29).

Excessive specialization is detrimental even to marital and family life. The contingencies of life—sickness, unavoidable absence of one spouse, unemployment, death—make it impossible for the spouses always to fulfill their different responsibilities; and even when both are present and functioning well, they often need each other's help. So, each should be able when necessary to carry out the most urgent elements of the other's role. For example, when a wife-mother is ill, the husband-father should be able to care for her and the children, and when a husband dies, his wife should be able to make urgent decisions about the family's financial affairs.

7. The Husband-Father Has a Special Role in Decision Making

Human action presupposes decision. Family life involves cooperative action, and so it requires unified decisions. To make decisions for any group is to function as the authority in that group. In some respects and in many decisions, the differences between the spouses' roles should not affect the working of authority in the family, and each family member has authority in his or her proper sphere. But in certain cases, the husband-father should make a decision, and his wife and children should obey. In this exercise of authority, the husband-father always should subordinate his individual interests to the family's common good. For, as has been explained (in 7.E.2), genuine authority is not domination, which is incompatible with cooperation, but is a necessary principle of cooperation and thus a role of service to the community.

a) All family members should contribute to deliberation. Good decision making presupposes careful deliberation: thinking of possible courses of action and

159. For example, Vatican II teaches that parents and teachers "in every phase of education should give due consideration to the difference in sex and the special role divine providence assigns each sex in the family and society" (GE 8); see also DS 3698/2215.

examining their potential advantages and disadvantages. Anyone who will be affected by an action, and especially anyone who will cooperate in it, is likely to have some information to contribute to this examination. Thus, wide participation in deliberation is desirable.

The spouses should communicate as fully as possible regarding actions affecting the family's common good, so that they will take adequate account of each other's thoughts and feelings. Children also should contribute to deliberation insofar as they are able. If decisions affecting the common good of the family are made without taking into account every member's ideas and wishes, good options sometimes will be overlooked, and some pros and cons of options under consideration will be ignored. Moreover, if each member's right to participate in deliberation is not respected, decisions will not be well understood and enthusiastically carried out.

b) **Family members should have authority in their proper spheres.** Each spouse has the primary and proper responsibility for a substantial part of the action required to serve and realize the family's common good. Each is better able to make decisions within his or her proper sphere, and so should make them, while the other should obediently cooperate in carrying them out. The Christian tradition recognizes this distribution of authority in the family: married women are to be "good managers of the household" (Ti 2.5; cf. 1 Tm 5.14). Children, especially in a large family, also have their own responsibilities and spheres of activity, in which they should make decisions; they will not mature toward adult responsibility unless their parents respect and cooperate with the decisions that are theirs to make.

c) **Sometimes authority in the family is exercised by consensus.** Some matters affecting the family's common good require cooperation transcending the various spheres of activity. Such matters can be major (for example, moving a long distance) or minor (going on a picnic). Decisions on such matters not only affect the whole family but require the exercise of authority for the family as a whole. In such cases, common deliberation is especially appropriate.

Sometimes deliberation leads to general agreement, resulting in many cases from a recognition by one of the spouses that the other is better equipped to make a particular decision, so that his or her proposal becomes the consensus upon which the whole family can undertake to act. That decision is the exercise of the authority of the family as a whole. Each member should obey, that is, faithfully carry out his or her part in what the family has undertaken.

d) **Sometimes one person must exercise authority for the family.** Consensus does not always emerge. Sometimes an emergency calls for quick action, and there is little or no time for deliberation and the development of consensus. Or, faced with two or more morally acceptable alternatives, different family members lean toward different decisions, and neither spouse recognizes special competence in the other to make the decision. Unless a single decision is made for the family as whole, however, the members will be unable to cooperate, and the elements of the common good which are at stake will not be realized or protected.

The family's good requires that authority be exercised in emergencies and in other cases when consensus does not emerge. But even though the model of democratic politics might seem to suggest that then the morally correct solution is majority rule, in families that will not work. For the children's competence to make decisions affecting the family's common good cannot reasonably be equated with that of the parents; and if voting is limited to the spouses and they do not agree, the result obviously will be an impasse.

e) In such cases, the husband-father ordinarily should decide. The authority of the husband-father in precisely such cases is the irreducible core of the traditional Christian teaching which Pius XI summarizes as "the primacy of the husband with regard to the wife and children, the ready subjection of the wife and her willing obedience" (see 2.b, above).

What has already been explained about the differentiation of the spouses' roles and the problem of authority in the family provides a basis for understanding the reasonableness of that teaching. The spouses' complementary roles are not limited to their biological bases, since the couple share in the marital good as complete persons, male and female. Authority is not domination but decision making, in which both spouses share, and its exercise almost always involves common deliberation and often is accomplished by consensus. Even when there is no consensus, if leadership is both exercised and followed lovingly, everything proceeds so smoothly that family members are hardly conscious of exercising authority and practicing obedience. Still, authority sometimes must be exercised by one spouse or the other, and the differences between their complementary roles are relevant for determining which it should be.

That plainly is so in emergencies. The identity of the leader who will exercise authority must be clear to everyone when an emergency arises. Authority in family emergencies calling for cooperation which transcends the members' distinct spheres of activity must therefore pertain to the status of one of the family members. Now, such family emergencies ordinarily require quick action by the husband-father, and several of his attributes can be crucial: his size, strength, and aggressiveness, and, very often, his experience in dealing with the world outside the family and his technical skill in selecting means and ordering them to goals. Thus, when emergencies arise requiring the cooperation of both spouses (and perhaps the children as well), very often the husband-father is best equipped to make decisions and take the leading role in carrying them out. Consequently, he should be recognized as the authority in such situations.

Because authority in family emergency situations should pertain to the status of the husband-father, it is appropriate that he also exercise authority for the family as a whole in the other cases that require it—where cooperation is needed transcending the family members' distinct spheres of activity, but no consensus emerges and neither spouse recognizes the other as better equipped to make the decision. For the husband-father's status as authority in emergency situations will shape habitual patterns of family cooperation, and that cooperation will proceed more efficiently in both kinds of cases if habitual patterns are accepted and followed. Also, in the concrete, emergency situations are not always clearly distinguished from others, and a decision about any one situation is likely to affect, and so require coordination with, what is to be done in other situations.

f) The proper exercise of authority is a service to the family. If a husband-father rightly exercises authority for the family as a whole and fulfills his other responsibilities as the family's leader, he does not dominate his wife and children. Rather, taking into account their ideas, desires, and feelings, he serves the family's common good to everyone's benefit. Indeed, for his own self-fulfillment as head of the family, he must subordinate his other individual interests, since he does well as the family's leader only if the whole family flourishes.

For example, a man is offered a promotion and increase in salary if he moves to another city, but judges that his present position is adequate to provide for his family and that the move would be detrimental to them. The family's common good will be better served if he refuses the offer, and so, if he rightly uses his authority as the head of the family, he will refuse, even though his individual interests, apart from his role as husband and father, would lead him to accept it.

Many men make such unselfish decisions precisely because their love for their families includes their commitment to fulfill the responsibilities of leadership. But men have more opportunities than women to act irresponsibly, and so, in the fallen human condition, they are more often tempted to be irresponsible, to exploit and dominate. Far from mitigating this situation, setting aside the husband-father's rightful headship in the family is likely to exacerbate it.

g) The authority of the husband-father is limited in various ways. Authority in the family is limited in the same ways as authority is in general (see 7.E.3–4). A decision of the husband-father that the family will do something wrong in itself has no authority and should not be obeyed. Moreover, even sound policies that he sets for the family can lead to conflicts of duties or otherwise call for exceptions when unexpected conditions arise.

Most important, as any authority's range is determined by the common good it serves, so authority in the family extends only to decisions about action bearing on the good of marital and familial communion. Neither spouse is subject to the other's authority in matters unrelated to that common good. If, then, there is a conflict of interests between the spouses in such a matter and they fail to reach a consensus, the decision falls outside the husband's authority. For example, if a childless couple, both pursuing careers, face a decision between living in two places, both equally suited to their common life but each advantageous to the professional interests of only one of them, neither has the authority to decide. They can make the necessary decision by using any fair and mutually agreeable method, for example, flipping a coin.

In some cases, the husband-father cannot fulfill his leadership role because he is absent, ill, or otherwise incapacitated. In other cases, he could fulfill his role but fails or even refuses to make needed decisions. The family's common good still requires that authority be exercised, and it usually falls to the wife-mother to do so.

h) Either spouse should be unselfish when the other is selfish. When the husband-father abuses his authority or the wife-mother wrongly refuses to submit to it, the other spouse should not respond by acting in a similarly selfish way. He or she instead should do faithfully what the common good, unbroken marital and familial communion, requires in that bad situation. For the common good of the spouses centers in the marital union itself, which they cannot dissolve but can only safeguard and share in more or less perfectly; also, if there are children, parental responsibilities are inescapable. Thus, when it best serves the common good, the more committed spouse should yield to the less responsible one. For example, if a husband-father decides for his own professional advancement to move his family to a distant city, though even he recognizes that this will be bad for the family as a whole, his wife and children should go along with him to avoid breaking up the family. Similarly, if a husband-father decides for the family's good to move to a distant city but his spouse refuses, though admitting that the move would be good for the family as a whole, he should stay with her, not move.

Question E: What Sexual Acts Are Appropriate for Christians?

Sexual act refers to any act whatsoever—whether thought, word, or deed—in which someone intends, either as an end in itself or as a means to some other end, to bring about or maintain sexual arousal and/or to cause incomplete or complete sexual satisfaction, whether in himself or herself, in another, or both.

Since sexual capacity enables human persons to participate in the good of marital communion, Christian married couples should engage in sexual acts which are conducive to that good and are otherwise reasonable, but should avoid all other sexual activity. If a sexual act is not marital, it violates the good of marriage, and so is not appropriate for any Christian.

All intentional sexual acts that violate the good of marriage—and this includes *all* intentional sexual acts of the unmarried—are grave matter. However, not all acts leading to sexual satisfaction are intentional. Moreover, not all sins which intentionally violate the marital good are mortal, since mortal sin requires not only grave matter but sufficient reflection and consent.

Chastity subordinates sexual desire and activity to love and reason, that is, to self-giving and the requirements of relevant intelligible human goods. Grace empowers every Christian to pursue chastity and attain it.

In this question, the norms of chastity will be articulated only insofar as they follow from the good of marriage itself. Some wrongful sexual acts, whether done by married couples or others, violate one or more goods in addition to the good of marital communion; for example, contraception always is a contralife act (see 8.E.2, above). Therefore, the treatment of such acts here should be studied in conjunction with their treatment in other chapters.[160]

---

160. For a more extensive treatment of some of the matters dealt with in this question, including a chapter on the biblical teaching on sex and critiques of opposed, contemporary views, see Ronald Lawler, O.F.M.Cap., Joseph M. Boyle, Jr., and William E. May, *Catholic Sexual Ethics: A Summary, Explanation, and Defense* (Huntington, Ind.: Our Sunday Visitor Publishing Division, 1985); William E. May and John F. Harvey, O.S.F.S., "On Understanding Human Sexuality: A Critique of the C.T.S.A. Study," *Communio* 4 (1977): 195–225. A brief, synthetic treatment of many of the ethical arguments developed in this question: John Finnis, "Personal Integrity, Sexual Morality and Responsible Parenthood," *Anthropos* (now *Anthropotes*) 1 (1985): 43–55; a valuable study from a different, but sound and complementary, theological perspective: Quay, *The Christian Meaning of Human Sexuality*.

1. Married Couples Should Engage in Chaste Marital Acts

Marital intercourse and sexual acts preparatory to it often are not only suitable but obligatory for married couples. But since even married couples can have various reasons for not engaging in sexual acts, the obligation is subject to exceptions. Moreover, not all sexual acts within marriage are conducive to the good of marriage, and only those fully integrated with commitment to this good are chaste. Hence, Christian married couples should not consider themselves entitled to any and every sexual activity which they find mutually agreeable, but should engage in chaste acts of marital intercourse.

a) **A married couple's sexual act can fail to be a marital act.** The first marital intercourse consummates the marriage by making the husband and wife actually to be one flesh. Subsequent acts of marital intercourse express and foster conjugal love:

> This love is uniquely expressed and perfected through the marital act. The actions within marriage by which the couple are united intimately and chastely are morally good and fitting. Expressed in a manner which is truly human, these actions signify and foster that mutual self-giving by which spouses enrich each other with joyful and grateful hearts. (GS 49)

Considering how marital intercourse expresses and fosters marital communion makes clear precisely what is required for a marital act.

Since the unselfish cooperation of a society's members for its common good is the mutual self-giving which expresses and fosters its unity, the sexual acts of a married couple express and foster their communion primarily because they contribute to the common good of marriage, which realizes their specific potentiality as husband and wife. But, as has been explained (in A.2), the organic complementarity of man and woman in respect to reproduction is the necessary condition for the very possibility of marriage, and the requirements of human parenting specify the characteristics of marriage as an open-ended community. Therefore, marital acts must realize both the spouses' open-ended community and their organic complementarity.

The married couple's open-ended community depends on their mutual consent, by which each spouse, in willing their common good, wills the other's good for his or her own sake. Genuine marital acts therefore must be performed willingly and lovingly. They cannot involve coercion of either party by the other or of both by a third party; nor can they involve one party's mere use of the other for selfish satisfaction or one's mere manipulation of the other to attain some extrinsic end.

At the same time, the couple's willing and loving behavior must constitute the cooperation appropriate to realize their organic complementarity in respect to reproduction. In most instances, of course, physiological conditions preclude conception. However, those conditions are not part of the human act of intercourse, for they are neither included in the couple's behavior nor subject to their choice. So, the appropriateness of their human act of sexual intercourse to realize their organic complementarity depends, not on its being able to cause conception, but only on its being the pattern of behavior which, in conjunction with other necessary conditions, would result in conception. In Church teaching, this relationship between marital intercourse and organic complementarity is expressed by saying that a true marital act is "of itself suited to procreating human life" or is "open to new life."[161]

Thus, a marital act expresses and fosters the couple's marital communion precisely because, when they willingly and lovingly cooperate with each other in an act of itself suited to procreating, their mutual self-giving actualizes their one-flesh unity. If one or both spouses engage in a sexual act which does not realize one-flesh unity in this way, that act is not marital.[162]

This point can be expressed in other terms. The marital act's character as willing and loving cooperation can be called its "unitive meaning," and its suitability for generation can be called its "procreative meaning." Using this terminology, the point is that the unitive meaning of marital intercourse includes its procreative meaning and is specified by it, just as the single good of marriage includes and is fulfilled by having and raising children.[163] Thus, because the marital act's procreative meaning is part of its unitive meaning, the two meanings are inseparable, for a whole cannot be without its parts.

Since, as has been explained, the definition of the marital act follows from what marriage is, and the part-whole relationship between the marital act's two meanings is a necessary implication of its definition, that relationship is determined by the features of human beings which determine what marriage is: the complementary capacities of male and female persons, the natural inclination of men and women to realize those capacities, and the principle of practical reason directing them to

161. See Paul VI, *Humanae vitae,* 11, *AAS* 60 (1968) 488, *PE,* 277.11 ("ad vitam humanam procreandam per se destinatus permaneat," translated "must of necessity retain its intrinsic relationship to the procreation of human life"); and John Paul II, *Familiaris consortio,* 29, *AAS* 74 (1982) 115, *OR,* 21–28 Dec. 1981, 6, following proposition 22 of the 1980 session of the Synod of Bishops (*"apertus ad novam vitam,"* translated "open to new life"). Also see: Karol Wojtyla, "La visione antropologica della 'Humanae vitae'," *Lateranum* 44 (1978): 125–45.

162. Moreover, when husband and wife cooperate in a sexual act which is not a marital act, what they do cannot be an act of conjugal love, that is, the reciprocal self-giving which brings about one-flesh unity. So, their action must have other motives, which, even if they include mutual affectionate feelings, are unintegrated with conjugal love and more or less at odds with it. Thus, John Paul II, *Familiaris consortio,* 32, *AAS* 74 (1982) 119, *OR,* 21–28 Dec. 1981, 7, teaches that "the innate language that expresses the total reciprocal self-giving of husband and wife is overlaid, through contraception, by an objectively contradictory language, namely, that of not giving oneself totally to the other. This leads not only to a positive refusal to be open to life but also to a falsification of the inner truth of conjugal love, which is called upon to give itself in personal totality." For another articulation of the same line of argument that contraception is incompatible with marital intercourse, see Cormac Burke, *Covenanted Happiness: Love and Commitment in Marriage* (San Francisco: Ignatius Press, 1990), 30–41.

163. This is implied by Vatican II when it teaches: "Marriage and conjugal love are by their nature ordained toward the begetting and educating of children" (GS 50). Francis X. Meehan, "Contemporary Theological Developments on Sexuality," in *Human Sexuality and Personhood* (St. Louis: The Pope John Center, 1981), 177, makes the same point: "Sexuality implies by its very bodily phenomenon a human-life dimension. What is often not understood, and what I would like to emphasize here, is that life and love are really not two separate meanings but are inherently connected and mutually conditioned. For this reason *Humanae Vitae* is more than a teaching on birth control: it is an anthropological insight suggesting that love calls for life—indeed so much so that any lack of orientation toward life actually flaws the love."

do so. Insofar as these features of men and women pertain to human nature, their source is God, the author of nature. Thus, as Paul VI teaches, God established the connection between the conjugal act's two inherent meanings, and people may not separate them.[164] If people do so in some sexual act, it simply is not a marital act.[165]

In sum, a married couple's sexual act can fail in either of two ways to be a marital act: (i) if at least one partner performs the act unwillingly or unlovingly (for example, if a third party compels a married couple to engage in intercourse, if a drunken husband forces his reluctant wife to submit, or if a wife has intercourse with her husband while deliberately wishing she were having intercourse with another man); or (ii) if either or both spouses do anything inconsistent with their act's being of itself suited to procreating (for example, if spouses unable to engage in intercourse due to the husband's impotence masturbate each other to orgasm, if a couple trying to prevent the transmission of disease use a condom, or if either or both spouses do something in order to impede conception).

Provided the couple willingly and lovingly do what is suited to cause conception when the other necessary causal factors are given, their human act is marital even if they know that those factors will not be given—that they are infertile, temporarily or permanently—due to causes extrinsic to their action. Moreover, provided the husband and wife do what is of itself suited to procreating, their will to engage in true marital intercourse is the only intention they must have to make what they do a marital act. They may also intend to procreate, but, even if conception is possible, they need not; it is sufficient if they simply intend to actualize their one-flesh unity so that they can experience and enjoy it.[166]

164. See Paul VI, *Humanae vitae,* 12, *AAS* 60 (1968) 488, *PE,* 277.12. John Paul II, *Familiaris consortio,* 29, *AAS* 74 (1982) 115, *OR,* 21–28 Dec. 1981, 6, cites proposition 21 from the 1980 session of the Synod of Bishops: "This Sacred Synod, gathered together with the Successor of Peter in the unity of faith, firmly holds what has been set forth in the Second Vatican Council (cf. *Gaudium et spes,* 50) and afterwards in the Encyclical *Humanae Vitae,* particularly that love between husband and wife must be fully human, exclusive and open to new life *(Humanae Vitae,* 11; cf. 9, 12)." To this the Pope appends the note: "Section 11 of the Encyclical *Humanae Vitae* ends with the statement: 'The Church, calling people back to the observance of the norms of the natural law, as interpreted by her constant doctrine, teaches that each and every marriage act must remain open to the transmission of life'." Also John Paul II, General Audience (18 July 1984), 4, *Inseg.* 7.2 (1984) 103, *OR,* 23 July 1984, 1, teaches "that the above-mentioned moral norm belongs not only to the natural moral law, but also to the *moral order revealed by God:* also from this point of view, it could not be different, but solely what is handed down by Tradition and the Magisterium and, in our days, the Encyclical *Humanae Vitae* as a modern document of this Magisterium."
165. See G. E. M. Anscombe, *Contraception and Chastity* (London: Catholic Truth Society, 1975), 18–21.
166. Many who dissent from received Catholic teaching claim that the Doctors of the Church who developed traditional sexual and marital morality, including St. Thomas, thought marital intercourse entirely free of sin for both spouses only if they chose it in order to procreate, since, these Doctors are alleged to have said, if one spouse engaged in intercourse for the other worthy motive—to render the debt (a phrase derived from 1 Cor 7.3)—the other spouse, seeking intercourse to avoid unchastity, would be guilty of venial sin. However, while Thomas thinks that a spouse who must seek intercourse to avoid unchastity sins venially, he says, *In Sent.,* 4, d. 31, q. 2, a. 2 (*S.t.,* sup., q. 49, a. 5), that the spouses are wholly excused from sin if their marital intercourse is a *mutual* rendering of the debt, which pertains to the good of fidelity ("quando conjuges conveniunt . . . ut sibi invicem debitum reddant, quae ad fidem pertinent, totaliter

b) **Marital chastity empowers couples both to act and to abstain.** Conjugal love is many faceted. It normally includes both erotic desire and emotional affection; moreover, for Christians living in God's friendship, it is transformed and elevated by charity. However, the essence of conjugal love is the husband's and the wife's mutual and unselfish willing of the good of marital communion, and, for the sake of that good, of each other's entire personal good (see GS 49). The willing of a good leads to the integration of acts with it, and the full integration of sexual acts in marriage with the good of marriage makes those acts reasonable and worthy. Hence, consistent and genuine conjugal love leads to reasonable and worthy sexual acts in marriage. Now, such sexual acts are chaste; so, conjugal love leads to marital chastity.[167]

Many people are attached to their personal independence, and some experience strong feelings of reserve and inhibitions against intimacy. Motivated by the unselfish willing of marital communion, marital chastity enables husbands and wives to overcome such attachments, feelings, and inhibitions, and so to engage in genuine marital acts and grow in marital communion. Marital chastity also enables a husband and a wife to abstain at appropriate times: when they are not together, when they lack privacy, when either reasonably prefers not to engage in intercourse, when intercourse might lead to new life but there are good reasons not to have a child (or another child), and so on.

c) **Marital chastity subordinates sexual pleasure to communion.** The pleasurable sensations of sexual activity culminating in orgasm are in themselves a private and incommunicable experience. Hence, to focus attention on this experience and strive to intensify it as much as possible tends to make the other person into a means, a "sex object." So, the Church teaches that spouses should pursue sexual gratification only in subordination to marital love.[168] Marital chastity, by

---

excusantur a peccato"). Thus, for Thomas, *rendering the debt* can refer to the spouses mutually giving themselves in marital communion, and on this matter his teaching is similar to Vatican II's: Germain Grisez, "Marriage: Reflections Based on St. Thomas and Vatican Council II," *Catholic Mind* 64 (June 1966): 4–19. See also Fabian Parmisano, O.P., "Love and Marriage in the Middle Ages," *New Blackfriars* 50 (1969): 599–608, 649–60.

167. Of course, it does so only if the couple make a serious and persevering effort. See GS 51; Paul VI, *Humanae vitae,* 25, AAS 60 (1968) 498–500, *PE,* 277.25. A helpful treatment of chastity in Christian marriage, with additional references to relevant theological sources: Lawler, Boyle, and May, *Catholic Sexual Ethics,* 128–43.

168. See Ford and Kelly, *Marriage Questions,* 169–207. Innocent XI condemned the proposition: "The marriage act performed for pleasure alone is completely free from all fault and venial defect" (DS 2109/1159, translation amended). The point is not that sexual pleasure is bad in itself or that it should not be part of the motive for marital intercourse. Sexual pleasure is morally indifferent in itself; the pleasure of a morally bad act is bad, but the pleasure of a morally good act is good. If married couples who abstain when appropriate at other times have marital intercourse if they are so inclined—that is, for the integral joy, which includes orgasmic pleasure, of experiencing their marital communion—their sexual urge is subordinated to their marital love; in that case, their habitual intention of living a good married life, sexually as in other ways, includes intelligible benefits, so that they do not act for pleasure *alone*. Thus, Pius XII, Address to Italian Catholic Union of Midwives, AAS 43 (1951) 851, *Catholic Mind* 50 (Jan. 1952): 62, teaches that sexual pleasure belongs to God's good creation and adds: "In seeking and enjoying this pleasure, therefore, couples do nothing wrong. They accept that which the Creator has given them"; but he

making the marital good itself central, makes it possible for the experience of loving cooperation in one-flesh communion to predominate and enjoyable sensations to take their proper, subordinate place in marital intercourse. Thus subordinated, erotic pleasure no matter how intense, is morally good (see *S.t.*, 2–2, q. 153, a. 2, ad 2).

The point is clarified by John Paul II's teaching that a man can commit adultery in his heart by looking lustfully at his own wife. He does not mean spouses may not look at each other with erotic desire or with the intention of arousing desire in themselves and each other. To *look lustfully* instead means to reduce "the riches of the perennial call to the communion of persons, the riches of the deep attractiveness of masculinity and femininity, to mere satisfaction of the sexual 'need' of the body." The person looked at in this way is made into a sex object. Hence: "Man can commit this adultery 'in the heart' also with regard to his own wife, if he treats her only as an object to satisfy instinct." And a woman likewise can commit this adultery toward her own husband.[169]

d) If reason calls for abstinence, intercourse cannot express love. Even when it is not appropriate to engage in marital intercourse, people often are tempted and constrained to do so by sexual excitement and desire. Of itself, however, sexual drive does not express love; it is no more communicative than any other biological drive. Outward behavior can express what is in one's mind and heart only insofar as it is, not the result of a biological drive, but a free self-communication. Thus, if an uncontrollable nervous condition causes a man from time to time to blurt out "Yes, yes!" everyone soon realizes that his "Yes, yes!" is meaningless. If his wife wants his agreement about anything important, she asks him to put it in writing. Likewise, to be expressive, sexual activity must be free, and to convey genuine love, it must tend to common benefit; unless freely chosen for the sake of common benefit, marital intercourse cannot express and nurture unselfish love.[170]

---

at once goes on to point out that pleasure must be subordinated to the ends of marriage and that marital happiness is proportionate to the couple's mutual respect, not to the pleasure they experience. Cf. Anscombe, *Contraception and Chastity*, 25–26.

169. John Paul II, General Audience (8 Oct. 1980), 3, *Inseg.* 3.2 (1980) 808–9, *OR,* 13 Oct. 1980, 7.

170. John Paul II, General Audience (23 July 1980), 3, *Inseg.* 3.2 (1980) 289, *OR,* 28 July 1980, 1, explains: "The 'heart' has become a battlefield between love and lust. The more lust dominates the heart, the less the latter experiences the nuptial meaning of the body, and the less it becomes sensitive to the gift of the person, which, in the mutual relations of man and of woman expresses precisely that meaning." Ibid., 6, *Inseg.* 291, *OR,* 12: "Concupiscence entails the loss of the interior freedom of the gift. The nuptial meaning of the human body is connected precisely with this freedom. Man can become a gift—that is, the man and the woman can exist in the relationship of mutual self-giving—if each of them controls himself. Concupiscence, which is manifested as a 'coercion "sui generis" of the body', limits interiorly and reduces self-control, and for that reason, makes impossible, in a certain sense, the interior freedom of giving. Together with that, also the beauty that the human body possesses in its male and female aspect, as an expression of the spirit, is obscured. There remains the body as an object of lust and therefore as a 'field of appropriation' of the other human being. Concupiscence, in itself, is not capable of promoting union as the communion of persons. By itself, it does not unite, but appropriates. The relationship of the gift is changed into the relationship of appropriation."

It follows that to be able to give oneself in marital intercourse so that the act means something, one needs self-control sufficient to be able to choose not to engage in intercourse when reason, considering all the relevant goods, calls for abstinence. At such times, love is expressed and fostered not by intercourse but by mutual support in abstaining cheerfully. Consequently, marital love requires a husband and a wife to develop marital chastity, that is, to subordinate genital arousal and satisfaction to the reasonable claims of all the aspects of their common good as a married couple. By enabling the couple both to come together when appropriate and to abstain when appropriate, marital chastity empowers them to engage in sexual acts which truly embody love, rather than merely manifest an urge for self-satisfaction.[171]

e) Marriage quiets concupiscence by subjecting desire to love. Having taught that it is good for the unmarried and widows to remain so, St. Paul adds: "But if they are not practicing self-control, they should marry. For it is better to marry than to be aflame with passion" (1 Cor 7.9; cf. 7.2, 5).[172] This norm is reflected by the traditional view that one of marriage's secondary ends is to serve as a "remedy for concupiscence" (see DS 3718/2241). *Concupiscence* here refers to sexual drive considered precisely insofar as it is affected by sin and tends toward satisfaction without regard to intelligible goods.

It is a mistake to suppose that marriage quiets concupiscence simply by providing a legitimate outlet for it, since experience shows that satisfying desire soon intensifies it, and that marriage does not automatically lessen one's sexual drive or focus it exclusively on one's spouse. The point rather is that for most Christians who wish to attain self-control but do not have the gift of complete continence for the kingdom's sake, marriage with its sacramental grace and conjugal love can provide a way of developing the virtue of chastity.[173]

f) Spouses should cooperate lovingly in marital intercourse. St. Paul teaches that spouses have an obligation to engage in marital intercourse:

> The husband should give to his wife her conjugal rights, and likewise the wife to her husband. For the wife does not have authority over her own body, but the husband does; likewise the husband does not have authority over his own body,

---

171. John Paul II, General Audience (12 Nov. 1980), 5, *Inseg.* 3.2 (1980) 1133, *OR,* 17 Nov. 1980, 9, contrasts the spontaneity of the sexual drive as such with the spontaneity of genuine love: "There cannot be such spontaneity in all the movements and impulses that arise from mere carnal lust, devoid as it is of a choice and of an adequate hierarchy. It is precisely at the price of self-control that man reaches that deeper and more mature spontaneity with which his 'heart', mastering his instincts, rediscovers the spiritual beauty of the sign constituted by the human body in its masculinity and femininity."

172. Michael L. Barré, S.S., "To Marry or to Burn: [To Burn] in 1 Cor 7:9," *Catholic Biblical Quarterly* 36 (1974): 193–202, argues that this verse does not mean that marriage is to be chosen by those who *cannot* be chaste. He points out that, while *cannot* is found in many translations, it is not in the Greek, and argues that the verse is addressed to those who both unreasonably resisted marriage and failed to practice self-control.

173. See St. Thomas, *In Sent.,* 4, d. 26, q. 2, a. 3, ad 4 (*S.t.,* sup., q. 42, a. 3, ad 4); cf. *In Sent.,* 4, d. 2, q. 1, a. 1, qu'la 2; John Paul II, General Audience (1 Dec. 1982), 3, *Inseg.* 5.3 (1982) 1486, *OR,* 6 Dec. 1982, 6–7. Those called neither to marriage nor to virginity or celibacy for the sake of the kingdom also can live chastely: see 8.f, below.

but the wife does. Do not deprive one another except perhaps by agreement for a set time, to devote yourselves to prayer, and then come together again, so that Satan may not tempt you because of your lack of self-control. (1 Cor 7.3–5)

Paul's formulation makes it clear that the obligation is mutual; in this matter, husband and wife are entirely equal. The reason is that in marrying, the two become one so truly that neither may regard his or her body as exclusively his or her own.[174]

Like all other affirmative obligations, this one has limits, and it must be understood correctly. Nobody can have an obligation to do what is wrong, and so there is no obligation to cooperate in intercourse if the couple morally ought to abstain, whether to avoid pregnancy or for some other reason. Again, the obligation is to engage in *marital* intercourse, and so there is no obligation to cooperate if contraception is used, or if one's spouse cannot engage in a human act, for example, due to alcohol or other substance abuse. Furthermore, as will be explained (in H.2.a), an adulterous spouse loses his or her right to marital intimacy.

If either party wishes for any reason not to have marital intercourse, the other manifests love and strengthens marital communion by complying with that wish, and so should abstain without resentment. At the same time, not every reason for abstaining is so morally compelling that it would be wrong for the couple to have marital intercourse if both are willing. For example, if one spouse has a serious disease that might be communicated through intercourse, the protection of the other's health is a reason for abstinence, yet the immediate contribution of chaste intercourse to marital communion can justify risks to health, even serious ones, especially if the alternative is prolonged abstinence. Consequently, assuming the couple do not have some additional reason (such as responsibilities to their children) to protect health, in such a case they may agree to have intercourse and accept the bad side effect of risk to health.[175]

g) Unreasonable refusal of marital intercourse is a grave matter. As has been explained, each spouse's right to intercourse has limits, and usually when either is reluctant to have intercourse, the other should not insist. Still, sometimes a spouse has no justifying reason for being unwilling to cooperate. Such unwillingness can be motivated by anger and hatred, an unreasonable desire to avoid

---

174. Thus, the feminist claim that a woman has an exclusive right to control her own reproductivity is false not only because it is taken to justify contraception and abortion but also, and more radically, because it presupposes an individualism at odds with the reality of marriage as a one-flesh communion of persons and so reduces the marital relationship to (at best) a contractual arrangement for mutual services.

175. Many approved authors held that marital intercourse is wrong when it involves a serious risk to health; see, for example, I. Aertnys, C. Damen, and I. Visser, C.Ss.R., *Theologia moralis,* ed. 18, 4 vols. (Turin: Marietti, 1967–69), 4:257–58. A recent argument along the same lines: John M. Haas, "HIV and Marriage," *Ethics and Medics* 16 (Feb. 1991): 1–3, (Mar. 1991): 3–4. However, St. Thomas, *In Sent.,* 4, d. 32, q. 1, a. 1, ad 4 (*S.t.,* sup., q. 64, a. 1, ad 4), holds that a wife should have intercourse with her leprous husband (although Thomas says that she need not share the same dwelling with him, since that more quickly leads to infection). Moreover, those who engage in chaste intercourse for the sake of marital communion can be as justified as people intending other goods in risking bad side effects (see 8.C.2.d, above). Today, some argue that, in order to avoid transmitting a disease, couples may practice so-called safe sex ("intercourse" with a condom). But that opinion is unsound, since a sexual act of that kind is not a marital act.

offspring, the manipulative use of marital intercourse to compel compliance in other matters, excessive preoccupation with other activities, and so on. Sometimes, too, one spouse without good reason travels alone or stays away from home for some time, thus depriving the other of the opportunity for marital intimacy. In all such cases, when the spouse deprived of marital intimacy makes it clear, by saying so or in any other way, that he or she desires it, the other should cooperate lovingly, and refusal is a grave matter.

The wrong of unreasonable reluctance to engage in marital intimacy admits of parvity but, like other injustices, only in cases in which, typically, the one who suffers the wrong considers it insignificant: for example, because intimacy is not denied for long and the unreasonable motive is not ill will but only some understandable weakness.

Of course, sometimes the spouses disagree about whether a refusal of marital intercourse is reasonable. Then both should try to find a harmonious solution, but if that is impossible, the spouse deprived of desired intimacy must remain faithful. Moreover, such a spouse should be tolerant, for even when a denial of intimacy is plainly unjustified, physical force, psychological coercion, nagging, and resentment are both incompatible with marital love and ineffective for obtaining the loving cooperation required for true marital communion.

h) Marital sexual acts short of intercourse can be chaste. Ejaculation by the male in the female's vagina is necessary for sexual intercourse insofar as it is a reproductive function, and so such ejaculation is necessary for a complete act of marital intercourse. However, within marriage various sexual acts short of complete intercourse can be chaste. Of course, like intercourse itself, such acts are chaste only insofar as spouses seek in them, not pleasure alone, but the wider good of marital communion in which pleasure is a subordinate element. Therefore, what is said here about acts short of intercourse should be understood, not as advising the married how they can maximize sexual gratification without committing mortal sins, but as clarifying some of the requirements of marital chastity.

Marital sexual acts short of intercourse are good in themselves if they (i) are necessary or helpful to marital intercourse and/or (ii) express and foster marital affection. Still, even if good in itself, an act short of intercourse can be bad due to a wrong intention or some circumstance. Thus, such acts become bad if they either (iii) are intended to bring about complete sexual satisfaction apart from marital intercourse or (iv) are in some other way at odds with the good of marital communion.[176]

i) Mutually agreeable erotic words, looks, gestures, and bodily contact of various sorts, including manual and oral stimulation of the genitals, can prepare psychologically and/or physiologically for marital intercourse, and can intensify the experience of communion and make it more gratifying. Self-stimulating acts also can prepare oneself for intercourse.

---

176. A sound treatment of these matters, including the morality of oral-genital contacts preparatory to intercourse: Ford and Kelly, *Marriage Questions,* 210–13, 224–34. Also see Aertnys, Damen, and Visser, *Theologia moralis,* 4:282–83, 290–94.

ii) In the intervals between marital intercourse, interaction leading to moderate sexual arousal can both bring about a continuing experience of one-flesh communion and prepare indirectly and remotely for eventual marital intercourse. Thus, when abstinence from intercourse is appropriate, married couples sometimes rightly express and foster their affection by sexually stimulating interaction.

iii) Any act of the wife or the husband intended to bring about his ejaculation outside her vagina cannot be ordered directly to marital intercourse, and so is not a marital act. As will be explained, every attempt to obtain sexual satisfaction in a nonmarital act is wrong, and so such nonmarital acts always are morally excluded. If such acts are intended to serve in some way as means to the marital good—by maintaining intimacy when intercourse is impossible, satiating the sexual urge during a period of separation and so lessening temptation to commit adultery, treating sexual dysfunction, and so on—they are morally bad means to an ulterior good end.[177]

The wife's complete sexual satisfaction (orgasm) is not necessary for sexual intercourse insofar as it is a reproductive function, but it does contribute to complete marital intercourse as a mutually satisfying experience of one-flesh communion. Hence, acts by the husband or the wife intended to intensify to orgasm her sexual arousal in continuity with any complete act of marital intercourse belong to that intercourse, and so they are marital, even if done during foreplay or after the husband's ejaculation and withdrawal. However, any act intended to bring about her orgasm through arousal in no way continuous with that involved in marital intercourse would be a nonmarital act, and therefore wrong.

iv) A couple's sexual acts short of intercourse can be incompatible with marital communion in various other ways: by being repugnant to either spouse (with the result that they do not express affection), by using pornographic material to bring about sexual arousal (thus arousing adulterous desire toward a third party), by involving significant and avoidable risk of causing the husband to ejaculate unintentionally outside his wife's vagina (thus interfering with complete intercourse and/or tempting him to intend the nonmarital satisfaction), by causing frustration and tension due to excessive arousal when intercourse is inappropriate, and so on.

Many acts that appear to meet the other criteria must be excluded inasmuch as they do not meet this one. For instance, some wives find oral stimulation of the penis repugnant, and for many men the practice leads to ejaculation outside the vagina. Again, any self-stimulation which does not pertain very closely to marital intercourse is likely to constitute masturbation or to be an occasion of that sin (see 2.f, below).

i) **The circumstances of marital sexual acts should be suitable.** Various circumstances can require abstinence. Couples should not neglect other serious

---

177. Moreover, as often is the case when bad means are chosen, such sexual acts are not likely to serve the end effectively. The impossibility of intercourse should occasion a quest for deeper intimacy by means such as conversation; masturbation during a period of separation is likely to occasion temptations to commit adultery, at least in the heart; and focusing attention on genital behavior may well worsen sexual dysfunction.

responsibilities requiring a temporary separation or brief delay of marital intercourse. Serious health risks that can be avoided by temporary abstinence from intercourse require couples to practice such restraint, for example, for a few weeks before and after childbirth. Usually, to avoid scandal and/or serious distraction from the experience of marital communion, intercourse and acts short of it involving any exposure of or contact with the genitals must be conducted in strict privacy, and so must be delayed if privacy is unavailable.

In order that marital intercourse provide a full and mutually satisfying experience of communion and not be reduced to a routine function, couples also should try to arrange favorable circumstances. These often include lessening the frequency of intercourse, engaging in conversation and/or recreational activities as a context for sexual intimacy, and arranging a time free of excessive fatigue, distractions, and pressure to hurry. For the same reason, couples may either try to achieve simultaneous orgasms, if they think the experience will enhance their intercourse as communion, or dispense with that effort, if they find it more distracting than helpful. All such wholesome efforts to enhance marital intercourse as an experience of communion must be distinguished from the hedonistic use of techniques focusing solely on the intensification of erotic sensations.

2. Married Persons Should Not Engage in Other Sexual Acts

The married should never seek sexual satisfaction with a person other than their spouse. Married couples should not seek complete sexual satisfaction apart from a genuine marital act. Apart from chaste marital acts, including those short of but appropriately related to marital intercourse, married persons should never choose to do anything in order to sexually stimulate themselves or others.[178]

a) Adultery in deed or in desire is always wrong. Whenever a married person engages in sexual intercourse, whether heterosexual or homosexual, with someone other than his or her spouse, and whenever a single person knowingly engages in sexual intercourse with someone who is married, both parties commit adultery and violate the good of marital communion. If both are married, they sin doubly by violating both their own and each other's marriages.

Adultery is bad for many reasons which are plain even to people who lack the light of faith. It tends toward either polygyny or divorce. Sometimes a wife tolerates her husband's habitual adultery, and he has one or more concubines, mistresses, or informal, transient, sequential relationships with other women. Such arrangements are somewhat like polygyny and impose similar disadvantages on the wife and children. But unlike wives and children in polygynous relationships, the families of habitual adulterers are not protected by commonly accepted social norms, and so are all the more likely to suffer harm.

Apart from such cases, either spouse usually experiences the other's adultery as a grave betrayal. Unless repented, the adulterous spouse's infidelity deprives his or her sexual acts within marriage of their capacity to express self-giving and

---

178. A helpful treatment of acts contrary to marital chastity, with additional references to theological sources: Lawler, Boyle, and May, *Catholic Sexual Ethics,* 146–75.

signify marital communion; and the innocent spouse who is aware of unrepented infidelity naturally finds intimacy, or even its prospect, repugnant. Moreover, by undermining the trust necessary for confident self-giving, adultery severely strains the whole marital relationship. Thus, unless the betrayal is repented and the relationship rebuilt, adultery often leads to divorce. As for secret adultery, it involves serious deception, which is inconsistent with openness and mutuality. Finally, when adulterous relationships result in conception, paternity may be uncertain and, in any case, the child, if permitted to survive, seldom is raised in a stable family (see *S.t.*, 2–2, q. 154, a. 8).

The light of faith makes the evil of adultery even clearer. Scripture severely condemns this sin.[179] Jesus teaches that to "look at a woman with lust"—that is, deliberately to entertain illicit sexual desire[180]—is sufficient to constitute the sin (see Mt 5.27–28). The Christian tradition also makes it clear that the norm excluding adultery is exceptionless. Since the ordinary, universal magisterium has proposed the traditional teaching on adultery as a revealed truth, this norm certainly has been infallibly taught and should be accepted with the assent of faith (see *CMP*, 35.D–E).

If one spouse commits adultery without the other's consent, the adulterous spouse violates his or her duty of faithfulness toward the betrayed spouse. But even if one spouse consents to the other's adulterous act, the sin remains adultery (see DS 2150/1200), inasmuch as both spouses violate their marital communion.

Acts intended to express or arouse sexual desire which are short of complete adulterous intercourse but involve a married person and any third party share the moral character of adultery. Moreover, even if adultery is only in the heart and remains hidden from the spouse, it gravely harms marital communion, because the will to commit adultery is inconsistent with marital love as an act of the will.

b) Incestuous adultery is an especially grave immorality. Many circumstances can add to the immorality of adultery. Several of these will be treated (in 3.f), since they also affect the moral character of sexual sins involving no married person. But one factor deserves mention here. Sometimes adultery involves a married person and someone in that person's family, for example, a married man has intercourse with his own daughter. Such adultery also is incest, and it violates not only the same goods as other adultery but also familial roles and relationships (see 3.f, below). Moreover, unless both parties consent, sexual intercourse is rape (see 8.G.2). Hence, incest involving a child too young to consent also is rape.

c) Bigamous relationships and remarriage after divorce are adultery. Once a person makes a marital commitment, any choice he or she makes to begin another sexually intimate relationship alongside or in place of the marriage radically violates the good of marital communion, and is adultery in an even more profound sense than particular acts of adulterous intercourse. A couple who attempt to

---

179. Like many other norms, the commandment proscribing adultery reaches its full scope and clarity only in the New Testament, where teaching on the matter is entirely consistent and firm: see Mt 5.27–28, 19.18; Mk 7.21–22, 10.19; Lk 18.20; Jn 8.3–4, 11; Rom 2.17–22, 13.9; 1 Cor 6.9; Heb 13.4; Jas 2.11; cf. *Theological Dictionary of the New Testament*, s.v. *moicheia*.

180. See St. Thomas, *Super evangelium S. Matthaei lectura*, on 5.27–28.

dissolve their marriage in order to make way for new relationships with others do not avoid the sin. Hence, Jesus teaches that divorce with attempted remarriage constitutes adultery for both parties (see Mt 5.32, Mk 10.11–12; cf. 1 Cor 7.10–11). Since any deliberate desire for a relationship alongside or in place of one's marriage is adultery, the deliberate wish that one's marriage did not exist so that one would be free to marry someone else also constitutes adultery.

d) Christian spouses should treat their marriage as sacred. Insofar as the marital union itself is the reality that is the sacrament, adultery which involves a Christian marriage is a sacrilege inasmuch as it violates the marital union.[181] Therefore, Christian spouses, who ought to regard their marriage as sacred, should avoid adultery not only out of fidelity to each other but also, and equally directly, out of fidelity to Jesus. They should personally resist, and help each other to resist, not only specific temptations to commit adultery in deed, but every desire to do so, every fantasy of a different partner, every temptation to consider their marriage dissoluble, every wish that they were not married to each other.

e) Spouses should not engage in complete, nonmarital sexual acts. True marital acts must be (i) a loving cooperation (ii) open to new life.

i) If a couple have sexual intercourse while one or both deliberately wish it were with a different partner, or if a couple are forced to engage in intercourse, it is not loving cooperation. If one spouse forces the other to submit to intercourse, the act cannot express and foster love, but rather damages marital communion. That is so even if the spouse using force is provoked by a wrongful denial of marital intimacy, since the violent act cannot realize marital communion, which requires loving cooperation.[182]

ii) As explained previously (in 1.a), the marital intercourse of a sterile couple can be open to new life. Sexual intercourse is open to new life when the couple do not intend to impede conception and their performance is such that conception would result if the physiological conditions were conducive to it. However, if either or both spouses seek complete satisfaction (orgasm) by cooperating in any sort of act which is not open to new life, that act is not marital.[183] That is so even if there

181. No explicit magisterial teaching supports this point, nor was it taught by the classical theologians. So, someone who denies that the marital union itself is the persisting sacrament can deny that adultery is a sacrilege without denying that it is always grave matter.

182. Edward J. Bayer, *Rape within Marriage: A Moral Analysis Delayed* (Lanham, Md.: University Press of America, 1985), 3, argues that "any sexual act of a husband, which is capable of impregnating his wife, and which is at the same time forced upon her by her husband against her objectively justified and serious refusal of consent" constitutes rape. However, although such a violent act is nonmarital, a grave injustice, and insofar as it violates marital love (other things being equal) worse than rape, it is specifically different from rape. For the married couple truly are one flesh, and so *sexual* violence within marriage does not violate *another* person's body. To call forcible intercourse within marriage "rape" is to use the word in an analogous sense, and this extension seems unwise inasmuch as it tends to support individualistic conceptions, according to which there is no one-flesh unity but only a dissoluble contract of marriage.

183. If the couple attempt to engage in marital intercourse and the husband unintentionally ejaculates outside his wife's vagina, their act is marital in intent even though not in fact a complete marital act. Provided the couple do what they can to avoid such accidents, acts of this kind have the same moral character as their other acts short of marital intercourse.

is no *intent* to impede new life, for example, if a husband uses a condom to prevent the transmission of disease, a couple engages in mutual masturbation for variety's sake, or a wife intentionally stimulates her husband to orgasm when the couple for some reason are incapable of intercourse.

Inasmuch as a sexual act involving complete satisfaction is not marital intercourse, it is wrong. It violates the sixth mode of responsibility (see *CMP,* 8.F) because, by diverting the couple's sexual behavior and experience from the good of marriage in its integrity, it damages that good and substitutes a merely apparent good: some of the psychological satisfactions or sentient pleasures pertaining to marital sex isolated from its wholeness. If such an act is chosen with the intent to impede new life, it also is contraceptive, and so is wrong because it violates the seventh or eighth mode of responsibility (see 8.E.3).

What about those cases, unfortunately not rare, in which the spouses are not of one mind, one wishing to engage in a sexual act not open to new life and the other wishing to have true marital intercourse? May the latter spouse cooperate in the act? The answer is that marital intercourse is a unitary act in which the spouses are united as a single, conjoint agent. Hence, it cannot occur as a moral act unless both spouses will it. Therefore, when either spouse wills that the act not be open to new life and the other knows it, he or she cannot cooperate without participating in a nonmarital act. Since such acts are wrong, formal cooperation in them also is wrong. (On the meaning of *formal cooperation,* see 7.F.1, above; *CMP,* 12.G.)[184]

f) Married persons never should seek independent sexual satisfaction. As has been explained, the married may engage in various marital acts short of intercourse and may stimulate themselves to prepare for marital intercourse (see 1.h). But if either husband or wife intentionally does anything to obtain sexual satisfaction without reference to his or her spouse, that act is contrary to the gift of self which realizes the good of marriage, and so violates marital communion. Such acts involve infidelity, because by them married persons treat their bodies, which they had dedicated to one-flesh communion, as if retaining authority over them.

An attempt to obtain sexual satisfaction plainly lacks reference to one's spouse in either of two cases: (i) if it is intentionally directed to complete sexual satisfaction apart from marital intercourse, and (ii) if it involves reference to some third

---

184. It seems to follow that initiating such an act or sharing in it as a sexual act (as distinct, say, from engaging in the relevant behavior under duress, not as a sexual act but in order to forestall physical abuse) always would be formal cooperation, and so is excluded. However, many sound moralists, with some support from the magisterium, think that, subject to various conditions, the spouse who wishes to engage in intercourse open to new life may share in, and perhaps even initiate, intercourse as a sexual act with his or her spouse, despite that spouse's choice to engage in an act not open to new life; see, for example, Aertnys, Damen, and Visser, *Theologia moralis,* 4:266–69; Pius XI, *Casti connubii, AAS* 22 (1930) 560–61, *PE,* 208.59; cf. Noonan, *Contraception,* 432–34, 506–8. But such moralists (and, undoubtedly, the magisterium) assume that the reluctantly cooperating spouse need only cooperate materially. They make that assumption because they think, I believe mistakenly, that under the conditions which they specify, such an act can remain marital intercourse (and perhaps they think this because they assume that each spouse's act can be an act of marital intercourse whether or not the other's is). If anyone really thinks that is true, he or she can follow the moral opinion which is based on it without in any way rejecting the Church's teaching.

party (whether or not it is directed to complete sexual satisfaction apart from marital intercourse). In these cases, the act is wrong not only specifically as infidelity, but also on the same basis (which will be explained) as masturbation or fornication for those who are not married.

Moreover, such acts cannot be justified by any sort of ulterior reference to the good of marriage—for example, as part of a program of treatment for sexual dysfunction or as stimulation to prepare for marital intercourse—since, even given such an ulterior reference, they are bad means to the good end.

g) The married sometimes commit venial sins against chastity. For the married, there can be light matter in sins of unchastity in two ways.

i) There can be some imperfection in the motivation for engaging in marital intercourse. Quite often, the emotional motivation underlying the choice to engage in it is not fully integrated with conjugal love, so that either or both spouses focus too much on individual satisfaction, with the bad result that the experience of marital communion is less perfect than it should be. And sometimes the spouses unreasonably choose to engage in or refrain from intercourse, but their un-reasonableness bears only on circumstances and does not involve any intention inconsistent with the marital good. For example, a wife seeks marital intercourse late in the evening, although realizing that she should not because her husband will be overly tired the next day. Again, a husband whose wife readily complies with his wishes about marital intercourse does not always attend as carefully as he knows he should to her tacit desire to engage in or abstain from it. Still, in such cases, the intention is to act for and enjoy the marital good and involves nothing at odds with that good. So, the matter can be light if the moral defect is not so great that the act seriously violates some other good.[185]

ii) As has been explained, incomplete sexual acts by the married can be good if they are oriented toward marital intercourse or, more generally, toward maintaining and fostering the ongoing marital communion, but are gravely bad if oriented toward any complete sexual act other than marital intercourse. However, some-times the married intentionally seek or maintain incomplete satisfaction in acts whose orientation is ambiguous, inasmuch as they serve neither the habitual intention of marital communion nor any intention at odds with it, but are motivated by inadequately integrated emotional sexual desire, which might eventually lead toward marital intercourse but also might constitute a temptation to violate the marital good. (While not grave matter in themselves, such sins will be grave matter if they are occasions of other sins: masturbation, adultery in the heart, and so on.)

In both (i) and (ii), there is no violation of the marital good because the intention is in no way contrary to it. But there is a violation of sexual morality, because the intention bears on sexual arousal and satisfaction, and the act is morally defective due to inadequately integrated desire. All such defects would be overcome by perfect marital chastity, but even spouses who never will anything at odds with marital love can be motivated by erotic feelings that are not integrated with their good will, and so sometimes commit venial sins against marital chastity.

---

185. See St. Thomas, *In Sent.*, 4, d. 31, q. 2, aa. 2–3 (*S.t.,* sup., q. 49, aa. 5–6).

3. The Unmarried Should Never Engage in Any Sexual Act

It is traditional Catholic teaching that "only in legitimate marriage does the use of the sexual faculty find its true meaning and its probity."[186] The basis of this teaching is that all human acts must be evaluated by objective criteria, based on the nature of human persons and human action, and all sexual acts must respect the full meaning of mutual self-giving and human procreation in the context of true love (see GS 51).

For the unmarried, all sexual acts are wrong because in one or another way they violate the good of marriage, that is, the good of fully personal one-flesh communion realized in true marital acts. Sexual acts outside marriage also may violate various other goods.

The explanations proposed in this section attempt only to show the primary reasons why sexual acts of the unmarried are wrong. How serious such sins are is another matter. It will be shown below (in 6) that no sexual sin which violates the good of marriage admits parvity of matter. Of course, such a sin might not be mortal, since there is no mortal sin without sufficient reflection and full consent.

a) Complete nonmarital sexual acts are of three basic kinds. A complete sexual act is one in which someone seeks complete satisfaction, that is, orgasm. Apart from adultery, which the unmarried also commit when they have intercourse with those who are married, the unmarried can engage in three basic kinds of complete sexual acts.

i) An unmarried individual can intentionally think, do, or undergo something other than intercourse to bring about his or her own orgasm.[187] Such an act is masturbation, regardless of the means used.

ii) An unmarried man and woman can willingly engage in sexual intercourse, intending that at least the man enjoy complete satisfaction by ejaculating in the woman's vagina. Such an act is fornication.

iii) Two unmarried men can willingly engage in anal or oral intercourse, intending that at least one of them enjoy complete satisfaction by ejaculating within the other's body. Such an act is sodomy, that is, homosexual intercourse.[188]

---

186. Congregation for the Doctrine of the Faith, *Persona humana*, 5, *AAS* 68 (1976) 82, Flannery, 2:489. For a helpful treatment of the requirements of chastity outside marriage, with additional references to theological sources, see Lawler, Boyle, and May, *Catholic Sexual Ethics*, 176–209.

187. Someone might object: According to this definition, which is necessary for the subsequent argument, not all deliberate genital stimulation of a man to the point of ejaculation is masturbation, for example, if the intention is not to experience orgasm but solely to provide a semen sample for analysis. Yet Pius XII, Address to the Second World Congress on Fertility and Sterility (19 May 1956), *AAS* 48 (1956) 472–73, *The Pope Speaks* 3 (1956–57): 195–97, rejects this practice as an unnatural abuse of the generative faculty. The answer is: While self-stimulation to obtain a semen sample is physically the same as any other masturbation, it is morally different. However, even if Pius XII's argument on this matter is not cogent, obtaining a semen sample in this way is grave matter, for it is a proximate occasion of grave sin (the more or less probable sexual fantasy and willing of the experienced sexual satisfaction) which is easily avoidable, since any semen sample required for any morally compelling reason can be obtained in some other way.

188. The word *sodomy* is used, not as a term of reproach, but in its descriptive sense, precisely to distinguish between the act of homosexual intercourse and the disposition toward it. One should

Other complete sexual acts involving two or more unmarried individuals are reducible to one or more of these three basic kinds. They are of two sorts.

i) Some are nothing more than cooperation in masturbation, in the sense that the intention of everyone involved is only that all or some of them reach orgasm. For example, a group of boys whose orientation is heterosexual play a game which involves sexually arousing one another. Such acts have the same moral character as masturbation (apart from any additional sins of thought and scandal involved).

ii) Others, for at least one participant, either substitute for or approximate to intercourse. For example, a boy and a girl stop short of fornication but fondle each other's genitals until at least one has an orgasm; a lesbian couple stimulate each other to orgasm. Such acts have essentially the same moral character as the relevant kind of intercourse, although differences in the likelihood of extramarital pregnancy, the possibility of transmitting disease, or other factors may make them more or less seriously wrong than fornication or homosexual intercourse.

b) All acts of these three kinds violate the good of marriage. As was explained in treating adultery, sexual intercourse involving a married and an unmarried person always is adultery for both parties, and masturbation by a married person is a specific kind of infidelity. Hence, the acts under consideration here are done by the unmarried; and since they need not be interested in the good of marriage, it might seem that their acts cannot violate that good. But even though the sexual acts of the unmarried can be wrong for other reasons, and the seriousness of their acts can depend more on other factors than on the ways in which they violate the good of marriage, the three basic kinds of complete nonmarital sexual acts do violate that good, each in its own special way.

c) Masturbators violate the body's capacity for self-giving. In the choice to masturbate, the immediate intention is to have a sentient and emotional experience: the sensation of orgasm and the accompanying emotional satisfaction. In this respect, masturbation differs from urination and defecation, where the motive is the need to expel waste materials, and the conscious awareness of the process—the sensation and felt satisfaction of desire—is incidental.[189] Of course, masturbation

---

not allow sentiment to cloud the truth about this act. John Paul II, Address to the Bishops of the United States (Chicago), 6, *AAS* 71 (1979) 1224–25, *OR*, 29 Oct. 1979, 9, makes the point clearly: "As 'men with the message of truth and the power of God' (2 Cor 6.7), as authentic teachers of God's law and as compassionate pastors you also rightly stated: 'Homosexual activity . . . as distinguished from homosexual orientation, is morally wrong'. In the clarity of this truth, you exemplified the real charity of Christ; you did not betray those people who, because of homosexuality, are confronted with difficult moral problems, as would have happened if, in the name of understanding and compassion, or for any other reason, you had held out false hope to any brother or sister. Rather, by your witness to the truth of humanity in God's plan, you effectively manifested fraternal love, upholding the true dignity, the true human dignity, of those who look to Christ's Church for the guidance which comes from the light of God's word."

189. Someone might argue that, since some animals masturbate, it is a natural function. That may be true for animals, and also for the spontaneous behavior of very small children. But here masturbation is considered, not simply as a pattern of behavior, but as a freely chosen act, whose intentional structure reveals its moral significance. This act's outward similarity to animal behavior is as irrelevant to morality as is the similarity of a parent's deliberate infanticide to the behavior of an animal killing its own young.

can be directed to some ulterior end, such as a night's rest, to be obtained by relieving sexual tension. But, while *relieving sexual tension* refers in part to tension (the pain of unsatisfied desire), it also refers to relieving (the experience of satisfying desire). Thus, the choice to masturbate as a means to an ulterior end, such as a night's rest, remains the adoption of a proposal to have the sentient and emotional experience of masturbating.

In choosing to actuate one's sexual capacity precisely in order to have the conscious experience of the process and its culmination, one chooses to use one's body as an instrument to bring about that experience in the conscious self. Thus, the body becomes an instrument used and the conscious self its user. In most cases, using one's body as an instrument is not problematic. This is done when one works and plays, and also when one communicates, using the tongue to speak, the finger to point, the genitals to engage in marital intercourse. In such cases the body functions as part of oneself, serving the whole and sharing in the resulting benefits. By contrast, in choosing to masturbate, one does not choose to act for a goal which fulfills oneself as a unified, bodily person. The only immediate goal is satisfaction for the conscious self; and so the body, not being part of the whole for whose sake the act is done, serves only as an extrinsic instrument. Thus, in choosing to masturbate one chooses to alienate one's body from one's conscious subjectivity.

Of course, this self-alienation from the body in no way affects the metaphysical unity of one's person, since no choice can alter a person's metaphysical constitution. However, the self-alienation is an existential dualism between the body and the conscious self, that is, a division between the two insofar as they are coprinciples of oneself considered as an integrated, acting, sexual person. Therefore, to choose to masturbate is to choose a specific kind of self-disintegrity, and, since choices determine the self unless and until the person makes another, incompatible choice (see *CMP*, 2.E.6–7), the choice of self-disintegrity damages the basic good of self-integration. But choosing to damage any basic human good violates the eighth mode of responsibility, and so is always wrong (see *CMP*, 8.H). Therefore, to choose to masturbate is always wrong.

The self-integration damaged by masturbation is the unity of the acting person as conscious subject and sexually functioning body. This specific aspect of self-integration, however, is precisely the aspect necessary so that the bodily union of sexual intercourse will be a communion of persons, as marital intercourse is. Therefore, masturbation damages the body's capacity for the marital act as an act of self-giving which constitutes a communion of bodily persons.[190] But to damage

---

190. The capacity in question is what John Paul II calls the "nuptial meaning of the body." He also has articulated a central point in the argument presented here: General Audience (4 June 1980), 4, *Inseg.* 3.1 (1980) 1681, *OR,* 9 June 1980, 19: " 'The love that is in the world', that is, lust, brings with it an almost constitutive difficulty of identification with one's own body; and not only in the sphere of one's own subjectivity, but even more with regard to the subjectivity of the other human being: of woman for man, of man for woman." With this point in mind, one can see why the dualistic attitude is manifested in attempts to rationalize sexual acts which cannot be integrated into authentic conjugal love. For treatment of an important instance involving the majority of Paul VI's Commission on Population, Family and Birthrate, see Germain Grisez, "Dualism and the New Morality," *Atti del congresso internazionale Tommaso*

an intrinsic and necessary condition for attaining a good is to damage that good itself. Thus, masturbators violate the good of marital communion by violating the body's capacity for self-giving. Moreover, since the choice to masturbate is wrong inasmuch as it is a choice of self-disintegrity, the choice remains wrong whether or not one has some reason to make it. Therefore, to make this choice for an ulterior good, such as a night's rest, is to choose a bad means to a good end.

d) Fornicators achieve only the illusion of marital communion. Sometimes one party to fornication is merely using the other to masturbate, and very often both parties' motives include a masturbatory component. Again, sometimes one party is treating his or her body as a mere instrument, either to motivate the other to do something—for example, to pay money or propose marriage—or to provide emotional and/or social satisfactions, such as a confirmation of masculinity or femininity, the thrill of conquest, and/or popularity. Such uses of the body as an instrument differ from masturbation in their motives but are like it in their moral character, since they violate the body insofar as it is a capacity for the self-giving which constitutes a communion of bodily persons.

Sometimes, however, the motive for choosing to fornicate is both different and impossible to satisfy except by fornicating. The couple are engaged to be married or are involved in a genuine interpersonal relationship more or less similar to marital friendship—or at least one party is trying to establish such a relationship. They choose sexual intercourse precisely insofar as it brings about the intimate communion pertaining to the good of marriage. Thus, they seem to begin to realize that good. Perhaps they also hope sexual intimacy will deepen and enrich their relationship as a whole. Moreover, if the act is open to new life, the couple become a complete organism with respect to the function of reproduction and perhaps actually become parents. But however that may be, they do not make the marital commitment essential to the complete realization of the good of marriage.

Of course, fornicators realize that they do not fully achieve the good of marriage. But they may be about to marry, or have good reasons not to marry, or not be interested in marriage, either for the time being or at all. Thus, they might argue that they do nothing unreasonable, for by engaging in sexual intercourse they share in the relevant good as fully as they now can or wish to—and is not that better than not sharing in it at all? However, the part of the good of marital communion which fornicators choose, bodily union, is not an intelligible good apart from the whole. Although bodily union provides an experience of intimacy, by itself it realizes only the natural capacity of a male individual and a female individual to mate. Sexual mating contributes to an intelligible good, which fulfills persons, only insofar as it is one element of the complete communion by which a man and a woman become, as it were, one person. Another element is necessary to bring about that communion: marital consent which conjugal intercourse fulfills.[191]

---

d'Aquino nel suo settimo centenario, vol. 5, L'agire morale (Naples: Edizioni Domenicane Italiane, 1977), 323-30.

191. Some try to justify "preceremonial" intercourse, meaning the act of a couple who seriously intend to marry and have a "growing commitment" to each other: Anthony Kosnik et al., Human Sexuality: New Directions in American Catholic Thought (Garden City, N.Y.:

Thus, although fornicators do choose the bodily union and experience of intimacy pertaining to the good of marriage, that good cannot be the immediate motive of their choice. Assuming their act is neither masturbatory nor manipulative, its immediate motive is only an emotional desire to share together in the experience of intimate communion. In choosing to act on that motive, they ensure that whatever experience of communion they achieve is only illusory, not an experience of the reality in which they are interested.

In choosing to do something which is capable of yielding only an illusion of participation in the good in which one is interested, a person forgoes choosing to do what would here and now really participate either in that good or some other available in the situation. For example, it may be that the couple who choose to fornicate forgo choosing to participate in the good of marriage by developing a chaste romantic relationship with a view to marriage. In any case, they choose to act for an illusory good instead of a real one, and such a choice always is unreasonable. In short, insofar as it is neither masturbatory nor manipulative, the choice to fornicate violates the sixth mode of responsibility (see *CMP*, 8.F).

"Trial marriage" is an illuminating example of fornication. Marriage can neither exist nor be experienced without mutual, permanent commitment. Attempting to sample marriage, as it were, means experiencing something entirely different: living together without commitment—and that experience cannot be a representative sample of married life. Hence, so-called trial marriage is self-defeating and unreasonable.[192]

Someone may object: While the appearance-reality argument is cogent in some cases, what if the couple are interested, not in marital communion, but only in some other sort of real and intimate communion, such as friendship, which they presently enjoy and which their sexual intercourse nurtures by communicating good will, affection, and so on? In part, the answer is that psychologically healthy couples who fornicate ordinarily do desire at least something of the experience of marital intimacy. Even in those who have no interest in marriage, there is a sign of that motivation in something many young couples learn by sad experience: very often,

---

Doubleday, 1979), 183–84, 188. Marital consent, however, does not grow; it is a definite cooperative performance. Until it is given, the couple are free to change their minds about marrying. Others try to justify "preceremonial" intercourse in a different sense, on the ground that a couple can fully consent to marriage without waiting for the public celebration: Paul Ramsey, "A Christian Approach to the Question of Sexual Relations Outside of Marriage," *Journal of Religion* 45 (1965): 112–13. Even for non-Catholics, this notion is questionable, since marriage is not simply a private agreement but a social act; still, it must be admitted that in the past the Church considered to be married a couple who, after a formal engagement, had sexual intercourse: see St. Thomas, *In Sent.*, 4, d. 28, q. 1, a. 2 (*S.t.*, sup., q. 46, a. 2). In any case, for Catholics today, valid marriage is *impossible* without witnesses (and normally requires an authorized representative of the Church); see *CIC*, c. 1108, §1.

192. See John Paul II, *Familiaris consortio*, 80, *AAS* 74 (1982) 180–81, *OR*, 21–28 Dec. 1981, 16. For a development of the essential argument against fornication and trial marriage, with pastoral guidance, see Bishops' Committee for Pastoral Research and Practice, National Conference of Catholic Bishops, *Faithful to Each Other: A Catholic Handbook of Pastoral Help for Marriage Preparation* (Washington, D.C.: United States Catholic Conference, 1989), 33–38, 71–77.

one partner sooner or later seeks a deeper commitment than the other is prepared to give. The other part of the answer concerns the fact that the unitive meaning of sexual intercourse, insofar as it makes the couple into a single reproductive principle, is part of the good of marriage; but precisely insofar as intercourse is not chosen for any aspect of that good, it does not communicate anything definite by itself, and therefore can communicate good will, affection, and so on only insofar as the couple use their own and each other's bodies as one uses one's tongue to speak, one's finger to point, and so on. But the motive for choosing sexual intercourse to communicate is not that it is especially apt for expressing good will and affection, since modes of communication commonly used by friends—conversation joined with actions conferring benefits (that is, real instantiations of one or more intelligible goods)—are far more expressive. The true motive is sexual desire and the pleasure of satisfying it. Hence, insofar as fornicators are not interested in the marital good, their intercourse is masturbatory. A sign of this masturbatory character is found in another thing many young couples learn by sad experience: nonmarital sexual intimacy obstructs friendship rather than nurturing it.

e) **Sodomites use their bodies in a self-defeating attempt at intimacy.** Like everyone else, sodomites have sexual urges and a natural inclination toward intimate, one-flesh communion. Thus, insofar as they are nonmarried persons who engage in sexual intimacy, their possible motivations and their choices are similar to those of fornicators, and are wrong for the same reasons.

Someone will object: Individuals who find themselves with a homosexual disposition cannot satisfy their sexual urges and natural inclination toward intimate communion in any more adequate way than by establishing a more or less permanent and exclusive relationship, including sexual intimacy. Therefore, while such partners' sodomy allows them only a feeling of intimacy, in choosing to have that experience they do not forgo the choice of the good of marriage, which simply is not accessible to them. Hence, the objection will conclude, sodomites need not choose an illusory good *instead* of a real one, and so their choice need not be unreasonable as that of fornicators is.

However, although it is true that partners in sodomy also could conceivably share in a committed relationship with sincere mutual affection and express their feelings in ways that would be appropriate in any friendship, the coupling of two bodies of the same sex cannot form one complete organism and so cannot contribute to a bodily communion of persons. Hence, the experience of intimacy of the partners in sodomy cannot be the experience of any real unity between them. Rather, each one's experience of intimacy is private and incommunicable, and is no more a common good than is the mere experience of sexual arousal and orgasm. Therefore, the choice to engage in sodomy for the sake of that experience of intimacy in no way contributes to the partners' real common good as committed friends.

Someone who admits that sodomy necessarily lacks the unitive significance of heterosexual intercourse which makes a couple a single reproductive principle might nevertheless suggest that a couple can choose such sodomitic intercourse as a way of communicating good will and affection. However, just as with fornicators, sexual intercourse is not chosen by sodomites in preference to conversation and mutually beneficial acts because it is the more expressive means of communicating good will and affection.[193] Rather, it is chosen because it provides subjective satisfactions otherwise unavailable. Consequently, while sodomites may not choose, as fornicators do, an illusory good *instead* of a real one, they do choose to use their own and each other's bodies to provide subjective satisfactions, and thus they choose self-disintegrity as masturbators do. Of course, while masturbators can be interested exclusively in the experience of sexual arousal and orgasm, sodomites also are interested in the illusion of intimacy.

Thus, those who engage in sodomy can be interested in some aspects of the good of marriage, including satisfaction of the inclination toward sexual intimacy and, perhaps, ongoing partnership in a common life. However, in choosing sexual intercourse for its subjective satisfactions, sodomites violate the body's capacity for self-giving as masturbators do. At the same time, in choosing to act for an experience which they know cannot fulfill that capacity, they act on their inclination toward one-flesh communion in a self-defeating way, and in this respect sodomy is similar to fornication, though more unreasonable.[194]

The preceding explanation has shown what is characteristic of sodomy: an experience of intimacy which cannot be the experience of a real communion of persons, inasmuch as the coupling of two bodies of the same sex cannot form one complete organism. Heterosexual activities deliberately not open to new life provide nothing better than a similar experience of intimacy without any real communion of persons. Thus, such heterosexual activities—including contracepted intercourse, within or outside marriage—are morally similar to sodomy.

f) Complete, nonmarital sexual sins can involve additional evils. Acts which basically are masturbation, fornication, or sodomy can have additional features which cause them to be specifically different kinds of sins. The basic immorality remains, and the additional features add to it.

---

193. James P. Hanigan, *Homosexuality: The Test Case for Christian Sexual Ethics* (New York: Paulist Press, 1988), 97–104, explains this point well, though not all parts of this book can be recommended.

194. Some say that for those with a homosexual orientation, sodomy is natural and therefore good. However, a homosexual disposition is natural only in the sense that any handicap for which an individual is not personally responsible is natural. Recent psychological work on homosexuality makes clear its pathological character and fits well with the argument against sodomy proposed here. See Bartholomew Kiely, S.J., "The Pastoral Care of Homosexual Persons: A Psychological Note," *OR*, 12 Jan. 1987, 6–7, for a useful bibliography and clear summary of relevant literature; Elizabeth R. Moberly, *Homosexuality: A New Christian Ethic* (Cambridge, England: James Clarke, 1983), for fuller development of one plausible psychological account of the homosexual condition and the possibility of healing it. Also see Congregation for the Doctrine of the Faith, *Letter to Bishops of the Catholic Church on the Pastoral Care of Homosexual Persons*, 2–7, *AAS* 79 (1987) 543–47, *OR*, 10 Nov. 1986, 2. The C.D.F.'s use of Scripture regarding sodomy often is criticized, but there are cogent criticisms of the common arguments offered in defense of sodomy: Manuel Miguens, O.F.M., "Biblical Thoughts on 'Human Sexuality,' " in *Human Sexuality in Our Time: What the Church Teaches*, ed. George A. Kelly (Boston: Daughters of St. Paul, 1979), 115–18; P. Michael Ukleja, "Homosexuality and the Old Testament," *Bibliotheca Sacra* 140 (1983): 259–66; Lynne C. Boughton, "Biblical Texts and Homosexuality: A Response to John Boswell," *Irish Theological Quarterly* 58 (1992): 141–53.

Complete sexual acts involving an animal (bestiality) probably often are wholly or mainly masturbatory in their motivation. Insofar as desire for bodily union motivates them, however, they violate human dignity in a unique way by putting human and animal bodies on the same level.

Any of the three basic kinds of act can involve the intentional infliction or undergoing of pain (sadomasochism). Insofar as pain is used to facilitate and/or intensify a sexual experience, the reduction of the body to the status of an object and the quest for satisfaction precisely in doing so increases the self-alienation inherent in masturbation and sodomy. Moreover, while pain itself is not an intelligible evil, the intentional infliction and undergoing of pain often involve some unjustifiable damage or risk to the body, and so violate the good of health.

Any illicit sexual intercourse that could result in conception involves readiness to do injustice to the possible child. Sometimes the couple is open to new life; the injustice lies in accepting the risk that the child will come to be without the stable parental principle necessary for a human being's full development. In other cases a baby is not wanted, and the injustice lies in accepting the risk of a child's coming to be as unwanted, and then perhaps being aborted or else resented and abused after birth. If contraception is used to prevent the coming to be of an unwanted child, still the couple accept the risk of the child's coming to be as unwanted, and also have a contralife will (see 8.E). Whether or not contraception is used, if there is an intention to abort an unwanted child, that intention is homicidal.

Intentionally to tempt and lead another to engage in an illicit sexual act is to commit the sin of sexual seduction, which is a specific form of the sin of scandal (see 4.E.2). Seduction often involves grave deceit, for example, when a man persuades a woman to fornicate by insincerely promising to marry her if she should become pregnant. The seduction of a virgin, other things being equal, is especially wrong, since she loses both the intrinsic and social value of her virginity (see *S.t.,* 2–2, q. 154, a. 6).

Rape adds to illicit sexual intercourse the grave injustice of sexual assault (see 8.G.2; cf. *S.t.,* 2–2, q. 154, a. 7). Since the lack of appropriate consent by either party to any sexual act makes that act sexual assault, fornication and sodomy involving children and others who are incapable of giving the necessary consent always is rape.

Both prostitutes and their clients commit the sin of sexual seduction toward each other. Prostitution also very seriously offends the dignity of the person of the prostitute, by reducing him or her to the status of a mere object of use (see GS 27). When people prostitute themselves out of desperate need, anyone who knows this and uses them both rapes them and commits an additional sin of exploitation, since the need should be dealt with without exacting any immoral and degrading service.

When partners to illicit sexual intercourse are members of the same family, they commit incest. Not only is some incest adultery and/or rape (see 2.b, above), all incest violates familial communion.[195]

---

195. St. Thomas, *In Sent.,* 4, d. 41, q. 1, a. 4, qu'la 1, locates the specific deformity of incest in its violation "naturalis foederis"; also see *S.t.,* 2–2, q. 154, a. 9.

Any illicit sexual act which involves the abuse of anything or anyone dedicated to God is a specific kind of irreverence, and so is a kind of sacrilege. Thus, if an illicit sexual act involves the body of a person vowed to chastity, all who knowingly choose to participate in it commit a sacrilege (see *S.t.*, 2–2, q. 154, a. 10).

g) Incomplete acts take their moral character from complete ones. Incomplete sexual acts are sexual acts—someone intends to bring about or maintain sexual arousal and/or to cause some degree of sexual satisfaction—but they do not involve orgasm. Such acts are not incomplete as human acts, since they carry out a choice, but are incomplete realizations of the body's sexual capacity. *Provided they are intended* to bring about sexual arousal and incomplete satisfaction, the following are among incomplete sexual acts: to imagine sexually stimulating performances by oneself or others, to look at sexually stimulating pictures, to engage in sexually stimulating conversation and behavior—which can include kissing, embracing, and virtually any other sort of bodily contact.

Some incomplete sexual acts are chosen as the certain or possible beginning of complete acts, and so plainly involve the same motivations as the complete acts. Thus, just as incomplete marital acts share in the moral character of marital intercourse, any nonmarital incomplete sexual act directed toward a complete one shares in all the factors that make the corresponding complete act wrong.

Other incomplete, nonmarital sexual acts are intended to remain incomplete. The choice is to bring about or maintain a certain level of sexual arousal and satisfaction, but not to carry the process to its natural culmination. However, erotic desire, which is the emotional motive for seeking sexual satisfaction, always motivates toward some kind of complete act. This is not to say that in choosing an incomplete act one necessarily chooses or even risks a complete act. But it does follow that the choice to seek only limited satisfaction has two objects—(i) the limit and (ii) the satisfaction—and these must be analyzed.

i) The choice is to limit the sexual process: *not* to "go all the way." There can be many motives for doing so, ranging from the wish to avoid pregnancy or disease to qualms of conscience. However, whatever the motives to limit the sexual process might be, they in no way conflict with the motives to engage (within limits) in the act, and those motives (the limits apart) would lead to the complete act.

ii) The choice is to do (within limits) the same kind of thing which one would do if pursuing the process to its culmination, for example, to engage in sexually arousing activities of sorts that usually precede intercourse. Thus, the choice of the incomplete act bears on sexual desire and its satisfaction, one's own body (and the body of anyone else involved), and the good of marriage in the same way that the choice of the corresponding complete act would bear on them.

Consequently, the moral character of the incomplete act, insofar as it is a sexual act, is exactly the same as that of the corresponding complete act (see *S.t.*, 2–2, q. 154, a. 4). The choice of the incomplete act differs morally only in respect to the content of its limiting object, which is irrelevant to the act as sexual, and only relevant to it as a pregnancy-avoiding act, a disease-avoiding act, as less troublesome to conscience than a complete act would be, and so on.

4. Sexual Thoughts Take Their Moral Character from Sexual Acts

Sexual thoughts can refer to two diverse kinds of thing: (i) to memories, images, or perceptions that lead to sexual arousal; (ii) to thoughts of specific sexual acts that provide objects for acts of the will.

i) Intentional sexual arousal is an incomplete sexual act, which has the same moral significance as the act that would complete it. Thus, intentionally to entertain any thought in order to cause or maintain sexual arousal has the same moral significance as the act in which it would culminate. Since the only good complete sexual act is marital intercourse, a choice to entertain thoughts tending toward any other complete sexual act is wrong in the same way that act would be.

ii) Whether sexually arousing or not, thoughts of specific sexual acts can themselves become objects of the will. It is good in itself, though it can be bad as an occasion of sin, to will any good sexual act of which one thinks, for example, for anyone to approve the marital intercourse of a honeymooning couple, for those who are engaged to wish they already were married and could engage in marital intercourse, and so on. Similarly, to will any bad sexual act is a sin of thought of one or another kind (see *CMP,* 15.G). Since one hardly is likely to choose any incomplete sexual act without at least conditionally willing the complete act to which it would lead, a sin of thought of this kind almost always is involved in any sinful incomplete sexual act. However, a sin of thought of this kind can be committed without engaging in an incomplete sexual act. For example, without experiencing any personal arousal or satisfaction, or even wishing for it, one can intentionally approve of someone else's sexual sins.

5. Sexual Satisfaction Can Occur without an Intentional Sexual Act

Sometimes, sexual arousal and even orgasm spontaneously occur. Such an occurrence in itself has no moral significance. Anyone aware of it can rightly be pleased to notice the healthy functioning of his or her body; there is no moral problem unless that functioning causes temptation or results from some earlier sexual sin (see *S.t.,* 2–2, q. 154, a. 5).

Sometimes, sexual arousal and even orgasm occur only as an unwanted side effect of some act chosen for a morally acceptable reason. Such acts must be distinguished from acts in which one intentionally does something to cause or maintain sexual arousal and/or bring about satisfaction. For when sexual arousal and satisfaction are only a side effect, it need not be sinful to accept them in making another, morally good choice. The moral importance of such acts is that they often are occasions of sexual sins (see 8.h, below).

6. All Intentional Sexual Acts Violating the Marital Good Are Grave Matter

As has been explained, apart from acts in which sexual arousal and satisfaction are not intended but only accepted as a side effect, all sexual acts by the unmarried violate the marital good in one or both of two ways: by abusing the body as a capacity for self-giving or by seeking an illusion of one-flesh communion. It is obvious how adultery, both for the married and for any unmarried person involved in it, violates the same good.

Complete solitary acts by the married not only violate the marital good as masturbation always does, but also involve the infidelity of treating the body as one's own, contrary to the gift of it to one's spouse. Complete nonmarital acts by the spouses, including contraceptive intercourse, are wrong in much the same way that fornication or sodomy is and they also involve a masturbatory element; thus, for the married, such acts also are at odds with the marital commitment. When the married intentionally seek or maintain incomplete sexual satisfaction with a view to—or as a partial substitute for—complete satisfaction in any act which would violate the marital good, that incomplete act likewise violates it.

That an act is morally wrong, however, does not automatically make it grave matter. Thus, it remains to explain why the Congregation for the Doctrine of the Faith, despite much contrary contemporary opinion, insists: "According to Christian and the Church's teaching, and as right reason acknowledges, sexual morality encompasses such important human values that every violation of it is objectively grave [note omitted]."[196]

This statement must be understood as referring to intentional sexual acts by the unmarried and to sexual sins of the married which violate the good of marriage. For the document in which the statement occurs focuses exclusively on intentional acts and primarily concerns sexual sins outside marriage. Thus, it is reasonable to suppose that the Congregation neither meant to assert that wrongly accepting sexual arousal or satisfaction as a side effect always is grave matter nor to reject the position, already explained (in 2.g), that within marriage imperfections of chastity that do not violate the marital good are only venially sinful.[197]

In explaining the Church's teaching about gravity of matter, which the Congregation restates, the explanations already given of the *wrongness* of the acts will be presupposed. The point of what follows is that, given their wrongness, they are *gravely* wrong and do not admit parvity of matter.

a) **This teaching of the Church has been proposed infallibly.** Through several centuries, approved Catholic theologians unanimously agreed in teaching that every intentional sexual sin outside marriage is grave matter admitting no parvity, and that the same is true of every intentional sexual sin committed by married persons that involves either the use of contraception, complete satisfaction apart from marital intercourse, or incomplete satisfaction by one spouse unambiguously directed toward complete satisfaction apart from the other.[198] The only kind

---

196. Congregation for the Doctrine of the Faith, *Persona humana,* 10, *AAS* 68 (1976) 89, Flannery, 2:494.

197. The position was articulated by St. Thomas—see *De malo,* q. 15, a. 2, c.—and held by all the approved authors. See, for example, Aertnys, Damen, and Visser, *Theologia moralis,* 2:175–76, 4:256–59, 4:290–94; Marcellinus Zalba, S.J., *Theologiae moralis summa,* 3 vols. (Madrid: Biblioteca de Auctores Cristianos, 1957–58), 2:138–43, 3:721–23; Benedictus H. Merkelbach, O.P., *Summa theologiae moralis,* 4 ed. (Paris: Desclée de Brouwer, 1942), 2:955–58, 3:950–53.

198. Patrick J. Boyle, S.J., *Parvitas Materiae in Sexto in Contemporary Catholic Thought* (Lanham, Md.: University Press of America, 1987), 31–44, provides references to the literature

of intentional sexual act which both violates the marital good and was not explicitly mentioned by the classical moralists is sexual intercourse between a married couple which fails to be marital because it is not performed freely and lovingly. However, their teaching extends to such intercourse just insofar as it is nonmarital, for in that case the sexual satisfaction is sought apart from true marital intercourse.

This theological consensus both reflected and shaped the belief of the whole Catholic Church. All the faithful, from the bishops to the least of the laity, held the same sexual morality. Moreover, they accepted it as part of the faith, for it was taken to be implicit in the sixth and ninth commandments and to be illustrated by various other texts of sacred Scripture. Now, the faithful as a whole cannot err when they all agree on what they take to be God's revealed word about a matter of faith and morals (see LG 12). Therefore, this teaching on sexual morality, although never solemnly defined, cannot be mistaken. It is guaranteed by the Holy Spirit's gift to the Church of infallibility.

Moreover, in teaching this sexual morality, the theologians did not act on their own authority. The authors of the manuals were approved authors, because the popes and bishops authorized their texts for use in teaching seminarians, who as priests would put into pastoral practice what they had learned. The popes and bishops themselves fulfilled their responsibility to teach sexual morality mainly in this way. (On other matters, of course, where theologians disagreed or treated obscure questions or dealt with explanations and details with little or no pastoral impact, their approved status did not imply that the popes and bishops themselves taught what the theologians taught.) Having once been seminarians themselves, the popes and bishops knew the teaching; they also knew the difficulty many of the faithful experienced trying to live by it. Therefore, in matters of sexual morality with great pastoral impact, about which all the approved authors agreed, the popes and bishops of the whole world clearly intended to teach precisely what they authorized their theologians to teach. This universal, constant, and most firm teaching of the popes and the bishops in communion with them around the world meets the conditions which Vatican II articulated for the infallibility of the ordinary magisterium. Although the Church has not solemnly defined the teaching excluding parvity of matter with respect to all intentional sexual sins against the good of marriage, that teaching has been infallibly taught.[199]

---

which substantiate this fact (especially in respect to extramarital acts), although Boyle goes on to reject the classical teaching. For substantiation regarding teaching on contraception: John C. Ford, S.J., and Germain Grisez, "Contraception and the Infallibility of the Ordinary Magisterium," *Theological Studies* 39 (1978): 277–80.

199. See LG 25. See Ford and Grisez, "Contraception and the Infallibility of the Ordinary Magisterium," for the full development of this line of argument. See Francis A. Sullivan, S.J., *Magisterium: Teaching Authority in the Catholic Church* (New York: Paulist Press, 1983), 119–52 for a critique of the Ford-Grisez argument; and Germain Grisez, "Infallibility and Specific Moral Norms: A Review Discussion," *Thomist* 49 (1985): 248–87, for the response to Sullivan's critique. For a summary of other theological debate, see Germain Grisez, "General Introduction," in John C. Ford, S.J., et al., *The Teaching of "Humanae Vitae" : A Defense* (San Francisco: Ignatius Press, 1988), 13–18.

b) **Trent definitively taught the core of this sexual morality.** Against Luther, the Council of Trent solemnly defined that unbelief is not the only mortal sin (see DS 1577/837). Trent showed this by pointing out that, according to St. Paul, divine law also excludes from the kingdom "those with faith who are fornicators, adulterers, effeminate [molles], sodomites, thieves, covetous, drunkards, eviltongued, greedy (see 1 Cor 6.9–10), and all others who commit mortal sins" (DS 1544/808).[200] By this use of Paul's text, the Council implicitly defined the proposition which Paul asserts there. For, in refuting one proposition by asserting another logically incompatible with it, one necessarily asserts the second proposition at least as firmly as the first is rejected. Trent's solemn definition against Luther's notion that unbelief is the only mortal sin implicitly defines as a truth of Catholic faith the Pauline proposition Trent invoked.

Plainly, Trent did not thereby implicitly define all the propositions about sexual acts that are infallibly taught by the ordinary magisterium, for most do not follow with logical necessity from St. Paul's text. It says nothing about incomplete acts and sins of thought, and mentions no sexual sin involving the married except adultery. Also, the word *molles,* which many moral theologians subsequently took to refer to masturbation, often was understood prior to Trent as referring to the receptive role in sodomy.[201] More important, the text from Paul also refers to "thieves, the greedy, drunkards, revilers, robbers," thus including in its list of sins which exclude from the kingdom some admitting of parvity. Thus, considered by itself, this text and the Council's use of it leave open the question—which only Scripture and tradition as a whole settle—whether there can be parvity of matter in sexual sins.[202]

Nevertheless, by the use it makes of 1 Cor 6.9–10, Trent's definitive teaching that unbelief is not the only mortal sin does show that it is a matter of faith that fornicators, adulterers, and sodomites are excluded from the kingdom—in other words, that their typical acts are in themselves grave matters.[203] Other elements of

---

200. Some deny that the New Testament's Greek word, *porneia,* refers to what is meant by *fornication* today, but see John J. O'Rourke, "Does the New Testament Condemn Sexual Intercourse Outside Marriage?" *Theological Studies* 37 (1976): 478–79; Joseph Jensen, O.S.B., "Does *Porneia* Mean Fornication? A Critique of Bruce Malina," *Novum Testamentum* 20 (1978): 161–84.

201. For example, see St. Thomas, *Super primam epistolam ad Corinthios lectura,* on 6.10; *S.t.,* 2–2, q. 138, a. 1, ad 1.

202. It is important to note that, when Church teaching focused on sexual morality itself, New Testament passages other than the one Trent cites against Luther often were used as illustrative. For example, Eph 5.3–12 was cited because it seems to teach the gravity of *all* intentional sexual sins. Warning against "fornication and impurity of any kind" (Eph 5.3), the sacred writer says nobody committing these sins "has any inheritance in the kingdom of Christ and of God" (Eph 5.5). Such sins are "unfruitful works of darkness" (Eph 5.11), completely unsuitable for children of light. Alternative views are excluded: "Let no one deceive you with empty words, for because of these things the wrath of God comes on those who are disobedient" (Eph 5.6). To whom does *no one* refer? Barth, *Ephesians: Chapters 4–6,* 566, mentions several views, but says Abbott's is to be preferred: "Eph 5:6 refers to 'Christians who made light of sin.'" Thus, dissent from Christian teaching on sexual matters began in New Testament times, and is not exclusively a twentieth-century phenomenon.

203. Someone might object that the use Trent makes of 1 Cor 6.9–10, does not show it is a matter of faith that *all* the kinds of sinners Paul mentions are excluded from the kingdom,

the tradition excluded parvity of matter. Thus, one can see why the Catholic Church in modern times developed the firm and uniform teaching concerning sexual acts summarized by the Congregation for the Doctrine of the Faith.

c) **The teaching concerning sexual sins' gravity is reasonable.** Many Catholics who accept and faithfully try to live according to the Church's teaching concerning sexual acts nevertheless are puzzled by it. Why are all sorts of intentional sexual acts which violate the good of marriage the matter of grave sin? Why, moreover, is there no parvity of matter in this whole area as there generally is in others, for example, in most kinds of sin of injustice?

Insight into these matters can help one to see that the Church's teaching on sexual acts is not merely a collection of rules, to appreciate its truth and value, and to live by it. For this reason, it is important not only to accept what the Church teaches but to grasp its reasonableness. That requires reflecting on two things: first, the important human and Christian values at stake in sexual acts, due to which they are in general grave matter; and second, the dynamic factors involved in human sexuality, due to which no kind of sin that violates the good of marriage and no single instance of such a sin will be morally insignificant.

d) **The human values at stake in sexual acts are very important.** While people differ about which values are at stake in sexual acts, nobody seriously denies that they are very important. It hardly needs saying that sex is one of the central human concerns. Considering human inclinations from an evolutionary perspective, this is understandable; otherwise, the human species would have become extinct. For unlike activities essential to the survival of each individual, whose value everyone quickly learns by experience, sexual activity serves a sociobiological purpose which individuals could ignore or even overlook. Thus, the sexual inclination necessarily is both powerful and deeply rooted in the human psyche. One need not agree with psychologists who reduce all human motivation to the erotic drive, in order to hold that sexuality colors every aspect of a man's or a woman's personality.

Moreover, while people differ about the moral norms of sexual activity, few who wish to be morally upright deny that marrying, having children, and raising them are among the best things in human life, those prized for their own sakes, and that it is important to integrate one's sexuality with other elements of one's personality. Faith both confirms and clarifies these human insights in its teaching on the goodness of marital communion, procreation, the raising of children, and chastity.

Even people who reject most of Catholic sexual morality can see how much harm is done by the kinds of acts its norms indicate to be sins.[204] The facts are

---

but only that at least one kind is, because a single counterexample falsifies Luther's position, so that for Trent's purpose it was sufficient if at least one of the kinds of acts Paul mentions is grave matter. However, although Luther indeed is refuted if any kind of act other than unbelief is a mortal sin, he is not refuted by Paul's proposition unless that proposition is asserted, and the proposition is that *all* the kinds of sinners mentioned are excluded from the kingdom, not that at least one kind is.

204. A telling critique of many permissive opinions from a strictly humanist viewpoint: Maggie Gallagher, *Enemies of Eros: How the Sexual Revolution Is Killing Family, Marriage, and Sex and What We Can Do about It* (Chicago: Bonus Books, 1989).

plain: women abandoned and left alone to care for children, children unwanted and aborted or abused, marriages and other intimate relationships strained and destabilized. These evils follow directly from extramarital and premarital intercourse. But most such intercourse is not motivated only by the desire to experience intimate communion; usually an important element in the motivation is the elementary desire for sexual satisfaction. Sexual desire is natural, and chastity is not easily achieved by fallen humans. But the devastating power of undisciplined sexual desire is the fruit of the theory that everyone is entitled to regular orgasms and of putting that theory into practice: masturbatory sexual activity as an accepted part of many people's lives.

That theory and practice also lead to the success of enterprises built on manipulating men by arousing their lust, pandering to them, and making women into sex objects. These enterprises usually also encourage and exploit a dark fascination with violence, and thus reinforce the reduction of personal bodies to the status of mere objects, to be used and abused for the sake of psychological satisfactions.

The promoters of sexual liberation thought it would eliminate the pain of sexual frustration and make society as a whole more joyful. What has happened instead shows how wrong they were. The pain of sexual frustration is slight in comparison with the misery of abandoned women and unwanted children, of people lonely for lack of true marital intimacy, of those dying wretchedly from sexually transmitted disease. Moreover, unchastity's destructive effects on so many families impact on the wider society, whose stability depends on families. The social costs not only are immense, but reinforce the personal problems that give rise to them. Boys and girls coming to maturity without solid formation in a stable family are ill prepared to assume adult social responsibilities. Public assistance to those who suffer private abandonment or neglect is both costly and inefficient; and people accustomed to self-indulgence find repugnant the sacrifices which providing adequate help for those in need would require. Thus, public attempts to mitigate the damage lead to the vigorous promotion of contraception, programs of sex education that take for granted and even encourage the masturbatory motive, and the legalization and public funding of abortion.

e) **The Christian values at stake are even more important.** Since central truths of Christian faith employ concepts drawn from marital and familial relationships, no one can accept the faith who does not understand well the human significance of a father, a child, a brother or sister, a faithful spouse. Indeed, the sounder people's experience of these realities is, the more easily they understand and accept God's tender mercy and absolute faithfulness. Underlying these revelatory realities is human sexuality and God's plan for its right use. Human sexuality might be said to be part of the language God uses to reveal himself. God did not learn this language from his creation; he invented it, among other reasons, to serve his revelatory purpose; and every abuse distorts the meanings of this "language" of God and garbles the message he wishes to communicate as much to every man and woman of today as to people of all nations and all times.

At the heart of the revelatory function of human sexuality is the natural sacramentality of marriage. This is the foundation for its specifically Christian sacramentality, which gives Christian marriage its special firmness and holiness. The sacramentality of marriage foreshadows the ultimate fulfillment of the human body as a capacity for self-giving: communion in the one-flesh reality of Jesus' risen life (see C.4, above). Since this is the human body's ultimate end, every abuse of human sexuality violates not only the natural marital good but an infinitely greater good: the body of Christ.

> The body is meant not for fornication but for the Lord, and the Lord for the body. And God raised the Lord and will also raise us by his power. Do you not know that your bodies are members of Christ? Should I therefore take the members of Christ and make them members of a prostitute? Never! Do you not know that whoever is united to a prostitute becomes one body with her? For it is said, "The two shall be one flesh." But anyone united to the Lord becomes one spirit with him. Shun fornication! Every sin that a person commits is outside the body; but the fornicator sins against the body itself. Or do you not know that your body is a temple of the Holy Spirit within you, which you have from God, and that you are not your own? For you were bought with a price; therefore glorify God in your body. (1 Cor 6.13–20; cf. 1 Thes 4.1–8; GS 14)

St. Paul's argument against fornication tells against other sexual sins.[205] For example, masturbation is not merely self-abuse, but abuse of the body of Christ; in damaging the body as a capacity for self-giving in genuine interpersonal communion, masturbation damages the Christian's capacity for sharing in the communion of the new covenant.

Besides, just as sexual immorality damages civil society, so it also weakens the body of Christ insofar as that body is a visible human community: the Church. For the large Church depends on stable families, its little domestic Churches, to provide new members, well prepared to live apostolic lives. Habitual unchastity nips in the bud not only vocations to priesthood and religious life, but also vocations to marriage, since people who cannot subordinate sexual desire to marital love are hardly prepared to accept marriage as a vocation.

Moreover, as explained earlier, much sexual immorality involves objectifying the body and alienating it from the conscious subject. When a Christian habitually degrades his or her own body and the bodies of others to the status of mere sex objects and instruments of satisfaction, he or she tends to carry this attitude over into other relationships, eventually depersonalizing everyone's body and the human body as such. Once depersonalized, the body seems to lack personal significance, to be only an instrument, perhaps dispensable and, if so, better dispensed with. Gradually this implicit acceptance of body-soul dualism makes it difficult to see why one should hope for one's own bodily resurrection, center one's faith on Jesus' resurrection, regard his bodily presence in the Eucharist as real, consider his virgin birth significant, or even regard as meaningful the teaching that original sin

---

205. For the generalization of the argument, see John Paul II, General Audience (11 Feb. 1981), *Inseg.* 6.1 (1981) 258–61, *OR,* 16 Feb. 1981, 3, 12. An illuminating commentary on the relationship between charity and chastity in St. Paul: Barnabas Mary Ahern, C.P., "Christian Holiness and Chastity," in *Declaration on Certain Questions Concerning Sexual Ethics: II, Commentaries* (Washington, D.C.: United States Catholic Conference, 1977), 111–19.

is transmitted by propagation. Indeed, once the body is depersonalized, it no longer seems credible—unless one supposes that God himself is a mere object and instrument—that a bodily human individual could be divine, that "the Word became flesh and lived among us" (Jn 1.14), and that one should live in the hope of seeing and touching "what we have seen with our eyes, what we have looked at and touched with our hands" (1 Jn 1.1).[206]

Thus, when sexual immorality becomes an accepted part of a Christian's life, it subverts the incarnationalism and sacramentalism at the heart of Catholic faith. More than that, it subverts faith in God the creator. For insofar as sense satisfaction is so highly valued that one is willing to violate intelligible goods for its sake, one tends to regard only two realities as important: the conscious experience in which that satisfaction is obtained and the instruments—the alienated body and desacralized world—used to bring about the satisfaction. Everything transcending immediate experience, including truth and virtue and God himself, begins to seem less real, perhaps completely irrelevant and even unreal.

Furthermore, insofar as the person is alienated by sexual immorality from his or her own body, its meaning and value seem to arise from the conscious subject's plan in using it and satisfaction resulting from that use. But deriving the human body's meaning and value from these sources directly contradicts its divinely given meaning and value, its capacity for self-giving, which sexual immorality violates. Consequently, sexual immorality makes it very difficult to believe that the human body and the natural world of which it is a part have meaning and value independent of human use, and so makes it very difficult to believe in the source of that meaning and value: God the creator. Although St. Paul did not explain how sexual immorality leads to unbelief, he saw the essential relationship between them, for he pointed out that unbelief leads to sexual immorality (see Rom 1.18–28).

f) The evil of sexual sins is never merely private. It is clear from the preceding that even solitary sexual sins are social sins insofar as they violate the body's capacity for self-giving and the sacramental significance of human sexuality. Moreover, if one considers masturbation not as an abstract kind of act but concretely, its social significance is even more unmistakable, for people are hardly likely to regard others' bodies with more respect than they regard their own. Also, it is questionable whether anyone can masturbate without some fantasy of a partner with whom sexual inclination would be more adequately satisfied. Thus, masturbation tends to make everyone's body into a sex object and predisposes masturbators to treat their sexual partners as masturbatory tools. But sexual intercourse cannot be a communion of persons if it is little more than the juxtaposition of instruments used by isolated self-conscious subjects to reach individual and incommunicable enjoyable sensations. Therefore, masturbation is essentially a social sin against interpersonal communion.

Then too, the kinds of sexual sins that most plainly have socially destructive consequences—adultery, fornication, and sodomy—would be committed far less

---

206. See Germain Grisez, "Turmoil in the Church," *Homiletic and Pastoral Review* 85 (Nov. 1984): 12-22.

often if it were not for the masturbatory component in their motivation. And that motivation would not be so prevalent if the practice of masturbation were not considered a minor moral evil, if that.

Besides, other areas of the masturbator's life are bound to be affected by the fact that he or she treats sensory satisfaction as a—perhaps, *the*—basic good, and also by his or her handicap with respect to sexual communion and attitude toward the body. If people habitually subordinate the marital good to the experience of sexual satisfaction, they are hardly likely to exercise self-mastery for the sake of relevant intelligible goods in their use of drugs, alcohol, food, play activities, and so on. If they habitually regard their own bodies, not as integral components of their selves but as mere instruments of their real selves, they are hardly likely to understand the self-alienation involved in lying and are likely to perceive other human bodies— other people—as instruments to be manipulated. Little wonder if living human persons who are not yet, or else no longer are, conscious subjects are regarded as mere objects, which, if not useful, may be disposed of.

The sensate culture manifests and also serves the masturbatory personality. Not only the professional prostitute and the pornographer but a very substantial proportion of those involved in socially accepted media employ them not so much to communicate with audiences as to manipulate them by appealing to and encouraging the masturbatory component in each individual's personality. Thus, the whole society becomes polluted, with the bad result that chastity, always difficult, becomes almost humanly impossible for children as well as for repentant adults struggling to achieve sexual self-control, and is very difficult even for the virtuous. Moreover, the sensate culture's impact goes far beyond its explicitly sexual content. Even in watching a seemingly innocent cartoon, children are likely to imbibe false beliefs and attitudes about the value of sensory satisfaction, how to regard one's own body and other persons, and all the human and Christian values at stake in sexual activity.

g) No individual sexual sin is a merely transient evil. While isolated, individual sexual sins are possible, they seldom occur in practice, except as lapses on the part of those who consider them gravely wrong and usually manage to avoid them. Temptations to commit many other kinds of sins—for example, lying and most kinds of injustice—spring from circumstantial factors, not from any deep, constant, strong human motive. But the sexual appetite is active and powerful through a long part of one's life, and so sexual sins are very likely to become habits. Satisfying the appetite intensifies it; sex is very habit forming. To try sex, focusing on the enjoyable experience itself, is to like it and want more of it. As time goes by, satisfying this habit, like a drug habit, demands more intense and fresh sexual stimuli. That is why the masturbatory component in sexual motivation always demands new partners and new thrills, and is the implacable foe of fidelity and normal heterosexual intercourse.

Even if sexual acts done solely or primarily for the enjoyable experience were not so strongly habit forming, someone who considered isolated sexual sins not seriously wrong never would be strongly motivated to repent them. Instead, he or she frequently would be strongly tempted to commit them, since the motivation and opportunity to enjoy the experience are nearly always present. Hence, failing to appreciate the gravity of each individual sexual sin is very likely to lead to a habit of sinning. Individual sexual sins which are not considered seriously wrong are not likely to be repented, and are almost certain to contribute to and share in all the evils of habitual sexual sins.

Some argue that, at least in the case of masturbation, very little is at stake in any particular act, so that isolated acts can be considered light matter and, even if fully deliberate, only venial sins. This argument makes two key assumptions which have already been criticized: that at least this kind of sexual sin is not grave and that it makes sense to talk about isolated sexual acts motivated by the desire for the enjoyable experience. Even if these two key assumptions were granted, however, the argument still would fail. For someone who masturbates is likely to fantasize some kind of sinful intercourse with a partner; and to consent to that fantasy would be a grave sin of thought. So, each act of masturbation—even supposing, though not conceding, that it otherwise would only be light matter—is grave matter insofar as it is a proximate occasion of a grave sin of thought (see 4.D.3.c).

h) The evil of sinful incomplete sexual acts is not merely partial. Some offer an argument along the same lines for parvity of matter in the sinfulness of incomplete sexual acts. The answer also is along the same lines. Moreover, an incomplete sexual act involves some sexual arousal, and emotional desire for and enjoyment of any sexual arousal tends toward complete satisfaction. Thus, sinful incomplete sexual acts occasion not only sins of thought but also sinful complete sexual acts. There can be no more justification for entering this proximate occasion of sin than for entering the other one.

It will be objected that the preceding argument assumes that the incomplete sexual acts in question are at least venially sinful, whereas many incomplete sexual acts should be considered different in kind from the complete sexual acts to which they correspond, so that, for example, even a passionate kiss is an entirely different thing, morally speaking, from fornication. The first thing to notice in answer to this objection is that there are passionate kisses which are not sinful incomplete sexual acts, for example, some kisses of chaste engaged couples (see I.3.a, below). But if experiencing passion is included in the choice carried out by the passionate kiss, and if the passion would find its complete satisfaction in fornication, then, as has been shown above, although the two plainly do differ greatly as outward performances, the moral act of passionate kissing is the same in kind as the moral act of fornicating. In that case, the passionate kiss is grave matter (see DS 2060/1140), for what one chooses is morally determinative, even though one for some reason forgoes complete satisfaction.

i) Sins intentionally violating the marital good admit no parvity. The considerations in f–h explain why parvity of matter in sexual sins is not to be found where some have looked for it: in supposedly private, isolated, or incomplete sexual acts. Still there remains a general reason for puzzlement. The classical moralists had a saying: "No parvity of matter in the sixth and ninth commandments." Yet it seems odd that almost any deliberate sexual sin is mortal while deliberate sins of other kinds often are only venial, even if they involve unfairness and manifest lack of Christian mercy and love of neighbor. A fully satisfactory solution to this puzzle would require articulating a complete theory of gravity and parvity of matter, and applying it to every kind of sin. But even without that, the previous explanations and a few additional considerations can throw a good deal of light on the matter.

To begin with, "No parvity of matter in the sixth and ninth commandments," is an oversimplification. As has been explained in the introduction to this seciton, there can be parvity of matter (and thus only venial sin) in sexual sins which do not intentionally violate the marital good: some sinful accepting of sexual satisfaction as a side effect and the imperfections in the chastity of spouses who nevertheless engage in essentially upright marital acts. At the same time, parvity also is excluded from some kinds of grave sin outside the sexual domain, for example, kidnapping, enslaving, and murdering someone. Moreover, there are many other kinds of sinful acts, such as sacrilege, whose definitions do not distinguish between an intentional violation of the good at stake and harm to it which is accepted as a side effect. In such cases, the intentional violation of the good sometimes excludes parvity of matter (for example, intentional irreverence toward God), but parvity is possible in other cases (certain cases of slight irreverence accepted as a side effect). Thus, the idea that the other commandments are altogether different from the sixth and ninth in regard to parvity is to some extent merely the result of how kinds of sins happen to be defined: the definitions of the various kinds of sexual sins imply an intentional violation of the marital good, while the definitions of many other kinds of sins do not imply the intentional violation of any basic human good.

If a sin grave in kind admits parvity, that must have a cause. In matters of justice, as was explained (in 6.A.7), the cause of parvity is that unfairness begins as soon as one does not do unto others as one would have them do unto oneself and those for whom one cares, while grave injustice only begins when one does not do unto others as one would have them *held* to do. While that does not explain the possibility of parvity in sins such as sacrilege, still the cause of parvity in sins against God is analogous: revelation, as interpreted by the tradition, makes it clear that, although certain sins against God are intolerable, in his tender love he is prepared to overlook some offenses even in matters of religion where the harm is only accepted as a side effect. But there is nothing analogous to cause parvity in intentional violations of the marital good. Although these sins never are merely private, their sinfulness is not primarily in offending against God or neighbor considered as persons distinct from oneself, but against oneself—"the fornicator sins against the body itself" (1 Cor 6.18)—and only thereby against God and neighbor, insofar as one should be in communion with them. Thus, in sexual sins, there can be no cause for parvity of matter analogous to the factors which account for it in sins of injustice and irreverence. If sins intentionally violating the marital good were to admit parvity, there would have to be an altogether different kind of cause.

Several factors sometimes suggested as causes of parvity in the sexual domain were examined in f–h and found not to be so, because sexual activities constitute so tightly knit a fabric. That tightness of knit also has been clarified. All the sins in question not only violate the basic good of marital communion but flow from the same nonrational motive: sexual desire unintegrated in a way of life bearing on that good in accord with reason. Sexual appetite is a powerful, continuing motivator, not easily restrained and not naturally opposed by other emotional motives. Insofar as a person becomes resigned to any kind of sexual sin, rational motivation no longer curbs sexual appetite. And insofar as virtue remains imperfect, no constant emotional motive opposes the satisfaction of nonintegrated sexual desire. By contrast, the various activities in which injustice occurs do not constitute so tightly knit a fabric. Some emotional motives for treating others wrongly—anger and hatred—are not constant, and are elicited only by some factor outside oneself. Although desire for goods, for oneself and those one cares about, as well as fear of threats to those goods, are constant motives which easily lead to injustice, they encounter constant opposition at their own level: the natural desire for community and fear of isolation. Hence, if an injustice is not grave, on the basis that makes for parvity of matter in matters of justice (explained in 6.A.7), it need not be grave on another basis: by carrying out a choice to act on the very motives underlying great injustices. Therefore, someone striving in large matters to fulfill the command to love one's neighbor as oneself can resign himself or herself to some kinds of petty unfairness, without giving free reign to unreasonable motivations of the sorts that lead to grave injustices. But someone who hopes to achieve chastity cannot intentionally make even the smallest unreasonable concession to sexual appetite.

Finally, although the evil in sexual sins is not primarily in any injustice they may involve, they should not be supposed to be compatible with love of neighbor. As has been explained, these sins are never merely private and always violate that basic human good in which love of neighbor is realized in a very fundamental and clear way: marital communion and the whole network of intimate relationships flowing from and depending on it. Moreover, sexual sins violate the requirements of neighbor love not only insofar as it bears on the natural goods of human persons and their communion, but also, as has been explained, insofar as it directs Christians toward a life of grace and heavenly communion. Indeed, since love of God depends on faith in him, and sexual sins inevitably pose a threat to faith, they never can be considered insignificant violations of charity toward God.

Grave sins are grave because incompatible with faith and its specific require-ments (see *CMP,* 16.G.7–12). Christian tradition recognized that any intentional violation of the marital good has this character. While theological explanations were not as clear as they might have been, traditional talk about the daughters of lust—the observed effects on Christian life of habitual, sinful sexual indulgence—shows that the opposition between sexual sin and faith was known sufficiently well.[207] Consequently, "No parvity of matter in the sixth and ninth command-ments" is no mere rule.

---

207. See, for example, St. Thomas, *S.t.,* 2–2, q. 15, a. 3; q. 20, a. 4; q. 53, a. 6; q. 153, aa. 4–5; *De malo,* q. 15, a. 4.

7. While Subjective Factors Can Mitigate Guilt, Sex Sins Remain Serious

Since grave matter is not the only condition for mortal sin, not all sins intentionally violating the marital good are mortal. Sufficient reflection and full consent also are necessary (see *CMP*, 15.C). Therefore, even if one does something which of itself violates the marital good, it is possible that one commits only a venial sin due to lack of full consent or sufficient reflection. But their frequent absence should not be presumed, on the basis that it is hard to control sexual appetite. On the contrary, even those enmeshed in quasi-compulsive sins of weakness should be presumed to be acting with sufficient knowledge and freedom (see *CMP*, 17.E). And in examining one's own conscience, one must be aware that, having judged a certain matter to be grave and simultaneously having chosen to do it, one has committed a mortal sin, despite choosing reluctantly, being motivated by intense passion, and hoping, even while sinning, for the grace of repentance.

Moreover, such a sin remains serious even when it is venial due to lack of sufficient reflection and/or full consent. Though compatible with charity, like any venial sin, it still carries with it the evil that makes sins of its kind grave: it still abuses the body and violates the marital good, still undermines the Christian attitude toward the body and so weakens faith.

Eventually, too, this abuse and violation are very likely to lead to mortal sins. For example, those who commit sexual sins of thought or incomplete acts, not realizing them to be grave matter, will surely be tempted to commit complete acts of masturbation, fornication, sodomy, or adultery, and almost surely will do so. Again, adolescents misled into thinking that isolated acts of masturbation are not grave matter will surely be tempted, and almost certainly will sin again and again, until a habit of yielding to unchaste desire is formed. This habit probably will lead at least to later heterosexual or homosexual sex play, if not to fornication or sodomy. In very many cases, it also will manifest itself in marriage: spouses not only will find it difficult to abstain when there is a reason to do so, but will engage in marital intercourse with seriously mixed motives, so that its power to express and nurture conjugal love will be greatly weakened. When marital difficulties arise, old habits of unchastity will reassert themselves, leading to the practice of contraception, recurrent masturbation, the use of pornography and fantasies of adultery, acts of adultery, and the marital instability and conflict which all too often end with divorce.

8. Grace Empowers Christians to Pursue Chastity and Attain It

Plainly it is difficult, even humanly impossible, for people to avoid sexual sins. But what fallen men, women, and children cannot do by themselves can be done with the Holy Spirit's assistance. It is a truth of faith that grace enables every Christian to avoid mortal sin. Quoting St. Augustine, the Council of Trent definitively teaches: " 'God does not command the impossible; but in commanding he cautions you both to do what you can and to pray for what you cannot,' and he helps you so that you can do it" (DS 1536/804, translation amended; cf. DS 1568/828). For mortal sinners to tell themselves that this truth is not true for them—that they no longer can count on God to enable them to live blamelessly in his sight—is the sin of despair.

Despair, however, is not the only sin against hope. It is presumption to suppose God will save someone who ignores his caution to do what can be done. Grace does not substitute for doing what one can. Rather, God's good will is so great that he wishes his gifts also to be human merits (see DS 1548/810; cf. 1582/842). So, the realities to which *grace* refers include the gift of the desire for holiness, the power to act, the awareness of what should be done, the free choice to do it, the doing of it, the merit for so doing, and the reward for that merit.

Consequently, since grace empowers Christians to attain chastity by doing what they can, it is important to recall and apply some of the things said elsewhere about organizing one's Christian life and overcoming sin. Here as in other areas of life, of course, the Christian is not a Stoic engaged in a lonely quest for moral perfection, but part of the body of Christ, whose members, enlivened by his Spirit, should work and grow together in holiness by bearing one another's burdens.

The general program for avoiding and overcoming sin was spelled out (in 4.D): keep relevant truths in mind, pray, deny oneself, serve others, avoid occasions of sin, anticipate and resist temptations, seek and accept help and support from a person or group capable of providing it. What is said here presupposes that program, while focusing on mistakes to be avoided and steps to be taken in dealing with sexual sins.[208]

a) **One must not use a self-defeating strategy to overcome sin.** Certain misconceived pastoral attempts to help people deal with sins of weakness involve strategies which not only fail to help but make matters worse. Sometimes pastors give advice which is sound as far as it goes—for example, to pray for grace and receive the sacraments regularly—but omits other things (treated in 4.D and below) essential for success. Those who try to follow the advice are likely to fail repeatedly, and as a result to lose confidence not only in themselves but in God.

Not only that, discouraged sinners, and even inexperienced children, sometimes receive not only inadequate but pernicious advice about dealing with sexual temptation. Some teachers and pastors say, for example, that virtually everyone sometimes commits sexual sins, that too much should not be made of them, that the only thing really necessary is to struggle against temptations to impurity, so that gradually sexual sins become less frequent and eventually perfect chastity is achieved.[209] For two reasons, this advice guarantees failure at least as surely as would similar advice given to someone with a habit of abusing alcohol or some other psychoactive substance.

First, it implicitly assumes that intentional sexual sins admit parvity of matter. But they do not; and part of the reason why—the dynamic factors at work in this area of life—guarantees that the advice, far from helping in the eventual achievement of chastity, will lead to a continuing and even stronger habit of impurity.

---

208. A sound work offering helpful insight and many suggestions for nurturing chastity: Benedict J. Groeschel, O.F.M.Cap., *The Courage to Be Chaste* (New York: Paulist Press, 1985).

209. See F.1.i, below, for a very clear response by John Paul II to advice along these lines given married couples in respect to the practice of contraception.

Second, and even more pernicious, an unstated but real component of this bad advice is: do not have a firm purpose of amendment—in other words, do not repent. Similar-sounding advice can rightly be given to people struggling with habits of venial sin, which they commit nondeliberately, that is, without sufficient reflection or full consent or both. But those struggling against temptations to commit sexual sins must be presumed to be sinning deliberately. They are, or should be, acutely aware of the evil to which they are tempted, and their surrender to the temptation generally is a fully conscious choice against conscience (see *CMP*, 17.E). Someone who attempts to reduce sexual sins gradually has an effective will to continue committing some such sins; not committing them at all remains only an inefficacious wish (see 4.C.3.b). Even if the wish remains when temptation arises, the effective will takes specific shape in the choice to sin again. For achieving any virtue, however, a will consistent with itself is absolutely essential, since a virtue's core is precisely the steady volitional love of the goods at stake and hatred of the evils that mutilate them. Advice to follow a gradual program of reducing sexual sins is therefore certain to be disastrous. The only way to stop committing sexual sins is simply to stop committing them, at once and forever, and the only hope of doing that is to have, not merely the wish for eventual chastity, but a firm and efficacious commitment to be chaste today, tomorrow, the next day . . . .[210]

b) **One should always keep in mind what is at stake in sexual sin.** For several reasons, it is very difficult to keep in mind the human and Christian values at stake in sexual acts. Human sexuality itself is mysterious, and sexual appetite tends to distract attention from intelligible goods. Moreover, the surrounding sensate culture insistently conveys an ideology which conceals the real values at stake, while rationalizing their habitual and even systematic violation. It is not surprising if even Catholics who accept the Church's teaching in this area and try to live by it sometimes see it as a kind of penance, something like the old Friday abstinence but more burdensome. Then even the gospel's plain norms concerning sex can seem to be an odd bit of bad news, to be accepted along with the good news, while, at least in this matter, people who do not accept any of the Church's teaching are better off because they can enjoy guilt-free sex.

As the preceding sections of this question make clear, this attitude is entirely mistaken. In particular, Catholic teaching concerning sexual morality is not a set of rules made up and imposed by the Church. St. Paul already encountered that error and firmly rejected it, blocking legalists' evasions by using language they would understand:

> This is the will of God, your sanctification: that you abstain from fornication; that each one of you know how to control your own body in holiness and honor, not with lustful passion, like the Gentiles who do not know God; that no one

---

210. It follows that many frequently employed pastoral strategies are disastrous. For a sound pastoral strategy, to which Vatican II made reference (in DH 14, n. 36 [n. 57 in Abbott]), see Pius XII, *De conscientia christiana in iuvenibus recte efformanda, AAS* 44 (1952) 270–78, *The Pope Speaks: The Teachings of Pope Pius XII*, ed. Michael Chinigo (New York: Pantheon Books, 1957), 93–99. Also see Germain Grisez et al., " 'Every Marital Act Ought to Be Open to New Life': Toward a Clearer Understanding," *Thomist* 52 (1988): 418–26.

wrong or exploit a brother or sister in this matter, because the Lord is an avenger
in all these things, just as we have already told you beforehand and solemnly
warned you. For God did not call us to impurity but in holiness. Therefore
whoever rejects this rejects not human authority but God, who also gives his Holy
Spirit to you. (1 Thes 4.3–8)

Thus, Christian sexual morality is an essential part of God's wise and loving plan,
which also includes the gift of the Holy Spirit. Moral truth and the Spirit's power
liberate Jesus' followers from the degradation of the unbelieving world and enable
them to live with honor and holiness: human fulfillment in Jesus together with a
share in his divine sonship. "The fruit of chastity," John Paul II teaches, "is the
interior harmony of the person, the capacity to realize a generous and unselfish
love, in freedom of spirit and with a more lively sensitivity to the value of divine
and transcendent goods."[211]

In practice, moreover, a legalistic attitude makes it virtually impossible to live
chastely. Anything felt to be an imposed restraint on one's deeply rooted appetites
provokes anger and rebelliousness; and if sexual self-indulgence is regarded as a
very desirable but unfortunately forbidden fruit, one is likely to look for some way
to reconcile its enjoyment with Christian faith and life, for example, by a repeated
round of sinning, "repenting," confessing, and sinning again. Consequently, it is
very important to understand, reflect on, and regularly call to mind what really is
at stake and how much one stands to lose if one commits sexual sins. Both love of
God and love of neighbor require that chastity be regarded as something worth
working for, and, insofar as one has it, something to be prized and cherished.

c) **One's sexuality should be integrated with one's personal vocation.** Christian love's general requirement of chastity is specified for each individual by his
or her personal vocation; moreover, the latter must provide the necessary emotional
motivation to channel sexual appetite. This it does by establishing a set of commitments toward particular goods and particular persons which implement faith and
love. In carrying out those commitments, one sensibly experiences the persons to
whom one wills goods, their enjoyment of them, and their suffering through
privation of them; and one good result is that these emotions are experienced in
harmony with faith and love. In this way, personal vocation generates the emotions
required to motivate a consistent Christian response to the values concretely at stake
in sexual acts as well as in other areas of life.

d) **For spouses, conjugal love is the principle of chastity.** Marriage remedies
concupiscence, not merely by providing a legitimate opportunity for sexual gratification, but by making available the sacramental grace of the Holy Spirit so that
spouses can integrate their sexual desire with the good of marriage (see 1.e, above).
Constant prayer for the Spirit's help, fidelity practiced from the beginning of
marriage, and chaste marital intercourse, as well as other acts of good family life,
strengthen both volitional and emotional love. Conjugal love, the central principle
of sexual morality, does not will the marital good as an abstract value but as it is

---

211. John Paul II, Homily at the Tomb of St. Maria Goretti, 6, *Inseg.* 9.2 (1986) 738, *OR,*
20 Oct. 1986, 10. Cf. Georges Cottier, O.P., "La conception chrétienne de la sexualité," *Nova
et vetera* 52 (1977): 1–21.

concretely realized in one's own marriage. Thus, the principle of sexual morality becomes, and is experienced as, an important part of one's own fulfillment and that of one's spouse.

One's responsibilities in the situation are obvious, and chastity is developed in fulfilling them as well as one can. By doing what is appropriate as a spouse and parent, a person serves those to whom he or she is committed. Their needs, and the benefits they enjoy from one's service, are not abstractions but realities, seen and felt and shared in. This experience involves and elicits powerful emotions—not only erotic affection but other feelings—which can limit, even oppose, sexual desire at its own level, thus harnessing and channeling it toward the intelligible goods at stake.

As the couple's chastity grows, they appreciate and rejoice in each other, their love remains lively even when difficulties arise, and, even in a psychological sense, adultery and divorce become unthinkable. Thus, Vatican II teaches:

> Sealed by mutual faithfulness and hallowed above all by Christ's sacrament, this [conjugal] love remains indissolubly faithful in body and in mind, in bright days or dark, and so it entirely excludes adultery and divorce. Firmly established by the Lord, the unity of marriage will radiate from the equal personal dignity of wife and husband, a dignity acknowledged by mutual and total love. The constant fulfillment of the duties of this Christian vocation demands notable virtue. For this reason, strengthened by grace for holiness of life, the couple will painstakingly cultivate and pray for endurance in love, largeheartedness, and the spirit of sacrifice. (GS 49)

e) For priests and religious, chastity rechannels sexual energy. Those called to celibacy or virginity for the kingdom's sake must not view sexual continence as a mere means to fulfilling their vocation, much less an arbitrary condition for ordination or sharing in the mission of a religious community. How they use sexual capacity is at the heart of their vocation, which for them must play the role which marriage plays for the married. Their commitment also requires them to interact with and benefit particular persons. If they properly fulfill their responsibilities, they rightly and richly realize their bodies' capacity for self-giving, and others receive their persons, not merely their services. In such selfless giving to the wider family of God, they receive benefits analogous to those of spouses and parents. Espoused to Jesus and spiritually parenting the children of the Church, those who live in perfect continence for the kingdom's sake also can develop the emotions necessary to transform sexual desire, not by satisfying or repressing it, but by rechanneling its energy into affection for a particular group of persons: these parishioners, this group of students, these patients . . ..[212]

This use of sexual capacity by no means negates its human and personal value. Indeed, in cherishing certain particular persons, and Christ in them, chaste priests and religious make present important features of heavenly communion which are absent from the sacrament of marriage. While in marriage two persons are so truly

---

212. See John Paul II, General Audience (28 Apr. 1982), *Inseg.* 5.1 (1982) 1344–48, *OR,* 3 May 1982, 3, 12.

united that they become, as it were, one new person, even so their distinctive bodily communion is limited to themselves and based on only one human capacity: reproduction. By contrast, the priest or religious can love and serve an indefinite multitude and realize the body's capacity for self-giving in a wide range of interpersonal relationships. In this way, continence for the kingdom's sake truly becomes an effective sign of the coming kingdom and its perfect communion of risen humankind in Jesus with God.[213]

f) **Anyone's present vocation can provide this integrating principle.** For part or, in some cases, all of their lives, all Christians lack the integrating principle of commitment to marriage or to complete continence for the kingdom's sake. But none ever lacks a personal vocation capable of integrating sexual appetite.

Since those who are neither married nor committed to complete continence for the kingdom's sake usually can and should look forward to making one commitment or the other, their vocation now is to prepare to fulfill whichever they may eventually make. This requires not only maintaining their bodies' capacity for self-giving by not abusing them sexually but employing that capacity, somewhat as faithful priests and religious do, in unselfish interpersonal relationships. In doing this, they should not suppose their effort to be chaste will bear fruit only in the future, in relation to those with whom they will enter into more specific communion later; for it has present benefits for those with whom they live now in the general communion of Christian life.

Moreover, their unselfish relationships and sexual self-control already manifest the value of the kingdom for which they hope and the power of the Spirit by whom they walk. Of course, that is true of every aspect of a faithful Christian's life, but it is especially true of this one. Not every Catholic adolescent, for instance, has occasion to bear witness as St. Maria Goretti did, yet the example of unembarrassed chastity given by a cheerful and outgoing Catholic boy or girl is a powerful proclamation of the gospel in the contemporary world and a great encouragement to other Christians, not least those already committed to marriage or complete continence for the kingdom's sake.

What about those who are married but apparently permanently separated from their spouses and those, including some with a homosexual orientation, who apparently lack the gifts for either marriage or a life of committed continence? Though such people suffer under a serious obstacle to living a good Christian life, their condition is not in itself a moral evil. Perhaps they never will achieve a habit of chastity so stable that they will no longer need to struggle against sexual temptations. But if they faithfully do what they can to remain continent, making determined, persevering use of the same means that others struggling against temptation must use, they need not commit any mortal sin.

After all, no one commits a mortal sin without freely choosing to do so, and the necessary grace to support one's freedom *always* is available to one who asks for it. To doubt this would be to doubt God's honesty, since he has promised: "My

---

213. See Paul Conner, O.P., and Basil Cole, O.P., *Christian Totality: Theology of Consecrated Life* (Bombay: St. Paul Publications, 1990), 59–88.

grace is sufficient for you, for power is made perfect in weakness" (2 Cor 12.9; cf. Mt 7.7–11, 21.22; Mk 11.24; Lk 11.9–13; 1 Jn 5.14–15). Keeping up this struggle, even if it turns out to be lifelong, belongs to the proper vocation of such people; like other vocations, it too bears constant fruit, not only in their own spiritual growth but also in their outstanding witness to the truth, both about the values at stake in sexuality and about the Holy Spirit's power to sanctify every person who seeks and accepts his grace.

Due to the fallen human condition, *everyone* suffers from some spiritual and moral handicaps, and is more or less disabled in the matter of sexuality. Often enough, those less disabled in this area suffer under some great handicap in another, perhaps involving matters which are less sympathetically viewed by others. Whatever one's handicap, that is one's cross: not only a burden but a grace, inasmuch as it is one's way of following the Lord Jesus, sharing in his redemptive work, providing material for the heavenly kingdom, and there attaining everlasting life.

g) Every available means must be used to avoid sexual sins. Previous paragraphs treated the specific truths which must be kept in mind to avoid sexual sins and spoke of the necessity of serving others in relationships determined by one's personal vocation in order to develop chastity.

The classic advice to pray for purity, especially to the Blessed Virgin, also remains sound, because she is both a perfect model of chastity and a loving mother who understands her children's weakness and wishes to nurture them in holiness. Another patron also might well be chosen for one's struggle—St. Augustine, say, who had the same struggle. By itself, however, prayer of petition is not enough. One also needs meditative prayer, by which an intimate personal relationship with Jesus is developed and sustained, and God's love is experienced. Only in this way can those striving to be chaste live in God's presence, feeling not threatened but accompanied, protected, and strengthened.

Deliberately frustrating other appetites by fasting and other forms of bodily self-denial helps integrate sexual appetite by subordinating sensory appetites to reason, and thus reintegrating reason, good will, conscious experience, and bodily performances. This has the good result of helping to heal the self-alienation of the masturbatory component of sexual sins. For a similar reason, serving others by corporal works of mercy, especially those which involve close personal contact, contributes in a special way to chastity's growth, since these corporal works involve experience based on an upright attitude toward the bodily person. Squarely facing challenges encountered in studies or work, and in this way having the satisfaction of overcoming difficulties, also builds sound self-confidence and develops the courage needed to endure the pain of frustrated sexual desire.

When sexual temptations arise, the strategy for dealing with them necessarily is indirect: stop attending to the temptation and turn to some other, absorbing, decent matter unrelated to the temptation's source. While experiencing a temptation, one should not try to get rid of it by praying about it, since that keeps it alive.[214]

---

214. For a constructive approach to overcoming habitual sodomy: John F. Harvey, O.S.F.S., *The Homosexual Person: New Thinking in Pastoral Care* (San Francisco: Ignatius Press, 1987).

h) Nonsexual acts that cause sexual arousal are occasions of sin. More serious sexual sins very often result from less serious ones, and complete sexual sins from those which are incomplete. Sinfully choosing to go somewhere or do something with the anticipation of sexual arousal frequently triggers a chain of such sins. Here it is easy to see what must be done: not commit the prior sins which lead to the additional sexual sins. But one must go beyond this, since nobody can hope to be chaste without practicing modesty, that is, systematically avoiding nonsexual actions and omissions which are occasions of sexual sins.

People often imagine they cannot avoid occasions of sexual sin, since the temptation arises from within and the opportunity to commit the sin, at least by desire, always is present; but that reflects a misunderstanding of what an occasion of sin is. (See 4.D.3, above, regarding occasions of sin in general.) The occasions of sexual sins are other actions or omissions that bring about or fail to avoid sexual arousal or things which cause it. To be sure, in these acts or omissions a person neither intends to bring about or risk sexual arousal as an end nor chooses it as a means (otherwise, the act or omission would be in itself a sexual sin, not only the occasion of one). Rather, sexual arousal and incomplete (or even complete) satisfaction, or their risk, are foreseen and accepted in choosing some other act, which, considered in itself (that is, apart from this side effect), might be morally good. For example, those doing some kinds of work—fitting clothing, doing physical examinations, studying certain sorts of material, and so on—sometimes know by experience that in doing their job they will be sexually aroused. Again, cleansing one's own or another's body can cause sexual arousal, and certain forms of legitimate exercise can have a like effect. Of course, the act of which sexual arousal and satisfaction are a side effect also can be morally bad, for example, a wasteful, self-indulgent act done for entertainment or amusement.

In either case, the side effect's occurrence constitutes an occasion of mortal sin, and so must be dealt with like any other occasion of mortal sin. Accepting sexual arousal or/and satisfaction as a side effect can be morally good or bad, and, if bad, can be grave or light matter, depending on the reason for choosing the act of which these are side effects and on the measures taken or omitted to ensure not giving in to any temptation.

It is a mistake for someone with sufficient experience to anticipate occasions of sexual sin to ignore the question until already deliberating about doing something which might be such an occasion. People instead should shape their lives in such a way that, insofar as possible, they are filled with worthwhile activities which carry out their personal vocations and involve few or no occasions of sin. For example, most people have no need to deal with the occasions of sexual sin presented by much contemporary literature and entertainment, since there is an adequate supply of wholesome literature, entertainment, and other recreational activities of a superior quality among which to choose.[215]

---

215. An excellent treatment of the responsibility of Christian families entirely to exclude pornography: Burke, *Covenanted Happiness,* 126–48; a collection of insightful, nontheological essays (not all of which are sound): *The Case against Pornography,* ed. David Holbrook (La Salle, Ill.: Open Court, 1973).

i) In one way, impurity is relative to individuals and situations. The impurity of intentional sexual acts in no way is relative. However, the same behavior may or may not be sinful or an occasion of sexual sin for particular individuals and in particular situations. Similar behavior not only can carry out very different intentions but also can have different effects on different people, or even on the same person under different conditions.

For example, kissing and embracing plainly are not always the same sorts of behavior but differ insofar as they involve different amounts and intensities of bodily contact. But even two kisses or embraces that are exactly the same outward behavior can be entirely different morally. Sometimes, due to the intention, they are incomplete sexual acts; sometimes, although not sexual acts at all, they cause sexual arousal or otherwise lead to sexual temptation; sometimes they neither are sexual acts nor lead to any sexual temptation.

Consequently, to avoid impurity a person must not only avoid intending any sexually sinful act but must pay careful attention to the actual effects of various kinds of acts and the foreseeable risks of sexual temptation. Because many of those effects and risks are relative, one person often may not do something entirely innocent for another.

Likewise, it is foolish and harmful to imagine that outward behavior which is virtuous in some cases will be virtuous in all, or to try to draw morally helpful lines on the basis of descriptions of outward behavior. In matters of purity, people often make too much depend on which parts of the body make contact or falsely imagine they are settling things by saying it is permissible to kiss and embrace "according to the customs of one's country" or "as chaste people do in showing affection for relatives and friends."

j) Christian communion and cooperation are needed for chastity. Someone pursuing chastity must cooperate closely with a confessor whose pastoral approach is sound. One also can benefit from the help of others, for example, a mutual support group or an individual who has fought and won the battle for chastity.

Beyond these obvious forms of cooperation, it is very important to try to enter or establish some sort of genuine Christian community larger than the nuclear family and, unlike most parishes today, something like an old-fashioned neighborhood. In such a community there are many close and easy personal relationships; people never struggle with their problems alone, for someone else quickly sees they need help and moves to supply it. Adults and children of different ages and both sexes have plenty of companions who share their faith and moral commitments. There are many opportunities to do good things with others, and strong social motives to avoid doing bad things, either with others or alone. Without becoming a ghetto, such a Christian community can provide a field, not completely overgrown with the weeds of sensate culture, in which the wheat of Christian life can grow. One approach would be for groups of devout young Catholic couples to purchase or rent homes close together, so that they could build up good neighborhoods of the sort seldom found today.

Even without such a community, families and single persons can try to establish and carry on chaste friendships, which are valuable in themselves (see 7.D.3.a) and helpful in achieving and persevering in chastity.[216] Lacking these, an individual is likely to be lonely, and a lonely person is likely to experience sexual temptations. With them, one engages in activities which serve intelligible goods and so provide real benefits for those involved, including many of the emotional satisfactions of a good marriage. Moreover, through nonsexual communication, friendships directly contribute to chastity by helping people resist or overcome the self-alienation resulting from the masturbatory element of sexual sins. Last, but not least, all the delightful experiences involved in such friendships can serve as absorbing, decent matters to which someone experiencing sexual temptation can redirect his or her attention.

9. One Has Responsibilities with Respect to Others' Chastity

One's primary responsibility bearing on other people's chastity is to practice modesty. And as modesty in relation to oneself is avoiding the occasions of sexual sins, so in relation to others it is avoiding, insofar as possible, communicating wrongful sexual thoughts and doing anything likely to arouse wrongful sexual desires. One also should do what one can to resist others' immodesty and promote others' chastity.

Immodesty sometimes takes the form of sexual manipulation and sexual aggression. Understanding both kinds of behavior and their interrelationship helps clarify the meaning and moral significance of so-called sexual harassment.

a) Justice and love call for modesty toward other people. People often, and in different ways, lead others into sexual sins. Plainly, that should not be done; it is scandal in the strict sense, and a grave violation of justice and love of neighbor (see 4.E.2). Thus, one must not ask others to commit sexual sins and must avoid giving bad example in this matter.

It also is necessary to avoid unnecessarily doing or saying anything which, even if innocent in itself, is likely to be an occasion of sexual sin for others. For instance, one should avoid not only public nudity and patently obscene behavior but unnecessarily dressing and/or acting in any way which proves likely to provoke anyone else's lustful thoughts and desires. Moreover, unless by way of admonition, no one should tell someone else of the inappropriate sexual thoughts, feelings, or reactions he or she arouses; married couples should be careful about what they do in their children's presence; girls and women should bear in mind that behavior which is not sexually arousing for them may well be so for a boy or man.

A person can be immodest by persisting in behavior which provokes an unexpected sexual response. Even though the behavior was not deliberately immodest, persisting in it will be a mortal sin if one chooses to persist after coming to know that doing so is gravely evil, or if the behavior's bad effect is willingly accepted due to some other unrepented mortal sin. Otherwise, immodesty of this kind is not a mortal sin, though greater love of neighbor often would preclude it by making one more sensitive to others' moral welfare and more careful to safeguard it.

---

216. With respect to religious life, Vatican II exhorts: "Let all, especially superiors, remember that chastity is guarded more securely when true brotherly or sisterly love flourishes in the common life of the community" (PC 12).

b) One should resist others' immodesty and promote their chastity. To cooperate in sexual sins or give in to those, such as pornographers, who intentionally try to arouse and serve sinful sexual desire provides these other sinners with part of what they seek in committing their own sins and so reinforces their bad motives. Even though such elements of one's own sexual sins may not constitute a distinct sin, they do harm others, and so provide an additional reason for avoiding them.[217]

Responsibility toward others does not end with being careful to avoid unnecessarily doing anything that might harm their chastity. One also should do what one can to help them achieve and maintain chastity. That includes admonishing those who appear to be committing sexual sins (see 4.E.1), as well as communicating the relevant truths, when possible, and bearing witness to their importance, especially by openly and firmly holding Catholic teaching and living according to it. In today's world, what St. Paul says about Christian life in general applies here with special appropriateness: "Do all things without murmuring and arguing, so that you may be blameless and innocent, children of God without blemish in the midst of a crooked and perverse generation, in which you shine like stars in the world" (Phil 2.14–15).

c) Sexual manipulation and aggression are forms of immodesty. If immodesty toward others is deliberate and not unwelcome, it is sexual manipulation: the purposeful motivating of another by wrongful sexual desire. Sometimes, sexual manipulation is intended to lead to a wrongful sexual act; then the manipulation itself is an incomplete sexual act of the sort to which it is meant to lead and also of seduction. Sometimes, however, sexual manipulation is intended to elicit some nonsexual behavior, and sexual desire is used only to attract attention and motivate the desired response. Then, while not itself a sexual act, it is a grave sin of scandal. Such scandal is common in advertising, but also occurs in interpersonal relationships, for example, when a woman uses "feminine charms," intending to motivate a man to satisfy some other desire of hers by sexually stimulating him. Men, of course, similarly manipulate women, and people also manipulate those susceptible to homosexual temptations.

If someone's deliberate immodesty toward another is unwelcome, it is sexual aggression. When intended as seductive—to arouse another's desire so that initially unwelcome sexual advances will be accepted—sexual aggression is wrong not only as an incomplete sexual act and as deliberate scandal, but as an imposition contrary to the other's upright will. But not all such behavior is intended to motivate the person toward whom it is directed, for sometimes those engaging in it seek only a sort of self-satisfaction, for example, when a man, regarding a woman as a sex object, manifests a masturbatory attitude by directing immodest and unwelcome words and gestures toward her. Women and homosexuals, of course, can engage in similar aggression.

---

217. Carl Hoffman, "A Psychiatric View of Obscene Literature," *Bulletin of the Guild of Catholic Psychiatrists* 8 (1961): 3–13, argues that pornography does affect behavior with detrimental social consequences.

Sometimes an attempt at sexual manipulation meant to motivate nonsexual behavior misfires and provokes an unwelcome sexual response. For example, an employee seeking a promotion deliberately stirs up a manager's sexual interest, and the manager, while not giving the promotion, responds with unwelcome sexual advances. In such cases, both parties act immodestly and do each other a grave injustice.

d) So-called sexual harassment is largely a problem of immodesty. *Harassment* connotes a pattern of behavior intended to disturb or annoy. Thus, the concept of sexual harassment is complex. Systematic insults bearing on someone's gender or sexual characteristics constitute sexual harassment even if no immodesty is involved (see 7.B.5.k–l). Isolated acts of sexual assault do not, strictly speaking, constitute harassment (see 8.G.2), though a practice of unwelcome sexual touching does.

For the most part, however, sexual harassment involves immodesty but stops short of sexual assault. Very often it takes the form of persisting in sexual aggression after it has been made clear that it is unwelcome (or when, at least, that ought to be presumed). Inasmuch as the immodest activity is ongoing, such harassment is worse than an isolated act of sexual aggression, which is more likely to be a sin of weakness.

Nevertheless, the emphasis placed by feminists on men's sexual harassment of women is confusing because of what it overlooks. In the first place, all deliberate immodesty toward others is a grave injustice; only a society which in general accepts immodest behavior is compelled to draw the line when it persists despite being unwelcome. Thus, trying to end sexual harassment while tolerating other immodesty in interpersonal relations sets too low a standard. In the second place, women and homosexuals sometimes sexually harass men and boys.

More often, of course, a woman's immodesty toward a man is welcomed, so that, by definition, it is not sexual aggression and cannot constitute harassment. Still, such immodesty always is gravely wrong insofar as it is likely to lead to sexual sins and gravely unjust insofar as it is scandalous; and it is still more seriously unjust when it is manipulative.

No doubt, many victims of sexual harassment, whether women or men, boys or girls, are entirely innocent; despite behaving modestly, they become the objects of others' habitual immodesty. The injustice in such a case is obviously very grave. Sometimes, though, a victim of harassment has provoked it by his or her own immodesty, or even by sexual manipulation which has misfired. The harassment then remains grave matter and should not be condoned; but the injustice is less than when similar harassment is directed at an innocent victim.

In sum, focusing attention on sexual harassment while ignoring sexual manipulation leaves out of consideration a factor which in some cases is essential to a fair judgment on the harassment's injustice. Moreover, since most sexual harassment involves immodesty, and since immodesty often provokes harassment, vigorous action against harassment, while necessary and good in itself, is unlikely to repress that evil unless modesty in general also is promoted.

Question F: What Are the Responsibilities of Spouses
                in Regard to Children?

Marriage unites the couple as a principle for handing on human life, and they
should procreate responsibly. Since a human person's life is complex, children
grow and develop over many years. Thus, the responsibilities of parents are
similarly complex and prolonged, though it may be said, in general terms, that
they should raise their children to be good persons, good citizens, and good
Christians. It is important to treat children fairly, and to exercise parental authority
within its limits. Parents have special responsibilities for their children's religious
formation and should see to it that Christian principles shape all other aspects
of their upbringing.

1. Married Couples Should Procreate Responsibly

Parenthood is an essential part of the vocation of marriage. The practice of
responsible parenthood means acting in accord with all the relevant moral norms.
To implement these, couples should both abstain from and engage in marital
intercourse when appropriate. Even couples who cannot or should not have children
can fulfill their marital communion by acting in a fatherly and motherly way toward
people who need love and help.

a) **The vocation of marriage includes parenthood.** As has been explained (in
A.1.j, above), marital communion is a basic human good. A man and a woman share
in this good by initiating the conjugal covenant and fulfilling it by becoming one
flesh, a bodily union which makes them in effect a single human organism
for the function of reproduction. Thus, the initiation of new life is not a good
extrinsic to marriage; it is the intrinsic perfection of the marital communion itself.
So, John Paul II teaches:

> In its most profound reality, love is essentially a gift; and conjugal love, while
> leading the spouses to the reciprocal "knowledge" which makes them "one flesh"
> (cf. Gn 2.24), does not end with the couple, because it makes them capable of
> the greatest possible gift, the gift by which they become cooperators with God
> for giving life to a new human person. Thus the couple, while giving themselves
> to one another, give not just themselves but also the reality of children, who are
> a living reflection of their love, a permanent sign of conjugal unity and a living
> and inseparable synthesis of their being a father and a mother.[218]

This explanation illuminates Scripture's account of how man and woman were
created for each other and in God's image and likeness (see Gn 1.27–28). One
aspect of their God-likeness is their sharing in his creative work, their cooperation
with him in completing the human race, which is the culmination of his whole
creative project: "Be fruitful and multiply, and fill the earth and subdue it" (Gn
1.28).[219] The fullness of God's revelation in Jesus makes clear the ultimate

---

218. John Paul II, *Familiaris consortio*, 14, *AAS* 74 (1982) 96, *OR*, 21–28 Dec. 1981, 3.

219. Pius XII, Address to Newlyweds (5 Mar. 1941); *Discorsi e radiomessaggi* 3 (1941–42):
7; *Papal Teachings: Matrimony*, 322, teaches: "It will depend on you also whether those 'innocent
souls, who know nothing' (Dante, *Purgatorio*, 16.87) shall come to the threshold of life, whom

significance of the married couple's work of procreation: each of their children is called to be a member of God's kingdom and to share in his happiness forever.

Since the good of children is intrinsic to the good of marriage, the vocation of marriage includes the vocation to parenthood. Thus, Vatican II teaches that the *particular mission* of spouses is to transmit human life and raise children (see GS 50; cf. GS 47, 48, 49, 51); Paul VI teaches that the transmission of human life is a most serious *office* of spouses, in which they offer a free and conscious service to God; and John Paul II explicitly teaches: "With the vocation to love, in fact, there is inseparably connected the *vocation* to the gift of life [emphasis added]."[220]

b) Procreative responsibility calls for conscientious judgment. Except for those who know they are sterile, the vocation to the gift of life included in the vocation to marriage has direct practical implications. Every fertile Christian married couple should have children unless some extraordinary responsibility forbids their doing so. Yet in this matter, as in any other, vocations differ; different couples have different responsibilities with regard to how many children to have and when to have them. But each has definite moral responsibilities in this area, for, as Paul VI teaches, spouses

> are not free to do as they like in the service of transmitting life, on the supposition that it is lawful for them to decide independently of other considerations what is the right course to follow. On the contrary, they are bound to ensure that what they do corresponds to the will of God the Creator.[221]

In times past, some faithful Catholics thought (and a few still do), that a couple can be sure of acting in accord with God's will by entirely rejecting family planning and trusting in providence. Certainly married couples should trust in providence. But providence has given the Christian couple reason enlightened by faith and the power to act in accord with it. Neglecting these gifts would not be pious submission to God's will, but presumptuous irreverence.

Therefore, questions of procreative responsibility call for a couple's conscientious reflection, in which they should take into account everything that might in any way be relevant: their physical, psychological, economic, and social conditions; the good of their present and future children; the needs of their extended families, of society as a whole, and of the Church.[222]

---

the embrace of infinite Love desires to call from nothing to make of them one day his chosen companions in the eternal happiness of Heaven. But if, alas! they remain but magnificent images in God's mind when they could have been rays of Sun that illuminates every man who comes into this world, they will forever be but lights extinguished by men's cowardice and selfishness."

220. John Paul II, Address to Participants in Congresses on the Family (7 Dec. 1981), 2, *Inseg.* 4.2 (1981) 857, *OR,* 18 Jan. 1982, 5. Paul VI, *Humanae vitae,* 1, *AAS* 60 (1968) 481, *PE,* 277.1, uses the word *munus,* which means an office or gift, a vocation, a mission. On this word's rich significance, see Janet E. Smith, "The *Munus* of Transmitting Human Life: A New Approach to *Humanae Vitae,*" *Thomist* 54 (1990): 385–427.

221. Paul VI, *Humanae vitae,* 10, *AAS* 60 (1968) 488, *PE,* 277.10 (translation amended); cf. GS 51. Helpful discussions of NFP drawn from experience: *Natural Family Planning: Nature's Way–God's Way,* ed. Anthony Zimmerman, S.V.D. (Milwaukee: De Rance, 1980), 5–76.

222. See GS 50, 87; Paul VI, *Humanae vitae,* 10, *AAS* 60 (1968) 487, *PE,* 177.10. Holy See, *Charter of the Rights of the Family,* art. 3, *EV* 9 (1983–85) 474, *OR,* 28 Nov. 1983, 3, summarizes:

Nobody else can make this judgment for them: "With docile reverence toward God, they will form for themselves a right judgment by mutual agreement and working together" (GS 50). It must be made by mutual agreement, because carrying it out will require that they have intercourse at certain times and abstain at others, and in these matters neither spouse can make unilateral judgments without violating the other's marital rights. They must make the judgment "with docile reverence toward God," keeping in mind his plan and will for them, and their responsibility to provide members for his family.

c) **The vocational perspective should shape the couple's judgment.** People who do not consider parenthood from the point of view of vocation are likely to suppose that spouses can rightly base their judgment simply on whether a child or children are among the things they happen to want out of life. However, Christian spouses should judge in the light of their vocational responsibilities, considered as a whole. In doing so, husband and wife respond not only to their common vocation to marriage and family life but to the total personal vocation of each. In this decision, as in others touching on vocation, they should focus on their gifts and limitations, and on the needs and opportunities calling for their service.

This means trying to discover whether, all things considered, they can have a child with a reasonable hope of raising him or her to be a good person, a good citizen, and a good Christian. Do any of the relevant factors make that hope unrealistic? And even if the hope is reasonable, do any of those factors constitute serious reason not to have a child, or another child, either now or, perhaps, ever? Reasons to limit family size are serious, however, only if they arise from responsibilities which at least one of the spouses should fulfill and which it would be impossible or difficult to fulfill if the couple have a child or another child.

d) **Different couples' responsible judgments can be different.** A couple who have the gifts necessary to raise a very large family, and whose other vocational commitments will help rather than hinder them in doing so, can rightly decide to have many children, even though they will not be able to give them every advantage in life, such as higher education, travel, and so on.[223] Another couple marry despite the fact that the man is afflicted with a serious disease; foreseeing that the wife will have her hands full caring for her husband and that any children they might have would grow up without their father's care and guidance, they can rightly forgo having children.[224]

"The spouses have the inalienable right to found a family and to decide on the spacing of births and the number of children to be born, taking into full consideration their duties towards themselves, their children already born, the family and society, in a just hierarchy of values and in accordance with the objective moral order which excludes recourse to contraception, sterilization and abortion."

223. See the commendation of couples who have large families in GS 50 and in the address of Pius XII to which the Council refers in its n. 13 (n. 171 in Abbott).

224. Pius XII, Address to the Italian Catholic Union of Midwives (29 Oct. 1951), *AAS* 43 (1951) 844–45, *Catholic Mind* 50 (1952): 56–57, teaches that a couple could rightly marry with the intention of limiting marital intercourse to infertile periods provided they have sufficient and sound moral grounds to avoid parenthood, and are willing to accept and raise any child they have despite their precautions.

Still another couple, capable of raising a large family but living in a society with a severe population problem, can rightly decide to limit their own family's size in order to use their gifts and resources to help other couples nurture and educate their numerous children. Their judgment is entirely different from that of a similar couple, living in an affluent society with a birthrate below the replacement level, who think the ecological effects of their nation's way of life or population problems in other parts of the world justify limiting their family to two children, even while they use the savings to maintain their high standard of living and do little or nothing to promote social justice in other counties.

e) **The couple should use upright methods to carry out their judgment.** The couple should exclude from the outset all methods "found blameworthy by the teaching authority of the Church in its unfolding of the divine law" (GS 51). Immoral methods—*in vitro* fertilization, artificial insemination, infanticide, abortion, sterilization, and contraception—not only violate the good of life and/or other goods, but directly violate the good of marriage itself. Used to implement decisions about family planning, they either render nonmarital the sexual activity which they facilitate between the spouses (sterilization and contraception), radically betray the responsibility to care for children (abortion and infanticide), or replace the marital act with a technique which renders offspring objects of production (*in vitro* fertilization and artificial insemination).[225] Spouses who fully understand and accept that marriage is their Christian vocation will reject all such methods.

By contrast, those who regard marriage as an arrangement for obtaining many of the things they want in life are likely to consider themselves entitled both to the children they want and to regular sexual satisfaction. As they see it, irresponsible procreation simply means having children whom their parents—or others—do not want; responsible parenthood does not require carrying out the vocation of marriage but merely doing what is necessary to prevent, or dispose of, "unwanted" children and have only those who are "wanted."

f) **To carry out their judgment, a couple need fertility awareness.** Since truly responsible parenthood precludes using immoral methods, a couple who have correctly decided to have or not have a child will carry out their decision by engaging in or refraining from marital intercourse when appropriate.

If the decision is to have a child, generally they need only have marital intercourse whenever that is opportune, and pregnancy soon will result. If not, however, they should use one of the available methods for identifying the days during the wife's menstrual cycle when conception is more likely.

If the decision is not to have a child, the couple could abstain entirely from marital intercourse; this in fact should be done if they conscientiously judge that they are strictly bound not to have a child and can be certain of that only by abstaining indefinitely. Still, few couples need do so. A woman is fertile only briefly during any cycle, and almost every couple can avoid having a child by abstaining

---

225. Congregation for the Doctrine of the Faith, *Instruction on Respect for Human Life in Its Origin and on the Dignity of Procreation: Replies to Certain Questions of the Day*, 2, *AAS* 80 (1988) 85–97, *OR*, 16 Mar. 1987, 4–6. On *in vitro* fertilization, see 5.D.4.c, above.

only during part of each cycle. How large a part depends on circumstances. If they judge that at present it would be seriously wrong to have a child, they should abstain except when morally certain conception will not occur. But if they have less stringent reasons—for example, good reasons for spacing births—they could rightly decide to be less cautious. In either case, the couple can engage in marital intercourse at other times during the cycle (unless there happens to be some other reason to abstain) without in any way being irresponsible, and sometimes they should do so to express and nurture conjugal love.[226]

g) **Such birth regulation by periodic abstinence is not contraception.** This alternation of periods of marital intercourse and periods of abstinence sometimes is called "periodic abstinence" or "natural family planning." As has been explained (in 8.E.2.e), periodic abstinence which implements a truly responsible judgment is different, morally speaking, from contraception, since under those conditions periodic abstinence, while it avoids *causing* a baby, is not *contralife,* as contraception inevitably is. To that explanation, only a few additions need be made here.

First, Pius XII and Paul VI indicate that periodic abstinence is appropriate precisely to implement a morally upright judgment, for they say it is rightly used only if there are "sufficient moral grounds" or "serious reasons" for avoiding conception or spacing births.[227]

Second, by carrying out an intention to impede procreation, spouses who contracept mutilate their sexual intercourse so that it is not truly marital (see E.1.a, above). Thus, contraception within marriage not only is contralife, as it is even for the unmarried, but contrary to marital love. By contrast, couples practicing periodic abstinence engage either in integral marital acts or none at all. With the practice of periodic abstinence, "The dynamics of self-giving and acceptance of the other person, which are proper to the conjugal act, are not denied." But the choice of contraception "denies the intrinsic meaning of the giving and receiving which is proper to the conjugal sexual act and closes it arbitrarily to the dynamics of transmitting a new human life."[228]

Third, John Paul II also tries to clarify the fundamental anthropological as well as moral difference between contraception and periodic abstinence:

> It is a difference which is much wider and deeper than is usually thought, one which involves in the final analysis two irreconcilable concepts of the human

226. Sound and useful practical treatments of natural family planning: John Kippley and Sheila Kippley, *The Art of Natural Family Planning,* 3rd ed. (Cincinnati: Couple to Couple League, 1984); Evelyn Billings and Ann Westmore, *The Billings Method: Controlling Fertility without Drugs or Devices* (New York: Ballantine, 1983). On the scientific aspects of NFP, also see *Natural Family Planning: Nature's Way–God's Way,* ed. Zimmerman, 81–140.

227. Pius XII, Address to the Italian Catholic Union of Midwives (29 Oct. 1951), *AAS* 43 (1951) 846, *Catholic Mind* 50 (1952): 57, teaches: "There are serious motives, such as those often mentioned in the so-called medical, eugenic, economic and social 'indications,' that can exempt for a long time, perhaps even for the whole duration of the marriage, from the positive and obligatory carrying out of the act." Also see Paul VI, *Humanae vitae,* 16, *AAS* 60 (1968) 492, *PE,* 277.16.

228. John Paul II, Address to Participants in a Training Course on Natural Family Planning (10 Jan. 1992), 3; *L'Osservatore Romano,* It. ed., 11 Jan. 1992, 5; *OR,* 22 Jan. 1992, 2.

person and of human sexuality. The choice of the natural rhythms involves accepting the cycle of the person, that is the woman, and thereby accepting dialogue, reciprocal respect, shared responsibility and self-control. To accept the cycle and to enter into dialogue means to recognize both the spiritual and corporal character of conjugal communion, and to live personal love with its requirement of fidelity. In this context the couple comes to experience how conjugal communion is enriched with those values of tenderness and affection which constitute the inner soul of human sexuality, in its physical dimension also. In this way sexuality is respected and promoted in its truly and fully human dimension, and is never "used" as an "object" that, by breaking the personal unity of soul and body, strikes at God's creation itself at the level of the deepest interaction of nature and person.[229]

The final sentence makes the point that periodic abstinence, when practiced with upright intentions, promotes marital chastity and overcomes the masturbatory attitude which so often contaminates sexual activity even within marriage.

Considered as a whole, the explanation is helpful, provided marital intercourse is thought of as an act by which the couple realize and share in the good of marriage and periodic abstinence is viewed as a practice by which they serve that same good. The explanation will seem unintelligible, however, to someone who thinks of sexual intercourse as a way of satisfying sexual desire, assumes that married couples are entitled to regular sexual satisfaction, realizes that on this assumption most couples' natural fertility would lead to the problem of unwanted births, and regards periodic abstinence as a solution to that problem—but one which, on those assumptions, hardly seems acceptable since it requires couples to forgo the regular satisfaction to which they supposedly are entitled.

h) The practice of abstinence to regulate births involves chastity. Abstinence is not always easy even for couples who correctly understand marital intercourse and the appropriateness of sexual abstinence to regulate births. Sometimes even for them, and more often for those without their insight, abstinence seems to have bad consequences. Vatican II notes this fact: "Where the intimacy of married life is broken off, its faithfulness often can be imperiled and its quality of fruitfulness undermined, for then the upbringing of the children and the courage to accept new ones are both endangered" (GS 51). Thus, the Council Fathers make it clear that they have paid attention to the evidence that in many cases, when sexual abstinence is prolonged, a husband and a wife become irritable with each other and express their feelings by treating the children badly; they may be tempted to commit adultery, at least in thought; their love cools, and they are unlikely to welcome another child.

Still, these evils are not inevitable, for they do not stem precisely from not engaging in marital intercourse but from one or both spouses' frustrated desire to engage in it. Many couples whose sexual urges are subordinated to their marital love do not suffer bad consequences when they abstain: "The power of love— authentic in the theological and ethical sense—is expressed in this, that love *correctly unites 'the two meanings of the conjugal act'*, excluding not only in theory

229. John Paul II, *Familiaris consortio,* 32, *AAS* 74 (1982) 120, *OR,* 21–28 Dec. 1981, 7.

but above all in practice the 'contradiction' that might be evidenced in this field."[230] Hence, whether briefly or even for a rather long period, such a couple can abstain when they should—to carry out a conscientious decision to avoid having a baby, or during necessary separations, illnesses, and so on—without experiencing distressing frustration.

Consequently, Vatican II, having noted that abstinence *can* have bad consequences, does not conclude that couples should not abstain when necessary. Instead, the Council teaches that conjugal love and the responsible transmission of life *can* be harmonized; but it points out: "Such a goal cannot be achieved unless the virtue of conjugal chastity is sincerely practiced" (GS 51).

While the Council does not explain how that should be done, its teaching certainly assumes that, from the beginning of their marriage, each couple should cooperate in doing it. All too often, a couple take little thought of parental responsibility and indulge their desire for sexual gratification without restraint, until urgent problems result. Instead they should practice chastity from their wedding day on. If so, they will avoid any abrupt, and perhaps unilateral, breaking off of the intimacy of married life.

Of course, conjugal chastity does not mean complete abstinence. As the core of the virtue of chastity for all Christians is a firm commitment to subordinate sexual desire to the intelligible goods served in carrying out their personal vocations, so, for the married, that means subordinating it to the good of marriage. Thus, conjugal chastity involves having marital intercourse when that truly serves the good of marriage; and even when abstinence is necessary, marital chastity does not mean breaking off intimacy but limiting sexual acts to the extent required to integrate them with other aspects of marital love.

i) **Periodic abstinence contributes to conjugal love.** Many couples who, judging that they should not have another baby, abstain for ten to twenty or more days each cycle bear witness to the benefits periodic abstinence has for their marital relationship. The explanation is that this practice not only calls for chastity but fosters it, by integrating the sexual urge with the good of marriage, and so making marital intercourse a more genuine act of mutual love, with a deeper and more lasting satisfaction. The self-discipline necessary to foster chastity, Paul VI teaches,

> brings to family life abundant fruits of tranquility and peace. It helps in solving difficulties of other kinds. It fosters in husband and wife thoughtfulness and loving consideration for one another. It helps them to repel inordinate self-love, which is the opposite of charity. It arouses in them a consciousness of their responsibilities. And finally, it confers upon parents a deeper and more effective influence in the education of their children.[231]

Thus, periodic abstinence can and should be experienced as enhancing conjugal love, rightly understood as the principle of marital communion fulfilled in the couple's cooperation with God in the service of life; it should not be considered,

---

230. John Paul II, General Audience (10 Oct. 1984), 4, *Inseg.* 7.2 (1984) 846–47, *OR,* 15 Oct. 1984, 8.
    231. Paul VI, *Humanae vitae,* 21, *AAS* 60 (1968) 496, *PE,* 277.21.

and so experienced, as a frustrating deprivation of conjugal love, mistakenly reduced to regular sexual satisfaction.[232]

Attaining marital chastity can be difficult, and can require real heroism, as John Paul II points out. It does not follow that it is beyond the reach of any Christian married couple, for the new covenant's grace, which all receive in the sacrament of marriage, enables all to act heroically when they must.

> The *real* difficulty is that the *heart* of man and woman is prey to concupiscence: and concupiscence urges freedom not to consent to the authentic demands of conjugal love. It would be a very serious error to conclude from this that the Church's teaching in this matter is in itself only an "ideal" which must then be adapted, proportioned, graduated to the so-called concrete possibilities of man: according to a "balancing of the various goods in question". But what are the "concrete possibilities of man"? And of *which* man are we speaking? Of the man *dominated* by lust or of the man *redeemed by Christ?* Because this is the matter in question: the *reality* of Christ's redemption.
>
> *Christ has redeemed us!* This means: he has given us the possibility of realizing *the entire* truth of our being; he has liberated our freedom from the *domination* of lust. And if the redeemed man still sins, this is not due to an imperfection of Christ's redemptive act, but to man's *will* not to avail himself of the grace which flows from that act.[233]

Therefore, married couples should not consider the requirement of marital chastity "as merely an ideal to be achieved in the future; they must consider it as a command of Christ the Lord to overcome difficulties with constancy."[234]

j) Chastity can be developed by practicing periodic abstinence. The practical measures which married couples, like all other Christians, can and must take to attain chastity have been treated (in E.8, above). Only a few additional specifications are needed with respect to periodic abstinence.

A couple whose chastity is imperfect will foresee that abstinence might be an occasion of sin, inasmuch as one spouse or both might be tempted to seek sexual

---

232. John Paul II, General Audience (21 Nov. 1984), 3, *Inseg.* 7.2 (1984) 1258, *OR,* 26 Nov. 1984, 1, teaches: "Respect for the work of God contributes to seeing that the conjugal act does not become diminished and deprived of the interior meaning of married life as a whole—that it *does not become a 'habit'*—and that there is expressed in it a sufficient fullness of personal and ethical content, and also of religious content, that is, veneration for the majesty of the Creator, the only and the ultimate depositary of the source of life, and for the spousal love of the Redeemer. All this creates and enlarges, so to speak, the interior space for the mutual freedom of the gift in which there is fully manifested the spousal meaning of masculinity and femininity. The obstacle to this freedom is presented by the interior *constriction of concupiscence,* directed to the other 'I' as an object of pleasure. Respect for what is created by God gives freedom from this constriction, it frees from all that reduces the other 'I' to a mere object: it strengthens the interior freedom of the gift."

233. John Paul II, Address to Participants in a Course on "Responsible Parenthood" (1 Mar. 1984), 4, *Inseg.* 7.1 (1984) 582–83, *OR,* 2 Apr. 1984, 7; cf. John Paul II, Address to Participants in a Seminar on "Responsible Parenthood" (17 Sept. 1983), 4, *Inseg.* 6.2 (1983) 564, *OR,* 10 Oct. 1983, 7. For a fuller and very clear presentation of the relevant teaching on this matter, see Pius XII, Address to the Italian Catholic Union of Midwives (29 Oct. 1951), *AAS* 43 (1951) 846–47, *Catholic Mind* 50 (1952): 58–59.

234. John Paul II, *Familiaris consortio,* 34, *AAS* 74 (1982) 123, *OR,* 21–28 Dec. 1981, 7.

satisfaction apart from marital intercourse. If the abstinence implements a genuinely conscientious judgment concerning birth regulation, however, the couple will already have taken this into account and, often, will not attempt to abstain for too long a time; in this way, they almost entirely forestall the occasion of sin.

But what if the reasons for not having a baby are very serious, so that they cannot forestall the occasion of sin by limiting abstinence? Then they should work together to change the situation, so that the temptation can be avoided or, if it arises, resisted. On the one hand, they can increase expressions of affection that are not sexually arousing. For example, a wife whose husband finds it hard to abstain can do many kindly, gentle things to intensify his feelings of affection, so that the latter will oppose his unruly sexual desire and help him control it. On the other hand, the couple can take special care to avoid experiences and thoughts, even though licit at other times, which lead to intense sexual arousal and so increase frustration. For example, a husband who finds it hard to abstain not only should avoid entertainment which leads to temptations to seek sexual satisfaction apart from marital intercourse (every husband should do that), but also as much as possible should avoid incomplete sexual acts, except those he is confident eventually will be completed in marital intercourse without departing from the practice of abstinence as it is required by the couple's conscientious judgment.

Finally, couples striving for the chaste practice of periodic abstinence should seek help from other couples who have been successful at it. Those who have already achieved greater maturity can provide good example and encouragement, as well as practical guidance in the techniques of interpreting the signs of fertility and infertility. Some dioceses and parishes have organized such couple-to-couple apostolates, and many more should.

k) All couples can perfect their marriage by parenthood. While some couples conscientiously conclude that they should not have children, others who think they should are disappointed by not having them. They can and should try to deal with this condition just as with any other health problem, using reasonably available medical help to make their marital acts fruitful. But if that does not help, they, like couples who judge that they should not have children, should recognize that begetting and giving birth to natural children is not, after all, part of their vocation as a married couple: God is calling them to some other form of service to life.

While they cannot realize and enjoy that fulfillment of marital communion which comes about when one-flesh unity is blessed with its proper fruit, they nevertheless can perfect their marriage by true parenthood. For parenthood is far more a moral than a biological relationship: its essence is not so much in begetting and giving birth as in readiness to accept the gift of life, commitment to nurture it, and faithful fulfillment of that commitment through many years.

The most obvious way for such couples to exercise parenthood is by adopting children. In adopting, a couple should take the same attitude as a couple engaging in marital intercourse with the right openness to new life. Just as these latter should always be ready to love and cherish any child God gives them, so, in adopting, a couple should not try to find the child who meets just those specifications they happen to feel are important, but the one God is calling them to accept. As is always true for people discovering an element of vocation, they first must recall that God's grace will enable them to overcome whatever difficulties they encounter in doing his will. Then they will identify the child God wishes them to accept by considering their own gifts and limitations, and matching these with the opportunities for adoption and the needs of babies and children who lack parents. For example, a couple who proceed as they should in identifying the right child will not be daunted by the prospect of adopting a severely handicapped child whom no one else wants and will be open to doing so, unless there are compelling reasons (not mere emotional motives) excluding that possibility.

Some couples with natural children of their own also can and should adopt. But what about those who not only should not or cannot have natural children but also cannot or should not adopt children? Fruitfulness and parenting are not limited to having and raising children, whether natural or adopted. They take other forms to which every Christian family is called:

> Family fecundity must have an unceasing "creativity", a marvelous fruit of the Spirit of God, who opens the eyes of the heart to discover the new needs and sufferings of our society and gives courage for accepting them and responding to them. A vast field of activity lies open to families: today, even more preoccupying than child abandonment is the phenomenon of social and cultural exclusion, which seriously affects the elderly, the sick, the disabled, drug addicts, ex-prisoners, etc.
>
> This broadens enormously the horizons of the parenthood of Christian families: these and many other urgent needs of our time are a challenge to their spiritually fruitful love.[235]

Couples who cannot be parents even by adopting children are called to perfect their marriages by parenting in these other ways.

2. Christian Parents Should Raise Children to Be Good Christians

To understand the specific elements of Christian parents' responsibility in raising children, it is necessary to understand both its end—the coming to be of good people who also are good Christians—and the reason why parents have the primary and inalienable right and responsibility to bring up their own children.

a) The end of raising a child is a good, Christian person. Parenting is cooperating with God in bringing new people to be and, even more, to maturity. Since God loves children and wants what is good for them—that they should become good and holy—Christian parents should want the same. Children who grow up to be good and holy people will, however, be good members both of human society and of the kingdom; thus, in working for their children's best interests, good Christian parents also serve these larger communities, as Pius XI teaches:

> The proper and immediate end of Christian education is to cooperate with divine grace in forming the true and perfect Christian, that is, to form Christ himself in those regenerated by Baptism, according to the emphatic expression of the Apostle: "My little children, of whom I am in labour again, until Christ be

---

235. John Paul II, *Familiaris consortio*, 41, *AAS* 74 (1982) 133, *OR*, 21–28 Dec. 1981, 9.

formed in you" (Gal 4.19). For the true Christian must live a supernatural life in Christ: "Christ who is your life" (Col 3.4), and display it in all his actions: "That the life also of Jesus may be made manifest in our mortal flesh" (2 Cor 4.2).

For precisely this reason, Christian education takes in the whole aggregate of human life, physical and spiritual, intellectual and moral, individual, domestic and social, not with a view of reducing it in any way, but in order to elevate, regulate and perfect it, in accordance with the example and teaching of Christ.[236]

b) **Raising a child includes nurturing, training, and educating.** To the extent that children are naturally endowed with their own dynamisms toward healthful growth, they need only be nurtured and allowed to develop spontaneously to become what they can and should be. To some extent, too, children must be trained, very much as pets are, though also with obvious differences, not least that pets are trained solely to domesticate them while children are trained for their own sake, that is, trained to do what will contribute to their development and flourishing as persons. Insofar as raising children involves training them, it produces something: a well-trained child.

Some theorists, however, overemphasize either nurture or training, or both, and try to reduce raising children to these parts of the larger process. But neither nurturing nor training addresses what is specific to a human person: practical intelligence and freedom.

The point of nurture should be the child's healthy growth. The point of training a child is twofold: to protect life and health, and to prepare the child for education in exercising specifically human capacities. The point of education, then, is the child's human goodness and Christian holiness, and nurture and training only provide the basis for it, while its heart lies in helping children to deliberate soundly and encouraging them to make good free choices. To accomplish this, parents and teachers should engage in constant, careful, and sympathetic communication with children, always keeping in mind their difficulties, ignorance, and inexperience, never shrinking from using authority, yet not using it harshly or rigidly but gently, to guide and encourage each child's own efforts to act responsibly.[237]

c) **Education should be directed toward the child's vocation.** "Children should be so educated that as adults they can, with a full sense of responsibility, follow their vocation, including a religious one, and choose their state of life" (GS 52). Parents should nurture and train children so that their specifically human potentialities can come into play and be realized for good, not bad. Good Christian children eventually will seek, accept, commit themselves to, and faithfully carry out their personal vocations. The overarching goal of all education should be to help them, in two ways, to do that: by preparing them, and by advising and encouraging them regarding the specific acts involved.

Children are prepared by facilitating and encouraging the acts that bring their capacities and gifts into play, by helping them share in true human goods and experience the delight of knowing truth, appreciating beauty, working well, making

---

236. Pius XI, *Divini illius Magistri, AAS* 22 (1930) 83, *PE,* 206.94–95.

237. See Pius XII, *Apostolic Exhortation to an International Congress of Teaching Sisters* (13 Sept. 1951), *AAS* 43 (1951) 739–41, *Catholic Mind* 50 (1952): 376–78.

friends, and so on. Having prepared children to take up their personal vocation, parents should help them to reflect on their gifts and opportunities, and understand how everything in their lives is related to the principle of vocation.

The vocational principle makes it clear that parents should not provide children with everything they want, and sometimes should provide them with things they do not want. Nor should it be parents' main aim that their children enjoy themselves and have possessions, success, and status. All these must be subordinated to being a good Christian person, one who finds and fulfills his or her unique vocation.

d) Parents should cooperate in children's personal formation. To bring children's capacities and gifts into play is to form them as persons, to develop their more or less good or bad character, and to shape their relationships with others. Since each parent makes a distinctive and irreplaceable contribution to this development, a father and a mother should cooperate. Negatively, they should avoid making incompatible demands and undercutting each other's efforts; positively, they should plan a coherent strategy for raising their children, discuss problems together, encourage each other to do what is appropriate, and then each personally do his or her part.[238]

In technologically advanced societies, economic and cultural factors tend to limit the father's contribution. Most men work and carry on many of the activities they take seriously away from their homes and children, while at home many waste much time in rather passive entertainment like watching television, rather than in activity involving interaction with their children. To fulfill their responsibilities, fathers should reduce passive entertainment to a minimum, converse with their children regularly about their own concerns and activities and the children's, and enlist the children's cooperation, for example, by getting them to help with chores around the house, helping them with their studies, and joining with them in church or civic projects, as well as in various active forms of recreation.[239]

e) In raising children, the responsibility of parents is primary. Vatican II teaches: "Since parents have given life to their children, they have a very grave duty to educate them, and so are to be recognized as their primary and principal educators" (GE 3).[240]

---

238. Two valuable works on the moral formation of children and adolescents: C. G. de Menasce, *The Dynamics of Morality,* trans. Bernard Bommarito (New York: Sheed and Ward, 1961); David Isaacs, *Character Building: A Guide for Parents and Teachers* (Blackrock, Ireland: Four Courts Press, 1984). Helpful booklets: James B. Stenson, *Preparing for Peer Pressure: A Guide for Parents of Young Children* (New Rochelle, N.Y.: Scepter, 1988); idem, *Preparing for Adolescence: A Parents' Guide* (New Rochelle, N.Y.: Scepter, 1990).

239. A helpful booklet on the father's responsibilities: James B. Stenson, *Successful Fathers* (New Rochelle, N.Y.: Scepter, 1989).

240. John Paul II, *Familiaris consortio,* 36, *AAS* 74 (1982) 126, *OR,* 21–28 Dec. 1981, 8, explains the conciliar teaching: "The right and duty of parents to give education is *essential,* since it is connected with the transmission of human life; it is *original and primary* with regard to the educational role of others, on account of the uniqueness of the loving relationship between parents and children; and it is *irreplaceable and inalienable,* and therefore incapable of being entirely delegated to others or usurped by others." The Church's law also is very clear on this matter: *CIC,* c. 793, §1: "Parents as well as those who take their place are obliged and enjoy the right to educate their offspring; Catholic parents also have the duty and the right to select those means and

This important teaching can be explained more fully as follows. A child comes to be and matures by gradually separating off from his or her parents and becoming independent. To the extent children have separated from their parents, they can and should function independently; and everyone, beginning with the parents themselves, should respect children's fundamental rights, which do not differ from anyone else's. But to the extent children have not yet separated off and cannot yet function independently, they are more closely tied to their parents than to anyone else, and their status in the larger society is not unlike that of a special part of their parents.[241] Now, everyone has the primary responsibility and right to care for himself or herself. Consequently, parents, rather than other interested parties, have the primary responsibility and right to nurture, train, and educate children.[242]

f) The sacrament of marriage helps parents to raise their children. Since the parental mission of raising children is a service to God and the Church, parents can count on the grace of the sacrament of marriage to help them fulfill this great responsibility. The sacrament

> consecrates them for the strictly Christian education of their children: that is to say, it calls upon them to share in the very authority and love of God the Father and Christ the Shepherd, and in the motherly love of the Church, and it enriches them with wisdom, counsel, fortitude and all the other gifts of the Holy Spirit in order to help the children in their growth as human beings and as Christians.[243]

Therefore, parents should not lack confidence, especially when they encounter difficulties and their best efforts seem to fail. Remembering that they are not alone, they should ask the Holy Spirit for his light and power, and confidently hope that if they continue to do their best, their loving effort will bear good fruit.

g) The parents' responsibility is limited and shared in certain ways. Since the Church and civil society exercise legitimate authority over everyone, they have legitimate authority over children and, insofar as children depend on their parents, over the raising of children (see GE 3). Parents, however, sometimes cannot fulfill their responsibility or fail to do so, and if they cannot or will not properly care for

---

institutions through which they can provide more suitably for the Catholic education of the children according to local circumstances"; c. 1136: "Parents have the most serious duty and the primary right to do all in their power to see to the physical, social, cultural, moral and religious upbringing of their children."

241. People's recognition of this truth no doubt is one reason why many feel it right to leave the abortion decision to the pregnant woman. That solution to the problem, however, does not follow from the principle, partly because abortion bears on the unborn precisely insofar as they are alive and growing human individuals, in these respects distinct from their parents from fertilization onward (see 8.D.1), and partly because abortion is radically opposed to the parental role, which is to promote the development of the child to maturity and independence.

242. See Leo XIII, *Rerum novarum, ASS* 23 (1890–91) 646–47, *PE,* 115.14; St. Thomas, *S.t.,* 2–2, q. 10, a. 12, c. Some recent secular thinking challenges the role of parents by regarding children as entirely autonomous individuals; the effect of such thinking is to increase the involvement of civil society in intimate family matters. A criticism of such thinking in the interests of family intimacy: Ferdinand Schoeman, "Rights of Children, Rights of Parents, and the Moral Basis of the Family," *Ethics* 91 (Oct. 1980): 6–19.

243. John Paul II, *Familiaris consortio,* 38, *AAS* 74 (1982) 129, *OR,* 21–28 Dec. 1981, 8; cf. *CIC,* c. 1134.

their children, others should do what they can. Thus, some can and should adopt children or provide foster care, while society should provide care, support, and protection for children who are orphaned, abandoned, neglected, or abused.

Moreover, parents cannot do everything necessary to nurture, train, and educate their children, any more than they can to care for themselves, and so they should make use of appropriate helps in raising children.[244] Still, they have the right to decide what helps to use, and should never abdicate this responsibility to others or to society.

Parents who give children up for adoption are not obtaining help in raising them, but are transferring the very role of parenting. They can rightly do this if they judge that the children's best interests require it. Sometimes adoption can be carried out within an extended family or other close community, and the natural parent can help raise the child. However, since children need the security of a unified parental principle, parents who do not retain parental responsibility should accept a strictly subordinate role rather than trying to divide it with others.

h) Children's good should limit the help obtained in raising them. In judging what help to obtain, parents should have their children's good in view. To have a strong sense of identity and basic security, children need a warm, close, and stable relationship with their parents and those who help care for them; this also is essential so that those raising children will be able to recognize each child's personal needs and gifts.

Moreover, children's personal formation comes about largely by the example and conversation of those who raise them. Nobody involved in raising children is perfect, but all involved should try hard to hand on only what is good in themselves, and to remedy, insofar as possible, the harm they inevitably do to children. Instead of rationalizing their defects, they should admit them and try to change for the better, like loving parents who thereby enjoy an important benefit of parenthood. Unfortunately, not everyone involved in caring for other people's children is sufficiently motivated to become a better person or to be honest about his or her faults. Parents therefore should personally care for their children, especially when small, and should educate them in matters where others might do them great and lasting harm.[245]

---

244. Schools are among *helps* to parents in fulfilling the educational task which, as both right and duty, pertains primarily to parents. Thus, *CIC*, c. 796, §1, declares: "Among educational means the Christian faithful should greatly value schools, which are of principal *assistance* to parents in fulfilling their educational task" (emphasis added).

245. Pius XII, Address to Women of Catholic Action (26 Oct. 1941), *AAS* 33 (1941) 452–53, *Clergy Review* n.s. 22 (1942): 134, teaches that the upbringing of children in the first months and years is entrusted especially to mothers, and urges mothers to nurse babies unless it is practically impossible to do so. John Paul II, Meeting with Unemployed Youth at Willson Training Centre (Hobart), 4, *Inseg.* 9.2 (1986) 1688, *OR,* 9 Dec. 1986, 5, teaches: "Children need care, love and affection. This attention must be given if children are to develop into secure, responsible persons, with moral, religious and psychological maturity. While the responsibility for family development rests on both mother and father, still very much depends on the specific mother/child relationship (cf. *Laborem Exercens,* 19; *Familiaris Consortio, 23*)."

Thus, parents do their children a grave wrong if they evade the parental role by unnecessarily turning over their responsibilities to others. Those who need help should be very careful to get it from people who will nurture, train, and educate their children out of love, not simply as a job. They also should consider what it will take to remedy, insofar as possible, the damage the child inevitably will suffer, and should work systematically to that end.

For example, unless absolutely necessary, parents should not resort to a day care center operated for profit and staffed by employees whose motivation is doubtful and who use dubious approaches to the care and education of children. Even if adequately nurtured, children often are badly trained and wrongly educated in such centers.[246] If day care is unavoidable, parents should prefer a care giver who shares their own values and is, or is likely to become, emotionally attached to the children—a grandparent, aunt, good friend, or neighbor. Some church-sponsored and community centers also provide child care by devoted people who share the parents' beliefs and values, are morally upright and psychologically balanced, and are more interested in the children's welfare than in earning a salary or making a profit. If there is no alternative to employing strangers mainly motivated by money, parents should look into the options available and choose carefully. Then they should drop in unexpectedly on the care giver from time to time or have a relative or friend do so, and be alert for any sign of trouble.

3. Parents Should Treat Their Children Fairly

Parents should use their position and the power it gives them for their children's real benefit. They can abuse it in two ways: by exploiting a child for their own selfish interests, and by practicing favoritism among their children. Parents also can be unfair to children by neglecting them.

a) **There are special reasons to be fair to children.** While serious unfairness to anyone is a grave matter, even slight unfairness in dealing with one's children is likely to be serious, since it has especially bad consequences. Children treated unfairly by their parents are likely to take this as a lesson to treat others unfairly. Moreover, they will not have the experience they need to conceive of God as a loving and faithful Father.

b) **Parents should be fair between themselves and their children.** Parents should not use a child to serve their own interests. While they sometimes do this in gross ways, such as by making children do heavy work or submit to incest, more often it happens in subtle, psychological ways, for example, by expecting children to compensate for parental failings and defects, by taking out hostilities on them, and so on. A deplorably common form of parental unfairness is arbitrary and harsh treatment of guiltless, but naughty and annoying, small children, motivated by negative parental feelings, unshaped by reason and unrestrained by love—which, perhaps, is absent.

---

246. Even the adequacy of nurture, especially in its psychological aspects, is questionable: Bryce J. Christensen, "Day Care: Thalidomide of the 1980's?" *The Family in America,* 1 (Nov. 1987), 1–8; Dwight P. Campbell, "Daycare as Child Neglect," *Homiletic and Pastoral Review* 91 (Oct. 1990): 12–21.

Sometimes parents rightly prefer what immediately benefits them to what immediately benefits their children. That is so when, but only when, the child would choose the same thing, supposing he or she could reason and chose rightly. For example, parents of a large and poor family, having met their children's essential needs, rightly prefer an adequate diet and medical care for themselves to some of the advantages for their children—say, music lessons and summer camp—which more affluent parents can and should provide for theirs.

But if the parents' interests conflict with needs of the child which the child would reasonably put first, the parents, for the sake of their own fulfillment as good parents, must sacrifice their interests.

c) **Parents should not practice favoritism among their children.** Many things can tempt parents to practice favoritism, but, whatever the motive, they should not.[247] If their resources for parenting—time, energy, and material means— are sufficient, they should try to give each child an equal share. This does not mean treating all the children alike, since children's needs and gifts differ; on the contrary, using equal portions of resources for the children often will result in treating each differently. Also, if parents with limited resources have a child whose extraordinary needs or gifts call for a larger portion, they can fairly depart from strict equality, provided they can honestly say they would do the same no matter which of their children received the advantage.

Factors that could lead to unfairness in dividing resources often are relevant to the question of how to use them. For instance, while it is wrong to do more or less for children depending on their sexes, it is not wrong to provide them with suitably different educational opportunities depending on sex (see GE 8). Again, while parents should not do less for a child who behaves badly, they should provide a well-behaved child with opportunities a badly-behaved child would waste, and should use the latter's fair share of available resources in efforts to overcome the causes of the bad behavior.

Of course, it is hard to allocate equal shares to different children, since most family resources vary over time and some, such as parental time and energy, are hard to measure. Parents need only try to do the best they can. Moreover, if their resources increase over time, they need not try to compensate, after the children are grown, for unavoidable differences while they were being raised. Parents who are fair in each decision they make while raising their children do not owe any child special treatment as an adult.

d) **Parents should not neglect their children.** In becoming a parent, one assumes a very extensive responsibility: to do everything in one's power, consistent

---

247. Pius XII, Address to Women of Catholic Action (26 Oct. 1941), *AAS* 33 (1941) 457, *Clergy Review* n.s. 22 (Mar. 1942): 137–38, teaches: "The whole education of your children would be ruined were they to discover in their parents—and their eyes are sharp enough to see—any signs of favouritism, undue preferences or antipathies in regard to any of them. For your own good and for the good of the family it must be clear that, whether you use measured severity or give encouragement and caresses, you have an equal love for all, a love which makes no distinction save for the correction of evil or for the encouragement of good. Have you not received them all equally from God?"

with meeting other grave moral responsibilities, to see to it that all of the child's genuine needs are met, until he or she is able to meet these needs without parental action. *Genuine needs* refers to much more than what is essential for survival (see 10.E.b); it includes everything necessary for psychological health and normal development in every respect.

Failure to fulfill this responsibility is neglect, whether or not that failure falls under the legal concept of *child neglect*. Such neglect is in itself a grave matter—a serious injustice—though it admits of parvity, for example, if generally conscientious parents occasionally fall short in small ways.

4. Parental Authority Is Exercised in Different Ways and within Limits

Since parents are primarily responsible for raising children, they must exercise authority. In doing so properly, they share in the authority of God the Father and help children to learn how wise it is to obey his loving plan for their lives. They should always be gentle and never arbitrary: "Do not provoke your children to anger, but bring them up in the discipline and instruction of the Lord" (Eph 6.4; cf. Col 3.21).

Nurture, training, and education require different methods. Since neither nurture nor training appeals to the child's intelligence and freedom, neither involves the use of authority in the strict sense, which always is a matter of making decisions to shape properly human actions. Parental authority in the strict sense therefore extends only to supplying for children's inability to judge for themselves what they should do.

In a wider sense, however, all initiative by parents in raising children can be considered an exercise of their authority. Moreover, parents exercise authority over the family as a community, so that even adult children living at home should obey their parents' reasonable decisions in matters affecting the whole family.

a) Parents should exercise their authority, not abdicate it. Because egalitarian ideology denigrates authority in general and consumerist culture encourages children to be insubordinate, many parents in the affluent Western nations are reluctant to exercise authority. Moreover, easily tempted by laziness and cowardice to abdicate their authority, and often feeling little discomfort or distress in the face of their children's self-centeredness, laziness, self-indulgence, or cowardice, parents frequently ignore, or even nurture, their children's moral weaknesses, rather than challenging them to behave better and develop strength of character. A child makes things difficult, the parents give in; a child argues that other children are allowed to do something, the parents compromise. And while wisely accepted advice can help parents make their own judgments, too often they unquestioningly accept the judgments of priests, teachers, and others about what children should do, or even uncritically take advice from psychologists and other so-called experts whose world views may not be consonant with Christian faith. In behaving like this, parents fail to fulfill their responsibility. Instead of using their authority as necessary to promote their children's true good, they neglect to use it, or even abuse it, to suit their own comfort and convenience.

b) Parental authority should serve children's true fulfillment. While parents are responsible for their children's nurture and training, they can exercise *authority* strictly so-called only in regard to education, where children cooperate in their own upbringing. Like any other, the authority of parents is not simply power; and although parents plainly can abuse and exploit children, they exercise no authority whatsoever in doing so. Like all other authority, parental authority is rooted in a common good. But the common good here is unusual, since the child is subject to parental authority in the strict sense just insofar as he or she is still incompletely separated from the parents. Therefore, the common good of parent and child as such, as distinct from their common good as members of the community of the family, is the child's good considered insofar as it also perfects the parent precisely as parent. In other words, in exercising parental authority in the strict sense, a mother and a father rightly seek only one thing for themselves: the fulfillment of becoming and being a good mother and a good father.

Since raising children involves separating them from their parental source, parents in educating should direct children only to the extent they cannot direct themselves. In doing this, parents should assume that their children would judge reasonably and choose rightly, if they could. Consequently, they should not lead a child to pursue his or her own self-interest, narrowly or selfishly conceived, since that harms the child. Rather, they should try to lead the child to do what is reasonable and good, which includes the generosity and unselfishness characteristic of good family members, thoughtful neighbors, and so on. Indeed, one of the best ways for parents to exercise their authority is by including children in family projects and encouraging them, from an early age, to contribute actively to the family's well-being.

c) Nurture and education set the proper standards for training. Training is the use of technique to shape children without their free cooperation. Although some training is legitimate, children are persons, not things, and so its use must be limited. In overstepping the limits and trying to shape a child as a person in accord with their own preferences, parents treat the child as no more than a product.

Training can serve nurture by establishing safe and healthy patterns of behavior; and parents should not prefer their own convenience and their satisfaction in a child's rapid progress to what is really safe and healthy. Training serves education in a more complex way, by establishing patterns of behavior that develop a child's capacities and enable him or her to experience goods which later will motivate human actions.

Training sometimes must use conditioning by sensory rewards and punishments arbitrarily connected to satisfactory and unsatisfactory performance. For example, small children can be rewarded by being given certain toys to play with for a brief time when they have behaved well; light spanking may be used as a punishment. Such motivations should serve training's legitimate purposes and not be used merely to control the child's behavior here and now. Moreover, an attempt at training should not be extended to behavior which a child could and should, but will not, perform as an act of responsible obedience. Thus, it is hard to see any justification for corporally punishing children whose misbehavior seems to stem from a free choice to disobey, that is, to reject a directive of parental authority, strictly so-called. (Rather than punishment by sensory pain, such wrongdoing calls for punishment which brings home to the child the badness of wrongdoing both in itself and by virtue of the effects that naturally flow from it.)

d) Parents should exercise control by providing suitable means. To some extent, parents can channel children's behavior by controlling their environment. Since inactivity is boring and intolerable for children, parents should provide them with the means appropriate for good actions while depriving them of means for bad actions. To some extent, all parents follow this principle—for example, giving babies safe rattles and taking away small objects they might choke on—but it should be followed systematically.

When children begin to reason and make choices, parents should continue to try to control their environment; but as they develop this becomes less effective in channeling their behavior, since they often can find ways of doing whatever they wish and always can abuse the means which their parents provide for doing good actions. Even so, until children become entirely independent, able to make their way without parental support, parents bear some responsibility in this matter. They should know how the means they provide their children are to be used and should not facilitate anything they judge wrong.

e) Parental authority presupposes love and reasonableness. Parental authority in the strict sense arises from parents' responsibility for their child's well-being and their superior ability to make judgments in his or her true interests. If parents love their children and treat them unselfishly and with consistent reasonableness, the children soon come to realize that parents generally do know best: it is good to follow their judgment and foolish to disobey. So, until their ability to reason practically is fully developed, children of good parents are aware that they should obey them and other adults who share their authority. This recognition of authority harmoniously complements a more elementary motivation which children who are well cared for develop in infancy: an awareness of dependence and a bond of affection, inclining them to enjoy giving pleasure to their parents and to fear displeasing them.

Nevertheless, even when good parents exercise authority properly, children can choose to disobey. Parents simply cannot make good choices for their children.

f) Parents should help children engage in human acts. Adults of normal intelligence can engage in practical reasoning, beginning from principles they understand or accept from some credible authority, and ending with judgments of conscience, which they then can freely choose to follow or violate. That ability is called "the use of reason." Small children do not have it; they develop it gradually, with respect to simple matters before more complicated ones. Therefore, for many years parents must supply children with more or less of the practical reasoning they need. In doing this, they naturally and rightly try to lead their children to do what they think is right and appropriate.

Sometimes the parent must do all the practical reasoning to reach the precise judgment regarding what the child should do and not do. But often, especially as children grow older, the parent need only work out the reasoning and present it, to help children understand what is right. It may even be sufficient to call attention to something relevant by raising a question. Since the long-range goal is that the child gain and rightly exercise full responsibility, the parent should supply only as much as necessary; hence, Vatican II teaches that "children and young people have the right to be stimulated to appraise moral values with right conscience and embrace them with personal commitment, and to know and love God more perfectly" (GE 1).

Therefore, in guiding a child's action, a parent should call attention to as much of the relevant sound motivation as the child can understand. When he or she cannot understand all the reasons, the parent should point to those elements the child can grasp. For example, one may appeal to sensible motives which really are part of the reasonable motivation of the act: "You should take this bitter medicine because it will make you feel better."

Parents should not appeal to authority as a motivation unless other motives are entirely beyond the children's understanding. Those who prefer the simplicity of authority to the complexity of explanation are shirking their duty to help their children grow in responsibility. Good parents are patient and careful in responding to children's "Why should I?" They are very reluctant to answer, "Because I said so."

Even when very small, a child should be allowed to choose between entirely acceptable alternatives identified by the parent, for example, between having chocolate or vanilla ice cream. The same principle also should be followed with regard to important matters such as vocation. Children may need help in reflecting on such matters and identifying possibilities to be considered, but parents should not try to practice discernment for them.

g) **Parental authority is limited by the child's true good.** Parents have no authority to require children to serve parental interests unless that really is beneficial to the children themselves. For example, parents may not require a child to work around the house except insofar as the work is the child's fair contribution to the family's common good, and so perfects the child as a responsible family member. If more work than that is required, the parents are exploiting the child; and if it harms the child's health or displaces other things he or she should be doing, the injustice is grave. Exploitative parents usually try to motivate a child by appealing to their authority and the child's dependence and affection. Unjust in itself, that also undermines parental authority, so that the child no longer has an adequate motive for accepting whatever sound guidance the parents offer.

h) **Parents should appeal only to appropriate motives.** Parents sometimes arbitrarily attach rewards and punishments to children's actions in order to motivate their obedience: "If you do well in school this year, next summer we will reward you with that trip you want to take." That is wrong, for by motivating children in this way, parents teach them to act simply to get what they happen to want, rather than on the basis of reason and sound discernment, in accord with their personal vocation. Plainly, too, if what is promised or threatened is not good for the child, it should not be done; whereas if it is good for the child and suitable for the parent to do, it should not be made contingent on irrelevant aspects of the child's behavior.

This mistake must be distinguished from other, legitimate uses of parental authority. Parents rightly insist on intrinsic connections—as distinct from arbitrarily attached rewards and punishments—and require children to organize their activities in a reasonable way: "You may not have dessert if you do not eat your vegetables," "You may not go out to play until you finish your homework." Again, parents rightly link a child's direct contributions to the family's common good with some direct benefit he or she receives from the family: "You must do your chores to obtain your allowance." Parents also rightly impose punishments of the sort chosen by self-disciplined people as ascetical practices: "Yesterday you rode your bicycle where it is too dangerous; so, today you may not take it out." Then too, in relating to their children not as authorities but as friends, parents rightly provide optional treats, which they also may promise under some condition, just as friends do: "When you pass your exams, I'll treat you to dinner and the theater!" Finally, parents should praise children for their good acts, honor their accomplishments, and offer them tokens of recognition, provided these are kept in their proper place and not enlarged to the point of being a principal motive for children's action.

i) **Parental authority ends when children can reason for themselves.** Eventually a child can do all of his or her own practical reasoning, and can rightly judge that mother and father do not always know best. As friends, parents still should offer advice they consider helpful; and in advanced cultures, the child still will need parental support, perhaps for many years (though the parents should judge for themselves whether the support a child desires will be in his or her true interests). Beyond this residue of parental authority, however, parents should deal with their conflicts with an autonomously functioning child in the same way as with marital troubles (see below, H.1).

The relationship which mature children who continue to live at home have with their parents is similar to that of other members of the extended family—a grandparent, uncle, or aunt—who may live there. The heads of the household rightly provide the direction required for its smooth functioning, and others should comply. But such direction is specifically distinct from parental authority.

5. Parents Have Special Responsibilities for Religious Formation

Since Christian parents should raise their children to be good Christians, they should take special care with religious formation, and should personally attend to it at every stage.[248] The sacrament of marriage consecrates Catholic parents for this work, a ministry of the Church directed toward building up her new members. In particular, parents fulfill this ministry by the example they give of following the

---

248. *CIC*, c. 226, §2, prescribes: "Because they have given life to their children, parents have a most serious obligation and enjoy the right to educate them; therefore Christian parents are especially to care for the Christian education of their children according to the teaching handed on by the Church." A study of many of the points treated in this section: Donald Martin Endebrock, *The Parental Obligation to Care for the Religious Education of Children within the Home with Special Attention to the Training of the Pre-school Child* (Washington, D.C.: The Catholic University of America Press, 1955).

way of Jesus: "By virtue of their ministry of educating, parents are, through the witness of their lives, the first heralds of the Gospel for their children."[249]

a) **Parents should not delay religious formation.** Some people argue that religious formation violates a child's autonomy and religious liberty: it is wrong, they say, for parents to indoctrinate a child with their personal religious beliefs; instead, the child should be allowed to make an unhampered choice about religion when he or she is old enough.

This view is contrary to the basic principles of parenting. Good parents naturally do their best to communicate to their children every good they themselves enjoy. But parents who do not raise their children in the faith not only deprive them of an important part of their Christian lives but leave them vulnerable to the secular humanism permeating contemporary culture. One therefore suspects that those who urge parental abstention from religious formation simply do not put a high value on religious faith and practice or even take a negative view of them.

Considered on its own terms, the argument against religious formation also fails. In bringing a child up to be a good Catholic, parents do not violate his or her autonomy; rather, they help the child enjoy the freedom of God's children from sin's consequences, which dreadfully burden people who lack faith and the sacraments.[250] Nor does religious formation violate religious liberty. To be sure, that liberty excludes coercive interference in anyone's religious quest and religious practice; but parents who provide religious formation, far from coercing their child, are doing what they can to initiate his or her personal religious quest and practice.

Of course, in this matter as in others, when children are ready to assume their own responsibility, parents should respect their right to do so, while providing good advice and encouragement, and hoping and praying for the best, but never resorting to coercion.

b) **Children should be baptized within the first weeks of life.** Since baptism is necessary for salvation, parents should arrange to have a child who is in danger of death baptized at once or should do it themselves. Otherwise, they should arrange for baptism within the first few weeks.[251]

In naming the child, the parents should confer with the pastor who will baptize him or her and should avoid any name that offends Christian sensibilities.[252] While the name need not be that of a saint, parents should consider the benefit to the child of bearing the name of a saint who will be his or her patron. In this matter, too, as in all the rest of their parenting, parents should give priority to what will be in the

---

249. John Paul II, *Familiaris consortio*, 39, *AAS* 74 (1982) 131, *OR*, 21–28 Dec. 1981, 8. *CIC*, c. 774, §2, prescribes: "Parents above others are obliged to form their children in the faith and practice of the Christian life by word and example; godparents and those who take the place of parents are bound by an equivalent obligation."

250. For a fuller refutation of arguments against parental religious formation, see Congregation for the Doctrine of the Faith, *Instruction on Infant Baptism*, *AAS* 72 (1980) 1137–56, Flannery, 2:103–17.

251. See *CIC*, c. 867.

252. C. 761 of the 1917 *Code of Canon Law* required that those who are baptized be given a "Christian name," but *CIC*, c. 855, says only: "Parents, sponsors and the pastor are to see that a name foreign to a Christian mentality is not given."

child's interests, and think about how names are used and abused, not least during the school years.

The parents ordinarily should choose as godparents two practicing Catholics, a man and a woman, who are at least sixteen and who have made their first Communion and been confirmed. One qualified Catholic is sufficient, however, and, together with a Catholic sponsor, a non-Catholic Christian can serve as a witness, though not strictly speaking as a sponsor.[253] Godparents should not be selected for their potential as gift givers or on trivial social considerations, but in light of their willingness and ability to "help the baptized to lead a Christian life in harmony with baptism, and to fulfill faithfully the obligations connected with it."[254]

c) **Parents should provide religious formation for preschool children.** Parents should begin religious formation while the child is still a baby and should continue it, mainly by their own personal efforts, during all the preschool years. The home should be enriched with concrete expressions of faith—objects such as statues and sacramentals, actions such as prayers and hymns—so that these will be among the first things of which the baby becomes aware. As soon as the child begins to respond to the parents' efforts to communicate, they should begin to communicate religious truths about Jesus along with other important truths. They not only should pray for their small children but, as soon as possible, encourage them to join in simple family prayers.

As a child grows, parents should give more extensive religious instruction in keeping with his or her capacity. They should take seriously any religious and moral question which the child asks, and should answer it with care. They should encourage the child to pray alone as well as with the family, and should suggest things to pray for, following the usual principle of directing what the child would wish to do if he or she were self-directing, for example, "Keep me safe, and help Mama and Daddy to be better parents."[255]

Blessings are sacramentals of a special and important kind. The *Book of Blessings* includes many blessings which lay persons can administer. Parents should make good and regular use of some of these, especially in blessing their own children and saying grace before and after meals. When a priest or deacon visits the home, he should be invited to administer some appropriate blessing.

At least occasionally, children should be taken to Mass even when they are small. Parents should use the opportunity for catechesis by explaining what goes on at church. With good parental instruction and example, children quickly learn to love the Eucharist and wish to participate. While being considerate of others in the congregation, parents should not be inhibited by the fact that, because of their

253. See *CIC,* cc. 873–74.
254. *CIC,* c. 872.
255. On the catechesis of infants, see John Paul II, *Catechesi tradendae,* 36, *AAS* 71 (1979) 1308, Flannery, 2:784–85. A helpful work on the religious education of children from ages three to six: Sofia Cavalletti, *The Religious Potential of the Child,* trans. Patricia M. Coulter and Julie M. Coulter (New York: Paulist Press, 1983).

short attention span, even children who wish to attend Mass sometimes misbehave and cause distractions.[256]

d) First confession should precede first Communion. The Church's law is that children should be prepared for first Communion and should receive it as soon as possible after they begin to reason, that is, around seven years of age. This reception should be "preceded by sacramental confession."[257] Bringing children to the sacrament of penance before first Communion is a sound practice. St. Paul's precept—one should examine oneself before receiving the Eucharist (see 1 Cor 11.28)—applies even to children. For even though some people argue that small children never commit mortal sins and so do not need the sacrament of penance, small children certainly do commit venial sins.[258] Preparing for and receiving the sacrament of penance will awaken their consciences and help them examine themselves, correctly evaluate the moral significance of whatever troubles them, and so receive Jesus with the greatest possible purity and peace of heart.

Children who begin to receive the sacrament early will be inclined to receive it when appropriate throughout their lives. If they do not begin before first Communion, however, some will not go to confession during their entire childhood, and that will be a formidable obstacle to their eventually doing so, even if absolutely necessary, when adolescents and adults.[259]

e) Parents bear the chief responsibility in this matter. Parents have the right and responsibility to see to it that their children are adequately prepared for the sacraments and are introduced to them when they should be.[260] They should begin fulfilling this responsibility when the children are very small, by providing an example of devout and frequent reception of the sacraments. Well in advance of formal preparation for the sacrament of penance, they should teach their children

---

256. On parents' responsibility to initiate children into prayer and to take them to Mass when they wish to go, see Congregation for Divine Worship, *Directory on Children's Masses,* 10, *AAS* 66 (1974) 32–33, Flannery, 1:257.

257. *CIC,* c. 914. See Congregations for the Clergy and for the Discipline of the Sacraments, *Sanctus Pontifex, AAS* 65 (1973) 410, Flannery, 1:241; Congregations for the Sacraments and Divine Worship, and for the Clergy, *Reply to a Query, AAS* 69 (1977) 427, International Commission on English in the Liturgy, *Documents on the Liturgy, 1963–1979: Conciliar, Papal, and Curial Texts* (Collegeville, Minn.: Liturgical Press, 1982), 990–91.

258. The argument that children of six or eight lack the sufficient reflection necessary for mortal sin is appealing, but does not prove its point beyond all reasonable doubt. It also overlooks the important possibility that even small children commit very serious venial sins in grave matter. A more ambitious argument against introducing children to the sacrament of penance rests on the assumption—sometimes bolstered by a misinterpretation of St. Thomas (*S.t.,* 1–2, q. 89, a. 6)— that they cannot commit any sins at all until old enough to make a "fundamental option" and the claim that they do not make such an option until adolescence. Against this argument's premises, see *CMP,* 16.D–E, 16.1.

259. See Congregations for the Sacraments and Divine Worship, and for the Clergy, *In quibusdam Ecclesiae partibus* (31 Mar. 1977), *EV* 6 (1977–79) 132–39, *Documents on the Liturgy,* 988–90. Some rationalize gross disobedience to the Church's norms concerning preparing children for the sacrament of penance by saying that encouraging them to receive it leads them to form a bad self-image, gives them an overly negative experience of the life of faith, and so on. Such assertions are gratuitous, grounded neither in faith, nor in a sound philosophy of moral responsibility, nor in competent and sound psychology.

260. See *CIC,* c. 914.

to examine their consciences, repent sins, and ask Jesus for forgiveness. They also should provide a model of repentance and reconciliation in their own marital relationship.

When the time comes for formal sacramental preparation, parents are entitled to seek help and to look for suitable confessors for their children, whether in their own parish or elsewhere. A suitable confessor is faithful to the Church's moral teaching and able to communicate it to children in a way they can grasp. Taking into account both the reality and the limits of children's moral responsibility, a priest of this sort tries to take children's sins as seriously as God does and help them understand just how seriously that is, which may well be less than they think.

Of course, if a child were prepared and encouraged to receive the sacrament of penance but were unwilling to do so, it would be wrong to prevent him or her from receiving first Communion when ready. This is hardly likely to happen, however, if parents, pastors, and catechists proceed according to the spirit of the Church's law.

f) **Parents must arrange systematic instruction in faith and morals.** For religious formation to succeed, parents must initiate it during the preschool years and continue it in the home even after children are in school. Besides providing informal catechesis, however, they should see to it that their children receive a thorough and sound formal catechesis in all the essential elements of Catholic faith and life. This requires a planned, organized program of instruction throughout the school years. While some parishes provide sound programs, whether in parish schools or otherwise, in others either there is no program or it is unsound. Parents then should seek other means: a sound program elsewhere or regular, systematic home instruction using sound materials.

Of course, in judging the soundness of any program, parents should recognize their own limitations and not jump to conclusions. If need be, they should seek advice from someone faithful to the Church's teaching and competent in theology and catechetics. But even then, they should not abdicate their responsibility before God and their duty to judge which of the acceptable catechetical programs should be used in instructing their children; only they can judge which will best complement their own efforts.

The judgment of the parents should prevail in this matter, because the principle of subsidiarity (see 6.E.5.c) applies: pastors and catechists should help parents, not replace them, in the work of religiously forming children.

g) **Parents should prepare children for confirmation and apostolate.** Children are confirmed at somewhat different ages in different dioceses. Parents nevertheless should see to it that their children are prepared for confirmation and receive it at the appropriate time.[261] They also should prepare for and/or follow up on this sacrament by guiding the children's thinking about vocation. Even if confirmation is administered toward the end of the grammar school years or later, parents should begin speaking about vocation soon after the children make their first Communion. In this way, they will be well prepared for confirmation, which

261. See *CIC*, 890.

will strengthen them to commit themselves to the various elements of their vocation and to carry out such commitments (see 2.B.4, above, and *CMP*, 31.D).

In developing the idea of vocation, parents should help children see as clearly and richly as possible the connections between their particular good choices and their Christian hope for the kingdom's coming and their personal share in it. They should teach children that whatever good they do has a value which goes beyond this world, while it is literally and utterly hopeless to waste this life seeking possessions, pleasure, and status.

As early as possible, too, parents should begin to tell children of their duty to help Jesus with his work of bringing the good news to all people and building up his kingdom, and to point out that each will have his or her own unique opportunities and ways of doing this. As children grow, this elementary concept of personal vocation should be developed. John XXIII teaches:

> Please carry on with your mission tirelessly and especially try to instill in youngsters from their earliest years—this is an area in which your apostolate can be particularly effective—a deep conviction that life is not just a lark, not just some kind of aimless wandering, not a search for some passing success and even less for easy money; instead, it means daily dedication of oneself; it means serving one's neighbor; it means a spirit of sacrifice applied to the hard work of a conquest that is always going on. This is the right way: and not the one that is sometimes suggested and urged by a mentality that deforms consciences and offers them a distorted view of reality.
>
>   You must also teach them that a person will enjoy true joy and peace of mind only if he lives up to his obligations generously and develops to their fullest the talents that God has hidden away in the mind and heart of each and every individual; you must make them realize that looking upon life as a vocation and living it in the light of that awareness is the one thing that will bring them the greatest satisfaction as well as being the secret of interior peace and of edification of neighbor.[262]

Children should be helped to understand not only their gifts and limitations but also the needs and opportunities of the Church and the world. They also should be encouraged to pray for discernment, so that in due time they will discern and commit themselves to their personal vocations. Parents should explain Jesus' counsels about poverty, chastity, and obedience, pointing out that, for those with the necessary gifts, life according to the counsels or in priestly celibacy for the kingdom's sake is preferable to marriage.

  h) Parents should respect children's vocational discernment. Parents should not press their children to choose one vocation or another; that requires discernment, and everyone must do his or her own discerning (see GS 52).[263] Still, parents

---

  262. John XXIII, Address to the Second National Congress of the Children's Association of Catholic Action (14 July 1961), *Discorsi, messaggi, colloqui del Santo Padre Giovanni XXIII*, vol. 3 (Vatican City: Tipografia Poliglotta Vaticana, 1962), 361; *The Pope Speaks* 7 (1961–62): 267–68; cf. John Paul II, Homily in Miraflores Park (Cuenca, Ecuador), 7–9, *Inseg.* 8.1 (1985) 309–11, *OR*, 11 Mar. 1985, 5–6.

  263. *CIC*, c. 219, declares: "All the Christian faithful have the right to be free from any kind of coercion in choosing a state in life."

can and should help their children understand their vocational options (see AA 11), and should use their judgment about whether to permit young children to take definite steps toward one or another vocation. For example, if convinced that an underage child is not ready, parents should forbid him or her to marry or enter a religious community. Similarly, when a child in grammar school or high school has the option of choosing, subject to parental approval, between different programs and courses, parents should approve or disapprove particular choices based on their own judgment regarding the child's gifts and probable vocation. As usual, though, the child should be allowed to make his or her own choices among possibilities which the parents deem acceptable.

i) **Even in religious matters, parental authority has limits.** At what age should a child's personal choices be respected in religious matters, such as Mass attendance? There is no single answer, but several things can be said.

First, children are never too old to be exhorted and admonished to fulfill their religious and other responsibilities.

Second, a preadolescent child's whimsical refusal to go to Mass with the family should be dealt with for what it is, not treated as an exercise of mature free choice.

Third, just as public officials may restrict or prevent outward religious behavior that disrupts public order (see DH 7), so parents may take appropriate steps to deal with the outward religious behavior of anyone in the household if it disrupts the whole household or the rights of any of its members. Deliberately missing Mass, however, even if it involves refusing to go to Mass with the family, is not disruptive behavior and it does not violate the rights of other family members. When such a failure or refusal to worship carries out a free choice of a kind that could be either a mortal sin or in accord with an erroneous conscience, no human power has the right to coerce anyone (see DH 2). Moreover, parents should realize that coercion in such a case, at best, will elicit only temporary and religiously meaningless outward conformity and, at worst, will provoke lasting resentment.

6. Christian Principles Should Shape a Child's Whole Upbringing

Raising children includes many other specific elements besides religious formation. Most present no moral problem for parents with a sound general understanding of their responsibilities. Here only a few matters are treated about which parents are likely to have moral questions.

a) **Parents should teach children the true value of material goods.** As explained above, as long as children depend on their parents, the latter can and should judge what to provide so that the children will become good people and good Christians. Knowing that some means are likely to be used badly and others well, good parents act accordingly. Catholic parents should consider means in the light of faith and pay careful attention to every aspect of their moral impact: "Children must grow up with a correct attitude of freedom with regard to material goods, by adopting a simple and austere life style and being fully convinced that 'man is more precious for what he is than for what he has' (GS 35)."[264]

---

264. John Paul II, *Familiaris consortio,* 37, *AAS* 74 (1982) 127, *OR,* 21–28 Dec. 1981, 8.

Often, for instance, children, lured by skillful advertisements, want toys and games which seem innocent but neither develop their capacities, nor exercise them in a healthy way, nor promote sociability.[265] Though tempted to provide such playthings simply to keep children occupied and out of physical danger, parents should not give in to demands for such things, which not only displace more worthwhile activities and waste resources but teach false values, for instance, that being entertained or having what others have is good in itself.[266] Instead, they should provide toys and games which will promote activities that benefit children while displacing not only obviously harmful but even seemingly harmless activities that do nothing better than keep them busy.

But even though the toy industry, like other aspects of culture, often does not serve children's true needs, are not parents better advised to provide the toys and games children want as long as they are not harmful, inasmuch as the practical alternative is that they feel deprived, become resentful, and sneak off to play at the homes of friends better supplied with popular items? No; for if parents use their ingenuity and persist in teaching sound values, children learn that beneficial activities are interesting and enjoyable.

However, the objection does point up something treated previously (E.8.j): conscientious parents need to seek or develop a wider community in which to live and raise children. In the midst of an alien culture, it is virtually impossible to bring children up as Christians if, for most of their time and from their tenderest years, they are fully immersed in its greediness and wastefulness.

b) **Parents should teach children the right use of the media.** The media of communication which parents allow in the home, and whose use outside the home should be a matter of parental guidance (see IM 10), are of very great importance in forming children. Excessive use of the media for passive entertainment displaces conversation and other activities, such as reading and handicrafts, and so stunts children's development.[267] Moreover, much of the content of television, radio, the cinema, popular music, and the print media is likely to have bad effects on children. The problem is not limited to elements patently immoral because they arouse lust and/or fascinate by representing brutality and violence. Sex and violence aside, much media content is objectionable because it conveys the secular world view and implicitly teaches that human happiness lies in possessions, status, success, and enjoyment. John Paul II teaches:

> It is wise to be alert to the growing influence which the mass media, and especially television, are exercising on the developing minds of the young, particularly as

265. See Eric Clark, *The Want Makers: The World of Advertising: How They Make You Buy* (New York: Viking, 1989), 185–201.

266. Paul VI, Address to the Eleventh Congress of the European Institute of Toys (7 May 1969), *Inseg.* 7 (1969) 953, *OR,* 15 May 1969, 2, teaches: "We likewise believe that it is Our duty to remind you that choice of toys has great pedagogical importance; luxury games establish certain habits, weapons develop aggressivity; others excite cruelty toward animals, and others again suggest dangerous attitudes. And everyone knows what influence has been exerted ever since ancient times by dice and cards."

267. Marie Winn, *The Plug-In Drug: Television, Children, and the Family* (New York: Viking, 1977), provides evidence and cogent analysis supporting this point.

regards their vision of man, of the world and of relationships with others; for the vision furnished them by the media often differs profoundly from that which the family would wish to transmit to them. Parents, in many cases, do not show sufficient concern about this. Generally they pay vigilant attention to the type of friends with whom their children associate, but do not exercise a similar vigilance regarding the ideas which the radio, the television, records, papers and comics carry into the "protected" and "safe" intimacy of their homes.[268]

Motion pictures and television have a special power and significance. Easily accessible and delightful in various ways, they provide a sense of immediacy, render viewers rather passive, and communicate much by suggestion, so that they bypass critical reflection.[269] Parents should exercise very tight control of small children's access to the media, for example, by making television available only for certain programs they judge beneficial for the children. Often, to accomplish this, they will have to protect younger children from experiences they rightly allow to older ones, and sometimes they will have to forgo entertainment which would be harmless to themselves.

As soon as possible, parents must begin teaching children to use the media moderately and to discriminate among the things the media provide. Instead of allowing children to accept media content passively, they should make it a subject for conversation and a means for education: for example, by pointing out the more and less satisfactory aspects of the media content which they permit the children to experience. In sampling promising new media content, parents should encourage growing children to apply standards critically, so that they will learn early to make their own sound choices.[270]

But no single family can censor everything the media present, and families therefore should cooperate in sharing information about their experiences and evaluations. They also should urge the bishops of the country to provide a sound, well-organized, and well-publicized service for rating the content of all the media for various age groups.

c) **Parents should prefer a Catholic school if it is sound.** Sound Catholic schools are a great help to parents in fulfilling their responsibilities regarding their children's religious formation and moral education. In such schools, moreover, other elements of formal education are correctly related to religion. The Church's

---

268. John Paul II, Message for World Communications Day (1 May 1980), *Inseg.* 3.1 (1980) 1042–43, *OR,* 19 May 1980, 11. Cf. Paul VI, Message for the World Day of Social Communications, *AAS* 70 (1978) 341–45, *OR,* 4 May 1978, 2, 12; Pius XI, *Vigilanti cura, AAS* 28 (1936) 254–57, *PE,* 217.16–26. A forceful, evangelical Protestant treatment of the problem: Donald E. Wildmon, *The Home Invaders* (Wheaton, Ill.: Victor Books, 1985).

269. See Pius XII, *Miranda prorsus, AAS* 49 (1957) 800–803, *PE,* 260.152–66. Also see Jerry Mander, *Four Arguments for the Elimination of Television* (New York: William Morrow, 1978), 192–260.

270. Pontifical Commission for the Instruments of Social Communication, *Communio et progressio,* 67, *AAS* 63 (1971) 618–19, Flannery, 1:316, teaches: "Parents and teachers should urge children to make their own choice even if the educators should reserve at times the final decision to themselves. And if they find themselves forced to disapprove of the way their children are using some aspect of the media, they must clearly explain the reasons for their objections. Persuasion works better than prohibition, and this is especially true in education."

law therefore directs parents to send their children to Catholic schools if they can.[271] But since the law's underlying intent is that parents fulfill their responsibility for the sound formation of their children, epikeia not only permits but requires them to avoid unsound Catholic schools if they can fulfill their responsibility more adequately in some other way (on epikeia, see *CMP*, 11.E.10, 11.G.6).

Of course, that is not so easy as might be thought. A secular school not only communicates some bad specific content and the secular world view, but may denigrate religion by treating it as not worth studying. Often, too, Catholic children in such a school have few if any companions who share their faith and way of life. Thus, secular schooling often succeeds in secularizing Catholic children or, at least, in convincing them that religion is only a private matter of secondary importance in life.[272]

Parents without access to sound Catholic schools therefore face a hard choice. Some can undertake the task of formal education themselves, sometimes in cooperation with one or several other families, and many parents should consider this possibility. Taking under consideration all the possibilities and their own capacity to remedy the defects of each, parents should judge which approach is likely to be best for their children.

d) **Parents should provide timely education in sexuality.** Children should not be told everything about sexuality all at one time; instead, as with most other matters, some things must be explained repeatedly and in diverse ways as they mature. The most basic point to communicate is that children are secure in parental love; parents also should manifest and teach great reverence for persons in their bodiliness. But, as is true in everything else, when a child of whatever age asks a question about sex, parents should answer honestly, not indulge in evasions or falsehoods: "Especially in the heart of their own families, young people should be aptly and seasonably instructed about the dignity, vocation, and exercise of married love" (GS 49). But parents need not and should not tell their children more than they can understand.

By the time children go to school, their parents should have taught them how to recognize and resist various improper advances they may encounter. A twelve-year-old child of average intelligence can understand, and should be told, why marital intercourse is good and sexual acts outside marriage are bad. As a child reaches

---

271. See *CIC*, c. 798; cf. GE 8. C. 796, §2, directs parents and teachers to cooperate closely with one another. Since the primacy of parental responsibility in educating children is emphasized in the Church's teaching and law (several instances have been quoted or cited), c. 798 probably should not be interpreted as curtailing the freedom of parents to educate their children at home, provided they are able adequately to do so, even if they could send their children to satisfactory Catholic schools; see Edward N. Peters, *Home Schooling and the New Code of Canon Law* (Front Royal, Va.: Christendom College Press, 1988), 39–46.

272. Pius XII, *Sertum laetitiae, AAS* 31 (1939) 639 and 650, *PE,* 223.20, teaches: "We raise Our voice in strong, albeit paternal, complaint that in so many schools of your land [the United States] Christ often is despised or ignored, the explanation of the universe and mankind is forced within the narrow limits of materialism or of rationalism, and new educational systems are sought after which cannot but produce a sorrowful harvest in the intellectual and moral life of the nation." DH 5, GE 6, and *CIC,* c. 797, assert the right of parents against civil society to a choice of schools in harmony with faith.

puberty, parents should explain personally what sexual differentiation and sexual desire are, how sexual intercourse is carried out, and its possible consequences. Girls should be taught about menstruation and boys about nocturnal emissions before they experience them. Pius XII, addressing mothers, teaches:

> With the discretion of a mother and a teacher, and thanks to the open-hearted confidence with which you have been able to inspire your children, you will not fail to watch for and to discern the moment in which certain unspoken questions have occurred to their minds and are troubling their senses. It will then be your duty to your daughters, the father's duty to your sons, carefully and delicately to unveil the truth as far as it appears necessary, to give a prudent, true, and Christian answer to those questions, and set their minds at rest. If imparted by the lips of Christian parents, at the proper time, in the proper measure and with the proper precautions, the revelation of the mysterious and marvelous laws of life will be received by them with reverence and gratitude, and will enlighten their minds with far less danger than if they learned them haphazard, from some unpleasant shock, from secret conversations, through information received from over-sophisticated companions, or from clandestine reading, the more dangerous and pernicious as secrecy inflames the imagination and troubles the senses.[273]

The point is that a child needs to know how to respond to sexual desire when he or she experiences it. Parents therefore should explain to children reaching puberty the sacredness of sex, the wrongness of masturbation and premarital sexual intercourse, the goodness of self-control, and the ways of dealing with temptation. This parental instruction should continue throughout adolescence.[274]

As John Paul II teaches, education in sexuality offered in schools should complement sound parental instruction, not conflict with it:

> Sex education, which is a basic right and duty of parents, must always be carried out under their attentive guidance, whether at home or in educational centres chosen and controlled by them. In this regard, the Church reaffirms the law of subsidiarity, which the school is bound to observe when it cooperates in sex education, by entering into the same spirit that animates the parents.[275]

Sometimes sound elements of sexual education are included in religious-formation programs and in courses in other fields, such as science or hygiene. Often, though, conscientious parents find real defects in programs of sexual education, such as imprudent timing and administrative arrangements, the unnecessary use of erotically arousing materials, erroneous teaching, and bad moral advice. In such cases,

273. Pius XII, Address to Women of Catholic Action (26 Oct. 1941), *AAS* 33 (1941) 455–56, *Clergy Review* n.s. 22 (Mar. 1942): 136.

274. A sound and clear little book intended to help parents fulfill their responsibilities as sexual educators: H. Vernon Sattler, C.Ss.R., *Challenging Children to Chastity: A Parental Guide* (St. Louis: Central Bureau of the Catholic Central Verein of America, 1991). Parents also might find it helpful to obtain and study (or read and discuss with their children) a sound treatment of Catholic sexual morality written for adolescents, for example, Robert J. Fox, *Charity, Morality, Sex, and Young People* (Manassas, Va.: Trinity Communications, 1987).

275. John Paul II, *Familiaris consortio*, 37, *AAS* 74 (1982) 128, *OR*, 21–28 Dec. 1981, 8. A clarification of parental responsibilities and standards for judging the quality of school programs: Congregation for Catholic Education, *Educational Guidance in Human Love: Outlines for Sex Education*, *EV* 9 (1983–85) 420–56, *OR*, 5 Dec. 1983, 5–9.

they should try to see to it that the defects are eliminated, or else should arrange for their child to be exempted from participating. Teachers and school administrators should recognize that parental judgment takes priority over theirs and respect that judgment, since their proper role is to serve as the parents' helpers.

Still, parents should not focus so much attention on one issue that they overlook or tolerate other questionable aspects of their children's formal education. Rather, they should fulfill their personal responsibility to give sexual education to their child, pay careful attention to what he or she is being taught by others, and do what they can to prevent or remedy the harm done by unsound teaching.

e) **Parents should monitor children's hobbies and friends.** Children need recreation, hobbies, and friends, and the three tend to go together. It is often the case that parents can responsibly allow a child considerable freedom, even autonomy, in these matters before many others. Doing so is important in order that the child can begin to develop personal interests, discover and try out his or her unique gifts, make personal friends, and so on.

Sometimes, though, parents who are conscientious about religious formation and formal education are too permissive about their child's recreation, hobbies, and friends. Aware of something definitely harmful, they are quick to intervene; but they also should be alert to subtle harms. For example, friends convey their families' values, which may not be good ones, and some hobbies and recreations can lead children to be overcompetitive, exclusively concerned with attaining goals, enamored of possessions, or absorbed in gaining status. At the same time, parents should respond affirmatively to all of a child's wholesome interests, not disdaining any, even if they seem rather insignificant, since any wholesome interest is an aspect of a child's development.

f) **Parents should try to find or form a suitable community.** Since a hostile social environment makes it far more difficult for parents to fulfill their responsibilities, they should try, if possible, to raise their children in a community friendly to their faith. It need not be entirely Catholic, not even entirely Christian, but it must be made up predominantly of faithful Christians or others committed to living their faith and handing it on to their children. In such a community, people with faith will set the trends in children's and young people's activities, and will greatly influence what goes on in school. Some parents can find a suitable community and sacrifice other things to move into it; others can build up such a community or, at least, some elements of one. In any case, when weighing options about where to live, parents should give very high priority to this factor.

Question G: What Are the Other Responsibilities of Family Life?

The previous questions have treated the responsibilities of spouses to each other and of parents to their children. Two other sets of responsibilities included in family morality remain to be treated: those of children to honor, help, and obey their parents, and those of the family as a whole. Of course, most responsibilities of the family as a whole also are responsibilities of individuals, for example, to bear witness to faith and to practice mercy toward everyone. But two problems require special treatment: the death of a family member and out-of-wedlock pregnancy involving a family member.

1. Children Should Honor, Help, and Obey Their Parents

Parents undertake many responsibilities toward their children. For their part, the children should cooperate fully in their own upbringing and respond to their parents with love and gratitude.

Honor can include love, reverence, respect, and obedience. While Christians are bound to love and respect every person, even enemies, and to obey every legitimate authority, parents deserve special love and reverent respect (see Sir 3.1–11). In partnership with God, they are the sources of their children's very being and of many other benefits:

> With all your heart honor your father,
> and do not forget the birth pangs of your mother.
> Remember that it was of your parents you were born;
> how can you repay what they have given to you? (Sir 7.27–28)

Hence, the divine precept: "Honor your father and your mother" (Ex 20.12, Dt 5.16; cf. Lv 19.3, Mt 19.19, Mk 10.19, Lk 18.20, Eph 6.2).

a) The duty to honor parents is both affirmative and negative. Affirmatively, children should love their parents and hope they will enjoy long and happy lives. They should pray for their parents, that they may be holy and good; they should strive to please their parents and be a credit to them by imitating their good example and fulfilling their good hopes and upright plans; they should express reverence and gratitude to their parents by speech and action. Grown children should continue to visit their parents, listen respectfully to their advice, celebrate their special occasions, give them gifts, and so on.[276]

Negatively, the sins anyone can commit against another take on a special malice when a child commits them against his or her mother or father. Old Testament precepts made this clear: "Whoever strikes father or mother shall be put to death" (Ex 21.15); "Whoever curses father or mother shall be put to death" (Ex 21.17; cf. Lv 20.9, Prv 30.17, Mt 15.4, Mk 7.10). Looking forward to greater freedom or their inheritance, children sometimes wish their parents would die, and that surely is a grave matter. But any thought, word, or deed against a parent is more likely to be a grave matter than is a similar act against someone else.

b) Children should protect and promote their parents' welfare. In practice, perhaps the most important way for children to honor their parents is by supporting them when they become dependent and seeing to it that they are decently cared for when they no longer can care for themselves (see Sir 3.12–16). This responsibility is a matter of justice.[277] If two or more of the children can help fulfill it, they should.

---

276. A thoughtful philosophical reflection on the relationship between adult children and their parents: Joseph Kupfer, "Can Parents and Children Be Friends?" *American Philosophical Quarterly* 27 (1990): 15–26.

277. Raymond F. Collins, "Obedience, Children and the Fourth Commandment: A New Testament Note," *Louvain Studies* 4 (1972–73): 157–73, argues that the commandment that one honor one's father and mother primarily requires adults to support their aged parents.

If one provides a home or daily care, the other or others should contribute what they can, for example, enough money to compensate for the related expenses. If one or more children evade the responsibility, the other or others should use every morally acceptable means to induce them to repent and do their share. Conscientious children sometimes can forestall difficulties of this kind by working with their parents, well before help is needed, to plan how it will be provided when the time comes. In any case, children should begin to provide help before their parents are utterly impoverished and helpless, without demanding that the parents surrender their possessions and give up control over their daily lives.

A sign of this responsibility's importance is that Jesus strongly condemned an attempt to evade it (see Mt 15.4–5, Mk 7.10–11). Moreover, New Testament catechesis forcefully affirms it: "If a widow has children or grandchildren, they should first learn their religious duty to their own family and make some repayment to their parents; for this is pleasing in God's sight" (1 Tm 5.4). "And whoever does not provide for relatives, and especially for family members, has denied the faith and is worse than an unbeliever" (1 Tm 5.8). Children fail in this responsibility not only by entirely neglecting it, but by fulfilling it minimally and grudgingly, so that parents are demeaned by being treated as beneficiaries of undeserved generosity.

In other respects too, the dignity of dependent parents and other elderly family members should be protected. Despite the inevitable diminishing of personal autonomy and functioning, an elderly person should be treated neither like a boarder in the household nor, except insofar as good care requires it, like a child.

Aging family members should provide an example of confident faith, thus making clear to others that their self-esteem is not based on what they can do, have, and enjoy but on who they are and on the heavenly fulfillment for which they hope. Moreover, due to their experience and long years of reflection, the elderly often have a special wisdom which they should make available, and the young should listen to them respectfully (see Sir 8.9, 25.5–6).[278]

c) **Children should obey their parents' legitimate judgments.** Like other authority, that of parents is limited in various ways (see 7.E.3–4, above). But within those limits, children not yet able to judge what is in their own interests should obey any command or prohibition given for their good by a parent; and, as long as children live within their parents' household, they should obey the parents' rules and decisions as heads of the family for its common well-being: "Children, obey your parents in everything, for this is your acceptable duty in the Lord" (Col 3.20; cf. Eph 6.1). Moreover, children should obey not only their parents' direct commands and prohibitions, but the reasonable directives of teachers and others whom parents authorize to care for and educate them.

This does not mean unthinkingly doing whatever they are told, however, for the responsibility of children to obey their parents and others, such as teachers, in their parents' place corresponds precisely to the responsibility and limits of parental

---

278. See John Paul II, *Familiaris consortio*, 27, *AAS* 74 (1982) 113–14, *OR*, 21–28 Dec. 1981, 6; John Paul II, Message for World Communications Day (10 May 1982), 2–3, *Inseg.* 5.2 (1982) 1476–78, *OR*, 24 May 1982, 3.

authority (see F.4.g, above). Moreover, parental authority in the strict sense, as distinct from the authority of the parents as heads of the household, gradually ends as children grow up (see F.4.i, above).

Children obey initially by listening carefully and being willing to hear what their parents are asking of them. If what they are told to do seems impossible or unreasonable or wrong, they should discuss the problem calmly and respectfully with their parents. That usually will resolve the problem, and children will be able to obey. But if a child remains convinced that obeying really would be wrong, he or she must not do so (see Acts 5.29).

Children's obedience should be motivated not by servile fear but by humble awareness of their need for direction, and by gratitude and love (see Sir 7.27–28). Thus, as they grow up, they will continue to respect their parents and wish to please them, but increasingly will make their own decisions. In this way, by age eighteen or so they will be ready to settle those matters which no one else should try to settle for them, such as questions concerning their own personal vocation and adult life (see GS 52).

d) Children's disobedience can be a grave matter. It is a grave matter for a child, rejecting parental authority, to decide to conform to parental commands only when he or she considers it more convenient than nonconformity. For this reason, the Mosaic law prescribed that a stubborn and rebellious son be put to death by stoning (see Dt 21.18–21). But even apart from general contempt for parental authority, disobedience to particular judgments can be grave matter. That will be so when the commanded or forbidden act is very important in itself or in its likely consequences. For instance, children are gravely bound to obey their parents' reasonable judgment concerning avoiding the proximate occasions of grave sin, serious risks to life, health, and safety, and so on. Even adult children living in the parental household are gravely bound to obey their parents' reasonable judgments concerning matters which seriously affect the well-being of the family as a whole.

Often, though, children's sins contrary to their parents' will in grave matters are not mortal sins of disobedience.

Sometimes children disobey without sufficient reflection concerning their duty to obey, so that, even if the act they do is a mortal sin, they do not commit an additional mortal sin of disobedience. For example, the father of a fourteen-year-old girl, fearing she will be seduced, clearly and firmly tells her not to date a seventeen-year-old young man who has behaved irresponsibly with other girls; the girl disobeys and fornicates with the young man; in doing so, she overlooks the gravity of her disobedience but is conscious of the gravity of fornication; thus, while committing a mortal sin of fornication, she does not commit an additional mortal sin of disobedience.

At other times children act contrary to their parents' will in a grave matter but do not disobey, since, fully able to make their own judgments in the matter, they are no longer under parental authority in respect to it. For example, the mother of a nineteen-year-old young man exhorts him to break off his sexually intimate relationship with a girl; he fully understands his moral responsibility, but is obdurate in his sin; still, he does not commit a sin of disobedience, since parental authority is no longer operative for the young man in the matter, and his mother's exhortation is the admonition of a fellow Christian, not the command of a parent.

2. The Family Should Be a Community of Love and Service

While family members rightly give one another special love and service, the home should not be a closed circle, where charity, if one can call it that, ends. Instead of regarding itself as a limited and closed communion of mutual love and caring, the family should accept its responsibilities of service to others and in the Church's apostolate. It fulfills this responsibility by sharing its spiritual riches with those to whom it extends hospitality and in neighborly fashion with other families (see AA 11, GS 48).

a) Familial love should extend beyond the primary relationships. The husband-wife and parent-child relationships are the primary ones constituting a family. Initially incapable of fully human personal relationships, children only gradually grow in responsibility and love. But since brothers and sisters are united in and through their parents, their relationships increasingly should acquire the characteristics of a good friendship, so that eventually they will fulfill in the most exemplary way the commandment: "Those who love God must love their brothers and sisters also" (1 Jn 4.21).

In a large family, the elder children share in some ways in their parents' responsibilities toward the younger, and the younger children should respond with appropriate respect and obedience. Moreover, the love among parents and children should expand to embrace in-laws (see Tb 10.12, 14.13) and others in the older and younger generations, not least grandparents and grandchildren.

b) Family members should love, forgive, and serve one another. Family life calls for the constant practice of mercy. Emotional bonds often facilitate this practice, but even when they are strained, each family member should contribute whatever he or she can to the good of the others and should readily seek reconciliation and offer forgiveness. A heartfelt "I am sorry" and a sincere "I forgive you" should be among the most common expressions of love among members of a Christian family, imperfect but drawn toward perfection by the Holy Spirit.

The family should be animated by mutual love, submission, and service. Family members should not keep careful accounts of what they contribute and receive, as if they were partners in a business. Rather, each should contribute according to his or her ability and receive according to his or her needs:

> The relationships between the members of the family community are inspired and guided by the law of "free giving". By respecting and fostering personal dignity in each and every one as the only basis for value, this free giving takes the form of heartfelt acceptance, encounter and dialogue, disinterested availability, generous service and deep solidarity.
>
> Thus the fostering of authentic and mature communion between persons within the family is the first and irreplaceable school of social life, an example and stimulus for the broader community relationships marked by respect, justice, dialogue and love.[279]

---

279. John Paul II, *Familiaris consortio*, 43, *AAS* 74 (1982) 134, *OR*, 21–28 Dec. 1981, 9.

In this way the family makes its primary contribution to society: forming its members for interpersonal relationships which humanize and personalize the wider society of which families are the living cells.

c) **A family should work to maintain and build up communion.** Familial communion has a specific quality, which shapes the actions necessary to sustain and perfect it. Somewhat as marital intercourse perfects the one-flesh communion of the couple, the family meal actualizes familial communion. Family members should participate in it and be generous and patient in sharing not only the food but themselves through conversation. Family members also should do their part in providing and maintaining their common dwelling and property. They should share the use of things liberally and should mutually serve one another by accepting a share of the chores, perhaps taking turns in doing the more onerous ones. Each has a special responsibility to respect the privacy and keep the secrets of the rest. The family should celebrate special occasions and sometimes recreate together. If a family member lives a sinful life, even abandons the faith, others should maintain the bonds of family communion insofar as possible, although they may never formally cooperate in sin and must take care that any material cooperation does not encourage obduracy and impede repentance.

d) **Families should be neighborly and hospitable to those in need.** Families have a specific capacity for neighborliness, that is, for assisting and supporting one another. Offering one another good example, encouragement, and practical assistance, they also should welcome such offers and gratefully accept the help they receive. Since neighboring families should be shown not only fairness but mercy, Christian families should hold no grudges, readily forgive faults, insist on rights only when necessary, and be kind and generous even toward difficult neighbors.

A family as a unit can engage in all sorts of works of mercy, but, being organized and equipped to meet the basic bodily, emotional, and spiritual needs of its own members, it can serve others in a unique way by providing hospitality, that is, welcoming and embracing outsiders in need as if they were family members (see AA 11). *Hospitality* should not be understood narrowly; it extends from "opening the door of one's home and still more of one's heart to the pleas of one's brothers and sisters, to concrete efforts to ensure that every family has its own home, as the natural environment that preserves it and makes it grow."[280]

3. The Family Should Deal with a Member's Death in a Christian Way

Christians' responsibilities in preparing for death were treated in a previous chapter (see 4.F). A death in a family creates an unusual and inescapable crisis, and every member should accept his or her responsibilities and fulfill them in a Christian way. In doing so, family members can transform their difficult situation into a time of grace for themselves and of Christian witness toward others.

a) **The family should participate in the Church's prayers and rites.** The prayers for the dead and the funeral rites which the Church provides manifest the

---

280. John Paul II, *Familiaris consortio*, 44, *AAS* 74 (1982) 136, *OR*, 21–28 Dec. 1981, 9.

true Christian attitudes and values which should shape the family's response to a loved one's death.[281] Death is horrible; the loss of the family member is real and irremediable; grief is appropriate. Yet a person who has lived and died in Jesus is not lost forever. Prayer for the deceased is needed and will be effective. Moreover, united with Jesus through baptism and the Eucharist, survivors can remain, through him, in communion with their departed loved ones, while looking forward to the resurrection of the dead and everlasting reunion in heaven. Therefore, family members should do their best to participate attentively in the Church's prayers and funeral rites. In this way, they fulfill their most important responsibility toward the one who has died, while at the same time gaining for themselves sound consolation.

If a member of the family arranges the funeral liturgy, he or she should avoid anything distasteful to any of the others in selecting among options, such as the music to be used. While the homily at a funeral Mass may refer to the deceased person's virtuous life, the homily should not turn into a eulogy.[282] Therefore, the family should neither expect nor encourage the homilist to deliver a tribute to their loved one. Any speech or speeches honoring the deceased person should come at some other suitable time, for example, on the eve of the funeral or after the burial, or, at least, after the completion of the funeral liturgy but before leaving the church.

b) **Family members should treat one another kindly and mercifully.** When a death occurs in a family, usually it is clear which family member should make necessary decisions, and others should support that person and help do what must be done. If difficulties arise, everyone should be ready to yield on matters of taste and personal preference. The parties to an important disagreement should agree on someone to mediate it, for example, the parish priest or a prudent and trusted family friend.

Fatigue and strong emotion sometimes lead to outbursts of anger and recrimination. Family members should understand and readily forgive one another such inappropriate words and behavior. Indeed, being together during a period of shared grief affords an opportunity for reconciliation to family members who have quarreled or become alienated from each other, and they should take advantage of this opportunity.

c) **Christian funerals should be simple and economical.** The Church proposes a norm for the conduct of Catholic funerals: "The bodies of the faithful, which were temples of the Holy Spirit, should be shown honor and respect, but any kind of pomp or display should be avoided."[283]

In former times, a family member or friend prepared the corpse, a simple box was used as a coffin, a brief wake was held at home, funeral rites were completed promptly, and burial was in the churchyard or nearby cemetery. During the twentieth century, new and costly practices became widespread: a professional

---

281. *CIC*, c. 1176, §1, prescribes: "The Christian faithful departed are to be given ecclesiastical funeral rites according to the norm of law." C. 1177 states that as a rule the funeral should be celebrated in the parish Church of the departed, but may be celebrated in another church with the consent of the person in charge of that church and after informing the departed person's pastor.
282. See *General Instruction of the Roman Missal*, 8.338.
283. *The Rites*, 652.

mortician prepares the corpse for viewing, a fine hardwood or metal casket is provided, a prolonged reception is conducted at a funeral home, funeral rites are delayed and people travel long distances to attend, and burial is in an elaborately landscaped and perpetually maintained memorial park.

Of course, the value of bringing family and friends together sometimes justifies travel impossible in earlier times, and some other elements of current funeral practices inevitably follow. Moreover, the wake retains its important religious and human functions, and a funeral home sometimes is the only reasonable place for it. However, in many respects current funeral practices are neither reasonable nor Christian. In affluent societies, even families of modest means often succumb to the sales techniques of the funeral industry, unreasonable social expectations, and confused emotions, for example, a feeling of guilt unless they provide a lavish funeral.

Christian families should not feel compelled to conform to prevailing secular standards and should consider alternatives. In some places, funeral societies or memorial associations help arrange dignified but inexpensive funerals; Catholic families might join such a group or establish one in their parish or diocese. Prudent and competent individuals preparing for death could work with their families to plan and arrange their own funerals, thus encouraging simplicity and economy. Even if this is not done, a family member or friend can shop for an inexpensive coffin and moderately priced funeral arrangements. Sometimes, by omitting a prolonged reception and the viewing of the corpse, its professional preparation and the use of the funeral home can be avoided.

Longstanding Catholic practice favors burying or entombing the corpses of the faithful departed, since doing so provides a fitting sign of the hope that those now resting in death will soon rise to everlasting life. Nevertheless, cremation has been permitted in the past when necessary for a grave reason, such as control of a contagious disease. Today, while the Church's law still encourages burial or entombment, it no longer forbids cremation, provided it is not chosen to express disbelief in the resurrection of the dead or for some other reason at odds with the faith.[284] Therefore, a Catholic family may choose cremation if there is any other motive for preferring it.

4. Families Should Deal Responsibly with a Pregnancy out of Wedlock

If nonmarital intercourse by either spouse or a dependent child results in conception, the family has important responsibilities to the unborn child and faces difficult choices. Relevant moral norms should be kept in mind in making them.

a) Certain choices must be excluded entirely. In this situation, the temptation for men and youths, as well as for their families, is to deny responsibility, even if they are morally certain of it, and do nothing more than they legally must. This is an unacceptable evasion of responsibility, unfair to both the mother and the child, for whom the father bears equal responsibility. By the same token, a woman or girl

---

284. See *CIC*, c. 1176, §3.

pregnant out of wedlock has no exclusive right to decide what she will do with her child. If a girl is dependent on her parents for care and support, she cannot unilaterally decide to keep and raise the child. The child's father and/or his parents also have the right to be heard and to have their views considered seriously.

Abortion is likely to come to mind and even be suggested as a solution. Firmly rejecting it, everyone concerned should give the pregnant woman or girl the loving support she needs to resist any such temptation. The baby has no responsibility whatsoever for the situation and has an absolute right to live, to be loved, and to be cared for as adequately as possible.

b) Certain other attractive choices often are imprudent. If the unborn child's parents are free to marry, and especially if they already wished to, that is likely to seem the best solution. Even so, to avoid making so serious a commitment under pressure and/or without adequate preparation, it generally is wise to postpone marriage until after the baby is born. Moreover, if the couple would not marry except for the pregnancy, if they are very young, or if there are other considerations arguing against marriage, marrying is imprudent, since marriages under these conditions usually are badly troubled and often end in divorce.

In recent years, many women who have had babies out of wedlock have decided to keep and raise them without marrying. This also has several grave disadvantages. The child is deprived of a father and, often, cared for much of the time by a series of strangers. In some cases, the maternal grandparents are compelled to shoulder much of the responsibility of parenthood, even though they had sound and even compelling reasons not to adopt the child. The unmarried mother also is less likely to be able to develop a sound relationship with a man who is free to marry her, and so is less likely ever to enter a good marriage.

c) If possible, the child should have a normal family life. Like any other child, the child conceived out of wedlock needs two parents who are truly and happily married, who fully accept him or her as their own, and who firmly commit themselves to carrying out their lifelong responsibilities as father and mother. Whenever possible, families should try to meet these needs; they can do so in various ways.

One is by arranging for adoption by another suitable family, who will love and care for the child, and raise him or her in the faith. Though the arrangements often are made through an adoption agency, sometimes well-qualified relatives, friends, or neighbors are prepared to adopt the baby, and arrangements can be made directly. The mother sometimes rejects adoption out of emotional motives, for mothers naturally are attached to their babies. However, emotional attachment should not prevail over a reasonable judgment concerning the child's best interests.

In other cases, the family itself can accept the child as its own. In particular, husbands whose wives conceive through adulterous intercourse should consider this solution and ask themselves whether Christian mercy does not require them to cooperate with it.

A family whose dependent son fathers a child out of wedlock or a man who does so should contribute to the child's support to the extent possible and necessary to provide the child with a normal family life.

Question H: What Should Spouses Do If Their Marriage Is Troubled?

While every married couple experiences many difficulties—for example, illness, a child's death, economic hardship—the marriage itself cannot be called troubled unless one or both spouses are not properly fulfilling their roles as spouses and/or parents. Of course, nobody is perfect, and so most couples experience some problems more or less regularly. These amount to trouble for the marriage only when the couple find them hard to handle, and their efforts seem not to make things any better as time goes by. Then they are likely to be tempted to regret having married each other.

With the help of prayer and good advice, nevertheless, a married couple willing to work together can deal with and overcome the difficulties troubling their marriage. Yet sometimes serious marital difficulties justify or even require a separation. Unfortunately, separation, whether justifiable or not, sometimes becomes permanent, and then often ends with divorce and attempted remarriage by one or both spouses. Even in such cases, the couple remain married to each other, and should fulfill relevant marital and familial responsibilities.

1. Couples Should Do All They Can to Overcome Marital Trouble

Sometimes it is said that a marriage has broken down, that a couple's love has died and their marriage with it, that a relationship has been torn apart so completely that nothing could possibly heal it. The suggestion is that marriage can cease to be before either spouse dies. But marriage is absolutely indissoluble. Therefore, to think about marriage as such expressions suggest is implicitly to deny the very reality of marriage and the truth about it which pertains to Catholic faith.

Mental illness can impair people's functioning to such an extent that they are not responsible for their behavior and are unable to rectify the difficulties it causes others. If one spouse is afflicted with such a pathology, the other must do his or her best for the good of everyone concerned. Typically, however, marital trouble results from a combination of moral failings, usually on both sides, and nonmoral factors. Since grace and freedom can overcome all serious sins, the moral failings which lead to serious marital difficulties can be overcome. Of course, the couple must cooperate in using available means and in dealing with nonmoral factors which occasion conflict. Moreover, venial sins can result in difficulties which a couple never can entirely overcome, but must live with.

a) **Moral failings lead to or aggravate marital difficulties.** Assuming freedom from psychopathology serious enough to interfere with deliberation and free choice, a perfectly virtuous husband and wife would be able to deal with anything which happened to them and would never be tempted to wish they were not married to each other. Even if such a couple disagreed about some very important matter, they would find an appropriate way of dealing with whatever divided them without compromising their deep marital harmony.

Of course, no couple is perfectly virtuous. Typically, difficulties begin to trouble a marriage when at least one spouse is doing something he or she should not do, or not doing something he or she should do, and this displeases the other, so that the couple find themselves in a conflict of wills. A difficulty troubling a marriage, therefore, almost always involves a moral conflict rooted in some sin of at least one spouse, and often rooted in ongoing, more or less serious sins of both. (Of course, many difficulties involve nonmoral factors as well, and those will be discussed in d, below.)

Among the sins that lead to or aggravate marital difficulties, failure to fulfill the responsibility to communicate—to express feelings and thoughts carefully and gently, and to listen attentively and sympathetically—has a special importance, since failure to communicate makes it impossible for the couple to cooperate effectively in building their friendship and dealing with other difficulties.

b) A couple who cooperate can overcome serious moral failings. A husband and wife who are prepared to cooperate in overcoming their difficulties must be ready to repent and stop committing any sin or sins troubling their marriage. If the trouble is serious, the sin also is serious; no matter what the character of the act in itself, the fact that it causes serious marital trouble makes it grave matter. Now, the Council of Trent definitively teaches that grace is sufficient so that Christians willing to repent and cooperate with it can avoid mortal sin (see DS 1536/804; cf. 1568/828). Moreover, if both spouses are Christians, their marriage is sacramental, so that they enjoy a special guarantee of "the grace that brings natural love to perfection, and strengthens the indissoluble unity, and sanctifies the spouses" (DS 1799/969). Therefore, a couple willing to cooperate with each other and with God's grace can successfully deal with any moral failings troubling their marriage.

c) The spouses should repent, forgive, and admonish each other. As soon as serious difficulties trouble a marriage, the couple should talk matters over calmly and fully. No doubt, angry words have been exchanged; perhaps they have nagged and threatened each other. Now they should set aside a time to reflect together about the underlying difficulties. Insofar as these involve moral failings, the remedy is in recognizing and repenting them. To this end, both self-examination and admonition have a role to play, but the former should precede the latter: "First take the log out of your own eye, and then you will see clearly to take the speck out of your neighbor's eye" (Mt 7.5, Lk 6.42).

So, having begun by praying for each other and praying together for the light to see what they are doing wrong and the strength to amend, each spouse should refrain for the time being from criticizing the other, and both should instead examine themselves. This self-examination should include recalling and thinking carefully about any accusations the other has made. Even accusations blurted out in anger often include important elements of truth. These must not be rejected defensively, but accepted with openness as important helps to self-reformation and growth in true marital love. Each spouse should repent his or her own sins, ask the other's pardon, and obtain forgiveness and grace in the sacrament of penance.

When the spouses have done this, if either thinks the other has not repented some sin causing serious trouble, he or she should admonish the apparently sinful spouse. But anyone admonishing an apparent sinner must proceed in a way appropriate to the relationship and in a manner likely to help rather than aggravate (see 4.E.1.h);

so, a spouse who engages in admonition should proceed lovingly and gently. It can sometimes be done almost tacitly, by noticing and showing appreciation for instances of good behavior and ignoring instances of the troubling behavior.

Someone admonishing his or her spouse should appeal to the common good of the marriage and show how the apparently sinful behavior is harming it in specific ways, at the same time reaffirming his or her love and making it clear that no grudge is held. Emphasis should be placed upon hope for a better and happier marriage once the present difficulty is overcome. Any sign of repentance and any effort the spouse makes to cooperate in improving matters should be greeted with gratitude.

There are three serious mistakes to avoid in admonishing. First, no matter how wronged one feels, admonition must not be used as a means of striking back; even the appearance of retaliation must be avoided, for to act, or seem to act, out of anger and hatred will only further damage communion and harden the sinner—if, indeed, he or she is one. Second, no matter how urgent it is that the apparent sinner change his or her ways, one should not try to induce change by appealing to selfish interests; that is wrong not only insofar as it is manipulative but also insofar as it is likely to alter behavior without inducing repentance, thus blocking the needed growth in love (see D.4.f–g, above). Third, no matter how discouraged one feels about the prospect that one's spouse will change, he or she never should be condemned as hopeless. If there really is a moral failing, repentance remains possible, but if there is not, the spouse's difficulty deserves understanding and sympathy, not condemnation.

d) The spouses should try to deal with nonmoral sources of trouble. If the effort to deal rightly with the moral dimension of serious marital troubles does not yield entirely satisfactory results, the spouses again should talk matters over, calmly and fully, trying to identify nonmoral sources of difficulty and how to deal with them. For, although marital troubles typically involve moral conflicts, many moral conflicts are occasioned by other things that are not as they should be.

Sometimes physical or psychological illness leads a spouse to behave badly: a husband with an ulcer is always irritable, a wife who is neurotic is upset if the house is not kept perfectly neat. This leads to venial sins, for example, of verbal abuse, sulkiness, refusal to cooperate in small matters. Although such sins very often are neither deliberate nor serious in themselves, the other spouse recognizes them as evil and is likely to react sinfully. So, the spouses' wills come into conflict, and when this conflict seriously disturbs marital communion, the wrongful acts for that reason become grave matter, though not mortal sins if they remain nondeliberate.

A similar process can be triggered by many other nonmoral evils. Due to defects in knowledge of the other sex or lack of communication skills, spouses can fail to understand each other. They can encounter any of the difficulties that even a perfectly virtuous couple would—financial problems, lack of adequate living space, things wearing out or breaking down, and so on—and any such difficulty can occasion conflict of wills, with consequent marital trouble.

Even if a nonmoral evil would be insignificant and tolerable in itself, a couple who see that it is occasioning serious marital trouble have a grave obligation to try to deal with, and so prevent, its continuing harmful effect on their relationship.

Once the source of trouble is recognized, the spouses themselves can deal with it in some cases. But often they will need appropriate help: medical or psychological care, counseling to improve mutual understanding and communication, training to acquire needed skills, and so on. Couples who see the need for such help have a grave obligation to make any sacrifices necessary to obtain it; they should not delay in the vain hope that the trouble will go away with the mere passage of time.

e) **Spouses whose troubles persist should seek counseling.** If a couple's serious marital trouble persists despite their best efforts to talk matters over and deal with the underlying difficulties, they should obtain help from someone experienced in dealing with marital difficulties and faithful to the Church's teaching about marriage and its responsibilities. Often, this will be a priest or deacon, but sometimes the needed help can be obtained from some happily married couple friendly to both spouses but not especially close to either. While the couple should look primarily for moral guidance in seeking such help, they often will receive other useful advice and help as well.

With the advantage of objectivity, suitable counselors can see through self-deception and rationalization, thus helping the spouses to discover sins their self-examination has overlooked. Counselors must be strictly impartial, since partiality would further divide the spouses and render ineffective the moral guidance and exhortation directed to the less-favored spouse. Both spouses should be encouraged to explain fully their views of the trouble and its causes. (A counselor often prudently judges it best to meet with the spouses separately at this stage.) He or she should listen carefully and ask sufficient questions to understand the specific conflict of wills and the sins involved in it, while paying special attention to inadequacies in the couple's understanding of the marital relationship and its responsibilities. For many marital troubles arise because one party or both falsely suppose that marriage in some respects is an arrangement for obtaining what one wants out of life or a partnership in which neither spouse need contribute more than the other and both are entitled to equal benefits.

Counselors also should try to identify and call to the spouses' attention any nonmoral sources of trouble, help them learn how to deal with those matters, encourage them to do so promptly, and, if possible, provide needed help or assist them in finding it.

f) **Couples should learn to live with less serious difficulties.** Even when couples do what they should to overcome serious marital troubles and what they can to overcome minor ones, every marriage has its less serious difficulties. Every Christian sometimes commits at least nondeliberate venial sins (see DS 228/106, 891/471, 1537/804, 1573/833), and some of these inevitably lead to a conflict of wills between the spouses. The residue of sin is not insignificant, and can always provoke serious trouble unless the couple persevere in trying to deal with it. Each spouse must strive to overcome his or her own faults, and both must practice mutual understanding, tolerance, and ready forgiveness.

If the spouses do everything they can, in most cases their troubles will subside, and their life together will be as happy as can be expected in this fallen world. In any case, they will experience the most important sort of happiness: peace within themselves and with God. But even a good marriage may never be happy by conventional standards, and obviously cannot be so if there are major, irremediable, nonmoral sources of difficulty, such as severe mental illness. Thus, even if a couple fulfill all the essential responsibilities of marriage and remain faithful until death, they may experience much hardship and suffering.

Those who receive this cross should accept it as part of their particular vocations, realizing that Christians are not entitled to expect conventionally successful and happy lives in this world. Rather, they should faithfully fulfill their responsibilities in order to prepare material for the kingdom, where alone all evils will be overcome and all goods securely enjoyed.

2. Sometimes Spouses May or Should Initiate a Marital Separation

Generally, spouses should remain together and deal as best they can with marital troubles and other problems. Under some conditions, however, one spouse may, or even should, intentionally break off common life, including marital relations, and establish residence apart from the other. For the most part, separation is justified only as a last resort and usually should be carried out in a way which leaves open the possibility of reconciliation.

During a separation, spouses must be especially conscientious about fulfilling their responsibilities to their children, while avoiding any relationship that might lead to marital infidelity.

a) Generally, one may separate from an adulterous spouse. A married person who, with sufficient reflection and full consent, engages in sexual intercourse, whether natural or sodomitic, with a third party commits a mortal sin of adultery. Someone morally certain, not merely suspicious, that his or her spouse has committed such a sin generally has the right to break off common life.

A spouse is not justified in separating on this basis if he or she also committed adultery, consented to the other's adultery, or provoked it, for example, by deserting, unreasonably refusing marital intercourse, or deliberately failing to provide support, with the result that desperate need led to prostitution.

Also, the innocent spouse, without approving the other's adultery, sometimes decides to accept it and continue married life. This is done either explicitly, when an innocent spouse agrees to continue or resume conjugal relations with his or her repentant, adulterous spouse, or tacitly, when a spouse morally certain the other party has committed or continues to commit adultery nevertheless tolerates it by freely continuing to engage in marital intercourse. Once one spouse has explicitly or implicitly accepted the other's adultery, it no longer provides a ground for separation. If, however, adultery recurs, the innocent spouse need not continue accepting it.

b) The innocent spouse should consider the good of marriage. In deciding whether to exercise the right to separate, the innocent spouse should take into account the requirements of Christian mercy and the inherent importance of the good of marriage, which remains despite the damage adultery has done to it.

If the adulterous spouse is truly repentant, mercy and concern for the good of marriage strongly argue for forgiving the infidelity and maintaining or restoring marital communion.[285] If the adulterous spouse is not repentant and the innocent partner judges that separation might induce repentance, the same factors seem to require that the latter initiate a separation while leaving the way open for reconciliation.

What about cases in which the sinning spouse is obdurate and the innocent spouse sees no realistic hope that separating will induce repentance? The innocent party should take into account all the responsibilities of his or her vocation, not least to any minor children and to the marriage itself. He or she remains entitled to marital intercourse, and perhaps other elements of the good of marriage can be salvaged even if it seems unlikely that mutual, faithful communion will be maintained. After prayerful discernment, therefore, the innocent spouse may either separate or tolerate the adultery, depending on which course seems best, all things considered. In separating, though, he or she should not entirely foreclose the possibility of reconciliation, and the separation should be reconsidered if the adulterous spouse eventually repents.

c) A spouse should separate when necessary to avoid grave harms. Sometimes one spouse leads or even pressures the other, or a child, into committing grave sin. Again, a spouse's behavior might pose a serious threat to the life, health, or bodily integrity of his or her spouse and/or child. Sometimes the one causing the harm is not morally responsible—for example, if the harmful behavior results from psychosis—but, more often, there is at least some moral responsibility.

If the threat of grave harm is such that delay in separating would be dangerous, immediate separation is the only right course.[286] In other cases, other means of preventing the harm should be tried first. Since separation itself usually seriously harms the good of marital communion, this harm should not be accepted without first making a serious effort to avoid it. Moreover, Christian mercy requires that the spouse suffering harm try not only to prevent it but to help the spouse who is behaving badly change for the better; and alternatives to separation often are more effective ways of achieving this end.

That is especially so when the bad behavior is more or less the product of psychological illness or serious moral weakness. So, for example, the wife of a brutal, alcoholic husband should consider having him arrested, so that the public authorities will force him to enter rehabilitation; for even though separation might seem a less aggressive measure, in many cases it also is less effective. Again, the spouse of someone who becomes seriously mentally ill should prefer to have him or her committed for treatment rather than separate and allow the illness to remain untreated.

Quite often, when the injury is spiritual or moral rather than physical or psychological, spouses wrongly tolerate grave harm to themselves or their children, or even cooperate in grave sin, instead of separating. But if, for example, a wife and mother abandons her faith and begins to undermine the children's faith, and the husband can only prevent this harm by separating, he should separate; or, if a

---

285. See *CIC*, c. 1152, §1; cf. c. 1695.
286. See *CIC*, c. 1153.

husband persistently perverts the marital relationship by pressuring his wife to engage in nonmarital sexual acts, and she cannot deal with this occasion of grave sin except by separating, she should separate.[287]

d) A spouse may separate if the other makes common life too hard. The traditional treatment of marital separation, reflected in the Church's law, considers separation justified not only on the ground of adultery and to avoid grave harm but in some additional cases in which one spouse makes "common life too hard."[288]

Plainly, that does not provide justification for those who decide to separate simply in order to compel their spouses to submit to their will. It is gravely wrong to use even temporary separation simply as a manipulative device against one's spouse, not only because it violates the responsibility to carry on common life but because it is an exercise of coercion contrary to conjugal friendship. Moreover, those who separate merely because they think it is in their personal interests proceed just as if they were not married, which gravely violates the responsibility to maintain common life.

A decision to separate temporarily may well be reasonable when common living is very difficult if it seems the good of marriage might be served in this way by leading the other party to reflect seriously and repent. Harder to justify is a decision to separate for an indefinite time, even as a last resort to escape unresolved serious marital troubles, except because of adultery or to avoid grave harm—situations already treated above. For marital consent is a commitment to pursue the good of marriage not only for better but for worse, whereas an indefinite separation is very likely to lead to very serious harm, including adultery by at least one of the spouses, to the already-damaged marital communion. Still, in some rare cases one spouse may cause the other or the children such great difficulties that the other can rightly judge it too hard to continue common life. This decision is properly made, however, only if it is based on prayerful and conscientious discernment, taking into account all the relevant goods and all the person's responsibilities.

e) Marital separation is subject to the Church's authority. Since Christian marriage is a service to the Church and subject to her authority, Catholic spouses

---

287. Bayer, *Rape within Marriage,* argues that a wife may use contraception if the couple should not have a child but her husband forces her to have intercourse. If correct, that view would allow such a wife to avoid separation by materially cooperating in nonmarital intercourse while defending herself against the harm of conception, on the analogy of the defense which any woman may rightly make against pregnancy which would be caused if she were raped by a man other than her husband. In reality, however, a wife in that situation will be strongly tempted to cooperate formally, though reluctantly, in nonmarital intercourse and also is likely to intend, not to defend herself against the fullness of one-flesh communion, but to prevent the coming to be of the child which the couple should not have. Bayer himself unwittingly verifies this point when he defines *intra-marital rape* to mean "any sexual act of a husband, which is capable of impregnating his wife, and which is at the same time forced upon her by her husband against her objectively justified and serious refusal of consent" (3). Plainly, the sexual acts of husbands which are analogous to rape include many which are not capable of impregnating their sexually oppressed wives. So, in defining *intra-marital rape* as he does, Bayer manifests the real point of his argument: to justify such a wife's use of contraception precisely insofar as it is contralife. But that is always wrong (see 8.E.3).

288. *CIC,* c. 1153, §1.

with justifiable reasons to separate should comply with Church law in doing so.[289] The innocent party who judges it best not to forgive or tolerate adultery may separate at once without first obtaining Church authorization. But if the separation is prolonged or permanent, he or she should consult a priest within the first few months (the Church's law requires that formal authorization be sought within six months).[290] Apart from separations justified on the basis of adultery, authorization to separate should be obtained in advance, unless there is danger in delaying. In that case, authorization should be obtained soon after separation; moreover, if the reason for separation ceases to exist, common life should be resumed unless authorization is obtained not to do so.[291]

Civil divorce cannot dissolve a Christian marriage, and generally spouses should not seek one. It makes reconciliation very unlikely and often opens the way to a new and enduring adulterous relationship, while further damaging the effectiveness of the real and indissoluble marital union as a sign of the unbreakable union of Christ and the Church. Still, in some cases there is virtually no hope of reconciliation and civil divorce is necessary to deal with important legal matters, such as property rights or the enforcement of a man's financial responsibilities toward his wife and children. Only in such cases is a Catholic justified in deciding to obtain a civil divorce, and even then he or she should not begin legal proceedings without first obtaining the Church's authorization.[292]

f) **Separated spouses still have marital and familial responsibilities.** Since separation does not alter the fact that the couple are married, they still must fulfill all their marital and familial responsibilities other than those pertaining to sexual acts and common life, which now is broken off. This includes fulfilling certain affirmative responsibilities toward each other: to pray for each other, to communicate insofar as that is necessary to keep open the possibility of reconciliation, to cooperate in caring for their children, and so on.

Moreover, the spouses should remain completely faithful to each other, entirely avoiding any romantic relationships with third parties. This may require severely limiting previously unexceptionable relationships with members of the opposite sex, since a separated person all too often becomes romantically involved with someone who up until then had been only a friend, coworker, good neighbor, or the like.

No matter which spouse provoked or initiated a separation, both remain fully responsible for their children's care.[293] Indeed, separated parents must work even

---

289. Those attempting to do so in accord with the relevant canons cited below may find that the Church's law in this matter is not in use in their diocese. Where that is so, it does not lessen moral responsibilities not to separate except for justifiable reasons, to avoid civil divorce if possible, to fulfill parental responsibilities, to avoid involvement in a new romantic relationship, and so on.

290. See *CIC*, c. 1152, §3.

291. See *CIC*, c. 1153.

292. See *CIC*, c. 1692.

293. *CIC*, c. 1154, prescribes: "After the separation of the spouses, suitable provision is to be made for the adequate support and education of the children." Archibald D. Hart, *Children and Divorce* (Waco, Tex.: Word Books, 1982), a professional psychologist writing from an evangel-

harder to do everything they can for the children's good. Separation of itself tends to deprive children of the parenting and security they need, and they are likely to suffer grave and permanent harm unless both spouses do their best to prevent it.

During a separation, serious failures of parental responsibility are very common and always are grave matter. In many cases, one spouse, due to hostility, makes it difficult for the other to have reasonable access to the children; husbands often irresponsibly fail, or even refuse, to provide child support; sometimes both spouses exploit and damage children by using them to conduct their hostilities against each other.

g) Despite separation, spouses can live good Christian lives. Abandoned or justifiably separated spouses bear a very heavy cross. But that cross belongs to their vocation: "In such cases their example of fidelity and Christian consistency takes on particular value as a witness before the world and the Church."[294] Like all other Christians, they should hope confidently in God's grace, which always is available to them for the asking. They should use every available means to fulfill their responsibilities, and should not let shame or false self-respect prevent them from seeking and accepting any help civil society can provide. When necessary, they should demand help from the Church, while other Catholics should recognize their special responsibility, not only to encourage these brothers and sisters in their hard situation but to aid them materially when necessary: "Bear one another's burdens, and in this way you will fulfill the law of Christ" (Gal 6.2).

3. Troubles Related to a Doubt about Validity Can Be Overcome

Sometimes serious trouble can be a sign that, even though a relationship seemed to be a marriage, in fact it was not, since the couple were not validly married. While it always is wrong for a married person to wish he or she were not married, someone whose marriage could be invalid does nothing wrong in recognizing a reason for doubting its validity; and once such a reason is recognized, it should be looked into.

a) Any doubt about the validity of a marriage should be resolved. Sometimes relationships considered marriages by everyone, including those involved, actually are invalid: either the parties were not free to marry each other, or one or both failed to give adequate consent, or some requirement of the Church for validity was not met. If one or both parties to a valid marriage doubt that they are married, the marriage will be troubled unless the doubt is put to rest; and if a couple who

---

ical-Christian standpoint, makes clear many of the damaging effects of divorce on children, but also, without condoning divorce, offers helpful advice for dealing with these bad effects.

294. John Paul II, *Familiaris consortio,* 83, *AAS* 74 (1982) 184, *OR,* 21–28 Dec. 1981, 17. Also, John Paul II, Homily at the Mass for Families (York, England), 6, *Inseg.* 5.2 (1982) 2010–11, *OR,* 7 June 1982, 9, teaches: "Let us not forget that God's love for his people, Christ's love for the Church, is everlasting and can never be broken. And the covenant between a man and a woman joined in Christian marriage is as indissoluble and irrevocable as this love (cf. *AAS* 71 [1979], p. 1224). This truth is a great consolation for the world, and because some marriages fail, there is an ever greater need for the Church and all her members to proclaim it faithfully. Christ himself, the living source of grace and mercy, is close to all those *whose marriage has known trial, pain, or anguish.* Throughout the ages countless married people have drawn from the Paschal Mystery of Christ's Cross and Resurrection the strength to bear Christian witness—at times very difficult—to the indissolubility of Christian marriage."

are not married are confident that they are, that is a bad state of affairs. Many factors which cause invalidity also result in serious trouble between the couple, but the results often will be unsatisfactory if it is dealt with simply as marital trouble. Moreover, a couple actually not married to each other lack some essential benefits of real marital communion, especially the sacrament of marriage. Since, then, the possible invalidity of a marriage is a very serious matter, everyone should be alert to its signs, and, if they appear, should acknowledge the doubt they raise and deal with it.

Still, even if a doubt arises, a Catholic who, so far as he or she knows, entered into marriage in accord with the Church's law should presume that the marriage is valid and should continue to act accordingly until the opposite is proved. However, Catholics in putative marriages who are morally certain that they are not married have no marital rights, and so may not engage in sexual intercourse with their putative spouses; nor should they consider themselves free to marry unless and until the Church so determines.

b) Various facts can reasonably give rise to such a doubt. If a Catholic attempts marriage without a Catholic ceremony and without obtaining the bishop's authorization, the couple very probably are not married.[295] If a couple agreed before marriage that one of them would be sterilized or that they would always practice contraception so as never to have children, their relationship is not a valid marriage.[296] If either partner was involved in a previous relationship which had any semblance of marriage, and the problem of that prior relationship was not cleared up before attempting a Catholic marriage, that partner probably was not free to marry.[297] If a couple have tried but failed to consummate their marriage, it may be null; if not, it possibly is dissoluble.[298]

If either or both partners were reluctant to marry but were forced to do so because of some pressure—for example, by parents concerned about the woman's pregnancy, or by one party's desperate need to emigrate or obtain a place to live—the consent required for marriage might have been lacking.[299] If after marriage either partner learns of some pre-existing circumstance which would have deterred him or her from consenting had it been known at that time, the consent may not have been sufficiently informed to make a marital commitment, particularly if the matter was an important one bearing on the marriage itself, such as the other party's attitudes about matters of religion or about marriage and its responsibilities.[300] Moreover, in general, if either party deserts or judges it justifiable to separate, the possibility should be considered that the trouble is caused by a factor which renders the putative marriage invalid. For desertion and separation signal profound trouble in a relationship, and sometimes the trouble results from one or another factor which also could render the relationship invalid as a marriage.

295. See *CIC*, cc. 1108–17.
296. See *CIC*, c. 1055, §1; c. 1101, §2.
297. See *CIC*, c. 1085.
298. See *CIC*, c. 1084, §1; c. 1142.
299. See *CIC*, c. 1103.
300. See *CIC*, cc. 1097–98; c. 1102, §2.

Threats of divorce early in a marriage can indicate that there was no consent to an indissoluble union. Many other more or less clear-cut signs can indicate either defects in consent or, possibly, incapacity at the time of marriage to assume and fulfill some of its essential responsibilities. Among these are indications of gross irresponsibility early in marriage: the man refuses to support the woman; she rejects the responsibilities of homemaking; either or both come and go as they please; or the man shows no interest in the woman's pregnancy and regards their baby as her exclusive responsibility. Other signs bear on the sexual activity of one or both partners: infidelity early in the marriage, ongoing use of pornography both before and after marriage, homosexual behavior, a demand by one party that the other engage in repugnant sexual behavior, use of contraception from the beginning of marriage because one partner would prefer never to have children or repeatedly insists on postponing them. Sometimes, too, serious substance abuse or a severe psychological problem around the time of marriage indicates an invalidating condition. Serious difficulties early in marriage centering around one or both partners' manipulative behavior and insistence on their rights can indicate that the consent in this case was only to a more or less fair arrangement rather than a genuine communion of life.

c) **By resolving doubts, the trouble can be dealt with appropriately.** Many of the signs which point to possible invalidity do not establish it as a fact, for they also could manifest one or both spouses' unreadiness to fulfill their responsibilities in a valid marriage.

Nevertheless, when there is doubt, the parties must neither presume the marriage to be invalid nor live with the doubt.

If the couple still wish to be married, most doubts about consent can be resolved by reaffirming consent to marriage.[301] Whatever marital trouble they might have, they are no less able to overcome it than any other married couple. But when a couple have separated and do not wish to be married, doubts about validity must be resolved by determining whether the putative marriage is or is not a real one. The matter should be taken to a diocesan tribunal or to a priest, who will help initiate tribunal proceedings.

A sound conclusion that a marriage is invalid can be reached only if the facts are truthfully presented and the Church's law is properly applied. This requires that the case be presented to the appropriate Church authority.[302] Since only the

---

301. See *CIC,* cc. 1156–59. Precisely *how* consent must be reaffirmed varies in diverse cases; the priest or Church official helping the spouse or couple with the problem will explain what is necessary. But in any case, the spouse or couple need not fear embarrassment, since there is no need to make the situation public.

302. *CIC,* c. 1671, prescribes: "Marriage cases of the baptized belong to the ecclesiastical judge by proper right." The judge in question usually is that of the tribunal of the diocese in which the marriage occurred, or in which one of the parties is living, or in which relevant evidence can most easily be gathered (see c. 1673). Certain cases are reserved to the Holy See. While an attempted marriage by a Catholic without a Catholic ceremony or a dispensation from that requirement is not even a putative marriage in the Church's eyes, a Catholic who has attempted marriage with one person is no longer free to marry another unless declared by the Church to be so.

Church's judges can settle marriage cases involving Catholics, no individual can determine his or her own freedom to marry, even with a priest's advice and help.

4. Spouses Who Attempt Remarriage Have Special Responsibilities

Neither partner in a valid marriage should attempt a second marriage while the other is living. Any sexual activity by the parties to a union of that kind is adulterous, not marital. Catholics who persist in adulterous relationships nevertheless have many of the responsibilities of marriage and family life, not only to their true spouses and all their children, but even to the partner with whom they live. If they fulfill these and other responsibilities, the Church is confident that God's grace of repentance and merciful forgiveness will be available to them if ever they are willing to accept it.

a) Such spouses should stop committing adultery. To call a relationship a "second marriage" suggests that, even though one party or both were previously married to others, they now are truly married to each other. Of course, when such a union is confirmed by civil marriage following civil divorce, society considers it to be a marriage. Moreover, so-called second marriages commonly differ in important ways from casual relationships or the less stable unions of couples merely living together: the partners can desire a loving and stable union, and can act as good parents. But even so, since marriage is absolutely indissoluble, neither partner in a real marriage can enter a second marriage as long as both are living. Thus, despite appearances and decent desires, the partners in such unions are not actually spouses. They should accept that fact and its implications in accord with the truth Jesus teaches: "Whoever divorces his wife and marries another commits adultery against her; and if she divorces her husband and marries another, she commits adultery" (Mk 10.11–12; cf. Mt 5.6, 1 Cor 7.10–11). And since adultery is always gravely wrong, they should break off their sexual relationship at once.

Generally, too, they should separate. Not doing so is almost certain to be an occasion of grave sin for them, while to others it is a sign of marital communion which does not actually exist and a possible source of scandal. But what if the couple have very grave reasons for continuing to maintain a common household, for example, they have small children who might not be properly cared for if they separate? Perhaps they can rightly continue to reside together, but only if they "take on themselves the duty to live in complete continence, that is, by abstinence from the acts proper to married couples."[303] In any case, such a couple are not in an impossible situation. Perhaps they can separate and still fulfill their essential responsibilities to their children and each other; if not, they certainly can live chastely, provided they pray for the necessary grace, repent their past sins, and use all the available means.

b) So-called internal forum solutions solve nothing. Church law provides that, when necessary, certain acts of Church governance and jurisdiction can be

---

303. John Paul II, *Familiaris consortio,* 84, *AAS* 74 (1982) 186, *OR,* 21–28 Dec. 1981, 17. On the conditions under which such cohabitation is permissible: Bernard O. Sullivan, *Legislation and Requirements for Permissible Cohabitation in Invalid Marriages* (Washington, D.C.: The Catholic University of America Press, 1954).

carried out in a private or secret way. Although such acts then cannot have all their usual legal consequences, they can affect someone's moral status and so enable him or her to live with a good conscience. Such acts are said to be carried out "in the internal forum."[304]

Some theologians, canonists, and pastors try to help Catholics who have attempted remarriage by advising them that they can rightly treat their second union as a valid marriage if only a single condition is met: they have reached a confident judgment of conscience that they are not living in an ongoing adulterous relationship. Sometimes such advice implicitly assumes that it does not matter whether the first union was a valid marriage, because outwardly it seems that nothing of it remains, while the second union has all the conventional appearances of a real, and perhaps good, marriage. Sometimes the assumption is that the marriage's objective validity is not important, provided those concerned are not acting against their consciences. And sometimes it is thought that those involved in or contemplating a second union are competent to judge whether the first union was a valid marriage. Regardless of the assumption, those offering such advice often call this way of acting an "internal forum solution."[305]

304. See *CIC*, c. 130; c. 1079, §3; c. 1082.

305. See James H. Provost, "Intolerable Marriage Situations Revisited," *Jurist* 40 (1980): 141–96. In support of this use of the so-called internal forum, some point out that the Prefect of the Congregation for the Doctrine of the Faith (Cardinal Seper) sent a circular letter, not published at the time, to bishops, 11 Apr. 1973 (*Canon Law Digest* 9 [1978–81]: 503–4), on the indissolubility of marriage and "abuses against the prevailing discipline concerning the admission to the sacraments of those who are living in an irregular union," and that the concluding paragraph of this letter stated: "As regards admission to the sacraments, the local Ordinaries will likewise please urge observance of the prevailing discipline of the Church on the one hand, and, on the other hand, however, take care that pastors of souls follow up with special solicitude those also who are living in an irregular union, applying in the solution of such cases, in addition to other correct means, the approved practice of the Church in the internal forum." However, in answer to a request for a clarification of the phrase, "approved practice of the Church in the internal forum," Archbishop Hamer, Secretary of the Congregation (who had countersigned the letter of 11 Apr. 1973), wrote to Archbishop Bernardin, President of the National Conference of Catholic Bishops, 21 Mar. 1975 (ibid., 504–5): "I would like to state now that this phrase ['probata praxis Ecclesiae"] must be understood in the context of traditional moral theology. These couples may be allowed to receive the sacraments on two conditions, that they try to live according to the demands of Christian moral principles, and that they receive the sacraments in churches in which they are not known so that they will not create any scandal." Again, in answer to an inquiry from the Scandinavian Episcopal Conference, 19 Feb. 1976 (ibid., 507), about the possibility of readmitting to the sacraments Catholics "convinced in their formed conscience that their fidelity to their second marriage is not a sin despite the objective contradictions with the Church's teaching and marriage discipline" and also "convinced that they are not obliged to give up sexual relations," the Congregation replied, 14 Apr. 1976 (ibid., 508): "With regard to the admission to the sacraments of the previously divorced and remarried, the Congregation requests that you not introduce any innovation. In case you propose theological arguments for a change of practice, the Congregation is gladly ready to investigate them." Finally, referring to one instance of the misinterpretation of the 1973 letter, Joseph Cardinal Ratzinger, Prefect, Congregation for the Doctrine of the Faith, "Church, Pope and Gospel" (letter to the editor), *The Tablet* (London), 26 Oct. 1991, 1311, explains: "Cardinal Seper's mention in his letter of 1973 of the 'approved practice in the internal forum' which Fr Davey cites was not referring to the so-called internal forum solution which properly understood concerns a marriage known with certainty to be invalid but which cannot be shown to be such to a marriage tribunal because of a lack of admissible proof. Cardinal Seper for his part was not

In reality, however, those who give such advice are neither exercising Church authority nor applying Church law; they are replacing these with subjectivist conscience and their own opinions and feelings about marriage and divorce. They may think that the law's inadequacy, as they see it, and the failure of Church leaders to remedy it justifies them in doing so for what they consider to be an overriding good: the peace of conscience of divorced Catholics living in second unions.

Of course, a Catholic who in the past entered into a marital relationship under the Church's authority sometimes is free to marry despite the fact that both parties to that relationship are still alive. In virtually all such cases, the relationship would have been a sacramental and consummated marriage had it been valid, but, for some reason, it was not. However, any marriage should be presumed valid by all concerned unless and until the contrary is proven according to the Church's law.[306]

This presumption is not peculiar to marriage cases. All important, socially significant acts should be presumed valid, provided those who undertake them appear to meet the usual conditions for doing them. Without this presumption, one never would know how to respond to such acts, what various persons' rights and duties were, and so on. Thus, if it were not reasonable to presume the validity of an apparent marriage involving a Catholic, neither would it be reasonable to maintain the more general presumption without which social life as a whole would be impossible.

According to the Church's law, only a Church judge can deal with marriage cases.[307] Of course, those who wish to enter into a new relationship often think, and perhaps even firmly believe, that their earlier relationships were not true marriages. But they are interested parties, and no one is likely to be a good judge of a matter which, besides involving the rights of others and the community's common good, has such a profound and direct impact on his or her own interests as this one does.

It will be said, however, that a so-called internal forum solution is justified in at least one sort of case: a putative marriage cannot be proved invalid, but a party to it knows for certain that he or she never has been married; such a person, it will be argued, is objectively free to marry, and therefore can do so in good conscience. However, marriage is not the act of a single individual, but of a couple and even, in a certain sense, of the wider community to which the couple belongs, inasmuch as people cannot marry without doing what is considered necessary in their community to do so. If an individual's putative marriage cannot be proved invalid, his or her putative and prospective spouses and the Church must consider it valid,

---

addressing the question of the validity of a prior marriage, but rather the possibility of allowing persons in a second, invalid marriage to return to the sacraments if, in function of their sincere repentance, they pledge to abstain from sexual relations when there are serious reasons preventing their separation and scandal can be avoided."

306. See *CIC,* c. 1060, c. 1085, §2.

307. See *CIC,* c. 1671. If extraordinary circumstances justified handling some case in the internal forum without meeting all the relevant requirements of canonical procedure, still the case would not really be resolved (but only seem to be) unless someone having jurisdiction correctly applied the Church's law. See Francisco Javier Urrutia, S.J., "The 'Internal Forum Solution': Some Comments," *Jurist* 40 (1980): 128–40.

and so that individual, even if unmarried, is not *objectively* free to marry. Joseph Cardinal Ratzinger, Prefect, Congregation for the Doctrine of the Faith, explains:

> By the way, as far as the "internal forum solution" is concerned as a means for resolving the question of the validity of a prior marriage, the magisterium has not sanctioned its use for a number of reasons, among which is the inherent contradiction of resolving something in the internal forum which by nature also pertains to and has such important consequences for the external forum. Marriage, not a private act, has deep implications of course for both of the spouses and resulting children and also for Christian and civil society. Only the external forum can give real assurance to the petitioner, himself not a disinterested party, that he is not guilty of rationalisation. Likewise, only the external forum can address the rights or claims of the other partner of the former union, and, in the case of the tribunal's issuance of a judgment of nullity, make possible entering into a canonically valid, sacramental marriage.[308]

The fundamental error of the so-called internal forum approach lies in trying to reduce a problem about the validity of a marriage to a private problem of individual conscience, even though marriage is ineluctably social as a human reality and ineluctably ecclesial as a saving mystery.

The practice of so-called internal forum solutions also is pastorally disastrous. Even though someone whose problem has been dealt with in this way may really believe he or she is not living in sin, the practice itself cannot reasonably be expected to bring about that state of conscience. For it invites self-deception and rationalization, and peace of conscience attained by such means is not a reliable sign of freedom from the guilt of grave sin (see *CMP*, 3.C).[309] Moreover, a supposedly pastoral solution which sets aside a previous union in favor of the partners in a current relationship disregards other parties. That includes not only those directly involved—for instance, abandoned spouses and children—but Jesus himself, other Catholic couples whose marriages are troubled, young people who interpret what is going on to mean marriage is dissoluble and who will later attempt marriage on that basis, and so on.

c) **Those in bad marriages should accept the truth of their situation.** If Catholics who have attempted remarriage think their first union might not have

---

308. Ratzinger, "Church, Pope and Gospel," loc. cit.

309. For insight into how the practice of so-called internal forum solutions invites self-deception and rationalization, see the criteria proposed by John R. Connery, S.J., et al., "Appendix B: The Problem of Second Marriages: An Interim Pastoral Statement by the Study Committee Commissioned by the Board of Directors of the Catholic Theological Society of America: Report of August 1972," *Proceedings of the Catholic Theological Society of America* 27 (1972): 236–37. Some of the proposed criteria are plausible, although, used by an interested party apart from any careful process, they plainly would result in frequent erroneous judgments. But one suggested criterion is "tolerance or intolerance of common life," which invites the following line of practical reflection: "In that first relationship, which I once thought was a valid marriage, my partner and I did not tolerate common life well. If we had, we would be happily married today. But, in fact, she deserted me [or I found life with him unbearable, or eventually neither of us wanted to go on with it]. So, we clearly lacked tolerance of common life. Therefore, plainly it was not a valid marriage." Indeed, *intolerance of common life* could translate "molestam cohabitationem," which Trent definitively teaches *cannot* be said to justify divorce (see DS 1805/975).

been valid, they should put that doubt to the test in a Church court. If they have no real doubt or do not wish to seek a decree of nullity—or if they have sought such a decree but their marriage was not proved invalid—they should abstain entirely from sexual intercourse and other sexual acts. Indeed, even if they do not choose to do so, they still are better off in avoiding self-deception and rationalization, accepting the truth of their situation, and continuing to fulfill all the responsibilities they are willing and able to fulfill.

That, obviously, includes their responsibilities as parents to all their children, as well as responsibilities with regard to matters such as support toward both (or all) their former and present partners. Moreover, such people should not consider themselves separated from the Church, but should listen to the word of God, persevere in prayer, attend Mass, contribute to works of charity, help in efforts to promote justice, and do penitential works. However, they should not participate fully in the Eucharist by receiving Holy Communion, for "their state and condition of life objectively contradict that union of love between Christ and the Church which is signified and effected by the Eucharist."[310]

---

310. John Paul II, *Familiaris consortio*, 84, *AAS* 74 (1982) 185, *OR*, 21–28 Dec. 1981, 17; cf. John Paul II, *Reconciliatio et paenitentia*, 34, *AAS* 77 (1985) 271–72, *OR*, 17 Dec. 1984, 13, where the position is restated. For a helpful commentary, see Dionigi Tettamanzi, "The Pastoral Care of the Family and Irregular Situations," *OR*, 30 Aug. 1982, 6–8; cf. E. Gagnon, "Pastoral Care of the Divorced and Civilly Remarried Catholic," in *Contemporary Perspectives on Christian Marriage*, 205–14; Bertrand de Margerie, S.J., *Remarried Divorcees and Eucharistic Communion* (Boston: St. Paul Editions, 1980). Some who argue that such persons may receive Holy Communion cite theological opinion from the early 1970s, including that of certain theologians, such as Joseph Ratzinger, who are undoubtedly faithful to the Church's teaching; see, for example, Ladislas Örsy, S.J., *Marriage in Canon Law: Texts and Comments, Reflections and Questions* (Wilmington, Del.: Michael Glazier, 1988), 292–93, citing and quoting brief passages from Joseph Ratzinger, "Zur Frage nach der Unauflösigkeit der Ehe," in *Ehe und Ehescheidung*, ed. Franz Henrich and Volker Eid (Munich: Kösel, 1972), 55–56. However, such theological opinion must be read in its historical context: a discussion which took place in the decade or so before the session of the Synod of Bishops which met in 1980 (for a brief chronology of that discussion, see Provost, "Intolerable Marriage Situations Revisited," 174–78). During its second period, which began in 1974, the International Theological Commission (of which Ratzinger was then a member) took up this issue; the Commission's conclusion (International Theological Commission, "Propositions on the Doctrine of Christian Marriage," 5.3, in *Texts and Documents, 1969–85*, 173–74), adopted in *forma specifica* (that is, with an absolute majority subscribing not only to the ideas but to the very wording), was firm and clear: "The incompatibility of the state of remarried divorced persons with the precept and mystery of the Paschal love of the Lord makes it impossible for these people to receive, in the Eucharist, the sign of unity with Christ. Access to eucharistic Communion can only be had through penitence, which implies detestation of the sin committed and the firm purpose of not sinning again (cf. *DS*, 1676)." Subsequently, the issue was discussed in the 1980 session of the Synod of Bishops; the teaching of John Paul in *Familiaris consortio* gathers up and responds to that discussion, reaffirming the exclusion from the Eucharist of the divorced who have attempted remarriage, and using terms similar to those of the International Theological Commission's document to explain the matter. Thus, the cited theological opinions of Ratzinger and others have been superseded, and now should be recognized as having been erroneous. The error was in attempting to hold at once two inconsistent positions: that marriage not only should not be dissolved but is indissoluble (which implies that those who have attempted a second marriage are living in adultery), and that those who continue to live as if they were spouses in an attempted second marriage can be reconciled (which implies that they are not living in adultery). Ratzinger himself, "Church, Pope and Gospel," loc. cit., comments on an attempt to draw norms from his

Those who accept the truth of their situation and do their best to live a Christian life within its limits can continue to hope for salvation. Although they are unwilling now to repent and amend their lives, being honest with themselves enables them to remain aware of their guilt, and without that awareness they could not repent. Assuring such Catholics that God is ready to forgive them whenever they are ready to repent, the Church looks forward as a loving mother to their repentance rather than their obduracy until death.

Question I: What Are the Responsibilities of Those Preparing for Marriage?

In contemporary, Western societies, people who decide they are ready to marry generally base that decision largely on the fact that they have found someone they want to marry. There is nothing wrong with that—unless one considers the matter in the light of faith and the perspective of vocation. But Christians shaping their lives as they should will proceed differently; they will not develop romantic relationships without knowing beforehand that they and their prospective partners are ready and free to marry.

Even early in adolescence, many young people can discern confidently that their vocation includes marriage; but whether it happens early or late, at that point an individual should begin preparing to undertake this vocation and fulfill its responsibilities. Judging himself or herself ready to marry, a person should begin to look for a suitable spouse, bearing in mind not only the qualities required in a spouse if the marriage is to be good and happy, but his or her own gifts and limitations. Finding someone with whom, both agree, the vocation to marry is shared, an individual should enter into an engagement. The engaged couple should work together to overcome any obstacles and prepare to marry, while also remaining open to signs that their judgment was mistaken and they should not marry.

Unfortunately, as in other matters, many Christians approach marriage just as nonbelievers do. That is taken into account in the following treatment of responsibilities regarding marriage preparation, and norms are articulated for those ready at any stage to begin to approach the matter as conscientious Christians should.

1. Some Should Discern a Vocation to Marriage and Prepare for It

Not all Christians are called to marriage, and those who are, need to discern this element of their vocation. Appropriate preparation should then begin, even if marriage will be possible only far in the future.[311] It should include developing and carrying on chaste friendships with persons of both sexes.

---

earlier theological work: they "are not norms in any official sense at all. They formed part of a *suggestion* (*'Vorschlag'*) I made as a theologian in 1972 [note omitted]. Their implementation in pastoral practice would of course necessarily depend on their corroboration by an official act of the magisterium to whose judgment I would submit. . . . Now, *the* magisterium subsequently spoke decisively on this question in the person of the present Holy Father in *Familiaris Consortio*."

311. John Paul II, *Familiaris consortio*, 66, *AAS* 74 (1982) 160, *OR*, 21–28 Dec. 1981, 13, outlines this early preparation for marriage.

   a) **Many should accept the vocation to prepare for marriage.** Sexual capacity is an important gift which Christians can use in different ways to contribute to the kingdom. On becoming fully aware of this capacity at puberty, each should begin to consider how he or she will integrate it into a good and holy life. Some also will need to reconsider this question later in life, for example, after a spouse dies.

   The starting point should be the fact that for some Christians it is better not to marry, since the unmarried who have the gift of complete continence can more easily grow in holiness and serve the kingdom in special ways (see Mt 19.11–12; 1 Cor 7.8, 38; *CMP,* 27.H; C.4.e, above).

   Still, many Christians will discern signs that they do not have the gift to use their sexual capacity in a dedicated single life in the world, or in a committed life of celibacy or virginity for the kingdom's sake. For some, the sign will be the one St. Paul indicates: "It is better to marry than to be aflame with passion" (1 Cor 7.9). If they are to live good Christian lives, they will conclude, sexual desire must be integrated with conjugal love and so subordinated to the good of marriage. Many of these people, and others too, will discern another sign: a felt need for a spouse and, if possible, children, a need experienced as a profound sense of personal incompleteness which they cannot accept peacefully.[312]

   The consideration of how sexual capacity fits into personal vocation next should focus on physical, mental, and psychological limitations and defects, to see if any preclude marriage. For example, some people will find themselves with a seemingly unalterable homosexual tendency or incurable impotency—that is, inability to engage in marital intercourse—and others will suffer from other health problems incompatible with fulfilling the responsibilities of marriage and family life.

   Some of those who discern signs pointing to marriage and see nothing precluding it are in a position to marry at once. At once, then, they should begin to seek a suitable partner. But others, including adolescents, should conclude only that they probably eventually will be called to marry. Their present vocation is to prepare for marriage, while keeping open the possibility that they never will be called to it.

   b) **This preparation consists in developing gifts and gathering resources.** In contemporary affluent societies, adolescents and young people who have no sense of personal vocation often live irresponsibly: they do willingly only what gives them immediate self-gratification, care little for others, are uncooperative, work only at what happens to interest them, set about greedily acquiring whatever

---

312. Even mature and holy people committed to a dedicated single life in the world or to virginity or celibacy for the kingdom's sake sometimes experience sexual desire and, perhaps even more strongly, as some testify, a sense of personal incompleteness. But they plainly have the gift for the life they live, and so such experiences indicate the lack of that gift only if accompanied by a feeling of inability ever to accept *peacefully* the renunciation involved in forgoing marriage and parenthood. While some Christians—for example, most people who have an unalterable homosexual tendency or who have been abandoned by their spouses—are called to forgo all sexual satisfaction and some or all the satisfactions of family life *whether or not they can do so peacefully,* Christians who enjoy the gift for the evangelical renunciation can accept it peacefully, so that they need not live with constant tensions, which would impede their apostolate and detract from their value as witnesses to the kingdom.

they desire, and wastefully mistreat and discard things. But the day-to-day lives of young people are important not only for their present satisfaction but for their future happiness. As Pius XI teaches, "the basis of a happy wedlock, and the ruin of an unhappy one, is prepared and set in the souls of boys and girls during the period of childhood and adolescence."[313] Everything they do should shape good character and develop Christian modes of response, for their intrinsic value and also for their possible future benefits for marriage and family life. Parents should do all they can to exemplify the relevant virtues and encourage their children to develop them.

Since genuine personal fulfillment in a good marriage does not come from self-gratification but from personal service to others, those looking forward to marriage should use their gifts to help and care for others as opportunity offers. For example, they should help care for the elderly and ill, look after and instruct younger children—whether their own brothers and sisters or others—and do what they can to lighten the burden of their parents' work around the house. Instead of regarding interpersonal relationships only as sources of benefit to themselves, they should consider their relationships, including those with parents and teachers, as opportunities to contribute to the well-being and happiness of others. By cooperating gladly and gratefully in others' plans and projects, they develop their capacity for teamwork, so important in marriage, while giving those with whom they cooperate the satisfactions of success and gratitude for their efforts.

Marriage and family life call not only for the education and training necessary to make an adequate living but also for the development of the skills and knowledge required to conduct married life, maintain and manage a household, and raise children. Those preparing for possible marriage should make choices about their education with the requirements of marriage and family life in mind, and should diligently pursue their studies. Still, formal education alone will never suffice. Prayer, Scripture reading, personal study, and discussion with parents and others who have experience of marriage also are needed, as is thoughtful observation of real families, both happy and miserable, to see how to fulfill the vocation and avoid common pitfalls.

Marriage and family life require good use of material things. People preparing for this vocation should share unselfishly and care well for their family's home and goods, acquire only what they really need, help those in need, and, if possible, save money or gather other material resources necessary to start a family.

c) **Those preparing for marriage should develop chaste friendships.** Everyone should have friends, because friendship is good in itself and also helps psychological and moral growth (see 7.D.3.a), including the development of the virtue of chastity (see E.8.j, above). Moreover, genuine friendships with people of both sexes bring specific benefits for adolescents and young people who are preparing for marriage: growth in self-awareness, knowledge of others' traits, including their masculinity and femininity, and practice in open and cooperative relationships with peers. The distinguishing marks and responsibilities of friendship have been treated above (in 7.D.3).

---

313. Pius XI, *Casti connubii, AAS* 22 (1930) 584, *PE,* 208.112.

Like any other relationship between individuals who can be sexually attracted to each other, a friendship between an adolescent boy and girl or a young man and woman normally differs from a relationship in which sexual attraction is entirely absent. Still, normal adolescents and young people can develop chaste friendships with persons of the opposite sex, just as faithful, heterosexual priests, religious, husbands, and wives can. If such friendships are to develop, however, friendship must not be displaced by romantic relationship. Romantic relationships are those whose quality as a whole is specified by erotic attraction: the couple are drawn to bodily contact and enjoy being together so that they can touch each other; contact is likely to lead to genital arousal; the erotic affection tends to exclude other similar relationships; and the relationship becomes absorbing, leads to daydreaming, and tends of itself to grow more intense (see 7.D.3.j–k).

Healthy adolescents and young people often experience intense erotic feelings; they should learn to recognize these for what they are and accept them, like other normal feelings, as good in themselves. But, like more mature men and women who are chaste friends, adolescents and young people need not allow romance to replace their friendships. To maintain and develop a genuine friendship, they must avoid acting on erotic feelings, and since sharing erotic feelings with those who excite them usually leads to acting on them, even such communication usually must be avoided. Young couples also will need to be careful about the time, place, and frequency of their meetings. To enjoy each other's company without running risks, they do well to share most of their activities with one of their families or a suitable group of friends.[314]

d) When marriage is not in prospect, romance is inappropriate. In affluent Western nations, people generally take it for granted that boys and girls will carry on a series of romantic relationships beginning in early adolescence. Television and the other media consistently communicate cultural standards which approve such relationships and take it for granted that they will include sexual activities. Most Catholics and other Christians have been influenced by the dominant culture to take an increasingly permissive attitude in this matter.

But a romantic relationship is appropriate only when it can lead to engagement and marriage. Otherwise, it provides no real benefits, but only certain satisfactions proper to engagement and marriage, while at the same time displacing the activities characteristic of friendship, which the partners might be able to develop and enjoy. In carrying on a romantic relationship for its illusory intimacy, people act for an apparent good which blocks true benefits of a real human good. To carry on a romantic relationship when marriage is not in prospect is therefore wrong.

Almost inevitably, too, such a relationship soon becomes gravely wrong. Even if it were not wrong in itself, it certainly is not morally necessary and so, at best, would be permissible. But as soon as such a relationship begins to intensify, the underlying erotic emotion leads to significant temptation, and so continuing the

---

314. For a sound and helpful guide to dealing with erotic feelings and forming chaste friendships, see Mary Rosera Joyce, *Friends: For Teens* (St. Cloud, Minn.: LifeCom, 1990). While intended as a text to be used with the guidance of a parent, teacher, or counselor, adolescents could profit from studying this book on their own.

relationship becomes an occasion of grave sin. Since this occasion of sin is easily avoided—by terminating the relationship—continuing it is a grave matter.[315]

Consequently, those preparing for marriage but not yet ready to seek a potential marriage partner should try to develop and carry on many chaste friendships while entirely avoiding romantic relationships, which are an obstacle to real friendship and a grave and unnecessary threat to chastity.

2. Those with Marriage in Prospect Should Seek Suitable Partners

A person who not only thinks his or her vocation includes marriage but is ready to become engaged should seek a suitable potential spouse, applying reasonable standards and practicing careful discernment in doing so. Pius XI teaches:

> To the proximate preparation of a good married life belongs very specially the care in choosing a partner; on that depends a great deal whether the forthcoming marriage will be happy or not, since one may be to the other either a great help in leading a Christian life, or, a great danger and hindrance. And so that they may not deplore for the rest of their lives the sorrows arising from an indiscreet marriage, those about to enter into wedlock should carefully deliberate in choosing the person with whom henceforward they must live continually: they should, in so deliberating, keep before their minds the thought first of God and of the true religion of Christ, then of themselves, of their partner, of the children to come, as also of human and civil society, for which wedlock is a fountain head.[316]

The best way to deal with intractable marriage problems is to forestall them by being very careful about whom one marries. It is important not to be guided by an image—acquired without reflection—of an ideal mate or to be carried along by romantic feelings, developed before taking serious thought about marriage. Having recognized that a particular individual cannot reasonably be considered a potential spouse, a person should realize that marriage to that individual cannot possibly be part of his or her vocation.

a) **Further steps should be taken to prepare for marriage.** At this stage, the preparation for marriage appropriate for adolescents should be continued and intensified. Those who have not yet done so should study Christian marriage and family life in some detail, with particular emphasis on acquiring a mature knowledge of marital sexual activity, including natural family planning, and sound techniques of child raising.[317] They also should try to develop relevant talents

---

315. See Aertnys, Damen, and Visser, *Theologia moralis,* 4:117. In affluent nations, many adolescents and young people who have no prospect of marriage are involved in romantic relationships. The most obvious are those described as "going steady," but most of what is called "dating" is part of, or is intended to lead to, such a relationship. Some nonromantic pairing off, particularly within the context of a larger group's social activities, also may be called "dating." In any case, what is important for moral evaluation is the character of the relationship, not what it is called.

316. Pius XI, *Casti connubii, AAS* 22 (1930) 585–86, *PE,* 208.115.

317. See John Paul II, *Familiaris consortio,* 66, *AAS* 74 (1982) 160–61, *OR,* 21–28 Dec. 1981, 13. If she has not already done so, a fertile woman should begin at this time to chart her menstrual cycles, noting the various signs of fertility and infertility.

further—for instance, in homemaking and caring for a home—and should gather necessary financial and other resources. If they have any doubts about their physical or psychological capacity to fulfill the responsibilities of marriage, they should obtain any necessary medical or other assistance to resolve them.

b) **One should not carry on untimely romantic relationships.** Since marriage is the only good fulfillment of a romantic relationship, a person should not have such a relationship with anyone whom he or she either should not or does not wish to marry. This requires making certain that someone meets other criteria of suitability as a marriage partner before allowing any romantic relationship to develop. If a romantic attachment is formed prematurely—that is, before reasonable standards are applied and discernment is exercised to exclude the possibility that one should not marry that person or would not wish to do so—one's emotions will interfere with good judgment.

Furthermore, even for those who have marriage in prospect, romantic relationships remain wrong until a suitable potential spouse has been identified. Romantic activities with anyone not thus identified are an easily avoidable occasion of grave sin, and so are themselves grave matter.

c) **One should consider only those truly available for marriage.** Even before seeking a suitable potential partner, a person should exclude anyone already married, pledged to celibacy or vowed to complete continence, too young or immature for marriage, a member of his or her own family, or known to be incapable of marital intercourse.[318] People unwilling to consider marriage or unable to marry in the reasonably near future also should be excluded.

d) **Only those who are morally well qualified should be considered.** Anyone of bad character should be excluded as a potential partner. Such a person is unlikely to fulfill marital and familial responsibilities, and his or her faults are virtually certain to cause grave moral difficulties, not only for a spouse but for any children. Although grave sinners through weakness can and perhaps will reform, it would be imprudent to treat such a person as a potential partner with a view to reforming him or her. All too often, such plans succeed only temporarily, and the habit of sinning returns after marriage.

Besides these general moral considerations, before considering anyone a potential marriage partner, a person must be certain of his or her attitudes concerning

---

318. A couple may not contract marriage if there is or may be a prior marriage bond unless it can be dissolved or determined to be null (see *CIC*, c. 1085), nor if either party is in orders or vowed permanently to chastity (see cc. 1087–88). Canon law also excludes marriage by boys under sixteen and girls under fourteen (see c. 1083), discourages marriage by anyone under the age accepted in the region (see c. 1072), and forbids marriage of anyone under eighteen without either parental consent or the local ordinary's permission (see c. 97, §1; c. 1071, §1, 6°). Divine law absolutely excludes the marriage of an ancestor (i.e., parent, grandparent) to a descendent (child, grandchild), legitimate or not, and of blood siblings (brother, sister, half-brother, and half-sister) (c. 1091, §§1–2). The marriage of persons similarly related by adoption, of certain close relatives by a prior marriage, of an uncle and niece or aunt and nephew, and of first cousins is prohibited by canon law (see c. 1091, §§1–2; c. 1092; c. 1094), but dispensations sometimes are given. Permanent inability to engage in marital intercourse at the time of an attempted marriage would invalidate that apparent marriage (see c. 1084, §1).

marriage and its specific responsibilities—that marriage is absolutely indissoluble, that abortion is unthinkable, that any necessary birth regulation must be by marital abstinence. Someone who does not share one's beliefs and commitments on these matters should be excluded as a marriage partner, since wrong attitudes would either render any attempted marriage invalid or else make it very hard to carry on in marriage without grave sin.[319]

Before anyone is considered as a potential marriage partner, it also is necessary to know about his or her attitudes concerning the religious formation of any children who might be born. An individual who is not prepared to have babies baptized soon after birth and brought up as practicing Catholics is not a good prospect for marriage, since he or she would raise very serious obstacles to fulfilling the most important responsibility which parents have toward their children.[320]

e) If possible, one should consider only those who share one's faith. Since marriage should be a full communion of life suited to handing on that whole life to children, a Catholic should marry a Catholic who completely shares his or her faith and moral commitment. Differences in religion detract greatly from unity of mind and heart while impairing parental unity in a most important respect.[321] Moreover, someone who does not fully share Catholic faith and moral commitment is unlikely to be morally well qualified to be a Catholic's spouse, since he or she, even if a person of genuine good will, is likely to have beliefs and commitments incompatible with the truth the Catholic Church teaches concerning marriage, its specific responsibilities, and the raising of children. Where otherwise suitable potential partners are available who completely share one's faith, anyone who does not should therefore be excluded.

Sometimes, however, no such suitable potential partner can be found. Then a Catholic's preference should be for baptized persons who firmly hold and faithfully practice Christian faith, even though in a church or ecclesial community not in full communion with the Catholic Church. Of course, only those may be considered whose beliefs and commitments about marriage, its specific responsibilities, and raising children are compatible with the truth the Catholic Church teaches. Marriage even with such a person still will involve difficulties, and the Catholic party will have to make special efforts to keep and grow in his or her faith; but the couple will have the great benefit of the sacramentality of the marriage, and, if they

319. Certainty about a potential spouse's beliefs and convictions on these matters is equally necessary whether the person is Catholic or not. There can be no valid marriage if either party excludes absolute indissolubility, exclusivity (i.e., no polygamy), or readiness to accept at least some children (see *CIC*, c. 1056; c. 1101, §2; c. 1125, 3°). Someone prepared to engage at times in marital intercourse open to life but also to use abortion or contraception as methods of birth regulation can marry validly, but his or her spouse may not formally cooperate in any sexual act facilitated by those methods.

320. *CIC*, c. 1086, cc. 1124–25, requires that if a Catholic marries a non-Catholic, the Catholic must make a sincere promise to do everything in his or her power to have any children baptized and brought up in the Catholic Church, and that the non-Catholic party be informed of this promise.

321. See Congregation for the Doctrine of the Faith, *Matrimonii sacramentum, AAS* 58 (1966) 235–36, Flannery, 1:474–75; Paul VI, *Matrimonia mixta, AAS* 62 (1970) 257–59, Flannery, 1:508–10.

overcome their special difficulties, their marriage can contribute to the ecumenical movement by manifesting unity in moral and spiritual values.[322]

Lacking a suitable potential Christian partner, a Catholic with marriage in prospect should try to find an upright non-Christian suitable in other respects, not least in beliefs and attitudes about marriage, its specific responsibilities, and the raising of children. Even if these criteria are met, such a marriage will involve more serious difficulties, require greater efforts, and lack sacramentality.[323] However, it can truly realize the essential good of marital communion, which includes the natural holiness of marriage; it also provides a special apostolic opportunity for the Catholic who lives a faithful and exemplary life, since in this way his or her non-Christian spouse will receive a very effective communication of the gospel and a certain real link with Jesus and his Church.

f) **One should prefer those with whom more perfect unity is likely.** While religious differences detract from unity of mind and heart, and impair parental unity in the most important respect, less important factors can pose serious problems for marital communion and cooperation in raising children. To become one flesh in marriage, not only must two persons differ by being of opposite sexes, but they also can differ fruitfully in other ways, provided these also are complementary, that is, like the difference in sexuality, they contribute to the unity of a functioning whole. Still other differences, however, contribute nothing to unity and, indeed, impede it. So, except for differences which are, or can be made, complementary, someone seeking a suitable potential spouse should prefer those as similar as possible to himself or herself in all respects. Often, of course, differences which will not help build a happy marriage lead to superficial attraction; but otherwise suitable potential partners who differ in ways which are only likely to lessen compatibility should be excluded from consideration if possible.

g) **One should seek a potential partner by forming real friendships.** People who live in a rather homogeneous and sound Catholic community or have been educated in such a community often have one or more apparently suitable potential marriage partners among their acquaintances. However, those who lack the benefits of such a community must make suitable acquaintances in other ways. In either case, only by developing a close interpersonal relationship can anyone acquire the information and carry out the discernment necessary to identify a suitable potential marriage partner.

For several reasons, that close relationship should be a real friendship without a romantic element. As already explained, the latter is excluded until an otherwise suitable potential partner has been identified. The only legitimate way to acquire

---

322. For Catholics, marriage to a non-Catholic Christian is forbidden without express permission of competent authority (see c. 1124), precisely so that measures can be taken to forestall dangers to the faith of the Catholic spouse and children (see *CIC*, c. 1125). On the ecumenical potential of such a marriage, see John Paul II, *Familiaris consortio*, 78, *AAS* 74 (1982) 179, *OR*, 21–28 Dec. 1981, 16.

323. According to *CIC*, c. 1086, a marriage between a Catholic and a non-Christian is invalid without a dispensation; therefore, to enter such a marriage, the Catholic party must fulfill the conditions for the necessary dispensation and obtain it.

intimate knowledge about other persons is sincere friendship; and even if a friend is found unsuitable as one's potential spouse, the friendship remains worthwhile, and it can be continued indefinitely if the romantic element has been excluded. Moreover, when the time comes for romance, it can provide a richer and more secure basis for marriage if real friendship has preceded and accompanies it.

3. An Engagement Should Be the Fruit of Both Romance and Reflection

Rightly, a man and a woman looking toward marriage to each other as part of their vocations develop a romantic relationship, but as they do, they also should reflect and discern together whether they really are called to marry. If they conclude that they are, they should become engaged.

The following articulation of norms for developing a relationship leading to engagement and marriage inevitably sounds overly rational, cold, and perhaps even calculating. In real life, however, proceeding in an upright way will not deprive the couple of the warmth and joyful spontaneity of being in love, for passion is a gift of nature. When this gift is received, it need not be prescribed, and so is taken for granted here.

a) **Romance and discussion of marriage should begin together.** If the parties to a real friendship come to see each other as suitable potential marriage partners, the friendship often will develop spontaneously into a romantic relationship. Erotic desire will be felt and expressed by bodily contact: holding hands, kisses, and embraces. While these contacts can and should be very restrained, insofar as they are expressions of erotic desire they point toward eventual fulfillment in one-flesh communion. If romance does not develop spontaneously, a person may rightly instigate it by similar expressions, although the possibility of marriage also can be raised without any such prior expression.

In any case, the beginning of conversation about the possibility of marriage and the initiation of a romantic relationship should take place together. Marriage is established by two things: mutual consent and consummation. Mutual consent presupposes common deliberation, and so requires conversation about the possibility of marriage. Consummation presupposes erotic affection, which should be fully integrated with the volitional element of conjugal love, that is, the mutual and unconditional will to be married to each other. So, erotic affection appropriately is expressed and nurtured in harmony with the deliberation and choices leading to marital consent.

Consequently, someone who becomes aware of the beginning of a romantic relationship should make certain, if not already so, that he or she is free to marry, that the other person is a suitable potential marriage partner, and that marriage will be possible in the reasonably near future. If all these things are so, the necessary conversation should be carried on.

b) **The relationship's romantic element should be chaste.** The process leading to marriage necessarily has a romantic element: the couple must think and talk about marriage and imagine themselves married; in doing so, they will experience erotic emotion toward each other. Some contacts inappropriate between persons with no prospect of marrying each other now become appropriate. These contacts, even if light enough to seem modest to any chaste person who observes them, inevitably point toward eventual marital intercourse; if they did not, they would not express erotic affection. If either party should find such contact repugnant and refuse it entirely, that is a clear sign that the couple are unsuited for marriage to each other.

Still, since a couple considering marriage are not yet married, any intentional sexual act is grave matter. They may not intend to bring about any sexual arousal whatsoever, that is, they may not seek and enjoy any experience of bodily contact precisely insofar as it includes such arousal. Rather, they should seek and enjoy that experience only insofar as it expresses and assists their actual present relationship: that of friends interested in marriage and considering marrying each other. Sexual arousal can only be accepted as a side effect, and its potential for being an occasion of sin, whether of action or of thought, must be taken into account and dealt with as the unmarried always must deal with it.

If the couple engage in bodily contact or other sexually arousing activity beyond the minimum legitimate and necessary to express erotic affection in a way true to their present relationship, they can hardly help intending that arousal, and so it will not be a side effect. For instance, prolonged kisses and embraces, the uncovering of the genitals, and genital touches are not clearer or more firm expressions of erotic desire than the less arousing forms of bodily contact that first begin to point toward eventual sexual intercourse. Thus, someone choosing the more arousing activities does not do so for the sake of expressing and eliciting affection, but for the sake of their natural effect: the bodily and psychic process which naturally ends in sexual intercourse. Consequently, while couples considering marriage may and should engage in light bodily contact to express and elicit erotic affection, they should limit such activity to what is necessary for its legitimate purpose and firmly commit themselves to blocking the natural dynamism of the erotic process. As their affection grows and their friendship becomes more intimate, the couple may not proceed to more arousing activities; indeed, they should be increasingly careful.

In some cases, those involved in a legitimate romantic relationship come to realize that marriage is no longer in prospect. Then they should not continue the relationship, since it no longer serves an intelligible purpose, will only block real friendship with each other and/or suitable romantic relationships with others, constitutes an unnecessary occasion of grave sin, and so is sinful.

c) **In persuading someone to marry, some means should be excluded.** If someone who raises the question of marriage finds that the other party neither entirely rejects the idea nor is persuaded that it is worth pursuing, he or she may try to motivate an affirmative response. This can involve not only articulating the reasons for thinking marriage to each other would be good, but trying to prove the point by appropriate actions, for example, doing things that show one's potential as an adequate provider or good homemaker. Moreover, affection may be expressed and nurtured in the ways suited to any good friendship as well as those appropriate in a romantic relationship within the limits already explained.

But not every effective means may be used in trying to persuade another to marry. Since insincerity here bears on a very important choice, any lying or deception about plans or intentions for marriage and family life is a very grave matter. A person must absolutely exclude any conscious pretense of sharing interests he or she does not really share, of intending to change in ways in which change is unlikely, and so on. Nor should the other party be offered unrelated goods, like wealth or status, as inducements to marry, since marital consent should be a free and mutual self-giving, not a giving of oneself or one's services in exchange for some other good.

Finally, lust must not be used by instigating or permitting any illicit sexual activity. Gravely sinful in itself and manipulative in the same way as any appeal to an irrelevant rational motive, this approach also is altogether self-defeating, for it elicits the transient desire for sexual satisfaction rather than the permanent will for communion of life, which is essential to marriage.[324]

d) Cooperation in discernment should precede engagement. Even though a couple believe marriage to each other may be their vocation and find that prospect appealing, they should not become engaged at once. Instead, they should further examine the idea of marrying each other and eliminate any doubt either might have—in other words, they should exercise discernment. This means taking the time and trouble to follow out relevant norms for discernment (see 2.E.3.e and 5.J).

As always, discernment here presupposes that there is no reason to think the possible commitment would be wrong. But even then, prayer and reflection are needed to exclude the possibility that the couple actually have some other vocation. Unless already on friendly terms with each other's families, they should become well acquainted with their possible in-laws, since marriage will bring each of them into the familial community to which the other will continue to belong.

Both also should ask for and listen carefully to the reactions and advice of their parents and other family members. The couple must make the decision, but their families are likely to provide wise and friendly advice, and the families' interest in the possible marriage demands that their contribution to the couple's deliberation be taken seriously.

Still, marriage will unite the couple, and the most relevant facts are those which have to do with them. Unless they have known each other for some time—for example, as schoolmates or neighbors—they will need time to relax, set aside the manner they assume for special occasions and new relationships, and manifest their usual feelings and habits. No matter how well they have known each other before thinking about marriage, they now must share their hopes and dreams, their concerns and expectations about marriage and family life, until confident that they can share the rest of their lives together and wish to do so.

---

324. Leo XIII, *Arcanum, ASS* 12 (1879) 401, *PE*, 81.41, points out that divorce and permanent separation seldom would occur "if men and women entered into the married state with proper dispositions, not influenced by passion, but entertaining right ideas of the duties of marriage and of its noble purpose; neither would they anticipate their marriage by a series of sins drawing down upon them the wrath of God."

If either has any specific doubts, the couple should try to resolve them. If one continues to feel some attraction to an alternative to the marriage, he or she should explore that other possibility. If either has any specific, persisting reason to doubt that the marriage will be a good one, the couple should take that as a sign that they are not called to marry and should terminate their romantic relationship.

Of course, many couples will come to the firm conviction that they should marry. Nothing else any longer has the slightest appeal, and no specific motive for hesitation remains. The only possible motives for not becoming engaged are the general anxiety every thinking person feels about the unknown future and the general reluctance every responsible person feels about taking on lifelong obligations. Setting aside these motives, the couple should become engaged. In doing so, each should promise to marry the other on one condition: that, at the moment they mutually consent to marriage, both enjoy the same confident discernment they now have achieved that this is their vocation.

4. The Engaged Should Prepare Themselves for Married Life

Engagement often is regarded as a time of preparation for marriage considered as an event rather than a common life. Thinking of themselves as all but married, the couple act more or less as if they already were. The marriage preparation required by the Church may be viewed as a mere hurdle to be cleared, while the emphasis is on making plans and arrangements for parties, the wedding ceremony, and the honeymoon. These events certainly must be planned, but the couple should focus more on the many years ahead than on their wedding day and the events connected with it. Moreover, they should live their engagement not merely as a time of transition but as a portion of their Christian lives, whose every moment is inherently valuable. For the engaged, engagement is their present vocation; they should respond in such a way that it will be a worthwhile and beautiful part of their lives even if they never marry.

Conscientious couples often ask: How long should an engagement last? The question admits of no straightforward answer. In two or three months, one couple can do everything necessary to prepare well for marriage, while another needs a year or two. Military service or studies can require that an engaged couple be separated for a time, making it prudent to delay marriage; so can other conditions—one party suffering an acute illness, loss of a job, and so forth. Still, those who do not have a reasonable prospect of marrying at some fairly definite time should not enter an engagement, and couples with no compelling reason for delay, but unable to agree on a date for marriage, should not prolong their engagement.

a) **An engaged couple should see a priest at once.** Before setting the wedding date, spreading the news of their engagement, or making any firm plans, the couple should see a priest, if possible a priest at the parish to which one or both belong. He will ask them various questions to make certain they are free to marry, and all these questions must be answered truthfully; lying would be grave matter. He also will provide information about the marriage preparation program required by the diocese. The couple should cooperate with this program, discuss the experience fully with each other, and so draw from it everything they can to prepare for a good marriage and family life.[325]

The interview with the priest and the marriage preparation program often make it clear to an engaged couple that they have left undone something which should have been done before they became engaged. If so, they should regard their engagement as tentative until it is established that there is no reason why they cannot or should not marry, and that neither has any doubts about whether he or she wishes to marry. If it becomes clear they cannot or should not marry, or if either party no longer wishes to do so, marriage to each other clearly is not their vocation, and, no matter how painful it may be, they should terminate their romantic relationship at once. If either has doubts, planning for the marriage should be postponed until all doubts are resolved.

b) Engaged couples have special reasons to be chaste. Having pledged their love, the engaged couple should avoid solitary sexual acts and sexual acts involving any third person. Not only are all such acts grave matter in themselves, but now they would violate the faithfulness each owes the other in virtue of their engagement promises. With their engagement, the couple should begin the lifelong faithfulness they will pledge to each other on their wedding day.

Moreover, if the couple have sinned together against chastity before their engagement, they should repent and commit themselves to perfect continence until married. Since they are not yet married, the norms explained above (in 3.b) continue to apply. Indeed, the engaged have an additional reason to avoid intentional sexual acts: sinning with someone cannot express love toward that person, and to commit sins against chastity with the person one is about to marry raises the question whether one wishes to marry that person, or only desires to have and make use of him or her. By abstaining from intentional sexual acts, the engaged couple practice an important element of marital sexuality, which often requires abstinence; and by helping each other abstain, they manifest their love—their will to be truly married—in an unmistakable way. In fact, perfect continence is the only way for them to manifest their love adequately, since by it they integrate their erotic affection with their future marriage.

Far from opening the way to intimacies previously excluded, then, engagement calls for greater caution to maintain perfect continence, since erotic desire naturally intensifies as marriage approaches. One important example of the caution necessary is that in planning to be together, an engaged couple should make sure they are never so entirely alone that they can be certain nobody will interrupt them. Of course, they need privacy for conversation, but they should not deceive themselves on that ground and unnecessarily expose themselves to temptation. The privacy

---

325. In some cases, unfortunately, official marriage preparation programs contain false teaching and bad advice. Couples should realize that nothing in such a program can alter the truth the Church teaches or free them from their responsibilities to be faithful to that teaching. Those who suspect or realize that the official program has been corrupted by dissenting opinions should seek better instruction wherever they can find it, even if they are compelled to undergo the required preparation as well.

they need for conversation can always be found in a public place or a room accessible to others.

c) **Engaged couples should settle several important questions.** Because a couple can set certain legitimate limits to their marital cooperation, and because different couples can adopt somewhat different methods for handling recurrent problems, the engaged should fully discuss and settle important matters which will determine the general shape of their married and family life.[326]

For example, unless they know they are sterile, they should make sure they share the same ideas about the number and spacing of children, and that they can agree about the technique of natural family planning they will use and how they will use it. They also should reach a clear understanding about whether both will work outside the home (and, if so, for how long and under what conditions), what part each will take in caring for children, and how they will divide and share other household duties. Again, because relationships with in-laws and the handling of finances often cause serious problems, engaged couples should discuss these matters thoroughly and agree on how they will deal with them. They also should come to an understanding on important practical issues that must be settled so that they can begin life together, for example, initial financial arrangements and setting up a common household.

In discussing these matters vital to building a good marriage, the engaged have a grave obligation not only to avoid deception but to be completely open and forthright. Cooperation here provides practice in what they will have to do throughout married life and is a good test of their compatibility. A couple who cannot settle some of these issues should accept that as a sign that they should not marry.

d) **Wedding arrangements should serve the relevant goods.** Marriage and the events surrounding it should be joyful. The beauty and grandeur of marriage itself, as well as the occasion's importance for the couple and their loved ones, call for a celebration suited to serve as a metaphor for heaven. Still, the essentials specified by the Church's rites for entering marriage and those determined by nature for consummating it are very simple. All other elements of the celebration and honeymoon are nonessential; and while they can serve the good of marriage, communion with the couple's families of origin, and friendship, they also can be given too much importance. As a result, wedding and honeymoon may exemplify consumerism while the relevant goods are harmed rather than served.

Specifically, concern with the trappings should not lead a couple to pursue appearances which interfere with the reality of the good of marriage itself. That can happen in various ways. Planning the wedding can distract them from essential elements of their preparation for marriage: prayer, study, coming to agreement on important issues, and so on. Sometimes lavish wedding and honeymoon preparations make it difficult for a couple with unresolved problems or doubts to break off their engagement. Resources sometimes are wasted which could better be used for establishing a household and having children. Perhaps most important, the reality

---

326. In doing this, couples might read and discuss a sound book, for example: Michael P. Penetar, *Building a Happy Marriage* (Boston: St. Paul Editions, 1986).

of married life often is a disappointing experience after the glamour of the wedding and honeymoon, and, with the excitement over, each partner may seem to the other no longer the same person he or she was during the engagement. Then they were comrades in a wonderful project; now they are companions in life, which must be lived ordinary day by ordinary day.

In making wedding arrangements, an engaged couple should try to strengthen rather than harm communion with their parents and families. That includes not asking for nonessentials which their families will find it hard to provide and respecting their parents' authority within their households and their wishes regarding their roles in the affair. Nor should the arrangements impose unreasonable burdens on other family members or friends, whose contributions to the celebration should be entirely voluntary and gratefully accepted. Finally, while a wedding is rightly considered an occasion for a major celebration, the conspicuous consumption often involved in lavish weddings and honeymoons is a grave abuse of resources, which violates social justice and love of neighbor. Occurring in connection with the celebration of a sacrament, this borders on sacrilege.

e) The engaged couple should prepare spiritually for marriage. An engaged person who has not already received the sacrament of confirmation should do so before marriage, if possible, because confirmation strengthens Christians to carry out their personal vocations. Also, to enjoy the full fruits of the sacrament of marriage, a Catholic couple should take steps to make certain not only that they are in the state of grace but that their love of Christ is deepened, and so they should make good confessions and receive Holy Communion.[327]

Throughout the period of engagement, the couple should pray for each other and pray together for a good and happy marriage. They might use various passages of Scripture—for example, "Grant that . . . [we] may find mercy and that we may grow old together" (Tb 8.7).

The couple may benefit greatly from studying and discussing together the liturgy for marriage, especially the readings provided in the lectionary for a nuptial Mass. They can enrich their spiritual preparation by prayerfully considering the relevance of these liturgical materials to their own future marriage. They also can help plan the liturgy, suggesting to the priest who will officiate those readings and other liturgical options they find most meaningful.

f) The engaged should prepare to commit themselves absolutely. While it is a grave matter for married persons intentionally to wish they had not married their spouses, the engaged have a grave obligation to remain open to the thought that they should not marry. Although they should not have become engaged unless firmly convinced they are called to marry each other, the process of marriage preparation, especially their own discussion of important matters, often raises fresh questions. That is why the mutual promise that forms the engagement is conditional and remains binding only if neither party has doubts when the time to marry comes. Questions that arise during the engagement period should not be regarded as temptations to be unfaithful to their mutual promise to marry, but as possible signs

---

327. See *CIC*, c. 1065.

that, after all, they are not called to do so. If it becomes clear that there is some reason why they should not marry, they should accept the fact that this is not their vocation, and promptly terminate the engagement.

Just before marrying, furthermore, the engaged couple should ask themselves, individually and together, whether they are still firmly convinced they should marry, or whether either has any unresolved doubts. At this point, of course, even more than when they made the engagement, they are likely to be feeling some anxiety about the unknown future and some reluctance to give up their freedom. Those feelings are not doubts, and should be set aside. But if either party has any specific motive for hesitation, the couple should either cancel the wedding or postpone it until the doubt is resolved. It would be wrong to go on with the wedding simply to avoid disappointment or embarrassment. Nor should either try to hold the other to the engagement, since the reluctance of either to marry should be recognized as a clear indication that marriage to each other is not part of their vocations.

This final discernment is necessary to exclude all doubts, because in exchanging marital consent the couple should commit themselves absolutely to be faithful spouses until death parts them. Marriage is for better or for worse; there should be no conditions whatsoever concerning anything that might happen in the future.[328] Thus, marital consent must exclude the thought that, if worse comes to worst, divorce and remarriage could be a solution. Moreover, in exchanging marital consent, not only do the couple give themselves to each other in a covenant which becomes absolutely indissoluble when fulfilled by marital intercourse, but together they accept their common vocation to be a sacred sign of the unbreakable unity of Christ with his Church, and so commit themselves to Christ to carry out this vocation faithfully.

---

328. *CIC,* c. 1102, §1, prescribes: "Marriage based on a condition concerning the future cannot be contracted validly."

CHAPTER TEN

WORK, SUBHUMAN REALITIES, AND PROPERTY

Summary

The Church's social doctrine embodies a rich development of thinking about responsibilities regarding work and subpersonal creation, including those regarding property and ownership.

Work is a basic human good through which people realize themselves as acting persons, and workers also have responsibilities toward their employers and toward others. These include trying to do good work, being loyal to employers, treating fellow workers fairly and mercifully, and not seeking unfairly high payment. For their part, employers have responsibilities toward workers: to treat them as associates, to recognize the priority of work over capital, to provide appropriate working conditions and just remuneration, to respond fairly to merit, to treat both men and women fairly, and to make special provisions for the disabled. Justice requires either that employers pay a family wage or that social measures meet the needs of workers with families to support. Workers' associations also have responsibilities. While they should not unfairly limit access to work, strikes can be justified within narrow limits.

Subpersonal creation neither is mere material for exploitation nor is it sacred in itself. Christians should treat subpersonal things as God's good creatures, and should see their dominion over nature as limited by moral norms. Both good and bad human use of subpersonal creation transform it; and, as the subhuman world was adversely affected by Adam's fall, so now Christians should help renew it. In enjoying and using nature, one should revere its creator. One also should use natural things reasonably and with restraint. As for animals, they do not have rights, but they should be treated kindly and used reasonably.

The ownership of property always remains subordinate to the universal destination of goods: God gives all material goods to humankind as a whole in order that everyone's needs might be met. Both private and public property are morally justifiable, but the universal destination of goods limits the rights of owners. Insofar as it is just, each society's property system specifies many moral responsibilities regarding material goods.

The Christian concept of property implies two basic moral norms applying to owners: they should share the use of their property with others and should practice conservation. A number of specific moral norms also must be observed in acquiring things, in caring for material goods, in seeing to their use and disposal, in returning lost or stolen property, and in regard to saving and insuring. Gambling can be morally acceptable but often is an abuse of property. Sins of thought bearing on property also should be avoided.

One also should help others to fulfill their responsibilities in regard to acquiring and using things, and should not unfairly take their property from them. Many acts which are not usually considered theft really are theft, morally speaking.

A person also has responsibilities in transactions. Giving and receiving gifts should promote interpersonal communion. Lenders should be generous and borrowers honest. Exchanges should be truly just, not merely mutually accepted. Seeking and accepting interest on a loan can be just.

Prologue to the Chapter

While dealing at length with responsibilities regarding property, classical moral theology paid little or no attention to responsibilities regarding work and subpersonal creation in general. The Church's modern social teaching richly develops this subject matter. In doing so, it greatly clarifies the moral conditions and requirements of property, which presupposes God's gift of the material world to humankind and people's work in response to that gift, as John Paul II teaches:

> The original source of all that is good is the very act of God, who created both the earth and man, and who gave the earth to man so that he might have dominion over it by his work and enjoy its fruits (Gn 1.28). God gave the earth to the whole human race for the sustenance of all its members, without excluding or favouring anyone. This is *the foundation of the universal destination of the earth's goods.* The earth, by reason of its fruitfulness and its capacity to satisfy human needs, is God's first gift for the sustenance of human life. But the earth does not yield its fruits without a particular human response to God's gift, that is to say, without work. It is through work that man, using his intelligence and exercising his freedom, succeeds in dominating the earth and making it a fitting home. In this way, he makes part of the earth his own, precisely the part which he has acquired through work; this is *the origin of individual property.* Obviously, he also has the responsibility not to hinder others from having their own part of God's gift; indeed, he must cooperate with others so that together all can dominate the earth.[1]

This succinct statement articulates and organizes all the topics which will be developed and treated in this chapter.

Question A: What Are One's Responsibilities with Respect to Work?

Some good human activities are done for their own sakes: worship, play, friendly conversation, and so on. Most others develop those who engage in them while bringing about some ulterior good result. *Work* here refers to any human activity—

---

1. John Paul II, *Centesimus annus,* 31, *AAS* 83 (1991) 831–32, *OR,* 6 May 1991, 10.

paid or unpaid, in the home or outside it, manual or intellectual—chosen and carried out at least partly for the sake of some good result beyond the activity itself. Thus, work includes the activity of civil servants, soldiers, priests, and educators; of property owners improving and maintaining property, homemakers, and parents caring for children; of Peace Corps volunteers helping people in less developed nations; as well as of people making their living. But work does not include recreational activities insofar as these are done for their own sake, nor does it include physical exercise done solely for self-development rather than partly or wholly for some good result beyond the acting person.

Much work is done as a contribution to a community's cooperative pursuit of some common good. Family members do some or most of their work not only for the family but within the household. In contemporary society, most people do much of their work in some kind of voluntary association, that is, as contractors with customers, as professionals with clients, or as employees of a business, a nonprofit organization, a governmental unit (which forms a voluntary association with its employees), or some other employer. Of course, all the responsibilities pertaining to activities in voluntary associations (treated in 7.D.1–2) apply to work done in such a context.

Here it remains to treat a few specific responsibilities which apply to work in general and a number of others applying to work done for remuneration: the responsibilities of workers to employers and others, of employers to employees, and of associations of workers. To understand these responsibilities adequately, however, the nature and ultimate significance of work must first be considered.

1. Responsibilities in Respect to Work Have a Theological Basis

The book of Genesis provides the theological foundation of all human responsibilities regarding work. Since God creates humans in his own image and likeness (Gn 1.27), they are to share in his own creative work by procreating offspring and ruling subpersonal creation: "God blessed them, and God said to them, 'Be fruitful and multiply, and fill the earth and subdue it; and have dominion over the fish of the sea and over the birds of the air and over every living thing that moves upon the earth' " (Gn 1.28; cf. Ps 8.5–8, Sir 17.1–4). Therefore, human persons should work because they are called to share in God's activity and continue his work of creation (see GS 34).[2]

All specific responsibilities in respect to work are grounded in the several basic human goods for which persons act in response to God's calling to take dominion over material creation and cooperate with him in carrying on his creative and redemptive work.[3] The relevant goods are not only human persons' very survival

---

2. See John Paul II, *Laborem exercens,* 4 and 25, *AAS* 73 (1981) 584–85 and 638–41, *PE,* 280.13 and 112–17. A useful commentary on John Paul II's theology of work: José Luis Illanes, "Trabajo, historia y persona: Elementos para una teología del trabajo en la 'Laborem exercens'," *Scripta theologica* 15 (1983): 205–31; a helpful scriptural study: Göran Agrell, *Work, Toil and Sustenance: An Examination of the View of Work in the New Testament* (Lund: Verbum—Hakan Ohlssons, 1976).

3. On the basic human goods, see *CMP,* 5.D.

and well-being, mutual service, and service to God, but their self-realization as acting persons, which includes both the fulfillment through good work of the skillful and careful worker and the moral goodness of the person who works justly and lovingly.

Despite the intrinsic value of work and its importance in human life as a whole, persons unable to work nevertheless retain their dignity and can live worthy and holy lives.

a) Work is a basic human good. Many people, especially those whose lives are dominated by consumerism or whose work is onerous, regard work as a necessary evil, something which must be done to get the money required either to obtain what they want or to meet genuine needs (*genuine needs* is clarified in E.1.b, below). Those who take this view of work empty a large part of their lives—the whole part devoted to work—of its intrinsic meaning. Even though most people rightly work to earn a living, nobody should regard work as a necessary evil, because work and play together constitute a category of basic human good (see *CMP*, 5.D). Work, therefore, need not be a mere means to other ends; in and of itself, it can and should fulfill the worker.

It is easy to see that play activities, which often are chosen for their own sake, in and of themselves fulfill persons. One might suppose that play is intrinsically fulfilling because immediately gratifying, but that misses the point: authentic play is enjoyable because it employs a person's or a group's capacities and skills in doing something which meets some standard of execution and accomplishment. But because work always is directed at least in part to some result beyond the activity itself, people less easily see that in and of itself work fulfills persons. However, it can do that insofar as it realizes the human capacities, special gifts, and acquired skills of persons in performances meeting standards. Workers intend this good when they seek to be good at what they do; sharing in this good, they take satisfaction in their work.

b) In working, people should realize themselves as acting persons. Since work is a basic human good, people also realize themselves while they carry out God's command to subdue the earth (see GS 35). Therefore, quite apart from the economic and other objective values of its product or service, all work should be recognized by workers and others as having a personal good as its intrinsic and most immediate value, and in that sense its primary value:

> The primary basis of the value of work is man himself, who is its subject. This leads immediately to a very important conclusion of an ethical nature: However true it may be that man is destined for work and called to it, in the first place work is "for man" and not man "for work." Through this conclusion one rightly comes to recognize the pre-eminence of the subjective meaning of work over the objective one. Given this way of understanding things and presupposing that different sorts of work that people do can have greater or lesser objective value, let us try nevertheless to show that each sort is judged above all by the measure of the dignity of the subject of work, that is to say, the person, the individual who carries it out.[4]

---

4. John Paul II, *Laborem exercens*, 6, *AAS* 73 (1981) 591, *PE*, 280.27.

Most people do not hold prestigious jobs, and many take little or no satisfaction in their work. But every worker should appreciate the value of his or her own work and take satisfaction in it, since "the basis for determining the value of human work is not primarily the kind of work being done, but the fact that the one who is doing it is a person."[5]

c) **One should work for survival and mutual service.** Of course, Christians also should work because work generally is necessary for survival and well-being, and one should do what one can to take care of oneself (see 1 Thes 4.10–12, 2 Thes 3.10, Ti 3.14; cf. *S.t.,* 2–2, q. 187, a. 3). Moreover, most workers support or contribute to the support of others, and one also should work in order to have something to share with the needy (see Acts 20.34–35). Furthermore, in a complex and highly organized economy, much work provides goods and services to others in exchange for payment. Justice and love therefore require that people shape their work in view of others' true goods.[6]

d) **Christians should work to carry on Jesus' redemptive work.** A Christian should undertake work as an important part of his or her personal vocation (see 2.E.2.a). Integrated with the commitment of faith and implementing the responsibility of apostolate, work thus becomes cooperation in Jesus' redemptive work, to be offered to God as an important part of one's self-oblation in communion with Jesus. By working, Christians in many ways both sanctify themselves and make amends for sin. Engrossing work forestalls temptations arising from idleness; hard work chastises the flesh; cooperating with others and meeting their requirements develop meekness and obedience; problems with work and unemployment are occasions for humility, prayer, and trust in God's providence.

Although work not only serves other basic human goods but is self-realizing, in the fallen human condition it often is burdensome: it tends to become toil. This is true not only of hard labor, but of much other work, for example, jobs reluctantly accepted, boring jobs, work which must satisfy an overly demanding employer or client, and work done under adverse conditions. Without negating work's inherent value, its toilsome character often makes it repugnant. Nevertheless, considered in the perspective of the redemptive significance of all work carried out in accord with one's Christian vocation, this toilsome aspect takes on the meaning of Jesus' cross.[7]

---

5. John Paul II, *Laborem exercens,* 6, *AAS* 73 (1981) 591, *PE,* 280.26. John XXIII, *Mater et magistra, AAS* 53 (1961) 422, *PE,* 267.84, quotes from a message of Pius XII (*AAS* 36 [1944] 254) an implication, important for structuring the economy, of the principle that people need to realize themselves in their work: "The small and average sized undertakings in agriculture, in the arts and crafts, in commerce and industry, should be safeguarded and fostered. Moreover, they should join together in co-operative associations to gain for themselves the benefits and advantages that usually can be gained only from large organizations. In the large concerns themselves there should be the possibility of moderating the contract of work by one of partnership."

6. John Paul II, *Laborem exercens,* 16, *AAS* 73 (1981) 619, *PE,* 280.73, teaches: "Man must work out of regard for others, especially his own family, but also for the society he belongs to, the country of which he is a child and the whole human family of which he is a member, since he is the heir to the work of generations and at the same time a sharer in building the future of those who will come after him in the succession of history."

7. John Paul II, *Laborem exercens,* 27, *AAS* 73 (1981) 645–46, *PE,* 280.127, teaches: "Sweat and toil, which work necessarily involves in the present condition of the human race, present the

And someone who shares in Jesus' cross by his or her work also will share by it in his resurrection, since work and its good results are materials for the heavenly kingdom, in which all the good fruits of human nature and of the efforts of those who are faithful will be found again, purified and glorified (see GS 38–39).[8]

e) Those who cannot work can live worthwhile lives. There are so many kinds of work that most people, however handicapped or debilitated, can make some good use of their limited gifts or residual powers. Still, some people—very small children, the severely retarded and demented, those suffering from grave illnesses, the elderly at some point—are unable to work. Because work is so important a part of life, people easily overvalue its significance, and so fail to appreciate the inherent dignity of those who cannot work, while overlooking the ways in which they still can carry on personally fulfilling and socially valuable activities.

Work is for persons, not persons for work; and people who simply cannot work, fully retain their personal dignity. Those temporarily or permanently unable to work should not feel worthless, but should accept this element of their vocation with resignation. By prayer and by showing their appreciation for the care they receive from others, they still can grow in holiness and benefit others.

2. Workers Have Responsibilities toward Employers and Others

Whether employed by others or not, Christians should regard work as an important part of their apostolate, and all workers should try to do good work. Employers are due obedience and loyalty, and workers should treat their co-workers fairly and mercifully. Fairness also sets a limit to how much pay a worker may demand, while mercy can call for doing unpaid work.

a) One's work should be a major part of one's apostolate. Since work is an important element of personal vocation, all the responsibilities in respect to personal vocation (treated in 3.E) come to bear on one's working life.[9] Thus, people have apostolic responsibilities toward the wider community and their fellow workers not only when deciding what kind of work to do or whether to accept a particular job, but also in their conduct as workers. A Christian should strive always to work and to act in work situations in a way which manifests God's truth and love revealed in Jesus; when occasion offers, he or she should bear explicit witness to faith.

Above all, it should be kept in mind that ultimately work can provide good material for the heavenly kingdom (see GS 38–39). People who fail to regard their

---

Christian and everyone who is called to follow Christ with the possibility of sharing lovingly in the work that Christ came to do (cf. Jn 17.4). This work of salvation came about through suffering and death on a cross. By enduring the toil of work in union with Christ crucified for us, man in a way collaborates with the Son of God for the redemption of humanity. He shows himself a true disciple of Christ by carrying the cross in his turn every day (cf. Lk 9.23) in the activity that he is called upon to perform."

8. See John XXIII, *Mater et magistra, AAS* 53 (1961) 462, *PE,* 267.259; John Paul II, *Laborem exercens,* 27, *AAS* 73 (1981) 646–47, *PE,* 280.129–30.

9. A valuable treatment of work as a central element of personal vocation, together with a rich theology of work: José Luis Illanes, *On the Theology of Work: Aspects of the Teaching of the Founder of Opus Dei* (New Rochelle, N.Y.: Scepter, 1982).

work as part of their vocation lose an important opportunity to give this dimension of life its richest meaning.

b) **Workers always should try to do good work.** Various motives sometimes lead workers purposely to do poor work or, at least, not to try to do their best. They may dislike their jobs because they are inherently hard or boring, or not fully suited to their abilities and interests, or involve difficult working conditions. Sometimes, too, they dislike their employers, superiors, or clients, who are unfair, too exacting, or personally disagreeable. Despite all such adverse motives, there are several reasons why workers should set and try to meet high standards for themselves.

In the first place, because work pertains to one's vocation, faithfulness in doing it is service to God. Every Christian worker should apply to himself or herself the New Testament's catechesis to slaves: "Whatever your task, put yourselves into it, as done for the Lord and not for your masters, since you know that from the Lord you will receive the inheritance as your reward; you serve the Lord Christ" (Col 3.23–24; cf. Eph 6.7–8).

Besides, since all work not only brings about some valuable result beyond itself but realizes the capacities of those who do it, workers harm themselves by not trying to do good work. They should cultivate their skills and be industrious for the sake of their own self-realization as acting persons. Work also can be offered as penance, especially if it is good work done despite motives for not doing it or not doing it so well. Sharing in this way in Jesus' cross, workers can integrate their working lives with faith and love, and so grow in holiness.

Moreover, since almost all work provides products or services for other people, fairness requires that workers serve others as everyone wishes to be served. Despite contrary motives, they should try to provide a good product or service. For example, a teacher harried by an incompetent principal should try to do a good job for the students' sake; an automobile assembly-line worker bored with the job should try to do it well for the eventual drivers' sake. Christian mercy, furthermore, requires that workers try to do good work for the sake of others even if they suffer serious injustices.

c) **Workers should work steadily during working hours.** Many people, whether employees or not, commit themselves to a certain schedule for work but fail to fulfill it. They begin late and quit early, take extra time off for rest periods and meals, socialize excessively during working hours, purposely work more slowly than is reasonable, shirk the work to which they have committed themselves while occupying themselves with other work, and so on. Such practices are a serious waste of time for any worker, and for employees, they usually are a serious injustice to the employer.

While this matter admits of parvity, employees should not gauge their responsibility by any lax standard set by what their co-workers do, but by the reasons, already stated, why workers should strive to meet high standards for their personal performance as well as by putting themselves in the employer's place and applying the Golden Rule.

d) **Workers should obey and be loyal to employers.** Workers should respect the authority of employers and obey them—of course, within the usual limits of the responsibility to obey (see 7.E.3–4). Obedience does not mean grudgingly doing the minimum required, but trying to understand and carry out the employer's or supervisor's intentions and plans for the work to be done.

Employees also should take care to fulfill their responsibilities with respect to keeping promises and secrets. Insofar as employers are generous, going beyond the requirements of justice in their dealings with employees, employees should show gratitude, especially by loyally supporting their employers in hard times. Workers hired, trained, and treated well by a conscientious employer should not change jobs for the sake of the advantages which another employer is able to provide by evading responsibilities toward other actual and potential workers.

e) Workers should treat their fellow workers fairly and mercifully. The responsibilities which fellow members of a voluntary association have toward one another apply when people work together. Each should do his or her part, not shirk it and impose added burdens on others. People should take credit only for their own work and accept responsibility for their mistakes, rather than claiming credit for others' work and blaming them for their own mistakes. Of course, disputes about such matters are nearly inevitable, and Christians should act mercifully, making concessions when possible and not being fussy about their rights.

Moreover, when opportunities for work are limited, mercy favors generosity in sharing them with others—co-workers or potential employees—who otherwise will suffer from lack of work. For example, workers who do not need more money but whose seniority gives them priority for working overtime rightly forgo the extra work if needier workers will benefit. Again, when their jobs are needed by others, workers who can afford it should consider taking early retirement and using their talents, time, and energy in response to some other, perhaps entirely new, element of their vocation.

f) Workers should support co-workers' just demands. Since individual workers often are vulnerable to injustice, workers' solidarity is important. Workers who benefit from worker solidarity but selfishly refuse to contribute to it do grave injustice to their fellows. Therefore, workers should join—or, if necessary, help to establish—a sound union or other workers' association and actively participate in it. They also have a special obligation to stand by others who are unjustly treated and to support their struggle for justice. Thus, workers usually should respect picket lines and not replace others who are on strike.

Two situations, however, justify making an exception.

(i) While workers should begin by presuming that others' strikes are just—a presumption usually hard to overcome due to the complexity of most situations in which a strike occurs—they should not support a particular strike if careful examination of the issues convinces them that it is more likely unjust than just. Under the same condition, those in need of work may accept an offer to replace the strikers.

(ii) When solidarity with presumably justly striking workers would impose very great burdens on an individual because of his or her extreme and urgent need, the Golden Rule can permit the individual to cross the picket line (for example, to obtain a vital product or service otherwise unavailable) or even to replace a striking worker (for example, to obtain the means necessary for survival, when the strikers have other alternatives).

The responsibilities of worker solidarity extend not only to fellow workers in one's own country, but to those in less affluent nations.

g) Workers should not seek unfairly high payment for their work. Just as workers sometimes are compelled by their needs to accept inadequate wages and other unfair terms, so they sometimes take advantage of others' needs and seek excessive payment for their work. Sometimes the unfairness is obvious—for example, when a disaster occurs and people with needed tools and/or skills overcharge for their desperately needed work—but often it is more subtle.

With work bought and sold like any other commodity and some salaries and fees driven up by market rigging and monopolistic structures, some people (for example, some executives, physicians, and lawyers) whose work is intrinsically rewarding are paid many times more than others (for example, clerks and typists, food-service and sanitation workers, police officers and taxi drivers) whose socially necessary work is boring, onerous, or even dangerous. The difference may in part have legitimate bases, such as costs of education, career uncertainties, and business expenses; but much of it plainly results from the working of employment markets, often within a framework of structural injustices, such as arbitrary limits on access to professional training and discrimination which excludes some able individuals from competing for certain positions. Professionals and others with high earnings might argue that their incomes are not excessive by comparison with the incomes of certain other people whose work yields little or nothing of real human worth. But the compensation lavished on these latter hardly sets a just standard.[10]

Thus, workers should seek only fair remuneration. They deserve compensation proportionate to the economic contribution their work makes, provided that contribution is evaluated by a just standard: the furthering of true human goods through cooperation in a justly structured economy.[11] By this standard, workers rightly seek payment sufficient to support themselves and their families (see 3.f–g, below), and are entitled to compensation for overhead, costs of employment, investment in education or training, use of their own tools and supplies, and so on. Moreover, those whose work is unusually onerous or dangerous deserve correspondingly high compensation.

h) Free service to the needy does not justify overcharging others. In some cases, structural injustices set a scale of fees or salaries above the level which would

10. John XXIII, *Mater et magistra, AAS* 53 (1961) 418–19, *PE,* 267.70, points out: "In economically developed countries, relatively unimportant services, and services of doubtful value, frequently carry a disproportionately high rate of remuneration, while the diligent and profitable work of whole classes of honest, hard-working men gets scant reward."

11. John XXIII, *Mater et magistra, AAS* 53 (1961) 419, *PE,* 267.71, after treating the requirement of a living wage, teaches: "Other factors too enter into the assessment of a just wage: namely, the effective contribution which each individual makes to the economic effort, the financial state of the company for which he works, the requirements of the general good of the particular country—having regard especially to the repercussions on the overall employment of the working force in the country as a whole—and finally the requirements of the common good of the universal family of nations of every kind, both large and small."

obtain in a just economic order. Individuals then may accept the usual and customary payment for their service or product from employers, clients, or customers entirely able and willing to pay; but they should redress the balance toward those adversely affected by the structural injustices, for example, by working without charge for those who cannot pay or transferring excess income to people who are in need.

But when some employers, clients, or customers are able and willing to pay only what is just, people charging unjustly high rates for their services or products may not justify that by pointing to the "charity" (or "pro bono") work they also do. Granting (for the sake of argument) that they are doing many works of mercy, those works do not justify charging others rates higher than otherwise justified, since nobody can be charitable at the expense of others.

i) Christians sometimes should do work for those who cannot pay. People who can earn an adequate income without using all the time and energy which might reasonably be devoted to work have the capacity to do additional work, either of the same kind or some other kind. Justice or mercy can then require that they use their surplus capacity for work by serving without charge those in need who cannot pay. Leo XIII teaches:

> Whoever has received from the divine bounty a large share of temporal blessings, whether they be external and material, or gifts of the mind, has received them for the purpose of using them for the perfecting of his own nature, and, at the same time, that he may employ them, as the steward of God's providence, for the benefit of others. "He that hath a talent," said St. Gregory the Great, "let him see that he hide it not; he that hath abundance, let him quicken himself to mercy and generosity; he that hath art and skill, let him do his best to share the use and the utility hereof with his neighbor."[12]

Of course, the specification of this responsibility is complex. Having conscientiously considered whether one has surplus capacity with which to meet real need, one sometimes may correctly judge that one's Christian responsibility lies elsewhere (see *S.t.*, 2–2, q. 71, a. 1). But if the conclusion is that one has a responsibility to do work for someone who cannot pay, doing so is not merely optional. Even if it is a call of mercy rather than a demand of strict justice, one should respond, since mercy is the justice of the kingdom (see 6.F.4).

3. Employers Have Responsibilities toward Workers

Employers here refers not only to those who put others to work for wages or salary but those who engage professionals for their services or arrange with independent contractors to obtain their work or products. Moreover, those who substantially influence the conditions of employment in the interests of anyone other than employees share in an employer's responsibilities; they can be called "indirect employers."[13]

---

12. Leo XIII, *Rerum novarum, ASS* 23 (1890–91) 652, *PE,* 115.22; the internal reference is to St. Gregory the Great: *Hom. in Evang.* 9.7, *PL,* 76:1109.

13. See John Paul II, *Laborem exercens,* 17, *AAS* 73 (1981) 620–22, *PE,* 280.77–81. In speaking of "indirect employers," the Pope is mainly concerned with governments, international

a) **Employers should recognize the priority of work over capital.** John Paul II teaches that work has priority over capital, that is, the whole collection of means of production, including the natural resources provided by God's gift as well as the processed materials and tools provided by previous human work. For work has personal dignity, while capital, considered as such (rather than as the embodiment of previous work), has only the value of material things. Moreover, work is the principal efficient cause of valuable results, while capital is only an instrumental and material cause. Thus, employers should not regard work as a mere part of their capital resources, another instrument which they purchase or rent, and use for their own purpose.[14]

Failure to recognize the priority of work leads to the practical error of evaluating it solely by the economic value of its results, an error John Paul II calls "economism."[15] Common to both laissez faire capitalism and socialism, economism at least implicitly includes a practical materialism: the belief that material realities may be given priority and superiority over spiritual and personal ones. This error leads employers who own or control the material means of production to treat work as a mere commodity, to be purchased at the lowest possible price, and to deal with employees as mere means to the employers' own ends: increasing profits by maximizing production and minimizing costs, and/or expanding a nation's economy. Plainly, this prevents employees from being associates in a common effort, and it frequently leads employers to the systematic abuse of their authority, to low wages, long hours, and bad working conditions.

b) **Employers' authority is to be used for the common good.** The common good of employers and employees is justice in their relationship and the value of the work done. The value of the work is divided and shared. The employer's share and proper good is the work's result: the thing produced or service rendered. The employee's share is self-realization in the work and just compensation for it. Since the work must be ordered to its result, which is the employer's proper good, he or she has authority to choose the result to be sought. Moreover, if employers are capable of it, they have the right to choose among the morally acceptable and technically feasible means available for bringing about the result they seek, and to direct the employee in using those means. But, like all authority (as distinct from mere power over others), the authority of employers is limited by its purpose and should be exercised for the common good: the value for all concerned of the work to be done and justice in the relationship.

c) **Employers should treat employees as associates.** Since employers and employees enjoy equal personal dignity, employers should care about their employees as persons and not treat them merely as means of obtaining the results of their work. Specifically, since the authority of employers is limited and exists to serve the common good, they should not treat employees like part-time slaves or mere means to the production of goods and services. Insofar as possible, they

---

organizations, and multinational corporations. However, the concept is broad enough to have important implications for the responsibilities of most Christians as consumers and/or investors.

14. See John Paul II, *Laborem exercens*, 12, *AAS* 73 (1981) 605–8, *PE*, 280.52–57.

15. See John Paul II, *Laborem exercens*, 13, *AAS* 73 (1981) 608–12, *PE*, 280.28–31, 58–62.

should help employees understand the significance of their work, the result they are to bring about, and the reasons for using particular means, so that, to the degree practicable, employees can direct their own work. Since self-directing workers are likely to be more energetic and efficient, employers taking this approach also usually benefit.

Moreover, employers should provide employees with appropriate ways of sharing in the management of the common enterprise:

> In economic enterprises it is persons who work together, that is, free and independent human beings created to the image of God. Therefore, with due regard to the functions of each—owner, contractor, manager, or worker—and while maintaining the necessary unity of direction, the active participation of everyone in the running of an enterprise should be promoted [note omitted]. (GS 68).[16]

At a minimum, employers should welcome employees' suggestions, especially about problems connected with their work, and consult them before making decisions affecting the common enterprise. In treating employees as true associates in the common effort, employers act not only in accord with employees' dignity, but with the value which work should have for them insofar as it is self-realizing. Employees whose dignity is fully respected also are more likely to do good work and less likely to be tempted to evade their responsibilities, with obvious benefits not only to the employer but to others whom the work serves.

d) Employers can abuse their authority in various ways. While employers always have the right to determine the result to be brought about by work, and sometimes to choose among technically feasible means and direct their use, they never should demand that workers compromise sound and relevant standards for doing good work. The temptation does arise. For example, the manager of an automobile service department might order the mechanics to finish jobs so quickly that they cannot be done well. Apart from the injustice to customers, the manager's order is a grave abuse of managerial authority inasmuch as it requires the mechanics to compromise their standards, thus depriving them of part of their proper good as employees: their fulfillment in doing good work.

Employers can take a legitimate interest in employees' activities outside working hours insofar as these significantly impact on performance at work or otherwise tend to harm the employer. Sometimes, though, employers exceed their authority by demanding that employees entirely subordinate their other activities to their work or by paternalistic meddling in employees' personal affairs, for example, their family life, recreational activities, and so on. Again, employers can abuse their

---

16. John XXIII, *Mater et magistra, AAS* 53 (1961) 423, *PE,* 267.91, teaches that "employees are justified in wishing to participate in the activity of the industrial concern for which they work. It is not, of course, possible to lay down hard and fast rules regarding the manner of such participation, for this must depend upon prevailing conditions, which vary from firm to firm and are frequently subject to rapid and substantial alteration. But We have no doubt as to the need for giving workers an active part in the business of the company for which they work—be it a private or a public one. Every effort must be made to ensure that the enterprise is indeed a true human community, concerned about the needs, the activities and the standing of each of its members."

authority by using employees' need for work and/or hope of advancement to manipulate them into doing more than was agreed upon, providing personal services or favors, and so on.

e) **Employers should provide appropriate working conditions.** Since work is for people, not people for work, employers should provide suitable employee benefits and should arrange work schedules with a view to employees' need for rest and vacation, while organizing and adapting the working situation itself to their needs. Insofar as possible, this involves excluding occasions of sin from the workplace and protecting employees' health and safety.[17] If work is repetitive and tiring—for example, the work of assemblers on a production line in a factory—assignments should be arranged and the pace of production set in such a way as to safeguard the physical and psychological health of every employee, not just in the short run, but against the cumulative bad effects of such work.

Different workers and groups of workers have additional, special needs, perhaps arising from personal limitations or from responsibilities in other areas of their lives. All workers also need—in a less strict sense—arrangements to make their work interesting and pleasant. Employers should take all these needs into account and, insofar as possible, provide for them in ways fair to everyone concerned.

f) **Employers should provide just remuneration for work.** Because of urgent need, ignorance, or other factors, workers sometimes freely agree to terms of remuneration which are not fair. This often happens during periods of high general unemployment, but it also regularly happens to certain classes of workers. For example, migrant workers and illegal immigrants often are exploited, and women with skill, seniority, and other qualifications equal to those of men often have been paid less for doing the very same work.[18] Treating work merely as a commodity to be purchased at minimum cost, the employer in all such cases takes advantage of the employee's need for work, sometimes paying even less than a living wage.

People who think of justice simply as the fulfilling of contractual duties see no injustice in such arrangements; but they are unjust, because the terms of remuneration should be governed by the Golden Rule, which plainly excludes taking advantage of either party's special needs.[19] The Golden Rule requires that the needs of both parties be considered, as well as the kind and amount of work done, working conditions, and the wider common good of society (see GS 67).

---

17. See Leo XIII, *Rerum novarum, ASS* 23 (1890–91) 649, *PE*, 115.20; John Paul II, *Laborem exercens*, 19, *AAS* 73 (1981) 628–29, *PE*, 280.93.

18. On migrant workers, see GS 66. Pius XII, Address to Catholic Associations of Working Women (15 Aug. 1945), *AAS* 37 (1945) 214, *Papal Teachings: The Woman in the Modern Church*, ed. Benedictine Monks of Solesmes (Boston: St. Paul Editions, 1959), 126, states: "We need not remind you, with your wide experience of social affairs, how the Church has always supported the principle that to the working woman is owed, for the same amount of work and production, a salary equal to that of the working man; that it would be an injustice, and contrary to common good, to profit without consideration from the work of the woman, only because it is available at a lower price. This would harm not only the working woman, but also the man, who would thus be exposed to the danger of unemployment."

19. See John XXIII, *Mater et magistra, AAS* 53 (1961) 405–6, *PE*, 267.18.

In applying the Golden Rule to determine fair terms of remuneration, the parties should use the market as a standard while recognizing its possible inadequacies. On the one hand, there is no justification for an employment contract which falls short of the standard because the employer is taking advantage of characteristics of the employee and his or her situation which are irrelevant to the value of the work. On the other hand, structural injustices which distort the employment market must be considered (see 6.B.4.b); and where these adversely affect both parties, fairness between them requires that they share the burden.

g) **Justice requires a family wage or adequate social measures.** Vatican II affirms the Church's teaching that payment for work must be such as to provide workers with the means for worthily cultivating their own and their dependents' material, social, cultural, and spiritual life (see GS 67).[20] Thus, if a full-time employee is responsible for a family, his or her personal and family needs are an especially important consideration in determining just remuneration.

The underlying reason is that an economic system's most basic purpose is to provide for everyone's needs, and so all who contribute their fair share should receive enough to meet their needs. But since children, especially when small, require constant parental attention and nurture (see 9.D.6.a, 9.F.2.h), it is not good for both parents to be forced to work, and so a worker's needs often are those of an entire family, while the worker's fair contribution is his or her full-time work. Therefore, fairness requires either a family wage—that is, "a single salary given to the head of a family for his work, sufficient for the needs of the family without the other spouse having to take up gainful employment outside the home"[21]—or, failing that, social measures adequate to provide every family with income equivalent to a family wage.

It is easy to see why this requirement of justice is complex. Besides trying to meet the needs of their workers, employers must avoid discriminating among their employees and should compensate every worker in proportion to the value of the work he or she does. Since the value of the work of different workers does not vary with their states of life and degrees of family responsibility, justice requires employers who can afford it to pay at least a minimally adequate family wage to all full-time adult employees, whether or not they have family responsibilities or

20. See also teachings cited in GS 67, n. 6 (n. 217 in Abbott). *CIC*, c. 231, §2, prescribes that lay people who work for the Church "have a right to a decent remuneration suited to their condition; by such remuneration they should be able to provide decently for their own needs and for those of their family with due regard for the prescriptions of civil law; they likewise have a right that their pension, social security and health benefits be duly provided."

21. John Paul II, *Laborem exercens*, 19, *AAS* 73 (1981) 627, *PE*, 280.90. Also, John Paul II, Address to Residents of Barrios (Bogotá), 5, *Inseg*. 9.1 (1986) 100–101, *OR*, 4 Aug. 1986, 6, points out that the Church's "social doctrine teaches that there must be no creation of hateful distinctions in respect to the work that men and women can carry out, and in respect to their just remuneration. It also teaches, however, that a just salary for the family must permit the woman who is a mother to dedicate herself to her inalienable duties of the care and upbringing of her children, without finding herself obliged to seek outside the home a complementary payment which would be at the cost of her maternal functions: due value must be attributed to these in society for the good of the family and of society."

are the sole wage earners in their families. If employers cannot do so, however, the principle of subsidiarity (see 6.E.5.c) indicates that the larger society should adopt some method—for example, tax advantages for workers supporting families, grants to women working full time as mothers and homemakers, family allowances, and/or public subsidies to poor families—of making up the difference between a family wage and an adequate individual wage.[22]

Of course, like other specific affirmative norms of justice, those which require a living wage and family wage are defeasible. If, under disastrous economic conditions, employers cannot pay a living wage and/or the larger society cannot provide the supplement required for a family wage, fairness requires wages and supplements sufficient that the deprivation suffered by workers and their families will be no greater than that suffered by employers, government officials, and so on, and their families.

h) Employers should respond fairly to their employees' merit. Employees differ in how well they do their work and, therefore, how much they contribute to the common good of their employer and themselves. Since excellent work is more valuable, those who do it deserve special recognition and compensation. This can take various forms: an expression of gratitude, some token of appreciation, an increase in autonomy in planning and carrying out the work, an increase in pay, promotion to a more desirable job, and so on.

Often, however, employers fail to recognize merit. If only one person is employed to do a specific kind of work, the employer may ignore the responsibility to reward this individual according to his or her merit, assuming instead that excellent work is the employer's right. Again, those who employ two or more people to do the same kind of work may fail to respond to their merit, either to avoid the difficulties of carefully judging and fairly rewarding each, or in the mistaken belief that fairness requires no more than fulfilling the contractual conditions to which employees agreed—conditions which often make no allowance for differences in merit.

Since work should fulfill the worker and excellent work usually is a sign that an employee acts with that motive, an employee generally experiences an employer's or manager's failure to recognize and fairly respond to merit as a serious disregard of his or her personal worth. While injustices of this sort could be slight, an instance clearly identifiable as such is likely to be a grave matter. Moreover, since failure by an employer or manager to recognize and respond fairly to merit diminishes the employee's sense of self-worth and takes away an important motivation for doing excellent work, it very often happens that this wrong sooner or later results in serious detriment to the employer.

i) Employers should treat both women and men fairly. If the requirement for a family wage is met, the family's economic needs never compel a married woman with children requiring care to work outside her home. Moreover, since making a home and raising children are at least as important and self-realizing as any other work available to either men or women, women who are full-time

---

22. See John Paul II, *Laborem exercens,* 19, *AAS* 73 (1981) 627, *PE,* 280.90.

homemakers and mothers do work which is both valuable in itself and personally fulfilling.[23] However, not all women are homemakers and mothers, and even some who are—for various reasons, good or bad—seek employment outside the home.

Employers should not exclude women from any job for which they are qualified and should not discriminate against them; nor should they yield to unjust pressures to discriminate in their favor. Fairness in employment opportunities and in pay means sameness of treatment for women and men, just as it does for persons in any other categories which divide them by criteria unrelated to the work to be done and its value. Nevertheless, members of either sex sometimes have physical or other limitations seldom experienced by members of the other sex. If such factors limit a particular individual's suitability for a certain job or his or her productivity in it, employers may fairly take the facts into account and either prefer another person for that job or make fair adjustments in compensation.

Moreover, since it is unlikely that a woman's plan of life as a whole will be exactly the same as a man's, fairness toward a woman sometimes requires that she be treated differently from men, so that requirements structured to accommodate men will not compel her, especially if she is a mother, to abandon other responsibilities in society at large and in her family.[24]

j) **Employers should make special, fair provisions for the disabled.** Most disabled people are capable of working, and work has the same importance for them as for anyone else. But their range of opportunities always is limited by their disability and sometimes also by discrimination. It is especially important that employers not exclude the disabled from any job for which they are qualified. Fairness also sometimes requires special attention to their working conditions and an effort to overcome various obstacles to their satisfactory job performance.[25]

k) **Indirect employers share in all the preceding responsibilities.** Those who manage businesses are direct employers, but investors in a business's securities and customers who purchase its products or services sometimes can exercise significant

---

23. John Paul II, *Familiaris consortio*, 23, *AAS* 74 (1982) 108–9, *OR*, 21–28 Dec. 1981, 5, teaches: "While it must be recognized that women have the same right as men to perform various public functions, society must be structured in such a way that wives and mothers are *not in practice compelled* to work outside the home, and that their families can live and prosper in a dignified way even when they themselves devote their full time to their own family. Furthermore, the mentality which honours women more for their work outside the home than for their work within the family must be overcome. This requires that men should truly esteem and love women with total respect for their personal dignity, and that society should create and develop conditions favouring work in the home." On the personal fulfillment available to the full-time mother and homemaker: Connie Fourré Zimney, *In Praise of Homemaking: Affirming the Choice to Be a Mother-at-Home* (Notre Dame, Ind.: Ave Maria Press, 1984).

24. See John Paul II, *Laborem exercens*, 19, *AAS* 73 (1981) 628, *PE*, 280.92. While the Pope does not indicate how this requirement should be fulfilled in concrete social and economic conditions—no doubt because they are too diverse and rapidly changing—one can easily think of arrangements in accord with it. For example, employers who can do so should offer women with school-age children jobs with work schedules corresponding to those of the schools, not as part-time employment with reduced rates of pay and few or no added benefits, but as a new type of employment with pay and benefits proportioned to that of full-time employees.

25. See John Paul II, *Laborem exercens*, 22, *AAS* 73 (1981) 634–35, *PE*, 280.105–6.

influence on policies and practices affecting workers. In this way, almost everyone sometimes acts as an indirect employer and shares in the employer's responsibilities toward workers. Still, the responsibilities of investors and customers, as indirect employers, are limited by their knowledge of a business's activities and their power to affect them. In some cases they fulfill their responsibilities by being alert to the possibility of injustice to employees and urging management to rectify injustices when they arise. But sometimes more direct action is called for; for example, when the workers have a just cause, customers should cooperate in boycotts of products, in just strikes (see 4.b, below) by respecting picket lines, and so on.

4. Workers' Associations Have Special Responsibilities

A workers' association is a structured voluntary association—a trade union, a professional association, or the like—directed to the common good of some group of workers. The Church teaches that workers have a right to form and participate in such associations (see GS 68). A member of a workers' association has all the responsibilities common to members of any structured voluntary association (see 7.D.1–2): to participate actively, to promote the association's true common good, and so on.

Participants in workers' associations should resist the temptation of group egoism. They should try to promote their own interests only insofar as these are just, not seek their own benefit at the expense of others' legitimate interests, for example, by demanding pay increases which are likely to lead to significant inflation and harm the economy as a whole.[26] Through their associations, workers should promote and support policies and actions which meet this wider requirement of justice.

a) **Workers' associations should not unfairly limit access to work.** Some workers' associations have the power to limit how many exercise a certain skill or practice a certain trade or profession. This power can be used legitimately—for example, to evaluate those seeking admission to the same field and screen out the unqualified—or it can be used to protect the interests of association members against the legitimate interests of others potentially capable of doing the same work and of consumers who wish to obtain fairly priced products or services. Members should consider whether an association's exclusionary power is being used fairly; if they judge it is not, they should promote or support its elimination or reform. For example, those in a profession which exercises strict control on entry and charges high fees should consider whether the entry limitations really are necessary to maintain professional standards—as is claimed—or are an abuse intended to

---

26. Pius XII, *Sertum laetitiae, AAS* 31 (1939) 643 and 685, *PE,* 223.40, lays down the relevant norm with respect to associations of producers, workers, and farmers: "Let them act in such a manner that in their care for the interests of their class they violate no one's rights; let them continue to strive for harmony and respect the common weal of civil society." John Paul II, *Laborem exercens,* 20, *AAS* 73 (1981) 631, *PE,* 280.97, explains: "Union demands cannot be turned into a kind of group or class 'egoism,' although they can and should also aim at correcting—with a view to the common good of the whole of society—everything defective in the system of ownership of the means of production or in the way these are managed."

maintain unjustly high fees; members of a trade union which limits the number of apprentices accepted should consider whether that is justified by the amount of work available or is merely a method of preventing others who, with or without union membership, will work in the same trade, from fairly competing for work and benefits.

b) Within narrow limits, a strike can be justified. Just as individual workers can legitimately enforce their demands for fair pay or working conditions by refusing to work, so associations of workers can legitimately conduct organized work stoppages—strikes. On the other hand, even if the cause is just, not every refusal to work is justified (see GS 68). An individual's refusal or an association's strike is justified only if four conditions are met: (i) the cause is just; (ii) methods of communication and/or mediation have failed to settle the issue; (iii) the side effects of refusing to work or striking can be accepted fairly; and (iv) some serious responsibility requires overcoming the injustice rather than patiently suffering it.[27]

i) An employer's unwillingness to remedy unnecessarily dangerous working conditions or maintain just wages during a period of inflation would constitute a just cause; but not the desire of well-paid workers to stay ahead of inflation or of workers with a rather light schedule to obtain still shorter hours, more vacation time, and additional holidays.

ii) Generally, people should settle disagreements by using cooperative methods of communication: reasoning and persuasion, perhaps with the help of a suitable mediator. These should be given a serious chance to work before resorting to the unilateral method of refusing to work or striking.

iii) A refusal to work or a strike has bad side effects: cooperative effort within the business or enterprise comes to a halt, and the goods to which it is directed will not be realized; relationships are likely to be strained and may be permanently damaged; sometimes there is a risk of violence against persons and property; and innocent third parties, such as consumers, often are harmed. In the absence of reasonable hope of remedying an injustice, these side effects cannot be accepted fairly. But even if there is reasonable hope, the fairness of accepting the side effects must be evaluated, as always, taking into account the points of view of all who will be affected. Moreover, certain sorts of side effects never can be fairly accepted, for example, the very grave harm to large numbers of people resulting from disruption of essential community services, the injury inflicted on society at large by paralyzing the whole economy.[28]

---

27. Leo XIII, *Rerum novarum, ASS* 23 (1890–91) 659, *PE,* 115.39, deplored strikes and taught that public authority should forestall them, but he did not condemn them. The magisterium has not articulated fully the conditions for a just strike. However, the four conditions stated here are implied by the teachings of Leo, GS 68, and John Paul II (see the next note), when these teachings are considered in the light of general requirements of justice and Christian mercy.

28. John Paul II, *Laborem exercens,* 20, *AAS* 73 (1981) 632, *PE,* 280.100, affirms that a strike or work stoppage "is recognized by Catholic social teaching as legitimate in the proper conditions and within just limits," but warns: "While admitting that it is a legitimate means, we must at the same time emphasize that a strike remains, in a sense, an extreme means. It must not be abused; it must not be abused especially for 'political' purposes." He then mentions the need to ensure essential services and to protect the common good.

iv) Even if the three previous conditions are met, unless some other grave responsibility requires that the injustice be resisted, Christian mercy calls for patiently suffering it rather than using a method which disrupts community and has bad side effects. For example, workers seeking a just wage in order to meet family responsibilities have a grave reason to resist injustice; but perhaps workers denied the degree of participation in management to which they are entitled should patiently suffer injustice in order to maintain and build up the imperfect community which exists.

c) **Workers' associations should promote genuine work.** Sometimes members of workers' associations are no longer able or willing to do their work yet wish to keep their jobs. Not infrequently, technological changes eliminate the need for certain kinds of work or reduced economic activity also reduces the work to be done. Whatever the cause of the problem, workers' associations should do what they can to help their members resume or continue using their abilities in a genuinely fruitful way.

Workers who are disabled, alcoholic, or have other problems should be helped to overcome their difficulties or to work to their full capacity despite them. Those whose jobs have been lost to technological change should be assisted in qualifying for other work. Those without enough to do because of reduced economic activity should be encouraged to devote their free time to something useful, and perhaps an association can provide opportunities for doing so.

Sometimes, however, workers' associations misuse their power by seeking to maintain the jobs of members no longer able or willing to do them, retain job categories which no longer involve real work (so-called featherbedding), or keep workers idle rather than allowing them to be assigned to work outside their usual job description.

Economically wasteful practices like these are unfair to employers and degrading to workers. Members of workers' associations should oppose them and support constructive alternatives.

Question B: How Should People Relate to Subpersonal Creation?

Human beings should neither despise subpersonal creation nor esteem it more than it deserves; they should respect it and treat it in accord with its true value. The right attitude is compatible with using and consuming subpersonal realities. Human use of material things transforms the world, humanizing and personalizing it in the case of morally good use, alienating it from humans and harming it in the case of abuse. The intrinsic goodness of subpersonal realities and their significance for human fulfillment imply some general norms.

Because human beings are by nature social and most human actions involve some sort of cooperation, human relations with subpersonal things usually are not individualistic but interpersonal and communal. Often, the agent who uses something is not a single person but a couple, a family, a group working together, or some larger society. This is assumed throughout the remainder of this chapter, even though, for simplicity's sake, statements relevant both to individuals and groups often speak only of the former.[29]

1. Christians Should Resist False Views of Subpersonal Reality

Vatican II observes: "According to the almost unanimous opinion of believers and unbelievers alike, all things on earth should be related to humankind as their center and crown" (GS 12). Still, before creating humans, God looks on the other parts of his creation and finds them good (see Gn 1.4, 10, 12, 18, 21, 25); and faith teaches that God creates all his works in wisdom and loves everything he makes (see Ps 104.24, Prv 8.25–31, Wis 11.24–25). Thus, each creature has inherent meaning and value which it can never lose.

Most people of all times and places have acknowledged that human action can achieve good results only with God's help, but the contemporary secularized world denies this truth. While some nonbelieving humanists rightly acknowledge human responsibility for the environment without falling into nature worship, the denial of the reality of God the creator removes the basis for a correct appreciation of subpersonal realities and a sound view of how humans should relate to them. Thus, false opinions on these matters flourish in the secularized world, and Christians who become forgetful of God as creator tend to absorb them.

a) **People should not regard nature as mere material for exploitation.** Many people who do not believe in God imagine that human beings are the sole source of meaning and value in the universe. Supposing subpersonal realities to lack intelligibility and value of their own, which humans can grasp and ought to respect, they think of nature as being at humankind's disposal: individuals, businesses, and governments may do with it whatever they please. Then scientific research is pursued mainly in order to discover ways of controlling nature by technology; technology is applied to serve not only genuine human needs (see E.1.b, below) but insatiable and often perverse human desires; and natural beauty is considered nothing more than a feature of things which happens to occasion subjective satisfaction in human beings.

This irreligious view provides a rationale for treating nature without piety, that is, without limits grounded in deep respect for subhuman things. *Development* then means unrestricted exploitation, which leads to irreversible changes in the natural world and tends to exhaust natural resources. Yet many people pursue this sort of development without recognizing any limit except self-interest, which, at best, embraces the long-term welfare of themselves and those they care for. As they treat the world without reverence toward God the creator, those enjoying the fruits of such development are further enriched and the poor further impoverished.[30]

---

29. Working in the Calvinist tradition, Peter De Vos et al., *Earthkeeping in the Nineties: Stewardship of Creation,* ed. Loren Wilkinson, rev. ed. of *Earthkeeping: Christian Stewardship of Natural Resources* (Grand Rapids, Mich.: William B. Eerdmans, 1991), provide a careful and well-informed treatment of the matters dealt with in this question. While a few positions in the book are inconsistent with Catholic teaching, as a whole it is theologically sound, balanced, and worth careful reading.

30. John Paul II, *Centesimus annus,* 37, *AAS* 83 (1991) 840, *OR,* 6 May 1991, 11, teaches that at the root of the destruction of the natural environment is an anthropological error: "Man, who

Of course, people generally claim to be acting within their rights in pursuing self-interest. But the so-called rights claimed by people who think they are the sole source of meaning and value often have nothing to do with justice; instead, the powerful decide which claims will count as fair and even which human individuals will count as persons. For example, while ignoring the misery of the poor, the wealthy and powerful, a mere handful of the world's population, not only engage in wanton waste and the spoliation of the earth but kill millions of unborn children every year.[31]

b) People should not regard nature as if it were sacred in itself. Even some who deny or are forgetful of God the creator recognize the intelligibility and value immanent in subpersonal realities, whose meaning and beauty arouse their wonder and awe. Feeling a quasi-religious reverence for nature and a kinship with subhuman things, they may even go so far as to ascribe rights to them (see C.1, below). On this view, any human intervention in nature is, as it were, a sacrilege if it markedly alters the world or destroys any unusual feature of the landscape or any species of living thing; while contemplation is the only unquestionably legitimate human use of the subhuman world which, insofar as possible, should be preserved intact and allowed to develop according to its own dynamics and without technological intervention.

This view has led to radical proposals to limit and even reduce world population. It also tends to obstruct some uses of natural resources which are necessary to serve the needs of already-living people. Since the affluent are more likely to have the time and money for study and recreation, their interests in these activities tend to prevail over the interests of less developed nations and poorer people in using natural resources to satisfy their basic needs. Thus, some proposed environmental policies take no account of the burdens they would impose by eliminating jobs or increasing the cost to the poor of food, shelter, home heating, transportation, and so on.[32]

---

discovers his capacity to transform and in a certain sense create the world through his own work, forgets that this is always based on God's prior and original gift of the things that are. Man thinks that he can make arbitrary use of the earth, subjecting it without restraint to his will, as though it did not have its own requisites and a prior God-given purpose, which man can indeed develop but must not betray. Instead of carrying out his role as a co-operator with God in the work of creation, man sets himself up in place of God and thus ends up provoking a rebellion on the part of nature, which is more tyrannized than governed by him [note omitted]."

31. John Paul II, *Centesimus annus*, 38, *AAS* 83 (1991) 841, *OR*, 6 May 1991, 11, points out: "Although people are rightly worried—though much less than they should be—about preserving the natural habitats of the various animal species threatened with extinction, because they realize that each of these species makes its particular contribution to the balance of nature in general, too little effort is made to *safeguard the moral conditions for an authentic 'human ecology'*. Not only has God given the earth to man, who must use it with respect for the original good purpose for which it was given to him, but man too is God's gift to man." The Pope goes on to affirm (in 39, *AAS* 841–42, *OR*, 12): "The first and fundamental structure for 'human ecology' is the family"; in this context he points out: "Human ingenuity seems to be directed more towards limiting, suppressing or destroying the sources of life—including recourse to abortion, which unfortunately is so widespread in the world—than towards defending and opening up the possibilities of life."

32. National Conference of Catholic Bishops, "Renewing the Earth" (14 Nov. 1991), *Origins* 21 (12 Dec. 1991): 426, points out: "Too often the structure of sacrifice involved in environmental

c) **In dealing with nature, people must cooperate with its creator.** Even people who practice a non-Christian religion can see the falsity of these ways of regarding the subhuman world, insofar as they ignore God the creator, on whom human dealings with subhuman creatures always depend. In dealing with nature, people ordinarily seek some benefit, some element of human fulfillment, for themselves and, usually, for others; but the realization of the anticipated benefit always depends not simply on them but on the concurrence of factors beyond their control. For example, a farmer plants in order to harvest, but the harvest also depends on the weather; a researcher works on a problem in order to find a solution, but the solution also depends on "inspiration." In acting, one must always hope for the best; but, falsely supposing the outcome to depend on chance, contemporary unbelievers regard all action as something of a gamble in which the only really accurate expression of encouragement is: "Good luck!"

Except for people schooled in the systematic nonbelief of post-Christian culture, however, not only Christians but people of virtually every time and place have realized more or less clearly, and realize now, that the hope essential to human action involves reliance on God. From the greatness and beauty of created things—not least, from their own being and actions—people become aware of the creator. Moreover, people are aware that, like their being as a whole, the principles of their practical reasoning, directing them to the good, are the creator's gift. They realize, at least in some confused and inarticulate way, that in acting for the goods to which those principles direct them, they are only doing part of what is necessary to achieve the benefits they hope for, and that they must count on God to give success to the work of their hands. This is to say that, in acting, human beings naturally experience themselves, not as autonomous agents, but as cooperators with the creator (see 1.C.1.d, above). This experience is an important source of the various religions, of prayers for the favor of God or the gods, of sacrifices to acknowledge gifts received and share the fruits of efforts with the unseen power whose cooperation contributed to bringing them about.[33]

d) **Technology tends to obscure human cooperation with the creator.** Today, the prevalence of technology, along with other factors, causes even firm believers to have less sense of cooperating with God than people had in times past. But technological instruments and processes not only presuppose created nature but remain part of it, entirely dependent on God's providence and conserving power.

Moreover, technological performances are not complete human actions; and while technology systematically organizes outward behavior to achieve definite goals, the goals achieved do not always constitute benefits, that is, contributions to the fulfillment of persons as such. To achieve benefits, the technology must be used properly, in accord with sound judgments which take into account the whole good of all the persons and communities affected. Yet fascination with technology tends

---

remedies seems to exact a high price from the poor and from workers. Small farmers, industrial workers, lumberjacks, watermen, rubber-tappers, for example, shoulder much of the weight of economic adjustment."

33. See John Finnis, "On Creation and Ethics," *Anthropotes* 5 (1989): 199–201.

to focus attention on it, while distracting attention from other aspects of a complete human act: its moral sources in the heart and its contribution or detriment to the fulfillment of persons. In a culture pervaded by technology, even Christians often overlook the fact that they can do nothing to achieve any good except by cooperating with God, in accord with the law which he has written on the human heart.

2. Christians Should Treat Subpersonal Things as God's Good Creatures

Placed by God in charge of subpersonal creation, human beings are responsible to him for how they treat these creatures. Respecting the meaning and value God has placed in his humbler creatures, humans should treat them as his gifts, which are not to be abused, and should use them to give God glory and fulfill genuine human needs (see E.1.b).[34]

a) God calls human beings to subdue the earth by their work. "Man is the image of God partly through the mandate received from his creator to subdue, to dominate, the earth. In carrying out this mandate, man, every human being, reflects the very action of the creator of the universe."[35] From the beginning, then, as was explained above (in A.1), people have been called to fulfill themselves by work, which always more or less directly involves interacting with and transforming subhuman things.[36]

In their work, humans share in God's superiority over subhuman creation. They are responsible for it, but not to it, as if it shared in the dignity and fundamental rights which they themselves enjoy as persons made in God's image. Rather, they are responsible to God and one another—not least, future generations—for their treatment of the things God has given to all humankind.

b) Human dominion over nature is limited by moral norms. What is the dominion which Genesis says God has given to humans? The sacred writers do not view it as unrestricted power, but make it clear that, in God's eyes, subhuman things and human beings form, as it were, a community of creatures, for which humans bear responsibility.[37] Thus, human sin provokes a disaster which affects the entire earth, but God preserves from the cleansing flood not only humans (Noah and his family) but other creatures, so that they can make a new beginning. The covenant God grants the survivors is inclusive: "I have set my bow in the clouds, and it shall be a sign of the covenant between me and the earth" (Gn 9.13)—"between me and all flesh that is on the earth" (Gn 9.17).

Consequently, the divine mandate to have dominion by no means authorizes people to do whatever they please with God's good and beautiful subhuman

---

34. A unique attempt to provide a theological account of the meaning of nature: Robert Faricy, S.J., *Wind and Sea Obey Him: Approaches to a Theology of Nature* (London: SCM Press, 1982). While some methodological presuppositions and conclusions of Faricy's work are arguable, it includes many sound insights and is well worth critical study.

35. John Paul II, *Laborem exercens*, 4, AAS 73 (1981) 585, *PE*, 280.13.

36. See John Paul II, *Laborem exercens*, AAS 577–78, *PE*, 1.

37. See Thomas F. Dailey, O.S.F.S., "Creation and Ecology: The 'Dominion' of Biblical Anthropology," *Irish Theological Quarterly* 58 (1992): 1–13.

creatures. John Paul II points out three ecological considerations: the need to take into account each thing's nature and place in the cosmos, the limits and non-renewability of natural resources, and the impact of some kinds of development on the quality of human life. Then he teaches:

> The dominion granted to man by the Creator is not an absolute power, nor can one speak of a freedom to "use and misuse", or to dispose of things as one pleases. The limitation imposed from the beginning by the Creator himself and expressed symbolically by the prohibition not to "eat of the fruit of the tree" (cf. Gn 2.16–17) shows clearly enough that, when it comes to the natural world, we are subject not only to biological laws but also to moral ones, which cannot be violated with impunity.[38]

c) **God makes humans responsible for subhuman creation.** It follows that *dominion* expresses not only the superiority of human beings over subpersonal creation but their divinely given responsibility with regard to all material creatures. God has, as it were, appointed people his agents: "The Lord God took the man and put him in the garden of Eden to till it and keep it" (Gn 2.15); they are to govern subhuman creation on God's behalf, administering "the world in holiness and righteousness" (Wis 9.3).[39] Thus, John Paul II teaches:

> Certainly humanity has received from God himself the task of "dominating" the created world and "cultivating the garden" of the world. But this is a task that humanity must carry out in respect for the divine image received, and, therefore, with intelligence and with love, assuming responsibility for the gifts that God has bestowed and continues to bestow. Humanity has in its possession a gift that must be passed on to future generations, if possible, passed on in better condition.[40]

Elsewhere he sums up the point: "It was the Creator's will that man should communicate with nature as an intelligent and noble 'master' and 'guardian,' and not as a heedless 'exploiter' and 'destroyer.' "[41]

Secularized culture fails to see the human relationship to nature in the wider context of the relationship of both human and subhuman creatures to God, while technology tends to obscure the constant need for human cooperation with God. Today, therefore, Christians must make a special effort to bring the light of faith to bear in understanding their responsibilities for subhuman creation.

d) **Contemplation of natural beauty fulfills both human beings and nature.** The beauty of nature should lead people to know and praise God: "Look at the rainbow, and praise him who made it; it is exceedingly beautiful in its brightness. It encircles the sky with its glorious arc; the hands of the Most High have stretched it out" (Sir 43.11–12). The universe manifests God's wisdom and love: "The heavens are telling the glory of God; and the firmament proclaims his handiwork" (Ps 19.1). This manifestation has an important result: "Ever since the creation of

---

38. John Paul II, *Sollicitudo rei socialis*, 34, *AAS* 80 (1988) 560, *OR*, 29 Feb. 1988, 9.

39. See David Winston, *The Wisdom of Solomon: A New Translation with Introduction and Commentary*, Anchor Bible, 43 (Garden City, N.Y.: Doubleday, 1979), 200–202.

40. John Paul II, *Christifideles laici*, 43, *AAS* 81 (1989) 477, *OR*, 6 Feb. 1989, 14.

41. John Paul II, *Redemptor hominis*, 15, *AAS* 71 (1979) 287, *PE*, 278.45.

the world his eternal power and divine nature, invisible though they are, have been understood and seen through the things he has made" (Rom 1.20). "For from the greatness and beauty of created things comes a corresponding perception of their Creator" (Wis 13.5).

Hence, one way for Christians to use subpersonal things is as a mirror in which to contemplate God's beauty and goodness (see *S.c.g.,* 2.2).[42] For its part, nature too is called on to praise its creator (see, for example, Ps 148.3–10). Lacking intelligence and freedom, however, subpersonal creatures cannot know and worship their creator by themselves; they need the help of human beings, as Vatican II teaches: "The human person is a unity of body and soul. By one's bodily condition, one gathers in oneself the elements of the material world, so that, through the human person, these elements reach their most exalted condition and raise their voice in free praise of the creator (cf. Dn 3.57–90)" (GS 14). Therefore, in contemplating the beauty of nature, people fulfill not only themselves but natural things, without in any way harming them.

e) God provides subhuman things for good human uses. Included in the dominion God gives humans over subpersonal creatures is the authority to use them to meet human needs. In completing the account in Genesis of God's original gifts to man and woman, the sacred writers make this point by referring to God's provision to meet the paradigmatic need for food: "God said, 'See, I have given you every plant yielding seed that is upon the face of all the earth, and every tree with seed in its fruit; you shall have them for food" (Gn 1.29; cf. Ps 104.14–15). Again, in the renewal of the covenant:

> God blessed Noah and his sons, and said to them, "Be fruitful and multiply, and fill the earth. The fear and dread of you shall rest on every animal of the earth, and on every bird of the air, on everything that creeps on the ground, and on all the fish of the sea; into your hand they are delivered. Every moving thing that lives shall be food for you; and just as I gave you the green plants, I give you everything." (Gn 9.1–3; cf. *S.t.,* 2–2, q. 64, a. 1)

A subsequent sacred writer having a more analytic bent of mind offers a fuller list of human needs (see Sir 29.21, 39.26), then, speaking in comprehensive terms, declares God to have provided subhuman creatures to meet these needs: "All the works of the Lord are good, and he will supply every need in its time" (Sir 39.33), and "How desirable are all his works, and how sparkling they are to see! All these things live and remain forever; each creature is preserved to meet a particular need" (Sir 42.22–23).

Of course, the human use of nature was to be limited to serving human needs within the framework of God's plan. Thus, the law required the Israelites to allow the land itself to share in the rest of the sabbatical year (see Lv 25.1–5; cf. Ex 23.10–13). Failure to keep the law would result in many dire consequences,

---

42. John Paul II, *Centesimus annus,* 37, *AAS* 83 (1991) 840, *OR,* 6 May 1991, 11, teaches that one should take toward nature a "disinterested, unselfish and aesthetic attitude that is born of wonder in the presence of being and of the beauty which enables one to see in visible things the message of the invisible God who created them. In this regard, humanity today must be conscious of its duties and obligations towards future generations."

including the expulsion of the Israelites from the land, so that it would enjoy the rest they had not allowed it (see Lv 26.33–35).

3. Human Use of Subpersonal Creation Transforms It

As soon as human persons exist, they occupy a particular territory, and this portion of the material world becomes their home. Moreover, as soon as people use things to serve their purposes, they begin to transform the world of nature into a world of culture. Entering into relationship with a portion of the world by occupying it or with a particular thing by using it, human beings as it were draw that portion or thing to themselves or put themselves into it, so that it becomes in some fashion linked with their own bodies.

In this way, subpersonal creation becomes humanized and personalized. Pieces of territory and things acquire new meaning and value; they are no longer merely parts of the natural world, but pertain to the human subject, whether individual or communal. Thus, in being humanized and personalized, they become *mine* and *ours*. Although it can be a principle of property, this basic appropriation of subpersonal things is far wider than any sort of ownership. For it includes things such as "my rock" (a particular rock where I regularly stop and rest while walking in the woods) and "our sunset" (an especially beautiful sunset which my wife and I enjoyed together).

The concept of property will be clarified (in D.1). The point here is that human use of subpersonal creation transforms it for good or ill, depending on whether that use is morally good or bad. The different implications of morally good and bad acts for the subhuman creatures involved in them can be articulated both in the language of philosophical analysis (in a and b) and in the language of faith (in c).

a) Good use of a subpersonal creature transforms it in one way. In doing what is morally good, a human agent acts as an integrated whole: reason, freedom, and the outward performance are at one (see *CMP,* 7.F, 13.D, 25.B). Consequently, in linking a subpersonal creature with a human agent's body, a good act links that thing with the person as a whole; and since the whole, integrated person is present in the act, the subpersonal entity is humanized and personalized in an unqualified sense.

Moreover, the meaning and value given the entity by a good human act in no way conflict with its inherent meaning and value. Rather, because the good human act is in accord with the God-given direction of practical reason, such an act fulfills the subpersonal creature's inherent meaning and value. If the action is morally good, culture perfects nature as the garden replaces the wilderness, for then God, working through good human actions, completes the creative work which he began without human cooperation.

Finally, good human acts involving subpersonal things perfectly link those things to the human agents. For the morally upright agent accepts and treats subpersonal creatures as gifts of God, and so fully realizes the dominion which God gives humans over them.

b) Bad use of a subpersonal creature transforms it in another way. In doing what is morally bad, a human agent acts more or less against reason rather than as an integrated whole. Hence, in linking a subpersonal creature with a human agent's body, a bad act fails to link that thing with the person as a whole; and since the whole person is not present in the immoral act, the subpersonal entity is not humanized and personalized in an unqualified sense. The new meaning and value it receives are of a limited and distorted sort, corresponding to the self-mutilation an immoral choice brings about in the wrongdoer, whose freedom and reason are subordinated to his or her unintegrated feelings and fantasies.

Moreover, while the new meaning and value given the entity by the human act are logically compatible with its inherent meaning and value, misusing anything harms it, for, rather than completely fulfilling the thing's divinely given potentialities, immoral use always partly displaces and blocks their fulfillment. Thus, because the bad human act conflicts with the God-given direction of practical reason, it violates the subpersonal creature's inherent meaning and value. If the action is morally bad, culture damages nature as devastation replaces the wilderness, for in this case bad human acts fail to cooperate with and complete God's creative work.

Finally, while bad human acts involving subpersonal things link the latter in some way to human agents, they also alienate those who do them from the entities which are misused. Linked to the wrongdoer's body, the misused entity either causes the latter to share in its alienation from reason or shares in the body's own alienation from the rational self. In either case, a subpersonal thing is not perfectly appropriated by being misused in a morally bad act. Even though a person feels that the thing is completely dominated by his or her wayward will, in reality the individual is failing to accept and exercise the dominion God has given humankind over it. Insofar as the person does not accept the thing as God's gift, he or she refuses it, thus losing the opportunity to make it fully and rightly his or her own.

c) As the earth shared in Adam's fall, it shares in redemption. Revelation also teaches that human sin harms the earth itself: "Cursed is the ground because of you; in toil you shall eat of it all the days of your life" (Gn 3.17; cf. 4.12). The prophets develop this idea:

> The earth dries up and withers, the world languishes and withers;
> the heavens languish together with the earth.
> The earth lies polluted under its inhabitants;
> for they have transgressed laws, violated the statutes,
> broken the everlasting covenant.
> (Is 24.4–5; cf. Jer 5.24–25, 12.4; Hos 4.1–3)

Correspondingly, the prophecies of postexilic restoration include the promise of the earth's renewal (see Is 30.23–26, Jer 33.10–13, Ezk 36.8–12).

St. Paul teaches that the whole of creation has been subjected to futility, so that it "has been groaning in labor pains until now" (Rom 8.22), but now it waits expectantly for redemption (see Rom 8.18–21). John Paul II, after calling attention to the relevant teaching of Scripture, comments:

> These biblical considerations help us to understand better *the relationship between human activity and the whole of creation.* When man turns his back on the Creator's plan, he provokes a disorder which has inevitable repercussions on

the rest of the created order. If man is not at peace with God, then earth itself cannot be at peace.[43]

Precisely how subpersonal creation will exist in the kingdom remains mysterious; but that it is to share in redemption is certain. For in Jesus, all things are to be saved and reintegrated (see Eph 1.9–10, Col 1.19–20) to form new heavens and a new earth (see 2 Pt 3.13; cf. Rv 21.1–5; GS 39).

d) **Christians should help to renew the subhuman world.** The liberation of subpersonal creation does not happen automatically. Rather, Christians are called to deal with nature according to God's plan, and in this way to reintegrate it with themselves; and material goods employed by persons in living their lives of faith according to their particular vocations share in the holiness of those lives, and so are restored to God through Christ.

The Church often invokes God's blessing not only on things and places related to the liturgy and other specifically religious acts but also on those involved in the work of the faithful and their other daily activities. These blessings, of course, praise and thank God for his gifts, and seek his help in achieving the good purposes to which the faithful mean to put them. But a blessing also signifies and contributes to the process by which Christians help to renew the subhuman world, so that by God's grace it will share in his salvific plan for the whole of creation. Consequently, it is appropriate to use blessings, which the Church provides, for dwellings and other places, means of transportation, tools and other equipment, animals, fields, flocks, seeds, and so on. The Church has made it easier to use many of these blessings by authorizing any layperson to administer them.[44]

4. Norms for Using Subpersonal Things and How They Are Violated

The two norms to be stated here flow directly from the preceding considerations. Additional norms, specifically concerned with property, will be articulated in questions D through G. Still, these two general norms apply to actions bearing on subhuman realities in general, whether or not they are anyone's property, and a violation of one or both of them underlies any injustice regarding property.

a) **In enjoying and using nature, one should revere its creator.** Since the meaning and value immanent in natural things and their source in God should be acknowledged, God should be praised by someone enjoying nature's goodness and beauty. A person should pray for the material goods he or she needs, accept what he or she receives as God's gift, use this gift according to the directions God provides through reason illumined by faith, and thank God while using and enjoying things.

Since eating is a paradigmatic use of natural goods, Christians traditionally have prayed before and after meals. For this prayer, the Church now provides several forms of blessing, with appropriate variations for the liturgical seasons.[45] Chris-

---

43. John Paul II, Message for World Day of Peace (1 Jan. 1990), 5, *AAS* 82 (1990) 149, *OR*, 18–26 Dec. 1989, 1.

44. See *The Roman Ritual: Book of Blessings,* trans. International Committee on English in the Liturgy (Collegeville, Minn.: Liturgical Press, 1989), General Introduction and Part II.

45. See *The Roman Ritual: Book of Blessings,* ch. 30.

tians today also should make a habit of looking to the reality which technology tends to obscure; and so they will strive to be conscious of constantly using natural goods even in the most highly processed products—for instance, medications, synthetic fabrics, and electronic devices—not neglecting to praise and thank God for his gifts when using such things.

b) **One should use natural things reasonably and with restraint.** To abuse any gift shows contempt for the giver, and material creation is God's gift to humankind. Reverence for the creator therefore requires respecting his subpersonal creation and using his gifts as he intended. Since beautiful and good natural things serve as objects of contemplation leading to God, there always is a reason to leave nature undisturbed. At the same time, God subordinated subpersonal nature to persons, and people constantly have reasons to use things to meet human needs. Therefore, people should never disturb natural things except to serve some human good, their own or others', in a reasonable way; but they always may deal with nature as that purpose requires.

c) **People have diverse motives for violating the preceding norms.** Many violations of the preceding norms result, not from a moral defect bearing specifically on the use of material things, but from some more general vice. Unbelief and irreverence toward God lead to the wrong attitudes described above (in 1); as also has been explained, it is an abuse to use a material thing in any sinful act. But diverse nonrational motives bearing specifically on the use of material things also account for various characteristic ways of misusing them.

Since material things have their own natures and dynamisms, using them and limiting their use require attention and effort. Often, though, laziness leads to waste: people prepare too much food and throw away leftovers, allow doors and windows in heated or cooled buildings to remain open, fail to maintain automobiles and appliances, and so on.

Subhuman things lack the rights of persons. People can and often do treat them with contempt, without risking punishment or retaliation; for example, a man vents his rage by kicking his dog.

Some material things correspond to human bodily appetites; thus, their use can be unreasonable because it is at odds with some true human good and motivated only by an emotional desire for sensory gratification: for pleasure, people eat and drink in unhealthy ways (see *S.t.*, 2–2, q. 148; q. 150).

Material goods can serve as means for bringing about or protecting various goods intrinsic to persons; thus, people can be led by experience to imagine that these extrinsic entities are in themselves fulfilling for persons, even though at the intellectual level they know better. As a result, emotional desire comes to focus on potentially instrumental goods, which are sought or retained without being ordered rationally to any basic human good. For instance, people seek and amass wealth as if it were an end in itself; the irrational "logic" is: some is good, more is better. In the absence of rational ordering, the desire for wealth becomes insatiable (see *S.t.*, 1–2, q. 30, a. 4; 2–2, q. 118).

In a somewhat similar way, a use which initially was ordered to realizing or protecting some true human good becomes unreasonable when emotional desire or fear motivates excess, even without the illusion that the instrumental good is an end in itself. Some collectors amass good and beautiful things—which certainly can be used and enjoyed—until they have more than will ever provide any real benefit to themselves or anyone else. Again, people anxious about possible deprivation and eventual death are tempted to accumulate goods—diverse forms of wealth and property— which they probably never will be able to use, piling up more and more in a vain quest for absolute security. "Surely for nothing they are in turmoil; they heap up, and do not know who will gather" (Ps 39.6; cf. Sir 14.3–10, Lk 12.15–21).

Last but not least, because using subhuman things links them with the bodily person and appropriates them, people frequently try to establish and experience, or confirm and manifest, their own importance or power by possessing, dominating, or destroying material things. But the motive is unreasonable because the good pursued is only apparent. For example, people want fine clothing in order to think of themselves as persons of quality; a woman drives a large automobile, impractical for her, to show her status; a man panels his office with a rare wood as a sign of his power. The point is not that people should never dress well, drive large automobiles, or have attractive offices, but that they should do so only for good reasons.

d) Only right uses of natural things fulfill human beings. Violations of the basic norms for using subpersonal things often are rationalized by the thought that merely possessing things and/or merely using them, whether reasonably or not, somehow makes humans better as persons. But that plainly is not so. People only become better as persons by willing and acting in accord with integral human fulfillment, so that they participate individually and in communion with others in basic human goods (see *CMP*, 5.D–H, 7.F). Possessing money and property does nothing whatever of itself to make people better, while the wrong use of natural things impedes their true fulfillment. Thus, Vatican II teaches: "People are more valuable for what they are rather than for what they have [note omitted]" (GS 35), and John Paul II explains: "To 'have' objects and goods does not in itself perfect the human subject, unless it contributes to the maturing and enrichment of that subject's 'being', that is to say, unless it contributes to the realization of the human vocation as such."[46]

Question C: How Should People Treat Nonrational Animals?

The general norms for dealing with other subpersonal realities apply in dealing with nonrational animals, but animals' special characteristics and human persons' special feelings toward them also require some specific norms.

---

46. John Paul II, *Sollicitudo rei socialis,* 28, *AAS* 80 (1988) 549, *OR,* 29 Feb. 1988, 7; cf. John Paul II, *Centesimus annus,* 36, *AAS* 83 (1991) 838–40, *OR,* 6 May 1991, 11. An extended contrast between "being" (the "personal form") and "having" (the "commodity form"), together with a telling critique of the consumerist culture which is prevalent in the United States: John F. Kavanaugh, *Following Christ in a Consumer Society: The Spirituality of Cultural Resistance,* rev. ed. (Maryknoll, N.Y.: Orbis, 1991).

1. Animals Themselves Do Not Have Rights

Some philosophers argue that animals have rights just as people do. As it is most commonly explained, the position is that humans have rights because they have interests which others' actions can fulfill (leading to satisfaction) or frustrate (leading to pain); but animals in various degrees—higher animals more, lower ones less—also have interests whose fulfillment or frustration causes them pleasure or pain; so, animals too have rights.[47]

Ascribing rights to animals leads directly to showing them deference even to the detriment of humans, for instance, some proponents of animal rights have interfered with the use of animals in medical and pharmacological research. Perhaps even more important, the theory of rights presupposed by most animal-rights proponents implies that, while any mature and normal mammal has some rights, unborn and newborn human individuals have none whatsoever.[48] Since the theory of animal rights has such implications, it is useful to explain why animals have no rights.

a) **Proponents of animal rights reject the Christian view of persons.** According to the Christian view, humans differ from subpersonal creation because God creates them in his own image, which includes the capacities of reason and free choice, and calls them to heavenly communion (see GS 12–22). Each human individual's fundamental rights necessarily flow from this natural and supernatural dignity, and his or her other rights presuppose it (see 6.B.6 and 7.A.2). In other words, the God-given meaning and value of human persons is the source of their fundamental rights and the foundation of any rights they acquire.

Thus, fundamental human rights in no way depend on meaning and value given by humans themselves; while even acquired rights depend on human reasoning and commitments, not on the sort of interests, reducible to sensory awareness and emotional desire, which human beings have in common with animals. According to this Christian view, animals are incapable of having rights, although animals of

47. See Peter Singer, *Animal Liberation*, 2nd ed. (New York: New York Review of Books, 1990), 6–9, 17–20; basically similar but more nuanced: S. F. Sapontzis, *Morals, Reason, and Animals* (Philadelphia: Temple University Press, 1987). Tom Regan, *The Case for Animal Rights* (Berkeley, Cal.: University of California Press, 1983), offers a different articulation of the view that animals have rights; he argues (232–65) that at least any normal mammal one year of age or older is like a person (including one who is not a moral agent, such as a one-year-old child) in being a subject of a life, so that all such individuals' inherent value entitles them to be included in the "others" to whom the Golden Rule applies. However, while Regan convincingly argues that moral agents are not the only bearers of rights, he fails to show that rights flow from the inherent value of every being that is a subject of a life in the sense that this is common to all normal mammals one year of age or older. Moreover, while Regan's position differs significantly in its philosophical details from the more common, utilitarian view, his argument is developed by dialectic with the more common view and so depends on it; and all theories supporting animal rights have more in common with one another than with any moral theology rooted in Christian faith or any ethical theory compatible with it. Hence, in the present context, Singer's articulation of the more common view is treated as typical.

48. See Singer, *Animal Liberation*, 81–82, 236–43. Regan, *The Case for Animal Rights*, 394–98, also is certain that animals' rights require vegetarianism and the cessation of experiments on mature mammals, but (319–20) he considers the rights of soon-to-be-born and even newborn humans a special problem to which he offers only a tentative solution.

each kind, like all other subpersonal creatures, do have their specific, God-given inherent value which humans should respect.

Proponents of animal rights at least implicitly reject this entire Christian view.[49] They deny that humans are endowed by God with fundamental rights, deny or minimize the significance of the difference between human reason and animal cognition, and hold that any difference between human interests and those of other animals provides, not a reasonable basis for denying rights to the latter, but only a basis for specifying which rights various individuals can have, inasmuch as animals of lower species develop only limited interests.[50]

b) Proponents of animal rights cannot account for moral obligation. Animal-rights proponents presuppose a theory of human rights and moral obligation which is not self-evident and is vulnerable to philosophical criticism. Even without appealing to their faith, Christians can argue cogently against the notion that animals have rights. If animals had rights, humans would have corresponding duties. However, told that important interests of their own should yield to rights ascribed to animals, people of common sense spontaneously respond: "If rats and skunks have rights, so much the worse for rights!" Thus, proponents of animal rights are challenged to give an account of moral obligation adequate to show why—given *their* understanding of rights—any moral agent ought to respect anyone else's rights.

Proponents of animal rights overlook this challenge, for their view of rights, which grounds rights in interests, renders moral obligation as such mysterious. On their view, each agent naturally acts egoistically in accord with his or her own interests, while naturally serving others' interests only insofar as they coincide with or are embraced in his or her own, as, for example, the interests of friends and family often are.

In this view, however, moral obligation is the demand that agents act altruistically when such a natural motivation is lacking and even when doing so seems to them contrary to their own interests.[51] But in that case, why should anyone be moral? Psychological and sociological attempts to account for moral feelings and practices do not begin to answer this question. At best they can explain only why some people in fact feel or think they ought to be altruistic. But the question is: Why *should* egoists repent and become altruists?

No thinker sharing the general world view of the proponents of animal rights ever has offered a plausible answer. For them, moral obligation remains inexplica-

---

49. The view that animals have rights is not new. The Manichaeans held it, and St. Augustine criticizes it: *De civitate Dei* 1.20; cf. St. Thomas, *S.c.g.,* 3.112.

50. See Singer, *Animal Liberation,* 187–98. Regan never mentions any Christian moral theology or natural law theory compatible with Christian faith.

51. The view being criticized is common in the empiricist tradition stemming from Hume. Regan, *The Case for Animal Rights,* proposes a metaethical theory which is not vulnerable to the criticism proposed here. For him, morality is a given; he holds (126–40 and 185–93) that purported moral principles are criticized by logical tests and by comparing them with considered moral intuitions. This approach, however, is equally incapable of answering the radical question: If animals have rights, why should anyone respect others' rights? Moreover, the thesis that animals have rights is inconsistent with most people's considered moral intuitions.

ble. Often, of course, moral obligation can be taken for granted, since all parties to a particular discussion may agree in presupposing it. But those who advocate animal rights cannot take moral obligation for granted, since they are trying to extend the previously accepted limits of altruism to animals, and that calls moral obligation itself into question.

c) **A sound account of moral obligation excludes animal rights.** One can account plausibly for moral obligation by reducing it to the first principles of practical reason, which shape human actions toward the basic intelligible human goods; these goods are aspects of the full being of bodily persons, and so they provide ultimate reasons for choosing actions that truly fulfill not only the agent, but other persons as well, in interpersonal communion (see *CMP,* 5, 7; above, 6.B.6).[52] Given an account of moral obligation along these lines, the moral ought is not reducible to anything antecedent, whether individuals' subjective interests or general characteristics of human nature. Rather, it is an irreducible part of human nature itself, an element of the God-given meaning and value constituting the essential dignity of human persons. Hence, the question, "Why should one be moral?" makes no more sense than the question: "Why are human beings human?"

This account of moral obligation explains why unborn and newborn human babies have rights. Other people have responsibilities toward these persons, not on the basis of anything actual about them beyond their being human individuals, but precisely on the basis of their human potentialities and needs, whose fulfillment depends as much on the love and care of their parents and others as on their own eventual interests. But this account excludes animal rights, since the first principles of practical reason, which underlie all rational motivation and every moral responsibility, direct action only toward intelligible human goods, and lower animals simply cannot be fulfilled by sharing in those goods. Thus, humans' responsibilities toward animals must be grounded in human goods—either in the good of human friendship with God or in other aspects of integral human fulfillment.

2. Humans Should Treat Animals Kindly and Use Them Reasonably

Although animals have no rights, humans should treat them kindly. While animals can be used in accord with moral norms to serve any basic human good, they often are misused, and all uses of animals can become wrong. Moved by emotion, people often treat animals unreasonably.

a) **People should not treat animals cruelly.** Because animals are sentient and responsive, people can be tempted to treat them with intentional contempt. Also, animals often are hurt and made to suffer by being used in actions which are morally wrong on other grounds. Either kind of mistreatment involves more or less

---

52. Inasmuch as the basic human goods are intelligible aspects of the potential fulfillment of humans as bodily persons, the principles of practical reasoning would provide the same basis for promoting and protecting the well-being of bodily persons of other biological species, if such exist, as of biological humans. Hence, if humanoids landed on earth or were encountered elsewhere in the universe, they would have rights. However, it does not follow that nonhuman animals have rights, but only that the community of bodily persons might include diverse biological species. See Germain Grisez, "When Do People Begin?" *Proceedings of the American Catholic Philosophical Association* 63 (1989): 40–41.

cruelty—something impossible in dealing with nonsentient creatures. Cruelty to animals should be avoided for two reasons.[53]

First, as has been explained, subhuman entities should be respected insofar as they are parts of God's good creation. They should not be disturbed without a good reason; and doing so in the absence of such a reason is irreverent toward God and pointlessly reduces their availability for others' appreciation and possible use. These considerations apply more strongly to animals than to nonsentient creatures, since animals enjoy greater inherent meaning and value. Cruel treatment of animals, insofar as it harms them without any good reason, violates these norms.

Second, cruelty towards an animal often manifests either unreasonable anger and hatred or a desire to derive satisfaction from the animal's suffering. Feelings of both kinds are contrary to people's natural sympathy for animals, and so manifest some disintegrity within the person experiencing them. In acting on such feelings, the underlying disintegrity increases, and so one harms oneself. Since there can be no reason for accepting this harm, it is always wrong to do so.

Cruelty to animals also often predisposes the agent or others to act cruelly toward people. Moreover, to take satisfaction in an animal's suffering sometimes is part of a sin of sadistic lust or leads to such a sin.

b) People should protect animals and treat them kindly. The two main reasons for avoiding cruelty to animals also are reasons to protect them and treat them compassionately whenever there is no reason for doing otherwise. On this basis, people who can easily provide harmless birds and animals with what they need to survive should do so. Since animals' lives are not sacred as human life is, and since their suffering cannot have the spiritual and moral meaning human suffering has, they should be killed when necessary to end their misery, unless one has some reason not to do so.

Inasmuch as the members of each species of living thing constitute a special object of human study, appreciation, and other possible future uses, there is a significant reason to protect endangered species. Of course, that reason can be overridden if some human good calls for actions which will cause the extinction of a subhuman species. In the absence of such a countervailing reason, however, one should support and cooperate in measures which are necessary to protect endangered species.

c) People may use animals as they may use other subhuman entities. Since animals are part of the subpersonal creation over which humans have dominion, they may be used in any way which truly and justly serves the basic goods of persons. In principle there is nothing wrong with using animals for human food, clothing, shelter, scientific and medical experimentation, ornamentation, art materials, games and sports, religious sacrifice, and so forth (see *S.c.g.*, 3.112). Provided animals are used for such a human benefit and the act is not morally wrong on some other ground, a person may kill them, harm them, and/or inflict pain on them to the

---

53. St. Thomas, *S.c.g.*, 3.112 (near end), briefly indicates reasons why people should not be cruel to animals; he overlooks the irreverence toward God implicit in mistreating animals, inasmuch as they have inherent goodness as creatures.

extent either necessary for the purpose or unavoidable without imposing significant burdens on human beings.

However, inefficiency and waste in using animals violate the norm requiring people to protect them, and so are more serious than similar irrationality in the use of nonsentient creatures. It is cruel to cause animals pain by misusing them in activities which serve no basic good of persons, for example, purported experiments which offer no reasonable prospect of advancing scientific knowledge and forms of entertainment which appeal to base passions. Likewise, someone who negligently causes animals to suffer while using them violates the specific norm to treat them kindly.[54]

Moreover, every nonrational motive which can lead to violations of the general norms for using subhuman entities also can lead to violations of the special norms for using animals. For example, some of the feeding and slaughter of animals for meat misuses them because that meat is not part of a healthy diet and/or because the agricultural capacity used in producing meat could be used more efficiently to provide more people with an adequate vegetarian diet. Again, it is an abuse of animals when a woman wears a fur coat for the sake of vain and ostentatious display rather than for its suitability as clothing or a man hunts and kills wild animals for mere self-magnification, not for food or even for sport involving real skill and, perhaps, fellowship.

3. One Should Not Keep Domestic Animals Unreasonably

Not long ago, most families kept domestic animals in order to meet basic human needs, but few did so, or could afford to do so, apart from need. Hence, classical moral theology did not treat the matter. As urban-industrial economy and culture developed, however, the practice of keeping pets became widespread; in affluent societies, a vast industry promotes and serves this practice. Most people do not think there is any moral issue in having domestic animals, and Christians have accepted the common view uncritically. But the matter calls for a conscientious judgment, which often should be negative.

a) One can have an adequate reason to keep domestic animals. While the main reasons of the past for keeping domestic animals seldom are operative today, even city-dwelling people still can have sufficient reasons to keep animals. Sometimes the use is straightforward: guide dogs lead the blind; guard dogs protect people and property; cats can prevent infestation with rodents; and a tank of tropical fish in a waiting room is decorative and entertaining. Sometimes the animal is a

---

54. Since Scripture, tradition, and the magisterium provide no basis for the thesis that vegetarianism is obligatory, arguments for that position originate from other sources. Some arguments begin from true premises but do not validly establish the position. For instance, vegetarians often point out morally indefensible practices in raising, handling, and slaughtering animals, but those practices can be reformed without imposing vegetarianism on human beings. Again, health considerations and the conservation of natural resources support restrictions, perhaps severe ones, on the use of animals for food, but do not exclude it entirely. Other arguments avoid logical fallacies but presuppose animal rights or some other premise at odds with Christian faith as a basis for an absolute norm excluding eating meat.

pet, not kept for obvious utility, yet it really serves a human good; for example, parents can use pets to teach children important lessons; people who live alone can derive benefits to their psychological health from having and caring for pets; and hobbyists can develop themselves in various ways by spending leisure time training and caring for animals.

Nevertheless, every nonrational motive which can lead to acquiring and keeping other subhuman things also can motivate one to keep domestic animals. In addition, specific feelings toward animals often lead people to acquire and care for pets despite good reasons for not doing so. For example, some people use a pet as a substitute for the child or friend whom they could and should have or cultivate.

b) Keeping pets without an adequate reason is wrong. To justify keeping a pet, a reason is needed (as distinct from a merely emotional motive), and it must be adequate: such that one can act on it without infringing other responsibilities or being unfair to other people. Keeping a pet without an adequate reason is wrong in at least three ways.

First, although this misuse of an animal usually involves excessive kindness rather than cruelty, it is like any other abuse of a subpersonal entity in its irreverence toward God. The irreverence is especially marked in those who invert God's order, which subordinates animals to human beings made in God's image, by substituting concern about animals for concern about people, care of animals for care of people, and psychological bonding with animals for interpersonal communion.

Second, devoting quantities of goods and services to pets is unjustifiable in the absence of an adequate reason for keeping them, since providing these goods and services uses natural resources and human work, and imposes environmental costs. This economic capacity ought to be devoted to promoting and protecting human goods, either in pet owners themselves or others. Thus, while pets seldom compete directly with the poor for food, medical care, and so on, unreasonably keeping pets does contribute indirectly to economic injustice.

Third, this misuse of animals often has a bad environmental impact, not only through the indirect effects of what is done to feed and care for them but also through the direct effects of animals' natural functions and behavior, for example, defecating and urinating, making noise, posing hazards to human health and safety, and so on.

For anyone who has an adequate reason to keep a pet, doing so is right and good. For anyone without an adequate reason, keeping a pet is wrong, and, considering the significance of the human goods at stake, the wrong seems likely to be a grave matter. However, the Church has not yet considered this issue.

Question D: What Are the Foundations of Moral Norms about Property?

Property usually refers to a portion of the world which someone occupies or to some thing which someone can use. Unless the context requires a narrower reference, however, *property* will be used in the rest of this chapter to refer not only to land, what is permanently attached to it, and other goods, but to money and whatever it can buy, including claims to services, entities such as stock certificates and insurance policies, and so on.

The common human dominion over subpersonal creation is more basic than property, which is merely a mode of sharing that dominion. Property ownership implies not only rights but also, and more fundamentally, responsibilities. Both private and public property are morally necessary. Moreover, each society needs to develop and implement a property system.

1. Property Should Serve the Providential Purpose of Material Things

God gives the whole human family dominion over subpersonal creation for everyone's reasonable use. People's occupancy of places and uses of things, together with the requirement of fairness, cause many territories and things to become property, that is, to be morally tied in a special way to a particular person, family, or other community. Nevertheless, property ownership always remains subordinate to the more basic truth that humankind as a whole receives all material goods from God as his gift.[55]

a) **God intends material goods for everyone's reasonable use.** Repeating constant and very firm Catholic teaching,[56] Vatican II articulates the fundamental truth about material goods:

> God has destined the earth and all it contains for the use of all human individuals and peoples, in such a way that, under the direction of justice accompanied by charity, created goods ought to flow abundantly to everyone on a fair basis [note omitted]. One must always bear this universal destination of goods in mind, no matter what forms property may take as it is adapted, in accordance with diverse and changeable circumstances, to the legitimate institutions of peoples. (GS 69)[57]

John Paul II emphasizes the importance of this point: the "principle of the common use of goods" is the "fundamental principle of the moral order in this [socioeconomic] sphere" and is "the first principle of the whole ethical and social order."[58]

55. A relevant study: Robert Gnuse, *You Shall Not Steal: Community and Property in the Biblical Tradition* (Maryknoll, N.Y.: Orbis Books, 1985); although some of the author's views are arguable, this work deserves careful study.

56. For a summary of recent magisterial teaching, see John Paul II, *Centesimus annus,* 30, *AAS* 83 (1991) 830–31, *OR,* 6 May 1991, 10.

57. The omitted note (n. 8 in the Council's text, n. 221 in Abbott) refers first to Pius XII, *Sertum laetitiae, AAS* 31 (1939) 642 and 653, *PE,* 223.34: "The fundamental point of the social question is this, that the goods created by God for all men should in the same way reach all, justice guiding and charity helping"; also to John XXIII, Consistorial Address, *AAS* 52 (1960) 5–11; John XXIII, *Mater et magistra, AAS* 53 (1961) 411, *PE,* 267.43. Matthew Habiger, O.S.B., *Papal Teaching on Private Property: 1891–1981* (Lanham, Md.: University Press of America, 1990), shows that papal teaching from Leo XIII to John Paul II on property followed St. Thomas and has been consistent; while some aspects have been clarified and some new points added, the positions taken by Leo have been maintained; differences in emphasis, which some mistakenly interpret as inconsistencies, are accounted for by differences in the situations the popes confronted, since each pope's situation posed the particular questions he addressed.

58. John Paul II, *Laborem exercens,* 18 and 19, *AAS* 73 (1981) 623 and 626, *PE,* 280.82 and 89.

Again: "It is necessary to state once more the characteristic principle of Christian social doctrine: the goods of this world are *originally meant for all* [note omitted]."[59] Yet again: "The basis for the social doctrine of the Church is the principle of *the universal destination of goods.* According to the plan of God the goods of the earth are offered to all people and to each individual as a means towards the development of a truly human life."[60]

b) The universal destination of goods must be understood rightly. This principle does not mean that in the beginning human persons jointly *owned* the material world, with each having an equal share; no such primitive social order ever existed.[61] Therefore, the universal destination of goods does not imply even a basic or prima facie claim on the part of each individual to an equal portion of the world's goods.

The principle means, rather, that nothing in subhuman creation ever comes to be with a label saying: this good is meant for this person but not that one, this group but not that, people of this sort but not of that sort.[62] Instead, both in the beginning and now, God provides all the riches of the material world for all people to use as he directs. His directions are the moral norms flowing from the principles of practical reason, which human beings naturally know. Thus, God makes material goods available for all humans *to use reasonably,* that is, for the promotion and protection of true human goods, not only in the users but in others, by cooperating justly with their creator and with one another.

c) The universal destination of goods limits an owner's rights. As explained previously (in B.3), particular material things or portions of subhuman creation become linked with particular persons or groups as the latter use them, for instance, as a person gathers plants and animals to eat or as a group occupies the territory in which it lives. Still, the mere fact that such a link exists does not constitute the

---

59. John Paul II, *Sollicitudo rei socialis,* 42, *AAS* 80 (1988) 573, *OR,* 29 Feb. 1988, 11.

60. John Paul II, *Christifideles laici,* 43, *AAS* 81 (1989) 476, *OR,* 6 Feb. 1989, 14.

61. In an argument rightly rejecting the theory that ownership derives entirely from what an individual puts into things, George I. Mavrodes, "Property," *Personalist* 53 (1972): 245–62, seems to presuppose such a primitive social order, for he argues that owners must compensate the community for what they appropriate.

62. Leo XIII, *Rerum novarum, ASS* 23 (1890–91) 644, *PE,* 115.8, teaches: "God has granted the earth to mankind in general, not in the sense that all without distinction can deal with it as they like, but rather that no part of it was assigned to any one in particular, and that the limits of private possession have been left to be fixed by man's own industry, and by the laws of individual races." The point might seem obvious. However, some thinkers deny or at least overlook it. For example, Robert Nozick, *Anarchy, State, and Utopia* (New York: Basic Books, 1974), 160, thinking of human products, holds: "Things come into the world already attached to people having entitlements over them"; he treats as a mere "limit case" the emergence of objects "from nowhere, out of nothing." The truth which faith confirms, however, is that Nozick's so-called limit case is the fundamental truth about all material goods, and that this truth limits and qualifies all human entitlements, including those of producers to their products. For the human makers of the most complex products of advanced technology, such as computers, no less than farmers harvesting their crops, begin with God-given materials and depend at every moment of their productive activity on the action of God in nature, not least in their own human nature, to achieve the benefits they anticipate. See John Finnis, *Natural Law and Natural Rights* (Oxford: Oxford University Press, 1980), 186–88.

relationship of owner to property. That relationship is a moral one differentiating the owner's role and responsibilities from those of other people. Like any other moral relationship, it must be governed by fairness. Not everyone who possesses something, but only one who possesses it fairly, can be that thing's owner in a moral sense (though obviously a person with no moral right to something can hold a legal title to it).

For possession to be fair, it must be consistent with the universal destination of goods, which requires that they be available for everyone to use reasonably. It follows that ownership cannot of itself entail an exclusive moral right to use. So, immediately after laying down the principle of universal destination (in the passage quoted in a), Vatican II adds: "For this reason, in using those goods, people should consider the exterior things which they legitimately possess not only as their own but as common, in the sense that their possessions should benefit not only themselves but others as well" (GS 69).

d) St. Thomas distinguishes the right to use from ownership. At the end of the sentence just quoted, the Council refers in a note to two passages in St. Thomas, clarifying the Christian teaching it reaffirms.[63]

In the first passage (*S.t.,* 2–2, q. 32, a. 5, ad 2), Thomas answers an argument that, because people have the right to keep what is their own, almsgiving is never a matter of precept, a strict duty in justice. Previously in the same article, he has pointed out that failure to give alms can result in eternal punishment (see Mt 25.41–46) and has argued that almsgiving is a matter of precept if two conditions are met: (i) one has more than enough to meet one's own needs and those of one's dependents, and (ii) some other person or persons cannot survive unless one makes one's surplus available. In this context, his answer to the objection is that any earthly good which God gives people is theirs in the sense that they own it, but not in the sense that they alone may use it; for insofar as they do not need it to satisfy their own needs, others should be able to use it to satisfy theirs. He supports this by making reference to a striking statement of St. Ambrose, which he had already quoted and which Vatican II also quotes: "Feed those who are dying of hunger, for if you have not fed them, you have killed them [note omitted]" (GS 69).[64]

In the second passage to which Vatican II refers (*S.t.,* 2–2, q. 66, a. 2), St. Thomas gives three reasons why owning property is morally licit and even necessary. First, people tend to take better care of what is theirs than of what is common to everyone or to a group, since individuals shirk a responsibility which

---

63. Vatican II here follows prior papal teaching; it refers to Leo XIII, *Rerum novarum, ASS* 23 (1890–91) 651, *PE,* 115.22, who also quoted St. Thomas. Cf. relevant passages in Thomas which the Council does not mention: *S.t.,* 1–2, q. 105, a. 2; 2–2, q. 66, a. 7; q. 87, a. 1, ad 4.

64. For further support from Scripture and the Fathers for the thesis that justice requires owners to use their excess property to satisfy others' needs, see John C. Cort, *Christian Socialism: An Informal History* (Maryknoll, N.Y.: Orbis, 1988), 19–41; Charles Avila, *Ownership: Early Christian Teaching* (Maryknoll, N.Y.: Orbis, 1983). For a broader introduction to the Fathers' social teaching, with representative selections: Peter C. Phan, *Social Thought,* Message of the Fathers of the Church, 20 (Wilmington, Del.: Michael Glazier, 1984); also see Igino Giordani, *The Social Message of the Early Fathers,* trans. Alba I. Zizzamia (Paterson, N.J.: St. Anthony Guild Press, 1944), 253–320. On what constitutes a genuine human need, see E.1.b, below.

is nobody's in particular. Second, if everyone were responsible for everything, the result would be sheer confusion. Third, dividing things up generally makes for harmony, while sharing common things often leads to tension. Owning property, understood as the capacity to care for and distribute things, therefore is justified. The capacity to use things, however, is an entirely different matter. In regard to use, a person is not justified in holding anything as proper but only as common, in the sense that he or she must be ready to share it with others in need.[65]

e) **Ownership is subordinate to the universal destination of goods.** Having quoted Vatican II's formulation (in GS 69) of the Church's constant and most firm teaching concerning the universal destination of material goods, Paul VI adds:

> All other rights, whatever they may be, including the rights of property and free trade, are to be subordinated to this principle. They should in no way hinder it; in fact, they should actively facilitate its implementation. Redirecting these rights back to their original purpose must be regarded as an important and urgent social duty.[66]

f) **Analogies do not adequately express the concept of property.** Because no human being owns anything which was not first God's gift to all humankind, property ownership is more like what most people would call "trusteeship" or "stewardship" than "ownership," and so many Christian writers employ such analogies.[67] However, no analogy with a legal institution adequately expresses what property truly is, and so none corrects the fundamental misunderstanding of property widespread even among devout Christians. Instead of resorting to analogies such as stewardship, therefore, it seems better directly to criticize the unsound concept of property and to articulate the implications of a sound concept more fully.

2. Private and Public Property Are Both Morally Grounded

Given that caring for property and seeing to its just availability to meet human needs come first among the functions associated with property ownership, it might be supposed that Christians ought to favor public ownership over private; in this way, it might be argued, public servants would function as trustees in carrying out the responsibilities of ownership, while the tendency of private owners to usurp exclusive use would be blocked. However, even though the Church's teaching acknowledges that public ownership of property can be justified, the Church also

---

65. For these arguments, Thomas clearly draws on Aristotle, *Politics* 2.5. But although Aristotle, too, says, "It appears, therefore, that it is better for possessions to be private but for their use to be common" (1263a38–39), Thomas's argument for this key point is essentially theological rather than philosophical. A summary of relevant New Testament teaching: Aquinata Böckmann, O.S.B., "What Does the New Testament Say about the Church's Attitude to the Poor?" in *The Poor and the Church,* ed. Norbert Greinacher and Alois Müller, Concilium, 104 (New York: Seabury, 1977), 36–45.

66. Paul VI, *Populorum progressio,* 22, *AAS* 59 (1967) 268, *PE,* 275.22; also, John Paul II, *Christifideles laici,* 43, *AAS* 81 (1989) 476, *OR,* 6 Feb. 1989, 14, teaches: "At the service of this destination of goods is *private property,* which—precisely for this purpose—possesses an *intrinsic social function.*"

67. John Paul II, *Sollicitudo rei socialis,* 42, *AAS* 80 (1988) 573, *OR,* 29 Feb. 1988, 12, uses another analogy: "Private property, in fact, is under a 'social mortgage' [note omitted]."

teaches that private property is morally necessary and sanctioned by divine law.[68] Thus, private property usually should not be socialized; most abuses of private property instead should be remedied by public regulation and a more just distribution of the responsibility of private ownership.

a) **Private ownership often is social rather than individual.** Individualism sometimes leads people to assume a false opposition between private property and common use. In reality, most human actions employing material things are cooperative; for example, a family shares a dwelling and the necessities of life; many stockholders own a corporation, and many workers use its productive facilities; an academic community shares a campus. Thus, public ownership, the holding of property by a civil society, is not the only form of social ownership, and collectivism not the only alternative to individualism (see 6.E.4–5).[69]

In the Church's social doctrine, the basic model of private social ownership is family ownership: property from which a family draws all or some of its livelihood, the land on which it lives, its home.[70] Since the family, unlike the individual, continues beyond one lifespan, the right of inheritance follows necessarily from the family's right to own property.[71] (Of course, this right is not infringed by taxes on the estates of those who leave more than enough to meet their families' needs and give their children a start in life.)

b) **The moral effect of ownership should determine the form it takes.** The responsibilities of ownership—proper care of property and its availability to meet human needs—pertain whether the property is public or private and, if the latter, social or individual. The responsibilities may go unfulfilled under any form of ownership; but if they are fulfilled, different forms of ownership can have very similar results with respect to the availability of goods for use. Yet private and public ownership of property differ essentially in how they distribute decision making and responsibility. In judging what forms ownership should take, therefore, it is necessary to consider the moral impact of ownership on the owner as a responsible moral agent.

c) **The moral well-being of persons calls for private property.** The Church's social doctrine firmly defends private ownership because of its potential moral benefits to the acting person.[72] In a predominantly agricultural economy, the

68. Leo XIII, *Rerum novarum, ASS* 23 (1890–91) 645, *PE,* 115.11, teaches that divine law implies the legitimacy of private property in forbidding coveting: Ex 20.17, Dt 5.21, Rom 13.9.

69. See Pius XI, *Quadragesimo anno, AAS* 23 (1931) 192, *PE,* 209.46.

70. See especially Pius XII, Pentecost Message, *AAS* 33 (1941) 202–3, *Catholic Mind* 39 (8 June 1941): 12–13.

71. Leo XIII, *Rerum novarum, ASS* 23 (1890–91) 646, *PE,* 115.13, teaches: "It is a most sacred law of nature that a father should provide food and all necessaries for those whom he has begotten; and, similarly, it is natural that he should wish that his children, who carry on, so to speak, and continue his personality, should be by him provided with all that is needful to enable them to keep themselves decently from want and misery amid the uncertainties of this mortal life. Now, in no other way can a father effect this except by the ownership of productive property, which he can transmit to his children by inheritance." Leo goes on to insist that family rights are at least equal to and in some respects prior to those of civil society.

72. See Jean-Yves Calvez, S.J., and Jacques Perrin, S.J., *The Church and Social Justice: The Social Teaching of the Popes from Leo XIII to Pius XII (1878–1958)* (Chicago: Henry Regnery,

paradigm of ownership is having one's own piece of land and the tools to work it. In a more developed economy, John XXIII noted, the ownership and management of productive goods often are distinguished; many people rely for security on insurance and pension schemes, and on various public programs; and some are far more interested in acquiring skill in a trade or competence in a profession than in having material goods as their property. Nevertheless, he reaffirmed the moral right to own private property and its personalistic foundation.[73]

d) Vatican II reaffirms the Church's teaching on this matter. While recognizing the complex forms which human dominion over material goods can take, Vatican II endorses prior Church teaching on private property:

> Because ownership and other forms of private dominion over material goods contribute to the expression of personality, and since, moreover, they give one an occasion for exercising one's role in society and in the economy, it is very important to promote the access of both individuals and communities to some ownership of of material goods.
>
> Private ownership or some other kind of dominion over material goods provides everyone with a wholly necessary area of personal and familial independence, and should be regarded as an extension of human freedom. Finally, since it adds incentives for carrying out one's vocation and responsibility, it is one prerequisite of civil liberties [note omitted]. (GS 71)

This very compact summary makes four points.

i) Private property helps people express their personalities: they can realize themselves in the things they own. A house, for example, becomes a home through the work family members put into maintaining and improving it to serve their common life. Ownership also enables people to express love and build up interpersonal communion by giving and sharing.

ii) Private ownership encourages people to strengthen the larger society and contribute to the common welfare. It does this in two ways: first, the prospect of having something of their own motivates people to work, to invent, and thus to create wealth; second, experiencing ownership challenges people to fulfill their social responsibilities by seeing to it that the goods they control benefit others as well as themselves.

iii) Control over some material goods is necessary for self-reliance, and self-reliance is necessary for appropriate autonomy. As only nations with adequate resources can develop their own economies, so only individuals and families owning suitable property can provide for themselves. Lack of self-reliance has an impact on those who depend on public subsidies: decisions about many personal and family matters inevitably are made for them by public agents.

iv) It is no accident that, as a matter of historical fact, widespread private ownership and recognition of civil liberties go together. Motivated to do their social

---

1961), 190–209, for a summary of the teaching through Pius XII; also see Jean-Yves Calvez, S.J., *The Social Thought of John XXIII: Mater et magistra,* trans. George J. M. McKenzie, S.M. (Chicago: Henry Regnery, 1965), 15–28. See Habiger, *Papal Teaching on Private Property,* for a more detailed treatment of the teaching from Leo XIII to John Paul II.

73. See John XXIII, *Mater et magistra, AAS* 53 (1961) 426–28, *PE,* 267.104–11.

duty, responsible owners can be entrusted with considerable liberty. Conversely, eliminating private ownership in favor of public ownership means decisions are made by public authorities, who must implement them by constant involvement in the details of everyone's life.[74]

e) **Public ownership of property also sometimes is justified.** Although the Church's teaching defends the private ownership of property, it also approves of public property (see GS 71). Of course, nobody questions the right of a civil society to own the material goods absolutely essential for carrying on its functions—such things as public buildings, official papers, and safety or military equipment—and certain things which all or most people use in common: roads, public parks, a postal system, and so on. But the Church's teaching goes further. It holds that some kinds of property are best reserved to the state, since allowing them to be privately owned would give their owners too much power over others, to the detriment of the common good.[75]

Moreover, for the sake of the moral and social goods which property should serve, the state can and ought to regulate the use of private property and even, if necessary, expropriate it, with just compensation to the former owners.[76]

f) **Two things must be noted to understand this teaching.** First, even if public ownership of certain productive property is justified, the property need not always be owned and managed directly by the state, as public buildings are. Other forms of public ownership are possible, for example, control by semi-independent, publicly regulated, nonprofit corporations. Hence, the Council's teaching speaks of "various forms" of public ownership (GS 71).

Second, when expropriation is justified, the just compensation often will be much less than what the former owner could have obtained by selling the property privately. For if private owners profit by using their property to the detriment of the common good, part of the property's market value will derive from the unjust profit it is expected to yield, and the owners deserve no compensation for losing that. In some cases, in fact, there need be no compensation at all, for owners who seriously and persistently violate justice in retaining and administering property might be justly punished by being compelled to forfeit what they have abused.

3. A Just System Specifies Moral Responsibilities Regarding Property

The responsibilities treated in chapters eight and nine bear directly on goods intrinsic to human persons, as individuals and in community: life, health, bodily

---

74. Dario Composta, S.D.B., "La persona umana e la proprietà privata," *Divinitas* 23 (1979): 62–87, defends the Church's teaching on private property against opposing views, especially those of Hegelian and Marxist inspiration.

75. See Pius XI, *Quadragesimo anno, AAS* 23 (1931) 214, *PE*, 209.114–15.

76. See Pius XII, Radio Message (1 Sept. 1944), *AAS* 36 (1944) 254, *Catholic Mind* 42 (Oct. 1944): 582; John Paul II, Address to Gathering at Cuilapan (Mexico), 6, *AAS* 71 (1979) 209, *OR*, 12 Feb. 1979, 7. Vatican II deals with a particular case in which expropriation might be justified: some large landowners keep much of their land unproductive and exploit hired labor; if necessary, the land should be divided and distributed to those who can make it fruitful (see GS 71); cf. Paul VI, *Populorum progressio,* 24, *AAS* 59 (1967) 269, *PE*, 275.24.

integrity, marriage, and family. So, the principles of practical reason and of morality, directing action toward integral human fulfillment, specify those responsibilities, in the sense that many relevant norms can be derived from moral principles alone.

Property rights and responsibilities are less fully determined by the principles of practical reason. Wealth and property are not goods intrinsic to persons. Rather, the realities constituting them are subpersonal things which become personalized through human occupancy and use, with the latter depending on human creative intelligence and freedom. While moral principles require that subpersonal things be used for morally good ends, with reverence toward God, and with justice toward other people, those principles by themselves do not imply any norms referring to property insofar as it is specified by human creativity. Consequently, human decisions can rightly specify property rights and responsibilities in diverse ways.

Every society therefore has a property system shaped by its own laws and customs: a set of rules and practices concerning the acquisition, use, and exchange of material things. Efficiency and fairness require such a system: it defines legitimate acquisition and creates the complex forms of ownership found in the community. Insofar as the system is just, it specifies many of one's moral responsibilities regarding property. But no actual property system is perfectly just, and the defects in the system under which someone lives must be taken into account in identifying responsibilities.

a) Socially established property systems do several things. Every society's property system presupposes the reality of ownership; ownership is not created by laws and social customs. However, each society's property system does spell out what will count in that society as legitimate acquisition, thus making it easy to recognize items of property and identify the owner of each. The system also settles otherwise unclear limits of ownership: boundaries of land, distinct aspects of complex things which can be used in different ways, when ownership lapses through disuse, and so on.

As a society's economy develops, it establishes conventions for a more complex property system. Rules are developed for dividing ownership and sharing the use of property, and sharp distinctions are introduced between ownership and legitimate custody and control, for example, by tenants or trustees. Elements of the responsibilities of ownership and the rights to use can be distributed among various people at different times and even at the same time. With the establishment of some commodity or symbol of value as a commonly accepted medium of exchange (money), it becomes possible to assign a comparative value to everything which can be exchanged. Symbolic tokens of ownership, such as titles to property and share certificates, are created. The relationship between owner and property no longer need involve any actual physical control; a token of ownership can be bought and sold, deposited to guarantee a loan, and so on. Laws make clear what counts as an enforceable agreement or contract to exchange property, the conditions under which a contract is no longer enforceable, and so on.

b) A property system is justified by serving the common good. It is possible to imagine a small group of fair-minded people who could own and use things properly without any established property system; they would settle all problems on a case-by-case basis. But since settling problems takes time and effort, and many problems are recurrent, regular practices soon would develop, even among such people, and these would become accepted as binding customs. A simple property system tends to become more complex in order to achieve further benefits by facilitating economic activities which are not possible without the system's additional features.

In many cases, moreover, even fair-minded people would find it very difficult to solve problems without the commonly accepted rules of a property system. For example, when property is fortuitously damaged or destroyed, the owner suffers the loss, and such losses often occur during a transfer of ownership, when it is unclear who is owner. Without rules to settle the precise moment at which a change of ownership occurs, even fair-minded people often would be unable to agree about which party must accept a loss.

By benefiting all or most members of a society without directly harming anyone, a property system can be morally justified, so that its rules and conditions become morally binding on all.

c) **Fairness also requires the development of a property system.** Even when rights and responsibilities could be determined without the clear rules of a property system, not only efficiency but fairness demands such a system. This is so because people differ greatly in assertiveness and ability to discern their own interests, so that lack of clear rules would put some at a constant disadvantage. Although such people inevitably suffer some disadvantage—for example, in buying and selling they negotiate less shrewdly than others—a property system often can save them from being exploited, by making them conscious of their rights and making others conscious of their responsibilities.

A property system also can serve justice insofar as its rules make it possible or easier for authorities to identify unfairness and rectify it by enforcing rules, requiring specific performance of undertakings, awarding damages to injured parties, and so on.

d) **The justice of the accepted property system should be presumed.** In general, one should presume that laws and binding customs are just (see 11.D.4.a). So, unless it is morally more probable that one may act contrary to a norm specified by the accepted property system, the norm should be followed.

Of course, even if a property system is entirely just, epikeia can come into play (see *CMP*, 11.E.10; below, 11.D.2.a). That will be so when unusual circumstances require an exception to the system's norms in order to serve ends any reasonable lawmaker would have intended the law to serve. For example, when need is so urgent that human life is at stake, one may openly or covertly take what is needed from anyone who can spare it, although that violates the letter of the law. For no reasonable lawmaker could intend the property system to prevent the use of available goods to satisfy someone's urgent needs, since all property is subordinate to the fundamental principle that God has destined material goods to meet human needs (see 1, above).

However, a norm should not be judged unfair or set aside merely because following it in a particular case will result in a state of affairs which seems unfair considered apart from the particular property system. For example, any law prescribing the distribution of the property of persons who die intestate—that is, without a valid will—sometimes leads to results which plainly are not those the deceased should, and quite possibly would, have brought about by making a will. Yet such a law can be just inasmuch as it provides a fair solution to the general problem, and some such solution is needed to prevent prolonged and wasteful conflicts among the possible heirs of people who die intestate. Moreover, epikeia seldom will come into play in such cases, since usually it will not be clear that lawmakers could not have reasonably intended the law to apply to them. Ordinarily, therefore, the administrator of the estate of someone who has died intestate should not try to circumvent the law, even though it prescribes what seems like an unfair distribution.[77]

e) **A property system's unjust norms sometimes may be ignored.** In this fallen world, any property system will be unfair in some respects, insofar as it embodies biases in favor of the society's dominant groups. Moreover, some property systems are based on false principles, such as an individualist or collectivist ideology, with the bad result of systematically violating, rather than implementing, the fundamental principle of the universal destination of material goods and/or the right of all families to the goods they need for their independence and security. Of course, even the most unjust property system includes norms which are just at least in regulating relationships among members of the same socioeconomic class. Hence, even if certain that the property system of his or her society is fundamentally defective, a person cannot assume that all its norms lack moral force. If, however, one is morally certain that a particular norm of the property system is unjust, that norm cannot of itself bind in conscience. Still, one often should comply with legal requirements which do not of themselves bind in conscience (see 11.D.3.b–c).

f) **Owners should avoid the injustices that the law permits.** Some people wrongly assume that whatever is lawful is morally acceptable. Even some Christians who recognize that as false with respect to other matters—for example, religious duties and sexual morality—assume its truth in forming their consciences about property matters. But while the just and applicable norms of an accepted system should not be violated, merely obeying the law is not sufficient to fulfill one's moral responsibilities. For those who legitimately exercise ownership in a just property system may nevertheless lack moral grounds for doing so. Moreover, as will be explained (in E.1.a), although owners should share the use of their property with others, many people in contemporary, affluent, secular societies do not recognize this obligation, and the property systems accepted in such societies more or less ignore it.

---

77. The administrator should call the apparent unfairness to the attention of those who stand to benefit from it, and they should make and follow a conscientious judgment on the matter. They, of course, in no way violate the law if they forgo a distribution to which they are legally but not morally entitled.

Consequently, conscientious Christians must always bear in mind that even though violating the norms of the accepted property system seldom is justified, those norms by themselves are not sufficient to guide responsible choices. Often, there is a duty in strict justice either to forgo material goods to which one is legally entitled or to use one's possessions to benefit others in ways to which they have no legal right.

g) **Moral reflection must attend to every form of property.** Any advanced property system provides for forms of property with no direct relationship to a material reality which could be possessed: conditional claims to insurance payments, copyrights, benefits due from social welfare funds, and so on. People who recognize their responsibilities and respect others' rights in regard to more concrete forms of property sometimes ignore relevant moral norms when dealing with such more abstract forms. Other things being equal, however, injustices such as theft and the retention of goods which should be used to meet others' urgent needs are the same no matter what form of property happens to be involved. Hence, the more abstract character of some forms of property should not be allowed to obscure relevant moral responsibilities.

4. Injustices as to Property Generally Constitute Grave Matter.

Violations of the norms concerning property which will be articulated in the balance of this chapter always involve some unfairness, either to particular persons, to a particular community, or to humankind at large. As with other matters of justice, it should be assumed that sins in this area are grave matters. The matter is correctly judged to be light in particular cases only if it is morally certain that the harm done to those wronged is so minor that people generally regard similar harm, suffered by themselves or those they love, as insignificant and tolerable (see 6.A.7).

Most people realize that they do a serious wrong in violating certain of these norms, such as that forbidding theft. In violating some others, however, even most Christians fail to realize that they do any wrong at all, much less that the matter is grave. Catechesis about these sins seldom has been as clear, forceful, and frequent as about those which violate exceptionless norms in matters admitting no parvity.

Moreover, considering what is now known about the environmental impact of many activities, the harm a person does others by maintaining a wasteful, consumerist style of life can no longer be judged insignificant as it once was. Even if particular instances do little harm, the choice—and so the moral responsibility—usually does not concern those individual instances, since they result from the habits and policies of one's style of life. In view of the harm to others resulting from one's whole way of life, the choice not to undertake the practice of conservation and change one's habits can hardly be a light matter.

Question E: What Are People's Responsibilities with Respect to Their Own Property?

Before considering responsibilities regarding others' property (question F) and in transactions (question G), the present question focuses on responsibilities in regard to acquiring, caring for, using, and disposing of property. Certain specific and important ways of using wealth—insurance, savings, and gambling—require special attention.

While the responsibilities treated here apply both to individual agents and to groups, such as families, for simplicity's sake what follows usually speaks only of individuals.

1. The Christian Concept of Property Implies Two Basic Moral Norms

Some general norms were set out (in B.4.a–b) for human use of subpersonal creation. Those norms apply to acquiring and holding property, and the motives for violating them account for owners' abuse of their property. But since ownership is subject to the requirements of fairness, the abuse of property by its owners not only is irreverent toward God but unfair to other people.

In addition, the Christian conception of property implies two basic norms applying only to owners: they should share the use of their property with others and should practice conservation.

a) Owners should share the use of their property with others. Contemporary secular opinion and Catholic teaching agree that in deciding about the use of things, owners may give preference to meeting their own needs and those of their dependents. Beyond that, however, the contemporary world's understanding of owning property stands in sharp contrast with the Christian understanding.

Most people in affluent, contemporary societies think owning property primarily means enjoying the right to do whatever one pleases with it. Of course, people recognize some limits, for example, that owners must pay taxes and not use property in ways which hurt others or impose unfair risks on them. But most people do not think owners have a strict duty to care for and conserve their property, and then, having met their own and their dependents' needs, to use it to meet others' needs. It is taken to be commendable charity, not strict justice, when even the wealthiest choose to help even the poorest.

In contrast, as has been explained (in D.1), the Church teaches that ownership always presupposes and is limited by the universal destination of goods, that is, by the fact that the material world is God's gift to humankind as a whole. Owning property means being responsible for the care and management of part of this gift. People do not have the right to do as they please with their property; they cannot assume that what they own is theirs to keep indefinitely and use just as they like, provided only they pay their taxes and do no harm to others. Rather, every owner has a constant, serious responsibility to make certain his or her property fairly serves genuine human needs. Having satisfied their own needs and those of their dependents, owners should do what they can to meet the needs of others. Consequently, under certain conditions almsgiving is so grave an obligation in strict justice that failure to feed the hungry can be a form of homicide (as has been explained in D.1.d).

Moreover, for Christians aware of having received the gift of God's love, this obligation in strict justice also is an unconditional requirement of mercy:

We know that we have passed from death to life because we love one another. Whoever does not love abides in death. All who hate a brother or sister are murderers, and you know that murderers do not have eternal life abiding in them. We know love by this, that he laid down his life for us—and we ought to lay down our lives for one another. How does God's love abide in anyone who has the world's goods and sees a brother or sister in need and yet refuses help? (1 Jn 3.14–17; cf. Mt 25.41–46)

To refuse help to others in need is to evict God's merciful love from one's heart and so to abide in that death which precludes eternal life.

b) **Genuine needs are more than the bare minimum for survival.** Since the concept of genuine human needs is essential to the preceding norm, it is necessary to explain what these are. On the one hand, they do not include whatever people think they need, since many people, especially in affluent countries, think they need all the comforts and luxuries they are accustomed to, plus any new ones they strongly desire. On the other hand, genuine human needs are not limited to the conditions for bare survival, since in merely surviving human beings cannot fulfill all their specifically human potentialities and are tempted by their misery to sin against others and their own dignity.[78]

Genuine human needs are marked out by the basic intelligible human goods (see *CMP*, 5.D; and above, 9.A.1.j), considered as the object of a will toward integral human fulfillment (see *CMP*, 7.F). Thus, *genuine* excludes not only mere objects of emotion but anything which would be obtained, used, or enjoyed sinfully; at the same time, *genuine needs* includes everything to be used in living a morally good life. Thus, in condemning certain inequalities as morally unacceptable, John Paul II uses a broad concept of necessities: "As regards necessities—food, clothes, housing, medico-social assistance, basic instruction, professional training, means of transport, information, possibility of recreation, religious life—there must be no privileged social strata."[79]

c) **The practice of conservation is a moral obligation.** Since God gave humankind as a whole dominion over lower creation, everyone should acquire property and use it conservatively. John Paul II teaches:

---

78. John Paul II, *Centesimus annus*, 36, *AAS* 83 (1991) 838–39, *OR*, 6 May 1991, 11, explains the problem of qualifying needs: "The manner in which new needs arise and are defined is always marked by a more or less appropriate concept of man and of his true good. A given culture reveals its overall understanding of life through the choices it makes in production and consumption. It is here that *the phenomenon of consumerism* arises. In singling out new needs and new means to meet them, one must be guided by a comprehensive picture of man which respects all the dimensions of his being and which subordinates his material and instinctive dimensions to his interior and spiritual ones. If, on the contrary, a direct appeal is made to his instincts—while ignoring in various ways the reality of the person as intelligent and free—then *consumer attitudes* and *life-styles* can be created which are objectively improper and often damaging to his physical and spiritual health. Of itself, an economic system does not possess criteria for correctly distinguishing new and higher forms of satisfying human needs from artificial new needs which hinder the formation of a mature personality."

79. John Paul II, Homily at Mass in Recife (Brazil), 5, *AAS* 72 (1980) 929, *OR*, 4 Aug. 1980, 10.

Make the most of the goods of nature: ensure that they will yield more in favour of man, the man of today and of tomorrow. As regards the use of God's gift of the land, it is necessary to think a great deal of the future generations, to pay the price of austerity in order not to weaken or reduce—or worse still, to make unbearable—the living conditions of future generations. Justice and humanity require this too [note omitted].[80]

Thus, conservative use means taking into account the adverse side effects one's actions might have on other people, not only those now living but future generations. Conservation requires restraint in using resources known to be nonrenewable and avoiding insofar as possible contributing to irreversible changes in nature, since any such change could interfere with potential future uses not now foreseen.

Consequently, individuals and groups should acquire only what they really need; use carefully whatever they acquire; when possible, reuse things or pass them on for others' use; when feasible, salvage usable parts and recycle materials; and carefully dispose of things which cannot either be reused or recycled.

Affluent people are especially obliged to practice conservation. As the Synod of Bishops points out, the essential conditions for human life on earth would suffer irreparable damage if everyone consumed and polluted at the same rate as people living in the wealthier nations do.[81] Therefore: "Those who are already rich are bound to accept a less material way of life, with less waste, in order to avoid the destruction of the heritage which they are obliged by absolute justice to share with all other members of the human race."[82]

d) One should consider how serious are violations of these norms. The gravity of these two basic moral norms regarding property is seldom sufficiently appreciated. Understanding why that is so can clarify a person's sense of justice in these matters.

As to the norm requiring owners to share their property with others, the common contemporary view of property is so pervasive that even Christians who know about the norm often fail to take it seriously. Indeed, even victims of injustice in this matter often take it for granted that owners act within their rights in adhering to conventional standards. That people do not see themselves as victims does not mean the harm they suffer is insignificant and tolerable. Even if not conscious of being victims of injustice, those deprived of their just share of the world's goods are well aware that the harm they suffer is great.

---

80. John Paul II, Homily at the Mass for Farmers (Legazpi City, Philippines), 4, *AAS* 73 (1981) 386, *OR,* 2 Mar. 1981, 11.

81. Synod of Bishops, Second General Assembly (1971), *Justice in the World, EV* 4 (1971–73) 804–7, Flannery, 2:697.

82. Synod of Bishops, Second General Assembly (1971), *Justice in the World, EV* 4 (1971–73) 834–35, Flannery, 2:709. John Paul II, Homily in Yankee Stadium (New York), 6, *AAS* 71 (1979) 1172, *OR,* 22 Oct. 1979, 5, likewise teaches against "consumerism, exhausting and joyless": "It is not a question of slowing down progress, for there is no human progress when everything conspires to give full reign to the instincts of self-interest, sex and power. We must find a simple way of living. For it is not right that the standard of living of the rich countries should seek to maintain itself by draining off a great part of the reserves of energy and raw materials that are meant to serve the whole of humanity."

As for the practice of conservation, classical moral theology never discussed it; few Catholics feel a moral obligation in the matter, and some dismiss it as a merely fashionable cause. The norm may seem rather puritanical, because the Catholic moral and ascetical tradition does not regard the exuberant and even lavish use of material goods as wrong in itself. Also, some leading conservationists are secular humanists, whose erroneous views on other matters diminish the credibility of their sound moral judgments and public policy proposals on this matter.

Even when Catholics recognize their duty to practice conservation, they, like other people, are likely to ignore its seriousness. Most of those whose interests require this practice make up a seemingly faceless, nameless multitude, including people of distant lands and future generations, whom only clear-eyed faith, not clouded common sense, recognizes as neighbors to be loved and treated fairly. Then too, it is easy to think of particular acts of waste and consumption as very small, and so people overlook their responsibility to commit themselves to a "less material way of life" and to change habits whose effects over time are great.

2. Christians Should Subordinate Possessions to the Kingdom

In deciding whether to acquire or retain anything, some people take into account only the comparative strength of their desire for that thing and others, and the limits of their ability to satisfy their desires. The desires usually include not only rational ones—for instance, for the necessities of life—but also merely emotional motives (listed in B.4.c, above). The latter, often stimulated and nurtured by advertising, always are virtually without limit, since no matter what one has, it is always possible to imagine having something more or better.[83] Also, for some people the measure of their ability to satisfy their desires is how much cash and credit they have currently available; they give little or no thought to meeting future responsibilities.

Christians should take a very different attitude, free from slavery to desire for possessions. An individual's personal vocation or a group's proper mission provides the standard for judgments about acquiring, holding, and disposing of things.

a) **Jesus requires his followers to give up their possessions.** After a rich man refuses Jesus' invitation to sell his possessions, give the proceeds to the poor, and become his disciple, Jesus tells his followers that wealth is a humanly insuperable obstacle to salvation (see Mt 19.16–26, Mk 10.17–27, Lk 18.18–27). Not everyone is called precisely as the rich man was, but every Christian life presupposes renunciation, which at least means detachment from material goods (see Lk 14.1–32): "So therefore, none of you can become my disciple if you do not give up all your possessions" (Lk 14.33).

The problem is that material goods offer quick gratification, which provides an illusion of happiness; thus, people set their hearts on having and using things rather than on sharing in the heavenly communion of persons:

> Do not be afraid, little flock, for it is your Father's good pleasure to give you the kingdom. Sell your possessions, and give alms. Make purses for yourselves that do not wear out, an unfailing treasure in heaven, where no thief comes near

83. See Eric Clark, *The Want Makers: The World of Advertising: How They Make You Buy* (New York: Viking, 1989).

and no moth destroys. For where your treasure is, there your heart will be also. (Lk 12.32–34)

Wealth tends to enslave, and possessions compete with God for a would-be disciple's allegiance: "No slave can serve two masters; for a slave will either hate the one and love the other, or be devoted to the one and despise the other. You cannot serve God and wealth" (Lk 16.13).

Consequently, the gospel challenges Christians either to live in evangelical poverty (see LG 42) or entirely to subordinate to their faith any necessary acquiring, retaining, and using of material goods. All Jesus' followers must give up everything they have, in the sense of investing all their material goods in God's kingdom. In doing so, as Jesus points out, they act with truly enlightened self-interest ("make for *yourselves*"); their investment will yield its return endlessly in heaven.[84]

b) Personal vocation or a group's mission provides the standard. Christians should implement their faith and organize their lives by committing themselves to doing God's will as they concretely discern it. In other words, they should respond to their personal vocations (see 2.E). Vocation must not be understood narrowly or individualistically; it extends to the whole of life, including such matters as friendships and legitimate recreation, and it specifies all the individual and social responsibilities of a Christian. Therefore, to devote material goods to the service of Jesus' kingdom means acquiring, using, and retaining them precisely insofar as they are necessary for survival or are suitable for fulfilling responsibilities pertaining to one's personal vocation.

Desiring and clinging to things which exceed this limit, whether by their quantity or their quality, is inconsistent with the total giving of self which Jesus requires of every one of his disciples. May I own an automobile? Perhaps. Do I need it for transportation? Not if public transportation (or a bicycle), perhaps supplemented by occasionally borrowing or renting an automobile, will do. Is the transportation a necessary and suitable part of an integrally Christian life? Not if I can forgo it while fulfilling all my responsibilities. May I buy a new, or an expensive, or a second automobile? Not if the old, or less expensive, or first one will meet my needs. Thus, while giving up all their possessions, Jesus' disciples may retain the things they need to follow him.[85]

Christians need not reject new technology or forgo improved facilities which really enable them better to fulfill their responsibilities. But they must not become

> slaves of "possession" and of immediate gratification, with no other horizon than the multiplication or continual replacement of the things already owned with others still better. This is the so-called civilization of "consumption" or "consum-

---

84. A useful commentary: Robert F. O'Toole, S.J., "Poverty and Wealth in Luke-Acts," *Chicago Studies* 30 (Apr. 1991): 29–41.

85. See *S.t.*, 2–2, q. 188, a. 7, for St. Thomas's explanation along these lines of the poverty appropriate to the various kinds of religious life which existed in his day. While that poverty differed from the detachment required of every Christian in permitting only communal possession of goods, the standard for judging what to possess is the same; see Jacques Leclercq, *Christianity and Money,* trans. Eric Earnshaw Smith, Twentieth Century Encyclopedia of Catholicism, 59 (New York: Hawthorn Books, 1959).

erism", which involves so much "throwing-away" and "waste". An object already owned but now superseded by something better is discarded, with no thought of its possible lasting value in itself, nor of some other human being who is poorer.

All of us experience firsthand the sad effects of this blind submission to pure consumerism: in the first place a crass materialism, and at the same time a *radical dissatisfaction,* because one quickly learns—unless one is shielded from the flood of publicity and the ceaseless and tempting offers of products—that the more one possesses the more one wants, while deeper aspirations remain unsatisfied and perhaps even stifled.[86]

One must obtain and keep things not in the vain pursuit of satisfaction in possession but in the reasonable pursuit of true goods.

Just as personal vocation sets the limit for the individual Christian, each community's proper mission provides the standard for its acquiring, using, and retaining material goods (see *S.t.,* 2–2, q. 188, a. 7). Parents may try to obtain what they need to bring up and educate their children; families may keep what they need to care for their disabled and elderly members. (In 6 below, specific norms for saving and ensuring will be treated.) But Christian families must not try to keep up with their materialistic neighbors. Likewise, the Church herself and each voluntary association may have the material goods necessary to carry out their missions. Still, it is an evasion of the gospel standard if a cleric, religious, or any of the faithful who is a leader or member of a prosperous parish, religious community, or other association enjoys a luxurious life-style, even without holding personal title to any of the property or money he or she uses and spends.

c) Leo XIII's teaching on this matter must be understood correctly. In clarifying the limits of the obligation of almsgiving, St. Thomas distinguishes two modes of what is needed: the first is what is absolutely necessary for one's own survival and the survival of one's dependents; the second is what is needed to live decently and provide for dependents according to one's social condition and status (see *S.t.,* 2–2, q. 32, a. 6, c.). Referring to this distinction, Leo XIII said the Christian is not required to give away "what he himself needs to maintain his station in life becomingly and decently."[87] This papal teaching sometimes has been taken to mean that Christians may retain all the wealth they need to maintain their standard of living, no matter how high. However, that interpretation is inconsistent with other elements of the Church's teaching. For example, Vatican II points out that some of the Fathers and Doctors of the Church teach that "one is obliged to come to the relief of the poor, and to do so not merely out of one's superfluous goods."[88] Therefore, it is reasonable to interpret Leo's teaching in the light of Thomas's, and to interpret the latter in its historical and textual context.

---

86. John Paul II, *Sollicitudo rei socialis,* 28, *AAS* 80 (1988) 548–49, *OR,* 29 Feb. 1988, 7; see Drew Christiansen, S.J., "Social Justice and Consumerism in the Thought of Pope John Paul II," *Social Thought,* Spring-Summer 1987, 60–73.

87. Leo XIII, *Rerum novarum, ASS* 23 (1890–91) 651, *PE,* 115.22 (translation supplied).

88. GS 69. An appended note (n. 10 in the Latin text, n. 223 in Abbott) refers to St. Basil, Lactantius, St. Augustine, St. Gregory the Great, St. Bonaventure, St. Albert the Great, and John XXIII, but neither to St. Thomas nor to Leo XIII.

As to the historical context: in Christian societies, someone's station in life could limit the material goods he or she needed, for it was mainly determined, not by wealth, but by social function and responsibilities—one's station and its duties. In contemporary affluent societies, however, station in life is largely determined by wealth, and so it can set no limit on one's standard of living. As to the text to which Leo referred, Thomas makes a point which Leo did not explicitly mention: that what one needs to live decently and meet one's responsibilities is not rigidly fixed but somewhat elastic; very often, someone with enough to make do could have considerably more without having an obvious surplus or considerably less without suffering a serious deficiency.

Transposing Thomas's standard to today, one can judge how much wealth one needs by considering all one's responsibilities, which are specified by one's personal vocation. In living by this standard, a person can fulfill the obligation indicated by Vatican II—to use even goods which are not superfluous to help the poor—since the limit defining the superfluous remains elastic, and allows what is reasonably considered necessary at one moment to become available the next to meet someone's unanticipated need. Consequently, Church teaching does not approve a standard of living higher than that set by the limit of an individual's personal vocation or a community's mission.[89]

3. Specific Norms to Be Followed in Acquiring Things

Besides the basic norms flowing from the Christian concept of property and the general norm that material goods should be subordinated to the kingdom, there are specific norms for acquiring, using, caring for, and disposing of property. The following norms guide one in acquiring material goods, both as to what to acquire and how to acquire it.

a) **Before acquiring anything, one should consider all the costs.** In many cases, acquiring something is only the beginning of a whole series of costs or further acquisitions. Even if these are easily foreseeable, the tendency is to ignore them and focus exclusively on the prospective benefits of having the thing.

So, before anything is acquired, all the costs and burdens of having, caring for, and using it should be considered, and the impact of all these factors should be measured against the thing's prospective use in meeting genuine needs. For example, offered an appealing free puppy, a family is attracted by the prospective benefits of having it as a pet; consideration also should be given to the cost of dog food, veterinary care, installing a fence, and so on, as well as the time and energy, otherwise available for other uses, which will be used in seeing to the animal's

89. John Paul II, *Sollicitudo rei socialis*, 31, *AAS* 80 (1988) 555, *OR*, 29 Feb. 1988, 8, teaches: "Thus, part of the *teaching* and most ancient *practice* of the Church is her conviction that she is obliged by her vocation—she herself, her ministers and each of her members—to relieve the misery of the suffering, both far and near, not only out of her 'abundance' but also out of her 'necessities'. Faced by cases of need, one cannot ignore them in favour of superfluous church ornaments and costly furnishings for divine worship; on the contrary it could be obligatory to sell these goods in order to provide food, drink, clothing and shelter for those who lack these things." A note refers to St. John Chrysostom, St. Ambrose, and Possidius.

needs. One also should consider whether one will be satisfied with the thing itself, or whether acquiring it will make one want still other things. For example, someone who buys a television set may need to subscribe to a cable service, probably will "need" a video cassette recorder, and then will "need" to rent or buy movies, and so on.

b) **In acquiring things one should consider ownership responsibility.** Since owning anything entails responsibility for its right use, not only by its owner but by others who might benefit from using it, nothing should be acquired unless one expects to be able to use it fully to meet legitimate needs or see to its right use. That responsibility can be fulfilled in various ways. In some cases, where there is a choice between acquiring something and borrowing or renting it to serve a temporary or occasional need, borrowing or renting should be preferred. In other cases, where it seems best to acquire something, its potential future use by others should be taken into account. In building a house, for example, one should try to make it serviceable for future occupants; in other words, its marketability should be considered, even if one does not expect to sell the house. Again, in purchasing clothing which one will not completely wear out, extremes of style should be avoided for the benefit of someone who will use it as secondhand clothing.

c) **In choosing things, one should take side effects into account.** Having and using anything will have various sorts of foreseeable side effects, and these should be considered in judging whether to acquire it. Among the side effects are those affecting the environment. Will using this fertilizer or automobile have a more serious environmental impact than using that one? Will a pet be a nuisance to neighbors, or will a noisy appliance disturb them? Even more important are moral side effects. Will having or using the thing be an occasion of sin? Will it scandalize others? Even if consumption is justified, conspicuous consumption should be avoided. Those things should be preferred which manifest Christian detachment and cannot reasonably be expected to arouse others' avarice or envy.

d) **One should prefer the simpler even if it is not cheaper.** Because mass production and mass marketing provide economies of scale, it may happen that, among material goods which differ little in price and would meet the same need equally well, one is simpler, involving fewer natural resources and less energy to produce. The temptation then may be to choose the more complex product, which typically promises to satisfy some additional desires, although it will not better serve any purpose in fulfilling vocation and carrying out mission.

In such cases, Christians should resist the temptation and prefer the simpler product, for they practice conservation by doing so. Moreover, by preferring the simpler way of meeting their authentic needs, they act on Jesus' norm—to give up possessions—and bear witness to their primary allegiance to God. Finally, preferring the simpler product, if it happens often enough, will tend to undermine the structures of the consumerist economy, by reducing the market for more complex products and encouraging more efficient production and better distribution of simpler goods.

e) **It can be better to gather, beg, or borrow than to buy or rent.** Many people in affluent societies feel that the only proper way to acquire things is by buying or renting them. However, the Christian principle of the universal destination of goods and the basic norms calling for shared use and conservation can favor gathering, begging, and borrowing.

Gathering is simply taking things which can be used and which no one owns or owners plainly have left for the taking; of course, due care must be exercised not to violate just property claims. In rural areas, food and fuel sometimes can be gathered from uncared for fields, streams, and forests; in urban areas, useful things often can be gathered from what others discard; employers sometimes allow employees to take leftovers, scrap, and other things which otherwise would be wasted. Gathering is a way of practicing conservation and it also saves money which can be put to other uses.

Begging and borrowing obtain from owners the gift or gratuitous use of things they can spare; of course, beggars and borrowers may not exaggerate their needs or falsely suggest that they lack resources to meet them. The beggar or borrower will find it easy to remember that all material goods are God's gifts to the whole of humankind, and so will be disposed to humility. Owners who respond favorably are helped to fulfill their responsibility to put their property to good use. Beggars and borrowers should show gratitude to benefactors, repaying material goods with spiritual ones. In this way, interpersonal communion grows more easily than it does between buyers and sellers. Members of a parish or neighbors could facilitate borrowing by cooperating in maintaining a catalogue of possessions which they are prepared to lend to one another.

f) In buying, shopping should be carefully planned. In affluent societies, many merchants and retail complexes promote shopping as a pastime, doing everything possible to stimulate shoppers' desires to buy. However, shopping as entertainment and impulse buying violate the Christian standard: a person should acquire only what is needed to fulfill his or her responsibilities. Therefore, insofar as possible, one should plan one's shopping, using advertising only as a source of factual information while resisting its persuasions. Genuine needs should be articulated as clearly as possible, products should be studied to discern how well they will meet those needs, and decisions should be based on real value for price, not on the superficial appeal of transient fashion or new style.

g) In borrowing money, future responsibilities should be taken into account. Plainly, it is always wrong to borrow money for uses which are not in themselves morally good. Therefore, money never may be borrowed for uses that are merely emotionally motivated, for example, to indulge unreasonable appetites or seek illusory self-fulfillment in possessions. Some families go heavily into debt in this way, with the bad result that both parents unnecessarily work outside the home, while leaving the care of their small children to others or leaving somewhat older children without the guidance and supervision they need.

Moreover, even when the use of the money would be morally good in itself, prospective borrowers should consider how the burden of repaying a debt will affect their ability to fulfill other responsibilities. For the most part, people whose incomes will not increase greatly during the period of a loan do better to avoid using part of their limited income to pay interest. Owing money also limits the ability to help others in need and to respond to new elements of one's vocation which might emerge. Therefore, borrowing which is not required to fulfill urgent responsibilities usually is unreasonable.

Many merchants and banks promote borrowing, veiling its cost by encouraging the use of charge accounts and credit cards, while emphasizing how small a payment is required to carry the balance from month to month. Actually, however, this involves borrowing money at rather high rates of interest. Most such borrowing can and should be avoided by prudent saving to provide for necessities and by self-restraint in forgoing unnecessary goods and services.

Still, provided one borrows to achieve a reasonable purpose and foresees that repaying the debt will not stand in the way of meeting other responsibilities, borrowing can be justified, for example, by a young person to obtain the education needed to fulfill his or her personal vocation or by a family to obtain a home.

4. Specific Norms about Caring for Material Goods

Time, effort, and resources should be devoted to caring for one's property and money in proportion to their true value. The value of material goods should be judged in reference not only to oneself and one's dependents, but to others as well.

a) Due care should be given to material goods. Some people, including some who are poor, fail to care for their property and money. They waste food and other consumables; neglect necessary maintenance of their homes, automobiles, and other equipment; damage and ruin things by careless use and avoidable accidents; regularly lose money and other valuables, or carelessly allow them to be stolen; and so on. The wealthy for their part often are prodigal, selfishly disregarding the inherent worth of material goods and their responsibilities to others.

People are especially prone to neglect things which they do not themselves need, no longer want, or plan to dispose of. They ignore their responsibility to other potential users or future owners. Many also are careless with things which are not their private property: public or community property, an employer's equipment and supplies, a rented dwelling or automobile, and so on. They selfishly disregard others' rights in this way, needlessly increasing their costs or impeding their potential benefits from using the things.

The basic norms concerning shared use and conservation require that all material goods receive due care. People should take the trouble to know how to care properly for things, disciplining themselves to make the necessary effort. Poor people who do not do this often fail seriously in their responsibilities to care for themselves and their dependents. Others also should be considered: potential or future users of things one does not need or plans to dispose of, fellow users of public or community property, owners and future users of things one rents and borrows, all those who must share the costs of employees' wastefulness, and so on. One seldom knows such people or experiences the effects of one's behavior upon them; but whether they are considered or ignored, they too are one's neighbors.

b) Excessive care should not be lavished on material goods. Some people put so much time, effort, and resources into caring for their property and money that they neglect other responsibilities, impede other people from making reasonable use of their things, or even fail to make good use of the things on which they lavish so much care. In some cases, excessive care for material goods shows inordinate attachment to them; in others, it manifests perfectionism, which may be more a psychological than a moral problem. In any case, the underlying problem should be addressed, and instrumental goods such as property and money should be subordinated to intrinsic human goods. Things should not receive so much care that genuine interpersonal communion or proper care for oneself is neglected.

c) **One should protect others' interests in family property.** People often hold legal title to things—real property, investments, insurance policies, and so on—which, morally, belong not to them individually but to their marital community or family as a whole. They should do what is legally necessary to protect other family members' interests in such property, so that, for example, inheritance and tax laws will not adversely affect those interests. Usually that requires that adults make a last will and testament or establish a trust, and review it periodically; often, too, executors, trustees, beneficiaries of insurance policies, and so on should be named. In all these matters, a person should take the care necessary to be morally certain that the provisions he or she makes are sound and legally effective. One's responsibilities to all the persons involved should be honored, without favoritism or antagonism toward any.

Of course, not everything one controls is automatically family property or should be given to family members when one dies. For example, in an affluent society offering many economic opportunities, parents, having helped their children get a start in life, might rightly judge that their remaining goods are not family property. Someone who conscientiously concludes that family members are not morally entitled to part or all of the things at his or her disposal should consider other just claims, such as the needs of the poor.

5. Specific Norms for Seeing to the Use of Material Goods

The following norms guide one in using material goods and administering them for others' use. Some special cases of using money will be treated separately below: insurance and savings (in 6) and gambling (in 7).

Two relevant norms require no further explanation: one should use material goods to meet one's own genuine needs and those of one's dependents, and one never should use anything in any immoral action.

a) **One should try to use things as fully as possible.** Affluent people often use things inefficiently, not only by neglecting to care for them and being careless in using them, both of which lead to waste, but by having available more than they need and/or using things only partially, then discarding them without regard to their remaining potential utility. For example, many people throw away large amounts of leftover food and discard clothing which is far from worn out; but the basic norm concerning conservation implies trying to use things efficiently by carefully limiting what one prepares for use and attempting to realize the full potential utility of anything one owns.

That does not mean the owners themselves always should realize the full potential utility. Very often, things partly used no longer serve their owners' purposes, but can meet others' needs. In such cases, owners should not throw things away, thinking only of their own convenience, but should take the trouble to sell or give the things they no longer need to someone who can use them.

Of course, there is a point at which it becomes wasteful to try to avoid waste: squeezing the last bit of toothpaste from the tube can take more time than it is worth. Sometimes, too, even though others might put something to use, it would be wasteful to go to the trouble of finding those potential users.

b) Using one's property to meet others' needs often is obligatory. Just as owners should use their money and consumable goods to meet their own needs and those of their dependents, they also should use these things to meet others' needs.[90] As has been explained, this responsibility sometimes binds gravely in strict justice. That certainly is so in a situation treated by classical Catholic moral theology: when an owner with superfluous goods can use them to meet someone's urgent and grave needs. However, as explained above (in 2.c), the obligation sometimes goes further, since the concepts of the superfluous and of needs are somewhat elastic.

Admittedly, individuals and families cannot by themselves overcome unjust economic structures, so that oftentimes there is no practical way to help those in urgent need by forgoing something here and now. Sometimes, however, the alternative of using property to meet others' needs is available. No very specific norm can be articulated to guide choices in such cases. Rather, one should recall Jesus' teaching about wealth, including the lesson of the parable of Dives and Lazarus (Lk 16.19–31; cf. GS 27, 64); one should recall too how Jesus identifies with those in need, and the consequences for those who do not succor him in the poor: " 'Just as you did not do it to one of the least of these, you did not do it to me.' And these will go away into eternal punishment" (Mt 25.45–46). One should bear in mind the universal destination of goods and the basic norm requiring owners to use their goods to meet not only their own and their dependents' needs but those of others. One should consider what others can do to meet their own needs, what is likely to be done by third parties, what one can do oneself, and all other relevant circumstances. Then one should apply the Golden Rule.

In doing so, it is right to take into account the priority which one's responsibility for dependents enjoys. But the temptation to make a virtually absolute presumption against others' claims must be resisted. That plainly is discriminatory, since goods are no less suitably used to meet *their* (outsiders') needs than *ours* (one's own and one's dependents'). The issue calling for discernment is how an upright and disinterested person, such as Jesus, would evaluate competing claims: for example, a famine victim's need for food and one's own need for foods and beverages beyond a well-balanced and healthful diet, third-world children's need for education and one's own children's need for the latest toys and electronic equipment, a pagan community's need to hear the gospel and a Christian community's need for a grand celebration on the occasion of a new bishop's installation.

---

90. Having stated the obligation of the faithful to support the Church, *CIC*, c. 222, §2, adds: "They are also obliged to promote social justice and, mindful of the precept of the Lord, to assist the poor from their own resources."

c) **Several factors should be considered in making this judgment.** In evaluating competing claims, differences in kinds of needs and in each need's urgency obviously should be considered. So should the question of whether there are alternative ways of meeting a need. The duty to honor a claim for help is greater if one is uniquely equipped to do so or if it is unlikely that anyone else will. (It is irrelevant to one's own responsibility that others who will not meet the need should do so.) Again, needs due to some sin or defect of a community to which one belongs (for example, misery in a region one's own nation has devastated by unjust military action) deserve special consideration even if in no way one's own fault (one did what one could to prevent the injustice).

A Christian also should consider how serving (and not serving) each need would affect all those involved, not only as individuals or distinct groups, but as interrelated members of the one body of Christ. Therefore, the order of charity must be taken into account: other things being equal, the claims of those with whom one has special and more intimate bonds—relatives, friends, members of the local community, and so on—are rightly preferred (see *S.t.,* 2–2, q. 32, a. 9; 6.A.1.f).

Someone willing and able to meet others' needs quickly finds that there are too many potential beneficiaries, for example, too many starving people in the world. Clear needs take priority over questionable ones, but often it is not feasible to try to determine whose needs take precedence, and one may do what one can to help those whose clear needs come to one's attention. For this reason, the needy person in one's path seems to have a special claim.

> In our times, the obligation is pressing to make ourselves the neighbor of absolutely every person, and of actively helping others when they come across our path, whether they be [in need in various other ways] or the hungry who disturb our conscience by recalling the voice of the Lord: "Just as you did it to one of the least of these who are members of my family, you did it to me" (Mt 25.40). (GS 27)

Modern means of communication bring many needy people across one's path, however. Here also it is necessary to appeal to the principle that clear needs take priority. Thus, a reputable relief agency working to improve agricultural methods so as to mitigate recurrent famines in a far-off land has a better claim on one's resources than do many people who personally seek one's help.

d) **One should resist rationalizing evasions of this obligation.** Even if someone does all he or she can to meet others' needs, human misery as a whole is reduced only infinitesimally. If the intractable mass of human poverty is regarded as a problem calling for a solution, it becomes clear that any solution would require, not just that individuals use their money and goods to meet others' needs, but that nations create a new social and economic order which would eliminate unjust structures and establish, everywhere in the world, programs to deal with poverty more effective than those now in operation anywhere.

Then too, some proponents of radical change argue that traditional ways of trying to meet people's urgent needs are only anodynes, which do more harm than good by hiding the need for radical social changes and impeding effective action to bring them about. Some of these people use all their time, energy, and resources in serious efforts to promote radical social change, and are prepared to lay down their lives in that cause. Insofar as they hunger and thirst for justice, they must be respected, whether or not one judges their ideology and methods sound. One also must be prepared to cooperate in using every morally acceptable means to mitigate or overcome structural injustices which lead to human misery.

It can happen, however, that, their social consciousness having been raised, affluent people and communities, including churches and church groups, find thinking about poverty as a vast problem and talking about the radical changes needed to solve it an attractive alternative to using their wealth to meet others' needs. Catholics who live very comfortably can employ the Church's social doctrine to sketch out magnificent plans for economic justice, verbally support public programs to implement those plans, condemn the selfishness of people who prevent their implementation, and think themselves more righteous than others who seem to lack social conscience and care only about personal salvation.

These are evasions of the obligation in strict justice to use one's wealth to meet others' needs. For an individual to fulfill this obligation will neither change the world nor solve the problem of poverty, but it will make a difference to each person he or she helps—a real person whose real misery really will be mitigated. Even though the mass of human misery will be reduced only infinitesimally, that will be of immeasurable value because of the immeasurable dignity of each person whose need is met. Moreover, fulfilling the obligation will prepare material for the heavenly kingdom (in which alone human misery will be definitively overcome) and will allow a Christian to have a social conscience without belittling anyone else's concern about personal salvation. Finally, Christians who use their wealth to meet others' needs bear credible witness to the gospel—witness which might contribute to effective political action to implement plans for the economic justice which the Church's social doctrine calls for.[91]

e) **Mercy calls Christians to do more than justice requires.** Although, other things being equal, responsibility for one's dependents requires satisfying their needs before others', Christian mercy, the justice of the kingdom, urges doing what can be done to satisfy others' needs rather than one's own. Such self-sacrifice contributes to Jesus' redemptive work of building up the kingdom, not only by its witness value but by overcoming the alienation which sin causes and so promoting interpersonal communion. Therefore, when only the claims of legitimate self-

---

91. See John Paul II, *Sollicitudo rei socialis,* 38, *AAS* 80 (1988) 564–66, *OR,* 29 Feb. 1988, 10. A Protestant theologian, Ronald J. Sider, "A Biblical Perspective on Stewardship," in *The Earth Is the Lord's: Essays on Stewardship,* ed. Mary Evelyn Jegen, S.N.D., and Bruno V. Manno, S.M. (New York: Paulist Press, 1978), 18–19, points out the necessary relationship between committed witness and political action: "Central to any Christian strategy on world hunger must be a radical call for the Church to be the Church. One of the most glaring weaknesses of the churches' social action in the past few decades is that the Church concentrated too exclusively on political solutions. In effect, Church leaders tried to persuade government to legislate what they could not persuade their Church members to live. And politicians quickly sensed that the daring declarations and frequent Washington delegations represented generals without troops. Only if the body of Christ is already beginning to live a radically new model of economic sharing will our demand for political change have integrity and impact."

interest are at stake, a Christian should make a strong presumption in favor of others' claims. For example, provided other responsibilities do not argue against self-sacrifice, someone in a situation of common, extreme, life-threatening need, rather than claiming his or her rightful share of the goods and opportunities required for survival, rightly gives up that share so that someone else might survive.

f) Some are called to administer material things for others' use. Sometimes, although its owners could give away property or money, they have such a gift for administering material goods that they should accept that as an element of their personal vocation. For example, people with both surplus wealth and skill in management can rightly set up or invest in businesses which provide just wages for gainful work and useful goods and services at fair prices, along with enough profit to compensate them reasonably for their work, which contributes to society's economic common good.[92] It is wrong to allow one's resources to remain unproductive when they could be put to work contributing to the economic development of one's community (see GS 65).

g) Sometimes owners should not reclaim property which had been stolen from them. Thieves and dishonest merchants often sell stolen property to innocent third parties. Both the original owner and the person who acquired it in good faith then seem to have a claim to it. The classical moralists, regarding ownership as a moral bond which endures when property is taken against an owner's just will, held that the possessor in good faith has no moral claim to property identified as stolen, and so must return it (or what remains of it) to the original owner.

The legal provisions of property systems generally seem to reflect the same view, although perhaps they are shaped in part by other considerations: the good faith of someone possessing stolen property often is hard to prove or disprove, and the rule excluding the claim of one who possesses in good faith discourages theft by making people careful not to acquire stolen property.

Unless the contrary is more probable, those who find themselves possessing stolen property should assume that relevant legal provisions are just and should conform to them.

If it is clear that the possessor really was in good faith, however, it may be that the original owner should not reclaim the property. Since the right of ownership is subordinate to the universal destination of material goods, the need of both—original owner and possessor in good faith—should be considered. Both were victimized; the harm each stands to suffer is relevant in judging what resolution will be fair. Sometimes the original owner can easily yield part or all of stolen property which is greatly needed by the possessor in good faith. Therefore, owners sometimes should forgo all or part of their legal right to reclaim stolen property.

h) The use of common property should be shared fairly. Members of families and other communities with property in common should be considerate of one another in using it. If one or several treat an item as their individual property, others are blocked from enjoying their fair share of its use. For example, one child refuses to allow others to take their turn playing with a toy; while others wait,

---

92. See Pius XI, *Quadragesimo anno, AAS* 23 (1931) 194 and 222, *PE,* 209.51 and 209.136.

someone uses a public restroom for reading; in a crowded picnic area, one small family occupies two tables; ignoring recall notices, a professor who is not subject to fines keeps books borrowed from the university library.

Often, such unfairness not only gravely violates others' rights but leads to serious tensions. An especially odious form occurs when someone retains continuous possession of something which he or she needs only occasionally or temporarily, thus requiring other members of the community to beg for its return to common use—a reasonable request all too often met with hostility.

i) **One should attend to the side effects of using things.** Rather often, a use otherwise morally acceptable becomes wrong because it leads to side effects which should not be accepted. Some are morally significant directly and in themselves: using something may be an occasion of sin for oneself or may scandalize others. Such side effects will not be overlooked by anyone seriously trying to live a Christian life. Others harm oneself—for example, smoking is bad for the smoker's health—or other persons.

Where the impact is on others, the question is whether the harm can be accepted fairly. For example, using amplifiers and speakers to play music can disturb others who do not wish to be disturbed; using poisons around the house and garden can endanger neighbors' children and pets; using gasoline and electricity usually has a negative environmental impact. Sometimes the use is fair despite the side effects, and other times the activity can be modified to prevent or sufficiently mitigate them; but sometimes one should forgo the use to avoid them.

In considering the fairness of accepting side effects, relevant circumstances must be taken into account. Although, to avoid severe environmental damage, some things should no longer be manufactured or brought into use, the cost of replacing similar things already in use may warrant continuing to accept their bad effects on the environment. Again, because poor individuals and societies have fewer alternatives, they may rightly accept side effects wrong for the wealthy to accept. Thus, the affluent should willingly accept greater burdens in preventing and correcting pollution, rather than favoring measures which overburden the poor by imposing identical burdens on rich and poor alike.

6. Specific Norms for Saving and Insuring

Saving and insuring are ways of preparing to meet future needs, and even though some insurance contracts include substantial elements of saving, the two differ in principle. Saving is suited to meet needs which are certain or very probable; insuring is suited to meet needs which might result from an unpredictable but serious loss. Although Jesus' teaching about wealth in the Sermon on the Mount might seem to exclude both (see Mt 6.19–34), at times they plainly are necessary to meet serious responsibilities. Thus, Catholic tradition and current exegesis uniformly interpret Jesus' teaching as not entirely excluding saving and insuring, but as warning Christians against seeking security and happiness by such means rather than looking to God for them (see *S.t.,* 1–2, q. 108, a. 3, ad 5; 2–2, q. 55, a. 7). Trusting God, Christians should be free of the anxiety which leads to miserliness and an endless quest for so-called financial security.

a) Solidarity should limit the need for saving and insuring. Much of the need for saving and insuring results from the institutionalization of individualism and non-Christian attitudes about property. In this matter as in others, Christians should try to increase family and community solidarity, which would limit the need for saving and insuring. Nevertheless, prevailing attitudes shape the property system and social programs in various ways, for example, by providing or not providing tax advantages for certain ways of meeting needs, requiring various kinds of insurance, and so on. Such provisions affect the options open to every reasonable person and family. Therefore, even where family and community bonds are strong, Christians today rightly save and insure more extensively than would be justifiable in a less individualistic society.[93]

b) In saving and insuring, one should consider every responsibility. People who are very poor need make no decisions about saving and insuring, because they must use everything available to meet urgent present needs. People who are neither poor nor wealthy must consider their responsibilities to meet their own and their dependents' needs, both at present and for the foreseeable future. They should save and insure insofar as future needs demand and present responsibilities permit. People who can meet their own and their dependents' present and future needs should consider their responsibility to others, especially the poor whose present needs are urgent, and should strike a just and merciful balance.

c) One should save and insure reasonably to meet future needs. It is not uncommon for people who are not poor and may even be wealthy to ignore future needs. Their attachment to material goods has less to do with anxiety and the quest for illusory security than with desires for immediate satisfactions and/or a quest for illusory self-fulfillment in having things, and they may spend all their available funds, and even go deeply into debt, indulging their fancies (see *S.t.*, 2–2, q. 119). Such people have no savings and little or no insurance beyond what the law or the conditions of their employment require. They make no provision to meet predictable needs; and their unfulfilled responsibilities wrongly deprive others of what is due them or shift the burden of meeting needs to society at large.

Plainly, unreasonable self-indulgence should yield to reasonable provision to meet future needs. Moreover, sometimes the less well-to-do should forgo even some current spending which would be justifiable in itself in order to provide for more important future needs. For example, young people usually should save to establish themselves, parents to educate their children, and working people to support themselves after retirement. A father of small children usually should carry the life insurance necessary to provide for their care should he die. Again, the

---

93. John Paul II, *Centesimus annus*, 49, *AAS* 83 (1991) 855, *OR*, 6 May 1991, 14, points out: "In order to overcome today's widespread individualistic mentality, what is required is *a concrete commitment to solidarity and charity*, beginning in the family with the mutual support of husband and wife and the care which the different generations give to one another. In this sense the family too can be called a community of work and solidarity. It can happen, however, that when a family does decide to live up fully to its vocation, it finds itself without the necessary support from the State and without sufficient resources." He draws the conclusion that it is urgent to promote family-oriented public policies.

possibility of causing others some serious, inadvertent harm usually requires that one carry liability insurance, both to protect assets needed to meet other responsibilities and to fulfill the possible responsibility to those whom one might harm.

d) The affluent should avoid excessive saving and insuring. Future needs always are more or less uncertain and open-ended; it is reasonable to provide for them only within limits, rather than trying to save enough to meet every possible need and trying to insure against every possible loss. As St. Thomas teaches: "One should not consider every case that might possibly occur in the future, for this would be to think about the morrow, which our Lord forbade (Mt 6.34), but one should judge what is superfluous and what is necessary according as things probably and usually occur" (*S.t.*, 2–2, q. 32, a. 5, ad 3). Due to the anxiety and attachment to material goods against which Jesus warned, however, affluent people are tempted to the miserliness of excessive saving and the self-indulgence of wasteful insuring. Those who succumb to this twofold temptation never think they have any surplus.

Sometimes, like the rich fool in Jesus' parable (see Lk 12.13–21), the affluent hoard goods, depriving others of what they themselves never will need. When investing savings, they often consider only safety and yield; otherwise, they are unconcerned about the use to which their capital is put, or perhaps even prefer to invest in businesses which maximize profits by exploiting employees and/or pandering to people's sinfulness. In buying insurance, instead of limiting coverage to an amount they conscientiously judge necessary to fulfill serious responsibilities, they may instead seek illusory protection against the inevitable. For example, in buying life insurance, a man may not be rationally motivated by an intention to provide for his dependents but irrationally motivated by fear of death itself, which no amount of insurance can prevent or undo.

e) One should consider the use to which invested money will be put. In investing savings, one must consider potential return and be careful about safety, so as to serve the purpose which justifies using the money in this way rather than in meeting someone's more or less urgent present needs. However, one also should try to avoid turning over the management of one's savings to people who will use them in unjust or otherwise immoral activities, and should try instead to invest in something morally acceptable. Of course, an individual's responsibility is limited by his or her ability to know about alternative possibilities and to choose reasonably among them. Moreover, as in other aspects of investing, one should not be too trusting in this matter, for while certain investment vehicles are advertised as "socially responsible," the notion of social responsibility here may not reflect a judgment conformed to Christian principles.

f) One should be honest and fair in insurance matters. Dishonesty and carelessness on the part of those insured directly harms insurers, but indirectly harms all buyers of similar insurance, to whom this cost of doing business eventually will be passed on.

Because insurance is intended to cover unpredictable losses, it is unfair to deceive a potential insurer about foreseen risks. So, in applying for any kind of insurance, one should answer questions honestly. Having obtained insurance, one should not be negligent, so that the likelihood of the loss insured against is markedly increased, but instead should make every reasonable effort to avoid or minimize that loss. In making any claim, a person rightly seeks every benefit to which he or she is entitled under the insurance contract, without exaggerating the loss or lying about relevant facts in order to obtain a larger settlement.

7. Gambling Can Be Reasonable but Often Is an Abuse of Property

While someone can have a morally acceptable reason to gamble, gambling is often wrong, especially when the stake is large.

a) **Gambling is specified by the gambler's intention.** Like some investing or insuring, gambling is an agreement between two or more parties in which at least one of them puts a sum of money or some other good at risk with the expectation, contingent on a future event, of either gaining more or losing the stake. Gambling differs from the responsible investment of savings to meet a foreseen future need in that gamblers do not accept a risk of loss as a side effect of making provision for the future but choose to take a risk for the sake of the gain they expect if they win. Similarly, using insurance as the vehicle for gambling, by staking its cost on the chance of a profit if the event insured against occurs, differs from responsible insuring in that gamblers do not pay to provide against some unavoidable risk but choose to risk the cost of the insurance for the sake of the anticipated gain.

Because the difference between investing or insuring and gambling sometimes is nothing more than the volition shaping the acts, the behavior usually character-istic of investing or insuring can carry out a desire to gamble, and so can be gambling from a moral point of view. Still, the property system and social conventions classify only those specific forms of behavior as gambling which usually serve that purpose.

b) **Gambling can enhance other rationally justified activities.** Gambling on a game one is playing, a sporting event one is observing, or something else in which one is involved can intensify interest and participation, thus making one's involve-ment deeper and more gratifying. If the activity constitutes good recreation, there can be a reason to seek that deeper involvement and enjoyment. Hence, if the gambling is not otherwise wrong, it can be justified for this reason. For example, provided they violate no law, wager modest amounts consistent with their other responsibilities, and avoid both addiction and scandal, friends competing in games of skill may bet on their performance, and co-workers or neighbors may operate a pool to wager against one another in predicting the winners of sporting events in which they are interested. When, as in these examples, the gamblers are friends or members of a community who fairly share the risks and rewards, such morally innocent gambling often also contributes to their interpersonal relationships.

c) **Gambling can contribute to psychological well-being.** The excitement of gambling can contribute to psychological well-being, not only when it enhances another rationally justified activity but even when engaged in by itself. For example, playing bingo sometimes helps elderly, retarded, or debilitated people to overcome their lethargy; a game of chance can be a welcome distraction for a family awaiting the resolution of some unusually tense situation. In such cases, too, gambling can have a valuable social dimension.

d) A gambling contract can be a vehicle for other good purposes. In certain circumstances, a gambling contract could be a morally acceptable investment vehicle. For example, a poor working-family, able to provide for current needs but unable to save significantly for the children's education or for retirement, might spend a small amount each week on a ticket in a state-run lottery, not choosing the high risk of losing, but only accepting it in the hope of winning enough to meet some of their future needs. For them, the lottery is a very high-risk investment, since no other investment they can make will serve their legitimate purpose.

A raffle or lottery also can be a means of donating to and raising funds for a church or charitable organization, or some other worthy purpose, private or public. However, to avoid scandal (in the strict sense defined in 4.E.2.a), churches and other organizations should not sponsor gambling which is forbidden by just laws or legal gambling in which participants risk significant amounts, for such gambling is very likely to lead many people into sin.

e) In gambling, one should not take unfair advantage of others. Experienced gamblers sometimes take unfair advantage by enticing people to compete in games at which they are unskilled. Moreover, gambling often involves outright fraud. People not uncommonly imagine that dishonesty somehow is justifiable when linked to gambling, perhaps because it is so widespread, or because its victims suffer it patiently, or because gambling is thought of as recreation rather than as serious business. However, lying never is justifiable.

Fraud, of course, must be distinguished from the bluffing and deception allowed by the rules of some games and mutually accepted as fair play by all participants (see 7.B.6.d).

f) Gambling motivated entirely by emotion is always wrong. Because of the element of risk and the prospect of gain, gambling always is exciting and sometimes emotionally satisfying, so that many people experience some emotional desire to gamble. However, there always is a reason not to gamble: other possible good uses for what is staked, such as meeting the needs of the poor and productive investment. Therefore, unless motivated by some reason grounded in an intelligible human good, gambling is always wrong.

While gambling motivated by emotion alone is in itself only light matter, the emotional motivation tends to lead those who indulge in it to become addicted. Thus, some people not only gamble without a justifying reason but do so despite grave consequences for themselves and/or their dependents. But even if people who gamble without a justifying reason do not become addicted and do no material harm to anyone, their action, even if not gravely wrong in itself, is likely to give scandal, by bad example or by cooperation, to people whose gambling is gravely wrong. Therefore, the obligation not to gamble without a justifying reason always is serious and often a grave matter.

g) Gambling a stake which should be used otherwise is wrong. Addicts often gamble stakes which should be used to meet their own or their dependents' needs, to pay just debts, or to help the poor. Often, too, gambling leads affluent people, including some not addicted to it, self-indulgently to waste assets which should be given to the poor or invested in enterprises promoting the common good. Since such gambling is likely to lead to—or actually involves—significant injustice, the matter is grave.

People with a good reason to save often wrongly gamble by choosing a riskier investment than necessary. Although the added risk is not necessary to obtain the return their good purpose requires, they give in to greed and court disaster. Quite often, too, people playing the markets use investment contracts as vehicles for gambling with large amounts of money which should be employed otherwise, for example, as capital for a worthwhile enterprise. Moreover, using investment contracts for gambling impedes the attainment of their morally good and necessary end by distorting markets and contributing to economic instability. Therefore, this form of gambling involves an especially grave social and economic evil.

h) Illegal gambling is almost always wrong. Much gambling is illegal. The general presumption that laws are just and must be obeyed (see 11.D.4.a) is hard to overcome in the case of laws against gambling, which in itself often is morally wrong and seldom a moral duty. Participating in gambling organized by racketeers is likely to scandalize the weak by bad example and those who organize it by cooperation. The illegal gambler should foresee these evils, cannot ascertain that they will be slight, and so should presume that they will be grave. Therefore, illegal gambling is wrong unless one is morally certain—which is very unlikely—that the relevant law is unjust or inapplicable, and participating in gambling organized by racketeers is grave matter.

8. Specific Norms for Disposing of Unneeded Property

Owners often dispose of property which they no longer need by selling it or bartering it for something they can use. Disposing of property in that way is a transaction, and transactions will be treated (in G). Also, as explained above (in 5.a), owners should consider others' needs before discarding anything which still might be useful. Here it remains to consider only those cases in which the owner does not need something, and nobody else can use it or, at least, trying to make it available to someone who could use it would be wasteful.

a) Sometimes one should keep things nobody currently needs. While people generally tend to throw away something when they do not foresee that preserving it will benefit themselves or someone they especially care about, they ought not to be too hasty. Instead, they should consider the possibility that things entirely useless now will be useful at some time in the future, evaluate their responsibility toward those who might then benefit, and make reasonable efforts to provide for possible future use. For example, before disposing of photographs, papers, and records, one should consider their possible historical value, if only for one's descendants. In some cases, a person can provide for possible future use of such things by donating them to a museum or library.

b) When feasible, parts should be salvaged and materials recycled. When owners judge that something considered as a whole has no current or potential future utility worth preserving, they should consider the potential utility of its parts or materials. Practicing conservation, a person should consider it better that a totally wrecked automobile be dismantled for its parts and melted down as scrap steel than allowed to rust away; when reasonably convenient, leaves should be used for compost instead of being burned; and so on. Public and private agencies, including some businesses, carry on mandatory or voluntary recycling programs, and these should be given the benefit of the doubt: one should participate in them unless it is counterproductive or too burdensome to do so.

c) **Useless things should be disposed of carefully.** When items of property not only are entirely useless but are in some way burdensome to keep, owners are tempted to consider only their own interests in disposing of them, and thus to solve the problem in the way least costly and most convenient for themselves. But what is cheap and easy for the owner often imposes burdens and costs on others. To some extent, governments try to limit these bad effects by laws against littering, dumping trash on vacant land, pouring engine oil into sewers, and so forth. Because such laws serve an important purpose, they should be obeyed, unless, of course, they are unjust or inapplicable. But owners disposing of useless things should go beyond the letter of relevant laws to consider what burden their action would impose on others and whether that burden can fairly be imposed. If not, they should either find a better alternative or arrange fair compensation for those affected. For ownership continues to entail responsibilities even when property has become entirely useless and burdensome.

Question F: What Are One's Responsibilities as to Others' Property?

Others here refers to other individuals, families, businesses, or communities of which one is not a member. One should borrow others' property responsibly, respect their property rights, and help them fulfill their property responsibilities. Not only outward sins but sins of thought bearing on material goods should be avoided.

1. One Should Help Others in Matters of Property

Others should be helped both to meet their responsibilities as owners and to protect, use, and care for their property.

a) **One should encourage others to be reasonable about property.** Injustice and lack of mercy about property are widespread; and in affluent societies owners often fail to grasp all that justice toward those in need requires of them. By word and example, a person should help others understand and fulfill their responsibilities in matters of property. Jesus does teach that his followers should avoid hypocritical display in giving alms (see Mt 6.2–4). Nevertheless, he also teaches that they should allow the light of their good works to shine for others' edification and God's glory (see Mt 5.14–16). Consequently, false modesty should not inhibit one's effective witness to the requirement of justice that owners use their property fairly to meet others' needs.

Sometimes Christians not only fail to encourage sound attitudes about property but even encourage unsound ones. Indeed, those who wish to sell things often do this deliberately by arousing and nurturing merely emotional motives in potential buyers so that they waste money which should be put to other uses.

Moreover, in a consumerist society, people often show great interest in others' property, commend them for it, praise its good features, and so on; while proud owners often display their wealth and glory in it, soliciting appreciation from friends and acquaintances. These practices may manifest good intentions of friendliness and sociability, but one should be cautious about engaging in them, for they may also manifest materialistic attitudes and support the sinful social practice of consumerism.

b) **Others should be helped to acquire and use things well.** This can be done in various ways, especially by providing accurate information and offering sound, disinterested advice. Due to misleading advertising and the variety and complexity of available goods, some people need help to discern the real quality and value of available products and learn how to use and care for things. For example, some purchase computer equipment they never learn to use; but someone experienced with computers and their uses can help others avoid unnecessary purchases and obtain what they truly need, then show them how to set up the equipment and learn to use it.

One may also help owners meet their responsibilities by informing them about others' needs which they might be able to satisfy and encouraging them to consider whether they can and should do so.

c) **Others should be helped to protect and care for property.** Opportunities sometimes arise to help others maintain or protect their property. For example, noticing that an automobile is leaking oil, or that the owner has forgotten to turn the lights out or lock the doors, one may be able to call his or her attention to the matter. Again, someone who notices signs of a fire or a possible burglary at an absent neighbor's home has a strict duty to call the fire department or the police.

d) **Lost property usually should be returned to its owner.** Protecting and returning lost property constitute a special and important case of helping its owner. Plainly, a finder who can return a lost item to its readily identifiable owner without significant trouble should do so. Even if this is not possible, one should make a reasonable effort to prevent other, possibly dishonest finders from stealing a lost item, by taking it into custody or turning it over to appropriate authorities, such as a lost-and-found office or the police.

Finders who fulfill these responsibilities are entitled to nothing more than fair compensation for their trouble and expense. However, owners rightly express their gratitude by rewarding finders who return lost property, and those who promise rewards should keep their word.

When finders have done all they should without locating the owner of lost property, they may consider it their own. What if the original owner subsequently comes to light? If the item is consumable or can wear out, and the finder has used it up or worn it out, the original owner has no claim to compensation. However, if the item remains useful, both the former owner and the finder have some claim to it, which must be resolved by the property system's provisions, if any, and by directly applying the Golden Rule. Again, sharing the item or its value often will be the appropriate resolution.

e) **The duty to return lost property admits of certain exceptions.** If obviously lost property—for example, small change lying on a sidewalk—is of little worth and its ownership would be difficult to determine, the finder may appropriate it. If finders would suffer unfair burdens or risks by returning lost property or safeguarding it, they need do no more than what is fair: what they and other reasonable owners would expect honest finders to do.

When special diligence and risk are needed to recover lost property and its owner declines to attempt recovery, another finder has a reasonable claim to the item; the conditions and limits of such a claim usually are specified by the property system.

Occasionally the finder of a lost item would have been justified in taking it without the permission of its legal owner (see 3.a, below). In such a case, the finder becomes its true owner in taking possession of it.

f) **One should take good care of property entrusted by others.** Someone who agrees to hold others' property in safekeeping, to serve as a guard, to manage investments, or something of the sort, should fulfill that promise just like other promises. It is beside the point whether one is employed to do the service or is doing it gratuitously. In using an employers' tools and materials, a person not only should resist any temptation to express hostile feelings by abusing them but should comply with all reasonable instructions and avoid waste.

2. One Should Not Unfairly Harm Others in Respect to Their Property

Material goods are extrinsic to persons, but serve them; moreover, property often pertains in some way to its owners' bodily reality, insofar as it has been personalized by their use of it. For these reasons, damaging or destroying property or impeding its owner's use and enjoyment of it harms the owner. That harm never should be intended, but sometimes may be accepted as a side effect.

a) **One should not purposely harm others through their property.** Hostile feelings toward others often are related to their property: one envies people their fine possessions or is indignant about their economic domination. Sometimes, however, the cause of hostile feelings is unrelated to property; for example, one's honor is attacked or one's friendship betrayed. In either case, the temptation can arise to try to harm others by damaging or destroying their property, or by impeding their use of it. Even if one has a just grievance, it is always a grave wrong to give in to this temptation, for that involves a will directly contrary to love of neighbor, just like any other act chosen precisely out of malice. Of course, when people act out of petty spite without sufficient reflection and/or consent, as often happens, they do not sin mortally.

b) **One should not purposely harm property without a reason.** Even apart from hostile feelings toward any particular person or group, merely emotional motives such as generalized hostility or mischievousness sometimes tempt people to harm property—to throw stones at passing vehicles, make graffiti, set fire to abandoned buildings, spread destructive computer viruses, and so on. Though no harm may be intended, such behavior always does harm people or, at least, risks harming them, and these bad effects cannot be justified, since the behavior has no rational point. Moreover, those affected seldom are likely to consider the harm insignificant, and so such acts usually are grave matter. Of course, children and immature adults who do such things often lack sufficient reflection.

c) **Others' property should not be harmed unfairly.** It is possible to choose to harm another's property or to do something which incidentally harms it without intending either to harm the owner or acting on a merely emotional motive. A person might kill someone's animal to protect a child, destroy timber to limit a fire, damage an automobile to prevent a criminal's escape, and so on. Of course, if anything else about the act makes it wrong, the property damage cannot be justified; but even if nothing else makes the act wrong, it can be unfair, for instance, if one would pursue the same end differently if one's own property were at stake. Even when there is a reason for deliberately damaging another's property, fairness may require compensation to the owner.

d) **One should be careful not to harm others' property by accident.** While no level of care can exclude accidents entirely, people generally want others to exercise a certain level of care to avoid harming their property, and so are bound in fairness to exercise like care to avoid harming the property of others.

In many circumstances, too, people want compensation from anyone who accidentally harms their property, and so they are bound in fairness to compensate another in similar circumstances for harming his or hers. Unless the damage is minor, it is a grave matter to evade this responsibility, for example, by driving away without leaving a note after negligently damaging someone's parked car.

3. One Should Not Unfairly Take Others' Property

While legal systems typically, and reasonably, define *theft* narrowly, as a moral category it should be understood broadly, so as to include every unfair taking, that is, all appropriation or use of the property of another individual or family, or of any organization or society, contrary to the owner's reasonable will.[94]

"You shall not steal" is one of the Ten Commandments (Ex 20.15; cf. Lv 19.11, 13; Dt 5.19; Jer 7.9–10; Zec 5.3–4). Like the others, it is endorsed by Jesus and presented in New Testament catechesis as an essential requirement of love of neighbor (see Mt 15.19, 19.18; Mk 7.21, 10.19; Lk 18.20; Rom 13.9; 1 Cor 6.10).

a) **Taking and using against a legal owner's will may be justified.** In general, it should be assumed that no property may be taken or used without the legal owner's express consent or, at least, a reasonable presumption of that consent. Still, there are two kinds of cases in which this general assumption can be set aside.

Sometimes epikeia applies (see D.3.d, above). Even though the owner has legal title to the property according to the norms of just law and has not consented to its being taken or used, one's need is grave and urgent, and one is morally certain the lawmaker would have authorized an exception to the law to meet that need. In such a case, the owner should consent to the taking or use of the property required to

---

94. See *Catechismus ex decreto Ss. Concilii Tridentini ad parochos (The Catechism by Decree of the Holy Council of Trent)*, Latin text with trans. by J. Donovan (Rome: 1839), 3.8.5–14 (2:164–74).

meet the need, and so the owner's right is not violated and the necessary taking or using is morally justified (see *S.t.,* 2–2, q. 66, a. 7).

At other times the owner's legal title to the property is morally defective, because granted or sustained by an unjust legal norm. If other relevant conditions are met (see 11.D.3.b–c), the property system's unjust norm may be set aside, and the legal owner's morally groundless claim may be ignored. In this way, even though the need is not grave and urgent enough to justify an exception to a just norm of a property system, the reason may be serious enough to justify ignoring an unjust norm.

Thus, if someone certainly owes one something in strict justice but, relying on the property system's inadequate justice, refuses to render what actually is due, one may stealthily take it.[95] Moreover, in a society whose unjust property system carefully protects the rights of powerful owners while ignoring the basic needs of the powerless, with the bad result that the wealthy live luxuriously while the poor, even with parsimony and hard work, cannot meet all their basic needs, the poor can be morally justified in using or taking what legally belongs to the wealthy, not just to survive, but to meet any genuine need which cannot otherwise be met. (*Genuine need* was clarified in E.1.b, above.)

Of course, no one ever is justified in taking anything against its legal owner's will in order to put it to some use wrong in itself. For example, a destitute drug addict may not steal from the rich to support his or her self-destructive habit. Even if taking and using property against the owner's will is justified, moreover, it does not follow that someone who does so is justified in employing bad means, such as threats of bodily harm, lying, and so on. Nor may one ignore foreseen bad consequences—whether to society at large, to innocent persons, or to oneself—which often cannot be rightly accepted.

b) Many acts not usually considered theft are theft morally. Although differing in various ways, some of them morally significant, various kinds of acts are easily recognized as sharing the common malice of theft: burglary, robbery, embezzlement, misappropriation of funds, and unauthorized appropriation of an employer's supplies or products. In general, all obtaining of money, goods, and services by fraud or unjust coercion involves the same injustice as theft: falsifying something's value in selling it, lying in order to obtain a more favorable contract, taking bribes or kickbacks, padding expense accounts, overstating the hours one has worked, charging for work not done, knowingly passing forged checks or counterfeit bills, incurring debts with the intention of declaring bankruptcy, concealing assets in order to obtain undue payments or benefits, rigging markets, fixing competitions so that prizes or gambling winnings will accrue to certain persons, extortion, blackmail, and so on. Moreover, all wrongful retention amounts to unfair taking: deliberately not returning what one has borrowed, neglecting or refusing to

---

95. This norm, called "occult compensation" by the approved authors, applies only to cases in which a particular owner is unwilling to meet a definite obligation, for example, an employer refuses to pay a just wage to a worker. The next sentence in the text broadens this norm to cases which the approved authors failed to consider, in which the wealthy in general fail to meet their obligations to the poor as a class.

pay just debts, keeping articles which have been found and should be returned, deliberately accepting something (such as change or a delivery) which one receives by mistake, concealing assets (for example, in a bankruptcy proceeding) in order to avoid making due payments, and so on.[96] Finally, failure to compensate fairly for the use of others' property or for damage to it also has the character of theft: infringement of patents and copyrights, purchasing goods with the intent of returning them for full credit after having used them, evading liability for accidents, and so on.

c) **Such acts should not too quickly be regarded as light matter.** Like most other injustices, many forms of wrongful taking can admit parvity of matter. Casuists have discussed this question so often that legalistically minded thieves may be able to find opinions which seem to treat what they are doing as light matter. Before judging that one can engage in such an injustice without committing a mortal sin, however, a person should bear several things in mind.

First, the matter is not light if it is likely to cause serious harm to anyone. For example, stealing a very small amount from a child or a poor person can cause great distress; taking something of little value in itself can lead to considerable trouble and inconvenience. The matter cannot be judged light if a reasonable person in the circumstances of any individual harmed would consider the harm significant, that is, would be noticeably saddened or angered by harm of that kind and amount (see *S.t.*, 2–2, q. 66, a. 6, ad 3). In evaluating the significance of harm suffered, however, one may take into account that a reasonable person might be less attached to property than some owners in fact are. For example, a wealthy individual of a miserly disposition might be very distressed if it appears that a cashier has shortchanged him or her by one dollar.

Again, even if an act or practice of wrongful taking does not harm any one person significantly, it may be gravely unjust because of its effect on the community as a whole. For example, petty cheating by some merchants in classifying, adulterating, weighing, and measuring goods can render honest competition impossible. Similarly, petty shoplifting can increase the costs of doing business so greatly that it cannot reasonably be considered insignificant; a sign of this is that public opinion generally supports the enforcement of laws forbidding it.

Given that an act is wrongful taking, doubts about its seriousness should be settled by presuming the matter grave. Someone who is willing to do wrong while doubtful about how serious the wrong will be, is willing to do the more serious wrong (see 5.I.2.a).

d) **Circumstances can aggravate the seriousness of wrongful taking.** Some forms of unfair taking—for instance, robbery, blackmail, and extortion—involve coercion or threats, which are likely to do the victim direct physical or psychological harm (see *S.t.*, 2–2, q. 66, a. 9). Other forms, such as burglary, involve violating privacy. In many cases, too, those who engage in wrongful taking should foresee

---

96. St. John Chrysostom points out that failure to use one's surplus to meet others' needs is theft and robbery, even if those resources were inherited: *De Lazaro concio, PG*, 48.987–88 (*On Wealth and Poverty*, trans. Catherine P. Roth [Crestwood, N.Y.: St. Vladimir's Seminary Press, 1984], 49–50).

that their acts will harm innocent persons by casting suspicion on them or will impose additional burdens on those who suffer the loss, for example, emotional distress, the trouble of verifying the loss and reporting it to police, and so on. Also, lying often facilitates or is part of an act of wrongful taking. Because of such circumstances, many acts of wrongful taking harm persons and social relationships far beyond the material loss itself.

The wrongful taking of Church property is irreverent toward God, and so is a sacrilege (see 1.K.6).

e) **A bad end always aggravates the seriousness of wrongful taking.** Although a thief generally is interested in possessing what he or she steals, not in harming the owner, and may even regret that harm and impose it only reluctantly, sometimes the very point of wrongful taking is to harm the owner. Motivated by hatred, such wrongful taking is far more serious than that in which stealing is a means to some other end, for it is directly contrary to love of neighbor.

Also, whenever intended to provide the means for some other immoral act, wrongful taking not only does injustice to the owner but abuses the material good.

f) **Circumstances can lessen the seriousness of wrongful taking.** Since wrongful taking presupposes moral claims and intentions, not all acts are clear-cut. The conditions which can justify taking against a legal owner's will are subject to judgment, which can be honest without being as careful as it should be. It makes sense to speak of family members stealing from one another, yet their property rights vis-à-vis one another often are unclear. Owners can be more or less reluctant to allow the taking of their property, for example, businesses often allow employees to make personal use of some facilities within unspecified limits. The obligation to pay the full price when a purchased good or service is not entirely satisfactory can be unclear. These and other circumstances can affect some of the essential elements of wrongful taking, thus perhaps lessening the seriousness of whatever wrong is done.

4. One Should Avoid Sins of Thought Bearing on Property

God's commandments exclude not only wrongly taking others' property but wrongly desiring it—coveting (see Ex 20.17, Dt 5.21). This sin can be committed by thinking of taking something illicitly, deliberately wishing to do so, and refraining only out of fear of the consequences. It also can be committed by deliberately hoping others will suffer some loss or harm from which one will benefit. For example, professionals covet if they hope more people will have problems so that they can raise their fees; merchants covet if they hope for a natural disaster which will cause shortages and higher prices.[97]

Besides coveting, a person also sins if, moved by envy or anger, he or she deliberately rejoices in losses others suffer in respect to their just possessions.

Moreover, it is sinful deliberately to long for wealth and possessions not in order to be able to fulfill one's responsibilities but for merely emotional gratification. Perhaps one envies prosperous evildoers (see Ps 73.2–12); perhaps one imagines

---

97. See *Catechismus ex decreto Ss. Concilii Tridentini*, 3.10.23 (2:228–29).

oneself equally prosperous and self-indulgent without being wicked. Perhaps one only daydreams about having wealth or possessions, without ill will toward the wealthy or a desire to take what is theirs; perhaps one resents class differences and looks forward to a time when the rich will be dispossessed. In any case: "Those who want to be rich fall into temptation and are trapped by many senseless and harmful desires that plunge people into ruin and destruction" (1 Tm 6.9). The heart is enslaved by inordinate wishes for wealth and possessions (see *S.t.*, 2–2, q. 118, a. 1); and so, while it is "hard for a rich person to enter the kingdom of heaven" (Mt 19.23), St. Thomas, following St. John Chrysostom, holds that it "is impossible for those who set their hearts on riches" to do so (*S.t.*, 2–2, q. 186, a. 3, ad 4).

Such sins of thought often involve grave matter, but are probably seldom committed with sufficient reflection. However, it is important to be aware of them and to resist temptations to commit them, since they distort one's attitude toward material goods, thus easily leading to other sins.

Question G: What Are One's Responsibilities in Transactions?

Transactions are cooperative acts bearing on the transfer of the ownership and/or use of property and money: giving and receiving gifts, gratuitous lending and borrowing, bartering, buying and selling, leasing and renting, and borrowing and lending money at interest. Insofar as any transaction involves acts already treated—acquiring and disposing of property, more or less fairly dealing with others' property, and so on—it should be carried out in accord with the norms relevant to those acts. Here it remains only to treat the responsibilities proper to transactions insofar as they are cooperative acts.

1. Giving and Receiving Gifts Should Promote Interpersonal Communion

The concept of gift giving is analogous; the central case is that of a transaction in which the transfer of the possession and use of material goods is solely a means to the good of interpersonal communion between the parties. This central case will be treated first; it clarifies by analogy secondary cases in which gift giving is used to acknowledge or strengthen other relationships.

a) **The giving of a gift should express sincere love.** To understand the moral ground of gift giving, it helps to recall what interpersonal communion is: a union of persons by mutual volitional love—the willing of one another's good for the sake of a common good which is or includes their interpersonal relationship itself. The initiation and continuation of this requires expression, and among its appropriate expressions are actions by at least one person intended to benefit another or others in a way to which they have no right. Transferring without compensation the ownership of mutually desirable material goods—that is, giving a gift—is one such action. (A gratuitous loan or an uncompensated service can be called "gift giving" in a wider sense.) Thus, while there never is a duty to give a gift,[98] using

---

98. On certain occasions, gift giving is obligatory to express gratitude, congratulations, and so on. Nevertheless, even on such occasions, it is not a duty in the strict sense, for the ground of

money and things for this purpose is morally right just insofar as the gift sincerely expresses love with the intention of initiating or building up interpersonal communion and does not violate other responsibilities.

b) This moral ground of gift giving implies several specific norms. In the absence of the relevant sort of love, a person should not give anything as a gift (using *gift* in the central sense). Similarly, to express that love, nothing should be given as a gift which would be given even in love's absence, nor should anything be given which will not both truly benefit the recipient and be experienced as beneficial. Therefore, it is wrong to give anything *as a gift* (i) that is known to be unwanted by the recipient, (ii) that the giver owes the recipient as compensation or on some other ground, (iii) instead of fulfilling some duty or in place of reparation for failing to fulfill a duty, (iv) in order to motivate the recipient otherwise than through the relevant sort of mutual love, or (v) on any merely emotional motive.

These norms often are violated. (i) Trying to cheer up his depressed friend, Jill, who lives alone, Jack gives her a puppy, although he knows Jill hates dogs ("Surely," Jack thinks, "Jill will become attached to this dog, and caring for it will do her a lot of good"). (ii) Sweatshop Garments Company does not pay its employees a just wage, but gives each a turkey at Thanksgiving and a ham at Christmas. (iii) Pete, who is engaging in an adulterous affair, salves his conscience by showering his wife with presents. Sally seldom visits her aged parents who live nearby in a retirement community, but on Mothers' Day and Fathers' Day she makes it up to them by sending them fashionable clothing and accessories from the very best stores. (iv) Kate, who owns a specialty store, seeks to improve business relationships and so increase profits by using surplus items as "gifts" for her employees and suppliers; while legitimately charging these items off as an expense of doing business, she often misrepresents them as personal gifts by insincerely pretending that her largess is motivated by affection. (v) Phil gives people expensive presents because doing so makes him feel superior to them. Martha gives presents mainly because she enjoys the recipients' appreciative reaction.

Such violations vitiate gift giving by falling short of sincerity, adequacy to express love, or both. Moreover, as in all other cases in which material goods are abused, violating these norms is unjust, insofar as what is thus abused should be put to some other just use.

People often violate several of these norms at once. The Jacksons agreed on their agenda before getting married, and they have been very successful in carrying it out. Both have good jobs, and they have a fine house, enjoy their vacations, and so forth. They also have two children, who have been brought up mainly by others, since neither parent ever has had much time for them. However, the Jacksons lavish presents on the children at Christmas, on birthdays, and on every other suitable occasion. Not only is this their way of being "good" parents, but it is also intended to motivate the children to be "good" children and make it clear to relatives, friends, and neighbors that the Jackson family is enjoying the "good" life.

---

the obligation is the good of communion, which demands that one manifest good will that transcends justice.

c) **Analogous sorts of gift giving are subject to other norms.** Sometimes, of course, as in (iv), behavior which abuses material goods insofar as it is insincere gift giving could be a right use if intended as a sincere expression of the good will appropriate to the business relationship (such expressions of good will also are called "gifts" in an analogous sense).

Similarly, disposing of surplus items by giving them to people who can put them to good use is a just use of property, which, however, is vitiated if misrepresented as an instance of gift giving in the central sense.

d) **In accepting a gift, a person assumes obligations to the giver.** Gifts in the central sense call for gratitude, acknowledgment, reciprocal love. Believing that a proffered gift expresses the relevant sort of good will, therefore, one should not accept it unless prepared to respond suitably. For example, if John is not open to a romantic relationship with Mary, he should not accept her costly Valentine's day gift. If Mary prefers not to develop friendships with co-workers, she should not accept the friendly invitation of a co-worker, Sarah, to go to a concert.

Again, sometimes a gift is offered subject to some condition, such as that it be used in a specific way. The gift should not be accepted unless the condition may rightly be met and one intends to meet it. However, if a gift offered subject to a legitimate condition has been accepted with the intention of meeting the condition, the obligation to do so is defeasible in the same ways as other promises (see 7.C.1.d). Of course, the obligation may not be set aside if just and applicable law requires that the condition be met.

2. One Should Be Generous in Lending and Honest in Borrowing

Borrowing often is a good and even better way of acquiring the things one needs (see E.3.e, above). People's frequent failures to fulfill the specific responsibilities which borrowing involves have the bad result of making most owners more resistant to lending their property than they otherwise would be.

a) **Owners should allow others to use their goods temporarily.** Owners and their dependents very often can realize only part of the potential usefulness of nonconsumable goods—real property, furniture, tools, and so on—from whose use others could benefit. Many owners who rightly retain possession of such goods mistakenly take it for granted that they may allow such things' potential utility to remain unrealized.

To realize that utility, owners should be ready to lend out things. They not only should deal fairly with any request to borrow but should offer the use of things to those who need them. Many owners are understandably anxious that their property will not be returned or will be damaged if they lend it. But in some cases they can afford to accept these risks and should do so; in other cases, they should require security, such as a damage deposit, to motivate renters or borrowers to fulfill their responsibilities.

b) **In seeking to borrow, one should be entirely forthright.** Owners must judge their responsibility to lend their property, and that cannot be done correctly unless they know all the relevant circumstances. Potential borrowers therefore should be not only truthful in answering questions but forthcoming in supplying the necessary information: what need they hope to meet by borrowing the property, and how great the need is; any unusual risks that the property will be harmed; any special provisions they will make to care for it; when and how they plan to return it; and so on.

Sometimes, someone who wishes to borrow something seeks to motivate the owner to lend it by resorting to emotional pressure and concealing or even lying about relevant circumstances. That is unjust because it impedes owners in fulfilling their responsibility to judge the request by the standard of fairness.

c) **One should carefully abide by agreements made in borrowing.** All the explicit and implicit conditions of agreements made in borrowing things should be fulfilled faithfully. These include limits of use, for instance, not to put what is borrowed at risk in certain ways, not to lend it to a third party, and so on.

In keeping and using borrowed items, the responsibility to care for them is at least as great as if one owned them. Often it is greater, for example, if the owner has taken especially good care of the item, if it is of sentimental value to the owner, or if the owner is due special gratitude for having lent it. Moreover, one should avoid unnecessarily lessening the potential future utility of that which is borrowed, for example, by marking up a borrowed book.

The explicit or implicit understanding about a borrowed item's return is especially important. Borrowers should return borrowed items as soon as is mutually convenient and, unless they seek and obtain an extension, not later than promised.

3. Exchanges Should Be Just, Not Merely Mutually Accepted

By *exchange* here is meant a transaction mutually transferring ownership and/or use of money, goods, and/or services: bartering, buying and selling, renting and leasing, hiring and providing services.

Even though an exchange is accepted by both parties, it may not be just. No exchange is just if someone thereby acquires something he or she should not or which he or she intends to use wrongly. Similarly, an exchange is unjust if it is intended (rather than merely accepted as a side effect) that others obtain something they should not have or mean to put to bad use.

The prospect of serving genuine human needs must motivate every just exchange. Moreover, a just exchange must be fair. That requires mutual informed consent, and such consent presupposes honesty. Many people imagine that only an even exchange is fair—equal things must be exchanged, resulting in a precise balance of the advantages gained. However, while fairness often requires equality, uneven exchanges also can be fair.

The norms articulated here apply to all exchanges, from those among neighbors to those among huge corporations in international trade. Employer-employee relations involve additional responsibilities, treated in question A.

a) **Both parties should seek a genuine understanding and fulfill it.** The parties to any exchange should seek an agreement based on mutual understanding, so that neither will enter into it with false expectations. Sellers, for example, should not set terms and limits in language which buyers cannot understand, nor should contracts be presented in fine print to discourage people from reading them.

Someone who makes an agreement to exchange anything should abide by it, just as by any other promise. Although many contracts provide remedies if the agreement is not kept, a provision of this kind is not a justification for choosing arbitrarily between keeping the agreement and allowing the remedy to take effect. If a person cannot keep an agreement or judges it fair not to keep it, he or she should inform the other party promptly and arrange for fair compensation. For example, buyers who cannot pay the agreed price at the agreed time act unfairly if they delay by giving false assurances that payment will soon be made, evade attempts to repossess goods, and so on.

b) One should never seek profit as if it were good in itself. Profit is the gain or advantageous return resulting from an exchange. Since exchanges can be mutually advantageious, both parties can profit. The prospect of profit can rightly be taken into account in deciding whether to cooperate in an exchange.

Nevertheless, in any exchange one should seek to increase one's own and/or others' capacities to act for basic human goods, which truly fulfill persons (see GS 64). Acquiring wealth and property by no means guarantees that one will use them rightly to serve persons, since avarice—that is, unreasonable emotional desire for gain—can motivate people to seek profit endlessly without benefiting anyone. Thus, in every exchange the end sought should be not only profit but the fulfillment of genuine human needs. Moreover, one should hope to fulfill those needs, not by any and every means, but only by means morally acceptable in every way.

Hence, while the profit motive of itself is neither morally good nor evil, it does tempt to avarice and in isolation is never a morally adequate motive, since it needs to be subordinated to an upright intention. Consequently, in exchanges, people should intend not only profit but also justice in the relationship and some morally good use to which any profit will be put (see *S.t.*, 2–2, q. 77, a. 4).

c) Sellers should be honest, not manipulative. Persuasion, including advertising, often is manipulative, in that it attempts to arouse emotional motivation irrelevant to any possible sound reason for acting as the persuasion would have others do.[99] Those attempting to sell anything should abstain entirely from manipulative persuasion, and instead should provide sound reasons for consideration by potential buyers. Plainly they should not lie or otherwise attempt to deceive (see *S.t.*, 2–2, q. 77, a. 2). For example, accurate weights and measures should be used; goods should not be adulterated and their quality should not be misrepresented.

Nevertheless, sellers may focus attention on a thing's better features and advantages, and, unless there is a contrary law or custom, need not point out its shortcomings, provided these are not concealed and the asking price takes them fairly into account (see *S.t.*, 2–2, q. 77, a. 3).[100]

Where it is the custom for sellers to allow for bargaining by initially asking a higher price than they expect to receive, that is not dishonest. But if a potential

99. A critique of advertising: Pontifical Commission for the Instruments of Social Communication, *Communio et progressio*, 59–62, *AAS* 63 (1971) 615–17, Flannery, 1:313–14.

100. However, having completed the transaction, a seller might have an obligation to point out a previously unmentioned defect, for example, if ignorance of it might lead to some significant harm.

purchaser offers more than the seller judges, all things considered, to be the maximum fair price, the latter should not accept the excess.

d) **Market or legally fixed prices often can be regarded as fair.** At the start, the fairness of a market price or a price fixed by law can tentatively be assumed, but this assumption is rebuttable. Sometimes one knows a market has been manipulated or is biased in one's favor due to underlying structural injustices, while a price set by law can be so ruinous to one party that it is manifestly unfair; and it is wrong to take advantage of a price known to be unfair. Instead, one must be willing to pay more or take less, and should proceed as one would if there were no relevant market or law.

To determine the fair price in such a case, the Golden Rule must be applied to the facts. The parties cooperate in doing so by honestly bargaining to a price which both freely accept, provided they are nearly equally well informed and motivated to do business. If one knows the other to be less informed, however, or under special pressure to come to terms, he or she should set a price more favorable to the other than that which bargaining biased by ignorance or special need would produce.

e) **Sometimes one should moderate an otherwise fair price.** Using one's money and things to meet others' needs can be an obligation in strict justice, while mercy can call for subordinating one's own needs to those of others (see E.5.b–f, above). In view of these responsibilities, someone dealing with the less wealthy, the unemployed, and so on sometimes should moderate the price that otherwise would be fair, and give a discount or pay a premium. The transaction then will be a compound of two elements: in part, a fair exchange; in part, a just use of money or property to meet the other's needs.

Arranging such a compound transaction should be considered whenever someone judges that his or her wealth should be used to meet others' needs. Such a transaction, involving the element of exchange, is more likely to protect the self-esteem and encourage the self-reliance of the less wealthy party, and so to promote stronger bonds of human community and charity.

4. Seeking and Accepting Interest on a Loan Can Be Just

Lending money at interest raises a special question due to the historical controversy over usury. Church teaching condemned usury, and a superficial reading of economic history suggests that *usury* referred in earlier times to what today is called "interest."[101] However, money itself no longer is what it once was. Thus, while the Church's teaching of earlier times remains true, today it can be just to charge interest on a loan.[102]

101. For a more careful reading of the history: John T. Noonan, Jr., *The Scholastic Analysis of Usury* (Cambridge, Mass.: Harvard University Press, 1957); Thomas F. Divine, S.J., *Interest: An Historical and Analytical Study in Economics and Modern Ethics* (Milwaukee: Marquette University Press, 1959), 3–116; Odd Langholm, *The Aristotelian Analysis of Usury* (New York: Columbia University Press, 1984).

102. Some argue that since the Church's teaching on usury developed, her teaching on contraception and other matters could change. For a reply, see *CMP*, 36.G.10; Matthew Habiger, O.S.B., "Is the Magisterium a Reliable Moral Guide? The Case of Usury," *Social Justice Review*, May-June 1989, 73–79.

a) **The Church's teaching on usury must be understood correctly.** The Church never taught that all charging of interest is wrong, but only that it is wrong to charge interest on a loan in virtue of the very making of the loan, rather than in virtue of some factor related to the loan which provides a basis for fair compensation (see DS 1442/—, 2546–47/1475–76).

Charging interest on a loan simply in virtue of making it takes advantage of the difference in need between lender and borrower. The assumption was that during the period of the loan, lenders can do without their money, for otherwise they would not lend it; but borrowers need the money, for otherwise they would not borrow it. Applying the general norm that surplus wealth should be used to satisfy others' needs, people with extra money should lend it without charge to those who need it. However, those who deposit or lend money can fairly charge for various other factors: costs incurred in making and administering the loan, the risk of nonpayment, probable inflation, taxes, the forgoing of other legitimate uses to which the money otherwise would be put, and so on.

b) **The possibility of investing money may be taken into account.** "Other legitimate uses" refers to the possibility of productive investment. This is not the same thing as lending, since one who invests becomes a sharer in the productive enterprise and so is entitled to share in its profit. St. Thomas already realized this (see *S.t.*, 2–2, q. 78, a. 2, ad 5). Still, viewing the prospect of profit on an investment as too uncertain to deserve consideration (see ad 1), he held that the existence of this alternative did not justify charging interest by those who instead chose to lend their money. If that argument was sound in the thirteenth century, however, it no longer is today, for anyone can invest in productive enterprises (for example, by buying high-grade corporate bonds) with moral certainty of preserving the principal and making a profit.

c) **It can be assumed that market rates of interest are usually fair.** Due to the change in the nature of money, every modern economy includes extensive money markets. Here most borrowers and lenders differ little in their information and their need, and it is reasonable to assume that market rates of interest reflect legitimate grounds for seeking and accepting the payment of interest. This is so even though structural injustices probably affect interest rates, since the effects of such injustices are impossible to assess, and might well offset one another.

In making personal loans to less wealthy people, however, one sometimes should lend at lower than market rates, just as one should moderate other prices, so that one's surplus wealth will be put to use satisfying genuine needs.

5. Transactions Often Offer Opportunities for Christian Witness

The Christian conception of property differs widely from the modern individualistic conception. Thus, since many people pay close attention to others' behavior in transactions, it often is possible to bear witness to the moral truth which faith affirms and clarifies by behaving in transactions according to Christian standards and indicating why one is doing so, instead of acting in the usual, expected way.

+   +   +

CHAPTER ELEVEN

PATRIOTISM, POLITICS, AND CITIZENSHIP

Summary

Patriotism, love for one's country, is a moral obligation for citizens. (Love for the other regional communities of which one is a member is analogous to patriotism, and also is an obligation.) But patriotism is love for the true good of one's country; it is not immoderate nationalism.

Patriotism requires that citizens fulfill a variety of relevant responsibilities. Among these, for Catholics, is defending and spreading the faith in their own nations, as is resisting the dominance of secular humanism, which harms the nation by destroying community.

Citizens are obliged to be dutiful and law-abiding. The moral claims of citizenship should neither be slighted nor overestimated. The common good shapes political society and also limits it; and it is the common good which grounds authority and all the duties of citizens.

As citizens, Catholics should take an active part in public affairs, adhering to the principles of Catholic social teaching. While this political role is primarily the responsibility of the laity, the Church's teaching specifies a number of purposes they should pursue, including religious liberty, equal justice for all, justice with respect to human life, the protection of marriage and the family, economic justice, and international justice and peace. Citizens also have a duty to vote conscientiously, and sometimes to participate more actively in politics.

All just and applicable laws should be obeyed, but even a just law can be inapplicable in unusual circumstances. One should not comply with an unjust law which is at odds with moral obligation, but otherwise various goods sometimes require complying with unjust laws. However, there is a presumption, not easily rebutted, that laws are just and applicable.

Citizens should cooperate with the criminal justice system, reporting probable crimes, cooperating in official investigations of crimes, giving testimony in court, and serving conscientiously on juries. While supporting the just punishment of criminals, Christians should oppose the use of the death penalty. Citizens ought to pay their taxes. The fact that tax laws are more or less unjust or that some public funds are misused usually does not justify nonpayment.

No war can be just unless several requirements are met, and a development of the Christian tradition in modern times makes it clear that aggressive war is excluded; but a war can be just if all the conditions are met, and citizens should participate in such a war as the law requires. However, participants in a just war should not choose to kill or harm anyone. Moreover, a nation's deterrent strategy can make its military actions unjustifiable. Christians almost always should refuse to serve in an unjust war.

Question A: What Are One's Responsibilities with Respect to Patriotism?

All individuals and families naturally and inevitably belong to larger communities: a local community (the town, city, or rural region), perhaps some intermediate community such as a province or state, and a country or nation. Patriotism is love for one's country or nation and loyalty to it.[1] This question clarifies the duty of patriotism itself, its distinction from immoderate nationalism, and some specific responsibilities flowing from patriotism. But since love for and loyalty toward the smaller, local community is analogous to patriotism, what is said here can be applied with appropriate qualifications to one's attitude and duties toward both the local community and any intermediate community, such as the state or province.[2]

As will be explained, the large community which is the primary object of patriotism is prior, at least logically, to its own political organization, so that it is helpful to distinguish between the large community and the political society (or "state"), although normally the same people and groups belong to both. Also, a political society is distinct from its government: its apparatus for making decisions and implementing them. Finally, the government is distinct from any one regime, which is a particular set of people who fill the government's offices.

The development of the United States illustrates these distinctions: during the seventeenth and early eighteenth centuries, many of the British colonists in North America gradually became a new nation as they formed an increasingly unified community with interests distinct from those of their homeland; this nation organized itself as a new political society with the Declaration of Independence (1776) and the Articles of Confederation (1781); later, this political society reorganized its government by adopting the Constitution; since 1789, the regime has changed to some extent with each national election and each change in the make up of the Supreme Court.

---

1. This statement about the object of patriotism is not intended to beg political questions. Conflicts often arise over how to identify and delimit the larger community, and wars are fought over the issue of which of two or more communities of different scope will control the political organization of a region. In such cases, what proponents of the claims of the larger community regard as a nation is considered by proponents of the claims of the smaller community to be an imperialistic imposition or, at best, a confederation of nations, each of which is or should be self-governing.

2. A sound and helpful scholarly work on the matters treated in this question as a whole: John J. Wright, *National Patriotism in Papal Teaching* (Westminster, Md.: Newman Press, 1956). The study was Cardinal Wright's dissertation for the S.T.D. at the Gregorian University in Rome; completed in 1939, it treats papal teaching from Leo XIII through Pius XI.

1. Patriotism Is Both a Natural Attachment and a Moral Obligation

Patriotism has significant emotional components, but centrally it should be a volitional love: the steady willing of the true good of one's nation. The Catholic Church teaches that patriotism is a duty. People, of course, have an analogous duty to will the good of their local community. Patriotism primarily bears on the underlying, large community and only secondarily on the state, which politically organizes the large community for the pursuit and protection of certain aspects of its common good.

a) **Individuals and families naturally belong to larger communities.** All people live with others in a particular region, so that they inevitably form a community, larger than even the most extended family, whose members are bound together in various ways. They share a common history and culture, usually including a common language; they work, play, and do business together; moreover, many of the families, neighborhoods, and other groups living in a region are tied together by intermarriages.

Such a regional community can exist at various levels; with the development of agriculture and industry, humankind formed cities and other local communities, and then formed nations. Since regional communities serve a broad set of continuing interests, they are not deliberately developed to carry out a specific act or set of acts but are open-ended (on open-ended community, see 6.C.2.d). At the same time, they also are limited, since their members' primary attachment is to the smaller and more intimate community of the family, and since individuals and families generally also belong to various voluntary associations in which they pursue important interests not shared by all, or even many, other people living in the same region.

b) **Political society is not the primary object of patriotism.** As will be explained, the protection and promotion of the common interests of members of any regional community call for political organization. Hence, nations tend to develop and/or maintain the laws and institutions of political society. However, since the large community has a natural basis in the network of nonpolitical relationships among the individuals, families, and other communities dwelling together or operating in a certain region, people can will their nation's good even apart from its political fortunes. For example, the Ukrainians maintained their national identity and patriotism through a long period despite lacking political independence and national sovereignty. Moreover, the common good of a national community usually includes important interests—for example, in culture and religion—which may be more suitably served by nonpolitical than political means. Therefore, the large community itself is the primary object of patriotism, which extends to political society and its government only insofar as these serve the common interests of the nation's members and their families, including the interests of the various nonpolitical communities to which they belong.

c) **People usually are attached to their regional communities.** Most people have strong feelings of affection and gratitude toward their local community and their country. They sprang from this community; it is the land of their forebears, their fatherland/motherland. They were shaped by its culture and feel at home in it, sharing as they do in its common life. Not only does their land's soil sustain them and their families but its natural features—these forests and fields, these hills and valleys, these rivers and shores, these skies and this weather—provided their first experience of natural beauty and their first insight into the natural world's inherent meaning and value. That inherent meaning and value show that the natural world is created and thus direct responsive minds toward God the creator. Hence, patriotic and religious feelings are closely related and intertwined.

d) **Patriotic feelings must be shaped by sound judgment and good will.** Provided it is integrated with the steady willing of the true good of the community, emotional attachment to one's nation is a powerful motive for fulfilling the responsibilities of authentic patriotism. Unless patriotic feelings are shaped by sound judgment and integrated with an upright will, however, they easily lead to moral failings of various kinds. Some people mistakenly think emotional attachment suffices to make them patriots, although they fail to fulfill their essential responsibilities to the community. Others allow themselves to be swept along by nationalistic feelings into supporting injustices toward other communities or violating the rights of some members of their own community, for example, by joining in the persecution of those who legitimately criticize commonly held opinions and widely accepted practices.

e) **Catholics should be patriots, loving their country's true good.** Catholic teaching makes it clear that patriotism, in the sense of love for the true good of one's nation, is a grave obligation.

Using patriotism as a pattern for the love which Catholics should bear toward the Church, Leo XIII teaches: "The natural law enjoins us to love devotedly and to defend the country in which we had birth, and in which we were brought up, so that every good citizen hesitates not to face death for his native land."[3] Again, he holds that patriotism, like love of the Catholic faith, is a duty "of paramount importance, and from which, in this life, no man can exempt himself."[4] Pius XII clearly articulates the ground and character of the obligation of patriotism: faith not only teaches that love should extend to every human being but that "we must follow a God-given order, yielding the place of honor in our affections and good works to those who are bound to us by special ties." And Pius supports this point by citing the example of Jesus' attachment to his own country, a bond he manifested by weeping over the coming destruction of Jerusalem.[5]

St. Thomas explains that patriotism belongs to a virtue akin to religion; this virtue, which he calls "pietas," disposes one to dutifulness, gratitude, and reverence toward one's parents and native land. For humans depend on their parents as procreators and their homeland as the source of their cultural and historical identity in ways somewhat analogous to that in which they depend on the Creator for their very being and every other good they enjoy (*S.t.*, 2–2, q. 101, a. 1).

3. Leo XIII, *Sapientiae Christianae*, ASS 22 (1889–90) 387, *PE*, 111.5.
4. Leo XIII, *Au milieu des sollicitudes*, ASS 24 (1891–92) 519, *PE*, 119.3.
5. Pius XII, *Summi Pontificatus*, AAS 31 (1939) 430, *PE*, 222.49.

2. Immoderate Nationalism Is Not Authentic Patriotism

While patriotism necessarily involves preferential love for one's own country, it does not exclude good will toward other national communities. Vatican II teaches: "Citizens should cultivate their patriotism generously and loyally, but without being narrow-minded, so that they always should look simultaneously to the good of the whole human family, which is united by various links among races, peoples, and nations" (GS 75; cf. AG 15). Thus, while unselfishly willing the true good of their own nation, Christians should not be jingoists or chauvinists, unconcerned about the welfare of other nations. Much less should they be ready to will other nations' destruction, subjugation, or humiliation.

a) **Christian patriots should limit nationalism by internationalism.** Humans are by nature social; their communal reality is as essential to their fulfillment as their individuality is (see GS 25; 6.C.1). God created the whole of humankind to be one community; he provided his gifts—material creation, human resources, and his self-revelation—for all peoples; and he calls all to enter into his kingdom. Human interdependencies extend beyond national boundaries, and there is a common good of humankind as a whole, to which every smaller human community should contribute (see GS 84–85). So, just as true self-love and love of neighbor are not only compatible but mutually implicit, so true patriotism and sound internationalism go together.

If a nation is to be truly great, therefore, it must treat other nations justly and generously. Moreover, unless a nation recognizes the need for international community and contributes to its realization, necessary cooperation will be impeded and conflicts will occur (see GS 83). Thus, patriotism itself demands a love comprehensive enough to include the people of all other nations, since without such inclusive love one's own community will remain unfulfilled in goods requiring wider cooperation, and international peace will be imperiled, at the risk of great harm to one's own nation.

b) **Christians should support justice in their nation's foreign relations.** Immoderate nationalism often leads people to the false view that, provided they act unselfishly toward their compatriots, they may share in their nation's selfishness in its relationships with other nations.[6] By contrast, while Christians cannot disown their country even when it does wrong they should do what is in their power both to prevent it from doing wrong and to bring it to repent and correct whatever wrongs it does, and should support it only when it does right.

c) **Christians should discern their nation's providential mission.** Pride and selfishness time and again have distorted the sense of mission of nations, so that it has come to form part of an ideology rationalizing imperialism: "manifest destiny," "the white man's burden," and so on. Still, such ideological distortions do not negate the truth that, just as individuals have a personal vocation, so nations, like other communities, have a proper mission. The divine gifts found within each nation and its homeland have been given to that people not only for them to exploit and enjoy, but for the use and service of others. Thus, the people of each nation

---

6. See Pius XI, *Caritate Christi compulsi, AAS* 24 (1932) 179–80, *PE*, 213.4.

should recognize both its strengths and its weaknesses, consider the needs of other nations, and support policies not only of mutual collaboration, when that is possible, but of unilateral assistance, if the means are available, whenever it is desperately needed by another nation.

3. Patriotism Is Realized by Fulfilling Relevant Responsibilities

As the steady willing of the true good of one's homeland, patriotism bears fruit and is manifested in action: the fulfillment of relevant responsibilities. These are twofold: some pertain to members of the large community independently of its being a political society, and some pertain to citizens as such. The former will be treated in the remainder of this question. Question B will explain the general ground of the duties of citizens, and questions C through E will treat the specific duties.

4. Patriotism Requires the Fulfillment of Many Other Responsibilities

The flourishing of most smaller communities contributes to the well-being of the nation. For example, good families provide good citizens, and good businesses both meet the nation's needs and make it prosperous. Thus, while one's responsibilities as a family member, a participant in the economy, and so on have their own proper grounds, they also should be fulfilled for the sake of the common good of the nation as a whole. In this way, patriotism provides an additional motive for fulfilling many other responsibilities.

5. Patriotic Catholics Should Defend and Spread the Faith in Their Own Nation

As baptized and confirmed members of the Church, Catholics are called to share in her apostolate by living the Christian life and bearing witness by their words, whenever appropriate, to the gospel's truth (see 2.D.4.a–b). Patriotism reinforces this general responsibility insofar as it bears on one's compatriots. Obviously, it is comparatively easy to contribute to the apostolate in one's own nation, since one is in contact with fellow community members and shares with them many common interests, which can provide points of departure and opportunities for dialogue. But more than this, precisely because patriots seek their nation's true good, patriotic Catholics should hope, pray, and work for their compatriots' conversion to the Catholic faith.[7]

a) **Patriotic Catholics should resist the dominance of secular humanism.** Conscious of their nation's religious traditions, Catholics should recognize all the sound elements in them as among the most precious of God's gifts to their homeland. They should do their best to safeguard, perfect, and hand on this heritage, in order that their nation will play the role which providence has assigned it in God's redemptive work in Christ: the spreading of the gospel and the growth of the kingdom. In societies whose culture is strongly influenced by secular humanism,

---

7. See Wright, *National Patriotism in Papal Teachings,* 93–139, for many references to the teaching of the popes from Leo XIII to Pius XI articulating and explaining this patriotic responsibility.

Catholics should work with other religious citizens to resist the privatization of religion and the dominance of unbelieving ideologies in public affairs, the media, and education.

In societies where secular humanism more or less prevails, those who still believe in God's revelation and try to live by it suffer various forms of discrimination. For example, while careful to treat more fashionable groups with great deference, the media often insult people who hold fast to faith traditions and treat their beliefs disparagingly; likewise, both in making faculty appointments and in determining course content, the academic world's open-mindedness and tolerance frequently do not extend to the convictions of orthodox Jews, evangelical Protestants, and faithful Catholics. Catholics should point out such instances of religious discrimination and seek remedies, not only insofar as they are afflicted with this injustice, but also insofar as it affects others who are striving to hold fast to divinely revealed truth.

b) **Secular humanism harms the nation by destroying community.** Secular humanists hold that there is no source of meaning and value transcending human thoughts and desires. People who accept this view tend no longer to believe they should conform to objective norms entailed by the truth about what is good. So, they can neither base community on what is good in reality nor settle differences by appealing to what is truly right. Instead, individuals who happen to have intense common interests of any kind form blocs to promote those interests, regardless of the welfare of other individuals and the wider community.[8]

As interest groups become blocs in this way, they no longer engage in real dialogue with outsiders. For rational discourse presupposes common, objectively true starting points, and no such starting points are acknowledged. Denying objective truth and dismissing appeals to it as attempts to impose arbitrary restrictions on freedom, the articulate members of each bloc manipulate ideas and words to promote their particular ends. Moral judgment gives way to rationalization, philosophy and theology to ideology, and thoughtful debate to propaganda. As a result, national community degenerates into a multitude of contending blocs, sharing no vision of the common good and no will to promote it. And even these blocs themselves are unstable and shifting, since their unity arises solely from their members' coincidence of interests, and interests can and do change from time to time. In this way, the abuse of freedom and the denial of objective truth weaken and eventually destroy community.

c) **Faith benefits a nation by developing and strengthening community.** Just as a nation is harmed by its citizens' denial of a transcendent source of meaning and value, so it is benefited by their obedience of faith, which recognizes and

---

8. John Paul II, *Centesimus annus*, 44, *AAS* 83 (1991) 848–49, *OR*, 6 May 1991, 13, teaches: "If there is no transcendent truth, in obedience to which man achieves his full identity, then there is no sure principle for guaranteeing just relations between people. Their self-interest as a class, group or nation would inevitably set them in opposition to one another. If one does not acknowledge transcendent truth, then the force of power takes over, and each person tends to make full use of the means at his disposal in order to impose his own interests or his own opinion, with no regard for the rights of others."

submits to the full truth about humankind's condition, dignity, and possibilities.[9] The truth of Catholic faith includes a sound morality, and sound morality harmonizes and integrates various interests in forms of cooperation which realize true community. Love of neighbor demands justice and mercy toward others, and justice and mercy toward compatriots bring about the solidarity of community.

Most sorts of differences within any nation are desirable, inasmuch as they enrich the community with their complementary contributions. So-called pluralism, however, is desirable only insofar as it leads to genuine dialogue which moves toward unity in truth. Considered in itself, ongoing division about ultimates does not express complementarity and is not good for community; it is only tolerable at best. The historical examples of Nazism and Leninism make it clear how a false ideology can be a serious threat to a community's human well-being. The same thing is true in general, since beliefs do have practical consequences: if part of a community is dedicated to a more or less false world view and way of life, whether religious or not, the error will threaten the well-being not only of that part but of the community as a whole. Consequently, precisely insofar as they love their country, Catholics should strive by witness, honest dialogue, and prayer to win all their compatriots to the faith.

But, someone might object, does that not violate religious liberty, as taught by Vatican II, and entangle church and state to the detriment of both? By no means. Religious liberty is immunity from coercion in matters religious (see DH 2); its point is to allow people to seek religious truth and freely embrace it (see DH 3). Hence, far from violating religious liberty, noncoercive efforts to share one's faith with others appropriately exercise that right (see DH 5, 14). As for the concern about church-state entanglement: while history shows that it is dangerous for the Church and political society to become officially or institutionally involved in each other's affairs, that is not in question here. The point, rather, is that Catholics should use nonpolitical means to share their faith with their compatriots.

6. Patriotic Catholics Should Promote the Common Good in Other Ways

Besides working for their compatriots' conversion to the true faith, patriotic Catholics should work in other nonpolitical ways to promote not only public morality, which includes social justice, but community solidarity and their nation's self-respect and honor.

a) One should foster virtue in one's nation. In liberal democratic societies, prevailing conceptions of liberty and disagreements among different segments of the community about various moral issues severely limit what government can do to enforce public morality, even insofar as it includes unpopular requirements of social justice. For this reason, it is especially important that upright members of the community fully use all the nonpolitical means available to them for fostering

---

9. See Pius XI, *Mit brennender Sorge, AAS* 29 (1937) 158–59, *PE,* 218.29. Though Pius responded in this 1937 encyclical to the challenge Nazi ideology presented to Catholics, his analysis is applicable with little adaptation to the impact of secular humanism on liberal democratic societies at the end of the twentieth century.

virtue. Individuals and families can do certain things by themselves, and they also can and should form or join appropriate organizations and movements. This kind of nonpolitical work for the common good becomes all the more necessary when a government makes bad laws and pursues morally unsound policies.

In any community, good example and sound admonition, manifesting moral truth and love of neighbor, are the most basic and powerful means of fostering virtue. Even large and diverse communities can be inspired by the stories of saints and heroes who provide relevant models, and upright people not only should give their own good example but should discern other models and do their best to make them known. Not everyone can be a Malcolm Muggeridge telling the world about a Mother Teresa, for most people do not have the gifts required to work profession-ally in the media of communication, the arts, and education. However, many Catholics can make some small contribution in such sensitive and culturally influential fields, and the cumulative impact of their modest contributions will be very important.

Even if Catholics do not use publicly financed schools, they should take an interest in the educational policies, programs, and personnel of these schools; they should work with other like-minded people and groups to support what is morally sound in both course content and the educational process, and to oppose moral relativism and decadence.

While wholesome entertainment should be praised and supported, Catholics should criticize immoral entertainment by sound standards. This always can be done by communications to editors or managers of the media and sometimes by directly contributing to the content of media, for example, by letters to editors and telephone calls to radio and television programs which accept and broadcast expressions of opinion by listeners and viewers. Organizations working against abuses such as pornography often deserve support, and organized boycotts and other methods of exerting pressure sometimes are appropriate.

Similar methods often can and should be used to promote social responsibility on the part of enterprises which pursue their private interests without regard to the common good by mistreating employees or customers, polluting the environment, and so on. The work of many people in defense of the lives of the unborn provides an example of what can be done, when necessary, to protect and promote essential elements of social justice by nonpolitical means, such as the dissemination of information, public demonstrations, and so on.

b) One should work for local and national solidarity. Patriotism and its analogues toward local community reinforce many responsibilities in strict justice or in mercy, insofar as their conscientious fulfillment, required on other grounds, also is demanded by the common good.

By impeding the full participation of some members in the community's cooperation, unjust discrimination against any class, region, racial or ethnic group, religious minority, or the like harms not only the individuals directly wronged but the common good. Instead of sharing in, condoning, or tolerating such injustice, a person should consider it a patriotic duty to work to surmount unreasonable lines of division in order to promote collaboration for the common good.

Similarly, as a member of any voluntary association—business, educational institution, professional group, trade union, or the like—a person should do everything he or she rightly can to cause the association's actions and policies to conform to the Golden Rule. Certainly, that will mean resisting any tendency for the group to engage in irresponsible pursuit of its narrow interests, for this is detrimental to the legitimate interests of other segments of the community, and thereby damaging to the common good. Of course, even a group organized precisely to promote some special interest can serve the common good, provided it represents and pursues its members' point of view and interest in an honest and fair-minded way, consonant with wider social harmony and with due regard for the particular interests of other segments of the community.

Many nonpolitical community activities contribute in different ways to a local region's or a country's solidarity and sense of identity. These include community charities, historical associations, museums, cultural centers and groups, sports teams, fairs, celebrations, and so on. People should appropriately participate in and support such community activities, since each can help in its own way to build up community. For example, spectator sports not only harmlessly entertain many people but provide an object of common interest and enjoyment for individuals and families who differ in many ways, and so significantly contribute to each local community's and country's regional and national spirit, which in turn facilitates cooperation in more important matters; hence, the amateur and professional athletes and teams representing cities or nations deserve some support, even if professional athletes and team owners are more interested in personal status and/or profit than in the common good.

c) **One should protect the honor of one's local community and nation.** While not boasting about one's community and being ready to give and accept constructive criticism of it, one should not slander it and should be prepared to defend it against lies and mistaken opinions. When dealing with outsiders and visiting other communities, people should bear in mind that their behavior is likely to be taken as representative, and so should avoid verifying negative stereotypes—the ugly American whose blatant consumerism offends the poor of other nations, the snobbish Parisian who thinks culture ends at the peripheral highway, and so on.

Question B: Why Should One Be a Dutiful and Law-Abiding Citizen?

Membership in a political society, citizenship, involves many specific responsibilities, which will be treated in questions C through E. The present question will clarify these responsibilities' general ground in the common good. Then it will show how to apply the standard of the common good to decide whether a governmental measure is just or a supposed civic duty a true moral obligation.[10]

---

10. On the matters treated in this question, see Yves R. Simon, *Philosophy of Democratic Government* (Chicago: University of Chicago Press, 1951), 1–71.

1. Certain Common Attitudes toward Political Society Must Be Rejected

Many people, including many Christians, take one or the other of two erroneous attitudes toward political society and the responsibilities of citizenship. Contrasting the right attitude with the two wrong attitudes sheds light on this part of moral life, which is an important part of a Christian's personal vocation.

a) **Some people overlook or deny the moral claims of citizenship.** Political society sometimes is regarded as a reality with great power, which the prudent, of course, will take into account, but which of itself makes no moral claim on its citizens. On this view, those in power cannot be ignored, and what governments do often has an important impact for good or ill. But one's respect for the state is not essentially different from one's respect for natural forces such as fire, floods, and winds. If this view were sound, membership in civic community plainly would involve no commitment but would merely be a given, to be arranged to one's convenience as much as possible.

The amorality, or even immorality, of many public officials and public policies, as well as the flagrant appeal of contemporary democratic politics to economic self-interest, nurture this attitude by suggesting that political society is merely an arrangement enabling individuals and groups, not least the wealthy and powerful, to pursue their self-interest. For Christians, the neutrality (and, very often, the antireligious bias) of the liberal democratic state with regard to things of ultimate importance contributes to this attitude. It also finds fertile ground in the experience of many unsophisticated people, not significantly involved in the political process, who passively experience governmental action as the impact upon their lives of an alien force: *they* are doing this to us and demanding that of us.

b) **Some people overestimate the moral claims of citizenship.** In denying the irreducible distinction between God and creatures, the German philosopher, G. W. F. Hegel (who died in 1831), replaced the Christian doctrines of creation and redemption with a metaphysical theory of reality as a single, evolving whole. He secularized the Christian concept of the Mystical Body and held that the state is a quasi-divine superperson in which the human essence, which he identified as rational freedom, is most fully realized. It follows that the state embodies an unconditioned end and has absolute authority over both its individual citizens and the nonpolitical communities which make it up. On this view, the state is the first principle of morality for its members; its customs and laws specify their duty; and there is no higher standard by which they could evaluate its claims on them. Indeed, the only limit on a state is that set by the power of other states, and the moral sovereignty of every state makes wars among them not only inevitable but indispensable for human progress.[11]

---

11. For an introduction to Hegel's theory of the State: Frederick Copleston, S.J., *A History of Philosophy*, vol. 7, *Modern Philosophy*, part I, *Fichte to Hegel* (Garden City, N.Y.: Doubleday Image, 1965), 252–61. The most important primary source: G. W. F. Hegel, *Philosophy of Right*, trans. T. M. Knox (Oxford: Oxford University Press, 1942); see especially 215 (§ 337).

While few people today accept Hegel's view, some who are both morally serious and politically sophisticated do think of citizenship as holding the supreme (or, if they are devout, the almost supreme) place among all their commitments. Such people typically believe that, in promoting their nation's interests and defending their political society, the regime is exempt from the moral requirements binding both individuals and other communities. Thus, they consider it morally permissible for officials of their government to lie under oath and even to kill the innocent, provided such acts are motivated by reasons of state rather than by personal considerations. This mistaken attitude leads to an intense desire to be a good citizen and an excessive deference toward governmental authority. Excessive deference often takes the form of unquestioning submission or a practically irrebuttable presumption that laws are just, commands must be obeyed, and when duties conflict, civic responsibilities always deserve priority.

c) **A Christian attitude avoids both of the preceding extremes.** As the next section explains, a Christian attitude agrees in part with (a): some exercises of governmental power altogether lack authority; and, while political society facilitates or obstructs Christians' pursuit of the most important things, it does not directly concern those things: "For here we have no lasting city, but we are looking for the city that is to come" (Heb 13.14), and so "our citizenship is in heaven" (Phil 3.20; cf. Col 3.1–3). But a right attitude also disagrees with (a) and agrees in part with (b): political society does make a direct moral claim on its members—"One must be subject, not only because of wrath but also because of conscience" (Rom 13.5; cf. *S.t.,* 2–2, q. 104, a. 6)—so that the responsibilities of citizenship are an important part of one's personal vocation, as Vatican II teaches:

> May all Christians be aware of their special and personal vocation in the political community. This vocation requires that they offer a shining example of devotion to duty and of service in promoting the common good, so that they also show by their deeds how authority can be harmonized with freedom, personal initiative with the interrelationships and bonds of the whole social body, and appropriate unity with beneficial diversity. (GS 75)

At the same time, contrary to (b), a Christian should not treat citizenship as inherently more important than other central elements of vocation (such as work and family) and should not defer unduly to the government's authority, much less regard the state as the first principle of morality. What the state demands can and sometimes does conflict with moral truth, and when that happens the Christian affirms: "We must obey God rather than any human authority" (Acts 5.29; cf. DH 11; *S.t.,* 2–2, q. 104, a. 5).

2. The Common Good both Shapes and Limits Political Society

Nations and lesser regional communities have a common good which calls for everyone's cooperation; the structuring of the community for that universal cooperation makes it a political society. But far from the common good of political society being the unconditioned end of its citizens and of the lesser communities within it, political society in fact has an instrumental character. Still, in the morally upright acts of persons as citizens, the basic human good of harmony among persons, justice and neighborliness, is realized and in this respect the common good of political society is not merely instrumental to other goods of its members, but is a constitutive part of their fulfillment. At the same time, since justice and neighborliness also are realized in nonpolitical relationships, not everything should be politicized, and so political society's common good does not include every moral good, although there are several ways in which government rightly promotes virtue and opposes vice.

a) **Certain common interests require or call for political society.** Individuals and families living in the same region have many diverse interests—religious, cultural, economic, and so on—which they pursue either by themselves or, more often, in and through various special associations, to which not all their neighbors belong. But those sharing a common homeland also have many important common interests, which demand or call for their cooperation.

The protection and promotion of certain of these common interests require or call for organizing the community as a whole with suitable structures and agencies. Such interests, shared by all individuals and families living in a region, include the following: avoiding or mitigating conflict among themselves, preventing insofar as possible the mischief of community members who might seriously violate others' rights, vindicating justice by imposing punishment on wrongdoers, dealing with other regional communities, protecting their own regional community against unwelcome intrusions or other interference by hostile outsiders, meeting common responsibilities of distributive justice by drawing fairly on community members' surplus resources to meet the needs of those lacking adequate resources, setting up cooperative arrangements to help families and other groups meet their responsibilities in matters such as education and health, and defining and supporting the responsibilities which pertain to certain important relationships (such as the duties of parties to contracts, of owners and others with regard to items of property, and of harm doers to those they have harmed) by making available regular forms and processes to shape action in such relationships and to provide remedies when responsibilities are not met. All these interests are operative in civilized nations with modern economies, and most are at work in all regional communities.

These and similar interests shared by members of a regional community constitute a distinctive common good. Since organizing the community in view of the various elements of its common good plainly is urgently necessary or very desirable, participation in that process is not morally optional for anyone (see GS 74). The necessary organization constitutes political society; a political society's machinery for making and implementing decisions is its government, with its military and police forces, its systems of criminal and civil law, its taxing and spending, its programs to support hospitals and schools, and its many public facilities, such as a monetary system, roads, a postal service, and so on.

b) **This common good also limits political society.** While showing the moral foundation of political society's common good, the preceding account simultaneously makes it clear that political society is only one community among others and should be limited so that it will not displace or absorb the others. In a variety of ways, individuals, families, and other groups pursue their own happiness, that is, the ends motivating those activities which they reasonably consider most worthwhile, such as the appreciation and understanding of nature, cultural pursuits, close personal relationships including marriage and parenthood, and friendship with God. A political society's common good is not the overarching and all-inclusive end (the unconditioned end) of its citizens, their families, and their other associations. On the contrary, political society's common good is instrumental and subordinate: "the sum of those conditions of social life which allow social groups and their individual members relatively thorough and ready access to their own fulfillment" (GS 26; cf. GS 74, DH 6).[12]

Understood in this way, political society is absolutely incompatible with totalitarianism of every kind. Rather than ruling a real state, a totalitarian regime strives totally to substitute its secularized caricature of the kingdom of God for political society and every other authentic human community.[13] Moreover, inasmuch as a political society's common good not only grounds but limits it, Aristotle's notion of the state as a quasi-organic whole of which citizens are parts must be criticized.[14] According to that notion, to attain the common good is greater and more godlike than to attain the good of any individual.[15] But the attainment of the common good, understood as instrumental to the fulfillment of individuals and social groups, cannot be superior to the attainment of their fulfillment itself.

c) **The common good contributes directly to citizens' fulfillment.** While the common good of political society is instrumental, it does not follow that it includes nothing intrinsically good or that the actions of citizens as such offer them no personal fulfillment other than what they attain as individuals, as family members, and as participants in other nonpolitical communities. An instrumental good also can be good in itself: people often rightly act for something intrinsically valuable and realize themselves in doing so although some ulterior good provides the reason for acting. For example, a person can do intrinsically valuable and fulfilling work in order to support his or her family; a person can seek theoretical knowledge for its technical applications; Christians can and should direct all their activities to the coming of God's kingdom without in the least derogating from the intrinsic value and humanly fulfilling character of secular activities (see GS 36, 72).

Similarly, political society's common good includes important aspects of the good of interpersonal harmony. A central purpose of political society is to establish

---

12. Papal teaching on the common good is diffuse, so that many passages must be studied and compared to gather its full sense. See, for example, John XXIII, *Mater et magistra; AAS* 53 (1961) 410, 417, 421, 438–39; *PE,* 267.40, 65, 78–81, 151; John XXIII, *Pacem in terris; AAS* 55 (1963) 272–73, 280–81, 293–94, 298; *PE,* 270.55–56, 84–85, 136–39, 154–55. For references to the teaching of previous popes on the matter and a summary: Jean-Yves Calvez, S.J., and Jacques Perrin, S.J., *The Church and Social Justice: The Social Teaching of the Popes from Leo XIII to Pius XII (1878–1958)* (Chicago: Henry Regnery, 1961), 114–24.

13. See Pius XII, *Summi Pontificatus, AAS* 31 (1939) 431–34, *PE,* 222.52–63; GS 73. A brief explanation of totalitarianism, with a helpful bibliography: *New Catholic Encyclopedia,* s.v. "totalitarianism."

14. See Aristotle, *Politics* 1.2.1253a18–29.

15. See Aristotle, *Nicomachean Ethics* 1.2.1094a26–b10. By contrast, consider the position articulated and defended by Jacques Maritain, *The Person and the Common Good,* trans. John J. Fitzgerald (New York: Charles Scribner's Sons, 1947), 5–20.

or protect justice in various relationships, and to shape and assist the mutually beneficial cooperation which enriches justice with neighborliness. But interpersonal harmony is one of the basic human goods (see *CMP*, 5.D.7, 5.2), and so the justice and neighborliness included in a political society's common good are intrinsically good, not good solely as means to ulterior good ends. It follows that when individual citizens, families, and other groups rightly fulfill authentic civic responsibilities, their morally good actions immediately and of themselves realize a basic human good and thereby contribute directly to their individual, familial, and other communal fulfillment.

While the earthly city must not be confused with the heavenly kingdom, all the justice and neighborliness imperfectly realized in the earthly city will be among the good fruits of human nature and effort which the blessed will find again in the kingdom (see GS 39). Consequently, a good Christian should be a good citizen, not only because political society's common good is a necessary means to other parts of Christian life but because the responsibilities of citizenship pertain to each Christian's personal vocation.

d) The common good does not include all justice and neighborliness. While political society's common good includes some aspects of the good of interpersonal harmony, other aspects of justice and neighborliness fall outside the common good.

In the first place, as explained in A.5–6 above, patriotic Catholics should spread and defend the faith in their nation and should promote the national common good in other nonpolitical ways. In fulfilling these responsibilities, they protect and strengthen authentic social solidarity—which involves mercy, justice, and other aspects of interpersonal harmony—in their national community as such, not only or precisely insofar as it is or could be a state. An example helps make the point clear: While Ukraine was subjugated, Ukrainian patriots who fostered their people's faith contributed to Ukraine's national solidarity, and so to various aspects of interpersonal harmony within the nation; yet they did not contribute to any political common good, since their subjugated national community was deprived of organization as a political society, and their national solidarity did not contribute to the common good of the political society of which the subjugated nation was an unwilling part. Analogously, patriots in a liberal democratic country who spread and defend their faith contribute to their nation's moral quality—which includes various aspects of mercy, justice, and so on—not insofar as their nation is a state but insofar as it is a people whose potential for community is prior to the political and transcends it.

Moreover, in the second place, the basic good of interpersonal harmony should be realized in every interpersonal relationship: in friendships, in marriage and family life, in the Church, and in schools, businesses, clubs, and other groups of all kinds. For the most part, justice, neighborliness, friendship, intimate love, and/or mercy can and should be realized in such interpersonal relationships without any intervention by any regional community and without any action by any government. In some cases, of course, political society rightly intervenes, not only to prevent grave injustices in nonpolitical relationships but to help families and other groups fulfill their proper responsibilities and to create conditions which favor their flourishing. For the most part, however, the various aspects of interpersonal harmony within families and other nonpolitical groups do not pertain to political society's common good. There are two reasons for that. First, the promotion and protection of those aspects of interpersonal harmony which have limited impact beyond the people actually involved are not matters of great interest to other members of the regional community. Second, governmental interference often would be more detrimental than conducive to the goods proper to families and other nonpolitical groups.

Consequently, while the autonomy of families and other nonpolitical groups is limited, within the necessary limits the state should respect the liberty and privacy of the communities within it. If, in pursuit of perfect justice, a government were to attempt to vindicate every right of every individual which is violated in every relationship, and/or, for the sake of neighborliness, were to attempt to assure the flourishing in every respect of every family and other group; then that government not only would exceed its authority, which is grounded in political society's common good, but would harm families and other nonpolitical groups. Indeed, such governmental excess would tend to displace all other communities and absorb them into political society. In doing so, it would violate the common good of political society itself, insofar as that is subordinate and instrumental not only to the fulfillment of citizens as isolated individuals but to their integral fulfillment in friendships, in marriage and family life, in the Church, and in other kinds of nonpolitical community.

e) The common good limits the ways government may promote virtue. Even though a political society cannot flourish without virtuous citizens, it plainly cannot be government's proper end directly to promote virtue in general, since not even all justice and neighborliness are included in political society's common good. Moreover, both the limits of political society's common good and its instrumentality in relation to the good of citizens as individuals and as members of nonpolitical communities set analogous limits on the extent to which government can rightly concern itself with other aspects of morality, especially insofar as they concern the interior acts and affections of hearts rather than the outward behavior which directly affects other people.[16]

Nevertheless, governments rightly do promote virtue and oppose vice in several ways. First, by forbidding harmful behavior and facilitating the cooperation of the nation as a whole in its common tasks, making and enforcing just laws directly promote the justice and neighborliness which pertain to the political society's common good. Second, this direct moral effect of just laws usually also has significant morally good side effects. These include reducing the competitive advantages available through wrongdoing and so making good citizens' upright

---

16. See *S.t.*, 2–2, q. 104, a. 5. Still, Aristotle, *Nicomachean Ethics* 10.9.1179a32–1180b28, and St. Thomas, *De regno*, 15 (or 2.4), hold that the general promotion of virtue and suppression of vice should be the main component of the common good of political society; in this, they overlook limits on the competence of the state which have been clarified by recent Church teaching regarding the instrumental character of political society's common good, the principle of subsidiarity (see 6.E.5.c, above), and religious liberty (see DH 2–8).

actions less burdensome and more rewarding to them, and removing or lessening certain occasions of sin; for example, governmental action for distributive justice reduces both excessive affluence and excessive poverty, thus reducing the temptations incidental to both conditions, and the outlawing of pornography reduces occasions of sins against chastity.[17] Third, by providing appropriate help to families and other nonpolitical communities, including churches, so that they can fulfill their proper responsibilities, governments indirectly promote virtue insofar as those communities do so.

3. The Common Good Grounds Authority and All the Duties of Citizens

The Christian teaching that "there is no authority except from God" (Rom 13.1) must be understood correctly. It points to authority's moral ground, due to which civic duties are moral responsibilities, which may not be set aside without adequate reasons. The correct understanding of authority's origin in God excludes three widely held, incompatible, but equally erroneous views: the theory that civil authority is delegated divine authority, the contract theory of authority, and the theory which confuses public authority with coercive power.[18]

a) *Authority is from God* means it is morally grounded in the common good. St. Paul teaches: "Let every person be subject to the governing authorities; for there is no authority except from God, and those authorities that exist have been instituted by God. Therefore whoever resists authority resists what God has appointed, and those who resist will incur judgment" (Rom 13.1–2; cf. 1 Pt 2.13–17). This teaching sometimes has been taken to mean that all civil authorities have a direct and personal authorization from God to exercise ruling power on his behalf within their assigned jurisdictions. On this view, of which the theory of the divine right of kings is one example, just as prophets speak for God and priests preach the gospel and administer the sacraments *in persona Christi,* so civil authorities rule as God's agents and on his behalf.

However, Catholic tradition and the Church's teaching exclude this interpretation of the scriptural text. St. Paul means, not that rulers are appointed by God, but that the authority-obedience relationship as such belongs to God's plan, according to which humans by nature are social beings, morally required to pursue the common good, for which authority is necessary.[19]

This teaching can be explained as follows. Society is natural: human persons are endowed by nature with practical reason, which calls them to pursue their true

---

17. Freedom of communication necessary for cooperation in worthwhile activities should be legally protected (see 7.B.4), but governments can justly outlaw pornography insofar as it degrades those depicted, tempts children and the sexually addicted, and contributes to a depraved cultural environment, which is conducive to sexual harassment (see 9.E.9.d).

18. A helpful philosophical analysis of the moral ground of authority: John Finnis, *Natural Law and Natural Rights* (Oxford: Oxford University Press, 1980), 231–59.

19. See Leo XIII, *Immortale Dei, ASS* 18 (1885) 162–63, *PE,* 93.3–5; John XXIII, *Pacem in terris, AAS* 55 (1961) 269–73 and 293, *PE,* 270.46–56 (with quotations from St. John Chrysostom, Leo XIII, and Pius XII) and 270.136.

good and to avoid evil; they also are so constituted by nature that, for the most part, they can pursue what is truly good only as a common good, in and through ongoing cooperative action; and the union of persons in ongoing cooperation is society. But authority is natural just as society is: since cooperation carries out a choice, and the capacity to make that choice is authority, society cannot exist without authority (see 7.E.1). Consequently, authority comes from God in this sense: it is grounded in the moral order, which comes from God.

b) **Governmental authority is not derived from a social contract.** According to the social contract theory, individuals are driven by self-interest to form the state, whose government they set up by their mutual agreement and promises, so that a government's authority comes from the citizens' delegation of their personal right to pursue their own interests in their own way. The American Declaration of Independence drew on a version of contract theory, which, however, incorporated the belief that humans are created by God and endowed with natural rights, which they reasonably seek to preserve and implement by entering into a social arrangement. Some other versions dispense with God and natural rights; post-Christian versions, assuming that humans are the sole source of meaning and value in reality, regard authority as nothing but a concession of arbitrary decision-making power—a concession necessary for people to obtain some of the things they happen to want.

A contract theory of the latter kind plainly cannot be reconciled with the Christian conception of authority as morally grounded. But Catholic teaching rejects as inadequate even versions of contract theory which presuppose a God-given moral order and natural rights. Although they acknowledge moral objectivity and include God, they miss elements essential to the Church's understanding of the truth that authority comes from God, namely, that humans are naturally social and that authority is immediately grounded in the moral implications of the common good. On the contract theory, society is artificial and authority is created by a prudent delegation by the people—"the consent of the governed"—a delegation which, it is worth noting, is a mere fiction rather than a real, historical act.[20]

In rejecting contract theory, however, the Church does not reject democracy. For, while authority comes from God, just government must be *for* the people inasmuch as it must serve the common good, which is the good of the people as a whole. Moreover, government normally should be *by* the people since they should participate insofar as possible in the exercise of authority by helping to choose public officials. Thus, as John Paul II points out, it is important for the rule of law (as against the arbitrary rule of a regime) that there be a distinction between and balancing of the legislative, executive, and judicial branches of government.[21] He likewise affirms the value of democratic elections: "The Church values the democratic system inasmuch as it ensures the participation of citizens in making political choices, guarantees to the governed the possibility both of electing and holding accountable those who govern them, and of replacing them through peaceful means

20. See Leo XIII, *Diuturnum, ASS* 14 (1881) 4–8, *PE,* 84.5–14. For a criticism of the contract theory, including St. Robert Bellarmine's transmission theory, see Finnis, *Natural Law and Natural Rights,* 246–54.

21. John Paul II, *Centesimus annus,* 44, *AAS* 83 (1991) 848, *OR,* 6 May 1991, 13.

when appropriate [note omitted]."[22] In electing those who will govern, citizens themselves share in making political choices; they shape cooperation for the common good, and so act as public officials at the highest level. Thus, in the democratic system, citizens exercise authority, which nonetheless comes from God.

Still, if the democratic system is impossible or breaks down, government remains necessary, and another form of government can be morally justified and deserve obedience. This point has a constant practical importance, since all just governments deserve the obedience of many people who in no way share in their authority: minors and various groups of noncitizens within their jurisdiction. Moreover, even a regime which wrongly holds power, such as the victor in an unjust war, or which abuses it, as the Roman emperors did, in many ways serves the common good, for example, by maintaining order and providing some essential services. Insofar as it serves the common good, such a regime exercises authority, which comes from God, and so deserves obedience, just as the New Testament affirms with respect to the Roman *imperium*.[23] (Of course, insofar as such a regime does not serve the common good, it exercises no authority, deserves no obedience, and should be opposed [see D.6, below].)

c) **Citizens' duties are not measured by government's coercive power.** Here *coercive power* means the government's capacity to enforce laws, ultimately by physical force and by penalties such as fines and prison terms. Even some people who are conscientious about their responsibilities in more intimate relationships take the view that, as citizens, they are morally required to do only what the government can compel them to do, and always are free to do as they please, provided they are willing to suffer the consequences. This confuses public authority with the coercive power of the government; such people overlook or disregard authority's moral claim, and so fail to understand and accept their own responsibility as citizens.

Still, civil authority and coercive power are closely related. Unlike any other community, political society embraces everyone in a certain region and is necessary to their well-being; yet, in any region, some people residing or sojourning there are unwilling to respect the common good or to contribute fairly to it. Thus, certain elements of the common good cannot be secured without the use of coercion, and so governments must be able and ready to use it. At the same time, the kinds of coercion regularly used in political societies seldom should be used in the family and other nonpolitical communities. They are hardly ever apt means for promoting

22. John Paul II, *Centesimus annus,* 46, *AAS* 83 (1991) 850, *OR,* 6 May 1991, 13; cf. GS 75.

23. Thus, Leo XIII, *Au milieu des sollicitudes, ASS* 24 (1891–92) 525, *PE,* 119.19, writing to the French about their history after 1788, distinguishes between the French nation's civil authority (an "immutable power" coming from God) and the various governments, which emerged from chaos after violent and often bloody crises, and draws the conclusion: "Consequently, when new governments representing this immutable power are constituted, their acceptance is not only permissible but even obligatory, being imposed by the need of the social good which has made and which upholds them. This is all the more imperative because an insurrection stirs up hatred among citizens, provokes civil war, and may throw a nation into chaos and anarchy, and this great duty of respect and dependence will endure as long as the exigencies of the common good shall demand it, since this good is, after God, the first and last law in society."

or protecting such communities' common goods, which, by comparison with that of political society, depend less on outward behavior and more on inward dispositions.[24] Consequently, political society has a virtual monopoly on the justified use of physical coercion.

Nevertheless, a government's coercive power neither is identical with nor the source of its authority. Coercion is a mere instrument of authority, and its use is justified only when authority is ignored and only insofar as the common good requires. In a perfectly virtuous world, officials always would make decisions fully in accord with the common good, and citizens, patriotically loving the common good, would willingly do their fair share in cooperating to promote and protect it. Even guests in the community, respecting their hosts' rights, would obey the laws. No one ever would violate a law while keeping an eye out for the police; no coercion ever would be needed; and the role of the police would be limited to directing traffic, helping people in distress, and so forth. Obviously, the real world is not perfectly virtuous, but the point is that no citizen should measure his or her civic duties by the government's capacity to enforce them.

d) **The duties of citizenship are moral responsibilities.** Not understanding the true sense in which authority comes from God, even many Christians who are fairly conscientious in other matters fail to take seriously their civic duties. They might argue: Many leaders are corrupt, many laws are more or less unjust, and no individual's dutifulness makes much difference.

The answer is: Participating in political life and obeying just laws are necessary for the common good; everyone should work for the common good and should be fair to others in this obligatory undertaking. Even though some officials are more or less corrupt and not all laws are perfectly just, fulfilling civic responsibilities contributes to the community's cooperation for its common purposes. One obeys laws, not lawmakers, and laws deserve obedience insofar as they are just, even if more or less corrupt officials do not deserve respect or gratitude. Moreover, one hopes other people will be good enough citizens that society will continue to provide the essential services one needs; it therefore is unfair to neglect to do one's share in fulfilling civic responsibilities.

Insofar as leaders and laws are imperfect, being a citizen is like living in a town where there is only one primary employer, a factory where most townspeople make their living. Even if the factory's manager cheats the employees and treats them harshly, and their struggle for justice meets with little success, the workers owe it to one another to do good work so that the business will make profits and survive. For if the factory fails and closes, everyone in town will suffer far worse evils. Similarly, everyone should keep faith with his or her compatriots by being a good citizen and obeying just laws, even though leaders and laws are never perfect.

e) **Hardship does not easily excuse one from fulfilling civic duties.** Sometimes a government tries to impose unfair burdens on certain citizens or groups of citizens; in such cases, citizens can rightly evade those burdens. Moreover, some-

---

24. The justifiable use of force by parents and guardians in raising small children is another matter; coercion is used because the small child simply is not capable of cooperating, so that community is limited, and parents or guardians must act unilaterally for the good of children.

times a conflict of duties can be resolved fairly by not fulfilling one's civic duty. However, civic duties can be very burdensome without being unfair. Meeting responsibilities to others always requires self-sacrifice, and so one is not excused from genuine civic responsibilities merely because it is hard to fulfill them. When unusual self-sacrifice is called for, very often everyone has a similar motive for not responding. For example, when violent crime terrorizes a neighborhood, nobody can identify the criminals and testify against them without running great risks, yet the neighborhood never will be safe unless some citizens take those risks. There-fore, nobody is excused from fulfilling civic duties by the vague and general claim that fulfilling them would be too hard.

4. The Common Good Is a Standard Which Governments and Citizens Can Use

In questions C through E, the common good of political society—which from now on usually will be referred to simply as *the common good*—will be pre-supposed as the most important principle for evaluating governmental measures and identifying civic responsibilities. However, many people find the notion of the common good obscure and confusing. Both the general idea of *common good* and the relationship between the common good and the good of the individual were treated in a previous chapter (6.C.1.d, 6.D), but one might still wonder: In practice, how can the common good be used as a standard?

The list (in 2.a, above) of common interests requiring or calling for the organi-zation of a regional community as a political society constitutes a sketch of such a society's common good. That sketch includes various instrumental goods, such as protection against hostile outsiders, systems of criminal and civil law, and a variety of public facilities. As was explained (in 2.c), the common good also includes something which is not only instrumental but intrinsically good: justice and neighborliness in certain relationships among compatriots. Proceeding from this understanding, together with general moral norms, especially the Golden Rule and moral absolutes, one can easily formulate the questions by which to determine whether political actions and policies truly serve the common good.

While that determination is necessary, it is not sufficient to answer questions about a citizen's responsibility to comply with the law in various kinds of cases. Therefore, other considerations essential for answering those questions will be treated below (in D and E).

a) **To use the common good as a standard, one must answer six questions.** Each of these questions bears on political actions and policies, and so on what officials are doing. But the point of asking the questions is to find out whether what they are doing truly serves the common good, and so deserves citizens' cooperation. Since this is the point of the questions, each focuses on one way in which a political policy or action sometimes fails to serve the common good: (i) it can be directed toward something other than the common good; (ii) it can unfairly distribute burdens and benefits among citizens; (iii) it can violate subsidiarity; (iv) it can be unfair to other nations; (v) it can be unfair to other individuals or groups; and (vi) it can violate a moral absolute.

i) Because officials sometimes abuse their power in order to pursue purely private benefits, and interest groups sometimes try to secure their own advantages by political means and public action, not all governmental measures which are morally acceptable in themselves deserve the cooperation of citizens as such. To determine whether citizens are morally required to cooperate in the action (or all the actions in the complex set) under consideration, one must ask: Precisely how would this action (or these actions) contribute to a purpose or purposes which pertain to the common good? If, for example, it is suggested that a public program be initiated to support the arts by providing grants to a small number of artists and subsidizing their work for the benefit of a small portion of the population with a taste for it, the question is: How would this program contribute to the culture of the nation as a whole? Again, if elected officials accept financial support from certain economic groups, one must ask: Has that support purchased favors for those groups' private interests?

ii) Any cooperation involves various burdens and offers various prospective benefits for different individuals, families, and other nonpolitical groups. Inequalities in wealth, education, and so on lead to differences in political power, and these can lead to violations of the Golden Rule as some members of a political society gain unfair advantages at others' expense. Thus, one must ask: Would the burdens and benefits involved in and resulting from this action (or these actions) be distributed fairly among the members of the community? For example: Does a law levying the same percentage of tax on all income unfairly burden people of modest income? Again: Do citizens eligible to vote do their fair share toward assuring their political society of sound government if they fail to vote conscientiously?

iii) Excessive action by political society can weaken the self-reliance of individuals and the solidarity and effectiveness of families and other nonpolitical communities. Then public action, rather than serving the common good, becomes self-defeating, since its undue expansion is inconsistent with the common good's instrumental character. Thus, one must ask: Would this action (or set of actions) violate the just liberties of individuals, families, and smaller communities or absorb functions which, perhaps with suitable public funding and/or other help, they themselves could and should fulfill?[25] For example: Does this public school system respect the primacy of the right and responsibility of parents to educate children?

iv) Differences in national power can lead to violations of the Golden Rule in international relations, and, as has been explained (in A.2.a), a nation guilty of such violations harms its own common good. Thus, one must ask: Would this action (or this set of actions) unfairly harm or selfishly fail to help any other nation or group of nations? For example: Will these regulations on international trade tend further to impoverish less developed trading partners?

v) A political society can ignore with impunity the legitimate interests of outside individuals and groups when these interests are not supported by another

---

25. This test is the so-called principle of subsidiarity (see 6.E.5.c). The politicization of the economy characteristic of even democratic socialism is not entirely acceptable: see the quotation from John Paul II in 6.E.5.d.

power. Here, too, violating others' rights harms the common good. Thus, one must ask: Would this action (or set of actions) violate the rights of any outsider? For example: Does this immigration policy selfishly refuse to welcome refugees who could and should be granted asylum?

vi) Sometimes it happens that basic human goods other than those included in the common good are at stake in political action. Then the action's bearing on these goods must be considered and can be morally decisive independently of any direct consideration of the common good. For example, since killing the innocent is always wrong, the Nazi program of genocide was immoral in itself, so that participation in it could not have been anyone's civic responsibility. Indeed, the official program and the activity of all Germans who wrongly cooperated in it violated their nation's common good. And in general, when members of a political society acting as such do anything wrong in itself, their action violates the common good precisely because it involves the society in something wrong in itself. Thus, one cannot use the common good as a standard for evaluating governmental measures and identifying citizens' responsibilities without asking: Is the action (or any one or more of the complex set of actions) under consideration morally excluded as always wrong?

b) **False conceptions of the common good should be avoided.** Many people ignore or misinterpret the specific justice and neighborliness which are central to the common good. In place of the relevant aspects of the good of interpersonal harmony, they focus on other things.

Some, perhaps assuming something like Hegel's organic theory of the state, emphasize the nation's power and status in the international community, its military success and maintenance of peace on its own terms, as if greatness of these sorts were good in itself. They think members of a political society do as they should insofar as history will judge their actions to have contributed to their nation's glory.

Others, presupposing a form of consequentialism (criticized in *CMP*, 6), hold the common good (which they sometimes call the "general utility" or "common interest") to be nothing but the greatest good for the greatest number of individual citizens. In explaining what constitutes the common good, they emphasize instrumental goods, for example, a prosperous national economy and good public facilities. Indeed, they think that even social justice and the protection of the fundamental rights of persons are objects of social concern only insofar as they are instrumental. According to this utilitarian view, members of a political society do as they should insofar as their actions tend to bring about a state of affairs in which such instrumental goods are realized, so that people can enjoy a rich and satisfying life, as individuals and in private associations, with a minimum of unpleasantness.

Still others, taking an individualistic approach, reject or qualify utilitarianism, for they regard personal liberty and equality as good in themselves. Such theorists emphasize individual rights, even at the expense of the diverse roles necessary for community and the aspects of justice which cannot be reduced to equality.[26] On

---

26. See Mary Ann Glendon, *Rights Talk: The Impoverishment of Political Discourse* (New York: Free Press, 1991), for an extended critique of views of this sort.

this view, citizens do as they should insofar as their actions maximize the equality of all members of the political society in doing as they please and obtaining whatever they need and want.

Elements of one or more of these erroneous views often are introduced into discussions of public policies and civic responsibilities. Hence, in applying the measure of the common good, one must avoid allowing such misconceptions to confuse matters.

Question C: What Are One's Responsibilities with Regard to Political Activity?

Citizens participate in government not only when they hold an elective or appointive office but also when they vote or otherwise engage in the political process, for example, by working in someone's political campaign, or by supporting or opposing proposed laws or governmental activities.

As in other fields, a person's actions in these matters should be guided by both relevant negative norms and general affirmative norms, for example, not to lie, not intentionally to harm opponents, not to violate just laws, to integrate commitments with other elements of one's personal vocation, to work to overcome divisions, and to treat others not only fairly but mercifully. Since such norms are dealt with elsewhere, the treatment here will focus on specific, affirmative responsibilities in the political sphere.

Some jurisdictions require that eligible citizens vote, but, generally speaking, affirmative responsibilities with regard to political activity are legally optional. Morally, however, one's duty to participate in government is extensive and can be serious. Citizens should try to understand the major issues and take positions on them in line with the requirements of justice. Every eligible voter should prepare and vote conscientiously. Some should participate in party politics and accept public office.

1. Catholic Citizens Should Participate Actively in Public Affairs

Vatican II teaches specifically that Catholics have affirmative responsibilities with regard to political matters: "In loyalty to their country and in faithful fulfillment of their civic obligations, Catholics should feel themselves obliged to promote the true common good. Thus, they should make the weight of their opinion felt, in order that civil authority may act with justice, and legislation may conform to moral precepts and the common good" (AA 14; cf. LG 36, GS 43, 75). Politics can be a dirty business, but if good people fail to do their duty in the political field, they abandon it to those who are less conscientious, and if faithful Christians and other believers keep clear of politics, they weaken the social position of their faith by allowing secular humanists to increase their power. Hence, while avoiding formal cooperation in anything immoral, Catholics should bring Jesus' truth and love to bear in the healing of the body politic.[27]

---

27. See Leo XIII, *Immortale Dei*, ASS 18 (1885) 177–78, *PE*, 93.44–45.

a) One should adhere to the principles of Catholic social teaching. In political activity as in any other, one should be guided by a Christian conscience, conformed to God's law and submissive to papal and episcopal teaching insofar as it authoritatively articulates that law in the gospel's light (see LG 24–25, 36; GS 50; AA 7). Thus, one should advocate or oppose public actions, policies, and programs by the standard of what is truly morally right and in accord with the common good (see AA 5–8, 14; GS 43).[28]

While the unrestrained pursuit of special interests is contrary to the common good, it is fully in accord with the common good to seek justice for various interest groups, for example, one's region, one's economic group, and the Church as one social body among others. The state should serve all legitimate interest groups in a balanced way, and prevent any from gaining unfair advantages over others. Hence, one also should oppose pressures for the government to favor one interest group against another to the detriment of the common good.

In line with the Church's teaching that government's proper role is to regulate social and economic affairs, and coordinate them for the common good, one should reject the view summed up by the slogan: "the less government the better." Governmental activities must be appropriately limited, but one should not support a general policy of deregulation, which would allow unlimited scope for the selfish pursuit of private ends.

At the same time, in accord with the principle of subsidiarity, the state should not be encouraged to assume the responsibilities of families and other nonpolitical groups; instead, measures which will provide them with appropriate funding and other forms of help should be supported.[29]

Those who oppose injustices and support what the common good requires often will appear impractical and unrealistic. However, by challenging entrenched injustices and standing against powerful trends threatening the common good, even a small number of principled and persistent people can make important contributions to public debate. They call attention to truths and values which otherwise would be ignored entirely, help conscientious politicians do what they can to mitigate evil, and perhaps lay a foundation for success in subsequent debates.

b) One should not propose one's personal views as Church teaching. On some matters, only one position is acceptable for faithful Catholics (see GS 43). For example, abortion and the use of embryonic humans as experimental material

---

28. See *CIC,* c. 222, §2.

29. By the same token, larger governmental units should not assume the responsibilities of regional and local governments, but should support them as necessary in meeting responsibilities. John Paul II, *Centesimus annus,* 48, *AAS* 83 (1991) 853–54, *OR,* 6 May 1991, 13, affirms that the state has competence in the economic sphere, namely, to create favorable conditions, to regulate for the common good, and even at times to substitute temporarily for private enterprise. He then criticizes the excesses of the welfare (or social assistance) state, explaining (854): "Here again *the principle of subsidiarity* must be respected: a community of a higher order should not interfere in the internal life of a community of a lower order, depriving the latter of its functions, but rather should support it in case of need and help to coordinate its activity with the activities of the rest of society, always with a view to the common good [note omitted]." The passage quoted in 6.E.5.d follows immediately.

should never be permitted by law.[30] In such cases, someone who calls fellow Catholics to cooperate in a course of political action and admonishes any who fail to do so, acts rightly in pointing out the Church's relevant teaching.

On many matters, however, faithful Catholics can legitimately disagree. In some situations, those exercising political power are open only to options incompatible with the Church's teaching, and the question is which of those options should be considered worse and so opposed in order to mitigate the evil. In other situations, there are two or more positions, incompatible with one another but compatible with the Church's teaching. In both kinds of cases, even though someone has arrived at a position by applying the Church's teaching to the facts of the problem as carefully as possible, he or she should not propose that opinion as the Church's teaching.[31] Moreover, a person should respect the views of others legitimately differing from his or her own and avoid bitter conflicts, which tend to damage both the common good and the Church's unity.

c) **The laity are primarily responsible for action in political matters.** In political matters, rather than looking to bishops and priests to lead the way, the laity should take the initiative:

> The laity must take on the renewal of the temporal order as their own mission; led by the light of the gospel and the mind of the Church, and motivated by Christian charity, they must act in that order directly and in a distinct way, cooperating as citizens with other citizens, using their own expertise, and acting on their own responsibility, everywhere and in everything seeking the justice of God's kingdom. (AA 7; cf. GS 43)

Having formed their consciences properly, the laity should make and act on their own judgments about which morally acceptable alternatives to support, which morally acceptable methods to use, and so on. Only in this way can they effectively cooperate as citizens with other like-minded citizens and avoid becoming, and being seen to be, agents of the Catholic Church, with all the inhibitions and burdens that status would involve.

d) **In policy debates, one should be honest, courteous, and firm.** One should be scrupulously honest and accurate, never arguing from premises one considers false or in ways one considers fallacious. A good end does not justify bad means, and dishonesty and manipulation destroy community. But when, as often happens, one's view is grounded in both faith and reason, there is nothing dishonest in proposing only those reasons which anyone of good will can understand and should accept. Moreover, when others' principles which one considers faulty happen to imply a true conclusion, one may point out what consistency with those principles requires. In public controversies, while maintaining civility and charity, and avoiding animosity and contentiousness, one should not fear to be divisive by pressing hard for what is right (see *S.t.*, 2–2, q. 38, a. 1). If adversaries attempt to suppress one's contribution to public discussion by labeling it an attempt to

---

30. See Congregation for the Doctrine of the Faith, *Instruction on Respect for Human Life in its Origin and on the Dignity of Procreation: Replies to Certain Questions of the Day*, 3, *AAS* 80 (1988) 99–100, *OR*, 16 Mar. 1987, 7.

31. See *CIC*, c. 227; cf. GS 43.

"establish religion" or "legislate morality," two things should be pointed out: first, proposals and arguments deserve to be considered on their merits, not dismissed by such labeling; and second, citizens committed to a traditional religious faith have the same right and duty as those who have adopted a secular humanist ideology to promote what they believe is for the true good of the society as a whole.

2. The Church's Teaching Specifies Many Purposes for Political Action

Since moral principles and the common good provide the standard for deciding whether to support or oppose particular public actions, policies, and programs, the Church's teaching, by articulating moral norms and clarifying the common good, helps Catholics to make morally sound political judgments. When relevant Church teachings are gathered together and formulated as norms for political action, the result somewhat resembles a political party's agenda or platform, but the point is different: to assist Catholics' prudent judgment by specifying many of the purposes by which their actions in the political sphere should be guided—actions which, with rare exceptions, will contribute to political processes not structured along confessional lines.

The Church's teaching, of course, must be applied prudently to discern which concrete options to support or oppose. Moreover, not all the following norms flow directly and clearly from first principles of practical reason, and not all pertain to Catholic faith or the Church's constant and very firm moral teaching. Thus, it probably will seem to most Catholics that one or another of these norms is questionable; in such cases, the documents cited should be studied and, where faith is not at issue, the weight of their teaching evaluated in light of the requirements and limits of the responsibility to give religious assent (see 1.I).

a) **Catholics should support religious liberty and its implementation.** Vatican II teaches that "in religious matters no one is to be forced to act against conscience or impeded from acting, within due limits, according to conscience, whether privately or publicly, whether alone or in association with others" (DH 2). The Council explains what is meant by "due limits": morally grounded legal norms necessary to protect the rights of all citizens, to settle conflicts of rights, to maintain genuine public peace, and to safeguard public morality (see DH 7). Within these limits, Catholics should support religious liberty for every person and religious group. For example, if a governmental policy not justified by relevant norms prevented Buddhists from building a temple, Catholics should support changing the policy so that the Buddhists' project would be treated in the same way as a proposal to build a church or synagogue.

However, religious liberty by no means requires an absolute or strict separation of state and church (see DH 6). Catholics may and should support not only laws protecting the freedom of religious bodies but measures, such as tax exemptions, favoring religious activities.[32] Moreover, they should insist that church-related

---

32. See Leo XIII, *Immortale Dei, ASS* 18 (1885) 163–64, *PE,* 93.6; United States Hierarchy, "Pastoral Letter on Mexico" (12 Dec. 1926), 23, in *Pastoral Letters,* ed. Nolan, 1:346–47.

schools and other institutions be protected against laws and social policies which pressure them to secularize. So, for example, provisions requiring religiously oriented schools, hospitals, and other agencies to compromise their religious character in order to receive their fair share of public subsidies should be opposed.

b) Catholics should support equal justice for all. With respect to human dignity and the fundamental rights of the person flowing from it, discrimination cannot be rational; it always violates love of neighbor and is contrary to God's intent (see GS 29, NA 5). Catholics therefore should support laws and social policies which protect everyone's fundamental rights and exclude every form of unfair discrimination against persons of any sort, for example, discriminatory practices in labor markets, educational systems, and electoral politics which create obstacles for certain racial groups.[33] They should support laws and policies to overcome discrimination not only against women in general—for example, with respect to educational opportunities and wages—but against "particular categories of women, as for example childless wives, widows, separated or divorced women, and unmarried mothers."[34]

John Paul II teaches: "Since disabled people are subjects with all their rights, they should be helped to participate in the life of society in all its aspects and at all the levels accessible to their capacities."[35] Laws and policies should be favored which protect the rights of the handicapped and enable them to fulfill themselves as much as possible and contribute what they can to the common good. For example, Catholics should urge government officials to protect handicapped babies who "are sometimes denied ordinary and usual medical procedures."[36]

Within limits consistent with the common good, a nation should receive immigrants, especially those, such as political and economic refugees, who have been compelled to leave their homeland.[37] Catholics therefore should support a just and merciful immigration policy and governmental action to prevent the exploitation of immigrants and migrant workers.[38] They also should support public policies to lessen the hardship of immigration by helping to reunite divided families as soon as possible (see AA 11) and by enabling more workers to find employment in their own countries so that they will not be forced to migrate.[39]

---

33. See National Conference of Catholic Bishops, "Economic Justice for All," 182, in *Pastoral Letters,* ed. Nolan, 5:434.

34. John Paul II, *Familiaris consortio,* 24, *AAS* 74 (1982) 110, *OR,* 21–28 Dec. 1981, 5.

35. John Paul II, *Laborem exercens,* 22, *AAS* 73 (1981) 634, *PE,* 280.104.

36. United States Catholic Conference, "Pastoral Statement of the United States Catholic Bishops on Handicapped People" (15 Nov. 1978), 8, in *Pastoral Letters,* ed. Nolan, 4:269.

37. John XXIII, *Pacem in terris, AAS* 55 (1963) 286, *PE,* 270.106, teaches: "And among man's personal rights we must include his right to enter a country in which he hopes to be able to provide more fittingly for himself and his dependents. It is therefore the duty of State officials to accept such immigrants and—so far as the good of their own community, rightly understood, permits—to further the aims of those who may wish to become members of a new society."

38. For example, by regularizing the status of as many undocumented immigrants as possible; see Administrative Committee of the National Conference of Catholic Bishops, "Together, a New People: Pastoral Statement on Migrants and Refugees" (8 Nov. 1986), 23, in *Pastoral Letters,* ed. Nolan, 5:340.

39. See John Paul II, *Familiaris consortio,* 77, *AAS* 74 (1982) 176, *OR,* 21–28 Dec. 1981, 16.

Human persons have rights not only as individuals but insofar as they associate in various communities. Laws and policies implementing an egalitarian and exclusively individualistic conception of rights can unjustly interfere with the liberty to form and cooperate in nonpolitical communities. Thus, Catholics should support the right of every legitimate association to use relevant criteria for membership and to regulate its own internal affairs.[40] On the same basis, they should oppose governmental actions which threaten the integrity of legitimate associations in the name of individual rights, for example, by using laws against discrimination to require Catholic institutions to entrust sensitive positions to people who are not the best qualified precisely as Catholics.

c) **Catholics should support justice with respect to human life.** Since the intentional killing of the innocent is always wrong, all innocent persons have an absolute right to life. Catholics should support laws which protect that right by forbidding abortion, infanticide, and the killing, whether by commission or omission, of handicapped, debilitated, or aged persons. They also should oppose the legalization of assisted suicide, euthanasia, and other intentional killing of any person with or without his or her consent.

If unjust laws permit wrongful killing, Catholics should support amendments or supplementary laws guaranteeing every person's right to refuse all involvement in such killing without incurring any criminal or civil liability, or suffering loss of employment or professional status.

Catholics should oppose public funding and other policies facilitating abortion while supporting legislation to promote morally acceptable alternatives.[41] They should support laws and public policies excluding the use and destruction of aborted human embryos and those created in the laboratory, for example, in scientific experiments or in treating someone else's disease.[42] Likewise, they should support laws forbidding "all interventions on the genetic heritage of the human person that are not aimed at correcting anomalies."[43]

Catholics also should support laws and public policies to mitigate unnecessary threats to human life.[44] Likewise, they should support public programs to ensure

40. See John XXIII, *Pacem in terris, AAS* 55 (1963) 262–63, *PE,* 270.23.

41. For example, expanded assistance to disadvantaged parents and their children; on this, see National Conference of Catholic Bishops, "Pastoral Plan for Pro-Life Activities: A Reaffirmation" (14 Nov. 1985), 37, in *Pastoral Letters,* ed. Nolan, 5:207.

42. Congregation for the Doctrine of the Faith, *Instruction on Respect for Human Life in Its Origin and on the Dignity of Procreation: Reply to Certain Questions of the Day,* 3, *AAS* 80 (1988) 99, *OR,* 16 Mar. 1987, 7, teaches: "The law cannot tolerate—indeed it must expressly forbid—that human beings, even at the embryonic stage, should be treated as objects of experimentation, be mutilated or destroyed with the excuse that they are superfluous or incapable of developing normally."

43. Holy See, *Charter of the Rights of the Family,* art. 4.c, *EV* 9 (1983–85) 475, *OR,* 28 Nov. 1983, 4.

44. The Committee on Social Development and World Peace, United States Catholic Conference, "Handgun Violence: A Threat to Life" (11 Sept. 1975), 9, in *Pastoral Letters,* ed. Nolan, 4:67, urges the eventual elimination of handguns with exceptions "for the police, military, security guards, and pistol clubs where guns would be kept on the premises under secure conditions."

that nobody dies of starvation, lack of shelter, the unavailability of emergency medical care, and so on.

Substance abuse not only endangers individuals' lives but threatens society as a whole.[45] Moreover, those who sell drugs to abusers exploit their weakness.[46] Catholics therefore should oppose legalizing the possession, distribution, and use of nontherapeutic drugs; they also should support public action to promote drug education and rehabilitation.

The Church teaches that everyone has a right to health care, and that it should be available to people of limited means, insofar as possible, at little or no direct cost.[47] Catholics therefore should support laws and policies suitable to ensure that everyone, including the poor and the unemployed, will have access to basic health care, including both preventative care and treatment.[48] In accord with the principle of subsidiarity, health care is best provided through voluntary associations formed for that specific purpose, with necessary public help and subject to appropriate governmental regulations. Catholics therefore should support such a system, including governmental action to increase the availability and efficiency of health care and to control its costs. They also should support legal safeguards to ensure that no health care provider will be compelled to do anything whatsoever contrary to his or her conscience.

d) **Catholics should support measures to protect marriage and the family.** Concerning marriage and the family, Vatican II teaches: "Public authority should regard it as a sacred duty to recognize, protect, and promote their authentic nature, to safeguard public morality, and to favor the prosperity of domestic life" (GS 52; cf. AA 11). Catholics therefore should support governmental protection and support for marriage and family life and oppose abandoning or weakening existing laws and policies which favor them. That includes opposing permissive laws on divorce and remarriage,[49] and resisting efforts to extend the legal status and privileges of marriage and family to homosexual relationships and other nonmarital unions.[50]

Catholics should oppose public programs promoting contraception, sterilization, and/or abortion, whether at home or abroad; especially they should oppose governmental coercion which would make the acceptance of illicit methods of birth limitation a condition for receiving public assistance or foreign aid.[51] Prostitution and pornography not only degrade the human person by treating her or his body as

---

45. See John Paul II, Address at the Therapeutic Center of San Crispino (Viterbo), 2–4, *Inseg.* 7.1 (1984) 1538–41, *OR,* 11 June 1984, 8–9.

46. See John Paul II, *Centesimus annus,* 36, *AAS* 83 (1991) 839, *OR,* 6 May 1991, 11.

47. See John XXIII, *Pacem in terris, AAS* 55 (1963) 259–60, *PE,* 270.11; John Paul II, *Laborem exercens,* 19, *AAS* 73 (1981) 628, *PE,* 280.93.

48. National Conference of Catholic Bishops, "Health and Health Care" (19 Nov. 1981), 5.56–63, in *Pastoral Letters,* ed. Nolan, 4:483–85, is more specific and calls for the development of a national health insurance program.

49. See Pius XI, *Casti connubii, AAS* 22 (1930) 571–73, *PE,* 208.84–85.

50. See Holy See, *Charter of the Rights of the Family,* art. 1.c, *EV* 9 (1983–85) 473, *OR,* 28 Nov. 1983, 3.

51. See John Paul II, *Familiaris consortio,* 30, *AAS* 74 (1982) 116–17, *OR,* 21–28 Dec. 1981, 6; *Sollicitudo rei socialis,* 25, *AAS* 80 (1988) 544, *OR,* 29 Feb. 1988, 6.

a mere thing to be used by others for their sexual gratification but impede the development and maintenance of the virtue of chastity, and especially hinder the education of children in this virtue.[52] Catholics therefore should support laws and vigorous law enforcement restricting prostitution and pornography as much as possible, especially to protect children and prevent prostitutes and purveyors of pornography from soliciting those who prefer not to be tempted. (On toleration of prostitution, see 4.E.2.j.)

All persons have the right to a good general education, so that they can use their gifts to serve others and reach the fulfillment to which they are called (see GE 1). Parents have the primary right and duty to educate their children (see GE 3, 6). Catholics therefore should support the laws, programs, and public policies necessary to assist parents in exercising their right and fulfilling their duty to educate. In particular, laws and policies should be supported which ensure that the children of the poor receive adequate education and that all children receive moral and religious education in accord with their parents' conscience.[53]

This means supporting not only parents' freedom to select the schools their children will attend but the steps required for this freedom's actual exercise, including adequate public subsidies, so that poor parents will enjoy at least as much public help in carrying out their educational role as those who are wealthy, and parents who choose religious schools will not suffer economic disadvantages on that account:

> There is a need for Christian families to be guaranteed the right to enjoy, without any discrimination on the part of the public authorities, the freedom of choosing a school for their children according to their own convictions, without this choice imposing upon them economic burdens that are too heavy.[54]

Catholics also should support the right of parents who can adequately educate their children at home to do so.

Similarly, Catholics should support provisions ensuring parental freedom to choose the provider in any public program of child care outside the home. They also should support legal protection of parental rights to determine what kind of education in sexuality their children will receive, and should oppose the imposition of programs of sexual education against the parents' will.[55] They should oppose

---

52. See John Paul II, *Familiaris consortio*, 24, *AAS* 74 (1982) 109, *OR*, 21–28 Dec. 1981, 5; Paul VI, *Humanae vitae*, 22, *AAS* 60 (1968) 496–97, *PE*, 277.22.

53. See *CIC*, c. 799; cf. GE 7.

54. John Paul II, Address to Catholic School Pupils, 4, *AAS* 78 (1986) 1032, *OR*, 24 Mar. 1986, 10. Also see DH 5, GE 6; *CIC*, c. 797; cf. Edward N. Peters, "Canonical Responsibilities for Public Aid to Private Education," *Faith and Reason* 16 (Spring 1990): 13–22; National Conference of Catholic Bishops, "Economic Justice for All," 343, in *Pastoral Letters*, ed. Nolan, 5:485.

55. Holy See, *Charter of the Rights of the Family*, art. 5.c, *EV* 9 (1983–85) 476, *OR*, 28 Nov. 1983, 4, declares: "In particular, sex education is a basic right of the parents and must always be carried out under their close supervision, whether at home or in educational centres chosen and controlled by them." Cf. John Paul II, *Familiaris consortio*, 37, *AAS* 74 (1982) 128, *OR*, 21–28 Dec. 1981, 8.

school-based clinics which provide children with contraceptives and sometimes even facilitate abortion.[56]

Catholics should support public policies recognizing the true value of work within the home and public action to ensure that wives and mothers will not in practice be compelled to work outside the home.[57] Laws and public policies should therefore be supported which assure families an adequate income, either through a family wage or through adequate social measures (see 10.A.3.g).[58] Provisions in laws or public programs making it economically advantageous for parents to separate should be opposed.[59] Catholics should support firm and effective governmental enforcement of fathers' duty to support their children.

"The family has the right to decent housing, fitting for family life and commensurate to the number of the members, in a physical environment that provides the basic services for the life of the family and the community."[60] Homeless individuals also need shelter. Catholics therefore should support public programs and policies to ensure that none will be deprived of adequate housing, that available housing and the resources needed to provide additional housing will be justly distributed, and that families will not be prevented by the cost of housing from moving whenever necessary to fulfill their responsibilities to earn a living, obtain education, and so on.[61]

Sometimes public policies, laws, and law enforcement result in the division of families. This is likely to be detrimental to the family, especially to children. So, unless a public action leading to the division of families is required by the common good or the protection of individuals from abuse or neglect, Catholics should oppose it. Where public actions which divide families may be necessary for some reason, Catholics should support measures to mitigate its bad effects, for example, provisions in penal law and policy allowing prisoners to maintain contact with their families and ensuring that the latter are not deprived of support.[62]

e) **Catholics should support justice in economic matters.** "The right to a share of earthly goods sufficient for oneself and one's family belongs to everyone" (GS 69). Since property is only a way of implementing it, this right is more basic

---

56. See National Conference of Catholic Bishops, "Statement on School-Based Clinics" (18 Nov. 1987), 13–16, in *Pastoral Letters,* ed. Nolan, 5:602–3.

57. See John Paul II, *Familiaris consortio,* 23, *AAS* 74 (1982) 108–9, *OR,* 21–28 Dec. 1981, 5.

58. See John Paul II, *Laborem exercens,* 19, *AAS* 73 (1981) 627–28, *PE,* 280.90–91.

59. For example, provisions which condition public assistance to poor children on the absence of the father; see National Conference of Catholic Bishops, "Economic Justice for All," 207 ("The nation's social welfare and tax policies should support parents' decisions to care for their own children") and 214 (on the working of a major welfare program), in *Pastoral Letters,* ed. Nolan, 5:442–43.

60. Holy See, *Charter of the Rights of the Family,* art. 11, *EV* 9 (1983–85) 480, *OR,* 28 Nov. 1983, 4.

61. See Pontifical Justice and Peace Commission, *What Have You Done to Your Homeless Brother? The Church and the Housing Problem* (Document on the Occasion of the International Year of Shelter for the Homeless), 3, *OR,* 8 Feb. 1988, 11–12.

62. See Holy See, *Charter of the Rights of the Family,* art. 9.d, *EV* 9 (1983–85) 479, *OR,* 28 Nov. 1983, 4.

than any right of ownership (see 10.D.1). Thus, public policies and programs necessary to ensure that nobody lacks the necessities of life should be supported: "As regards necessities—food, clothes, housing, medico-social assistance, basic instruction, professional training, means of transport, information, possibility of recreation, religious life—there must be no privileged social strata."[63] Normally, the most important, appropriate governmental action will lie in encouraging and regulating private enterprise, by means of public policies which promote balanced economic activity, so that nobody able and willing to work will lack employment at just wages.[64] However, insofar as additional public measures are necessary, they also should be supported.[65]

Catholics should support laws and public policies, including reasonable limits on taxation, which will foster a very wide distribution of material goods and encourage those who must work for a living to save so that they might own durable consumer goods, houses, land, tools, equipment, and/or share in the ownership of the businesses which employ them.[66] They should support public laws and policies which secure property rights—for example, noninflationary monetary policy—so that workers and investors can enjoy the fruit of their efforts.[67] They also should support laws and policies protecting and favoring small and medium-sized enterprises in agriculture, the arts and crafts, and commerce and industry—for example, the craftsman's business and the family farm, and cooperatives formed by such independent enterprises—rather than the increasing concentration of wealth and economic power, and the domination of the entire economy by a comparatively few large corporations.[68]

While recognizing both the proper roles of a business's owners and managers and the need for unity in decision making, Vatican II teaches that employees should actively participate in some appropriate way in running a business (see GS 68).[69] So, Catholics should support laws and public policies which will discourage the

63. John Paul II, Homily at Mass in Recife (Brazil), 5, *AAS* 72 (1980) 929, *OR*, 4 Aug. 1980, 10.

64. See John Paul II, *Centesimus annus*, 15, AAS 83 (1991) 812–13, *OR*, 6 May 1991, 7; National Conference of Catholic Bishops, "Economic Justice for All," 119–24 and 136–69, in *Pastoral Letters*, ed. Nolan, 5:415–17 and 420–30.

65. For example, unemployment benefits, job training or retraining programs, subsidies for jobs in the private sector, and the creation of public service jobs. In addition to the places cited in the previous note, see John Paul II, *Laborem exercens*, 18, AAS 73 (1981) 622–23, *PE*, 280.82.

66. See Leo XIII, *Rerum novarum*, ASS 23 (1890–91) 662–63, *PE*, 115.46–47; John XXIII, *Mater et magistra, AAS* 53 (1961) 420–21 and 428–29, *PE*, 267.75–77 and 113–15.

67. John Paul II, *Centesimus annus*, 48, AAS 83 (1991) 852–53, *OR*, 6 May 1991, 13, teaches that, especially in a market economy, economic activity "presupposes sure guarantees of individual freedom and private property, as well as a stable currency and efficient public services. Hence the principal task of the State is to guarantee this security, so that those who work and produce can enjoy the fruits of their labours and thus feel encouraged to work efficiently and honestly."

68. See Pius XI, *Quadragesimo anno, AAS* 23 (1931) 210–11, *PE*, 209.105–8; John XXIII, *Mater et magistra, AAS* 53 (1961) 422, *PE*, 267.84–85.

69. The papal teachings cited in the Council's n. 7 (n. 219 in Abbott) make it clear that what is at stake here is some form of institutionalized participation in planning and decision making. See also National Conference of Catholic Bishops, "Economic Justice for All," 298–301, in *Pastoral Letters*, ed. Nolan, 5:470–72.

unilateral management of enterprises by executives responsible exclusively to owners or stockholders, and should encourage some active involvement of employees in planning and decision making.

Catholics, of course, should support governmental respect for the right of workers, companies, and consumers to organize in order to pursue their common interests by morally acceptable means.[70] But they also should support the public regulation required to prevent such organizations from using their power to the detriment of the common good and to protect their members against corrupt leadership, for example, against criminals taking over labor unions.

"In a system of taxation based on justice and equity it is fundamental that the burdens be proportioned to the capacity of the people contributing."[71] Catholics should support distributing the tax burden so that the wealthier will be taxed more heavily and the poorer more lightly, if at all, and should oppose taxes which are especially hard on the poor.[72]

Because God created the world and its resources for all humankind, human dominion over the earth is limited by moral norms, which require not only respect for the rights of everyone now living but preservation of the common heritage for future generations (see 10.B.2.b–c). Catholics should support laws and public programs to conserve natural resources, especially nonrenewable ones, and to regulate activities with an aim to eliminating or mitigating damage to the environment. However, measures should be opposed which have an unfair impact, for example, on the poor or on people living in certain regions or engaging in certain occupations; instead, the burdens of sound ecological policies should be distributed fairly among those able to bear them.[73]

f) Catholics should support international social justice. Since there is a universal common good, the good of humankind as a whole, which neither national governments nor existing international organizations adequately serve, Catholics should support the self-limitation of its sovereignty on the part of their nation and its collaboration in developing a worldwide political authority capable of discerning and evaluating problems which affect the universal common good, and effectively directing international cooperation toward their just resolution.[74]

Pending the development of such an authority, Catholics should support the participation of their government in existing international organizations to the extent the activities of the latter seem to serve the international common good.

---

70. See Leo XIII, *Rerum novarum, ASS* 23 (1890–91) 663–68, *PE,* 115.48–58; John Paul II, *Centesimus annus,* 7, *AAS* 83 (1991) 801–2, *OR,* 6 May 1991, 6.

71. John XXIII, *Mater et magistra, AAS* 53 (1961) 434, *PE,* 267.132.

72. For example, sales or excise taxes on necessities; see National Conference of Catholic Bishops, "Economic Justice for All," 202, in *Pastoral Letters,* ed. Nolan, 5:440.

73. See National Conference of Catholic Bishops, "Renewing the Earth" (14 Nov. 1991), *Origins* 21 (12 Dec. 1991): 426.

74. See GS 82; John XXIII, *Pacem in terris, AAS* 55 (1963) 291–96, *PE,* 270.130–45; John Paul II, *Centesimus annus,* 58, *AAS* 83 (1991) 863–64, *OR,* 6 May 1991, 15; National Conference of Catholic Bishops, "Economic Justice for All," 322–24, in *Pastoral Letters,* ed. Nolan, 5:478–79. Also see Rodger Charles, S.J., and Drostan Maclaren, O.P., *The Social Teaching of Vatican II: Its Origin and Development* (San Francisco: Ignatius Press, 1982), 256–60.

However, international organizations sometimes do unjust acts or adopt unjust policies, for example, impose excessive sanctions on some nation or establish programs to foster immoral methods of population control. In such cases, Catholics should oppose their nation's cooperation in the injustice and support its efforts to prevent or rectify it.

Like individuals, nations are equal in their human dignity and basic rights. Thus, Catholics should urge their nation to follow the Golden Rule in its relations with other nations: to respect every other nation's right to independence, and to fulfill faithfully treaties and other agreements made in accord with international law.[75] They should support their government's respect for the identity of each people, with its own history and culture, and should oppose treating any nation as inferior, due to its comparative military or economic weakness, smaller size, or the different character of its people.[76]

Since strict justice requires those with adequate means not to allow others' basic human needs to go unmet, Catholics living in affluent nations should support public programs and policies to assist poorer nations: to help them develop themselves in accord with their own national character and identity, to regulate trade relations with them so that they will receive what they need in exchange for what they can supply, and to restructure or even cancel debts which they cannot pay without undue hardship to their people.[77] Catholics also should support the equitable inclusion of the poorer nations in all bodies which will make decisions about world trade, international monetary arrangements, and other matters which will affect their economic interests.[78]

If one foreign power has unjustly attacked another, Catholics should oppose abandoning the victim of unjust attack and support assisting it.[79] If their government favors one party to an international conflict against the just claims of another, Catholic citizens should oppose that unjust foreign policy.

"The arms race wounds humankind most gravely, and injures the poor to an intolerable degree" (GS 81).[80] For their own nations, therefore, Catholics should support arms limitation and mutual disarmament (see GS 82). They also should oppose foreign policies which encourage poorer nations to use their limited resources on armaments. International trade in armaments often is carried on for purely economic motives; laws and policies to eliminate the arms trade should be supported except insofar as that trade is a necessary means to maintaining or restoring just peace.[81]

75. See Pius XII, *Summi Pontificatus, AAS* 31 (1939) 438, *PE*, 222.74.

76. See John Paul II, *Sollicitudo rei socialis, 33, AAS* 80 (1988) 558, *OR*, 29 Feb. 1988, 8–9.

77. See GS 85–86; Paul VI, *Populorum progressio*, 43–50, *AAS* 59 (1967) 278–82, *PE*, 275.43–50; John Paul II, *Centesimus annus*, 33–35, *AAS* 83 (1991) 834–38, *OR*, 6 May 1991, 10–11.

78. See Synod of Bishops, Second General Assembly (1971), *Justice in the World*, 3.4, *EV* 4 (1971–73) 832–33, Flannery, 2:708.

79. See Pius XII, Christmas Message (24 Dec. 1948), *AAS* 41 (1949) 12–13, *Catholic Mind* 47 (Mar. 1949): 184–85.

80. See also John XXIII, *Pacem in terris, AAS* 55 (1963) 286–88, *PE*, 270.109–13.

81. See John Paul II, *Sollicitudo rei socialis*, 24, *AAS* 80 (1988) 541–42, *OR*, 29 Feb. 1988, 6.

3. One Should Vote Conscientiously

Many citizens regard voting as a privilege which, morally speaking, they are entirely free to exercise or not, just as they please. But Vatican II, having taught that it is in accord with human nature that all citizens should be able to participate freely and actively in shaping political structures and choosing leaders, draws the conclusion: "Therefore, all citizens are to bear in mind that it is both their right and duty to use their free vote to promote the common good" (GS 75).[82]

Perhaps because major, general, national elections receive great attention from the media, some people vote in them but omit voting in other elections and/or in primaries. Similarly, some people vote for candidates for office but omit voting on the issues which have been placed on the ballot. As a rule, however, an election's outcome is likely to affect many people in significant ways, so the duty to vote is not limited to elections which draw more attention and seem more important.

Totalitarian regimes sometimes conduct elections for mere show, and even in democratic societies an election occasionally offers no option which makes any detectable difference to the common good. In such cases, there is no obligation to vote and there may even be an obligation to refuse to do so.

a) **The limited impact of one vote is not an excuse for failing to vote.** Since elections are almost never decided by a single vote, many people think their vote will make little difference, and use this as an excuse for not voting. This excuse is unsound for two reasons.

First, even if one's single vote made no difference, one should vote in order to be fair to more conscientious fellow citizens. If the thoughtful and conscientious do not vote, elections will be decided by those whose motives are not rational or are purely selfish, with disastrous results for the common good. Since any rational person wants others who are thoughtful and conscientious to vote, it is unfair then to excuse oneself from voting because a single vote will not make a difference.

An analogy will help to make the point clear. Many people are tempted to pick a single flower from a lovely display in a public park, but if many give in to the temptation, the display will be spoiled. Therefore, all who enjoy the flowers as they stroll through the park hope that others will not pick them and resent it if they notice someone doing so. Thus, if one makes an exception in favor of oneself—"This blossom will make a fine boutonnière and nobody will miss it"—one violates the Golden Rule.

Second, since politics is an ongoing process, votes can have important political effects even when not decisive. The size of the vote by which a candidate wins often affects the candidate's power while in office. Hence, it usually is worthwhile to use one's vote to widen the margin by which a good candidate wins or narrow the margin by which a bad one wins. Moreover, the size of a losing candidate's vote often determines whether he or she will again be nominated or run for the same office or another one. From this perspective, too, it often is worthwhile to use one's vote for a good candidate or against a bad one.

---

82. A helpful study: Titus Cranny, S.A., *The Moral Obligation of Voting* (Washington, D.C.: The Catholic University of America Press, 1952).

b) **One should prepare adequately before voting.** Since voting is a duty which must be carried out in view of the common good, responsible voting requires careful consideration of what really is at stake in any particular election. What one-sided advertisements say about issues and candidates seldom provides a sufficient basis for judgment.[83] Instead, one should critically consider available information, and then judge which choice is more likely to promote the common good. It is not sufficient to weigh how voting for a particular candidate or position on an issue will benefit oneself, since self-interest need not coincide with the common good.

In considering candidates, a voter should assess their qualifications for the office they are seeking. Their past experience and intellectual gifts are relevant. Pleasing personality can help a public official deal effectively with people, but should not be overrated as a qualification; good character is far more important. Candidates who say they are personally opposed to grave injustices but could not refuse to cooperate in them manifest readiness gravely to violate their victims' rights and, thus, the common good. They are either badly confused, gravely dishonest, or both. For, as John XXIII teaches,

> It is quite impossible for political leaders to lay aside their natural dignity while acting in their country's name and in its interests. They are still bound by the natural law, which is the rule that governs all moral conduct, and they have no authority to depart from its slightest precepts.[84]

Therefore, one should not vote for a candidate who says, "I'm personally opposed to such-and-such an injustice, but . . .," unless the alternative is even worse.

Sometimes the best way to judge how to vote is to follow someone else's advice. As on any other matter, however, no one should trust the advice of others without good reasons for thinking they have the resources to make a sound judgment and no motive for providing unsound advice. Plainly, these conditions often are not met by those who offer unsought advice about how to vote.

Sometimes, one's deliberation leads to incommensurable reasons for and against each option. In such cases, however, it usually is possible to make a choice supported by reasons and guided by discernment, and this should be done. But if, having done what can and should be done to prepare to vote, one still finds no firm, rational basis for making a choice, it is right to abstain from voting on that office or that matter.

c) **One should not vote unquestioningly for a party.** Some people follow the recommendations of a certain political party by voting for all its candidates and positions on ballot questions. Even if one party is plainly preferable, however, no

---

83. See Eric Clark, *The Want Makers: The World of Advertising: How They Make You Buy* (New York: Viking, 1989), 291–314.

84. John XXIII, *Pacem in terris, AAS* 55 (1963) 279–80, *PE,* 270.81. Likewise, Leo XIII, *Immortale Dei, ASS* 18 (1885) 179, *PE,* 93.47, teaches: "It is unlawful to follow one line of conduct in private life and another in public, respecting privately the authority of the Church, but publicly rejecting it; for this would amount to joining together good and evil, and to putting man in conflict with himself; whereas he ought always to be consistent, and never in the least point nor in any condition of life to swerve from Christian virtue."

party is perfect, and unquestioning adherence to any party is unreasonable. Rather, both the parties and the candidates, as well as any specific issues which will be decided by vote should be considered on their merits.

Parties have different degrees of importance in different constitutional systems. In parliamentary systems, stability often requires that one party win a majority, so that it can organize the government; members of parliament often must vote with their party leaders on important issues. Voters must therefore take into account that in voting for a certain candidate they are likely to be supporting the positions of that candidate's party and may be voting for government by that party.

In the United States, it is likely to be somewhat less important what party has a majority in a legislative body. But candidates for the chief office in the executive branch—president, governor, mayor—often urge the election of legislators of their party, on the ground that the legislature's support will be needed for effective government. That argument can be sound in some cases, and insofar as it is, voters should look beyond the merits of particular candidates and consider how the election of each individual would affect each party's impact, for good or ill, on the common good.

Still, a particular candidate's election always affects the common good to some extent by empowering not only his or her party but the candidate personally. Therefore, even in a parliamentary system, and more so in a system where parties are less important, the merits of both the parties and the candidates should be considered. A candidate should not be preferred on the basis of his or her party without reconsidering the merits of each party, which, of course, partly depend on the merits of the whole slate of candidates of each.

d) One sometimes should vote for the less bad of two unworthy candidates. As explained above (in a), one usually should vote for good candidates even if they seem certain to lose. However, sometimes there are three or more candidates, no worthy candidate has any chance of winning, and the race is close between two unworthy candidates, one clearly worse than the other. Then, instead of voting for a worthy candidate as a mere gesture which will have little significant effect on the common good, one should try to prevent the election of the worse of the unworthy candidates by voting for his or her less bad opponent.

e) The responsibility to vote can be a grave matter. There can be adequate excuses for omitting to prepare for an election and to vote, such as serious illness or the press of other responsibilities. Moreover, the guilt of many who fail to vote undoubtedly is mitigated by lack of clarity about the duty and/or by the fact that their omission results from inattention rather than from choice.

Yet even though the duty to prepare oneself and vote in certain elections might be light matter, the responsibility is grave in principle, since the common good is very important and will be seriously affected if people fail to vote conscientiously.[85] When the duty to vote is grave, it is even more clearly a grave matter to

---

85. See Pius XII, Address to the Lenten Preachers of Rome (16 Mar. 1946); *Discorsi e radiomessaggi,* 8 (1946–47): 19; *Papal Teachings: Directives to Lay Apostles,* ed. Benedictine Monks of Solesmes, trans. E. O'Gorman, R.S.C.J. (Boston: St. Paul Editions, 1963), 89.

violate conscience or ignore the common good in deciding how to vote, for example, deliberately to vote on the basis of self-interest against the common good or to disregard the common good and sell one's vote.

4. One Sometimes Should Participate More Actively in Politics

In most situations, most Christians have no obligation to contribute money or services to a political party, work in any candidate's campaign, promote the approval or defeat of a measure on the ballot, or seek or accept any public office. Many people lack the resources and gifts for such activities, and Christians whose lives are organized, as they should be, in accord with their personal vocations are likely to be preoccupied with other responsibilities.

In some situations, nevertheless, there is an obligation to become more actively engaged in politics. That will be so if one judges that the common good is seriously at stake, the need for one's contribution is urgent, and involvement will not require doing something wrong in itself or unjustifiably neglecting other responsibilities.

a) **Public office should be accepted as a service.** Anyone who might seek or accept public office will be encouraged by Vatican II's affirmation: "The Church considers worthy of praise and respect the work of those who, as a service to others, devote themselves to the public good and accept the burdens of this role" (GS 75). That can include a rather large number of people at some point in their lives, since offices differ greatly in the gifts they require and the burdens they impose. Membership on a local school board or library committee might well be within the capacity of someone unsuited for higher offices; similarly, temporary service in some office might well be compatible with other elements of the vocation of a person not free to make public service a career.

b) **Active participation in politics can be virtuous.** Typically, someone who takes a proportionalist approach will rationalize particular political acts at odds with the common good on the ground that they are indispensable means of serving it more adequately on the whole: "I must try to satisfy that group's unjust demands in order to gain (or retain) office so that I can work for social justice" or "To gain the votes necessary to pass this good program we must support an amendment whose whole purpose is to satisfy that group's unjust demands."

Nevertheless, someone motivated by a spirit of service to the common good can engage in politics without moral compromise.

> To accomplish this requires a full-scale battle and a determination to overcome every temptation, such as recourse to disloyalty and to falsehood, the waste of public funds for the advantage of a few and those with special interests, and the

---

Subsequently, facing the possibility that a Marxist regime would be elected in Italy, Pius restated the norm even more forcefully (Address to the Pastors of Rome [10 Mar. 1948], *AAS* 40 [1948] 119, *Papal Teachings: Directives to Lay Apostles,* 89–90): "In the present circumstances it is a strict obligation for all who have the right, both men and women, to take part in the elections. Whoever abstains from voting, especially through indolence or laxness, is guilty by that fact of a grave sin, a mortal offense." Also see Wright, *National Patriotism in Papal Teaching,* 175–76; John H. Schwarz, "The Moral Obligations of Voting," *American Ecclesiastical Review* 105 (Oct. 1941): 289–304.

use of ambiguous and illicit means for acquiring, maintaining and increasing power at any cost.[86]

Of course, the refusal to compromise generally will lead to the loss of some political support and sometimes will result in the loss of an election. Thus, someone uprightly engaging in politics must detach himself or herself from success and be prepared to yield power.

Even when others use dishonest methods, faithful Christians sometimes can cooperate to some extent, provided they avoid formal cooperation in wrongdoing. But no Christian may support any political organization whose main purpose is to further partisan interests at the expense of the common good or whose ideology is at odds with Christian faith and morals. (However, political parties can rightly promote particular interests insofar as these are likely to contribute to the common good, and, while the platforms of parties in liberal democracies often include morally unacceptable proposals, most parties avoid major ideological commitments incompatible with Christian faith.)

Question D: What Are One's Responsibilities with Respect to Laws?

In general, just laws should be obeyed, but sometimes a law just in itself is inapplicable to one's action. Sometimes compliance with an unjust law is morally required, but other times such compliance would be morally wrong. Ordinarily, it should be presumed that compliance with any law, just or unjust, is morally required, but under certain conditions this presumption can be overcome. In itself, the duty to obey just laws is a grave matter, but the responsibility admits of parvity. Insofar as laws are unjust or imperfect, citizens should work to reform them. Citizens often should resist bad laws, and in certain circumstances may, or even should, work for the replacement of a bad regime.

1. One Should Obey Conscientiously All Just and Applicable Laws

Laws are directives given by those exercising authority in a community in order to guide its members' cooperation toward their common good (see *S.t.*, 1–2, q. 90, aa. 1–3). Just laws are those which fully conform to the standard of the common good set out above (in B.4.a). As will be explained in the next section, a law just in itself sometimes is inapplicable.

A person should make a reasonable effort to find out what laws are in force and how they apply to his or her actions. Every just law should be obeyed in accord with its spirit, not minimalistically, even if it is not being enforced, or has some injustice associated with it, or might well be better.

a) There are special reasons why citizens should be law-abiding. The primary moral grounds of the responsibility to obey just and applicable laws are the reasons, already stated (in B.3.a, d), why civic responsibilities in general should be fulfilled: the obligation to pursue and protect the goods which constitute the

86. John Paul II, *Christifideles laici*, 42, AAS 81 (1989) 473–74, *OR*, 6 Feb. 1989, 14.

common good and the duty to be fair to others. But there are additional factors requiring conscientious obedience to just and applicable laws: the more or less probable bad consequences of failing to obey. The potential bad consequences for oneself, one's family, and one's associates are obvious: punishment, shame, ill repute, and so forth. Less obvious, but very important, are indirect bad consequences for the common good.

Not only do those who disobey a law directly withhold their cooperation and perhaps interfere with others' action for the common good, but they also indirectly affect others' actions. Some who observe lawbreaking will be tempted to follow the bad example, and even those who do not are nevertheless likely to be discouraged and less generous in fulfilling civic responsibilities. The inevitable antagonism between the more and less law-abiding strains the mutual good will necessary for community. Resources that could be put to other uses must be expended on law enforcement. The authorities, taking account of the limited will to community manifested by limited obedience to the laws, often are inhibited from choosing ways of pursuing and protecting the common good which would be preferable if only citizens were more dutiful.

b) **One should obey laws whose existence and relevance are obvious or probable.** In general, people know what the law is and what it requires. Still, doubts do sometimes arise, due to the lack of adequate information about the law or incompatible interpretations of its relevance to one's actions. When conditions change, for example, it may happen that a law which once effectively guided cooperation toward the common good no longer does so. Since it now is pointless, the authorities no longer enforce it and even the most law-abiding citizens no longer heed it. Yet it remains in the code as a dead letter, no longer in force. Confronted with a law which seems archaic, one therefore might wonder whether it still is in force. Again, studying the directions provided by the government's tax office to see whether a certain kind of income must be reported, one might find the topic treated in two different places, one seeming to say no, the other yes.

To direct action effectively toward the common good, lawmakers must see to it that most citizens can determine what rules of law are in force and how they should be applied to their actions. Some means usually is available to settle doubts, and it should be used: ask some conscientious and well-informed fellow citizen, seek guidance from an appropriate public official, consult a lawyer, and so forth. If this leads to the conclusion that a norm of law more probably is in force than not and/or more probably requires one thing than another, one should act accordingly.

Sometimes, however, doubt persists even after a reasonable effort to overcome it: it seems no more likely that the law is in force than not or requires this rather than that. Now, a person's moral responsibility is to obey laws, not anything and everything which might be a law, and to do what the law in fact requires, not anything and everything it might require. Law's function is to shape cooperation toward the common good; but if, having made a reasonable effort, citizens cannot determine what the law requires of them, they cannot effectively cooperate. Consequently, when a rule of law remains doubtful, citizens simply cannot cooperate in accord with it, and so it does not bind in conscience.

c) **Not the law's letter but its intent specifies one's duty to obey.** In many cases, if the law's wording is not definite, clear, and simple, its effectiveness in shaping cooperation is impeded. However, in some cases its purpose can be served without precise compliance with its letter, so that reasonable citizens do not expect precise compliance and public officials usually are satisfied with substantial compliance, which implies some noncompliance.

For example, speed limits must be definite, and the precise limit established is more or less arbitrary. Due to variations in the road, the environment, and the performance of vehicles, drivers could not consistently avoid exceeding the limit except by very carefully maintaining a speed well within it. Moreover, traffic officers must allow a margin for their own errors and so cannot fairly charge a driver with speeding unless there is evidence that the vehicle's speed exceeded the limit by more than that margin. In view of these factors, most people regard speeds slightly in excess of the limit as acceptable, and officers do not intentionally charge those whose speed is within that margin. Since those setting speed limits take these facts into account and set them at a somewhat lower level than they think the common good requires, the speed limit indicated by the letter of the law is consequently both more precise and lower than the legislature actually intends.

In cases of this kind, citizens are not morally bound to comply with the letter of the law; instead, they may shape their behavior in accord with the reasonable and common understanding of the law's intent. Still, within the margin between the law's letter and its intent, violations sometimes are officially noticed, and the law is enforced. That need not be due to any unfairness; indeed, it is inevitable if the law is to be enforced and its intended purpose served. Citizens who obey the law according to its intent but do not comply with its letter should therefore be prepared to accept and cooperate with its enforcement against their noncompliance. Noncompliance with the letter of the law is not morally wrong in such cases, but seeking to resist or evade the just penalty for that noncompliance is wrong.[87]

d) **Just laws should be fulfilled according to their spirit.** Many people approach all laws with a legalistic mentality, seeing them primarily as limitations on their freedom to do as they please and examining each law closely to try to discover the absolute minimum required to avoid liability for lawbreaking. Such legalism and minimalism manifest defects both in commitment to the common good and in fair-mindedness and mercy toward fellow citizens.

Instead of approaching laws this way, one should try to understand their purpose and shape one's action by them toward that purpose, while encouraging the same attitude in others and hoping everyone's cooperation will bear fruit in the common good. Recognizing that everyone sometimes falls short of doing what he or she

---

87. In general, one's moral obligation is not merely to accept the penalty if one disobeys a law (as the so-called purely penal law theory holds) but rather to obey the law: see Matthew Herron, T.O.R., *The Binding Force of Civil Laws* (Paterson, N.J.: St. Anthony Guild Press, 1952); Finnis, *Natural Law and Natural Rights,* 325–32. However, if the law's letter differs from its intent, compliance with the intent is obeying the law. The duty to accept the penalty for noncompliance with the letter flows from the relationship between law enforcement and the common good, not from the legislator's *fiat,* as in the purely penal law theory.

should, Christians should make an extra effort, so that mercy will overcome evil and redeem the benefit for all which will be lost if the law fails of its purpose. The proper approach to traffic laws, for instance, begins with understanding that they regulate driving for everyone's safety and convenience. When conditions are bad, good citizens are more careful than the law requires. When traffic is snarled, they are courteous: they give other drivers a chance to proceed. When other drivers are inept, confused, careless, drunk, or reckless, Christian citizens should be merciful: they should yield their rights in order to compensate for others' shortcomings.

e) **False standards should not be used to judge a just law nonbinding.** Even citizens who generally approach laws with the right attitude sometimes use a false standard in evaluating particular laws. Thus they risk mistakenly excusing themselves from obeying a just law. Three false standards are widely used.

Sometimes a law remains in force and is not a dead letter, but often is violated and seldom enforced. For example, in many places drivers disregard a seldom-enforced law against entering an intersection unless it will be possible to pass through it without blocking it. Noticing that they can do this with impunity, those with a strictly legalistic attitude for that reason alone consider the law nonbinding. But even many who are more fair-minded feel relieved of the duty to obey the law, for they notice that others disobey it, hastily generalize that nobody is obeying it, and feel they need not treat others better than others treat them. This standard is false; the common good remains the correct standard. The law's purpose is to facilitate efficient traffic movement; and even if many people violate it, obeying it usually does something toward serving its purpose, while the more often it is violated, the worse traffic is snarled.

Again, injustice sometimes is associated with a law. Perhaps procedural injustices occurred in its making; perhaps it is not enforced evenhandedly; perhaps lawmakers give bad example by violating it themselves; perhaps the regime is corrupt; perhaps the government is unjust. Many people mistakenly think these associated injustices subvert the law and render it nonbinding. What is relevant, however, is the justice of the law itself: Does it meet the standard of the common good? If so, it deserves obedience even if, to take the most extreme case, the government itself is unjust: "Where public authority, going beyond its competence, oppresses citizens, they should not be unwilling to do what the common good objectively demands" (GS 74). For example, in nations conquered by the Nazis and governed by their puppet regimes, many just laws—such as those forbidding various serious forms of wrongdoing, regulating traffic, and so forth—were maintained from codes previously in force or even were newly enacted. Despite the injustice of such puppet governments, their just laws served the common good, and so deserved obedience.

Finally, sometimes conscientious and thoughtful citizens think a law does not serve the common good as well as some alternative would. Since they would amend the law or replace it if they could, they conclude that they will meet their responsibility by doing what a better law would require, even when that involves violating the existing law. This misapplies the standard of the common good, which is not that the decision of those exercising authority must be the best possible—an impossible ideal—but only that it be good and not in any way evil. Moreover, those who substitute their own judgment about how to serve the common good for what the law requires abandon communal cooperation for individualistic action and presume what they are unlikely to know: that their judgment is better than that of those entrusted with authority.

2. In Unusual Circumstances, Even a Just Law Can Be Inapplicable

Sometimes a law just in itself should not be applied in given circumstances, and one rightly does not obey it because something else, which happens to be incompatible with obedience, ought to be done. The conflicting duty can have two different sources: the common good itself or some other morally upright interest.

a) **The common good can call for an exception to a just law.** A just law shapes cooperation toward the common good in the situations to which it is meant to apply. Still, because no lawmaker can foresee and provide for every eventuality, in unusual circumstances a law which is just in itself can become counterproductive. Thus, a conscientious and thoughtful citizen, without arrogantly presuming the superiority of his or her personal judgment, sometimes can judge that the common good requires an act or omission contrary to what the law specifies. For example, a town's ordinance forbids ringing church bells between midnight and six in the morning; but in the middle of the night a church sexton notices that a large prairie fire is about to engulf the town; rightly judging that he must warn the townspeople, he sets the bells to clanging. The sexton's judgment, which pertains to an aspect of the virtue of justice called epikeia (see *CMP*, 11.E.10; *S.t.*, 1–2, q. 96, a. 6; 2–2, q. 120), is not that the common good would be better served by a different law—say, one more flexible about the ringing of church bells—but that in these unusual circumstances, here and now, the law's spirit requires setting aside its letter.

Where it is right to make an exception on this basis, the law could not reasonably have been meant to apply in that situation. One is confident that, were the authorities aware of the circumstances and functioning properly, they not only would see that one's course of action is objectively reasonable but would prescribe it. For the law's force comes from the common good, and here the common good itself requires that the law not be applied.

b) **A conflict of duty can call for an exception to a just law.** As was explained above (in B.3.e), hardship does not easily excuse one from fulfilling civic duties, including the duty to obey laws. However, just as certain unusual circumstances can require setting aside the letter of the law for the sake of the common good, so other unusual circumstances can make abiding by the law so burdensome that an exception is justified for the good of some person, family, or other group. In its usual application, the law is just, but in some circumstances it would be unfair for the authorities to require obedience.

If possible, a citizen should seek an official dispensation from the law in such a case (see *S.t.*, 1–2, q. 97, a. 4). But even when that is impossible, it sometimes is fair for the citizen to act contrary to the law. The test is: Would conscientious, fair-minded members of the community agree that anyone in such circumstances should make the exception? If so, one will be confident that a jury chosen at random would not convict one for violating the law, and will agree that anyone confronted with a similar situation should act in the same way. For example, laws protecting property often may be set aside when human life is at stake, and the courts recognize the reasonableness of doing so by accepting the so-called necessity defense.

Since there can be no duty to do anything sinful, however, avoiding sin, no matter how burdensome that may be, never can generate a conflict of duty and render a law inapplicable. Thus, no conflict of duty can justify doing anything wrong in itself, or with a wrong intention, or in a way unfair to others. Moreover, since everyone ought to make some sacrifices for the common good, the burden justifying an exception must be grave. Unless one has a moral obligation to avoid the burden, it plainly is not grave.

3. The Proper Response to Unjust Laws Varies

Insofar as a law is unjust, there is a sense in which it is no law at all: it is not a proper exercise of authority shaping cooperation toward the common good. Yet unjust laws have more or less the same social and institutional causes, features, and effects as just laws, and in that sense they are laws.[88] Therefore, from a moral point of view, one's responsibilities do not end with the judgment that a law is unjust; one may not proceed as if the unjust law were nothing at all. Rather, it is a fact posing a special moral problem.

Insofar as a law is unjust, obedience is not strictly speaking called for. The question thus is, not whether to obey an unjust law, but whether to comply with it, that is, conform one's behavior to it. Sometimes one should not comply, and sometimes one should practice civil disobedience (see 6.a, below). But sometimes either the common good or some personal responsibility requires compliance despite the law's injustice. When there are reasons both for and against complying, but no obligation to do either, a person should discern which is preferable and choose accordingly.

a) **One should not comply with a law at odds with a moral obligation.** Sometimes a law is radically unjust because it directs doing some act excluded by a moral absolute or prohibits an act which citizens not only have a general right but a strict duty to do. For example, a law or directive might require the killing of certain innocent persons (see Ex 1.16) or forbid the preaching of the gospel (see Acts 5.28). In such cases, Christians rightly judge: "We must obey God rather than any human authority" (Acts 5.29; cf. DH 11; *S.t.*, 2–2, q. 104, a. 5) and do what is morally required rather than comply.[89]

In such a case, is there an obligation to be open about one's noncompliance with the law and/or to accept the penalty? In general, no. The goods at stake very often require that noncompliance be as stealthy as possible and that every morally acceptable means be used to evade punishment. Sometimes, though, specific circumstances require that noncompliance be open and punishment be accepted.

---

88. For a fuller treatment of some aspects of this matter, together with references to the theological tradition, see Finnis, *Natural Law and Natural Rights*, 351–68.

89. See Leo XIII, *Sapientiae Christianae, ASS* 22 (1889–90) 388–89, *PE,* 111.10; Pius XII, *Ad Apostolorum Principis, AAS* 50 (1958) 606–7, *PE,* 261.20–24.

Stealthy noncompliance may be scandalous (see 2 Mc 6.18–31); open refusal to comply may be necessary to bring about an unjust law's rectification; concealing noncompliance may be possible only by using immoral means such as lying; evading punishment might unfairly cause others to suffer; and so on.

b) **Sometimes the common good requires compliance with an unjust law.** If an unjust law requires nothing at odds with moral obligation, the common good may well require compliance (see GS 74). That can be so for different reasons.

Sometimes the law's injustice lies in unfairly distributing burdens and benefits among citizens, in violating the rights of other nations, or in wrongly taking over the responsibilities of individuals, families, or other nonpolitical groups; even so, the law does direct cooperation toward an element of the common good. In such cases, the responsibility of citizens to pursue or protect the common good can require them to obey the law while accepting injustice to themselves and perhaps also materially cooperating in injustice to others. Suppose, for example, that the regulations governing air traffic unfairly favor the convenience and safety of the private aircraft of influential citizens of a few powerful nations, while imposing unfair burdens on both commercial aviation and other nations. People will still have serious reasons to fly, and, if they do, the common good of air safety will require them to comply with the unjust regulations. In doing so, they need not choose or intend the injustice to others, any more than that to themselves, as either means or end. Rather, they could accept both injustices as inevitable side effects of acting on good reasons to fly and meeting their responsibilities to the common good.

Sometimes the law's injustice is more radical, and it does not direct action toward the common good. Yet even then, the common good can require compliance. Suppose, for example, that a military government imposed by the victor in an unjust war enacts laws exacting reparations from the defeated nation and credibly threatens its destruction if citizens refuse to comply. The nation's common good requires compliance, just as an individual's good usually requires compliance with a robber's demand: "Your money or your life." Again, suppose that, on the one hand, certain laws purportedly made for the sake of public safety do not shape cooperation toward any common good but were enacted only for the unfair convenience of certain groups, while, on the other hand, citizens can comply at the cost only of slight personal inconvenience. In such a case, one should consider the likely effect of noncompliance on others' attitudes toward all laws and tendencies to disobey even entirely just laws. Since widespread contempt for law gravely harms the common good, in the situation described a person might be required to comply with the unjust law so as not to contribute to that harm.

c) **Another responsibility can require compliance with a law which is not just.** Whether or not the common good calls for compliance with an unjust law, responsibility for one's own well-being or some duty toward others can require it. That obviously is so in the example of the unjust regulations governing air traffic. In many cases, too, the penalties risked by violating an unjust law would impede one from fulfilling other important responsibilities—for example, toward dependents, work associates, or clients—and there is no justification for taking the risk: one therefore should comply.

In some cases, all the members of an oppressed group should comply with unjust laws in order to avoid provoking greater injustices against the group's weaker members. Sometimes, too, laws providing and regulating the use of public facilities are unjust, but people must comply if they are to use those facilities, and some responsibility requires their use. For example, prior to 1954, only racially segregated schools were available to many families in the United States, and so parents, to meet their responsibility to educate their children, were compelled in that matter to comply with segregation laws.

4. There Is a Presumption, Not Easily Rebutted, in Favor of the Law

Patriotic and fair-minded citizens are ready to obey the laws, not predisposed to look for reasons which might negate that duty. But sometimes it is warranted to examine the duty to comply.

a) One should presume that laws are both just and applicable. If aware of a law relevant to his or her action, a person generally should take for granted that it is just and applicable, and act as it directs, without delaying to investigate the possibility that it need not, or even should not, be complied with. Although those subject to a law frequently have some reason for thinking noncompliance would be preferable, by itself that provides no adequate ground for not complying or for deferring compliance. Such reasons usually seem plausible because of the individual's limited viewpoint and special interests, which lead to overlooking considerations that justify the law's directive and exclude exceptions. Thus, for the most part, reasons for questioning whether to comply with a law do not point to the conclusion that one should not. Moreover, if citizens were not in the habit of unhesitating compliance, civic cooperation would collapse amidst endless hesitations, reflections, debates, and frustrations. Consequently, everyone should make a general presumption in favor of compliance with the law: compliance often is morally required even if a law is unjust; and usually laws are just; exceptions are unwarranted; and failure to obey promptly will undermine effective cooperation for the common good.

b) Sometimes one should investigate whether to comply with a law. Since there is a general presumption in favor of compliance, one has no general duty to question whether particular laws should be complied with; indeed, a general tendency to do that wastes time, fosters temptations not to comply, and manifests, at best, lack of community spirit and, at worst, rebelliousness.

Still, questioning a law's justice or applicability sometimes is appropriate. Investigation is morally required and blind compliance is excluded (see GS 79) when one has, not merely a vague suspicion, but a definite reason for thinking that following the law would be morally wrong—that the act it requires is wrong in itself, that complying would unfairly cause harm to someone or some group, or that the circumstances morally require making an exception. While not morally required, investigation also can be warranted on various wider grounds, for example, evidence that in making a law the authorities were motivated by self-interest rather than concern for the common good, the very great burdensomeness of complying, indications that a law is not bringing about fruitful cooperation, and so on.

c) **The presumption in favor of the law is not easily rebutted.** The mere fact that investigation is warranted or even morally required does not at once overturn the presumption in favor of compliance, and the law should not be violated while inquiry proceeds. Still, if the law and the circumstances admit delaying compliance, one may be justified in delaying and should do so if the question is whether complying would be wrong.

Investigation often does not reach a definitive conclusion. Sometimes it leads to a probable conclusion that there is no obligation to comply, yet one is confident no wrong will be done by complying and is not morally certain that noncompliance will not be wrong. In such cases, the presumption in favor of compliance stands, and one should comply.[90] A mere personal preference cannot prevail over the presumption in favor of compliance.

Sometimes, however, the investigation whose outcome is not definitive was morally required: the question is not whether noncompliance would be morally permissible but whether compliance would be morally wrong. In such a case, if it seems more likely than not that one should comply, the presumption in favor of the law stands, and one should comply. But if, having considered everything, including the grounds for the presumption in favor of the law, one judges it more probable that it would be wrong to comply, then one ought not. Rather, as in any other case of uncertainty about moral obligations, one should fulfill what more likely is one's true moral responsibility (see *CMP,* 12.C.7).

5. In Itself the Duty to Obey the Law Is Grave but Admits Parvity

Law shapes cooperation toward the common good, and those exercising public authority seldom make laws about insignificant matters. Disobedience to a law is thus likely to have significant bad consequences for someone—indeed, in most cases, for many people—and disobedience to any just and applicable law therefore usually is a grave matter. Even though, as often happens, what a law requires may appear at first sight trivial or even ridiculous, careful consideration generally shows that more is at stake than meets the eye. Moreover, lawbreaking's indirect effects must be taken into account, not least the fact that violating any law weakens the general habit of obedience, which is vital to the common good. Furthermore, since lawbreaking involves unfairness to fellow citizens, an important sign of its gravity is the seriousness with which people take others' violations, even in comparatively small matters. To be inconvenienced even by someone else's parking violation strikes few people as insignificant.

Nevertheless, sometimes a violation can be a light matter because a law's subject matter makes it possible that even if small violations become common, neither significant harm nor significant indirect bad effects will result. A sign of such parvity is that even citizens who do not themselves violate the law consider

---

90. St. Alphonsus Maria de Liguori, *Theologia moralis,* ed. L. Gaudé, 4 vols. (Rome: Ex Typographia Vaticana, 1905–12), 1:80–81, shows that the tradition supports a strong presumption in favor of the law. However, not all of those cited seem to distinguish clearly between cases in which one is confident that compliance is morally permissible and cases in which there are reasons for thinking that obeying a law would be wrong.

violations insignificant. The violation might be merely technical, not an action wrong in itself, and so minor that nobody would expect it to be punished. Or, again, it might be something wrong in itself but subject to parvity, for example, slight trespassing of a kind reasonable property owners easily tolerate and never seek to prevent by asking officials to enforce the law.

Sometimes police or other officials are bribed to facilitate sinful lawbreaking. Bribery not only itself violates the law, but involves scandal; other things being equal, it is a graver matter, morally speaking, than other lawbreaking. Moreover, bribery quickly corrupts legal processes, so that, without giving bribes, nobody can obtain from officials what he or she deserves. Poor people who cannot afford to pay bribes then suffer great injustices. (What about corrupt regimes in which bribery is officially tolerated and necessary to do things which are entirely legitimate? Assuming the end is good and the means chosen morally acceptable in all other respects, the paying of bribes in that kind of situation is material cooperation in wrongdoing, which may or may not be morally acceptable; see 7.F.4–5.)

6. One Should Work for Just Laws and against Governmental Injustices

Obeying God rather than complying with a demand of human authority whenever the two conflict, obeying just and applicable laws, and complying when appropriate with unjust laws do not exhaust one's responsibilities with respect to laws. Good citizens also should do what they can to change unjust laws and prevent or remedy governmental injustices.

In this struggle for justice, of course, actions wrong in themselves may never be chosen as means. Always, too, Christians should proceed in accord with specifically Christian principles, including love of enemies. And, as has been explained, even in a context of officially sanctioned injustice, just and applicable laws should be obeyed and unjust laws often should be complied with. Therefore, citizens should try first to achieve justice by strictly lawful means: publicity, political action, the courts, referenda, peaceful demonstrations, and so on. Whenever an injustice is great and there is a real prospect of overcoming it by lawful means, one should cooperate in the effort as fully as one can without neglecting other serious responsibilities.

a) Sometimes one should practice civil disobedience. Civil disobedience is a method of public protest against a law, public policy, or governmental act. It involves three things: (i) openly violating some law to focus attention on an injustice as a means toward overcoming it; (ii) avoiding doing anything wrong in itself, damaging to the common good, or unfair to fellow citizens; and (iii) showing sincerity and respect for authority by willingly suffering the penalty for violating the law. Sometimes those engaged in civil disobedience can violate a law whose injustice is (or is included in) the precise object of their protest. For example, some people violated laws requiring racially segregated seating on public transportation in order to protest the injustice both of those laws and the entire system of segregation. In other cases, it is either practically or morally impossible to focus civil disobedience on the injustice being protested, and so some related law is violated as a symbolic gesture. For example, civil disobedience has sometimes been practiced by carrying out demonstrations on public property slightly within the boundaries of zones from which demonstrations were excluded.

Civil disobedience should not be used as a substitute for lawful means of pursuing justice, but only as a supplement to them and only when there is good reason to hope that it will help overcome injustice rather than provoke its deeper entrenchment. Those engaging in civil disobedience should manifest neither hatred of anyone nor contempt for rational argument. The tactic also should be avoided if it seems likely to harm the common good, for example, by contributing to a general breakdown of public order.

Rightly conducted in suitable circumstances, however, civil disobedience is morally acceptable. By combining illegality with evidence of serious concern for the common good, it can effectively call attention to officially sanctioned injustices. Even when it involves violating some just law as a gesture, it can be morally justified, provided no moral norm independent of law is violated. For in such a case, the letter of the law does not apply, since the merely symbolic violation is meant to serve the common good, and reasonable lawmakers, even those holding a contrary position on the matter at issue, should appreciate that intention and recognize the service.

Consequently, for those whose other responsibilities permit them to accept punishment for civil disobedience, this practice can be morally good. Indeed, if grave injustices cry out for remedy, in appropriate circumstances Christians should engage in civil disobedience and, other things being equal, plainly should prefer it to measures involving more risks to the common good and/or to innocent persons.

b) Sometimes substantive and covert lawbreaking is warranted. Strictly lawful means and civil disobedience often are sufficient to carry on an effective struggle for justice, but in some cases they are inadequate. Of course, nothing can justify doing anything wrong in itself, damaging to the common good, or unfair to fellow citizens. But under certain circumstances, lawbreaking is warranted which is not merely symbolic but substantive, and those who engage in it need not act openly and accept punishment. Rather, they may rightly act covertly and try to avoid being caught.

Perhaps a regime has seized power contrary to the provisions of a just constitution, in order to protect special interests against the common good. Or perhaps a government has been imposed unjustly, for example, by the victors in an unjust war. In such cases, patriotic citizens often are justified in carrying on a systematic campaign of nonviolent resistance, in order to bring about reforms or the replacement of the usurping regime or unjust government. Such resistance can include the violation of many laws, for example, those forbidding the movement of persons, restricting publication, regulating certain forms of economic activity, and so on.

Sometimes, too, a government which on the whole is just has laws which unjustly permit the violation of a certain group's fundamental human rights, for example, laws permitting abortion. Now, in general, if citizens observe one person killing another, they may use the minimum force necessary to defend the victim's life, and in such a case, laws against trespassing, the destruction of property, and so forth should not keep anyone from doing what is required. Considered in themselves, moreover, acts morally acceptable in defending someone's life against a violation forbidden by a just law do not become immoral when they are necessary to defend someone's life against a violation permitted by an unjust law. In sum, when fundamental human rights are at stake, those engaged in their defense are not always morally bound to remain within the limits of civil disobedience.[91] In such cases, of course, the use of illegal means to defend the victims' rights might well be excluded by concern for the common good (for example, the danger of wide-spread public disorder) or one's other responsibilities (for example, the likely effects on one's family if one were sent to prison).

c) **Rarely, force may be used to replace a bad regime.** When regimes repress justified action for nonviolent reform and use institutionalized violence to maintain structural injustices, they and their supporters are chiefly responsible for revolutionary outbreaks which occur when people in desperation resort to arms in their pursuit of justice.[92] Moreover, since bad rulers who systematically pursue ends at odds with a nation's common good have no real authority, their status is the same as that of rebels against a just government (see *S.t.,* 2–2, q. 42, a. 2, ad 3). Therefore, the Church's teaching admits the possible moral justification of recourse to armed struggle as a last resort "to put an end to an obvious and prolonged tyranny which is gravely damaging the fundamental rights of individuals and the common good [note omitted]."[93]

Nevertheless, Christians should be very cautious about supporting the use of force against those in power, for, in practice, attempts to overthrow a bad regime are likely to be morally flawed. The side effects and risks involved in the use of force cannot be justified so long as there is any reasonable hope of attaining the end without armed struggle, and nonviolent action's capacity for effecting change should not be underestimated.[94] No use of force is justified unless the prospect of

91. Thus, it is a mistake to apply the standards of civil disobedience to illegal actions taken to protect human life. This mistake underlies the view that people involved in direct action against abortion are morally obliged to show respect for public authority by cooperating with arresting officers, paying fines, and so on. It also leads to arguments which are beside the point, for example: Direct action against abortion is counterproductive, because it alienates law-abiding people rather than winning them to the prolife cause. In fact, direct action against abortion aims not at changing public opinion but at saving babies; its bad side effects on public opinion may be accepted unless doing so is more probably unfair than fair to others affected, including other babies at risk. (Also, it is hard to know whether direct action against abortion is counterproductive, for even though it alienates some law-abiding people, it bears witness to the truth and makes it more difficult for people to forget that abortion kills babies.)

92. See the Medellín Conference document: Second General Conference of Latin American Bishops, *The Church in the Present-Day Transformation of Latin America in the Light of the Council,* vol. 2, *Conclusions,* 2nd ed., 2.15–19 (Washington, D.C.: Division for Latin America, United States Catholic Conference, 1973), 60–63.

93. Congregation for the Doctrine of the Faith, *Instruction on Christian Freedom and Liberation,* 79, *AAS* 79 (1987) 590, *OR,* 14 Apr. 1986, 7; cf. papal teachings cited in the Congregation's n. 119.

94. John Paul II, *Centesimus annus,* 25, *AAS* 83 (1991) 822–23, *OR,* 6 May 1991, 9, explains: "The events of 1989 are an example of the success of willingness to negotiate and of the Gospel spirit in the face of an adversary determined not to be bound by moral principles. These events

success is sufficient to warrant the inevitable costs. Furthermore, if force is used against a bad regime, its military capabilities and readiness to use them are likely to make bad means seem necessary—terrorism, torture, provocations intended to create martyrs, and so on—but nothing can justify using such means.[95] Finally, even if the bad regime is overcome, the common good may not be served; the new regime may be as bad as the old or even worse.[96]

Consequently, Catholic teachers often speak out against revolutionary violence. For example, even though the Latin American bishops clearly recognized widespread, entrenched injustices in their region and morally condemned them, they rejected the option of political violence and instead held: "Our responsibility as Christians is to use all possible means to promote the implementation of nonviolent tactics in the effort to re-establish justice in economic and sociopolitical relations."[97] Considering that the bishops took this position despite the authoritarian

---

are a warning to those who, in the name of political realism, wish to banish law and morality from the political arena. Undoubtedly, the struggle which led to the changes of 1989 called for clarity, moderation, suffering and sacrifice. In a certain sense, it was a struggle born of prayer, and it would have been unthinkable without immense trust in God, the Lord of history, who carries the human heart in his hands. It is by uniting his own sufferings for the sake of truth and freedom to the sufferings of Christ on the Cross that man is able to accomplish the miracle of peace and is in a position to discern the often narrow path between the cowardice which gives in to evil and the violence which, under the illusion of fighting evil, only makes it worse." P. Régamey, O.P., *Non-violence and the Christian Conscience* (London: Darton, Longman and Todd, 1966), articulates a Catholic theology of nonviolent action; Gene Sharp, *The Politics of Nonviolent Action* (Boston: Porter Sargent, 1973), provides an extensive treatment of the theory, methods, and dynamics of nonviolent struggle. While neither of these works is acceptable in every respect, both are valuable and deserve careful study.

95. Paul VI, *Mense maio, AAS* 57 (1965) 356, *PE,* 272.8, notes "that there is very often no respect for the sacred and inviolable character of human life" and condemns "secret and treacherous warfare, terrorist activities, the taking of hostages, and savage reprisals against unarmed people." Congregation for the Doctrine of the Faith, *Instruction on Certain Aspects of the "Theology of Liberation"*, 11.7, *AAS* 76 (1984) 904–5, *OR,* 10 Sept. 1984, 4, teaches: "The truth of mankind requires that this battle be fought in ways consistent with human dignity. That is why the systematic and deliberate recourse to blind violence, no matter from which side it comes, must be condemned (cf. *Doc. de Puebla,* II, c. II, 5, 4). To put one's trust in violent means in the hope of restoring more justice is to become the victim of a fatal illusion: violence begets violence and degrades man. It mocks the dignity of man in the person of the victims and it debases that same dignity among those who practice it." Also Congregation for the Doctrine of the Faith, *Instruction on Christian Freedom and Liberation,* 78–79, *AAS* 79 (1987) 589–90, *OR,* 14 Apr. 1986, 7, teaches: "The fight against injustice is meaningless unless it is waged with a view to establishing a new social and political order in conformity with the demands of justice. Justice must already mark each stage of the establishment of this new order. There is a morality of means [note omitted]." Hence, although armed struggle could be justified as a last resort to put an end to obvious and longstanding tyranny, "because of the continual development of the technology of violence and the increasingly serious dangers implied in its recourse, that which today is termed 'passive resistance' shows a way more conformable to moral principles and having no less prospects for success."

96. The popes frequently stress this point; see, for example, John XXIII, *Pacem in terris, AAS* 55 (1963) 301, *PE,* 270.161–62.

97. Third General Conference of the Latin American Episcopate, *Evangelization in Latin America's Present and Future,* 2.5.4.533, in *Puebla and Beyond: Documentation and Commentary,* ed. John Eagleson and Philip Scharper, trans. John Drury (Maryknoll, N.Y.: Orbis, 1979), p. 198; in 2.5.1.509–10, pp. 194–95, the document frankly points out the origin of the violence:

character of many of the regimes then holding power in their nations, it is even less likely that armed struggle could be justified to remedy injustices in nations living under freely elected regimes.

Question E: How Should Citizens Meet Certain Difficult Civic Responsibilities?

With respect to most matters, the general clarifications already provided will suffice for good citizens to understand their civic responsibilities, including their duty to obey relevant laws. However, the requirements of the criminal justice system, tax laws, and military service in war raise special moral problems, many of which have been treated by Catholic moral theologians. These problems, which often puzzle good citizens, merit special treatment in view of their importance as well as their difficulty.

1. All Citizens Should Cooperate with the Criminal Justice System

All citizens appreciate the importance of the criminal justice system when they need it for their own protection or want it to bring especially odious criminals to justice. At other times, however, people tend to take this system for granted and to think the whole responsibility for making it work rests on public officials: police, district attorneys, judges, and so on. But that view is mistaken. For the sake of the common good, everyone should contribute to the effectiveness of the criminal justice system.

The following treatment assumes that the laws violated are just and that the criminal justice system uses just processes and serves the common good. If criminal laws and/or processes are unjust, citizens' responsibilities might be different, as has been explained (in D.3, above).

a) Citizens should support the primary end of criminal law. The chief purpose of criminal law, and of the entire criminal justice system, is not to apprehend and punish criminals but to forestall crimes, for criminal acts are gravely harmful to the common good, usually by being grave injustices in themselves. In making laws, public authorities seek to prevent these injustices and other harms, and to encourage potential criminals to resolve problems fairly, respect the rights of others, live peaceably, and employ morally acceptable means to seek any benefits they might anticipate from committing crimes. Consequently, the basic way in which every citizen should cooperate with the criminal justice system is by supporting virtuous living and sound community, primarily by giving good example always and sound admonition when appropriate.

Citizens also should support public and private educational efforts to make clear the inherent harmfulness of criminal behavior not only to innocent victims but to criminals themselves. The regular, evenhanded, well-publicized apprehension,

---

"The violence is generated and fostered by two factors: (1) what can be called institutionalized injustice in various social, political, and economic systems; and (2) ideologies that use violence as a means to win power. The latter in turn causes the proliferation of governments based on force, which often derive their inspiration from the ideology of National Security."

trial, and punishment of criminals is an effective method of moral education, and citizens should urge that the processes of criminal law be conducted for the sake of this end as well as others.

Appropriate action for social justice also contributes to criminal law's purpose, by improving the options available to many people who otherwise would be more severely tempted to commit crimes.

b) Criminals may not use all possible means of defending themselves. If accused of a crime, one should not try to protect oneself by lying; to do so is a grave injustice (see *S.t.,* 2–2, q. 69, aa. 1–2). However, it is not lying for the guilty to plead not guilty, since this plea is not a denial of guilt but only an indication that the accused wishes to exercise the right to stand trial. Similarly, to plead guilty to a lesser crime than that actually committed is not lying, but only an indication of readiness to resolve the case on that basis.

Those accused of crimes of which they are guilty can be morally bound not to exercise their legal right to remain silent, even though confessing guilt will lead to punishment. In many cases, they serve both the common good and their own interests by admitting their guilt, cooperating with the authorities, and seeking mitigation of punishment. In some cases, the common good requires this, for example, when necessary in order to provide the authorities with information they need to halt the ongoing criminal activity of others and/or a prolonged and very costly investigation. Sometimes fairness to others requires a criminal to confess, for example, to prevent an innocent person from being prosecuted and/or punished for the crime, or to put an end to some harm being suffered by its victim. In still other cases, the criminal's own authentic self-interest requires a confession, either to support his or her commitment to reform or to avoid living with anxiety about possible exposure.

c) One ought to report probable crimes to the proper authorities. In general, children understandably consider it a serious betrayal when one member of their group tells parents or teachers about another's misbehavior. For children do not always form a single community with their parents or teachers, since adult authority over them extends to each child for his or her own good, while the group of children forms an independent community for whose common good they cooperate. Like informers in a totalitarian state, tattlers are loathed because they typically act out of self-interest rather than concern for others. However, as people grow up and take their place in adult society, they should put aside children's ways and begin to cooperate under the direction of public authorities for the common good of all. Therefore, if they live under a government which on the whole is just, their general sense of fellowship with one another as subjects of authority should not inhibit them from reporting probable crimes.

Someone who thinks a crime is being planned or committed, or has been committed, should inform the police or other relevant authorities of his or her reasons for believing this (see *S.t.,* 2–2, q. 68, a. 1). In providing this information, the person should take pains to be accurate, neither exaggerating nor understating anything, and distinguishing between conjecture and direct knowledge, and should answer any questions fully and precisely (see a. 3). Indeed, facts supporting even a reasonable suspicion of criminal activity should be reported if this might prevent serious harm to the common good or to some person.

d) This norm admits of exception in four kinds of cases.

First, there is no obligation to provide information if doing so would be pointless, for example, if a criminal law is enforced only when an official notices a violation as it is occurring or if the authorities make it clear that they cannot or will not act on information regarding a certain kind of violation.

Second, public policy, if not the letter of the law, sometimes allows a crime's victim to decide whether the violator will be prosecuted. In such cases, a victim persuaded that prosecution will not be in the true interests of those concerned need not inform authorities of the crime, and others aware of the crime also have no responsibility to report it.

Third, upright people aware of illegal activities by members of their own families, friends, and so on often put off informing the public authorities while admonishing the criminal to repent, make amends, and abide by the law in the future. This seems justifiable provided all the goods at stake are adequately safeguarded. In many cases, though, either the common good, fairness to others, or the criminal's own true self-interest requires that he or she confess the crime, and no exception to the duty to report criminal activity is justified if the criminal ought to confess but refuses. Moreover, if private admonition proves ineffective, indefinite delay in reporting criminal activity is unjustifiable, since the goods at stake must be safeguarded.

Fourth, special duties of confidentiality, among which the seal of confession holds a unique place, sometimes conflict with the duty to report criminal activities. (On solving conflicts of duties, see 5.K.3.)

Still, when officials seek a citizen's help in resolving a criminal case, he or she has a special duty to cooperate with the investigation, and exceptions are harder to justify. Moreover, concealing relevant evidence and lying to protect a criminal not only are morally wrong in themselves but generally are legal offenses.

e) Sometimes one should testify in court. Courts often require individuals to testify. But even if not required, one should offer to testify, unless prevented by some overriding responsibility, if doing so seems likely to contribute to a just verdict. Witnesses sometimes have just grounds for declining to answer certain questions, but they should never misrepresent facts for the sake of bringing about what they happen to think would be the right outcome. They should testify not only truthfully but with care to be accurate and to provide relevant information.

f) If called upon, a citizen should serve conscientiously on a jury. If serving on a jury would conflict with some other important responsibility or involve great hardship, a person may have adequate grounds to be excused, and those grounds should be presented honestly to the officers of the court. Plainly it is wrong to evade jury duty by exaggerating possible grounds in hopes of being excused or by dishonestly trying to provoke dismissal as unsuitable or undesirable; it is doubly wrong to omit registering to vote in order to evade jury duty.

When serving on a jury, one should attend carefully not only to the evidence presented but also to the judge's instructions about the law and its proper application to the case. During the jury's deliberations, one should be open to the arguments of other jurors, but should never agree to a verdict one considers unsound.[98]

g) The preceding responsibilities constitute grave matter. Lying which impedes the working of the criminal justice system seriously harms the common good and sometimes also seriously harms individuals. Moreover, none of the preceding specific norms (in b through g) ever is clearly relevant unless something important is at stake. Thus, if aware of one of these responsibilities and tempted to evade it by lying or to omit fulfilling it without a sufficient reason, one should not regard the matter as light.[99]

Confessing one's own crime, reporting the probable crime of another, cooperating in a criminal investigation, testifying in court, or serving on a jury regularly involve certain burdens and inconveniences, but that is not a sufficient reason to neglect these responsibilities. Nor, generally, is fear of possible retaliation by criminals, since everyone should make substantial personal sacrifices for the sake of the common good. However, if the authorities do not take reasonable measures to protect citizens who try to do their part, the latter sometimes can reasonably judge that their responsibilities in these matters are limited. Even so, they may not evade them by lying, and should do what they safely can, for example, by anonymously providing the authorities with information.

h) Christians should support the view that crime involves guilt. As deterministic theories of human behavior have become dominant in psychology and the social sciences, some people, including many involved in administering the criminal justice system, have come to deny that anyone ever freely chooses to break the law. Crime is reduced to the broad category of *antisocial behavior,* all of it attributed to psychological and/or social determining factors, which inevitably render those who misbehave more or less dysfunctional. This reductionistic view is based on the denial (not necessarily self-conscious, of course) of the truth which faith teaches concerning the dignity of human persons as self-determining beings, made in the image of God (see *CMP,* 2.B). Christians should oppose it, while upholding the distinction between crime and its guilt, on the one hand, and guiltless dysfunctional behavior, on the other.

Lawbreakers who lack moral responsibility for their misbehavior should not be treated as criminals, but as handicapped or mentally ill persons. If possible, they should be helped to overcome their handicap or recover from their illness; if necessary, they should be restrained to protect others and for their own good. But those who choose to violate the law should be treated as free and responsible persons, who bear guilt for their crimes. Of course, the guilt of some criminals is mitigated by factors limiting their capacity to deliberate and/or their options for choice, and such mitigating factors should be taken into account, either in specifying their crimes—for example, the distinction between premeditated and non-premeditated homicide—or in imposing penalties.

---

98. People called to testify or to serve on a jury in civil cases have the same responsibilities as those in criminal cases.

99. On false testimony, see *S.t.,* 2–2, q. 70, a. 4.

i) Christians should support just retributive punishment of criminals. Those who take revenge are motivated by anger or hatred to answer evil with evil. Retributive punishment, however, is not revenge, but the restoration of justice. Since crime is not merely antisocial behavior but freely committed injustice, it calls for retribution. For, besides whatever substantive harm they do, criminals freely prefer their own interests to the rights of others and the common good, and in doing so they seize more than their fair share of the liberty to do as one pleases. This overreaching requires steps to restore a just balance between criminals and law-abiding people.[100] Therefore, it is right that criminals be made to suffer what does not please them by being deprived of some of the liberty to do as one pleases which law-abiding citizens enjoy. This deprivation is the essence of punishment as retribution. That is why governments, as means of punishment, use fines, prison terms (see *S.t.,* 2–2, q. 65, a. 3), and other measures which more or less limit convicted criminals' freedom to pursue their own interests. In suffering punishment, criminals lose their advantage over law-abiding citizens who have restrained themselves and limited their self-interest for the sake of the common good and out of respect for others' rights.[101]

If criminals were no different from those who engage in guiltless antisocial behavior, punishing them to prevent social harms, even if effective, would not be justifiable. Given that retributive punishment is just, however, it also can rightly serve to prevent future social harms, by deterring the criminal and others from committing additional crimes, providing an opportunity for the criminal to reform, and so on. Therefore, Christians can support punishment for such purposes provided it does not exceed the limits of just retribution. However, they should oppose punishments which demean criminals as persons or intentionally attack the basic human goods instantiated in them.

The factors which determine how severely various crimes are punished are not always rationally defensible. Partly that is because people find certain kinds of crimes more repugnant than others, and most are less upset by the kind of crimes typically committed by members of the community considered more respectable. Such prejudices, and the differences in punishment to which they lead, are unjust, and Christians should support reforms to eliminate that injustice.

j) Christians should oppose the use of the death penalty. While acknowledging that "Catholic teaching has accepted the principle that the state has the right to take the life of a person guilty of an extremely serious crime," the bishops of the United States hold that "there are serious considerations which should prompt Christians and all Americans to support the abolition of capital punishment."[102] Among these considerations, the bishops explain, are certain values:

> We maintain that abolition of the death penalty would promote values that are important to us as citizens and as Christians. First, abolition sends a message that

---

100. See *S.t.,* 1–2, q. 87, a. 6; *S.c.g.,* 3.140, 146; cf. Pius XII, Address to the Italian Association of Catholic Jurists (5 Dec. 1954), *AAS* 47 (1955) 60–71, *Catholic Mind* 53 (June 1955): 364–73.

101. See Finnis, *Natural Law and Natural Rights,* 260–64.

102. National Conference of Catholic Bishops, "Statement on Capital Punishment" (Nov. 1980), 1.4, 9, in *Pastoral Letters,* ed. Nolan, 4:428, 430.

we can break the cycle of violence, that we need not take life for life, that we can envisage more humane and more hopeful and effective responses to the growth of violent crime. . . .

Second, abolition of capital punishment is also a manifestation of our belief in the unique worth and dignity of each person from the moment of conception, a creature made in the image and likeness of God. . . .

Third, abolition of the death penalty is further testimony to our conviction, a conviction which we share with the Judaic and Islamic traditions, that God is indeed the Lord of life. It is a testimony which removes a certain ambiguity which might otherwise affect the witness that we wish to give to the sanctity of human life in all its stages. . . .

Fourth, we believe that abolition of the death penalty is most consonant with the example of Jesus, who both taught and practiced the forgiveness of injustice and who came "to give his life as a ransom for many" (Mk 10.45).[103]

These are cogent reasons.

Indeed, grounded in moral and Christian principles, as they are, these reasons point beyond the bishops' expressed purpose of supporting the abolition of capital punishment, and they tend to show that Catholic teaching no longer should accept "the principle that the state has the right to take the life of a person guilty of an extremely serious crime."[104]

Of course, many arguments against capital punishment are misleading, even fallacious. They may involve the denial of criminal guilt and just retribution, overlook the opportunity to repent which capital punishment offers to habitual criminals, manipulate inadequate statistics regarding the effects of various forms of punishment, and/or manipulate feelings of sympathy by focusing on the sufferings of criminals while ignoring those of their innocent victims.

Moreover, provisions of the law recorded in the Old Testament authorized the death penalty for many crimes and mandated it for some (especially see Gn 9.6; cf. *CMP*, 8.H.7); St. Paul speaks of the divine basis of governmental authority in terms which, on their face, include authorization of capital punishment (see Rom 13.1–7); and the Church required reconverting Waldensians to make a profession of faith which included the affirmation: "The secular power can without mortal sin carry out a sentence of death, provided it proceeds in imposing the penalty not from hatred but with judgment, not carelessly but with due solicitude" (DS 795/425).

Nevertheless, since New Testament teaching abrogated many provisions of the law recorded in the Old Testament, its stipulations regarding capital punishment cannot be presumed to pertain to divine revelation (see *CMP*, 8.H). The Israelites' understanding of what justice requires in regard to punishment seems to have been imperfect: Jesus not only personally prevented the carrying out of the death penalty in a case for which the law of Moses prescribed it (see Jn 8.3–11), but radically criticized the law of retaliation: "eye for eye, tooth for tooth" (see Mt 5.38–41; cf.

---

103. National Conference of Catholic Bishops, "Statement on Capital Punishment" (Nov. 1980), 2.10–13, in *Pastoral Letters,* ed. Nolan, 4:430–31.

104. Also see Commission Sociale de l'Episcopat Français, "Éléments de réflexion sur la peine de mort," *La documentation catholique,* 75 (1978), 108–15, which also opposes the use of the death penalty with a theological argument which points to its unacceptability in principle.

Ex 21.23–25, Lv 24.19–20, Dt 19.21). St. Paul offers a like critique immediately before speaking of the divine source of human rulers' penal power (see Rom 12.17–21).[105] And Pius XII teaches that

> the words of the sources [of revelation] and of the living teaching power do not refer to the specific content of individual juridical prescriptions or rules of action (cf. particularly Rom 13.4 [where Paul speaks of the sword borne by public authority]), but rather to the essential foundation itself of penal power and of its immanent finality.[106]

In the past, capital punishment sometimes may have seemed justified as a defensive measure which public officials, lacking an alternative such as a prison system, felt compelled to use against current, imminent, or habitual violations of public order. Today, however, this defensive function plainly can be served in other ways. Thus, it is hardly possible to see how the use of the death penalty can be reconciled with Christian conceptions of human dignity and the sanctity of every human life.[107]

It is arguable whether the profession of faith required of reconverting Waldensians constitutes a solemn definition, but if it does, it concerns only the subjective morality of the act of capital punishment.[108] Moreover, the position that capital punishment can be just does not seem to have been proposed infallibly by the ordinary magisterium, for, unlike moral teachings on actions most Christians might do, the received position on this matter seems to have been taken for granted in theology and catechesis rather than proposed universally as a truth to be accepted as certain by the faithful.[109] Therefore, it seems that Catholic teaching on capital

105. Also see John Paul II, *Dives in misericordia,* 12, *AAS* 72 (1980) 1216, *PE,* 279.121.

106. Pius XII, Address to the Italian Association of Catholic Jurists (5 Feb. 1955), *AAS* 47 (1955) 81, *Catholic Mind* 53 (June 1955): 381. By denying that Rom 13.4 refers to a specific rule of action, Pius is able to insist on the perennial necessity of retribution for a just system of criminal law without thereby seeming to criticize Italy's policy (save during the period of fascist government) on the death penalty, which Italy had renounced in 1889, reintroduced in 1928, and abolished in 1944.

107. Unlike most theologians, St. Thomas confronts this problem. However, although he holds that sinners should be loved with charity insofar as they remain human beings capable of beatitude (see *S.t.,* 2–2, q. 25, a. 6), when he faces the objection that it is evil in itself to kill human beings and that the end does not justify the means, he fallaciously argues that killing criminals does not violate their human dignity because they have fallen from that dignity by sinning, and that they can be killed for the sake of the common good just as diseased parts of the body can be cut off for the good of the whole (see *S.t.,* 2–2, q. 64, a. 2, c. and ad 3). Also see Germain Grisez, "Toward a Consistent Natural-Law Ethics of Killing," *American Journal of Jurisprudence* 15 (1970): 66–73; however, John Finnis, *Fundamentals of Ethics* (Washington, D.C.: Georgetown University Press, 1983), 129–30, argues that capital punishment need not be regarded as an attack on human life; he holds that only justice, not the criminal's death, need be intended.

108. The profession affirms explicitly only that officials need not commit a *mortal sin* when they carry out a death sentence; similarly, there was a time when Christians, unaware of the objective morality of their acts, need not have committed a mortal sin when they coerced a heretic into recanting or marketed a slave's child. On coercion in religious matters, compare DH 2–7 with *S.t.,* 2–2, q. 10, a. 8; q. 11, a. 3; on slavery, compare GS 27 and 29 with *S.t.,* 2–2, q. 57, a. 3, ad 2, and a. 4 (but see, too, 2–2, q. 104, a. 5, where Thomas invokes the principle, "all human persons are by nature equal," to set some absolute limits to a master's dominion over a serf).

109. A general historical-theological survey: M. B. Crowe, "Theology and Capital Punishment," *Irish Theological Quarterly* 31 (1964): 24–61, 99–131.

punishment can develop, just as Catholic teachings on coercion in matters of religion and on slavery have.[110]

Even if capital punishment is considered morally acceptable in principle, however, no truth of faith or morals requires Christians to support its use. The considerations which the American bishops articulate seem adequate to show that Catholics should oppose it in practice.

2. Citizens Ought to Pay Their Taxes

The government needs material resources to carry out its essential services for the common good and to contribute to various private activities—such as education, health care, and aid to the poor—which also serve the common good. Fairness requires that citizens contribute to supplying what the government needs in proportion to their own financial resources, and just taxes exact that fair contribution. Consequently, the responsibility to pay just taxes is both real and serious, and it has been explicitly included in Christian moral instruction from New Testament times down to the present day (see Rom 13.7; cf. Mt 22.21, Mk 12.17, Lk 20.25; see DH 11, GS 30).[111]

Yet many Christians do not take this responsibility as seriously as they should. Moreover, certain questions about the obligation deserve consideration.

a) One may not lie to evade taxes, even if they are unjust. Since lying is always wrong (see 7.B.6), and a bad means may never be used even to attain a good end (see *CMP*, 8.H), lying is excluded even when it is the only way of avoiding unjust taxes. All the more, lying to evade just taxes is morally wrong and, since the lie facilitates a serious violation of law, gravely so. One therefore should be honest in answering official questions and filling out forms on which taxes are based, and if the authorities lawfully require that relevant records be produced, they should not be concealed or altered.

In some jurisdictions, nevertheless, the letter of some tax laws must be interpreted in the light of a virtually universal custom of not reporting property or income on which certain taxes are assessed. Almost all citizens who are familiar with the custom will understate their tax basis to the customary extent. Since public officials are aware of the custom but do nothing to change it, they obviously take it into account in setting tax rates and in interpreting citizens' statements regarding their tax liability. Consequently, in such cases, it is neither violating the law's spirit nor lying to understate one's tax basis in accord with the custom.

b) Lawful methods of minimizing the tax burden may be used. There is nothing inherently wrong in taking advantage of loopholes and shelters provided

---

110. See Commission Sociale de l'Episcopat Français, "Éléments de réflexion sur la peine de mort," 115; "Editoriale: Riflessioni sulla pena de morte," *La civiltà cattolica* 132 (1981): 417–28.

111. On the conditions for justice in taxation, see Pius XII, Address to the International Association for Financial and Fiscal Law (2 Oct. 1956); *Discorsi e radiomessaggi* 18 (1956–57): 507–10; *The Pope Speaks* 4 (1957–58): 77–80. A study of the various theological theories regarding the duty to pay taxes: Martin T. Crowe, C.Ss.R., *The Moral Obligation of Paying Just Taxes* (Washington, D.C.: The Catholic University of America Press, 1944).

in tax laws.[112] Nor is it wrong to seek expert advice about lawful ways to minimize one's taxes.

Sometimes the tax laws are so complex that even people who make a reasonable effort to find out how to apply them, using available sources of information, cannot tell whether or not something is taxable income or how large a tax to pay. For example, the law might not make it clear how certain income should be classified, and so leave it doubtful whether tax is due on it. If it seems no more likely that the law requires paying the tax than not, one is not morally required to pay it, since rules of law which remain doubtful after reasonable effort to discover what they require do not bind in conscience (see D.1.b, above).

Using lawful methods to minimize the tax burden sometimes leads to a dispute with tax officers. Those who know, or come to realize, that their position is unsound should not prolong the dispute, but those convinced they are in the right may use all morally acceptable means, such as appeals, to obtain a favorable resolution. In any case, assuming the tax law is just and the process is fair, citizens should be prepared to pay any additional tax, interest, and/or penalty owing if the dispute is resolved unfavorably.

c) Bartering must be distinguished from gratuitous exchanges. Family members, friends, and neighbors often provide various services and goods to one another, and in some cases do so very regularly, on a genuinely gratuitous basis: the service is done or the good loaned or given without counting its economic value, and no accounts are maintained. While some degree of reciprocity is common and even expected in such relationships, it is based on family solidarity, friendship, or neighborliness, not on the market value of the goods and services exchanged. It is a sign of this that those who can give more tend to do so.

Bartering is similar to gratuitous exchange insofar as both activities involve trading goods and/or services without the exchange of money. However, the parties to bartering do count the economic value of the goods and/or services each provides; if their relationship is a continuing one, reciprocity on the basis of market value is expected, and accounts (at least unwritten ones) are maintained. And nobody involved expects the parties to provide goods and services gratuitously and without reciprocation.

Often, either the law's letter or its customary interpretation exempts gratuitous exchanges from sales and/or income taxes, but taxes bartering on the same basis as economic activity in which money is exchanged. Obviously, where such legal provisions obtain, nobody is morally required to report gratuitous exchanges or pay taxes on them, and people may rightly take care to avoid making a gratuitous exchange appear to be bartering. But those who do engage in bartering should not evade the application of just tax laws to their activity, despite its similarities to gratuitous exchange. Trying to make their bartering look like gratuitous exchange is deception, a lie; while evading taxes on bartering is no less serious a moral offense

112. While those favored may take advantage of even those provisions of tax law which they judge to be plainly unjust, they should make just use of such tax savings, as of all their wealth, and should do what they can to rectify the injustice.

than other tax evasion, even though it might be less obvious, and so less easily detected and more easily rationalized.

d) **Taxation to finance public aid to the poor can be just.** Some more or less well-to-do people rationalize tax evasion by arguing that the tax they evade is unjust because it will fund public programs to aid the poor. To be sure, particular tax laws and particular programs for the poor may be unjust, but the general argument is not sound. People with surplus wealth should use it to aid the poor, and their obligation is a grave one in strict justice (see 10.E.5.b–d). Therefore, taxing surplus wealth to fund public welfare programs not only can help meet the needs and vindicate the rights of the poor but can help those with surplus resources to fulfill their grave responsibilities toward those in need.[113]

e) **Citizens usually should comply with more or less unjust tax laws.** Many people argue, on diverse grounds, that various tax laws are unjust. For example, sales or value added taxes are criticized as regressive, that is, as imposing heavy burdens on those least able to bear them. Similarly, income taxes often are criticized as insufficiently progressive, that is, as requiring too little from the most affluent, perhaps by allowing them various loopholes and shelters, and thus imposing unfair burdens on the middle class. The unfair distribution of certain public subsidies also is cited, for example, public funding of schools which denies assistance to parents who send their children to religiously sponsored schools. Such arguments often are plausible and sometimes are sound. But even so, it does not follow that citizens in a position to evade taxes can rightly do so.

Many people of modest incomes cannot evade taxes, while many who can—professionals, owners of small businesses, independent contractors, landlords, and so on—enjoy greater than average incomes. Such people may well be taxed less than justice requires, even allowing for those injustices which affect them as well as others. Moreover, if those able to evade taxes do so, people of modest income who cannot evade taxes are likely to suffer greater injustice by being required to pay higher taxes, being deprived of public subsidies, suffering the bad economic consequences of public debt, or some combination of these. Thus, tax evasion by those capable of it hardly is likely to serve the common good by making the government's taxing and spending as a whole more just.

Consequently, either the common good or the duty to avoid unfairly harming others, or both, usually will require a citizen to comply with a tax law which either

---

113. For this reason, National Conference of Catholic Bishops, "Economic Justice for All," 202, in *Pastoral Letters,* ed. Nolan, 5:440, states the following principles which should guide the moral evaluation of the tax system: "First, the tax system should raise adequate revenues to pay for the public needs of society, especially to meet the basic needs of the poor. Second, the tax system should be structured according to the principle of progressivity, so that those with relatively greater financial resources pay a higher rate of taxation. . . . Third, families below the official poverty line should not be required to pay income taxes." Earlier in the same document (sec. 183–85, pp. 434–36), the bishops show the vast inequalities in the distribution of wealth and income in the United States, explain that some degree of inequality is both justifiable and desirable for economic and social reasons, but find the actual inequalities unacceptable, because they are both unfair to the poor and detrimental to social solidarity and community.

is more or less unjust in itself or is a means of raising public funds which are more or less unjustly distributed.[114]

f) Misuse of some public funds usually does not justify nonpayment of taxes. Even in those nations which have generally just governments and laws, some public funds are likely to be used for bad purposes, such as abortion or armaments with no possible just use. In such cases, some conscientious citizens think it justified, or even obligatory, not to pay taxes or, at least, not to pay the portion which, in their judgment, would be misused. Sometimes, of course, nonpayment could be chosen as an act of civil disobedience, and as such might be justified under the conditions previously explained (in D.6.a). Apart from civil disobedience, however, the prospective misuse of some public funds does not justify, much less morally require, nonpayment of all or any part of the taxes which otherwise ought to be paid. For, since citizens cannot designate the purposes for which their tax payments will be used, nonpayment will withhold support from all the good uses of public funds, to which they owe support, as well as from any misuses. Moreover, like any other evasion of taxes, this one will hurt fellow citizens of modest means who cannot evade taxes.

3. Citizens Can Be Morally Obliged to Fight in a Just Defensive War

Catholic teaching and practice make several points clear. On the one hand, nations should seek their own security and world peace by diplomacy and international collaboration rather than constant preparations for war, which always involve an arms race, often accompanied by universal conscription.[115] On the other hand, military service can be a morally acceptable profession for a Christian; nations may justly require military or other public service of citizens even in peacetime; and Christians may rightly volunteer to serve in a just war. The present treatment will not deal with these points, but only with a citizen's responsibility regarding required service in a just war.

Every decent person detests war insofar as it causes much death, injury, and suffering, along with extensive destruction, damage, and dissipation of material goods. However, Christians should be even more concerned about the injustice war involves and the many moral evils to which it leads.

Any just war must be defensive, but not every defensive war is just, since other conditions also must be met. Still, in principle just war remains possible. Moreover, neither magisterial teachings on conscientious objection, nor those condemning violence and calling for an end to war, nor pacifist elements in the Christian tradition exclude the possibility that a Christian might be morally bound to

---

114. Many classical moralists take for granted that if tax laws are unjust, the taxes need not be paid, and some, while arguing for a strong presumption for laws generally, argue for a presumption against the justice of tax laws. D. F. O'Callaghan, "Theology: Duty to Pay Income Tax," *Irish Ecclesiastical Record* 104 (1965): 302–6, in a generally sound treatment, errs by overlooking the impact of tax evasion on many people of modest means, and so fallaciously argues that a certain level of tax evasion is justified. Some arguments for a stricter view: Philip S. Land, S.J., "Evading Taxes Can't Be Justified in Conscience," *Social Order* 5 (1955): 121–25.

115. See Wright, *National Patriotism in Papal Teaching,* 177–92.

participate in a just war. At the same time, particular wars often are unjust, and most ways of cooperating even materially in an unjust war are likely to be immoral. Christian citizens therefore should inquire whether their nation's military actions are justified, and should refuse to participate insofar as such refusal is necessary to avoid not only formal cooperation but all morally unacceptable cooperation.

a) **No war can be just unless several conditions are met.** Wars include myriad actions of individuals and various groups, all with their own moral responsibility. But each belligerent power also is engaged in a single, great social act, for which that power as a unified moral agent bears moral responsibility. While that social act's justice or injustice is not the sole determinant of a citizen's responsibility to participate or not participate in a war, it is a very important one. Hence, while officials contemplating or directing a war may not be concerned about relevant moral requirements, it is important to articulate the moral norms which should shape the choice to wage war.[116]

Wars often are unjust simply because those planning or directing them ignore relevant implications of the Golden Rule. They may unfairly harm the enemy by choosing means which are cruel and wantonly destructive, in the sense that they cause more death, damage, and suffering than necessary to achieve military objectives. They may take unfair advantage by treachery, for example, prepare the way for a surprise attack by pretending to negotiate to prevent war or insincerely agreeing to an armistice.[117] They may unfairly bring about harm not only to the enemy but to their own people by initiating or continuing a war with no reasonable hope of success or by initiating a war which could be avoided by alternatives short of war, such as negotiation and nonviolent action.[118] They may initiate or carry on a war with a bias in favor of those who stand to benefit and against those who stand to lose from it, thus unfairly bringing about destruction of life and other goods, on either or both sides, which any fair-minded person would consider either entirely unreasonable or more extensive than reasonable.[119]

116. The choice to engage in war includes both the choice to conduct it (which not only is made at the outset but repeatedly reaffirmed) and the choice of means (which not only is made after the war starts but is presupposed by preparations for war). Sometimes the conditions required for justly going to war (*ius ad bellum*) are distinguished from the conditions required for justly engaging in military action (*ius in bello*); see, for example, National Conference of Catholic Bishops, "The Challenge of Peace: God's Promise and Our Response," 80–110, in *Pastoral Letters*, ed. Nolan, 4:515–23. However, neither that distinction nor the precise list of conditions has deep roots in Catholic tradition; "Challenge of Peace" draws on works by Ralph Potter and James Childress, two contemporary Protestant theologians (see n. 35, pp. 516–17), who sum up the results of the nonsystematic reflections of various modern theologians. Most of the substance of those reflections, which is rooted in Catholic tradition, is incorporated in the present analysis; however, here the conditions are drawn systematically from moral principles.

117. While deceptions involving lying and breaking promises are wrong, in warfare ambushes (and, by implication, other stratagems) are morally acceptable, as St. Thomas points out (*S.t.*, 2–2, q. 40, a. 3), since in such cases enemies are deceived only by what is concealed from them.

118. John Paul II, *Centesimus annus*, 25 and 51–52, *AAS* 83 (1991) 822–23 and 857–58, *OR*, 6 May 1991, 9 and 14, commends nonviolent action as an alternative to warfare. On nonviolent action, see the works of P. Régamey and Gene Sharp, cited in a note to D.6.c, above.

119. St. Thomas does not state but takes for granted the requirements of fairness in warfare (see *S.t.*, 2–2, q. 40, a. 1). Like many modern treatments of the conditions for a just war, National

Those planning or directing a war sometimes consider it necessary or useful to choose as means acts which are evil in themselves, such as "taking no prisoners" or torturing or killing prisoners, taking and abusing hostages, directly attacking noncombatants, and engaging in indiscriminate destruction.[120] The choice of such means is not only wrong in itself but incompatible with love of enemies and, specifically, with the will to secure just and lasting peace with them. Thus, while unauthorized wrongdoing by some or many participants in a war does not by itself render the war as such unjust, no war can be just if those responsible for initiating or conducting it include intrinsically evil acts in their general strategy.[121]

Nations sometimes take the initiative in using military force, or carry on a war, in order to resolve an international dispute or promote some national purpose. Pius XII teaches that such aggressive wars cannot be just.[122] War can be just only if defensive military action is necessary to prevent, halt, or limit others' unjust use of force.[123] So, for a war to be just, its objective cannot include the enemy's total

---

Conference of Catholic Bishops, "Challenge of Peace: God's Promise and Our Response," 92–94 and 96–100, in *Pastoral Letters*, ed. Nolan, 4:518–20, sets out several requirements of fairness (comparative justice, last resort, probability of success, and proportionality) without articulating their underlying common principle. However, this document does make it clear (sec. 105, p. 522) that proportionality must be understood in terms of fairness: "We know, of course, that no end can justify means evil in themselves, such as the executing of hostages or the targeting of noncombatants. Nonetheless, even if the means adopted is not evil in itself, it is necessary to take into account the probable harms that will result from using it and the justice of accepting those harms. It is of utmost importance, in assessing harms and the justice of accepting them, to think about the poor and the helpless, for they are usually the ones who have the least to gain and the most to lose when war's violence touches their lives."

120. Vatican II explicitly deals with the paradigmatic example of the last: "Any act of war aimed indiscriminately at the destruction of entire cities or of extensive areas along with their population is a crime against God and man himself. It merits unequivocal and unhesitating condemnation" (GS 80; see also GS 79).

121. To choose intrinsically evil acts as means is to will contrary to the good of the persons whom those acts are meant to harm; such a will is inconsistent with love of neighbor and excludes what St. Thomas calls "right intention," which he clarifies, following St. Augustine, as conducting war for the sake of peace and excluding various forms of hatred—the desire for harm, revenge, and so on (see *S.t.*, 2–2, q. 40, a. 1). Moreover, in and of themselves, intrinsically evil acts, such as attacking noncombatants, cannot counter others' unjust use of force, but can at best only motivate or facilitate other acts which can directly affect combat; so, the choice of any intrinsically evil act as part of a general strategy indicates a defective intention: the injustice either of the war's objective, or of the political policy it implements, or of both.

122. Pius XII, Christmas Message (24 Dec. 1944), *AAS* 37 (1945) 18, *Catholic Mind* 43 (Feb. 1945): 72, teaches that there is a duty to ban "wars of aggression as legitimate solutions of international disputes and as a means toward realizing national aspirations"; in Christmas Message (24 Dec. 1948), *AAS* 41 (1949) 12–13, *Catholic Mind* 47 (Mar. 1949): 184, Pius XII also teaches: "Every war of aggression against those goods which the Divine plan for peace obliges men unconditionally to respect and guarantee, and accordingly to protect and defend, is a sin, a crime, and an outrage against the majesty of God, the Creator and Ordainer of the world."

123. Pius XII, Christmas Message (24 Dec. 1948), *AAS* 41 (1949) 13, *Catholic Mind* 47 (Mar. 1949): 185, teaches that some human goods are so important that their defense against unjust aggression can be fully justified and even obligatory: "A people threatened with an unjust aggression, or already its victim, may not remain passively indifferent, if it would think and act as befits Christians"; in Address to the Eighth Congress of the World Medical Association (30 Sept. 1954), *AAS* 46 (1954) 589, *Catholic Mind* 53 (Apr. 1955): 244, he teaches that under certain conditions even atomic, bacteriological, and chemical war could be justified "where it must be

destruction or unconditional surrender, and any war directed to such an objective is unjust throughout its course.[124]

A private group such as a gang might start or carry on a war, or someone lacking the necessary authority might order a nation's military forces into war. Such a private or unauthorized war cannot be just; indeed, it is not a war in the sense relevant here, for it is not the social act of a nation. That also is the case if war is authorized only within certain limits as to methods, place, or time, and an unauthorized extension beyond those limits changes the real character of what is going on, so that it no longer is the sort of thing that can be a just war.[125]

b) Pius XII's exclusion of aggressive war develops Christian tradition.
St. Thomas, following St. Augustine, does not think only defensive warfare can be just. The two doctors indicate that nations can rightly wage war in order to punish outlaw nations, just as they rightly use their police power within their jurisdiction to bring criminals to justice (see *S.t.*, 2–2, q. 40, a. 1). If that view were correct, just wars, rather than always countering an enemy's unjust use of force, sometimes would attempt to achieve retributive justice. For example, a superpower might rightly make war on a small power to punish it for attacking and annexing its even smaller neighbor, despite the fact that the neighbor, ruled by an oppressive regime, deserved no defense. Hence, one might wonder whether Pius XII's statements that only defensive war can be just express a judgment contingent on contemporary problems or, instead, propose a doctrine solidly grounded in Christian tradition. At least three considerations support the latter view.

First, contemporary problems were a factor, but traditional principles also were in play. In obvious respects, modern war is very different from any war Augustine and Thomas could have imagined. By the end of the nineteenth century—well before atomic, bacteriological, and chemical weapons became available—modern technology and industry had greatly increased war's carnage and devastation. The intertwining of industry with military power, together with the new weapons and new strategies for using them—climaxing in the terror bombing of World War II and the subsequent development of nuclear deterrence strategies and systems— somewhat blurred the line between combatants and noncombatants, made discrimination increasingly difficult, and made it more and more likely that virtually any aggressive war would be or become indiscriminate. Thus, the idea of using military

---

judged as indispensable in order to defend oneself" and with "limits on its use that are so clear and rigorous that its effects remain restricted to the strict demands of defense"; in Christmas Message (23 Dec. 1956), *AAS* 49 (1957) 19, *Catholic Mind* 55 (Mar.–Apr. 1957): 178, he teaches that under certain conditions "every effort to avoid war being expended in vain, war—for effective self-defense and with the hope of a favorable outcome against unjust attack—could not be considered unlawful."

124. Any nation aware that its enemy seeks its total destruction or unconditional surrender faces different and harder options than it would if its enemy sought only to counter some particular use or uses of force by it, and a nation facing harder options must be expected to fight not only longer but more ferociously and tenaciously from the outset.

125. St. Thomas, *S.t.*, 2–2, q. 40, a. 1, states as the first condition for a just war the authorization of the sovereign, who is responsible for the common good; private parties should call on the public authorities rather than conduct private wars.

power to rectify injustices no longer seemed plausible, and the analogy between military power and domestic police power no longer seemed valid. Increasingly, too, combatants were no longer professionals but citizens forced to fight, sometimes at gunpoint, so that it more and more was the case that aggressive war punished most severely those who had little or no responsibility for the policies and actions of the political and military leaders of a nation considered outlaw. These modern developments called for a fresh application of traditional principles, drastically limiting the situations in which military action could be morally justified. Indeed, many people began to say, with reason, that war had changed its very nature, and the magisterium shared this view. John XXIII teaches: "In this age which boasts of its atomic power, it no longer makes sense to maintain that war is a fit instrument with which to repair the violation of justice."[126] Noting John's point, Vatican II, explains how "the horror and perversity of war are immensely magnified by the addition of scientific weapons," and draws the conclusion: "All these considerations compel us to undertake an evaluation of war with an entirely new attitude" (GS 80, with n. 2 [n. 258 in Abbott]).

Second, there is another way, less obvious but more profound, in which nondefensive war in modern times differs in nature from what Augustine and Thomas had in mind.[127] Because in their days there was, at least in theory, a supreme, worldwide authority—the Roman emperor, the pope—to whom every other human ruler was subject, they could think about nondefensive war on the analogy of law enforcement within a nation. However, the development of the modern state robs this idea of whatever plausibility it may have had in earlier times. In a world of independent states, each jealous of its sovereignty and none recognizing any legitimate authority higher than its own, war is something like the self-help measures to which individuals and families resort in the absence of public authority capable of maintaining law and order. In such a situation, however, any self-help beyond that strictly necessary for self-defense provokes reprisals and endless feuds. Those involved may not always be subjectively guilty of vengefulness and murder, but objectively their feuding is wrong. In the absence of public authority, their real duty is, not to do their best to do justice without it, but to establish the commonly recognized authority they obviously need.[128] The same thing plainly is true of the modern world, and, beginning with Leo XIII, the popes have come, step by step, to this conclusion.[129] Thus, aggressive war must be

126. John XXIII, *Pacem in terris, AAS* 55 (1963) 291, *PE,* 270.127.

127. See Augustine Regan, C.Ss.R., "The Worth of Human Life," *Studia Moralia* 6 (1968): 242–43.

128. John Paul II, *Centesimus annus,* 52, *AAS* 83 (1991) 857–58, *OR,* 6 May 1991, 14, exhorts: "No, never again war, which destroys the lives of innocent people, teaches how to kill, throws into upheaval even the lives of those who do the killing and leaves behind a trail of resentment and hatred, thus making it all the more difficult to find a just solution of the very problems which provoked the war. Just as the time has finally come when in individual States a system of private vendetta and reprisal has given way to the rule of law, so too a similar step forward is now urgently needed in the international community."

129. Leo XIII, "Nostis errorem," *Acta Leonis XIII,* vol. 9 (Rome: 1890), 48, having pointed out the futility of the arms race, adds significantly (translation supplied): "And so there should be

excluded as unjust, not only because such war no longer can be carried on justly but because in principle it is not the right way to deal with international injustice and pursue world peace.[130] Modern history, if not the whole of history, makes it clear that aggressive war not only leads to endless and total strife but is a side effect of the nations' collective evasion of their common responsibility to establish real world community.

Third, insofar as wars intended to punish outlaw nations seemed justifiable by analogy with capital punishment, the arguments which the American bishops propose for discontinuing the use of capital punishment point to the injustice in principle of such aggressive wars, just as they point, without the bishops' intending it, to capital punishment's unacceptability in principle (see 1.j, above).

c) **If all the conditions are met, war can be just.** Vatican II first recalls "the permanent binding force of universal natural law and its all-embracing principles" (GS 79), condemns as criminal all actions which violate those principles, and insists that international agreements making war less inhuman should be honored and strengthened. Then the Council goes on to teach:

> As long as the danger of war remains and there is no competent and sufficiently powerful authority at the international level, governments cannot be denied the right to legitimate defense once every means of peaceful settlement has been exhausted. Government authorities and others who share in public responsibility have a duty, therefore, to protect the safety of the peoples for whom they are responsible, while acting with seriousness in such serious matters. But it is one thing to undertake military action for the just defense of the people, and something else again to seek the subjugation of other nations. Nor does the possession of war potential make every military or political use of it lawful. Neither does the fact that war has unhappily begun mean that everything becomes permissible between the warring parties. (GS 79)

Thus, though not all defensive wars are just, since other conditions also must be met, defensive war remains in principle justifiable, and in some circumstances can be a nation's duty.[131]

---

sought for peace foundations both firmer and more in keeping with nature: because, while it is allowed consistently with nature to defend one's right by force and arms, nature does not allow that force be an efficient cause of right. For peace consists in the tranquillity of order, and so, like the concord of private persons, that of rulers is grounded above all in justice and charity." Still, the popes were slow to draw the obvious conclusion that the nations should establish a real world government, and when John XXIII finally draws it explicitly, he suggests that the need for an effective international authority has only recently emerged: *Pacem in terris, AAS* 55 (1963) 291–94, *PE,* 270.130–38.

130. Thus, Pius XII explains his sharp distinction between the absolute condemnation of aggressive war and his qualified approval of defensive war in the context of his articulation of the concept of Christian peace: see Christmas Message (24 Dec. 1948), *AAS* 41 (1949) 11–13, *Catholic Mind* 47 (Mar. 1949): 183–85. Also see "Editoriale: Coscienza cristiana e guerra moderna," *La civiltà cattolica* (6 July 1991): 3–16; trans. William Shannon, "Modern War and Christian Conscience," *Origins* 21 (19 Dec. 1991): 450–55.

131. John Paul II, Message for the Celebration of the Day of Peace (1 Jan. 1982), 12, *AAS* 74 (1982) 336–37, *OR,* 4 Jan. 1982, 7, teaches: "Christians, even as they strive to resist and prevent every form of warfare, have no hesitation in recalling that, in the name of an elementary requirement of justice, peoples have a right and even a duty to protect their existence and freedom

d) If a war is just, one should participate insofar as law requires. Having taught that war to defend against unjust attack can be justified, Pius XII draws the conclusion that, in the event of such a war, a Catholic citizen would be morally obliged to serve as law requires:

> If, therefore, a body representative of the people and a government—both having been chosen by free elections—in a moment of extreme danger decides, by legitimate instruments of internal and external policy, on defensive precautions, and carries out the plans which they consider necessary, it does not act immorally. Therefore a Catholic citizen cannot invoke his own conscience in order to refuse to serve and fulfill those duties the law imposes.[132]

If a defensive war is just, the defense of the common good makes it not only permissible but required for a nation to go to war, and so all citizens have a grave responsibility to cooperate. Those designated by law for military service should fulfill their duty, despite personal inconvenience and jeopardy to their lives. It would be a grave matter to invoke conscience in order to evade the duty to serve one's country in a just defensive war. (Still, if called on to fight, one should judge whether the war is just: see g, below.)

e) The magisterium and tradition do not support the contrary view. Certain elements of magisterial teaching might be thought to support conscientious objection to military service even in a just war.

First, Vatican II teaches that "it seems right that laws make humane provisions for the case of those who for reasons of conscience refuse to bear arms, provided however, that they agree to serve the human community in some other way" (GS 79). However, this teaching says nothing about the objective morality of conscientious objection to bearing arms in some or all wars. Rather, considering that some people, including some Christian pacifists, sincerely believe themselves obliged to refuse military service in all or in some wars, the Council expresses the opinion ("it seems") that it is only fair that they be given the option of some other form of service instead of being coerced into taking up arms contrary to their conscience.[133]

Similarly, Vatican II teaches "that the arms race, to which so many countries have recourse, is not a safe way to preserve a steady peace" (GS 81). But the

---

by proportionate means against an unjust aggressor (cf. Constitution *Gaudium et Spes,* 79)." Cf. Pius XII, Christmas Message (24 Dec. 1948), *AAS* 41 (1949) 12–13, *Catholic Mind* 47 (Mar. 1949): 184–85.

132. Pius XII, Christmas Message (23 Dec. 1956), *AAS* 49 (1957) 19, *Catholic Mind* 55 (Mar.–Apr. 1957): 179.

133. This opinion is closely related to Vatican II's teaching that "in religious matters no one is to be forced to act against conscience" (DH 2), because, while bearing arms is not a religious matter, conscientious objection to doing so often is deeply rooted in religious faith. United States Catholic Conference, "Declaration on Conscientious Objection and Selective Conscientious Objection" (21 Oct. 1971), 11, in *Pastoral Letters,* ed. Nolan, 3:285, asserts: "In the light of the Gospel and from an analysis of the Church's teaching on conscience, it is clear that a Catholic can be a conscientious objector to war in general or to a particular war 'because of religious training and belief.'" However, this declaration also reaffirms the obligation of citizens to serve the common good and the possibility of a just war (see sec. 4–7, p. 284). Thus, unless the bishops meant that, due to a blameless error of conscience, an upright Catholic can object to war in general, their statement was internally inconsistent, as well as at odds with the teaching of Pius XII.

magisterium's teaching against the arms race, often repeated by the popes from Leo XIII to John Paul II, articulates the common responsibility of nations to develop better ways of resolving disputes, so that war can be completely outlawed and international justice maintained without it (see GS 82). Until the nations fulfill that common responsibility, a particular nation and its citizens can be morally required to fight a defensive war.

Likewise, passionate papal statements against war must be understood, not as excluding the possibility of a just defensive war, but as appeals to the nations to fulfill their common responsibility to work for peace.[134] Again, when John Paul II unqualifiedly condemns violence as "not the Christian way" and calls for its replacement with "peace and forgiveness and love; for they are of Christ," he must be understood as rejecting any unjustified resort to arms, not as excluding the possible just use of military power.[135]

Admittedly, the Christian tradition includes significant pacifist elements, that is, either or both of two closely related positions: that war always is sinful and that the gospel allows Christians to use only nonviolent methods of defense.[136] However, since the magisterium, in accord with the far greater part of the Christian tradition, continues to teach clearly and firmly that there can be just defensive wars in which citizens should serve, pacifist elements in the tradition provide no adequate theological ground for contradicting that teaching but only point to the need that it be complemented with other truths, often overlooked or even denied, to which pacifists call attention.

Among these truths are that mercy can require Christians as individuals to suffer injustice instead of fighting back, that nonviolent methods of resolving disputes often can be effective and always should be preferred, that no aggressive war can be just, that many defensive wars are unjust, that participants in any war are tempted to hate their enemies and do various wicked things, that in any war some participants succumb to those temptations, and that choosing to kill or harm any person is incompatible with loving that neighbor as oneself.[137]

f) Participants in a just war should not choose to kill or harm anyone. Obviously, if a war is just, participants need never choose to do most of the wicked acts often done in war, and upright participants never will so choose. Loving their

---

134. See, for example, Paul VI, Address to the General Assembly of the United Nations (4 Oct. 1965), *AAS* 57 (1965) 881, *The Pope Speaks* 11 (1966): 51, 54: "*Never again one against the other,* never, never again! . . . Never again war, never again war!" But the whole situation and context makes the meaning clear.

135. Compare John Paul II, Address at Drogheda (Ireland), 10, *AAS* 71 (1979) 1082, *OR,* 8 Oct. 1979, 10, which includes the quoted phrases, with the passage previously quoted from his subsequent Message for the Celebration of the Day of Peace (1 Jan. 1982).

136. See National Conference of Catholic Bishops, "Challenge of Peace: God's Promise and Our Response," 111–21, in *Pastoral Letters,* ed. Nolan, 4:523–25; cf. Louis J. Swift, *The Early Fathers on War and Military Service,* Message of the Fathers of the Church, 19 (Wilmington, Del.: Michael Glazier, 1983); David G. Hunter, "A Decade of Research on Early Christians and Military Service," *Religious Studies Review* 18 (Apr. 1992): 87–94.

137. Most Catholic theologians have denied the last proposition, which excludes intentional killing not only of innocents but of anyone under any conditions. For the argument for this proposition, see *CMP,* 8.H, 26.K.

enemies, they will not be moved by hatred or expediency to cause them more harm than necessary or treat them treacherously, to refuse to allow them to surrender or abuse them if they do, to make war on noncombatants or engage in indiscriminate attacks, and so forth.

The point here, however, is not obvious: if a war is just, participants need never choose to kill or harm even enemy military personnel. Both pacifists and proponents of just war assume that in combat such choices are inevitable; given this common assumption, their views are irreconcilable, since pacifists hold that choices to kill or harm enemies are incompatible with loving them, while proponents of just war, in maintaining that defensive military action can be morally obligatory, are compelled to maintain that loving enemies does not exclude choosing to kill or harm them. Nevertheless, as has been explained in a previous chapter (8.B.1), a person can knowingly cause someone's death without intending it, that is, without willing it as an end or means; so, sometimes people can rightly defend themselves and/or others with deadly force, accepting as a side effect the death thus caused, but not seeking it as an end or choosing it as a means (see 8.C.1.d; cf. *S.t.*, 2–2, q. 64, a. 7).

Since upright participants in a just war will engage in military action only insofar as necessary to prevent, limit, or halt some unjust use of force by the enemy, they will employ military force only against those who pose an imminent and morally unavoidable threat of grave harm to themselves, their comrades, compatriots, or cobelligerents. Therefore, in each and every military act participants in a just war can choose precisely to counter the unjust threat confronting them; they need never choose precisely to destroy or harm either the lives or other basic human goods of enemies. Often, of course, they will foresee that their military acts, if successful in countering the unjust threat, also will bring about death and destruction; but they will accept these evils as side effects, not choose them as means.[138]

Since just warriors need not choose precisely to destroy or harm their enemies' lives or other basic human goods, they should never make that precise choice. If they do, their will toward their enemies will not be loving, and truly just warriors love their enemies. Indeed, as soon as enemy personnel cease to pose an unjust threat, an upright participant in a just war will stop using force against them, will treat them humanely, and even will do what is possible to mitigate their suffering.

Someone might argue that if the leaders and members of an armed force chose only to counter unjust threats confronting them, they could take action only against an enemy actually engaged in the use of force; and this would put them at such great disadvantage that they could not win—thus making just war impossible, since it certainly is not just to bring about the bad results of war without reasonable hope of winning. However, the unjust threat in such a case is posed not only by enemy personnel actually engaged in the use of force but by those being brought into position, held in readiness, or trained for combat; it continues to be posed by enemy personnel in retreat if they are unwilling to surrender, since presumably they will

---

138. For another statement of this view of just war, see Regan, "The Worth of Human Life," 240–43.

return to fight another day; it includes not only weapons in use by the enemy force but all the bases, depots, and war plants which now support and supply it or will do so in the future. Therefore, while choosing only to counter unjust threats confronting them, the leaders and members of an armed force can do everything militarily possible—subject to the limitation of not using means which are evil in themselves—to prevent, limit, or halt the enemy's unjust use of force, comprehensively understood.

g) If called on to fight, one should judge whether the war is just. It might seem that Pius XII's teaching that "a Catholic citizen cannot invoke his own conscience" to refuse required military service forbids Catholics called to participate in a war to inquire whether it is just or, at least, frees them from the responsibility to do so. But that is not so. For only after specifying several conditions does Pius exclude conscientious refusal to obey a legal requirement to participate in military action, and he makes it clear that he intends the specified conditions to imply all the conditions for a just war, for he says that under those conditions the regime authorizing war "does not act immorally."

Therefore, Pius should be understood as teaching only that Catholics should not invoke conscience to evade their moral responsibility to serve in a just war; his teaching does not mean anyone should or may blindly carry out orders commanding actions contrary to a judgment of conscience derived from principles of natural law—something the whole Christian tradition, including Vatican II, emphatically warns against (see GS 79).

As with any other legal requirement, if the law requires citizens to fight in a war, they should presume that they ought to comply. However, blind compliance is excluded and investigation is morally required whenever there is a definite reason to think complying would be morally wrong. But people required to fight in a war do have a definite reason for thinking compliance would be wrong: it will involve killing and causing grave harm to others, and that hardly will be morally acceptable unless the war is just; no war is just, however, unless several conditions are met; and history makes it clear that these conditions often are not met, either from a war's outset or from some point in its course. Therefore, if called on to fight, a person should judge whether the war is just, and if engaged in military action, he or she should remain alert for evidence that it no longer is just.[139]

Still, as with any other case in which blind compliance with a law is excluded, the mere fact that investigation is required does not at once overturn the presumption in favor of complying. Mere doubts do not justify refusal to serve. The state of affairs always is complex, and citizens generally lack much relevant information. But if not morally bound to comply with the law, one certainly is morally bound

---

139. Administrative Board of the United States Catholic Conference, "Statement on Registration and Conscription for Military Service" (14 Feb. 1980), 6, in *Pastoral Letters,* ed. Nolan, 4:361, states: "While acknowledging the duty of the state to defend society and its correlative right to use force in certain circumstances, we also affirm the Catholic teaching that the state's decision to use force should always be morally scrutinized by citizens asked to support the decision or to participate in war." Also see J. M. Cameron, "Obedience to Political Authority," in *Problems of Authority* ed. John M. Todd (London: Darton, Longman and Todd, 1962), 199–214.

not to comply, since what is at stake is no mere personal preference. Sometimes, too, official statements of policy, declarations by military leaders, unchallenged reports about the war's conduct or course, or other factors strongly indicate that a war is not, or has ceased to be, just. In such cases, if citizens consider everything— the possibility that they are being misled by propaganda, the limitations of their access to relevant information, the grounds of the presumption in favor of the law's requirement, their possible moral responsibility to engage in certain forms of material cooperation in a war even if it is unjust, and so on—and judge it more probably wrong to comply with the law and participate or continue participating in the military action, then they ought not to comply.

h) A nation's deterrent strategy can make its military actions unjustifiable. Since a potential enemy often can be deterred by threats which could be justly carried out ("We have superior forces and are prepared to defend our freedom, so if it comes to war, we will defeat you in battle"), deterrence as such need not be immoral. Moreover, referring to nuclear deterrence, John Paul II has stated: "In current conditions 'deterrence' based on balance, certainly not as an end in itself but as a step on the way toward a progressive disarmament, may still be judged morally acceptable."[140] However, this general statement does not mean that actual ways of exercising nuclear deterrence are morally acceptable.[141] Indeed, examination of the facts and analysis of relevant concepts show that the nuclear deterrence which the United States, Britain, and France maintained for years against the Soviet Union included threats of final retaliation and city swapping, and that those threats expressed real choices to kill many innocent persons if certain conditions ever were fulfilled.[142] The same was true of the deterrence policy of the Soviet Union and other nuclear powers.

Whether now or in the future, deterrence by similar threats—whether by the same or other nations, and whether based on nuclear or other capabilities of mass destruction—will involve choices of the same kind. Plainly, any such choice (that is, to kill the innocent under certain conditions) is gravely immoral, and nobody may formally cooperate in any action carrying it out. Moreover, within the limits of their other responsibilities, citizens should oppose their nation's acquiring or maintaining such a deterrent; no citizen ever should support doing so.

The responsibility to avoid formal cooperation has implications for many policies and acts—not only military but political, economic, and other—of any nation with a morally unacceptable deterrent. For the deterrent will affect other

140. John Paul II, Message to Special Session of the United Nations Organization for Disarmament (7 June 1982, delivered by Cardinal Casaroli, 11 June 1982), 8, *AAS* 74 (1982) 879, *OR*, 21 June 1982, 4.

141. Thus, Cardinal Agostino Casaroli, Address at University of San Francisco, 12, *OR*, 28 Nov. 1983, 7, after quoting John Paul II's statement on deterrence, nonofficially explains: "This statement is of a general nature, and, with regard to the actual ways of exercising this deterrence, one has to have recourse to the familiar principles of moral teaching: taking into due consideration what is at stake, that is to say the values that may be endangered and which have to be protected."

142. See John Finnis, Joseph M. Boyle, Jr., and Germain Grisez, *Nuclear Deterrence, Morality and Realism* (Oxford: Oxford University Press, 1987), 3–174; on John Paul II's statement on deterrence: 97–98, 103.

things the nation does, so that without its deterrent it would be unable rationally to retain, plan, or carry out certain other policies and acts. But nobody can rationally will the attainment of an end without willing all the means necessary to it. Therefore, the willing of any policy or act with an immoral deterrent as its underpinning will include the choice expressed by that threat. It follows that such a nation's military actions, even if otherwise entirely justifiable, will be unjustifiable if they presuppose and rely on the balance of power maintained by a morally unacceptable deterrent. Except for morally necessary material cooperation, citizens should not participate in or support such military actions, or any other of their nation's policies or acts relying on a morally unacceptable deterrent.

   i) **Four considerations tell against material cooperation in an unjust war.** As explained in a previous chapter (7.F), while one may never cooperate formally in an immoral action, sometimes one may, or even should, cooperate materially. Since citizens often are strongly motivated, whether by emotions or reasons, to participate in various ways in unjust wars, one wonders: To what extent may Christians materially cooperate in a war they judge unjust? Like other questions about material cooperation, this one admits of no simple answer. However, the following four considerations should be helpful.

   First, an unjust war, with its combination of great moral evil and vast human misery, is a paradigmatic instance of the fallen human condition. As such, it calls in a special way for effective witness to God's redemptive truth and love. To those choosing the darkness of violence and thereby deepening the shadow of death, Christians should point out the way of Christ: self-sacrifice, reconciliation, and life in peace. But they cannot do this by words alone; their deeds must exemplify and confirm what they say. However, if the intentions hidden in the hearts of material cooperators in evil were not upright, they would be formal cooperators. So, to the degree that Christians materially cooperate in an unjust war, they are impeded from exemplifying the truth and love they proclaim and confirming them by their deeds, since, despite their good intentions, those deeds in fact contribute to the very way of evil opposed to the gospel. Therefore, if Christian citizens judge that their nation is waging an unjust war, their responsibility to bear witness to the gospel argues that they should take an unambiguous stand for justice, love, and peace by avoiding even material cooperation.

   Second, an unjust war is a terrible disaster for the nation waging it. Both the war's moral evil and all the human misery it brings on the nation's own people gravely wound the common good. Patriotic citizens should do what they can, not only to avoid contributing to the disaster, but to prevent or put an end to it. Not only does material cooperation in an unjust war always contribute to it, however, but many forms of material cooperation are inconsistent with working to oppose it. This is so partly for the same reason that material cooperation undercuts Christian witness: to oppose the war, citizens must speak out, yet their argument will ring hollow if their deeds seem to belie it. But there also is another reason. Citizens very often have no other way or, at least, none more effective, of compelling a regime to consider the question of the justice of a war it is initiating or waging, than to withhold their legally required cooperation and provoke governmental enforcement action. They then can use any available legal processes to make their case against the war and to call into question the regime's case for it. Especially in a democratic society, if large numbers of conscientious citizens do this, their action is likely to bring about a rectification of national policy.

Third, an unjust war wrongly inflicts terrible harm on the enemy nation and its people, and this is so even if, as often happens, the war is unjust on both sides. Anyone suffering that harm will wish that citizens of the enemy nation who consider the war unjust would withhold most forms of cooperation from it and do what they can to prevent or end the harm it is inflicting. But the Golden Rule requires those who would materially cooperate in the war to put themselves in the place of its victims among the enemy. Therefore, fairness forbids most forms of material cooperation in an unjust war and requires citizens to do what they can to oppose so grave an injustice.

Finally, participating in an unjust war often is an occasion of sin for citizens who materially cooperate, and some forms of material cooperation are likely to be proximate occasions of grave sin. Of itself war is a social act; participants become dependent on one another. So, involvement in war tends to elicit commitment, if not to the nation's cause, at least to one's compatriots and, especially, one's more immediate comrades. But the immediate welfare of compatriots and comrades often will depend heavily on the success of the war effort, unjustifiable though it is, and that success will require that others do actions which, objectively, are gravely wrong. Hence, this commitment to compatriots and comrades will tempt those who initially participate in an unjust war by cooperating materially to will that others do things which, objectively, are gravely wrong. But to will this would be to cooperate formally, and so certainly sinfully, in the war's immorality. Therefore, material cooperation in an unjust war often occasions the sin of formal cooperation.

j) Material cooperation in an unjust war often is immoral. In view of the preceding considerations, Christians plainly should not materially cooperate in a war they judge unjust unless confident that some moral responsibility requires them to do so. For example, an engineer employed in reducing air pollution should not set to work making poison gas simply because the war work pays better.

Nevertheless, some upright Christians will judge that they should materially cooperate in an unjust war. Chaplains and medical personnel, for example, may well judge that, while their care of the souls and bodies of military personnel will contribute to the war effort, the needs of those they serve morally require them to exercise their ministries.

Also, many on the home front who do the same work during war as in peacetime—farmers, bankers, utility workers, many civil servants, and so forth—may well judge that, while doing their usual jobs will help the war effort, they should continue to do them in order to fulfill their responsibilities both to support their families and to serve noncombatants and even the nation's common good, insofar as it remains intact despite the unjust war. And, as explained above (in 2.f), citizens usually should pay their taxes even if some public funds are used for bad purposes, and so upright citizens usually will materially cooperate in an unjust war by helping to pay for it.

Although, in many wars, most members of the armed services never engage in combat, those who do can hardly avoid formally cooperating in the war. But even if they could, engaging in combat in a war one judged unjust surely would be wrongful material cooperation, since one would be accepting grave harms to the enemy not as side effects of a choice to counter an unjust threat to the common good of one's nation, but of some other choice, such as doing what is necessary to avoid punishment.

But would blameless material cooperation in a war judged unjust be possible for someone cooperating only to the extent of serving in the armed forces in some role—for example, personnel, communications, or food service—which did not involve engaging in any actual combat? In view of the four general considerations stated above, it hardly seems possible, especially because anyone serving in the armed forces (with some exceptions such as chaplains and medical personnel) might in some circumstances be reassigned and called on to engage in combat, and then be subject to very great pressure to do so. Moreover, even if a government does not recognize the legitimacy of conscientious objection, the penalty imposed on those who refuse to serve in the armed forces usually is not so grave as that imposed on those who refuse to obey orders after having undertaken to serve.

k) Christians almost always should refuse to serve in an unjust war. If, as has now been argued, only certain special groups such as chaplains and medical personnel can blamelessly serve in an unjust war, all other Christians should either evade the requirement to serve (for example, by hiding or fleeing to a place of refuge) or refuse service in the armed forces in any war they judge more probably unjust than just. Moreover, those already in the armed forces should not engage in combat when they judge that a war is unjust. If already engaged, they should surrender to the enemy or refuse to go on fighting. If not engaged in combat, they should desert, seek a discharge, or in some other way ensure that they do not go into combat; they also should avoid materially cooperating in the war effort in any way they judge probably wrong.

Anyone judging he or she should not comply either with the law's requirement to serve in a war or with some particular order—for example, to attack noncombatants—should be prepared to suffer the consequences: being required to do morally acceptable alternative service, however difficult or hazardous, or to undergo punishment, however severe. The alternative is to violate conscience, and in this situation Christians say: "We must obey God rather than any human authority" (Acts 5.29; cf. DH 11; *S.t.*, 2–2, q. 104, a. 5).[143]

The law of most nations either does not allow for the legitimacy of conscientious objection to military service or does so only within narrow limits. If the limits are too narrow to cover one's case, one of course may not lie to obtain the benefit which the law provides to others. Catholics should support laws which adequately provide for every conscientious objector by allowing all of them to carry out some kind of service to society which they can do in good conscience (see GS 79).

---

143. See Gordon C. Zahn, *In Solitary Witness: The Life and Death of Franz Jägerstätter*, rev. ed. (Springfield, Ill.: Templegate, 1986).

l) Christians should pray for peace. Peace is the fruit of that justice which includes mercy (see 6.F.7). Even if Christians work to promote justice and encourage mercy, they know that peace, like every good, depends primarily on God's kindness and, in this fallen world, on his mercy, which alone can overcome hatred and reconcile enemies. Therefore, Christians should pray earnestly and persistently for peace, and should perfect their prayers with penitential works, especially works of mercy, which directly contribute in some small way to reconciliation and peace, but whose greater efficacy lies in their being humble offerings united with Jesus' sacrifice. For the fruit of that sacrifice is the risen Savior's gift of the reconciling Spirit and his peace (see Jn 20.19–23).

Still, as long as this world remains sinful, peace will be imperfect and fragile. The peace the world seeks will be granted only when Jesus returns in glory and hands over his kingdom to his Father (see GS 38–39). Therefore, we must pray not only that the Lord bless us and protect us from all evil, but that he bring us to everlasting life.

"Come, Lord Jesus!" (Rv 22.20).

INDEXES

Unlike those in volume one, references in all of these indexes *are* to the book's pages. The indexed material may appear either in the text, or in one or more of the footnotes, or in both.

There are seven separate indexes. Six are to the work's sources in (1) Sacred Scripture, (2) the teachings of the Church gathered in the handbook edited by Denzinger and Schönmetzer, (3) the Vatican II documents, (4) documents of popes and the Holy See, (5) the Code of Canon Law, and (6) various works of St. Thomas Aquinas. (See pages xviii–xxi of the Preface and User's Guide for information about these sources and for the abbreviations used in referring to them.) The seventh index is a list of names and subjects, which includes all authors quoted or mentioned in the book and a guide to locating treatments of topics.

These indexes have been designed primarily as an aid to review, or for recapturing information after one has become familiar with the book. Readers wishing to explore only a limited subject might find the Contents and the summaries at the beginning of the chapters more helpful for locating the part of the book in which they are interested. Such readers should bear in mind that a complete question usually is the smallest unit in which they can expect to find everything needed for an accurate understanding of any smaller unit, and that the summaries and the introductory materials at the beginning of questions and the numbered sections within them never stand on their own.

In most cases, only some of the pages on which a topic is mentioned are listed in the names and subjects index, and the topics mentioned in the summaries are never indexed. Likewise, the entries in the names and subjects index under *Thomas Aquinas, St.* and the names of particular popes and councils include only a few of the many places where their teachings are cited, quoted, or discussed. The places indexed are those where an especially noteworthy or characteristic teaching is discussed or comes into play in a special way.

Readers familiar with volume one may wonder why they do not find here a list of key words. The reason is that this volume presupposes volume one, and the words listed there are used here with the same meanings. No new technical vocabulary is introduced here except in connection with particular topics, where necessary explantions are provided as needed. It remains true that readers may find it helpful to have at hand, besides their *Webster's,* a reference work such as the *Modern Catholic Dictionary,* by John A. Hardon, S.J.

1: Sacred Scripture

Genesis

1.4: 772
1.10: 772
1.12: 461, 772
1.18: 461, 772
1.21: 461, 772
1.25: 461, 772
1.26–30: 461
1.26–27: 597
1.27–28: 557, 681
1.27: 557, 573, 755
1.28: 569, 597, 681, 754, 755
1.29: 777
1.31: 461
2.15: 776
2.16–17: 776
2.18–24: 597
2.18–23: 556, 597
2.18: 333, 556, 569, 573
2.23–24: 575, 604
2.24: 556, 570, 574, 587, 598, 599, 681
3.1–6: 219
3.3: 462
3.16: 387, 622
3.17: 779
3.19: 462
4.1: 597
4.12: 779
5.1–3: 597
9.1–3: 777
9.5–7: 461
9.6: 475, 892
9.13: 775
9.17: 775
11.1–9: 333
12–22: 8
12.2: 597
17.1–14: 78
17.16: 597
22.2–18: 478
22.15–18: 434
26.24: 597
30.1: 597
37.20–22: 237

Exodus

1.16: 879
1.17: 407
1.18–21: 407
1.21: 407
20.2–4: 64
20.7: 75

20.8–9: 146
20.11: 146
20.12: 713
20.13: 474, 475
20.15: 824
20.16: 410
20.17: 257, 793, 827
21.15: 318, 713
21.17: 318, 713
21.23–25: 893
23.1: 410
23.4–5: 311
23.7: 474
23.10–13: 777
23.20–22: 311

Leviticus

18.6–18: 589
19.3: 713
19.11: 824
19.12: 75
19.13: 824
19.18: 138, 306, 307, 311, 366
19.33: 311
20.9: 318, 713
24.19–20: 893
25.1–5: 777
26.33–35: 777–78

Deuteronomy

5.6–8: 64
5.11: 75
5.16: 713
5.17: 474, 475
5.19: 824
5.20: 410
5.21: 793, 827
6.4–5: 133
6.5: 138, 306
7.1–6: 311
7.1–2: 474
10.19: 311
13.12–18: 474
19.10: 474
19.13: 474
19.15–19: 410
19.21: 893
20.1–4: 311
20.16–18: 311, 474
21.8–9: 474
21.18–21: 715
24.1–4: 599
27.25: 474

30.15–16: 462
30.19: 462
32.4: 24

Joshua

6.16–21: 311
6.18–21: 474
10.22–25: 311
10.28–40: 311
10.40: 474
11.10–23: 311
11.14: 474
24.14–27: 78

1 Samuel

1.6: 597
15.1–3: 311
15.2–32: 474
15.22: 434
18–20: 424–25

1 Chronicles

10.13–14: 65

2 Chronicles

20.29: 311

Tobit

4.15: 307
8.7: 751
10.12: 716
12.8–10: 192
14.13: 716

Job

31.15: 597
38.1–42.6: 22

Psalms

3.8: 78
8.5–8: 755
13.1–6: 78
13.5: 78
14.1: 26
16.1–2: 78
18.30–35: 78
19.1: 776
31.1–2: 78
31.5: 240
31.14–24: 78
33.4: 24
33.18–22: 78
36.5–10: 78

2: Denzinger–Schönmetzer

3: The Second Vatican Council

4: Documents of Popes and the Holy See

5: The Code of Canon Law

6: Works of St. Thomas Aquinas

7: Names and Subjects

life of, 460–69; social nature of, 332–34, 467, 557; work and, 756–58

Personal vocation: in general, 113–29, 276, 280, 705–7; particular vocations, 170–71, 737–38; and specific responsibilities, 193–94, 373–76, 419, 421, 527–28, 610–11, 672–75, 681–90, 691–92, 758–59, 804–6, 846. *See also* Apostolate; Marriage; Political Society; Work

Peruvian Episcopal Conference, 102, 259

Peter, C. J., 210

Peters, E. N., 710, 865

Petrine privilege, 590–95

Pets. *See* Animals

Pettirsch, F. X., 149

Phan, P. C., 791

Pharisaical scandal, 234

Phillips, R., 575

Philo, 557

Physicians, right use of, 523–32

Pilgrimages, 194

Pinckaers, S., 84

Pius XI: on choice of spouse, 739, 741; on conjugal love, 564; on divorce, 590. 591–92; on ends of marriage, 562–63; on gravity of contraception, 517; on properties of marriage, 604; on roles of spouses, 615, 616–17, 618, 631; on sacramentality of marriage, 596, 601. *See also* entry in separate index of references to Documents of Popes and the Holy See

Pius XII: on abortion, 498; on capital punishment, 893; on Church's mission, 100; on conscientious objection to military service, 903, 906; on ends of marriage, 563; on frequent confession, 201; on intentional killing, 477; and "outside the Church nobody is saved," 20; on periodic abstinence, 685; on sex education, 711; on war, 899–903. *See also* entry in separate index of references to Documents of Popes and the Holy See

Planned Parenthood Federation of America, 500

Plantinga, A., 22

Plato, 252

Pleading not guilty, 888

Pleasure, health and, 520, 781; as a motive, 8, 34, 98, 110, 349, 350, 352, 612, 706; sexual, 637–38, 641, 646, 653

Pluralism in the Church, 163–64

Police, cooperating with, 888–89

Political parties, 871–72

Political society, responsibilities in, 844–911

Polygamy, 559, 574–77, 603–4, 643

Pontifical Biblical Commission, 18

Pontifical Commission on Population, Family, and Birthrate, 467, 650

Poor, the, 101–2, 120, 376–78, 772, 805–6, 811–14, 896

Pope, teaching authority of, 19–21, 38–39, 46–55

Population and contraception, 515–16

Pornography, 394, 398, 642, 665, 669, 676, 679, 731, 843, 851, 864–65

Positivism, legal, 323

Posner, R. A., 323–24

Pospishil, V. J., 590

Possidius, 806

Potter, R., 898

Potterie, I. de la, 38

Praxis, moral truth and, 259–60

Prayer: chastity and, 675; for Church, 168; death and, 241, 717–18; discernment and, 293; by the divorced, 736; ecumenism and, 177; by the engaged, 751; faith and, 56–58; family, 612–13; hope and, 87–89; indulgences and, 198; liturgical, 152; by the married, 625, 639–40; with non-Catholics, 157; overcoming sin by, 216–19; for peace, 911; as penance, 192–93; and prudence, 247; teaching children, 703; vocation and, 121–22; as worship, 62–63

Preferential option for the poor, 101–2, 376–77

Pregnancy out of wedlock, 719–20

Pregnancy wastage, 497

Premarital intercourse, 652–53

Presumption: in favor of the law, 881–82; in favor of the personhood of the unborn, 497–98; about matters of fact, 269; sin of, 95–97

Price, just, 324–25, 833

Pride, 34–35, 349–50

Priests: chastity of, 673–74; duty to support, 170–71

Privacy, 551–52

Private property, 791–95

Prizefighting, 550–51

Procreation. *See* Marriage, parenthood and

Profanity, 67

Profession of faith, 65–66

Profit, 832

Promises, 70–74, 74–76, 264–65, 412–14, 831

Property: definition of, 788–89; family, 717; private and public, 791–95;